This book is dedicated in honor of all political science scholars who, from a multitude of perspectives and using diverse methodologies, strive to increase knowledge and understanding of politics and political life.

Table of Contents

Preface

This project has its origin in the Spring of 1981, shortly after Seymour Martin Lipset, then president of the American Political Science Association, asked me to be program chair for the 1982 Annual Meeting. In undertaking that job, I made a fateful decision -- that it might be interesting and useful to encourage a substantial number of political scientists to turn their attention to one particular issue by having a "theme" for the meeting. The theme I chose was "The State of the Discipline." The idea was well received; interest in serious evaluation of research and knowledge in the discipline was very high, and President Lipset and Thomas Mann, then executive director of the Association, asked me to collect the theme papers that had been presented at the meeting into what became the first edition of this book. This second edition retains the same overall goal of reviewing important recent research in various subfields of political science. All of us connected with the project share the hope that this edition will be as useful as was the first for students, teachers, researchers, and others who are interested in the cumulation of knowledge in our discipline.

In the years since the first edition was published, we were pleased to learn that teachers throughout the profession used that volume in a variety of different courses, and that many researchers were using it to get an overview of both their own and other areas of research. About two years ago, therefore, the current executive director, Catherine Rudder, and deputy director Robert J-P. Hauck, thought it must surely be time to do an update. This edition, however, did not begin as a series of papers for an annual meeting but, rather, "from scratch." To provide the opportunity for different perspectives on research to be expressed, we assembled a new set of chapter authors. In addition, these authors were asked to provide a perspective on the research literature that was as international and comparative as their expertise and the research literature itself permitted. The story of how this transition occurred may be of some interest to members of the profession.

At the time we began to plan for the second edition, Theodore Lowi was the president of the Association. Since we did not have an existing group of papers already prepared as we had had for the first edition, President Lowi and the Publications Committee asked me to consult with colleagues in the profession before deciding on the final group of authors for the new edition. As I recall those early conversations with Cathy, Rob, and Ted, I think we all assumed that we were going to ask the scholars who had written for the first edition to update and revise their chapters, and that the consultation I was to do would be primarily about the new chapters that would be added to cover some major areas that had not appeared in the first edition. I think we all envisioned a project that would be completed fairly quickly and with few of the coordination complexities that usually accompany volumes involving large numbers of authors -- certainly that was my understanding!

As with any project that involves consultation, however, one does not always anticipate the ideas of those one consults. And when the ideas that come forth are good ones, one may wind up with a project that is considerably different from that envisioned by its initiators. That is certainly the history of this edition.

To comply with the request for consultation, I wrote to perhaps a hundred colleagues who had recently served in positions in which they would have had the need and the opportunity to think about the state of the discipline, either in general or in their own particular research areas. My correspondence list included current and past section chairs for the Annual Meetings, officials of the "organized sections," officers of the Association, and other colleagues and friends whom I knew to be especially concerned about the state of the discipline. I expected few replies. Instead, I received numerous thoughtful, concerned, and extraordinarily helpful letters from colleagues of every disciplinary persuasion. Most often, people were generous with kind remarks about the first edition and numerous suggestions for coverage and authors for the new one. There were also, of course, those who were less happy and wanted important changes to be made.

These letters had a profound effect on the further course of planning and, ultimately, the book itself. In the end, it is in large part this input that was responsible for the direction the new book has taken, and the ways in which it departs from the first edition. The many specific suggestions about coverage and content were all interesting and helpful and very many resulted in specific charges to authors about materials that should be covered in their chapters. Many of the authors whose chapters are included were suggested to me initially by these correspondents.

My informal content analysis of the letters also yielded several more general themes that came up with some frequency.

First, both as researchers and as teachers, colleagues did want updates on what was going on in their own areas and also for areas that they did not have the time or the responsibility to follow on a regular basis. The advice here was yes, do another volume, but then be sure to do a third before another ten years goes by. The literature advances too rapidly to have such long intervals between editions.

Second, many writers pointed out that the research literature is so specialized, and so many new areas of research have achieved critical mass status, that many more chapters were needed. Surely the new edition would have to have a chapter on (insert your favorite research area here; for sure, someone mentioned it).

Third, political science is a worldwide endeavor. Not only do we need more comparative chapters than there were in the first edition, but *all* the chapters should be comparative. (The people who made *this* suggestion were a particularly intense minority, who tended to express themselves with somewhat more passion than many others...)

Fourth, the chapter by (insert your favorite first edition chapter author here) was truly outstanding but what you must do now is give (insert a new name here) a chance to write on this field so that other perspectives, other approaches, and other bodies of literature have a chance to be highlighted.

In short order, I realized that I had gotten much more advice than I had bargained for, and that all of these common themes represented worthwhile ideas that I wanted to take seriously. It soon became clear that this would not be the relatively expeditious undertaking that had been envisioned. But it would be an opportunity for the resulting book to respond to at least some of these ideas and perhaps to have an even broader impact than we had imagined.

There was not much I could do about the first two of these themes. It was not my task at the moment to plan for future volumes. And, for the present, the Publications Committee and the Council had approved funding for one volume whose size would limit the number of chapters that could be included. But despite the fact that they departed from our original informal planning, I decided that the third and fourth themes were within my purview as editor, and that I would try to implement them.

More comparative approaches and coverage appealed to me for two principal reasons: first, I thought that chapters that made a serious effort to cast our research in an international, cross-national, or cross-cultural perspective could be very useful in encouraging the development of more general theories of politics. And, second, I hoped that a comparative perspective would make the book more useful in other countries and thereby serve to broaden the scope of shared ideas and perspectives, and stimulate additional cross-national discussion and research.

If the comparative theme were to be taken seriously, however, I realized that many of the chapters would have to be substantially different than the versions that had appeared in the original volume, in which this was not a special consideration. At the same time, many writers had commented on how useful the original chapters had been. Ultimately, I saw that if I were to encourage a comparative perspective, and invite at least some new authors, that the original chapters would not, in fact, be superseded by the new ones. The new chapters would of course include a more recent set of materials, but to the extent that they also provided different approaches, including the possibility of a comparative perspective, they would not necessarily supplant or revise the perspectives and materials discussed in the original chapters. And if having a new author with a different perspective was a good idea for one or two areas, why not for all?

Thus began the "second," rather than the "revised," edition of this book, a two year project that would involve an entirely new set of authors whose charge would be to review, discuss, and assess the literature in each area, from a world-wide, cross-national, or cross-cultural perspective, in whatever ways and to the extent that the research in each field lent itself to this goal. I hope that others will share the view that the new goals of this current edition were worthwhile ones, even if their accomplishment has been uneven or incomplete. And because the papers in the original edition really are different in focus and perspective, they remain valuable research and teaching tools. For this reason, the Table of Contents to the first edition of *Political Science: The State of the Discipline* is presented as an appendix to the present volume.

Telling the story of how this book came to be will make clear that while the Association is publishing it, it is in no way an "official" or "authorized" guidebook to our discipline. If a field is omitted, it is because of space problems rather than any decision as to its importance or relevance to the discipline, or the quality of research it produces. Nor, however, do I want to take all the responsibility for fields that do not appear. There were several cases where the person who was invited to write a particular chapter never did so and by the time it became clear that the chapter in question would not materialize, it was too late to invite someone else. And in a couple of cases, authors who did submit first drafts were unable in the short time available to revise their chapters in time for publication. On the positive side, I am pleased that we were able to bring to completion as many of the chapters that were originally planned as do appear in the book.

I hope researchers and teachers in fields that are not covered in this edition will find useful material in the other political science research reviews that have been published in recent years, and that together all of these efforts will contribute to the nourishment and flowering of all of the diverse branches of our discipline. But there may be more that we can do to encourage this process, which brings me back to the first two themes that emerged from the letters of which I spoke above: more frequent updates in a larger number of areas.

Both the letters I received and the chapters that appear in this book suggest to me that political science is in a period of great vitality and increasingly rapid research development. But to turn a proliferation of ideas, information, and research findings into knowledge and theory requires intellectual synthesis and integration. Literature reviews can contribute in an important way to this process.

As I noted above, a few other handbooks and volumes of literature reviews for our discipline have appeared in recent years. Each of these has been a large undertaking that took years to complete. Moreover, because virtually all have been self-contained efforts, the need to draw all of the chapters together for publication at a fixed time in a pre-defined amount of space means that coverage will almost surely be incomplete. Certainly that is the case with this volume. Limited size prevents the inclusion of chapters in each area in which vigorous research is occurring. Fixed and infrequent publication dates mean that chapters that are commissioned but not finished in time do not appear, and that fields growing rapidly may not be reviewed as often as the literature warrants. As knowledge proliferates and research becomes more specialized, such omissions may leave unrepresented in any one collection important fields of research and growing numbers of researchers.

Therefore, in addition to stimulating research and discussion in the areas that are covered, I hope the publication of this volume will also encourage more attention to the utility of having literature reviews published on a more regular basis and in a wider variety of areas. The most efficient way to do this is through serial publication. Our journal editors might consider whether they can do more of this than they have in the past, although the increasing quantity of the primary research itself creates space pressures that may make this solution improbable. A new journal devoted to literature review also suggests itself. Another possibility might be for the Association to develop a monograph series of literature reviews.

An ongoing series in paperback format would mean that there would be no artificial (i.e., space and time) limitations on the subfields and areas that could be covered, and that fields could be reviewed as frequently as the growth of research or diversity of perspectives in each area warranted. Each of us contributes only a very small part to the enterprise of developing a science of politics and political life. Keeping abreast of what others are doing and getting perspective on how our own work fits into or departs from the larger effort can help in important ways to make that part as productive as possible. For teaching purposes, smaller and relatively inexpensive monographs could be useful in an even larger number of courses. I therefore hope serious discussion of these possibilities will take place in the near future.

The story of how this book came to be would be entirely incomplete if I did not say how important a role was played by the reviewers of all of these chapters. It is understandable that an editor goes first to friends and acquaintances for such a task because it tends to be unheralded and anonymous and one hesitates to impose on those one doesn't know personally. But how many people in so many different fields can one editor know personally? Thus, I found myself at the door, the telephone, the FAX machine or the E-mail port of friends and colleagues, both personally known and known only by name and reputation, at work, on vacation and about to leave for field research. Not only were these colleagues generous in their advice the first time around but many of them graciously assisted again when I called to ask for a second reading of a revised manuscript. The journal editors in our profession probably already know that so many of our colleagues are such good citizens; for me, on a once in every ten-years basis, it was a pleasure to be reminded that I had found this out once before.

My own colleagues at Michigan State, being handier than any others, are the largest contingent of reviewers from any one University and they are due a special note of thanks for their generous counsel, numerous suggestions, and willingness to talk on a moment's notice. Special thanks are due to the department chair, Brian Silver, for marshalling substantial material support for the project.

The American Political Science Association, of course, has borne the major part of the expenses of the project. More than this, however, we are all fortunate to have an Association whose staff is truly dedicated to serving the needs of the discipline, as well as the profession. I want to thank Cathy Rudder for her overall support and encouragement of the project. Joanne Dunkelman managed to take computer disks from twenty different contributors and through the marvel of desktop publishing, and a great deal of personal skill, turn them into the pages of this book. Pat Spellman's careful proofreading was a great help to all. Most of all I want to thank Rob Hauck, who facilitated the project in myriad ways and always with great good humor. As well as supervising the physical production of the book, Rob was always there with phone calls reminding me about deadlines and press dates. Had it not been for his support and assistance, the book might have been a twenty-year rather than a ten-year update.

Without the assistance and encouragement of many other colleagues throughout the discipline the project would have been both more difficult and less rewarding. I want especially to thank the following individuals who either served as reviewers of the individual chapters or who wrote me with advice and suggestions for the book:

Paul R. Abramson, Michigan State University
Robert H. Bates, Duke University
John Brigham, University of Massachusetts
Thad A. Brown, University of Missouri
Gary Bryner, Brigham Young University
Bruce Bueno de Mesquita, Hoover Institution on War, Revolution and Peace
Aage R. Clausen, Ohio State University
Fred Dallmayr, University of Notre Dame
Rodolfo O. de la Garza, University of Texas
Michael Doyle, Princeton University
Heinz Eulau, Stanford University
Morris Fiorina, Harvard University
Richard E. Flathman, Johns Hopkins University
Timothy Fuller, The Colorado College
F. Chris Garcia, University of New Mexico
G. David Garson, North Carolina State University
Scott Gates, Michigan State University
James Granato, Michigan State University
Joel Grossman, University of Wisconsin
Peter A. Hall, Harvard University
Matthew Holden, Jr., University of Virginia
Gretchen Hower, Michigan State University
Richard Hula, Michigan State University
Shanto Iyengar, University of California-Los Angeles
Herbert Jacob, Northwestern University
Robert W. Jackman, University of California-Davis
M. Kent Jennings, University of California-Santa Barbara
Mack H. Jones, Prairie View A&M University
John Kincaid, Advisory Commission on Intergovernmental Relations
Gary King, Harvard University
Jack H. Knott, Michigan State University
Stephen D. Krasner, Stanford University
David C. Leege, University of Notre Dame
Seymour Martin Lipset, George Mason University
Theodore J. Lowi, Cornell University
Robert C. Luskin, University of Texas
Jane Mansbridge, Northwestern University
Lawrence Mayer, Texas Tech University
David R. Mayhew, Yale University
Arthur Melzer, Michigan State University
Gary Miller, Washington University
Warren E. Miller, Arizona State University
Kristen Monroe, University of California-Irvine

James D. Morrow, Hoover Institution on War, Revolution and Peace
Michael Nelson, Vanderbilt University
M. J. Peterson, University of Massachusetts
Samuel Popkin, University of California-San Diego
Austin Ranney, University of California-Berkeley
Jorgen Rasmussen, Iowa State University
Jeffrey Riedinger, Michigan State University
Wilma Rule, University of Nevada-Reno
Virginia Sapiro, University of Wisconsin
Martin Schain, New York University
Joseph A. Schlesinger, Michigan State University
Byron E. Shafer, Oxford University
Kenneth Shepsle, Harvard University
Brian Silver, Michigan State University
Harold Spaeth, Michigan State University
Kaare Strom, University of California-San Diego
Frank J. Thompson, State University of New York at Albany
Michael W. Traugott, University of Michigan
Nicolas van de Walle, Michigan State University
Hanes Walton, Jr., Savannah State College
Mark E. Warren, Georgetown University
Jerry Weinberger, Michigan State University
Susan Welch, Pennsylvania State University

Of course, many ideas were offered and not all were accommodated, and some of these individuals were critical in a variety of ways. Therefore none of those listed bear responsibility for what follows but all have my gratitude for participating.

Ada W. Finifter
East Lansing, Michigan
February 1, 1993

Theory and Method

1

Texts and Canons:
The Status of the "Great Books" in Political Theory

Arlene W. Saxonhouse

The arguments have flown fast and free over the last several years, rocking the academic world: canon or no canon? Is it Western imperialism, misogyny, and racism, or is it the core of civilized discourse over the ages? Are the texts we study and assign to our students culture and time bound, reproducing the white, patriarchal past in a multicultural present or are they to be preserved as the focus of common discourse lest we and our students drown in a sea of relativism? The rhetoric on both sides of the debate has been powerful; moderation has been a forgotten virtue. And the subdiscipline of political theory as the study of great texts written by earlier generations has not been immune to the swirling debates. Indeed, it was a political theorist, Allan Bloom, in his best-selling *Closing of the American Mind* (1987), who did much to bring this issue to public attention and to set the tone for the debate. While this debate has addressed the broader field of the role of education in contemporary American society, challenges from within the discipline of political theory have been launched as well, questioning the claimed apotheosis of certain classic readings: the works of authors such as Plato, Aristotle, Machiavelli, Hobbes, Locke, Mill, and Marx. Others have defended this core as being at the foundation of our ability to theorize about the value, purpose, and meaning of political life, and the courses in which students read Plato et al. continue to be included in the curricula of most political science departments.

Political theory as a field managed, though barely, to survive the assaults of the 1950s and 1960s. On the one hand, there was positivism, which denied validity or meaning to the conceptual core of a field that used such inaccessible terms as justice, duty, freedom; on the other hand, there was behavioralism, which dismissed the normative in favor of the empirical. The severest and most powerful assaults of the last decade, though, have come from within. John Gunnell, for instance, claims that the core of authors and readings traditionally included in the study of political theory is simply a "myth," constructed by modern theorists with particular

agendas; others argue that those works that have become part of the so-called "myth" survived by chance rather than because of their status as great works, worthy of careful reading, from which we might learn about the nature of politics (Condren 1985). Yet others have turned political theory into a subfield of history, especially intellectual history, embedding the classic texts in an historical setting of language usage on one side or political experiences on the other. To borrow the language of David Miller describing this movement: "[T]exts that we now regard as classic sink into the landscape" (1990, 425).

Such attacks arise since in many ways political theory *is* an artificial construct that lacks an independent identity, caught as it is at the cross-roads of a multitude of disciplines. While political scientists may see political theory as a subfield of their own discipline, political theory draws from (and is claimed by) history, philosophy, sociology, literary studies, linguistics, and women's studies.[1] At home in none, but enriched by all, political theory during the last decade has confronted the new threat of the centrifugal force of interdisciplinary connections which have often led to sharply divided communities of discourse. Beyond the isolation from mainstream political science, the sub-specialties of political theory informed by their various inter-disciplinary connections have become isolated from one another. Thus, at the same time that the very texts we might have defined as the unifying basis of political theory are under assault, the activity of studying those texts has itself been drawn in different directions.

It is the argument of this essay, though, that the texts that have come under such powerful and (usually) articulate attack and that have been appropriated by other disciplines have weathered the assaults and remain a central part of the discipline of political science -- though recent trends suggest that their survival is in no sense assured. In part, these texts have survived the attacks of the last decade because political theorists have not established a simply defensive stance asserting the validity of the old and established; rather, they have expanded the readings to include a far more varied corpus of works. Further, what I shall call the "instrumental" approach to political theory has allowed for new questions to be addressed to these texts and, precisely because of the inherent richness of these texts, they can help us address such questions. The texts explore what may be called the "perennial questions" that confront all political communities, e.g., how to organize and distribute (i.e., develop principles of justice), what goals to define or deny (i.e., develop justificatory principles). Thus, they have been able to clarify how contemporary questions arising from contemporary events are illuminated by reflection on the fundamental questions of political life with which the classic authors deal.[2]

The survival of texts as the basis of the study of political theory, though, depends on the continued ability of these works to respond to the questions posed by a variety of schools. I emphasize the importance of this response since, of late, the discourse of conflict between the various schools in political thought may have mellowed in tone, but perhaps only because of the absence of a continued engagement; the subfields within political theory seem to suffer from the "separate tables" syndrome diagnosed by Gabriel Almond as plaguing the discipline at large (1988). To argue for the survival of texts at the core of the discipline, though, I must try to integrate the two major, but warring approaches within the subfield and suggest how the newer trends can serve to aid and not undermine one another. The integration may not be possible, but the attempt is essential if political theory is not to lose its status as the normative foundation from which political science gains its significance.

R.G. Collingwood in his sensitive and engaging *Autobiography* introduces his chapter entitled "Question and Answer" with the story of his confrontation with the Albert Memorial in Kensington Gardens. Passing it every day on his way to work, he was struck:

> Everything about it was visibly mis-shapen, corrupt, crawling, verminous; for a time I could not bear to look at it...recovering from this weakness, I forced myself to look, and to face day by day the question: a thing so obviously, so incontrovertibly, so indefensibly bad, why had Scott done it? To say that Scott was a bad architect was to burke the problem with a tautology; to say that there was no accounting for taste was to evade it....What relation was there...between what he had done and what he had tried to do. Had he tried to produce a beautiful thing?...If so, he had of course failed. But had he perhaps been trying to produce something different?...If I found the

> monument merely loathsome, was that perhaps my fault? Was I looking in it for qualities it did not possess, and either ignoring or despising those it did (1929, 28-29)?

Collingwood's tale can be read, as one school of thought does, as only allowing the old questions to be asked of artifacts, whether they be the bowl made by the ancient Corinthian potter or the dialogues written by Plato. Anything more would impose on the texts a meaning never intended. And one finds support for this view in Collingwood's claim that: "Now, the question 'To what question did So-and-so intend this proposition for an answer?' is an historical question, and therefore cannot be settled except by historical methods" (1929, 39).[3] Or, his tale may be read as urging us not to ask our own questions; thus, we may remove ourselves from the specificity of our own time and place, and learn from the insights offered to us by those whose questions may have been different, but who, precisely by their different questions, make us attend to universals rather than the particularities of our own time and place. The latter reading of Collingwood's message would keep the study of texts as political theory within the discipline of political science as a guide to its practice. The former may transfer the reading of such texts to a subfield of history or make it of curious interest to the political scientist, but hardly the stuff out of which a discipline is made. The conflict between these two approaches and their numerous variants have dominated the last decade. Political theory concerned with the classic texts must confront that conflict both substantively and methodologically.

The Construction of a Canon in Political Theory

In the earlier edition of *The State of the Discipline* and in two articles in the *American Political Science Review*, one from 1978 and a more recent one in 1988, John Gunnell analyzed the "reified analytic construct[ion]" of what he called the "chronologically ordered canon of classic texts" (1988, 72) or "a reconstructed tradition [that] has become the principal context for understanding the meaning of past texts, and the significance attributed to a work that has become largely a matter of its role in this historical narrative" (1978, 122). In the earlier essay, Gunnell uses Leo Strauss's writing as an example of many who "presuppose the tradition of datum." "Strauss articulates a distinctive traditional myth; but the myth of the tradition, in one form or another, has been a pervasive feature of most scholarship in the history of political philosophy" (1978, 131). Gunnell here sets forth an important challenge for those in political science who study texts: not simply, how do we study the texts that we do (the most important methodological controversies within the subfield which over the last decade have threatened civilized discourse among its practitioners), but why study texts. Both questions need to be addressed in an assessment of the state of political theory.

The debate over the "canon" that has in the last several years come to infiltrate the study of political theory may find its origins in the writings of Matthew Arnold, who in his turn drew heavily from the German authors concerned with *Bildung*, the moral and character education of the young. Confronted with the emerging challenge to the Bible as the primary source of moral education, Arnold proposed the turn to literature as the new guide to the moral education of the young in a democratic regime. What had been canonical in terms of Church-related doctrine becomes canonical in terms of a secular literature that teaches the virtues of the new secular age. Reading texts is not merely illuminating, historically enlightening; for Arnold speaking to the world of nineteenth century England, the careful reading of literature is the source of our humanity and identity.

Quite in contrast to such a role for the canon, George Sabine published his volume, *A History of Political Thought* in 1937 and thereby established for American students of political science the sub-field based on the title of his book, distinct from intellectual history and a part of the study of politics. Unconcerned with the history and writing of texts as the source of education for the upright man or citizen, he introduces his volume by noting that "theories of politics are themselves part of politics," and by firmly asserting that "they do not refer to an external reality but are produced as a normal part of the social milieu" (1949, xi), he made it clear that his study had nothing to do with virtue, truth, or moral education. By the time of the second edition in 1949 Sabine asserts that the author (i.e., himself) is "even more convinced than he was in 1937 that neither he nor any man can stand apart from the values and conventions of the culture in which he was read" (1949, ix). Thus, his volume is a selection of authors who have interesting things to say about certain political issues of their times and may have also had an influence on subsequent authors. Sabine's firm assertion that the texts studied were exemplars of political thought of the past granted them no particular status beyond localized expressions and analyses of political circumstances. They were no more than that, not eye-opening documents, not works that might transform the reader as Arnold envisioned in his campaign to create a literary canon. Sabine's selection process, however arbitrary we may consider it,

has had a primary role in defining the canon for the discipline. For example, he includes Seneca and Ambrose, John of Salisbury and Dante, John Knox and Thomas More, but not Aeschylus or Tacitus or Shakespeare or Mary Wollstonecraft or Simone Weil or Hannah Arendt. All in the latter group have become in the last decade or are in the process of becoming, part of the ever expanding, though seldom contracting, core of works read and studied by political theorists.

Sabine's choice of whom to include depended on Sabine's assessment of who said interesting things about politics, but also the degree to which he could set a particular author within his particular milieu: "The fact that a man exists or that a book was written is, in itself, no part of the history of political theory as here conceived" (1949, xiii).[4] In stark contrast to Sabine's approach to the history of political thought stands the work of Leo Strauss and many of his followers. For Strauss, the texts that we include in our canvass of what has been said about political life in the past have an entirely different status; far from being simply the expression of the political circumstances of a particular time, they have become in his writings works to be plumbed for the truths that they may tell about political life, its goals, its possibilities, and especially its limits. In his concern for natural right, these are not truths that depend on the political circumstances of a particular time. They are not simply "produced as a normal part of the social milieu." The study of texts goes beyond learning what interesting things were said about politics in the past to the search for what these texts, though written long ago, can tell us about politics in a world confronted by the crises of self-doubt, historicism, and relativism. They play the moral, educative role Arnold praised, not so much because they teach what to think, but how to think about the political world. As Strauss phrases it in his essay "What is Liberal Education?," "We cannot be philosophers, but we can love philosophy; we can try to philosophize. This philosophizing consists...in listening to conversations between the great philosophers...the greatest minds, and therefore in studying the great books" (1989, 7).[5] Thomas Pangle and Nathan Tarcov put it this way in the newly added "Epilogue" to the 1987 edition of the Strauss-Cropsey volume *History of Political Philosophy*: "Strauss's study of the history of political philosophy therefore presupposed a radical dissatisfaction with contemporary thought and a resulting interest in that earlier thought which did not start from the premises responsible for the present crisis" (1987, 912). In this sense Strauss is, as Gunnell claims, "thoroughly instrumental...in that he utilizes the history of political philosophy to mount an attack on what he believes to be the philosophic foundation of contemporary politics" (1978, 130). There was nothing instrumental about

Sabine's readings; he simply told us what men thought about politics. There is something profoundly instrumental inherent in Strauss' study of the texts.

To Strauss and Sabine can be attributed what I see as the two dominant approaches to the study of texts of political theory in the last decade, though the variants are many.[6] On the one hand, there are those who turn to political theory for enlightenment about our condition in the contemporary world, for guidance about the normative choices that we as political creatures confront, for a sense of who we as political actors are or can be, for the conversations we must have about the meaning of political life.[7] On the other hand, there are those who deny that the texts of the past can provide us with insights of that sort, who demand that we see the history of political theory as a way of studying the foundations of our political language and concepts, of learning how texts and concepts emerge from political and linguistic practices and how they in their turn come to govern our understandings and analyses of political life.[8] Such differing goals for the study of political theory have generated further (but, I would suggest, subsidiary) debates about how one goes about studying a particular text. These methodological debates may have caused firestorms of controversy a decade or so ago; more recently, the methodological concerns have led to a series of self-exploratory reviews of methods within, rather than across, approaches. This has had the consequence of taming the discourse at the same time as unfortunately dividing the discipline.

Gunnell may be justified in claiming that the canon has been constructed in the case of political theory, but the challenge is to assess how we as scholars are to respond to this construction. Are we to follow what Gunnell has pejoratively called the instrumental approach? Are we to find in this construction of texts an historical challenge, both of origins and of impact? What methodological implications do such approaches entail? Are we to escape the texts whose language constrains us within antiquated and/or oppressive conceptual frameworks? Before I turn to a discussion of the two major approaches to political theory, let me try to frame the discussion in part by addressing what, in answer to this last question, is perhaps one of the most radical challenges to political theory as the study of texts. This challenge finds its origins in Hegelian thought and is carried forward by such continental authors as Nietzsche and Heidegger and on to Foucault and Derrida; it raises questions not about the text insofar as it serves as a source of enlightenment about what was thought in the past or what ought to be thought in the present, but about whether the text as object is capable of study by a subject and whether the text imprisons the reader in the particular language an author (or the tradition) uses, thereby limiting the nature of our discourse about political life. It

is to the latter point that I wish to turn first, in particular in its expression in feminist theory, as an aid to understanding the controversy between the two schools that I have identified.[9]

Feminist political theory, often drawing on literary criticism of the last decade and the continental thought emerging from the Hegelian legacy, has asked on occasion whether feminist scholars can even write about the canon of classic texts without themselves being co-opted by the masculine language that has been used in those texts. Does the decision to study the text commit a scholar to a pre-determined masculine discourse? Should the old texts and the study of them, then, simply disappear because of their oppressive analytic frameworks which we must endeavor to escape? Linda Zerilli (1991) in a recent article in *Political Theory* raises issues about the attachment of political theorists to the canon of old texts and sees those texts as restraints upon transformative discourse. Focusing on an earlier debate between two feminist scholars, Jean Bethke Elshtain and Mary Dietz, about the proper reading of Sophocles' *Antigone*, Zerilli castigates each author for speaking in predetermined language. Elshtain (1982) had turned the powerful figure of Antigone into the expression of familial concern within the context of the city. Dietz (1985) preferred to see Antigone in her role as citizen concerned about the public welfare of Thebes. Calling on the language of the French feminist Luce Irigaray (but echoing the concerns I shall discuss below that Quentin Skinner has raised about imposing our own paradigms on the thought of the authors of the past), Zerilli raises the problem: "If Elshtain and Dietz translate, finally, the foreign, dissonant voice of Antigone into the more familiar, reassuring voice of mothers and/or citizens, it is because their readings have been 'framed,' so to speak, by the larger political conversations: a 'perennial' dialogue which requires that the authors articulate feminist politics by situating themselves in relation to the accepted terms of debate (public/private), and by defending a particular reading of canonical texts" (1991, 257). She proposes a new strategy of "mimesis" as a means of transcending "discourse which now admits women as conversants but whose unspoken symbolic terms require that, when women speak, they continue to disguise themselves as men and deny their origins in the house" (1991, 259).

Zerilli, by introducing these challenges to the study of texts, brings not only the deconstructive language of our literary siblings to the discussion; she raises as well the challenge first popularly posed by Carol Gilligan's 1982 book, *In A Different Voice*, the challenge of whether males and females speak differently on moral issues. Though a whole industry has emerged in the social science literature addressing the adequacy or

inadequacy of Gilligan's studies of young men and women, the broader issue that was raised forces readers of texts to question whether the gender of the author -- and perhaps even the reader -- determines the way in which that text can speak and the way in which it will be used. When Zerilli asks whether female scholars working in the field of the history of political thought are forced, as she puts it, to "cross dress," to talk in masculine language filled with "masculine images" which enslaves rather than liberates women, she is engaging in the broader debate about whether political theory is universal or particularized, or in Zerilli's and by extension Gilligan's view gendered, whether women authors reflecting on the principles of political life perceive those principles differently from men and whether women caught up in exploring the ideas of male authors become themselves the exponents of male values and the articulators of male perspectives.

The challenge posed is one that must be answered differently by the two major approaches I identified above and discuss below. If a text is particularized -- located in the gender of the reader or the author or in historical or linguistic space -- it will be lost as the speaker of a universal truth or as the object of commentaries through which we can educate ourselves and others. It will "sink into the landscape," in Zerilli's view, of body or of gender, as well as of language and historical circumstance. If the texts are to be read as universal educators, as the "instrumental approach" suggests, then they must abstract from the peculiar qualities of the author (and the reader) -- be they of historical place, gender, or psychological make-up. Feminist theory, drawing on what has come to be part of the post-modern discourse, has helped to clarify this opposition, making us confront the degree to which we need to see a text as embodied or abstracted from particularity. It is an opposition of underlying epistemological and methodological principles that needs to be remembered for the following discussion.

The "Instrumental" Approach

What I shall call the instrumental approach, without the pejorative overtone implicit in Gunnell's language, is captured in the language of the Preface of the first edition of the Strauss-Cropsey volume and reprinted in the second and third: "The authors and editors have done their best to take political philosophy seriously, assuming throughout that the teachings of the great political philosophers are important not only historically...that the questions raised by the political philosophers of the past are alive in our own society" (1987, xiii). Jacob Klein observed in the preface to his

classic commentary on Plato's *Meno*, "In the past, for long stretches of time, writing commentaries was a way of expounding the truth. It may still be that" (1965, 3). This is not so much "hiding behind the text" (a not infrequent assessment of such commentaries) as allowing for reflection on the text to raise questions and pose possible answers that neither scholar nor reader may have asked before. The text, as an object, becomes the impetus to reflection, the spur to curiosity, and the commentary becomes the report of where that reflection and curiosity has led, as well as a guide to others about what they can learn from such a reading. The tradition of such writing is well rooted in a past filled with Biblical commmentaries; it is clearly secularized in the more recent traditions, but the expectation that commentaries can reveal important truths remains at the heart of most such commentaries today, though unfortunately few works can ever reach the depth of analysis that Klein achieved in his slim volume.

Klein, however, along with Strauss, was exceptional for making such claims in books written 20 or so years ago. The language that I will suggest is so prevalent today proclaiming the usefulness of texts for learning truths about politics does not fill the prefaces of some of the finest work in political theory from the period of the 1960s when positivism and behavioralism may have restrained more open claims, though such assumptions may have been implicit. Michael Walzer, for instance, modestly presents his classic *The Revolution of the Saints* as "a supplement [to] other interpretations of seventeenth century history" (1965, vii). He adds, "My only object is to make Puritan radicalism, so unattractive to my contemporaries, humanly comprehensible" (p. ix). It is we who must recognize the profound insights into the nature of religious movements, indeed all movements that entail self-sacrifice, inherent in his analysis. Though Judith Shklar's study of Rousseau, *Men and Citizens: A Study of Rousseau's Social Theory*, from 1969 has much to say about the psychological foundations of political life, she avoids any introductory assertions about "lessons" or "truths" and leaves it simply at: "Since the title of this book announces its contents quite accurately, I shall not detain the reader with any further explanations" (1969, vii). It is only in the brilliant postscript that she allows herself to reflect on why write such a commentary in the first place and why we may choose "to read and to respond to [Rousseau, Montesquieu, Machiavelli] and to the even more distant Plato and Aristotle with a vigor that few other authors have been able to arouse. In fact, they educate us and that is why they are interpreted and re-interpreted" (p. 218). Today, such language would be prominently and forcefully articulated at the beginning of any such book rather than appended as an apparent after-thought.[10] Joseph Hamburger's study of

Intellectuals in Politics: John Stuart Mill and the Philosophical Radicals focuses on the "ideas the Philosophical Radicals thought relevant to their activities as politicians" (1965, vii) and in tracing through the political odyssey of their principles, he does not ask us to assess or learn from those arguments as much as from the success and failures of political philosophy brought to the political arena. Moving even to books of the late 1970s we find classic works such as Julian Franklin's book on *John Locke and the Theory of Sovereignty: Mixed Monarchy and the Rights to Resistance in the Political Thought of the English Revolution* which begins with the claim only to describe and explain the "transformation in the theory of sovereignty which entered the modern tradition via Locke" (1978, ix). In giving this explanation, he turns attention to an author not part of the canon, George Lawson, whose work Franklin is eager to resurrect for its argument asserting the reversion of power to the people upon the dissolution of government. The book entails detective work, but in its praise for Lawson it also indicates Franklin's own interest in the power of radical democratic theory.

A canvass of the many books of commentary on the texts of the "constructed" and expanded core written by political theorists over the last decade frequently reveals a willingness to articulate strikingly different expectations about what either textual commentary or historical research and detective work will reveal.[11] There is now the open assertion that commentary leads to truth, whether the authors identify themselves with the "teachings" of Strauss or not, and that history can lead to a profound understanding of the possibilities or limits of our own political situations. Peter Euben, for example, in *The Tragedy of Political Theory: The Road Not Taken* (1990), a book that primarily works from ancient Greek texts, tragedies, and Platonic dialogues, begins by noting that perhaps because of Allan Bloom's best-selling book and I.F. Stone's *The Trial of Socrates* (1988) "issues central to our identity as a nation -- the place of education in a democratic polity...the question of moral relativism and the status of knowledge...are deliberated in terms of Socrates' death and Plato's *Republic*"; he goes further: "The principal object of this book is to consider Greek tragedy insofar as it provides a preface for understanding classical political theory and to suggest that the tragedians and those theorists provide in turn a ground for contemporary theorizing" (1990, 4). In contrast to any Straussian reading of the texts he studies, Euben finds in the classical authors the critical questioning of a culture's reifications, the theoretical awareness of the dangers of theorizing which "subjugat[es] or marginaliz[es] parts of the self or others or history" (1990, 304), all of which perspectives certainly derive more from Foucault than from Strauss. Thus, Plato's *Republic*, Thucydides'

History, Euripides' *Bacchae* teach of the tragic recognition that is so much a part of our contemporary world: the certainties of the universal truths we so desperately desire may lead to indifference "to the particularities of time, place and person" (1990, 270). There are lessons to be learned, though certainly not Strauss's.

Stephen G. Salkever's *Finding the Mean: Theory and Practice in Aristotelian Political Philosophy* (1991) works largely through analyses of Aristotelian texts. The commentary he offers suggests "that Aristotelian theorizing can produce a more attractive and useful picture of modern liberal democracy -- its problems and its possibilities -- than those yielded by classical republicanism or individualistic democratic theories." Salkever returns to the Aristotelian conceptual structure because "it allows us to overcome our unhappy preoccupation with the distinction between public and private realms." The case he wishes to make is that "Aristotelian practical philosophy [is] a source of education...for a better understanding of ourselves as moderns and liberals" (1991, 8). Aristotle then becomes the guide to the re-examination of the place of virtue in a liberal democracy without the burden of republicanism. Or Thucydides' History in Steven Forde's *The Ambition to Rule: Alcibiades and the Politics of Imperialism in Thucydides* (1989) has an "educational task," namely to show citizens similar to the law-abiding, pious Athenian general Nicias "the inadequacies of some of their most cherished beliefs" (1989, 10), the profound contradiction between nature and politics, the contradiction between human virtue and morality and human nature and the political community. Forde's study of how Athens depends on Alcibiades becomes a discourse on a democratic regime's dependence on anti-democratic principles and frightens us into a recognition of the victories that may destroy us.

The "instrumental" approach is not, by any means, limited to those writing on the ancient Greek authors.[12] Indeed, hostility to the Greek philosophers explicitly informs some of the scholarship in this mold. Stephen Holmes's early essay worried precisely about the educative role that a return to Greek political theory might pose for modern liberal, highly differentiated societies. His essay "Aristippus in and out of Athens" published in the 1979 volume of the *APSR*, albeit overdrawn and a bit cranky, fretted about the normative power and appeal of the classical Greek authors as presented by Arendt and especially Strauss. The argument that if we allow the Greek texts to be our teachers, we face the worst sort of tyranny lies at the heart of Holmes's concern about relying on authors writing in a society so profoundly alien to our own. One is not just studying an historical artifact when one reads

Aristotle's *Politics*, Holmes suggested, or the interesting thoughts of someone who happens to have been particularly bright and perceptive about political matters. One is being educated in how to think about, and especially how to evaluate, the political world in which we live. This is a serious activity. The polemical tone of Holmes's essay is almost necessitated by the seriousness of the threat he envisions. Sabine's texts require no such polemicism.[13] In Holmes's subsequent book on Benjamin Constant, he makes clear that he writes about this thinker not only because of "the subtlety and sheer intelligence of Constant's thinking about modern society and the kind of freedom it makes possible," but because Constant's insights "suggest a major re-assessment of the categories that still dominate the debate about liberalism" (1984, 1-2). In particular, in contrast to his earlier assessment of the Greek authors, "Constant's political theory cannot be considered entirely passe" and we ought to take "Constant's position seriously even today "since his articulation of the key roles of political deceit and truth, of governmental neutrality, of public and private can serve as an alternative to both communitarian and anti-political ideals" (1984, 260).

Holmes uses his analysis of Constant to address the contemporary controversy in the wider field of political theory (and indeed in the public discourse in numerous widely read journals) between so-called liberals and so-called communitarians that characterizes much of the recent works on the great and sometimes lesser texts. One might see such writing as simply appeals to authority: Plato supports this and therefore (depending on our attitude towards Plato) we should (or should not) support that view too. Though this sort of argument may be characteristic of lesser studies, it does not capture the way in which the texts are used by those more skilled in analysis and commentary. The claim is not simply to give greater weight to one's own argument, but to help in analyzing the consequences and educating in the questions raised by the communitarian challenge launched against the liberals. One thinks here, for example, of Nancy L. Rosenblum's *Another Liberalism: Romanticism and the Reconstruction of Liberal Theory* (1987). Though hardly a close study of or commentary on text, Rosenblum draws on the arguments and insights primarily of nineteenth century European authors to argue for a "reconstructed liberalism" that acknowledges "historical individuals" and allows for the "affective, personal, and expressive" (1987, 3-4). Having introduced romanticism into liberalism and arguing that such an integration is possible without transforming liberalism into communitarianism, Rosenblum admits that her Romantic liberalism speaks to needs that are "historically contingent and not universal" (1987, 190). Here truths from textual

study need not be true across time and space, but their contingency makes them no less significant, as Rosenblum sees it, for "justify[ing] political life and reconcil[ing] men and women to it" (1987, 190).

While Holmes and Rosenblum have explored the meaning of liberalism through commentaries on texts from the sixteenth to nineteenth centuries, defenders of a more communitarian vision of the political world or of one which encourages political participation and engagement in the public realm have turned to such authors as Aristotle or Rousseau to present "truths" about the possibilities of politics. Alasdair MacIntyre's *After Virtue* (1981) and Benjamin Barber's *Strong Democracy* (1984) are examples here. It took an article such as that of Bernard Yack's (1985) to suggest that Aristotle's polis was hardly the place where a seeker of community should turn or where "political friendship shares the character of personal intimacy" (1985, 104). Yack's commentary, beyond correcting a widespread misconception of Aristotle's political thought, warns about the tendency of "contemporary political theorists…to look to Aristotelian political concepts for a counterimage to liberalism's image of political society" (1985, 109). The correction by Yack is necessary precisely because he sees the inadequate use of texts for teaching values. If we are to learn from Aristotle, then we must read him for what he says, not for what we may want him to say. Commentaries must be truly commentaries and recasting an author to gives one's own view of an issue is merely to call forth witnesses, not to take the opportunity to engage in conversations such as Strauss enjoins us to do. The challenge that historians, literary theorists, feminist theorists, pose is whether such conversations are possible if readers are the creators of their texts or if the texts are dependent on the particularized gender or historical location of their authors or if the texts themselves enslave.

Use of textual analysis as a way of ferreting out the truth and of educating ourselves and others is hardly new. It extends at least as far back as the Platonic interpretations of the Homeric poems. But the explicitly didactic role of explications and textual readings in recently published volumes suggests both why political theory has been caught up in the so-called battle of the books or the crisis of the canon and why the behavioral and positivist attacks so prominent two decades ago appear today more quaint than threatening. With the demise of positivism and the demands for verification as the only philosophic stance for the human sciences, with the rejuvenation of normative discourse in a society concerned with the dangers of an unleashed science, abstraction from evaluative questions no longer can characterize the entire discipline. While social sciences have mostly moderated earlier claims of scientific precision and have increasingly recognized the more subjective nature of the categories employed, political scientists in general and political theorists in particular are no longer willing to adopt uncritically the distinction of fact and value that controlled the social sciences for several generations and certainly did so when Sabine was writing his influential volume. Political theorists can now turn to texts for normative purposes as these texts are recognized as helping us to clarify our understandings of the good and the bad, the just and the unjust, the beautiful and the ugly.

The threat to this normative approach to political theory comes not from the exponents of a value-free social science as it did two decades ago, but from those who deny that the "texts of the canon" can be read normatively without commentators imposing their own views and paradigms, i.e., that we can ever be in a position to learn from these texts freed from the encrustation of our personal, social, political, and gendered histories. Rousseau in his search to learn who we are by nature had suggested we remember the statue of the sea god Glaucus which could barely be seen under all the disfigurements that seas and storms had brought to it over time. If we are, indeed, so laden with our history, commentaries cannot be "a way of expounding the truth" as Klein had suggested, but the simple expression of personal values imported back to the text commented upon. Insofar as we deny texts the capacity to educate and to commentary the search for truth, political theory reduces to either a subspecies of history where we engage in asking only what the questions were and deny that we can assess the status of those questions, much less the answers given, or it becomes a subspecies of certain forms of literary analysis and feminist theory where the text simply disappears and the reader, the subject, the centered self, replaces the author and all investigation of truth about politics -- or anything else -- becomes meaningless. Should this occur, the intense battles of an earlier generation when political theory confronted political science would fade not because of science's victory, but because of theory's withdrawal from the battle.

The "Historical" Approach: Critique, Transformation -- and Secession?

Texts in Context

Despite Sabine's introduction of the subfield of the history of political thought to the discipline of political science, the study of political theory remained part of a much larger and more ancient tradition of intellectual history. Studies of particular authors who wrote on political topics of their own time that may have had signficance for contemporary times; studies of concepts such as natural law, or representation, or justice that traced terms across the centuries; studies of the influence of one author upon another or of who said what first; all these filled the landscape of political theory. Interpretations were offered; clarifications of meaning identified; sequences of ideas followed. This tradition found a home in both history and political science departments. In the latter, behavioralism, focussing on current practices rather than institutions or the historical conditions that may have given rise to those practices, tolerated the history of political thought largely because of tradition. But it remained isolated, of little more than antiquarian interest giving a touch of literacy and sophistication to an article or essay, but hardly any significance to work in the discipline at large.

All such work, however, became the object of attack by what we may now call the "Cambridge School" or those who advocate the study of "ideas in context."[14] Cambridge University Press has recently embarked on a publication series called simply "Ideas in Context," edited by Richard Rorty, J.B. Schneewind, and Quentin Skinner. The policy statement at the front of the first volume articulates concisely the perspective of this school: "The books in this series will discuss the emergence of intellectual traditions....The procedures, aims, and vocabularies that were generated will be set in the context of the alternatives available within the contemporary framework of ideas and institutions....it is hoped that a new picture will form of the development of ideas in their concrete contexts" (Rorty et al. 1984, ii). We have here the definition of the new "historical" approach to texts, whether of political theory or not.

At an earlier time, such language about "ideas in context" would have evoked images of a Marxist contextualism that often finds in the classic texts an ideological content deriving from contemporary sociological, economic and political conditions -- and in a few books, such as those of Neal Wood, still does. Wood's Marxist contextual approach controls the 1978 book he wrote with Ellen Meiskins Wood, *Class Ideology and Ancient Political Theory*, a work which endeavors to put Socrates, Plato, and Aristotle into their social contexts and claims: "Their political thought can be conceived as the supreme intellectual expression of the increasing class consciousness of the aristocracy during the fourth century" (1978, 3).[15] Wood's Marxist contextualism, however, has not had the widespread impact of the new contextualism of the Cambridge School.[16] The new contextualism, as Wood recognizes and criticizes, is that of language and of agency drawing from what has been generally called the "linguistic turn" of philosophy during the last half century. While the work of the historian John Pocock brought to the field of political theory the core principles at the base of the new contextual approach (Pocock 1962), it was Quentin Skinner's 1969 essay "Meaning and Understanding in the History of Ideas" that became the flagship statement calling for scholars "attempt[ing] to arrive at an understanding of the work" (1988, 29)[17] to embed a philosophical text in the discursive context of the age in which it was written.[18] Dismissing studies whose "whole point is conceived in terms of recovering the 'timeless questions and answers' posed in the 'great books' and so of demonstrating their continuing relevance'" (1988a, 30) Skinner argues that we must cast off the controlling paradigms of our own age which are inappropriately applied to the thought of the past and search instead for what, borrowing from J.L. Austin, he calls in the early essay, the "illocutionary force" of any text, i.e., the intention of the author writing such a text, something that can only be derived from a "delineat[ion of] the whole range of communication which could have been conventionally performed on the given occasion by the utterance" (1988a, 63-64). Such an approach can at most give us insight not into perennial questions, much less perennial truths, but rather into the "essential variety of viable moral assumptions and political commitments" (1988a, 67).

While this was a tentative first statement, more destructive with its arrows cast at virtually all previous work in the history of ideas (of which the history of political thought was but a part) than constructive, twenty years have brought its share of adamant adherents as well as critics. More significantly, though, there has been a refinement that sets the principles of this approach into a larger theoretical framework that addresses the role of language in the construction of our political environment. Skinner has moved to what he himself admits is a "less polemical statement of the central claims" found in his earlier "avowedly polemical essays" (1974, 278, 279) and acknowledges an interest in "the classic texts [as] worthy of study in themselves," (p. 279) though on the next page he worries about the "distorting perspective" they bring to our study of history. In language reminiscent of Sabine's dictum of including whoever said something interesting, Skinner comments: "To speak of a text as a classic is to imply that there may be special reasons for wishing to understand it" (p. 281). One cannot make that judgment, he suggests, prior to having ascertained the intention and context. In language that he himself does not use, but which we often hear from colleagues in the humanities, to judge a text as a classic is "to privilege" it without the certainty that it deserves that privilege. Or to borrow the image of the sacred geese on the Roman acropolis from the Dedicatory Epistle of *Leviathan*, we

study texts not because they are they, but because they are there.

Skinner comes to question his earlier use of Austin's phrase "illocutionary force" by recognizing the complexity of trying to assign intentions on the basis of words. He claims (to cite again the prevailing jargon) that we need to ask what is the range of speech acts that can standardly be performed by a given writer when he makes use of a given set of concepts and terms (p. 289). With this perspective Skinner now claims to introduce the possibility of change and revolutionary force to the texts he assesses, always reminding us, though, of the necessity that "Every revolutionary is...obliged to march backward into battle. To legitimate his behavior, he is committed to showing that it can be described in such a way that those who currently disapprove of it can somehow be brought to see that they ought to withhold this disapproval after all" (p. 296). Skinner seems to be suggesting that somehow the author can, after all, rise above language as a restraint, but that to effect change, the speaker must speak in language understood by the listeners of his times.

The initial revision of his argument cited in the previous paragraph appeared in the 1974 volume of *Political Theory* which featured a symposium on Skinner's methodology. The two commentators included in the symposium were profoundly sympathetic to Skinner's contextualist approach, but complain that Skinner is too limited in his understanding of context. Jonathan M. Weiner takes on Skinner's innovative early work on Hobbes in which Skinner had argued that Hobbes was far less original or outside of common discourse than usually acknowledged and that he was indeed a participant in a particular intellectual circle where his political ideas were hardly radical (Skinner 1966). Skinner had thus suggested that Hobbes's ideas -- like them or not -- were simply not as offensive to his own generation as previous scholars had thought. Weiner's concern was with the limited nature of Skinner's "context," in particular that it avoided the social and the political, and that by understanding context only in terms of ideas Skinner may not provide an adequate basis for assessing the radical nature of Hobbes's thought. Gordon Schochet in his turn raised two separate questions: whether Skinner's goals of total immersion can ever be achieved and whether Skinner's assertion that the "tradition" is simply artificially constructed means that we cannot tell the difference between a greater and lesser work. This is a point to which I will return below.

By 1988 James Tully was able to collect from a wide selection of published criticisms a series of highly provocative and thoughtful essays on Skinner's method in the Polity Press volume *Meaning and Context: Quentin Skinner and His Critics*. The epigraph for the volume comes from Wittgenstein's *Culture and Value* and captures the essence of Skinner's method: "Words are deeds." Though Skinner's essays in this volume build on the philosophic and literary examinations of such terms as "meaning" and "interpretation," he reiterates his commitment to focus on "not just the issues or themes with which the text is concerned" (1988a, 77), but to shift the emphasis off the "discussion of the idea of the text as an autonomous object, and on to the idea of the text as an object linked to its creator, and thus on to a discussion of what its creator may have been doing in creating it" (1988a, 78). After reprinting the most significant of Skinner's methodological essays, Tully prints the criticisms that confront Skinner with questions about how intent can be identified when the "real reasons" of an individual or a group are hardly accessible (Tully 1988), about whether his methods "render history gratuitously barren" (Femia 1988, 174), or whether Skinner has turned intellectual history into the history of ideologies and burdened and restrained it with excessive philosophical baggage (Minogue 1988).

Skinner defends himself in the final chapter of Tully's volume against the critiques printed in the volume and those published elsewhere in part by arguing again that the history of thought "should be viewed not as a series of attempts to answer a canonical set of questions, but as a sequence of episodes in which the questions as well as the answers have frequently changed" (1988, 235). The goal of recovering the meaning of a text itself, he asserts, must be rejected "in the name of the need to recover, at the same time, what the author of the text may have meant by it" (1988b, 282). In particular, he now responds to the "many critics" who have accused him of relativism, an accusation he rejects since he claims not to be interested in truth anyway: "I have merely observed that the question of what it may be rational to hold true can vary with the totality of one's beliefs. I never put forward the reckless and completely different thesis that truth itself can vary in the same way" (1988b, 256). Most significantly, at the end of his essay, he defends himself against accusations that his own work is motivated purely by antiquarian interests, telling us that the "alien character" of the beliefs of those whose ideas he studies "constitutes their 'relevance'." Reflecting on such alternative possibilities, "we provide ourselves with one of the best means of preventing our current moral and political theories from degenerating into uncritically accepted ideologies." His studies, he tells us, enable us to strengthen "our present beliefs by way of testing them against alternative possiblities, or else improving them if we come to recognize that the alternatives are both possible and desirable" (1988b, 287).

The language here, surprisingly, almost seems to recall Strauss's plea that we read with seriousness the texts of old so that we may see ourselves and the possible limits of our own beliefs. For Strauss "constant intercourse with the greatest minds...is...a training in boldness....the boldness implied in the resolve to regard the accepted views as mere opinions, or to regard the average opinions as extreme opinions which are at least as likely to be wrong as the most strange or the least popular opinions....Liberal education supplies us with experience in things beautiful" (1989b, 8). One has no doubt that Skinner would not particularly care to be associated with Strauss in this fashion and the differences between the two perspectives certainly cannot be denied. But the conversation that Strauss seeks is there in Skinner's most recent claim as he tries to move beyond historicism and antiquarianism. The profound difference, though, lies in that Strauss seriously expects the texts and the conversations they provoke to help in the recovery of the "beautiful," while Skinner poses this as only the faintest of possibilities and perhaps only to assure his readers of the relevance of his studies against accusations of mere antiquarianism. It says much about the more recent role of the history of political thought that Sabine would never even have felt the need to answer such concerns.

Amidst all the methodological essays expounding the need to study meaning in the context of authorial intent, Skinner has produced his two-volume work *Foundations of Modern Political Thought* (1978). The work carries out in part the promise to "surround these classic texts with their appropriate ideological context" as Skinner searches for the origins of the modern concept of the state. Nevertheless, while detailed summaries of the content of minor works are a large part of the study, these minor texts continue to circulate around just those major authors familiar to those who study the canon that has become traditional over the last five decades. The texts may begin to sink into the landscape of discourse, but they never disappear and we never lose sight of the text or the author. Indeed, on almost every page we learn of a text that may be of wide interest to us for more than its discursive content. Skinner's work, though, is not without its own problems of interpretations. Tarcov (1982) in his review of the treatment of Machiavelli in Skinner's first volume gives one of the numerous critiques evoked by the reading of texts Skinner offers. For Tarcov, Skinner takes Machiavelli too readily at his word, sees him as engaging only with his contemporaries and not with the political philosophers of the past; thus, by setting Machiavelli only in the context of his own times, Skinner fails to recognize the equivocations and paradoxes in the texts. The contextual method, as Tarcov analyses it, leaves the writing as timely only for the writers' own time and not for ours. Skinner thus may fail to recognize what may be Machiavelli's intention or the true "illocutionary force" of his writings: to speak past his time and to us.

Apart from Skinner's and Pocock's work there are few examples of how all the methodological discourse about authorial intent and textual meaning affects the practice of study of texts. Strauss's approach to political theory, at least two academic generations older than the Cambridge School, has spawned an ever increasing number of works that pay homage to his methods of analysis and his philosophic concerns, revealing both the benefits of the careful and imaginative use of his approach as well as the profound defects of its simplistic application. We must await a comparable set of works before we can assess the success of the Cambridge School's approach and its potential contributions to political theory -- or its abstraction and secession from the enterprise of political theory. The evidence on this will emerge from the "Ideas in Context" series, the first volume of which was yet another collection of largely methodological essays by philosophers, historians, and political theorists about the possibilities of a history of ideas (Rorty et al. 1984). The second volume, *Virtue, Commerce, and History*, is primarily a compilation of Pocock's essays published from 1976-82 (1985). With regard to issues of direct concern to political theorists, there is only Pocock's book and David Lieberman's *The Province of Legislation Determined: Legal Theory in Eighteenth Century Britain* (1989). We are left to wonder, however, about the degree to which these studies, wonderfully intriguing with their detailed presentations of political language at work, help us address the questions political theorists address, i.e., the degree to which they will ever allow us to transcend the level of historical curiosity despite the methodological baggage. The richness of the works that have been written is truly impressive and the range of scholarship wide. Nevertheless, the methodological essays may raise the more theoretically interesting questions about the political power of language, its control and creation of environments, while that same methodology tells us that the vast scholarly endeavors cannot lead to theoretically interesting questions precisely because of their embeddedness in time and place.

Despite the ambivalence expressed in Skinner's response to Schochet's 1974 question about how to identify greater or lesser works, Skinner is part of an editorial team including Raymond Geuss and Richard Tuck that is editing the "Cambridge Texts in the History of Politics" from the Cambridge University Press. While the "Ideas in Context" series immerses the texts in the linguistic landscape, the "Cambridge Texts in the History of Political Thought" is a much more active and ultimately probably more important endeavor, making available to scholars and students a wide variety of "the most important texts required for understanding the history of political thought." The advertisement for the series does indicate that the "scholarship of the present generation has greatly expanded our sense of the range of authors indispensable for such an understanding" and that the series will include "a number of less well-known works, in particular those needed to establish the intellectual contexts that in turn help to make sense of the major texts;" so far, the series is giving us at a steady pace fresh, accessible, well-bound paperback editions of a large number of previously difficult to acquire, but key texts of "canonical" authors edited by top-flight scholars.

In an earlier article (1988) I made note of a Committee of Political Theorists constituted by the American Political Science Association that met in Washington in 1943 to discuss the state of political theory. That committee concluded that despite "broad differences" among political theorists about the principles and ontological foundations necessary for the study of political science, the committee as a whole was unified in its conclusions that the profession as a whole must continue to study Plato, Aristotle, Augustine, Cicero, and scores of others because "they make us conscious of the content of our own minds" (1944, 730). The specific, though rather mundane, concern that emerged from the meeting of these political theorists was the lack of current editions of the great thinkers such as Marsilius, Bodin, and Sidney for both teaching and scholarship. This was a problem to be remedied once the war ended. Now, almost 50 years later, that problem is finally being addressed most significantly by the Cambridge series (and, we must note, by the publications series of the Liberty Fund, whose volumes are not only well produced and well bound, as are the Cambridge University Press volumes, but also deliciously inexpensive).[19] Access to these texts should in fact do much to bolster the status of the texts. There almost seems something contradictory between the two Cambridge series, but perhaps the series of texts indicates, in fact, that the texts we use for reflecting on politics will hardly slide into the landscape and will instead remain at the core of the study of political theory, whether one adheres to the instrumental approach or not.

Variations on Texts in Context

John Dunn, identified by Richter, for example, as part of the Cambridge School (1986, 620), certainly an advocate of the principal methodological approaches of that school and included in compilations of scholarly work of that group, is willing to go beyond the recovery of the discursive meaning to claim that his scholarship will help in the badly needed "rethinking" of political theory. Modern political theory requires this rethinking, Dunn claims, "because it is philosophically so feeble and politically so maladroit," a condition he describes as "becoming increasingly hazardous both for particular human collectivities and for the species as a whole" (1985, 1). His studies of Locke are to aid modestly in reversing this trend by exploring the source and the role of trust in Locke's political thought. While he finds that source in the "simple frame of Puritan values which Locke inherited from his father," Dunn goes further to claim "there is simply no conceptual truth in political theory more fundamental than the truth that men trust in what they can" (1985, 33). Indeed, in his essay comparing Locke, Hume, and Smith he recognizes in Locke's anguish about the possiblity of rationality without theocentricism that Locke points us to "an anguish which we still have coming to us." "It has taken us nearly three centuries to catch up with him" (1985, 67). However much Dunn may embed his Locke in his discursive history, Dunn still turns to Locke for the truths he may tell us about ourselves, our political possibilities and limits. The contradiction between text as educator and text as historical construct and datum seems to fade here as commentary turns into forewarning.

Don Herzog, who is not at all a part of the "Ideas in Context" perspective and who spends little time engaging in methodological debates, does illustrate in his *Happy Slaves: A Critique of Consent Theory* (1989) how the study of texts, of social history, of political discourse can all help us to reflect on the construction of some of the critical concepts of political theory, in his case, consent. His work emphatically denies the possibility of discovering truths in the texts we read, but he reads the texts as suggesting creative solutions to the political and social problems of the time in which they were written. Thus, he discovers in the text's confrontation with political circumstances aids in puzzling through the questions with which a political theorist must deal. Thus, for example, his reading of Hobbes ignores (for the most part, at least) the standard reconstructions of Hobbes's thought as self-interest properly understood leading to civil society; instead he finds that Hobbes's concern is to generate a language in which the arguments for disobedience disappear or become incoherent. Rather than searching for a consistency which Herzog asserts is not there, we must recognize that "Hobbes' brilliance lies partly in his ability to step back from political disputes...[H]e asks himself, what conceptual frameworks make these disputes possible? Then he tries to design new frameworks to replace old ones" (1989, 109). The reading of the text here is only part of the endeavor, one chapter out of several which are to explore consent theory, but by embedding the text in the political and

social crises of seventeenth century England, Herzog is able to explicate both Hobbes and consent theory from the novel perspective which focuses on challenges to reasons not to obey rather than on reasons for obedience. The text here is neither an oracle of truth nor another datum in an historical tale, but a powerful prod to reflection on a key political concept.

Concepts in Context

Herzog's study of consent theory in Hobbes draws on the concept of consent in the seventeenth century, but Herzog is not interested in tracing the history of the concept; rather he wants to puzzle through the concept itself. A concern with conceptual history that may or may not lead to conceptual clarification for our own time, though, is re-emerging especially among a community of German scholars under the leadership of Reinhart Koselleck who is supervising the production of a multi-authored, multi-volume resource tracing the historical development of political concepts in Germany.[20] Melvin Richter in a series of articles (1986, 1990) has attempted to alert English and American scholars to the significance of this major cooperative endeavor that "provide[s] synchronic analyses of language, situation, and time, as well as diachronic analyses of continuity, alteration, and innovation in these political vocabularies" (1990, 42), and to suggest a possible compatibilty between the approaches of the Cambridge School and the German conceptual historians. Distinctive about this work in Germany is the project's concern with placing concepts, rather than texts, in context. While analytic and ordinary language philosophy had illustrated the inadequacy of certain political concepts by looking at them in their use in conversations, the German scholars see the concepts not only in the present; they are studied as well in their move across time. In this endeavor, the interpretive activity is less in the texts than in the language of the period and the social history under examination. Thus, we find attention to dictionaries, encyclopaedias, handbooks, and thesauri (Richter 1990, 47). Insofar as this project studies the language of politics, the questions that arise about intentions and illocutionary force characteristic of the Cambridge School or about truth and moral education that motivates Strauss and his students cannot and do not surface. Rather, as Koselleck himself puts it: "Concepts do not only teach us the uniqueness of past meanings but also contain the structural possibilities, treat the concatenations of difference, which are not detectable in the historical flow of events....It is only concepts that demonstrate persistence, repeatable applicability, and empirical validity...which indicate that a once 'real' history can today appear generally possible" (1985, 90).

Nevertheless, Richter sees this scholarly endeavor as a valuable, but largely unrecognized, resource for scholarship in the history of political thought: "Historians concerned with political theory written in English might well consider the feasiblity of an analogous enterprise...of such a conceptual history of political concepts in English. [This would offer] the possibility of engaging in a comparative history of leading concepts in political theory written in English, French, and German" (1986, 634). In asking Anglophones to follow the example of the German scholars, Richter envisions an integration of the methodologies of the German project and the interests of John Pocock and Quentin Skinner, or as he puts it: "How compatible are these German and the Anglophone modes of treating political language by rigorously historical methods." The compatibility lies in the benefit the Anglophones would get from the German method of "non-reductive use of social history" and recognizing units larger than the individual theorist or school of thought, while the Germans would learn from the Anglophones the importance of the issues raised about "political thought and theorizing as forms of linguistic action" (1990, 69). In proposing this mutual education, Richter appears to forget the "text." While Strauss and Skinner certainly approach texts in a diametrically opposed fashion, they still acknowledge the primacy of the text as the window through which they discover their respective goals; for the German school, the text becomes just one of many resources for discovery of the conceptual history.[21] The text is neither an actor as in Skinner's understanding, nor a conversational partner who will lead us to question and grow morally and philosophically as in Strauss's. The text becomes only datum.[22]

Terence Ball, nevertheless, tries to follow through on Richter's plea in his book *Transforming Political Discourse* (1988) where he makes an effort to integrate all three of the above approaches, without fully acknowledging the theoretical oppositions. Arguing that our "political discourses help to transform us making us who and what we are as political agents and citizens...[A]s the concepts constitutive of our speech change, so do we" (1988, ix), he suggests the power of language to control us. In contrast to Strauss here, the language does not illuminate or reveal truths freeing us from accepted opinions, nor does it enable us to reflect more deeply on the puzzles of political concepts. Rather, we become in Ball's argument creatures of our own language instead of its creators. For precisely this reason he is interested in the transformation of language and applauds the fact that, "[a] static and ahistorical view is at last giving way among Anglo-American philosophers to a more historical approach to the study of language and in particular the language of political theory" (1988, 6).

Skinner's and Pocock's approach presents a host of challenges to political theory if it is to remain a part of political science. If the study of the text is simply to learn of authorial intention, does it give us insight into political phenomena? Does it aid us in the exploration of the normative goals of the political communities? The approach is explicitly hostile to the normative concerns of political theory since the texts give no lessons about good and bad, just and unjust, only about the way such language may be used by authors. Meaning is not plumbed for truth, but for intent, and the question may rightly be raised about what this has to say to political scientists. Ashcraft's work (1986), which goes beyond authorial intent alone, though that is very much part of his endeavor, to the exploration of political movements and the political theorist as a participant in those movements, goes back to some of the issues that made Walzer's book on the Puritan saint a classic. But without that sensitivity to the potential political consequences of texts and their engagement in the crises of the time, the danger exists that the study of texts as part of discursive contexts will look in upon itself and remain a subfield isolated in history departments away from and not speaking to the concerns of political scientists or political theorists. Strauss's approach, with its numerology and searches for hidden meanings, with its elevation of ancients over moderns, with its fierce challenge to a study of politics he saw as eviscerated by social science, provoked firestorms of controversy and made its presence vividly felt in the discipline for better or worse. Text as historical datum sinking into the landscape allows the political scientist to ignore the normative issues raised by the texts.

The Texts, the Canon, and the Question of Gender

Linda Zerilli's article challenging feminist scholars to dismiss the masculine texts and discourses that imprison us in a traditional world view can help to frame the discussion of the two dominant strands of political theory by questioning the possibility of an abstract truth such as Straussian commentary strives to achieve and by making radical claims about both the text and the reader as enmeshed in time, place, and gender. By even raising these broad methodological questions, Zerilli's article illustrates how significant a transformation has taken place in the study of gender and the history of political thought over the last two decades. When feminist concerns first hit political theory in the 1970s, the goal often was to document the dreadful history of misogynist statements by one male author or another, statements that have served to justify the exclusion of women from the political realm and confine them to the private world of the family. Plato (everywhere except in Book V of the *Republic*), Aristotle, Aquinas, Machiavelli, Rousseau, Hegel all were ready targets for such attacks. The title of a 1979 edited volume, *The Sexism of Social and Political Theory: Women and Reproduction from Plato to Nietzsche*, captures well the tenor of such work.[23] Over the last decade, however, feminist scholars have engaged the texts of the past far more seriously -- both to learn from them and to understand how these texts might give insight into the presumptions underlying the liberal, democratic regimes. While American feminist scholars in political theory have not for the most part changed so much that the texts formerly castigated as oppressive documents responsible for all womankind's suffering are now wholly welcomed, the vitriol is gone. A recognition of the need to learn from these texts and what I have labeled the "instrumental" approach surfaces more often than not; the acknowledgement that introducing questions of gender can yield new insights into our political understanding characterizes much of the recent work in this area. Zerilli's concern is that such scholarship traps women in the vise of masculine political concepts and language.

My own work (Saxonhouse 1980, 1984, 1985, 1986) has aimed at turning attention away from the theorist bashing language of the earlier generations of feminist scholars to show how attention to gender can give us new insights into the arguments of authors from the Greek playwrights to Machiavelli. Those new insights, I argue, enable us to recognize the dangers of exclusion, of demands for uniformity, and the dismissal of the private as relevant for analyses of political life. Thus, the ancient authors may illuminate for us the limitations of our use of gender in our understanding of political life. Similarly, Jean Elshtain in her *Public Man, Private Woman*, the first half of which traces the concepts of public and private through the history of political thought, begins, "To condemn or praise the thinker and ignore the thought is not the way a theoretical mind works" (1981, xv). In urging us to be theoretical, Elshtain urges us to read in order to learn, e.g., from Plato or Aristotle or Augustine, what each one has to say about the relation of the family to city, rather than simply to condemn.

Wendy Brown in her work *Manhood and Politics: A Feminist Reading in Political Theory* (1988), which takes a profoundly different perspective than mine and Elshtain's, notes as well, however, "Certainly it is easy enough to declare every well-known political theorist 'wrong' on the nature of man, manhood, woman, and womanhood. Such a declaration is also uninteresting. Far more interesting and important are the sources, permutations, power, tenacity, and implications of such

formulations" (1988, 14). Brown's work ranges chronologically from ancient Greece through Weber looking not so much for the exclusion of women themselves from politics and their "relegation to subordinate spheres and statuses." This is well-known. Rather, the texts she studies "offer a rich articulation of masculinist public power, order, freedom, and justice" (1988, ix). Accepting this richness of the texts of political theory, she argues that the politics she finds in the great texts over the last two and a half millennia are "gendered" in their alienation of the head (male), which is intellect and reason, from the body (female), which is dirty necessity. She calls for the re-integration of the body into the political world. The texts in the analyses they receive from Brown give us no universal truths; rather, they have been responsible for profoundly disturbing divisions within society and yet "from each [of the texts] we can learn not only what is wrong with a politics rooted in a masculine tradition, but what is compelling about it such that it calls for transformation rather than thoroughgoing condemnation" (1988, 7). Brown's plea for the re-gendering of politics by giving it a "feminine" body may obfuscate a need we have to remove from our discourse the language that gives genders to such concepts, but her argument forces us to return to texts and their language, to re-think our use of gender-laden terms. In Zerilli's understanding, however, Brown is still captured by the masculine discourse, relying on male texts to set the agenda for her reformed politics.

In the mode of studying male authors from the perspective of gender, not to condemn but to learn, Hanna Pitkin (1984) offers an extensive analysis of Machiavelli's texts since, as she puts it, "For me, thinking about politics and thinking about Machiavelli have become interconnected enterprises, each illuminating and obscuring the other" (1984, 3). She goes on to describe the "dual intent" of her book making clear her own adherence to the instrumental approach, despite the gender and misogyny of Machiavelli. Her book is to address two issues: "The narrowly specific one of interpreting a particular thinker on the basis of a body of texts and the more general one of understanding the subject matter those texts address: ourselves as political creatures" (1984, 3). But to engage in this discovery about ourselves as political creatures, Pitkin insists that the category of gender be introduced and that Machiavelli's insights and the lessons he can teach us depend on "his anxiety about being sufficiently masculine." Thus, her study is permeated with the images of women that lace Machiavelli's pages whether in the political treatises or in the comedies or in the histories and biographies. Pitkin's concerns are the profoundly political concerns of citizenship and foundings. But neither, as she learns from her reading and analysis of Machiavelli, can be addressed without attention to gender, as the political concepts (well beyond the dominant one of Fortune as a woman) of public and private, mastery, autonomy all appear to depend on perceptions of the relations between the sexes and in particular the fear of the female. Pitkin's work is among the most profound of this genre, making evident the gender relations previously unrecognized in studies of Machiavelli, and, more importantly, making clear the significance of those relations. Studying the possible sources of Machiavelli's language, she does not allow the language or the texts to "sink into the landscape;" rather, they reveal the possibilities of a collectivity of civic virtue as well as the profound dangers that misogyny may pose to that collectivity and a "best" political world.

Carole Pateman in *The Sexual Contract* also returns to the classic canon of political theory, not so much to learn about ourselves as citizens as does Pitkin, but to uncover gender-related terms so as to reveal the sinister hidden assumptions lurking behind the forcefully articulated arguments of some of the heroes of liberal theory. Writing primarily on the origins of liberalism in the works of the seventeenth century, she discovers there what she describes as the "repressed dimension of contract theory" (1988, ix), namely the sexual contract that is the title of her book. Analyses of the writings of Hobbes, Pufendorf, Locke, and Rousseau suggest that a hidden or unacknowledged conjugal contract, which does not depend on equality, precedes the social contract. This means, according to Pateman, that women are never participants in the social contract and therefore must continue in liberal society as subordinates even as men are free. These studies yield insights into the origins of what she calls modern patriarchy where men remain masters. In her more detailed discussion of Hobbes' role in the construction of modern patriarchy (1989) she carefully glosses Hobbes' text to draw out the inherent difficulties in Hobbes' theories for a contract theory that avoids the assumptions of male domination over the female. Pateman's approach, while reminiscent of the earlier theorist bashing noted above in its condemnation of liberal theorists for not providing for a truly equal and free political community for women, goes further than the early efforts and, whether or not one agrees with her conclusions, shows, as Catherine Zuckert has put it, "how deeply rooted, far-reaching and complex the problems are" (1990b, 662).

To the degree that scholarship concerned with gender has remained wedded to texts in political theory, it has often clustered around particular figures in the canon. By his almost unique willingness to write in favorable terms about the prospect of women as active participants in the political realm, John Stuart Mill has been the focus of considerable scholarship, both favorable and critical, by feminist scholars. When he published his *On the Subjection of Women* in 1869, he became the first major political theorist from the traditional canon since Plato in the *Republic* to welcome the prospect of women as equal participants in the public life of the community. Nevertheless, while Mill's *On Liberty* and *On Representative Government* and *Utilitarianism* all were widely acknowledged as part of the discipline of political theory, important works to be included in any tradition of political theory texts, it was only in the 1970s with the rise of the most recent feminist movement that *On the Subjection of Women* gained recognition as a text worthy of consideration and perhaps as a contribution to our assessment of the role of women in the life of the political community.[24] Though the essay has been subjected to criticism for its failure to carry the principles of equality in the public sphere back into the private sphere (Okin 1979, chap. 9) or its methodological commitment to an "impossibly 'pure' empiricist methodology" (Ring 1985, 28; also 1991, chaps. 3, 4), it was also welcomed as an all too unusual expression of theoretical interest in the public role of women. Mary Lyndon Shanley (1981) found in it a plea for the equality and friendship in marriage that had not previously surfaced within the tradition of political theory.

While Mill and Plato have been the objects of much debate among those interested in gender and political theory, virtually all of the others included in the traditionally constructed canon have been subjected to similar analysis. A recent volume, *Feminist Interpretations and Political Theory*, edited by Shanley and Pateman (1991), reprints a whole series of articles and chapters written mostly during the 1980s on authors from the "canon" -- Plato, Aristotle, Hobbes, Locke, Rousseau, Hegel, Marx. Analyses of these authors are expanded by the introduction of gender into the way that they are interpreted. No uniform or dominant readings characterize these essays as did the essays included in the 1979 *The Sexism of Social and Political Theory* mentioned above. Rather, the implications of an author and his or her arguments for gender issues are extracted and the consequences of ignoring gender explored.

The introduction of gender into the readings of these texts, though, is not necessarily to bring to them questions that they did not address. One could argue that the study of politics necessitates an awareness of gender insofar as politics entails the distinction between public and private (or the denial of such a distinction) and that the liberal forgetfulness of gender, while not necessarily implying Pateman's sexual contract, blinds us to the multitude of issues raised by the public and private spheres and by the questions of difference in a political theory founded on fundamental principles of equality. Jean Elshtain's 1981 book, *Public Man, Private Woman*, set the tone for this investigation of theories articulated in the works we read when she prefaced her own study by commenting: "Although few of the thinkers I shall examine felt compelled to explain or speculate as to why a public-private demarcation had emerged in the first place, each seems under an obligation to justify and to explain the particular division that exists in his own epoch and sustains ongoing social forms, whether to defend it or as a contrast to his own alternatives" (1981, 9). Or Jennifer Ring's more recent work (1991) shows how the epistemological principles of any political theory must confront the challenge of gender and the claims of some feminist writers that gender entails differences in the manner in which each sex is able to know. Are there different ways of knowing and thus different understandings of political life? The analyses of Mill, Hegel, and Marx in Ring's book focussing on whether there is a "gendered" epistemology again suggest how far we have moved from simply pointing the finger at the misogyny of the past.

It is not that the questions, let's say of public and private and epistemology, are being imposed now that we have discovered gender as a significant category, bringing, as e.g., Skinner might say, our own paradigms to the texts we read; rather, crises of modern times enable -- or force -- us to recognize issues. We then find in the works of the great philosophers not that these issues are the new construction of modern times, but that the previous generations of scholars working in the field of political theory have simply not bothered to ask questions that the authors of the classic texts had asked themselves. Pateman herself notes this problem; having written about political participation (1970) and political obligation (1979) through reflection on writers such as Hobbes, Rousseau, and Mill, she writes in the preface to a recent collection of her essays how some of those essays, written before she recognized the importance of gender, remain framed within the traditional masculine assumptions about the character of political theory. We may be in a position to learn from the authors of the past because we are prepared to ask forgotten questions, whether about gender, opinion, justice, equality, and so forth. It is only by the careful reading of the texts that we can learn whether those before us posed these questions and what their answers might have been. Collingwood warned about bringing our questions to the past, but changes in our own social structures may enable us to recognize questions asked previously which we ourselves have denied as legitimate or, more likely, forgotten how to ask. To make this argument, though, we must reject the principle underlying Zerilli's critique, namely that there is a different discourse for male writers and for female writers, that women caught up in exploring the ideas of male authors become themselves the exponents of male value and the articulation of male

perspectives. The writings of scholars such as Pitkin on Machiavelli suggest how much will be lost if we allow ourselves to read these texts as particularized according to gender and race.

Pateman concludes her essay on Hobbes with the telling quote from the eighteenth century feminist Mary Astell: "If *all men are born free*, how is it that all women are born slaves" (1989b, 463)? Pateman's reference to Astell raises the question, but does not answer, whether women authors reflecting on the principles of liberal theory at its foundings perceive those principles from a fundamentally different perspective. In the volume of essays that she and Shanley have edited, Plato, Aristotle, and Rousseau are side by side with Mary Wollstonecraft, Simone de Beauvoir, and Hannah Arendt, authors unnoted by Sabine or Strauss and Cropsey. The structure of the Shanley-Pateman volume thus introduces the female voices, but does not deny the need to engage the male authors as well, nor does it raise the worry about the co-optation that may come from such engagement. The recovery of forgotten women theorists has meant the addition of new voices to the general discourse of political theory and not just the recovery of a feminine voice. Mary Dietz's work on Simone Weil (1985) and the multitude of recent writings on Hannah Arendt suggests that the study of these female authors has far less to do with gender than with the larger (can I say, universal?) questions that confront all students of political theory concerned with violence, political action, political will, and so forth. The challenge, however, does remain to integrate authors who because of our own limited vision of whose works deserve study, whatever time, place, or body they may inhabit or in whatever genre they may write, have not been part of the discipline, though they may have much to say to us about our political world. The concern among some feminist scholars has been with those who have been unfortunately excluded only because of gender. Their inclusion ought not be based on gender, but on their ability to make us engage in conversations from which we can learn.

The plea, now often heard, to include women authors, whether because they speak with a different voice or not, makes us consider as well the more general question of who -- and what -- is to be included in the study of political theory.

Who's Included

In writing his book on the history of political thought, Sabine chose to include whoever said interesting things about politics, and he produced a long list that includes minor authors of minor pamphlets next to authors, who, however much they may be liked or disliked, are recognized as profound thinkers. There seems to have been little self-conscious reflection about who would make it into the history of political thought and who would be left out. Gunnell's concern about Strauss was the opposite, that the inclusion was too self-conscious thereby creating a false sense of a gigantomachy between moderns and ancients that never took place and thus idiosyncratically excluded and included texts. Skinner's methodology denying privilege to one text over another raised the question of how we might go about deciding which texts to study if we did not have the capacity ahead of time to identify those which were worthy of such study. It poses the problem stated so well in Plato's *Meno*. If we do not know the truth, how will we recognize it when we find it?

How, indeed, do we identify out of the vast philosophical and political literature of our intellectual past those texts which we ought to study, whether we wish to use them "instrumentally" as sources of education and moral training, or to set them into their historical and discursive setting? Allan Bloom, dismissing with an exclamation point any talk of canons, responds to this issue of who ought to be read by serious students by looking to the list of texts "generated immanently by the [great] writers themselves" (1980, 123-24). Spinoza supposedly alerts us to Machiavelli, and Hobbes to Aristotle, and more significantly (since we would most likely take Machiavelli and Aristotle seriously anyway), Rousseau to Xenophon. But Bloom's method here is not very satisfying since it leads to the exclusion of those who may not have been readily accessible (e.g., Antiphon) or who may have been dismissed for frivolous reasons, such as being of the wrong sex, to have been taken seriously as an author even by the "great writers." Nor does this help us to clarify where this chain of "greats" begins. Strauss himself was aware of the problem of generating this list of whom to include in our conversations when he commented: "It is merely an unfortunate necessity which prevents us from listening to the greatest minds of India and of China; we do not understand their languages, and we cannot learn all languages" (1989b, 7). This he wrote in 1959 well before the calls for multi-culturalism in the university became the coin of common discourse. Were we to have access to those works, we should read them alongside those from our Western culture. This seems to be one of the few programs set forth by Strauss not followed through by his students.[25] Strauss further warns us that while "we may think that the possible alternatives are exhausted by the great thinkers of the past...we cannot exclude the possibility that other great thinkers might arise in the future -- in 2200 Burma -- the possibility of whose thought has in no way been provided for in our schemata" (1989a, 30).

Admittedly we cannot look that far into the future, but still characteristic of the study of texts over the last decade or two has been the enormous expansion of texts beyond the Hobbes-Locke-Rousseau schema, not so much in terms of non-Western authors as Strauss himself had envisioned, but in terms of previously unstudied Western authors and, in particular, literary genres usually assigned to other academic disciplines but now recognized as part of political theory. Whoever says interesting things about politics need not so identify himself or herself as doing so. In part, it was the work of Strauss himself that led to this vastly expanded corpus. Sabine's list was long and apparently inclusive, but because of his narrow understanding of the meaning of what is political, the authors he included were narrow in their approaches and understood politics only in terms of public affairs and openly acknowledged public concerns. Strauss's willingness to expand the object of political philosophy to the considerations of the best life, of the gods and politics, of virtue, of nature, of family enabled him to resurrect authors who had been dismissed as second-rate (Xenophon), as belonging to a different discipline (Thucydides), as merely comic, bawdy playwrights (Aristophanes), or as from so different a culture they were beyond the interest of students of Western Civilization (Al-Farabi). As his study of Plato's *Euthyphro* shows, a Platonic dialogue that appears to be concerned with piety really enables us to consider the relation between the legislative art, the gods, justice, and the "half-truth" of the gods as superfluous for legislation (Strauss, 1988a: Chap. 8).[26] Or he explains how a comedy about ancient tragedy (*The Frogs* by Aristophanes) is really about the the poet's role as the educator of citizens (1966, chap. 8).

We can find evidence even in the *American Political Science Review* that the list of texts now read as political theory has expanded dramatically. There now are articles on Homer (Dobbs 1987), on Thucydides (Orwin 1984, 1989) and on Aeschylus (Euben 1982); none of these authors made it into the pantheon of political theorists identified by Sabine in 1937.[27] Peter Euben, justifying the publication of a collection of essays on the ancient playwrights entitled *Greek Tragedy and Political Theory*, writes, "As the very idea of juxtaposing Greek tragedy and political theory implies, I regard the former as analogous to, if not itself a kind of theoretical activity" (1990, xi). To study ancient tragedy is to practice political theory precisely because those tragedies written as a lesson for the citizens of Athens force their audiences, whether in the modern or the ancient world, to question the most basic principles of human organization and justice. The *Oresteia* brings us face to face with the dreadful need for, as well as the dehumanizing consequences of, the judicial system, or Euripides' *Ion* explores the forces that drive political systems towards xenophobia, or his *Bacchae* points to the problem of defining membership that confronts all communities, political or otherwise.

Similarly, novelists and playwrights help Judith Shklar on her ramble through the issues she confronts in *Ordinary Vices*, a work which builds primarily on reflections on the essays of Montaigne (who also failed to make it into Sabine and the Strauss and Cropsey compendia). Stephen Salkever's analysis of Aristotle (1991) introduces a discussion of E.M. Forster's *Howards End* to develop his analysis of Aristotle's understanding of the relationship between psychological theory and political practice, thus bringing together a twentieth century novelist and a fourth century B.C. philosopher to teach about the relations of political practice and practical wisdom.[28] And beyond the plays and the novels we find published in *Political Theory*, George Kateb's analysis of Walt Whitman's "Song of Myself" as a poem that makes us aware that individuality conjoined with connectedness is necessary for democratic society. The boundaries that previously defined whom to incorporate in the schema of political theory discourse now seem to have disappeared, and we are left with only the imagination of the current practitioners as the limit on which authors and works are to be plumbed for their insights into the problems of political life.

Skinner's work has meant the expansion of sources in a quite different direction. He has turned not so much to alternative literary genres, but to authors who may not be the first-rate minds with whom one would want to carry on a Straussian conversation, but who become part of the corpus because their writing gives insights into the use of language at the time at which they wrote. Virtually every page of Skinner's two-volume *Foundations of Modern Political Thought* is filled with summaries of authors known only to the most erudite scholars. Meanwhile, the German school of Koselleck is bringing in dictionaries and documents that make no pretense to argument but only serve as historical resources for study.

The expansion in genres studied, the recovery of authors previously forgotten (or consciously ignored) by political theorists is matched as well by the emergence of twentieth century authors whose works have come to serve the same role as the texts studied by Sabine and Strauss and Wolin. Strauss's works, his commentaries, his essays, his speeches, have themselves become the object of intense analysis. Drury's (1988) attack is thus far the only book-length analysis directly on his writings, though *The Review of Politics* (1991, 53, 1) put out a rare special issue devoted exclusively to articles about Strauss's thought. In a prefatory note by the editors, they note that "over the past decade, scholars of his

writings have inquired of his writings whether his teachings contribute to a more 'free' society, to a more 'responsible' society, or a cult of 'godlike' philosophers" (Deutsch and Nicgorski 1991).[29] Others of the twentieth century whose works have become part of the conversation of political theorists and their writings are becoming the object of the type of textual engagement previously reserved for authors of the stature of Plato and Hobbes. The next decade will reveal whether they continue to reward this level of intellectual plumbing for meaning and insight. Most conspicious here are those -- Heidegger, Arendt, and Foucault -- who have challenged any complacency engendered by enlightenment philosophy, who have taken the modern world to task for its political and epistemological assumptions. The challenges are serious -- and often frightening -- but to understand those challenges requires serious engagement with the texts of these authors. That is beginning and making its way to the center of the subfield. While at least with Heidegger and Foucault much of the academic attention has come in other disciplines (especially philosophy and literature) the importance of their thought as a challenge to the traditionally accepted modes of political action, of political analysis, of textual analysis is confronting the discipline at large.

Without avoiding or excusing Heidegger's support of National Socialism in the Germany of the 1930s, authors like Dallmayr (1984), Newell (1984), Gillespie (1984 chap 5), Zuckert (1990c), and White (1990) have been and are exploring how Heidegger's works help us grapple with the modern political experience of nations, community, freedom, technology, and science in a world that must be defined by time and by history. Studies of Arendt are multiplying almost daily. There may be something of a desire among feminist scholars to bring Arendt into the pantheon of male authors as a female intruder, despite what may be seen by some as the masculinity of her language and her thought, but there is as well the widely acknowledged power and clarity of her vision of the crises of the modern world and a sympathy for her attempt to re-introduce a politics of action and speech into an unadorned world of labor.[30] While Foucault's books, essays, and published interviews confront us with the serious challenge of whether texts can have any meaning that does not derive from a set of power relations outside the text itself, the challenges he has posed go well beyond the problems of textual meaning to questions of power, epistemic and linguistic, questions of the meaning of subject and actor, of freedom and discipline, and much more. He thus presents us with challenges to the very activity of reading in the field of political theory, of engaging in any analysis of power and social relations, of evaluating social practices and regimes. The very meaning of, responses to, and effects of those challenges has prompted the exploration of how we are even to read the texts he has left, as political theorists are beginning to bring him into the ken of their interpretative efforts (e.g., Phelan 1990; Miller 1990; Thiele 1990).

The expansion of the corpus in all directions is important for deepening our knowledge and resources. As with every field of study, however, as it expands the practitioners become more and more separated and conversations among scholars more difficult. A smaller core of texts means a more focused conversation among political theorists, but also a conversation that can become constricted and narrow, looking only in on itself. The wider the core of readings, the more difficult it becomes to carry on the conversation. Insofar as political theory is conversation about the just and the unjust, the best regime and the worst, legitimacy and illegitimacy -- the expansion of readings and the possibilities of new understandings of these questions are to be welcomed. The challenge, though, is to maintain the conversation despite the expansion. It is not clear that the last generation of scholars has been able to achieve this.

Conclusion

R.G. Collingwood, faced with the ugliness of the Albert Memorial, was forced to confront the meaning of beauty for himself and for the architect of the memorial. He claimed that he could not understand the memorial or appreciate it if he used his own standards of beauty; he needed to understand how the memorial met the standards of a different time and a different person. In this way, perhaps, he learned the limits of his own conception of beauty and was led to discover a beauty that transcended the expectations of his own set of experiences. The texts that we include in the study of political theory likewise cannot be understood insofar as we go to them only with our own questions and our own standards. To this extent we must be able to set them in a context, to see them as having authors, as speaking in a language that a particular set of a past population could understand. But this need not leave them as simply artifacts of the past -- curiosities of long faded values. Collingwood recognized that Scott's standards of beauty may not have been his own, that the role of this memorial may not have matched his own conception of that role, but in so doing he need not learn the relativity of all standards of beauty. The challenge may be Socratic: to raise questions about the opinions precisely by showing that those opinions may not be universal. But as with Socrates, to learn that our truths may not themselves be universal does not lead to the impossibility of searching for truths. It leads rather

to the *aporia*, the admission of ignorance, that is at the foundation of all learning.

To be able to learn about the limits of our opinions we need to understand the context of the works we read; if we do not, we are left with our questions unanswered. Despite the attacks on texts launched by those critical of their "gendered" language, of their status as object rather than subject, of their psychological and historical distance from us, we have seen no lessening over the last decade of commentary on and engagement with texts. What we have seen is the increased willingness to acknowledge the educative role of these texts -- a role that may make them more dangerous than they were when they were read simply to set the record straight about who said what, when, and first. Socrates was executed by the Athenians for corrupting the young as he goaded them to ask new questions of their established norms and perhaps find those norms wanting. The return to texts for this normative education does entail a certain degree of danger. Though theorists today have no illusions that the hemlock is likely to confer martyrdom's immortality on them, they are prepared to confront the profoundly discomforting conclusions that a Nietzsche or a Heidegger may force us to acknowledge, the undermining of the enlightenment foundations of knowledge and the political consequences of that critique. If anything, it is likely that the next decade will see continued and increased attention to precisely those texts that do force us to question some of our most casually accepted assumptions. It is the unsettling quality of these texts that make them far more powerful educational tools than perhaps even Matthew Arnold envisioned in his pleas for a literary canon. What has appeared to be given in any society may not be; but that is precisely why we read these texts and why they are at the center of so much academic debate of late.

On the other hand, the historical debates that set those texts into a discourse of a time and place so distant from our own, that assume fundamental discontinuities rather than continuities, that force us to spend our time learning a new language can make these works seem sterile. Yet, as Strauss recognized and as Collingwood warned us, we cannot read those texts without language skills, broadly conceived. Sophocles' *Antigone*, for example, is not about fighting for the rights of self-expression of the individual, as it is far too often understood to be. To read the play in that way is not to learn from Sophocles. But if we know nothing about the absence of a language of individual rights to self-expression or of the centrality of the conflict between household and the establishment of the polis in ancient Athens, we may make this mistake. The overwhelming challenge for the next generation is then to resist the appeal of a too comfortable isolation between the two major approaches to political theory -- the first, in which commentary fails to acknowledge that the lessons of any text will be bound up in the language and conceptual framework of particular times, and the second, in which history will diminish texts to mere historical data lacking the powerful educative role they have played in the past. While we may leave the Cambridge School to debate the methodological possibilities of recovering the "illocutionary force" or "meaning," we ignore to our detriment their guidance about language.

For sure, to read and spend our time reflecting on and writing commentaries about a Plato or a Thucydides or a Nietzsche or a Simone Weil represents a leap of faith that these works will repay our efforts. At times we may be disappointed. But to deny the possibility that we may learn is to lose an opportunity to rethink our opinions and to forget what scholarship and education is all about.

Notes

Thanks for help on this essay are owed to a number of people. John E. Jackson's skepticism about texts helped me define the initial structure of this essay and his comments on an early draft helped me refine it. Don Herzog, Tim Fuller, and an anonymous reviewer gave sage advice about some inaccuracies and made me excruciatingly aware of all that I have had to leave out. Shanetta Paskel provided invaluable bibliographic help.

1. Gunnell introduces his contribution to the first edition of *Political Science: The State of the Discipline* by distinguishing between PT (political theory as a subfield of the discipline of political science) and pt (political theory as a more general interdisciplinary body of literature, activity, and intellectual community) (1983, 3). If anything, the interdisciplinary nature of political theory has expanded enormously in the last decade.

2. There are two chapters in this volume dealing with political theory. The subfield does not divide itself easily -- or indeed at all. The artificial line drawn between the two chapters is contemporary and perennial issues. Clearly the political theory confronting the contemporary political world draws on the traditions articulated in the history of political thought and the way in which we read that history depends on our contemporary concerns. Attempts not to overstep the artificial boundaries should not be construed as avoidance of the issues with which the other chapter is dealing.

3. See Skinner (1974, 283-4) for an acknowledgement of his debt to the thought of R. G. Collingwood.

4. Condren (1985) takes this history of the study of political thought back to an 1855 volume by a Robert Blakey entitled *A Brief History of Political Literature from the Earliest Times* and a 1902 book by W. Dunning, *A History of Political Theories*. Nevertheless, for American political theorists it was Sabine's volume that defined the field and especially located the texts studied as epiphenomena of the age in which they were written.

5. Strauss is certainly aware of the problems inherent in such an injunction. In his essay on Heidegger, he comments: "The only question of importance, of course, is the question whether Heidegger's teaching is true or not. But the very question is silent about the question of competence -- of who is competent to judge" (1989a, 29).

6. In this construction I have not focused on the role of Sheldon Wolin's influential volume, *Politics and Vision* (1960). Wolin adopts, as he puts it, an historical approach, though one far more limited than we find in Sabine or the Strauss and Cropsey *History of Political Philosophy*, but he does so with the "conviction that an historical perspective is more effective than any other in exposing the nature of our present predicaments" (1960, v). Though Wolin's perception of those "predicaments" contradicts Strauss's version on almost every point, the study of texts for both is the means to address their determination to aid in the recovery of meaning for political life.

7. A constant stream of republications of Strauss's work and new collections of his lectures and essays, sympathetically introduced by Pangle (Strauss 1983 and 1989a) and Gildin (Strauss 1989c) attests to the continued impact of Strauss on a whole generation of political theorists in America, though clearly not in Europe. This is not the place to explore the divisions within that generation, east coast and west coast Straussians, etc., who while debating the reading even of Strauss himself do not deny the power of Strauss or the texts he studied. Meanwhile, Strauss has been the object of a particularly hostile reading by Drury (1988), but see Timothy Fuller's review of Drury's book for a telling and moderate response (1991).

8. In no way is the following meant to suggest a direct link between Strauss and the authors who see political theory as instrumental or Sabine and those who engage in the historical pursuit of political theory. Indeed, many of the scholars would be horrified to see themselves identified with one or the other. My point is simply that there is a common intellectual drive that motivates scholars who may appear to have significantly different orientations.

9. I have structured this essay in terms of the debate between the approaches of Strauss and the Cambridge School. To do so, as the anonymous reviewer pointed out, I have not engaged some of the more serious threats to the text and our capacity to read them whether instrumentally *or* historically that have come from Nietzsche, Heidegger, and Foucault. My failure to address these challenges is not to diminish their importance -- only to admit the limits of an essay of this sort, as well as its author's level of comfort with and competence in the works of these thinkers.

10. Compare here Shklar's colloquy with Montaigne in *Ordinary Vices* (1984) in which she makes clear the moral purpose of her work; despite a self-effacing description of the work as "a ramble through a moral minefield, not a march toward a destination" (1984, 6) and her comments at the end of the "ramble" that "I have contributed nothing to homiletic literature, and I have not harangued 'modern man,'" there lies behind these disclaimers the deep concern that citizens of a liberal society understand that they must "put cruelty first."

11. The survey of works presented here can in no way pretend to be comprehensive. It is not. The list of books and articles published in the area of the history of political theory and political thought is vast. Reflection on the last ten years can only allow for reference to a small number of works as exemplars of trends rather than offer a comprehensive statement of what has been done. Thus, the larger corpus of writing about Hume, Hegel, Oakeshott, Voegelin, and many others will not be addressed -- not because such work is any less important to the understanding of the trends in political theory, but because of limits of time, space, and my own expertise.

12. It should not surprise us, though, that many of the first and second generation of students of Strauss continue to write on the classical authors whose insights into things political Strauss repeatedly favored, e.g., Nichols's two books (1987, 1992) or Coby (1987), but in response to Strauss's broad interests we find other favored periods or authors as well. For just a beginning, see Weinberger (1985); Melzer (1990); Kelly (1987); Schwartz (1984); Gildin (1983) on Rousseau,

Tarcov (1984) and Grant (1987) on Locke; Danford (1990) on Hume; Smith (1989) on Hegel; Gillespie (1984) on Hegel and Heidegger.

13. As James Nichols points out, however, in his comment on Holmes's piece, Holmes may greatly exaggerate the danger by misreading Strauss to be a crude instrumentalist engaging in "'the imprudent importation of doctrines there [ancient Greece] espoused into the context of a highly differentiated society,'" (1979, 130) despite Strauss's firm assertion that "We cannot reasonably expect that a fresh understanding of classical political philosophy will supply us with recipes for today's use" (Strauss, *City and Man*, quoted by Nichols, 1979, 129). See also Strauss's review of John Wild where he comments: "[T]he teaching of the classics can have no immediate practical effect, because present day society is not a *polis*" (quoted in Tarcov 1991, 3).

14. Richter (1990, 49) apologizes for using the label "Cambridge School" since the phrase may not describe "a group as cohesive as that name implies." I make no such apologies.

15. More recent books by Neal Wood on Locke (1984) and Cicero (1988) reiterate the importance of embedding "a classic text...in the appropriate social, political and economic context" (1984, 2). According to Wood, since most classic texts in political theory are "histories from above" and thus written by a member or client of the ruling classes the work must be read in the context of history from below. From this perspective, Wood criticizes the exponents of the Cambridge School for recognizing only ideas and paradigms as history rather than seeing in history the major social and economic forces of the past. For Wood, those of the Cambridge School fit well into the philosophic rather than the historical camp and by implication are of less interest to those concerned with politics (1984, 10-12).

16. Of quite a different order, perhaps standing all on its own, is the monumental work of Richard Ashcraft (1986) on John Locke. Ashcraft sets Locke's *Two Treatises* firmly into the intellectual context of the seventeenth century, but is particularly interested in placing Locke in the political world of the dissidents of Restoration England. As such, the volume goes beyond recovering "the subjectively intended meaning of Locke's action in writing the *Two Treatises of Government*" (1986, 12) to the study of political movements. The Cambridge School's methodology can only contribute partially to this endeavor (1986, 12 note 12) which takes Ashcraft more deeply into historical intrigues than a study of seventeenth century discourse would.

17. The references that follow are to the reprint of the essay in Tully (1988).

18. Skinner comments in note 2 that his theories apply to any practice of the history of ideas. He just happens to use examples from political thought because that "reflects my own specialisation" (1988, 291 note 2). But it could just as easily have been the the study of esthetics or of ethics. For a consideration of the expansion of Skinner's views in precisely that direction see the series of essays in Rorty et al. (1984).

19. The most recent list of texts in the Cambridge series includes Aristotle, Bentham, Constant, Hooker, Leibniz, Locke, Machiavelli, J.S. Mill, Montesquieu, More, and Paine, hardly authors of "lesser known works." The Liberty Fund has reprinted important (but perhaps lesser known) classics such as Mandeville's *Fable of the Bees*, Algernon Sidney's *Discourses*, Lord Acton's Essays, Hume's Essays, and much more.

20. A Collection of Koselleck's essays, *Futures Past*, has been put out in translation by MIT Press (1985).

21. In a very different endeavor Harvey Mansfield's new book (1989) on the executive claims to resemble a "conceptual history," but a conceptual history that emphatically learns from texts, especially Machiavelli, not for clarification of the use of a term, but to raise serious questions about the nature of current practice.

22. Richter's original article in *Political Theory* in 1986 drew forth two rejoinders from Jeremy Rayner (1988, 1990) with an intervening response from Richter (1989) in which the two debated the compatibility proposed by Richter in terms of the implications of the philosophy of language and semantic analysis for the respective schools.

23. O'Brien (1981) is an example from this earlier period of a far more thoughtful work critical of "male-stream political thought" for its denigration of the importance of reproductive labor within any political community.

24. We can note that Sabine (1937, chap. 32), for example, writes of the *Autobiography*, of the essays on Bentham and Coleridge, of the *Logic*, of *Utilitarianism*, *On Liberty*, *On Representative Government*, but makes no mention of *On the Subjection of Women*. The chapter on Mill by Henry M. Magid (1987, 784-801) in the Strauss and Cropsey volume does not mention the essay at all, neither in the text nor in the appended list of recommended readings. Nor does it surface in Wolin's book. It took almost 60 years after Carrie Chapman Catt put out an edition of the work in 1911 (New York: Frederick A. Stokes Company) for the work to be republished by Alice Rossi and MIT Press. Now there are a multitude of collections in which this essay appears.

25. Though see the paper by Salkever and Nylan presented at the 1991 APSA meetings for a start in this direction.

26. My own work on the *Euthyphro* (1990) and the *Symposium* (1984b) gets its inspiration from Strauss's insistence that all Platonic dialogues are about politics, not just the *Republic*, *Statesman*, and *Laws*.

27. This is not even to begin to catalogue such articles that now regularly fill *Political Theory*, *Interpretation*, *Journal of Politics*, *Review of Politics*, *Polity*, and other such journals where we find numerous articles in political theory.

28. Although I have not discussed American political thought in this essay, in the context of the present point I should note Catherine Zuckert's book with the wonderful double entendre title *Natural Right and the American Imagination: Political Theory in Novel Form* (1990a) in which the classics of American literature are explored for insights into the political philosophy of the American regime.

29. See also the volume edited by Alan Udoff (1991). Though this volume is subtitled "A Critical Engagement," Udoff's concluding comment in his introductory remarks, "It is a blessing that Leo Strauss lived and wrote" (22), suggests that it isn't quite that.

30. The writing on Arendt has exploded recently. A few citations must suffice: Kateb (1983), Benhabib (1988), Jacobitti (1988), Honig's (1988) criticism of Jacobitti, Bradshaw (1989), Dossa (1989), Ring (1989); even this does not capture the flurry of panels at meetings and works in progress on Arendt's thought.

Bibliography

Almond, Gabriel. 1988. "Separate Tables: Schools and Sects in Political Science," *PS: Political Science and Politics* 21:828-42.

Ashcraft, Richard. 1986. *Revolutionary Politics and Locke's "Two Treatises of Government."* Princeton: Princeton University Press.

Ball, Terence. 1988. *Transforming Political Discourse and Critical Conceptual History*. Oxford: Basil Blackwell.

Barber, Benjamin R. 1984. *Strong Democracy: Participatory Politics for a New Age*. Berkeley: University of California Press.

Benhabib, Seyla. 1988. "Judgment and the Moral Foundations of Politics in Arendt's Thought." *Political Theory* 16:29-52.

Bloom, Allan. 1980. "The Study of Texts." In *Political Theory and Political Education*, ed. Melvin Richter. Princeton: Princeton University Press.

Bloom, Allan. 1987. *The Closing of the American Mind: How Higher Education Has Failed Democracy and Impoverished the Souls of Today's Students*. New York: Simon and Schuster.

Bradshaw, Leah. 1989. *Acting and Thinking: The Political Thought of Hannah Arendt*. Toronto: University of Toronto Press.

Brown, Wendy. 1988a. *Manhood and Politics: A Feminist Reading in Political Theory*. Totowa, NJ. Rowman & Littlefield.

Brown, Wendy. 1988b. "Supposing Truth Were a Woman.....: Plato's Subversion of Masculine Discourse." *Political Theory* 16:594-616.

Clark, Lorenne M. G., and Lynda Lange, eds. 1979. *The Sexism of Social and Political Theory: Women and Reproduction from Plato to Nietzsche*. Toronto: University of Toronto Press.

Coby, Patrick. 1987. *Socrates and the Sophistic Enlightenment: A Commentary on Plato's "Protagoras."* Lewisburg: Bucknell University Press.

Collingwood, R.G. 1929. *Autobiography*. Oxford: Oxford University Press.

Condren, Conal. 1985. *The Status and Appraisal of Classic Texts: An Essay on Political Theory, Its Inheritance and the History of Ideas*. Princeton: Princeton University Press.

Dallmayr, Fred. 1984. "Ontology of Freedom: Heidegger and Political Philosophy." *Political Theory* 12:204-34.

Danford, John W. 1990. *David Hume and the Problem of Reason: Recovering the Human Sciences*. New Haven: Yale University Press.

Deutsch, Kenneth, and Walter Nicgorski. 1991. Special Issue on Leo Strauss. *The Review of Politics* 53.

Dietz, Mary. 1985. "Citizenship with a Feminist Face: The Problem with Maternal Thinking." *Political Theory* 13:19-37.

Dietz, Mary. 1988. *Between the Human and the Divine: The Political Thought of Simone Weil*. Totowa, NJ: Rowman and Littlefield.

Dobbs, Darrell. 1987. "Reckless Rationalism and Heroic Reverence in Homer's *Odyssey*." *American Political Science Review* 81:491-508.

Drury, Shadia. 1988. *The Political Ideas of Leo Strauss*. Basingstoke, Hampshire: Macmillan.

Dunn, John. 1985. *Rethinking Modern Political Theory: Essays 1979-83*. Cambridge: Cambridge University Press.

Elshtain, Jean Bethke. 1982. "Antigone's Daughters." *Democracy* 2:46-59.

Euben, J. Peter. 1982. "Justice and the *Oresteia*." *American Political Science Review* 76:22-33.

Euben, J. Peter. 1986. *Greek Tragedy and Political Theory*. Berkeley: University of California Press.

Euben, J. Peter. 1990. *The Tragedy of Political Theory: The Road Not Taken*. Princeton: Princeton University Press.

Femia, Joseph V. 1988. "Historicist Critique of 'Revisionist' Methods." In *Meaning and Context*, ed. James Tully. Oxford: Basil Blackwell.

Forde, Steven. 1989. *The Ambition to Rule: Alcibiades and the Politics of Imperialism in Thucydides*. Ithaca, NY: Cornell University Press.

Franklin, Julian. 1978. *John Locke and the Theory of Sovereignty: Mixed Monarchy and the Right of Resistance in the Political Thought of the English Revolution*. Cambridge: Cambridge University Press.

Fuller, Timothy. 1991. "Review of *The Political Ideas of Leo Strauss*." *Political Theory* 19:137-41.

Gildin, Hilail. 1983. *Rousseau's "Social Contract": The Design of the Argument*. Chicago: University of Chicago Press.

Gillespie, Michael. 1984. *Hegel, Heidegger, and the Ground of History*. Chicago: University of Chicago Press.

Gilligan, Carol. 1982. *In a Different Voice: Psychological Theory and Women's Development*. Cambridge: Harvard University Press.

Grant, Ruth. 1987. *John Locke's Liberalism*. Chicago: University of Chicago Press.

Gunnell, John G. 1978. "The Myth of the Tradition." *American Political Science Review* 72:122-34.

Gunnell, John G. 1983. "Political Theory: The Evolution of a Sub-Field." In *Political Science: The State of the Discipline*, ed. Ada Finifter. Washington, DC: American Political Science Association.

Gunnell, John G. 1988. "American Political Science, Liberalism, and the Invention of Political Theory." *American Political Science Review* 82:71-87.

Hamburger, Joseph. 1965. *Intellectuals in Politics: John Stuart Mill and the Philosophical Radicals*. New Haven: Yale University Press.

Herzog, Don. 1989. *Happy Slaves: A Critique of Consent Theory*. Chicago: University of Chicago Press.

Holmes, Stephen Taylor. 1979. "Aristippus in and out of Athens." *American Political Science Review* 73:113-28.

Holmes, Stephen. 1984. *Benjamin Constant and the Making of Modern Liberalism*. New Haven: Yale University Press.

Honig, B. 1988. "Arendt, Identity and Difference." *Political Theory* 16:77-98.

Jacobitti, Suzanne. 1988. "Hannah Arendt and the Will." *Political Theory* 16:53-76.

Kateb, George. 1983. *Hannah Arendt: Politics, Conscience, Evil*. Totowa, NJ: Rowman and Allenhead.

Kateb, George. 1990. "Walt Whitman and the Culture of Democracy." *Political Theory* 18:545-71.

Kelly, Christopher. 1987. *Rousseau's Exemplary Life: The Confessions as Political Philosophy*. Ithaca: Cornell University Press.

Klein, Jacob. 1965. *A Commentary on Plato's "Meno."* Chapel Hill: University of North Carolina Press.

Koselleck, Reinhart. 1985. *Futures Past: On the Semantics of Historical Time*. Trans. Keith Tribe. Cambridge: MIT Press.

Lieberman, David. 1989. *The Province of Legislation Determined: Legal Theory in Eighteenth-Century Britain*. Cambridge: Cambridge University Press.

MacIntyre, Alasdair. 1981. *After Virtue: A Study in Moral Theory*. Notre Dame: Notre Dame University Press.

Mansfield, Harvey, Jr. 1989. *Taming the Prince: The Ambivalence of Modern Executive Power*. New York: The Free Press.

Melzer, Arthur M. 1990. *The Natural Goodness of Man: On the System of Rousseau's Thought*. Chicago: University of Chicago Press.

Miller, David. 1990. "The Resurgence of Political Theory." *Political Studies* 38:421-37.

Miller, James. 1990. "Carnivals of Atrocity: Foucault, Nietzsche, Cruelty." *Political Theory* 18:470-91.

Minogue, Kenneth. 1988. "Method in Intellectual History." In *Meaning and Context*, ed. James Tully. Oxford: Basil Blackwell.

Newell, W.R. 1984. "Heidegger on Freedom and Community: Some Political Implications of His Early Thought." *American Political Science Review* 78:775-84.

Nichols, James H. Jr. 1979. "Comment on Holmes." *American Political Science Review* 73:129-33.

Nichols, Mary. 1987. *Socrates and the Political Community: An Ancient Debate*. Albany: State University of New York.

Nichols, Mary. 1992. *Citizens and Statesmen: A Study of Aristotle's "Politics"*. Savage, MD: Rowman and Littlefield.

O'Brien, Mary. 1981. *The Politics of Reproduction*. Boston: Routledge & Kegan Paul.

Orwin, Clifford. 1984. "The Just and the Advantageous in Thucydides: The Case of the Mytilenian Debate." *American Political Science Review* 78:485-94.

Orwin, Clifford. 1989. "Piety, Justice and the Necessities of War: Thucydides' Delian Debate." *American Political Science Review* 83:233-39.

Okin, Susan Moller. 1979. *Women in Western Political Thought*. Princeton: Princeton University Press.

Pangle, Thomas L., ed. 1987. *The Roots of Political Philosophy: Ten Forgotten Socratic Dialogues*. Ithaca: Cornell University Press.

Pateman, Carole. 1970. *Participation and Democratic Theory*. Cambridge: Cambridge University Press.

Pateman, Carole. 1985. *The Problem of Political Obligation: A Critique of Liberal Theory*. Cambridge: Polity Press.

Pateman, Carole. 1988. *The Sexual Contract*. Stanford: Stanford University Press.

Pateman, Carole. 1989a. *The Disorder of Women: Democracy, Feminism and Political Theory*. Stanford: Stanford University Press.

Pateman, Carole. 1989b. "'God Hath Ordained to Man a Helper': Hobbes, Patriarchy and Conjugal Right." *British Journal of Political Science* 19:445-63.

Phelan, Shane. 1990. "Foucault and Feminism." *American Journal of Political Science* 34:421-40.

Pitkin, Hannah Fenichel. 1984. *Fortune is a Woman: Gender and Politics in the Thought of Niccolo Machiavelli*. Berkeley: University of California Press.

Pocock, J.G.H. 1962. "The History of Political Thought: A Methodological Inquiry." In *Philosophy, Politics, and Society*. 2nd series, ed. Peter Laslett and W.G. Runciman. Oxford: Basil Blackwell.

Pocock, J.G.H. 1985. *Virtue, Commerce, and History*. Cambridge: Cambridge University Press.

Rayner, Jeremy. 1988. "On *Begriffgeschichte*." *Political Theory* 16:496-501.

Rayner, Jeremy. 1990. "On *Begriffgeschichte* Again." *Political Theory* 18:305-307.

Richter, Melvin. 1986. "Conceptual History (*Begriffsgeschichte*) and Political Theory." *Political Theory* 14:604-37.

Richter, Melvin. 1989. "Understanding *Begriffsgeschichte*: A Rejoinder." *Political Theory* 17:296-301.

Richter, Melvin. 1990. "Reconstructing the History of Political Languages: Pocock, Skinner, and the *Geschichtliche Gundbegriffe*." *History and Theory* 29:38-70.

Ring, Jennifer. 1985. "Mill's *The Subjection of Women*: The Methodological Limits of Liberal Feminism." *Review of Politics* 47:27-44.

Ring, Jennifer. 1989. "The Pariah as Hero: Hannah Arendt's Political Actor." *Political Theory* 19:433-52.

Ring, Jennifer. 1991. *Modern Political Theory and Contemporary Feminism: A Dialectical Analysis*. Albany: State University of New York Press.

Rorty, Richard, J.B. Schneewind, and Quentin Skinner, eds. 1984. *Philosophy in History: Essays on the Historiography of Philosophy*. Cambridge: Cambridge University Press.

Sabine, George. [1937] 1953. *A History of Political Theory*. New York: Henry Holt and Company.

Salkever, Stephen G. 1991. *Finding the Mean: Theory and Practice in Aristotelian Political Philosophy*. Princeton: Princeton University Press.

Salkever, Stephen G., and Michael Nylan. 1991. "Teaching Comparative Political Philosophy: Rationale, Problems, Strategies." Presented at the annual meeting of the American Political Science Association, Washington.

Saxonhouse, Arlene W. 1984a. "Aeschylus' *Oresteia*: Misogyny, Philogyny, and Justice." *Women and Politics* 4:11-32.

Saxonhouse, Arlene W. 1984b. "Eros and the Female in Greek Political Thought: An Interpretation of Plato's *Symposium*." *Political Theory* 12:5-27.

Saxonhouse, Arlene W. 1985. *Women in the History of Political Thought*. New York: Praeger.

Saxonhouse, Arlene W. 1986. "From Hierarchy to Tragedy and Back Again: Women in Greek Political Thought." *American Political Science Review* 80:403-18.

Saxonhouse, Arlene W. 1988. "Of Paradigms and Cores." *Polity* 21:409-18.

Saxonhouse, Arlene W. 1990. "The Philosophy of the Particular and the Universality of the City: Socrates' Education of Euthyphro." *Political Theory* 16:281-99.

Schochet, Gordon. 1974. "Quentin Skinner's Method." *Political Theory* 2:261-76.

Schwartz, Joel D. 1984. *The Sexual Politics of Jean-Jacques Rousseau*. Chicago: University of Chicago Press.

Shanley, Mary Lyndon. 1981. "Marital Slavery and Friendship: John Stuart Mill's *The Subjection of Women*." *Political Theory* 9:229-47.

Shanley, Mary Lyndon, and Carole Pateman, eds. 1991. *Feminist Interpretations and Political Theory*. University Park, PA: Pennsylvania State University Press.

Shklar, Judith N. 1969. *Men and Citizens: A Study of Rousseau's Social Theory*. Cambridge: Cambridge University Press.

Shklar, Judith N. 1984. *Ordinary Vices*. Cambridge: The Belknap Press of Harvard University Press.

Skinner, Quentin. 1966. "The Ideological Context of Hobbes's Political Thought." *Historical Journal* 9:286-317.

Skinner, Quentin. 1969. "Meaning and Understanding in the History of Ideas." *History and Theory* 8:3-53.

Skinner, Quentin. 1974. "Some Problems in the Analysis of Political Thought and Action." *Political Theory* 2:277-303.

Skinner, Quentin. 1978. *Foundations of Modern Political Thought*. 2 vols. Cambridge: Cambridge University Press.

Skinner, Quentin. 1988a. "Meaning and Understanding in the History of Ideas." In *Meaning and Context*, ed. James Tully. Oxford: Basil Blackwell.

Skinner, Quentin. 1988b. "A Reply to My Critics." In *Meaning and Context*, ed. James Tully. Oxford: Basil Blackwell.

Smith, Steven B. 1989. *Hegel's Critique of Liberalism: Rights in Conflict*. Chicago: University of Chicago Press.

Steinberger, Peter. 1990. "Hannah Arendt on Judgment." *American Journal of Political Science* 34:803-21.

Stone, I.F. 1988. *The Trial of Socrates*. Boston: Little, Brown and Company.

Strauss, Leo. 1966. *Socrates and Aristophanes*. New York: Basic Books.

Strauss, Leo. 1983. *Studies in Platonic Political Philosophy*. Chicago: University of Chicago Press.

Strauss, Leo. 1989a. *The Rebirth of Classical Rationalism*. Chicago: University of Chicago Press.

Strauss, Leo. [1959] 1989b. "What is Liberal Education?" In *Liberalism Ancient and Modern*. ed. Leo Strauss. Ithaca: Cornell University Press.

Strauss, Leo. 1989c. *An Introduction to Political Philosophy: Ten Essays by Leo Strauss*, ed. Hilail Gildin. Detroit: Wayne State University Press.

Strauss, Leo, and Joseph Cropsey. 1987. *History of Political Philosophy*. 3rd edition. Chicago: University of Chicago Press.

Tarcov, Nathan. 1982. "Quentin Skinner's Method and Machiavelli's *Prince*." *Ethics* 92:692-710.

Tarcov, Nathan. 1984. *Locke's Education for Liberty*. Chicago: University of Chicago Press.

Tarcov, Nathan. 1991. "On a Certain Critique of Straussianism." *The Review of Politics* 53:3-18.

Thiele, Leslie Paul. 1990. "The Agony of Politics: The Nietzschean Roots of Foucault's Thought," *American Political Science Review* 84:907-925.

Tully, James. 1988. *Meaning and Context: Quentin Skinner and His Critics*. Cambridge: Polity Press.

Udoff, Alan, ed. 1991. *Leo Strauss's Thought: Toward a Critical Engagement*. Boulder: Lynne Rienner.

Walzer, Michael. 1965. *The Revolution of the Saints: A Study in the Origins of Radical Politics*. Cambridge: Harvard University Press.

Weinberger, J. 1985. *Science, Faith and Politics: Francis Bacon and the Utopian Roots of the Modern Age*. Ithaca: Cornell University Press.

Weiner, Jonathan M. 1974. "Quentin Skinner's Hobbes." *Political Theory* 2:251-60.

White, Stephen K. 1990. "Heidegger and the Difficulties of a Postmodern Ethics and Politics." *Political Theory* 18:80-103.

Wilson, Francis G. 1944. "Report of the Political Theory Panel." *American Political Science Review* 38:726-33.

Wolin, Sheldon. 1960. *Politics and Vision*. Boston: Little, Brown and Company.

Wood, Ellen Meiskins, and Neal Wood. 1978. *Class Ideology and Ancient Political Theory*. New York: Oxford University Press.

Wood, Neal. 1984. *John Locke and Agrarian Capitalism*. Berkeley: University of California Press.

Wood, Neal. 1988. *Cicero's Social and Political Thought*. Berkeley: University of California Press.

Yack, Bernard. 1985. "Community and Conflict in Aristotle's Political Philosophy." *The Review of Politics* 47:92-112.

Zerilli, Linda. 1991. "Machiavelli's Sisters: Women and 'the Conversation' of Political Theory." *Political Theory* 19:252-276.

Zuckert, Catherine. 1990a. *Natural Right and the American Imagination: Political Philosophy in Novel Form*. Savage, MD: Rowman and Littlefield.

Zuckert, Catherine. 1990b. "Review of Carol Pateman's *The Disorder of Women*." *The Review of Politics* 52:660-62.

Zuckert, Catherine. 1990c. "Martin Heidegger: His Philosophy and His Politics." *Political Theory* 18:51-79.

2

Political Theory in the 1980s: Perplexity Amidst Diversity

William Galston

The topic of this survey, even narrowly defined, encompasses an unmanageably large literature, and I must begin by announcing what I have been allowed, or compelled, to exclude. Unlike its predecessor, this volume contains a separate chapter dealing with, inter alia, specific interpretations of historical figures in the "tradition" and general theories as to the nature of the interpretive activity; I will therefore touch on such matters only briefly and in passing. Nor (for reasons that I hope sections I and II will make clear) will I spend much time on the kinds of theorizing explicitly directed toward empirical research programs (which is not to say that political theory and political science can afford to proceed in isolation from one another -- or so I shall argue).

Nor, finally, can I do justice to the dramatic flowering of scholarship focused on American political thought during the past generation. I can hazard a few generalizations: As compared to the once-dominant Hartzian view, many current interpretations are more inclined to consider civic republican and theological supplements to Lockean liberalism, to advance revisionist views of the content of America's Locke, to revive and extol what might be called the transcendentalist/pragmatist tradition, and to bring to the fore the voices of all-but-forgotten dissenting movements. And as Judith Shklar suggested in her APSA presidential address, we are on the whole increasingly likely to see connections between American political thought and an American political science embodying in its empirico-statistical methods the democratic principle that the lives of ordinary people are intrinsically significant (Shklar 1991, 4). These manifestly inadequate remarks will have to stand in place of the fuller treatment this topic deserves (see also Kloppenberg 1987; Hirshman 1990; Pangle 1988).

Even within the circumscribed area I do try to cover, no brief survey can possibly do justice to the full variety of interesting and important work. As an alternative to silent or inadvertent omission, I have constructed a topically organized bibliography that, while necessarily less than comprehensive, is considerably fuller than a simple list of textual citations. Readers wishing to go farther than I could in a particular direction may find it useful to refer to the appropriate section of the bibliography with which this chapter ends.

I. Basic Narrative Strategies

The story of political theory during the past decade can be told from many different points of view, and the selection of any one is bound to prove in some measure arbitrary. Setting to one side, for the moment, substantive disagreements that inevitably affect the choice of plot line, there are at least three basic narrative strategies, not mutually exclusive, that might be employed. The trajectory of political theory can be seen as shaped by the shifting contours and imperatives of its disciplinary locations, by the political problems and conflicts on which it reflects (or, alternatively, of which it serves as ideological representation), and by the inner logic of its theoretical development and disputation. While observers of political theory disagree as to which should be given pride of place, most would agree that each has played a significant role. At the risk of getting ahead of my story, but in the hope of giving the reader some preliminary orientation, let me offer a brief characterization of political theory during the past decade under the three headings just enumerated.

Disciplinary Location

With regard to disciplinary location, the 1980s began with political theorists divided between departments of political science and philosophy, in fitful communication across the border but largely cut off from other members of their respective disciplines. These conditions persisted through the 1980s, with the added complication that political theory came to be practiced in, and opened itself to, other disciplines as well. For example, the quantity of political theory carried out within the legal academy escalated sharply (see for example Hirshman 1990; Perry 1988; Symposium 1988), and the impact of literary, psychological, and social theory (much of it of European provenance) on American political theory was substantial.

As disciplinary divisions grew more complex, geographical divisions eroded significantly. British and American theorists crisscrossed the Atlantic at record rates; while Jurgen Habermas tirelessly incorporated Anglo-American theory into a renewed European critical theory, Richard Rorty worked to bring Europeans such as Nietzsche and Heidegger into the American pragmatist fold.

This is not to say that the substantive implications of geography disappeared altogether. On the contrary: because political theory is increasingly a multinational discipline, it is more important than ever to reflect with some self-awareness on differences among political cultures that may have an impact on objects and styles of theorizing.

For example, it is familiar (but not incorrect) to suggest that in comparison to the U.K., the United States is more socially diverse and more affected by rights-based individualism. These contrasts do not determine theoretical outcomes, but they do help set theoretical agendas. For example, prompted by the many social and cultural differences in American society, American political theory has begun to ask whether universalism and impartiality may not often mask ignorance about, and even bias against, these differences. America, the land of individualism, has also become the battleground of a contest between defenses of individualism based on Kant's conception of autonomous moral agents and critiques of individualism inspired by Hegel's conception of individuals as socially embedded and constituted. Cultural diversity is linked as well to the fact that, compared to British liberals, Americans have been far more strongly drawn to theories that see the state as neutral with respect to competing conceptions of the good life and, therefore, as abstaining from promoting any particular idea of human perfection (see Barry 1990, li). Here, too, debate widened during the 1980s as dissenting theorists questioned the possibility and desirability of neutrality and anti-perfectionism, so understood.

Another key difference between the United Kingdom and the United States lies in the presence of a major left-wing party in the former and its absence in the latter. In this light, it is not accidental that many American theorists have opted for an aestheticized withdrawal from the standard political arena in favor of literary and cultural concerns.

One may also speculate that the greater residual appeal of utilitarianism in the U.K. vis-a-vis the U.S. is related to the contrast between (on the one hand) a unified civil service and plenipotentiary parliament, which can at least be imagined as performing aggregative calculations, and (on the other) the dispersion of political power and the omnipresence of rights-based thinking characteristic of America. (While surely suggestive, these reflections on plausible relations between theory and cultural context should not be taken to suggest any straightforward reduction or subordination of the former to the latter.)

Political Problems and Conflicts

With regard to the complex interplay of political theory and politics, a number of developments stand out. Chief among them was the diminished appeal of Marxism as political practice. To be sure, key Marxist categories such as alienation retained a measure of critical force, and theorists inspired by Marx continued to work at a high level of rigor (see especially Cohen 1988; Elster 1985; Reiman 1987; Roemer 1982, 1988). Still, for many the ties to Marx became increasingly attenuated.

The decline of Marxism coexisted, however, with a continuing desire in many quarters for a critical standpoint vis-a-vis various aspects of contemporary society. In both the United States and the U.K., the 1980s were dominated by a resurgent conservative politics that some theorists (primarily libertarians and social conservatives) applauded but that left many traditional liberals and social democrats stunned and disoriented. One possible response was a renovated liberalism more aware of, and responsive to, the weaknesses that had opened the door to conservative triumphs (see Rosenblum 1989, "Introduction"). Another possible response was a defense of classic socialist ideals more attuned to the demonstrable practical and moral advantages of market economies and democratic politics (e.g., Miller 1989). A third line of response was a critique of conservative politics framed in non-liberal, or antiliberal, terms: thus "virtue" was counterposed to "greed," and "community" was invoked against selfishness, against social isolation, against individualism run amok. This strategy could of course draw upon the enduring tropes and sentiments of antiliberalism (Holmes 1989). A fourth response drew upon the "postmodern" criticisms of the Enlightenment philosophical-political project launched by European thinkers such as Martin Heidegger, Jacques Derrida, Michel Foucault, and Jean-Francois Lyotard; political theorists mining this vein could be seen variously as proposing a critique, or intensification, of liberalism (see especially Connolly 1990).

The felt need for a critical vocabulary was augmented by the multiplication and growth of insurgent groups within liberal societies. During the 1980s, new movements based on ethnicity, gender, and sexual orientation came to the fore. These trends were particularly pronounced within the United States, with its relatively open immigration policies, surge of women into the non-domestic workforce (including academia), and legal system that encourages litigation as a vehicle of social change. Some theorists argued that liberalism, properly understood, offered the most promising framework for articulating and accommodating these new demands. For example, Susan Moller Okin argued that we can have a "humanist liberalism" that fully includes women, but only if we can devise "a theoretical basis for public policies that, recognizing the family as a fundamental political institution, extends standards of justice to life within it" (Rosenblum 1989, 53). Others argued that the liberal discourse of equality and diversity was a cloak for various forms of hierarchy and hegemony; they opted for theoretical expression through concepts such as multiculturalism, decentering, and difference (for the debate within feminism, see Rhode 1990).

More broadly, developments during the past decade have had the effect of calling into question the traditional focus of much political theorizing on the public institutions of the modern nation-state. This interrogation has taken place along numerous fronts -- within nations, among nations, and across national boundaries. In response to changing gender relations, feminist thought has moved to reject, or fundamentally reconfigure, the distinction between public and private life. The upsurge of ethnic identification has led some theorists to explore the moral claims of distinct subcommunities within nation-states (see especially Kymlicka 1989, chaps. 7-10).

Among nations, questions such as the international enforceability of basic rights and resource transfers in response to emergencies and the exigencies of democratization and development are clearly on the agenda. The renewed activism of transnational institutions such as the United Nations, the World Bank, and the European Community furnishes meaningful sites for the application of general principles (for a comprehensive survey, see O'Neill 1991).

Across national borders, we see the rise of multinational corporations and of technologies that transfer information instantaneously and globally. These and similar entities create new sites of power whose relation to the reach of national states, individually or jointly, is yet to be determined. The increased salience of transnational environmental issues such as ozone depletion, global warming, and the Chernobyl disaster is generating new issues of distribution and of agency.

More recently, the economic collapse and political breakup, first of the Soviet European empire and then of the Soviet Union itself, has exacerbated fears concerning massive refugee flows -- fears already widespread in nations such as France, Germany, and the United States that have experienced increased levels of immigration during the past decade (Schuck and Smith 1985). The Soviet collapse has also heightened the risk of proliferation of nuclear arms technology and expertise, raising new issues of national sovereignty and global responsibility.

Inner Logic of Theoretical Development

With regard, finally, to the inner logic of theoretical development and dispute, a number of developments stand out. To begin with, key figures from the past were reappropriated for contemporary purposes. To the Kantian revival already underway in the 1970s were added refurbished versions of, inter alia, Aristotle (representing deliberation and civic virtue), Hobbes (contractual origination), Locke (individual rights and property), Rousseau (direct democracy), Hegel (civil society and community), Wollstonecraft and Mill (the subjugation of women), and Nietzsche (subversion of the liberal self and social order). It was not difficult to deploy one's favorite against the competitors: communitarians reenacted Hegel's critique of Kantian formalism; participatory democrats repeated Rousseau's strictures against Lockean privacy; Foucauldians replayed Nietzsche's relentless critique of bourgeois society; and so forth.

To some extent, theoretical discussions occurred within rather than among the arenas demarcated by these selective reappropriations. Thus (to take but two examples), Will Kymlicka could write a first-rate Kant-inspired introduction to *Contemporary Political Philosophy* that made no mention whatever of thinkers such as Foucault, Derrida, Gadamer, and Heidegger (Kymlicka 1990) while William Connolly offered an equally meritorious Nietzschean meditation on *Political Theory and Modernity* with but one passing reference each to Rawls and Kant (Connolly 1988). This points to a broadly significant contrast: among analytical political theorists working within philosophy departments Nietzsche rarely rates more than a passing glance, while for many political theorists working within political science departments, he has come to occupy a strategic position. Indeed, as Jurgen Habermas has argued, the aspect of contemporary European thought that has had the greatest impact in America during the 1980s represents, in one way or another, a reworking of Nietzschean themes (Habermas 1987, chap. IV).

I do not mean to suggest, however, that the parallel revivals of Kant and Nietzsche have altogether failed to intersect. On the contrary: the broad tendencies they represent became locked in one of the major theoretical conflicts of the past decade, between Enlightenment modernity and its "postmodern" critics.

This conflict is worked out on at least three levels. First, contemporary Nietzscheans are deeply mistrustful of the idea of "truth," seeing truth-claims as occurring within systems of thought and practice that represent either the effects of power or the distortions and exclusions of metaphysically laden discourse. While contemporary philosophers working within the Anglo-American tradition do not typically embrace objectivist or realist accounts of truth, they do tacitly assume that rational discourse serves functions other than self-assertion or the maintenance of given power relations.

Second, non-Nietzscheans affirm, while Nietzscheans deny, the utility of some concept of the "self" as a more or less transparent, unified, and self-governing entity. Throughout the 1980s, for example, John Rawls has rested his reconstructed theory of justice on a specific understanding of "moral personality" -- individuals as agents endowed with the moral powers of acting in accordance with principles of justice and of shaping and revising their own conceptions of the good. Nietzscheans, by contrast, have declared the "death of man" understood as the autonomous sovereign ego, emphasizing instead individuals as sites of language, power relations, and the unconscious.

Third, Nietzscheans are far more likely than are non-Nietzscheans to understand "modernity" as a unified and questionable historical phenomenon -- that is, to focus on the most dubious features of bureaucratic rationalization and bourgeois life and to interpret them as the progressive self-undermining of Western rationalism. While most Nietzscheans, at least in America, see their efforts as bolstering a less hierarchical and more democratic egalitarian order (Connolly 1988, 168-75), their critique of modernity nonetheless recapitulates many nineteenth-century conservative and aristocratic animadversions against the emerging liberal order (Holmes 1989, 245-47). Non-Nietzscheans, by contrast, tend to criticize contemporary society not as relying on untenable views of reason, justice, and society, but rather as failing to live up to those ideals. The rational/moral superiority of modernity is assumed; the problem lies not with our norms, but in our deeds.

The rise of postmodernism, and in particular the increasing influence of Michel Foucault on political thought, contributed to a reorientation of critical theory during the 1980s. While Habermas, for example, has continued to develop his analysis of communicative rationality as the basis of social legitimacy and to criticize the traditionalist hermeneutic enterprise of Gadamer and other German neo-Aristotelians (McCarthy 1978; White 1988), he has also embarked on a comprehensive critical examination of postmodernism (Habermas 1986, 1987). While postmodernism is typically identified with the non-Marxist left criticism of liberal democracy, Habermas has redescribed it as a form of covert conservatism with roots in the aesthetic-aristocratic antiliberalism of the nineteenth century (Habermas 1980).

The clash between modernists and postmodernists was but one of the issues that configured political theory in the 1980s. Another, triggered in the early 1980s by the publication of Michael Sandel's *Liberalism and the Limits of Justice*, Alasdair MacIntyre's *After Virtue*, Michael Walzer's *Spheres of Justice*, and a series of essays by Charles Taylor, was the "communitarian" critique of liberalism as (among other flaws) abstract, unhistorical, hyperindividualist, resting on an unsustainable metaphysic of the self, indifferent to virtue, and blind to the kinds of human goods that are enjoyed only in the company of our fellow human beings. This communitarian critique, inspired in considerable measure by Hegel, overlapped significantly with the "civic republican" critique inspired by J. G. A. Pocock's *Machiavellian Moment* (Pocock 1975) and by Hannah Arendt. Key civic republican theses such as the primacy of direct political activity oriented toward the common good were deployed against (what was taken to be) the liberal defense of privacy and self-interest.

As we shall see (Section III), the liberal response throughout the 1980s was complex. By the end of the decade, many liberals were turning back toward "civil society" -- the complex weave of groups, associations, and subcommunities -- as a mediation between individuals and state institutions. This move, inspired variously by Tocqueville, Hegel, Catholic social thought, and successful movements such as Poland's Solidarity and Czechoslovakia's Velvet Revolution, enabled liberals to recognize the emotional and moral possibilities of collective action while preserving their commitment to individual liberty. Indeed, some liberals had begun to argue that liberal autonomy was not only compatible with, but required, state action that protects subcommunities, sometimes through special legal status (Raz 1986; Kymlicka 1989, 1992; Kukathas 1992).

Parallel to the rediscovery of civil society came a third important theoretical development, the rediscovery of the "state." Theorists conducted a multi-front war against pluralism, structural-functionalism, and classical Marxism, all interpreted as modes of reducing the state to (at best) a dependent variable of social processes. In the face of this social reductionism, state theorists sought to restore an understanding of public institutions as at least quasi-autonomous and to show how this perspective could illuminate a range of empirical issues (see especially

Krasner 1984; Nordlinger 1981; Skocpol 1982; Skowronek 1984). In response, leading figures from the previous generation of theorists contended that the state had never really been expelled from political theory and research (Almond 1988; Lowi 1988) or, more pugnaciously, that its reemergence would mean reemersion in the conceptual morass from which political analysis had extricated itself only recently and with such great difficulty (Easton 1981).

A fourth key development of the past decade was the renewed interest in pragmatism, sparked by thinkers such as Richard Rorty and Richard Bernstein. Pragmatism was interpreted, first, as an alternative to philosophical "foundationalism." Rather than looking outside to metaphysics, natural science, epistemology, or theology for its fundamental propositions, social theory was free to proceed by reflecting on its own characteristic problems; the point was context, coherence, practical testing, or even imaginative projection, not linear movement from premises to conclusions (Rorty 1982, 1989; Bernstein 1985b). Pragmatism served, second, as a way of reinvigorating the idea of democratic participation through deliberation; John Dewey's understanding of "social intelligence" came increasingly to the fore (Bernstein 1985a, 1992; Anderson 1990, 1991; Westbrook 1991).

Finally, no story of political theory in the 1980s would be complete without stressing the extraordinary development and vitality of feminist thought. Its explorations ramified into all aspects of politics, society, personality, and inquiry: the constitution and construction of gender differences; the retrieval of neglected writers, agents, and questions, and the corresponding expansion or reconstitution of what political theory theorizes about; the exploration of covert gender assumptions in theoretical categories such as the public/private distinction, rights, and justice; the examination of bias and discrimination in practical spheres structured by such categories; and the questioning of entire modes of philosophy and social inquiry (those based on, e.g., abstraction and "objectivity") as gender-based and partial. Overlying this ramification of subject matter is the reenactment within feminist theory of debates across the range of social thought: feminism is now practiced in liberal-humanist, democratic, Marxist, post-structural, psychoanalytic, social-constructionist, and biological-essentialist modes, among others. Whatever the next key steps may be, it seems safe to predict that feminist thought will play a central role in the political theory of the 1990s. (For clear summaries of recent trends see Coole 1990; Randall 1991; Phillips 1991, chap. 2; Kymlicka 1990, chap. 7. More generally, see Additional Bibliography, section 2.)

II. The Chronological Beginning: The 1980s

To the diversity of narrative lines corresponds the multiplicity of possible points of departure for the telling of the tale. I have chosen to begin at what, given my assignment, is the chronological beginning -- to wit, the early 1980s -- and with a document that is at least institutionally appropriate, namely, John Gunnell's historically based contribution to the predecessor volume in this decennial series (for a comprehensive account of recent disciplinary histories of political science, see Farr 1988).

At the outset of a detailed account stretching over nearly a century, Gunnell distinguishes between "Political Theory as a subfield of the discipline of political science (PT) and political theory as a more general interdisciplinary body of literature, activity, and intellectual community (pt)" (Gunnell 1983, 3). For much of the century, the theoretical discourse of politics was intimately connected with political science, either as the framework of its research program or (especially during the 1950s and 1960s) as its ardent critic. During the 1970s, however, both these forms of connection became attenuated, PT withered, and pt flowered as a more or less autonomous endeavor with its own journals and characteristic concerns.

This shift, the separation (if not outright divorce) of political theory from political science, is the first of Gunnell's principal theses. The others concern the nature of the theoretical activity itself. In Gunnell's view, the political theory of the 1970s was characterized by a variegated *dispersion* of issues and concerns and by an *alienation* from real political life. He writes, with something approaching nostalgia, about the vanished epic struggle between behavioralists and their traditionalist critics. He describes, with something approaching contempt, what he regards as pt's metatheoretical self-absorption and deliberate self-distancing from actual political phenomena. And he predicts that these three features of pt -- divorce, dispersion, alienation -- will continue through the 1980s and beyond (Gunnell 1983; see also Gunnell 1986, chap. 1).

Of these three predictions, that of divorce has been borne out in only a qualified sense. A number of leading democratic theorists have appropriated, or critically encountered, empirical findings (see, inter alia, Beitz 1989; Dahl 1989; Fishkin 1991; Gutmann 1987; Mansbridge 1990); students of civic education have of necessity examined concrete social processes (Murchland 1991); rational choice theorists have increasingly used their deductive conclusions as hypotheses guiding empirical research (for a useful summary, see McLean 1991; Grafstein 1992); and liberal theorists are getting down to cases (Kymlicka 1989). By and large, however, theorizing directed toward the practice of political inquiry has been limited compared to the 1950s and 1960s, and the reintegration many hoped might occur after the termination of the behavioralist/traditionalist conflict has failed to materialize.

Following David Easton's 1969 call for a "post-behavioral" political science more oriented toward practical issues, "policy studies" was heralded as the arena for the new synthesis (or eclecticism, or at least truce). But in a recent survey of the first two decades of the *Policy Studies Journal*, Ethan Fishman concludes that the promise of greater integration has gone largely unfulfilled. Few students of public policy have sought to avail themselves of the conceptual and normative insights offered by the philosophical tradition; and while some political theorists have tried to engage pressing issues of contemporary American politics (notably abortion and affirmative action), few have translated their arguments into publicly accessible terms. As reasons for this disappointing result, Fishman cites "mutual antagonism": on the one hand, the lingering positivism and technical incrementalism of most empirical policy researchers, and on the other, the enduring self-absorption and hyper-textualism of many political philosophers (Fishman 1991).

With regard to Gunnell's second prediction -- continued dispersion within political theory -- I have already mentioned the proliferation of theoretical genres during the past decade. There has been a fair amount of sniping across genre borders, but notably less cross-fertilization. For example, many accounts of "democratic deliberation" tacitly presuppose either that under conditions of full deliberative equality, something approaching unanimity is to be expected or, failing a full consensus, that the results of a majoritarian decision procedure are unproblematic. But there is little empirical support for the former assumption, and the latter has been called into question (to say the least) by the line of inquiry Kenneth Arrow and others initiated some decades ago. One may seek to resolve these difficulties by reducing the centrality of majoritarianism for democratic theory (see Beitz 1989, chap. 3); one is not free simply to ignore them (for more extended remarks along these lines, see Iain McLean's essay in Held 1991, 172-96).

Let me now inspect the issue of dispersion through a somewhat wider-angled lens. Writing in the context of British political theory, David Miller focuses on three principal shifts of emphasis during the past two decades. Critical studies of classic texts were largely replaced by "conceptual history" as practiced by Quentin Skinner, J. G. A. Pocock, John Dunn, Terence Ball, James Farr, and others (see Pocock 1985; Tully 1988; Ball 1988; Ball, Farr, and Hanson 1989). Analyses of specific concepts (freedom, obligation, and so forth) were

largely replaced by more systematic normative political theories, many in the liberal and/or contractarian mode. Finally, theories exploring and justifying political institutions such as parliamentary government were replaced by theoretical analyses of public policy -- especially welfare state policies, at least in the British case (Miller 1990).

While not sharply dissenting from this description, David Held offers an historical account emphasizing addition rather than substitution. For example, he suggests that analysis of specific concepts remains viable as a mode of theorizing, coexisting with (and sometimes shading into) the elaboration of more comprehensive normative structures. (Consider, inter alia, Richard Flathman's careful inquiries into concepts such as freedom, authority, and citizenship; Flathman 1987.) Similarly, he suggests that normative-theoretical reflection on institutions is supplemented, but hardly replaced, by parallel analyses of public policy issues. And he emphasizes the importance of developments in the form of "model-building" political theory drawing on the resources of theoretical economics, game theory, and rational choice theory (Held 1991, 16-18; see also Elster 1991 and McLean 1991a).

The inevitable question is how (or whether) these lines of theorizing fit together. A generation ago, Brian Barry suggested that if the (then just barely beginning) upsurge of systematic normative theory constituted a return to traditional political philosophy's concern with the nature and conditions of good forms of government, the development of the theorizing Held dubs model-building should be viewed as "technical aids to clear thinking about this subject matter" (Barry 1989, 17).

There was, and is, much good sense in this proposal. As I have already suggested, however, theorists in both modes have been notably slow to embrace it. One reason, perhaps, is that model-building typically presents itself as more than technical. As Jon Elster has recently put it, "Rational choice theory is first and foremost normative. It tells us what to do in order to achieve our aims as closely as possible. It does not, in the standard version, tell us what our aims ought to be" (Held 1991, 116-17). Rational choice theory, then, addresses its normative assessment to the nexus between individual aims and collective choice procedures (or institutions); it is uncritical regarding individual aims themselves. But this last point is ambiguous: it can be read as saying that no form of theory can rationally assess individual aims or, alternatively, that only forms of theory other than model-building can do so. The former represents not a Barry-style technical aid for, but rather a direct challenge to, normative theories that seek to appraise and where necessary modify individual goals and attachments. The latter tacitly proposes a division of labor between theories of preference-formation and theories of preference-aggregation, an arrangement that would at least make possible some synthesis along Barry's lines (for further remarks along this line, see Miller 1990, 432-33).

Gunnell's third prediction, concerning alienation, raises even more complex questions. To begin with, the standard for engagement with "real politics" is hardly self-evident. This much is clear: political theory is located somewhere between philosophy and politics, partaking of both, identical with neither. No doubt much contemporary theory is too abstract and self-contained to shed much light on politics. Still, to have any chance of providing its distinctive form of illumination, theory must stand at some distance from the practice of politics; accusations of excessive distance are always contestable and not infrequently unfair.

Beyond this relatively easy step, matters quickly become more complex; the distance between theory and practice cannot be measured as the crow flies. Michael Walzer has argued for a kind of "connected" criticism that confronts the practices of a specific community with its own immanent norms. On inspection, he suggests, it turns out that these norms are quite concrete, embedded in specific functional "spheres" of overall community life (Walzer 1983, 1987). John Rawls has proposed a normative structure whose basic building blocks -- inter alia, conceptions of a well-ordered society and of moral personality -- are drawn from the public culture of a liberal democratic community. This too is a form of connection, albeit at a higher level of generality than Walzer thinks appropriate (Rawls 1980). Even more general, yet still in some measure connected, is Habermas's effort to draw norms transcending (but valid for) specific social contexts out of the commitments immanent in undistorted communicative practice (Habermas 1987, lecture XI).

To be sure, the link between these various normative standpoints and concrete political problems is not always straightforward. But it seems unreasonable to expect theory by itself to do all the work. At its best, theory can establish a general framework that helps us pick out, and put in order, the features of actual institutions and policies needed for their assessment. Even when concrete phenomena do not directly inform the discovery (or construction) of principles of judgment, they will form indispensable elements of their meaning and application.

However abstractly political theory presents itself, it is seldom as far removed from politics as it may appear. On the contrary, it may well be characterized as the continuation of politics by other means. To repeat a theme already broached: many contemporary theories represent varieties of discomfort with life in liberal democratic/bureaucratic welfare states. That these theories become elaborate and even abstruse does not mean that they wholly lose touch with, or fail to explicate, the experiences out of which they arise. That they employ unfamiliar vocabularies and grammars of criticism reflects the special situation of contemporary antiliberalism -- namely, the eroding credibility of Marxism as alternative practice.

This much, though, must be conceded to Gunnell: many theoretical disputes reach the point of diminishing or even negative returns long before they grind to a halt. Theoretical discourse may begin as rooted, but it can (as Gunnell suggests) end as aimlessly self-referential, as a gear spinning without connection to any other machinery. This is the phenomenon inspiring Brian Barry's "nightmarish feeling that 'the literature' has taken off on an independent life and now carries on like the broomsticks bewitched by the sorcerer's apprentice" (Barry 1989, 18). It can be ameliorated only by book publishers and journal editors more prepared than are many today to blow the whistle on exhausted topics and to take chances on less entrenched or faddish approaches.

At roughly the same time that Gunnell was composing his trenchant account, *Political Theory* published a special issue entitled "Political Theory in the 1980s: Prospects and Topics." Two of the seven essays dealt with political theory as a discipline. Douglas Rae offered a Gunnellish critique: rather than boldly theorizing about politics, imperatives of security and career led academics instead to "theorize about theories about politics." The result was a lush profusion of "conceptual essays, genetic theories of theories, biographies of theorists, reductions of theories, projective transformations of theories, cryptographies of theories, consequentialist surveys of theories, structural analyses of theories, deconstructions of theories" (Rae 1981). Writing in a similar vein (if somewhat more affirmative tone), Brian Barry noted the difference between political theory as practiced in departments of political science and of philosophy: driven in each case by distinctive intradisciplinary career pressures, the former tends toward bloated and repetitive exegeses of other theories, while the latter tends toward subtle distinctions and ingenious arguments that are largely evidence-free and add little to our substantive understanding (Barry 1981).

There was much truth in these disciplinary descriptions, and not much change in the decade since (although, as I suggested earlier, these stylistic differences have been overlain with substantive ones). Still, one wonders whether these phenomena are specific to political theorists, or rather are endemic in the life of modern academics generally. The institutionalization of intellectual life in the university has fostered disciplinary parochialism and careerism and has in some ways reinforced a perennial intellectual tendency toward disengagement from serious practice. But the historical alternatives for intellectuals -- the whims of aristocratic or haute-bourgeois patrons, the petty tyrannies of editors and publishers, the unsubtle coercion of parties and movements -- have not been so inspiring either. There is a tension between freedom of inquiry and the imperatives of any institutional structure -- that is, between the life of the mind and the felt necessities of physical and social existence -- that cannot be fully overcome. The most that can reasonably be expected is constant awareness of, and struggle against, those aspects of practical context that deform thought.

Whatever their exaggerations, the arguments of Rae, Barry, and Gunnell can be understood as bracing antidotes to the mood of self-congratulation that had settled over political theory in the early 1980s in the wake of its phoenix-like rebirth. The standard account goes something like this: The "death" of constructive political theory and its replacement with the history of political thought was in fact murder by positivism. But with the dwindling plausibility of positivism through both external challenge and internal critique, the possibility reemerged of a political theory sobered by the demolition of earlier naivete but confident of its ability to engage in non-emotivist, adequately defensible normative discourse. The space thus opened was occupied with the publication of John Rawls's *Theory of Justice*, which triggered a period (not yet ended) of intense activity and palpable progress (see especially Plant 1991).

This story was too simple to be entirely true. As Barry has recently argued, few of the mid-century philosophers fingered as the hitmen were actually positivists, and it is just as plausible to ascribe the decline of political theory to a mushy but pervasive utilitarianism (Barry 1990, xxxii-xxxviii). This then yields the Revised Standard Version: Rawls is still at the heart of the story, but now as an anti-utilitarian who presupposes and builds upon the discrediting of logical positivism.

Still, doubts could be, and were, raised, concerning the viability of this entire theoretical style. John Dunn, for example, wondered whether the new breed of normative anti-utilitarians (among whom he included Robert Nozick, Ronald Dworkin, and Bruce Ackerman as well as Rawls) were "utopian" in the negative sense of overlooking inescapable questions of political possibility. Political theory, he declared, "is not principally an exercise in the appraisal and grading of the comparative ethical merits of different societies. Rather, it is a segment of human practical reason." Among other implications, this means that political theory cannot simply impose itself upon, but must directly take into account, the constraints of practice; for political theorists,

sociological innocence is utterly debilitating (Dunn 1985, 154-55, 159-160).

Granting, arguendo, the good sense of Dunn's general point, one may wonder whether it is wholly fair to all the theorists he reproaches. Rawls for one has contended throughout the 1980s that political theory must be political through and through: it must be rooted in the public culture of the societies it addresses, and it must build upon basic features of those societies -- in the case of liberal democracies, on the fact of pluralism. Doubts can be raised as to the adequacy of the "commonsense political sociology" on which Rawls relies, but its central place in recent iterations of his theory can hardly be denied.

Yet this fact does not by itself suffice to meet the deeper thrust of Dunn's criticism, which calls into question not just the relationship between theoretical norms and empirical facts, but the currently popular characterization of political theory as the development and justification of normative propositions. Rather, Dunn insists, political theory is principally an attempt to understand what is really going on in society, and its agenda is therefore set (or ought to be set) by developments in a "historically given practical world" (Dunn 1985, 1).

Dunn's counterproposal has the merit of highlighting the fact that the demise of positivism spawned more than renewed normative activities. It also legitimized a conception of interpretation as a distinctive feature of social inquiry -- specifically, an interpretive practice carried on within traditions and history and with a keen self-reflective awareness of the interpreter's specific, though open and malleable, finitude (Held 1991, 13-16). Granting the legitimacy of interpretation, however, the proposed substitution of understanding for appraisal cannot be fully executed. As Dunn himself points out, "the question of whether an existing assemblage of human practices is essentially appropriate as it stands or whether it requires drastic and systematic reconstitution is at the core of social and political theory." For this reason, "a simple appeal to the authority of practice has no determinate content and is necessarily either evasive, insidious, or vacuous." The critique of philosophical detachment launched by Oakeshott and Wittgenstein among others serves as a necessary corrective to naive or vicious abstraction, but "it hardly makes a very adequate philosophical approach to the rational critique and prudent revision of human practices" (Dunn 1985, 174-75). What we seem to be left with, then, is the more measured if less challenging view that while concrete political practice provides the proper objects of political philosophy, such practice cannot directly resolve the choice it regularly sets between change and the status quo. Political philosophy is not free to disregard the phenomena of (e.g.) political economy and ethnic division, but the questions they raise of appraisal and response are at least distinguishable from those of understanding *simpliciter* (for related features of this issue, see Galston 1980, 25-27 [on Oakeshott]; Bernstein 1985b, 154-55 [on Gadamer]; Beiner 1989 [on the Gadamer/Habermas debate]).

It is harder to set aside another of Dunn's objections. The new wave of anti-utilitarian theories, he insists, lacks the means essential for its self-justification: while deeply Kantian in inspiration, the theories offer "a Kantian ethics without any convincingly characterized defense of or surrogate for a Kantian ontology." To be sure, the quasi-Kantians are not alone in this; the past decade has also yielded neo-Aristotelianism without teleological metaphysics and neo-Hegelianism without History or Totality. Still, the thinkers among whom modern theorists scavenge for inspiration were at least addressing serious problems, which we are avoiding: "to raid their philosophical creations, like magpies, for odd bits of more or less sparkling material to adorn our own less ambitious intellectual domiciles is to display a particularly unreflective intellectual indolence" (Dunn 1985, 179-80).

This criticism reflects an important feature of contemporary theory, much discussed during the 1980s. Since the publication of Richard Rorty's *Philosophy and the Mirror of Nature* in 1979, the rejection of "foundationalism" has gathered strength. Since Descartes (the argument runs), both natural science and social theory were bewitched by the false metaphor of solid (indubitable) foundations as giving strength to otherwise rickety (that is, contestable) propositions. But now that we "know" that no such foundations are available, that the very idea of such foundations is incoherent, we can get on with the business of theorizing as a self-consciously social enterprise rooted in the beliefs and practices of the enterprising community (Rorty 1979).

Many critics of contemporary anti-foundationalism believe that these Rortean arguments proceed too briskly (not to say blithely). We are not faced, they insist, with the stark choice between Cartesian first principles and Wittgensteinian "forms of life" as sources of normative judgment; there are coherent alternatives to both objectivism and relativism (Bernstein 1985b; Herzog 1985). The internal critique of socially established practices can yield surprising results. Moreover, the rejection of X as a basis for political theory does not entail the rejection of all relation between X and theory: certain political-theoretical theses may turn out to be inconsistent with (say) particular metaphysical views of the self, and vice-versa (Galston 1991b, chap. 2). If so, the heart of Dunn's objection is sustained.

While we may no longer be able to do political theory in the grand metaphysical style of previous centuries, we are not free to assume that it is an autonomous and self-sufficient endeavor.

III. Contemporary Liberal Democracy

As I noted earlier, the proliferation of political theory during the 1980s renders the selection of any single narrative line to some extent arbitrary. I want to suggest, however, that one plausible way of telling the story is to focus on contemporary liberal democracy -- in particular, on the diverse ways in which it has been attacked and defended.

In the hope of bringing some rough order into the thrust-and-parry, let me offer a schematic description of the political system at issue. Contemporary liberal democracy includes, at a minimum, the following features: constitutional government, based on popular consent and operating through representative institutions; a market economy subject to some degree of political restriction and regulation; a system of welfare provision and social insurance; a diverse society with a wide range of individual opportunities and choices, and of independent groups and associations ("civil society"); and a substantial, strongly protected sphere of privacy and individual rights. What follows is a brief review, seriatim.

Constitutional Government

During the 1970s it was widely argued that liberal democracies were excessively responsive to their publics -- whence "overload," inflation, and crises of governance. Far from being historical accidents, many thought, these trends represented an unfolding inner logic -- a democratic corrosion of previous hierarchical and cultural restraints on public demands. During the 1980s, by contrast, the emphasis shifted to the inadequate responsiveness of representative institutions. This indictment included numerous counts: the insulation of political elites from ordinary citizens; excessive reliance on courts at the expense of a more majoritarian, citizen-based politics; the disproportionate impact of organized "special interests" on the legislative process; the diversionary and demagogic manipulation of public dialogue, tactics magnified by modern communications technology; and, most fundamentally, the exclusion of the citizen-body from direct involvement in the institutions of self-government.

Underlying these specific indictments could be discerned three democratic standards allegedly violated in everyday practice: equality, deliberation, and participation. It is by no means clear, however, that these standards are in practice harmonious -- that reforms intended to enhance any one of them will necessarily promote the others (see Fishkin 1991). Nor is it clear what each, considered separately, in practice requires. Take democratic equality: Does it apply to individuals or groups? Does it require only fair opportunity, or in addition some attention to results? These and related issues have arisen in the context of interpreting and enforcing the U.S. Voting Rights Act (for the most thorough discussion, see Beitz 1989, chaps. 6 and 7). There is somewhat more agreement on the general proposition that inequalities of money and private power should not be allowed to distort the political articulation of competing views within the democratic community, but the practical requirements of this proposition are disputed (see, e.g., Beitz 1989, chap. 9; Fishkin 1991, 29-34, 99-101).

Reflecting in part the low level of contemporary political discourse, the past decade has witnessed an explosion of interest in democratic deliberation (see Additional Bibliography, section 4). Many theorists would agree with Jane Mansbridge that "the quality of deliberation makes or breaks a democracy" (Murchland 1991, 125); many have offered normative descriptions of improved deliberations; the impact of pragmatist and Deweyan analogies between scientific and political communities has been substantial. Practical and institutional proposals have, however, lagged behind, in part because deliberative ideals run up against some harsh realities of campaigns and representation in mass democracies, but also because, taken to extremes, the emphasis on deliberation can turn into a romantic escape from politics. Sound deliberation will improve the articulation of differences, but it will not necessarily erase them. Not all deliberation will be conducted as a quest for the common good, and unforced consensus will rarely be its product. Deliberation is an indispensable aspect of politics, but not (in most circumstances) a full substitute for the exercise of power.

Rising interest in deliberation is in some respects an aspect of the broader concern with direct citizen participation in democratic governance. While the necessity of some sort of representation in the modern nation-state can hardly be denied, some theorists have taken this fact as proof of the superiority of smaller political units, and many have looked to local politics, grassroots organizations, and group rights as counterweights to large-scale representative institutions. The classic Madisonian argument that representation enhances deliberation is not much in vogue; the perfectionist Arendtian claim that only direct participation develops and expresses citizens' humanity has carried the day (for quintessential statements, see Barber 1984 and

the essay by Pitkin and Shumer in Murchland 1991, 106-14; for a thoughtful dissent on behalf of representation and a more skeptical view of politics generally, see Kateb 1981).

One difficulty with the participatory ideal, evident in practice but underexplored in theory, is its tendency to shift power toward those with greater inclination and opportunity to invest substantial time and energy in political activity. As students of post-1968 Democratic Party presidential nominating processes have long argued, this shift does not necessarily lead to results that are more representative of all interests and views within the relevant community.

Cutting across specific debates about equality, deliberation, and participation is the broader question of how far democracy's writ runs. Some theorists have argued that the existence of a hierarchically organized corporate economy is incompatible with the principles of a democratic polity (e.g., Walzer 1983) while others offer a less unitary view (e.g., Miller 1989, chap. 9). This is one manifestation of the wide-ranging disagreement concerning the amount of differentiation that does, or should, exist within a liberal democracy; compare, for example, Stephen Macedo's characterization of liberalism as a comprehensive regime with Charles Larmore's critique of that "expressivist" idea (Macedo 1990, chap. 2; Larmore 1987, chaps. 4 and 5).

Markets

During the past generation, the long-running theoretical debate between friends and foes of market economies has been enriched by practical experience in the advanced industrialized West, in nations struggling with the legacy of Stalinism, and in post-colonial regions experimenting with different models of development. We are now in a position to evaluate what has been gained, lost, and learned (or relearned).

The market, it is now widely acknowledged, is what its staunchest defenders always insisted: a remarkable mechanism for transmitting information and for inducing change. It promotes efficiency, generates wealth, fosters individual mobility and opportunity, and increases personal freedom (see Miller 1989, part II). These are not inconsiderable advantages; they help explain the rise of conservative parties throughout the West during the 1980s, the delegitimation of command economies in Eastern Europe and the former Soviet Union, the attack on state influence over the economy throughout Latin America, and the increasing influence of the Asian model of development vis-a-vis the Tanzanian socialist model so popular in the 1970s.

But as recent experience suggests, there are important entries in the debit column as well. The market is insensitive to the distribution of income and wealth among economic classes and geographical locations; indeed, there are indications that under contemporary conditions it tends to exacerbate preexisting disparities. Left to its own devices, the market does little to alleviate the burdens of the dislocations it induces: witness the struggles of communities and regions dependent on declining economic sectors. To individuals as well as firms, the market presents various barriers to entry that are bound to have unequal impacts on different social groups, especially when (as today) educational attainment commands an increasing wage and mobility premium. As currently organized, the market does little to ameliorate tensions women experience between workplace and family or to reduce persistent inequalities flowing from this tension as well as from continuing discrimination in pay and promotion. The market is structured by rules that it neither creates nor enforces, so if the political sphere does not exercise its authority appropriately vis-a-vis the market, inefficiencies and scandals result. The market does not achieve a self-regulating balance between consumption and investment or, for that matter, between short-term and long-term interests. And added to these difficulties rediscovered in recent years are the classic kinds of market failure known (if sometimes underestimated) all along: imperfect information, externalities not factored into perceived prices, and inadequate provision of the public goods that undergird sustainable economic growth.

To the extent that the liberal democratic project is bound up with rising material aspirations, its historic link to (suitably regulated) market economies cannot be regarded as accidental. But that is not the end of the matter. To begin with, most theorists deny any easy identification of distributive justice with the outcome of unadjusted market processes. Whether one invokes the criterion of need, or desert, or equal respect, or equality of opportunity, the operation of the market is bound to seem in some measure morally arbitrary, if not repugnant. The issue of how the imperatives of aggregation and distribution are related is one of the staples of contemporary theory. Rawls's "difference principle" represents an influential proposal for balancing these two imperatives, seen as partially opposed. It is also possible to argue, as do some libertarians, that distribution has no standing independent of the market (see Kymlicka 1990, chap. 4; Miller 1989, chap. 2); with Ronald Dworkin, that aggregate growth has no independent normative status (Dworkin 1985, chap. 12); or, with some advocates of workplace democracy, that the motivational effects of a more just distribution will simultaneously promote enhanced productivity and growth (Reich 1989, chaps. 9 and 23).

A second objection to markets goes deeper. The commitment to growth can be questioned on both empirical and normative grounds: empirically, as resting on counterfactual assumptions about resources, technology, and the global "carrying capacity"; normatively, as embodying a rapacious and exploitative attitude toward a nature whose beauty is to be cherished and integrity respected. These considerations have sparked the rise of "Green" parties in Europe and of a worldwide environmental movement, and they have helped revive the centuries-old tradition of anti-modernist thought, the latest wave of which seems inspired by Heidegger. It remains to be seen, however, what will happen if democratic majorities come to see a conflict between the maintenance of the environment as a public good and the opportunity to acquire private goods historically afforded by economic growth. I might add that as the walls separating the capitalist West and socialist East fell, it became apparent that polities linked to market economies had been far more responsive than were those of command economies to issues of environmental degradation.

The third, perhaps most fundamental, objection to markets focuses on the quality of human relationships it entails, within the process of production and for society generally. This critique, propounded in overlapping ways by Marxists, utopian socialists, and traditionalists, emphasizes the dehumanizing effects of specialized labor, the cash nexus, the relentless destabilization of established communities, and the loss of understanding and control summed up in the term "alienation."

This objection persists because it reflects real problems. The division of labor is indeed humanly problematic; Adam Smith himself argued that "The man whose whole life is spent in performing a few simple operations...generally becomes as stupid and ignorant as it is possible for a human creature to become." Materialism is unattractive and hardly conducive to moral depth; the constant dynamism of markets undercuts the desire for security and stability; and so forth.

But what is the standpoint from which these criticisms are launched? A central teaching of the biblical tradition is that human labor is alienated, not accidentally or temporarily but intrinsically. From this standpoint, which deserves more theoretical consideration than it usually receives, the demand for an end to alienation represents a covert desire for the (impossible) return to Eden. Or if we wish to remain on the purely secular plane, we may remind ourselves of the old joke: What is the difference between capitalism and communism? Capitalism is the exploitation of man by man; communism is just the reverse.

To repeat, this is not to say that the underlying normative concern -- for the development of healthier individuals and societies -- is beside the point. Indeed, the liberal reform impulse in the West during the past 150 years has worked to make market relations of both production and exchange more decent and humanizing, while preserving (as Marx also sought to do) the most dynamic, productive, and liberating elements of market systems. The results are imperfect, the effort incomplete and ongoing. But what is the alternative? The return to artisanship and small-scale production represents at best an option within, not a substitute for, the market; and as the work of Robert Lane, among others, suggests, there is little evidence that in practice (as opposed to ideology) nonmarket systems score higher along key normative dimensions than do markets (Lane 1978, 1986, 1989).

Welfare

At the heart of the liberal effort to mitigate the less desirable effects of the market lies the modern welfare state, the practice of which has spawned a significant theoretical literature (Gutmann 1988; Moon 1988). It has been justified variously as the protection of the most vulnerable members of society, as the provision of basic human needs, as the reflection of the liberal commitment to autonomy and consent, or as recognition of basic communal cohesion and shared fate (Miller 1990, 435). Judgments concerning its practical adequacy within any particular community will reflect expectations, frequently competing, as to the purposes it should serve (for a discussion within the U.S. context, see Marmor et al. 1990, chaps. 2 and 7). Welfare policies have been criticized by libertarians, as illegitimate state interference with property and personal freedom; by neo-conservatives, as fostering dependency and thereby perpetuating the ills they are intended to counteract; by egalitarians, as paternalistic and dehumanizing; by traditional leftists, as social pacification masquerading as humanitarianism; and by Foucauldians, as an aspect of the insidious extension of social discipline throughout modern life.

In contemporary U.S. politics, the characteristic bureaucratic mechanisms for the delivery of welfare services have come under attack (from dissidents in both major parties) as cumbersome, inefficient, and diversionary, and an effort is now underway to think through less bureaucratic alternatives. This practical development gives rise to an intellectual challenge, the elaboration of a theory of what might be termed "market welfare," similar to that faced by theoreticians of market socialism.

Social Diversity

Central to the self-understanding of liberalism is the conviction that it provides the widest possible scope for diversity -- that is, for conceptions of the good and ways of life that individuals and groups may select, or to which they may adhere, without bias or interference. This conviction has evoked a range of objections. Some feminists and multiculturalists argue that in practice liberalism tacitly endorses and enforces a constraining (patriarchal, racist, Eurocentric) vision of human life. This raises the question, much debated among these critics, whether the cure for the diseases of liberalism is more liberalism -- a society more aware of and responsive to the full claims of diversity -- or rather a break with liberalism in the name of some version of separatism.

Within liberal theory, the discussion of diversity has revolved around the issue of "neutrality." Can liberalism be understood as a generalization of the idea of religious toleration, neutral with respect to ways of life and conceptions of the good? On which understanding of neutrality is this claim most plausible? During the 1980s, the pro-neutrality arguments of liberals such as Rawls, Dworkin, and Ackerman have been countered by liberals who believe that neutrality is not possible or, if possible, not obviously desirable. Still others argue that the issue is not universal theory but rather contextual commitment: neutrality means opposition to historically specific kinds of state intervention. Amidst this proliferating debate, a rough-and-ready consensus may be shaping up: while no form of political community can be fully neutral in any sense, liberal communities are more capacious and accommodating than any others, and they possess the inner resources to reflect on, and in some measure rectify, their historic biases and constraints (on neutrality, see generally Additional Bibliography, section 9).

The neutrality discussion led to, or joined with, the question of community. During the 1980s, communitarians suggested the liberal emphasis on diversity came at the expense of devotion to the common good and that, taken to an extreme, it might undermine patriotic identification with, and even the viability of, liberal societies. The liberal response took three forms. It was argued, first, that the rhetoric of the common good had historically functioned as a cloak for elitism, militarism, and state oppression and that suspicion of this category was amply warranted; second, that liberalism embodied a conception of justice that all citizens could reasonably embrace and that could serve as an adequate basis for shared commitments and common endeavors; and third, that over and above justice, there was a distinctively liberal conception of the good that informed liberal communities.

Another count in the communitarian indictment was the claim that liberalism could not accommodate any adequate account of virtue. In the wake of the relentless liberal corrosion of shared beliefs and practices on which the virtues depend, we were now living "after virtue;" but life under such circumstances was barren, conflict-ridden, and degrading (MacIntyre 1981). A related thesis, of civic republican inspiration, was the charge that the privileged position of self-interest within liberal thought (and life) ruled out virtue understood as selfless devotion to the common good.

Once again, the liberal response was complex. Influenced by an interpretation of early modern history, some liberals argued that the distinction between selfishness and selflessness does not map neatly onto the distinction between good and bad; piety can produce more cruelty, and idealism more evil, than selfishness ever did (Holmes 1989, 233). Others argued that liberalism was by no means devoid of an understanding of virtue, one distinguished from the contemplative, republican, and Christian conceptions, to be sure, but not without its own dignity and integrity (Galston 1991a; Macedo 1990; Shklar 1984). It does appear that it is easier for liberal theory to accept a conception of the virtues as instrumental to the preservation of liberal societies than as intrinsic to human excellence. But in circumstances of deep practical and philosophical disagreement as to the content of intrinsic excellence, this inclination is not obviously a disadvantage.

Privacy and Individual Rights

Beginning with its effort to decouple political life from intractable religious disputes, liberalism has employed a distinction between the public and private spheres. As Nancy Rosenblum has observed, the boundary has been anything but fixed and inflexible. Still, its existence (and corresponding arguments about its location) has been constitutive for liberal thought. Therein lies a perennial liberal vulnerability: it can always be charged that a matter of public concern has been erroneously immunized from public scrutiny or that a matter deemed "private" illicitly influences public deliberation (Rosenblum 1989, 5, 7).

In past generations this charge was most likely to be leveled by Marxists against the privatization of economic relations; today its most usual provenance is feminists critical of the privatization of gender and family relations. It can be argued that gender inequalities distort liberal politics, or that liberal politics defines and defends such inequalities; at any rate, that the liberal state cannot remain neutral with regard to them (Okin 1989). The difficulty is to determine, if the personal is truly the political, how the public/private distinction is to be preserved in any form. This is one reason why many contemporary feminists have altogether rejected the liberal problematic.

Another reason is the liberal focus (critics would say fixation) on rights. Here many feminists close ranks with communitarians, of whom they are otherwise quite critical. Rights are abstract, but life is concrete; rights are individual, but life is interpersonal and social; rights are defensive and conflictual, while what we need is connection, care, and cooperation; rights pretend to universal validity, when they are at best dubious social constructions (Gilligan 1982; Pateman 1988; Ruddick 1984).

The liberal defense of rights has historically taken fear of disaster as its point of departure: rights may be, or do, much of what their critics allege, but where would we be without them? In our desire for a more caring society and more meaningful politics, let us not forget the danger of tyranny. Besides (it may be said in a more affirmative mode), rights help secure the possibility of true individuality, pluralism, and shifting involvements. If we really prize the opportunity to shed traditional roles and undertake various experiments in living, rights are needed to secure the structure of liberty (see the essays by Shklar, Kateb, and Rosenblum in Rosenblum 1989). In a more theoretical vein, defenders of rights argue that they are far more than "nonsense upon stilts," as charged by classical utilitarians, or fictions on a par with belief in unicorns and witches, as alleged by contemporary communitarians (for a survey, see Galston 1991b).

The debate over rights is part of a larger dispute over the appropriate way of conceiving the relation between individuals and communities. During the 1980s, communitarians typically charged liberals with embracing the myth of the presocial individual, of overlooking the myriad ways in which individuals are socially constituted, and therefore of overestimating the extent to which individuals can separate themselves from social aims and attachments. Liberals counterattacked, charging communitarians with historical inaccuracy and philosophical ineptitude: liberalism has never been so foolish as to deny that we become human only in society, but it does not follow that society must be organic or solidaristic. The liberal idea of individualism is political, not metaphysical, directed at illicit forms of public or private power based on unsustainable claims to knowledge and personal superiority.

By the end of the 1980s, however, the debate had subsided somewhat and was in the process of being reconfigured. One of its initiators, Charles Taylor, suggested (some would say conceded) that the contending parties had talked past one another. "Ontological" issues divide individualists from holists, while "advocacy" issues divide (say) partisans of individual rights from defenders of solidaristic communities. Taylor's thesis is that while there is at least some connection between them, one's stand on the former set of issues does not rigidly determine any position on the latter: for example, it is possible to combine holism at the ontological level with individualism on the political plane (Taylor 1989). If the dispute does not completely disappear, it is to say the least radically reconfigured. In particular, attention can shift to the arena of advocacy, in which (as many commentators have observed) communitarians have been remarkably reticent about advancing substantive counterproposals to classic liberal positions.

This lengthy chronicle of controversies between supporters and detractors of liberalism could leave the impression that recent liberal thought is more monolithic than it is. In fact, as in so many other parts of political theory, liberalism witnessed a notable proliferation during the 1980s. There were numerous disagreements over the scope of liberal rights, the requirements of liberal equality, and the content of liberal justice. Deontological liberalism was developed and denounced. Some theorists revived Millean utilitarianism as a basis for modern liberalism, while others sought support in Hegel, Aristotle, Montaigne, or Emerson, among many others. Following Isaiah Berlin, some argued that liberalism expresses, or requires, the existence of plural and incommensurable values, no one of which enjoys clear priority; others pursued Ronald Dworkin's suggestion that liberalism represents the working out of a single master value, a distinctive conception of human equality.

The variety of substantive liberal positions was almost matched by the range of justificatory strategies. Rawls was thought by many to have shifted from an argument offered as valid regardless of time and place, appealing to general features of human rationality and conditions of existence, to an argument presenting itself as an interpretation of democratic public culture (Galston 1991a, chap. 7). Richard Rorty followed up his critique of foundationalism with an unabashed account of liberalism as ethnocentric (Rorty 1983). Critics of particularist liberalism (e.g., Waldron 1987) countered by arguing that liberalism is unintelligible without some kind of universalist claim. Pursuing this strategy, some thinkers inspired by Habermas, Dewey, and Aristotle systematically explored the structural parallels between the scientific conditions of free inquiry and the political conditions of a free society (Anderson 1990; Salkever 1990; Spragens 1990). Still others favored a mid-range, contextualist approach, presenting liberalism as the outcome of a series of specific historical choices between better and worse political alternatives, understood deliberatively and prudentially (Herzog 1989; Holmes 1984). At present there is arguably more agreement among liberals (indeed, between liberals and non-liberals)

concerning concrete political judgments than concerning justificatory strategies; but whether this fact suggests the need to abandon, or rather to reemphasize, the process of justification is itself the subject of controversy.

IV. The Future Agenda of Political Theory

While not exactly unjudgmental, the preceding remarks have been as nearly descriptive as I could manage. In this final section I wish to take up the editor's charge to discuss the future agenda of political theory, which will necessarily (she notes) "reflect a more personal view of the field."

As a general matter, I believe, theorists should try harder to take real political controversies as their point of departure and to attend to the terms in which these debates are conducted. There should be less top-down theorizing or, to put it another way, more of an effort to employ the method of reflective equilibrium -- judgment of abstract principles in light of concrete political realities, not just vice-versa -- that Rawlsians often preach but seldom practice (see Gutmann 1989, 342). Theorists should also reduce their reliance on a characteristic method of analytical moral philosophy: the employment of micro-examples either forcibly extracted from their real-world contexts of meaning, or invented outright.

If theorists are to begin with actual political issues, they must work harder at the outset to be empirical. By this I mean two things. The theoretical agenda must be set to a greater extent by the major practical questions now before us, and we must try to see the issues as they are, not as ideologically prepackaged. This is not to say that political theory can return to the epistemology of immaculate perception; it is to say that the basic contours of most issues are marked out by some combination of empirical research and common sense that political theorists (and for that matter political leaders) ignore at their peril.

The night before I wrote this paragraph, for example, Mikhail Gorbachev resigned as president of the defunct Soviet Union, acknowledging among other errors his inability to see the forces of disintegrative nationalism at work in the empire he ruled. The ideology of socialist universalism had blinded him to what was happening before his eyes. During the 1990s, political theorists will render themselves as irrelevant as Gorbachev if they ignore the global nationalist tide -- not to mention the shared language, ethnicity, history, and religion so often at its heart.

Even when ideology does not lead to denial, it can generate distortion. The Marxist picture of liberal democratic society as comprehensively exploitative began, and ended, as a caricature; so too the Foucauldian picture of liberal democratic society as comprehensively disciplinary. To be sure, each of these orientations provokes thought and casts light onto previously darkened areas. But both mistake a part for the whole; both offer a totalizing interpretation of social reality based on that part; and neither in the last analysis can validate its preferred counterproposal without referring to the liberal norms it seeks to expunge. As Nancy Fraser has argued, "By claiming that panoptical autonomy is not the horror show Foucault took it to be, the Habermassian humanist challenges him to state, in terms independent of the vocabulary of humanism, exactly what is wrong with this ...society and why it ought to be resisted" (Fraser 1985).

Theorists too often assume that pointing to flaws, real or alleged, in the theoretical justification of a particular political system suffices as a critique of practices within that system. It is not difficult, for example, to uncover difficulties in various philosophical accounts of rights. But that is hardly the end of the matter; we must also attend to the ways in which rights function in practice, and to the real-world consequences of trying to do without them. Empirically sensitive theory will reason from politics to texts and arguments, not just the other way around. The alternative is the political equivalent of the aeronautical proof that bumblebees cannot fly.

If theory does become more empirically aware, we may expect a diminished role for what Ian Shapiro has called "gross concepts" (Shapiro 1989). We will spend much less time arguing about liberalism versus communitarianism (or civic republicanism), foundationalism versus contextualism, and so forth. Our theoretical disagreements will be finer-grained; they will illuminate, rather than substitute for, political controversies. Rather than going on holiday, our words will get to work.

Admittedly, the task of thinking empirically involves more than common sense and is greatly complicated by the sheer proliferation of research. As David Miller has noted, perhaps the greatest practical dificulty that now faces political theory "is simply the immense body of empirical material that modern political science has collected" (Miller 1987, 385). But this is an argument for intelligent selection, not blithe obliviousness. Political theorists could do worse than read this volume cover to cover before returning to their business.

This is not to say that political theory should adopt a merely passive or receptive stance toward political science. Theorists can perform an important critical function by pointing out the role of unacknowledged conceptual and normative commitments in empirical research programs. In some cases, theory can play a constructive role in the formulation of such programs (consider the impact of Arrovian theorems on research into agenda-setting processes within legislative bodies). Theory can even shape sophisticated empirical techniques to test the validity of its own internally generated hypotheses, as in the case of simulated "veil of ignorance" experiments (Frohlich and Oppenheimer 1992). The plea is only for a greater receptivity to the world on the part of theorists all too ready to distance themselves critically from it, or to impose themselves imaginatively upon it.

This should not be interpreted as a call for quietism, let alone for the abandonment of the task of critical appraisal central to political theory since its inception. It is a proposal as to how these tasks can be carried out more effectively. Another proposal in the same vein rests on the proposition that criticism is not enough. Theorists dissatisfied with the status quo have an obligation to set forth an alternative that is both preferable and practicable. In political theory, as in public life, the operative question must always be, "Compared to what?" Whether or not it is substantively correct, Winston Churchill's famous comment -- that democracy is the worst form of government except for all the others that have ever been tried -- has methodological force for theory as well as practice. It is one thing to point out incompleteness or imperfection in a political system, quite another to conclude (on that basis) that we should refrain from supporting it. Political theorists must take more seriously the possibility that our most cherished ends conflict with one another and that even under the most favorable circumstances, neither individuals nor societies can "have it all" (Barry 1990, xxxix-xliv; Lukes 1989). A simply utopian critical standpoint -- one resting, for example, on an unrealizable vision of complete liberation or perfect harmony -- is worse than useless.

An implication is that normative theory must have definable consequences. In this vein, let me propose a new "difference principle": every theorist should be required to ask, If what I say were adopted as valid or true, what difference would it make? The answer to this question need not take the form of new policies or institutions or (r)evolutionary movements; it may involve only a changed stance toward politics on the part of the theorist and others similarly situated; but it must be definable and (if the theorist is acting responsibly) explicitly defined.

Another is that political theory must be made more publicly intelligible than much of it is today. This is not to say that every argument can or should be conducted non-technically. It is to say that the principal conclusions of theory, and the considerations supporting them, must be translated into forms of expression open to scrutiny by a wider audience. The alternative is a mandarin enterprise sealed off from political life, neither nourishing nor nourished by nonacademic perspectives. In this regard, indications of seriousness would be, on the one hand, an increased propensity on the part of individual theorists to publish in semi-popular journals such as *The New Republic*, *The American Prospect*, *Dissent*, *The Atlantic*, and *Commentary*, and on the other, a greater disposition on the part of the profession generally to honor and reward a more generally accessible style of theorizing. On the former front, anyway, some recent developments have been encouraging; but it is too soon to declare the long-awaited return of the public intellectual.

With regard to the substantive agenda of future political theory, let me offer a few proposals that go beyond the general injunction of increased empirical and political awareness.

During the 1980s, neo-pragmatic attacks on "foundationalism" combined with the Nietzschean hermeneutics of suspicion and the skeptical residue of positivism to call into question the rational status of normative assessment. The result was not what one might have expected -- diminished quantity of, and confidence in, such assessment -- but the very opposite, a kind of blithe normative self-assertion. The "self" doing the asserting could be individual (the Rortyean "strong poet") or collective (the Rawlsian "democratic public culture"), but in either case it was regarded as self-sufficient. But this view of the matter is patently insufficient, for the simple reason that when self-assertions come into conflict it provides no way of adjudicating among them.

Armed with the anti-Cartesian insight that absolute certainty and verification are not to be expected, political theorists should apply themselves once again to the task of developing reasonable support for the principles they espouse. This process might involve the kind of sophisticated naturalism invoked by contemporary neo-Aristotelians. It might also involve a cautious reengagment with processes of inquiry that have historically influenced political theory, but which the contemporary revival has set aside -- in particular, metaphysics, the natural sciences, and religion. Along these lines, theorists would scrutinize, more systematically than heretofore, the proposition that our public principles can be "political, not metaphysical." And they would pay more attention to the kinds of inquiries now conducted within the American Political Science Association under the organizational rubrics of "Politics and Life Sciences" and "Politics and Religion." At the very least, a political theory practiced in this way would no longer be so unself-consciously (hence

dogmatically) secular or so thoughtlessly confident that recent biological discoveries leave our understanding of political behavior and institutions untouched.

Under the influence of *A Theory of Justice* and analytical moral philosophy, political theory during the past two decades has emphasized the assessment of public policy outcomes and of individual orientation toward public choices; Kymlicka's survey goes so far as to identify contemporary political philosophy with "theories of justice" (Kymlicka 1990, 3-5). These were hardly insignificant concerns, but they pushed into the background questions of institutional design and assessment. (Remarkably, a major influence of Rawls's *Theory of Justice*, which concentrates on the question of designing just institutions, has been to push to the background questions of institutional design and assessment.) There are some welcome signs that this imbalance is now being addressed (Brennan and Lomasky 1989; Elster and Slagstad 1988; Phillips 1991; Rothstein 1992), and one hopes that this countertrend will continue to gather strength. One of the defining characteristics of politics, after all, is the embeddedness of individual behavior within humanly contrived, and revisable, institutional structures; their assesment and reform has now, in the wake of the collapse of communism, assumed an urgent importance without precedent in recent history.

Also shoved aside by the focus on distributional issues were questions of individual character as both formed by, and sustaining, public institutions and policies. Here again there are welcome signs of a turning tide. The easy belief that the efficacy of public endeavors is unaffected by citizens' character (to be determinedly old-fashioned, by their virtue and vice) is giving way to a more complex interplay of social structure and individual agency in which the latter is seen as something more than negligible, and other than a dependent variable (Galston 1988; Wilson 1991). Theorists are increasingly interested in problems of both explicit civic education and undesigned but potent processes of character development. Here as elsewhere, it is vital to rejoin theoretical concerns to empirical political inquiry; for example, many ideologically driven propositions (from both left and right) about the effects of markets on personality turn out to be of at best questionable validity (Lane 1989).

Related to questions of character is the even wider issue of human psychology and its relation to politics. During the 1970s the impact of Freud on political theory, so profound in the 1950s and 1960s, perceptibly diminished. Much liberal theory of the past two decades has deployed a relatively thin and abstract psychological vocabulary, in which motivations of morality and self-interest have largely displaced attention to the passions. In this respect, at least, the recent resurgence of interest in Nietzsche seems likely to have a salutary effect on our understanding of phenomena such as fear, anger, and resentment (Connolly 1990); so too efforts to explore the political significance of psychologists such as Melanie Klein (Alford 1989, 1990). In general, today's political theorists would do well to remember that many of the most enduringly important theorists of the past achieved their impact in no small measure by bringing stunning visions of human desires and passions to center stage.

Another issue that must be more fully joined in the 1990s is the relation between group identity and liberal democracy. This issue arises both on the Right, with the claims of tradition and fundamentalist communities, and on the Left, with claims based on (inter alia) race, gender, and ethnicity. Specific controversies from multicultural education to affirmative action to free exercise of religion are at stake; so too is the adequacy of a mode of political theorizing that restricts itself to individuals and public structures as core elements. A range of materials could well be brought to bear on these questions -- among others, constitutional conflicts, classic discussions of civil society, feminist arguments, and forms of comunitarianism that abandon the identification of cultural community with political community. Most fundamentally, theorists will have to debate the extent to which the public principles of a liberal democratic order should be extended to, and if necessary imposed upon, the inner workings of its multiple and diverse subcommunities (for an important start see Kukathas 1992; Kymlicka 1992).

The final item in this informal agenda for the 1990s is the nature and limits of political authority. This is an issue that arises in the context of American political culture, historically torn between mistrust of, and need for, central authority. And it is an issue woven in various ways through the fabric of contemporary political theory, in the work of libertarians, liberal skeptics such as Michael Oakeshott, Isaiah Berlin, and Richard Flathman, liberal proceduralists such as Stuart Hampshire and H. L. A. Hart, and democratic dissenters such as George Kateb (drawing on the Emersonian tradition) and William Connolly (drawing on Foucault). The problem, as Flathman puts it, is that while we cannot possibly do without authority altogether, we must never lose sight of the ways in which it (necessarily) restricts the processes of free reflection and judgment (Flathman 1989). The challenge, which is both moral and institutional, is to find ways of chastening authority, of maximizing spaces for unforced individuality and commonality, that do not render authority incompetent to perform its essential tasks -- in particular, the necessarily institutional protection of the very space for freedom that can seem, but is not, wholly independent of the practice of authority (for a provocative effort to meet this challenge, see Flathman 1992).

As I have stressed throughout this essay, the 1980s have witnessed both a continued gap between political theory and political science and an enormous proliferation of theoretical agendas and styles. To some considerable extent these trends are inevitable. Still, I cannot avoid the suspicion that the ratio of synthesis to analysis in contemporary theory is far too low. Parallel to developments within separate theoretical arenas, we need more discussion about how they might fit together into a more systematic theory of politics. This amounts to a plea for something less than Kantian architectonic but more than postmodernist bricolage, perhaps along the lines of the medieval "order of the sciences."

I referred earlier to Brian Barry's proposal a generation ago that welfare economics, game theory, and rational choice should be used to clarify traditional questions of political value. No doubt some today would wish to amend this proposal, and others to reject it outright. It would surely have to be broadened to include the significant theoretical developments of the past thirty years. But it is at least headed in the right direction. In our theory as well as our politics, we should devote as much attention to the "unum" in the 1990s as we gave to the "pluribus" in the 1980s.

Notes

I want to express my gratitude to the readers of previous drafts of this essay, whose extensive comments helped me produce a final draft more nearly representative of the full range of political theory during the 1980s. These readers include William Connolly, James Farr, Richard Flathman, Michael Lacey, Jane Mansbridge, Henry Richardson, and Nancy Rosenblum. I am especially grateful to Ada Finifter, whose firm but gentle editorial hand helped make the essay far more user-friendly than it would otherwise have been. The remaining omissions and infelicities are mine alone.

Bibliography

Alford, C. Fred. 1989. *Melainie Klein and Critical Social Theory: An Account of Politics, Art, and Reason Based on Her Psychoanalytic Theory*. New Haven: Yale University Press.

Alford, C. Fred. 1990. *The Self in Social Theory: A Psychoanalytic Account of Its Construction in Plato, Hobbes, Locke, Rawls, and Rousseau*. New Haven: Yale University Press.

Almond, Gabriel A. 1988. "The Return to the State." *American Political Science Review* 82:854-74.

Anderson, Charles W. 1990. *Pragmatic Liberalism*. Chicago: University of Chicago Press.

Anderson, Charles W. 1991. "Pragmatism & Liberalism, Rationalism, and Irrationalism: A Response to Richard Rorty." *Polity* 23:357-371.

Ball, Terence. 1988. *Transforming Political Discourse*. Oxford: Basil Blackwell.

Ball, Terence, James Farr, and Russell Hanson, eds. 1989. *Political Innovation and Conceptual Change*. Cambridge: Cambridge University Press.

Barber, Benjamin. 1984. *Strong Democracy: Participatory Politics for a New Age*. Berkeley: University of California Press.

Barry, Brian. 1981. "Do Neighbors Make Good Fences? Political Theory and the Territorial Imperative." *Political Theory* 9:293-301.

Barry, Brian. 1989. *Democracy, Power, and Social Justice: Essays in Political Theory*. Oxford: Clarendon Press.

Barry, Brian. 1990. *Political Argument: A Reissue with a New Introduction*. Berkeley: University of California Press.

Beiner, Ronald. 1989. "Do We Need A Philosophical Ethics: Theory, Prudence, and the Primacy of Ethos." *Philosophical Forum* 20:230.

Beitz, Charles. 1989. *Political Equality*. Princeton: Princeton University Press.

Bernstein, Richard J. 1985a. "Dewey, Democracy: The Task Ahead of Us." In *Post-Analytic Philosophy*, ed. John Rajchman and Cornel West. New York: Columbia University Press.

Bernstein, Richard J. 1985b. *Beyond Objectivism and Relativism: Science, Hermeneutics, and Praxis*. Philadelphia: University of Pennsylvania Press.

Bernstein, Richard J. 1992. *The New Constellation: The Ethical-Political Horizons of Modernity/Postmodernity*. Cambridge: MIT Press.

Brennan, Harold G., and Loren Lomasky, eds. 1989. *Politics and Process: New Essays in Democratic Thought*. Cambridge: Cambridge University Press.

Cohen, G. A. 1988. *History, Labour, and Freedom: Themes from Marx*. Oxford: Oxford University Press.

Connolly, William E. 1988. *Political Theory and Modernity*. Oxford: Blackwell.

Connolly, William E. 1990. "Identity and Difference in Liberalism." In *Liberalism and the Good*, ed. R. Bruce Douglass, Gerald M. Mara, and Henry S. Richardson. New York: Routledge.

Coole, Diana. 1990. "Feminism and Politics." In *New Developments in Political Science*, ed. Adrian Leftwich. Aldershot: Edward Elgar.

Dahl, Robert A. 1989. *Democracy and Its Critics*. New Haven: Yale University Press.

Dunn, John. 1985. *Rethinking Modern Political Theory*. Cambridge: Cambridge University Press.

Dworkin, Ronald. 1985. *A Matter of Principle*. Cambridge: Harvard University Press.

Easton, David. 1981. "The Political System Beseiged by the State." *Political Theory* 9:303-25.

Elster, Jon. 1985. *Making Sense of Marx*. Cambridge: Cambridge University Press.

Elster, Jon. 1991. "The Possibility of Rational Politics." In *Political Theory Today*, ed. David Held. Stanford: Stanford University Press.

Elster, Jon, and R. Slagstad, eds. 1988. *Constitutionalism and Democracy*. Cambridge: Cambridge University Press.

Farr, James. 1988. "The History of Political Science." *American Journal of Political Science* 32:1175-95.

Fishkin, James S. 1991. *Democracy and Deliberation*. New Haven: Yale University Press.

Fishman, Ethan. 1991. "Political Philosophy and the Policy Studies Organization." *PS: Political Science and Politics* 24:720-23.

Flathman, Richard. 1987. *The Philosophy and Politics of Freedom*. Chicago: University of Chicago Press.

Flathman, Richard. 1989. *Toward A Liberalism*. Ithaca: Cornell University Press.

Flathman, Richard. 1992. *Willful Liberalism: Voluntarism and Individuality in Political Theory and Practice*. Ithaca: Cornell University Press.

Fraser, Nancy. 1985. "Michel Foucault: A 'Young Conservative'?" *Ethics* 96:165-84.

Frohlich, Norman, and Joe A. Oppenheimer. 1992. *Choosing Justice: An Experimental Approach to Ethical Theory*. Berkeley: University of California Press.

Galston, William A. 1980. *Justice and the Human Good*. Chicago: University of Chicago Press.

Galston, William A. 1991a. *Liberal Purposes: Goods, Virtues, and Diversity in the Liberal State*. New York: Cambridge University Press.

Galston, William A. 1991b. "Practical Philosophy and the Bill of Rights: Perspectives on Some Contemporary Issues." In *A Culture of Rights: The Bill of Rights in Philosophy, Politics, and Law -- 1791 and 1991*, ed. Michael Lacey and Knud Haakonssen. Cambridge: Cambridge University Press.

Gardbaum, Stephen A. 1992. "Law, Politics, and the Claims of Community." *Michigan Law Review* 90:685-760.

Gilligan, Carol. 1982. *In a Different Voice: Psychological Theory and Women's Development*. Cambridge: Harvard University Press.

Grafstein, Robert. 1992. "Rational Choice Inside and Out." *The Journal of Politics* 54:259-68.

Gunnell, John. 1983. "Political Theory: The Evolution of a Sub-Field." In *Political Science: The State of the Discipline*, ed. Ada W. Finifter. Washington, D.C.: The American Political Science Association.

Gunnell, John. 1986. *Between Philosophy and Politics: The Alienation of Political Theory*. Amherst: University of Massachusetts Press.

Gutmann, Amy. 1987. *Democratic Education*. Princeton: Princeton University Press.

Gutmann, Amy, ed. 1988. *Democracy and the Welfare State*. Princeton: Princeton University Press.

Gutmann, Amy. 1989. "The Central Role of Rawls's Theory." *Dissent* Summer 1989:338-42.

Habermas, Jurgen. 1980. "Modernity versus Postmodernity." *New German Critique* 22:3-14.

Habermas, Jurgen. 1986. "Taking Aim at the Heart of the Present." In *Foucault: A Critical Reader*, ed. David Couzens Hoy. Oxford: Basil Blackwell.

Habermas, Jurgen. 1987. *The Philosophical Discourse of Modernity*. Cambridge: MIT Press.

Held, David, ed. 1991. *Political Theory Today*. Stanford: Stanford University Press.

Herzog, Don. 1985. *Without Foundations: Justification in Political Theory*. Ithaca: Cornell University Press.

Herzog, Don. 1989. *Happy Slaves: A Critique of Consent Theory*. Chicago: University of Chicago Press.

Hirshman, Linda R., ed. 1990. "Symposium on Classical Philosophy and the American Constitutional Order." *Chicago-Kent Law Review* 66:1-242.

Holmes, Stephen. 1984. *Benjamin Constant and the Making of Modern Liberalism*. New Haven: Yale University Press.

Holmes, Stephen. 1989. "The Permanent Structure of Antiliberal Thought." In *Liberalism and the Moral Life*, ed. Nancy Rosenblum. Cambridge: Harvard University Press.

Kateb, George. 1981. "The Moral Distinctiveness of Representative Democracy." *Ethics* 91:357-374.

Kateb, George. 1989. "Democratic Individuality and the Meaning of Rights." In *Liberalism and the Moral Life*, ed. Nancy Rosenblum. Cambridge: Harvard University Press.

Kloppenberg, James T. 1987. "The Virtues of Liberalism: Christianity, Republicanism, and Ethics in Early American Political Discourse." *Journal of American History* 74:9-33.

Krasner, Stephen. 1984. "Approaches to the State: Alternative Conceptions and Historical Dynamics." *Comparative Politics* 16:223-46.

Kukathas, Chandran. 1992. "Are There Any Cultural Rights?" *Political Theory* 20:105-39.

Kymlicka, Will. 1989. *Liberalism, Community, and Culture.* Oxford: Oxford University Press.

Kymlicka, Will. 1990. *Contemporary Political Philosophy: An Introduction.* Oxford: Clarendon Press.

Kymlicka, Will. 1992. "The Rights of Minority Cultures." *Political Theory* 20:140-46.

Lane, Robert E. 1978. "Markets and the Satisfaction of Human Wants." *Journal of Economic Issues* 12:799-827.

Lane, Robert E. 1986. "Market Justice, Political Justice." *American Political Science Review* 80:383-403.

Lane, Robert E. 1989. "Market Choice and Human Choice." In *Markets and Justice: Nomos XXXI*, ed. John W. Chapman and J. Roland Pennock. New York: New York University Press.

Larmore, Charles. 1987. *Patterns of Moral Complexity.* Cambridge: Cambridge University Press.

Lowi, Theodore. 1988. "The Return to the State: Critique." *American Political Science Review* 82:885-91.

Lukes, Steven. 1989. "Making Sense of Moral Conflict." In *Liberalism and the Moral Life*, ed. Nancy L. Rosenblum. Cambridge: Harvard University Press.

Macedo, Stephen. 1990. *Liberal Virtues: Citizenship, Virtue, and Community in Liberal Constitutionalism.* Oxford: Clarendon Press.

MacIntyre, Alasdair. 1981. *After Virtue: A Study in Moral Theory.* Notre Dame: University of Notre Dame Press.

McLean, Iain. 1991a. "Rational Choice and Politics." *Political Studies* 39:496-512.

McLean, Iain. 1991b. "Forms of Representation and Systems of Voting." In *Political Theory Today*, ed. David Held. Stanford: Stanford University Press.

Mansbridge, Jane, ed. 1990. *Beyond Self-Interest.* Chicago: University of Chicago Press.

Mansbridge, Jane. 1991. "Democracy, Deliberation, and the Experience of Women." In *Higher Education and the Practice of Democratic Politics*, ed. Bernard Murchland. Dayton, OH: Kettering Foundation.

Marmor, Theodore, Jerry Mashaw, and Philip Harvey. 1990. *America's Misunderstood Welfare State.* New York: Basic Books.

McCarthy, Thomas. 1978. *The Critical Theory of Jurgen Habermas.* Cambridge: MIT Press.

Miller, David. 1987. "Political Theory." In *The Blackwell Encyclopedia of Political Thought*, ed. David Miller. Oxford: Basil Blackwell.

Miller, David. 1989. *Market, State, and Community: Theoretical Foundations of Market Socialism.* Oxford: Oxford University Press.

Miller, David. 1990. "The Resurgence of Political Theory." *Political Studies* 38:421-37.

Moon, J. Donald, ed. 1988. *Responsibility, Rights, and Welfare: The Theory and Practice of the Welfare State.* Boulder: Westview Press.

Murchland, Bernard, ed. 1991. *Higher Education and the Practice of Democratic Politics.* Dayton, OH: Kettering Foundation.

Nordlinger, Eric. 1981. *On the Autonomy of the Democratic State.* Cambridge: Harvard University Press.

Okin, Susan Moller. 1989. "Humanist Liberalism." In *Liberalism and the Moral Life*, ed. Nancy L. Rosenblum. Cambridge: Harvard University Press.

O'Neill, Onora. 1991. "Transnational Justice." In *Political Theory Today*, ed. David Held. Stanford: Stanford University Press.

Pangle, Thomas L. 1988. *The Spirit of Modern Republicanism.* Chicago: University of Chicago Press.

Pateman, Carole. 1988. *The Social Contract.* Stanford: Stanford University Press.

Perry, Michael J. 1988. *Morality, Politics, and Law.* New York: Oxford University Press.

Phillips, Anne. 1991. *Engendering Democracy.* University Park, PA: Pennsylvania State University Press.

Pitkin, Hanna Fenichel, and Sara Shumer. 1991. "On Participation." In *Higher Education and the Practice of Democratic Politics*, ed. Bernard Murchland. Dayton, OH: Kettering Foundation.

Plant, Raymond. 1991. *Modern Political Thought.* Oxford: Basil Blackwell.

Pocock, J. G. A. 1975. *The Machiavellian Moment.* Princeton: Princeton University Press.

Pocock, J. G. A. 1985. *Virtue, Commerce, and History.* Cambridge: Cambridge University Press.

Rae, Douglas W. 1981. "Political Theory and the Division of Labor in Society: Asleep Aboard the Titanic and Steaming into Halifax." *Political Theory* 9:369-78.

Randall, Vicky. 1991. "Feminism and Political Analysis." *Political Studies* 39:513-32.

Rawls, John. 1980. "Kantian Constructivism in Moral Theory." *Journal of Philosophy* 77:515-72.

Raz, Joseph. 1986. *The Morality of Freedom.* Oxford: Clarendon Press.

Reich, Robert B. 1989. *The Resurgent Liberal.* New York: Random House.

Reiman, Jeffrey. 1987. "Exploitation, Force, and the Moral Assessment of Capitalism: Thoughts on Roemer and Cohen." *Philosophy and Public Affairs* 16:3-41.

Rhode, Deborah, ed. 1990. *Theoretical Perspectives on Sexual Difference.* New Haven: Yale University Press.

Roemer, John. 1982. *A General Theory of Exploitation and Class.* Cambridge: Harvard University Press.

Roemer, John. 1988. *Free to Lose: An Introduction to Marxist Economic Philosophy.* Cambridge: Harvard University Press.

Rorty, Richard. 1979. *Philosophy and the Mirror of Nature.* Princeton: Princeton University Press.

Rorty, Richard. 1982. *Consequences of Pragmatism.* Minneapolis: University of Minnesota Press.

Rorty, Richard. 1983. "Postmodern Bourgeois Liberalism." *Journal of Philosophy* 80:583-589.

Rorty, Richard. 1989. *Contingency, Irony, and Solidarity.* Cambridge: Cambridge University Press.

Rosenblum, Nancy L., ed. 1989. *Liberalism and the Moral Life.* Cambridge: Harvard University Press.

Rothstein, Bo. 1992. "Social Justice and State Capacity." *Politics & Society* 20:101-26.

Ruddick, Sarah. 1984. "Maternal Thinking." In *Mothering: Essays in Feminist Theory*, ed. Joyce Trebilcot. Totowa, NJ: Rowman and Allanheld.

Salkever, Stephen G. 1990. *Finding the Mean: Theory and Practice in Aristotelian Political Philosophy.* Princeton: Princeton University Press.

Sandel, Michael. 1982. *Liberalism and the Limits of Justice.* Cambridge: Cambridge University Press.

Schuck, Peter H., and Rogers M. Smith. 1985. *Citizenship Without Consent: Illegal Aliens in the American Polity.* New Haven: Yale University Press.

Shapiro, Ian. 1989. "Gross Concepts in Political Argument." *Political Theory* 17:51-76.

Shklar, Judith N. 1984. *Ordinary Vices*. Cambridge: Harvard University Press.

Shklar, Judith N. 1989. "The Liberalism of Fear." In *Liberalism and the Moral Life*, ed. Nancy L. Rosenblum. Cambridge: Harvard University Press.

Shklar, Judith N. 1991. "Redeeming American Political Theory." *American Political Science Review* 85:3-15.

Skocpol, Theda. 1982. "Bringing the State Back In." In *Items*, vol. 36. New York: Social Science Research Council.

Skowronek, Stephen. 1984. *Building a New American State*. Cambridge: Cambridge University Press.

Spragens, Thomas A., Jr. 1990. *Reason and Democracy*. Durham, NC: Duke University Press.

Symposium. 1988. "The Republican Civic Tradition." *The Yale Law Journal* 97:1493-1723.

Taylor, Charles. 1989. "Cross-Purposes: The Liberal-Communitarian Debate." In *Liberalism and the Moral Life*, ed. Nancy L. Rosenblum. Cambridge: Harvard University Press.

Tully, James, ed. 1988. *Meaning and Context: Quentin Skinner and His Critics*. Cambridge: Polity Press.

Waldron, Jeremy. 1989. "Particular Values and Critical Morality." *California Law Review* 77:561-89.

Walzer, Michael. 1983. *Spheres of Justice*. New York: Basic Books.

Walzer, Michael. 1987. *Interpretation and Social Criticism*. Cambridge: Harvard University Press.

Westbrook, Robert B. 1991. *John Dewey and American Democracy*. Ithaca: Cornell University Press.

White, Stephen K. 1988. *The Recent Work of Jurgen Habermas: Reason, Justice, and Modernity*. Cambridge: Cambridge University Press.

Additional Bibliography

1. General
2. Feminist Thought
3. Democracy/Critical Theory
4. Utilitarianism
5. Community/Republicanism/Virtue
6. State and Civil Society
7. Socialism/Marxism
8. Liberalism
9. Liberal Neutrality
10. Liberal Justice/Equality of Opportunity
11. The Nietzschean/Postmodern Controversy

1. General

Ball, Terence, ed. 1987. *Idioms of Inquiry: Critique and Renewal in Political Science*. Albany: State University of New York Press.

Barber, Benjamin, ed. 1981. "Political Theory in the 1980s: Prospects and Topics." *Political Theory* 9:291-424.

Baynes, Kenneth, James Bohman, and Thomas McCarthy, eds. 1987. *After Philosophy: End or Transformation?* Cambridge: MIT Press.*

Bluhm, William. 1984. *Force or Freedom? The Paradox in Modern Political Thought*. New Haven: Yale University Press.

Brown, A. 1986. *Modern Political Philosophy: Theories of the Just Society*. Harmondsworth: Penguin.

Dunn, John. 1990. *Interpreting Political Responsibility*. Princeton: Princeton University Press.

Elster, Jon. 1983. *Sour Grapes: Studies in the Subversion of Rationality*. Cambridge: Cambridge University Press.

Gunnell, John. 1988. "American Political Science, Liberalism, and the Invention of Political Theory." *American Political Science Review* 82:71-88.

Gutmann, Amy. 1982. "Moral Philosophy and Political Problems." *Political Theory* 10:33-48.

Horton, John. 1990. "Weight or Lightness: Political Philosophy and Its Prospects." In *New Developments in Political Science*, ed. Adrian Leftwich. Aldershot: Edward Elgar.

Mansbridge, Jane, ed. 1990. *Beyond Self-Interest*. Chicago: University of Chicago Press.

Masters, Roger. 1989. *The Nature of Politics*. New Haven: Yale University Press.

Masters, Roger. 1990. "The Resurgence of Political Theory," *Political Studies* 38:421-37.

Miller, David, and Larry Siedentop, eds. 1983. *The Nature of Political Theory*. Oxford: Clarendon Press.

Nagel, Thomas. 1986. *The View from Nowhere*. New York: Oxford University Press.

Nelson, John S., ed. 1983. *What Should Political Theory Be Now?* Albany: State University of New York Press.

Parfit, Derek. 1984. *Reasons and Persons*. Oxford: Oxford University Press.

Pettit, Philip. 1980. *Judging Justice: An Introduction to Contemporary Political Philosophy*. London: Routledge and Kegan Paul.

Rae, Douglas, et al. 1981. *Equalities*. Cambridge, MA: Harvard University Press.

Rajchman, John, and Cornel West, eds. 1985. *Post-Analytic Philosophy*. New York: Columbia University Press.

Reiman, Jeffrey. 1990. *Justice and Modern Moral Philosophy*. New Haven: Yale University Press.

Schaar, John W. 1981. *Legitimacy in the Modern State*. New Brunswick, NJ: Transaction Books.

Shapiro, Ian. 1990. *Political Criticism*. Berkeley: University of California Press.*

Strong, Tracy B. 1990. *The Idea of Political Theory*. Notre Dame: University of Notre Dame Press.

Taylor, Charles. 1985. *Philosophy and the Human Sciences: Philosophical Papers, ii*. Cambridge: Cambridge University Press.

Walzer, Michael, ed. 1989. "The State of Political Theory." *Dissent* (Summer):337-70.*

Williams, Bernard. 1985. *Ethics and the Limits of Philosophy*. Cambridge: Harvard University Press.

[*Note: The starred items in this section contain useful bibliographies or bibliographical essays.]

2. Feminist Thought

Allen, A. 1988. *Uneasy Access: Privacy for Women in a Free Society*. Totowa, NJ: Rowman and Allenheld.

Baier, Annette. 1986. "Trust and Antitrust." *Ethics* 96:231-60.

Baier, Annette. 1987. "The Need for More Than Justice." *Canadian Journal of Philosophy* supp. vol. 13:14-56.

Benhabib, Seyla. 1989. "On Contemporary Feminist Theory." *Dissent* (Summer):366-70.

Benhabib, Seyla, and Drucilla Cornell, eds. 1987. *Feminism as Critique*. Minneapolis: University of Minnesota.

Blum, Lawrence. 1988. "Gilligan and Kohlberg: Implications for Moral Theory." *Ethics* 98:472-91.

Broughton, J. 1983. "Women's Rationality and Men's Virtues." *Social Research* 50:597-642.

Charvet, J. 1982. *Feminism.* London: J. M. Dent.

Code, L., S. Mullett, and C. Overall, eds. 1988. *Feminist Perspectives: Philosophical Essays on Method and Morals.* Toronto: University of Toronto.

Dietz, Mary. 1985. "Citizenship with a Feminist Face: The Problem with Maternal Thinking." *Political Theory* 13:19-37.

Eisenstein, Z. 1984. *Feminism and Sexual Equality: Crisis in Liberal America.* New York: Monthly Review Press.

Elshtain, Jean Bethke. 1981. *Public Man, Private Women: Women in Social and Political Thought.* Princeton: Princeton University Press.

Elshtain, Jean Bethke. 1990. *Power Trips and Other Essays: Essays in Feminism as Civic Discourse.* Madison: University of Wisconsin Press.

Flanagan, Owen, and Kathryn Jackson. 1987. "Justice, Care, and Gender: The Kohlberg-Gilligan Debate Revisited." *Ethics* 97:622-37.

Fraser, Nancy. 1985. "What's Critical about Critical Theory? The Case of Habermas and Gender." *New German Critique* 35:97-131.

Fraser, Nancy. 1989. *Unruly Practices.* Minneapolis: University of Minnesota Press.

Friedman, Marilyn. 1987. "Beyond Caring: The De-moralization of Gender." *Canadian Journal of Philosophy* supp. vol 13:87-110.

Gould, Carol, ed. 1984. *Beyond Domination.* Totowa, NJ: Rowman and Allanheld.

Green, K. 1986. "Rawls, Women, and the Priority of Liberty." *Australasian Journal of Philosophy* supp. to vol. 64:26-36.

Greschner, D. 1989. "Feminist Concerns with the New Communitarians." In *Law and the Community*, ed. A. Hutchinson and L. Green. Toronto: Carswell.

Grimshaw, Jean. 1986. *Philosophy and Feminist Thinking.* Minneapolis: University of Minnesota Press.

Harding, Sandra. 1982. "Is Gender a Variable in Conceptions of Rationality? A Survey of Issues." *Dialectica* 36:225-42.

Hartsock, Nancy C. M. 1983. *Money, Sex, and Power.* Boston: Northeastern University Press.

Held, Virginia. 1987. "Non-Contractual Society." In *Science, Morality and Feminist Theory*, ed. Marsha Hanen and Kai Nielsen. *Canadian Journal of Philosophy* supp. to vol 13:111-38.

Hirschmann, Nancy J. 1989. "Freedom, Recognition, and Obligation: A Feminist Approach to Political Theory." *American Political Science Review* 83:1227-44.

Jaggar, Alison. 1983. *Feminist Politics and Human Nature.* Totowa, NJ: Rowman and Allanheld.

Kearns, Deborah. 1983. "A Theory of Justice -- and Love: Rawls on the Family." *Politics* 18:36-42.

Kennedy, E., and Susan Mendus. 1987. *Women in Western Political Philosophy.* Brighton: Whitesheaf Books.

Kittay, Eva Feder, and Diana T. Meyers, eds. 1987. *Women and Moral Theory.* Savage, MD: Rowman and Littlefield.

MacKinnon, Catharine. 1987. *Feminism Unmodified: Discourses on Life and Law.* Cambridge: Harvard University Press.

MacKinnon, Catharine. 1989. *Towards a Feminist Theory of the State.* Cambridge: Harvard University Press.

Nicholson, Linda. 1986. *Gender and History: The Limits of Social Theory in the Age of the Family.* New York: Columbia University Press.

Nunn-Winkler, Gertrud. 1984. "Two Moralities? A Critical Discussion of an Ethic of Care and Responsibility versus an Ethic of Rights and Justice." In *Morality, Moral Behavior, and Moral Development*, ed. W. Kurtines and J. Gewirtz. New York: Wiley.

Noddings, Nel. 1984. *Caring: A Feminine Approach to Ethics and Moral Education.* Berkeley: University of California.

Nye, A. 1988. *Feminist Theory and the Philosophies of Man.* London: Croom Helm.

O'Brien, Mary. 1981. *The Politics of Reproduction.* London: Routledge and Kegan Paul.

Okin, Susan Moller. 1979. *Women in Western Political Thought.* Princeton: Princeton University Press.

Okin, Susan Moller. 1990. *Justice, Gender, and the Family.* New York: Basic Books.

Olsen, F. 1983. "The Family and the Market: A Study of Ideology and Legal Reform." *Harvard Law Review* 96:1497-1578.

Pateman, Carole. 1987. "Feminist Critiques of the Public/Private Dichotomy." In *Feminism and Equality*, ed. Anne Phillips. Oxford: Blackwell.

Pateman, Carole, and Elizabeth Gross, eds. 1986. *Feminist Challenges: Social and Political Theory.* Boston: Northeastern University Press.

Phelan, Shane. 1989. *Identity Politics.* Philadelphia: Temple University Press.

Pitkin, Hannah. 1984. *Fortune Is a Woman.* Berkeley: University of California Press.

Schwartz, Joel. 1984. *The Sexual Politics of Jean-Jacques Rousseau.* Chicago: University of Chicago Press.

Siltanen, Janet, and Michelle Stanworth, eds. 1984. *Women and the Public Sphere.* London: Hutchinson.

Spelman, Elizabeth. 1989. *Inessential Woman.* Boston: Beacon Press.

Stiehm, Judith Hicks. 1983. "The Unit of Political Analysis: Our Aristotelian Hangover." In *Discovering Reality*, ed. Sandra Harding and Merrill B. Hintikka. Dordrecht: D. Reidel.

Stiehm, Judith Hicks, ed. 1984. *Women's Views of the Political World of Men.* Dobbs Ferry, NY: Transnational Publishers.

Sunstein, Cass R., ed. 1989. *Symposium on Feminism and Political Theory. Ethics* 99:219-406.

Taub, N., and E. Schneider. 1982. "Perspectives on Women's Subordination and the Role of Law." In *The Politics of Law*, ed. D. Kairys. New York: Pantheon.

Tong, Rosemarie. 1989. *Feminist Thought: A Comprehensive Introduction.* Boulder: Westview Press.

Tronto, Joan. 1987. "'Women's Morality': Beyond Gender Difference to a Theory of Care." *Signs* 12:644-63.

Vetterling-Braggin, Mary, Frederick A. Elliston, and Jane English, eds. 1981. *Feminism and Philosophy.* Totowa, NJ: Littlefield, Adams.

Wendell, S. 1987. "A (Qualified) Defense of Liberal Feminism." *Hypatia* 2:65-93.

Wilson, L. 1988. "Is a 'Feminine' Ethic Enough?" *Atlantis* 13:15-23.

Young, Iris Marion. 1990. *Justice and the Politics of Difference.* Princeton: Princeton University Press.

Young, Iris Marion. 1990. *Throwing Like a Girl and Other Essays in Feminist Philosophy and Social Theory.* Bloomington: Indiana University Press.

Zaretsky, E. 1982. "The Place of the Family in the Origins of the Welfare State." In *Rethinking the Family: Some Feminist Questions*, ed. B. Thorn and M. Yalom. New York: Longman.

3. Democracy/Critical Theory

Barber, Benjamin. 1988. *The Conquest of Politics: Liberal Philosophy in Democratic Times.* Princeton: Princeton University Press.

Barry, Brian. 1979. "Is Democracy Special?" In *Philosophy, Politics, and Society*, Fifth Series, ed. Peter Laslett and James W. Fishkin. New Haven: Yale University Press.

Beiner, Ronald. 1983. *Political Judgement*. London: Methuen.

Benhabib, Seyla. 1986. *Critique, Norm, and Utopia*. New York: Columbia University Press.

Benjamin, Roger, and Stephen L. Elkin, eds. 1985. *The Democratic State*. Lawrence: University Press of Kansas.

Bowles, Samuel, and Herbert Gintis. 1986. *Democracy and Capitalism: Property, Community, and the Contradictions of Modern Social Thought*. New York: Basic Books.

Braybrooke, David. 1983. "Can Democracy Be Combined with Federalism or with Liberalism?" In *Liberal Democracy (Nomos XXV)*, ed. J. Roland Pennock and John W. Chapman. New York: New York University Press.

Chapman, John W., and Alan Wertheimer, eds. 1989. *Majorities and Minorities (Nomos XXXII)*. New York: New York University Press.

Cohen, Joshua. 1989. "Deliberation and Democratic Legitimacy." In *The Good Polity: Normative Analysis of the State*, ed. Alan Hamlin and Philip Pettit. Oxford: Blackwell.

Cohen, Josh, and Joel Rogers. 1983. *On Democracy: Toward a Transformation of American Society*. New York: Penguin.

Dahl, Robert. 1979. "Procedural Democracy." In *Philosophy, Politics, and Society*, Fifth Series, ed. Peter Laslett and James W. Fishkin. New Haven: Yale University Press.

Deutsch, Kenneth, and Walter Soffer, eds. 1987. *The Crisis of Liberal Democracy: A Straussian Perspective*. Albany: State University of New York Press.

Dryzek, John S. 1990. *Discursive Democracy*. Cambridge: Cambridge University Press.

Duncan, G., ed. 1983. *Democratic Theory and Practice*. Cambridge: Cambridge University Press.

Elkin, Stephen L. 1987. *City and Regime in the American Republic*. Chicago: University of Chicago Press.

Ely, John Hart. 1980. *Democracy and Distrust: A Theory of Judicial Review*. Cambridge: Harvard University Press.

Fishkin, James. 1987. "Ideals without an Ideal: Justice, Democracy and Liberty in Liberal Theory." In *Individual Liberty and Democratic Decision-Making*, ed. Peter Koslowski. Tubingen: J. C. B. Mohr.

Gilbert, Alan. 1990. *Democratic Individuality*. Cambridge: Cambridge University Press.

Gould, Carol. 1988. *Rethinking Democracy: Freedom and Social Cooperation in Politics, Economy, and Society*. Cambridge: Cambridge University Press.

Graham, Keith. 1982. "Democracy and the Autonomous Moral Agent." In *Contemporary Political Philosophy: Radical Studies*, ed. Keith Graham. Cambridge: Cambridge University Press.

Graham, Keith. 1986. *The Battle of Democracy: Conflict, Consensus, and the Individual*. Totowa, NJ: Barnes & Noble.

Gutmann, Amy. 1980. *Liberal Equality*. Cambridge: Cambridge University Press.

Gutmann, Amy. 1983. "How Liberal Is Democracy?" In *Liberalism Reconsidered*, ed. Douglas MacLean and Claudia Mills. Totowa, NJ: Rowman and Allanheld.

Habermas, Jurgen. 1985. *The Theory of Communicative Action, Vol. 1: Reason and the Rationalization of Society*. Boston: Beacon Press.

Habermas, Jurgen. 1989. *The Theory of Communicative Action, Vol. 2; Lifeworld and System: A Critique of Functionalist Reason*. Boston: Beacon Press.

Held, David. 1987. *Models of Democracy*. Stanford: Stanford University Press.

Held, David. 1990. *Foundations of Democracy*. Cambridge: Polity Press.

Manin, Bernard. 1987. "On Legitimacy and Political Deliberation." *Political Theory* 15:338.

Mansbridge, Jane. 1980. *Beyond Adversary Democracy*. New York: Basic Books.

Mansfield, Harvey Jr. 1985. "Constitutional Government: The Soul of Modern Democracy." *The Public Interest* 81:3-16.

Mapel, David. 1989. *Social Justice Reconsidered*. Urbana, IL: University of Illinois Press.

Nelson, William N. 1980. *On Justifying Democracy*. London: Routledge and Kegan Paul.

Oakeshott, Michael. 1991. "Political Discourse." In Michael Oakeshott, *Rationalism in Politics and Other Essays*. Indianapolis: Liberty Press.

Offe, Claus. 1987. "Democracy against the Welfare State?" *Political Theory* 15:501-37.

Offe, Claus, and Ulrich K. Preuss. 1991. "Democratic Institutions and Moral Resources." In *Political Theory Today*, ed. David Held. Stanford: Stanford University Press.

Pennock, J. Roland. 1979. *Democratic Political Theory*. Princeton: Princeton University Press.

Pennock, J. Roland, and John W. Chapman, eds. 1983. *Liberal Democracy (Nomos XXV)*. New York: New York University Press.

Riker, William. 1982. *Liberalism against Populism*. San Francisco: W. H. Freeman.

Sartori, Giovanni. 1987. *The Theory of Democracy Revisited*. Chatham, NJ: Chatham House.

Shapiro, Ian. 1989. "Three Fallacies Concerning Majorities, Minorities, and Democratic Politics." In *Majorities and Minorities (Nomos XXXII)*, ed. John W. Chapman and Alan Wertheimer. New York: New York University Press.

Thompson, J. B., and David Held, eds. 1982. *Habermas: Critical Debates*. London: Macmillan.

Thompson, Dennis F. 1980. "Moral Responsibility of Public Officials: The Problem of Many Hands." *American Political Science Review* 74:905-16.

Thompson, Dennis F. 1983. "Bureaucracy and Democracy." In *Democratic Theory and Practice*, ed. Graeme Duncan. New York: Cambridge University Press.

Turner, Bryan. 1990. "Outline of a Theory of Citizenship." *Sociology* 24:189-217.

Walzer, Michael. 1981. "Philosophy and Democracy." *Political Theory* 9:379-99.

White, Stephen K. 1988. *The Recent Work of Jurgen Habermas: Reason, Justice, and Modernity*. Cambridge: Cambridge University Press.

Wolin, Sheldon S. 1989. *The Presence of the Past: Essays on the State and the Constitution*. Baltimore: Johns Hopkins University Press.

Wolin, Sheldon S. 1985. "Revolutionary Action Today." In *Post-Analytic Philosophy*, ed. John Rajchman and Cornel West. New York: Columbia University Press.

4. Utilitarianism

Brink, D. 1986. "Utilitarian Morality and the Personal Point of View." *Journal of Philosophy* 83:417-38.

Fishkin, James. 1983. *The Limits of Obligation*. New Haven: Yale University Press.

Frey, R., ed. 1984. *Utility and Rights*. Minneapolis: University of Minnesota Press.

Goodin, Robert. 1982. *Political Theory and Public Policy*. Chicago: University of Chicago Press.

Griffin, James. 1986. *Well-Being: Its Meaning, Measurement, and Moral Importance*. Oxford: Oxford University Press.

Hare, R. M. 1982. "Ethical Theory and Utilitarianism." In *Utilitarianism and Beyond*, ed. Amartya Sen and Bernard Williams. Cambridge: Cambridge University Press.

Hare, R. M. 1984. "Rights, Utility, and Universalization: Reply to J. L. Mackie." In *Utility and Rights*, ed. R. Frey. Minneapolis: University of Minnesota Press.

Harsanyi, John. 1985. "Rule Utilitarianism, Equality, and Justice." *Social Philosophy and Policy* 2:115-27.

Hart, H. L. A. 1979. "Between Utility and Rights." In *The Idea of Freedom*, ed. Alan Ryan. Oxford: Oxford University Press.

Haslett, D. 1987. *Equal Consideration: A Theory of Moral Justification*. Newark: University of Delaware.

Kymlicka, Will. 1988. "Rawls on Teleology and Deontology." *Philosophy and Public Affairs* 17:173-90.

Mackie, J. L. 1984. "Rights, Utility, and Universalization." In *Utility and Rights*, ed. R. Frey. Minneapolis: University of Minnesota Press.

Railton, Peter. 1984. "Alienation, Consequentialism, and the Demands of Morality." *Philosophy and Public Affairs* 13:134-171.

Riley, Jonathan. 1988. *Liberal Utilitarianism: Social Choice Theory and J. S. Mill's Philosophy*. Cambridge: Cambridge University Press.

Sen, Amartya, and Bernard Williams, eds. 1982. *Utilitarianism and Beyond*. Cambridge: Cambridge University Press.

Singer, Peter. 1979. *Practical Ethics*. Cambridge: Cambridge University Press.

Williams, Bernard. 1973. "A Critique of Utilitarianism." In *Utilitarianism: For and Against*, ed. J. J. C. Smart and Bernard Williams. Cambridge: Cambridge University Press.

5. Community/Republicanism/Virtue

Beiner, Ronald. 1989. "What's the Matter with Liberalism?" In *Law and the Community*, ed. A. Hutchinson and L. Green. Toronto: Carswell.

Benhabib, Seyla. 1988. "Judgment and the Moral Foundations of Politics in Arendt's Thought." *Political Theory* 16:29-52.

Bradshaw, Leah. 1989. *Acting and Thinking: The Political Thought of Hannah Arendt*. Toronto: University of Toronto Press.

Budziszewski, J. 1986. *The Resurrection of Nature: Political Theory and the Human Character*. Ithaca: Cornell University Press.

Canovan, Margaret. 1985. "Politics and Culture: Hannah Arendt and the Public Realm." *History of Political Thought* 6:617-42.

Chapman, John W. and William A. Galston, eds. 1992. *Virtue: Nomos 34*. New York: New York University Press.

Crowley, B. 1987. *The Self, the Individual and the Community: Liberalism in the Political Thought of F. A. Hayek and Sidney and Beatrice Webb*. Oxford: Oxford University Press.

Dagger, Richard. 1985. "Rights, Boundaries, and the Bonds of Community: A Qualified Defense of Moral Parochialism." *American Political Science Review* 79:436-47.

Dossa, Shiraz. 1989. *The Public Realm and the Public Self: The Political Theory of Hannah Arendt*. Waterloo: Wilfred Laurier University Press.

Finnis, John. 1980. *Natural Law and Natural Rights*. Oxford: Clarendon Press.

Galston, William A. 1988. "Liberal Virtues." *American Political Science Review* 82:1277-92.

Galston, William A. 1989. "Community, Democracy, Philosophy: The Political Thought of Michael Walzer." *Political Theory* 17:119-30.

Gutmann, Amy. 1985. "Communitarian Critics of Liberalism." *Philosophy and Public Affairs* 14:308-22.

Herzog, Don. 1986. "Some Questions for Republicans." *Political Theory* 14:473-93.

Hirsch, H. N. 1986. "The Threnody of Liberalism: Constitutional Liberty and the Renewal of Community." *Political Theory* 14:423-49.

Honig, B. 1988. "Arendt, Identity, and Difference." *Political Theory* 16:77-98.

Kateb, George. 1984. *Hannah Arendt: Politics, Conscience, Evil*. Totowa, NJ: Rowman and Littlefield.

Kymlicka, Will. 1988. "Liberalism and Communitarianism." *Canadian Journal of Philosophy* 18:181-203.

Macedo, Stephen. 1988. "Capitalism, Citizenship, and Community." *Social Philosophy and Policy* 6:113-39.

MacIntyre, Alasdair. 1981. *After Virtue: A Study in Moral Theory*. Notre Dame: University of Notre Dame Press.

MacIntyre, Alasdair. 1988. *Whose Justice? Which Rationality?* Notre Dame: University of Notre Dame Press.

MacIntyre, Alasdair. 1990. "The Privatization of Good: An Inaugural Lecture." *Review of Politics* 52:344-61.

Paris, David. 1991. "Moral Education and the 'Tie That Binds' in Liberal Political Theory." *American Political Science Review* 85:875-901.

Post, Robert. 1989. "Tradition, the Self, and Substantive Due Process: A Comment on Michael Sandel." *California Law Review* 77:553-60.

Rosenblum, Nancy. 1984. "Moral Membership in a Postliberal State." *World Politics* 36:581-96.

Rorty, Richard. 1985. "Postmodernist Bourgeois Liberalism." In *Hermeneutics and Praxis*, ed. R. Hollinger. Notre Dame: University of Notre Dame Press.

Rorty, Richard. 1985. "Solidarity or Objectivity?" In *Post-Analytic Philosophy*, ed. John Rajchman and Cornel West. New York: Columbia University Press.

Sandel, Michael. 1982. *Liberalism and the Limits of Justice*. Cambridge: Cambridge University Press.

Sandel, Michael. 1984. "Morality and the Liberal Ideal." *The New Republic* (May 7, 1984):15-17.

Sandel, Michael. 1984. "The Procedural Republic and the Unencumbered Self." *Political Theory* 12:81-96.

Stout, Jeffrey. 1986. "Liberal Society and the Languages of Morals." *Soundings* 69:32-59.

Sullivan, William. 1982. *Reconstructing Public Philosophy*. Berkeley: University of California Press.

Taylor, Charles. 1986. "Alternative Futures: Legitimacy, Identity, and Alienation in Late Twentieth-Century Canada." In *Constitutionalism, Citizenship, and Society in Canada*, ed. A. Cairns and C. Williams. Toronto: University of Toronto Press.

Wallach, John. 1987. "Liberals, Communitarians, and the Tasks of Political Theory." *Political Theory* 15:581-611.

Walzer, Michael. 1990. "The Communitarian Critique of Liberalism." *Political Theory* 18:6-23.

Whelan, Frederick. 1981. "Citizenship and the Right to Leave." *American Political Science Review* 75:636-53.

Wilson, James Q. 1991. *On Character*. Washington, DC: American Enterprise Institute.

Yack, Bernard. 1985. "Community and Conflict in Aristotle's Political Philosophy." *Review of Politics* 47:92-112.

Yack, Bernard. 1988. "Does Liberal Practice 'Live Down' to Liberal Theory: Liberalism and its Communitarian Critics." In *Community in America: The Challenge of 'Habits of the Heart,'* ed. Charles Reynolds. Berkeley: University of California Press.

6. State and Civil Society

Alford, Robert R., and Roger Friedland. 1985. *Powers of Theory: Capitalism, the State, and Democracy*. Cambridge: Cambridge University Press.

Carnoy, Martin. 1984. *The State and Political Theory*. Princeton: Princeton University Press.

Cohen, Jean, and Andrew Arato. 1992. *Civil Society and Political Theory*. Cambridge: MIT Press.

Elkin, Stephen L. 1985. "Between Liberalism and Capitalism: An Introduction to the Democratic State." In *The Democratic State*, ed. Roger Benjamin and Stephen L. Elkin. Lawrence: University Press of Kansas.

Habermas, Jurgen. 1989. "The New Obscurity: The Crisis of the Welfare State and the Exhaustion of Utopian Energies." In *The New Conservatism: Cultural Criticism and the Historians' Debate*, ed. Shierry Weber Nicholsen. Cambridge: MIT Press.

Keane, John. 1988. *Democracy and Civil Society*. London: Routledge.

Keane, John, ed. 1988. *Civil Society and the State*. London: Routledge.

Offe, Claus. 1984. *Contradictions of the Welfare State*. London: Hutchinson.

Pierson, Christopher. 1984. "New Theories of State and Civil Society." *Sociology* 18:563-71.

Pierson, Christopher. 1991. *Beyond the Welfare State?* University Park, PA: Pennsylvania State University Press.

Skocpol, Theda. 1979. *States an Social Revolutions: A Comparative Analysis of France, Russia, and China*. Cambridge: Cambridge University Press.

Taylor, Charles. 1990. "Modes of Civil Society." *Public Culture* 3:95-118.

Wolfe, Alan. 1989. *Whose Keeper? Social Science and Moral Obligation*. Berkeley: University of California Press.

7. Socialism/Marxism

Arneson, Richard. 1981. "What's Wrong with Exploitation?" *Ethics* 91:202-27.

Arneson, Richard. 1985. "Marxism and Secular Faith." *American Political Science Review* 79:627-40.

Arneson, Richard. 1987. "Meaningful Work and Market Socialism." *Ethics* 97:517-45.

Ball, Terence, and James Farr, eds. 1984. *After Marx*. Cambridge: Cambridge University Press.

Brenkert, G. 1983. *Marx's Ethics of Freedom*. London: Routledge and Kegan Paul.

Buchanan, Allen. 1982. *Marx and Justice: The Radical Critique of Liberalism*. Totowa, NJ: Rowman and Littlefield.

Campbell, Tom. 1983. *The Left and Rights: A Conceptual Analysis of the Idea of Socialist Rights*. London: Routledge and Kegan Paul.

Carens, Joseph. 1986. "Rights and Duties in an Egalitarian Society." *Political Theory* 14:31-49.

Cohen, G. A. 1990. "Marxism and Contemporary Political Philosophy, or: Why Nozick Exercises Some Marxists More Than He Does Any Egalitarian Liberals." *Canadian Journal of Philosophy* supp. vol. 16:363-87.

Cunningham, Frank. 1987. *Democratic Theory and Socialism*. New York: Cambridge University Press.

Diegel, Len, and Ian Gough. 1991. *A Theory of Human Need*. New York: Guilford Press.

DiQuattro, A. 1983. "Rawls and Left Criticism." *Political Theory* 11:53-78.

Doppelt, G. 1981. "Rawls' System of Justice: A Critique from the Left." *Nous* 15:259-307.

Dunn, John. 1984. *The Politics of Socialism: An Essay in Political Theory*. Cambridge: Cambridge University Press.

Elster, Jon. 1983. "Exploitation, Freedom, and Justice." In *Marxism: Nomos 26*, ed. J. Roland Pennock and John W. Chapman. New York: New York University Press.

Elster, Jon. 1986. "Self-Realization in Work and Politics: The Marxist Conception of the Good Life." *Social Philosophy and Policy* 3:97-126.

Geras, A. 1989. "The Controversy about Marx and Justice." In *Marxist Theory*, ed. A. Callinicos. Oxford: Oxford University Press.

Keane, John. 1984. *Public Life and Late Capitalism: Toward a Socialist Theory of Democracy*. Cambridge: Cambridge University Press.

Keat, R. 1982. "Liberal Rights and Socialism." In *Contemporary Political Philosophy: Radical Studies*, ed. K. Graham. Cambridge: Cambridge University Press.

Laclau, Ernesto, and Chantal Mouffe. 1985. *Hegemony and Socialist Strategy*. New York: Verso.

Levine, Andrew. 1988. "Capitalist Persons." *Social Philososphy and Policy* 6:39-59.

Levine, Andrew. 1989. "What Is a Marxist Today?" *Canadian Journal of Philosophy* supp vol. 15:29-58.

Lukes, Steven. 1985. *Marxism and Morality*. Oxford: Oxford University Press.

Miller, David. 1989. "In What Sense Must Socialism Be Communitarian? *Social Philosophy and Policy* 6:51-73.

Miller, Richard. 1984. *Analyzing Marx*. Princeton: Princeton University Press.

Nielsen, Kai. 1987. "Rejecting Egalitarianism: On Miller's Nonegalitarian Marx." *Political Theory* 15:411-23.

Nielsen, Kai. 1989. *Marxism and the Moral Point of View*. Boulder: Westview Press.

Nove, Alec. 1983. *The Economics of Feasible Socialism*. London: George Allen and Unwin.

Plotke, David. 1989. "Marxism and Democratic Theory." *Dissent* (1989):343-49.

Reeve, Andrew, ed. 1987. *Modern Theories of Exploitation*. London: Sage.

Reiman, Jeffrey. 1981. "The Possibility of a Marxian Theory of Justice." *Canadian Journal of Philosophy* supp. vol. 7:307-22.

Reiman, Jeffrey. 1983. "The Labor Theory of the Difference Principle." *Philosophy and Public Affairs* 12:133-59.

Roemer, John. 1982. "New Directions in the Marxian Theory of Exploitation and Class." *Politics and Society* 11:253-87.

Roemer, John. 1985. "Should Marxists Be Interested in Exploitation?" *Philosophy and Public Affairs* 14:30-65.

Sadurski, Wojciech. 1983. "To Each According to His (Genuine?) Needs." *Political Theory* 11:419-32.

Schwartz, Adina. 1982. "Meaningful Work." *Ethics* 92: 634-46.

Smith, Steven B. 1985. "Althusser's Marxism without a Knowing Subject." *American Political Science Review* 79:641-55.

Wood, A. 1984. "Justice and Class Interests." *Philosophica* 33:9-32.

Wood, A. 1981. "Marx and Equality." In *Issues in Marxist Philosophy, 4*, ed. J. Mepham and D. H. Ruben. Brighton: Harvester Press.

8. Liberalism

Abbott, Philip and Michael B. Levy, eds. 1985. *The Liberal Future in America: Essays in Retrieval*. Westport, CT: Greenwood Press.

Ackerman, Bruce. 1980. *Social Justice in the Liberal State*. New Haven: Yale University Press.

Arthur, John. 1987. "Resource Acquisition and Harm." *Canadian Journal of Philosophy* 17:337-47.

Barry, Brian. 1989. *Theories of Justice*. Berkeley: University of California Press.

Barry, Norman. 1986. *On Classical Liberalism and Libertarianism*. London: Macmillan.

Benn, Stanley. 1988. *A Theory of Freedom*. Cambridge: Cambridge University Press.

Bogart, L. 1985. "Lockean Provisos and State of Nature Theories." *Ethics* 95:828-36.

Carens, Joseph. 1985. "Compensatory Justice and Social Institutions." *Economics and Philosophy* 1:39-67.

Christman, J. 1986. "Can Ownership Be Justified by Natural Rights?" *Philosophy and Public Affairs* 15:156-77.

Cohen, G. A. 1986. "Self-Ownership, World-Ownership, and Equality." In *Justice and Equality Here and Now*, ed. Frank Lucash. Ithaca: Cornell University Press.

Connolly, William. 1984. "The Dilemma of Legitimacy." In *Legitimacy and the State*, ed. William Connolly. Oxford: Basil Blackwell.

Damico, Alfonso J., ed. 1986. *Liberals on Liberalism*. Totowa, NJ: Rowman and Littlefield.

Diggs, B. 1981. "A Contractarian View of Respect for Persons." *American Philosophical Quarterly* 18:273-83.

Doyle, Michael. 1986. "Liberalism and World Politics." *American Political Science Review* 80:1151-70.

Dworkin, Ronald. 1981. "What Is Equality? Part I: Equality of Welfare; Part II: Equality of Resources." *Philosophy of Public Affairs* 10:185-246, 283-345.

Dworkin, Ronald. 1983. "In Defense of Equality." *Social Philosophy and Policy* 1:24-40.

Dworkin, Ronald. 1985. *A Matter of Principle*. Cambridge: Harvard University Press.

Dworkin, Ronald. 1987. "What Is Equality? Part III: The Place of Liberty." *Iowa Law Review* 73:1-54.

Dworkin, Ronald. 1988. "What Is Equality? Part IV: Political Equality." *University of San Francisco Law Review* 22:1-30.

Dworkin, Ronald. 1989. "Liberal Community." *California Law Review* 77:479-504.

Feinberg, Joel. 1986. *The Moral Limits of the Criminal Law, vol. 3: Harm to Self*. New York: Oxford University Press.

Feinberg, Joel. 1988. *The Moral Limits of the Criminal Law, vol. 4: Harmless Wrongdoing*. New York: Oxford University Press.

Franco, Paul. 1990. *The Political Philosophy of Michael Oakeshott*. New Haven: Yale University Press.

Fried, Charles. 1983. "Distributive Justice." *Social Philosophy and Policy* 1:45-59.

Gaus, Gerald. 1990. *Value and Justification: The Foundations of Liberal Theory*. Cambridge: Cambridge University Press.

Gauthier, David. 1986. *Morals by Agreement*. Oxford: Oxford University Press.

Gibbard, A. 1985. "What's Morally Special about Free Exchange?" *Social Philosophy and Policy* 2:20-28.

Goodin, Robert. 1988. *Reasons for Welfare*. Princeton: Princeton University Press.

Grafstein, Robert. 1990. "Missing the Archimedean Point: Liberalism's Institutional Presuppositions." *American Political Science Review* 84:177-93.

Gray, John. 1986. *Liberalism*. Minneapolis: University of Minnesota Press.

Gray, John. 1989. *Liberalisms: Essays in Political Philosophy*. London: Routledge and Kegan Paul.

Hampshire, Stuart. 1989. *Innocence and Experience*. Cambridge: Harvard University Press.

Harman, Gilbert. 1983. "Human Flourishing, Ethics, and Liberty." *Philosophy and Public Affairs* 12:307-22.

Holmes, Stephen. 1991. "The Liberal Idea." *The American Prospect* 7:81-96.

Lomasky, Loren. 1987. *Persons, Rights, and the Moral Community*. Oxford: Oxford University Press.

MacLean, Douglas, and Claudia Mills, eds. 1983. *Liberalism Reconsidered*. Totowa, NJ: Rowman and Allanheld.

Martin, Rex. 1985. *Rawls and Rights*. Lawrence, KS: University Press of Kansas.

Morris, Christopher. 1988. "The Relation between Self-Interest and Justice in Contractarian Ethics." *Social Philosophy and Policy* 5:119-53.

Nagel, Thomas. 1991. *Equality and Partiality*. New York: Oxford University Press.

Narveson, Jan. 1988. *The Libertarian Idea*. Philadelphia: Temple University Press.

Okin, Susan Moller. 1989. "Humanist Liberalism." In *Liberalism and the Moral Life*, ed. Nancy L. Rosenblum. Cambridge: Harvard University Press.

O'Neill, Onora. 1986. "The Public Use of Reason." *Political Theory* 14:523-51.

Paul, Ellen Frankel, et. al., eds.. 1987. *Equal Opportunity*. Oxford: Basil Blackwell.

Pelczynski, Zbigniew, and John Gray, eds. 1985. *Conceptions of Liberty in Political Philosophy*. New York: St. Martin's.

Pinkard, Terry. 1987. *Democratic Liberalism and Social Union*. Philadelphia: Temple University Press.

Pogge, Thomas. 1989. *Realizing Rawls*. Ithaca: Cornell University Press.

Rawls, John. 1982. "The Basic Liberties and Their Priority." In *The Tanner Lectures on Human Values III*, ed. Sterling McMurrin. Salt Lake City: University of Utah Press.

Rawls, John. 1982. "Social Unity and Primary Goods." In *Amartya Utilitarianism and Beyond*, ed. Amartya Sen and Bernard Williams. Cambridge: Cambridge University Press.

Rawls, John. 1985. "Justice as Fairness: Political Not Metaphysical." *Philosophy and Public Affairs* 14:223-51.

Rawls, John. 1987. "The Idea of an Overlapping Consensus." *Oxford Journal of Legal Studies* 7:1-25.

Rawls, John. 1989. "The Domain of the Political and Overlapping Consensus." *New York University Law Review* 64:233-55.

Riley, Jonathan. 1985. "On The Possibility of Liberal Democracy." *American Political Science Review* 79:1135-51.

Rowland, Barbara. 1987. *Ordered Liberty and the Constitutional Framework: The Political Thought of Friedrich A. Hayek*. New York: Greenwood.

Rosenblum, Nancy L. 1987. *Another Liberalism: Romanticism and the Reconstruction of Liberal Thought*. Cambridge: Harvard University Press.

Rosenblum, Nancy L., ed. 1989. *Liberalism and the Moral Life*. Cambridge: Harvard University Press.

Ryan, Alan. 1986. *Property and Political Theory*. Oxford: Basil Blackwell.

Sadurski, Wojciech. 1985. *Giving Dessert Its Due: Social Justice and Legal Theory*. Norwell, MA: Kluwer Academic.

Scanlon, T. M. 1982. "Contractualism and Utilitarianism." In *Utilitarianism and Beyond*, ed. Amartya Sen and Bernard Williams. Cambridge: Cambridge University Press.

Scheppele, Kim Lane, and Jeremy Waldron. 1991. "Contractarian Methods in Political and Legal Evaluation." *Yale Journal of Law and the Humanities* 3:195-230.

Sen, Amartya. 1980. "Equality of What?" In *The Tanner Lectures on Human Values I*, ed. Sterling McMurrin. Salt Lake City: University of Utah Press.

Sen, Amartya. 1985. "Rights and Capabilities." In *Morality and Objectivity*, ed. Ted Honderich. London: Routledge and Kegan Paul.

Sen, Amartya, and Bernard Williams, eds. 1982. *Utilitarianism and Beyond*. Cambridge: Cambridge University Press.

Shapiro, Ian. 1986. *The Evolution of Rights in Liberal Theory*. Cambridge: Cambridge University Press.

Smith, Rogers. 1985. *Liberalism and American Constitutional Law*. Cambridge: Harvard University Press.

Soltan, Karol. 1987. *The Causal Theory of Justice*. Berkeley: University of California Press.

Starr, Paul. 1991. "Liberalism after Socialism." *The American Prospect* 7:70-80.

Sterba, James. 1988. *How to Make People Just: A Practical Reconciliation of Alternative Conceptions of Justice*. Totowa, NJ: Rowman and Littlefield.

Sumner, L. W. 1987. *The Moral Foundation of Rights*. Oxford: Oxford University Press.

Taylor, Charles. 1985. *Philosophy and the Human Sciences: Philosophical Papers II*. Cambridge: Cambridge University Press.

Varian, Hal. 1985. "Dworkin on Equality of Resources." *Economics and Philosophy* 1:110-25.

Walzer, Michael. 1984. "Liberalism and the Art of Separation." *Political Theory* 12:315-30.

Weale, Albert. 1982. *Political Theory and Social Policy*. London: Macmillan.

9. Liberal Neutrality

Ackerman, Bruce. 1989. "Why Dialogue?" *Journal of Philosophy* 86:5-22.

Alexander, Larry, and Maimon Schwarzchild. 1987. "Liberalism, Neutrality, and Equality of Welfare vs. Equality of Resources." *Philosophy and Public Affairs* 16:85-110.

Arneson, Richard. 1990. "Neutrality and Utility." *Canadian Journal of Philosophy* 20:215-40.

Barry, Brian. 1990. "How Not to Defend Liberal Institutions." *British Journal of Political Science* 20:1-14.

Douglass, R. Bruce, Gerald M. Mara, and Henry S. Richardson, eds. 1990. *Liberalism and the Good*. New York: Routledge.

Galston, William A. 1982. "Defending Liberalism." *American Political Science Review* 76:621-29.

Goodin, Robert, and Andrew Reeve, eds. 1989. *Liberal Neutrality*. London: Routledge.

Gutmann, Amy, and Dennis Thompson. 1990. "Moral Conflict and Political Consensus." In *Liberalism and the Good*, ed. R. Bruce Douglass et al. New York: Routledge.

Larmore, Charles. 1990. "Political Liberalism." *Political Theory* 18:339-60.

Lloyd Thomas, D. A. 1988. *In Defense of Liberalism*. Oxford: Basil Blackwell.

Neal, Patrick. 1985. "Liberalism and Neutrality." *Polity* 17:664-84.

Neal, Patrick. 1987. "A Liberal Theory of the Good?" *Canadian Journal of Philosophy* 17:567-82.

Neal, Patrick. 1990. "Justice as Fairness: Political or Metaphysical? *Political Theory* 18:24-50.

Marneffe, Peter de. 1990. "Liberalism, Liberty, and Neutrality." *Philosophy and Public Affairs* 19:253-74.

Nagel, Thomas. 1987. "Moral Conflict and Political Legitimacy." *Philosophy and Public Affairs* 16:215-40.

Paris, David. 1987. "The Theoretical Mystique: Neutrality, Plurality, and the Defense of Liberalism." *American Journal of Political Science* 31:909-39.

Perry, Michael J. 1989. "Neutral Politics?" *Review of Politics* 51:479-509.

Rawls, John. 1988. "The Priority of Right and Ideas of the Good." *Philosophy and Public Affairs* 17:251-76.

Raz, Joseph. 1990. "Facing Diversity: The Case of Epistemic Abstinence." *Philosophy and Public Affairs* 19:3-46.

Rodewald, Richard. 1985. "Does Liberalism Rest on a Mistake?" *Canadian Journal of Philosophy* 15:231-51.

Spragens, Thomas A. Jr. 1986. "Reconstructing Liberal Theory: Reason and Liberal Culture." In *Liberals on Liberalism*, ed. Alfonso J. Damico. Totowa, NJ: Rowman and Littlefield.

Thigpen, Robert, and Lyle Downing. 1983. "Liberalism and the Neutrality Principle." *Political Theory* 11:585-600.

Waldron, Jeremy. 1987. "Theoretical Foundations of Liberalism." *Philosophical Quarterly* 37:127-50.

10. Liberal Justice/Equality of Opportunity

Bowie, Norman, ed. 1988. *Equal Opportunity*. Boulder: Westview Press.

Braybrooke, David. 1987. *Meeting Needs*. Princeton: Princeton University Press.

Brubaker, Stanley. "Can Liberals Punish?" 1988. *American Political Science Review* 82:821-36.

Carens, Joseph. 1986. "Rights and Duties in an Egalitarian Society." *Political Theory* 14:31-50.

Fishkin, James. 1983. *Justice, Equal Opportunity, and the Family*. New Haven: Yale University Press.

Goodin, Robert. 1986. *Protecting the Vulnerable: A Re-Analysis of our Social Responsibilities*. Chicago: University of Chicago Press.

Goodin, Robert. 1988. *Reasons for Welfare: The Political Theory of the Welfare States*. Princeton: Princeton University Press.

Green, S. J. D. 1989. "Competitive Equality of Opportunity: A Defense." *Ethics* 100:5-32.

Jencks, Christopher. 1988. "Whom Must We Treat Equally for Educational Opportunities to Be Equal?" *Ethics* 98:518-33.

Lucash, Frank, ed. 1986. *Justice and Equality: Here and Now*. Ithaca: Cornell University Press.

Paul, Ellen Frankel, Fred D. Miller, Jeffrey Paul, and John Ahrens, eds. 1987. *Equal Opportunity*. Oxford: Blackwell.

Sher, George. 1987. *Desert*. Princeton: Princeton University Press.

Thomson, Garrett. 1988. *Needs*. London: Routledge and Kegan Paul.

11. The Nietzschean/Postmodern Controversy

Araca, Jonathan, ed. 1989. *After Foucault: Humanistic Knowledge, Postmodern Challenges*. New Bruswick, NJ: Rutgers University Press.

Bernstein, Richard, ed. 1985. *Habermas and Modernity*. Cambridge: MIT Press.

Bernstein, Richard. 1987. "One Step Forward, Two Steps Backward: Richard Rorty on Liberal Democracy and Philosophy." *Political Theory* 15:538-63.

Blitz, Mark. 1981. *Heidegger's Being and Time and the Possibility of Political Philosophy*. Ithaca: Cornell University Press.

Blumenberg, Hans. 1983. *The Legitimacy of the Modern Age*. Cambridge: MIT Press.

Bowie, Malcolm. 1991. *Lacan*. Cambridge: Harvard University Press.

Connolly, William. 1985. "Taylor, Foucault, and Otherness." *Political Theory* 13:365-76.

Connolly, William. 1987. *Politics and Ambiguity*. Madison: University of Wisconsin Press.

Connolly, William. 1991. *Identity\Difference: Democratic Negotiations of Political Paradox*. Ithaca: Cornell University Press.

Corlett, William. 1989. *Community without Unity: A Politics of Derridian Extravagance*. Durham, NC: Duke University Press.

Dallmayr, Fred. 1989. *Margins of Political Discourse*. Albany: State University of New York Press.

Detwiler, Bruce. 1988. "Habermas and Rationality." *Political Theory* 16:553-79.

Detwiler, Bruce. 1990. *Nietzsche and the Politics of Aristocratic Radicalism*. Chicago: University of Chicago Press.

Farias, Victor. 1989. *Heidegger and Nazism*. Philadelphia: Temple University Press.

Gillespie, Michael A., and Tracy Strong, eds. 1988. *Nietzsche's New Seas: Explorations in Philosophy, Aesthetics, and Politics*. Chicago: University of Chicago Press.

Honig, B. 1991. "Declarations of Independence: Arendt and Derrida on the Problem of Founding a Republic." *American Political Science Review* 85:97-114.

Lyotard, Jean-Francois. 1984. *The Postmodern Condition*. Minneapolis: University of Minnesota Press.

Merquior, J. G. 1985. *Foucault*. Berkeley: University of California Press.

Norris, Christopher. 1987. *Derrida*. Cambridge: Harvard University Press.

Rabinow, Paul, ed. 1984. *The Foucault Reader*. New York: Pantheon.

Rorty, Richard. 1983. "Postmodern Bourgeois Liberalism." *Journal of Philosophy* 80:583-89.

Rorty, Richard. 1987. "Thugs and Theorists: A Reply to Bernstein." *Political Theory* 15:564-80.

Strong, Tracy. 1989. *Friedrich Nietzsche and the Politics of Transfiguration*. Berkeley: University of California Press.

Taylor, Charles. 1985. "Connolly, Foucault, and Truth." *Political Theory* 13:377-86.

Thiele, Leslie Paul. 1990. "The Agony of Politics: The Nietzschean Roots of Foucault's Thought." *American Political Science Review* 84:907-26.

Thiele, Leslie Paul. 1990. *Friedrich Nietzsche and the Politics of the Soul: A Study of Heroic Individualism*. Princeton: Princeton University Press.

Vattimo, Gianni. 1991. *The End of Modernity*. Baltimore: Johns Hopkins.

Warren, Mark. 1988. *Nietzsche and Political Thought*. Cambridge: MIT Press.

White, Stephen K. 1986. "Foucault's Challenge to Critical Theory." *American Political Science Review* 80:419-32.

White, Stephen K. 1991. *Political Theory and Postmodernism*. Cambridge: Cambridge University Press.

Wolin, Richard, ed. 1991. *The Heidegger Controversy: A Critical Reader*. New York: Columbia University Press.

3

Feminist Challenges to Political Science

Susan J. Carroll and Linda M. G. Zerilli

The study of women and politics within the discipline of political science was stimulated by and has evolved simultaneously with the contemporary feminist movement. Prior to the emergence of the feminist movement in the mid-1960s, few books or articles pertaining to women were written by political scientists (a notable exception being Duverger 1955), and from 1901 to 1966 only eleven dissertations focusing on women were completed (Shanley and Schuck 1974). The Women's Caucus for Political Science, founded in 1971, began in 1972 to sponsor several papers on gender at the annual meetings of the American Political Science Association, and during the early to mid-1970s the first few path-breaking books on women and politics were published (e.g., Amundsen 1971; Kirkpatrick 1974; Jaquette 1974; Freeman 1975).

From such humble origins, the subfield of women and politics grew at a rapid pace. By the early 1990s the numbers of papers, articles, and books written by political scientists focusing on women and politics or feminist theory had grown considerably. For example, more than 60 gender-related papers were presented at the 1992 Annual Meeting of the American Political Science Association, and in 1991, *Women & Politics*, a scholarly journal devoted to publishing empirical and theoretical work on women and politics, published 24 articles and reviewed 21 books on women and politics and feminist theory. The growth of a body of scholarship focusing on women and gender within the discipline of political science has paralleled similar (although frequently more rapid) patterns of growth in other disciplines in the humanities and social sciences (DuBois et al. 1985). In addition, work on gender in political science has been strongly influenced by the rapid development of interdisciplinary work in women's studies.

The study of women and politics also became more institutionalized within the discipline throughout the 1970s and 1980s. Two of the most important developments were the establishment in 1981 of the journal, *Women & Politics*, and the formation of an Organized Section on Women and Politics Research within the American Political Science Association in 1986. In addition, in 1986 the political science department at Rutgers University became the first in the country to offer women and politics as both a major and minor field of study toward a Ph.D. Most of the larger political science departments now have at least one faculty member who specializes in gender politics, and many departments now offer women and politics courses as a regular part of their undergraduate curriculum.

The work being done in this rapidly growing field has important implications for all political scientists, not just those who are specialists in women and politics. Feminist scholarship poses a set of questions that challenge the theoretical and epistemological foundation on which the discipline is constructed. Sometimes implicitly and sometimes explicitly, the work being done by feminist scholars raises important questions about both *what* we study as political scientists and *how* we study it.

Framework

This essay will examine the questions posed by women and politics research about what we study as political scientists and how we study it in the context of three analytically distinct categories of research on women and politics. The first category consists of critiques of the ways in which political theory and empirical research in political science have traditionally excluded women as political actors and rendered them either invisible or apolitical. The second category consists of research that has attempted to add women into politics, to make them visible as political actors, while accepting the existing dominant frameworks of political analysis. The third category consists of research that calls existing frameworks and assumptions into question; work within this category suggests that our dominant frameworks cannot accommodate the inclusion of women as political actors and that many of the frameworks, assumptions, and definitions central to political science must be reconceptualized.

We would not argue that these categories of work on women and politics are chronologically distinct or that research in any one category is more important than research in another. Although much of the early research on women and politics falls into the first two categories while the third category is of more recent vintage, all three categories of research are apparent in current work. Similarly, all three have made important contributions to our understanding of the ways in which gender and assumptions about gender have permeated the discipline. While we treat these three categories of research as analytically distinct for purposes of this essay, the demarcations among them are admittedly fuzzy. One category tends to flow into another, and the work of a single scholar sometimes cuts across two or even all three categories.

We do not intend to provide a comprehensive review of the literature on women and politics; given the proliferation of work in recent years, such a review would be a monumental task, which fortunately is beyond the scope of this essay. Instead, in discussing the three categories of research, we draw largely on literature from political theory and from American politics both because our specializations are in those fields and because these are the two areas in political science where the greatest amount of work on gender has taken place. Through this review we hope to demonstrate that both feminist theory and more empirically oriented work on gender have posed serious and often similar questions about what we study in political science and how we study it.

Women as Invisible or Apolitical

In political science as in other disciplines, feminist scholarship had its origins in critiques of the ways in which the philosophical canon of political theory and the empirical canon of behavioral political science excluded women and women's activity from their subject matter, often rendered women invisible, and employed stereotypical assumptions about women's apolitical "nature" and their behavior. Although several important critiques appeared in the 1970s (e.g., Bourque and Grossholtz 1974; Shanley and Schuck 1974; Jaquette 1974; Iglitzin 1974; Goot and Reid 1975; Boals 1975; Okin 1979; Elshtain 1979a), recent critiques continue to add to our understanding of the ways that the discipline as a whole and specific subfields within the discipline either have failed to deal with women or have treated women in a stereotyped manner (e.g., Randall 1991; Ackelsberg and Diamond 1987; Nelson 1989; Sapiro 1989; Grant 1991; Halliday 1991).

Inasmuch as political science is interested in questions of citizenship, many feminists have turned their attention to the historical tradition of Western political theory to explain both the invisibility of women as political actors and the sexist attitudes toward women that have permeated much of the discipline. The earliest feminist critiques were concerned with breaking the silence about women that had characterized -- and to some extent still does characterize -- the scholarly literature on the canon of political theory. Even as feminists found that the majority of past political theorists had excluded women from participation in the public sphere, they also found that these theorists had not simply neglected women in their texts (Okin 1979; Elshtain 1981; Saxonhouse 1985; Eisenstein 1981; Shanley 1982). On the contrary, the classic theorists were deeply worried about what they deemed most often to be the disorderly influence of women on political affairs. Women were not simply missing in the canonical texts; rather, they had been read out of the Western tradition by political theory scholars (Jones and Jonasdottir 1988).

In important respects, then, feminist political theorists set out from the start to make visible what their academic colleagues had made invisible, namely women. Although women were present as a subject of no small concern for the classic theorists, they were absent as political actors. Thus feminists were intent to show, first, how the tradition has justified women's exclusion from participation in the public sphere, and, second, how that exclusion has defined what counts as citizenship across a wide historical range of political theories, up to and including modern democratic theory. Because women had been a virtual non-topic within the scholarly literature in political theory, many feminists were concerned initially with chronicling what past political theorists had said about women and showing how what they had said had been used to justify women's banishment from civic life. Focusing on the "patriarchal attitudes" of political theorists from Plato to Hegel, feminists found that most theorists had portrayed women as not fully human or fully rational or fully political beings (Figes 1970; Mahowald 1978; Brennan and Pateman 1979; Clarke and Lange 1979; Pateman 1980a). Whether women were defined in terms of their disruptive sexuality, lack of justice, incapacity for reason, or all of the above and more, the classic theorists had cast them as being utterly deficient in those qualities that were deemed necessary for active participation in the civic community. "Women *qua* women," in short, were "excluded from the public, political, and economic spheres" (Clarke and Lange 1979, viii).

Those feminists who focused on the "blatantly anachronistic or flatly misogynist elements" of the classic texts (Brown 1988, 11) decried "the sexism of political theory" and declared the Western tradition "utterly bankrupt" as a means for advancing feminist theories of citizenship and sexual equality (Clarke and Lange 1979, xvii; Figes 1970). Even feminists who did not advocate such an outright dismissal of the canon agreed that the classic theorists offered little in the way of a political analysis of the sexual division of labor in the family (Okin 1979; Elshtain 1981; Eisenstein 1981). Part of the problem, as Susan Moller Okin argued, was that political theorists naturalized the family and women's place within it. They viewed women in strictly functionalist terms: "Philosophers who, in laying the foundation for their political theories, have asked 'What are men like?' 'What is man's potential?' have frequently, in turning to the female sex, asked, 'What are women *for*?'" (Okin 1979, 10).

Susan Moller Okin was one among a growing number of feminists who came increasingly to view the less than flattering images of women found throughout the Western tradition as being more than merely incidental to representations of the political. What a theorist said about women, feminists came to argue, was absolutely crucial to how he conceptualized the terms of citizenship (Pateman 1980b; Eisenstein 1981; Elshtain 1981; Saxonhouse 1985). Not only were concepts such as justice, rights, and consent articulated in the absence of women as political actors, but also their meaning was constituted through that absence. This core insight, although not fully developed in the feminist literature of the late 1970s and early 1980s, was crucial for the scholarship on gender for at least three reasons: one, it enabled feminists to contest the "add women and stir" approach to political theory; two, it offered a way of thinking through women's contemporary status as second-class citizens; and, three, it suggested that the legacy of the Western tradition on the discipline of political science has been to treat women as political outsiders whose proper place is in the family.

Critiques of the empirical canon of behavioral political science research have in many respects echoed the themes that have characterized critiques of the political theory canon. Feminists have examined and found problematic the treatment of women in such classic works as: Angus Campbell et al., *The American Voter*; Robert Lane, *Political Life*; Fred Greenstein, *Children and Politics*; Gabriel Almond and Sidney Verba, *The Civic Culture*; Robert Dahl, *Who Governs?*; and Hans Morgenthau, *Politics Among Nations* (Bourque and Grossholtz 1974; Sapiro 1979; Tickner 1991).

Perhaps the most striking observation about the traditional behavioral political science literature is how seldom women are mentioned and how little serious and sustained attention is devoted to explaining their behavior. Regardless of whether women were physically present or absent among the population studied, they are invisible in much of the pre-feminist literature. Even when women

were present among the subjects studied, and even when an examination of their experiences would have contradicted the main conclusions of a study (as, for example, Virginia Sapiro maintains would have been the case for Robert Dahl's *Who Governs?*), women were most often ignored (Sapiro 1979).

Nevertheless, a clear and coherent picture of women and their behavior emerges from works in the empirical canon, including several of the books mentioned above, that do explicitly (even if only briefly) examine women's behavior. The portrait is one of women as apolitical at worst and politically deficient at best. Women are portrayed as lacking in political interest and involvement (e.g., Berelson, Lazarsfeld, and McPhee 1954, 25; Campbell et al. 1960, 489-90). They have low political efficacy and belief systems that lack conceptual sophistication (e.g., Campbell et al. 1960, 490-2). They vote less often than men, and when they do vote, they tend to defer to and vote like their husbands (e.g., Campbell et al., 485-6, 492-3). They "personalize" politics, paying more attention to personalities than to issues (e.g., Greenstein 1965, 108; Almond and Verba 1963, 535). They are more conservative in their political preferences and voting (despite the fact that they vote like their husbands) (e.g., Almond and Verba 1963, 535) and less tolerant of left-wing political groups such as Communists and socialists (e.g., Stouffer 1955, 131-55).

Feminist scholars have shown that this political portrait of women is based on research riddled with untested assumptions and methodological flaws (see especially Jaquette 1974; Bourque and Grossholtz 1974; Goot and Reid 1975). Because of the problems that characterize the analysis of women in much of this literature, it is impossible to ascertain fully the extent to which the research reflects an accurate portrayal of women's political behavior at the time and the extent to which the portrayal of women as far less politically engaged and sophisticated than men is a product of gender-related biases on the part of researchers. At a minimum, it seems fair to conclude that the assumptions and biases that are reflected in this research (as discussed below) led to an exaggerated portrayal of differences between women and men.

Early behavioral political scientists accepted unquestioningly the public-private split and the definition of woman as primarily oriented toward responsibilities and activities in the private sphere evident in much of Western political thought (Elshtain 1974). The family was viewed as a monolithic unit (Sapiro 1989; Goot and Reid 1975) with the male as the family head and dominant political representative. A woman's primary obligations were assumed to be to her roles as wife and mother. Men's political behavior became the norm against which women's political behavior was measured and found lacking (Bourque and Grossholtz 1974). These assumptions not only were untested, but also seem to have been accepted as "natural," with change in women's and men's roles viewed as either inconceivable or undesirable.

This series of interrelated assumptions affected both *what* questions were asked (and, more importantly, not asked) about women's political behavior and *how* women's political behavior was studied by pre-feminist behavioral political scientists. Because women were viewed as apolitical and oriented primarily toward the private sphere of home and family, findings about women's lower levels of involvement and interest in politics were not considered problematic. Political scientists did not empirically investigate the question of why women in the general population did not show higher levels of engagement with politics; rather, they assumed they knew why. Similarly, the near-absence of women from positions in political elites, particularly as public officeholders, was not a question that intrigued or disturbed political scientists. Rather, the under-representation of women among political elites became a question worthy of investigation only after the advent of feminism both outside and inside the discipline.

The ways in which the assumptions of pre-feminist behavioral political scientists affected their work are even more evident when it comes to *how* women's political behavior was studied. Feminist critics have devoted considerable attention to showing that the application of supposedly objective research methods to the study of women's political behavior in the empirical canon was hardly value-free.

Feminists have pointed to a number of ways in which behavioral political scientists can be accused of practicing "bad science" in investigating women's attitudes and involvement. Several scholars have provided examples demonstrating that political scientists exaggerated or even misconstrued their findings to fit their preconceived notions about women's nature and the ways that women and men differ (e.g., Goot and Reid 1975; Bourque and Grossholtz 1974).

When researchers found legitimate differences between females and males, they almost always interpreted the differences in such a way as to make females appear apolitical. For example, Fred Greenstein asked children what they would do if they could change the world; he noted that girls were more likely to suggest "a distinctly nonpolitical change" such as "Get rid of all the criminals and bad people" (Greenstein 1965, 116; Bourque and Grossholtz 1974, 243). Similarly, Susan C. Bourque and Jean Grossholtz pointed out that findings of lower levels of political efficacy for women when compared with men were interpreted as a sign of men's political competence and women's incompetence. They

suggested alternatively that such findings might reflect women's "perceptive assessment of the political process" and that perhaps men "express irrationally high rates of efficacy because of the limitations of their sex role which teaches them that they are masterful and capable of affecting the political process" (Bourque and Grossholtz 1974, 231).

Researchers sometimes asked questions which were clearly biased in such a way as to elicit responses that would construe males as political and females as apolitical. For example, Lynne B. Iglitzin, who examined questionnaires used in three classic political socialization studies (Greenstein 1965; Hess and Torney 1968; Andrain 1971), concluded that in many of the questions, "Politics is portrayed as a male-only world by the unvarying use of the male gender, the pictures chosen, and the limited and stereotyped choices of answers provided" (1974, 33).

Finally, political scientists engaged in a practice that Bourque and Grossholtz termed "fudging the footnotes" (1974). Bourque and Grossholtz found that some political scientists cited sources for statements about the political attitudes and behavior of women that, when checked, did not really say what had been attributed to them. For example, they noted how Robert Lane's contention in *Political Life* that political conflict between husbands and wives is usually resolved by the wife being persuaded by the husband was contradicted by the study he cited in support of his contention. Instead of persuasion by the husband, the study found mutual influence between husbands and wives and a tendency for children to follow the mother's partisan predisposition in cases where parents disagreed on political party preference (1974, 234-5). Bourque and Grossholtz provide other examples showing that early behavioral researchers sometimes "fudged the footnotes" by citing data from earlier studies without the qualifications and context that had accompanied them in the original text, thus misrepresenting the original findings.

While the "bad science" that characterized the examination of women's behavior in some of the classic studies can be corrected by eliminating the biases of the past and practicing "good science" in future research, some feminists have raised criticisms of behavioral political science research that are more fundamental and not nearly as easily addressed as are mere charges of bias. One of these critics is Jean Bethke Elshtain, who has claimed that the problem lies with an epistemology that separates facts and values. She has explained:

> The problem is more complex and
> fundamental than any charge of bias. *It is
> that every explanatory theory of politics
> supports a particular set of normative
> conclusions.* To have an explanatory theory,

the analyst must adopt a framework linked, implicitly if not explicitly, to notions of human nature and human purposes. This framework sets the boundaries of the phenomena to be investigated. Some factors of social life will be incorporated, and others will be expunged from view before research begins (1979a, 242).

In Elshtain's view (a view shared by many other feminist political scientists), behavioral political science has adopted a framework that excludes much of what women do from political analysis and relegates most women to a private realm outside of politics. Elshtain has observed:

> Within mainstream political science, what has been described traditionally as politics tends to factor women out of the activity and has excluded for many years the questions raised by feminists. Such questions are relegated to a sphere outside organized political activity and are dismissed as private "troubles" (1979a, 243).

Like Elshtain, Barbara Nelson has also pointed to problems with both the epistemology and the content of political science. While acknowledging that many feminist political scientists would wish to retain the systematic study of events as one type of research, she has argued that feminist critics raise questions about "the universalism of the findings and disinterestedness and unconnectedness of the observer" that cannot be corrected simply by acknowledging or attempting to remove values or biases from empirical research (1989, 22). She has observed:

> The study of gender is revolutionary because it threatens the belief that most existing research is gender neutral and universalistic. In political science, like the social sciences in general, women may not fit into existing social theories, which suggests that in many cases social knowledge believed to be cumulative may not be cumulative at all (1989, 22).

As for content, Nelson has concluded, based on her analysis of three popular introductory textbooks and two recent self-reflective volumes on the state of the discipline, that an overemphasis on electoral politics is one of the reasons why political science has devoted so little attention to women and their experiences. She has urged that as a discipline we must:

> ... include in the study of politics not only the recognition of the exclusion of women from what is traditionally political, but also

the inclusion of politics in what women have traditionally done. We shall have gone a long way to creating a more inclusive political discourse if we give attention to families, communities, voluntary groups, social movements, and the welfare state, just to name a few topics. The discipline needs a two-fold strategy, emphasizing that all political subjects are gendered while also giving attention to those areas and concerns where women have traditionally put their political energy (1989, 21).

Feminist critiques of both the philosophical canon of political theory and the empirical canon of behavioral political science suggest that contemporary political scientists should regard much of what was written about women prior to the 1970s with skepticism. The pre-feminist empirical literature is so heavily influenced by assumptions about women's apolitical nature that it is difficult to separate scientific fact from fiction. The end result is that we know relatively little about women's political behavior prior to the development of feminist scholarship both because women were so seldom studied in any serious and sustained way, and because when they were studied, they were examined through a biased lens.

The feminist critiques of the empirical canon also provide evidence that a positivist epistemology can (and perhaps always does) mask an underlying set of normative assumptions about human nature and, in particular, about women's nature. Many feminist scholars within the discipline today are very wary of claims to objective, value-free research and universal truths. Their wariness stems, in part, from the discovery of strong biases in pre-feminist scientific research regarding women's political behavior. Their wariness also stems, in part, from the realization that women's absence from the subject matter of much behavioral research means that the universal truths supposedly being discovered through this research are, in fact, gendered -- i.e., based on men's experiences of politics, not women's.

Finally, feminist critiques of the philosophical canon of political theory and the empirical canon of behavioral political science call into question our conception of politics with its foundation in the split between public and private life. Rather than take that split at face value, feminists have endeavored to analyze it historically and to show how a more critical conceptualization of it would significantly alter how we think about the meaning of citizenship and about women as citizens.

Debunking the Myth of the Invisible, Apolitical Woman

Much of the theoretical and empirical work undertaken by women and politics scholars during the 1970s and 1980s was aimed at making women visible in political theory and behavioral research and correcting the biases of the past; this type of work continues into the present. Women and politics scholars utilized existing disciplinary (and sometimes nongendered interdisciplinary) frameworks and approaches to examine both the portrayal of women in the works of major political theorists and women's political behavior at citizen and elite levels. These scholars attempted to dispel both the notion that women were apolitical beings and the idea that women's (and men's) roles in society were dictated by nature and thus immutable.

This body of women and politics literature is important because it demonstrates the importance of gender as a category of analysis within mainstream political theory and political science. However, it is also important for another reason. In subjecting women and women's experience to political analysis, in applying existing disciplinary frameworks and approaches to women, this research pointed to possible limitations and inadequacies in those frameworks and approaches. Focusing on women and women's experience in an attempt to fit women into the picture often revealed that important adjustments were necessary; women did not always fit simply and neatly into the existing picture. In some respects this research suggested that important material was left out and that the existing picture was only a partial representation of political reality; a wider-angle lens was needed. In other respects this research suggested that the picture itself needed to be recomposed in order to encompass women's experience.

In an effort to complicate the familiar image of public man and private woman, several feminist political theorists have rethought the development of the modern public sphere through the historical lens of women's political participation and experience. For example, Joan Landes (1988) has argued that the emergence of the bourgeois public sphere in enlightenment France cannot be understood adequately without attending to the enormous social influence of salon women in the Old Regime. No mere ornament to the Royal Court, the salon "belonged to a wider urban culture," and was "distinguished by its 'worldliness' and cosmopolitan character" (1988, 25). As key players in the "system of advancement for merit" (1988, 24), salon women were crucial to the social changes that brought about the demise of the landed aristocracy.

By making gender a central category of her analysis, Landes has enriched our understanding of the class struggles that altered the face of eighteenth-century Europe. She has shown that an ideology of female domesticity was crucial to the social ascendancy of the middle classes, and that the modern public sphere was historically constructed through the exclusion of women. When women and their interests are properly accounted for, Landes has argued, "enlightenment begins to look suspiciously like counterenlightenment, and revolution like counterrevolution" (1988, 204). The implications of her claim that the eighteenth-century citizen was not a generic but rather a gendered category are far-reaching: "the [contemporary] women's movement cannot 'take possession' of a public sphere that has been enduringly reconstructed along masculinist lines" (1988, 202).

The tension that Landes has located between political equality and sexual inequality has been taken up by several other feminist theorists, who have been concerned to challenge conventional tales about the historical emergence of modern democracies. Mary Lyndon Shanley (1989) has pursued a similar line of investigation into Victorian debates about universal suffrage and female domesticity. Shanley has found that political women challenged nineteenth-century liberalism to live up to its promise of equal rights for all. While recognizing the failure of most Victorian feminists to question the sexual division of labor in the family and to advocate economic equality for the laboring masses, Shanley has also called our attention to how they exploited the tenets of liberal ideology to serve a wide range of progressive ends. In contrast to Landes, she has suggested that the contemporary women's movement can continue to do so.

One of the most important contributions of feminists who have integrated gender into their work on the origins of liberal society has been to highlight the tension between women as rights-bearing citizens and women as an oppressed sex-class. Some scholars have argued that this tension is the very motor behind liberal feminism, and that it has the potential to radicalize the mainstream women's movement (Eisenstein 1981; Shanley 1989). As Zillah Eisenstein has observed:

> Liberal feminism involves more than simply achieving the bourgeois male rights earlier denied women, although it includes this. Liberal feminism is not feminism merely added onto liberalism. Rather, there is a real difference between liberalism and liberal feminism in that feminism requires a recognition...of the sexual-class identification of women as women....This recognition of women as a sexual class lays the subversive quality of feminism for liberalism because liberalism is premised upon women's exclusion from public life on this basis. The demand for the real equality

of women with men, if taken to its logical conclusion, would dislodge the patriarchal structure necessary to a liberal society (1981, 6).

In a later book, *Feminism and Sexual Equality* (1984), Eisenstein concluded that the more American liberal feminists radicalize their agenda in response to an unresponsive state -- which has sought, at least since 1980, to curtail the most fundamental political demands brought by the mainstream women's movement (e.g., the ERA and abortion rights) -- the more the tension between women as a sex-class and women as citizens would be exposed. Liberal feminists, in short, would be forced to recognize the limits of liberalism.

Other feminists have argued that the problem for liberal feminism lies in its appeal "to the bureaucratic apparatus of the state and of the corporate world to integrate women into the public sphere through programs seeking equal opportunity and affirmative action" (Ferguson 1984, 4). This reliance on the bureaucratic state to obtain feminist ends, critics have maintained, is antithetical to an anti-hierarchical "vision of individual and collective life" (Ferguson 1984, 5; Elshtain 1981; Ruddick 1989; Denhardt and Perkins 1976).

Many feminists are wary about enhancing the power of a state whose surveillance capacities, they have argued, are cause for alarm. According to Carole Pateman, liberal feminism comes into an uneasy alliance with the state when it relies on the idea of the contract to promote social equality for women. In a time when "the influence of contract doctrine is extending into the last, most intimate nooks and crannies of social life," Pateman has written, feminists have every reason to worry about "the conjuncture of the rhetoric of individual rights and a vast increase of state power" (1988, 232). Pateman rejects the notion that the liberal discourse of rights alone can further feminist struggles for social, economic, and political equality. The putatively autonomous individual who has property in himself and who makes contracts, she has argued, has never applied fully to women. On the contrary, the proprietal self is a masculinist construction that has historically assumed and continues to assume men's property in women. For women, the freedom to contract has always been constrained by their sexual subordination to and economic dependence on men. Arguing that "a free social order cannot be a contractual order," Pateman has urged feminists to develop "other forms of free agreement through which women and men can constitute political relations" (1988, 232).

In contrast to the skepticism of those feminist political theorists who maintain that the women's movement cannot attain its goals of sexual equality through mainstream politics, many empirical feminist

political scientists have suggested that women must enter the formal political arena in order to achieve equality. Thus, a significant body of empirical work conducted by women and politics scholars in the 1970s and 1980s focused on electoral politics. In particular, several of the first books to be published on women and politics focused on women public officials and party activists (e.g., Kirkpatrick 1974, 1976; Diamond 1977; Githens and Prestage 1977). Other early work focused on women's collective efforts to influence the policy-making process (e.g., Freeman 1975).

One of the primary tasks undertaken by the earliest research on women in political elites was that of challenging the near invisibility of women in the empirical canon of political science by demonstrating the presence of women among officeholders and activists. Thus, Jeane J. Kirkpatrick began the conclusion to her path-breaking study of 50 women state legislators serving in the early 1970s with the statement, "The most important finding of this study is that political woman exists" (1974, 217). Countering the image of women as apolitical, as by nature different from men, she then went on to assert that the political women she studied were similar in many respects to male politicians, in particular in their social backgrounds and psychological characteristics (1974, 220). However, to reassure those who at the time might have thought that any woman similar to a male politician could not be "normal," Kirkpatrick explained:

> ... *"political woman" is not grossly deviant from her female peers.* She is not necessarily "masculine" in appearance or manner; she has not necessarily rejected traditional female roles and interests. Quite the contrary. The political women on whom this book is based are... [almost all] wives and mothers.... Well-groomed, well-mannered, decorous in speech and action, these are "feminine" women in the traditional sex-stereotyped sense of that word (1974, 219).

When viewed from the perspective of the 1990s, Kirkpatrick's book, like other early empirical work on women and politics, appears cautious, conservative, and restricted in scope. However, when considered in its proper historical context, i.e., as a response to the invisibility and apolitical (or politically deficient) image of women within the existing behavioral political science research of the time, the importance and the (at least implicitly) challenging nature of *Political Woman* and other similar works are immediately apparent.

Women and politics scholars have attempted to make political women visible not only as individuals, but also as an organized, collective political force. Working within traditional disciplinary frameworks, women and politics scholars have analyzed both the feminist and anti-feminist movements and their successes and failures in affecting public policy outcomes (e.g., Freeman 1975; Costain 1980, 1982; Gelb and Palley 1982; Gelb 1989; Boles 1979; Mansbridge 1986; Mathews and De Hart 1990; Klatch 1987).

Like Kirkpatrick and others who studied women in political elites, women and politics scholars who studied mass political behavior conducted research that countered the image of women as apolitical or politically deficient. While some researchers continued to find evidence of notable differences between women and men in political orientations and behavior in the U.S. and other countries (e.g., Jennings and Farah 1980; Rapoport 1982, 1985), most researchers in the 1970s and early 1980s found little evidence that women in the United States differed greatly from men in their political orientations or behavior. In part, the findings of few sex differences in these studies resulted from the elimination of much of the gender bias which had influenced both the methodology and the interpretation of findings in earlier research and which had led to a portrayal of women as more politically different from men than they undoubtedly were. However, in part, the lack of significant sex differences in most of the studies conducted in the 1970s and 1980s also reflected actual changes in political behavior that had taken place as differences between men's and women's social roles, education, and employment decreased.

Research conducted in the 1970s and 1980s demonstrated that women were as likely or almost as likely as men to participate in political activities such as working in campaigns, writing letters to public officials, attending political meetings, and contributing money to candidates or parties (Hansen, Franz, and Netemeyer-Mays 1976; Welch 1977; Baxter and Lansing 1980; Beckwith 1986). In addition, Sandra Baxter and Marjorie Lansing found women in all age groups to be as interested as men in following campaigns -- a finding that they noted "contrasts sharply with the myth of nonpolitical woman" (Baxter and Lansing 1980, 46). Research on childhood socialization conducted during the 1970s suggested that politically relevant differences between boys and girls also seemed to be few in number and limited primarily to political interest and knowledge (Orum et al. 1974; Sapiro 1983, 38).[1] Berenice A. Carroll, writing in 1979, summed up the feminist empirical research on women in American politics as follows:

> ...the picture which emerges is...one...of women holding political attitudes and engaging in political behaviors very similar to those of men, at all levels from school

children to party activists and local officeholders. On almost all measures of voting, participation, efficacy, activism, ideology, and performance, sex differences between men and women, if present at all, are small (1979, 292).

In contrast to both the philosophical canon of political theory and the empirical canon of behavioral political science, which viewed differences between women and men as natural, women and politics scholars writing in the 1970s and 1980s generally attributed those sex differences which did occur to gender role socialization and/or adult gender roles. Differences between women and men, whether in elites or mass publics, were viewed as socially constructed and thus changeable rather than as natural and immutable. As the socialization of women and the opportunities and roles that were open to them in society changed, so too would their political behavior.

In this vein, studies of women's political orientations and participation examined the effects of education, finding increased education to be related to increased participation for women as well as to higher levels of political interest and efficacy (e.g., Sapiro 1983; Hansen, Franz, and Netemeyer-Mays 1976; Welch 1977; Baxter and Lansing 1983; Poole and Zeigler 1985). Working outside the home also was found to be related to women's involvement in conventional forms of participation, with employed women participating at rates similar to those of men, and women who were full-time homemakers participating at notably lower rates (Andersen 1975; Welch 1977, 724-5).[2] Finally, studies suggested that having children had an adverse effect on both political participation and various political orientations (Sapiro 1983, 177; Jennings and Niemi 1981, 296-7). The implication of these findings was that women's levels of participation would be likely to increase further as women increased their educational attainment, entered the labor force in larger numbers, spent a smaller proportion of their lives raising children, and received more help with child care. Thus, the few existing sex differences in political orientations and participation might well diminish as changes took place in women's roles and their socialization into those roles.

At the elite level, women and politics scholars devoted considerable attention to examining the question of why so few women held public office, and here, too, early feminist explanations often focused on gender role socialization and adult gender roles. Several studies focused on delegates to national party conventions and other party activists, who were considered a potential pool of future candidates for public office. These studies consistently found that women were less ambitious for public officeholding than their male counterparts

(Jennings and Thomas 1968; Costantini and Craik 1977; Kirkpatrick 1976; Fowlkes, Perkins, and Rinehart 1979; Sapiro and Farah 1980; Jennings and Farah 1981; Costantini and Bell 1984). Women's lower levels of political ambition were generally explained in terms of gender differences in political socialization and gender roles although the explanations were sometimes linked to lack of political opportunities. M. Kent Jennings and Barbara G. Farah, for example, observed, "For the present...cultural norms and structural conditions -- especially the dual demands of homemaking and career plus inequities in the opportunity structure -- continue to exert a dampening influence on the political life expectancies of women" (1981, 480).

The emphasis on gender role socialization and the effects of gender roles in explaining why few women held public office was prevalent in literature examining other politically active women as well. In a frequently cited study, Marcia Manning Lee examined the factors that kept women who were active in their communities from running for office. In addition to fear of sex discrimination, the two factors which held women back were their responsibility for care of young children (a factor that held few men back) and their perceptions of appropriate and inappropriate roles for women; most viewed holding public office as improper behavior for a woman (Lee 1976).

Research on women officeholders also emphasized the constraining effect of gender roles and gender role socialization (Diamond 1977; Stoper 1977; Mandel 1981). Kirkpatrick, for example, noted that traditional sex role requirements were the principal constraints preventing women from running for office. She observed that the women legislators in her study were remarkable precisely because they had managed to blend their political lives with traditional roles. She asked:

> If these women can do it, why can't/don't others? Perhaps because they lack high self-esteem and broad identifications, habits of participation, a desire to influence public policy, political skills needed to do so, a husband willing to cooperate, the empathy, flexibility, self-knowledge, and energy needed to live a busy and complicated life when so many less demanding alternatives are so readily available (1974, 240).

As this passage from Kirkpatrick's *Political Woman* illustrates, much of the literature stressing gender role socialization and gender roles implied that individual women themselves had to change their lives in order for women's representation in public office to increase. Observing this tendency in the literature, Berenice Carroll

wrote in 1979, "There is still a heavy focus on sex-role socialization, with its implicit tendency to 'blame the victim' (or her mother) and to place on women the burden of changing sex roles without changing the system which requires the existing sex-role patterns, rewards those who conform to it, and punishes those who defy it" (1979, 306). Whether in response to this observation by Carroll and others or for other reasons, a change in emphasis occurred in the 1980s within the literature on political elites, especially that material dealing with the question of why women were underrepresented numerically among public officeholders. Many researchers turned their focus away from examining how gender role socialization and adult gender roles kept women from being more like the "political men" who held public office. Instead, they focused squarely on the operation of the political system itself as an explanatory variable helping to account for women's underrepresentation (e.g., Carroll 1985; Darcy et al. 1987).

These researchers demonstrated that the staying power of incumbents and the lack of winnable open seats are major obstacles to women's electoral success in the United States and elsewhere (Andersen and Thorson 1984; Darcy et al. 1987; Carroll 1985; Studlar et al. 1988). Electoral arrangements also are very important (see Rule and Zimmerman 1992; see also Welch and Studlar 1990 for a particularly good review of the research on the impact of electoral arrangements on women's electability). At the state legislative level in the U.S., women run in a greater proportion of multimember than single-member districts, and women who run in multimember districts win at a higher rate than those who run in single-member districts (Darcy et al. 1987, 119; Carroll 1985, 110; Rule 1990). Moreover, when states change from multimember to single-member districts as several states have done during the past three decades, the proportion of women running and winning decreases compared to national trends (Darcy et al. 1987, 119-22). Although differences in electoral arrangements are probably less important at the municipal level, there is evidence that women fare slightly better when cities have at-large rather than district elections (Darcy et al. 1987, 117-8; MacManus and Bullock 1989; Welch and Karnig 1979).[3]

Comparative research has demonstrated that women's representation in national legislatures is greater in countries with proportional representation, especially those utilizing party lists, than in countries like the U.S., which elect representatives on the basis of plurality voting (Randall 1987, 140-2; Rule 1981; Norris 1985; Lovenduski 1986; Haavio-Mannila et al. 1985). The institution and implementation of quotas for women on the party list for election within some European political parties has further enhanced women's representation in those countries (e.g., Dahlerup 1988, 297; Kolinsky 1991; Phillips 1991, 84-5).

Although this research on the effect of electoral arrangements on women's representation has been conducted utilizing the frameworks, approaches, and techniques of mainstream political science, it nevertheless has important normative implications for behavioral political scientists. Barbara Nelson was quoted earlier in this essay as suggesting, "all political subjects are gendered." Research on the effect of electoral arrangements provides a good example by showing that certain supposedly gender-neutral features of the way the political system operates systematically discriminate against women. Certainly, the existing electoral arrangements of the U.S. are not gender neutral, although the experience of some Western European countries with quota systems suggests that electoral systems can be altered to make them more so. Political analysis that deals with proposed reforms in electoral systems or procedures (e.g., term limits, campaign finance), or that uncritically accepts existing electoral arrangements without explicitly examining the gender implications of those reforms or arrangements, may well end up, however unintentionally, perpetuating women's exclusion from public officeholding.

Empirical studies of women's behavior at mass and elite levels have also posed challenges to what we study as political scientists and how we study it by calling attention to previously unexamined variables and by arguing that in some cases gender-specific models are necessary to better explain political behavior. Empirical studies of women and politics have devoted considerable attention to the ways that women's so-called private lives, especially their responsibilities and connections to partners and children, influence and constrain their behavior. While generally finding family-related factors to be more important for women than for men, some feminist scholars made another important discovery: men have families too! And those families seem to have a significant impact on men's as well as on women's behavior. For example, Diane Kincaid Blair and Ann R. Henry found that family problems are the major factor leading to retirement from office for men as well as women serving in state legislatures; previous research had attributed legislative turnover primarily to low salaries and had failed to investigate the possible importance of family-related variables (Blair and Henry 1981). Similarly, Sapiro found that conflicts between family commitments and public commitments, although resolved differently by the two sexes, were experienced at least as often by men as by women among partisan elites (Sapiro 1982). Thus, the empirical women and politics literature would suggest that the possible influence of so-called

private life considerations be given more serious attention in future research on political behavior.

Although much of the research on women and politics has suggested that some variables have a more important influence on women's political behavior while others are more important for men, a few recent studies have taken this argument one step further. These studies have suggested that the *process* and *calculus* of political decision making differs for women and men; some factors are more critical to women's decisions and other factors are more critical to men's. An example of such work is a study conducted by Linda L. M. Bennett and Stephen Earl Bennett examining gender differences in political interest and the impact of apathy on voting behavior. They concluded:

> ...the process leading women to the voting booth differs from that of men. While men are motivated more out of interest and partisanship, age and SES are the prime determinants among women. The top political disposition discriminating among women is citizen duty. In short, while men went to the polls in 1984 mainly because they were interested, to the degree that political dispositions were involved in their calculus of voting, women went to the polls because they thought they ought to go (1989, 119).

There is evidence that women and men employ a different calculus not only in deciding whether to vote, but also in deciding how to vote. For example, Ethel Klein's analysis of 1980 election data indicated that the voting calculus of women and men was very different in that election, with women's rights issues influencing women's votes far more than they influenced men's (1984, 161-2). In a more recent study, Susan Welch and John Hibbing (1992) have demonstrated that economic considerations are less important in women's voting calculus than in men's; moreover, while men are more likely to vote on the basis of egocentric economic judgments, women more often utilize sociotropic economic considerations in making their voting decisions.

In a similar vein, Timothy Bledsoe and Mary Herring have argued that different factors affect the decisions of women and men serving on city councils regarding the pursuit of higher office. They have suggested, "If the situation of women in electoral politics is unique, the decision-making process for these women may be unique as well" (1990, 213). They found that the decisions of women were more likely than those of men to be influenced by the strength of their current political position and their self-perceptions of political vulnerability. However, women's decisions were not influenced by ambition; in fact, ambitious women were less likely than those without ambition to seek office. In contrast, men's decisions were little affected by their current circumstances but strongly affected by political ambition. In fact, ambition seemed to be the only variable that really mattered for men (1990).

Perhaps Janneke Van der Ros (1987) has carried the argument about differences in women's and men's political behavior and decision making farther than anyone else. She has suggested that gender-specific explanatory models be used whenever relevant in behavioral studies, and she has taken the first steps toward developing such models.

Not all women and politics scholars agree on the desirability of creating gender-specific models of political behavior. Some would rather see the development of nongendered models that would encompass all of human behavior. Others would suggest that we should reject completely the idea of models that try to generalize across all or even half of humanity and move instead in the direction of greater historical, cultural, and situational specificity in our investigation of political behavior. Nevertheless, studies which suggest that we need gender-specific models of political behavior are important because they call into question the universality of our existing knowledge and reveal it to be rooted in men's experience. Although feminist scholars may not be in agreement over the desirability of universals, they most certainly are in agreement that current empirical knowledge does not adequately reflect women's experiences.

Rethinking Traditional Frameworks and Assumptions

In recent years many women and politics scholars and feminist theorists have produced work that more explicitly confronts and challenges the dominant frameworks and assumptions of the discipline. Often influenced by the interdisciplinary perspectives of women's studies, these scholars have raised new questions and introduced new frameworks into the study of gender and politics. Their work suggests that we need to rethink and reconceptualize various approaches, assumptions, and concepts that are central to the discipline.

Empirically oriented feminist political scientists have challenged conventional definitions of politics by adopting an approach to their research that puts the perspectives of women and women's experiences at the center of their analysis. As one example, in contrast to earlier research that documented the effect that women's

private lives had on their public lives but nevertheless did not question the basic assumption underlying much of western political thought and practice that life is, and can be, divided into public and private spheres, some recent research has through its focus on women's experiences called into question this assumption of a split between public and private life. For example, examining women state legislators' decisions to run for office and their private life situations, Susan J. Carroll found no evidence of a split between public and private in these women's lives and suggested that we need a new conceptualization. Finding that women's personal life choices had affected public careers and that their public life choices had had an impact on their private life situations, Carroll concluded, "A dualistic conception of public and private as largely separate and mutually exclusive spheres of existence does not adequately portray the reality of these women's lives; rather, public and private in the lives of women officeholders seem to constitute a holistic system of interrelated social relations where any action taken or choice made has repercussions throughout the system" (1989, 63).

Although they have not focused as explicitly on the relationship between public and private, several other scholars have questioned dominant conceptions of politics by using women's perspectives as a point of departure for their analysis of politics. One example is Diane Fowlkes, who interviewed 27 white women activists with diverse political backgrounds. Fowlkes acknowledged that her purpose was "not to test theory but to present and explicate the political worlds of the diverse white women in this study," and that the generalizations that she drew from her interviews were "intended to explicate the various meanings that *these women* give to their political worlds and the various dynamics that shape their political actions" (1992, 27). As part of her study, Fowlkes allowed the women to speak in open-ended fashion about how they defined "the political." The ways in which these activists defined politics were both rich and varied. Some viewed the political as political scientists often do -- as working for candidates for public office, holding office, governing, or advocating issues. However, others viewed the political in ways that suggested a broader or an alternative conception of politics -- as linking the private and public spheres, as developing power to bring about change, and as bringing change through the lives they lead on a daily basis. While most of the women activists' conceptions touched in one way or another on the theme of power, Fowlkes noted that the themes of educating and consciousness-raising, perhaps less often considered to be part of politics by contemporary political scientists, also cut across their conceptions of politics (1992, 184-214). By allowing women to speak from their own perspectives in their own terms, Fowlkes's work suggests that the discipline of political science must expand its conception of politics if it is to encompass the ways that the women she interviewed think about the political.

Like Fowlkes, Cynthia Enloe in *Bananas, Beaches, and Bases* also used women's perspectives as a point of departure for rethinking politics -- in this case international politics. Enloe noted that she "began this book thinking about Pocahontas and ended it mulling over the life of Carmen Miranda" (1990, xi). She readily admitted that:

> These women were not the sorts of international actors I had been taught to take seriously when trying to make sense of world affairs. But the more I thought about Pocahontas and Carmen Miranda, the more I began to suspect that I had been missing an entire dimension of international politics -- I got an inkling of how relations between governments depend not only on capital and weaponry, but also on the control of women as symbols, consumers, workers and emotional comforters (1989, xi).

In some ways Cynthia Enloe's work does for international relations what the work of Jeane Kirkpatrick and others helped to do for American politics -- it makes women visible. However, Enloe's work differs significantly from that of Kirkpatrick and others discussed earlier in this essay in that Enloe has not adopted the dominant assumptions and frameworks of work in political science; rather, she has set them aside and used instead the perspective of women's experiences, specifically the experiences of Pocahontas and Carmen Miranda, as her point of departure for examining international politics. She has examined some topics (e.g., nationalism, diplomacy, militaries, and international debt) that are familiar to those who study international politics. However, all have been analyzed through the lens of gender and from the perspective of women's experiences with them. Enloe has concluded:

> Conventional analyses stop short of investigating an entire area of international relations, an area that women have pioneered in exploring: how states depend on particular constructions of the domestic and private spheres. If we take seriously the politics of domestic servants or the politics of marketing fashions and global corporate logos, we discover that international politics is more complicated than non-feminist analysts would have us believe. We especially have to take culture -- including commercialized culture -- far more seriously (1989, 197).

Like Carroll, Fowlkes, and Enloe, scholars who have taken women's experiences as a starting point for their analyses but adopted a more historical approach have suggested that we need to rethink and reconceptualize the way we view politics. Much of what women have done historically has been viewed as "philanthropy" or "service" or "disorderly conduct," but it has rarely been seen as politics (Lebsock 1990, 35). In large part, this has been the result of the public/private split; men's activities have been viewed as public activities while women's have been seen as extensions of their domestic roles. Mary Beth Norton has described the transition that took place in the field of women's history, where scholars initially accepted a "male definition of politics," one clearly linked to the public/private split. Historians who focused on women's experiences quickly discovered that this definition was too narrow to encompass women's political activities. As Norton has explained, "Drawing on the feminist movement's insight that 'the personal is political,' women's historians broadened the category to include women's attempts to gain control over their own lives -- both inside and outside marriage -- and to have an impact on the society in which they lived" (1986, 40). Consistent with this redefinition of the "political," feminist historians focused on women's participation in voluntary associations, the temperance movement, the women's club movement, the social settlement movement, and the trade union movement among other activities (Norton 1986; Lebsock 1990). Political scientists might well look to the experience of their colleagues in history for guidance in constructing a more gender-inclusive conception of politics.

Some empirical work has moved in a direction similar to the direction suggested by women's history. One example is *Women and the Politics of Empowerment* (1988), edited by Ann Bookman and Sandra Morgen. This volume includes several case studies of the activism of working-class women. It examines the activities of women who are household workers, social service agency workers, hospital union workers, and clerical workers in an insurance office. Included in the volume are studies of women who organized a clerical union, fought to reopen a prenatal and gynecology clinic, organized to obtain better quality education for their children, and led a campaign to obtain improved neighborhood services. While many of these activities might well be considered outside the domain of politics as traditionally defined, the editors have argued that all are politically relevant. As they have explained:

> The articles on community organizing document the political meaning and breadth of women's efforts to transform urban space and public policy. In contrast to the popular

view that sees these activities as "voluntary associations" or "mutual aid societies," these cases show women challenging the power of the state and the interests of landlords, developers, and other private institutions. These are certainly political activities (1988, 9-10).

In addition to challenging the ways in which political scientists have traditionally thought about politics, recent empirical work on women and politics has begun to use gender as a category of analysis for studying political structures and processes. This is a relatively new development because, as the previous sections of this essay illustrated, gender has generally been employed as a category of analysis only in studying the behavior of individuals. Perhaps the best example of the application of a gendered analysis to the study of political structures and processes is the recent work on the welfare state and welfare state formation (e.g., Gordon 1990; Sarvasy 1992; Nelson 1990; Diamond 1983). This research has demonstrated that the U.S. welfare state evolved in ways that were clearly gendered (Nelson 1990; Jenson 1990). For example, a two-channel welfare state developed in the U.S., one from the development of Mother's Aid, which was intended for women in the home who had lost their spouses, and the other from the development of Workmen's Compensation, which was intended for men who lost their pay because of work-related disabilities (Nelson 1990). This literature has also demonstrated that the welfare state reinforces inequities based on gender, race, and class at the same time that it provides material aid for those in need (Mink 1990). The welfare state is frequently portrayed as paternalistic and a means of exercising social control over women, but some have argued that it also constitutes a political resource which makes women more secure and less powerless than they otherwise would be (Piven 1990). Regardless, it is clear that the new feminist scholarship on the welfare state has challenged political scientists to think more seriously about the role that gender has played in its formation and operation.

Recent research on women's voting behavior and women in public office, while often employing the same behavioral methodologies that have traditionally characterized research on voting and officeholding, has nevertheless posed a new challenge to the discipline. While much of the earliest empirical research on women and politics worked to counter the image of women as different from men and to convince political scientists that women and men were in most respects politically similar, this new research challenges political scientists to think once again about gender difference. Unlike in its previous incarnation, in its new incarnation gender difference is generally viewed as an asset, not a

deficiency; women are seen as bringing perspectives to politics which are currently lacking.

For example, scholars who have examined the so-called gender gap in voting behavior and public opinion have frequently attributed it to differences in women's and men's values and priorities (Conover 1988; Frankovic 1982; Shapiro and Mahajan 1986; Klein 1985; Norris 1985; Mueller 1988). Although they disagree about whether the gender gap is caused by women's greater pacifism, compassion for the needy, nurturance, feminism, commitment to the welfare state, or other qualities, feminist researchers have generally agreed that the gender gap is a manifestation of differing perspectives between women and men (Carroll 1988). Similarly, research on women in public office has found that women public officials give greater priority than men both to so-called women's issues and to issues related to women's traditional roles as care-givers in the family and in society more generally (Dodson and Carroll 1991; Carroll, Dodson, and Mandel 1991; Dodson 1991; Saint-Germain 1989; Thomas 1991; Thomas and Welch 1991). The authors of these studies have suggested that women's greater involvement with policies in such issue areas as reproductive rights, violence against women, child care, health care, children's welfare, and education reflects the different experiences and perspectives that women bring to office with them. Moreover, the addition of these different experiences and perspectives to the policy-making process is viewed as a positive development that will enhance the overall quality of representation. Debra L. Dodson and Susan J. Carroll, for example, have argued:

> ...significant change is taking place — change that has important long-term implications. As more women enter legislatures, the policy agenda is being reshaped to better reflect the concerns brought into the legislature by women. The end result is likely to be an agenda that is more reponsive not only to the specific needs of women, but also to the needs of a broader cross-section of our society (including, for example, the economically disadvantaged, children and those who lack access to adequate health care) (1991, 94).

Empirically oriented political scientists who have examined the ways that women both as voters and as officeholders are bringing perspectives to politics that are currently underrepresented have been strongly influenced by the work of so-called "gender difference" theorists (e.g., Gilligan 1982; Chodorow 1978; Ruddick 1989) in women's studies. The work of Carol Gilligan on gender differences in moral reasoning has been especially important for many feminist political scientists. Taking on the scholarship in moral theory from Sigmund Freud to Lawrence Kohlberg, Gilligan challenged the claim that women achieve an attenuated stage of moral development in which "goodness is equated with helping and pleasing others" (1982, 18), and that women have therefore a stunted sense of justice (i.e., the capacity to make impartial judgments according to a set of universal rules). Curiously enough, Gilligan observed, "the very traits that traditionally have defined the 'goodness' of women, their care for and sensitivity to the needs of others, are those that mark them as deficient in moral development" (1982, 18). She drew on the work of Nancy Chodorow (1978) to argue that gender differences in moral reasoning are rooted not in biology but rather in childhood development, specifically in the contrasting relationships that boys and girls have to their primary care-giver, the mother. The abstract rules that govern men's moral reasoning, Gilligan held, reflect the achievement of masculine identity through a radical separation from the mother and the maintenance of firm ego boundaries. The context-based principles that govern women's moral reasoning reflect the achievement of feminine identity through a far less radical form of separation from the mother and the maintenance of empathetic relations to others.

Insofar as the traditional moral standard of impartiality takes for granted the masculine values of separateness and autonomy, wrote Gilligan, "women's failure to separate them becomes by definition a failure to develop [morally]" (1982, 9). Gilligan refuted the notion that the "quality of embeddedness in social interaction and personal relationships that characterize women's lives" was a "developmental liability" (1982, 9). She took that quality as an occasion to advance an alternative moral theory, one that would give legitimacy to women's "different voice":

> When one begins with the study of women and derives developmental constructs from their lives, the outline of a moral conception different from that described by Freud, Piaget, and Kohlberg begins to emerge and informs a different description of development. In this conception, the moral problem arises from conflicting responsibilities rather than from competing rights and requires for its resolution a mode of thinking that is contextual and narrative rather than formal and abstract. This conception of morality as concerned with the activity of care centers moral development around the understanding of responsibility and relationships, just as the conception of morality as fairness ties moral development to the understanding of rights and rules (1982, 19).

The argument that women have a different sense of morality grounded in a sense of everyday life and the web of human relationships (Belenky et al. 1986; Miller 1976; Gilligan 1982) has had a profound influence on the work of many feminist theorists who are concerned with challenging a wide variety of abstract models in the social sciences. As Sara Ruddick has put it in *Maternal Thinking*: "Given the value that is placed on abstraction in academic life, concreteness can become a combative insistence on looking, talking, and asking troublesome questions" (1989, 95).

Ruddick has maintained that "abstraction is central to militarist thinking." Like several other feminists working in the area of peace studies, she has argued that realism, as it is articulated by defense intellectuals, is grounded in universal rules of human behavior which assume that "people and nations will, if they can, dominate and exploit those who are weaker" (Ruddick 1989, 179; Elshtain 1987; Cohn 1987; Enloe 1989). Similarly, Jean Bethke Elshtain has written that the realist model of "professionalized IR discourse" focuses exclusively on the abstract entities called states and ignores the most material facts of human life: "No children are ever born, and nobody ever dies, in this constructed world. There are states, and they are what is" (1987, 91).

Both Elshtain and Ruddick have argued that women's experience, and especially maternal experience, provides the basis for political resistance to authoritarian regimes and for peace activism in democratic countries. Each has insisted that women's role in the maintenance of life offers a vital model of civic participation which treasures "the connectedness of self and other" (Ruddick 1989, 225). For example, the famous resistance of the Madres of Argentina challenges us to rethink conventional notions of peace politics and, not least, of femininity. Ruddick has observed:

> In their protests, these women fulfill traditional expectations of femininity and at the same time violate them....Women who bring to the public plazas of a police state pictures of their loved ones, like women who put pillowcases, toys, and other artifacts of attachment against the barbed wire fences of missile bases, translate the symbols of mothering into political speech. Preservative love, singularity in connection, the promise of birth and the resilience of hope, the implacable treasure of vulnerable bodily being -- these cliches of maternal work are enacted in public....They speak a 'woman's language' of loyalty, love, and outrage; but they speak with a public anger in a public place in ways they were never meant to do (1989, 229).

Clearly not all feminists espouse the model of "maternal thinking" or social feminism advanced by Ruddick and Elshtain, and some are intensely critical of it. The lively feminist debate over what is called "gender difference" turns in large part on the skepticism some critics have toward any effort to revalue women's traditional role in the family. Mary Dietz has argued that maternal thinking not only overvalues motherhood and the intimate relations of kin, but also devalues the relations among total strangers or mere acquaintances which are the very basis of large representative democracies. The good mother does not necessarily make the good citizen, and "the bond among citizens is not like the love between a mother and child" (1985, 31; Ferguson 1984). As "citizens are not intimately, but politically involved with each other," writes Dietz, "we look in the wrong place for a model of democratic citizenship if we look to the family" (1985, 31).

Perhaps the most difficult of balancing acts for feminist scholars is how to account for and give value to women's experience without reproducing socially ascribed gender roles. Still, many scholars worry that, so long as gender differences carry social significance, feminists downplay those differences at their peril. Feminist scholarship has clearly shown how the notion that "we are all just people" translates in political science discourse, not to mention in social practices, into "we are all just men." As Susan Moller Okin has argued in her most recent work, *Justice, Gender, and the Family*, gender-neutral language in contemporary political theory effaces the material reality of sexual inequality and reproduces "theories of justice [which], like those of the past, are about men with wives at home" (1989, 13). Like Ruddick, Gilligan, and Elshtain, Okin is critical of theories of justice that offer "some abstract 'view from nowhere'" (1989, 15). Like Dietz, however, she cannot accept the argument that "'justice' and 'rights' are masculinist ways of thinking about morality that feminists should eschew or radically revise, advocating a morality of care" (1989, 15). For one thing, the evidence that women have a different way of moral reasoning is debatable at best; for another, feminists who make such a claim, all disclaimers notwithstanding, risk playing into the familiar "stereotypes that justify separate spheres" (Okin 1989, 15).

The legal theorist Martha Minnow has captured the problem we have been describing as follows: "Both focusing on and ignoring difference risk recreating it. This is the dilemma of difference" (1984, 160). Negotiating the "difference dilemma" has been a particularly delicate matter in the area of feminist legal studies (Eisenstein 1988; MacKinnon 1987; Bower 1991). In an essay on the sex-discrimination suit brought by the

Equal Employment Opportunity Council in 1978 against the Sears, Roebuck & Company, the historian Joan Scott usefully summarized the "equality-versus-difference" conundrum as follows:

> When difference and equality are paired dichotomously, they structure an impossible choice. If one opts for equality, one is forced to accept the notion that difference is antithetical to it. If one opts for difference, one admits that equality is unattainable.... How then do we recognize and use notions of sexual difference and yet make arguments for equality? The only response is a double one: the unmasking of the power relationship constructed by posing equality as the antithesis of difference, and the refusal of its consequent dichotomous construction of political choices (1988, 172).

This is a difficult and tall order for feminist scholars. But Scott has insisted that to avoid treating masculinity and femininity as if they were unchanging essences, feminists must ask: "How are differences being constructed" in specific social, historical, and discursive contexts? (1988, 173).

Scott's suggestion that a "power relationship" is concealed in the difference/equality opposition has been forcefully argued by the feminist legal theorist Catherine MacKinnon. In *Feminism Unmodified*, MacKinnon has called for "a shift in perspective from gender as difference to gender as dominance" (1987, 44). What is taken as women's difference from men, she has maintained, is really the difference created through women's social, political, and economic subordination to men. Sexual difference is at bottom an unequal power relationship between women and men, one whose feminist dismantling is not a matter of asserting women's moral superiority; it is rather a matter of politics. Like Scott, MacKinnon has insisted that feminists need to challenge the idea that sexual difference is *the* fundamental social difference, and that they need to refuse the choice between difference and sameness:

> To define the reality of sex as difference and the warrant of equality as sameness is wrong on both counts. Sex, in nature, is not a bipolarity; it is a continuum. In society it is made into a bipolarity. Once this is done, to require that one be the same as those who set the standard -- those which one is already socially defined as different from -- simply means that sex equality is conceptually designed never to be achieved. Those who most need equal treatment will be the least similar [e.g., poor women], socially, to

those whose situation sets the standard as against which one's entitlement to be equally treated is measured (1988, 44).

So-called "sex equality," according to MacKinnon, is an oxymoron. To be sexed is to be a woman (or rather a wo-man) and to be a woman is to be unequal. As long as sexual difference remains unquestioned, social equality for women will remain impossible.

The only way out of the difference dilemma, these critics have argued, is to refuse sexual difference (man versus woman) and to affirm instead what Zillah Eisenstein has termed "the plurality of differences among women" (1988, 223). In *The Female Body and the Law*, she has called for "a radical pluralist and feminist theory of equality," one that would "recognize the specificity of the female body and the variety of ways this is expressed: individually (as in differences of health, age, body strength, and size) and in terms of a woman's race and economic class" (1988, 222). Eisenstein has taken up the most monolithic of all representations of the female body, the pregnant body, and has radically redeployed it throughout her book to undercut the sameness/difference opposition:

> A middle-class, black, pregnant woman's body is not one and the same as a working-class, white, pregnant woman's body. The pregnant body of a woman in her midthirties is not identical to the pregnant body of a woman in her early twenties. A welfare woman's pregnant body may not be the same as an upper-middle-class woman's pregnant body. [And so forth.] (1988, 222-223).

What Eisenstein has called for is a far more complicated approach to the very category of women and of sexual difference than that which has been advanced thus far in the scholarly literature on women and politics. She has asked feminists, in effect, to question the very terms that they use in their work because those terms tend to reproduce the very thing that feminists want to critique: sexual inequality. If one is a woman, surely that is not all that one is. And those other race and class identities (to name but two) shape how one experiences being a woman and -- this is crucial -- how one is seen by others as a woman. African-American women are not (and have not been) seen as "women" in the same way that white women are seen (hooks 1981; Spelman 1988). Working-class women are not (and have not been) viewed as "women" in the same way that domesticated middle-class women are viewed (Riley 1988; Zerilli 1993). We shall have more to say about the category "women" in our concluding section.

Another problem for feminist scholars who wish to advance a gender-sensitive approach to politics but are wary of monolithic claims about "women's difference" is how to theorize "women's experience." Nancy Hartsock has tackled this problem in her influential work on "feminist standpoint theory." Hartsock wanted to develop an epistemology and a theory of power that would take account of gender differences without universalizing them. She distinguished:

> ... between what Sara Ruddick has termed 'invariant or *nearly* unchangeable' features of human life, and those that, despite being '*nearly* universal' are 'certainly changeable'. Thus that women and not men *bear* children, is not (yet) a social choice, but that women and not men rear children...is clearly a social choice (1985, 223).

Hartsock read women's experience through the lens of Marxist historical materialism. She argued that it is not enough to talk about "women's standpoint," their sense of interconnectedness with others and with nature (*pace* Gilligan, Ruddick, or Elshtain); rather, one must examine the development of a "feminist standpoint" as it emerges in the context of political activism, that is to say, its "achieved character" and "liberatory potential" (Hartsock 1983, 232).

Hartsock's approach has the advantage of thinking through not only how women's experiences shape their political consciousness but also how their political consciousness shapes their experiences as women. It thus broaches the question of how feminine identity is socially constructed and radically challenged through political activism. Rather than treat "women's experience" as if it were a stable and unified category, she has called for a political analysis of how the experience of "being a woman" is given meaning in and through the political practices of feminism.

Some Thoughts on Challenges for the 1990s

We have argued that a persistent problem for feminist scholars has been how to develop alternative theoretical and empirical models that would take into account women's experiences and perspectives, but that would avoid both reproducing socially ascribed gender differences and effacing the social diversity among women. For these reasons, the category of women has come under question in the work of some feminist scholars.

Yet feminists have good reason to worry about throwing into question the very category that has enabled both their collective resistance to oppression and their scholarship. Giving voice to women "as women" in social life and political practice has been absolutely crucial for contesting women as invisible, apolitical, or simply as the (deficient) other from men. As Elizabeth Spelman has written, "Feminists have long been aware of the levels at which male privilege operates to erase women's lives and perspectives from view" (1988, 4). "Nevertheless," she has added, "our distancing ourselves from the views of blatant sexists keeps us from recognizing the extent to which we may in fact share elements of their views" (1988, 5). That is to say, feminists also often have a blind spot in their research -- one that ignores other categories of social difference (e.g., class, race, and sexual orientation) by working with the category of women *as if* it encompassed the experiences of all women. "This," Spelman has said, "leads us to the paradox at the heart of feminism":

> Any attempt to talk about all women in terms of something we have in common undermines attempts to talk about the differences among us, and vice versa. Is it possible to give the things women have in common their full significance without thereby implying that the differences among us are less important? How can we describe those things that differentiate women without eclipsing what we share in common? (1988, 3).

In our view, Spelman formulates precisely the key dilemma confronting feminist political science today. While enormous strides have been made by feminist scholars, few would doubt that there is still much work to be done. Can that work be accomplished if we treat the differences among women as if they were as significant as what women have in common? How can one make women visible, not to mention challenge the frameworks that render them invisible, if one overly complicates the term "women" that makes the feminist project possible?

There are, needless to say, no easy answers to these questions despite the fact that they are, in our view, some of the most important questions confronting feminist political scientists, and indeed feminist scholars across all disciplines, in the early 1990s. Nevertheless, in this concluding section, we would like to suggest why feminist scholars ought to keep asking these questions, to offer some possible ways of beginning to think through them, and to indicate why we think these questions are important to the discipline.

The first reason why feminists do well to interrogate the category (women) that seems at first glance to be the theoretical foundation of their own research concerns the matter of what is meant by "what women have in common as women." In her book, *Feminist Theory: From Margin to Center*, bell hooks has pondered this very phrase as follows:

> A central tenet of modern feminist thought has been the assertion that 'all women are oppressed.' This assertion implies that women share a common lot, that factors like class, race, religion, sexual preference, etc. do not create a diversity of experience that determines the extent to which sexism will be an oppressive force in the lives of individual women. Sexism as a system of domination is institutionalized but it has never determined in an absolute way the fate of all women in this society (1984, 5).

This "ideology of 'common oppression'" (1984, 8), hooks has argued, is based on a "one-dimensional perspective on women's reality" -- a white, heterosexual, middle-class woman's perspective (1984, 3). When feminists invoke phrases like women's oppression, women's experience, and women's difference, they "conflate the condition of one group of women with the condition of all women and…treat the differences of white middle-class women as if they were not differences" (Spelman 1988, 3). The term "women," in other words, effaces the diversity of its purported social referent; its true referent is a far more partial social reality.

As we argue in more detail below, even when feminists try to take account of women's diversity by factoring into their analyses such variables as race and class, they do not tackle properly the problem of the category of women that we have been describing. Just as feminists have shown that one cannot treat gender as a mere variable, neither can one treat race and class as mere variables. Just as feminists have shown that to make gender an analytic category of their research is to rethink traditional political science frameworks, so do critics like Spelman (1988), hooks (1984), Evelyn Brooks Higginbotham (1992), Patricia Hill Collins (1989), and Julianne Malveaux (1990) insist that when race and class are treated as analytic categories of feminist theory, then existing feminist frameworks themselves must be rethought.

For some feminist political theorists, this rethinking has entailed the development of new strategies for interrogating historical and contemporary inscriptions of sexual difference which examine the lived relation of social subjects to socio-symbolic configurations of masculinity and femininity (Brown 1988; Lorraine 1990; Di Stefano 1991; Zerilli 1991; Zerilli 1993). As Christine Di Stefano has written recently, "gender must be approached as simultaneously 'real' and 'false'; that is, as a set of representations that (in conjunction and tension with other representations [e.g., of race and class]) creates a world of fixed, yet also unstable, meanings, relations, and identities, which simultaneously produce and do violence to specific subjects in specific ways"

(1991, xiv). The challenge for feminists, she argues, is to disrupt cultural representations of an incommensurable sexual difference which organize "the world 'as if' women stood in a derivative (but also opposed) relation to 'man'" (1991, xiv), and, we would add, "as if" that relation were not only immutable but also more socially significant than the relations of race and class.

The instability of the category "women" and of naturalized sexual difference, as demonstrated in the works of feminist theorists, has important implications not only for political theorists, but also for more empirically oriented political scientists. Although these implications will become clearer as the debate over the category "women" continues to play itself out over the next several years, we can put forth a few preliminary observations from the vantage point of the early 1990s.

The work of feminist theorists suggests that researchers in the 1990s should be more cautious and self-reflective about their use of the category "women" than they have been in the past. Most empirical work focusing on women or gender (or even including sex as a control variable) has assumed that the category "women" has an inherent political meaning, that there is something politically relevant, most commonly "interests" (see Sapiro 1981 for a discussion of issues involved in defining women's interests), that all women share. Most empirical researchers believe that by controlling statistically for variables such as race, age, income, and education, they can isolate and measure the effects due to gender. However, applying statistical controls to isolate the effects of gender is not sufficient to deal with the problem of the category "women" as it is posed by feminist theorists. Rather, feminists who have interrogated the category "women" question whether such gender effects, free from the influence of other confounding variables, exist at all -- whether there is any commonality, any essence, or even any interests that all women share after variations in their race, age, education, income, and the like are taken into consideration. Instead, they suggest that race, class, and gender, for example, are so intertwined that all work together to shape identity (or, in this case, political identity). Women exist in an historical and cultural context, and to erase or ignore this context is to gloss over important differences among women.

What does this actually mean for those who do empirical research? First, it means that we should be less concerned with comparing women with men and more concerned with examining how different subgroups of women in different contexts behave politically. If we take the critiques of the category "women" seriously, our research is likely to become more contextual and more historical. It will make visible those women (e.g., women of color, poor women) whose experiences are often erased in the pursuit of scientific generalizations that purportedly apply to all women. Taking seriously critiques of the category "women" will likely move us in the direction of reducing our knowledge claims and our pursuit of universal truths. It will make us less likely to generalize across women (or men) of differing classes, races, cultures, nationalities, ethnicities, or generations. However, what we sacrifice in our ability to generalize (which those who theorize about the category of women would suggest has led only to false or misleading generalizations anyway) will be more than made up for in the depth and richness of our analysis and our understanding.

While empirical researchers who are sensitive to critiques of the category "women" may well become more reflective and self-conscious in their use of the term and more contextual and culturally specific in their approach to research, there are, as we noted earlier, good reasons for researchers not to abandon fully the category that has enabled their work. By using the category "women," feminist political scientists have been able to call into question some of the central assumptions and frameworks of the discipline. The concerted focus by feminists on women and women's experience has helped us as a discipline to see the biases and the blinders that characterized pre-feminist work and to improve our knowledge base by correcting for these biases and removing the blinders. In the same way, the current feminist interrogation of the category "women" may lead to research that will expand and improve our disciplinary knowledge base through greater historical and cultural specificity and more attention to heretofore neglected segments of the population. A major task for women and politics scholars in the 1990s will be to work through the many questions surrounding the category "women," perhaps finding some middle ground between uncritical acceptance and total abandonment of the category. In doing so, feminist scholars are likely to continue to pose new and important challenges to the discipline of political science.

Notes

We would like to thank Ada Finifter, Virginia Sapiro, Barbara Crow, Kathleen Casey, and an anonymous reviewer for their careful readings and constructive suggestions regarding this essay.

1. More recent research has suggested that we should not be so quick to discount the impact of childhood socialization in producing politically relevant differences between girls and boys. (See for example, Bennett and Bennett 1989; Owen and Dennis 1988.)

2. More recent research suggests the relationship between working outside the home and political participation may be less straightforward than once thought. For example, McDonagh (1982) has argued that social status variables are more important than employment per se, and Andersen and Cook (1985) failed to find a short-term impact from entry into the paid work force although their findings pointed to the possibility of a long-term impact.

3. In contrast to the results for women, multimember districts and at-large voting systems have been found in many cases to disadvantage African Americans and Latinos. See Persons (1991) and Fraga (1991) for reviews of this research. Unfortunately, most of the research on women and minorities has not examined the effects of electoral systems on women of color. Notable exceptions are: Karnig and Welch (1979) who found that African-American women do about as well in at-large as in district municipal elections, indicating that the findings for women (dominated by whites) and minorities (dominated by men) cannot be assumed to be true for minority women; Welch and Herrick (1992) who found that African-American, Latino, and white women all fare slightly better with at-large municipal electoral systems, although other factors are more important than electoral structures in explaining the representation of all three groups of women; and Rule (1992) who found that multimember state legislative districts benefit both African-American and white women.

Bibliography

Ackelsberg, Martha, and Irene Diamond. 1987. "Gender and Political Life: New Directions in Political Science." In *Analyzing Gender: A Handbook of Social Science Research*, ed. Beth B. Hess and Myra Marx Ferree. Newbury, California: Sage.

Almond, Gabriel, and Sidney Verba. 1963. *The Civic Culture*. Princeton: Princeton University Press.

Amundsen, Kirsten. 1971. *The Silenced Majority: Women and American Democracy*. Englewood Cliffs: Prentice-Hall.

Andersen, Kristi. 1975. "Working Women and Political Participation, 1952-1972." *American Journal of Political Science* 19:439-53.

Andersen, Kristi, and Stuart J. Thorson. 1984. "Congressional Turnover and the Election of Women." *Western Political Quarterly* 37:143-56.

Andersen, Kristi, and Elizabeth Cook. 1985. "Women, Work, and Political Attitudes." *American Journal of Political Science* 29:606-25.

Andrain, Charles F. 1971. *Children and Civic Awareness*. Columbus: Merrill.

Baxter, Sandra, and Marjorie Lansing. 1980. *Women and Politics: The Invisible Majority*. Ann Arbor: University of Michigan.

Beckwith, Karen. 1986. *American Women and Political Participation: The Impacts of Work, Generations, and Feminism*. New York: Greenwood.

Belenky, Mary Field et. al. 1986. *Women's Ways of Knowing: The Development of Self, Voice, and Mind*. New York: Basic Books.

Bennett, Linda L. M., and Stephen Earl Bennett. 1989. "Enduring Gender Differences in Political Interest: The Impact of Socialization and Political Dispositions." *American Politics Quarterly* 17:105-22.

Berelson, Bernard R., Paul F. Lazarsfeld, and William N. McPhee. 1954. *Voting*. Chicago: University of Chicago Press.

Blair, Diane Kincaid, and Ann R. Henry. 1981. "The Family Factor in State Legislative Turnover." *Legislative Studies Quarterly* 6:55-68.

Bledsoe, Timothy, and Mary Herring. 1990. "Victims of Circumstances: Women in Pursuit of Political Office." *American Political Science Review* 84:213-23.

Boals, Kay. 1975. "Review Essay: Political Science." *Signs* 1:161-74.

Boles, Janet K. 1979. *The Politics of the Equal Rights Amendment: Conflict and the Decision-Making Process*. New York: Longman.

Bookman, Ann, and Sandra Morgen. 1988. *Women and the Politics of Empowerment*. Philadelphia: Temple University Press.

Bourque, Susan C., and Jean Grossholtz. 1974. "Politics an Unnatural Practice: Political Science Looks at Female Participation." *Politics and Society* 4:225-66.

Bower, Lisa C. 1991. "'Mother in Law': Conceptions of Mother and the Maternal in Feminism and Feminist Legal Theory." *Differences: A Journal of Feminist Cultural Studies* 3:20-38.

Brennan, Teresa, and Carole Pateman. 1979. "Mere Auxiliaries to the Commonwealth: Women and the Origins of Liberalism." *Political Studies* 27:183-200.

Brown, Wendy. 1988. *Manhood and Politics: A Feminist Reading in Political Theory*. Totowa, NJ: Rowman & Littlefield.

Campbell, Angus, Philip Converse, Warren Miller, and Donald Stokes. 1960. *The American Voter*. New York: Wiley.

Carroll, Berenice A. 1979. "Political Science, Part I: American Politics and Political Behavior." *Signs* 5:289-306.

Carroll, Susan J. 1985. *Women as Candidates in American Politics*. Bloomington: Indiana University Press.

Carroll, Susan J. 1988. "Women's Autonomy and the Gender Gap: 1980 and 1982." In *The Politics of the Gender Gap: The Social Construction of Political Influence*, ed. Carol M. Mueller. Newbury Park, CA: Sage.

Carroll, Susan J. 1989. "The Personal Is Political: The Intersection of Private Lives and Public Roles Among Women and Men in Elective and Appointive Office." *Women and Politics* 9:51-67.

Carroll, Susan J., Debra L. Dodson, and Ruth B. Mandel. 1991. *The Impact of Women in Public Office: An Overview*. New Brunswick, NJ: Center for the American Woman and Politics.

Chodorow, Nancy. 1978. *The Reproduction of Mothering: Psychoanalysis and the Sociology of Gender*. Berkeley: University of California Press.

Clarke, Lorenne M. G., and Lynda Lange. 1979. *The Sexism of Social and Political Theory: Women and Reproduction from Plato to Nietzsche*. Toronto: University of Toronto Press.

Cohn, Carol. 1987. "Sex and Death in the Rational World of Defense Intellectuals." *Signs: Journal of Women in Culture and Society* 12:687-718.

Collins, Patricia Hill. 1989. "The Social Construction of Black Feminist Thought." *Signs* 14:745-73.

Conover, Pamela Johnston. 1988. "Feminists and the Gender Gap." *Journal of Politics* 50:985-1010.

Costain, Anne N. 1980. "The Struggle for a National Women's Lobby." *Western Political Quarterly* 33:476-91.

Costain, Anne N. 1982. "Representing Women: The Transition from Social Movement to Interest Group." In *Women, Power and Policy*, ed. Ellen Boneparth. New York: Pergamon Press.

Costantini, Edmond, and Kenneth H. Craik. 1977. "Women as Politicians: The Social Background, Personality, and Political Careers of Female Party Leaders." In *A Portrait of Marginality*, ed. Marianne Githens and Jewel L. Prestage. New York: McKay.

Costantini, Edmond, and Julie Davis Bell. 1984. "Women in Political Parties: Gender Difference in Motives Among California Party Activists." In *Political Women: Current Roles in State and Local Government*, ed. Janet Flammang. Beverly Hills: Sage.

Dahl, Robert. 1961. *Who Governs?* New Haven: Yale University Press.

Dahlerup, Drude. 1988. "From a Small to a Large Minority: Women in Scandinavian Politics." *Scandinavian Political Studies* 11:275-98.

Darcy, R., Susan Welch, and Janet Clark. 1987. *Women, Elections, and Representation*. New York: Longman.

De Lauretis, Teresa. 1987. *Technologies of Gender: Essays on Theory, Film, and Fiction*. Bloomington: Indiana University Press.

Denhardt, Robert B., and Jan Perkins. 1976. "The Coming Death of Administrative Man." *Women in Public Administration* 36: 379-84.

Diamond, Irene. 1977. *Sex Roles in the State House*. New Haven: Yale University Press.

Diamond, Irene, ed. 1983. *Families, Politics, and Public Policy: A Feminist Dialogue on Women and the State*. New York: Longman.

Dietz, Mary G. 1985. "Citizenship with a Feminist Face: The Problem with Maternal Thinking." *Political Theory* 13:19-37.

Di Stefano, Christine. 1991. *Configurations of Masculinity: A Feminist Reading in Modern Political Theory*. Ithaca, NY: Cornell University Press.

Dodson, Debra L. 1991. *Gender and Policymaking: Studies of Women in Office*. New Brunswick, NJ: Center for the American Woman and Politics.

Dodson, Debra L., and Susan J. Carroll. 1991. *Reshaping the Agenda: Women in State Legislatures*. New Brunswick, NJ: Center for the American Woman and Politics.

DuBois, Ellen Carol, Gail Paradise Kelly, Elizabeth Lapovsky Kennedy, Carolyn W. Korsmeyer, and Lillian S. Robinson. 1985. *Feminist Scholarship: Kindling in the Groves of Academe*. Urbana: University of Illinois Press.

Duverger, Maurice. 1955. *The Political Role of Women*. Paris: UNESCO.

Eisenstein, Zillah. 1981. *The Radical Future of Liberal Feminism*. New York: Longman Press.

Eisenstein, Zillah. 1984. *Feminism and Sexual Equality: Crisis in Liberal America*. New York: Monthly Review Press.

Eisenstein, Zillah. 1988. *The Female Body and The Law*. Berkeley: University of California Press.

Elshtain, Jean Bethke. 1974. "Moral Woman and Immoral Man: A Consideration of the Public-Private Split and Its Political Ramifications." *Politics and Society* 4:453-73.

Elshtain, Jean Bethke. 1979a. "Methodological Sophistication and Conceptual Confusion: A Critique of Mainstream Political Science." In *The Prism of Sex: Essays in the Sociology of Knowledge*, ed. Julia A. Sherman and Evelyn Tort Beck. Madison: University of Wisconsin Press.

Elshtain, Jean Bethke. 1981. *Public Man, Private Women: Women in Social and Political Thought*. Princeton: Princeton University Press.

Elshtain, Jean Bethke. 1987. *Women and War*. New York: Basic Books.

Enloe, Cynthia. 1990. *Bananas, Beaches and Bases: Making Feminist Sense of International Politics*. Berkeley: University of California Press.

Ferguson, Kathy E. 1984. *The Feminist Case Against Bureaucracy*. Philadelphia: Temple University Press.

Figes, Eva. 1970. *Patriarchal Attitudes*. Greenwich: Fawcett.

Firestone, Shulamith. 1970. *The Dialectic of Sex*. New York: Bantam.

Fowlkes, Diane, Jerry Perkins, and Sue Tolleson Rinehart. 1979. "Gender Roles and Party Roles." *American Political Science Review* 73:772-80.

Fowlkes, Diane L. 1992. *White Political Women: Paths from Privilege to Empowerment*. Knoxville: University of Tennessee Press.

Fraga, Luis Ricardo. 1991. "Latinos in State Elective Office: Progressive Inclusion in Critical Perspective." In *Women, Black, and Hispanic State Elected Leaders*, ed. Susan J. Carroll. New Brunswick, NJ: Eagleton Institute of Politics.

Frankovic, Kathleen A. 1982. "Sex and Politics -- New Alignments, Old Issues." *PS: Political Science & Politics* 15:439-48.

Freeman, Jo. 1975. *The Politics of Women's Liberation*. New York: Longman.

Gelb, Joyce, and Marian Lief Palley. 1982. *Women and Public Policies*. Princeton: Princeton University Press.

Gelb, Joyce. 1989. *Feminism and Politics: A Comparative Perspective*. Berkeley: University of California Press.

Gilligan, Carol. 1982. *In a Different Voice: Psychological Theory and Women's Development*. Cambridge: Harvard University Press.

Githens, Marianne, and Jewel L. Prestage, eds. 1977. *A Portrait of Marginality: The Political Behavior of the American Woman*. New York: McKay.

Goot, Murray, and Elizabeth Reid. 1975. *Women and Voting Studies: Mindless Matrons or Sexist Scientism?* Sage Professional Papers in Contemporary Political Sociology, no. 8. London: Sage.

Gordon, Linda, ed. 1990. *Women, the State, and Welfare*. Madison: University of Wisconsin Press.

Grant, Rebecca. 1991. "The Sources of Gender Bias in International Relations Theory." In *Gender and International Relations*, ed. Rebecca Grant and Kathleen Newland. Bloomington: Indiana University Press.

Greenstein, Fred. 1965. *Children and Politics*. New Haven: Yale Univerity Press.

Halliday, Fred. 1991. "Hidden from International Relations: Women and the International Arena." In *Gender and International Relations*, ed. Rebecca Grant and Kathleen Newland. Bloomington: Indiana University Press.

Hansen, Susan B., Linda M. Franz, and Margaret Netemeyer-Mays. 1976. "Women's Political Participation and Policy Preferences." *Social Science Quarterly* 56:576-90.

Hartsock, Nancy C. M. 1985. *Money, Sex, and Power: Towards a Feminist Historical Materialism*. Boston: Northeastern University Press.

Haavio-Mannila, Elina et al. 1985. *Unfinished Democracy: Women in Nordic Politics*. Oxford: Pergamon Press.

Hess, Robert D., and Judith V. Torney. 1968. *The Development of Political Attitudes in Children*. Garden City, NY: Doubleday Anchor.

Higginbotham, Evelyn Brooks. 1992. "African-American Women's History and the Metalanguage of Race." *Signs* 17:251-74.

hooks, bell. 1981. *Ain't I a Woman: Black Women and Feminism*. Boston: South End Press.

hooks, bell. 1984. *Feminist Theory: From Margin to Center*. Boston: South End Press.

Iglitzin, Lynne B. 1974. "The Making of the Apolitical Woman: Femininity and Sex-Stereotyping in Girls." In *Women in Politics*, ed. Jane S. Jaquette. New York: Wiley.

Jaquette, Jane S. 1974. "Introduction." In *Women in Politics*, ed. Jane S. Jaquette. New York: Wiley.

Jennings, M. Kent, and Norman Thomas. 1968. "Men and Women in Party Elites: Social Roles and Political Resources." *Midwest Journal of Political Science* 12:469-92.

Jennings, M. Kent, and Barbara G. Farah. 1980. "Ideology, Gender and Political Action: A Cross-National Survey." *British Journal of Political Science* 10:219-40.

Jennings, M. Kent, and Barbara G. Farah. 1981. "Social Roles and Political Resources: An Over-Time Study of Men and Women in Party Elites." *American Journal of Political Science* 25:462-82.

Jennings, M. Kent, and Richard G. Niemi. 1981. *Generations and Politics: A Panel Study of Young Adults and Their Parents*. Princeton: Princeton University Press.

Jenson, Jane. 1990. "Representations of Gender: Policies to 'Protect' Women Workers and Infants in France and the United States before 1914." In *Women, the State, and Welfare*, ed. Linda Gordon. Madison: University of Wisconsin.

Jones, Kathleen B., and Anna G. Jonasdottir. 1988. "Introduction: Gender as an Analytical Category in Political Theory." In

The Political Interests of Gender, ed. Kathleen B. Jones and Anna G. Jonasdottir. London: Sage.

Karnig, Albert, and Susan Welch. 1979. "Sex and Ethnicity in Municipal Representation." *Social Science Quarterly* 60:465-81.

Kirkpatrick, Jeane J. 1974. *Political Woman.* New York: Basic Books.

Kirkpatrick, Jeane J. 1976. *The New Presidential Elite: Men and Women in National Politics.* New York: Russell Sage Foundation.

Klatch, Rebecca E. 1987. *Women of the New Right.* Philadelphia: Temple University Press.

Klein, Ethel. 1984. *Gender Politics.* Cambridge: Harvard University Press.

Klein, Ethel. 1985. "The Gender Gap: Different Issues, Different Answers." *The Brookings Review* 3:33-7.

Kolinsky, Eva. 1991. "Women's Quotas in West Germany." *Western European Politics* 14:56-72.

Landes, Joan B. 1988. *Women and the Public Sphere in the Age of the French Revolution.* Ithaca, NY: Cornell University Press.

Lane, Robert. 1959. *Political Life.* New York: The Free Press.

Lebsock, Suzanne. 1990. "Women and American Politics, 1880-1920." In *Women, Politics, and Change,* ed. Louise A. Tilly and Patricia Gurin. New York: Russell Sage Foundation.

Lee, Marcia Manning. 1976. "Why Few Women Hold Public Office: Democracy and Sex Roles." *Political Science Quarterly* 91:296-314.

Lorraine, Tamasin E. 1990. *Gender, Identity, and the Production of Meaning.* Boulder, CO: Westview Press.

Lovenduski, Joni. 1981. "Toward the Emasculation of Political Science: The Impact of Feminism." In *Men's Studies Modified: The Impact of Feminism on the Academic Disciplines,* ed. Dale Spender. Oxford: Pergamon Press.

Lovenduski, Joni. 1986. *Women and European Politics: Contemporary Feminism and Public Policy.* Amherst: University of Massachusetts Press.

MacKinnon, Catherine A. 1987. *Feminism Unmodified: Discourses on Life and Law.* Cambridge: Harvard University Press.

MacManus, Susan A., and Charles S. Bullock III. 1989. "Women on Southern City Councils: A Decade of Change." *Journal of Political Science* 17:32-49.

Mahowald, Mary. 1978. *Philosophy of Women: Classical to Current Concepts.* Indianapolis: Hacket.

Malveaux, Julianne. 1990. "Gender Difference and Beyond: An Economic Perspective on Diversity and Commonality among Women." In *Theoretical Perspectives on Sexual Difference,* ed. Deborah L. Rhode. New Haven: Yale University Press.

Mandel, Ruth B. 1981. *In the Running.* New York: Ticknor and Fields.

Mansbridge, Jane J. 1986. *Why We Lost the ERA.* Chicago: University of Chicago Press.

Mathews, Donald G., and Jane Sherron De Hart. 1990. *Sex, Gender, and the Politics of ERA: A State and the Nation.* New York: Oxford University Press.

McDonagh, Eileen L. 1982. "To Work or Not to Work: The Differential Impact of Achieved and Derived Status upon the Political Participation of Women, 1956-1976." *American Journal of Political Science* 26:280-97.

Miller, Jean Baker. 1976. *Toward a New Psychology of Women.* Boston: Beacon.

Mink, Gwendolyn. 1990. "The Lady and the Tramp: Gender, Race, and the Origins of the American Welfare State." In *Women, the State, and Welfare,* ed. Linda Gordon. Madison: University of Wisconsin.

Minnow, Martha. 1984. "Learning to Live with the Dilemma of Difference: Bilingual and Special Education." *Law and Contemporary Problems* 48:157-211.

Morgenthau, Hans J. 1948. *Politics Among Nations.* New York: Knopf.

Mueller, Carol M., ed. 1988. *The Politics of the Gender Gap: The Social Construction of Political Influence.* Newbury Park, CA: Sage.

Nelson, Barbara J. 1989. "Women and Knowledge in Political Science: Texts, Histories, and Epistemologies." *Women & Politics* 9:1-25.

Nelson, Barbara J. 1990. "The Gender, Race, and Class Origins of Early Welfare Policy and the Welfare State: A Comparison of Workmen's Compensation and Mother's Aid." In *Women, Politics, and Change,* ed. Louise A. Tilly and Patricia Gurin. New York: Russell Sage Foundation.

Norris, Pippa. 1985. "The Gender Gap in Britain and America." *Parliamentary Affairs* 38:192-201.

Norton, Mary Beth. 1986. "Is Clio A Feminist? The New History." *New York Times Book Review,* April 13.

O'Brien, Mary. 1981. *The Politics of Reproduction.* Boston: Routledge & Kegan Paul.

Okin, Susan Moller. 1979. *Women in Western Political Thought.* Princeton: Princeton University Press.

Okin, Susan Moller. 1989. *Justice, Gender, and the Family.* New York: Basic Books.

Orum, Anthony, Roberta Cohen, Sherri Grasmuck, and Amy W. Orum. 1974. "Sex, Socialization and Politics." *American Sociological Review* 39:197-209.

Owen, Diana, and Jack Dennis. 1988. "Gender Differences in the Politicization of American Children." *Women & Politics* 8:23-43.

Pateman, Carole. 1980a. "'The Disorder of Women': Women, Love, and the Sense of Justice. *Ethics* 91:20-34.

Pateman, Carole. 1980b. "Women and Consent." *Political Theory* 8:149-68.

Pateman, Carole. 1988. *The Sexual Contract.* Stanford: Stanford University Press.

Persons, Georgia A. 1991. "Blacks in State Elective Office: The Continuing Quest for Effective Representation." In *Women, Black, and Hispanic State Elected Leaders,* ed. Susan J. Carroll. New Brunswick, NJ: Eagleton Institute of Politics.

Phillips, Anne. 1991. *Engendering Democracy.* University Park, PA: Pennsylvania State University.

Piven, Frances Fox. 1990. "Ideology and the State: Women, Power, and the Welfare State." In *Women, the State, and Welfare,* ed. Linda Gordon. Madison: University of Wisconsin Press.

Poole, Keith T., and L. Harmon Zeigler. 1985. *Women, Public Opinion, and Politics.* New York: Longman.

Randall, Vicky. 1987. *Women and Politics: An International Perspective.* 2nd ed. Chicago: University of Chicago.

Randall, Vicky. 1991. "Feminism and Political Analysis." *Political Studies* 39:513-32.

Rapoport, Ronald B. 1982. "Sex Differences in Attitude Expression: A Generational Explanation." *Public Opinion Quarterly* 46:86-96.

Rapoport, Ronald B. 1985. "Like Mother, Like Daughter: Intergenerational Transmission of DK Response Rates." *Public Opinion Quarterly* 49:198-208.

Riley, Denise. 1988. *Am I That Name? Feminism and the Category of 'Women' in History.* Minneapolis: University of Minnesota Press.

Ruddick, Sara. 1989. *Maternal Thinking: Towards a Politics of Peace.* Boston: Beacon Press.

Rule, Wilma, and Joseph F. Zimmerman, eds. 1992. *United States Electoral Systems: Their Impact on Women and Minorities.* New York: Praeger.

Rule, Wilma. 1992. "Multimember Legislative Districts: Minority and Anglo Women's and Men's Recruitment Opportunity." In *United States Electoral Systems: Their Impact on Women and*

Minorities, ed. Wilma Rule and Joseph F. Zimmerman. New York: Praeger.

Rule, Wilma. 1981. "Why Women Don't Run: The Critical Contextual Factors in Women's Legislative Recruitment." *Western Political Quarterly* 34:60-77.

Rule, Wilma. 1990. "Why More Women Are State Legislators." *Western Political Quarterly* 43:437-48.

Saint-Germain, Michelle A. 1989. "Does Their Difference Make a Difference? The Impact of Women on Public Policy in the Arizona Legislature." *Social Science Quarterly* 70:956-68.

Sapiro, Virginia. 1979. "Women's Studies and Political Conflict." In *The Prism of Sex: Essays in the Sociology of Knowledge*, ed. Julia A. Sherman and Evelyn Tort Beck. Madison: University of Wisconsin Press.

Sapiro, Virginia, and Barbara G. Farah. 1980. "New Pride and Old Prejudice: Political Ambitions and Role Orientations Among Female Partisan Elites." *Women & Politics* 1:13-36.

Sapiro, Virginia. 1981. "Research Frontier Essay: When Are Interests Interesting? The Problem of Political Representation of Women." *American Political Science Review* 75:701-16.

Sapiro, Virginia. 1982. "Private Costs of Public Commitments or Public Costs of Private Commitments? Family Roles Versus Political Ambition." *American Journal of Political Science* 26:265-79.

Sapiro, Virginia. 1983. *The Political Integration of Women: Roles, Socialization, and Politics*. Urbana: University of Illinois.

Sapiro, Virginia. 1987. "What Research on the Political Socialization of Women Can Tell Us About the Political Socialization of People." In *The Impact of Feminist Research in the Academy*, ed. Christie Farnham. Bloomington: Indiana University Press.

Sapiro, Virginia. 1989. "Gender Politics, Gendered Politics: The State of the Field." Presented at the annual meeting of the Midwest Political Science Association, Chicago.

Sarvasy, Wendy. 1992. "Beyond the Difference Versus Equality Policy Debate: Postsuffrage Feminism, Citizenship, and the Quest for a Feminist Welfare State." *Signs* 17:329-62.

Saxonhouse, Arlene W. 1985. *Women in the History of Political Thought: Ancient Greece to Machiavelli*. New York: Praeger.

Scott, Joan Wallach. 1988. *Gender and the Politics of History*. New York: Columbia University Press.

Shanley, Mary L., and Victoria Schuck. 1974. "In Search of Political Woman." *Social Science Quarterly* 55:632-44.

Shanley, Mary L. 1989. *Feminism, Marriage, and the Law in Victorian England, 1850-1895*. Princeton: Princeton University Press.

Shanley, Mary L. 1982. "Marriage Contract and Social Contract in Seventeenth-Century English Political Thought." In *The Family in Political Thought*, ed. Jean Bethke Elshtain. Amherst: University of Massachusetts Press.

Shapiro, Robert Y., and Harpreet Mahajan. 1986. "Gender Differences in Policy Preferences: A Summary of Trends from the 1960s to the 1980s." *Public Opinion Quarterly* 50:42-61.

Spelman, Elizabeth V. 1988. *Inessential Woman: Problems of Exclusion in Feminist Thought*. Boston: Beacon Press.

Stoper, Emily. 1977. "Wife and Politician: Role Strain Among Women in Public Office." In *A Portrait of Marginality*, ed. Marianne Githens and Jewel L. Prestage. New York: McKay.

Stouffer, Samuel A. 1955. *Communism, Conformity and Civil Liberties*. Garden City, NY: Doubleday.

Studlar, Donley T., Ian McAllister, and Alvaro Ascui. 1988. "Electing Women to the British Commons: Breakout from The Beleaguered Beachhead?" *Legislative Studies Quarterly* 13:515-28.

Thomas, Sue. 1991. "The Impact of Women on State Legislative Policies." *Journal of Politics* 53:958-76.

Thomas, Sue, and Susan Welch. 1991. "The Impact of Gender on Activities and Priorities of State Legislators." *Western Political Quarterly* 44:445-56.

Tickner, J. Ann. 1991. "Hans Morgenthau's Principles of Political Realism: A Feminist Reformulation." In *Gender and International Relations*, ed. Rebecca Grant and Kathleen Newland. Bloomington: Indiana University Press.

Van der Ros, Janneke. 1987. "Class, Gender, and Participatory Behavior: Presentation of a New Model." *Political Psychology* 8:95-123.

Welch, Susan. 1977. "Women as Political Animals: A Test of Some Explanations for Male-Female Political Participation Differences." *American Journal of Political Science* 21:711-30.

Welch, Susan, and Albert K. Karnig. 1979. "Correlates of Female Office Holding in City Politics." *Journal of Politics* 41:478-91.

Welch, Susan, and Donley T. Studlar. 1990. "Multi-Member Districts and the Representation of Women: Evidence from Britain and the United States." *Journal of Politics* 52:391-412.

Welch, Susan, and Rebekah Herrick. 1992. "The Impact of At-Large Elections on the Representation of Minority Women." In *United States Electoral Systems: Their Impact on Women and Minorities*, ed. Wilma Rule and Joseph F. Zimmerman. New York: Praeger.

Welch, Susan, and John Hibbing. 1992. "Financial Conditions, Gender, and Voting in American Elections." *Journal of Politics* 54:197-213.

Zerilli, Linda M. G. 1991. "Machiavelli's Sisters: Women and the 'Conversation' of Political Theory." *Political Theory* 19: 252-76.

Zerilli, Linda M. G. 1993. *Signifying Culture and Chaos: Women in Rousseau, Burke, and Mill*. Ithaca, NY: Cornell University Press.

4

Formal Rational Choice Theory: A Cumulative Science of Politics

David Lalman, Joe Oppenheimer, and Piotr Swistak

Formal political theory is commonly described as the analysis of rational choices and their aggregate consequences in non-market contexts. It resembles economic analysis which is concerned with rational behaviors in market contexts. In other words, the two fields share the same set of assumptions concerning individual choice. Hence they overlap methodologically and differ primarily in the contexts in which the choices are made. Whether the individual is considered as citizen or consumer, he is viewed as consistent in his behaviors. *Homo politicus* has rejoined *homo economicus*.

Early contributions to the area were made by researchers trained outside political science.[1] William Riker (1958, 1962) was one of the first in our discipline to recognize the importance of the approach for the understanding of politics. Increasing numbers of political scientists followed his lead. For more than a quarter century, the body of formal results and their empirical tests have grown steadily. A number of Nobel prizes awarded for work in the field have brought publicity and encouragement.[2] By now, the field of formal theory (a.k.a. positive theory, public choice, and collective choice) has grown into a major area of research in our discipline. Leading journals such as the *American Political Science Review*, the *American Journal of Political Science*, and the *Journal of Conflict Resolution* devote a substantial proportion of their pages to formal analyses of political processes.[3] The number of textbooks available at the graduate level has increased substantially over the last decade; many deal specifically with political applications.[4]

We recognize that a record of growth and success is not a sufficient recommendation; it certainly does not substitute for careful evaluation. In this essay, we try to describe in what ways formal theory has influenced our thinking about politics.

Our presentation is intended as an introduction for the sophisticated student of political science who may be untrained in deductive methods but who is nonetheless willing to handle abstractions. Our goal is to give the unfamiliar reader a set of simple yet firm intuitions about how formal theories advance our understanding of politics. We do not attempt to cover the field in its entirety. Social choice theory, for example, is not discussed explicitly. Rather, in the interest of portraying the methodological and epistemological factors which have contributed to the field's success, we have chosen to construct this essay around three major substantive areas: voting, collective action, and coalitional stability. Each is discussed separately, even though much of the analysis is in fact interrelated. This is not to say that the discussion is limited to the three areas. We also touch upon the uses of the rational choice approach in other areas such as institutional design, public policy analysis, and political philosophy.

The Distinctive Nature of Formal Theory as a Field

As compared to many fields of specialization within political science, formal theory is unusual. Formal theorists work neither on a particular set of institutions nor on a substantively defined set of political problems. Instead, they often purport to know something specific about what is going on in each of the widely ranging institutional contexts throughout the discipline.

A second distinctive feature of rational choice research is that it is often mathematical. What is more, over the decades much of the mathematics has been refined in its content and reified in its presentation. Today, even for the mathematician, a great deal of technical skill may be needed to comprehend papers in the field. And even with the mathematician's technical advantages, a great deal of reflection is required to comprehend the "political" content of the formulations and their solutions. Unfortunately, these are barriers to entry to *anyone* wishing to appreciate what has been produced in the field.

To understand why the field has these distinctive features, we begin by examining the epistemological goals of the practitioners and the general structure of the arguments they put forward.

The Goals of the Practitioners

The Reasons for a Formal Theory

The concept of formal theory in political science refers to a deductive method of theory construction. The deductive method, common throughout the sciences, guarantees that theories are consistent. Consistency, however, is only a prerequisite for the cumulative growth of knowledge; it does not, in itself, guarantee progress. Progress requires that our theories are in some way descriptive of real world processes. Thus theoretical constructions should lead to testable hypotheses. In short, then, formal theorists endeavor to develop testable, deductive theories of political behavior and institutions.

Formal theory is thus defined more by the *method* of the theory construction than by the *content* of its theories. This important point is taken for granted by the practitioners, but it is often missed by critics. As a method, deduction can be used to construct theories based on *any* set of assumptions, as long as this set does not include inconsistent statements. Deduction, when applied correctly, guarantees the logical validity of all of the derived propositions and, hence, the consistency of the entire theory. Formal theories are consistent in just this fashion. In most sciences the name "theory" is reserved for such constructs.

Necessary Truths or Testable Conjectures?

In any theory, some propositions are fundamental to the system, others are derivative. The fundamental propositions which form the premises of theories are referred to as assumptions or axioms. For the purposes of our discussion it is useful to distinguish between these two concepts. As in mathematics and normative theory, axioms are initial propositions assumed to be truths not correctable by the world of facts. Assumptions we will understand here as empirical conjectures. As such, premises are, in principle, testable. From these assumptions, other propositions are deduced. Such a description is open to misunderstanding, because the notions of "logically" and "derived" are often used neither carefully, nor consistently.

The use of logic, the set of rules which preserve the truth of an argument, guarantees that an argument is consistent. An argument can be thought of as a set of statements or propositions. Consistency among a set of statements is the property that all the statements can be

true simultaneously. That is, there exists some logically possible state of the world in which all the statements are true. An argument built with inconsistent statements can not possibly describe *any* state of the world. Such arguments are *necessarily* false. Hence consistency is an essential property of proper argument.

The relationship of logical derivation, or deduction, in argument is a relationship between two sets of statements, such as between premises and conclusions. A deductively valid argument requires that if the premises are true, then the conclusion *must* be true. If the premises are indeed true, then the statement of the deductive relationship between the premises and the conclusions *is* tautological. This is not a problem, however, if the premises are treated as conjectures.[5] In this case, the whole set of statements derived from the assumptions -- the entire theory -- constitutes a set of empirical conjectures. Thus, many of the criticisms of the work in formal theory as tautological are to some extent misplaced.

Normative or Descriptive Theories?

A further ambiguity fundamentally affects one's view of a theory's testability. Many theories can be perceived either as normative or descriptive. These perspectives imply different procedures when theoretical predictions do not conform well with the facts. In short, a normative theory addresses how an individual *should* behave (say to maximize profit), while a descriptive theory addresses how one *does* behave. Intuitively, only the latter, the "does," is testable.

For those who view a theory of rational action as normative, the fundamental propositions of the theory are indeed axiomatic. Testing the theory is irrelevant to their concerns. Facts would then only be important to assess how people deviate from what they should be doing. For those who view the same theory as descriptive, observation and experimentation play a fundamental role in theory development through the assessment of the theory's explanatory value. Because some researchers have treated some of the research as normative (e.g., Von Neumann and Morgenstern's expected utility theory), the theories were at times insulated from empirical tests. But we do not believe this is the mainstream use of formal theory in political science.

When a theory is treated as empirically testable, deductive methods of theory construction yield a great advantage. To the extent that the assumptions are true, all propositions derived from them are *detachable* from these assumptions and presumptively true.[6] This implies that each of the derived conclusions can be used to test the truth of any set of (possibly true) premises which implies them. Hence, the many testable conclusions derived in the theory are indirect tests of the assumptions. This is of fundamental importance when assumptions are difficult to test directly, as is often the case when modeling political phenomena with theories of choice. Those theorists interested in the truth value of the premises used in their arguments will be interested in generating and testing new conclusions from their premises. And they are -- regardless of the substantive field in which the inferences lie. Hence the intrusive quality of the field.

The Use of Mathematics

This discussion of the nature of theory, and its ties to logic can explain the general use of mathematics in the field. Because mathematics contains within it all the assumptions and techniques of logic, anything which has been shown to follow mathematically has been shown to follow logically.[7]

Mathematics or symbolic notation is by no means necessary to deductive theories. The theories of Downs (1957), Schelling (1963) and Coase (1960), for example, were developed practically without symbols and mathematics. But when performed in natural language, proper deduction is very difficult and full of traps. Definitions of terms can slip and improper inferences can be drawn. Symbolic notation and formalization guard against such problems.

While symbolic or mathematical arguments are often thought of as difficult and complex, we should recall that the very reason for formal modeling is precisely the opposite. The language of symbols and the use of mathematical tools are used because they provide the simplest form of precise description and the easiest method for carrying out complex deductive arguments. Thus the very point of formalization is to clarify, not to obfuscate.

The Role of Experimentation

Theoretical claims made about reality are assessed according to their correspondence with the facts and their coherence with our understanding of the facts.[8] For any correspondence to be replicable, the nature of the observations must be made with considerable care to reflect the details specified in the theoretical argument. In the physical sciences this led to the development of an experimental tradition. This tradition has also taken root in formal theory, and the results from many of these experiments are reported in the current issues of our leading journals.[9]

The core aspirations of the field, then, are logically inferred, theoretical arguments, tested in a particular research paradigm. That paradigm is characterized by a consensus regarding what counts as theory, and a rather intricate, often formalized and mathematical argumentation, to generate testable conjectures of substantive and theoretical interest. And the testing of the conjectures tends necessarily to mirror the intricate and careful nature of the theory, to insure against improperly accepting or rejecting the work.

The reader can now infer from the stipulated goals a number of the characteristics of formal theory. For example, the use of symbolic notation and mathematical methods, emphasis on testing through experimentation, the use of a small set of general assumptions in theory construction are obvious elements. But what of its substance? Since many of the behavioral assumptions used in formal theories come from a different discipline -- economics -- the reader may find it useful to get an overview of some of the specific content of the premises at the foundations of the theory before considering the areas in which they have spawned useful or insightful applications.

Foundational Premises

Rationality

The field's major premise is that politics is inextricably involved with the act of choosing. Theorists try to explain political phenomena by using the behavioral conjecture that actors (individuals, states, organizations, etc.) make purposive, goal-seeking choices based on their own preferences -- they are rational. It is assumed that an individual is able to rank alternatives from best to worst. Such a ranking will have the property of transitivity. Transitivity is the condition that if alternative *a* is better than alternative *b* and *b* is better than alternative *c*, then it is certain that *a* is better than *c*. Actors are thought to choose according to what is best for them given their *own* preferences or tastes.

This does not mean, though it is often misconstrued, that rationality precludes altruistic behavior. We can have a rational choice theory which helps explain the behavior of an actor who is exclusively concerned with helping others. Mother Teresa, considered as a symbol of perfect generosity, may well both calculate how best to accomplish her altruistic goals and behave rationally. Rationality, in itself, has nothing to say about whether the desires, or preferences, of an individual are benevolent or evil. Theories of rational action do not explain where preferences come from. In its most general form, rationality as a behavioral statement takes the goals of an individual as given and both describes how those goals would be attained efficiently and stipulates a consistency between preferences and actions. Individuals assess their available options and choose those which they expect to best achieve their goals. The silence of the rationality axioms on tastes can be seen in many results that make no restrictions on individual preference orders.[10] Typically, an actor's preferences are represented in the theory as a *utility* function which registers not only the order of an individual's preferences but their intensity as well.

Preferences and Expected Value

Quite often a course of action (let us say inserting money into a vending machine and pressing the Coke button) is not sufficient to guarantee a desired outcome. It may lead to numerous outcomes (let us say the wrong product, or nothing at all). When a course of action leads to a set of possible outcomes, it can be portrayed as a gamble and expose the decision maker to the risk that something less than the desired outcome will eventuate. Obviously, any successful theory, or even a description of choice, must take into account not only the utilities of the possible outcomes but their probabilities as well. Thus, expected utility theory is a form of contingency analysis that explicitly evaluates a decision in terms of both the desirability and the likelihood of the scenarios a course of action may lead to. The worst-case scenario is analogous to the down-side risk. It is not so disturbing to the decision maker when it is neither too bad, nor too likely. If a decision maker with values for the outcomes can assign a probability to each outcome occurring, then the value of the entire lottery can be expressed as an *expected utility* by summing the value of each outcome weighted by its probability of occurring.[11] Various lotteries can then be compared in terms of their expected utilities in order to make the best choice -- the course of action expected to return the greatest welfare.

Self-Interest and Other Value Constraints

Further conjectures are often added to the utility maximizing assumption which narrow (at times considerably) the types of interests actors are presumed to hold. These may be very general conjectures, or rather narrow ones for special actors, within a particular model. Such specification allows us to conjecture actors' preferences (or utilities) over a set of possible outcomes. By far the most widely employed is an assumption of *self-interest*. Self-interest is generally understood to mean that individuals do not directly care about the welfare of others.

Like the rationality conjecture, self-interest certainly is fundamental in economics, and has stood the test of time well in market contexts as applied to profit maximization. Its verisimilitude in other contexts may be looser. But the theory of self-interested behavior is particularly suited for deductive simplicity. After all, it assumes that i's preferences are not determined by j's preferences. To consider dropping or changing that assumption leaves us with a problem: If not self-interest, what? Beyond self-interest lies an infinity of alternative conjectures.

Other values are often imputed to classes of actors in models dealing with specific sorts of repeated choices. In economics it is frequently stipulated that suppliers are motivated only by pecuniary interests. For example, a firm is conjectured to maximize profit. In political models, Downs (1957) conjectured that political parties and politicians faced with competition in a plurality election system would seek to maximize votes to gain office. Frohlich et al. (1971) conjectured that politicians were interested in maximizing profit; Niskanen (1971) assumed that bureaucrats were interested in maximizing their budgets, and so on. It is through such conjectures that some abstract models yield substantive hypotheses about empirical phenomena. Of course, such conjectures are not without controversy. Does a candidate care only about election? Perhaps candidates have personal attitudes about the issues in their platforms. If so, perhaps the model will be less than perfectly predictive.[12] Nonetheless, we should not be too hasty in disregarding a model simply because we wish to include a more expansive notion of preferences or self-interest. Models are to be learned from. For example, models that postulate election (or reelection) to office as the politician's motivation can teach us something about the strength of the ballot as a tool for voters to control their representatives.

Main Features of Applications

Levels of Analysis

A hallmark of rational choice theories is the predominant (though not exclusive) focus on the *individual* as the actor making the decisions. This focus stems directly from two things. First, the foundational conjectures are obviously formulated with individual actors in mind, and many questions are specifically about how individuals behave in given contexts. Second, even if we assume that individuals can make rational choices, we cannot guarantee that groups will.[13] An example of how individual rationality can lead to group irrationality is discussed in the next section. Strong assumptions must be made in order to guarantee group rationality. Nonetheless, we still might ask how a system would operate *if* such strong assumptions were met. Thus, collective actors such as states, social classes, unions, etc., continue to be used as decision agents in the literature of formal theory. Some of these will be discussed further below, but to illustrate the range of collective actors in rationality models, we draw the reader's attention to a few examples.

Applications to international relations often begin with some notion of welfare maximizing states. One of the earlier ones (Olson and Zeckhauser 1966) was criticized from this point of view (Oppenheimer 1979b), but it clearly yields interesting, testable results regarding the likely distribution of benefits and costs from alliances and other international organizations. Similar assumptions about rational aggregate actors have been used to develop conditions which generate a stable international balance of power (Niou and Ordeshook 1986; Wagner 1986). Still others, interested in strategic choices leading to or away from interstate war, have confined their analyses to state decisions not involving collective decision making (Lalman 1988; Bueno de Mesquita and Lalman 1992).

Other formal theorists have developed models built on Marx's notions of class conflict. They assume that classes make choices to maximize the aggregate welfare of their members. These include Przeworski and Wallerstein (1982) who show that Marx's predictions of inevitable warfare, rather than compromise, was logically wrong. Indeed, arguments relying on class rationality were an early target of formal theorists. For example, Olson (1965) argued that, in the absence of other incentives, one cannot expect the members of any class to struggle for their collective interests to any significant degree. On the other hand, even Olson (1982) used a similar collective rationality assumption on the part of interest groups to develop arguments regarding constraints on economic development.

Institutional Constraints and Questions of Stability

Institutional contexts matter. Individuals acting rationally can arrive at different outcomes in different institutional settings. These institutions, then, act in some way as constraints on actions. Or, as Plott (1978, 207) puts it:

> "Institutions determine the rights and powers of individuals. In the game theory jargon institutions determine the acts available to players at the time they act as well as the consequences which result from any pattern of acts taken by players. Clearly, the consequences, in terms of the social choice from among the feasible alternatives depend upon both the preferences of individuals and the institutions which define the process. In the game jargon, we simply say that the outcome resulting from the game depends upon the set of feasible outcomes,

individuals' preferences, and the rules of the game. These rules, which govern, or at least influence the outcome of the overall game, form the basic institutions of the society."

The study of institutions and their effects on policy outcomes is, of course, a traditional concern of political scientists. However, we find that the prediction of a single, stable, good outcome, which is so often reached in economics, is rarely to be hoped for in political settings.

The outcomes produced from political institutions may not be a strict function of individual preferences and the rules of the institution. Indeed, policy alternatives may not be stable, in spite of the fixed preferences of the individuals. To understand this troubling aspect, let us define a concept of *stability*. An outcome would be stable if *no* group of actors has both the ability and the desire to change it. These outcomes are undominated by other outcomes, and they are commonly known as the *core*. In economics it has been shown that the general market outcome is, under a wide variety of conditions, such a stable outcome. That is, it is a member of the core (see Newman 1965, chap. 5). In contrast to this, many non-market decision problems can be shown to have no stable outcomes in the sense just described.

We can illustrate political instability with the classical example of the voters' paradox. The simplest form of the voters' paradox can arise with three individuals {*1, 2, 3*} using the simple majority decision method to select a winner from three alternatives {*a, b, c*}. Each voter can rank the alternatives from best to worst. Now suppose that the preferences of the voters are:

Ranking of Outcomes	Voter 1	Voter 2	Voter 3
First	a	c	b
Second	b	a	c
Third	c	b	a

In a vote between *a* and *b*, *a* wins, supported by the coalition of voters *1* and *2*. Between *b* and *c*, *b* is the majority winner, supported by the coalition of voters *1* and *3*. We might think that since *a* wins a majority over *b* and *b* wins a majority over *c*, that *a* would be able to win over *c*. Such would be the case if majority rule guaranteed transitive outcomes. But, paradoxically, we see that the coalition of voters *2* and *3* decides for *c* over *a* -- *a* defeats *b*, *b* defeats *c*, *c* defeats *a*.... As a group, decisions on the outcomes are cyclic. The three who could individually rank the alternatives from best to worst are unable to do so as a group. We can also see that the core is empty in this situation. For any of the three outcomes there is a winning coalition interested in overturning it. There is no equilibrium. And without an equilibrium, predictions in politics are tenuous, at best.

Although we have illustrated the lack of stability and the emptiness of the core with a specific example of a voters' paradox, we hope to make clear below that this deficiency is far more general.[14] Stability in political institutions is an elusive prey.

Major Findings

Voting Theory

The theory of rational voting in general, and the theory of majoritarian voting in particular, are probably the best developed theoretical results in all of political science. Even casual reading in the area is likely to impress one with an awareness that a substantial set of questions have been well formalized and answered. Specifically, a large number of questions on how and when majority rule can (or cannot) aggregate the preferences of voters in a coherent fashion, have been studied. Further, the normative values associated with the majority voting method have been identified and well formalized. Of course, research continues, but the research is ever more focused.

Majority rule is surely not the only voting method used in political gatherings. But it is the first to come to mind, and it is hard to think of a legislature, a corporate board, or even a social club that has not acted as a committee and used majority rule to decide an issue. Contained within the logic of the rule, though not immediately obvious, are a number of problems, including the potential for the cycle that arises from the voters' paradox. In such situations an alternative may well win but victory will not stem only from the preferences of the voters and the voting rule. Something beyond these factors would be required to stop the cycling and lead to a winner. To see this, and a number of other interesting aspects of the problem, we begin with a very simple case: one without cycles.

The Median Voter Theorem: A Case of Stability

In the late 1940s Duncan Black (see Black 1958) began investigating majority rule as a decision-making method. He asked what we might expect if
1. a group of individuals are to vote on policy alternatives represented as points on a line
2. each of the voters has a most preferred, or ideal, point (policy), and

3. for each voter, alternatives farther to the right (or left) of the ideal point are increasingly less preferred.[15]

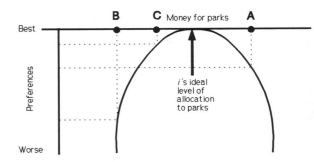

Figure 1: Displaying a Single-Peaked Preference

We begin the analysis with the utility function displayed in Figure 1. The horizontal axis represents allocations for a parks budget. The utility function represents the preferences of an individual who feels that one size of budget is preferred over all others -- an ideal policy. To spend less than the ideal is increasingly less preferred for smaller and smaller budgets. (In Figure 1, the individual's preferences are symmetric around the person's ideal point.) Also, to spend more than the ideal is increasingly less preferred. Such preferences are referred to as "single-peaked," for fairly obvious reasons. Of course, this individual will vote for the ideal point over any alternative opposing it. This individual's preferences are well defined across any pair. For example, budget C is preferred to budget A, which is in turn preferred to budget B. Notice also that the preferences are transitive across all budgets.

Now let us use this notion to illustrate the workings of majority rule under the circumstances stipulated by Black. Consider that the parks budget is to be decided upon by a committee of five voters {1, 2,...,5}, each with single-peaked preferences. Figure 2 illustrates the preferences of these individuals. What might interest us in such a situation? Imagine that voting leads to an outcome somewhere along the line beyond the ideal points of the most extreme voters 1 and 5: say alternative x. Any such outcome would be quite a poor choice for the group. After all, there are alternatives that *every* voter prefers over those such as x. Within the bounds of the extreme voter ideal points there would always be *some* point *everyone* could agree to over any point outside this set. This desired property is called *Pareto optimality,* and sets with this property are *Pareto sets.*[16] We see that the Pareto set for all the voters is the line segment connecting their ideal points, and against any outcome not in the set, some point in it could be supported by unanimity. For example, voter 5's ideal

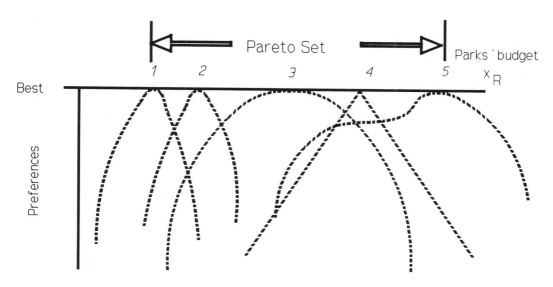

Figure 2: Pareto Set Given N, Single-Peaked Preferences, 1 Dimension

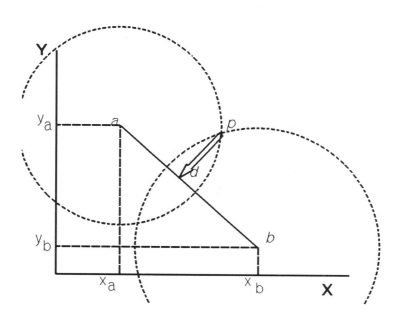

Figure 3: The Ability of 2 Voters to Agree to a Point on the Line Connecting Their Ideal Points, Rather Than a Point off It

alternative is supported unanimously against any alternative to the right of it, such as *x*. Similarly, there is unanimous support for voter *1*'s ideal alternative over any point to the left of it. But in a contest comparing any two points lying between the ideal points of voter *1* and voter *5* we could not get unanimity. So, in this simple case, majority rule supports Pareto optimality. This may not seem like a lot, but it is certainly a minimum which we would hope could be achieved. After all, why use a method that cannot deliver an outcome which everyone could agree upon if they but junked the procedure?

With this in mind, we might wonder what other properties majority rule delivers when it is employed in this simple, one-dimensional space. Does it lead to moderate or centrist policy outcomes within the Pareto set, or to extreme policies, for example? Under the circumstances of single-peaked preferences on a single dimension, Black showed that the *median voter,* who has an equal number of voters on either side (in this case, voter *3*), is in a privileged position. Just as we saw that the ideal policy of voter *5* is unanimously supported over policies to its right and *1*'s ideal is unanimously favored over motions to the left, there is *majority* support for the ideal policy of the median voter over any motion away from it. The median voter can form a coalition with voters *1* and *2* to vote down alternatives to the right. Motions to the left are defeated by the coalition of voter *3* together with voters *4* and *5*. We see then that the ideal point of the median voter is the equilibrium outcome under majority rule. This is Black's median voter theorem, a fundamental result in formal political theory.

Let us shift our focus and consider questions of coalitions on this committee. Analogously to the arguments above, a coalition's members can *unanimously* agree to restrict their proposals to the points which connect the extreme ideal points of its members. Notice that the median voter's ideal point is part of the line segment connecting the ideal points of any majority set of voters (i.e., the median voter is a member of all winning coalitions). The median voter's ideal point is therefore a member of all the possible proposals which winning coalitions would put forward. Indeed, it is the only such member. So if it were passed, there would be no possible winning subgroup of committee members who could agree to back any other alternative. No coalition would have the power and the desire to change the outcome. No other point can get the support of all winning coalitions, and therefore the ideal point of the median voter is in, and is the only element in, the core. Majority rule goes further (when there are single-peaked preferences along one dimension) than selecting the Pareto set. It selects the median ideal point as the equilibrium from the elements of the Pareto set.

Beyond One Dimension and the Median Voter

Black's median voter theorem gave us a description of conditions under which majority rule aggregates the preferences of voters to produce a stable, "moderate" outcome. In demonstrating the theorem he also gave us the spatial framework for analyzing voting. But Black went beyond this to research the consequences of majority rule when, though the preferences of the voters are single-peaked, the policies under consideration have more than a single attribute. An example would be voters considering not just the size of a single budget, but the allocation of a budget across multiple programs, such as money for parks and money for police. In these situations, one finds that we have reason to be less sanguine about majority rule (Black and Newing 1951).

Now to represent these policies we need more than points along a line. We must add dimensions to form a multi-dimensional policy space. Policies are now points in this space. Do we still get a stable outcome? Is it still the case that majority rule yields moderate results? If we are outside of the Pareto set, do we have reason to expect movement toward it? Do we have results in the core? These are typical formal theory questions, and each can be answered.

To illustrate these results, consider a simple example. Figure 1 represents two individuals whose ideal levels of **X** and **Y** are represented as the points *a* and *b*. For the sake of greater simplicity, assume each individual ranks all policies strictly by how close that policy is from her ideal point. It does not matter what the direction from the ideal point may be; greater distances are less preferred.[17] Notice that such preferences are still single-peaked. The analytical convenience of the restriction is that such an individual is indifferent among points that are equidistant from the ideal -- a circle with the center at the ideal point. Points within a circle are closer to the ideal point and hence more preferred; those outside are more distant and less preferred.

Our two individuals in Figure 1 agree that compared to the point *p* there are points they both would approve of. Constructing the indifference set (circle) for each person through *p* creates a lens-shaped area where they overlap. Points within this lens are mutually agreeable. For any point *p* off the line segment connecting *a* and *b* there is a point on the line segment (referred to as the *contract curve)* that both prefer.[18] That is, the line segment *ab* constitutes the Pareto set for the two individuals.

Consider now the situation with additional voters, in this case three: *a*, *b*, and *c*. In Figure 4, each has circular indifference curves. Analogously to the argument just made, they could unanimously agree that a

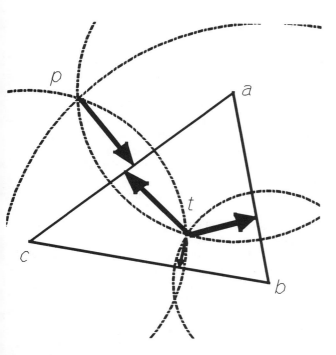

Figure 4: 3 Persons, 2 Dimensions. A Core Exists for Unanimity, but Not for MR

point outside the triangle made by their ideal points is not as good as *some* points on or inside the triangle. Thus the triangle and the points within it are the Pareto set. And, as must be the case for a point in the Pareto set (see above), when we consider points within the triangle there is no point able to garner unanimous support over any other point.

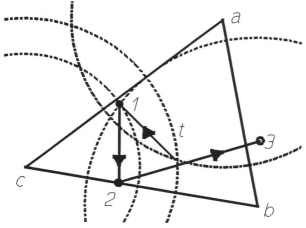

Figure 5: A Voting Trajectory out of the Pareto Set

With majority rule, are there any stable points analogous to the median voter's ideal point in the one-dimensional case? The preceding paragraph showed that we should search for any such point within the Pareto set. So consider a point inside the triangle *abc* such as *t* in Figure 4. We see that a variety of majority coalitions can upset any such point. There are three lenses containing the alternatives that represent possible improvements over *t* for each of the two-person, winning coalitions. Since with majority rule, any outcome obtained by a winning coalition can be outvoted by another coalition, *there is no core in this situation.*[19] In contrast to the median voter theorem, *t* and other such centrist policies are *not* stable. Also note that each of the lenses includes points outside the triangle *abc*; the lenses include non-Paretian, or *Pareto-dominated,* points. In Figure 5 we have duplicated the situation, but drawn one of many possible voting paths representing a series of three votes starting at *t*. *t* is unstable relative to the points in any of the lenses, and these points are in turn unstable themselves. Consider the majority voting path we have constructed from *t* to *1*, to *2*, to *3*. The coalition *ac* obviously prefers point *1* to *t*; *bc* prefers point *2* to *1*; and *ab* prefers *3* to *2*. This shows that majority rule can lead to a Pareto-dominated outcome. So majority rule in more than one dimension, even with single-peaked preferences, does not guarantee stable outcomes. Nor does it restrict outcomes to the Pareto set. We find that by relaxing just the restriction that the policy is one-dimensional, majority rule loses its nice, well-behaved properties. Indeed, majority rule appears grossly unstable. Outcomes can wander about, even if the decision rule and the preferences of the individuals remain fixed.

In one dimension, single-peaked preferences force a symmetry in the voting situation. At the median voter's ideal point, the voters to the left have the same voting strength and are diametrically opposed to those on the right. When the median ideal point is threatened, the median voter can turn either coalition from losing to winning. Such symmetry is missing in the two-dimensional case of Figure 4. This lack of symmetry is typical when there is more than a single dimension. The voter who is the median in one dimension is not generally the median voter in the other dimension. Indeed, in two dimensions there are an infinite variety of directions to go from any point, and in each direction we could have a different median. With this variety goes our majority rule equilibrium.

Figure 6 contrasts the condition of symmetry with that of asymmetry. The ideal points of five voters {*a, b, c, d, e*} with Euclidean preferences are contrasted with a very similar 5-person set {*a, b, c, d, e**}. For each of the three-person winning coalitions, the optimal

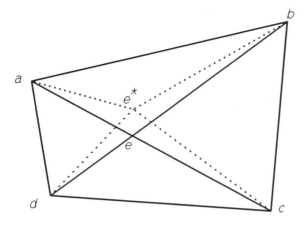

Figure 6: 5-Person, Two-Dimensional Majority
Voting: With, and Without, an Equilibrium

set of outcomes is the points on or in the triangle
constructed with their ideal points. In the first set, e has
an ideal point at the intersection of the lines connecting
the diagonal pairs of voter ideal points. Now e is in each
of the winning coalition's set of optimal points. And,
there is no three-person coalition which can agree to form
in order to upset the policy e. Thus, e is the core, the
equilibrium outcome in this example.

Notice how different the situation is if the central
ideal point, e, is replaced by a just slightly different ideal
point, e^*. Now e^*, though still near the center of the
diagram, is no longer in equilibrium. Two of the three-
person coalitions, bcd and acd, have an incentive to form
to upset e^*. e^* is not part of an optimal set for those
coalitions, since it is not in the triangle associated with
each.

Plott (1967) formalized a set of symmetry
conditions in a spatial context of any finite number of
dimensions which leads to a majority rule equilibrium.
Plott demonstrated that when there is a single point which
is a median in *all* directions, much like the hub of a
bicycle wheel, an equilibrium will exist. Note that e is
such a hub, but e^* is not. We have no reason to expect
such a demanding condition to be satisfied in the real
world. The apparent unlikeliness of these conditions
shows the fragility of majority rule. When there is no
radical symmetry, there is no stable outcome. So, in
Figure 6, there is no end to the coalitional cycling when
e^* is the fifth person's ideal point. Not comforting.

When Plott's symmetry conditions are not met,
how big a problem do we have? Still using only majority

rule and conditions on preferences, McKelvey (1976,
1979) and Schofield (1978) produced results indicating
that even a slight breakdown of the symmetry in
preferences leads to intransitivities that are not even
limited to any region of the policy space. Surely, for
normative theorists this lack of equilibrium is
discomforting. Yet, these results may not be the final
answer, and there may be reason to suspect some stability
in political outcomes in spite of the ubiquity of
disequilibrium and cycles. Theorists have shown that
political arrangements and institutions surrounding
majority rule can reduce the set through which outcomes
can wander.

To show that although intransitivities can cover
the space, does not lead one to conclude that political
outcomes will wander unchecked. For example, imagine
a committee with a chairperson. The chairperson might
be a strong agenda setter with extraordinary knowledge of
the preferences of the other voters. Such an image is not
very distant from what we think of as congressional
committees. The chairperson can indeed manipulate a
cyclical voting situation. But unless those manipulations
were made to her own disadvantage (not likely), she
would not leave off the process with the outcome outside
the Pareto set.[20] So the conclusions of how majority
rule is likely to play out must be thought about within the
context of our experience. We must ask, what are the
institutional parameters of the process under study?
Adding institutional and other features brings the models
more verisimilitude with politics as we experience it.

But other restrictions modify majority rule
instability. And since majority rule usually exists in a
richer institutional context, these arrangements are
usefully considered. For example, the common
legislative practice of separating alternatives on an issue-
by-issue basis is a restriction on the way majority rule is
employed. The fact that there are conditions under which
such issue-by-issue procedures promote stability is clearly
of political interest, in that it addresses how political
procedures affect outcomes.

Kramer (1972), Shepsle (1979), and Shepsle and
Weingast (1981) find that when preferences are *separable*
(i.e., preferences on one issue dimension are independent
of the outcome on the other), separating the issues can
stabilize outcomes and induce a regularity in politics.
Notice that such regularities depend upon an elaboration
of the majority rule method and a restriction on
preferences that is more than a representational
convenience.

Prisoners' Dilemma: The Problem of Collective Action, and the Developments of Non-Cooperative Game Theory

One of the main findings of economics is that purely selfish individuals can all profit from engaging in voluntary exchanges.[21] Hence, in a typical market exchange problem a buyer and a seller would contract with each other until there are no further possible gains from trade. The transactions would allocate the available gains among the two parties: neither the buyer, nor the seller, can get more benefits without a decrease in the benefits to the other -- the outcome is both optimal (see above) and stable. In these market exchanges, the object is assumed to belong solely to the purchaser. The nature of goods is sometimes quite different. Not only those who pay, but also those who do not, share the benefits. In such non-market situations, selfish motives no longer produce an optimal outcome. Indeed, this failure to generate satisfactory outcomes might be, as many would argue, the very reason for the existence of political institutions.

The above argument is not new. It has certainly been around since Hobbes. The fact that the common welfare may not be achieved as the consequence of purely selfish calculation underlies the classical call for the necessity of state. One formal model of such situations is the so-called Prisoners' Dilemma game: a specific model in the theory of games. From this perspective, politics is, in no small measure, "the study of ways of transcending the Prisoners' Dilemma" (Elster 1976). What, then, are game theory and the Prisoners' Dilemma game?

In short, the theory of games is an attempt to analyze the problem of choice in situations where choices are interdependent. These are often referred to as strategic situations. The theory of games is traditionally divided into non-cooperative and cooperative branches. In the theory of cooperative games, analysis focuses on situations where players can make binding commitments. There, the main analytical concepts involved are coalitions, side payments, and bargaining. The basic problems analyzed concern which coalitions will form, what payoffs they will obtain, and how the payoffs will be divided among the coalition members. Non-cooperative game theory, on the other hand, focuses on situations in which binding commitments are not possible, and where, therefore, individual actors, rather than coalitions, are central to the analysis.[22] We will take a closer look at the cooperative branch of game theory after finishing with the Prisoners' Dilemma. But first, we will use the case of the Prisoners' Dilemma game to exemplify the methods of and the results in the non-cooperative branch of the theory.

The Main Concepts of the Theory of Games and the Prisoners' Dilemma

The Prisoners' Dilemma (hereafter referred to as PD), together with the voters' paradox, is by far the most widely known and celebrated example of the use of formal theory in political science. The game has been used to seek insights, explain, and describe political interactions in virtually all areas of political science and public policy. Often the PD has been used as a model for the general problem of collective action (also called the free rider problem, or the "tragedy of commons"). Numerous applications (cf., Axelrod 1984) have an impressive range: from international politics and cooperation (Snidal 1985; Oye 1986), to international trade (Laver 1977), to problems of political philosophy (Taylor 1987). Below, we will use PD in yet another capacity -- to exemplify the steps involved in the construction and development of any formal theory. We will try to show what such a theory does and does not contain, how it relates back to the reality, how it generalizes beyond its simplest form, and how it grows into a cumulative body of research.

The name of the PD game is derived from the story told to motivate interest in the dilemma it presents: Two partners in crime are taken prisoner and face alternative prison terms depending on which one of them, if either, chooses to give the state evidence.[23] Between this story and the realization that much of politics is "the study of ways of transcending the Prisoners' Dilemma" lies a theory which needs development to lead to this insight. Like any theory, it begins with abstraction, the heart of any creative analysis.

The genuine insight in science remains in separating, from an infinitely complex web of reality, a small number of crucial factors. The first steps in theory construction involve therefore a generous use of Occam's razor. In the PD story the key components include the **players** (two suspects), their available **strategies** (to defect from each other by confessing, and to cooperate by not confessing), and **payoffs** (preferences on or utilities of outcomes). These three elements indeed comprise the fundamental concepts of game theory. The depiction of PD in the so-called normal or strategic form is presented in the table below. This otherwise simple conceptual and representational framework -- in which the PD strategic interaction is represented -- constitutes one of the main insights of the non-cooperative theory of games. There are the players: *Row* (her strategies are represented as rows) and *Column* (with strategies represented as columns). The outcomes are associated with strategy choices by the players and are shown as pairs of numbers in the four cells of the table. The players' preferences over the outcomes are further represented there by the two numbers in each of the cells: the first number representing the payoff to *Row*, the second to *Column*. Now, the fundamental assumption of the theory conjectures that players choose strategies to maximize their payoffs.

Table 1. A One-Shot Prisoners' Dilemma Game

	Column Cooperates with *Row*	Column Defects from *Row*
Row cooperates with *Column*	2, 2	0, 3
Row defects from *Column*	3, 0	1, 1

Payoffs, Rationality, and Self-Interest

Payoffs are part of the abstraction and they are considerably stripped here of their everyday meaning. In the simplest form of the game, numbers depicted in Table 1 would merely indicate the order of players' preferences on outcomes: from the best (3) to the worst (0). For some applications, however, it may be reasonable to interpret the numbers in the table as units of utility for the players. The utility interpretation is usually more natural and convenient; hence we use it (even though the "preference interpretation" is more general and sufficient to define the PD).

How will a rational player behave facing the PD situation? First note that any player is better off defecting, no matter what the other player does. To see this, consider the choice situation confronting *Row*, for example. *Row*'s strategy choice has to be made independently of that of *Column*. (This assumption can, for simplicity, be thought of as players making simultaneous choices.) The opponent, *Column*, could cooperate or defect. If *Column* were to cooperate, then *Row* could get 3 (**T**) or 2 (**R**) depending on whether she defects or cooperates; clearly, defection gives her a higher payoff. If *Column*, on the other hand, were to defect, then *Row* could get 1 (**P**) for defecting and 0 (**S**) for cooperating. Here again defection gives her a higher payoff. In short, no matter what the other player does, *Row*'s defect strategy yields a higher payoff. Technically, we say that the strategy of defection strictly dominates the strategy of cooperation: it is best under all circumstances. And since the same reasoning applies to the other player (their situations are purely symmetric),

rational players would both defect in this game, and each will end up with a payoff of 1. Thus, the "paradox": rationality leads to a suboptimal payoff. Had the players cooperated, they would each have received the payoff of 2.

Part of what seems paradoxical about the suboptimal solution to the PD is related to the assumption (in all non-cooperative games): players can make no binding contracts. While such agreements would obviously be useful to secure the cooperative payoff, enforceable contracts would lead us to model the situation differently and use different tools (those of cooperative game theory) to analyze it. In consequence, solutions to the cooperative form of the game may be different. Indeed, the cooperative version of the PD presents no dilemma at all. The optimal cooperative outcome is the sole solution of the game -- the only element of the core.[24]

From Simple Ideas to Complex Formalizations -- The Point and the Power of Formal Modeling

The Collective Action and Other Empirical Problems as Prisoners' Dilemmas

As a depiction of a real political interaction, Table 1 does not look very compelling. Even if some situations, like an arms race, seem to resemble a PD, the one-shot (no future interactions) assumption is often not a reasonable presumption. Arms races occur over time, with many non-binary decisions being made by parties that alter their responses in a sequence of moves. Likewise, collective action problems may intuitively seem to have a resemblance to a PD, but since they almost always involve many participants, a two-person matrix would be inadequate. Similar concerns are barriers to most direct applications. On one hand, many actual situations seem to share the core properties of the PD; on the other hand, their depiction as a one-shot, two-person, two-option game is inadequate. Applications require changes in the model. But do the changes fundamentally alter the analysis of the situation? Any such change of the model would have to involve, in one way or another, a more general depiction of the PD game. While there are a number of possible ways to define a PD, the following would be the core elements of all such definitions:

(i) Defection is the dominant strategy (for each of the players); hence the defection of all is the predicted equilibrium outcome.

(ii) The equilibrium outcome is not Pareto optimal; the payoffs from universal cooperation are higher for all players.

With these two definitional features, it should be much easier to see the scope and the generality of the PD problem. Note first that (i) and (ii) do not rely on the assumption of only two players. By generalizing beyond two persons, we are permitted more serious applications - - such as to collective action problems. Consider automobile emissions problems, as an example. Assume, for simplicity, that in a society of similar individuals, each must decide whether to install a catalytic converter in her car (cooperate) or not (defect). Suppose that the benefit of lead-free air (the outcome of all cooperating) is worth more to an individual than what it costs to install a converter. Will individuals install such devices in their cars? No matter what everyone else does (i.e., whether they all install, only some install, or nobody installs), any single person's choice will have but a negligible effect on the overall quality of air. Certainly, the marginal improvement in air quality would not outweigh the cost of the converter. Hence, the logic of the problem is clear: regardless of everyone else's behavior, an individual is better off defecting [property (i)]. Further, when all defect, everyone is worse off than if they all cooperated [property (ii)]. In this generalized PD, all players defect and all end up with an inefficient outcome: the central property of the dilemma.

Properties (i) and (ii) permit us to go further. They lift not only the constraint on the number of players, but also the limit on the number of strategies available to any player. To see this, consider the decision of how much money to contribute to a charity. Strategies in this case are numerous: every different amount of money constitutes a separate option or strategy. With some straightforward assumptions (similar to those used in the problem above), it is easy to conclude that the logic of the problem would result in conditions (i) and (ii). Hence, neither the number of players nor the number of actions available to them is essential for the PD effect; the simple two-person, two-strategy PD can be extended in a natural fashion to cover a large and important class of political phenomena (Hardin 1971).

Indeed, the generic PD problem is an aspect of the provision of all public goods: goods for which the market does not operate as an effective exclusion mechanism for those who do not pay. Such are the problems of cleaning up the environment, working for (or against) a revolution, contributing to a public radio station: goods which, once provided, can be used by all, including those who did not contribute to its provision. In all these cases, the benefits of any contribution are distributed widely, but the costs are incurred privately.

This is a generic property of what are called *public goods*. An argument which shows that selfish motives will not lead to the provision of a public good is often referred to as the problem of collective action. This view, called by Olson the "Logic of Collective Action," (Olson 1965) was revolutionary in the 1960s when it was proposed as a general characterization of problems facing political groups. By now it is a part of the foundations of the discipline. Indeed, the general mechanism behind the failure to cooperate turns out to be the same in the collective action problem as it was in the PD game.

Other views of the collective action, and public good, problem have been developed since Olson's classic. The PD is now but one of a set of alternative games developed to deal with the empirical domain of the problem. So, for example, Dawes and Orbell (1982), Frohlich et al. (1970, 1975), and Schelling (1978) model the situation without dominant strategies. Taylor (1987) develops alternative models quite fully and discusses their application to collective action problems. Many of these have since been subjected to extensive experimental tests.

Repeated Games

Above, we established that the essential properties of the PD do not vary as the number of either players or options increases. But there are other important extensions of the basic model. Most real-life situations are not isolated -- they are bound to repeat, often in the same or similar form. Suppose that a PD interaction is being repeated; what would be the predicted outcome? Are rational players doomed to end up with the inefficient equilibrium outcome again, or is there a possibility to do better?

To develop an analysis of repeated games, we must go beyond our simple tool of a dominant strategy to predict the game's likely outcomes. Indeed, a game -- like the one-shot PD -- in which both players have a dominating strategy, is not a good example to use to display the power, and methods, of game theory. After all, no theory is really needed to predict what happens in a one-shot PD -- the outcome is both obvious and robust.[25] When a player has a strategy which dominates all her other options, there is little ambiguity about what she should do. But such games are very unusual. In a typical game, a strategy may be "good" (i.e., maximizing) to play against *some* of the strategies of the opponent, but not all. It is for this more general circumstance that we must ask, how will rational players choose in the game? In all non-trivial repeated games, and certainly in the repeated PD game, there are usually no dominant strategies, and so one must search for an answer to this question.

Toward a More General Solution -- The Nash Equilibrium

A solution concept in the theory of games is simply a prediction of how the game will be played by rational players. Among many solution concepts, the concept of *Nash equilibrium* is the most fundamental. To illustrate it, consider yourself playing against a single opponent. If you choose strategy **A** and your opponent chooses **B**, we would want your choice to be stable (or in equilibrium) once you discovered the choice of your opponent. What does it mean for a pair of strategies, **A** and **B**, to be in equilibrium? Given the assumption of rationality, the reason for you to choose **A** must be that **A** is the best strategy to be used against the strategy chosen by your opponent. To interpret this, ask: "If my opponent chooses **B**, can I do better by choosing something other than **A**?" (The other player can reason analogously.) Now, if neither of you has an incentive (can get a higher payoff) to change your strategy *unilaterally*, then **A** and **B** are a pair of strategies in (Nash) equilibrium. The notion of no *unilateral* incentive to shift is the essential meaning of this equilibrium concept.[26] Nash (1953) has proved that every (finite) game has at least one such equilibrium.

The Possibility of Cooperation -- The Folk Theorems

Equipped with the general solution concept of the Nash equilibrium, we can now explore equilibria in the two-person repeated PD. Repetitions bring a new incentive structure to the game. Through repetitions players can condition their current moves on the past play of their opponent. Defections can be punished and cooperations rewarded. If players care about future payoffs and the game does not have a definite termination point,[27] it would seem that a threat of punishment (for example, a 'grim-trigger' strategy: "if you defect in any period of the game, I will defect forever after") should be sufficient to sustain stable cooperation in every period of the game. This simple intuition is essentially correct. It might be less obvious, however, that a whole spectrum of other behaviors, from pure cooperation to pure defection, can be in equilibrium as well. As it turns out, there are infinitely many possible Nash equilibrium outcomes and they can support any "amount of cooperation" in a stable state. Theorems which establish this have come to be known in game theory as the Folk Theorems.[28]

One important finding of the folk theorems for the general PD problem is that *cooperative equilibria are possible* and so the optimal (cooperative) outcome can be attained without external enforcement.[29] While this is the first good news, at least two related issues should still be addressed: First, which parameters of the model make the cooperative equilibrium possible, and second, what conditions, if any, make cooperation more likely? Folk Theorems, after all, merely state that all outcomes are possible in equilibrium; they do not say which ones are more likely. We now turn to these two questions.

The Importance of the Future

An important assumption in Folk Theorems concerns the expected value of the future payoffs: the theorems hold only if the "future is important enough." This means that only with sufficiently small discounting of the future, and sufficiently large probabilities of continuing the game, can the entire range of equilibrium states -- from pure defection to pure cooperation -- be attained. (If individuals heavily discount future payoffs and/or the probability of continuation is small, mutual defections constitute again, like in the one-shot case, the only Nash equilibrium.[30])

The Blessing of Bounded Rationality

By showing that any outcome is possible in equilibrium, Folk Theorems are practically useless for making predictions. Can further changes to the model make one of these equilibria more likely than others? Suppose that we "assume away rationality" and hypothesize that in a population of players a simple evolutionary mechanism, rather than rational calculation, leads to the adoption or abandonment of certain strategies. The so-called evolutionary theory of games is a very recent direction of research. (It takes its root in biology with the works of Maynard Smith and Price 1973; Maynard Smith 1982). Axelrod's (1984; Axelrod and Dion 1988) highly influential, and ingenious, simulations and findings suggest that cooperation can evolve from anarchy. Bendor and Swistak (1992a, 1992b) prove that the purely cooperative state is the most robust stable state: the easiest to attain and the hardest to disrupt. And so cooperation turns out to be the most likely equilibrium state -- bounded rationality helps in solving the notorious dilemma.

Other Real World Twists

Above, we developed generalizations of the original PD game. Each variation of the conditions of the game has generated its own form of analysis, consistent with the premises of the theory of games. Together they contribute to widen our storehouse of cumulative findings. There are more variations, and more results; some of these variations are nested in fairly autonomous branches of game theory. The listing in Table 2 exemplifies a few directions of research:

Table 2: Variations of Game Conditions and Families of Analysis

Variation of originally stated conditions	Resulting family of game analysis
players move in turns	extensive form games
interactions are repeated in the future	repeated games
players do not know payoffs to others	games of incomplete information
players use constrained maximization	bounded rationality, bounded complexity, and evolutionary games

This list, though far from being complete, symbolizes and reflects the power of formal theorizing: insights into the problem are sought at the most basic level (e.g., the one-shot PD game). But once this is achieved, one can bring back many of the factors which were initially abstracted away. One can then study the influence of these factors on the outcome of the game one at a time. Theoretical developments in formal theories thus resemble a robustness analysis. Even though some theorems may be very difficult to prove and theoretical progress may stretch over decades, each new result contributes a part to the theory as a cumulative endeavor.

Predicting Political Coalition Formation and Stability

As already pointed out, in non-market situations often no outcome enjoys stability. This means that for any coalitional structure, there is always some group whose members can do better by breaking away from the current arrangement and forming a new coalition. Then, no matter what the status quo, some group would have both the ability and an incentive to change it. In the language of cooperative game theory, we would say that there are no outcomes in the core or that the core of the game is empty. We have already shown the core to be usually empty in spatial voting problems. Below, we will see that such instability is a typical, rather that an exceptional, property of many political choice processes when considered without additional institutional and other environmental factors.

Empty Cores Reconsidered

If we agree with Lasswell, that politics consists of non-market deals to determine "who gets what, when, and how," the generic substance of politics can be seen as redistribution. If we now use game theory to address the issue of stability of various redistributional options, the answer, much as in voting games, turns out to be unsettling. In a large and important class of redistributional games, stable outcomes do not exist. More specifically, if we conceive of a problem as a purely redistributive (formally equivalent to a zero-sum) cooperative game (players can communicate and make and enforce contracts), we can show that no such game has outcomes in the core (cf., Luce and Raiffa 1957, 193-96). The simple game in Table 3 illustrates this general problem.

Table 3: Purely Distributional Game Showing Cyclical Coalition Problem

Line #*	Coalition	Payoffs	In the Bargaining Set?
1	123	1/3, 1/3, 1/3	Yes
2	12	1/2, 1/2, 0	Yes
3	13	2/3, 0, 1/3	No
4	32	0, 1/2, 1/2	Yes
5	12	1/4, 3/4, 0	No
6	13	1/3, 1/3, 1/3	Yes

* The first line is arbitrary. Each subsequent line represents a coalition, and proposed payoff structure, which beats the proposal above it.

The game consists of three persons who use majority vote to distribute one dollar. This means that any two (or three) person coalition that can agree to a distribution would also have power to enforce it. With this definition of the game in mind, we can now demonstrate that no distribution is stable in the sense previously mentioned. Table 3 illustrates the main steps in the reasoning. To see why the core of this game is empty, first assume that some group got together and considered a potential distribution. Suppose, to initiate the argument, that all three players agreed on an equal share. This is a situation depicted in line #1 of Table 3 (an analogous argument can be presented for any possible initial distribution). But now a two-person coalition, like the one on line #2, can clearly do better for itself and beat the first coalition. Thus, the coalitional arrangement of line #1 is unstable. Yet any potential two-person majority would not be stable itself, since the individual left out can strike a deal with one of the two coalition members. The outsider can propose something that both would prefer over the current arrangement (like the coalition of line three). But, this can again be beaten by the arrangement of line four, and so on. There are no incentives in the game to prevent the round robin from continuing.

The logic of this argument extends to the general case of distributive problems. As long as the rules of the game assure that a majority is decisive, the coalition of the whole would not be stable. A smaller group, suffice it constitutes a majority, would profit by forming a coalition and excluding everyone else from sharing in the distribution. Yet, the excluded minority would have incentives to make other deals which would further destabilize the arrangement, and so on. The conclusion generalizes to larger groups. It goes beyond majorities and voting. The general conclusion goes beyond the simple examples: *without further constraints, or further political arrangements, no coalitional struggle over a purely distributional matter has a stable outcome -- it is not possible for all coalitions to be satisfied at the same time.* Hence, no way of structuring the payoffs insures that all players get what they could guarantee themselves *if* they formed some other coalition; there is always a coalition able to improve the payoffs of all its members.

However, the problem of instability goes farther than that: empty cores turn up well outside the class of purely redistributional games.[31] And stability turns out to be an exceptional rather than a common property of cooperative games. Like Arrow's theorem, the common nonexistence of the core[32] helps us realize that many political outcomes and processes do not have the good properties that we would otherwise like them to have. Instability of all outcomes in games with empty cores means that no *single* outcome can be used as a prediction. Needless to say, there is something unsettling about this. After all, most of our theories (in the physical and life sciences, economics, demography, etc.) yield unique outcomes as predictions. Hence, an important insight from these models to political science is showing that political reality is, in this sense, a different type of reality: unique predictions are often not to be expected.

While theoretical models incorporate a relatively small number of variables, a large number of relevant, or potentially relevant, factors is always assumed away. In consequence, results which are obtained in such models are not directly applicable unless some additional methodological assumptions are specified. Most commonly, though rarely stated, the theorist assumes the effect of the factors which are not included in the model is negligible. Often one questions such assumptions (e.g., the negligible effect assumption) to investigate the robustness of a theoretical result. If, for instance, a game has an empty core, would it remain empty if the payoffs were altered by some small (epsilon [ϵ]) amount?

After all, payoffs in models are admittedly artificial: they do not include the small effects of the excluded factors.

This leads us to the following question: Can a non-empty core be obtained with a small shift in parameters? If so, a stable outcome can, after all, be empirically observed without contradiction of the theory. Second, if stability is not obtained, we may be able to induce it through small changes in payoffs. This second would be a crucial concern if payoffs can be effectively altered by policy decisions, even if the change would have to be substantial. These two important concerns, one methodological (robustness), the other political (altering payoffs via government intervention) motivate the so called ϵ-core (Shubik 1982, 153 et seq.) -- a generalization of the core concept.

Getting Stability with a Little Help -- The ϵ-Core

If the lack of stability is a serious problem for political arrangements and if the government can affect payoffs to coalitions, can this power be utilized to secure stability? Again, consider the distributional case as an example. Imagine that we imposed a tax on coalition reformulation in the division of a dollar case. If the tax were one dollar, the first coalition to form would be stable -- any reformulation would simply imply the loss of all gains. While the prospect of a 100% tax looks artificial, the point being made is quite practical -- there is always some level of taxation which stabilizes an outcome. A more realistic task would be to find the lowest tax needed to induce a non-empty core, and this may be an important policy problem. Given a fixed level of taxation, all outcomes which are stable under it are elements of the so-called ϵ-core (see Shubik 1982 for a precise definition and various refinements). If the tax which induces a non-empty ϵ-core is small, stability can be obtained cheaply. Of course, all kinds of transaction costs, as well as other forms of government coercion, would have an effect equivalent to that of taxation. So coalitional instability can be solved by external factors like coercion. Formal analysis can thus bring a new understanding to our observation of the pervasiveness of political coercion. Coupled with the empty cores in distributional politics, it can also help us understand a bit of the correlation between redistributive and coercive political regimes.

Other Perspectives

Game theory also points to a possibility of identifying feasible outcomes to the coalitional instability problem by analyzing the coalition formation process. Note that both the core and the ϵ-core predict the stable outcome (or the lack thereof) without modeling a process which leads to it. The "core-like" solutions were meant to identify coalitional structures with a balanced power among coalitions. Indeed, this is all they do. How a specific outcome is attained is a different type of question which requires a different line of inquiry. Such models will have to address the process of coalition formation in terms of the bargaining and the negotiations which are involved.[33]

Modeling the Process: Bargaining Sets and Competitive Solutions

Perhaps the most useful, and certainly the dean, of the solution concepts in the process oriented category, is the notion of the *bargaining set* (Aumann and Maschler 1964).[34] Aumann and Maschler conjecture that the bickering would start with an objection by one player against another coalition partner. They then ask whether the player being objected to has a compelling counter argument. To illustrate its approach we again use the example in Table 3. Consider the three-person coalition on line #1. Note that as we move to line #2 in the table, player #3 is being excluded from the coalition. Aumann and Maschler attempt to capture the coalitional bargaining which might occur *inside* the coalition, in the attempted dumping of player #3. To illustrate, let us say player #1 raises the following objection to player #3:

> Player #1 objects: I object to your being in the coalition. I could do a lot better without you getting 1/3 of the payoff. So I plan to make an offer to Player #2 that we form a coalition without you. I will offer him 50% of the dollar.

> Player #3 could counter: You are not in any privileged position in this argument. I can easily counter your objection. After all, I could do just as well as you by making a similar offer to Player #2, and then where would you be?

Hence the existence of a valid counter objection to player #1's objection might stabilize the situation of the equal payoff. A similar argument can be made for the coalition of line #2. In this arrangement, either player could object to their partner and propose a coalition with the third player which would improve both their payoffs. But any such objection could be met with a valid counter objection: the player being excluded in the proposal can point out that she too can make *as good an offer*, and be better off for it. Again, potential negotiations like that may make the coalition of line #2 stable. It is precisely such balance between possible objections and counter objections which motivates the concept of the bargaining

set: we say that an outcome belongs to the bargaining set if all objections can be validly countered.

We can also see now which outcomes *do not* belong to the bargaining set. Consider line #3, for example. With the coalition of players #1 and #3, and the payoffs split 2/3, 1/3, not all objections can be validly countered. If player #3 objects against player #1, the dialogue would start something like this:

> Player #3: I object to your being in the coalition. I could do a lot better without you getting 2/3 of the payoff. So I think that I am going to make an offer to Player #2 that we form a coalition without you. I will offer him 50% of the dollar. That will leave me better off.

Note that player #1 cannot counter this objection; to make a similar offer to the second player, she would have to take a *cut* in her payoff. In consequence, the outcome of line #3 is not in the bargaining set. Nor is that of line #5, for similar reasons. So in these cases, where there is an equality of power between the coalition participants, only the equal payoff patterns in the coalition which forms belong to the bargaining set. More generally, the bargaining set sees stability as bought with the payoffs in a coalition balancing the power of the coalition members to form alternative partnerships.

Given an obvious relevance of the bargaining set to many political problems, the concept has been widely used. Recently, Niou and Ordeshook (1986) have used it to get leverage over the problem of alliances in maintaining a balance of power in international arenas. Earlier, Oppenheimer (1979a) suggested a model of interest group coalitions using the concept, while Schofield (1980, 1982) has used it in analyzing parliamentary coalitions and voting problems. Indeed, the scope of the applications has been quite wide.

The process of negotiations which led to the bargaining set was assumed to have occurred among individual partners of the actual or the potential coalitions. Would we, however, get the same set of outcomes if we were to assume that it is coalitions who have to bid competitively amongst themselves to recruit and retain individual members? This led to the ingenious formulation of the *competitive solution* concept with its different stability patterns (McKelvey, Ordeshook, and Winer 1978). In some studies involving experimental results as well as some with data from actual political processes, the competitive solution predicts better than the bargaining set. For example, Ordeshook (1986, 429) uses data of parliamentary coalitions in Norway to show that the competitive solution is a better predictor. In general, however, the results are ambiguous: which bargaining models do best where is still an open issue. Looking at policy outcomes in coalitional governments, for instance, both the bargaining set and the competitive solution seem to do well (Ordeshook and Winer 1980). In addition, other considerations (such as communication patterns, equity, fairness, and universalism) seem to impinge on the performance of all the solution concepts, including the core (Miller and Oppenheimer 1982; Eavey and Miller 1984b; McKelvey and Ordeshook 1981). Indeed, it is useful to note that the permeability of all the solution concepts to external factors helps define the research frontiers of both cooperative and non-cooperative game theory.

Other Areas of Application and Success

Above, we presented the central findings of three major fields of formal theory. Yet other findings, which touch upon most corners of the discipline, abound. Although it is impossible to review them comprehensively, we can develop a casual overview by illustrating some of the more accessible applications. This yields a catalogue of some of the more important items. We begin with problems of institutional and policy design and analysis. This leads us to normative questions of political philosophy. Applications of rational choice theory to issues of policy and institutional design have been plentiful. Here we select a few works to illustrate the sort of leverage to be gained from the theory.

Institutional Design and Analysis

Affecting Outcomes with Structures

How structures or institutions affect the choices of individuals is the general question behind the institutional design problem. The problem of consolidation of urban governments serves as an early example of formal theory application to institutional design. Before the 1950s urban planners and other social scientists had serious intellectual arguments regarding the merits of consolidating urban jurisdictions. Planners, in part desiring increased simplicity of organization, advocated the unification of governments in urban areas. They saw the proliferation of municipalities as inefficient and diminishing the cities' abilities to supply services to the urban population. Commuters, as was argued, were "free riding" on the efforts of the city-dweller. Two early strands of formal theory were applied to the problem. First Tiebout (1956) showed that the proliferation of independent municipalities, differentiated by their service and tax programs, increased overall efficiency. Citizens migrate to the town which fits best

their values and supplies the mix of goods they most prefer. Tiebout saw governments as competing for citizens, and this process would decrease the inherent difficulty of revelation of the citizen's demand for services and alleviate the expected problems of suboptimal supply.[35]

As newer tools of analysis were invented (specifically, Buchanan's theory of clubs, 1965), the problem was looked at anew. Using the notion of clubs, Ellickson (1973) showed that the game of urban municipality creation and population migration has a stable outcome. Ellickson concluded that the equilibrium would involve the migration of populations to and from towns until there was segregation by income. Poor people would, in the end, cluster in the low service towns. Efficiency was to be gained only at a cost of fairness in distribution (also see Miller 1981). By specifying the problem or urban consolidation in terms of individual behavior, the theorists were able to sort out both the value conflicts and the projected effects of the alternative policies.

Another area which led to accessible and interesting findings stemmed from an apparent contradiction between theory and observation. As we discussed above, voting and democratic procedures have a propensity for instability. Yet, stability is commonly observed: certainly more than one might infer. In the eyes of the casual beholder, voting cycles are not common (cf. Tullock 1967). An interesting and important line of questioning examines which of the existing institutional arrangements induce stability. Trying to discover whether stability could be predicted by institutional details, theorists focused on the structure of voting rules. Romer and Rosenthal (1978) were among the first to show this in a context of a small committee reporting to a larger voting body (i.e., a school board suggesting a policy alternative to a legislature or an electorate). The work was soon replicated, for Congress and congressional committees, by Shepsle and Weingast (1981). As a result, some important political structures were shown to be capable of inducing a non-empty core and hence an equilibrium outcome.[36] Once it became clear that predictions could be generated by focusing more on the details of the institutions, it was only natural that the concept of the core was applied to macro, as well as micro, structures. This, for example, permitted a substantial reanalysis of the relative powers of the branches of the U.S. government (e.g., Miller and Hammond 1987, 1990).

Generating Incentive Compatible Institutions

As a final design concern, note that when individuals have little incentive to reveal their preferences (see note 35), it can be non-trivial to design an institution which generates acceptable results. Then theoretical applications may be quite practical and useful. One such case was faced by the American Public Broadcasting Network. The PBS affiliates had to express their evaluation of shows being considered for the next calendar period. The existing incentives led stations strategically to understate their evaluation of the most important and successful shows, like Sesame Street. Expecting shows like Sesame Street to gain sufficient support from others (i.e., they could get it as a free ride, without spending their "political capital"), many affiliates concentrated on preserving shows that they themselves produced, or shows which were of special interest to their region. This problem led to a temporary defeat of the most important shows and, in consequence, to the design of a less manipulable system by formal theorists brought in as consultants (see Ferejohn et al. 1979).

Public Policy Analysis and Design

Markets have two desirable properties: they are predictable and efficient, or at least more so than some of the bureaucratic and political environments. Hence, it is in general good news when markets can be created to reach policy goals which were previously sought by other means. Formal theorists have been at the forefront of designing such policy induced markets. A few exemplars of such policies have been accomplished through designs which harness the rational choice theorizing.

Developing Quasi Markets

As an example of the general problem, consider the issue of noxious industrial discharges: We can establish a market for permits of noxious substance discharges, so as to provide firms incentives to cut down their pollution levels. The design can roughly be described as follows. Instead of a "standards" policy, which sets the maximum level of emissions for each firm, the government sets the total level of the waste permitted. By distributing (or selling) a particular number of emission permits (each giving the owner a particular quantity of emissions) allowing permits to be traded, we create a market in which firms have incentives to be low polluters.[37] If, for example, a firm can decrease its emissions for less than the required cost of the permit, it can then sell any extra permits it does not need to others who have not yet efficiently decreased their emissions. Those who are least efficient at solving the pollution problem pay most. Meanwhile the government remains in full control of the market; if it wishes to "tighten up" the standard, it can regulate the quantity of permits on the market (e.g., it can repurchase and retire permits, or if permits expire annually, it can decrease the number of new permits issued). Of course, the inspections, to insure compliance, would not be different than in the previous regime.

More generally, this sort of shift in the design of an institution provides an incentive for the actor to work with the goal of the group or the society. Such policies are designed to be flexible in implementation at the individual level. They give the actor an incentive to adopt the most efficient response possible. Hence the general call for what we call *incentive compatibility* in the design of institutions. The price to be paid for the lack of such institutions may be very substantial. Plott (1983), for example, conducted an experimental study which showed very significant differences in efficiency levels and goal attainment under regulatory forms with and without incentive compatibility.

Deregulation and Efficiency

One of the most prominent economic policies in the Reagan decade was that of deregulation and for this general direction the theoretical work of Ronald Coase was not without influence. In what came to be known as the *Coase Theorem,* Coase showed (1960) that a situation involving externalities[38] does not need government intervention and can be left to the parties involved to settle; the optimal outcome would ensue as a result of bargaining. For example, a polluter in a residential area would either have to pay the damages to the community, or would receive payment from the community to stop the noxious activity. In either case, an efficient solution would occur. Who would pay whom would only depend upon the initial distribution of property rights.[39] A number of experimental studies confirmed this relationship (Hoffman and Spitzer 1986, 1982). However, Aivazian and Callen (1981) demonstrated a problem with a possible generalization of Coase's theorem. When the externality problem involves more than two parties the core may be empty and so, no stable bargain might ensue. If the bargaining cycle goes through suboptimal points, the efficiency of the outcome is threatened. Most recently, experimental work shows that Coasian solutions to cases with suboptimal points in a bargaining cycle cannot be expected to generate Paretian results (Guyton, Blake, and Leventhal 1991).

Political Philosophy

Given the leverage gained over the properties of democracy, voting, and institutional design, we would expect rational choice theory to have serious implications for political philosophy. It does.

Utilitarianism, Pareto, and Distributive Justice

The uncovering, by formal theorists, of some relationships between normative properties of collective outcomes, like Pareto optimality, and the assumptions of individual rationality was reported above. These findings are relevant to debates in political philosophy. To see this, consider that Pareto optimality is all that is left of utilitarianism if we remove the assumption of interpersonal utility comparisons (Soltan 1982). Further, Pareto optimality, all by itself, is insufficient to generate *any* distributive judgment (Sen 1973, chap. 1). We are left with the interesting conclusion that modern utilitarianism is insufficient to generate distributive judgments. Hence, the field of distributive justice must be motivated by other values.

Harsanyi (1955) was among the first to apply the tools of rational choice theory directly to problems of distributive justice. Later, however, it was mainly Rawls' work on justice which (while gaining a prominent position in political philosophy) attracted the attention of formal theorists (Rawls 1971). Two specific concerns regarding Rawls' conception of justice have produced interesting and important results. The first was the proof that his justice conditions implied a dictatorship (Plott 1978). The second line of work, by Howe and Roemer (1981), showed that only under extreme assumptions regarding risk aversion was the Rawlsian outcome, of maximizing the welfare of the worst off, stable (i.e., an element of the core).[40] Traveling down this path, we see that by taking utilitarianism, in its modern guise, and adding values regarding risk, we generate a family of possible notions of distributive justice (for a very nice exposition of this the reader may want to consult Wittman 1979). In addition to these, other notions of justice, based on yet different additions to the rationality stew, have been developed. They are discussed in some detail by Sen (1973). Finally, as came to be typical of the work in formal theory, experiments have been run to generate empirical evidence regarding what principles would be chosen behind a veil of ignorance (see Frohlich and Oppenheimer 1992).

Democracy

Given what we have said above, it may look like the lessons for democratic political philosophy are all negative. This is not quite so. Some limited, but quite attainable, positive properties of democracy have been identified. Thus, for example, if Schofield (1978) and McKelvey (1979) force us to let go of the hope that majoritarian democracy alone results in a maximization, or even an improvement in the welfare of the populace, we can still ask: "What are its other properties?" And

onto this, the findings of Kramer (1977) and Miller (1980, 1983a, 1983b) cast light. Although Schofield and McKelvey show majoritarian systems can lead us to wander anywhere in the policy space, Kramer and Miller show the dynamics of the path to be less debilitating: when the trajectory of voting leads from the Pareto set, it must turn around and come back toward it.

Yet another response to the lack of central tendency in majority election research has been proposed. It is based on a different behavioral model of the voter which assumes that voter's choice is probabilistic (first advocated by Luce and Raiffa [1957, appendix] and Hinich 1977; it has now been explored more fully by Coughlin et al. 1988). The model assumes voters to have different probabilities to vote for different candidates and the probability of voting for a candidate increases as the candidate gets "closer" to the voter's ideal point. With simple assumptions regarding the function which translates distances from ideal points into probabilities of voting for alternatives, Coughlin et al. have developed powerful results. Competing candidates, each interested in maximizing the expected value of the number of votes they receive, are shown to end up in equilibrium seeking relatively "central" positions in the utility space. The resulting equilibria turn out to be not only efficient (cf. Mueller 1989, 201-203) but also surprisingly similar to the sorts of aspirations of the utilitarian philosophers (Coughlin 1984, 1988).

Liberalism and Personal Responsibility

The notions of liberalism and human rights have been important in political philosophy. And the analysis of such rights (both alienable and inalienable), and how they can conflict with other values, has been aggressively developed by formal theorists (Sen 1970a, 1970b). Take, for instance, our discussion of how structure can induce equilibria (see note ?). We reported that some institutional structures were capable of stopping the nefarious cycles. These gains, however, are often obtained by giving particular institutions (legislative committees, for example) disproportionate rights or power to design policy on specific issues. Such a devolution of decision authority can lead to suboptimal outcomes. Indeed, the general problem is identical to that of the Liberal Paradox (Sen 1970b) -- a theorem which shows that conditions of optimality and liberalism are not compatible. In other words, optimality can, at times, be attained only by constraining liberty, and preserving liberty results in a potential loss of efficiency.[41]

A final illustration concerns our image of the responsible citizen. The collective action problem was shown often to leave individuals without incentive to take political action. Unable to greatly affect the outcome, citizens are left without incentive to stay informed regarding their political choices (Downs 1957). Such legal and philosophical concepts that link what we can hold people responsible for with their psychological state at the time of choice (e.g., *mens rea*) will be affected by showing that what we can reasonably expect from rational individuals is ignorance and lack of disposition to be involved. Hence, this generates arguments for a lessened individual ethical responsibility with regard to political matters (Oppenheimer 1985). If one can only marginally affect the outcome, then (given the modern philosophical adage "no ought without a can") the contours of the modern political philosophy scene must flow around the findings of the rational choice theories just as they flow around the findings of other modern sciences.

Concluding Comments

Our extended (though admittedly partial) tour of the findings of formal theory in political science puts the reader in a position to assess the current state of the field and some of the controversies within, and surrounding, the field. We temporize a bit about this task because controversies do get resolved and, in a developing field, the current state is passed before one can comment on it. We also offer some prognosis for the future of a science of politics and in what way formal theory conforms to the scientific standards we alluded to above.

Possible Limitations and a Prognosis for Further Contributions

If we conceptualize the field of formal theory as the combination of deductive methods and the basic conjectures of rationality, we might wonder how far such a thin reed can be pushed. Work continues at the foundational level and in expanding the range of applications. One of the healthy signs that the field will continue to grow and develop is the displayed willingness of its practitioners to explore the possibility of reformulating the foundational assumptions. These reformulation efforts have so far been pushed in two areas: choice under risk and self-interest.

Preferences, Expected Value

Over the last fifteen years or so, how people behave in the face of risk has become a topic of intense experimental research. Major, replicable discrepancies to the (von Neumann-Morgenstern) expected utility assumptions have shown up in the laboratory. These negative findings have implications, not only for the status of the expected utility theory as a valid descriptive

theory of choice, but also for the behavioral consequences of many formulations of rationality. Although a number of serious theoretical reformulations have been proposed, they have proved to be neither a reasonable normative, nor a reliable descriptive, alternative to the standard expected utility theory.[42]

Self-Interest

Like the rationality conjecture, narrow self-interest certainly is part of the foundational conjectures of economics, and has stood the test of time well in market contexts. On the other hand, the display of pure self-interest seems to be context dependent. In non-market contexts, significant non-self-interested behavior such as altruism has often been observed.[43] Such displays, often thought to have some political role, call for a theoretical explanation.

The theory of rationality does not restrict the values which an individual may have and which generate his or her preferences. But many models of rational behavior do stipulate narrowly self-interested preferences, assuming that preferences of an individual are independent of the preferences of others. And to consider dropping or changing that assumption leaves us with a problem. If preferences are not independent, then what is the specific form of their interdependence? Beyond self-interest lies an infinity of alternative conjectures. Behaviorally, although at times significant, this "deviant," non-self-interested behavior has not been found to be predominant (see the experiments reported in Frohlich et al. 1984). Simple "other-regarding" alternatives to theories of self-interest, such as a specific form of altruism, have theoretical problems themselves (see Margolis 1982) even though they do cover a considerable amount of the observations of non-self-interested behavior. Further, there is some evidence that individuals who hold these other-regarding values are quite consistently acting in a rational way (Frohlich and Oppenheimer 1984; Goetze and Galderisi 1986). Trying to understand the role of altruism has, however, led to the development of both non-self-interested models and tests of such arguments.

A Cumulative Record of Contributions

Perhaps most central to the evaluation of the field should be its record in generating a trail of claims to knowledge -- claims that are made so as to be correctable. Not only is it clear that a large number of topics central to the concerns of the discipline are now theoretically "understood," but the knowledge claimed about these topics is increasing. The field of formal theory has made indelible marks in such widely scattered areas of political interest as

    A. the level of participation and information we can expect of voters,

    B. the level of political organizing we can expect endogenous to a group,

    C. the expectations we can have of simple democratic processes,

    D. how to design better public policy and institutions,

    E. how to harness the power of markets for the use of policy goals.

We have not discussed the many non-experimental, empirical studies either conducted on or informed by formal theory. This too is an important part of the record of the field. Repeatedly, formal theory models have led to better specification of statistical models, even to the point of specifying the functional form to be estimated. Many new (at times non-obvious) relationships have been uncovered through the use of formal methods. What is important, of course, is that rational choice provides a unified theory of political behavior. Applications to different areas do not require a new theory. New applications are new contexts and as such are introduced as constraints on the basic theory. Though it continues to be improved and refined, the theory remains vibrant. As it leads to more and better knowledge claims in seemingly disparate areas of political life, our confidence in the theory improves.

By now, the field of formal theory has established itself. Its accumulated knowledge claims are relevant to practitioners who would wish to study disparate areas of the discipline. Increasingly, students of politics must be able to read, understand, and even manipulate the theoretical arguments of this field to understand the substantive claims of political analysis.

A Science of Politics

We have attempted here to present formal theory in a way that would make further comment unnecessary. But in the fear we have failed, we offer the following coda. The essence of any science is the explanation of the world around us. The motivations for seeking these explanations range from simple curiosity to pragmatic considerations of how to manipulate better our surroundings. The simply curious may be more attracted to the structure of the abstractions created than the more practically oriented. Good science is rigorous in its argumentation and in its testing, because it is the rigor that is most responsible for the truth value of the theory.

For practical matters, more than a bit of skepticism in matters of evidence is also well advised.

Formal theory, we have tried to indicate, has these features. The theory is constructed and interpreted to be correctable. Imprecise postulates, faulty proofs, ambiguous links between the theory and the real world all get challenged -- not on the basis that we do not like the answers so much as that we do not believe that the methods of science were used properly. After all, science is not an answer so much as it is a method of obtaining answers, tentative as they may be. In this way, science has the power to change what we believe about the world. The present authors agree on very little about the state of formal theory, or where it is going, but they do agree that rational choice theory has fundamentally changed how the discipline ought to proceed in studying politics and training students.

Notes

The authors wish to thank Michael Alberty, Norman Frohlich, John Guyton, and Kenneth Shepsle for their very timely and solid critiques of the first sketches of this paper.

1. These include John von Neumann and Oscar Morgenstern's game theory (1944), Duncan Black's rediscovery of the voter's paradox and his analysis of committees and elections (1958), Kenneth Arrow's general possibility theorem (1963), Anthony Downs's spatial model of party competition (1957), James Buchanan and Gordon Tullock's evaluation of constitutional forms (1962), and Mancur Olson's theory of collective action (1965).

2. These would include (the year in brackets is the year in which the Prize was awarded) Paul Samuelson [1970] and Kenneth Arrow [1972], who both received the Nobel Prize for a variety of contributions. Their respective contributions to the theory of social choice (see Arrow 1963, 1977) and public goods (see Samuelson 1955, 1954) were conspicuous, however. James Buchanan [1986], another Nobel laureate, was given the prize explicitly for his work in the public choice area (see Buchanan 1965, 1968; and Buchanan and Tullock 1962). Ronald Coase [1991] (see Coase 1960) and Gary Becker [1992] are the latest to receive the prize for work which most would consider in this field. Some would also include Herbert Simon [1978] and Maurice Allais [1988].

3. Other journals are devoted specifically to publishing results in formal theory. *Public Choice* (published since 1966) the pioneer journal in the field, has been joined in the last decade by *Social Choice and Welfare* (since 1981), *Rationality and Society* (since 1988), *The Journal of Theoretical Politics* (since 1988), and numerous others. Important articles in the field are scattered across journals in economics and the other social sciences, as well as a number of interdisciplinary journals. Barry and Hardin (1982, 387-390) provide a dated but useful guide to the classic readings and standard periodicals in the area.

4. Enelow and Hinich (1984) provides an introduction to spatial models of elections, Mueller (1989) gives an overview of non game-theoretic rational choice theory, Ordeshook (1986) explains game theory and how it can be used to explain political phenomena. Other texts in game theory include Fudenberg and Tirole (1991), Kreps (1990a, 1990b), Myerson (1991), Owen (1982), Rasmusen (1989), Shubik (1982), and Van Damme (1987). We should also note that the classic textbook by Luce and Raiffa (originally published in 1957) has

been brought out of retirement and republished in 1985. Undergraduate offerings in the area include Bonner (1986), Brams (1975, 1978, 1980, and 1985), Davis (1983), Elster (1989), Frohlich and Oppenheimer (1978), and Hamburger (1990). A growing number of departments have begun to include these materials in their undergraduate curriculum.

5. Some economists have regarded the fundamental assumptions about human action as non-correctable axioms protected from test (Friedman 1953; Von Mises 1957). Nagel (1963) has shown this position to be epistemologically flawed. In political science, it is common to view the fundamental propositions of theories of action as assumptions and not axioms. As a consequence these theories are regarded as falsifiable.

6. If we presume the premises to be true, we are also making the testable presumption that the conclusions are. The real strength of this property of deductive argument becomes clearer when it is properly compared with the nature of inductive arguments and statistical explanation (see Hempel 1965, 53-79, 394-406). Conclusions of inductive, statistical arguments are virtually never detachable from the informational content of the premises which are used to generate them.

7. The relationship between mathematics and logic is, itself, an interesting question. We refer the reader to Quine (1970, 98-101) for discussion of the relationship.

8. The issues we put aside here concern the presumptive nature of truth and the theory of truth that underlies efforts to test theories. White (1967) and Prior (1967) are good sources on this subject, and they have good bibliographies.

9. One of the leaders of this tradition in economics is Vernon Smith. Smith (1976) and Plott (1979) discuss the basic methodological issues surrounding experimentation.

10. Of course, some models include substantive claims about these values.

11. This notion of utility was developed by Von Neumann and Morgenstern (1944, chap. 2). Also see Luce and Raiffa (1957, chap. 2).

12. Alternative models have often been developed to deal with variations in precisely these sorts of conditions. For an example involving politicians who are motivated by policy as well as votes, see Wittman (1977).

13. Although space prohibits a full discussion of this central area of formal theory, there are a number of good texts on aggregation problems. For example, see Sen (1970a), Arrow (1977), Bonner (1986), and Schwartz (1986).

14. Our discussion focuses on majoritarian voting rules, but we should point out here that Arrow's General Possibility Theorem instructs us that this problem in aggregating preferences to form a social decision is not restricted to such rules.

15. Enelow and Hinich (1984) provide an excellent treatment of this representation of policies and preferences. We will usually further stipulate that the preferences are symmetric about the voter's ideal point. This is obviously a rather restrictive assumption, but the restriction is useful. Symmetric preferences over spatial options can be evaluated in terms of simple Euclidean distances.

16. A Paretian outcome is one from which no improvements can be made for some people without hurting others. In other words, if x is a Paretian outcome, then even if there are some people who prefer y to x, others prefer x to y and would be against such a move.

17. Unequally weighted distances would be important in many real-world applications, such as the evaluation of the siting of point-sources of air pollution given prevailing winds, etc. Extensions of the material in this manner are straightforward (see Enelow and Hinich 1984).

18. That the contract curve in this example is a straight line is an artifact of the fact that we have assumed circular indifference sets.

19. If the rule were unanimity, the Pareto set, points in and on the triangle, would constitute a core. Everyone in the group agrees that points in the triangular area are better than those outside it, and no movement from a point within it is unanimously supported.

20. An interesting, even amusing, study of the impressive power of a chairperson in a small club is reported in Levine and Plott (1977).

21. Schwartz (1981) proves that an element of coercion may be relevant for the stabilization of all trades.

22. In reality there often is a very thin line between cooperative and non-cooperative situations. Thus the distinction between the two branches of game theory remains fuzzy. One attempt to get around the problem, called the Nash program, was to reformulate all of game theory as a theory of non-cooperative games. While, in principle the reformulation is possible, in most cases it complicates rather than clarifies the problem.

23. In greater detail: two suspects for a major crime are taken into custody and separated. The police have enough evidence to convict them on a minor offense. The district attorney, believing correctly that they have committed the serious crime, lacks the evidence necessary to convict them. To strengthen her case, she offers each of the suspects: defect from your partner and confess, and we will be lenient. If you confess and your partner does not, you will be released (the best outcome -- the Temptation payoff: T) and your partner will get a maximum sentence (the worst outcome -- the Sucker's payoff: S); if the two of you continue to cooperate with each other, and neither of you confesses, you will both be convicted of the minor crime (the second best outcome -- the Reward payoff: R); if you both confess, you will both go to jail but the judge will be lenient (the third best outcome -- the Punishment payoff: P). What we have leads us to postulate that both prisoners (i and j) share preferences such that: $T >_{i,j} R >_{i,j} P >_{i,j} S$. This ordering of payoffs, the same for the two players, defines what is called a one-shot two-person PD game. Note that a different order of payoffs can be reasonably postulated (e.g., if not only jail terms but other factors matter). If this were the case, the game depicted would no longer be the PD (Rapoport 1992; Swistak 1992).

24. The PD is developed as a cooperative game in Ordeshook (1986, chaps. 7 and 8). The conclusion that the cooperative outcome is the sole element of the core requires an additional constraint: $T + S <_{i,j} 2R$, often included in the characterization of the PD.

25. For example, that neither information nor communication conditions matter when you play the PD game. Whether you know the payoffs to the other player, or not, you will defect. (Knowing your own payoffs is sufficient.) Similarly, players may negotiate, threaten, and promise, but if no binding commitments are possible, when it comes to the actual decision, no one has an incentive to keep their promise.

26. If we consider the Nash equilibrium as a reference point to compare with actual behavior, it often fails to predict accurately. A few reasons account for most of its failures. Two follow straight from the definition of the Nash solution: players fail to predict correctly, or they fail to maximize with respect to a prediction. Observations of these deviations have led to new directions of research and brought about many new solution concepts. The most important of these are reviewed and developed at length in any of the newer textbooks on game theory (see note ?). The analysis of these developments in non-cooperative game theory goes beyond the scope of the current essay. We should also note that there are justifications of Nash's notion which are not based on the correct prediction of the opponent's strategy. Concepts like minimax introduce some other constraints which get around the requirement of prediction as an essential aspect of rational calculation (see Frohlich and Oppenheimer 1978, chap. 3). Of course, Nash can fail as a predictor if a game, modeled as a non-cooperative situation, turns out to be a cooperative one. Then, as was the case with PD, a different outcome may result from the non-cooperative and the cooperative analyses.

27. These are often referred to as infinite-horizon games. They are modeled as infinitely repeated games with a "weighting"

parameter on future payoffs which may be interpreted as a probability of continuing the game in the next period, a discount parameter on future payoffs, or a parameter reflecting a joint effect of both.

28. If we define the "amount of cooperation" as an expected frequency of cooperative moves in a game, the folk theorems essentially state that any percent of cooperative moves, from 0% to 100%, can be attained in equilibrium. Folk Theorems derive their name from the fact that many game theorists believed them to be true before any formal proofs were published. They are reported to have been known (Aumann 1987) since the late 1950s or early 1960s. The plural form "theorems" is often used to indicate that the same proliferation of equilibria effects holds under various assumptions (e.g., Rubinstein 1979; and Fudenberg and Maskin 1986).

29. Alternative routes to a similar conclusion regarding the collective action problem can be seen in Hardin (1982) and Taylor (1987).

30. It should be noted that when we remove uncertainty about the future interactions and the exact termination period becomes known to both players, the possibility of cooperation is lost again. Mutual defections in all periods is the only equilibrium outcome of the game (cf. Luce and Raiffa 1957). The proof is based on the so-called backward induction argument, which hinges on a very demanding assumption of "common knowledge" (I know that he knows that I know that he knows ....). (Results related to common knowledge may be among the most important and consequential recent developments in game theory. The first formulation of the "common knowledge" concept is due to Lewis (1969). The first formalization was given by Aumann (1976).) While this deductive result was consistently in contrast with experimental observations, some recent theoretical results shed light on this discrepancy. In general, the "defect in all periods" solution turns out to be very vulnerable to small changes in the assumptions of the model. If, for example, the game is known to be finite but players do not know which period will be the last, the cooperative outcome is again a possible equilibrium (Basu 1987). Cooperation can also arise as an epsilon-equilibrium (Radner 1980; Fudenberg and Levine 1986) and as a result of a bounded complexity of strategies which players use (Neyman 1985). In short, the bad news here turned out not to be robust. The unique deficient equilibrium does not hold under small changes in the model.

31. To see how rare is the existence of the core, i.e., how demanding is the stability condition, consider a more general, yet still simple to analyze, class of games -- the so-called symmetric games. A game is called symmetric if the payoff to a coalition depends only on its size. This means that the payoff to all different but equal-size (e.g., two-person) coalitions is the same. In a symmetric game the core exists if, and only if, the payoff to the individuals in the equal share outcome is larger in the coalition of all than it is in any smaller coalition (Shubik 1982, 147). In other words, the core exists only if the coalition of all has the maximal per capita payoffs. For example, for any symmetric three-person game to have a core, a two-person coalition can get less than 2/3 of the payoff to the coalition of all three players. This is a very severe constraint on the payoffs. It is obviously not met in purely distributional games like the one in our example. The fact that the empty core shows up in all zero sum games, and in all symmetric games of the sort noted, sheds light on some more general mechanisms behind the difficulty with voting (i.e., that the problem does not stem from the spatial analogues). This, in turn, allows us to understand more fully the breadth and depth of what has come to be called the Arrow problem (again, see Shubik, *op. cit.*, for an interesting discussion).

32. Von Neumann and Morgenstern (1944, 260 et seq.), anticipating the problem of an empty core, adopted the so-called "stable set" as a solution concept in cooperative games. While stable sets usually exist, their problem is one of abundance, not scarcity: typically a game has many stable sets and, hence, the concept serves as a "weak" predictor of the outcome. Stable sets are often more useful for the purpose of seeing which outcomes will *not* be obtained. In the divide-a-

dollar game example, (1/2,1/2,0), (1/2,0,1/2), (0,1/2,1/2) are the only elements of the stable set. The reader who is intrigued why (1/3,1/3,1/3) is not predicted as a feasible outcome should consult any of the textbooks in the area for the definition and the discussion of this important solution concept (in Shubik 1982, cf. 157 et seq.).

33. One other important line of research was proposed by Shapley (1953), and is typically referred to as the Shapley value. It associates a unique payoff structure with every cooperative game. All the major value solutions are based on considerations of weighting and combining the values of possible outcomes.

34. Although Aumann and Maschler introduced this solution concept, they did not use it to predict which coalitions would form. Rather, they tried to predict which payoff structures would stabilize each of the possible coalitions. It took later work (Peleg 1963) to note how this can be extended to predict coalition formation. We should also note that the bargaining set is often large; such is the case in our example. Consequently, some refinements of the bargaining set have been developed. These include the kernel (a subset of the bargaining set), and the nucleolus (a single point in the kernel).

35. It should be noted that revelation of an individual's demand for a public good is a major problem: in general, individuals do not have an incentive to reveal their true preferences. When a person is thirsty and can buy a Coke, her choice to purchase the Coke is a revelation of her demand for the good. The same is not true, however, for public goods. The lack of voting for a candidate, for example, does not have to reflect the lack of desire for the candidate's victory; the voter might have simply conjectured that her preferred candidate will win regardless of her vote. In general, Samuelson (1954) argued that there was an inherent problem in getting a truthful or undistorted measure of individual demand for a public good. This problem was greatly embellished by a number of authors who were quite successful in inventing partial solutions (cf. Mueller 1989, chap. 8).

36. Such structurally induced outcomes are constrained by the status quo and the sets of preferences of the members of both groups. Formal analyses like the ones cited help to explain why membership on committees tends to be by those with the more intense interest in the issues governed by the committees. In experiments, Eavey and Miller (1984a) showed that the predicted distortion (toward the median voter of the committee and away from the median of the legislature) might not be as pronounced when there is solid bargaining between the two bodies.

37. Since some of the policies of the U.S. and foreign governments are now built on these ideas, discussion is often available in the popular press; see Weisskopf (1989). Some early work on the logical structure of the problem of using charges to manipulate environmental quality can be found in Kneese and Bower (1968, Part II).

38. Externalities are effects of market transactions which are not reflected in the market price. As such they can often be thought of as public goods.

39. Coase's theorem works under the assumption of negligible bargaining costs. It is often emphasized that "negligible bargaining costs" mean that Coase's theorem does not imply massive deregulation. But at least when the parties could, and would, be compensated for the costs of bargaining, and when these costs were less than those of regulation, Coase's result does imply deregulation.

40. It should be noted that any deductive proofs involving Rawls' conditions require specific formalization of his normative conditions. Since Rawls' own argument is a bit verbose, it cannot be known whether his argument is fully consistent with its formalization by Plott or Howe and Roemer. Regarding results on the attitudes towards risk, it is interesting to note that the core was shown to include Harsanyi's (1955) notions of maximizing the average when there was no risk aversion among the individuals.

41. The dilemma here may sound similar to the one in the Prisoners' Dilemma game. There too, the fact that each individual had

the right to choose led to the suboptimal result. Indeed, Bernholz (1976) and Miller (1977) show Prisoners' Dilemma to be a type of liberal paradox -- yet another unexpected connection in the complex labyrinth of results discussed here (also see the more general argument in Breyer and Gardner 1980).

42. Some major discrepancies between the axioms of the expected utility theory and the experimental data were found quite early (1950s and 60s). These early findings are usually associated with the so-called Ellsberg and Allais Paradoxes (see Schoemaker 1982 for an excellent review). A host of experimental studies followed in the 1970s and 80s (e.g., Lichtenstein and Slovik 1971; Grether and Plott 1979). Popular treatments of this technical material are available in Quattrone and Tversky (1988), Kahneman and Tversky (1982), and Tversky and Kahneman (1981). For some alternative directions of research see Kahneman and Tversky (1979), Machina (1989), Cox and Epstein (1987), and Holt (1986).

43. Experimental results in this area are varied. The main context in which a residual of non-self-interested behavior has continually shown up is that of Prisoners' Dilemma experiments (cf. Marwell and Ames 1981). But dissents are heard on this in later, better controlled experiments by Isaac et. al (1984 and 1985) and most recently, by Iwakura and Saijo (1992). Other studies like McKelvey and Palfrey (1991), show that in some non-market contexts one can generate a great deal of altruism.

Bibliography

Aivazian, V. A., and Jeffrey L. Callen. 1981. "The Coase Theorem and the Empty Core." *Journal of Law and Economics* 24:175-81.

Arrow, Kenneth. 1963. *Social Choice and Individual Values.* 2nd ed. New Haven: Yale University Press.

Arrow, Kenneth. 1977. "Current Developments in the Theory of Social Choice." *Social Research* 44:607-622.

Aumann, Robert J., and Michael Maschler. 1964. "The Bargaining Set for Cooperative Games." In *Advances in Game Theory*, ed. M. Dresher, L. S. Shapley, and R. Tucker. Princeton, NJ: Princeton University Press.

Aumann, Robert. 1976. "Agreeing to Disagree." *Annals of Statistics* 4:1236-39.

Aumann, Robert. 1987. "Game Theory." In *The New Palgrave: A Dictionary of Economics.* New York: Norton.

Axelrod, Robert. 1984. *The Evolution of Cooperation.* New York: Basic Books.

Axelrod, Robert, and Douglas Dion. 1988. "The Further Evolution of Cooperation." *Science* 242:1385-90.

Barry, Brian, and Russell Hardin. 1982. *Rational Man and Irrational Society.* Beverly Hills, CA: Sage.

Basu, Kaushik. 1987. "Modeling Finitely-Repeated Games with Uncertain Termination." *Economic Letters* 23:147-51.

Bendor, Jonathan, and Piotr Swistak. 1992a. "The Emergence and Stability of Cooperation." *Research Paper No. 1182.* Graduate School of Business, Stanford University.

Bendor, Jonathan, and Piotr Swistak. 1992b. "Characterization of Solution Concepts in Standard Evolutionary Games." *Research Paper No. 1183.* Graduate School of Business, Stanford University.

Bernholz, P. 1976. "Liberalism, Logrolling, and Cyclical Group Preferences." *Kyklos* 29:26-37.

Black, Duncan. 1958. *The Theory of Committees and Elections.* Cambridge: Cambridge University Press.

Black, Duncan, and R. Newing. 1951. *Committee Decisions with Complementary Valuations.* London: William Hodge.

Bonner, John. 1986. *Introduction to the Theory of Social Choice.* Baltimore: John Hopkins University Press.

Boyer, Mark. n.d. *International Cooperation and Public Goods: Opportunities for the Western Alliance.* Baltimore: Johns Hopkins University Press.

Brams, Steven J. 1975. *Game Theory and Politics.* New York: The Free Press.

Brams, Steven J. 1978. *The Presidential Election Game.* New Haven, CT: Yale University Press.

Brams, Steven J. 1980. *Biblical Games.* Cambridge, MA: MIT Press.

Brams, Steven J. 1985. *Superpower Games.* New Haven, CT: Yale University Press.

Breyer, F., and R. Gardner. 1980. "Liberal Paradox, Game Equilibrium, and Gibbard Optimum." *Public Choice* 35:469-81.

Buchanan, James. 1965. "An Economic Theory of Clubs." *Economica* 32:1-14.

Buchanan, James. 1968. *The Demand and Supply of Public Goods.* Chicago: Rand McNally.

Buchanan, James, and Gordon Tullock. 1962. *The Calculus of Consent.* Ann Arbor: University of Michigan Press.

Bueno de Mesquita, Bruce, and David Lalman. 1992. *War and Reason.* New Haven: Yale University Press.

Coase, Ronald H. 1960. "The Problem of Social Cost." *Journal of Law and Economics* 3:1-44.

Coughlin, Peter. 1984. "Probabilistic Voting Models." In *Encyclopedia of the Statistical Sciences: Vol. 6*, ed. Sam Kotz, Norman Johnson, and Campbell Read. New York: Wiley.

Coughlin, Peter. 1988. "Expectations about Voter Choices." *Public Choice* 44(1):49-59.

Coughlin, Peter, Dennis Mueller, and Peter Murrell. 1988. "Electoral Politics, Interest Groups, and the Size of Government." University of Maryland. Mimeo.

Cox, James C., and Seth Epstein. 1987. *Preference Reversals without the Independence Axiom.* Paper presented at Public Choice Meetings, Tucson, AZ.

Dawes, Roy, and John Orbell. 1982. "Cooperation in Social Dilemma Situations: Thinking about It Doesn't Help." In *Research in Experimental Economics*, Vol. 2, ed. Vernon Smith.

Davis, Morton D. 1983. *Game Theory: A Nontechnical Introduction.* Rev. ed. New York: Basic Books.

Downs, Anthony. 1957. *An Economic Theory of Democracy.* New York: Harper and Row.

Eavey, Cheryl L., and Gary J. Miller. 1984a. "Bureaucratic Agenda Control: Imposition or Bargaining?" *American Political Science Review* 78:719-33.

Eavey, Cheryl L., and Gary J. Miller. 1984b. "Fairness in Majority Rule Games with Core." *American Journal of Political Science* 28:570-86.

Ellickson, Bryan. 1973. "A Generalization of the Pure Theory of Public Goods." *American Economic Review* 63:417-32.

Elster, Jon. 1976. "Some Conceptual Problems in Political Theory." In *Power and Political Theory*, ed. Brian Barry. London: Wiley.

Elster, Jon. 1989. *Nuts and Bolts.* Cambridge: Cambridge University Press.

Enelow, James, and Melvin J. Hinich. 1984. *The Spatial Theory of Voting.* Cambridge: Cambridge University Press.

Ferejohn, John A., Robert Forsythe, and Roger G. Noll. 1979. "Practical Aspects of the Construction of Decentralized Decision-making Systems for Public Goods." In *Collective Decision Making: Applications from Public Choice Theory*, ed. Clifford S. Russell. Baltimore: Johns Hopkins Press for Resources for the Future.

Friedman, M. 1953. "The Methodology of Positive Economics." In *Essays in Positive Economics.* Chicago: University of Chicago Press.

Frohlich, Norman, Joe A. Oppenheimer, Tom Hunt, and Harrison Wagner. 1975. "Individual Contributions for Collective Goods: Alternative Models." *Journal of Conflict Resolution* 19:310-29.

Frohlich, Norman, and Joe A. Oppenheimer. 1970. "I Get By with a Little Help from My Friends." *World Politics* XXIII:104-21.

Frohlich, Norman, and Joe A. Oppenheimer. 1978. *Modern Political Economy.* Englewood Cliffs, NJ: Prentice Hall.

Frohlich, Norman, Joe A. Oppenheimer, and Oran Young. 1971. *Political Leadership and the Supply of Collective Goods.* Princeton, NJ: Princeton University Press.

Frohlich, Norman, Joe A. Oppenheimer, Pat Bond, and Irvin Boschman. 1984. "Beyond Economic Man." *Journal of Conflict Resolution* 28:3-24.

Frohlich, Norman, and Joe A. Oppenheimer. 1992. *Choosing Justice: An Experimental Approach to Ethical Theory.* Berkeley: California University Press.

Fudenberg, Drew, and David Levine. 1986. "Limit Games and Limit Equilibria." *Journal of Economic Theory* 38:261-79.

Fudenberg, Drew, and Eric Maskin. 1986. "The Folk Theorem in Repeated Games with Discounting or with Incomplete Information." *Econometrica* 54:533-54.

Fudenberg, Drew, and Jean Tirole. 1991. *Game Theory.* Cambridge, MA: The MIT Press.

Goetze, David, and Peter Galderisi. 1986. "A Place for Altruism in Political Theory." Paper presented at the 1986 Annual Meeting of the American Political Science Association, Washington, DC.

Grether, David M., and Charles R. Plott. 1979. "Economic Theory of Choice and the Preference Reversal Phenomenon." *American Economic Review* 69:623-38.

Guyton, John L., Elizabeth L. Blake, and Steven Leventhal. 1991. "An Experimental Test of Coasian Bargaining in Games with Empty Cores." Presented at Public Choice Society Annual Meeting, New Orleans, LA.

Hamburger, Henry. 1990. *Games as Models of Social Phenomena.* New York: W. H. Freeman, Inc.

Hardin, R. 1971. "Collective Action as an Agreeable N-Prisoners' Dilemma." *Behavioral Science* 16:472-79.

Hardin, R. 1982. *Collective Action.* Baltimore: Johns Hopkins University Press for Resources for the Future.

Harsanyi, John C. 1955. "Cardinal Welfare, Individualistic Ethics, and Interpersonal Comparisons of Utility." *Journal of Political Economy* 63:302-21.

Hempel, Carl G. 1965. *Aspects of Scientific Explanation.* New York: Macmillan Free Press.

Hinich, Melvin J. 1977. "Equilibrium in Spatial Voting: The Median Voter Result Is an Artifact." *Journal of Economic Theory* 16:208-19.

Hoffman, Elizabeth, and Matthew L. Spitzer. 1982. "The Coase Theorem: Some Experimental Tests." *Journal of Law and Economics* 25:73-98.

Hoffman, Elizabeth, and Matthew Spitzer. 1986. "Experimental Tests of the Coase Theorem with Large Bargaining Groups." *Journal of Legal Studies* 15:149-71.

Holt, Charles. 1986. "Preference Reversals and the Independence Axiom." *The American Economic Review* 76:508-13.

Howe, Roger E., and John E. Roemer. 1981. "Rawlsian Justice as the Core of a Game." *American Economic Review* 71:880-95.

Isaac, R. Mark, James M. Walker, and Susan H. Thomas. 1984. "Divergent Evidence on Free Riding: An Experimental Examination of Possible Explanations." *Public Choice* 43: 113-49.

Isaac, R. Mark, Kenneth F. McCue, and Charles R. Plott. 1985. "Public Goods Provision in an Experimental Environment." *Journal of Public Economics* 26:51-74.

Iwakura, Nobuyuki, and Tatsuyoshi Saijo. 1992. "Payoff Information Effects of Public Good Provision in the Voluntary Contribution Mechanism: An Experimental Approach." Paper presented at the 1992 Public Choice Meetings, New Orleans.

Kahneman Daniel, and Amos Tversky. 1982. "The Psychology of Preference." *Scientific American* 246:160-73.

Kahneman, Daniel, and Amos Tversky. 1979. "Prospect Theory: An Analysis of Decision Making under Risk." *Econometrica* 47:263-91.

Kneese, Allen V., and Blair T. Bower. 1968. *Managing Water Quality: Economics, Technology, Institutions.* Baltimore: Johns Hopkins University Press for Resources for the Future.

Kramer, Gerald. 1972. "Sophisticated Voting over Multidimensional Choice Spaces." *Journal of Mathematical Sociology* 2:165-80.

Kramer, Gerald. 1977. "A Dynamical Model of Political Equilibrium." *Journal of Economic Theory* 16:310-34.

Kreps, David. 1990a. *Game Theory and Economic Modeling.* New York: Oxford University Press.

Kreps, David. 1990b. *A Course in Microeconomic Theory.* Princeton NJ: Princeton University Press.

Lalman, David. 1988. "Conflict Resolution and Peace." *American Journal of Political Science* 32:590-615.

Laver, Michael, 1977. "Intergovernmental Policy on Multinational Corporations: A Simple Model of Tax Bargaining." *European Journal of Political Research* 5:363-80.

Levine, Michael, and Charles Plott. 1977. "Agenda Influence and Its Implications." *Virginia Law Review* 63:561-604.

Lewis, D. K. 1969. *Convention.* Cambridge, MA: Harvard University Press.

Lichtenstein, S., and P. Slovik. 1971. "Reversal of Preferences between Bids and Choices in Gambling Decisions." *Journal of Experimental Psychology* 89:46-55.

Luce, Duncan, and Howard Raiffa. [1957] 1985. *Games and Decisions.* New York: Wiley.

Machina, Mark J. 1989. "Dynamic Consistency and Non-Expected Utility Models of Choice under Uncertainty." *Journal of Economic Literature* XXVII:1622-68.

Margolis, Howard. 1982. *Selfishness, Altruism, and Rationality.* Cambridge: Cambridge University Press

Marwell, Gerald, and Ruth E. Ames. 1981. "Economists Ride Free, Does Anyone Else? Experiments on the Provision of Public Goods (IV)." *Journal of Public Economics* 15(4):295-310.

Maynard Smith, John. 1982. *Evolution and the Theory of Games.* Cambridge: Cambridge University Press.

Maynard Smith, John, and G. Price. 1973. "The Logic of Animal Conflict." *Nature* 246:15-18.

McKelvey, Richard D. 1976. "Intransitivities in Multidimensional Voting Models and Some Implications for Agenda Control." *Journal of Economic Theory* 12:472-82.

McKelvey, Richard D. 1979. "General Conditions for Global Intransitivities in Formal Voting Models." *Econometrica* 47:1085-11.

McKelvey, Richard D., Peter C. Ordeshook, and Mark D. Winer. 1978. "The Competitive Solution for n-Person Games without Transferable Utility." *American Political Science Review* 72:599-615.

McKelvey, Richard D., and Peter C. Ordeshook. 1981. "Experiments on the Core." *Journal of Conflict Resolution* 25:709-24.

McKelvey, Richard D., and T. Palfrey. 1991. "An Experimental Study of the Centipede Game." Mimeo. California Institute of Technology, Social Science Working Paper #739.

Miller, Gary J. 1981. *Cities by Contract: The Politics of Municipal Incorporation.* Cambridge: MIT.

Miller, Gary J., and T. H. Hammond. 1987. "The Core of the Constitution." *American Political Science Review* 81:1156-74.

Miller, Gary J., and T. H. Hammond. 1990. "Committees and the Core of the Constitution." *Public Choice* 66:201-28.

Miller, Gary J., and Joe A. Oppenheimer. 1982. "Universalism in Experimental Committees." *American Political Science Review* 76:561-74.

Miller, Nicholas R. 1977. "Social Preference and Game Theory: A Comment on the Dilemmas of a Paretian Liberal." *Public Choice* 30:23-28.

Miller, Nicholas R. 1980. "A New Solution Set for Tournaments and Majority Voting: Further Graph-Theoretical Approaches to the Theory of Voting." *American Journal of Political Science* 24:68-96.

Miller, Nicholas R. 1983a. "Pluralism and Social Choice." *American Political Science Review* 77:734-47.

Miller, Nicholas R. 1983b. "The Covering Relation in Tournaments: Two Corrections." *American Journal of Political Science* 27:382-85.

Mueller, Dennis C. 1989. *Public Choice II*. New York: Cambridge University Press.

Myerson, Roger B. 1991. *Game Theory: Analysis of Conflict*. Cambridge, MA: Harvard University Press.

Nagel, Ernest. 1963. "Assumptions in Economic Theory," *American Economic Review* (May):211-19.

Nash, J. F. 1953. "Two-person Cooperative Games." *Econometrica* 21:128-40.

Newman, Peter. 1965. *Theory of Exchange*. Englewood Cliffs: Prentice Hall.

Neyman, A. 1985. "Bounded Complexity Justifies Cooperation in the Finitely Repeated Prisoners' Dilemma." *Economic Letters* 19:227-30.

Niou, Emerson M. S., and Peter C. Ordeshook. 1986. "A Theory of the Balance of Power in International Systems." *Journal of Conflict Resolution* 30:685-715.

Niskanen, William. A. Jr. 1971. *Bureaucracy and Representative Government*. Chicago: Aldine.

Olson, Mancur. 1965. *The Logic of Collective Action*. Cambridge: Harvard University Press.

Olson, Mancur. 1982. *The Rise and Decline of Nations: Economic Growth, Stagflation, and Social Rigidities*. New Haven: Yale University Press.

Olson, Mancur, and R. Zeckhauser. 1966. "An Economic Theory of Alliances." *Review of Economics and Statistics* 48:266-79.

Oppenheimer, Joe A. 1979a. "Outcomes of Logrolling in the Bargaining Set and Democratic Theory: Some Conjectures." *Public Choice* 34:419-34.

Oppenheimer, Joe A. 1979b. "Collective Goods and Alliances: A Reassessment." *Journal of Conflict Resolution* 23:387-407.

Oppenheimer, Joe A. 1985. "Public Choice and Three Ethical Properties of Politics." *Public Choice* 45:241-55.

Ordeshook, Peter C. 1986. *Game Theory and Political Theory*. New York: Cambridge University Press.

Ordeshook, Peter C., and Mark Winer. 1980. "Coalitions and Spatial Policy Outcomes in Parliamentary Systems: Some Experimental Results." *American Journal of Political Science* 24:730-52.

Owen, Guillermo. 1982. *Game Theory*. New York: Academic Press.

Oye, Kenneth, ed. 1986. *Cooperation under Anarchy*. Princeton, NJ: Princeton University Press.

Peleg, Bezalel. 1963. "Bargaining Sets of Cooperative Games without Side Payments." *Israel Journal of Mathematics* 1:197-200.

Plott, Charles. 1967. "A Notion of Equilibrium and Its Possibility under Majority Rule." *American Economic Review* 57:787-806.

Plott, Charles R. 1979. "The Application of Laboratory Experimental Methods to Public Choice." In *Collective Decision Making: Applications from Public Choice Theory*, ed. Clifford S. Russell. Baltimore: Johns Hopkins Press for Resources for the Future.

Plott, Charles R. 1978. "Rawls's Theory of Justice: An Impossibility Result." In *Decision Theory and Social Ethics, Issues in Social Choice*, ed. Hans W. Gottinger and Werner Leinfellner. Dordrecht, Holland: Reidel.

Plott, Charles R. 1983. "Externalities and Corrective Policies in Experimental Markets." *The Economic Journal* 93:106-27.

Prior, A. N. 1967. "Correspondence Theory of Truth." *Encyclopedia of Philosophy*, vol. 2. New York: Macmillan.

Przeworski, Adam, and Michael Wallerstein. 1982. "The Structure of Class Conflict in Democratic Capitalist Societies." *American Political Science Review* 76:215-38.

Quattrone, George A., and Amos Tversky. 1988. "Contrasting Rational and Psychological Analyses of Political Choice." *American Political Science Review* 82:719-36.

Quine, W. V. O. 1970. *The Philosophy of Logic*. Englewood Cliffs, NJ: Prentice Hall.

Radner, Roy. 1980. "Collusive Behavior in Oligopolies with Long but Finite Lives." *Journal of Economic Theory* 22(2):136-56.

Rapoport, Anatol. 1992. "Game Theory Defined: What It Is and Is Not." *Rationality and Society* 4:74-82. (Special issue entitled *The Use of Game Theory in the Social Sciences*, ed. James S. Coleman)

Rasmusen, Eric. 1989. *Games and Information: An Introduction to Game Theory*. Oxford: Basil Blackwell.

Rawls, John. 1971. *A Theory of Justice*. Cambridge: Harvard University Press.

Riker, William. 1958. "The Paradox of Voting and Congressional Rules for Voting on Amendments." *American Political Science Review* 52:349-66.

Riker, William. 1962. *The Theory of Political Coalitions*. New Haven: Yale.

Romer, Thomas, and Howard Rosenthal. 1978. "Political Resource Allocation, Controlled Agendas, and the Status Quo." *Public Choice* 33:27-43.

Rubinstein, A. 1979. "Equilibrium in Supergames With the Overtaking Criterion." *Journal of Economic Theory* 21:1-9.

Samuelson, Paul. 1955. "A Diagrammatic Exposition of a Theory of Public Expenditure." *Review of Economics and Statistics* 37:350-56.

Samuelson, Paul. 1954. "The Pure Theory of Public Expenditure." *Review of Economics and Statistics* 36:387-89.

Schelling, Thomas C. 1963. *The Strategy of Conflict*. New York: Oxford University Press.

Schelling, Thomas C. 1978. *Micromotives and Macrobehavior*. New York: W.W. Norton.

Schoemaker, Paul J. H. 1982. "The Expected Utility Model: Its Variants, Purposes, Evidence, and Limitations." *Journal of Economic Literature* XX:529-63.

Schofield, Norman. 1978. "Instability of Simple Dynamic Games." *Review of Economic Studies* 45:575-94.

Schofield, Norman. 1980. "The Bargaining Set in Voting Games." *Behavioral Science* 25:120-29.

Schofield, Norman. 1982. "Bargaining Set Theory and Stability in Coalition Governments." *Mathematical Social Science* 3:9-31.

Schwartz, Thomas. 1981. "The Universal Instability Theorem." *Public Choice* 37(3):487-502.

Schwartz, Thomas. 1986. *The Logic of Collective Choice*. New York: Columbia University Press.

Sen, A. K. 1970a. *Collective Choice and Social Welfare*. New York: North Holland.

Sen, A. K. 1970b. The Impossibility of a Paretian Liberal." *Journal of Political Economy*. 78:152-57.

Sen, A. K. 1973. *On Economic Inequality*. New York: Norton.

Shapley, L. S. 1953. "A Value for N-person Games." In *Contributions to the Theory of Games*, vol. 2, ed. H.W. Kuhn and A. W. Tucker. Princeton, NJ: Princeton University Press.

Shepsle, Kenneth. 1979. "Institutional Arrangements and Equilibrium in Multidimensional Voting Models." *American Journal of Political Science* 23:27-59.

Shepsle, Kenneth, and Barry Weingast. 1981. "Structure Induced Equilibrium and Legislative Choice." *Public Choice* 37:503-20.

Shubik, Martin. 1982. *Game Theory in the Social Sciences*. Cambridge: MIT Press.

Smith, Vernon L. 1976. "Experimental Economics: Induced Value Theory." *American Economics Association: Papers and Proceedings* 66:274-79.

Snidal, Duncan. 1985. "Coordination versus Prisoners' Dilemma: Implications for International Cooperation and Regimes." *American Political Science Review* 79:923-47.

Soltan, Karol E. 1982. "Empirical Studies of Distributive Justice." *Ethics* 92:673-91.

Swistak, Piotr. 1992. "What Games? Why Equilibria? Which Equilibria? Three Problems with Game Theory." *Rationality and Society* 4:103-16. (Special issue entitled *The Use of Game Theory in the Social Sciences*, ed. James S. Coleman)

Taylor, Michael. 1987. *The Possibility of Cooperation*. New York: Cambridge University Press.

Tiebout, C. M. 1956. "A Pure Theory of Local Expenditures." *Journal of Political Economy* 64:416-24.

Tullock, Gordon. 1967. "The General Irrelevance of the General Impossibility Theorem." *Quarterly Journal of Economics* 81:256-70.

Tversky, Amos, and Daniel Kahneman. 1981. "The Framing of Decisions and the Psychology of Choice." *Science* 221:453-58.

Van Damme, Eric. 1987. *Stability and Perfection of Nash Equilibria*. Berlin: Springer-Verlag.

Von Mises, Richard. 1957. *Probability, Statistics, and Truth*. New York: George Allen and Unwin.

Von Neumann, John, and Oskar Morgenstern. 1944. *Theory of Games and Economic Behavior*. New York: Wiley.

Wagner, R. Harrison. 1986. "The Theory of Games and the Balance of Power." *World Politics* 38:546-76.

Weisskopf, Michael. "Free Market Strategy Puts Profits in Pollution Control: Clean Air Bill's Radical System of Incentives, Credits, Deadlines Could End 12-Year Statement in Congress." *Washington Post,* 12 November 1989, sec. H.

White, Alan R. 1967. "Coherence Theory of Truth." *Encyclopedia of Philosophy*, vol. 2. New York: Macmillan.

Wildavsky, Aaron. 1992. "Indispensable Framework or Just Another Ideology? Prisoners' Dilemma as an Antihierarchical Game." *Rationality and Society* 4:8-23. (Special issue entitled *The Use of Game Theory in the Social Sciences*, ed. James S. Coleman)

Wittman, Donald A. 1977. "Candidates with Policy Preferences: A Dynamic Model." *Journal of Economic Theory* 14:108-9.

Wittman, Donald. 1979. "Diagrammatic Exposition of Justice." *Theory and Decision* 11:207-37.

5

The Comparative Method

David Collier

Comparison is a fundamental tool of analysis. It sharpens our power of description, and plays a central role in concept-formation by bringing into focus suggestive similarities and contrasts among cases. Comparison is routinely used in testing hypotheses, and it can contribute to the inductive discovery of new hypotheses and to theory-building.

The forms of comparison employed in the discipline of political science vary widely and include those contained in statistical analysis, experimental research, and historical studies. At the same time, the label "comparative method" has a standard meaning within the discipline and in the social sciences more broadly: it refers to the methodological issues that arise in the systematic analysis of a small number of cases, or a "small N."[1] This chapter examines alternative perspectives on the comparative method that have emerged over roughly the past two decades. Although the primary focus is on discussions located in the fields of comparative politics and international studies, the application of the comparative method is by no means restricted to those fields.

The decision to analyze only a few cases is strongly influenced by the types of political phenomena under study and how they are conceptualized. Topics for which it is productive to examine relatively few cases include revolutions, particular types of national political regimes (e.g., post-communist regimes), or particular forms of urban political systems. This focus on a small number of cases is adopted because there exist relatively few instances of the phenomenon under consideration that exhibit the attributes of interest to the analyst. Alternatively, some analysts believe that political phenomena in general are best understood through the careful examination of a small number of cases. In the field of comparative and international studies, the practice of focusing on few cases has achieved greater legitimacy in recent years in conjunction with the rise of the school of "comparative historical analysis," in which small numbers of countries are studied over long periods. This close scrutiny of each country limits the number of national cases a scholar can consider.[2]

Choosing to study few cases routinely poses the problem of having more rival explanations to assess than cases to observe, or the quandary of "many variables, small N" (Lijphart 1971, 686). Elementary statistics teaches us that as the number of explanatory factors approaches the number of cases, the capacity to adjudicate among the explanations through statistical comparison rapidly diminishes. This problem has stimulated much discussion of how most productively to analyze a small N.

The late 1960s and early 1970s saw a boom in writing on comparative method (e.g., Merritt and Rokkan 1966; Kalleberg 1966; Verba 1967; Smelser 1968; Lasswell 1968; Przeworski and Teune 1970; Sartori 1970; Merritt 1970; Etzioni and Dubow 1970; Lijphart 1971; Vallier 1971; Zelditch 1971; Armer and Grimshaw 1973). This literature established a set of norms and practices for small-N research, proposed alternative strategies for conducting such analyses, and created a base line of understanding that has played an important role in the ongoing practice of small-N studies. This chapter assesses the issues of comparative method that have been debated in the intervening years and considers their implications for ongoing research. The point of departure is Arend Lijphart's (1971) article "Comparative Politics and Comparative Method." Among the studies published in that period, Lijphart's piece stands out for its imaginative synthesis of basic issues of comparison and of the relation between comparative method and other branches of methodology.[3] It therefore provides a helpful framework for examining, and building upon, new developments in the field.

A central theme that emerges in the discussion below is that refinements in methods of small-N analysis have substantially broadened the range of techniques available to comparative researchers. The most fruitful approach is eclectic, one in which scholars are willing and able to draw upon these diverse techniques.

Synopsis of Lijphart

Lijphart defines the comparative method as the analysis of a small number of cases, entailing at least two observations, yet too few to permit the application of conventional statistical analysis. A central goal of his article is to assess the comparative method in relation to three other methods--experimental, statistical, and case-study--and to evaluate these different approaches by two criteria: 1) how well they achieve the goal of testing theory through adjudicating among rival explanations, and 2) how difficult it is to acquire the data needed to employ each method (see Figure 1).

The experimental method has the merit of providing strong criteria for eliminating rival explanations through experimental control, but unfortunately it is impossible to generate appropriate experimental data for most topics relevant to political analysis. The statistical method has the merit of assessing rival explanations through the weaker but still valuable procedure of statistical control, but it is often not feasible to collect a sufficiently large set of reliable data to do this form of analysis.

The case-study method has the merit of providing a framework in which a scholar with modest time and resources can generate what may potentially be useful data on a particular case. Unfortunately, opportunities for systematically testing hypotheses are far more limited than with the other methods. Yet Lijphart (pp. 691-93) insists that case studies do make a contribution to testing hypotheses and building theory, and he offers a suggestive typology of case studies based on the nature of this contribution. He distinguishes among *atheoretical* case studies; *interpretative* case studies (that self-consciously use a theory to illuminate a particular case); *hypothesis-generating* case studies; *theory-confirming* case studies; *theory-infirming* case studies (that, although they cannot by themselves disconfirm a theory, can raise doubts about it); and *deviant case* analyses (that seek to elaborate and refine theory through a close examination of a case that departs from the predictions of an established theory). Lijphart emphasizes that "certain types of case studies can even be considered implicit parts of the comparative method" (p. 691), and to the extent that the assessment of hypotheses does occur in some case studies, it is often because the case studies are placed in an implicit or explicit comparative framework. Yet even within this framework, he emphasizes that findings from a single case should not be given much weight in the evaluation of hypotheses and theory (p. 691).

The comparative method, as defined by Lijphart, has an intermediate status in terms of both his criteria. It provides a weaker basis than the experimental or statistical method for evaluating hypotheses, due to the lack of experimental control and the problem of many variables, small N. Yet it does offer a stronger basis for evaluating hypotheses than do case studies. Despite the constraint of addressing more variables than cases, the comparative method allows systematic comparison that, if appropriately utilized, can contribute to adjudicating among rival explanations.

Although the data requirements of the comparative method may be much greater than for case studies, Lijphart argues that they are less demanding than for experimental or statistical research. He therefore views the comparative method as most appropriate in research based on modest resources, and he suggests that studies using the comparative method might often serve as a first step toward statistical analysis.

> If at all possible one should generally use the statistical (or perhaps even the experimental) method instead of the weaker comparative method. But often, given the inevitable scarcity of time, energy, and financial resources, the intensive comparative analysis of a few cases may be more promising than a more superficial statistical analysis of many cases. In such a situation, the most fruitful approach would be to regard the comparative analysis as the first stage of research, in which hypotheses are carefully formulated, and the statistical analysis as the second stage, in which these hypotheses are tested in as large a sample as possible. (1971, 685)

Lijphart also proposes solutions to both sides of the problem of many variables, small N (1971, 686 ff). With regard to the small number of cases, even if researchers stop short of a statistical study, they can nonetheless try to increase the number of cases used in assessing hypotheses. With regard to the large number of variables, he suggests two approaches. First, analysts can focus on "comparable cases," that is, on cases that a) are matched on many variables that are *not* central to the study, thus in effect "controlling" for these variables; and b) differ in terms of the key variables that *are* the focus of analysis, thereby allowing a more adequate assessment of their influence. Hence, the selection of cases acts as a partial substitute for statistical or experimental control. Second, analysts can reduce the number of variables either by combining variables in a single scale or through theoretical parsimony, that is, through developing a theory that focuses on a smaller number of explanatory factors.

Thus, Lijphart provides a compact formulation of the relationship between the comparative method and

Figure 1. Situating the Comparative Method as of 1971: Lijphart's Scheme

Case Study Method	Comparative Method	Experimental Method

Case Study Method

Merit: Permits intensive examination of cases even with limited resources

Inherent Problem: Contributes less to building theory than studies with more cases

Types of Case Studies:
1. Atheoretical
2. Interpretive
3. Hypothesis-generating
4. Theory-confirming
5. Theory-infirming (i.e., case studies that weaken a theory marginally)
6. Deviant case studies

Comparative Method

Defined as: Systematic analysis of small number of cases ("small-N" analysis)

Merit: "Given inevitable scarcity of time, energy, and financial resources, the intensive analysis of a few cases may be more promising than the superficial statistical analysis of many cases" (Lijphart, p. 685)

Inherent Problem: Weak capacity to sort out rival explanations, specifically, the problem of "many variables, few cases"

Potential Solutions:
1. Increase number of cases
2. Focus on comparable cases
3. Reduce number of variables
    a. Combine variables
    b. Employ more parsimonious theory

Experimental Method

Merit: Eliminates rival explanations through experimental control

Inherent Problem: Experimental control is impossible for many or most topics of relevance to field of comparative politics

Statistical Method

Merit: Assesses rival explanations through statistical control

Inherent Problem: Difficult to collect adequate information in a sufficient number of cases, due to limited time and resources

other methodologies, and he offers solutions to the characteristic dilemmas of the comparative method.

Further Perspectives on Small-N Analysis

The two decades following Lijphart's study have seen the emergence of new perspectives on small-N analysis, as well as a renewed focus on methodological alternatives already available before he wrote his article. Though many of these innovations appear in work explicitly concerned with the comparative method, conventionally understood, others appear in writing on the experimental, statistical, and case-study methods. The result has been an intellectual cross-fertilization of great benefit to the comparative method. Figure 2 provides an overview of these innovations.

Innovations in the Comparative Method

Innovations in the comparative method can be discussed in terms of the issues introduced above, encompassing the goals of comparison, the justification for focusing on few cases, and the problem of many variables, small N.

Goals of Comparison

A central and legitimate goal of comparative analysis is assessing rival explanations. However, as Theda Skocpol and Margaret Somers (1980) argue, comparative studies should be understood not merely in terms of this single goal, but in terms of three distinct, yet ultimately connected, goals.[4] The first is that considered above: the systematic examination of covariation among cases for the purpose of *causal analysis*.[5] The second is the examination of a number of cases with the goal of showing that a particular model or set of concepts usefully illuminates these cases. No real test of the theory occurs, but rather the goal is the *parallel demonstration of theory*. This use of comparison plays an important role in the process through which theories are developed. The third type of comparison is the examination of two or more cases in order to highlight how different they are, thus establishing a framework for interpreting how parallel processes of change are played out in different ways within each context. This *contrast of contexts* is central to the more "interpretive" side of the social sciences and reflects yet another way that comparison is frequently used.

In addition to providing a more multifaceted account of the goals of comparison, Skocpol and Somers suggest the intriguing idea of a research "cycle" among

these approaches (pp. 196-197). This cycle arises in response to the problems that emerge as scholars push each approach up to -- or beyond -- the limits of its usefulness. For example, a "parallel demonstration" scholar might introduce a new theory and show how it applies to many cases. "Hypothesis-testing" scholars, wanting to specify the conditions under which the theory does not hold, could make further comparisons with the goal of discovering these conditions. Hypothesis-testing studies that too brashly compare cases that are profoundly different might, in turn, stimulate "contrast of contexts" scholars to examine more carefully the meaning of the differences among the cases. It is thus useful to look beyond an exclusive focus on the role of comparison in broad causal analysis, to an understanding that encompasses the different elements in this research cycle.

This is not to say that assessing hypotheses does not remain a paramount goal of comparison, and many scholars insist that it is the paramount goal. Yet this broader perspective offers a valuable account of how comparative work proceeds within a larger research community, pointing usefully to the interaction among different goals of comparison.

Justification for Small N

A second trend is toward a more elaborate justification of a focus on relatively few cases. Lijphart's rationale seems in retrospect rather modest, in that it emphasizes only the problem of inadequate resources and treats the small-N comparison as a way station on the route to more sophisticated statistical analysis.

A very different defense of working either with a small N or with case studies had previously been available in arguments favoring a "configurative" approach (Heckscher 1957, 46-51, 85-107), and this perspective was elaborated a few years before the publication of Lijphart's analysis in Sidney Verba's (1967) review essay advocating the "disciplined configurative approach." In evaluating Robert A. Dahl's *Political Oppositions in Western Democracies* (1966), Verba points both to the sophistication of the hypotheses entertained in the book and to the difficulty of assessing them adequately, except through a close command of the cases, leading him to advocate this disciplined configurative mode of research. Verba's formulation is appealing because he is concerned with systematic hypothesis testing and theory building. At the same time, he links this priority with a more explicit appreciation of the difficulty of testing hypotheses adequately and the value of properly executed case studies in providing subtle assessments of hypotheses.

It might be claimed that the difficulty of adequately testing hypotheses ultimately derives from the

Figure 2. Innovations Relevant to the Comparative Method

Case Study Method

New Perspectives on Case Studies

1. New defense of the case study method (Campbell)
2. Refinements in Lijphart's typology of case studies (Eckstein, George)
3. Improvement of causal analysis in case studies through "process tracing" (George and McKeown)
4. Critique of value of case studies in assessing rational choice theory (Achen and Snidal)

Comparative Method

Broadened Understanding of Types of Comparative Studies

1. Emphasis on interpretive understanding
2. Idea of a "research cycle" among the types (Skocpol and Somers)

Further Justifications for Focus on a Small-N

1. To pursue "disciplined configurative approach" (Verba, reinforced by Almond and Genco)
2. To avoid problem of "conceptual stretching" (Sartori)
3. To facilitate "thick description" and other forms of interpretive understanding (Geertz and many others)
4. To achieve analytic depth of case-oriented approach (Ragin)

Debates on Solutions to Problem of Many Variables, Small-N

1. Value of increasing number of cases
2. Comparable cases versus contrasting cases (Lijphart versus Przeworski and Teune)
3. Reducing number of variables in conjunction with using stronger theory

Experimental Method

Diffusion of Older Ideas and Introduction of New Ideas on Quasi-Experimental Design

1. Methodology of quasi-experiments and interrupted time-series design becomes more widely known
2. Analysis of the Connecticut crackdown on speeding as exemplar of interrupted time-series analysis (Campbell and Ross)
3. Diffusion of ideas about quasi-experiments encouraged by codification of evaluation research
4. Proposed statistical solution to problem of selection bias in quasi-experiments (Achen)

Statistical Method

New Warnings and New Solutions

1. Criticism of standard statistical practice in the social sciences (Freedman)
2. New statistical techniques relevant to small-N analysis
3. Effort to refine statistical analysis of a small-N in the debate on corporatism and economic growth in Western Europe (Lange-Garrett-Jackman-Hicks-Patterson)

problem of limited resources discussed by Lijphart. If enough talented researchers worked long and hard, they could carry out a *Political Oppositions* study for many dozens of countries. Yet the problem here is somewhat different from that emphasized in Lijphart's initial formulation. It is not so much that resources are limited, but that constructing adequate comparisons has proved more difficult than had often been thought in the 1960s and early 1970s, in the initial days of enthusiasm for comparative statistical research. Among these difficulties, that of the valid application of concepts across diverse contexts has been especially vexing.

Within the literature on comparative method, a key step in elucidating these problems of validity, and thereby strengthening the justification for a small N, is Giovanni Sartori's (1970) classic discussion of "Concept Misformation in Comparative Politics," the basic themes of which are elaborated in his later book *Social Science Concepts* (1984). Sartori suggests that the application of a concept to a broader range of cases can lead to conceptual "stretching," as some of the meanings associated with the concept fail to fit the new cases. The concepts that can most easily be applied to a broad range of cases are often so general that they do not bring into focus the similarities and contrasts among cases that are essential building blocks in worthwhile comparative analysis. Consequently, a study focused on concepts that are carefully adapted to this "finer slicing" of a given set of cases should be extended to other cases only with great caution. From this perspective, it may be argued that the most interesting studies will often be those that focus on a smaller number of cases.

With regard to the problems of increasing the number of cases under study,[6] Adam Przeworski and Henry Teune's *The Logic of Comparative Social Inquiry* (1970) is a major source of insight. Although they argue that achieving a high level of generality should be a basic goal of social science, their framework is centrally concerned with the difficulties that can arise in generalizing beyond an initial set of cases. With regard to problems of validity, they advocate the use, when necessary, of "system-specific" indicators that serve to operationalize the *same* concept in *distinct* ways in different contexts (pp. 124-130). For the scholar seeking to move toward a larger set of cases, the potential need for system-specific indicators necessitates the close examination of every new case.

Przeworski and Teune also address the problem that as the analyst incorporates more cases into a study, distinct causal patterns may appear in the new cases. To deal with this problem, Przeworski and Teune advocate "replacing proper names" of social systems by identifying those systems in terms of the explanatory factors that account for why causal relations take a particular form within each system (pp. 26-30).[7] This approach makes the invaluable contribution of providing a theoretical, rather than an idiosyncratic and case-specific, basis for analyzing differences in causal patterns. However, extending an analysis to additional cases on the basis of this procedure again requires a painstaking assessment of each new context. Thus, Przeworski and Teune provide a valuable tool for adequately analyzing a larger number of cases, but their approach again shows that this must be done with caution.

Since 1970, the renewal of a Weberian concern with interpretive understanding, i.e., with deciphering the meaning of behavior and institutions to the actors involved, has also strengthened the justification for advancing cautiously with one or very few cases. Clifford Geertz's (1973) label "thick description" is commonly evoked to refer to this concern,[8] and this focus has appeared in many guises relevant to political research, including Gabriel Almond and Stephen J. Genco's analysis of "Clouds and Clocks" (1977) and Skocpol and Somers' "contrast of contexts" approach, which encompasses studies that use comparison to richly contextualize research findings. Charles C. Ragin's *The Comparative Method* (1987) explores another facet of this concern in his analysis of the "holistic" orientation of what he calls "case-oriented" research and the complex problems of "conjunctural causation" -- that is, causal patterns that vary according to the context -- to which configurative scholars are typically far more sensitive.

Finally, the intellectual success in recent years of the school of comparative historical analysis has played an important role in legitimating a focus on a small N. This approach was pioneered in works such as Reinhard Bendix (1964), Barrington Moore (1966), and Lipset and Rokkan (1967), and more recent works include Rokkan (1970), Tilly (1975), Paige (1975), Bendix (1978), Trimberger (1978), Skocpol (1979), Bergquist (1986), Luebbert (1991), Goldstone (1991), Collier and Collier (1991), and Rueschemeyer, Stephens, and Stephens (1992). Methodological statements focused on this tradition include Skocpol and Somers (1980), Skocpol (1984), Tilly (1984), and Ragin (1987).

The particular form of analysis in these studies varies considerably, as suggested by Skocpol and Somers' typology noted above. In varying combinations, these studies employ both rigorous qualitative comparisons that extend across a number of nations, and also historical analysis that often evaluates each national case over a number of time periods.[9] This tradition of research thus combines well-thought-out comparison with an appreciation of historical context, thereby contributing to an effort to "historicize" the social sciences.

Although the uses of comparison in this literature are diverse, as Skocpol and Somers emphasized, it may be argued that a major consequence of the growing importance of comparative historical studies is to further legitimate the approach that was Lijphart's original concern: the assessment of rival explanations, based on systematic, qualitative comparison of a small number of cases. In light of a spectrum of studies from Barrington Moore's (1966) pioneering analysis of the emergence of alternative forms of modern regimes, to Skocpol's (1979) study of revolution, to Luebbert's (1991) analysis of the emergence of liberalism, fascism, and social democracy in interwar Europe, it is evident that this literature has given new legitimacy to the use of broad historical comparison for systematic causal analysis. Efforts to codify procedures for assessing hypotheses in this type of analysis, such as that in Ragin's *Comparative Method* (1987), further reinforce the plausibility of insisting on the viability of small-N analysis as a middle ground between case studies and statistical studies.

Solutions to the Problem of Many Variables, Small N

The evolving debates on comparative method have suggested further refinements in Lijphart's original three solutions for the problem of many variables, small N, i.e.: 1) increasing the number of cases, 2) focusing on matched cases, and 3) reducing the number of variables.

1. *Increase the Number of Cases* At the time Lijphart wrote, it was believed in some circles that comparative social science would increasingly be oriented toward large-N comparative studies, based on extensive quantitative data sets and rigorous statistical analysis. Today there can be no question that, for better or worse, quantitative cross-national research in the subfield of comparative politics, and quantitative international politics in the subfield of international relations, have not come to occupy as dominant a position as many had expected. Within these two subfields, they hold the status of one approach among many.

Various factors have placed limits on the success of large-N research based on quantitative data sets, among which is certainly the renewed concern with closely contextualized analysis and interpretive studies. Broad quantitative comparison may have been set back as many scholars discovered how extraordinarily time-consuming it is to construct appropriate data sets, often out of proportion to the professional rewards that seem to be forthcoming. This is particularly a problem when the focus of analysis extends beyond the advanced industrial countries to regions for which it is often extremely difficult to develop reliable data. In addition, the quantitative-comparative approach has probably been hurt by the publication of too many studies in which concepts are operationalized with dubious validity and which employ causal tests that are weak, unconvincing, or inappropriate (Ragin 1987, chap. 4).

Yet the fact that broad quantitative comparison has not become a predominant approach should not lead scholars to overlook what has been accomplished. Robert Jackman (1985) insists that comparative statistical research has had more success than is recognized, and Lijphart's own recent work moves in this direction (1990). The failure to seize good opportunities to do quantitative research could certainly be viewed as being as much of a mistake as premature quantification, and the fruitful debate on corporatism and economic growth in Western Europe discussed below is one of many examples of how statistical methods can effectively address interesting analytic issues. Further, the availability of new statistical techniques (also discussed below) has made it far more productive to do quantitative analyses with as few as ten to fifteen cases. Consequently, the option of increasing the "N" at least to that level is still worth pursuing, and it should probably be pursued more often.

2. *Focus on Comparable Cases* The recommendation that analysts focus on carefully matched cases has been both reinforced and challenged. In a discussion published in the mid-1970s, Lijphart (1975) explores further the trade-off he noted in 1971 between the goal of increasing the number of cases and the goal of matching cases as a substitute for statistical control. Obviously, if a researcher is to select cases that are really similar, however that similarity is defined, the number of appropriate cases is likely to become limited. In the face of this trade-off, Lijphart opts in favor of the more careful matching of fewer cases, and he goes so far as to restrict the application of the term "comparative method" to analyses that focus on a small number of carefully matched cases. This emphasis parallels a much earlier perspective on the comparative method referred to as the method of "controlled comparison" (Eggan 1954). Arthur Stinchcombe's (1978) advocacy of the methodology of "deep analogy," i.e., the comparative analysis of very few, extremely closely matched, cases pushes this approach even further.

A contrasting strategy is advocated by Przeworski and Teune (1970, 32-39) and Przeworski (1987, 38-41). They suggest that even with careful matching of cases in what they label a "most similar" systems design, there remains a problem of "overdetermination," in that this design fails to eliminate many rival explanations, leaving the researcher with no criteria for choosing among them. They prefer instead a "most different" systems design, based on a set of cases which are highly diverse and among which the analyst traces similar processes of change.[10] Przeworski suggests that the strength of this design is in part responsible for important advances in the literature on democratization, such as the work of O'Donnell, Schmitter, and Whitehead (1986). Przeworski maintains that this literature addresses such a broad range of cases that analysts are forced to distill out of that diversity a set of common elements that prove to have great explanatory power.[11]

This discussion can be placed in perspective by recognizing that cases that are closely matched from one point of view may contrast sharply from another. My own recent work (Collier and Collier 1991) combines the two strategies by starting with a set of eight Latin American countries that are roughly matched on a number of broad dimensions. Among the eight countries, the analysis focuses on pairs of countries that are nonetheless markedly different. The overall matching assures that the contexts of analysis are analytically equivalent, at least to a significant degree, and the paired comparison places parallel processes of change in sharp relief because they are operating in settings that are very different in many respects.

In conjunction with the debate over the merits of most similar and most different systems designs, it is important to recognize that in many studies, the conclusions reached in the overall comparison of cases are also assessed -- implicitly and sometimes explicitly -- through within-case analysis. In the section on case studies below, the discussion of "pattern matching" and "process tracing" suggests some of the forms this takes. It is no coincidence that within the school of comparative historical analysis, findings are often reported in books, rather than articles. Part of the reason is that the presentation of detailed information on each case serves to further validate the conclusions drawn from comparisons across cases.

These within-case comparisons are critical to the viability of small-N analysis. As Stanley Lieberson (1991, 312-315) has correctly insisted, taken by themselves, comparisons across a small number of cases, using either a most similar or a most different systems design, provide a weak basis for causal inference. However, if one considers the role of these internal comparisons, the "N" is substantially increased, thereby strengthening causal analysis.[12]

This use of within-case comparison can also help protect the analyst from a problem that arises in the most different systems design, in which countries are matched on the dependent variable and differ in terms of a series of background variables. Barbara Geddes (1990) has shown that if cases are selected on the basis of scores on the dependent variable, which is how most different systems designs are often carried out, the lack of variance on the outcome to be explained introduces a "selection bias" that can greatly weaken causal inference. One way of mitigating this problem is to introduce greater variability through internal comparison.

The ongoing debate on most similar versus most different systems designs has implications for the status of area studies. Dankwart Rustow (1968) argued some time ago in favor of moving beyond an area studies approach, and many scholars agree that cases should be selected in response to the analytic requirements of particular research projects, rather than on the basis of a geographic proximity that at best is often a poor substitute for the analytic matching of cases. Recent "cross-area" studies on successful export-led growth and on democracy suggest that this alternative perspective is gaining ground.[13]

However, the area studies approach is a booming business today for a variety of reasons, including the impressive funding of area studies by U.S. foundations in recent decades, as well as institutional momentum. In fact, from the point of view of the theoretically oriented small-N comparativist, this is not a bad outcome. The country case studies produced by area specialists are crucial building blocks in most comparative work, and without them cross-area studies would be on far weaker ground. It is essential to recognize that these case studies benefit greatly from the intellectual leverage gained when individual scholars develop, over many years, a cumulative and well-contextualized understanding of a particular region. Particularly in light of current concerns that broad comparative studies should be attentive to the context of analysis, the contribution of area specialists is essential.

3. *Reduce the Number of Variables*: The third solution to the small-N problem is to reduce the number of explanatory factors, either through combining variables, sometimes referred to as "data reduction," or through employing a theoretical perspective that focuses on a smaller set of explanatory factors. One of the promising sources of parsimonious explanatory theory is the "rational choice" approach that has gained increasing attention among political scientists. Rational choice modeling offers a productive means of simplifying arguments that contain a multitude of interesting variables, but that may fail to specify the most critical ones. Within the field of comparative analysis, Geddes's (1991) study of administrative reform in Latin America, which models the impact of different electoral and party systems on the incentives of legislators to adopt reform, provides an excellent example of a productive simplification of a complex topic. As such models gain increasing acceptance in the comparative field, analysts will acquire a useful tool for addressing the small-N problem.[14]

More work on concept formation is also needed, notwithstanding the sustained contribution of Sartori

(1970, 1984, 1991, 1993, and Sartori, Riggs, and Teune 1975); the work of authors such as McKinney (1966), Kalleberg (1966), and DeFelice (1980); and also Burger's (1976) invaluable synthesis of the Weberian approach to concept formation. Comparativists do not devote enough attention to thinking through how well or poorly concepts are serving them and therefore may have insufficient ground for knowing whether they are making appropriate choices in the effort to achieve theoretical parsimony.

The field of cognitive science has recently provided insights into categorization that may be useful in refining the concepts employed in comparative studies. The application of these insights is illustrated by George Lakoff's (1987) challenge to frameworks, such as that of Sartori, that employ what Lakoff calls "classical categorization," in which the meaning of concepts is understood in terms of defining characteristics that are seen as giving the concepts well-defined boundaries. This understanding is crucial to Sartori's framework, in that the problem of conceptual stretching which he analyzes hinges on these boundaries. Cognitive scientists argue that in ordinary language, the meaning of concepts derives not from defining characteristics, but from an implicit "cognitive model" that underlies the concept and from "exemplar" cases that serve to anchor the concept's meaning and provide a point of reference for identifying better and worse cases. This perspective provides a different view of the question of boundaries, and hence of conceptual stretching. More work is needed to discover the degree to which these patterns in ordinary language are also present in social science usage, and if so, the implications for the use of concepts in comparative analysis (see Collier and Mahon 1993).

Innovations Suggested by Work on Other Methods

Experimental Method

Although the experimental method itself may be of little relevance to the topics addressed in most comparative research, ideas derived from the experimental method can improve small-N studies. Donald Campbell and Julian Stanley's classic *Experimental and Quasi-Experimental Designs for Research* (1963) shows how the logic of experimental design can be applied to "quasi-experiments," that is, to "observational" studies that include some event or innova-tion that has a form analogous to an experimental intervention, but that occurs in a "natural" setting. An example would be the initiation of a new public policy whose impact one wishes to assess.

Campbell and Stanley underline the great value in quasi-experiments of the "interrupted time series"

design. In this design the analyst looks at a long series of observations over time, so that the values of the observed variable are examined not only at two points immediately before and after the policy change or other innovation (which "interrupts" the series), but also well before and well after. To illustrate the risk of restricting the analysis to these two observations, the authors present several hypothetical configurations of data in which restricting the analysis to two observations leads to a finding of sharp discontinuity, whereas the full time series reveals continuity. Causal inferences about the impact of discrete events can be risky without an extended series of observations. Comparativists employing small-N analysis must heed this warning, since they routinely analyze the impact of discrete events, ranging from wars, revolutions, and military coups to specific public policies.

Donald Campbell and Laurence Ross's (1968) subse-quent analysis of the impact on traffic fatalities of the Connecticut crackdown on speeding in the 1950s provides a stunning "exemplar" of the imaginative application of a quasi-experimental design to public policy analysis. Indeed, Przeworski (1987, 31) has argued that methodology is influenced far more by exemplars than by formal attempts to "legislate" correct methods, and the Connecticut crackdown article has certainly played that role.[15]

The case appears to be a simple one. When the State of Connecticut initiated strict enforcement of the vehicular speed limit in the 1950s and traffic deaths dropped sharply, the cause and effect relationship seemed obvious. Yet in evaluating this causal link, Campbell and Ross do an impressive analysis of potential threats to its "internal validity" (was that really the cause in Connecticut?) and its "external validity" (can the finding be generalized?). No sensitive analyst can read this article without acquiring a more sober view of the problems of evaluating policy impacts.

Ideas about quasi-experimental and interrupted time series design have also been disseminated through the large body of writing on evaluation research. This includes studies that apply these ideas to the analysis of political development (Hoole 1978), as well as excellent treatments of experimental design and evaluation research in introductory textbooks on social science methodology, such as Babbie (1992).

Although much writing on quasi-experiments appears to offer helpful guidance and practical advice to small-N analysts, Christopher H. Achen's *The Statistical Analysis of Quasi-Experiments* (1986) may leave them feeling that the methodological challenges posed by this type of design are overwhelming. In studies of the impact of public policy, the core problem is the lack of "randomization" in the application of the policy, which may result in selection bias. For example, the benefits of a policy are commonly received by some groups and not by others, on the basis of certain attributes possessed by the groups, and it is possible that these prior attributes will themselves reinforce the outcomes that the policy seeks to promote. In the absence of true experimental data, this poses the challenge of disentangling the impact of the policy from the impact of these prior attributes. This causal riddle can be addressed by constructing a model of how citizens are selected to be recipients of the policy. This model then becomes a building block in the analysis of the policy's impact, in that these prior considerations can be "factored out" in assessing the policy. Achen shows that solving the riddle requires a complex form of "two-stage" statistical analysis.

The implications of Achen's book may be discouraging for analysts working with a small number of cases. An adequate solution to the lack of randomization requires a form of statistical analysis which can be applied to an elaborate quantitative data set, but this technique would be hard to apply in a small-N study. A more hopeful view might be that the literature on experiments and quasi-experiments at least provides useful warnings about the perils of analyzing discrete events as if they were true experimental interventions. In the absence of appropriate data sets, the researcher must exercise caution in making causal claims.

Innovations in Statistics

Recent work on statistical analysis has provided both new warnings about the risks of statistical studies and new opportunities for doing meaningful statistical work with relatively modest case bases. The statistician David Freedman has launched a major assault on the use of multivariate quantitative analysis in the social sciences (1987, 1991), which he claims fails because the underlying research design is generally inadequate and because the data employed fail to meet the assumptions of the statistical techniques. His criticism may bring considerable satisfaction to those who have been skeptical about statistics all along and who take comfort in the greater "control" of the material they feel derives from analyzing relatively few cases through more qualitative techniques. It is realistic to expect that we may go through a period of greater questioning of the use of statistics in the social sciences. However, as with the rejection of quantitative cross-national research discussed above, it would be unfortunate if a reaction against quantitative studies went too far.

The emergence of new statistical techniques that are helpful in the analysis of relatively few cases makes such a blanket rejection unwarranted. One example is the development of "resampling strategies" such as the "bootstrap" and "jackknife" (Diaconis and Efron 1983,

Mooney and Duval 1992). These techniques use computer simulation to create, from an initial set of real data, a large number of hypothetical replications of the study, which can then be used in statistical tests that are not as vulnerable to violations of distributional assumptions as are more conventional tests. These techniques may be especially useful when there is great heterogeneity among units, as may readily occur in cross-national comparisons.

The development of "robust" and "resistant" statistical measures (Hampel et al. 1987; Hartwig 1979; Mosteller and Tukey 1977) is promising in much the same way. These measures are relatively unaffected by extreme or deviant values and can therefore help overcome the problem in small-N analysis that findings may be seriously distorted by a single observation that is greatly in error.

Another set of techniques concerned with this same problem is "regression diagnostics" (Bollen and Jackman 1985; Jackman 1987). These are tests used in conjunction with conventional regression analysis to assess whether unusual values on particular observations, called influential cases, have distorted the findings. The advantage of regression diagnostics in comparison with robust and resistant statistics is that one can employ them with the more familiar coefficients associated with regression analysis.

The use of regression diagnostics is nicely illustrated in the recent debate on the relationship between corporatism and economic growth in 15 Western European countries (Lange and Garrett 1985, 1987; Jackman 1987, 1989; Hicks 1988; Hicks and Patterson 1989; Garrett and Lange 1989). The starting point of this debate is Peter Lange and Geoffrey Garrett's 1985 article, which presents an interesting and complex idea in a simple form. They argue that the organizational strength of unions in the labor market and the political strength of the left in the electoral and governmental arenas both have an impact on economic growth, but that this impact is shaped by a complex interplay between these two factors, which they represent through an "interaction" term in their regression analysis of the 15 cases.

In a reanalysis of their article, Robert W. Jackman (1987) employs regression diagnostics to examine certain influential cases that he believes distort their findings. In the ensuing discussions among these five authors, an expanded model with further control variables is proposed, this expanded model is both challenged and defended, and Lange and Garrett subsequently defend their original model and call for new data and further tests.

This scholarly debate brings together an important substantive problem, a high level of area expertise and knowledge of specific cases, the inventive use of a relatively straightforward statistical model, a constructive critique based on regression diagnostics, and a sustained process of cumulative knowledge generation based on the scrutiny of a shared data set. Just as the Campbell and Ross article on the Connecticut speeding crackdown is an exemplar of a quasi-experimental design, this debate should stand as an exemplar of a methodologically sophisticated effort by several scholars to solve an important problem within the framework of small-N quantitative analysis. This debate also shows that although an "N" of 15 might often be approached through qualitative small-N comparison, it can likewise be subjected to statistical analysis, with interesting results.

Another area in which potential problems of statistical analysis are amenable to solution concerns the issue of "average effects" in regression studies. The results of the simpler forms of regression analysis are based on an average of the strength of causal relations across the cases being studied. For the coefficients produced by regression analysis to be meaningful, it is necessary that these causal relations be homogeneous across the cases. Yet Ragin (1987, chap. 4), among others, has forcefully argued that this assumption commonly does not hold, given the complex forms of "multiple conjunctural causation" often encountered in comparative studies. In different contexts of analysis, the interaction among causal factors may vary.

However, solutions to this problem are available. John E. Jackson (1992) shows how it can be addressed with advanced statistical techniques, and the interaction term in the Lange-Garrett regression analysis, discussed above, deals with precisely this problem: that the effect of one explanatory factor varies depending on the value of another explanatory factor. Finally, Przeworski and Teune's procedure of "replacing proper names," also discussed above, takes this problem of causal complexity and turns it into an opportunity to deal more theoretically with the diversity of causal patterns.

Innovations in the Case-Study Method

When Lijphart wrote his 1971 article, he apparently felt some hesitation about including a discussion of case studies in an assessment of the comparative method.[16] Yet the two topics are closely linked, and his helpful typology of the uses of case studies in hypothesis testing and theory building set the stage for refinements in case study analysis later introduced by other scholars.

One of the most suggestive discussions of the case-study method is that of Campbell (1975). He dramatically recants the bold assertion he made in his earlier book with Stanley that "one-shot" case studies are

"of almost no scientific value" (1963, 7). He shows instead that case studies are the basis of most comparative research, that they offer many more opportunities than is often recognized for falsifying the researcher's main hypotheses, and that much can be learned from making explicit the comparisons that are often implicitly built into case studies. For example, any given hypothesis about a case has implications for many facets of the case. Campbell uses the label "pattern matching" to refer to the process of discovering whether these implications are realized. The analyst can thereby increase the "N" by multiplying the opportunities to test hypotheses within what may initially have been viewed as a "single" case.

This procedure of pattern matching is helpful in addressing the long-standing concern that case studies are useful for generating hypotheses, but that the same case cannot then be used to test the hypothesis because it offers no possibility of disconfirmation. This is sometimes referred to as the problem of ex post facto hypotheses.[17] The procedure of pattern matching opens the possibility that an hypothesis initially generated by a particular case could subsequently fail to be supported by the same case. Thus, the problem of ex post facto hypotheses can be partially overcome.[18]

Harry Eckstein (1975, 113-123) is likewise concerned with testing, as opposed to generating, hypotheses in case-study analysis, and he argues forcefully that many analysts have greatly underestimated the value of case studies for hypothesis testing. In particular, the carefully constructed analysis of a "critical case" -- for example, one about which the analyst has particularly strong expectations that it will fit the hypothesized causal pattern -- can provide an invaluable opportunity to falsify the relevant hypothesis.

Alexander George and Timothy McKeown (1985), building on George (1979), present a helpful synthesis of two key building blocks in the process through which hypotheses are tested in case studies. The first corresponds to the conventional approach to placing a case in comparative perspective, which they call the "congruence procedure." The scholar examines the values of an hypothesized independent and dependent variable for a given case and determines, in light of explicit or implicit comparison with other cases, whether these values are consistent with the predictions of the hypothesis under consideration (pp. 29-30). The second is "process-tracing," through which the researcher engages in a close processual analysis of the unfolding of events over time within the case (pp. 34-41). The goal is to assesses whether the dynamics of change within each case plausibly reflect the same causal pattern suggested by the comparative appraisal of the case in relation to other cases. Process tracing may be seen as a specific instance of Campbell's pattern matching, and as with pattern matching the analyst makes a series of within-case observations against which the hypothesis can be further assessed.

Overall, these articles, along with works such as Robert K. Yin's *Case Study Research* (1984), offer a systematization of case-study procedures that provide a valuable point of reference for scholars concerned with small-N analysis. At the same time, the debate continues on the proper role of case studies in assessing and building theory. An interesting part of this debate, published as a special issue of the journal *World Politics* (1989) focuses on the contribution of case studies to evaluating one application of rational choice analysis, i.e., rational deterrence theory in international relations. The opening article by Achen and Snidal (1989) argues that the case studies employed by many international relations specialists do not adequately address the central ideas of this body of theory, thereby raising an issue perhaps not often enough considered in discussions of the comparative method: How can the *methodological* concern with executing good comparisons be linked to the key analytic issues posed by the particular *theories* that are to be evaluated? Achen and Snidal also note the problem of selection bias in case studies of deterrence theory, that is, the problem that case studies usually focus on deterrence failure, whereas much or most of the time deterrence works. The issue of the journal includes a series of articles by scholars close to the case-study tradition who debate the issues raised by Achen and Snidal. These articles constitute a valuable effort to think through how case studies have functioned in relation to the assessment of a particular body of theory, a line of inquiry that should be taken up more often.

In this debate on deterrence theory, an intellectual tension emerges that has been a recurring theme in this chapter: between analyses that seek to achieve a generic understanding, based on relatively few variables and encompassing many cases, as opposed to analyses that seek to draw out the complexities of particular cases.

Conclusion

Among the diverse approaches discussed in this chapter, three major analytic alternatives stand out. First, new perspectives on the case-study method have strengthened the viability of that approach. Discussions of opportunities for within-case comparisons have in fact begun to blur the distinction between case studies and the comparative method, although the case-study approach does remain a distinct tradition. Interest in case studies has been reinforced by several factors, including the renewed concern with interpretive social science, the

continuing intellectual and institutional strength of area studies, and deep skepticism in some circles about the validity of broad comparison.

Second, it is evident that quantitative techniques employing a relatively small number of cases can successfully address important substantive questions. This approach merits attention in light of the new statistical tests suitable for small-N analysis. The opportunity for cumulative scholarly learning provided by statistical studies is nicely illustrated by the Lange-Garrett-Jackman-Hicks-Patterson debate. This debate is also relevant to the issue of linking rival research traditions, because it shows that insights derived from case studies and from more qualitative comparative work can, after all, serve as stepping-stones on the path toward statistical analysis.

The third alternative has been reinforced as well: the systematic comparison of a small number of cases, with the goal of causal analysis, which is the approach that Lijphart originally advocated. In this perspective, broad qualitative comparison is seen as both possible and productive. The growing influence of the school of comparative historical analysis has substantially enhanced the credibility of this approach, and it plays an important role as an analytic middle ground between the case-study tradition and small-N statistical analysis.

All three of these approaches will persist, and a key question is how well they can be linked. The tradition of research on Western Europe provides an encouraging model, in that the findings of quantitative comparative scholars play an important role in general debates in that field.[19] In research on Latin America, by contrast, quantitative comparative work receives considerably less attention from mainstream scholars. Yet the kind of cross-fertilization found in the West European field can make an important contribution to strengthening research. With good communication, country specialists and experts in qualitative small-N comparison can push the comparative quantifiers toward more carefully contextualized analysis. Likewise, the comparative quantifiers can push the country specialists and experts in qualitative comparison toward more systematic measurement and hypothesis testing. A central goal must be to sustain such communication.

The implications for graduate training are clear. If Ph.D. candidates are to be prepared to address these issues of comparison, they should have enough training in statistical methods to evaluate quantitative studies that employ old, and new, methods of statistical analysis and to use such methods when appropriate. Those more oriented toward statistical analysis should have enough background in qualitative small-N comparison and case study analysis to be able to build on the analytic contribution of those approaches. Both groups should have substantial exposure to basic writings on the philosophy of science and logic of inquiry that can provide the framework for more informed choices about these methodological alternatives.

In this way, the foundation can be laid for an eclectic practice of small-N analysis that takes advantage of opportunities that present themselves on both sides of what could otherwise be a major intellectual divide.

Notes

This is a revised and expanded version of an article earlier published in Dankwart A. Rustow and Kenneth Paul Erickson, eds., *Comparative Political Dynamics: Global Research Perspectives* (New York: Harper Collins, 1991). Permission to reprint granted by Harper Collins. Ruth Berins Collier, Kenneth Paul Erickson, Leonardo Morlina, Elizabeth Busbee, and Carol A. Medlin made particularly useful suggestions on earlier drafts. I also acknowledge comments from Christopher Achen, Stephen Collier, James Fearon, David Freedman, Deborah Norden, Robert Powell, Merrill Shanks, and Laura Stoker. Ada Finifter and two anonymous reviewers likewise made helpful comments. This research has been supported by a Guggenheim Fellowship, the Social Science Research Council, and the Institute of Governmental Studies at Berkeley. Finally, I would like to note a very promising manuscript (King, Verba, and Keohane 1992) that unfortunately came to my attention too late to be discussed in this chapter.

1. "N" is used to refer to the number of cases analyzed in any given study.

2. References to representative works of comparative historical analysis are presented below.

3. In his comparison of these methods, Lijphart acknowledges his debt to Smelser's (1968) excellent analysis that employed a parallel framework. See also Smelser (1976).

4. This perspective has been elaborated by Skocpol (1984, chap. 11), and a parallel formulation is found in Charles Tilly (1984, chap. 4).

5. Skocpol and Somers (1980, 181-87) refer to this as "macro-causal" analysis. Yet small-N studies that generate and test hypotheses can have both a macro and a micro focus, and it does not seem productive to exclude from this category those with a micro focus. Hence, this alternative label is used.

6. Although Przeworski and Teune are centrally concerned with issues that arise when additional cases are added to an analysis, the problems they discuss are also more likely to occur if one is dealing with a larger N to begin with.

7. For example, instead of referring to "Venezuela," one would refer to a country in which, due to the impact of massive oil revenues, a particular causal relationship assumes a distinct form.

8. "Thick description" is sometimes mistakenly understood to refer simply to "detailed description," which is not what Geertz intends.

9. Given that these studies often focus on long periods of time within each case, it might be argued that the number of cases could be greatly increased through comparison over time, thereby making them something other than small-N studies. However, since the goal of many studies in this tradition is to explain overall configurations of national outcomes as they are manifested over long periods, these outcomes often cannot be disaggregated into a series of longitudinal observations. Hence, the number of cases cannot realistically be increased through the use of comparison over time.

10. The most similar and most different systems designs correspond, respectively, to John Stuart Mill's (1974) method of difference and method of agreement. Whereas Przeworski and Teune's labels of "similar" and "different" refer to whether the cases are matched, as opposed to contrasting, on a series of *background* variables, Mill's labels of "difference" and "agreement" refer to whether the cases are contrasting, as opposed to matched, on the *dependent* variable.

11. Personal communication from Adam Przeworski.

12. Christopher Achen, personal communication, has long insisted on this point.

13. For example, Gereffi and Wyman (1990), Haggard (1990), Przeworski (1991), and Rueschemeyer, Stephens, and Stephens (1992).

14. For a discussion of strategic choice models (a closely related type of model) that have been applied to the analysis of political reform, democratization, and democratic consolidation in Latin America, and that likewise offer fruitful simplifications of complex phenomena, see Collier and Norden (1992).

15. The reprinting of this article in a reader on social science methodology (Tufte 1970) made it widely available to political scientists, and its influence has been substantial.

16. Personal communication from Arend Lijphart.

17. This problem is routinely discussed in introductory methodology texts, e.g., Babbie (1992, 24-25, 427).

18. Although pattern matching within the same case introduces the possibility of falsifying the hypothesis, it does not overcome all of the problems of ex post facto hypotheses. Thus, pattern matching will probably not overcome a problem of unrepresentativeness which may arise due to selection bias or to the chance selection of an atypical case.

19. See, for example, the debate on interest mediation and corporatism in Western Europe, including Wilensky (1976), Hibbs (1978), Schmitter (1981), and Cameron (1984). The debate started by Lange and Garrett (1985) is a continuation of this line of analysis.

Bibliography

Achen, Christopher H. 1986. *The Statistical Analysis of Quasi-Experiments*. Berkeley and Los Angeles: University of California Press.

Achen, Christopher H., and Duncan Snidal. 1989. "Rational Deterrence Theory and Comparative Case Studies." *World Politics* 41:143-69.

Almond, Gabriel A., and Stephen J. Genco. 1977. "Clouds, Clocks, and the Study of Politics." *World Politics* 29:489-522.

Armer, Michael, and Allen Grimshaw, eds. 1973. *Comparative Social Research*. New York: John Wiley.

Babbie, Earl. 1992. *The Practice of Social Research*, 6th edition. Belmont, CA: Wadsworth.

Bendix, Reinhard. 1964. *Nation-Building and Citizenship: Studies of Our Changing Social Order*. New York: John Wiley.

Bendix, Reinhard. 1978. *Kings or People: Power and the Mandate to Rule*. Berkeley and Los Angeles: University of California Press.

Bergquist, Charles. 1986. *Labor in Latin America: Comparative Essays on Chile, Argentina, Venezuela, and Colombia*. Stanford: Stanford University Press.

Bollen, Kenneth A., and Robert W. Jackman. 1985. "Regression Diagnostics: An Expository Treatment of Outliers and Influential Cases." *Sociological Methods and Research* 13:510-42.

Burger, Thomas. 1976. *Max Weber's Theory of Concept Formation: History, Laws, and Ideal Types*. Durham: Duke University.

Cameron, David R. 1984. "Social Democracy, Corporatism, Labour Quiescence, and the Representation of Economic Interest in Advanced Capitalist Society." In *Order and Conflict in Contemporary Capitalism*, ed. John H. Goldthorpe. New York: Oxford University Press.

Campbell, Donald T. 1975. "'Degrees of Freedom' and the Case Study." *Comparative Political Studies* 8:178-93.

Campbell, Donald T., and H. Laurence Ross. 1968. "The Connecticut Crackdown on Speeding: Time Series Data in Quasi-Experimental Analysis." *Law and Society Review* 3:33-53.

Campbell, Donald T., and Julian C. Stanley. 1963. *Experimental and Quasi-Experimental Designs for Research*. Chicago: Rand McNally.

Collier, David, and James E. Mahon. 1993. "Conceptual 'Stretching' Revisited: Alternative Views of Categories in Comparative Analysis." *American Political Science Review*.

Collier, David, and Deborah L. Norden. 1992. "Strategic Choice Models of Political Change in Latin America." *Comparative Politics* 24:229-243.

Collier, Ruth Berins, and David Collier. 1991. *Shaping the Political Arena: Critical Junctures, the Labor Movement, and Regime Dynamics in Latin America*. Princeton: Princeton University Press.

Dahl, Robert A., ed. 1966. *Political Oppositions in Western Democracies*. New Haven: Yale University Press.

DeFelice, E. Gene. 1980. "Comparison Misconceived: Common Nonsense in Comparative Politics." *Comparative Politics* 13:119-26.

Diaconis, Persi, and Bradley Efron. 1983. "Computer-Intensive Methods in Statistics." *Scientific American* 248:116-30.

Eckstein, Harry. 1975. "Case Study and Theory in Political Science." In *Handbook of Political Science*, vol. 7, ed. Fred Greenstein and Nelson W. Polsby. Reading, MA: Addison-Wesley.

Eggan, Fred. 1954. "Social Anthropology and the Method of Controlled Comparison." *American Anthropologist* 56:743-63.

Etzioni, Amitai, and Frederic L. Dubow, eds. 1970. *Comparative Perspectives: Theories and Methods*. Boston: Little, Brown.

Freedman, David A. 1987. "As Others See Us: A Case Study in Path Analysis." *Journal of Educational Statistics* 12:101-28.

Freedman, David A. 1991. "Statistical Models and Shoe Leather." In *Sociological Methodology 1991*, ed. Peter Marsden. San Francisco: Jossey-Bass.

Garrett, Geoffrey, and Peter Lange. 1989. "Government Partisanship and Economic Performance: When and How Does 'Who Governs' Matter?" *Journal of Politics* 51:676-93.

Geddes, Barbara. 1990. "How the Cases You Choose Affect the Answers You Get: Selection Bias in Comparative Politics." In *Political Analysis*, vol. 2, ed. James A. Stimson. Ann Arbor: University of Michigan Press.

Geddes, Barbara. 1991. "A Game Theoretic Model of Reform in Latin American Democracies." *American Political Science Review* 85:371-392.

Geertz, Clifford. 1973. "Thick Description: Toward an Interpretive Theory of Culture." In *The Interpretation of Cultures*, ed. Clifford Geertz. New York: Basic Books.

George, Alexander L. 1979. "Case Studies and Theory Development: The Method of Structured, Focused Comparison." In *Diplomacy: New Approaches in History, Theory, and Policy*, ed. Paul Gordon Lauren. New York: The Free Press.

George, Alexander L., and Timothy J. McKeown. 1985. "Case Studies and Theories of Organizational Decision Making." *Advances in Information Processing in Organizations*, vol. 2. Santa Barbara, CA: JAI Press.

Gereffi, Gary, and Donald L. Wyman, eds. 1990. *Manufacturing Miracles: Paths of Industrialization in Latin America and East Asia*. Princeton: Princeton University Press.

Goldstone, Jack A. 1991. *Revolution and Rebellion in the Early Modern World*. Berkeley and Los Angeles: University of California Press.

Haggard, Stephan. 1990. *Pathways from the Periphery: The Politics of Growth in the Newly Industrializing Countries*. Ithaca: Cornell University Press.

Hampel, Frank R., *et al.* 1987. *Robust Statistics: The Approach Based on Influence Functions*. New York: John Wiley.

Hartwig, Frederick, with Brian E. Dearing. 1979. *Exploratory Data Analysis*. Sage University Paper, Series No. 07-016. Beverly Hills, CA: Sage Publications.

Heckscher, Gunnar. 1957. *The Study of Comparative Government and Politics*. London: George Allen and Unwin.

Hibbs, Douglas A., Jr. 1978. "On the Political Economy of Long-Run Trends in Strike Activity." *British Journal of Political Science* 8:153-175.

Hicks, Alexander. 1988. "Social Democratic Corporatism and Economic Growth." *Journal of Politics* 50:677-704.

Hicks, Alexander, and William David Patterson. 1989. "On the Robustness of the Left Corporatist Model of Economic Growth." *Journal of Politics* 51:662-675.

Hoole, Francis W. 1978. *Evaluation Research and Development Activities*. Beverly Hills, CA: Sage Publications.

Jackman, Robert W. 1985. "Cross-National Statistical Research and the Study of Comparative Politics." *American Journal of Political Science* 29:161-82.

Jackman, Robert W. 1987. "The Politics of Economic Growth in Industrial Democracies, 1974-80: Leftist Strength or North Sea Oil?" *Journal of Politics* 49:242-56.

Jackman, Robert W. 1989. "The Politics of Economic Growth, Once Again." *Journal of Politics* 51:646-661.

Jackson, John E. 1992. "Estimation of Models with Variable Coefficients." In *Political Analysis*, vol. 3. ed. James A. Stimson. Ann Arbor: University of Michigan Press.

Kalleberg, Arthur L. 1966. "The Logic of Comparison: A Methodological Note on the Comparative Study of Political Systems." *World Politics* 19:69-82.

King, Gary, Sidney Verba, and Robert O. Keohane. 1992. *Scientific Inference in Qualitative Research*. Unpublished manuscript, Department of Government, Harvard University.

Lakoff, George. 1987. *Women, Fire, and Dangerous Things: What Categories Reveal about the Mind*. Chicago: University of Chicago Press.

Lange, Peter, and Geoffrey Garrett. 1985. "The Politics of Growth: Strategic Interaction and Economic Performance in Advanced Industrial Democracies, 1974-1980." *Journal of Politics* 47:792-827.

Lange, Peter, and Geoffrey Garrett. 1987. "The Politics of Growth Reconsidered." *Journal of Politics* 49:257-74.

Lasswell, Harold D. 1968. "The Future of the Comparative Method." *Comparative Politics* 1:3-18.

Lieberson, Stanley. 1991. "Small N's and Big Conclusions: An Examination of the Reasoning in Comparative Studies Based on a Small Number of Cases." *Social Forces* 70:307-20.

Lijphart, Arend. 1971. "Comparative Politics and Comparative Method." *American Political Science Review* 65:682-93.

Lijphart, Arend. 1975. "The Comparable Cases Strategy in Comparative Research." *Comparative Political Studies* 8:158-77.

Lijphart, Arend. 1990. "The Political Consequences of Electoral Laws, 1945-1985." *American Political Science Review* 84:481-96.

Lipset, Seymour Martin, and Stein Rokkan. 1967. "Cleavages, Structures, Party Systems, and Voter Alignments: An Introduction." In *Party Systems and Voter Alignments*, eds. Seymour Martin Lipset and Stein Rokkan. New York: Free Press.

Luebbert, Gregory M. 1991. *Liberalism, Fascism, or Social Democracy: Social Classes and the Political Origins of Regimes in Interwar Europe*. New York: Oxford University Press.

McKinney, John C. 1966. *Constructive Typology and Social Theory*. New York: Meredith Publishing Company.

Merritt, Richard. 1970. *Systematic Approaches to Comparative Politics*. Chicago: Rand McNally.

Merritt, Richard, and Stein Rokkan, eds. 1966. *Comparing Nations: The Use of Quantitative Data in Cross-National Research*. New Haven: Yale University Press.

Mill, John Stuart. [1843] 1974. *A System of Logic*. Toronto: University of Toronto Press.

Mooney, Christopher Z., and Robert D. Duval. 1992. "Bootstrap Inference: A Preliminary Monte Carlo Evaluation." Paper presented at the annual meetings of the American Political Science Association, Chicago.

Moore, Barrington. 1966. *Social Origins of Dictatorship and Democracy: Lord and Peasant in the Making of the Modern World*. Boston: Beacon Press.

Mosteller, Frederick, and John W. Tukey. 1977. *Data Analysis and Regression*. Reading, MA: Addison-Wesley.

O'Donnell, Guillermo, Philippe C. Schmitter, and Lawrence Whitehead, eds. 1986. *Transitions from Authoritarian Rule*. Baltimore: John Hopkins University Press.

Paige, Jeffrey. 1975. *Agrarian Revolution: Social Movements and Export Agriculture in the Underdeveloped World*. New York: Free Press.

Przeworski, Adam. 1987. "Methods of Cross-National Research, 1970-1983: An Overview." Meinolf Dierkes, Hans N. Weiler, and Ariane Berthoin Antal, eds. *Comparative Policy Research: Learning from Experience*. Brookfield, VT: Gower.

Przeworski, Adam. 1991. *Democracy and the Market: Political and Economic Reforms in Eastern Europe and Latin America*. Cambridge: Cambridge University Press.

Przeworski, Adam, and Henry Teune. 1970. *The Logic of Comparative Social Inquiry*. New York: John Wiley.

Ragin, Charles C. 1987. *The Comparative Method: Moving beyond Qualitative and Quantitative Strategies*. Berkeley and Los Angeles: University of California Press.

Rokkan, Stein. 1970. *Citizens, Elections, Parties: Approaches to the Comparative Study of Processes of Development*. New York: David McKay.

Rueschemeyer, Dietrich, Evelyne Huber Stephens, and John D. Stephens. 1992. *Capitalist Development and Democracy*. Chicago: University of Chicago Press.

Rustow, Dankwart. 1968. "Modernization and Comparative Politics: Prospects in Research and Theory." *Comparative Politics* 1:37-51.

Sartori, Giovanni. 1970. "Concept Misformation in Comparative Politics." *American Political Science Review* 64:1033-53.

Sartori, Giovanni, ed. 1984. *Social Science Concepts: A Systematic Analysis*. Beverly Hills, CA: Sage.

Sartori, Giovanni. 1991. "Comparing and Miscomparing." *Journal of Theoretical Politics* 3:243-57.

Sartori, Giovanni. 1993. "Totalitarianism, Model Mania, and Learning from Error." *Journal of Theoretical Politics*.

Sartori, Giovanni, Fred W. Riggs, and Henry Teune. 1975. *Tower of Babel: On the Definition and Analysis of Concepts in the Social Sciences*. International Studies Association, Occasional Paper No. 6, University of Pittsburgh.

Schmitter, Philippe C. 1981. "Interest Intermediation and Regime Governability in Contemporary Western Europe and North America." In *Organizing Interests in Western Europe*, ed. Suzanne D. Berger. Cambridge: Cambridge University Press.

Skocpol, Theda. 1979. *States and Social Revolutions: A Comparative Analysis of France, Russia, and China*. Cambridge: Cambridge University Press.

Skocpol, Theda. 1984. *Vision and Method in Historical Sociology*. Cambridge and New York: Cambridge University Press.

Skocpol, Theda, and Margaret Somers. 1980. "The Uses of Comparative History in Macrosocial Inquiry." *Comparative Studies in Society and History* 22:174-97.

Smelser, Neil. 1968. "The Methodology of Comparative Analysis of Economic Activity." In *Essays in Sociological Interpretation*, ed. Neil Smelser. Englewood Cliffs, NJ: Prentice-Hall.

Smelser, Neil. 1976. *Comparative Methods in the Social Sciences*. Englewood Cliffs, NJ: Prentice Hall.

Stinchcombe, Arthur L. 1978. *Theoretical Methods in Social History*. New York: Academic Press.

Tilly, Charles. 1975. *The Formation of National States in Western Europe*. Princeton: Princeton University Press.

Tilly, Charles. 1984. *Big Structures, Large Processes, Huge Comparisons*. New York: Russell Sage.

Trimberger, Ellen Kay. 1978. *Revolution from Above: Military Bureaucrats and Development in Japan, Turkey, Egypt, and Peru*. New Brunswick, NJ: Transaction Books.

Tufte, Edward R. 1970. *The Quantitative Analysis of Social Problems*. Reading, MA: Addison-Wesley.

Vallier, Ivan, ed. 1971. *Comparative Methods in Sociology: Essays on Trends and Applications*. Berkeley and Los Angeles: University of California Press.

Verba, Sidney. 1967. "Some Dilemmas in Comparative Research." *World Politics* 20:111-27.

Wilensky, Harold L. 1976. *The 'New Corporatism,' Centralization, and the Welfare State*. Professional Papers in Contemporary Political Sociology Series. Beverly Hills: Sage Publications.

Yin, Robert K. 1984. *Case Study Research: Design and Methods*. Applied Social Research Methods Series, vol. 5. Beverly Hills: Sage Publications.

Zelditch, Jr., Morris. 1971. "Intelligible Comparisons." In *Comparative Methods in Sociology: Essays on Trends and Applications*, ed. Ivan Vallier. Berkeley and Los Angeles: University of California Press.

6

The State of Quantitative Political Methodology

Larry M. Bartels and Henry E. Brady

In the first edition of this volume, Achen (1983a, 69) complained that "political methodology has so far failed to make serious theoretical progress on any of the major issues facing it." In the intervening decade, thanks in no small part to Achen's prodding, the field of political methodology has progressed significantly on several fronts. While political methodologists have still "done nothing remotely comparable" to the invention of factor analysis by psychometricians or structural equation methods by econometricians (Achen 1983a, 69), they have invented, adopted, or further developed an impressive variety of useful techniques for dealing with event counts (King 1989d), dimensional models (Poole and Rosenthal 1991; Brady 1985b, 1990; Enelow and Hinich 1984), pseudo-panels (Franklin 1990), model misspecification (Bartels 1991b), parameter variation (Rivers 1988; Jackson 1992a), aggregated data (Achen and Shively n.d.), selection bias (Achen 1986b), non-random measurement error (Brady 1985a; Palmquist and Green 1992), missing data (Mebane n.d.), and time series data (Freeman, Williams, and Lin 1989; Beck 1990).

Moreover, while the volume and sophistication of basic methodological research in political science have increased significantly in the decade since Achen surveyed the field, the impact of methodological research on empirical work throughout the discipline has probably increased even more significantly. In order to document that fact, in addition to describing recent methodological advances in a variety of areas, we point to innovative and important applications of quantitative methods in every part of political science. To that end, in addition to reviewing every issue of *Political Methodology* (1974-1985) and the four volumes of *Political Analysis* dated 1989-1992 (but published in the next year), we reviewed and classified according to methodology over 2,000 articles in other political science journals, including every article published in *The American Political Science Review* from 1981 to 1991 and every article published in *The American Journal of Political Science, Comparative Political Studies, Comparative Politics, Journal of Conflict Resolution*, and *International Studies Quarterly* from 1984 to 1991.[1]

Despite having cast so wide a net, we must emphasize that, due to inevitable limitations of space and expertise, our discussion of problems and techniques remains selective. Models and analyses based on computational, rather than statistical, logic are gaining a foothold (Alker 1988; Schrodt 1991). Data graphics, inspired by the ideas of Tufte (1983) and Cleveland (1985) and by the power and convenience of computer graphics packages, are becoming increasingly sophisticated. These strands of research and others have added significantly to the vitality and utility of political methodology in the last decade. We omit them here not because we consider them unimportant or uninteresting, but because we prefer to focus our finite attention upon what we consider the mainstream of contemporary political methodology: the armamentarium of techniques developed to relate statistical models to quantitative data of various sorts.

There is no one way to organize the many topics touched upon in our survey of the field. We have chosen to follow a rough logical progression from data collection through modeling to estimation. We begin in Section 1 with data collection, where there has been a notable resurgence in the use of experiments, innovations in survey design, and a proliferation of events data in a variety of research areas.

Sections 2 and 3 are organized around distinctive units of analysis. Time-series research has profited greatly from the development of Box-Tiao methods, vector autoregression, cointegration and error correction models, and the Kalman filter; these developments are described in Section 2. In Section 3 we survey innovations in the use of pooled time-series cross-sectional data, panel data, and auxiliary data sets, as well as the current state of aggregate data analysis.

Another familiar distinction is among nominal, ordinal, interval, and ratio data. Special methods are necessary for dependent variables that are not interval or ratio measures; in Section 4 we discuss methods for analyzing polychotomous "categorized" data such as standard Likert opinion questions, polytomous or multiple choice data such as choice of party or candidate, and event count and duration data such as the number of governments or wars in a period of time.

No matter what the measurement level, our variables are often measured with considerable error. In Section 5 we discuss some sources and consequences of measurement error. We also note some significant progress in dealing with random and non-random measurement error, sample selection bias, and missing data.

In Section 6 we turn to dimensional models, which have often been used to understand the factors underlying voter and legislative choice. Political scientists initially borrowed methods for dimensional analysis from psychology; but in the past twenty years, in this perhaps more than in any other area, political scientists have led the way in making methodological advances.

In Section 7 we survey some general problems of model specification. We outline some techniques for policing the consequences of specification uncertainty, including sensitivity analysis, cross-validation, and formal specification tests, and we describe some distinctive contributions by political scientists toward understanding and managing the statistical consequences of misspecification.

Finally, once the data are collected and the model specified, parameter estimates must be obtained. Political methodologists have now moved well beyond using ordinary least squares for every problem. In Section 8 we describe advances in estimation, including creative applications of maximum likelihood and other estimation methods.

Our view is that the subfield of political methodology exists to serve the needs of substantive political research and can be successful only to the extent that it facilitates progress in the various substantive subfields of the discipline. Thus, in Section 9 we review some of the many areas of political science in which methodological advances have led directly to important substantive advances in the past decade or so. We focus especially on two areas identified by Achen (1983a) as ripe for methodological contributions: the nature of the survey response and the phenomenon of economic voting.

1. Data Collection Methods

Political scientists' data collection strategies have been diversified and enriched in the past decade. Experimenters have created more realistic experimental settings and married experiments with survey research. Survey researchers have moved from strictly cross-sectional designs to repeated cross-sections, sophisticated panels, and other approaches designed to add time and context to the analysis. Events data have proliferated, and lengthy, high-quality time series involving many nations or other actors are now available for a wide range of phenomena.

While these new sources of data have improved our ability to generalize and to make causal inferences, they have also provided new challenges for political methodologists. Since some of the discipline's major data collection efforts have cost millions of dollars and decades of people's lives, it seems well worth our time and trouble to develop new techniques, and to train researchers in those techniques, in order to extract as much information as possible from these often heroic data collection efforts.

Experiments

In the past decade, political scientists have found many new and exciting ways to do experimental work. Samples are more representative and treatments are more realistic, increasing greatly the external validity of experimental work. Experimental methods have been built into opinion surveys to combine the advantages of both approaches. In addition, there is a strong commitment to using experiments to help develop and test formal theories of collective decision making, political psychology, and other important political phenomena. For example, whereas books on question-wording experiments (Schuman and Presser 1981; Sudman and Bradburn 1982) once seemed to be nothing more than catalogs of odd and even freakish phenomena, recent work has used similar experiments to understand how people think about politics (Tourangeau and Rasinski 1988; Sniderman et al. 1991; Sniderman and Piazza 1993). A new book on experimental research in political science (Kinder and Palfrey 1992) provides an excellent sample of the diverse and sophisticated work now being done in this area.

Although there is a long tradition of using experiments in public opinion research to determine the impact of political messages on people's opinions (Hovland, Janis, and Kelley 1953), these experiments typically involved unrepresentative samples (college students), limited treatments (sometimes just differences in written instructions), and often artificial treatments (hypothetical candidates, countries, or news reports). They showed that some people could be persuaded in some ways under some conditions, but they could not provide reliable evidence about the likely presence or magnitude of those effects in natural settings.

In the 1980s political scientists became more sensitive about the external validity of experimental research and started to develop more realistic experiments done in real time with real people. More representative samples were recruited from outside the university (Iyengar and Kinder 1987; Iyengar 1987, 1991), sometimes even regionally or nationally representative samples (Sniderman et al. 1991; Piazza, Sniderman, and Tetlock 1990; Johnston et al. 1992). Experiments also used more sophisticated stimuli such as entire news programs carefully edited to include or omit particular stories (Iyengar and Kinder 1987; Sullivan and Masters 1988; Masters 1988; Iyengar 1991). Finally, more complex designs have included re-interviews after a period of time to see whether effects persist (Iyengar and Kinder 1987; Sullivan and Masters 1988).

Another group of experimental researchers has not worried very much about representativeness or realism because they simply wanted to convince skeptics that citizens could make the seemingly complicated and sophisticated calculations required by theories of rational choice, bargaining, and justice, and that the equilibria predicted by rational choice theory would be attained under some conditions. In perhaps the most famous experiments in this tradition, Levine and Plott (1977) and Plott and Levine (1978) showed how committee agendas can be manipulated to reach a wide range of divergent outcomes. Riker (1986, chap. 3) provided a very readable summary of these results.

More recently, McKelvey and Ordeshook (1985) considered a sequence of two-candidate elections under incomplete information in which "voters have no contemporaneous information about the candidate positions, and candidates have no information about voter preferences. The only source of information is historical data on the policy positions of previous winning candidates and contemporaneous endorsement data" (1985, 480). The experimental data provided some support for a mathematical result predicting an equilibrium under these conditions equivalent to what would occur if voters had full information.

In another series of experiments, Frohlich and Oppenheimer (1990) showed that students do not adopt Rawlsian notions of justice in a simulated task, although they do choose a "safety net" for the least able of their members. They also showed that in a production environment where students must live with the distributive rule they have chosen, participation in choosing the rule leads to greater acceptance of it.

In this kind of research, the experimental situations are obviously artificial, but the surprise lies in finding out that relatively naive subjects can act in ways that are very sophisticated. McKelvey and Ordeshook (1990, 140-41) concluded that:

> the experimental research that this essay reviews gives us considerable confidence that the large body of theoretical research into spatial models of committees and

elections is not without sound empirical content. Certainly, those models may have to be elaborated before we can apply them directly to the study of, for example, the U.S. Congress, parliaments, and actual elections. But those same experiments, in addition to revealing fruitful avenues of opportunity for the theorist, also suggest how theoretical models can be adapted to environments outside the laboratory.

A recent edited volume (Palfrey 1991) provides another overview of laboratory research in political economy.

Perhaps the most innovative use of experimentation has been the effort of Sniderman and his collaborators to marry experimental research and representative sample surveys. In a series of studies of American racial attitudes and Canadian views of rights and freedoms, they designed variations in question wording to test for the impact of various considerations on people's attitudes. For example, they asked respondents whether certain kinds of people deserve government help, with random changes in the race, gender, age, marital-parental status, and "dependability" of the prospective recipient (Piazza, Sniderman, and Tetlock 1990). This complex experiment is made possible by a computer assisted telephone interviewing (CATI) system that can produce as many different interview "forms" as the researcher can devise.

Sniderman and his colleagues also described other possible experimental and non-experimental methods using CATI. Source attribution experiments vary the credibility of the source associated with a statement. This technique was used by Johnston et al. (1992) in an effort to simulate the rhetoric of the 1988 Canadian election campaign. By asking some randomly selected respondents about the "Canadian" free trade agreement and others about the "Mulroney Government's" free trade agreement, they found that Prime Minister Brian Mulroney was a rhetorical liability during the early part of the campaign but became an asset as his popularity increased towards the end of the campaign. Johnston et al. also used a "challenge" methodology advocated by Piazza, Sniderman, and Tetlock (1990) to determine which arguments were most likely to move public opinion about free trade as the campaign progressed.

These techniques and others like them provide new ways to do public opinion research, allowing researchers to learn about people's attitudes and beliefs by challenging them, by employing varying stimuli in unobtrusive ways, and by using experiments to test what really matters to people.

Survey Designs

Survey research now profits from having a history. There are more than 50 years of Gallup polls at almost monthly intervals, 40 years of American National Election Studies done every two years, 20 years of the annual General Social Survey, and many other valuable surveys. The chasm between time-series analysts using aggregate data and cross-sectional analysts using survey data has been filled over time with mountains of survey data. The limitations of the standard cross-sectional survey, discussed in detail by Mebane (1991), can now be overcome with a time series of cross-sections. Researchers can also use these surveys as time series to follow the dynamics of public opinion over long time periods (Mueller 1973; Carmines and Stimson 1989; Page and Shapiro 1992; Stimson 1991a; Mayer 1992). And mystifying differences between the results produced by time-series and cross-sectional analyses can be resolved by analyzing surveys over time, as we document in Section 9 below for the case of economic voting (Kramer 1983; Markus 1988).

Survey researchers have also developed new designs for surveys in the past 25 years. The 1978 and 1980 National Election Studies produced representative samples of around 20 people in each of 108 congressional districts, allowing researchers to study the linkages between public opinion, congressional elections, and the roll-call votes of members of Congress (Bartels 1991a). The 1988, 1990, and 1992 Senate election studies produced even larger samples of about 75 respondents in each of the 50 states, providing rich opportunities to study temporal, geographical, and candidate- and election-specific variations, often with the "campaign" as the relevant unit of analysis (Franklin 1991).

The 1980 National Election Study combined repeated cross-sections with a panel beginning in January and continuing through the election year (Markus 1982) to provide the most complete study of campaign dynamics since the classic Columbia studies (Lazarsfeld et al. 1944; Berelson et al. 1954). The 1984 National Election Study completed 70 interviews a week from January to November, facilitating "rolling-cross-section" analyses of election season dynamics (Brady and Johnston 1987; Allsop and Weisberg 1988; Bartels 1988). The 1988 Canadian Election Study used daily samples of 70 people to produce a study of the dynamics of a parliamentary election (Johnston et al. 1992).

The House, Senate, and rolling cross-section studies all provide small numbers of interviews by some discrete unit -- a congressional district, a state, a week, or a day. These units vary on a variety of contextual dimensions, including the degree of competitiveness in the election, media coverage, and autonomous events.

The challenge for political methodology is to make full use of the information contained in time- or place-specific samples that, treated individually and naively, are too small and error-laden to be of much use.

Events Data

Events data vary greatly in their substantive focus (alliances, cabinet dissolutions, presidential vetoes), units of observation (the international system, nations, presidencies), and time intervals (days, months, years). Yet they share a common structure, recording whether a particular event has occurred in each time interval in each relevant unit, and, if it has, recording attributes of the event, the unit, the time interval, or all of these.

The prototypical events data collections in political science are those dealing with war (Sorokin 1937; Wright 1942; Richardson 1944, 1960). Among the best known of these is the Correlates of War project of Singer and Small (1972; Small and Singer 1982), which includes data from 1816 to 1980 on various features of wars, civil wars, and interstate disputes. More recently, Levy (1983) has developed a similar data set for wars involving great powers from 1495 to 1975. In the 1980s, the Singer-Small, Levy, and other data sets have been extended as part of a National Science Foundation project on Data Development for International Research (DDIR); the interstate conflict databases funded by this project were described by Cioffi-Revilla (1990), and an overview of international data sets was provided by McGowan et al. (1988).

Many other forms of events data are available in political science. Within international relations, the term "events data" is often reserved for daily codings of newspaper reports on international interactions, such as Charles McClelland's World Events Interaction Survey (WEIS) and Edward Azar's Conflict and Peace Data Bank (COPDAB).[2] Several volumes have been devoted to methodological issues arising from these and similar data (e.g., Azar and Ben-Dak 1975; Burgess and Lawton 1972; Kegley et al. 1975), and a 1983 symposium in *International Studies Quarterly* (Howell 1983; Vincent 1983; McClelland 1983) raised questions of comparability between the WEIS and COPDAB time series. Goldstein and Freeman (1990) justified their use of events data to analyze conflict and cooperation among the United States, the USSR, and China in part by demonstrating convergence in their findings across three different sets of events data (WEIS, COPDAB, and Ashley [1980]).

Events data have also been gathered to study patterns at the national level. The best known and most widely used of these data sets (McGowan et al. 1988) is the *World Handbook of Political and Social Indicators* (Taylor and Jodice 1983a, 1983b).[3] Banks (1971) provided yearly attribute and events data, sometimes dating back to the early nineteenth century, for most of the countries of the world. Morrison, Mitchell, and Paden (1989) provided extensive data on events in African countries. Freedom House provides yearly ratings of the level of freedom in countries around the world (Starr 1991). Bienen and van de Walle (1989) have data on 165 African leaders from independence through 1987; Jackman (1978) has data on African coups from 1960 through 1975; Strom (1985) has extensive data on governmental coalitions in Western parliamentary democracies between 1945 and 1982; King and Ragsdale (1988) have data on the American presidency, including presidential vetoes, press conferences, and many other events.

The analysis of events data is not straightforward. There are significant measurement problems and complicated analytical issues arising from unreliability in the classification of events and the complexities of inherently multidimensional phenomena. This is most clearly seen in the difficulties of defining wars (Levy 1983, chaps. 3 and 4; Small and Singer 1982, chaps. 2 and 3; Levy 1985; Thompson and Rasler 1988), democratic transitions (O'Donnell and Schmitter 1986, chap. 2), episodes of deterrence (Huth and Russett 1988; Lebow and Stein 1990), or coups in Africa (Jackman et al. 1986). Even defining something as apparently simple as the duration of a government can raise difficulties (Lijphart 1984).

In response to difficulties like these, Collier and Mahon (n.d.) suggest a need for multidimensional conceptualizations of events and for analytical techniques allowing for multivariate dependent variables. Another, albeit little used, approach to measurement problems in events data is to employ multiple indicator methods borrowed from psychometrics (Achen 1987). For example, Faber (1987) used confirmatory factor analysis to study the measurement properties of the COPDAB data.

Analytical problems also arise in deciding whether to analyze events history, sequence, or counts data,[4] and in developing models appropriate to each alternative (Tuma and Hannan 1984). Sociologists (Tuma and Hannan 1984; Allison 1984), statisticians (Cox 1972), economists (Heckman and Singer 1982), epidemiologists (Gross and Clark 1975; Elandt-Johnson and Johnson 1980), and engineers (Kalbfleisch and Prentice 1980) have developed sophisticated methods for analyzing these different types of events data for marital, employment, and health statuses (including the reliability of machines and products). The challenge for political scientists is to adopt these methods when they are useful and to develop new ones to meet the special needs of our discipline.

2. Time-Series Analysis

Time-series data have come to play an increasingly prominent role in political science in the last decade, especially in empirical work at the intersection of politics and economics. The time-series methods first introduced by Hibbs (1974), including generalized least squares and autoregressive integrated moving average (ARIMA) models (Box and Jenkins 1976), are now adopted routinely to model a wide variety of trends, autoregressive errors, and moving average processes in time-series data.[5]

The econometric literature continues to be the major source of new techniques for analyzing time-series data.[6] But political scientists have become increasingly sophisticated in their efforts to adopt and adapt these techniques to studies of the political business cycle (Beck 1987), presidential popularity (Beck 1992; Ostrom and Smith n.d.), arms races (Williams and McGinnis 1988), and other political phenomena. Four techniques in particular have seen both rapid theoretical development and fruitful application in political settings: Box-Tiao intervention models, vector autoregression, cointegration, and the Kalman filter.

Box-Tiao Intervention Methods

Box-Tiao intervention methods (Box and Tiao 1975), introduced to political scientists by Hibbs (1977), have been used to show that the ideology of governing parties influences unemployment rates (Hibbs 1977), although world economic conditions also matter (Alt 1985); that wars influence economic growth rates, government expenditure, and taxes (Rasler and Thompson 1985a, 1985b); that bureaucratic interventions and outputs change with such political factors as legislation, appointments, and control of the presidency (Wood 1988; Wood and Waterman 1991); and that partisanship responds to presidential popularity and other political trends (MacKuen, Erikson, and Stimson 1989).

The results from these studies are fascinating stylized facts, but the interventions they consider (wars, political events like Watergate, and changes in the ideology of a governing party) are often very complex "treatments" for which simple causal claims ("wars increase taxes") seem dangerous. In addition, Box-Tiao methods are usually employed to estimate simple "reduced" forms with few covariates and little attention to causal sequence. More researchers should employ causality tests (e.g., MacKuen, Erikson, and Stimson 1992) to lend credence to their arguments, and more attention should be devoted to developing structural models. For example, Hibbs and Dennis (1988, 478), rather than simply following Hibbs' earlier (1977) lead analyzing how political partisanship affects income equality, built a structural model in which "unemployment, inflation, transfer spending, and inequality are determined endogenously, and they are driven politically by the party controlling the White House and the partisan balance in Congress."

Vector Autoregression

Vector autoregression is due primarily to Sims (1977, 1980). The excellent exposition by Freeman, Williams, and Lin (1989) is aimed at political scientists and includes an illustrative empirical analysis of government expenditures in Britain. Williams and McGinnis (1988), McGinnis and Williams (1989) and Williams (n.d.a) provided additional political applications.

The main feature of vector autoregression is that each variable in an equation system is regressed on a large collection of past values of all the variables in the system. The resulting parameter estimates may be thought of as reduced-form parameter estimates for some unspecified structural model including the same set of variables. This approach has two significant attractions. First, the problem of model specification is solved by simply including lagged values of all the variables in the system.[7] And, second, since current disturbances are uncorrelated by assumption with everything in the past, the problem of estimation has a simple solution: ordinary least squares is always the appropriate estimator.

But this simplicity has its price. The unrestrictive approach of vector autoregression to the selection of regressors entails a corresponding cost in the precision of the resulting reduced-form parameter estimates. Indeed, parameter estimates from vector autoregressions tend to be so imprecise that it is conventional not to interpret them individually but to test the significance of *sets* of parameter estimates for one or more variables simultaneously using an F-test or modified likelihood ratio test (Freeman, Williams, and Lin 1989, 845).[8]

Statistical tests on whole sets of parameter estimates can produce results that seem puzzling to analysts with specific ideas about the causal processes at work. For example, in Williams and McGinnis's vector autoregression of U.S. and Soviet military spending levels from 1949 to 1981 (1988, 984), F-tests failed to reject the null hypotheses that the two series are mutually exogenous ($p=.29$ and $p=.55$), despite the fact that the single parameter estimate most plausibly representing the reaction of U.S. spending to observed Soviet spending (with a three-year lag, as suggested by Ostrom and Marra 1986, 828) was large (.81) and clearly different from zero by conventional statistical standards (with a standard

error of .37, even in a regression with only 22 degrees of freedom, $p < .025$).

Since individual parameter estimates from vector autoregressions are not directly interpretable as estimates of structural effects, analysts commonly depict the dynamic relationships among variables by simulating the effects of random shocks, or "innovations," in one variable upon the future time paths of all the variables in the system. However, the results of this "innovation accounting" sometimes depend crucially upon the analyst's assumptions regarding the causal relationships among the contemporaneous innovations themselves. Typically, in order to interpret contemporaneous correlations among residuals from different equations, the analyst "must choose an ordering of the causal chain of contemporaneous effects, an ordering that should be given some theoretical underpinning" (Freeman, Williams, and Lin 1989, 847). When the pattern of responses in the dynamic system depends crucially upon such choices, the strong assumptions about causal structure that are supposed to be eschewed in vector autoregression must be let back in by a side door.

Nevertheless, proponents of vector autoregression argue that their approach reflects a more realistic attitude toward the uncertainties of model specification than does the conventional approach to specifying and estimating simultaneous equation models. As Freeman, Williams, and Lin (1989, 853-54) put it:

> SEQ [conventional simultaneous equation] and VAR [vector autoregression] modeling rest on different assumptions about what we presently know and what we can know about the nature of social reality. SEQ modelers presume that our theories are relatively well developed, or that we know quite a bit about social reality. For example, our theories tell us exactly how variables are interrelated, including the functional forms of these interrelationships. This knowledge is reflected in the strong, zero-order restrictions that SEQ modelers impose on their equations, for example, in the exogeneity and lag specifications in their equations. . . . VAR modelers assume, in contrast, that our theories are relatively undeveloped, or that our understanding of social reality is severely limited. . . . Only a weak set of restrictions about what variables to include in the model and about the contemporaneous relationships among variable innovations are theoretically justified, in their opinion.

One way to mitigate the imprecision of the results of vector autoregression is to incorporate prior beliefs about the structure of lagged relationships within a Bayesian framework. The use of informative priors in Bayesian vector autoregression (BVAR), especially to improve the precision of forecasts, has been advocated in economics by Todd (1984) and Litterman (1984), among others, and in political science by Williams (n.d.a; McGinnis and Williams 1989). Indeed, there is some reason to hope that the adoption of a Bayesian approach to vector autoregression may encourage the use of Bayesian methods by other analysts as well, perhaps contributing eventually to the sort of integration of complementary approaches envisioned by Zellner (1979).

Cointegration and Error Correction Models

Much economic theory and some in political science makes rich use of the notion of "equilibrium." Error correction models are methodologically attractive primarily because they can represent quite directly both theoretical expectations about equilibrium relationships and real-world deviations from those equilibrium relationships. For example, Ostrom and Smith (n.d.) distinguished between a set of "quality-of-life outcomes" (unemployment and inflation) expected to have "consistent and enduring effects on presidential approval" and a set of "dramatic political events" (foreign crises, scandals, health problems, and the like) expected to produce transitory "bumps and wiggles" in long-run trends of presidential approval. An error correction model captures the notion that dramatic events may make presidential approval at any given time somewhat higher or lower than is warranted by the underlying equilibrium relationship between quality-of-life outcomes and approval but recognizes that these transitory discrepancies will tend to erode over time as a political system returns to equilibrium.

In the past several years, time-series econometricians have made rapid strides in the development of error correction models, and of techniques for addressing the closely related phenomenon of "cointegration." The seminal article by Engle and Granger (1987) on cointegration has spurred a booming econometric literature (Phillips 1988, 1991; Engle and Granger 1991). Applications in political science include Beck (1992) and Ostrom and Smith (n.d.) on presidential approval, and Ostrom and Smith (1991) on defense spending.

A series of variables is said to be cointegrated if some linear combination of those variables is of lower order than the variables themselves. For example, two (or more) series X_{jt} may each be non-stationary (exhibiting mean drift), but with some cointegrating vector α producing a linear combination $Z_t = \alpha' X_t$ that is itself stationary (with constant mean and finite variance).

The relationship of cointegration implies "that both series individually have extremely important long-run components but that in forming Z_t these long-run components cancel out" (Granger and Newbold 1986, 225). As Granger and Newbold also pointed out (1986, 226), Z_t can be thought of as a short-run (stationary) deviation from an underlying equilibrium relationship $\alpha' X_t = 0$; "many economic theories are expressed in terms of equilibria of just this sort. Now Z_t can be interpreted as the equilibrium error, that is, the extent to which the economy is out of equilibrium."

The Granger Representation Theorem (Engle and Granger 1987) shows that the cointegrating relationship $Z_t = \alpha' X_t$ can be transformed into an equation relating current changes in any one variable to lagged changes in all the variables in the system, plus a moving average of current and lagged disturbances, minus some fraction of the previous equilibrium error Z_{t-1}. This transformation provides explicit connections not only between cointegration and error correction (since it allows for direct estimation of the error correction mechanism through the coefficient on Z_{t-1}), but also between cointegration and vector autoregression (since the transformed equation is essentially a vector autoregression in first differences, but with the additional regressor Z_{t-1}).

Engle and Granger (1987) proposed a sequential technique for estimating both the long-run equilibrium relationships among the variables in the system and the short-term dynamics of the error correction mechanism. The first step in this sequential technique is to estimate the long-run equilibrium relationship among variables by regressing levels of each variable on levels of all the other variables in the system. Thus, for example, Ostrom and Smith (n.d.) began by regressing monthly levels of presidential approval for the eight years of the Reagan administration on levels of inflation and unemployment (plus dummy variables for the 1981 assassination attempt and the Iran-contra scandal), and by regressing levels of inflation and unemployment on levels of the other variables as well. The second step is to test for cointegration in the relevant series. In the case of presidential approval, it is neccesary to establish that, although presidential approval levels themselves are not stationary, the residuals from the first-stage regression of approval on other variables in the system are stationary.

The third step in the Engle-Granger technique is to estimate the error correction model, which is essentially a vector autoregression of first differences but with an additional variable (a residual from the corresponding first-stage estimation) representing Z_{t-1}, the extent to which the system was in disequilibrium in the previous period. The parameter estimate associated with this lagged residual will lie between 0 and -1 if the error correction model makes substantive sense and can be interpreted as a measure of the strength of equilibrating forces in the system. For example, Ostrom and Smith (n.d.) estimated a coefficient on lagged residual popularity of -.58 (with a standard error of .09); the implication of this estimate is that shocks to Reagan's approval rating from dramatic political events had a half-life of about a month.

The econometric literature on cointegration continues to advance at a rapid pace. While this advance is itself impressive, the speed and sophistication with which political scientists have begun to apply these techniques are also impressive. Some recent developments are reflected in the exchange among Durr (n.d.), Beck (n.d.), Williams (n.d.b), and Smith (n.d.) in *Political Analysis*, and in a further exposition by Smith (1992).

The Kalman Filter

The Kalman filter was invented in engineering (Kalman 1960) and developed in economics by Harvey (1981), Watson and Engle (1983), and others. Harvey's (1989) book-length treatment covers both the basic theory and a variety of extensions. The expository survey for political scientists by Beck (1990) includes an accessible theoretical discussion, illustrative analyses of presidential approval and government investment data, and help with programming in GAUSS.

The Kalman filter is a tool for estimating a "state space model" combining a transition equation for latent endogenous variables with a measurement equation relating latent variables to observable indicators. For an Lx1 latent state vector γ_t, the transition equation can be written as:

$$\gamma_t = \Phi_t \, \gamma_{t-1} + B_t \, x_t + \Psi_t \, \epsilon_t \, ,$$

where x_t is a Kx1 vector of observed exogenous variables, ϵ_t is an Mx1 vector of stochastic disturbances, and Φ_t, B_t, and Ψ_t are matrices of parameters to be estimated.[9] An Nx1 vector of observed data y_t is related to the latent endogenous variables γ_t (and to the observed exogenous variables) by the measurement equation

$$y_t = \Lambda_t \, \gamma_t + \Xi_t \, x_t + \Omega_t \, \delta_t \, ,$$

where δ_t is an Nx1 vector of measurement errors and Λ_t, Ξ_t and Ω_t are matrices of parameters to be estimated. Thus, a useful way to think about the Kalman filter is as a structure-cum-measurement model for time-series data parallel to the general model of covariance structures developed by Jöreskog and others for cross-sectional data (Engle and Watson 1981).

The main attraction of the Kalman filter is its flexibility. For example, since all the parameters in the measurement model employed in the Kalman filter may in general be time dependent, missing data can be handled by assigning large measurement error variances to interpolated values (Harvey and McKenzie 1984). Beck (1990, 141-44) described an analysis of Reagan approval based on *New York Times*/CBS Poll data for which about 40% of the monthly data had to be interpolated. Although parameter estimates derived from the Kalman filter (with an assumed error standard deviation of four percentage points in months with interpolated data and zero in months with actual poll results) were generally similar to least squares estimates with the interpolated data treated at face value, the least squares analysis underestimated the (negative) effect of the lagged error term by about 50%.

In addition, the time dependence of the structural parameters in the transition equation make the Kalman filter suitable for estimating models with time-varying parameters (Beck 1983); indeed, Beck (1990, 135-36) noted that this has "probably been the principal application of the S[tate]S[pace]F[orm] in econometrics."

Since careful attention to measurement, time dependence, and error processes have all become increasingly important elements in sophisticated methodological work, the Kalman filter -- a powerful and flexible technique for dealing with all three -- seems destined to achieve increasing prominence in time-series research. As Beck pointed out (1990, 147), "The Kalman filter comes into its own when we actually care about the error process. There is no other technique that apportions the total error variance into measurement error and other sources of error. For evaluating theories such as rational expectations, which make strong predictions about error processes, the K[alman]F[ilter] is invaluable."

3. Time Series of Cross-Sections, Panels, and Aggregated Data

Aggregated Data and Ecological Inference

Political science data are often aggregated over time or units, and these data can present special problems for analysts. When aggregate outcomes can reasonably be thought of as having been produced by "unitary actors," it may be unproblematic to treat them as macro-level data. In cases where aggregate outcomes arise from more complicated individual-level processes, as with votes for political parties, aggregate presidential popularity, or political protests, aggregate-level analyses of covariation are less obviously appropriate, although nevertheless quite common. This has led some researchers to propose individual-level causal models, aggregate them, and develop techniques for estimating the underlying causal relationships. Both approaches have their place, but researchers are not always clear about which tack they are taking, and this can lead to confusion about whether they are testing individual-level causal theories or describing aggregate-level relationships.

One of the clearest examples of macro-level analysis of aggregated data is MacKuen, Erikson, and Stimson's (1989) article on "Macropartisanship," which proposed that, "Just as party identification is the key concept in studies of the individual voter, its aggregate -- what we term macropartisanship -- is central to theories of party system and voter alignment" (1989, 1125). MacKuen, Erikson, and Stimson examined the determinants of macropartisanship using a long time series constructed from individual-level survey data. Presidential popularity (Mueller 1973; Hibbs 1987), party vote share (Clubb, Flanigan, and Zingale 1980), seats in a legislature (Grofman 1983; King 1989b), and many other aggregate characteristics of political systems have been treated in this way. In some cases, the theoretical framework amounts to little more than a regression equation. In other cases, a macro-level model is proposed, as with Taagepera's (1986) generalization of the "cube law" relating seats to votes in legislative elections.

A related form of macro-level modeling involves using survey data to develop aggregated measures for geographical units. For example, Achen (1977, 1978) and others used survey data to study the relationship between the policy preferences of congressional constituencies and their representatives; Jackson (1990) developed an errors-in-variables method for estimating models using small area data; and Wright, Erikson, and McIver (1987) measured state partisanship and ideology using survey data.

In still other cases, a micro-level model of behavior is developed and then aggregated over individuals to suggest what the corresponding macro-level relationships should be. In these cases, the resulting models can be put to diverse uses. For example, King (1989b) developed a stochastic model of the relationship between seats and votes that relaxes the usual assumption of uniform partisan swing, allowing him to estimate a variety of characteristics of electoral systems. Although King also analyzed the impact of redistricting, his major goal was simply to characterize electoral systems in a useful and parsimonious fashion. In the political economy literature, Kramer (1983) took a different tack. He was fundamentally concerned with making individual-level causal inferences, and he developed an argument as to why aggregate data might provide a better estimate

than survey data of the impact of economic conditions on the vote.

Of all these enterprises, Kramer's best reflects the classic problem of "ecological inference," in which individual-level relationships are estimated directly from aggregate-level data. Most of the literature on ecological inference flows directly from Robinson's (1950) article on "the ecological fallacy" and Goodman's (1959) advocacy of "ecological regression." As Erbring (1990, 235) put it, "Ever since Robinson (1950) first shocked a whole generation of social scientists with his demonstration of the 'ecological fallacy,' much has been written about alleged fallacies, biases, pitfalls, and hazards of one kind or another lurking behind aggregate data and about strategies for circumventing them."

On one hand, researchers have attempted to clarify problems of ecological inference by starting from micro-level models and analyzing the difficulties that arise from various forms of aggregation. Hanushek, Jackson, and Kain (1974) identified aggregation bias as a specification error, clarifying in a familiar framework how ecological regression sometimes goes wrong and how aggregation bias can be reduced through careful attention to issues of model specification. Although their results have sometimes been interpreted to mean that ecological regression is consistent if the corresponding individual-level regression is properly specified, Achen (1986a, 2) showed that "coefficients in properly specified micro-regressions are generally biased when estimated with aggregate data." Erbring (1990) further clarified the relationship between specification bias and design effects, emphasizing the role of variance partitioning in aggregation and the connection between the problem of ecological inference and more general problems of research design. Finally, Freeman (1990) described some analogous statistical difficulties arising from temporal aggregation of time-series data, with references to the relevant econometric literature and an example focusing upon empirical studies of superpower rivalry in international relations.

A second approach has been to devise new techniques for mitigating the problems of ecological inference. Often, work of this sort begins with a critique of Goodman's ecological regression technique and then proposes modifications of Goodman's approach. For example, Ansolabehere and Rivers (1992) proposed a way to combine survey and aggregate data to get better estimates of racial voting patterns. Achen (1984) showed that ecological regression applied to constituency-level British election returns yields results that are wildly at odds with the results of individual-level analysis of survey data and proposed a new "quadratic" technique for ecological regression that produces results much closer to the individual-level results. Achen (1983a, 1983b, 1984,

1986a) and Shively (1969, 1974, 1985) have been leaders in efforts of this sort, and their forthcoming book (Achen and Shively n.d.) will no doubt serve as a valuable compendium of techniques for ecological inference.

We now have a better understanding of the problems involved in making inferences from aggregated data, as well as some workable, if imperfect, techniques for dealing with those problems. Achen's (1983a, 85) suggestion still holds: "Serious theoretical research on deriving an aggregate level contextual model from empirically verified assumptions about individual level interactions should have a high priority for students of social context." In the meantime, the fact that no technique can compensate fully for the absence of relevant individual-level data should not prevent analysts from utilizing the best available techniques for mitigating aggregation problems; nor should the ultimate intractability of ecological inference prevent us from continuing to strive for understanding in areas beyond the reach of ideally suitable data.

Time-Series Cross-Sectional, Panel, and Pseudo-Panel Methods

Time-series cross-sectional (TSCS) data vary both over units such as government agencies, nations, or individuals and over time. For example, Fischer and Kamlet (1984) studied budgetary allocations for three government agencies over a 27-year period, Pollins (1989) considered U.S. trade with 24 different partners over 24 years, and typical election panel studies (Markus 1982; Conover and Feldman 1989) include from two to five interviews with each of 1,000 to 2,000 people.[10] These designs increase the number of observations, vary both time and context, and provide the opportunity to control for idiosyncratic behavior through the inclusion of dummy variables or lagged endogenous variables. At the same time, they pose some significant methodological challenges.

Consider the most general TSCS linear regression:

$$y_{it} = a_{it} + x_{it} \, b_{it} + e_{it},$$

where y_{it} varies over I units indexed by i and over T time periods indexed by t; a_{it} is a set of intercepts varying by unit and time; x_{it} is a vector of J independent variables; b_{it} is a parameter vector varying by unit and time, and e_{it} is an error term. This model is woefully underidentified, with only IxT observations available to estimate IxT intercepts, IxJxT slopes, and at least one variance for characterizing the error term.[11] Additional assumptions are necessary, and the TSCS literature provides a smorgasbord of possible restrictions and tests for these

restrictions. If we assume, for example, that the slopes are constant over time and units, $b_{it} = b$, that the intercepts can be expressed linearly as $a_{it} = c_i + d_t$ to allow for idiosyncratic unit and time effects, that there is no serial or spatial dependence in the error, and that heteroskedasticity results from the varying ability of the independent variables to explain each unit's behavior, then only one slope, I+T intercepts, and I variances must be estimated -- a number less than IxT observations for modest values of I and T. Although TSCS methods have been developed almost exclusively by economists (Hsiao 1986; Judge et al. 1985, chap. 13), political scientists can now refer to the excellent overviews by Stimson (1985) and Sayrs (1989). Stimson's article has been widely cited in the literature, in part because it provides a useful distinction between time-serial dominant (T > I) and cross-sectional dominant (I > T) data.

Many other complications arise with TSCS studies. It often makes sense to include a lagged endogenous variable to control for prior opinions (Markus 1982), last year's budgetary decisions (Fischer and Kamlet 1984), or prior levels of economic development (Alvarez, Garrett, and Lange 1991; Bradshaw and Tshandu 1990). A lagged endogenous variable produces biased parameter estimates if it is measured with error (McAdams 1986), if there is autocorrelation in the equation (Hibbs 1974), or if the adjustment process is not Markov and depends upon more than the last value of the endogenous variable (Beck 1992).

Another difficulty can arise when there are interdependencies across units. In budgetary studies, for example, the sum of the allocations to all agencies is the total budget, so one agency must be dropped from the analysis when the total budget is also being modeled (Kamlet and Mowery 1987). Interdependencies also arise from diffusion or contagion across units. Diffusion and contagion can be considered nuisances and treated as a form of spatial autocorrelation, but they can also be addressed directly by including additional explanatory variables in the analysis (Ross and Homer 1976). Schneider and Ingraham (1984) used this strategy to study social policy innovations across nations. More generally, interrelations or interactions among units can create simultaneities. When the number of units is small, as with Fischer and Kamlet's (1984) two-category budget model, a simultaneous equation system can be estimated in which the dependent variable for each unit enters into the equation for every other unit, but when the number of units is large, as with most cross-national studies, the problem appears very difficult.

The most sophisticated TSCS models are found in the budgeting literature and in panel studies. Starting with theories of incremental budgeting, a great deal of attention has been paid to budgetary decision making (Berry and Lowery 1990), with simultaneous equation

Bartels and Brady   131

(Fischer and Kamlet 1984) and switching regressions (Kiewiet and McCubbins 1988) used to model the annual budgetary battle between the president and Congress.

In panel studies, simultaneities (Markus 1982) and errors in measurement (McAdams 1986) have been staples of concern, and sophisticated models have been developed to study opinion change (MacKuen 1984; Bartels n.d.). For example, Bartels (n.d.) used panel data from the 1980 American National Election Study to estimate the political impact of media exposure in a presidential election campaign. In addition to using the panel design to estimate and adjust for the effects of measurement error, he developed an estimation strategy in which opinion reports at two or more points in time could be used in the context of a simple Bayesian model of opinion change to characterize the "distinctive messages" received by those exposed to television news and newspaper coverage of the campaign in the intervening period. In this case, as in other cases where individual opinions are quite stable over relatively short periods of time, the availability of direct, individual-level measurements of prior opinion greatly increases our ability to relate opinion changes to individual differences in media exposure, political predispositions, physical location, and other factors.

Perhaps the most exciting opportunity for innovation by political scientists lies with analyzing repeated random cross-sections. Unlike standard time series of cross-sections or panel studies, in these survey designs different individuals are interviewed in each time period. The resulting data can be analyzed by simply taking aggregate statistics for each cross-section and treating them as a time series, as in Allsop and Weisberg's (1988) study of macro-partisanship over the course of the 1984 presidential campaign. Of course, this approach throws away a great deal of information that might be better exploited in a pooled TSCS analysis, but it is often hard to know how to use that information to full advantage. In their study of the 1988 Canadian campaign, Johnston et al. (1992, Appendix B) proposed two different TSCS methods for using this additional information.

More work is needed to develop methods that utilize the full power of this design. However, one such method has already been developed: Franklin's (1990) "two-stage auxiliary instrumental variables" estimator. In Franklin's approach, pseudo-panels are constructed by using common variables in two or more separate data sets. Suppose, for example, that we want to know the relationship between party identification in 1960 and 1964. We have no panel of respondents covering this period, but we do have separate cross-sections in the two election years. Using the 1960 data, we can estimate party identification as a function of a set of instrumental variables (demographic variables and other fixed characteristics) available in both data sets. Then, using the coefficients from the 1960 equation for party identification, we can construct estimates of 1960 party identification for each person in the 1964 cross-section. Finally, we can regress 1964 party identification on estimated 1960 identification to determine, for example, whether a realignment occurred in the intervening period. Franklin (1990) showed the conditions under which this procedure makes sense and also derived the standard errors of the resulting parameter estimates.

4. Techniques Tailored to Measurement Properties of Data

Polychotomous Data and Polytomous Choice

With the admonitions of Aldrich and Nelson (1984) in mind, political scientists confronted with dichotomous dependent variables now routinely use logit or probit, make Goldberger corrections for the linear probability model, or at least apologize for the limitations of ordinary least squares. In practice, these three methods often produce very similar results, and the OLS model has the great virtue of being easy to estimate and to interpret (Achen 1986b). In fact, given the difficulty of interpreting probit and logit estimates (Nagler 1991; Denk and Finkel 1992), there is a great deal to be said for OLS.

Dichotomous variables, of course, are only the simplest form of polychotomous or polytomous choice data. Jacoby's (1991) review of measurement theory surveys many other possibilities. Economists (Maddala 1983) and psychometricians (Muthen 1984; Rasch 1980) have developed a variety of methods for analyzing these kinds of data. Political scientists have begun to adopt some of the methods developed by economists: Tobit for truncated variables like the amount of welfare paid by local communities (Sharp and Maynard-Moody 1991), nested logit for multistage decision processes of international agencies and voters (Hansen 1990; Born 1990), switching regressions to capture presidential and congressional interaction over budgetary matters (Kiewiet and McCubbins 1988), and multivariate logit (Franklin and Jackson 1986; Jackson and King 1989) and probit (Ostrom and Simon 1988) for simultaneous equations. Techniques developed by psychometricians are not as widely known or used.

In addition to borrowing methods from other disciplines, political scientists have developed some innovative and important techniques of their own for analyzing polychotomous data. Most notably, McKelvey and Zavoina (1975) extended the familiar probit model to deal with ordinal, rather than simply dichotomous, dependent variables. The ordinal probit model has been used to study the partisanship of Latinos and Asian Americans (Cain, Kiewiet, and Uhlaner 1991), opinions on abortion (Franklin and Kosaki 1989), and many other political phenomena.

In an especially interesting application, Krehbiel and Rivers (1988) synthesized the ordinal probit model and an ideal point model of congressional roll-call voting. In Krehbiel and Rivers's approach, the ordinal information contained in a series of congressional roll-call votes, in combination with a set of observed covariates -- characteristics of legislators and districts -- makes it possible to obtain consistent estimates of individual legislators' ideal points in just the same way that ordered probit can be used to estimate scale values.[12] Krehbiel and Rivers presented both unidimensional and multidimensional variants of their method, and they developed approaches both for the case where there is some auxiliary information on the locations of bills (for example, the wage levels proposed in each of a series of minimum wage bills) and for the case in which no such information is available. Bartels (1991a) used Krehbiel and Rivers's model to estimate the impact of constituency opinion on congressional defense appropriations votes in the first year of the Reagan defense buildup, using the levels of spending proposed in each of a series of alternative appropriations bills to calibrate the spending preferences of members representing congressional districts with varying levels of public support for increased defense spending.

Several other innovations by political scientists are also worth noting. Rivers (1988) developed a method for estimating models with parameter heterogeneity using rank-preference data. Brady (1989, 1990) showed that standard factor analysis applied to interpersonally incomparable ordinal rankings produces misleading results and developed a model for the dimensional analysis of these data. Rivers and Vuong (1988) developed a new two-step maximum likelihood estimator for simultaneous probit models. And Brady and Ansolabehere (1989) developed a threshold model of paired comparison choices and estimated a trinomial probit model with the threshold parameterized by political knowledge and preferences parameterized by a vector of explanatory variables.

Thus, political methodologists, drawing in part upon the distinctive problems, data, and models of political science, have made significant contributions to the analysis of polychotomous data and polytomous choices. The methods they have developed, along with the various methods developed by econometricians and, especially, psychometricians, await fruitful application in a variety of areas of political research.

Event Count and Event History Models

Event counts are ubiquitous and important in political science. In order to understand the various statistical issues arising in analyses of these data, it is helpful to begin with a general statistical framework. Let y_i be the number of events recorded for each observation i, say the number of vacancies on the United States Supreme Court in each year since 1787 (King 1987), and let x_i be a vector of explanatory variables related to the count, such as the number of seats on the Supreme Court, the degree of electoral turnover, or the time since the last vacancy. The x_i might also be just a constant or a set of dummy variables for years. Then we can write:

$$y_i = f(x_i \ b) + e_i,$$

where f is a function, b is a set of parameters, and e_i is an error term. As written, almost any data can be fit to this non-linear model. To be of interest, we must make additional assumptions about the functional form f, the vector of independent variables, and the error term. The classic Poisson model is based upon three assumptions. First, the dependent variable y_i is assumed to follow the Poisson distribution with mean $f(x_i \ b)$. Second, the function f is assumed to be the exponential, so that $f(x_i \ b) = \exp(x_i \ b)$, ensuring that the expected number of events in each time period is positive. Third, there is assumed to be only one explanatory "variable" x_i with a constant value of one, so that every observation is generated by a Poisson process with the same mean, exp(b).

There is a substantial tradition, dating back at least to Wallis (1936) and Richardson (1944), of using the distribution of event counts produced by a Poisson process as a baseline model for studying events data.[13] The Poisson process is a good baseline model because it only requires a very simple set of assumptions about how events occur: that the probability of an event is constant over time (temporal homogeneity) and across units (actor homogeneity) and that events occur independently of each other (without diffusion or contagion) and with low probability in each time period. Under these assumptions, the number of events per time period can be shown to follow a Poisson distribution (see King 1988 for an accessible proof).

Of course, each of these assumptions will be implausible for many applications.[14] There are ample reasons to believe that the probabilities of events vary by time and unit of observation; this suggests that the homogeneity assumptions are too strong. Independence of events also seems implausible in many situations where diffusion is a strong possibility. Analyses of policy innovations in the American states (Walker 1969; Gray 1973), oil nationalization (Kobrin 1985), social security

(Collier and Messick 1975), and coups (Putnam 1967; Midlarsky 1970; Li and Thompson 1975) provide abundant evidence of diffusion. Thus, going beyond assumptions of homogeneity and independence has been the major challenge facing analysts of events data during the past fifteen years.

Fortunately, there are several ways to generalize the classic Poisson model, depending upon whether one focuses upon the error term e_i, the functional form $f(x_i b)$, or the vector of attributes x_i.

Until the last decade, the major focus has been on generalizing the error term.[15] As early as Richardson's (1944, 243-44) work, there was a realization that plausible violations of the Poisson process model, such as contagion or heterogeneity, would lead to other distributions, such as the negative binomial. By now there are many sophisticated and clever analyses of event counts in which alternative distributions are fit to data on war (Davis, Duncan, and Siverson 1978; Most and Starr 1980; Levy 1982; Siverson and Starr 1991), alliances (McGowan and Rood 1975; Siverson and Duncan 1976; Job 1976; Midlarsky 1983), terrorist acts (Hamilton and Hamilton 1983), urban riots (Midlarsky 1978), and elite turnover (Casstevens 1989).

However, this research strategy seems to us to face three insurmountable problems. First, since real data never fit any distribution exactly, it is hard to determine how good a fit is good enough to be useful. Second, some hypotheses (such as actor heterogeneity and addictive contagion) lead to identical distributions, so that it is impossible to distinguish them. And, third, fitting distributions does not provide any indication of what might be causing heterogeneity or contagion. (For a related discussion of diffusion, see Ross and Homer 1976.)

These difficulties lead naturally to a shift away from generalizing the error term e_i in favor of generalizing the functional form $f(x_i b)$. King (1988, 1989a, 1989c, 1989d) employed this strategy to develop an increasingly general set of "Poisson regression" models. In his first paper, King (1988) described the Poisson regression model, argued for the utility of the exponential functional form, demonstrated the biases that can arise from using ordinary least squares, and presented an empirical example. In this initial paper he argued (1988, 858-59) that "the underlying mathematical process generating event count data is driven by the Poisson distribution," but a year later (King 1989d, 763) he took the position that "the Poisson regression model...makes two key assumptions about the way unobserved processes generate event counts [homogeneity and independence] that are implausible in many applications....If these assumptions do not hold, but the Poisson model is applied anyway, parameter estimates will be inefficient and standard errors inconsistent, a situation analogous to heteroskedasticity in least squares models." King developed models allowing for temporal heterogeneity and contagion based upon the negative binomial for overdispersion and the continuous parameter binomial for underdispersion. The result is a generalized event count (GEC) distribution which produces estimates without any a priori assumption about under- or over-dispersion. Finally, in a wide-ranging paper on event count models for international relations, King (1989a) reviewed his earlier contributions and described several new models including a "hurdle" model in which the onset of war is modeled separately from its escalation, a truncated model in which only episodes of international sanctions are observed, an extension of this model in which the variance of the distribution is parameterized in terms of a vector of independent variables, and a model for Poisson regressions with correlated errors.

King generalized the basic Poisson model in all three directions noted above -- the error term, the functional form, and the vector of independent variables -- and also made some progress toward modeling multiple equation systems. His models provide a very useful package of techniques for dealing with event counts, especially since he has programmed his methods into a set of computer routines for the GAUSS statistical package.

At the same time, there is more work to be done in at least two directions. First, under- and over-dispersion might be considered specification problems in the same way that heteroskedasticity and autocorrelation are often considered failures of specification in regression models. From this perspective, the GEC model should be only a way-station to a better specification. Second, more work has to be done to derive event count distributions from first principles -- from the underlying stochastic processes generating the data. This is not an easy task; Tuma and Hannan (1984, 305) noted that "the probability mass function for the count of events...has apparently not yet been derived for a general...Markov model." Indeed, the difficulty of deriving event count distributions from more basic models led Tuma and Hannan to recommend using event histories in preference to event counts whenever the former are available.

Event history analyses have become more common in political science in the past decade. The study of cabinet durations illustrates both some of the pitfalls and some of the possibilities of these analyses. Initial efforts (Browne, Frendreis, and Gleiber 1984, 1986; Cioffi-Revilla 1984) failed to capitalize fully on the strengths of stochastic modeling, being based upon simple Poisson models with constant rates of dissolution. The simplicity of these models probably accounts for Strom's characterization of them as "disappointing and inadequate" (Strom et al. 1988, 929). King et al. (1990) went a long way towards meeting such objections by developing a stochastic model in which the probability of cabinet dissolution varies with a series of observable explanatory variables.

Event history methods have been applied in other areas as well. Bienen and van de Walle's (1989) proportional hazard model of leadership duration in Africa and Strang's (1991) analysis of decolonization from 1500 to 1987 both allowed for changes in the probability of events over time and as a function of measured covariates. In their study of state lottery adoptions, Berry and Berry (1990) used a pooled time-series cross-sectional probit method to estimate a discrete time hazard rate model described by Allison (1984). These efforts and others like them bode well for the future of stochastic modeling in political science. Useful book-length introductions to the relevant models and methods include Tuma and Hannan (1984), Allison (1984), and King (1989c).

5. Measurement Error and Missing Data

Problems of measurement were central to the intellectual agenda for political methodology set out by Achen a decade ago. "One thing political methodologists *have* done," he wrote (1983a, 70), "is to show that measurement does matter." Political methodologists have made significant additional progress on problems of measurement in the intervening decade. Explicit attention to measurement in the formulation and estimation of statistical models, though by no means standard, is an increasingly common feature of our best empirical work. Structural equation models with latent (unobserved) variables (Bollen 1989) have come into widespread use.[16] Jöreskog and Sörbom's LISREL software, now available within SPSS, is only one of several available computer programs (EQS, LISCOMP) for estimating such models. On the theoretical side, our understanding of proxy variables, though far from complete, is considerably more advanced than it used to be. And problems of measurement outside the classic errors-in-variables and scaling frameworks inherited from econometrics (Fuller 1987) and psychometrics (Jöreskog and Sörbom 1979) are beginning to be recognized and tackled.

The Consequences of Random and Non-Random Measurement Error

Achen (1983a, 71-74) provided a summary and extension of what was known at the time about the effects of random measurement error in explanatory variables. He cautioned against the false but widespread belief that measurement error simply attenuates regression coefficients, so that "if one can establish the existence of an effect in spite of measurement error, the true effect must be even larger." Explicit attention to the consequences of measurement error has recast our substantive understanding of many political phenomena, including the stability (Achen 1975; Erikson 1979) and generational transmission (Dalton 1980) of political attitudes, the role of party identification (Franklin and Jackson 1983; Green and Palmquist 1990), and the impact of media exposure (Bartels n.d.).

Achen also pushed political scientists to go beyond the standard assumption of random measurement error by showing (1983a, 75) that when measurement errors are not random, literally anything can happen: "for any arbitrary coefficient vector β^*, there exists a systematic error structure...that will generate it." This sweeping negative result demonstrated -- if any formal demonstration was necessary -- that it is futile to hope for a solution to the problems of inference inherent in analyzing data with non-random error, except insofar as we can bring to bear some specific knowledge of the relevant error structure.

Later, Achen (1985) identified a particularly perverse and previously unrecognized consequence of non-random measurement error. He showed that, if two proxies for a single latent variable are included in a regression model, the regression coefficient for the less reliable of the two proxies will tend to have the wrong sign, even in large samples, if the measurement errors in the proxies are sufficiently correlated. Only the combined effect of both proxies is interpretable in this case. What is worse, Achen showed that sign reversals can occur even when the measured variables are proxies for distinct latent variables (so that their individual effects are of direct substantive interest), if the measurement errors are sufficiently correlated and the latent variables themselves are also sufficiently correlated. Thus, "the common practice of using a long series of regression 'control variables' which are inexact proxies can be a misleading data-analytic technique. Such variables not only bias the estimated effect of non-proxy variables, as is well known, but in the presence of correlated errors, they may severely distort or even reverse their own estimated effects as well" (Achen 1985, 310).

Other analysts have derived the consequences of random and non-random measurement error in regression models of varying generality. Green (1991) analyzed the effects of measurement error in the context of a simultaneous equation model of party identification and political attitudes. Cowden and Hartley (n.d.) analyzed the effects of using complex measures that proxy for more than one latent variable in an ordinary regression analysis. And Palmer (1992) derived similar results from a somewhat more general model in which a source of correlated measurement error also appears (or belongs) as an explanatory variable in its own right in the structural equation of interest.

Guessing and Other Sources of Error in Survey Responses

These results of the consequences of random and non-random measurement error reinforce Achen's message (1985, 311) that in order to make any real progress surmounting the inferential problems posed by measurement error, we "must know something about the error structure a priori." One especially promising source of a priori information about the error structures of political data is careful consideration of our measuring instruments themselves. Rather than simply tacking an additive random error term onto an explanatory variable, as in the standard econometric approach, a few analysts have begun to develop models recognizing and exploiting the fact that some specific kinds of measurement error are more likely than others.

For example, Brady (1985a) and Green (1988) analyzed non-random measurement error resulting from response sets -- different people using response scales in idiosyncratic but consistent ways across items. The general setup used by Brady and Green is similar to the assumption of a linear transformation of true underlying opinion made by Aldrich and McKelvey (1977). In models of this sort, even if true responses are independent of one another, survey responses across two items may be correlated if some people always use the upper part of a scale and other people always use the lower part of the scale. Green (1988) corrected for these effects and found that liberalism-conservatism may be unidimensional and not multidimensional as argued by Conover and Feldman (1981). Brady (1990) showed that because rankings of candidates are neither interpersonally comparable nor interval measures, standard factor analysis methods can be very misleading. He proposed a method that just uses ranking information and applied it to candidate rankings collected from Democrats who attended the 1984 Iowa caucuses.

In a similar spirit, Brady and Sniderman (1985, Appendix 2) proposed a "guessing" model in which those without opinions on seven-point issue scales were assumed to choose responses centered on the midpoint of the scale. Their scaling method produced an estimate of 8.5% guessers. Jackson (1992b) took a somewhat different approach, modeling the probability of various observed survey responses -- or non-responses -- as a function of two unobserved variables representing, respectively, latent preferences and latent non-opinion. For example, Jackson's analysis of responses to an item about school integration in the 1956 American National Election Study survey found that a substantial proportion of respondents without real opinions nevertheless agreed or disagreed with the statement that "The government in Washington should stay out of the question whether white and colored children go the same school," despite the presence of both a filter question asking whether respondents had thought much about this issue and a "not sure" response option. What is especially interesting is that these "pseudo-responses" were not equally distributed between the "agree" and the "disagree" categories but were much more likely to be "agree" responses, producing a significant misrepresentation of the division of "genuine" public opinion on the issue.

On the surface, these guessing models might seem similar to standard measurement error models, but they can have substantially different implications. For example, it is not hard to show (Brady 1993) that in a population in which some fraction of the population follows a Wiley and Wiley (1970) autoregressive model with any arbitrary amount of attitude stability, and the remainder simply guess by choosing randomly from some distribution with a mean at the center of the scale, the standard Wiley-Wiley estimation procedure will produce parameter estimates that are indistinguishable from those produced when the entire population follows the Wiley-Wiley model. This is true as long as the fraction of non-guessers is not zero, and it is true no matter how many waves of data are available. In short, the Wiley-Wiley model is fundamentally unidentified, and stability measures of 1.0 are consistent with a population in which nearly everyone guesses.[17]

The implication of these results is that high estimated stability coefficients alone are not very informative about the substance of political opinion. Higher and higher piles of computer output demonstrating that attitudes are extremely stable in the sense measured by Wiley-Wiley and other measurement models -- as in Krosnick's (1991) industrious analysis of hundreds of correlations among issue items in three different data sets -- are completely consistent with the guessing model described above with an arbitrarily high fraction of guessers. At this point, we do not need more such data analyses, but better models of how measurement error arises and what it represents.

Non-Random Samples and Sample Selection Bias

Political scientists commonly work with sets of observations that are non-random samples from some population of interest. In opinion surveys, for example, an inappropriate sampling frame may make some people more likely than others to be selected for interviewing; differences in lifestyles may make some of those selected more likely than others to actually be contacted by an interviewer; differences in political interest may make some of these contacted more likely than others to cooperate. Comparable problems arise in many other research settings.

This non-random selection will generally bias the results of cross-tabulations, regressions, and other statistical analyses. The pitfalls of "selecting on the dependent variable" have been widely, if vaguely, understood for some time. But the broader significance of selection bias was unrecognized, and statistical corrections for its effects were unknown, until Heckman (1976, 1979) showed how to treat censoring as a specification error in the familiar econometric framework.

Heckman's technique proceeds from the observation that the mean of a dependent variable conditional upon selection into the sample may depend in a systematic way upon the sample selection process. If we can model this dependence, then we can distinguish between structural effects and sample selection effects. In much the same way that instrumental variables are required to distinguish reciprocal effects in simultaneous equation models, the key to successful application of Heckman's technique is that there must be available a variable (or set of variables) significantly related to selection into the sample, but unrelated to the dependent variable of substantive interest. Achen (1986b, chaps. 4 and 5) provided a thorough intuitive and technical treatment of the bias engendered by censoring and of Heckman's correction, as well as an extension from the probit framework to the linear probability framework.

Although much empirical work still proceeds regardless of the pitfalls of analyzing data from censored samples, sensitivity to these pitfalls has increased. In the field of survey research, designers and analysts of the 1984 American National Election Study went to some lengths to estimate the impact of non-response; Brehm (1990) provided a comprehensive report of the results in the context of a more general discussion of survey non-response. Gelman and King (1990) applied the logic of selection bias to the problem of estimating the electoral advantage of congressional incumbency from observed election outcomes. Jackman and Vella (1992) looked for selection bias in estimates of partisan bias and responsiveness in redistricting plans. Geddes (1991) described the pitfalls of making inferences from censored samples in cross-national comparative studies. And Achen and Snidal (1989) criticized the use of non-randomly selected case studies in the study of deterrence in international relations.

Missing Data

Sample selection bias of the sort addressed by Heckman and Achen is only one of a variety of missing data problems plaguing political research. It is the one most frequently addressed, not because it is necessarily the most important but because a coherent and reasonably straightforward solution is available within the familiar econometric framework. The more common case of partially missing data -- in which some but not all of the data for a given observation are available -- is both less well understood theoretically and less well handled empirically.

The simplest technique for dealing with missing data is probably also the most common in political science: throw out the observations for which any data are missing and analyze only complete observations. Of course, the resulting loss of information can be considerable. In a typical analysis of issue positions in an election survey, for example, half or more of the respondents may have data missing on one or more issues. What may be worse, the non-randomness of the subset of respondents for whom complete data are available may induce serious sample selection bias of the sort described above.

An alternative approach is to impute values for missing data. For example, analysts sometimes substitute the sample mean for any values that are missing -- mean imputation. Usually it is preferable to substitute some other value that makes use of the non-missing data for the observation, such as the conditional mean from a regression analysis -- regression imputation -- or the observed value from a matched observation in the sample -- hot deck imputation. When the dispersion of a distribution is of interest, it may make sense to impute missing values by random sampling from some appropriate distribution -- stochastic regression imputation.

As a discipline, we are remarkably ignorant of the benefits and pitfalls of these various approaches. The result is that imputation of missing data is relatively rare in political research and is seldom documented in sufficient detail to be replicable or justified on any good methodological grounds. Although the statistical theory of missing data has many unsolved problems, results of the sort provided by Little and Rubin (1987, chaps. 3 and 4) offer a considerable statistical basis for dramatic improvements in the current state of empirical work.

The most sophisticated treatment of missing data in the political science literature to date appears in Mebane's (n.d.) analysis of the effects of U.S. local government fiscal activity. The Census Bureau's Census of Governments data sets provide detailed information on intergovernmental transfers for 80,000 local governments at five-year intervals, while Surveys of Governments in other years provide similar information for samples of a fifth to a third of these local governments. In order to estimate the effects of local fiscal activity, Mebane had to pool these two sources of information to estimate total intergovernmental transfers for all local governments in a given area in each year.

Mebane implemented a three-step estimation procedure combining features of the sample selection and measurement error corrections proposed by Heckman (1976, 1979) and Fuller (1987), respectively. In the first stage, Mebane estimated the probability that a given local government would be included in a given annual Survey of Governments sample; given the Census Bureau's sampling procedures, these probabilities are influenced (but not entirely determined) by the size of the government and its level of fiscal activity. In the second stage, Mebane used the estimated probabilities of inclusion from the first stage to impute fiscal totals for each area from the incomplete observed data by reweighting the observed totals in each area by the ratio of expected to actual observations; in addition to providing an estimate of the total fiscal activity in each area, this stage provided estimates of the measurement error in these estimated totals (which varied with the proportion of governments actually observed in a given area). In the third stage, Mebane outlined a procedure for correcting parameter estimates from a simple regression model in which local fiscal totals appeared as explanatory variables for biases resulting from sample selection (for areas in which no governments happened to be selected for observation) and measurement error (in areas where some but not all local governments were selected for observation), using variants on the approaches of Heckman and Fuller, respectively.

Although the details of Mebane's analysis reflect many specific features of the substantive problem he set out to address, the general outlines of his approach are clearly relevant to a broader class of problems in which missing data play an important role.

6. Dimensional Analysis

Since the pioneering work of Rice (1928), Thurstone (1932), and Gosnell (1937), dimensional analysis has been used to study electoral preferences and legislative roll-call votes. The field continues to be driven by the availability of voting data, candidate evaluations (often "thermometer" scores), and issue placements of candidates from sample surveys and roll-call or interest group ratings from legislatures. In voting and legislative research, the major issues have been the fit of the models, their underlying dimensionality, the interpretation of these dimensions, their stability over time, and the centrality or non-centrality of the candidates with respect to the voters or the members (or committees) relative to the legislature as a whole. In each of these areas, political scientists have developed original methods for estimating these models, and they have used these methods to provide statistical tests of important political questions.[18]

Voting Studies

The point of departure for most voting studies has been the "ideal-point" model of preference inspired by the psychometric literature (especially Coombs 1964) and the spatial modeling literature (Downs 1957; Davis and Hinich 1966).[19] This model presumes that voter i's "utility" U_{ij} for a candidate j is a function of the distance between the voter's positions V_{it} on T different dimensions of concern, and the candidate's locations C_{jt} on these same issues:

$$U_{ij} = - \Sigma_{t=1,T} (V_{it} - C_{jt})^2 + e_{ij}$$

where e_{ij} is an "error" term including any idiosyncratic influences on voter i's evaluation of candidate j. In this equation, as the distance between the voter and the candidate increases, the voter's evaluation of the candidate gets lower. This simple model has been generalized to other functional forms, and variables for "valence" issues -- about which everyone agrees that more is better -- have been added in some versions. Thus, a more general formulation is

$$U_{ij} = - [\Sigma_{t=1,T} (V_{it} - C_{jt})^r]^s + a X_j + e_{ij}$$

where r and s are exponents providing a flexible functional form and X_j is a vector representing valence issues such as competence or character. The values of r and s define the way that distance is measured: if $r=2$ and $s=1/2$, then the distance is Euclidian; the value $s=1/r$ defines a more general type of distance called the "Minkowski" metric. Still other values are possible, such as the squared Euclidian distance ($r=2$, $s=1$). Research in the past twenty years varies in the kinds of assumptions that are made about the functional form, whether or not valence issues are included, the nature of the error term, and the properties of the measure used for utility. There is also variation in the degree to which these assumptions are made explicit.

Rabinowitz (1976, 1978) developed and applied a novel "line of sight" procedure to obtain unbiased similarity measures for candidate pairs, which were then used as the basis for non-metric multidimensional scaling (NMDS). Whereas previous authors had argued over whether Pearson, Spearman, or some other correlations should be used for scaling procedures (e.g., Weisberg 1974b), Rabinowitz started from specific ideal point models (Euclidian and more generally Minkowski metrics) and developed a new and more appropriate measure of similarity. This measure was the basis for a NMDS procedure (Rabinowitz 1976) using Kruskal's (1964) "stress" as a measure of fit. Rabinowitz (1978) reproduced Weisberg and Rusk's (1970) two-dimensional representation of candidate positions; using these candidate positions, he estimated voter ideal points and showed that, contrary to the expectations of the median voter theorem (Black 1958), there was no candidate located in the center of the distribution of voters. Kruskal's stress is an ad hoc measure of fit, so it is hard to evaluate these results, but Brady's (1985b) statistical framework for NMDS provides one way to obtain standard errors of estimates and tests for goodness of fit.

Hinich and his collaborators (Cahoon 1975; Cahoon, Hinich, and Ordeshook 1978; Enelow and Hinich 1984, Appendix 9.1) took a much different approach to estimating spatial models of elections. Unlike Rabinowitz, they made strong metric assumptions about the measurement properties of thermometer scores, and they then cleverly modified factor analysis methods to obtain statistically consistent estimates of candidate positions for a squared Euclidian model ($r=2$, $s=1$). Their empirical work confirmed the social and economic dimensions found by previous scholars, and in later work they provided evidence for a "valence" dimension such as "integrity, executive ability, compassion, and intelligence" (Enelow and Hinich 1984, 174) about which all voters feel the same way. After obtaining candidate positions in the space, Enelow and Hinich used a procedure analogous to the estimation of factor scores to estimate voter ideal points. Using these estimates, they argued (Enelow and Hinich 1984, 222) that "major American political figures are not far away from the center of the electorate."

Poole (1981, 1984) developed a metric unfolding method for the Euclidian model ($r=2$, $s=1/2$), and Poole and Rosenthal (1984) applied it to thermometer evaluations. Poole's technique locates voters and

candidates simultaneously, and it provides a very efficient algorithm for obtaining estimates. Rivers (1987) and Brady (1991b), however, have argued that this method can yield statistically inconsistent estimates for both candidate and voter positions. Intuitively, the difficulty is that voter positions are essentially factor scores and there is a well-known indeterminacy in their estimation (Macdonald 1985) that corrupts the estimates of candidate positions as well.[20]

These papers have made substantial advances in our understanding of the spatial structure of candidate evaluations. Yet, except for the use of stress and other similar R-squared kinds of measures for the adequacy of the scaling method, no statistical measures of fit and no standard errors are reported for these methods. Brady (1991a) provided a "computationally simple, statistically consistent, reasonably efficient, and statistically informative generalized least squares (GLS) estimator for a general class of nonlinear multidimensional scaling (MDS) models including the 'ideal-point' models of voters' and legislators' behavior proposed by Melvin Hinich, Keith Poole and others" (1991, 97). The approach described by Brady assumes that thermometers are metric ratings and provides a statistical framework for testing a wide range of hypotheses about these models, including their functional form, their dimensionality, and the values of specific parameters. Moreover, Brady showed that a T-dimensional squared Euclidian model can be estimated using LISREL as a constrained $T+1$ dimensional factor model. This provides a very simple way to estimate this model and to obtain all the statistical information provided by LISREL, including standard errors of parameter estimates and a χ^2 goodness-of-fit statistic.

Applying his method to 1980 National Election Studies data, Brady showed that the ideal point model outperforms a factor model and that candidates are far away from the median voter. Using LISREL, it would be a simple matter to use this model to perform a variety of statistical tests, including tests for the constancy of candidate positions and of the distribution of voter ideal points over several waves of a panel. In two other papers, Brady (1989, 1990) considered rankings of candidates for which metric techniques are clearly inappropriate. These papers also provide a statistical basis for analyzing these data.

Aggregate voting data have also been scaled using principal components analysis (Rabinowitz, Gurian, and Macdonald 1984; Rabinowitz and Macdonald 1986; Macdonald and Rabinowitz 1987). This work yields two basic dimensions representing ideology and party. Rabinowitz and Macdonald (1986) showed that this approach yields reasonable estimates if every voter across all the states and all the years makes ideal point calculations using the same dimensions, if there are no idiosyncratic factors like the e_{ij} above, and "if the distribution of the voters in each of the 50 states is multivariate normal, with states having different mean locations but identical covariance structures." These assumptions are a reasonable starting point, but there are good reasons to believe that idiosyncratic factors do matter and that covariance structures might differ substantially across states. For one thing, it is easy to show that a large number of precincts with different means and otherwise identical multivariate Normal distributions of voters will produce an aggregate distribution that is not multivariate Normal, but a mixture of Normals. This suggests that the multivariate Normal assumption is a very special assumption.

Perceptual Studies

Since the 1970s, the National Election Studies have asked citizens to place themselves and candidates on seven-point issue scales. These data provide a way of mapping how citizens perceive themselves and the candidates. They also provide a more direct way of determining whether vote choices can be explained in terms of voter distances from candidates, instead of generating candidate and voter positions indirectly from voter choices or candidate evaluations, as with the scaling methods described above. One disconcerting feature of these placements, however, is that for the same issue and candidate, perceptions vary substantially from one person to another. One person will see Ronald Reagan as tough on crime, while another will view him as easy on crime. This has led researchers to develop models of these responses. Aldrich and McKelvey (1977) developed the first sophisticated model of response in which a person i's placement Y_{ijm} of candidate j on issue m is a linear transformation of some underlying true position Y_{jm} of the candidate:

$$Y_{ijm} = a_{im} + b_{im} Y_{jm} + d_{ijm}$$

where a_{im} adjusts for the fact that different people may anchor the scale in different ways, b_{im} adjusts for differences in the range of the scale used by otherwise identical people, and d_{ijm} represents random error in perceptions of the candidate's position. Aldrich and McKelvey suggested a method that simultaneously estimated both the locations of candidates and the voter characteristics a_{im} and b_{im}, but they did not provide any proofs of its statistical properties. They found that, except for Wallace in 1968 and McGovern in 1972 on Vietnam, candidates were close to the median voter. Palfrey and Poole (1987) used the Aldrich-McKelvey method to consider the relationship between ideological extremism and voting behavior.

Enelow and Hinich (1989) modified the Aldrich and McKelvey model by assuming that a small number T of candidate positions C_{jt} underlie the true candidate positions Y_{jm} on each issue:

$$Y_{jm} = \Sigma_{t=1,T} C_{jt} f_{tm},$$

where f_{tm} is the degree to which dimension t underlies issue m. This is then substituted into the equation for Y_{ijm} above:

$$
\begin{aligned}
Y_{ijm} &= a_{im} + \Sigma_{t=1,T} b_{im} C_{jt} f_{tm} + d_{ijm} \\
&= a_{im} + \Sigma_{t=1,T} g_{imt} C_{jt} + d_{ijm},
\end{aligned}
$$

where $g_{imt} = b_{im} f_{tm}$. Enelow and Hinich assumed that the g_{imt} are produced by random variables that are independent across dimensions t for each issue m. Once a_{im} is subtracted off each observed candidate issue position, a factor analysis of the covariances across candidates for each issue should yield the same candidate positions C_{jt}. Enelow and Hinich (1989, 464) claimed that "very little change could be detected across these factor analyses," so they pooled the data across all issues to obtain estimates of the covariances for their final factor analysis. They found two dimensions and that "the candidates lie relatively close to the average voter and exhibit little movement over the campaign" (1989, 461).

Enelow and Hinich's model has the virtue of utilizing methods for which we have well-developed statistical theory; but that virtue has not yet been fully exploited. For example, Enelow and Hinich did not test for the stability of candidate positions across issues, as they could have done using LISREL for simultaneous factor analysis in several populations (Jöreskog and Sörbom 1979, chaps. 7 and 8). A more complete integration of available methods, with more attention to standard errors and statistical tests, will greatly facilitate substantive interpretation of the results of these analyses.

More generally, direct scaling of votes, candidate evaluations, or perceptual items almost invariably lead to two or three basic dimensions, but the interpretation of these dimensions varies markedly from study to study, with substantially different conclusions about whether or not candidates are near the median voter. Hinich and his collaborators have consistently found that candidates are near the median, whereas Rabinowitz, Poole, Brady, and others have found that candidates tend to be far away from the center of the voter distribution. To reconcile these different results and interpretations, we must pay more attention to statistical hypothesis testing, and we must extend our scaling models, possibly along the lines suggested by Brady and Sniderman (1985), to include more ancillary information -- voter issue positions, candidate perceptions, and socioeconomic variables -- in order to refine and better interpret our results.

Legislative Studies

The major strides in legislative roll-call analysis during the 1980s have been undertaken by Poole, Rosenthal, and their collaborators, who assembled some extraordinary datasets, overcame significant computational problems, and generally improved our understanding of the American Congress. Poole's metric unfolding technique (1981, 1984) has been used to analyze interest group scores of legislators (Poole and Daniels 1985).[21] Poole and Rosenthal (1985) have also utilized another scaling method for the direct analysis of roll-call votes. Their initial NOMINATE program assumes a one-dimensional space and that "each roll call is a choice between two points on the dimension -- one point represents the outcome corresponding to a yea vote and the other point represents the outcome corresponding to a nay vote" (1985, 360). Legislators calculate their utility for each point based upon an ideal point model, their own position on the one dimension, and idiosyncratic factors represented by an error term with a Weibull distribution. The probability that the legislator votes yes or no is given by an analytical expression involving exponentials, which is used to form a likelihood function across all legislators and all roll calls.

In later versions of this program, called D-NOMINATE, Poole and Rosenthal (1991) extended the method to consider multiple dimensions and change over time. As with the metric procedure, Poole and Rosenthal have only provided Monte Carlo simulations and not analytical proofs of the statistical properties of their method.[22]

In addition to concerns about the statistical properties of their methods, two other criticisms have been leveled at Poole and Rosenthal's work. First, Koford (1989, 1991) argued that their measures of fit overemphasize the role of the first dimension relative to later dimensions, although Poole and Rosenthal have disagreed (1991). Second, a formal model of legislatures proposed by Snyder (1992, with a reply by Rosenthal) implies that "If some committees are 'preference outliers' relative to the legislature as a whole...then roll call data are likely to be 'artificially unidimensional.'" The lessons of both these critiques are simple: we need better models undergirding our statistical techniques, and we need to work harder to develop the statistical properties of those techniques. At the same time, the critiques themselves signal the importance of Poole and Rosenthal's work, which offers one of the most prominent examples of methodological advance in political science in the past twenty years.

7. Model Specification[23]

In textbooks, "model specification" is sometimes taken quite narrowly to refer to the problem of choosing an appropriate list of explanatory variables in a regression model. Sometimes the scope of the topic is broadened to include questions of functional form and assumptions about the distribution of the disturbance term. But even this broader definition makes it easy to gloss over some important practical problems that are fundamentally similar in their causes and consequences to those encompassed in the usual formulation. The problem of choosing an appropriate population, for example, is essentially identical to the problem of choosing an appropriate set of explanatory variables (since two or more distinct populations can be represented in a pooled model by appropriate use of indicator variables and interaction terms). Problems arising in the use of aggregated data can be addressed using much the same framework used to address seemingly unrelated problems of model specification (Theil 1971, chap. 11; Hanushek, Jackson, and Kain 1974; Erbring 1990). Time series (Beck 1985) and simultaneous equation models (Bartels 1985, 1991b) generate fundamentally similar problems.

Specification Uncertainty and the Perils of Data Dredging

Statistical inferences always rest upon the assumptions embodied in a specific statistical model. In an ideal world, the specification of a model would be determined by strong theoretical expectations, together with accumulated knowledge of the measurement processes generating our data. But real political research is more often marked by very considerable uncertainty about which explanatory variables may be relevant, their functional forms, and the sources and nature of stochastic variation and measurement error.[24]

Ironically, as political methodologists have become more sophisticated, fundamental problems of specification uncertainty have become increasingly pressing. As we have already noted, complex simultaneous equation, factor analysis, and covariance structure models have become increasingly commonplace in various areas of political science. In most respects, this increasing complexity is well and good; but one costly side effect of complexity is to multiply the number of difficult, and often arbitrary, specification decisions upon which any empirical result depends. Too often we lack the strong theory necessary to specify clearly how observable indicators are related to latent variables, or which variables in a structural equation are exogenous and which are endogenous. "We are left with a plethora of loosely related, partially contradictory models in a single substantive area; one analyst's key endogenous variable is assumed by a second to be exogenous and totally ignored by a third, with substantive consequences that are completely unclear to all concerned" (Bartels 1985, 182). The result is that, even after we have estimated our complex models, we remain -- or at least, we should remain -- much less confident in our estimates of causal effects than classic statistical theory would lead us to expect.

Specification uncertainty is especially troubling to the extent that it invites "data dredging," an extensive exploration of alternative specifications in search of one that produces "significant" parameter estimates, a high R-squared value, or any other desired result. Even for relatively simple regression models, the range of possible alternative specifications is sufficiently large that really efficient data dredging requires the help of a computer equipped with a "stepwise regression" or other variable selection procedure; but humans can, and too often do, also engage in data dredging in their own slightly less efficient way. By "capitalizing on chance" -- overfitting the data to produce impressive results that reflect the peculiarities of the sample at hand more than the underlying causal structure of interest -- they knowingly or unknowingly mislead themselves about the strength and certainty of their results.

The perils of data dredging can be elegantly illustrated by the behavior of data analysts in simple controlled experiments. For example, Green (1990) presented the results of an experiment in which first-year graduate students estimated regression parameters from simulated data without knowing the exact form of the model used to generate the data. Three potential regressors were included in the students' data sets, but only two of these actually had non-zero parameters in the "true" model. Even this rather modest level of specification uncertainty was sufficient to produce errors in the estimated parameters far in excess of what would be expected on the basis of sampling variability: the observed root mean squared error of the parameter estimate Green focused upon was more than twice as large as the nominal standard error derived from classic regression theory.

In an interesting pedagogical wrinkle, Green compared the effects of data dredging among two distinct groups of students who were randomly assigned to somewhat different courses of statistical training. He found that "in comparison to students who were warned against atheoretical model specification, those whose training in regression emphasized classical F-tests and goodness-of-fit were more likely to misspecify their models by including endogenous regressors and excluding causally relevant, but statistically insignificant variables" (Green 1990, 7). Because the latter group "were quick to

abandon common sense when the opportunity arose" (Green 1990, 9), their observed root mean squared error exceeded the nominal standard error by 155%, while the observed root mean squared error in the former group exceeded the nominal standard error by a somewhat less harrowing 85% (computed from data presented by Green 1990, 8-9).

Sensitivity Analysis, Out-of-Sample Validation, and Cross-Validation

Green's experiment provides some limited support for his hopeful contention (1990, 9) that "data-dredgers are made, not born." Nevertheless, his results and others like them suggest that, even in the best homes, a latent predisposition toward data dredging leads empirical research seriously astray. The best safeguards against the inferential ill effects of data dredging are sensitivity analysis and out-of-sample validation. Unfortunately, neither has been common in political science.

Sensitivity analysis explores the robustness of key parameter estimates under plausible alternative specifications of a statistical model. When several plausible specifications produce similar results, we can have considerably more confidence in the validity of those results than when apparently minor changes in model specification produce essentially different conclusions. No competent researcher would be so oblivious to this fact as to run a single regression and trust the results it produced. Nevertheless -- whether due to the insecurity or lack of imagination of researchers or the space constraints of journals -- a single regression is often reported as if it were the only one run. Sometimes a footnote is included to the effect that "I tried something different and the results came out the same."[25] But it is seldom made really clear how far a model can be pushed before the results do change significantly. For the most part, we have preferred the false security of a single, implicitly unproblematic model specification to the messier but more enlightening truth that would emerge if extensive sensitivity analysis was a routine part of our published empirical research.

Another remarkably underutilized test of the extent to which the fit of a statistical model reflects data dredging or capitalizing on chance is its success in accounting for data outside the sample used to generate the original results. Kramer's (1971) analysis of economic voting in U.S. congressional elections is one of the very few statistical analyses in the political science literature to have been tested against new data. Kramer's model fit aggregate vote results for congressional elections from 1896 to 1964 with a standard error of about three percentage points (Kramer 1971, 140).

Atesoglu and Congleton (1982) applied Kramer's model to eight subsequent elections (1966-1980), producing an out-of-sample root mean squared forecasting error of about four percentage points (omitting the anomalous Watergate election of 1974 -- about six percentage points for the whole period). Atesoglu and Congleton (1982, 873, 875) concluded that "Kramer's equations have relatively good post-sample predictive ability" and discounted the allegation of "data mining" made by at least one of Kramer's critics. Political scientists unused to validating their models with independent data may be surprised that a "relatively good" result would produce out-of-sample forecast errors on the order of 30 to 100% larger than those produced in the original sample. What should be more surprising -- and embarrassing -- is how few important statistical relationships in political science have ever been validated, even to this degree of accuracy, on samples other than those used to generate them in the first place.

Even when independent data are not available to estimate out-of-sample forecast errors, it is still possible to get a more realistic estimate of the goodness of fit of a model by cross-validation (Geisser 1975). The cross-validation criterion is the square root of the sum of squared prediction errors for the available sample, where each prediction error is the difference between an observed value of y and the corresponding predicted value based on a regression omitting that observation. Thus, the cross-validation criterion differs from the usual standard error of the regression, $\hat{\sigma}$, in that the estimated error for each observation is derived from a regression omitting that observation, rather than from the overall regression with parameter estimates chosen, in part, to fit that observation as well as possible.[26]

Of course, cross-validation is not a panacea for all our problems of model specification. In particular, using cross-validation as a criterion for selecting a regression model (Beck and Katz 1992) reintroduces the familiar perils of data dredging in a new, slightly more sophisticated form. Nevertheless, it seems clear that model assessments based upon cross-validation are less prone to unrealistic optimism than those based upon more conventional techniques, especially in small samples. In addition to providing a useful exposition, Beck and Katz (1992) presented a series of political science examples applying the cross-validation criterion to regression, probit, and duration models estimated on small (15 to 314 observations) data sets.

Specification Tests

Restrictive assumptions are necessary elements of any model specification. But how restrictive should they be? Specification tests are intended to check the restrictive assumptions in a given model specification by treating them as statistical hypotheses to be tested. For example, Wald, likelihood ratio, or Lagrange multiplier tests may be used to decide whether a specific restriction "significantly" decreases the goodness of fit of a given model (Judge et al. 1985, chap. 21).

The explanatory variables in a regression model may be correlated with the disturbance term for a variety of reasons: for example, because other relevant explanatory variables are omitted from the regression, because included explanatory variables are measured with error or have the wrong functional form, or because the dependent variable has a simultaneous reciprocal impact on one or more of the explanatory variables. If misspecification of any of these sorts is suspected, it may be possible to specify an alternative model that is sufficiently general to avoid the suspected misspecification, but at some cost in terms of precision. For example, additional explanatory variables might be added to the regression, or an instrumental variables estimator might be used instead of ordinary least squares (if appropriate instrumental variables are available).

Hausman (1978) proposed a general family of specification tests applicable to situations of this kind, where an efficient but potentially inconsistent estimator can be compared with a consistent but less efficient alternative. In some simple cases, Hausman tests are equivalent to more familiar hypothesis tests. For example, a Hausman test comparing a more parsimonious (and thus more efficient) regression model with a consistent but less parsimonious alternative specification is equivalent to an F-test of the joint significance of the additional variables in the alternative model. The real power of Hausman's formulation lies in its generality, which has prompted applications in a variety of areas. For example, White's (1980, 1982) approach to testing for heteroskedasticity produced an estimator for the covariance matrix of regression parameter estimates that is consistent even when the regression disturbances are heteroskedastic. White's heteroskedasticity-consistent standard errors not only provide a benchmark for testing stronger assumptions, previously adopted uncritically, concerning the homoskedasticity of regression disturbances; they are also beginning to see widespread use in their own right in situations where the traditional assumptions are implausible.

Another useful byproduct of the specification testing approach has been to focus attention on the statistical properties of conditional estimation strategies, or "pretest estimators" (Judge and Bock 1978; Judge et al. 1985, chap. 3). Suppose we decide in advance to specify a restrictive model, test its adequacy against a more general alternative using some specification test, and then adopt the parameter estimates from either the restricted model (if the specification test fails to reject the null hypothesis at some prespecified confidence level) or the more general alternative (if the specification test results in rejection of the null hypothesis). For simple strategies of this sort, it is feasible to examine the statistical properties of the resulting parameter estimates much as we would those of the parameter estimates produced by either of the two alternative specifications themselves. Formally specified conditional estimation strategies are only a rough approximation to the complexity of actual data analysis. But in the absence of any fully developed theory of "ad hoc statistical inference" (Leamer 1978), rigorous analysis of pretest estimators is a useful first step toward accommodating statistical theory to statistical practice.

Finally, some analysts have advocated using specific batteries of specification tests on a routine basis as an integral part of the model-building process. For example, Granato (1992), following Hendry, Qin, and Favero (1989), proposed a specific 12-step "agenda for model building" based upon a battery of diagnostic tests for serial correlation, heteroskedasticity, non-Normality, omitted variables, inappropriate functional forms, and parameter variation. Granato advocated the use of these tests as criteria for successfully "reducing" a general model to a simpler, more parsimonious specification consistent with the data. Although systematizing the diagnostic process in some such way may help to avoid egregious misspecification, it is unclear what criteria should be used to balance the competing demands of parsimony and accuracy in the process of model reduction. "Reduction *does* involve a change in the original parameters," Granato wrote (1992, 134-35, emphasis in original), "but for valid reduction, the parameters *must be* constant and maintain the same sign as in the original model. Or, to put it another way, model reduction must not result in a loss of information."

The apparent contradiction between change and constancy is partially resolved by an explanatory footnote: "In other words, the parameter of the 'reduced' model is roughly the same as the 'general' model" (Granato 1992, 135). Nevertheless, the myriad complications bound up in the phrase "roughly the same" seem sufficiently daunting to hamstring this or any other mechanical formula for model specification. How rough is "rough"? Which restrictions should we test first, how stringently, and why? In the absence of some foolproof formula for managing the inevitable, various, and complex tradeoffs between unbiasedness and precision in real data analysis, model specification must continue to be guided more by statistical experience and substantive insight than by any all-purpose recipe.

Analyzing the Consequences of Misspecification

Specification tests can be very useful for establishing that a model is misspecified, but they are much less useful for understanding or managing the practical consequences of misspecification. A rather different approach to the uncertainties of model specification is reflected in the work of Bartels (1985, 1991b). "Often," as Bartels (1985, 181) put it:

> our existing stock of theorems allows us to specify with impressive rigor what the world would have to look like in order for our standard procedures to produce the right results. But theory of the usual sort too often provides little in the way of useful guidance to researchers who want to proceed, even though their data and models fail to satisfy the assumptions on which the impressive theorems are based. We need a different sort of theory capable of illuminating the practical consequences of the simplifications and approximations involved in everyday empirical research.

Bartels (1985) compared the consequences of three distinct sorts of misspecification in simultaneous equation models: omitting endogenous regressors, treating them as exogenous, and treating them as endogenous by introducing false restrictions on the effects of other (exogenous) variables. In addition to characterizing the inconsistencies in the parameter estimates resulting from each of these three sorts of misspecification, Bartels (1985, 190) derived a "rule of thumb" for choosing between the first and second strategies (in order to minimize the resulting inconsistency due to misspecification) based upon prior beliefs about the likelihood that a specific true parameter exceeds a specified critical value.

In much the same spirit, Bartels (1991b) analyzed the practical consequences of using "quasi-instrumental" variables that only approximately satisfy the textbook assumption of exogeneity. Bartels showed (1991b, 781, 786) that the true asymptotic mean squared error of an instrumental variables parameter estimate will be understated in this case by a factor of $(1 + N \rho_{zu|X}^2)$, where N is the sample size and $\rho_{zu|X}^2$ is the squared population partial correlation between the instrumental variable z and the disturbance u, holding constant any other (exogenous) explanatory variables in the regression. This result suggests that the inferential consequences of even fairly minor misspecification may be quite serious. For example, the true (asymptotic root mean squared) error of the instrumental variables parameter estimate will be more than twice as large as the nominal standard error if the sample size is 50 and the partial correlation between z and u is greater than .25, or if the sample size is 300 and the partial correlation between z and u is greater than .10.

In addition, Bartels derived a decision rule for preferring an instrumental or "quasi-instrumental" variables estimator to ordinary least squares by an asymptotic mean squared error criterion. He showed that a "quasi-instrumental" variables estimator will have a smaller asymptotic mean squared error than the ordinary least squares estimator if and only if

$$\rho_{xz|X}^2 > (\rho_{zu}^2 + 1/N)/(\rho_{xu}^2 + 1/N),$$

where ρ_{xu}^2 and ρ_{zu}^2 measure the endogeneity of the original regressor x and the instrumental variable z, respectively, and $\rho_{xz|X}^2$ is the squared population partial correlation between x and z, holding constant any other (exogenous) explanatory variables X in the regression. The importance of the squared population partial correlation $\rho_{xz|X}^2$ in this expression led Bartels (1991b, 798-800) to suggest that the corresponding squared sample partial correlation $R_{xz|X}^2$ should be reported as a matter of course in instrumental variables applications, since the more conventional practice of reporting the R^2 statistic from a purging regression of x on both z and X may greatly exaggerate the apparent efficiency of the instrumental variables estimator (since only that portion of z uncorrelated with X actually contributes to the efficiency of the instrumental variables parameter estimates).

8. Estimation

The increasing methodological sophistication of political research owes much to the explosion of computing technology. Researchers who once spent late nights at their university computer centers running batch jobs using SAS or SPSS can now perform much more complex analyses much more conveniently on increasingly powerful and inexpensive personal computers using increasingly powerful and specialized statistical software. Since software is being developed and disseminated at a rapid rate, any detailed discussion of specific packages would quickly be obsolete, so none will be attempted here. *The Political Methodologist*, the newsletter of the Methodology Section of the American Political Science Association, is a good source of current information.

One implication of these technological developments is that political methodologists have been able to adopt and develop increasingly complex models without sacrificing the ability to estimate the parameters of those models using real data. Two developments have been especially important. First, the increasing power of iterative algorithms to search large parameter spaces has facilitated the application of iterative estimation techniques, and thus of maximum likelihood estimation. Second, the ability of modern computers to engage in intensive resampling has facilitated the development of a variety of estimators based upon resampling, most notably bootstrap estimators.

Maximum Likelihood Estimation

A decade ago the vast majority of estimators used in political science research were based upon the least squares criterion, and maximum likelihood estimation was an exotic solution to special problems in which the least squares principle was inapplicable, including probit and logit models with individual-level data and factor analytic and covariance structure models (as, for example, in the very influential textbook treatment by Hanushek and Jackson 1977).[27]

Today the situation is quite different. Political methodology has its own survey of maximum likelihood estimation (King 1989c) comparable to those available in biometrics (Edwards 1972) and econometrics (Cramer 1986). And, thanks in part to King's advocacy, political scientists have applied maximum likelihood estimators to a growing variety of models, including measurement models, event count models, and generalizations of logit and probit models (Nagler 1992).

The extent to which applied research in political science has begun to utilize maximum likelihood estimation is heartening. Nevertheless, some persistent conceptual confusions have not been entirely dispelled. In particular, researchers and readers alike sometimes seem to forget that maximum likelihood is, properly speaking, an estimation criterion rather than either a model or an algorithm.

The familiar phrase "maximum likelihood model" is a misnomer, since model specification and estimation are logically distinct enterprises. It is certainly true, as King (1989c) has argued, that the maximum likelihood framework may facilitate the specification and estimation of more interesting and flexible models; but the models themselves must stand or fall on their substantive plausibility and utility. Whenever the "maximum likelihood" brand name serves to forestall rather than promote attention to real issues of model specification, the result is detrimental.

On the other hand, the term "maximum likelihood estimation" is sometimes misleadingly applied to any iterative estimation scheme. Although maximum likelihood estimation is almost invariably implemented using some iterative search algorithm, it certainly does not follow that any parameter estimates produced by any iterative search algorithm are, ipso facto, maximum likelihood estimates. Maximum likelihood estimates, with their attractive statistical properties, only result if the function being maximized is, in fact, a correctly specified likelihood function satisfying some non-trivial technical conditions.

Among other things, the full specification of a likelihood function requires specific distributional assumptions. However, it is worth noting (McCullagh and Nelder 1989) that "quasi-likelihood" estimators are also available for a broad class of "generalized linear models" (including linear regression, logit and probit, log-linear, count, and survival models). These estimators require less strong distributional assumptions, but they can still be shown to be optimal within the rather broad class of linear estimating functions.

Bootstrapping

Although resampling techniques of various sorts have a considerable history in statistics, developments in the field accelerated rapidly when Efron (1979) proposed the bootstrap technique. Bootstrapping "has been the subject of furious theoretical research and heated debate in the statistical community" (Mooney and Duval 1991, 1). Mooney and Duval's own exposition includes references to the relevant statistical literature, as well as a clear introduction and examples aimed at political scientists. The "leisurely" exposition by Efron and Gong (1983) is also especially useful in that it places bootstrapping within a broader array of resampling techniques.

The basic idea of the bootstrap is to estimate parameters repeatedly from independent samples drawn from the original sample of interest. For example, in a regression analysis based upon 100 observations, many samples of 100 observations each would be drawn (with replacement) from the original 100 observations, and the regression parameters would be estimated in each of those samples. Depending upon the complexity of the problem and the availability of computing power, for example, each regression parameter might be estimated independently in 1,000 different samples, each drawn randomly from the original sample of 100 observations. The empirical distribution of the 1,000 different estimates of each parameter would then serve as an estimate of the sampling distribution of that parameter.

Bootstrapping has two primary applications. First, since estimates of parameter variability often rely on different and more stringent assumptions than estimates of the corresponding parameters themselves, the possibility of dispensing with those more stringent assumptions and estimating the sampling distribution

directly is an attractive one. For example, in a regression model where the usual assumption of Normally distributed errors seemed implausible, bootstrapping could be used to estimate the sampling distribution of parameter estimates without recourse to that assumption.

Bootstrapping techniques are also useful for estimating parameters for which no simple analytic formulae exist. An especially important example for political scientists, as Mooney and Duval (1991) noted, is the difference between two sample medians. Formal theories of collective choice often predict an outcome reflecting the preference of the median voter in the relevant collectivity. Thus, for example, a congressional committee and its parent body would be expected to produce different policy outcomes if their respective median voters had different preferences, but not otherwise. The existence of "significant" differences between the positions of median legislators in committees and on the House floor has been a matter of some controversy in the literature on congressional politics, but it has usually been investigated without formal statistical testing or with difference-of-means tests instead of difference-of-medians tests as a matter of statistical convenience (Krehbiel 1990; Hall and Grofman 1990). Mooney and Duval (1991) pointed out that bootstrapping provides a straightforward technology for estimating directly the sampling distribution of the difference between the relevant medians in this problem and others.

9. Political Methodology and Political Science

Much of the scientific progress in any field occurs well behind the intellectual frontier, where yesterday's breakthroughs are consolidated and disseminated to become tomorrow's standard practice. Thus, the improvement in the state of political methodology during the past decade must be gauged not only from the best theoretical work in *Political Analysis*, but also from the best and less-than-best empirical work in the discipline's mainstream journals and books. By this standard, too, the state of quantitative political methodology looks better now than it did a decade ago.

The limitations of some once-popular techniques, such as stepwise regression and standardized regression coefficients, are better understood by workaday researchers, thanks to the pedagogical efforts of Achen (1982), King (1986), and others. Bivariate analyses have to a considerable extent been supplanted by more realistic multivariate specifications. And the careless practice of reporting regression parameter estimates without standard errors or t-statistics is fading, though it is by no means eliminated.

All these changes reflect a significant increase in the average level of methodological sophistication of empirical research in the field. But with what payoff? New and better methods and standards are of no intrinsic interest to political scientists who are not themselves methodologists; the discipline as a whole cares only -- and rightly so -- about the light political methodology can help to shed upon substantive questions about political phenomena. Thus, it is incumbent upon political methodologists to demonstrate that their techniques have made real contributions to the study of politics.

We believe that there are real contributions to point to in a variety of areas. Statistical analysis appears with increasing prominence and sophistication in the discipline's prize-winning books (Bartels 1988; Lewis-Beck 1988; Carmines and Stimson 1989; Freeman 1989), if not in its leading journal.[28] Empirical analyses explicitly derived from or shedding light upon rational choice or other formal theories of political behavior, though still rare, appear with increasing frequency (Poole and Rosenthal 1985; Enelow and Hinich 1985; Brady and Sniderman 1985; Bartels 1986; Krehbiel and Rivers 1988; Brady and Ansolabehere 1989; Krehbiel 1991). In the field of international relations, new methods have shed new light on the dynamics of great power rivalry (McGinnis and Williams 1989; Goldstein and Freeman 1991). In American politics, the conventional wisdom concerning presidential influence in Congress has been recast through more careful attention to the endogeneity of presidential requests (Rivers and Rose 1985). And in comparative politics, the literatures on cabinet durability in parliamentary democracies (King et al. 1990) and on leadership succession and regime stability (Londregan and Poole 1990, 1992) have been put on firmer statistical footing.

These advances and others like them are -- or should be -- familiar to scholars in the various subfields of political science. In this section, rather than simply multiplying examples, we describe in some detail two cases in which methodological advances have had clear and important substantive payoffs. For purposes of illustration we choose precisely the two problems Achen chose a decade ago to represent the untapped potential of political methodology: the nature of the survey response and the phenomenon of economic voting. The fact that political methodologists have made significant progress on both these problems in the intervening decade seems to us to suggest that further investment in basic methodological research will continue to pay handsome dividends in terms of our substantive understanding of politics.

The Nature of the Survey Response

Ever since the classic work of Converse (1964, 1970) demonstrated the remarkable instability of individual political opinions as measured over relatively short periods of time, analysts of public opinion have struggled to figure out "what survey responses are measuring" (Achen 1983a, 80). Achen's own earlier (1975) contribution and many others (Erikson 1979; Converse and Markus 1979; Jackson 1983; Judd, Krosnick and Milburn 1981; Kinder 1983; Norpoth and Lodge 1985) addressed, but did not resolve, the issue of whether response instability reflected the absence of stable attitudes or simply the vagaries of opinion measurement.

As Achen pointed out (1983a, 76-81), the persistence of disagreement in this debate may largely reflect the limitations of the mathematical models used to study response stability.[29] In particular, Achen pointed out that very different mathematical models -- including one allowing for random measurement error and implying almost complete stability in underlying political attitudes (Wiley and Wiley 1970) and another allowing for autocorrelated measurement error and implying almost complete *instability* (Wiley and Wiley 1974) -- could account equally well for the available data. This result was discouraging because each model was just identified, and a model incorporating both would require more information than was available in a three-wave panel.[30]

On the basis of that observation, Achen (1983a, 80-81) suggested that "a great deal could be learned by extending our current techniques to lengthier panel studies....A better understanding of the Converse problem would result, and more importantly, clues would be provided as to how mathematical modeling of survey responses might proceed." The course of subsequent research in the field has followed precisely Achen's prescription. Feldman (1990) and Palmquist and Green (1992) both used data from Thomas Patterson's five-wave panel study to estimate a more general model of response instability in which random and correlated error could be distinguished. Both found that the random error model "fit the observed data...very well" (Feldman 1990, 51), especially when the measurement error variances were allowed to vary across panel waves. Feldman's stability estimates for issue positions and party identification ranged from .85 to 1.00, and his reliability estimates ranged from .49 (for a tax item) to .90 (for party identification); candidate evaluations had similar reliabilities (from .63 to .94) but lower stabilities (as low as .37 and no higher than .89). Feldman (1990, 40) concluded that "there is nothing inherent in the Wiley and Wiley measurement model that automatically produces perfectly stable estimated true scores."

Feldman went on to examine whether individual level response instability is related to political knowledge or other characteristics. He found that "knowledgeable people do report more stable attitudes as the nonattitudes model would predict," but that "this relationship is *not* large enough to account for all or most of observed response instability" (1990, 51-52). He concluded that "neither of the major interpretations of response instability is sufficient to account for these findings." Feldman went on to propose a more complicated model in which observed instability results from a combination of pure measurement error and the variability produced by respondents reconstructing their specific opinions in each interview from essentially stable sets of information, beliefs, and values "rather than carrying around preformed and rehearsed positions on a host of issues, people can draw on their information, beliefs, and values to respond to policy questions as they arise" (1990, 52-53).

Drawing upon Feldman's results, a considerable accumulation of research on specific question wording and question placement effects, and psychological theory, subsequent analysis by Tourangeau and Rasinski (1988), Zaller and Feldman (1992), and Zaller (1992) has gone a long way toward developing and testing more realistic mathematical models of the survey response. In these models, respondents are assumed to construct opinions by sampling considerations from a store of relevant possibilities. Question wording and question placement are interpreted as influencing the probability of retrieving some considerations rather than others. And response instability represents neither an indictment of ordinary people's political sophistication nor a mere nuisance caused by imperfections of measurement, but a window upon the diversity and complexity of political considerations that are the basic building blocks of public opinion. The result is a methodological advance, but it is also a theoretical advance of profound importance to anyone who studies the nature or impact of public opinion.

Economic Voting

The literature on economic voting provides one of the clearest instances in which political methodology has contributed to significant empirical and theoretical advances in a research area of widespread substantive interest. A vigorous controversy regarding the relative importance of "sociotropic" and individual "pocketbook" effects of economic conditions on the vote (Kramer 1971; Kinder and Kiewiet 1979; and many others) has been largely resolved through a combination of sophisticated statistical modeling (Kramer 1983) and careful empirical work (Markus 1988).

The essential contribution of Kramer (1983) was to specify clearly the limitations of both time-series and cross-sectional data in the context of economic voting models. Individual-level cross-sectional analyses had typically found modest and inconsistent effects, Kramer argued, because "politically relevant" changes in individuals' personal income were swamped in the available survey data by politically irrelevant changes deriving from idiosyncratic individual circumstances (promotions, retirements, and the like). On the other hand, aggregate time-series analyses had found consistent and significant effects because they were much less subject to this sort of measurement error (at least given Kramer's assumption that politically irrelevant changes in economic circumstances cancel out across the population). But Kramer also pointed out that estimates based on aggregate time-series data necessarily confounded the effects of individuals' own economic circumstances and the effects of national economic conditions, making it impossible to disentangle "pocketbook" and "sociotropic" voting with the data at hand.

Markus overcame this logjam by pooling survey data from a series of presidential elections (1956-1984) in which aggregate economic conditions varied significantly.[31] The resulting variation in both aggregate economic conditions (across election years) and personal economic circumstances (both across and within election years) made it possible to distinguish the effects of national conditions and personal economic circumstances on vote choices. Markus's results demonstrated that both national and personal economic conditions significantly influenced presidential votes. According to Markus's (1988, 146) estimates, each 1% increase in aggregate real disposable personal income per capita increased the vote share for the presidential candidate of the incumbent party by 2.3%, of which 1.9% was a direct effect associated with national income changes and the remainder was an indirect effect produced by changes in personal circumstances. As for the relative weight of national and personal circumstances, Markus (1988, 148) estimated that an improvement in personal economic circumstances (being "better off than a year ago" rather than "about the same") increased a voter's probability of supporting the incumbent party's presidential candidate by about the same amount as a 3.6% increase in aggregate real disposable personal income per capita -- roughly, the difference in aggregate economic conditions between a boom year (1956, 1964, or 1972) and a year with no aggregate income growth (1960).

As with the work on the nature of the survey response, this brief history of research on economic voting illustrates clearly how careful methodological work can have significant substantive payoffs. The scholarly literature on economic voting has taken a permanent step forward, overcoming in the process conceptual and practical problems that seemed daunting only a decade ago. In view of these examples, and others like them, it hardly seems unduly optimistic to hope for similar gains in other substantive areas of political science in the decade to come.

Conclusion

Quantitative political methodology in the past decade has been a strong growth stock. We see no signs of a downturn in the intellectual vitality of the field or in the quantity or quality of research. On the contrary, there is every indication that further investment will pay even greater intellectual dividends. But what sort of investment is required at this stage? We see the same three glaring needs that Achen identified a decade ago. In each case there has been notable progress since he wrote, but in each case the underlying problem remains far from solved.

First, as Achen (1983a, 87) argued a decade ago, political methodologists and political theorists alike need to develop "formal theories with measurement models built into them." Where such theories have been developed, as in the fields of dimensional analysis, survey response, event counts, polytomous choice, and some areas of time-series analysis, significant methodological progress has followed. In the field as a whole, however, there is still far too much data analysis without formal theory -- and far too much formal theory without data analysis.

Second, "to provide for the future, much better mathematical training will have to be provided at both the graduate and undergraduate level" (Achen 1983a, 89). Our traditional patterns of undergraduate training demand reform; as the research literature throughout the discipline becomes more sophisticated methodologically (and theoretically), it will be increasingly difficult to pretend that an undergraduate curriculum with little or no formal analytical training can provide more than a superficial caricature of the field. The problem is even clearer at the graduate level, with the added difficulty that we must also devote sufficient intellectual resources to train new and more sophisticated generations of methodological specialists. As long as otherwise reputable political science departments rely upon economists, psychologists, and sociologists to supply their graduate coursework in methodology, it will continue to be the case that "the pages of our journals frequently have the look of living rooms decorated at garage sales" (Achen 1983a, 70).

Third, as Achen (1983a, 89) also argued a decade ago, "fundamental research must come to take

priority, at least some of the time, over applied work. It should be possible to get funding, publish respectably, and make a career studying the principal agenda of political methodology." In this respect there has been greater progress in the past decade. Young methodological specialists who were graduate students or assistant professors when Achen wrote now fill senior positions in leading political science departments; their students are entering the field's junior ranks in increasing numbers; and their teachers continue to publish not only respectably but with great distinction.

Progress on these fronts has been, and will undoubtedly continue to be, stimulated by the institutional development of political methodology as a subfield. The Methodology Section of the American Political Science Association, a goal when Achen wrote, is now a functioning organization with hundreds of dues-paying members. Its annual publication, *Political Analysis* (Stimson 1990, 1991b, 1992; Freeman n.d.), publishes a significant fraction of the best research in the field. And its newsletter, *The Political Methodologist*, is an increasingly ambitious forum for news, reviews, and intellectual debate. Summer methodology conferences at Michigan (1984), Berkeley (1985), Harvard (1986), Duke (1987), UCLA (1988), Minnesota (1989), Washington University (1990), Duke (1991), and Harvard (1992) have provided an important new forum for presenting and discussing methodological research. Many of the articles described in this review were first presented at these conferences. With funding from the host universities and the National Science Foundation, recent conferences have included dozens of graduate students in addition to faculty members from across the United States.

Nevertheless, any survey of the field must recognize that the number of political scientists working and thinking primarily as methodologists is still exceedingly small and that, in the long run, the number and energy of the field's part-time adherents cannot adequately compensate for a dire shortage of trained, committed specialists. As long as most political science departments have more Latin Americanists, urbanists, and voting behavior specialists than methodologists it cannot be surprising that we know more about the vicissitudes of politics in Nicaragua, New Haven, and the New Deal coalition than about the central methodological problems of our discipline. And as long as colleagues in other fields count anyone who does applied statistical work as a political methodologist, and vice versa, we cannot be surprised that our principal methodological agenda remains unconquered.

Notes

The authors thank Simon Jackman, Gary King, Bradley Palmquist, and Paul Sniderman for constructive criticism and advice, and Chris Downing, Lyn Lake, and Guy Whitten for able research assistance.

1. We chose these journals because they covered all the major subfields of empirical political science and because our colleagues suggested that they would be the best places to find innovative quantitative work.

2. These data sets cover somewhat different time periods (1966-1986 and 1948-1978, respectively) and use different coding procedures for actions (WEIS codes each event into one of 22 different categories and COPDAB uses a 15-point ordinal cooperation-conflict scale), but they are similar in that each identifies an originating nation, a target nation, and a date of the action.

3. The first volume of these data includes over one hundred "Cross-National Attributes and Rates of Change" circa 1975 for the major nations of the world, and repeated values, often back to 1950, at five-year intervals for over half the variables. The second volume includes "a record of political protest and violence, state coercive behavior, and formal governmental change and elections in the major countries of the world for the years 1948-1977" (1983b, xiii). Over 87,000 events are recorded in both daily and annual form, and attributes are coded for over 30,000 of these events.

4. The event history, the most complete description of the data, tells us the timing of all moves into and out of each possible status; the events sequence only records the sequence of states occupied by each sample member without the timings; event counts record only the number of relevant events in an interval.

5. When these methods are not employed, a Durbin-Watson statistic is usually reported to justify the use of ordinary least squares. Using the Durbin-Watson statistic makes sense because it is a relatively good test for both autoregressive and moving average errors (Judge et al. 1985, 322-32), but probably too many authors assume that a significant Durbin-Watson implies a first-order autoregressive process when there are, as Hibbs (1974) noted, many other possibilities.

6. Granger and Newbold (1986) offer a useful technical introduction to time-series methods in econometrics, albeit with a heavier emphasis on forecasting than has been common in the political science literature.

7. Of course, this rule presupposes that we have already decided which variables belong in the system on theoretical grounds. In addition, some discretion remains regarding appropriate lag lengths; here it is customary to rely upon one or another goodness-of-fit test rather than upon any theoretical presuppositions about the relevant dynamics (Freeman, Williams, and Lin 1989, 845).

8. Tests of this sort were originally motivated by the concept of Granger causality (Granger 1969; Freeman 1983). A variable X is said to Granger cause another variable Y if current values of Y can be predicted more accurately from the histories of both X and Y than from the history of Y alone. Thus, rejecting the null hypothesis that all of the parameters associated with lagged values of X in a vector autoregression are zero constitutes evidence that X Granger causes Y.

9. This framework can be further generalized -- for example, to include longer lags of endogenous variables -- by appropriately supplementing the state vector γ_t (Beck 1990, 130-31).

10. Time-series cross-sectional studies have considered defense burden sharing (Palmer 1990; Oneal 1990), determinants of military expenditures (Rosh 1988) and democratization (Gonick and Rosh 1988), diffusion of social policy innovations (Schneider and Ingram 1984), budgeting in the U.S. (McCubbins and Schwartz 1988; Kiewiet and McCubbins 1988; Kamlet and Mowery 1987), community expenditures (Schneider 1989), electoral results by state (Holbrook 1991; Chubb 1988), union political action (Delaney, Fiorito, and Masters 1988), and enforcement of environmental regulations by counties (Scholz, Twombly, and Headrick 1991).

11. Indeed, there may be a need for I separate variances due to heteroskedasticity across units, an additional I or more parameters for

autocorrelation, and one or more parameters to correct for spatial autocorrelation across units.

12. Wilkerson (1991) criticized this approach on two grounds. First, he doubted whether legislators always vote sincerely, as they are assumed to do in Krehbiel and Rivers's model. Second, he doubted whether a point, particularly in one dimension, can completely characterize legislators' assessments of a bill or amendment.

13. The Poisson distribution has been applied to a wide variety of political phenomena, including Supreme Court appointments (Wallis 1936; Ulmer 1982), wars (Richardson 1944; Houweling and Kune 1984), international alliances (McGowan and Rood 1975; Job 1976; Siverson and Duncan 1976), democratic transitions (Starr 1991), the circulation of elites (Casstevens 1989), and the duration of governments (Browne, Frendreis, and Gleiber 1986).

14. In addition, the Poisson has the peculiar property that its mean equals its variance, which seems odd in many applications.

15. The focus on the error term may seem odd to those versed in multivariate statistical procedures, but there were two compelling reasons for it. First, many interesting data series -- the number of wars, alliances, coups, or urban riots -- were collected without much attention to possible explanatory variables. Second, adding covariates to the Poisson model produces likelihood equations that must be solved iteratively, a daunting task before the advent of modern computers and packaged software programs. Although these limitations have handicapped research in this area, they have also meant that the literature on event counts is significantly more self-conscious than other literatures in political science about the underlying stochastic processes generating observed data.

16. Applications include multiple indicator structural or path models of citizen tolerance (Shamir and Sullivan 1983), welfare guarantees in the American states (Plotnick and Winters 1985), individual preferences for tax policy (Hawthorne and Jackson 1987), black belief systems (Allen, Dawson, and Brown 1989), the relationship between political participation and efficacy (Finkel 1985), state policy liberalism (Wright, Erikson, and McIver 1985) and spending by House challengers (McAdams and Johannes 1987), confirmatory factor analysis of emotional responses to candidates (Marcus 1988) and to the economy (Conover and Feldman 1986) and of the structure of core beliefs (Feldman 1988), and many others.

17. This result is reminiscent of the classic Converse "black-white" model in which some people have attitudes and others do not; but it has the virtue of "nesting" the Converse model and the Wiley-Wiley model within a larger model. Moreover, it can be shown that within the larger model, high stabilities and high reliabilities (low error variances) can coexist, and guessers can have an error variance that is no larger than that of non-guessers. These surprising results follow because the respondents who are guessing do have a "stable" point of reference -- the center of the scale -- which the Wiley-Wiley method treats as a stable true opinion.

18. One stimulus for these developments was a clever and very readable paper by Weisberg (1974a) entitled "Dimensionland: An Excursion in Spaces." Weisberg posed fundamental questions about the utility of scaling methods for political science data, explored the meaning of unidimensionality and the relationship between factor analysis and multidimensional scaling (MDS), and suggested that political scientists had to develop a distinctive set of scaling methods suitable to politics.

19. Although they did not use scaling procedures directly, Rabinowitz and Macdonald (1989) and MacDonald, Listhaug, and Rabinowitz (1991) developed a very interesting alternative to spatial modeling called a "directional theory of issue voting." Building upon Rabinowitz's (1978) finding that most candidates did not seem to be near the median voter, these papers argued that voters choose candidates who are on the same side of the issue as they are. This means that a candidate who is close to a voter based upon a distance measure might be shunned if the candidate is on the wrong side of an

issue that is important to the voter. A moderate pro-choice voter would prefer an extreme pro-choice candidate to a moderate pro-life candidate.

20. Brady (1991b) showed that a Poole-like estimator actually does produce statistically consistent estimates of both factor scores and factor loadings in a linear factor model. Rivers's (1987) result, then, is partly the result of the non-linearities inherent in ideal point models. It can also be shown that the Poole estimator would yield correct results if there were no error in the model. These results suggest that the Poole estimator may not produce much bias if the amount of error is small.

21. Jackson and Kingdon (1992) have criticized the use of interest group scores to explain congressional votes, but their argument does not bear on the debate about the number of dimensions in legislative votes.

22. Indeed, Poole and Rosenthal recognized that the standard proof of consistency for maximum likelihood does not apply, but they made the odd statement (1991, 272) that "At a practical level, this caveat is not important. The key point is that data is being added at a far faster rate than parameters." Yet there are many examples in statistics where adding data faster than parameters does not ensure consistency. The Monte Carlo reports in their paper are more convincing; but much more work still needs to be done to assay the statistical properties of their innovative method for scaling roll-call votes.

23. This section draws heavily upon Bartels (1990), where some related points are discussed in more detail.

24. Fascinating questions about the role of theoretical expectations in statistical inference were raised by a Box-Jenkins ARIMA analysis in the *Journal of Conflict Resolution* (Orme-Johnson et al. 1988), demonstrating that "a very small group practicing [the Maharishi technology of the unified field] in East Jerusalem appeared to influence overall quality of life in Jerusalem, Israel, and even in neighboring Lebanon." The editor of the journal (Russett 1988, 773) did not know what to make of the finding and admitted that "The hypothesis has no place within the normal paradigm of conflict and peace research. Yet the hypothesis seems logically derived from the initial premises, and its empirical testing seems competently executed." Schrodt (1990) questioned whether the research was, in fact, competently executed; but whatever the truth in this case, the original article raises significant questions about what scientific hypotheses we should be willing to entertain and what proof we should require for their demonstration. How strongly should theory incline us to believe or disbelieve that there are "long cycles" in the severity of war in the international system (Goldstein 1988, 1991; Beck 1991), or that postwar U.S. savings rates were influenced by changes in public perceptions of the threat of nuclear war (Slemrod 1986)? As we add new and more powerful techniques to our kitbag of tools, it is worth remembering that good inferences require more than powerful techniques and large t-statistics.

25. It is striking how seldom, in footnotes of this sort, trying something different makes the results come out different.

26. The cross-validation criterion is simply the square root of the PRESS (PRediction Error Sum of Squares) criterion of Allen (1971) and is also closely related to the jackknife and bootstrap techniques (Efron and Gong 1983).

27. Of course, the least squares and maximum likelihood criteria sometimes lead to the same estimator, as in the case of ordinary regression with normally distributed errors. In cases like this, researchers did maximum likelihood estimation in the same way they wrote prose, without knowing it.

28. King (1991, 2-3) reported the results of a content analysis in which the proportion of *American Political Science Review* articles using "quantitative data and methods in some way" has fluctuated around 50% since 1969.

29. Another approach to the problem of mass belief systems has been to reconceptualize political sophistication and ideological

constraint. Luskin (1987) provided a magisterial overview of various measures of political sophistication and some of his own suggestions. Peffley and Hurwitz (1985) and Hurwitz and Peffley (1987) suggested an interesting approach based upon a hierarchical structure of attitudes with core beliefs informing broad postures which, in turn, are the basis for specific beliefs.

30. Later, Palmquist and Green (1992, 128) showed that the identification problem is even worse than in Achen's telling because "standard errors for the measurement error parameters [of the Wiley and Wiley (1974) model with correlated errors] are typically so large that it is not hard to see how implausible values could result simply from sampling error." With three waves of data it is not only impossible to distinguish between the two models but also virtually impossible to get informative estimates of the parameter estimates of the correlated error model.

31. Rivers (1986) independently proposed a similar solution to the Kramer problem, albeit with a somewhat different model and estimation strategy.

Bibliography

Achen, Christopher H. 1975. "Mass Political Attitudes and the Survey Response." *American Political Science Review* 69:1218-23.

Achen, Christopher H. 1977. "Measuring Representation: Perils of the Correlation Coefficient." *American Journal of Political Science* 21:805-15.

Achen, Christopher H. 1978. "Measuring Representation," *American Journal of Political Science* 22:475-510.

Achen, Christopher H. 1982. *Interpreting and Using Regression.* Beverly Hills: Sage Publications.

Achen, Christopher H. 1983a. "Toward Theories of Data: The State of Political Methodology." In *Political Science: The State of the Discipline,* ed. Ada W. Finifter. Washington, DC: American Political Science Association.

Achen, Christopher H. 1983b. "If Party ID Influences the Vote, Goodman's Ecological Regression Is Biased (But Factor Analysis Consistent)." University of California, Berkeley. Typescript.

Achen, Christopher H. 1984. "How to Estimate Party Loyalty Rates from Aggregate Voting Data." University of California, Berkeley. Typescript.

Achen, Christopher H. 1985. "Proxy Variables and Incorrect Signs on Regression Coefficients." *Political Methodology* 11:299-316.

Achen, Christopher H. 1986a. "Necessary and Sufficient Conditions for Unbiased Aggregation of Cross-Sectional Regressions." Presented at the annual meeting of the Political Science Association, Washington, DC.

Achen, Christopher H. 1986b. *The Statistical Analysis of Quasi-Experiments.* Berkeley: University of California Press.

Achen, Christopher H. 1987. Statistical Models for Event Data: A Review of Errors in Variable Theory. Paper presented at the First DDIR (Data Development for International Research) Conference on Event Data, Columbus, OH.

Achen, Christopher H., and W. Phillips Shively. n.d. *Cross-level Inference: New Approaches.*

Achen, Christopher H., and Duncan Snidal 1989. "Rational Deterrence Theory and Comparative Case Studies." *World Politics* 41:143-69.

Aldrich, John H., and Richard D. McKelvey. 1977. "A Method of Scaling with Applications to the 1968 and 1972 Presidential Elections." *American Political Science Review* 71:111-30.

Aldrich, John H., and Forrest D. Nelson. 1984. *Linear Probability, Logit, and Probit Models.* Beverly Hills: Sage Publications.

Alker, Hayward R., Jr. 1988. "The Dialectical Logic of Thucydides'

Melian Dialogue." *American Political Science Review* 82:805-20.

Allen, D.M. 1971. "Mean Square Error of Prediction as a Criterion for Selecting Variables." *Technometrics* 13:469-75.

Allen, Richard L., Michael C. Dawson, and Ronald Brown. 1989. "A Schema-based Approach to Modeling an African-American Racial Belief System." *American Political Science Review* 83:421-42.

Allison, Paul D. 1984. *Event History Analysis*. Beverly Hills: Sage Publications.

Allsop, Dee, and Herbert F. Weisberg. 1988. "Measuring Change in Party Identification in an Election Campaign." *American Journal of Political Science* 32:996-1017.

Alt, James E. 1985. "Political Parties, World Demand, and Unemployment: Domestic and International Sources of Economic Activity." *American Political Science Review* 79:1016-40.

Alvarez, R. Michael, Geoffrey Garrett, and Peter Lange. 1991. "Government Partisanship, Labor Organization, and Macroeconomic Performance." *American Political Science Review* 85:539-56.

Ansolabehere, Stephen, and Douglas Rivers. 1992. "Using Aggregate Data to Correct for Nonresponse and Misreporting in Surveys." Presented at the Ninth Annual Political Methodology Summer Conference, Cambridge.

Ashley, Richard K. 1980. *The Political Economy of War and Peace: The Sino-Soviet-American Triangle and the Modern Security Problematique*. London: Frances Pinter.

Atesoglu, H. Sonmez, and Roger Congleton. 1982. "Economic Conditions and National Elections, Post-Sample Forecasts of the Kramer Equations." *American Political Science Review* 76:873-875.

Azar, E.E., and J.D. Ben-Dak. 1975. *Theory and Practice of Events Research*. New York: Gordon and Breach.

Banks, Arthur S. 1971. *Cross-Polity Time-Series Data*. Cambridge: MIT Press.

Bartels, Larry M. 1985. "Alternative Misspecifications in Simultaneous-Equation Models." *Political Methodology* 11:181-99.

Bartels, Larry M. 1986. "Issue Voting Under Uncertainty: An Empirical Test." *American Journal of Political Science* 30: 709-28.

Bartels, Larry M. 1988. *Presidential Primaries and the Dynamics of Public Choice*. Princeton: Princeton University Press.

Bartels, Larry M. 1990. "Five Approaches to Model Specification." *The Political Methodologist* 3:2-6.

Bartels, Larry M. 1991a. "Constituency Opinion and Congressional Policy Making: The Reagan Defense Buildup." *American Political Science Review* 85:457-74.

Bartels, Larry M. 1991b. "Instrumental and 'Quasi-Instrumental' Variables." *American Journal of Political Science* 35:777-800.

Bartels, Larry M. n.d. "Messages Received: The Political Impact of Media Exposure." *American Political Science Review*.

Beck, Nathaniel. 1983. "Time-varying Parameter Regression Models." *American Journal of Political Science* 27:557-600.

Beck, Nathaniel. 1985. "Estimating Dynamic Models Is Not Merely a Matter of Technique." *Political Methodology* 11:71-89.

Beck, Nathaniel. 1987. "Elections and the Fed: Is There a Political Monetary Cycle?" *American Journal of Political Science* 31: 194-216.

Beck, Nathaniel. 1990. "Estimating Dynamic Models Using Kalman Filtering." In *Political Analysis*, Vol. 1, ed. James A. Stimson. Ann Arbor: University of Michigan Press.

Beck, Nathaniel. 1991. "The Illusion of Cycles in International Relations." *International Studies Quarterly* 35:455-76.

Beck, Nathaniel. 1992. "Comparing Dynamic Specifications: The Case of Presidential Approval." *Political Analysis* 3:51-87.

Beck, Nathaniel. n.d. "The Methodology of Cointegration." *Political Analysis*.

Beck, Nathaniel, and Jonathan Katz. 1992. "Model Assessment via Cross Validation." Presented at the Ninth Annual Political Methodology Summer Conference, Cambridge.

Berelson, Bernard R., Paul F. Lazarsfeld, and William N. McPhee. 1954. *Voting*. Chicago: University of Chicago Press.

Berry, Frances Stokes, and William D. Berry. 1990. "State Lottery Adoptions as Policy Innovations: An Event History Analysis." *American Political Science Review* 84:395-415.

Berry, William D., and David Lowery. 1990. "An Alternative Approach to Understanding Budgetary Trade-Offs." *American Journal of Political Science* 34:671-705.

Bienen, H., and N. van de Walle. 1989. "Time and Power in Africa." *American Political Science Review* 83:20-34.

Black, Duncan. 1958. *Theory of Committees and Elections*. Cambridge: Cambridge University Press.

Bollen, Kenneth A. 1989. *Structural Equations with Latent Variables*. New York: John Wiley & Sons.

Born, Richard. 1990. "Surge and Decline, Negative Voting, and the Midterm Loss Phenomenon: A Simultaneous Choice Analysis." *American Journal of Political Science* 34:615-45.

Box, George E.P., and G.C. Tiao. 1975. "Intervention Analysis with Applications to Economic and Environmental Problems." *Journal of the American Statistical Association* 70:70-79.

Box, George E.P., and Gwilym M. Jenkins. 1976. *Time Series Analysis*. Oakland, CA: Holden-Day.

Bradshaw, York W., and Zwelakhe Tshandu. 1990. "Foreign Capital Penetration, State Intervention, and Development of Sub-Saharan Africa." *International Studies Quarterly* 34:229-51.

Brady, Henry E. 1985a. "The Perils of Survey Research: Inter-Personally Incomparable Responses." *Political Methodology* 11:269-91.

Brady, Henry E. 1985b. "Statistical Consistency and Hypothesis Testing for Nonmetric Multidimensional Scaling." *Psychometrika* 50:509-37.

Brady, Henry E. 1989. "Factor and Ideal Point Analysis for Interpersonally Incomparable Data." *Psychometrika* 54:181-202.

Brady, Henry E. 1990. "Dimensional Analysis of Ranking Data." *American Journal of Political Science* 34:1017-48.

Brady, Henry E. 1991a. "Traits versus Issues: Factor Versus Ideal-Point Analysis of Candidate Thermometer Ratings." *Political Analysis* 2:97-129.

Brady, Henry E. 1991b. "Statistical Properties of Alternating Least Squares and Maximum Likelihood Estimators for Vector and Squared Euclidean Functional Preference Models." Paper presented at the annual meeting of the Psychometric Society, Rutgers University, New Brusnwick, New Jersey.

Brady, Henry E. 1993. "Stability, Reliability, and Guessing." Paper presented at the Quantitative Methods Seminar, University of California, Berkeley.

Brady, Henry E., and Stephen Ansolabehere. 1989. "The Nature of Utility Functions in Mass Publics." *American Political Science Review* 83:143-63.

Brady, Henry E., and Richard Johnston. 1987. "What's the Primary Message: Horse Race or Issue Journalism?" In *Media and Momentum: The New Hampshire Primary and Nomination Politics*, ed. Gary R. Orren and Nelson W. Polsby. Chatham, NJ: Chatham House Publishers.

Brady, Henry E., and Paul M. Sniderman. 1985. "Attitude Attribution: A Group Basis for Political Reasoning." *American Political Science Review* 79:1061-78.

Brehm, John. 1990. "Opinion Surveys and Political Representation." Ph.D. diss. University of Michigan.

Browne, Eric C., John P. Frendreis, and Dennis W. Gleiber. 1984. "An 'Events' Approach to the Problem of Cabinet Stability." *Comparative Political Studies* 17:167-97.

Browne, E.C., J.P. Frendreis, and D.W. Gleiber. 1986. "The Process of Cabinet Dissolution: An Exponential Model of Duration and Stability in Western Democracies." *American Journal of Political Science* 30:628-50.

Burgess, P.M., and R.W. Lawton. 1972. *Indicators of International Behavior: An Assessment of Events Data Research.* Beverly Hills: Sage Publications.

Cahoon, L.S. 1975. "Locating a Set of Points Using Range Information Only." Ph.D. diss. Carnegie-Mellon University.

Cahoon, L.S., M.J. Hinich, and P.C. Ordeshook. 1978. "A Statistical Multidimensional Scaling Method Based on the Spatial Theory of Voting." In *Graphical Representation of Multivariate Data*, ed. P.J. Wang. New York: Academic Press.

Cain, Bruce E., D. Roderick Kiewiet, and Carole J. Uhlaner. 1991. "The Acquisition of Partisanship by Latinos and Asian Americans." *American Journal of Political Science* 35:390-422.

Carmines, Edward G., and James A. Stimson. 1989. *Issue Evolution: Race and the Transformation of American Politics.* Princeton: Princeton University Press.

Casstevens, R.W. 1989. "The Circulation of Elites: A Review and Critique of a Class of Models." *American Journal of Political Science* 33:294-317.

Chubb, John E. 1988. "Institutions, the Economy, and the Dynamics of State Elections." *American Political Science Review* 82:133-54.

Cioffi-Revilla, Claudio. 1984. "The Political Reliability of Italian Governments: An Exponential Survival Model." *American Political Science Review* 78:318-37.

Cioffi-Revilla, Claudio. 1990. *The Scientific Measurement of International Conflict.* Boulder: Lynne Rienner Publishers.

Cleveland, William S. 1985. *The Elements of Graphing Data.* Monterey, CA: Wadsworth.

Clubb, Jerome, William H. Flanigan, and Nancy H. Zingale. 1980. *Partisan Realignment: Voters, Parties and Government in American History.* Beverly Hills: Sage Publications.

Collier, David, and Richard E. Messick. 1975. "Prerequisites Versus Diffusion: Testing Alternative Explanations of Social Security Adoption." *American Political Science Review* 69:1299-15.

Collier, David, and James E. Mahon. n.d. "Conceptual 'Stretching' Revisited: Alternative Views of Categories in Comparative Analysis." *American Political Science Review*.

Conover, Pamela Johnston, and Stanley Feldman. 1981. "The Origins and Meaning of Liberal/Conservative Self-Identifications." *American Journal of Political Science* 25:617-45.

Conover, Pamela Johnston, and Stanley Feldman. 1986. "Emotional Reactions to the Economy: I'm Mad as Hell and I'm Not Going to Take It Anymore." *American Journal of Political Science* 30:50-78.

Conover, Pamela Johnston, and Stanley Feldman. 1989. "Candidate Perception in an Ambiguous World: Campaigns, Cues and Inference Processes." *American Journal of Political Science* 33:912-40.

Converse, Philip E. 1964. "The Nature of Belief Systems in Mass Publics." In *Ideology and Discontent*, ed. David E. Apter. New York: Free Press.

Converse, Philip E. 1970. "Attitudes and Non-Attitudes: Continuation of a Dialogue." In *The Quantitative Analysis of Social Problems*, ed. Edward R. Tufte. Reading, MA: Addison-Wesley.

Converse, P.E., and G.B. Markus. 1979. "Plus ça Change...The New CPS Election Study Panel." *American Political Science Review* 73:32-49.

Coombs, Clyde H. 1964. *A Theory of Data.* New York: John Wiley & Sons.

Cowden, Jonathan, and Thomas Hartley. n.d. "Complex Measures and Sociotropic Voting." *Political Analysis.*

Cox, D.R. 1972. "Regression Models and Life Tables." *Journal of Royal Statistical Society*, Series B 34:187-202.

Cramer, J.S. 1986. *Econometric Applications of Maximum Likelihood Methods.* New York: Cambridge University Press.

Dalton, Russell J. 1980. "Reassessing Parental Socialization: Indicator Unreliability Versus Generational Transfer." *American Political Science Review* 74:421-31.

Davis, Otto A., and Melvin Hinich. 1966. "A Mathematical Model of Policy Formation in a Democratic Society." In *Mathematical Applications in Political Science II*, ed. J. Bernd. Dallas: Southern Methodist University Press.

Davis, William W., George T. Duncan, and Randolph M. Siverson. 1978. "The Dynamics of Warfare: 1816-1965." *American Journal of Political Science* 22:772-92.

Delaney, John Thomas, Jack Fiorito, and Marick F. Masters. 1988. "The Effects of Union Organizational and Environmental Characteristics on Union Political Action." *American Journal of Political Science* 32:616-42.

Denk, Charles E., and Steven E. Finkel. 1992. "The Aggregate Impact of Explanatory Variables in Logit and Linear Probability Models." *American Journal of Political Science* 36:785-804.

Downs, A. 1957. *An Economic Theory of Democracy.* New York: Harper and Row.

Durr, Robert H. n.d. "An Essay on Cointegration and Error Correction Models." *Political Analysis.*

Edwards, A.W.F. 1972. *Likelihood.* New York: Cambridge University Press.

Efron, Bradley. 1979. "Bootstrap Methods: Another Look at the Jackknife." *Annals of Statistics* 7:1-26.

Efron, Bradley, and Gail Gong. 1983. "A Leisurely Look at the Bootstrap, the Jackknife and Cross-Validation." *American Statistician* 37:36-48.

Elandt-Johnson, R., and N. Johnson. 1980. *Survival Models and Data Analysis.* New York: Wiley.

Enelow, James M., and Melvin J. Hinich. 1984. *The Spatial Theory of Voting: An Introduction.* Cambridge: Cambridge University Press.

Enelow, James M., and Melvin J. Hinich. 1989. "The Location of American Presidential Candidates: An Empirical Test of a New Spatial Model of Elections." *Mathematical Computer Modeling* 12:461-70.

Enelow, James M., and Melvin J. Hinich. 1985. "Estimating the Parameters of a Spatial Model of Elections: An Empirical Test Based on the 1980 National Election Study." *Political Methodology* 11:249-68.

Engle, Robert F., and Clive W.J. Granger. 1987. "Co-integration and Error Correction: Representation, Estimation, and Testing." *Econometrica* 55:251-76.

Engle, Robert F., and Clive W.J. Granger, eds. 1991. *Long-Run Economic Relationships: Readings in Cointegration.* Oxford: Oxford University Press.

Engle, Robert F., and M. Watson. 1981. "A One Factor Multivariate Time Series Model of Metropolitan Wage Rates." *Journal of the American Statistical Association* 76:774-80.

Erbring, Lutz. 1990. "Individuals Writ Large: An Epilogue on the 'Ecological Fallacy.'" *Political Analysis* 1:235-69.

Erikson, Robert S. 1979. "The SRC Panel Data and Mass Political Attitudes." *British Journal of Political Science* 9:89-114.

Faber, Jan. 1987. "Measuring Cooperation, Conflict, and the Social Network of Nations." *Journal of Conflict Resolution* 31:438-64.

Feldman, Stanley. 1988. "Structure and Consistency in Public Opinion: The Role of Core Beliefs and Values." *American Journal of Political Science* 32:416-40.

Feldman, Stanley. 1990. "Measuring Issue Preferences: The Problem of Response Instability." *Political Analysis* 1:25-60.

Finkel, Steven E. 1985. "Reciprocal Effects of Participation and Political Efficacy: A Panel Analysis." *American Journal of Political Science* 29:891-913.

Fischer, Gregory W., and Mark S. Kamlet. 1984. "Explaining Presidential Priorities: The Competing Aspiration Levels Model of Macrobudgetary Decision Making." *American Political Science Review* 78:356-71.

Franklin, Charles H. 1990. "Estimation Across Data Sets: Two-Stage Auxiliary Instrument Variables Estimation (2SAIV)." *Political Analysis* 1:1-24.

Franklin, Charles H. 1991. "Eschewing Obfuscation? Campaigns and the Perception of U.S. Senate Incumbents." *American Political Science Review* 85:1193-1214.

Franklin, Charles H., and John E. Jackson. 1986. "Structural Estimation with Limited Variables." In *Political Science: The Science of Politics*, ed. Herbert F. Weisberg. New York: Agathon Press.

Franklin, Charles H., and Liane C. Kosaki. 1989. "Republican Schoolmaster: The U.S. Supreme Court, Public Opinion, and Abortion." *American Political Science Review* 83:751-71.

Franklin, Charles H., and John E. Jackson. 1983. "The Dynamics of Party Identification." *American Political Science Review* 77:957-73.

Freeman, John R. 1983. "Granger Causality and the Time Series Analysis of Political Relationships." *American Journal of Political Science* 27:327-58.

Freeman, John R. 1989. *Democracy and Markets: The Politics of Mixed Economies*. Ithaca, NY: Cornell University Press.

Freeman, John R. 1990. "Systematic Sampling, Temporal Aggregation, and the Study of Political Relationships." *Political Analysis* 1:61-98.

Freeman, John R., ed. n.d. *Political Analysis*, Vol. 4.

Freeman, John R., John T. Williams, and Tse-min Lin. 1989. "Vector Autoregression and the Study of Politics." *American Journal of Political Science* 33:842-77.

Frohlich, Norman, and Joe A. Oppenheimer. 1990. "Choosing Justice in Experimental Democracies with Production." *American Political Science Review* 84:461-77.

Fuller, Wayne A. 1987. *Measurement Error Models*. New York: John Wiley & Sons.

Geddes, Barbara. 1991. "How the Cases You Choose Affect the Answers You Get: Selection Bias in Comparative Politics." *Political Analysis* 2:131-50.

Geisser, S. 1975. "The Predictive Sample Reuse Method with Applications." *Journal of the American Statistical Association* 70:320-28.

Gelman, Andrew, and Gary King. 1990. "Estimating Incumbency Advantage Without Bias." *American Journal of Political Science* 34:1142-64.

Goldstein, Joshua S. 1988. *Long Cycles: Prosperity and War in the Modern Age*. New Haven: Yale University Press.

Goldstein, Joshua S. 1991. "The Possibility of Cycles in International Relations." *International Studies Quarterly* 35:477-80.

Goldstein, Joshua S., and John R. Freeman. 1990. *Three-Way Street, Strategic Reciprocity in World Politics*. Chicago: University of Chicago Press.

Goldstein, Joshua S., and John R. Freeman. 1991. "U.S.-Soviet-Chinese Relations: Routine, Reciprocity, or Rational Expectations?" *American Political Science Review* 85:17-35.

Gonick, Lev S., and Robert M. Rosh. 1988. "The Structural Constraints of the World-Economy on National Political Development." *Comparative Political Studies* 21:171-99.

Goodman, L. 1959. "Some Alternatives to Ecological Correlation." *American Journal of Sociology* 64: 610-25.

Gosnell, Harold F. 1937. *Machine Politics: Chicago Model*. Chicago: University of Chicago Press.

Granato, Jim. 1992. "An Agenda for Econometric Model Building." *Political Analysis* 3:123-54.

Granger, C.W.J. 1969. "Investigating Causal Relations by Econometric Models and Cross Spectral Methods." *Econometrica* 37:424-38.

Granger, C.W.J., and Paul Newbold. 1986. *Forecasting Economic Time Series*, 2nd ed. San Diego: Academic Press.

Gray, Virginia. 1973. "Innovation in the States: A Diffusion Study." *American Political Science Review* 67:1174-93.

Green, Donald Philip. 1988. "On the Dimensionality of Public Sentiment Toward Partisan and Ideological Groups." *American Journal of Political Science* 32:758-80.

Green, Donald Philip. 1990. "On the Value of Not Teaching Students to be Dangerous." *Political Methodologist* 3:7-9.

Green, Donald Philip. 1991. "The Effects of Measurement Error on Two-Stage Least-Squares Estimates." *Political Analysis* 2: 57-74.

Green, Donald Philip, and Bradley Palmquist. 1990. "Of Artifacts and Partisan Instability." *American Journal of Political Science* 34:872-902.

Grofman, Bernard. 1983. "Measures of Bias and Proportionality in Seats-Votes Relationships." *Political Methodology* 9:295-327.

Gross, A.J., and V.A. Clark. 1975. *Survival Distributions*. New York: Wiley.

Hall, Richard L., and Bernard Grofman. 1990. "The Committee Assignment Process and the Conditional Nature of Committee Bias." *American Political Science Review* 84:1149-66.

Hamilton, Lawrence C., and James D. Hamilton. 1983. "Dynamics of Terrorism." *International Studies Quarterly* 27:39-54.

Hansen, Wendy L. 1990. The International Trade Commission and the Politics of Protectionism. *American Political Science Review* 84:21-46.

Hanushek, Eric A., and John E. Jackson. 1977. *Statistical Methods for Social Scientists*. New York: Academic Press.

Hanushek, Eric A., John E. Jackson, and J.F. Kain. 1974. "Model Specification, Use of Aggregate Data, and the Ecological Correlation Fallacy." *Political Methodology* 1:87-106.

Harvey, Andrew C. 1981. *Time Series Models*. Oxford: Philip Allan.

Harvey, Andrew C. 1989. *Forecasting, Structural Time Series Models and the Kalman Filter*. Cambridge: Cambridge University Press.

Harvey, Andrew C., and C. McKenzie. 1984. "Missing Observations in Dynamic Econometric Models: A Partial Synthesis." In *Time Series Analysis of Irregular Observations*, ed. E Parzen. Berlin: Springer-Verlag.

Hausman, Jerry. 1978. "Specification Tests in Econometrics." *Econometrica* 46:1251-72.

Hawthorne, Michael R., and John E. Jackson. 1987. "The Individual Political Economy of Federal Tax Policy." *American Political Science Review* 81:757-74.

Heckman, James. 1976. "The Common Structure of Statistical Models of Truncation, Sample Selection, and Limited Dependent Variables and a Simple Estimator for Such Models." *Annals of Economic and Social Measurement* 5:475-92.

Heckman, James. 1979. "Sample Selection Bias as a Specification Error." *Econometrica* 47:153-61.

Heckman, J.J., and B. Singer. 1982. "The Identification Problem in Econometric Models for Duration Data." In *Advances in Econometrics,* ed. W. Hildenbrand. Cambridge: Cambridge University Press.

Hendry, David F., Duo Qin, and Carlo Favero. 1989. *Lectures on Econometric Methodology.* Oxford: Oxford University Press.

Hibbs, Douglas A., Jr. 1974. "Problems of Statistical Estimation and Causal Inference in Time-Series Regressional Models." *Sociological Methodology* 1973-74:252-308.

Hibbs, Douglas A., Jr. 1977. "On Analyzing the Effects on Policy Interventions: Box-Jenkins and Box-Tiao vs. Structural Equation Models." *Sociological Methodology* 1977:137-79.

Hibbs, Douglas A., Jr. 1987. *The American Political Economy: Macroeconomics and Electoral Politics.* Cambridge, MA: Harvard University Press.

Hibbs, Douglas A., Jr., and Christopher Dennis. 1988. "Income Distribution in the United States." *American Political Science Review* 82:467-90.

Holbrook, Thomas M. 1991. "Presidential Elections in Space and Time." *American Journal of Political Science* 35:91-109.

Houweling, H.W., and J.B. Kune. 1984. "Do Outbreaks of War Follow a Poisson-Process?" *Journal of Conflict Resolution* 28(1):51-61.

Hovland, C.I., Irvine Janis, and H.H. Kelley. 1953. *Communication and Persuasion.* New Haven: Yale University Press.

Howell, Llewellyn D. 1983. "A Comparative Study of the WEIS and COPDAB Data Sets." *International Studies Quarterly* 27:149-59.

Hsiao, Cheng. 1986. *Analysis of Panel Data.* Econometric Society Monographs, No. 11. Cambridge University Press: New York.

Hurwitz, Jon, and Mark Peffley. 1987. "How Are Foreign Policy Attitudes Structured? A Hierarchical Model." *American Political Science Review* 81:1099-1120.

Huth, Paul, and Bruce Russett. 1988. "Deterrence Failure and Crisis Escalation." *International Studies Quarterly* 32(1):29-46.

Iyengar, Shanto. 1987. "Television News and Citizens' Explanations of National Affairs." *American Political Science Review* 81:815-32.

Iyengar, Shanto. 1991. *Is Anyone Responsible?* Chicago: University of Chicago Press.

Iyengar, Shanto, and Donald R. Kinder. 1987. *News That Matters: Television and American Opinion.* Chicago: University of Chicago Press.

Iyengar, Shanto, Mark D. Peters, and Donald R. Kinder. 1982. "Experimental Demonstrations of the 'Not-So-Minimal' Consequences of Television News Programs." *American Political Science Review* 76:848-58.

Jackman, Robert W. 1978. "The Predictability of Coups d'Etat: A Model with African Data." *American Political Science Review* 72:1262-75.

Jackman, Robert W., et al. 1986. "Explaining African Coups d'Etat." *American Political Science Review* 80:225-50.

Jackman, Simon, and Francis Vella. 1992. "Electoral Redistricting and Endogenous Partisan Control." *Political Analysis* 3:155-71.

Jackson, John E. 1983. "The Systematic Beliefs of the Mass Public: Estimating Policy Preferences with Survey Data." *Journal of Politics* 45:840-65.

Jackson, John E. 1990. "An Errors-in-Variables Approach to Estimating Models with Small Area Data." *Political Analysis* 1:157-80.

Jackson, John E. 1992a. "Estimation of Models with Variable Coefficients." *Political Analysis* 3:27-49.

Jackson, John E. 1992b. "Attitudes, No Opinions, and Guesses." Presented at the annual meeting of the Midwest Political Science Association, Chicago.

Jackson, John E., and David C. King. 1989. "Public Goods, Private Interests, and Representation." *American Political Science Review* 83:1143-64.

Jackson, John E., and John W. Kingdon. 1992. "Ideology, Interest Group Scores, and Legislative Votes." *American Journal of Political Science* 36:805-23.

Jacoby, William. 1991. *Data Theory and Dimensional Analysis.* Newbury Park, CA: Sage Publications.

Job, Brian L. 1976. "Membership in Inter-Nation Alliances, 1815-1965: An Exploration Utilizing Mathematical Probability Models." In *Mathematical Models in International Relations,* ed. Dina A. Zinnes and John Gillespie. New York: Praeger.

Johnston, Richard. 1992. "Party Identification Measures in the Anglo-American Democracies: A National Survey Experiment." *American Journal of Political Science* 36:542-59.

Johnston, Richard, André Blais, Henry E. Brady, and Jean Crête. 1992. *Letting the People Decide.* Montreal: McGill-Queen's University Press.

Jöreskog, Karl G., and Dag Sörbom. 1979. *Advances in Factor Analysis and Structural Equation Models.* Cambridge, MA: Abt Books.

Judd, Charles M., John A. Krosnick, and Michael A. Milburn. 1981. "Political Involvement and Attitude Structure in the General Public." *American Sociological Review* 46:660-69.

Judge, George G., and M.E. Bock. 1978. *The Statistical Implications of Pre-Test and Stein Rule Estimators in Econometrics.* New York: North-Holland.

Judge, George G., et al. 1985. *The Theory and Practice of Econometrics.* New York: John Wiley and Sons.

Kalbfleisch, J.D., and R.L. Prentice. 1980. *"The Statistical Analysis of Failure Time Data."* New York: Wiley.

Kalman, R.E. 1960. "A New Approach to Linear Filtering and Prediction Problems. Transactions of ASME." Series D, *Journal of Basic Engineering* 82:35-45.

Kamlet, Mark S., and David C. Mowery. 1987. "Influences on Executive and Congressional Budgetary Priorities: 1955-1981." *American Political Science Review* 81:155-78.

Kegley, C.W., Jr., G.A. Raymond, R.M. Rood, and R.A. Skinner. 1975. *International Events and the Comparative Analysis of Foreign Policy.* Columbia: University of South Carolina Press.

Kiewiet, D. Roderick, and Mathew D. McCubbins. 1988. "Presidential Influence on Congressional Appropriations Decisions." *American Journal of Political Science* 32:713-36.

Kinder, Donald R. 1983. "Diversity and Complexity in American Public Opinion." In *Political Science: The State of the Discipline,* ed. Ada W. Finifter. Washington, DC: American Political Science Association.

Kinder, Donald R., and D. Roderick Kiewiet. 1979. "Economic Discontent and Political Behavior: The Role of Personal Grievances and Collective Economic Judgments in Congressional Voting." *American Journal of Political Science* 23:495-527.

Kinder, Donald R., and Thomas R. Palfrey. 1992. *Experimental Foundations of Political Inquiry.* Ann Arbor: University of Michigan Press.

King, Gary. 1986. "How Not to Lie with Statistics: Avoiding Common Mistakes in Quantitative Political Science." *American Journal of Political Science* 30:666-87.

King, Gary. 1987. "Presidential Appointments to the Supreme Court." *American Politics Quarterly* 15:373-86.

King, Gary. 1988. "Statistical Models for Political Science Event Counts: Bias in Conventional Procedures and Evidence of the Exponential Poisson Regression Model." *American Journal of Political Science* 32:838-63.

King, Gary. 1989a. "Event Count Models for International Relations: Generalizations and Applications." *International Studies Quarterly* 33:123-47.

King, Gary. 1989b. "Representation Through Legislative Redistricting: A Stochastic Model." *American Journal of Political Science* 33:787-824.

King, Gary. 1989c. *Unifying Political Methodology: The Likelihood Theory of Statistical Inference.* New York: Cambridge University Press.

King, Gary. 1989d. "Variance Specification in Event Count Models: From Restrictive Assumptions to a Generalized Estimator." *American Journal of Political Science* 33:762-84.

King, Gary. 1991. "On Political Methodology." *Political Analysis* 2:1-29.

King, Gary, James E. Alt, Nancy Elizabeth Burns, and Michael Laver. 1990. "A Unified Model of Cabinet Dissolution in Parliamentary Democracies." *American Journal of Political Science* 34:846-871.

King, Gary, and Lyn Ragsdale. 1988. *The Elusive Executive: Discovering Statistical Patterns in the Presidency.* Washington, DC: Congressional Quarterly Press.

Kobrin, Stephen J. 1985. "Diffusion as an Explanation of Oil Nationalization." *Journal of Conflict Resolution* 29(1): 3-32.

Koford, Kenneth. 1989. "Dimensions in Congressional Voting." *American Political Science Review* 83:949-62.

Koford, Kenneth. 1991. "On Dimensionalizing Roll Call Votes in the U.S. Congress." *American Political Science Review* 85:955-76.

Kramer, Gerald H. 1971. "Short-term Fluctuations in U.S. Voting Behavior, 1896-1964." *American Political Science Review* 65:131-43.

Kramer, Gerald H. 1983. "The Ecological Fallacy Revisited: Aggregate Versus Individual-Level Findings on Economics and Elections and Sociotropic Voting." *American Political Science Review* 77:92-111.

Krehbiel, Keith. 1990. "Are Congressional Committees Composed of Preference Outliers? *American Political Science Review* 84: 149-63.

Krehbiel, Keith. 1991. *Information and Legislative Organization.* Ann Arbor: University of Michigan Press.

Krehbiel, Keith, and Douglas Rivers. 1988. "The Analysis of Committee Power: An Application to Senate Voting on the Minimum Wage." *American Journal of Political Science* 32:1151-74.

Krosnick, J.A. 1991. "The Stability of Political Preferences: Comparisons of Symbolic and Nonsymbolic Attitudes." *American Journal of Political Science* 35:547-76.

Kruskal, J.B., 1964. "Multidimensional Scaling by Optimizing Goodness of Fit to a Nonmetric Hypothesis." *Psychometrika* 29:1-27.

Lazarsfeld, Paul F., Bernard Berelson, and Hazel Gaudet. 1944. *The People's Choice, How the Voter Makes Up His Mind in a Presidential Campaign.* New York: Columbia University Press.

Leamer, Edward E. 1978. *Specification Searches: Ad Hoc Inference with Nonexperimental Data.* New York: John Wiley & Sons.

Lebow, Richard Ned, and Janice Gross Stein. 1990. "Deterrence: The Elusive Dependent Variable." *World Politics* 42(3):336-69.

Levine, Michael E., and Charles R. Plott. 1977. "Agenda Influence and Its Implications. " *Virginia Law Review* 561-604.

Levy, Jack S. 1982. "The Contagion of Great Power War Behavior, 1495-1975." *American Journal of Political Science* 26:562-82.

Levy, Jack S. 1983. *War in the Modern Great Power System, 1495-1975.* Lexington: University Press of Kentucky.

Levy, Jack S. 1985. "Theories of General War." *World Politics* 37:344-74.

Lewis-Beck, Michael S. 1988. *Economics and Elections: The Major Western Democracies.* Ann Arbor: University of Michigan Press.

Li, Richard P.Y., and William R. Thompson. 1975. "The 'Coup Contagion' Hypothesis." *Journal of Conflict Resolution* 19:63-88.

Lijphart, Arend. 1984. "Measures of Cabinet Durability." *Comparative Political Studies* 17(2):265-79.

Litterman, Robert B. 1984. "Forecasting and Policy Analysis with Bayesian Vector Autoregressive Models." *Federal Reserve Bank of Minneapolis Quarterly Review* 8:30-41.

Little, Roderick J.A., and Donald B. Rubin. 1987. *Statistical Analysis with Missing Data.* New York: John Wiley & Sons.

Londregan, John B., and Keith T. Poole. 1990. "Poverty, the Coup Trap, and the Seizure of Executive Power." *World Politics* 42:151-83.

Londregan, John B., and Keith T. Poole. 1992. "The Political Economy of Growth, Nonconstitutional Rule, and Leadership Succession." Presented at the Ninth Annual Political Methodology Summer Conference, Cambridge.

Luskin, Robert C. 1987. "Measuring Political Sophistication." *American Journal of Political Science* 31:856-99.

Macdonald, Stuart Elaine, Ola Listhaug, and George Rabinowitz. 1991. "Issues and Party Support in Multiparty Systems." *American Political Science Review* 85:1107-31.

Macdonald, Stuart Elaine, and George Rabinowitz. 1987. "The Dynamics of Structural Realignment." *The American Political Science Review* 81:775-96.

MacKuen, Michael B. 1984. "Exposure to Information, Belief Integration, and Individual Responsiveness to Agenda Change." *American Political Science Review* 78:372-391.

MacKuen, Michael B., Robert S. Erikson, and James A. Stimson. 1989. "Macropartisanship." *American Political Science Review* 83:1125-42.

MacKuen, Michael B., Robert S. Erikson, and James A. Stimson. 1992. "Peasants or Bankers? The American Electorate and the U.S. Economy." *American Political Science Review* 86:597-611.

Maddala, G.S. 1983. *Limited-Dependent and Qualitative Variables in Econometrics.* Cambridge: Cambridge University Press.

Marcus, George E. 1988. "The Structure of Emotional Response: 1984 Presidential Candidates." *American Political Science Review* 82:737-62.

Markus, Gregory B. 1979. *Analyzing Panel Data.* Beverly Hills: Sage Publications.

Markus, Gregory B. 1982. "Political Attitudes During an Election Year: A Report on the 1980 NES Panel Study." *American Political Science Review* 76:538-60.

Markus, Gregory B. 1988. "The Impact of Personal and National Economic Conditions on the Presidential Vote: A Pooled Cross-Sectional Analysis." *American Journal of Political Science* 32:137-54.

Mayer, William G. 1992. *The Changing American Mind.* Ann Arbor: University of Michigan Press.

McAdams, John. 1986. "Alternatives for Dealing with Errors in the Variables: An Example Using Panel Data." *American Journal of Political Science* 30:256-78.

McAdams, John C., and John R. Johannes. 1987. "Determinants of Spending by House Challengers, 1974-84." *American Journal of Political Science* 31:457-84.

McClelland, Charles A. 1983. "Let the User Beware." *International Studies Quarterly* 27:169-77.

McCubbins, Mathew D., and Thomas Schwartz. 1988. "Congress, the Courts, and Public Policy: Consequences of the One Man, One Vote Rule." *American Journal of Political Science* 32:388-415.

McCullagh, P., and J.A. Nelder. 1989. *Generalized Linear Models.* 2nd ed. London: Chapman & Hall.

McDonald, Roderick P. 1985. *Factor Analysis and Related Methods.* Hillsdale, NY: Lawrence Erlbaum Associates, Publishers.

McGinnis, Michael D., and John T. Williams. 1989. "Change and Stability in Superpower Rivalry." *American Political Science Review* 83:1101-23.

McGowan, Patrick J., and Robert M. Rood. 1975. "Alliance Behavior in Balance of Power Systems: Applying a Poisson Model to Nineteenth-Century Europe." *American Political Science Review* 69:859-70.

McGowan, P., H. Starr, G. Hower, R. Merritt, and D. Zinnes. 1988. "International Data as a National Resource." *International Interactions* 14(2):101-13.

McKelvey, Richard D., and Peter C. Ordeshook. 1985. "Sequential Elections with Limited Information." *American Journal of Political Science* 29:480-512.

McKelvey, Richard D., and Peter C. Ordeshook. 1990. "A Decade of Experimental Research on Spatial Models of Elections and Committees." In *Advances in the Spatial Theory of Voting,* ed. James Enelow and Melvin Hinich. Cambridge: Cambridge University Press.

McKelvey, R., and W. Zavoina. 1975. "A Statistical Model for the Analysis of Ordinal Level Dependent Variables." *Journal of Mathematical Sociology* 4:103-20.

Mebane, Walter R., Jr. 1991. "Problems of Time and Causality in Survey Cross-sections." *Political Analysis* 2:75-96.

Mebane, Walter R., Jr. n.d. "Analyzing the Effects of U.S. Local Government Fiscal Activity I: Sampling Model and Basic Econometrics." *Political Analysis.*

Midlarsky, Manus I. 1970. "Mathematical Models of Instability and a Theory of Diffusion." *International Studies Quarterly* 16(4): 60-84.

Midlarsky, Manus I. 1978. "Analyzing Diffusion and Contagion Effects: The Urban Disorders of the 1960s." *American Political Science Review* 72:996-1008.

Midlarsky, Manus I. 1983. "Absence of Memory in the Nineteenth-Century Alliance System: Perspectives from Queuing Theory and Bivariate Probability Distributions." *American Journal of Political Science* 27:762-84.

Midlarsky, Manus I. 1988. "Rulers and the Ruled: Patterned Inequality and the Onset of Mass Political Violence." *American Political Science Review* 82:491-509.

Mooney, Christopher Z., and Robert D. Duval. 1991. "Bootstrapping: Computationally Intensive, Non-Parametric Statistical Inference." Presented at the Eighth Annual Political Methodology Summer Conference, Durham.

Morrison, D., R.C. Mitchell, and J.N. Paden. 1989. *Black Africa: A Comparative Handbook.* 2nd ed. New York: Irvington Press.

Most, Benjamin A., and Harvey Starr. 1980. "Diffusion, Reinforcement, Geopolitics, and the Spread of War." *American Political Science Review* 74:932-46.

Mueller, John E. 1973. *War, Presidents, and Public Opinion.* New York: Wiley.

Muthen, B. 1984. "A General Structural Equation Model with Dichotomous, Ordered Categorical, and Continuous Latent Variable Indicators." *Psychometrika* 49:115-32.

Nagler, Jonathan. 1991. "The Effect of Registration Laws and Education on U.S. Voter Turnout." *American Political Science Review* 85:1393-1406.

Nagler, Jonathan. 1992. "Scobit: An Alternative Estimator to Logit and Probit Allowing for Tests of Heterogeneity of Respondents and Interactive Effects in Models with Dichotomous Dependent Variables." Presented at the Ninth Annual Political Methodology Summer Conference, Cambridge.

Norpoth, Helmut, and Milton Lodge. 1985. "The Difference Between Attitudes and Nonattitudes in the Mass Public: Just Measurement?" *American Journal of Political Science* 29:291-307.

O'Donnell, G.A., and P.C. Schmitter. 1986. *Transitions from Authoritarian Rule.* Baltimore: Johns Hopkins University Press.

Oneal, John R. 1990. "Testing the Theory of Collective Action." *Journal of Conflict Resolution* 34:426-48.

Orme-Johnson, David W., Charles N. Alexander, John L. Davies, Howard M. Chandler, and Wallace E. Larimore. 1988. "International Peace Project in the Middle East: The Effects of the Maharishi Technology of the Unified Field." *Journal of Conflict Resolution* 32:776-812.

Ostrom, Charles W., Jr., and Robin F. Marra. 1986. "U.S. Defense Spending and the Soviet Estimate." *American Political Science Review* 80:819-42.

Ostrom, Charles W. Jr., and Dennis M. Simon. 1988. "The President's Public." *American Journal of Political Science* 32:1098-119.

Ostrom, Charles W., Jr., and Renée M. Smith. 1991. "Routinization and Reciprocity in U.S. Defense Expenditure Policy Making: An Analysis of Countervailing Forces." Michigan State University. Typescript.

Ostrom, Charles W., Jr., and Renée M. Smith. n.d. "Error Correction, Attitude Persistence, and Executive Rewards and Punishments: A Behavioral Theory of Presidential Approval." *Political Analysis* 4.

Page, Benjamin I., and Robert Y. Shapiro. 1992. *The Rational Public: Fifty Years of Trends in Americans' Policy Preferences.* Chicago: University of Chicago Press.

Palfrey, Thomas R., ed. 1991. *Laboratory Research in Political Economy.* Ann Arbor: University of Michigan Press.

Palfrey, Thomas R., and Keith T. Poole. 1987. "The Relationship Between Information, Ideology and Voting Behavior," *American Journal of Political Science* 31:511-30.

Palmer, Glenn. 1990. "Corralling the Free Rider: Deterrence and the Western Alliance." *International Studies Quarterly* 34(2): 147-64.

Palmer, Harvey. 1992. "Respondent Variation in Measurement Error." Presented at the annual meeting of the Midwest Political Science Association, Chicago.

Palmquist, Bradley, and Donald P. Green. 1992. "Estimation of Models with Correlated Measurement Errors from Panel Data." *Sociological Methodology* 22:119-46.

Peffley, Mark A., and John Hurwitz. 1985. "A Hierarchical Model of Attitude Constraint." *American Journal of Political Science* 29:871-90.

Phillips, P.C.B. 1988. "Regression Theory for Near-Integrated Time Series." *Econometrica* 56:1021-43.

Phillips, P.C.B. 1991. "Optimal Inference in Cointegrated Systems." *Econometrica* 59:283-306.

Piazza, Thomas, Paul M. Sniderman, and Philip E. Tetlock. 1990. "Analysis of the Dynamics of Political Reasoning." *Political Analysis* 1:99-120.

Plotnick, Robert D., and Richard F. Winters. 1985. "A Politicoeconomic Theory of Income Redistribution." *American Political Science Review* 79:458-73.

Plott, Charles R., and Michael E. Levine. 1978. "A Model of Agenda Influence on Committee Decisions." *American Economic Review* 68:146-60.

Pollins, Brian. 1989. "Does Trade Still Follow the Flag?" *American Political Science Review* 83:465-80.

Poole, Keith T. 1981. "Dimensions of Interest Group Evaluation of the U.S. Senate, 1969-78." *American Journal of Political Science* 25:49-67.

Poole, Keith T. 1984. "Least Squares Metric, Undimensional Unfolding." *Psychometrika* 49:311-23.

Poole, Keith T., and R. Steven Daniels. 1985. "Ideology, Party, and Voting in the U.S. Congress, 1959-1980." *American Political Science Review* 79:373-99.

Poole, Keith T., and Howard Rosenthal, 1984. "U.S. Presidential Elections, 1968-80: A Spatial Analysis." *American Journal of Political Science* 28:282-312.

Poole, Keith T., and Howard Rosenthal. 1985. "A Spatial Model for Legislative Roll Call Analysis." *American Journal of Political Science* 29:357-84.

Poole, Keith T., and Howard Rosenthal. 1991. "Patterns of Congressional Voting." *American Journal of Political Science* 35(1):228-78.

Putnam, Robert D. 1967. "Toward Explaining Miliary Intervention in Latin American Politics." *World Politics* 20:83-110.

Rabinowitz, George. 1976. "A Procedure for Ordering Object Pairs Consistent with the Multidimensional Unfolding Model." *Psychometrika* 41(3):349-73.

Rabinowitz, George. 1978. "On The Nature of Political Issues: Insights from a Spatial Analysis." *American Journal of Political Science* 22:793-817.

Rabinowitz, George, P.H. Gurian, and S.E. Macdonald. 1984. "The Structure of Presidential Elections and the Process of Realignment." *American Journal of Political Science* 28:611-35.

Rabinowitz, George, and S.E. Macdonald. 1986. "The Power of the States in the U.S. Presidential Elections." *American Political Science Review* 80:65-87.

Rabinowitz, George, and S.E. Macdonald. 1989. "A Directional Theory of Issue Voting." *American Political Science Review* 83:93-122.

Rasch, G. 1980. *Probabilistic Models for Some Intelligence and Attainment Tests.* Chicago: University of Chicago Press.

Rasler, Karen A., and William R. Thompson. 1985a. "War and Economic Growth of Major Powers." *American Journal of Political Science* 29:513-38.

Rasler, Karen A., and William R. Thompson. 1985b. "War Making and State Making: Governmental Expenditures." *American Political Science Review* 79:491-507.

Rice, Stuart A. 1928. *Quantitative Methods in Politics.* New York: Knopf.

Richardson, Lewis Fry. 1944. "The Distribution of Wars in Time." *Journal of the Royal Statistical Society* 107 (III-IV):242-50.

Richardson, Lewis Fry. 1960. *Statistics of Deadly Quarrels.* Pacific Grove, CA: Boxwood Press.

Riker, William H. 1986. *The Art of Political Manipulation.* Yale University Press.

Rivers, Douglas, and Nancy L. Rose. 1985. "Passing the President's Program: Public Opinion and Presidential Influence in Congress." *American Journal of Political Science* 29:183-96.

Rivers, Douglas. 1986. "Microeconomics and Macropolitics: A Solution to the Kramer Problem." Presented at the Political Methodology Society Meeting, Harvard University.

Rivers, Douglas. 1987. "Inconsistency of Least Squares Unfolding." Presented at the Political Methodology Society Meeting, Durham.

Rivers, Douglas. 1988. "Heterogeneity in Models of Electoral Choice." *American Journal of Political Science* 32:737-57.

Rivers, Douglas, and Quong H. Vuong. 1988. "Limited Information Estimators and Exogeneity Tests for Simultaneous Probit Models." *Journal of Econometrics* 39:1-20.

Robinson, W.S. 1950. "Ecological Correlations and the Behavior of Individuals." *American Sociological Review* 15:351-57.

Rosenthal, Howard. 1992. "Response to Snyder's 'Committee Power, Structure-Induced Equilibria, and Roll Call Votes': The Unidimensional Congress Is Not the Result of Selective Gatekeeping." *American Journal of Political Science* 36:31-35.

Rosh, Robert M. 1988. "Third World Militarization." *Journal of Conflict Resolution* 32:671-98.

Ross, Marc Howard, and Elizabeth Homer. 1976. "Galton's Problem in Cross-National Research." *World Politics* 29:1-28.

Russett, Bruce 1988. "Editor's Comment." *Journal of Conflict Resolution* 32:773-75.

Sayrs, Lois W. 1989. *Pooled Time Series Analysis.* Beverly Hills: Sage Publications.

Schneider, Mark. 1989. "Intermunicipal Competition, Budget Maximizing Bureaucrats, and the Level of Suburban Competition." *American Journal of Political Science* 33:612-28.

Schneider, Saundra K., and Patricia Ingraham. 1984. "The Impact of Political Participation on Social Policy Adoption and Expansion." *Comparative Politics* 17(1):107-22.

Scholz, John T., Jim Twombly, and Barbara Headrick. 1991. "Street-Level Political Controls over Federal Bureaucracy." *American Political Science Review* 85:829-50.

Schrodt, Philip A. 1990. "A Methdological Critique of a Test of the Effects of the Maharishi Technology of the Unified Field." *Journal of Conflict Resolution* 34:745-55.

Schrodt, Philip A. 1991. "Predicting Interstate Conflict Outcomes Using a Bootstrapped ID3 Algorithm." *Political Analysis* 2:31-56.

Schuman, Howard, and Stanley Presser. 1981. *Questions and Answers.* New York: Academic Press.

Shamir, Michal, and John Sullivan. 1983. "The Political Context of Tolerance: The United States and Israel." *American Political Science Review* 77:911-28.

Sharp, Elaine B., and Steven Maynard-Moody. 1991. "Theories of the Local Welfare Role." *American Journal of Political Science* 35:934-50.

Shively, W. Phillips. 1969. "'Ecological' Inference: The Use of Aggregate Data to Study Individuals." *American Political Science Review* 63:1183-96.

Shively, W. Phillips. 1974. "Utilizing External Evidence in Cross-Level Inference." *Political Methodology* 1:61-73.

Shively, W. Phillips. 1985. "A Strategy for Cross-Level Inference Under an Assumption of Breakage Effects." *Political Methodology* 11:167-79.

Sims, Christopher A. 1977. "Exogeneity and Causal Ordering in Macroeconomic Models." In *New Methods of Business Cycle Research: Proceedings from a Conference*, ed. Christopher A. Sims. Minneapolis, MN: Federal Reserve Bank of Minneapolis.

Sims, Christopher A. 1980. "Macroeconomics and Reality." *Econometrica* 48:1-48.

Singer, J. David, and Melvin Small. 1972. *The Wages of War 1816-1965, A Statistical Handbook.* New York: John Wiley & Sons.

Siverson, Randolph M., and George T. Duncan. 1976. In *Mathematical Models in International Relations,* ed. Dina A. Zinnes and John Gillespie. New York: Praeger.

Siverson, Randolph M., and Harvey Starr. 1991. *The Diffusion of War.* Ann Arbor: University of Michigan Press.

Slemrod, Joel. 1986. "Saving and the Fear of Nuclear War." *Journal of Conflict Resolution* 30:403-19.

Small, Melvin, and J. David Singer. 1982. *Resort to Arms.* Beverly Hills: Sage Publications.

Smith, Renée M. 1992. "Cointegration and Error Correction: A Look at 'New' Estimation Problems Through a Familiar Lens." Presented at the annual meeting of the American Political Science Association, Chicago.

Smith, Renée M. n.d. "Error Correction, Attractors, and Cointegration: Substantive and Methodological Issues." *Political Analysis* 4.

Sniderman, Paul M., and Thomas Piazza. 1993. *The Scar of Race.* Cambridge, MA: Harvard University Press.

Sniderman, Paul M., Thomas Piazza, Philip E. Tetlock, and Ann Kendrick. 1991. "The New Racism." *American Journal of Political Science* 35:423-47.

Snyder, James M., Jr. 1992. "Committee Power, Structure-Induced Equilibria, and Roll Call Votes." *American Journal of Political Science* 36:1-30.

Sorokin, Pitirim A. 1937. *Social and Cultural Dynamics.* Vol. 3 of *Fluctuation of Social Relationships, War, and Revolution.* New York: American Book Company.

Starr, Harvey. 1991. Democratic Dominoes. *Journal of Conflict Resolution* 35:356-81.

Stimson, James A. 1985. "Regression in Space and Time: A Statistical Essay." *American Journal of Political Science* 29:914-47.

Stimson, James A., ed. 1990. *Political Analysis.* Vol 1. Ann Arbor: University of Michigan Press.

Stimson, James A. 1991a. *Public Opinion in America.* Boulder, CO: Westview Press.

Stimson, James A., ed. 1991b. *Political Analysis.* Vol. 2. Ann Arbor: University of Michigan Press.

Stimson, James A., ed. 1992. *Political Analysis.* Vol. 3. Ann Arbor: University of Michigan Press.

Strang, David. 1991. "Global Patterns of Decolonization, 1500-1987." *International Studies Quarterly* 35:429-54.

Strom, Kaare. 1985. "Party Goals and Government Performance in Parliamentary Democracies." *American Political Science Review* 79:738-54.

Strom, Kaare, Eric C. Browne, John P. Frendreis, and Dennis W. Gleiber. 1988. "Contending Models of Cabinet Stability." *American Political Science Review* 82:923-41.

Sudman, Seymour, and Norman M. Bradburn. 1982. *Asking Questions.* San Francisco: Jossey-Bass Publishers.

Sullivan, Denis G., and Roger D. Masters. 1988. "'Happy Warriors': Leaders' Facial Displays, Viewers' Emotions, and Political Support." *American Journal of Political Science* 32:345-68.

Taagepera, Rein. 1986. "Reformulating the Cube Law for Proportional Representation Elections." *American Political Science Review* 80:489-504.

Taylor, C.L., and D.A. Jodice. 1983a. *World Handbook of Political and Social Indicators.* Vol. I. New Haven, CT: Yale University Press.

Taylor, C.L., and D.A. Jodice. 1983b. *World Handbook of Political and Social Indicators.* Vol. II. New Haven, CT: Yale University Press.

Theil, Henri. 1971. *Principles of Econometrics.* New York: John Wiley & Sons.

Thompson, William R., and Karen A. Rasler. 1988. "War and Systemic Capability Reconcentration." *Journal of Conflict Resolution* 32:335-66.

Thurstone, L.L. 1932. "Isolation of Blocs in a Legislative Body by the Voting Records of Its Members." *Journal of Social Psychology* 4:425-33.

Todd, Richard M. 1984. "Improving Economic Forecasting with Bayesian Vector Autoregression." *Federal Reserve Bank of Minneapolis Quarterly Review* 8:19-29.

Tourangeau, Roger, and Kenneth A. Rasinski. 1988. "Cognitive Processes Underlying Context Effects in Attitude Measurement." *Psychological Bulletin* 103:299-314.

Tufte, Edward R. 1983. *The Visual Display of Quantitative Information.* Cheshire, CT: Graphics Press.

Tuma, Nancy Brandon, and Michael T. Hannan. 1984. *Social Dynamics.* Orlando, FL: Academic Press.

Ulmer, S. Sidney. 1982. "Supreme Court Appointments as a Poisson Distribution." *American Journal of Political Science* 26:113-16.

Vincent, Jack E. 1983. "WEIS vs. COPDAB: Correspondence Problems." *International Studies Quarterly* 27:161-68.

Walker, Jack L. 1969. "The Diffusion of Innovations Among the American States." *American Political Science Review* 63:880-99.

Wallis, W. Allen. 1936. "The Poisson Distribution and the Supreme Court." *Journal of the American Statistical Association* 31:376-80.

Watson, Mark W., and Robert F. Engle. 1983. "Alternative Algorithms for the Estimation of Dynamic Factor, Mimic and Varying Coefficient Regression Models." *Journal of Econometrics* 23:385-400.

Weisberg, Herbert F. 1974a. "Dimensionland: An Excursion into Spaces." *American Journal of Political Science* 18:743-76.

Weisberg, Herbert F. 1974b. "Models of Statistical Relationship." *American Political Science Review* 68:1638-55.

Weisberg, Herbert F. 1970. "Dimensions of Candidate Evaluations." *American Political Science Review* 64:1167-85.

Weisburg, Herbert F., and Jerrold G. Rusk. 1970. "Dimensions of Candidate Evaluation." *American Political Science Review* 64:1167-85.

White, Halbert. 1980. "A Heteroskedasticity-Consistent Covariance Matrix Estimator and a Direct Test for Heteroskedasticity." *Econometrica* 48:817-38.

White, Halbert. 1982. "Maximum Likelihood Estimation of Misspecified Models." *Econometrica* 50:1-25.

Wiley, D.E., and J.A. Wiley. 1970. "The Estimation of Measurement Error in Panel Data." *American Sociological Review* 35:112-16.

Wiley, J.A., and M.G. Wiley. 1974. "A Note on Correlated Errors in Repeated Measurements." *Sociological Methods and Research* 3:172-88.

Wilkerson, John. 1991. "Analyzing Committee Power: A Critique." *American Journal of Political Science* 35:624-42.

Williams, John T. n.d.a. "Dynamic Change, Specification Uncertainty, and Bayesian Vector Autoregressive Analysis." *Political Analysis* 4.

Williams, John T. n.d.b. "What Goes Around Comes Around: Unit Root Tests and Cointegration." *Political Analysis* 4.

Williams, John T., and Michael D. McGinnis. 1988. "Sophisticated Reaction in the U.S.-Soviet Arms Race: Evidence of Rational Expectations." *American Journal of Political Science* 32:968-95.

Wood, B. Dan. 1988. "Principals, Bureaucrats, and Responsiveness in Clean Air Enforcements." *American Political Science Review* 82:213-36.

Wood, B. Dan, and Richard W. Waterman. 1991. "The Dynamics of Political Control of the Bureaucracy." *American Political Science Review* 85:801-28.

Wright, Gerald C., Jr., Robert S. Erikson, and John P. McIver. 1987. "Public Opinion and Policy Liberalism in the American States." *American Journal of Political Science* 31:980-1001.

Wright, Gerald C., Robert S. Erikson, and John P. McIver. 1985. "Measuring State Partisanship and Ideology with Survey Data." *Journal of Politics* 47:469-89.

Wright, Quincy. 1942. *A Study of War.* Chicago: University of Chicago Press.

Zaller, John. 1992. *The Nature and Origins of Mass Opinion.* New York: Cambridge University Press.

Zaller, John, and Stanley Feldman. 1992. "A Simple Theory of the Survey Response: Answering Questions vs. Revealing Preferences." *American Journal of Political Science* 36:579-616.

Zellner, Arnold. 1979. "Statistical Analysis of Econometric Models." *Journal of the American Statistical Association* 74:628-43.

Political Processes and Individual Political Behavior

7

Comparative Political Parties: Research and Theory

Kenneth Janda

This essay reviews the state of research on comparative political parties, which I define as the analysis of parties across nations. If your field is comparative politics, my focus should suit you. If you are primarily interested in American party politics, please continue reading. I intend to demonstrate that even students of American parties can benefit from a comparative perspective on their research.

This essay covers only publications since 1980 that take an explicitly comparative approach to the analysis of political parties. Although it refers to earlier writings and to some single-country studies, it does so only to make certain points. This essay does not pretend to cover all important articles before 1980 nor all examples of outstanding research on parties in individual countries. With two exceptions, every citation is in English, which distinctly limits the scope of this review. It does not consider the rich literature on comparative political parties that exists in other languages -- especially in the works of French, German, and Italian scholars. Fortunately, some important works in other languages have been translated into English, and -- even more fortunately for us mono-lingual Americans -- many foreign parties scholars (thankfully most of the Scandinavians) write and publish in English. In fact, more than half the citations herein were written by European scholars and about half were originally published outside the United States.

Because of scholarly ethnocentricity, much of the comparative parties literature escapes the attention of American academics. Consider the findings of Giles, Mizell, and Patterson (1989), who surveyed faculty in departments with graduate programs about professional journals. About half of American political scientists were familiar with *Comparative Politics* (55%) and *Comparative Political Studies* (46%), the leading U.S. journals in the comparative field.[1] Less than 7%, however, were familiar with the *European Journal of Political Research* -- a major source of articles on comparative political parties -- or even with *The British Journal of Political Science* -- another important source. Presumably, even fewer knew about the *International Political Science Review*, *Journal of Theoretical Politics*, and *West European Politics* -- all foreign publications and all frequently cited herein. LaPonce (1980) conducted an "import-export" analysis of citations in the *American Political Science Review* [APSR] compared with the official journals of the other four oldest political science associations (Canadian, Indian, French, and British). He found that all national journals are ethnocentric, but the *APSR* was particularly so. This supports McKay's statement, "Rarely do American scholars read, and therefore rarely do they cite, European journals" (1988, 1052).[2]

With some notable exceptions to be discussed below, the parties literature in the U.S. is not strong on comparative analysis. In contrast, the European parties literature reflects the great strength of European political science in structural comparative politics, which McKay defines as "the systematic study of political institutions and processes across several and sometimes many countries" (1988, 1054). The American literature deals mainly with home-grown political parties and makes relatively few comparisons with parties in other countries. Of course, the United States is a large country, arguably the world's oldest democracy, and a true superpower -- all of which support the case for studying American parties per se. I argue, however, that limiting focus to American parties limits understanding as well. It is the familiar problem of missing the forest for the trees. The best way to understand the peculiar nature of American parties (and they are peculiar) is to study them in a comparative framework -- which means reading more works of foreign scholars who do such analyses.

This essay on the field adjusts for this imbalance in scholarship in the United States by reviewing recent writings on the comparative analysis of political parties, emphasizing the conceptual bases of the research and theory. Readers are directed to two excellent reviews of writings on American parties -- one by Leon Epstein in 1983 and the other by William Crotty in 1991 -- for coverage of the American literature.

American Parties in Comparative Perspective

What can we learn from looking at American parties in comparative perspective? Viewed by scholars from abroad, American political parties have always been puzzling phenomena. Analyzing politics in the U.S. Congress around the turn of the century, Bryce "kept to the last the feature of the House which Europeans find the strangest. It has parties, but they are headless. There is neither Government nor Opposition. There can hardly be said to be leaders..." (1912, V.I, 151). Writing just after World War II, Maurice Duverger, the most influential European writer on political parties in this half of the century, remarked that "American parties have a very archaic structure" (1963, 22; originally published in 1951). Nearly twenty years later, he still described American parties as "traditional" and largely excluded them from his analysis of modern mass (European) parties (1972, 8-9).

U.S. scholars have also noted the peculiar character of the Democratic and Republican parties compared with parties in other countries. In his comprehensive U.S. parties textbook, Eldersveld (1982) devoted a chapter to "The Special Nature of American Party Organizations." He described their structure as a "stratarchy" -- a nonhierarchical system of layers of control with diffused power and limited lines of accountability (pp. 97-99). Leon Epstein, who had compared parties in Western democracies (1980) in a major work two decades earlier, titled his own text on U.S. parties, *Political Parties in the American Mold* (1986), implying that the "mold" was unique:

> The distinctiveness of American parties is old and well established. It is not mainly the product of the last few decades of widely perceived decline. As governing agencies, American parties have nearly always been less cohesive in national policy making than parties in parliamentary regimes. And as extragovernmental agencies, their strength, where it existed, was traditionally state and local rather than national. Moreover, American parties have ordinarily been without the dues-paying mass memberships characteristic of European parties (p. 4).

Similarly, Keefe (1991), in the sixth edition of his popular textbook, characterized American parties as being dispersed in power, consisting of coalitions of groups, displaying ideological heterogeneity, emphasizing inclusivity, and lacking a clear notion of membership.

In describing American parties, all these authors made explicit or implicit references to parties in other countries. They engaged in comparative analysis to explain the nature of the Democrats and Republicans. If such comparisons help us understand parties in the United States, we can understand even them better by expanding our comparative knowledge of political parties. One needs to know how scholars have defined and measured generalized concepts of party structure, cohesion, factionalism, ideology, strategy, and so on in order to make intelligent comparisons across parties and party systems. One also needs to know the results of comparative research on what causes these party properties, how they interrelate, and what effects they have on politics and government. On entering this literature on comparative political parties, one soon learns that it has a rich theoretical tradition and has maintained that tradition in developing party theory.

Party Theory and Party Definitions

In his sweeping review of the American parties literature, Crotty also indicted writings on comparative parties for lacking "any one approach or model to supply an adequate perspective for relevant analysis" (1991, 182). But in an earlier essay (1969), Crotty recounted the history of theoretical integration in European scholarship, notably in the work of Ostrogorski, Michels, and Duverger. Ostrogorski (1964, originally 1902) attributed the rise of parties to the industrial revolution and the extension of the franchise. Michels's famous Iron Law of Oligarchy (1962, originally 1911) accounted for the tendency of leaders to maintain power at the expense of their members' interests. Duverger's rich contribution (1963) linked party ideology to party structure and explained the nature of a nation's party system by the nature of its electoral system.

Contemporary European scholarship has maintained its leadership in the development of party theory. Of course, some important party theorists have been American, but most of the stimulating theorists have a European appointment or origin (e.g., Budge, Charlot, Duverger, Laver, Mair, Panebianco, Rokkan, Sartori, Schofield, and Strom). There are reasons for this European influence in party theory. Some might cite the juxtaposition of party systems in nearby countries. To interpret politics across common borders (the argument goes), scholars are encouraged to conceptualize more broadly about party politics, which spurs the development of party theory.

Unfortunately, an explanation of common boundaries does not travel well to the United States. Only a few party scholars -- e.g., Epstein (1964) and Schwartz (1991a and 1991b) -- have compared American with Canadian parties, much less with Mexican parties.

A more plausible explanation lies in the greater number and variety of parties within European countries compared with the United States. Because the Democrats and Republicans have duopolized U.S. politics for more than a century, American scholars have focused on the powerful, studying the only two parties with major impact on national politics. When third parties cast darker shadows on the two-party landscape, scholars have been encouraged to think more generally about parties and have devised typologies to accommodate the interlopers (Rosenstone, Behr, and Lazarus 1984). Otherwise, relatively few U.S. political scientists have been challenged by our party system to build party theory. Crotty's 50-page review of the American literature devoted only four pages to "The Search for Theory" and mostly dealt with the single book by Downs (1957) and various publications by Schlesinger -- which have been recently collected in a single volume (1991).

The very nature of the two major U.S. parties has also constrained the development of party theory due to the problem of defining the boundaries of a party to serve as a unit of analysis. In Europe, there is a better-developed sense of formal party membership, sometimes reflected in membership fees, that helps define who belongs to a party. Although most states record party registration for purposes of conducting primary elections, the concept of party members clearly has no national applicability, and the term, "dues-paying member," sounds foreign to our ears. American scholars have attempted to deal with this boundary problem by distinguishing among the "party in the organization" and "party in the government" as opposed to "party in the electorate." But this piecemeal attempt to resolve the problem has not proven to be theoretically fruitful (Schlesinger 1991, 3).

As Pomper noted, "American parties are a jumble of these three conventional forms, which cannot readily be separated" (1992, 146). Pomper's solution was to conceptualize parties in terms of their *goals* (collective or coalitional), *mode* of operation (instrumental or expressive), and breadth of *focus* (elite or mass). These three dimensions produced an eight-fold classification of party concepts. Accordingly, the U.S. Democrats and Republicans are predominantly coalitional and instrumental, with a mass focus -- which means they fit Pomper's concept of party as an "office-seeking rational team." Although his conceptualization produced seven other types of parties, the range of concepts is still not broad enough to encompass some parties in cross-national analysis. The issue hinges on choosing a narrow or a broad definition of a political party.

A Narrow Definition of "Party"

Schlesinger noted that some scholars "want to define party to include all the numerous political organizations that call themselves by the name" (1991, 6). He continued, "However useful a theory of party based on such a broad definition would be, the theory I propose to elaborate is less ambitious" and applies only to "parties that contest in free elections, and primarily those parties that are able to win elections over time" (p. 6). Accordingly, Schlesinger adopted the well-known definition by Downs: a party is "a team of men seeking to control the governing apparatus by gaining office in a duly constituted election" (1957, 25). Many scholars employ a comparably narrow definition, perhaps excluding entities that they would commonly regard as a party in other countries.

This contradiction was apparent in Neumann's *Modern Political Parties* (1956), one of the first collections of studies in comparative politics. In his concluding essay, Neumann wrote, "Only the coexistence of at least one other competitive group makes a political party real," and said, "A one-party system is a contradiction in terms" (p. 395).[3] Nevertheless, Neumann's reader included an article on the Communist Party of the Soviet Union. Despite the way he defined a party, even Neumann found it awkward not to regard communist parties as political parties (see also Epstein 1975, 233). To do otherwise would exclude a huge body of literature important to comparative politics (Fischer-Galati 1979; Szajkowski 1986; Timmerman 1987; Gilberg 1989; Narkiewicz 1990). Moreover, Randall (1984, 4) contended that this "Eurocentric" definition would exclude non-communist one-party systems in Third World countries, and, as Pempel pointed out in his book on one-party dominant regimes, "The vast majority of the nation-states in the world could be characterized as one-party states" (1990, 1).

Focusing on parties' functions in contesting elections tends to exclude the class of "anti-system" parties, which Sartori defined as parties that undermine the legitimacy of the regime (1976, 132-133). For example, communist parties in multiparty systems often participated only tactically in elections (Gilberg 1989; Narkiewicz 1990). A definition based in electoral competition would also exclude militant religious, ethnic, and regional parties that operate on the fringes of the political system. For instance, McDonald and Ruhl noted that only "a few" of the more than 125 active parties in Latin America play the roles "attributed to them in the general theoretical literature -- literature that is based on Western European and Anglo-American systems in which military obedience and legislative power are taken for granted" (1989, 3).

A Broad Definition

A truly general theory of political parties cannot be built on a narrow definition of party that precludes applications to one-party systems and anti-system parties. Duverger's classic *Political Parties* fruitfully discussed single party systems as well as multiparty systems, and it compared paramilitary parties with competitive parties. His scope of application was so general that he did not base his study on a definition of party. In a later book, Duverger defined parties as (1) having "their primary goal the conquest of power or a share in its exercise," and (2) drawing "their support from a broad base" in contrast to pressure groups, which "represent a limited number with a particular or private interest" (1972, 1-2). The first part of his definition implied that parties can exist without contesting elections. The second part attempted, rather unsuccessfully, to distinguish parties from pressure groups -- which is the critical issue in constructing a broad definition of a political party.

Sartori analyzed at length the conceptual issues in defining a party (1976, 60-64). He aimed for a "minimal definition" that treated as variables all properties that were not *required* of a party. Sartori defined a party as "any political group identified by an official label that presents at elections, and is capable of placing through elections (free or nonfree), candidates for public office" (p. 63). By indicating that elections need not be free, Sartori broadened the definition to include parties in party-state systems ruled by a single party. However, Sartori's definition did not admit for study those organizations that sought or obtained power outside the electoral process.

Still more broadly, a party can be defined as an organization that pursues a goal of placing its avowed representatives in government positions (Janda 1980b, 5). All organizations have multiple goals. To qualify as a party, an organization must have as *one* of its goals that of placing its avowed representatives in government positions. ("Government" here means in the U.S. sense of public office, not the British sense of the cabinet.[4]) Moreover, these individuals must be *avowed* representatives of the party, which means in practical terms that they must be openly identified with the party name or label. If an interest groups openly runs its own candidates, it becomes a party. In Epstein's words, "The recognizable label (which may or may not be on the ballot) is the crucial defining element" (1966, 104). Finally, the term "placing" should be interpreted broadly to mean through the electoral process (when a party competes with one or more others in pursuing its goal) *or* by a direct administrative action (when a ruling party permits no electoral competition) *or* by forceful imposition (when a party seeks to subvert the system and thereby capture the government). Thus, parties can pursue, respectively, *competitive*, *restrictive*, or *subversive* strategies to achieve their goal.

As opposed to Sartori's definition, this broader one accommodates the Bolshevik seizure of power in the 1917 revolution (Barghoorn 1956), the Cuban Popular Socialist Party's capitalization on Castro's rise to power (Griffiths 1988), the Iraqi Ba'th Party's takeover following the 1968 coup (Farouk-Sluglett and Sluglett, 1988), and the Mexican Institutional Revolutionary Party's practices in restricting electoral competition (Philip 1988). Obviously, these subversive and restrictive parties are different from competitive parties and require some different theory (LaPalombara and Weiner 1966, 29-33). Nevertheless, Duverger (1963) already demonstrated that revolutionary and authoritarian parties could be analyzed productively along with competitive parties, and other research productively compared parties in all regions of the world (Janda and Gillies 1983). It remains to be seen how much overlap there is in propositions covering different types of parties.

For comparative political parties, the basic issue in defining a party is whether parties are narrowly or broadly defined. The definition determines whether general theory is limited to explaining only the behavior of purely competitive parties in democratic systems or whether it aims at a broader universe, including parties in single-party systems and anti-system or subversive parties. Many American party scholars would, like Schlesinger, be satisfied with a narrow definition of party that supported a "general" theory that only applied to competitive parties. Even many European scholars would accept a definition that restricted study to party systems in Western democracies (von Beyme 1983, 2), but those studying the Third World would need a broader definition that supported theory about parties operating in their political systems. Even Epstein, who restricts his own study to competitive parties in western democracies admits that "there is no harm in maintaining the breadth of definition" (1975, 233).[5]

Concepts for Analyzing Political Parties

This review of literature on comparative political parties employs a broad definition of party. To skirt the vast comparative politics literature that is more interested in the nation as a unit of analysis, it slights writings on party *systems* in preference for those on individual parties. To structure my discussion, I rely on a conceptual framework employed in my cross-national survey of political parties (Janda 1980b). I contend that most of the important aspects of political parties, as opposed to party systems, can be embraced by ten broad concepts: institutionalization, issue orientation, social support, organizational complexity, centralization of power, autonomy, coherence, involvement, strategy and tactics, and governmental status. The literature on comparative political parties can be usefully reviewed under each of these conceptual headings.

Institutionalization

Institutionalization is the process by which parties become established and acquire value and stability (Huntington 1965, 394). As Welfling (1973, 13) pointed out, institutionalization is not only a process but a property or state. As a property, party institutionalization can be defined as the extent to which a party is reified in the public mind so that it exists as a social organization apart from its momentary leaders while regularly engaging in valued patterns of behavior (Janda 1980b, 19). In the United States, the two major parties are virtually identical in their state of institutionalization, but across the world, party institutionalization is highly variable. For example, Scott (writing in the mid-1960s) noted that in Latin America "little real political party machinery exists at the local level, and what does exist is seldom related directly to a national party. Instead, a few local notables build on their own personalistic organizations for each election, allying themselves with national leaders of so-called national parties for reasons of power or material advantage" (1966, 337). Pye saw parties in Southeast Asia in much the same light (1966), but Welfling's careful analysis found that even African parties varied in institutionalization (1973). Dix's recent research on Latin American parties also found that parties and party systems "were somewhat more institutionalized as the 1990s began than they were during Latin America's previous democratic heyday around 1960" (1992, 505).

Party institutionalization has been measured in various ways. Sometimes party age or counts of splits and mergers are used as indicators (Lane and Ersson 1991, 113; Dix 1992). It has also been measured on a scale built from measures of age, electoral stability, legislative stability, and leadership change.[6] More often, the concept has been tapped with simpler measures of minimum election strength and minimum durability. Rose and Mackie, for example, said, "a party is judged to have become institutionalized if it fights more than three national elections. A group that fails to do this is not an established political party, but an ephemeral party" (1988, 536). Applying their criterion to 19 democratic countries from electoral origins through 1983, they uncovered 369 parties that contested at least one national election and won at least 1% of the vote, but barely more than half of these became institutionalized.

Clearly, the numerous new parties in Eastern Europe and the Soviet Union face a challenge of institutionalization. In the 1989 Polish elections, Solidarity swept nearly all the offices it contested, but Jasiewicz (1992) attributed its success to anti-government voting rather than to pro-Solidarity sentiment -- a view supported by the regression analysis of election results by Heyns and Bialecki (1991). After the October 1991 elections to the Polish parliament, Jasiewicz reported that some 30 parties or groups were elected to the 460-seat chamber and the strongest party had only 62 seats. Speaking of Poland's new political situation, he said, "With the exception of the renamed communists and a few veteran opposition groups..., the parties are brand new. They have no tradition, no apparatus, no organizational history, no established rules of conduct" (1992, 66).

The situation was comparable in the former Soviet Union, which, according to Kelley (1992), demonstrated "behavioral" pluralism in 1991 with more than 60,000 political organizations. However, Kelely said it lacked "institutionalized" pluralism and certainly was not a multiparty system,

> at least inasmuch as that description commonly implies that the party structures channel political conflict, accurately reflect the views of and speak for particular constituencies, and take part in the functioning of government or opposition. In many ways, the evolution of the party and group structures has not reached that level of maturity" (1992, 31).

McFaul held that party development in Russia was hampered by citizens' obvious reasons to distrust and disdain political parties and by the new parties' reluctance in discarding old attitudes about the purposes and functions of political organizations. "Finally," McFaul said, "there are simply too many parties; democracy has been hindered by too much democracy" (1992, 32).[7]

Treating institutionalization as a dependent variable, Rose and Mackie identified four factors that increased the chances of a nascent party becoming institutionalized: (1) its origin at the founding of competitive elections, (2) a proportional representation system of elections, (3) being based on an organized social group, and (4) its initial success in winning votes. Three of these factors pertain to a party's "conditions of origin," which Duverger (1963) identified as a major predictor of party properties. Other scholars have owed party institutionalization to party origin. Panebianco (1988, 50-52) identified three important factors: (1) whether the party was organized by a "center" that "penetrated" the country or arose from local organizations that congealed into a national organization (i.e., territorial *penetration* or *diffusion*);[8] (2) whether the party was sponsored by an existing institution or arose on its own (i.e., *externally* or *internally* legitimated); (3) whether or not its founder stamped the organization with his *charisma*. Panebianco theorized that territorial penetration, internal legitimation, and the absence of charisma all predict to strong party institutionalization.

Institutionalization has a more interesting role in party theory as an independent variable. This is its prime function for Panebianco, who contended that "parties can be distinguished primarily according to the *degree of institutionalization* they attain" (1988, 55). For Panebianco, institutionalization not only predicts organization of internal groups, but it also is a major inhibitor of party transformation or change (p. 265). That is, highly institutionalized parties are more resistant to change. Moving from individual parties to the party system, Welfling theorized that the overall level of party institutionalization inhibited social conflict and promoted stability (1973, 54-58), and Dix (1992) viewed party system institutionalization as contributing to democracy in Latin America.

Issue Orientation

Comparative research on political parties pays great attention to parties' positions on issues with cross-national significance. Many such issues have been subsumed under the concept of ideology, but concern has also been given to issues that do not fit common ideological concepts. As Duverger demonstrated forty years ago, ideology has a central role in party theory, primarily as an *independent* variable that affects other party characteristics. He spoke primarily about ideological types -- communist, socialist, center, conservative, and fascist -- but implicitly viewed them as positions along a left-right scale.

The Left-Right Dimension

The theoretical centrality of ideology in party theory is demonstrated by the outpouring of empirical research on comparative party ideologies -- most of which has been done by European scholars (Mavrogordatos 1987, 335). Since Duverger, scholars have advanced beyond the simple typologies of parties as communist, socialist, and so on, while accepting the principle of a single left-right dimension. Laver and Schofield (1990, 51-52) identified several methods used to order parties along a left-right continuum, including old-fashioned reading of primary and secondary sources (Taylor and Laver 1973; de Swaan 1973; Dodd 1976), systematic surveys of experts (Castles and Mair 1984),

content analysis of party platforms (Budge, Robertson, and Hearl 1987), and dimensional analysis of mass survey data (Huber 1989).[9] Laver and Schofield conveniently summarize much of this research for 18 countries in an appendix (pp. 245-266).

The survey by Castles and Mair (1984) deserves discussion. They asked over 100 western political scientists to classify parties in 17 countries on an 11-point scale, ranging from Ultra-Left (0) to Ultra-Right (10). A total of 119 parties were rated, each by at least three country experts. Then Castles and Mair averaged their ratings to assign a left-right scale position to every party. They noted that "such a procedure necessarily does some damage to a multifaceted reality in which two or more political dimensions coexist and cross-cut each other" (p. 75). Nevertheless, they concluded that the parties' ideologies were judged by "general standards rather than purely national considerations" (p. 83), supporting the parties' placements on a single continuum.

Other cross-national research on party ideologies has uncovered at least two dimensions underlying parties' issue positions. One study used library research to code 150 parties in 53 countries on 13 different issues commonly identified with the left-right continuum, and then analyzed their intercorrelations to disclose the latent factors. Eleven of the issues came out on two distinct factors (Janda 1980b, 147-149). Seven mostly economic variables correlated with what was called a "Marxist" scale, and four "civil rights and liberties" variables correlated with a "liberalism" scale.

A "two-factor" interpretation of parties' issue positions was also supported in the most ambitious effort at analyzing party ideology. Budge, Robertson, and Hearl (1987) reported the results of a project sponsored by the European Consortium for Political Research to perform a content analysis of the election manifestos of all significant parties in 19 countries from 1945 to 1983. Rather than judging the political substance of the parties' statements, the group of country experts engaged in the more objective but controversial procedure of counting the number of sentences in the platform according to 54 categories in seven broad policy domains. "For this implies that the most important aspect of the documents is the degree of emphasis placed on certain broad policy areas, rather than each party's support for, or opposition to, a specific policy within these areas" (p. 24). Using factor analysis, this method of content analysis produced two major factors: "a central and clearly Left-Right cleavage in most of the countries under consideration -- 15 out of 20" (p. 392) and a second dimension that "often seems to reflect Left-Right contrasts in a modified form" (p. 395). So despite the possibility of great complexity in parties' issue positions across nations, existing research suggests that the variation can be accounted for with only two factors, both of which have some "left-right" elements. (See Silverman (1985) for a probing conceptual analysis of two dimensions in the left-right typology.)

In principle, parties can change their ideology, and Downs (1957) theorized that they do change in order to win votes. However, research on the spatial distribution of voters in European party systems disclosed that parties avoid the center of the left-right dimension, even though that area is dense with voters (Listhaug, Macdonald, and Rabinowitz 1990).[10] Despite instances of abrupt changes in party ideology for electoral gains -- the German SPD's transformation in 1959 is the stellar example (see Panebianco 1988, 253-257) -- the more common argument has been that parties change issue positions incrementally over time, becoming less ideological and more "catch-all" in nature (Kirchheimer 1966). Thomas' longitudinal study of 54 parties in 12 Western nations over nearly a century showed "a dramatic narrowing in the scope of domestic political conflict" over issue positions (1975, 46; Thomas 1980). Thomas also uncovered subtle variations of the "end of ideology" and the "convergence" hypotheses, some of which were not supported.

Most recently, scholars have focused on whether the conflict between "materialist" and "post-materialist" values has absorbed the classic left-right conflict in party cleavages, as Inglehart claimed (1977, 242; 1990, 296-298). Knutsen (1988; 1989) tested this "new politics" viewpoint with data on party preferences in ten countries and found that both cleavages existed, with neither dominating. In a related vein, Kitschelt (1990) explored the "new structural differentiation and polarity" introduced in Europe by Left-libertarian parties (p. 201).

Issue-Based Parties

While most major parties can be placed along a single left-right continuum, and still more can be comfortably accommodated with the introduction of a second dimension, some parties resist classification because of their commitment to a single issue or type of issue. Lane and Ersson (1991, 273) distinguish between *nonstructural* issues, which are based on notions of national policies, and *structural* issues, which are based in social groups and give rise to ethnic, religious, regional, and certain class-based parties (pp. 103-111). (Parties based on structural issues are treated below under social support.)

Considerable research has been done recently to identify parties that promote nonstructural issues, especially "new" issues promoted by new parties when existing parties fail to take up the issue (Lawson and Merkl 1988; Dalton and Kuechler 1990). The prime example is protection of the environment advocated by European "Green" parties (Müller-Rommel 1985; Schoonmaker 1988). In their study of 233 new parties formed in western countries from 1960 to 1980, Harmel and Robertson (1985) found that only 10% qualified as "new issue" parties "(i.e., those characterized as ecology parties, anti-nuclear or peace parties, anti-EEC parties, anti-NATO parties, or feminist parties)" -- despite the attention academics paid to them (p. 508). Nearly half of the new parties offered alternatives to "old" issues on the left-right dimension. They included "tax protest" parties and other parties on the new right (Lane and Ersson (1991, 108-111). Whether the purer "new politics" parties fit on the Left-Right dimension has been a subject of study (Müller-Rommel 1990). Kitschelt and Hellemans (1990) set forth the issues, and in a limited study of Belgian parties, concluded that economic leftism exists in contemporary politics but it does not exactly match the traditional left-right dimension.

Most research on issue orientation is concerned with measurement. When ideology and issues are involved in theoretical studies, they are mainly treated as independent variables. Scholars are less concerned with the causes of issue orientation than with its consequences for government process (coalition formation) and policy outcomes (e.g., economic and social programs). We review this literature later, for it involves other concepts that we need to discuss first.

Social Support

Parties are formed not only to promote policy issues in a Burkean fashion but also to secure social interests (Charlot 1989).[11] Lipset and Rokkan (1967) produced the most powerful comparative statement of parties as political expressions of social cleavages. They isolated four major cleavages -- center-periphery, state-church, land-industry, and owner-worker -- that gave rise to European parties with different social bases, e.g., regional, religious, occupational, and so on. Dalton (1988, 128-149) provided a concise and updated explanation of these cleavages. Although Dix (1989) argued that the Lipset-Rokkan historical cleavages did not apply to Latin American parties, there is evidence that the Lipset-Rokkan social bases do apply across cultures. More specifically, the six social dimensions -- economic status, religion, ethnicity (including language and race), region, urbanization, and education -- were used productively to analyze party support across a broad range of nations (Janda 1980b, 41).

The operating assumption of an early collection of voting studies was that "social differences structure party loyalties" (Rose 1974, 16). Smith (1989) described the difficulty in keeping straight the distinction between parties and party systems when discussing the subject of social cleavages, which "relates to the social make-up of support for individual parties -- not to the 'system,' not that is if we follow a definition based on interaction" (p. 351). For now, we restrict attention to parties, not to parties as they interact within a political system (Laver 1989). The major dimensions of party systems are discussed later.

Considerable research involving parties' social support was stimulated by the seminal study of Rose and Urwin (1975). They assessed the "social cohesion" of 76 parties in 17 Western nations by the degree to which their supporters come from a given region, religion, ethnic group, urban-rural area, or social class. Rose and Urwin found that parties were most cohesive on religion and class, in that order. Analyzing votes cast within regions for 93 parties in 16 Western nations over three elections, Ersson, Janda, and Lane (1985) found that region alone explained most of the variance in party support but also found strong influence of religion and class within regions.[12]

Parties that have broad social bases are assumed to aggregate diverse interests rather articulate specific ones. Presumably, parties differ from interest groups by aggregating rather than articulating interests (Almond and Powell 1966), but this distinction is not ironclad. Jankowski (1988) argued that broad interest groups do better at aggregation than political parties, and some parties rival interest groups in articulation. The narrower the social basis of a party's support, the more likely they are to articulate interests. Most studies of the social bases of party support have simply assumed that structural parties (those with strong bases) articulate structural issues Mair (1989a, 170-171). Some research has confirmed this assumption. The greater the concentration of party supporters from a single region, the stronger the party's opposition to national integration; and the greater the concentration of supporters from a given religion, the stronger the party's position on secularization of society -- depending on the religion (Janda 1989).

In their 1967 book, Lipset and Rokkan had also contended that the origins of cleavage resulted in a "freezing" of the European party system such that parties' support in the 1960s reflected their support 40 years earlier. In finding that European parties' electoral strength changed little from 1945 to 1969, Rose and Urwin (1970) supported the Lipset-Rokkan thesis of a frozen party system. For a time, this interpretation of stability in European party politics was accepted, but no longer. Mair (1983) recounted the many studies that demonstrated electoral volatility that occurred since 1970 (see also Maguire 1983; Pedersen 1983). In some countries, electoral volatility resulted in the systematic loss of support for certain parties, particularly for communist parties (Waller and Fennema 1988) and

socialist parties (Piven 1992). Challenging Lipset and Rokkan, Shamir's time series analysis (1984) showed that the party systems were never really frozen in the first place, and Lybeck (1985) contended that the Lipset-Rokkan hypothesis was inherently untestable anyway. However, Mair (1989b) contended that when Lipset and Rokkan discussed cleavages, they were not necessarily referring to specific political parties but to political opponents (e.g., left and right) more generally, which could save their hypothesis. This argument was developed in Bartolini and Mair (1990, 63-65), who analyzed electoral volatility in 303 elections in 13 Western European countries from 1885 to 1985 and found a "fundamental bias toward stability" that "became more pronounced over time" (pp. 287-288).

Scholars still use the Lipset-Rokkan framework for studying the declining importance of structural cleavages for party support, which some view as party dealignment (Knutsen 1988 and 1989). In their edited collection of studies, Dalton, Flanagan, and Beck (1984) reported the "common theme" of "shifts in the long-term bases of partisan support -- party identification and social cleavages" (p. 451). In *When Parties Fail*, Lawson and Merkl (1988) viewed these shifts as evidence of major party decline: "All over the world, single-issue movements are forming, special interest groups are assuming party-like status, and minor parties are winning startling overnight victories as hitherto dominant parties lose the confidence of their electorates" (p. 3). Reiter (1989) reviewed the literature that explained "party decline" according to various independent variables: "affluence, the growth of the state, the catch-all party, neo-corporatism, the mass media, new political issues and cleavages, problems with state performance, or post-industrialism" (p. 329). But neither Reiter nor Selle and Svåsand (1991) found systematic evidence of party decline in cross-national, longitudinal data on party support. Wolinetz (1988) said that evidence of party change was more likely to be found in organizational change as parties adapted to a changing environment.

Organizational Complexity and Power

There is very little contact between the vast organizational theory literature and the literature on political parties (Janda 1983).[13] For example, a computer search of the *Sociological Abstracts* file available in the DIALOG™ online information services found 905 abstracts that mentioned "political party" or "parties" in articles and conference papers from 1980 to 1991, but only three also mentioned "organizational theory" or some variant. Moreover, only two (Deschouwer 1986; Jankowski 1988) pertained specifically to political parties. Because few comparative party scholars draw on the well-developed organizational theory literature, the conceptualization of party structure has an ad hoc quality, with little attention paid to creating reliable measures of party organization (Janda 1983). In this case, the American literature on party organization has an earlier history (see Crotty 1968) and is better developed.[14] Creative measurement of party organization is evidenced in the collaborative work by Gibson et al. (1983) and Cotter et al. (1984) on comparative analyses of state and county party organizations, and in later work by Gibson et al. (1989). This research found a surprising amount of organizational strength among state and local parties in 1980 and, if anything, increased levels of strength when the parties were studied again in 1984. Unfortunately, these studies were rooted in the American context and do not help much in comparative cross-national analyses.

Wellhofer (1979) is one of the few scholars who devised measures of a broad organizational concept for application to parties across nations. Wellhofer proposed the concept of "organizational encapsulation," defined as "the elaboration of party sub-units to envelop as many of the day-to-day life activities of the membership as possible" (p. 206).[15] Encapsulation was measured with three objective indicators of party membership and local organizations for socialist labor parties in Argentina, Britain, Norway, and Sweden. He used time series analysis in a longitudinal study to demonstrate how these organizational inputs were linked to vote outputs (see also Wellhofer 1981). Unfortunately, Wellhofer dealt primarily with that one organizational concept. On the other hand, Panebianco (1988), conceptualized party organization more richly -- discussing its dominant coalition, institutionalization, and organizational complexity -- but was less clear on how to measure these concepts objectively.

Most of the empirical comparative research on party organization again draws inspiration from Duverger. He advanced propositions using such concepts as direct/indirect structure, basic elements, organizational articulation, and centralization of power. Lane and Ersson thoughtfully modified and applied these concepts in their study of European parties (1991, 123-128). Janda (1980b) interpreted Duverger through the organizational theory literature to differentiate two major dimensions of organizational structure: degree of organization and centralization of power. Degree of organization, which is similar to Duverger's articulation, referred to the complexity of structural differentiation. Centralization of power, following Duverger, referred to the location and distribution of authority. When measured by two highly reliable scales over more than 100 parties, these two dimensions were empirically unrelated.[16] Despite these findings, the distinction between organizational complexity and centralization of

power have not been widely recognized, which is why they are treated together in this section.

With few exceptions, the comparative parties literature has paid relatively little attention to conceptualizing party organization and even less to measurement issues. This is particularly true for the concepts of complexity and power. For example, Sartori (1976) simply talked of an undifferentiated "organization" dimension on which parties could be classified as "organized," "organizationless," or "half and half" (pp. 76 and 81). Lawson (1976) created a set of six types of organization based on the locus of power and involvement of active members (p. 78). Indeed, von Beyme despaired over the complicated network of organizational influences in European parties and said, "A typology of similar cases is the utmost that seems possible" (1983, 367).

Concepts of organizational structure are also not prominent in empirical party theory, with Duverger again an exception. He used organizational variables as both independent and dependent variables. For Duverger, centralization of power was a cause *of* party cohesion (discussed below) and was caused *by* leftist ideology. He also explained party organization by the conditions of origin (e.g., whether it began inside or outside the parliament; early or late in the nation's political development). Several scholars (Hodgkin 1961; LaPalombara and Weiner 1966) have used conditions of origin to explain party structure in the Third World and European parties, while Koelble (1989) cited both ideology and conditions of origin in explaining the West German Green Party's decentralized structure. Few scholars have used centralization as an independent variable in comparative research. An exception is Dalton (1985), who combined a European voter survey with a simple measure of party centralization to show that the more centralized the party, the more accurately voters perceived its cues.

Complexity of party organization and centralization of power are also caused by environmental factors. In their study of 95 parties in 28 democratic and quasi-democratic nations, Harmel and Janda (1982) found that parties in the same country tended to be similarly organized. For complexity of organization, 44% of the variance was explained with six environmental variables (modernity, population size, electoral system, restrictions on suffrage, recency of democratic experience, and lack of party competition). For centralization of power, 35% of the variance was explained with six variables (country size, federalism, and aspects of legislative-executive structure).

As noted earlier, Eldersveld, Epstein, Keefe, and others have characterized both major U.S. parties as extremely decentralized. A quantitative cross-national analysis of more than 100 parties documented their claim:

American parties are clearly less centralized than the European norm, and they are certainly among the most decentralized parties in the world. None of the Western European parties in the sample had a lower score on the centralization of power than did U.S. parties. Moreover, when the entire sample of the world's parties is considered, the American parties outrank only the Blancos and Colorados of Uruguay -- which some scholars would contend are not parties but coalitions, or groupings of parties -- and the Social Action Party of Chad, which terminated in 1962 . . . (Janda 1980a, 355).

However, the same study also showed that American parties did not lack in complexity of organization: "In point of fact, American political parties do tend to have as much if not more in the way of formal structure than most other parties in the world . . ." (p. 355). Since that cross-national comparison was made, most observers would contend that American national party organizations have become more professional and organizationally active, and somewhat more centralized (Herrnson 1990), but the Democrats and Republicans are still highly decentralized by world standards.

In analyzing the nature of American parties, Keefe held that "parties are less what they make of themselves than what their environment makes of them" (1991, 1). Clearly, the U.S. constitutional framework (especially the presidential system and federalism) has contributed to the decentralized nature of its parties compared with parties elsewhere (Janda 1992). But both the Democrats and Republicans have changed over time, as they adapted to a changing environment. Future scholars will be aided in studying organizational change with the publication of a major data handbook on indicators of party change from 1960 to 1990, edited by Katz and Mair (1992). The result of a coordinated cross-national research project involving scholars in 12 Western countries, this handbook provides time-series data on party membership, finance, staff size, and so on, and detailed information on party rules changes and on the relationship of political parties to other social organizations over time.

Autonomy

Autonomy can be defined as a party's structural independence from other institutions and organizations, whether in or out of the country (Janda 1980b, 91).[17] This concept figures prominently in writings of Sartori (1976, 45-46) and Panebianco (1988, 55-58), who said a party is autonomous to the extent that it is not dependent on resources controlled by other organizations, and it fits with Lagroye's comment (1989, 364-365) that parties are embedded in a "system of organizations," all of which are subject to changes affecting their parts of the system. Parties can sacrifice autonomy to other sectors of society by relying on them for funds, members, or leaders. Structural infringement on party autonomy can also come from relations with domestic parties or foreign organizations. Some research showed that all five sources of infringement are essentially unrelated (Janda 1980b, 152). Apparently autonomy, like virtue, can be compromised in a variety of ways.

Source of Funds

In an early article, Heidenheimer (1963) described the difficulty in obtaining data for comparative research on party finance. In his study of parties in eight countries, only the German SPD covered its normal expenses from party dues (p. 792-793). This fits with other findings that only about 25 % of the world's parties in the 1950s and 1960s relied on their own sources (mainly party dues) for most funding (Janda 1980b, 92). Since Heidenheimer, there has been relatively little cross-national research on party finance published in journals, especially in English.[18] However, some valuable studies have appeared in edited volumes on elections and campaign funding (particularly Alexander 1989a; Levush 1991). This research has focused on the trend toward public financing in western nations (Paltiel 1980 and 1981). Alexander reported that 18 of 21 nations introduced public funding after 1960 (1989b, 14), resulting in a decline in the importance of party dues. The effects of public funding on parties are complex. Strom (1990, 579-581) theorized that public finance increased the autonomy of party leaders vis-a-vis party activists, and Schlesinger (1991, 25) thought that public finance made parties more bureaucratic. Nassmacher's study (1989) of public subsidies to parties in Austria, Italy, Sweden, and West Germany tended to support both contentions, and Mendilow's research on party politics in Israel and elsewhere concluded that public funding "is capable of generating fundamental changes such as may lead to the restructuring of the entire party system" (1992, 113). One major result was an increased centralization of power "by the subordination of branches to the central headquarters and top leadership" (p. 112). Public funding was also addictive, and -- at least in Israel -- tended to increase the ideological stance of new parties.

Source of Members

Duverger distinguished between "direct" and "indirect" membership, depending on whether membership is a voluntary act of affiliation or a consequence of membership in another social organization, like a labor union (1963, 6). This is a meaningful distinction, for parties (like British Labour) with indirect membership are less autonomous than those with only individual members. Nevertheless, fewer than 10% of the world's parties in 1960 had any indirect members, while about 20% had no formal membership requirements (Janda 1980b, 93). Because party membership data are unreliable and often not applicable, Lawson advised paying more attention to the number of votes actually received by a party than the number of members it claimed (1976, 93). Alternatively, one can study party identification or "attachment" as a form of party affiliation (Richardson 1991). In the case of Europe, this research is facilitated by two decades of Eurobarometer surveys, which permit longitudinal, comparative research, albeit with some problems (Katz 1985). In several countries from 1974 to 1988, Schmitt (1989) found a decline in people who felt "close to" a party, but the pattern tended to be mixed elsewhere, and Germany even showed a slight increase of attachment. Formal party membership is discussed below under the concept of involvement.

Source of Leaders

Panebianco uses the term, "dominant coalition," for the group of leaders who control the principal power resources of a party organization (1988, 38). In slightly more than 25% of the parties in 1960, most leaders came from one sector of society, indicating a lack of autonomy (Janda 1980b, 94). Lawson (1976) analyzed diversity in party leadership in three countries, but this topic has not been studied heavily through comparative research. Everyone seems to agree on the importance of leadership, particularly in party change (Wilson 1980, 542-544), but it is notoriously difficult to study rigorously.

Relations with Domestic Parties

Duverger identified three types of cooperative interparty "alliances": electoral, parliamentary, and governmental (1963, 330-351). Electoral alliances infringe the least on autonomy, and governmental alliances the most. "Satellite" parties of ruling parties in Eastern Europe demonstrated the most severe loss of autonomy (Fischer-Galati 1979), but this subject drew little attention from party scholars.[19] Although there are other dimensions to research on party alliances (Gilberg 1989; Kolinsky 1987), the emphasis has been on governing coalitions in parliamentary democracies (Pridham 1986; Laver and Schofield 1990). The coalition literature, which relies heavily on rational choice theory, is reviewed below under party strategy. The concern here is whether coalition possibilities limited party autonomy, a concern that surfaced in the concept of

a "relevant" party. Sartori said that a party is relevant if it "affects the tactics of party competition" by having "coalition potential" or having "blackmail potential" -- possessed by an antisystem party or one that can veto political arrangements (1976, 123; see also Herzog 1987). Budge and Keman theorized about the effects of antisystem parties on party behavior (1990, 44), while Hofferbert and Klingemann (1990) contended that the FDP in Germany acts as a swing party due to its blackmail potential.

Relations with Foreign Organizations

Parties can have relationships (mostly but not exclusively) with international party organizations or foreign governments that can impinge on their autonomy. This was clear in the case of communist parties but it also applied to Socialists (Pelinka 1983, 108-124), Christian Democrats (Irving 1979), and Liberals (Hrbek 1988) -- all of whom maintained international organizations and demonstrated varying degrees of solidarity in international bodies (Pridham and Pridham 1981). Goldman (1983) has been the foremost scholar of such "transnational" parties, and the topic is certain to grow in importance with the growth of the European community. For example, Eijk and Oppenhuis (1991) analyzed the competition for votes among parties competing in direct elections to the European parliament in 1989.

Coherence

The concept of coherence was introduced into comparative politics by Huntington (1965, 403-405) and developed by Anderson (1968, 396-397) for the study of state and local parties. In comparative analysis, coherence has been defined as "the degree of congruence in the attitudes and *behavior* of party members" (Janda 1980b, 118). "Behavior" is emphasized because few cross-national studies have surveyed the attitudes of party activists or members -- as opposed to voters. One exception was the European Political Parties Middle-Level Elites Project, which collected questionnaires from activists attending more than 65 national party conferences in nearly all the European community countries (Niedermayer 1986). Most research from this project was published in German, with a typical study focusing on the representation of social groups within the party elites (Niedermayer and Schmitt 1983). This mammoth survey of middle-level party elites was criticized by Pierre (1986) for being done in isolation from other aspects of party organization.[20] In any event, there are few such studies (but see Dalton 1985) because massive research is required to compare attitudinal congruence among party members or activists. It is much easier to study coherence in party behavior, which is more open to inspection.

Cohesion

Party cohesion, defined as the extent to which parties vote together in legislative bodies, is readily amenable to study, and legislative voting has generated a huge literature in the United States. Despite the publication of such voting data in foreign countries, research on party cohesion is less common in cross-national analysis, although there are many studies in individual countries (Collie 1985). There has also been surprisingly little research on the effect of organizational attributes on party cohesion -- despite Duverger's early hypotheses. He said that "domination over the parliamentary representatives by the party" was due to the "general structure of the party and its general orientation" (1963, 202). His argument can be reformulated into three hypotheses: the more centralized the party, the higher the cohesion; the greater the leftism, the higher the cohesion; and the more ideologically extreme, the higher the cohesion.

Ozbudun (1970) conducted the most concerted effort at the comparative study of party cohesion. He and other scholars (Turner and Schneier 1970; Loewenberg and Patterson 1979) concentrated on six environmental factors in explaining party cohesion: presidential government, federalism, multiple parties, ideological polarization, single-member districts, and legislative effectiveness. Harmel and Janda (1982) found that 32% of the variance in legislative cohesion could be explained with only two variables (legislative-executive structure and legislative effectiveness). Their analysis supported Epstein's contention that separation of powers was the key variable in explaining the low cohesion of American parties compared with those elsewhere (1980, 315-350).

Factionalism

There is another aspect to coherence in party behavior, factionalism. In a pioneering article, Zariski (1960) defined a faction as "any intra-party combination, clique, or grouping whose members share a sense of the common identity and common purpose and are organized to act collectively -- as a distinct bloc within the party -- to achieve their goals" (p. 33).[21] Sartori (1976, 76-79) proposed a typology of factions based on their interest (power or spoils) and their principles (ideologies or ideas). Another approach distinguished between factionalism based on ideology, issues, leadership, and strategy (Janda 1980b). Over 100 parties were scored on

each type of factionalism on a seven-point scale. The ideological basis was somewhat more common than the others, but all types of factionalism tended to be interrelated; e.g., if a party had ideological factions, it also tended to have leadership factions.

Most research on factionalism has regarded it as a dependent variable in party theory. Belloni and Beller (1978) edited a collection of studies that sought to describe and explain factionalism. It included an article by Zariski (1978), who listed a "dozen most tenable and agreed-upon generalizations on factionalism" (p. 32). Most of his propositions linked factionalism to environmental factors, such as the nature of the electoral system. Nevertheless, Belloni and Beller concluded that factionalism was also due to the "sociological complexity of the party; ideological looseness of the party; the origin of the party in a merger of predecessor parties [i.e., its conditions of origin]; [and] the party's internal looseness or decentralized structure" (p. 435).

The Belloni and Beller book largely avoided regarding factions as independent variables. However, party factionalism is an important cause of low voting cohesion and needs to be included in any theory of party government. Factionalism's effect on party cohesion is apparent in American politics. Southern and Northern Democrats often opposed each other in Congressional voting until an ideological realignment began to occur in the South around 1970. Since then, party cohesion (as measured by *Congressional Quarterly* party unity scores), has almost steadily increased. Sinclair attributes this rise in voting cohesion to decreased ideological heterogeniety of the Democrats (1990, 241-242). Finally, factionalism and cohesion together (the general concept of coherence) are critically important in coalition theory, which -- with few exceptions (Luebbert 1986; Laver and Shepsle 1990) -- assumes that parties act as units (Laver and Schofield 1990, 17-22). Brady and Bullock (1985) provided a general review of literature on parties and factions in legislatures from the standpoint of legislative behavior. They saw "much to be done" in linking the legislative party to external components and in investigating the relationship "between the degree of fractionalization and/or factionalization of legislative parties and the way in which parties distribute task and power" (pp. 175-176).

Involvement

In a major section of his book, Duverger (1963) discussed at length the concepts of party membership, degree of participation, and nature of participation. Individually, these topics have drawn a great deal of attention in the parties literature, but there has been only mixed success in integrating the discussion. I prefer to subsume these topics under the concept of involvement, defined as the intensity of psychological identification with the party *and* as the commitment to furthering its objectives by participating in party activities (Janda 1980b). The italicized "and" distinguishes party involvement from mere party identification by requiring some degree of party activism (voting alone does not qualify). In comparative research, this concept has been measured with several types of variables: severity of membership requirements, membership participation, material incentives, and purposive incentives. Research has shown that these variables tend to intercorrelate and can be combined into a scale of involvement (Janda 1980b).[22]

Membership

The concept of formal membership in a political party has little meaning in the United States (Schlesinger 1991, 152), but it is important in comparative analysis. As Duverger noted, signing one's name to a membership form both signifies and produces commitment to the party (1963, 71). For Duverger, the notion of a "card-carrying" party member reflected his conception of a modern mass (usually leftist) party. He created the "membership ratio" -- the number of members to the number of electors -- and speculated about its meaning but did not really formulate much theory (p. 94). Merkl (1980) compared party members, voters and leaders, and Bartolini (1983) analyzed membership data and membership ratios over time. Bartolini formulated several hypotheses (e.g., party membership is more stable than the party electorate), tested them with data on socialist parties in about a dozen European countries, and found most of them worked better for the pre-war than the post-war period. He concluded that Duverger was reacting to the past and overestimated the role and future of mass parties (pp. 119, 213).

In contrast to Bartolini's pessimism about the future of political parties in contemporary society, Selle and Svåsand (1991) writing a decade later and analyzing a longer time series found that "aggregate membership figures for Western European parties do not show a general decline in party membership" (p. 460). Calculating party membership as a ratio to electors, however, Katz computed downward trends for 20 of 29 parties from 1945 to 1984 (1990, 149). Because party members can constrain leaders, Katz concluded that both leaders and members are finding formal membership less attractive, which raises questions about the linkage function of parties (pp. 158-159). Lawson's volume on party linkage also drew negative conclusions for the "policy-responsive" linkage function of parties (1980, 21-22). However, Dalton's study (1985) of 742 party candidates in nine countries for election to the European parliament in 1979 compared the candidates' attitudes toward policies with attitudes of party voters interviewed the same year, and contradicted Katz. Overall, Dalton found "substantial agreement between policy views of the Western European public and party elites," and he attributed a large portion of this agreement "to the interactive linkage between voters and parties" (1985, 293).

Incentives

Parties scholars have devoted considerable attention to incentives for party activists (Duverger's "nature" of participation) regardless of formal membership. A starting point for such analysis is Clark and Wilson (1961), who distinguished between "material" (economic benefits), "purposive" (party policies), and "solidary" (social) incentives as motivational factors in all organizations. In parties, these incentives translate into gaining personal benefits, implementing the party's program, or making friends and having fun. Early empirical studies, particularly in the U.S., sought to determine which motivation was dominant. Wilson (1962) said that "professional" party organizations (i.e., city machines) were primarily composed of activists motivated by material incentives, whereas "amateur" organizations had more activists motivated by purposive incentives. In a study of Republican and Democratic county leaders active in their candidate's 1988 presidential campaigns, Bruce, Clark, and Kessel (1991) determined that the purposive or "true believer" orientation predominated within both presidential party groups.

In an influential essay, Wright (1971) elaborated Wilson's distinction into the Rational-Efficient and the Party-Democracy models of political parties (pp. 6-7). American parties tend to be Rational-Efficient: concerned with performing their electoral function and winning elections. In contrast, traditional European socialist parties are "more policy-oriented, ideological, and concerned with defining policy" (p. 7). Wright believed that specific parties could possess some mix of these models, and he argued that "the development of theory and research on political parties has been hindered by adherence to one or the other" as either-or models (p. 7).

In recent years, the discussion of incentives has revived the distinction between party leaders and their rank-and-file that formed the basis of Michels's "iron law of oligarchy." In simple form, Michels's theory explained how leaders perpetuate themselves in power at the expense of their followers' interests (1962).[23] This distinction has surfaced in rational choice theory in the assumption that leaders seek "office" -- which can *only* come from winning elections -- while activists seek "benefits" -- which may or may not come from winning (Schlesinger 1991, 138). For Schlesinger, who views party leaders as pure office seekers, Wright has it all wrong: there are not "different kinds of parties but the same kinds of parties subject internally to the tensions provoked by the conflicting goals of office and benefits" differentially shared by leaders and activists (p. 145). May (1973) applied the term "curvilinear disparity" to the condition arising when top party leaders and party voters were congruent in their goal orientations while middle-level leaders differed. Kitschelt's analysis (1989) of "the curvilinear disparity of political incentives between voters, party activists and party leaders" (p. 401) contended that evidence of such disparity comes mainly from two-party systems and that "curvilinearity is a much less plausible trait of the micropolitics of party organization" in continental Europe (p. 421).

Nevertheless, Schlesinger uncovered a confusing question in the discussion of incentives: are incentives properties of individuals or of groups? He regretted that Downs, who defined a party as "a team" seeking office through election, assigned ambition to the party collectively rather than to party activists individually. To Schlesinger, Downs's approach led away from understanding party organization (Schlesinger 1991, 36). By shifting discussion from the motivational bases of party activists (incentives) to the nature of party goals, Wright shifted to the concept of party strategy.

Strategy and Tactics

Earlier, I favored defining "party" broadly to include restrictive and subversive parties as well as competitive parties. Instead of categorizing parties into different strategies, one can regard a party's strategy for obtaining its goal as a variable. For example, the French Communist Party, which competed in elections and won about a quarter of the vote during the 1950s, also operated as an anti-system party, using strikes and demonstrations to destabilize the government. Thus the PCF could be scored as following a mixed strategy: mostly competitive but somewhat subversive. The dominant Mexican PRI, on the other hand, followed a mostly competitive but somewhat restrictive strategy, hampering and even controlling its opposition. One study of a representative sample of 150 parties across the world in 1960 found that only about 50% followed a pure competitive strategy, 11% were pure restrictive, 3% were pure subversive, and the other third employed some mix of strategies (Janda 1980b, 78-90). Mixed strategies are consistent with Wright's view (1971) of competitive parties as combining elements of the Rational-Efficient and the Party Democracy models. As we will see, the concept of party strategy as a variable opens new avenues

in rational choice analyses of the behavior of competitive parties. Not only is the theory of party strategies best developed for competitive parties, but most of the world's parties (68% in 1960) have been purely or mostly competitive. So further discussion will deal only with competitive party strategies.

Competitive Strategies

Downs's seminal book (1957) is often viewed as belonging to the spatial theory of voting, but it is equally pertinent to the theory of parties. Downs assumed not only that parties seek to win office but that they seek to maximize votes (1957, 11,31). Arguing that parties formulate policies to win elections, rather than win elections to formulate policies, he theorized that parties in a two-party system with a unimodal distribution of voter preferences would locate their policies vaguely at the middle of the distribution. In so doing, Downs neatly accounted for the centrist two-party system in the United States. Downs's model of the vote-maximizing party has been especially influential for American party theorists, such as Schlesinger (1991, 143). In comparative research, however, Downs's work has been less important than that of Riker (1962). Riker also assumed that parties seek to win office, but they do not maximize their votes (see also Wellhofer 1990). Instead, they seek to win by the smallest possible margin, called the "minimum winning coalition" (1962, 32-33).[24]

Riker's work was important to comparative parties theory because it applied to the creation of parliamentary coalitions to form a government. Coalition theory assumed an "office-seeking" rather than "vote-seeking" strategy.[25] Early tests of coalition theory by De Swaan (1973) and Dodd (1976), and articles in Browne and Dreijmanis (1982) typically found minimum winning coalitions (measured by size of the legislative majority or by number of parties) forming less than half the time. Dodd also showed that minimum winning coalitions lasted longer than non-minimum winning coalitions, but his finding was challenged by Grofman (1989), who explained it by features of the party system. Laver and Schofield (1990) provided the most thorough nonmathematical discussion of coalition theory, comparing minimal winning coalitions (using various criteria) with minimal winning coalitions that are also ideologically "connected," with other versions that incorporate policy considerations, and with the game-theoretic concept of the "core point" in parties' preferred policy positions. They noted that while the best "policy blind" theory "is more often wrong than right about which coalition will form (making correct predictions in about 40% of all situations in which no party has a legislative majority), it does very much better than we would do by picking coalitions out of a hat" (Laver and Schofield 1990, 96).

Like Laver and Schofield, Budge and Keman (1990) reviewed the empirical research sparked by the pure office-seeking theory and concluded that the theory fit the data better when it permitted only coalitions that were ideologically "connected," which fits with findings by Franklin and Mackie (1984) about the importance of ideology in predicting coalition formation. However, that restriction modified the office-seeking assumption by introducing a policy-seeking strategy (pp. 17-19). Budge and Keman also reviewed results from pure policy-based theory (core theory) that predicted coalitions whose policies would be closest to those of its component parties but found no improvement in results (Laver and Schofield 1990, 19-26). In formulating their own theory of party government, Budge and Keman rely on a mixed strategy: parties seek office as a means of advancing policy (1990, 31).

In an important article, Strom (1990) outlined and critiqued three pure party strategies: vote-seeking, office-seeking, and policy-seeking. He then proposed seven hypotheses stating the effects of institutional features on competitive party behavior, for example:

> 1. The greater the degree of electoral competitiveness (the uncertainty of electoral contests), the more parties will pursue votes.
>
> . . .
>
> 7. The greater the office benefit differential between government and opposition relative to the policy influence differential, the greater the propensity of political parties toward office-seeking behavior" (pp. 588-589)

Strom incorporated his propositions concerning parties' internal organization into two causal models to explain the mix of strategies pursued by competitive political parties.

In the poetically titled, *Paper Stones*,[26] Przeworski and Sprague explored the strategic decision confronting democratic socialist parties that arises from this dilemma: "Socialism cannot be achieved without participation in democratic institutions, but participation erodes the will for socialism" (1986, 2). Przeworski and Sprague reported, moreover, that the proportion of the population employed as wage earners in industrial activities never surpassed 50% in any country. Because socialist parties regularly peaked at less than 50% of the vote, they needed to broaden their appeal beyond the proletariat. However, "By broadening their appeal, socialist parties dilute the general ideological salience of class and, consequently, weaken the motivational force of

class among workers" (p. 45). Przeworski and Sprague conducted a rigorous quantitative analysis of the consequences for socialist parties in opting for "pure supraclass and pure class-only strategies" in seven countries, saying "The difference between the shares resulting from pursuing pure strategies is the range of choice that a party faces when it decides which course of action to adopt" (p. 106). In most cases, they concluded that a pure supraclass strategy from the beginning would have been preferable, particularly in Denmark and Norway. Although such a strategy would have cost socialist parties some working-class votes, their net increment in voting support would have been positive.

Competitive Tactics

In military terminology, strategy refers to a plan for pursuing a goal while tactics refers to actions taken to implement the strategy. Similarly, party tactics refer to what parties actually do to carry out their strategy. The cross-national literature on party tactics that fulfill a competitive strategy is relatively small. Penniman (1981) studied campaign styles. Farrell and Wortmann (1987) analyzed parties in three countries for "political marketing" -- use of candidate packaging and communications media. Bowler (1990) examined the effects on voters of party movement on issues. Sainsbury (1990) edited a symposium on strategies and party-voter linkages in several countries, and noted that parties confronted a dilemma, in that "dwindling membership increased the difficulties of parties to mobilize and structure the vote, while less direct citizen involvement in parties made congruity between mass opinion and public decisions more difficult to achieve (p. 6)."

Governmental Status

The term "governmental status" refers to the nature and extent of a party's participation in national politics. This concept subsumes research on parties' electoral strength and political importance.[27] In keeping with a vote-seeking model of the party and our form of government, American scholars are apt to measure party dominance by percentage of votes won in elections and control of the executive. In keeping with an office-seeking model and a parliamentary form of government, European scholars look at percentages of seats won in parliament and participation in government -- i.e., the distribution of cabinet ministries. As Budge and Keman said, "Evaluations of office-seeking theory have concentrated on the emergence of government coalitions because it is here that the theory is most explicit and widely applied" (1990, 15). More definitively, Strom said that the "strategic interaction" among parties, so essential to coalition theory, simply "collapses" in two-party systems (1990, 586).

Electoral Strength

In party theory, measures of electoral performance occasionally serve as dependent variables in studies assessing the "effectiveness" of party organizations. Despite the popular academic opinion that party organization counts for little in turning out votes, practical politicians think otherwise. The expansion and strengthening of the Republican Party's national organization, particularly in the area of campaign finance, was done "to win elections and to maximize the number of elective offices won" (Sorauf and Wilson 1990, 199). Similarly, the strengthening of American state and local parties, observed by Gibson et al. (1989) and mentioned earlier, was aimed at being more effective, not less. As Huckfeldt and Sprague said, "If party activity is so ineffective, why do parties and candidates continue to invest their resources in the activity?" (1992, 84). Their detailed study of party mobilization in one U.S. community stressed the "catalytic function of party activity" in the neighborhood, not just its direct effects on individual voters. "Party organizations mobilize the faithful, and the activity of the faithful sends a message to the rest of the public (p. 84)."

As already noted, one study (Dalton 1985) found that centralized parties were more able to communicate their message to voters. Others have noted a tendency toward increased organization and centralization of power in certain conservative European parties as they employed the new campaign techniques of mass media and polling to combat the mass organization of leftist parties, which, in turn, responded in kind -- producing a "contagion from the right" (Epstein 1980, 257). Deschouwer (1986) sought to determine what type of party organization was most effective for parties across countries. He distinguished between "electoral" effectiveness, measured in votes won and "political" effectiveness, measured by both cabinet participation and governmental leadership. Relating these measures to various measures of party organization and the environment, Deschouwer found results consistent with the contingency model of organizations. It holds that there is no "best way" to organize for effectiveness, which is contingent on environmental factors.

Participation in Government

More commonly, however, the concept of governmental status has served as an independent variable in studies on the "impact" of political parties on governmental policies under the assumption of party government (Wildemann 1986; Katz 1987). A spurt of such research in the late 1970s used governmental status in conjunction with party ideology. (Small parties typically were ignored in this research; see Müller-Rommel and Pridham 1991.) Studying 25 Western industrial countries, Hewitt (1977) found a correlation between the strength of socialist parties in the legislature and expenditures for social services. In Hibbs's study (1977) of 12 nations, the longer socialist labor parties were in the executive from 1960 to 1969, the lower the mean unemployment rate but the higher the inflation rate.[28] Cameron's analysis (1978) of public expenditures in 18 countries found that "the dominance in government of leftist parties was a sufficient condition for a relatively large increase in the scope of public activity" (p. 1253). In a pair of articles (1978a and 1978b), Cowart looked over time at socialist dominance in government in seven nations and concluded that leftist governments were more likely than rightist governments to respond to changing economic conditions and to employ more diverse policy instruments.

Castles (1982) edited an important collection of cross-national studies of party impacts on policies in democratic states. Using various measures of the legislative and cabinet strength of leftist and rightist parties in analyzing public expenditures in 18 nations, Castles's own study found that the "best measure of partisan control typically 'explains' between 20 and 50% of the variance in expenditure" (p. 85). The other studies in his book showed fewer party effects. Schmidt's research (1982) on macroeconomic policies (tax base, unemployment, inflation) questioned how much party control really matters and looked to "extra-parliamentary" politics for explanation. Armingeon's article (1982) on redistribution of income also downplayed the role of leftist parties alone in the absence of the commitment by union wage negotiators to party goals (p. 269), and Arnhem and Schotsman (1982) reached a similar conclusion about the role of labor unions. In short, this set of studies loosened the linkage between leftist parties' governmental status and government policy made in the earlier studies. Lehner and Schubert (1984) and Weede (1990) addressed such mixed findings.

Budge and Keman (1990) advanced the study of party influence on government policy by separating cases in which the parties governed singly from those of government by party coalition. They rigorously set out a series of four general assumptions and some auxiliary ones (p. 42), from which they drew implications for policies pursued by governments. For example:

> (iv) Each party in the government will have some of its preferred policies put into effect: for instance, governments including an Agrarian party will pursue policies more

favourable to farmers and rural interests than governments without an Agrarian party . . . (Assumptions 2,3(c)).

(v) The direction of policy in specific areas will be influenced by party control of the competent ministries (Assumptions 1,2,3; Table 2.2 Assumption 3). (pp. 50-51)

Budge and Keman tested their theory with data on 20 Western governments and found that it fit the post-war experience. Their analysis of coalition government concluded that "parties exert a strong, and even determining, influence on government decision-making," and swung the evidence back to the "party matters" side (1990, 158).

Nevertheless, governments, not parties, remained the real units of analysis for Budge and Keman. Studying the policy impacts of individual parties requires examining their platforms or manifestos to see what particular parties propose and what they really pursue when given the opportunity. There are such studies that demonstrate party impacts in the United States (Pomper and Lederman 1980) and in Britain (Rose 1984), but there is little cross-national research on this complicated problem. However, Hofferbert was involved in similar studies of party impacts in two countries -- the United States (Budge and Hofferbert 1990) and Germany (Hofferbert and Klingemann 1990) -- using data from the ECPR party manifesto project. Both studies demonstrated specific impacts of party programs on government policy, with party influence in the U.S. coinciding most strongly with occupancy of the presidency and party influence in Germany working mainly through possession of cabinet ministries. Hofferbert and Klingeman warned, "Comparative policy studies, with their general focus on blunt indicators of party control are clearly in need of refinement and amendment." The party patterns "are but poorly revealed by contrasting the mere incumbency of one set of collective actors (parties of the 'left' or of the 'right') against one another and then seeking policy consequences of that contrast" (Hofferbert and Klingemann 1990, 300-301).

Concepts for Analyzing Party Systems

Although research on political parties is related to that on party systems, the two bodies of literature employ different concepts and theories. Duverger reflected this difference by dividing his classic *Political Parties* into "Book I: Party Structure" and "Book II: Party Systems." Sartori's *Parties and Party Systems* (1976) is similarly divided into two parts, with that on party systems more than twice as long as that on parties.

Whereas parties are studied by specialists interested in them as political institutions, party systems attract the larger group of scholars interested in politics across nations. Especially in the U.S., more articles have been published on cross-national studies of party systems than comparative analyses of parties. For the most part, the literature on party systems focuses on Western democratic nations, but there have been some efforts to build typologies of Latin American party systems (Wertz 1987; Collier and Collier 1991, 498-505).

Although the difference in the unit of analysis produces a different set of analytical concepts, party concepts and system concepts might seem to be identical in a one-party system. In a penetrating analysis, Sartori reasoned that parties make a system only when there are multiple parties (1976, 42-45). One party can relate to the state in a "party-state system," in which the party's properties figure in analysis, but there cannot properly be a one-party system. Despite the frequent usage of the terms "one-party" or "single-party" systems, Sartori's view holds in the literature, which requires at least two parties to make a party system.

In the first edition of their book, Lane and Ersson (1987b) carefully reviewed scholars' positions on definitional, conceptual, and analytical issues involved in studying party systems. All scholars agreed that a party system, like any system, consists of parts and relationships among those parts, such that the system is more than the sum of its parts. Accordingly, Lane and Ersson defined a party system as "a set of political parties operating within a nation in an organized pattern, described by a number of *party-system properties*" (1987b, 155). Scholars differ on what system properties are important concepts in theories of party systems, and their emphases are reflected in their research. Using Lijphart's set of important properties (1984), we find emphasis on (1) minimum winning coalitions (Dodd 1976; Laver and Schofield 1990), (2) government durability (Dodd 1976; Grofman 1989), (3) effective number of parties (Taagepera and Grofman 1985; Herzog 1987; Molinar 1991), (4) number of issue dimensions (Powell 1987; Listhaug, Mcdonald, and Rabinowitz 1990), and (5) electoral disproportionality (Rae 1971; Lijphart 1990). Others would add party competition (Laver 1989; Strom 1989; Ware 1989) and volatility (Pedersen 1983).

To establish the important dimensions of variations in party systems, Lane and Errson factor analyzed a set of 14 different indicators (along the lines of those proposed by Lijphart) for 272 elections in 16 European countries from 1920 to 1984. (The factor analysis was only reported in the first edition of their book, not in the second.) They concluded that the European party systems had five major dimensions:

1. *Fractionalization*, i.e., the variation in the number and strength of the constituent parts of the party systems
2. *Functional orientation*, i.e., the variation between traditional bourgeoisie parties and religious and ethnic parties
3. *Polarization*, i.e., the variation in the ideological distance between the political parties along the right-left scale
4. *Radical orientation*, i.e., the variation in the strength of leftist parties
5. *Volatility*, i.e., the variation in net mobility between political parties (Lane and Ersson 1987b, 177).

Lane and Ersson also concluded that the basic problem for the study of party systems is the analysis of change on these dimensions, which they defined as both fluctuations and trends.

In recent years, measurement of party system change has been one of the most important research topics in comparative politics (Mair 1983; Flanagan and Dalton 1984; Wolinetz 1988; Laver 1989; Mair 1989b; Smith 1989; Smith and Mair 1989; Smith and Mair 1990). Fewer writings, however, have tried to *explain* system change (Silverman 1985; Mair 1989a; Alber 1989; Carmines 1991). Those that have, as Reiter said, consider rising "affluence, the growth of the state, ... neo-corporatism, the mass media, new political issues and cleavages, problems with state performance, or post-industrialism" (1989, 329). Inglehart's work on postindustrialism (1990) and a new politics stressing the environment and quality of life is heavily featured in this literature. Poguntke (1987) for example, spelled out central elements of the new politics and suggested five possible effects on party systems: formation of new social movements, take-over of small parties, splitting of larger left-wing party into a post-material left party, alienation of new politics citizens and withdrawal of political support, and foundation of a new party (pp. 78-79). Party system concepts have figured most prominently as independent variables in cross-sectional analyses of political system performance. Powell's analysis of 28 party systems in the 1965-75 period found that those high in support for extremist parties had executive instability and mass rioting (1981). In a later study, he distinguished between effects on instability and those on rioting (1986). However, Lane and Ersson (1987a) found only indirect effects of party system fractionalization and polarization on social disorder and government instability.

The most developed theory about party systems is that on electoral systems, which usually treats party systems as dependent variables. Much of this theory originated in Book II of Duverger, and the proposition that single-member districts and plurality elections produce a two-party system has become known as "Duverger's Law" (Taagepera and Grofman 1985; Scarrow 1986). Fortunately, that vast literature has been admirably represented in some recent publications (Grofman and Lijphart 1986; Lijphart 1990). Blais (1991) also produced an excellent summary of the "debate" over electoral systems, complete with explanatory models of electoral effects. Reviewing the evidence on proportional representation, Blais says, "PR is not clearly superior to the plurality rule in promoting political order in advanced democracies and seems to be a risky choice in new ones" (p. 246).

With the fall of communism and the emergence of party competition in Eastern Europe, the effects of electoral systems on party politics assumed new political importance. Lijphart soon became the most prominent advocate of PR and multiparty politics for these emergent nations, arguing that PR and parliamentary government had a better record than alternative plurality systems, "particularly with respect to representation, protection of minority interests, voter participation, and control of unemployment" (1991a, 83). In reply, Quade defended plurality systems and criticized Lijphart's argument:

> Plurality voting encourages the competing parties to adopt a majority-forming attitude. The parties incline to be moderate, to seek conciliation, to round off their rough edges - - in short, to do *before* the election, in the public view, the very tasks that Lijphart applauds PR systems for doing *after* the election" (1991, 41).

Laryedret sided with Quade, saying, "Parties in plurality systems tend to be moderate because most votes are to be gained among the undecided voters of the center" (1991, 33). In his rejoinder, Lijphart (1991b) held that democracies often turned to PR to accommodate cleavages, that the superior economic record of PR systems was unquestioned, and that plurality systems produced distorted majorities that were seen as undemocratic.

In the midst of this academic debate, the new nations devised new electoral systems. Hibbing and Patterson (1992) described Hungary's complex system involving PR and plurality voting, and they favored its plurality features over straight PR. Analyzing the Polish situation, Jasiewicz (1992) found less fault with the electoral system than with its lack of established parties, although he was not convinced by Lijphart's case for PR. Later, Lijphart (1992) analyzed the choice of voting systems in Czechoslovakia, Hungary, and Poland during the collapse of communism, testing Stein Rokkan's hypothesis that old established bourgeois parties in the late 1800s (and communist parties in the late 1980s) favored PR as a way of retaining some power against new waves of voters. He concluded that it applied at least to Poland, which did adopt an extreme form of PR.

These exchanges of views on electoral impacts occurred outside any broad theoretical structure. Katz (1980) formulated a deductive theory "to explain the issue orientation, ideological style, and structural coherence (cohesion versus disintegration versus factionalism) of legislative parties" (p. 13). The thrust of his theory was that "parliamentary party organization will appear as an extension of campaign organization, and hence will reveal the same structural characteristics as a rationally organized campaign" dictated by electoral rules (p. 32). Based on eight assumptions of voters and electoral competition (pp. 17-18), Katz proposed twelve hypotheses, for example:

> 5. Parties in large district PR systems will be more likely to be ideologically oriented than those competing in plurality systems.
> 6. Parties competing in small districts will tend to be personalistically oriented or patronage oriented, whereas parties competing in larger districts will tend to be issue oriented. (pp. 33-34).

Katz tested his hypotheses in two ways, with an extensive test involving cross-national data on parties and with an intensive test involving in-depth analysis of parties in Britain, Ireland, and Italy. Both tests supported most of his hypotheses. Other scholars had advanced similar findings, but Katz said, "There is a difference between knowing something to be so and understanding why" (p.117). His theoretical structure helped explain why parties differed according to electoral systems.

The State of Party Theory

Our attention turns now to party theory, focusing on theories that involve individual parties as units of analysis. It is fashionable among party scholars at home and abroad to lament the lack of party theory. This complaint has a long and honorable history. Writing in French over fifty years ago, Duverger said:

> We find ourselves in a vicious circle: a general theory of parties will eventually be constructed only upon the preliminary work of many profound studies; but these studies cannot be truly profound so long as there exists no general theory of parties (1963, xiii).

Duverger then spun out scores of bivariate generalizations, scattered widely over 200 pages. Janda and King (1985) isolated 19 major hypotheses in

Duverger's book, tested them with cross-national data on approximately 100 parties, and found statistical support for 12.[29] The keystone of Duverger's theorizing was the concept of party ideology. Because Duverger viewed leftist parties as the "modern" type, Janda and King used the concept of leftism in formalizing his hypotheses. Of the 12 supported hypotheses, 11 involved leftism as either a direct or indirect causal factor. The driving force of ideology in Duverger's theory is seen in Figure 1, the causal diagram that Janda and King devised for all 12 confirmed hypotheses, with specific variables identified by the major concepts in this review.

According to Figure 1, ideology (leftism) is the initial cause of virtually all organizational attributes in Duverger's bivariate propositions about party structure. In general, leftist parties tend to demonstrate more involvement by their members in party doctrine, more complexity in organizational structure, and more centralization of power. They do so because leftist parties are agents of social change (Hamilton 1989, 219), and parties need stronger organization to effect change than to defend the status quo. Even today, Duverger's theorizing dominates party research (Sartori 1976, x).[30]

Despite Duverger's considerable success in his effort to "sketch a preliminary general theory of parties," scholars decades later still pleaded for party theory. In 1972, Mayer titled the chapter on parties in his comparative politics text, "The Search for a Theory of Parties." Acknowledging the stimulus of Duverger's book in 1976, Sartori observed that "there is still no general theory of parties" (1976, xi). Rewriting his comparative text nearly two decades later, Mayer still found that "research in any one aspect of parties tends to appear in isolation from other aspects of the topic without justification for the theoretical importance of the questions being asked" (1989, 142). In his recent review of the American parties literature, Crotty denied any "dominant perspective in the study of political parties" and saw party theory as "a goal to be sought" (1991, 148). In the English translation of his major book on political parties in Western democracies, von Beyme emphasized the importance of theory building to organize facts about parties, but sighed, "Complaints about a lack of satisfying theories are as old as party research itself and will certainly be directed against this study as well" (1985, 6).[31]

In contrast to the view that we lack party theory, Schlesinger contends, "A theory has lain embedded in most of our writing on parties. We have, however, failed to see it as a whole" (1991, 4). I agree that we have complained too long about the lack of party theory. Over the years, a substantial body of theory has been built, and it is time to recognize the accomplishments. Perhaps party scholars have been expecting too much by

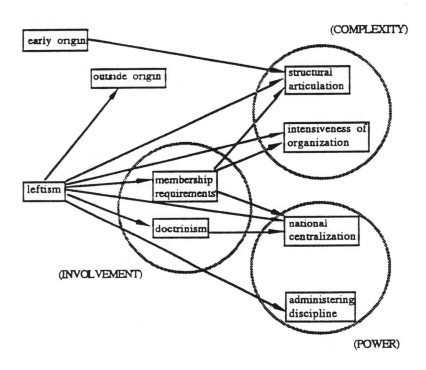

Figure 1: Causal Diagram of Twelve Confirmed Hypotheses from Duverger

calling for "a general theory." What would a general theory look like? We can try to envision this mythical object by speculating on its form and scope.

The Form of a General Theory

Must a general theory of political parties meet the rigorous requirements of a hypothetico-deductive system, complete with axioms, postulates, and mathematical expression? If so, rational choice theory applied to parties (Greenberg and Shepsle 1987; Holler 1987; Laver and Shepsle 1990; Baron 1991; Coram 1991) would seem to qualify. Judging by the scholarly style of some who have called for general theory (e.g., Sartori and von Beyme), this requirement is too demanding. For many, a general theory could consist of tightly organized verbal statements of theoretical propositions that were empirically testable. If so, examples can be found in Duverger, Katz (1980), Panebianco (1988), Budge and Keman (1990), Laver and Schofield (1990), Strom (1990), and Schlesinger (1991).

In discussing what it means to build party theory, Budge and Keman (1990) advanced "a series of hypotheses or propositions each of which can be examined and compared with what the collected information on that point actually tells us. Taken together, such propositions constitute the 'theory' or 'explanation' of why and how the parties act as they do, and if upheld should also enable us to anticipate what they are going to do in government, under given circumstances" (pp. 7-8). An important way to achieve theoretical clarity "is to put all this in mathematical form," but that narrows the focus because of restrictive and simplified assumptions (p. 9). They chose to favor broad coverage and practical relevance, relying on verbal expression of tightly reasoned propositions. Their work and other examples indicate that party theory need not be mathematized to be general.

Scope of Explanation

A truly general theory should also have a broad scope of application to political parties. There are two aspects to the scope of a theory: the types of parties to which it applies and the range of party phenomena that it explains. The scope of application depends on the definition of party that underlies the theory. The issue is whether the definition is narrow and theoretically *exclusive*, or broad and theoretically *inclusive*. If based on a broad definition of party, as used in this review, party theory should be applicable in principle to political parties everywhere, within the parameters of the theoretical conditions. We are left with the range of party phenomena encompassed by the theory.

What would a truly general theory of parties explain? For example, would a general theory about parties encompass voting behavior? As Schlesinger (1991) argues, that is excluded by defining parties as organizations; voters are choosers among parties, not the parties themselves. Although it is common to speak of parties as coalitions of voters, none are coalitions in the proper sense of the word. "None represent conscious, explicit agreements by members of these categories to pursue joint action" (p. 8). He states that this exclusion is a critical point. "Much of the difficulty political scientists have had in developing a theory of political parties has come from not knowing what to do with the voters" (p. 8). Excluding voting behavior from a theory of parties does not mean that party theory cannot include propositions about voting behavior. It simply means that party theory has no responsibility for explaining voting behavior, for its theoretical target is party organization and behavior.

Must a general theory of parties explain everything about parties? Furthermore, must it be a single integrated theory? If so, we will lack a general theory until we have a body of interrelated propositions that -- at a minimum -- explains (1) covariation among organizational characteristics within individual parties; (2) how and when parties form, change, and disappear; and (3) the effects of political parties on political life -- on its institutional and personal aspects. If this is the goal of general theory, then it is virtually certain that there will never be a general theory of political parties. Nor will there be a general theory of voting, or of legislatures, or of any other political institution or behavior, for we demand too much.

We should not expect a single general theory to explain everything about parties. Instead, we should acknowledge the existence of coherent bodies of explanation for broad segments of party phenomena as general theory. Our task should be to discover islands rather than look for continents. An analogy with voting behavior may be helpful: There are bodies of theory that explain voting turnout and bodies that explain voting choice. Turnout and choice theories share some points of contact, but they are essentially separate bodies of propositions. In the parties field, as I hope to have demonstrated in this review, we already have some bodies of theory that address distinct but important party phenomena.

Conclusion

In his recent and comprehensive review of literature on American parties, Crotty (1991) observed, "Political parties research, then, is more a uniting of a broad confederation of individual studies and research emphases with a tenuous relationship to one another than it is a highly focused, clearly demarked or well-integrated subfield of the discipline" (p. 138). In a section on "The Search for Theory," he characterized the American research as "self-consciously empirical and atheoretical" (p. 145). He saw special promise in the work of Schlesinger and said, "The more theoretical applications and conceptual developments that are attempted, the more models generated and explanations advanced, the better it will be for a field that has not been known for the quality or variety of its theorizing" (p. 148).

I agree with Crotty that research on American parties can benefit greatly from closer attention to theoretical applications, and there are other American theorists besides Schlesinger and Downs. Kamens (1989), for example, has proposed a theory of party development to account for the paradox that U.S. parties have grown stronger organizationally since the 1960s while becoming less important as vehicles for mass mobilization. His explanation focuses on the nationalization of politics and shifts in culture with the rise of higher education and the mass media. Nevertheless, there are many more examples of theorizing about parties in the comparative literature than in the American literature. For instance, I have already cited theoretical efforts by Duverger, Katz, Strom, and Budge and Keman. There is also Ware's flow-chart model of party behavior (1987, 108), Panebianco's theory of party transformation (1988, 262-273), the theories of candidate selection analyzed by Gallagher and Marsh (1988), Hamilton's well-developed model of determinants of socialist party radicalism (1989, 30-31), the exposition of coalition theory in Laver and Schofield (1990), and Schlesinger's theory of the multinuclear party (1991, 151-172). Party scholars can lament the lack of party theory no longer. Our challenge now is to assimilate, develop, and extend existing theory rather than wait for a general theory to descend from on high. Even if students are primarily interested in U.S. party politics, they could sharpen their analytical skills and theoretical insights by paying more attention to comparative political parties and by reading the European literature.

Notes

1. Virtually all those surveyed reported that they were familiar with the *American Political Science Review* (99%) and the *Journal of Politics* (91%).

2. LaPonce shows that all national journals are basically ethnocentric, with the *British Journal of Political Science* least so. Nevertheless, in a comparison of British and American journals, Crewe and Norris found that "the proportion of American political scientists

reading U.K.-based journals was two and a half times the proportion of British political scientists who read U.S.-based journals" (1991, 526).

3. Neumann's formal definition of a political party was "the articulate organization of active political agents, those who are concerned with the control of governmental power and who compete for popular support with another group or groups holding divergent views" (p. 396).

4. Ware (1987, 17) failed to recognize that "government" means "public office" in the United States in the context of this definition.

5. However, Schlesinger takes the opposite position: "I would argue that the compulsion to seek an all-inclusive definition of parties blinds us to the great varieties and types of political organizations that the restricted view allows us to identify in democracies, and therefore, the crucial distinctions that should be made between them" (1991, 203).

6. Intercorrelations among indicators of age, leadership competition, legislative stability, and electoral stability produced a single factor solution for 150 political parties and a scale with a Cronbach reliability coefficient of .79 (Janda 1980b, 143-144, 155).

7. Given the proliferation of parties in the former communist countries, one needs a reference guide to party politics, and some have already been published. Szajkowski (1991) listed more than 500 parties in 12 countries in the region, and other books by Pribylovskii (1992) and Abramov and Darchiyev (1992) described hundreds of parties and proto-parties in Russia alone.

8. Panebianco credited this distinction to an analytical framework proposed by Eliassen and Svåsand (1975).

9. Laver and Schofield actually listed another technique, dimensional analysis of parliamentary roll call votes, but this method has been primarily limited to party analyses in single countries, not in cross-national analysis.

10. In contrast to the traditional "proximity" theory of voting proposed by Downs, an alternative "directional" theory is proposed by Rabinowitz, Macdonald, and Listhaug (1991). This theory assumes that political issues are bipolar, and that voters decide according (1) to the direction of their preference and (2) to the strength of their preference. "Similarly, parties advocate different directions of policy and present them with different levels of intensity" (p. 149). Given a voter slightly left of center, "proximity theory predicts a preference for the party nearest the center, while directional theory predicts a preference for a party farther away" (p. 150). See also Macdonald, Listhaug, and Rabinowitz (1991).

11. Charlot (1989, 353) credits Seiler (1986) for distinguishing between two sequences of party formation. In one, the issue orientation precedes the laying claim to power and the resulting partisan alignment. In the other, the partisan alignment precedes the issue orientation and the laying claim to power. Seiler's work is in French.

12. In a later study of 108 parties in 19 elections over two widely spaced elections, Rose and Urwin (1975) found little support for regionalism as a basis of party cohesion.

13. One early, and lonely, exception is Anderson (1968), who worked to relate the organizational theory literature to the study of state and local parties.

14. Although the study of party organization is better developed in the American literature, even there it is a neglected topic. Epstein (1991) examined 238 articles and research notes published in the *American Political Science Review* from March 1986 through December 1990 and found only one item, a research note, on extra-governmental party organization.

15. This is similar to Duverger's concept of "community" (1963, 131).

16. The six-item scale for degree of organization (complexity) had a reliability of .82, as measured by Cronbach's alpha. The eight-item scale for centralization of power had an alpha of .83.

Over all the parties, the two scales were virtually uncorrelated, r=.03. (Janda 1980b, 156-157).

    17. Huntington (1965) defines autonomy in terms of interests rather than structure. He requires autonomous organizations to "have their own interests and values indistinguishable from those of other social forces" (p. 401).

    18. Out of 905 abstracts on political parties identified in a DIALOG™ search, only 25 mentioned finance or funding; only a few dealt specifically with party finance; and none that were remotely comparative were in English.

    19. Not only did the former "satellite" parties of ruling Communist parties in Eastern Europe (e.g., the four minor parties in the German Democratic Republic) clearly lack autonomy, but some scholars contended that they should not be regarded as separate parties. However, their survival after the collapse of the ruling party indicated that they had distinct organizations, albeit subservient ones.

    20. For a defense of the Middle-Level Elite project, see Reif, Niedermayer, and Schmitt (1986).

    21. A later definition by Belloni and Beller (1978), is conceptually identical. They define faction as *"any relatively organized groups that exists within the context of some other group and which* (as *political* faction) *competes with rivals for power advantages within the larger group of which it is a part"* (p. 419, emphasis in original).

    22. Five indicators of involvement -- severity of membership requirements, membership participation, material incentives, purposive incentives, and doctrinism -- were used to produce a scale with an alpha reliability coefficient of .78 (Janda 1980b, 154-155).

    23. Koelble (1989) has contended that Michels's "iron law" did not apply to the West German Green Party, when organization did not result in oligarchy.

    24. See Schlesinger (1991, 135-145) for a trenchant analysis of these opposing positions.

    25. Although Schlesinger used the term "office-seeking" in referring to his theory (1991, 143), it is really a "vote-seeking" theory when compared to the European usage of office-seeking. See Strom (1990).

    26. Przeworski and Sprague explain their title, *Paper Stones*, with this statement: "Barricades were no longer needed when workers could cast ballots: votes were 'paper stones.'" (1986, 1).

    27. Duverger's chapter on "Strength and Alliances" (1963, 281-351) dealt with indicators of governmental status.

    28. But Hibbs's research drew criticism from Payne (1979) for biased selection of cases, and other methodological issues, to which Hibbs replied (1979).

    29. In keeping with Duverger's own broad view of comparative party analysis, these linkages were empirically supported by data that included restrictive and subversive parties in communist and Third World countries along with the larger group of mostly competitive parties in democratic regimes (Janda 1979). The numbers of parties underlying each proposition varied from 79 to 135 (Janda and King 1985).

    30. For a dissent on the value of Duverger's work, see Daalder (1983, 10-12).

    31. Von Beyme was replying to an earlier review of the German edition of his book, which found "incomprehensible" his "lack of interest in general theory" (Raschke 1983, 109).

Bibliography

Abramov, Yury K., and Alexander N. Darchiyev. 1992. *Political Parties and Movements in Russia, 1985-1992.* Moscow: Synovya I. Docheri.

Alber, Jens. 1989. "Modernization, Cleavage Structures, and the Rise of Green Parties and Lists in Europe. In *New Politics in Western Europe: The Rise and Success of Green Parties and Alternative Lists.* ed. Ferdinand Muller-Rommel. Boulder, CO: Westview Press.

Alexander, Herbert E., ed. 1989a. *Comparative Political Finance in the 1980s.* Cambridge: Cambridge University Press.

Alexander, Herbert E. 1989b. "Money and Politics: Rethinking a Conceptual Framework." In *Comparative Political Finance in the 1980s.* Cambridge: Cambridge University Press.

Almond, Gabriel, and G. Bingham Powell. 1966. *Comparative Politics: A Developmental Approach.* Boston: Little, Brown.

Anderson, Lee. 1968. "Organizational Theory and the Study of State and Local Parties." In *Approaches to the Study of Party Organization*, ed. William J. Crotty. Boston: Allyn and Bacon.

Armingeon, Klaus. 1982. "Determining the Level of Wages: The Role of Parties and Trade Unions." In *The Impact of Parties: Politics and Policies in Democratic Capitalist States,* ed. Francis G. Castles. London: Sage Publications.

Arnhem, J. Corina van, and Geurt J. Schotsman. 1982. In *The Impact of Parties: Politics and Policies in Democratic Capitalist States,* ed. Francis G. Castles. London: Sage Publications.

Barghoorn, Frederick C. 1956. "The USSR: Monolithic Controls at Home and Abroad." In *Modern Political Parties: Approaches to Comparative Politics*, ed. Sigmund Neumann Chicago: University of Chicago Press.

Baron, David P. 1991. "A Spatial Bargaining Theory of Government Formation in Parliamentary Systems." *American Political Science Review* 85:137-164.

Bartolini, Stefano. 1983. "The Membership of Mass Parties: The Social Democratic Experience, 1989-1978." In *Western European Party Systems*, ed. Hans Daalder and Peter Mair. London: Sage Publications.

Bartolini, Stefano, and Peter Mair. 1990. *Identity Competition, and Electoral Availability: The Stabilisation of European Electorates 1885-1985.* Cambridge: Cambridge University Press.

Belloni, Frank P. and Dennis C. Beller. 1978. *Faction Politics: Political Parties and Factionalism in Comparative Perspective.* Santa Barbara, CA: ABC Clio Press.

Blais, André. 1991. "The Debate over Electoral Systems." *International Political Science Review* 12: 239-260.

Bowler, Shaun. 1990. "Voter Perceptions and Party Strategies: An Empirical Approach." *Comparative Politics* 23:61-83.

Brady, David W., and Charles S. Bullock, III. 1985. "Party and Factions Within Legislatures." In *Handbook of Legislative Research*, ed. Gerhard Lowenberg, Samuel C. Patterson, and Malcolm E. Jewell. Cambridge: Harvard University Press.

Browne, Eric C., and John Dreijmanis, ed. 1982. *Government Coalitions in Western Democracies.* London: Longman.

Bryce, James. [1893] 1912. *The American Commonwealth.* Vol. I, II. New York: Macmillan.

Bruce, John M., Johan A. Clark, and John H. Kessel. 1991. "Advocacy Politics in Presidential Parties." *American Political Science Review* 85:1089-1105.

Budge, Ian, David Robertson, and Derek Hearl. 1987. *Ideology, Strategy and Party Change: Spatial Analyses of Post-War Election Programmes in 19 Democracies.* Cambridge: Cambridge University Press.

Budge, Ian, and Richard I. Hofferbert. 1990. "Mandates and Policy Outputs: U.S. Party Platforms and Federal Expenditures." *American Political Science Review* 84:111-131.

Budge, Ian, and Hans Keman. 1990. *Parties and Democracy: Coalition Formation and Government Functioning in Twenty States.* Oxford: Oxford University Press.

Cameron, David R. 1978. "The Expansion of the Public Economy: A Comparative Analysis." *American Political Science Review* 72:1243-1261.

Carmines, Edward G. 1991. "The Logic of Party Alignments." *Journal of Theoretical Politics* 3:65-85.

Castles, Francis G., ed. 1982. *The Impact of Parties: Politics and Policies in Democratic Capitalist States*. London: Sage Publications.

Castles, Francis G., and Peter Mair. 1984. "Left-Right Political Scales: Some 'Expert' Judgments." *European Journal of Political Research* 12:73-88.

Charlot, Jean. 1989. "Political Parties: Towards a New Theoretical Synthesis." *Political Studies* 37:352-361.

Clark, Peter B., and James Q. Wilson. 1961. "Incentive Systems: A Theory of Organizations." *Administrative Science Quarterly* 6:129-166.

Collie, Melissa P. 1985. In *Handbook of Legislative Research*, ed. Gerhard Lowenberg, Samuel C. Patterson, and Malcolm E. Jewell. Cambridge: Harvard University Press.

Collier, Ruth Berins, and David Collier. 1991. *Shaping the Political Arena*. Princeton, NJ: Princeton University Press.

Coram, Bruce T. 1991. "Why Political Parties Should Make Unbelievable Promises: A Theoretical Note." *Public Choice* 69:101-108.

Cotter, Cornelius P., James L. Gibson, John F. Bibby, and Robert J. Huckshorn. 1984. *Party Organizations in American Politics*. New York: Praeger.

Cowart, Andrew T. 1978a. "The Economic Policies of European Governments, Part I: Monetary Policy." *British Journal of Political Science* 8:285-311.

Cowart, Andrew T. 1978b. "The Economic Policies of European Governments, Part I: Fiscal Policy." *British Journal of Political Science* 8:425-439.

Crewe, Ivor, and Pippa Norris. 1991. "British and American Journal Evaluation." *PS: Political Science & Politics* 23:524-531.

Crotty, William J., ed. 1968. *Approaches to the Study of Party Organization*. Boston: Allyn and Bacon.

Crotty, William J. 1969. "The Quest for Scientific Meaning in Analyses of Political Parties." In *A Methodological Primer for Political Scientists*, ed. Robert T. Golembiewski, William A. Welsh, and William J. Crotty. Chicago: Rand McNally.

Crotty, William J. 1991. "Political Parties: Issues and Trends." In *Political Science: Looking to the Future, Volume 4: American Institutions*, ed. William J. Crotty. Evanston: Northwestern University Press.

Daalder, Hans. 1983. "The Comparative Study of European Parties and Party Systems: An Overview." In *Western European Party Systems*, ed. Hans Daalder and Peter Mair. Beverly Hills: Sage Publications.

Dalton, Russell J. 1985. "Political Parties and Political Representation: Party Supporters and Party Elites in Nine Nations." *Comparative Political Studies* 18:267-299.

Dalton, Russell J. 1988. *Citizen Politics in Western Democracies: Public Opinion and Political Parties in the United States, Great Britain, West Germany, and France*. Chatham, NJ: Chatham House.

Dalton, Russell J., Scott C. Flanagan, and Paul Allen Beck, ed. 1984. *Electoral Change in Advanced Industrial Democracies: Realignment or Dealignment?* Princeton, NJ: Princeton University Press.

Dalton, Russell J., and Manfred Kuechler. 1990. *Challenging the Political Order: New Social and Political Movements in Western Democracies*. New York: Oxford.

Deschouwer, Kris. 1986. "Political Parties as Organizations: A Contingency Approach." Paper delivered at the World Conference of the International Sociological Association.

De Swaan, A. 1973. *Coalition Theories and Cabinet Formation*. Amsterdam: Elsevier.

Dix, Robert H. 1989. "Cleavage Structures and Party Systems in Latin America." *Comparative Politics* 21:23-37.

Dix, Robert H. 1992. "Democratization and the Institutionalization of Latin American Political Parties." *Comparative Political Studies* 24:488-511.

Dodd, Larry C. 1976. *Coalitions in Parliamentary Government*. Princeton, NJ: Princeton University Press.

Downs, Anthony. 1957. *An Economic Theory of Democracy*. New York: Harper.

Duverger, Maurice. [1951] 1963. *Political Parties*. New York: Wiley.

Duverger, Maurice. [1966] 1972. *Party Politics and Pressure Groups: A Comparative Introduction*. New York: Thomas Y. Crowell.

Eldersveld, Samuel J. 1982. *Political Parties in American Society*. New York: Basic Books.

Eliassen, Kjell A., and Lars Svaasand. 1975. "The Formation of Mass Political Organizations: An Analytical Framework." *Scandinavian Political Studies* 10:95-121.

Eijk, Cees van der, and Erik V. Oppenhuis. 1991. "European Parties Performance in Electoral Competition." *European Journal of Political Research* 19:55-80.

Epstein, Leon. 1964. "A Comparative Study of Canadian Parties." *American Political Science Review* 58:46-59.

Epstein, Leon. 1966. "Political Parties in Western Democratic Systems." In *Essays in Political Science*, ed. Edward H. Burehrig. Bloomington: Indiana University Press.

Epstein, Leon. 1975. "Political Parties." In *Handbook of Political Science, Volume 4: Nongovernmental Politics*, ed. Fred I. Greenstein and Nelson W. Polsby. Reading, MA: Addison-Wesley.

Epstein, Leon. 1980. *Political Parties in Western Democracies*. New Brunswick, New Jersey: Transaction Books.

Epstein, Leon. 1983. "The Scholarly Commitment to Parties." In *Political Science: The State of the Discipline*, ed. Ada W. Finifter. Washington: American Political Science Association.

Epstein, Leon. 1986. *Political Parties in the American Mold*. Madison: University of Wisconsin Press.

Epstein, Leon. 1991. "Overview of Research on Party Organization." Paper prepared for the Local Parties Workshop at the Annual Meeting of the American Political Science Association, Washington, DC.

Ersson, Svante, Kenneth Janda, and Jan-Erik Lane. 1985. "Ecology of Party Strength in Western Europe: A Regional Analysis." *Comparative Political Studies* 18:170-205.

Farrell, David M., and Martin Wortmann. 1987. "Party Strategies in the Electoral Market: Political Marketing in West Germany, Britain and Ireland." *European Journal of Political Research* 15:297-318.

Farouk-Sluglett, Marion, and Peter Sluglett. 1988. "The Iraqi Ba'th Party." In *Political Parties in the Third World*, ed. Vicky Randall. London: Sage Publications.

Fischer-Galati, Stephen, ed. 1979. *The Communist Parties of Eastern Europe*. New York: Columbia University Press.

Flanagan, Scott C., and Russell J. Dalton. 1984. "Parties Under Stress: Realignment and Dealignment in Advanced Industrial Societies." *West European Politics*. 7:7-23.

Franklin, Mark N., and Thomas T. Mackie. 1984. "Reassessing the Importance of Size and Ideology for the Formation of Governing Coalitions in Parliamentary Democracies." *American Journal of Political Science* 28:671-692.

Gallagher, Michael, and Michael Marsh, ed. 1988. *Candidate Selection in Comparative Perspective: The Secret Garden of Politics*. London: Sage Publications.

Gibson, James L., Cornelius P. Cotter, John F. Bibby, and Robert J. Huckshorn. 1983. "Assessing Party Organizational Strength." *American Journal of Political Science* 27:193-222.

Gibson, James L., John P. Frendreis, and Laura L. Vertz. 1989. "Party Dynamics in the 1980s: Changes in County Party Organizational Strength, 1980-1984." *American Journal of Political Science* 33:67-90.

Gilberg, Trond, ed. 1989. *Coalition Strategies of Marxist Parties.* Durham: Duke University Press.

Giles, Micheal W., Francie Mizell, and David Patterson. 1989. "Political Scientists' Journal Evaluations Revisited." *PS: Political Science & Politics* 22:613-617.

Goldman, Ralph M., ed. 1983. *Transnational Parties: Organizing the World's Precincts.* Lanham, MD: University Press of America.

Greenberg, Joseph, and Kenneth Shepsle. 1987. "The Effect of Electoral Rewards in Multiparty Competition with Entry." *American Political Science Review* 81:525-537.

Griffiths, John. 1988. "The Cuban Communist Party." In *Political Parties in the Third World*, ed. Vicky Randall. London: Sage Publications.

Grofman, Bernard. 1989. "The Comparative Analysis of Coalition Formation and Duration: Distinguishing Between-Country and Within-Country Effects." *British Journal of Political Science* 19:291-302.

Grofman, Bernard, and Arend Lijphart, ed. 1986. *Electoral Laws and Their Political Consequences.* New York: Agathon Press.

Hamilton, Malcolm B. 1989. *Democratic Socialism in Britain and Sweden.* New York: St. Martin's.

Harmel, Robert, and Kenneth Janda. 1982. *Parties and Their Environments: Limits to Reform?* New York: Longman.

Harmel, Robert, and John D. Robertson. 1985. "On the Study of New Parties." *International Political Science Review* 4:403-418.

Heidenheimer, Arnold J. 1963. "Comparative Party Finance: Notes on Practices and Toward a Theory." *Journal of Politics* 25:790-811.

Herrnson, Paul S. 1990. "Reemergent National Party Organizations." In *The Parties Respond: Changes in the American Party System*, ed. L. Sandy Maisel. Boulder, CO: Westview Press.

Herzog, Hanna. 1987. "Minor Parties: The Relevancy Perspective." *Comparative Politics* 19:317-329.

Hewitt, Christopher. 1977. "The Effect of Political Democracy and Social Democracy on Equality in Industrial Societies: A Cross-National Comparison." *American Political Science Review* 42:450-464.

Heyns, Barbara, and Ireneusz Bialecki. 1991. "Solidarność: Reluctant Vanguard or Makeshift Coalition?" *American Political Science Review* 85:351-370.

Hibbing, John R., and Samuel C. Patterson. 1992. "A Democratic Legislature in the Making: The Historic Hungarian Elections of 1990." *Comparative Political Studies* 24:430-454.

Hibbs, Douglas A. 1977. "Political Parties and Macroeconomic Policy." *American Political Science Review* 71:1467-1487.

Hibbs, Douglas A. 1979. "Reply to Payne." *American Political Science Review* 73:185-190.

Hodgkin, Thomas. 1961. *African Political Parties.* London: Penguin Books.

Hofferbert, Richard I., and Hans-Dieter Klingemann. 1990. "The Policy Impact of Party Programmes and Government Declarations in the Federal Republic of Germany." *European Journal of Political Research* 18:277-304.

Holler, Manfred J., ed. 1987. *The Logic of Multiparty Systems.* Dordrecht, The Netherlands: Kluwer Academic Publishers.

Hrbek, Rudolff. 1988. "Transnational Links: The ELD and Liberal Party Group in the European Parliament." In *Liberal Parties in Western Europe*, ed. Emil J. Kirchner. Cambridge: Cambridge University Press.

Huckfeldt, Robert, and John Sprague. 1992. "Political Parties and Electoral Mobilization: Political Structure, Social Structure, and the Party Canvass." *American Political Science Review* 86:70-86.

Huntington, Samuel. 1965. "Political Development and Political Decay." *World Politics* 17:386-430.

Huber, John D. 1989. "Values and Partisanship in Left-Right Orientations: Measuring Ideology." *European Journal of Political Research* 17:599-621.

Inglehart, Ronald. 1977. *The Silent Revolution: Changing Values and Political Styles Among Western Publics.* Princeton, NJ: Princeton University Press.

Inglehart, Ronald. 1990. *Culture Shift in Advanced Industrial Society.* Princeton, NJ: Princeton University Press.

Irving, Roland Eckford Mill. 1979. *The Christian Democratic Parties of Western Europe.* London: Allen and Unwin.

Janda, Kenneth. 1979. *Comparative Political Parties Data, 1950-1962 (ICPSR Study 7534).* Ann Arbor: Inter-University Consortium for Political and Social Research.

Janda, Kenneth. 1980a. "A Comparative Analysis of Party Organization: The United States, Europe, and the World." In *The Party Symbol: Readings on Political Parties*, ed. William J. Crotty. San Francisco: W.H. Freeman.

Janda, Kenneth. 1980b. *Political Parties: A Cross-National Survey.* New York: The Free Press.

Janda, Kenneth. 1983. "Cross-National Measures of Party Organizations and Organizational Theory." *European Journal of Political Research* 11:319-332.

Janda, Kenneth. 1989. "Regional and Religious Support of Political Parties and Effects on their Issue Positions." *International Political Science Review* 10:349-370.

Janda, Kenneth. 1992. "The American Constitutional Framework and the Structure of American Political Parties." In *The Constitution and American Political Development: An Institutional Perspective*, ed. Peter F. Nardulli. Urbana: University of Illinois Press.

Janda, Kenneth, and Robin Gillies. 1983. "How Well Does 'Region' Explain Political Party Characteristics?" *Political Geography Quarterly* 12:179-203.

Janda, Kenneth, and Desmond King. 1985. "Formalizing and Testing Duverger's Theories on Political Parties." *Comparative Political Studies* 18:139

Jankowski, Richard. 1988. "Preference Aggregation in Political Parties and Interest Groups: A Synthesis of Corporatist and Encompassing Organization Theory." *American Journal of Political Science* 32:105-125.

Jasiewicz, Krysztof. 1992. "From Solidarity to Fragmentation." *Journal of Democracy* 3:55-69.

Kamens, David H. 1989. "A Theory of American Political Party Development, 1960-1986," *Journal of Political and Military Sociology* 17:263-290.

Katz, Richard S. 1980. *A Theory of Parties and Electoral Systems.* Baltimore: Johns Hopkins.

Katz, Richard S. 1985. "Measuring Party Identification with Eurobarometer Data: A Warning Note." *West European Politics* 8:104-108.

Katz, Richard S., ed. 1987. *Party Governments: European and American Experiences.* Berlin: Walter de Gruyter.

Katz, Richard S. 1990. "Party as Linkage: A Vestigial Function?" *European Journal of Political Research* 18:143-161.

Katz, Richard S., Peter Mair, eds. 1992. *Party Organizations: A Data Handbook on Party Organizations in Western Democracies, 1960-1990.* London: Sage Publications.

Kelley, Donald R. 1992. "The Democratic Revolution in the U.S.S.R.: Can the System Cope with Pluralism?" *Midsouth Political Science Journal* 13:27-49.

Keefe, William J. 1991. *Parties, Politics, and Public Policy in America*. Washington, DC: Congressional Quarterly.

Kirchheimer, Otto. 1966. "The Transformation of the Western European Party Systems." In *Political Parties and Political Development* ed. Joseph LaPalombara and Myron Weiner. Princeton, New Jersey: Princeton University Press.

Kitschelt, Herbert. 1989. "The Internal Politics of Parties: The Law of Curvilinear Disparity Revisited." *Political Studies* 3:400-421.

Kitschelt, Herbert. 1990. "New Social Movements and the Decline of Party Organization." In *Challenging the Political Order: New Social and Political Movements in Western Democracies*, ed. Russell J. Dalton and Manfred Kuechler. New York: Oxford.

Kitschelt, Herbert, and Staf Hellemans. 1990. "The Left-Right Semantics and the New Politics Cleavage." *Comparative Political Studies* 23:210-238.

Koelble, Thomas A. 1989. "Party Structures and Democracy: Michels, McKenzie, and Duverger Revisited via the Examples of the West German Green Party and the British Social Democratic Party." *Comparative Political Studies* 22:199-216.

Kolinsky, Eva, ed. 1987. *Opposition in Western Europe*. New York: St. Martin's.

Knutsen, Oddbjørn. 1988. "The Impact of Structural and Ideological Party Cleavages in West European Democracies: A Comparative Empirical Analysis." *British Journal of Political Science* 18:323-352.

Knutsen, Oddbjorn. 1989. "Cleavage Dimensions in Ten West European Countries: A Comparative Empirical Analysis." *Comparative Political Studies* 21:495-533.

Lagroye, Jacques. 1989. "Change and Permanence in Political Parties." *Political Studies* 37:362-375.

Lane, Jan-Erik, and Svante O. Ersson. 1987a. "Multipartism." In *The Logic of Multiparty Systems*, ed. Manfred J. Holler. Dordrecht, The Netherlands: Martinus Nijhoff.

Lane, Jan-Erik, and Svante O. Ersson. 1987b. *Politics and Society in Western Europe*. London: Sage Publications.

Lane, Jan-Erik, and Svante O. Ersson. 1991. *Politics and Society in Western Europe*. 2nd ed. London: Sage Publications.

LaPalombara, Joseph, and Myron Weiner, ed. 1966. *Political Parties and Political Development*. Princeton: Princeton University Press.

LaPonce, J. A. 1980. "Political Science: An Import-Export Analysis of Journals and Footnotes." *Political Studies* 28:401-419.

Lardeyret, Guy. 1991. "The Problem with PR." *Journal of Democracy* 2:30-35.

Laver, Michael. 1989. "Party Competition and Party System Change: The Interaction of Coalition Bargaining and Electoral Competition." *Journal of Theoretical Politics* 1:301-324.

Laver, Michael, and Kenneth A. Shepsle. 1990. "Government Coalitions and Intraparty Politics." *British Journal of Political Science* 20:489-508.

Laver, Michael, and Norman Schofield. 1990. *Multiparty Government: The Politics of Coalition in Europe*. Oxford: Oxford Press.

Lawson, Kay. 1976. *The Comparative Study of Political Parties*. New York: St. Martin's Press.

Lawson, Kay, ed. 1980. *Political Parties & Linkage: A Comparative Perspective*. New Haven, CT: Yale University Press.

Lawson, Kay, and Peter H. Merkl, ed. 1988. *When Parties Fail: Emerging Alternative Organizations*. Princeton: Princeton University Press.

Lehner, Franz, and Klaus Schubert. 1984. "Party Government and the Political Control of Public Policy." *European Journal of Political Research* 12:131-146.

Levush, Ruth, ed. 1991. *Campaign Finance of National Elections in Foreign Countries*. Washington, DC: Law Library of Congress.

Lijphart, Arend. 1984. *Democracies: Patterns of Majoritarian and Consensus Government in Twenty-one Countries*. New Haven, CT: Yale University Press.

Lijphart, Arend. 1990. "The Political Consequences of Electoral Laws, 1945-85." *American Political Science Review* 84:481-496.

Lijphart, Arend. 1991a. "Constitutional Choices for New Democracies," *Journal of Democracy* 2:72-84.

Lijphart, Arend. 1991b. "Double-Checking the Evidence," *Journal of Democracy*, 2:42-48.

Lijphart, Arend. 1992. "Democratization and Constitutional Choices in Czecho-Slovakia, Hungary and Poland 1989-91." *Journal of Theoretical Politics* 4:207-233.

Lipset, Seymour Martin, and Stein Rokkan. 1967. *Party Systems and Voter Alignments*. New York: Free Press.

Listhaug, Ola, Stuart E. Macdonald, and George Rabinowitz. 1990. "A Comparative Spatial Analysis of European Party Systems." *Scandinavian Political Studies* 13:227-254.

Loewenberg, Gerhard, and Samuel C. Patterson. 1979. *Comparing Legislatures*. Boston: Little, Brown.

Luebbert, Gregory. 1986. *Comparative Democracy: Policy Making and Governing Coalitions in Europe and Israel*. New York: Columbia University Press.

Lybeck, Johan A. 1985. "Is the Lipset-Rokkan Hypothesis Testable?" *Scandinavian Political Studies* 8:105-113.

Macdonald, Stuart Elaine, Ola Listhaug, and George Rabinowitz. 1991. "Issues and Party Support in Multiparty Systems." *American Political Science Review* 85:1107-1131.

Maguire, Maria. 1983. "Is There Still Persistence? Electoral Change in Western Europe, 1948-1979." In *Western European Party Systems: Trends and Prospects*, ed. Peter H. Merkl. New York: Free Press.

Mair, Peter. 1983. "Adaptation and Control: Towards an Understanding of Party and Party System Change." In *Western European Party Systems*, ed. Hans Daalder and Peter Mair. London: Sage Publications.

Mair, Peter. 1989a. "Continuity, Change and the Vulnerability of Party." *West European Politics* 12:169-187.

Mair, Peter. 1989b. "The Problem of Party System Change." *Journal of Theoretical Politics* 1:251-276.

Mavrogordatos, George T. 1987. "Downs Revisited: Spatial Models of Party Competition and Left-Right Measurements." *International Political Science Review* 8:333-342.

May, John D. 1973. "Opinion Structure of Political Parties: The Special Law of Curvilinear Disparity." *Political Studies* 21:135-151.

Mayer, Lawrence C. 1972. *Comparative Political Inquiry*. Homewood, IL: Dorsey Press.

Mayer, Lawrence C. 1989. *Redefining Comparative Politics: Promise Versus Performance*. Newbury Park: Sage Publications.

McDonald, Ronald H., and J. Mark Ruhl. 1989. *Party Politics and Elections in Latin America*. Boulder, CO: Westview Press.

McFaul, Michael. 1992. "Russia's Emerging Political Parties." *Journal of Democracy* 2:25-40.

McKay, David. 1988. "Why Is There a European Political Science?" *PS: Political Science & Politics* 21:1051-1055.

Mendilow, Jonathan. 1992. "Public Party Funding and Party Transformation in Multiparty Systems." *Comparative Political Studies* 25:90-117.

Merkl, Peter H. 1980. "The Sociology of European Parties: Members, Voters, and Social Groups." In *Western European Party*

Systems: Trends and Prospects, ed. Peter H. Merkl. New York: Free Press.

Michels, Robert. [1911] 1962. *Political Parties: A Sociological Study of the Oligarchical Tendencies of Modern Democracy*. New York: Free Press.

Molinar, Juan. 1991. "Counting the Number of Parties: An Alternative Index." *American Political Science Review* 85:1383-1391.

Muller-Rommel, Ferdinand. 1985. "The Greens in Western Europe: Similar but Different." *International Political Science Review* 6:483-499.

Muller-Rommel, Ferdinand, ed. 1989. *New Politics in Western Europe: The Rise and Success of Green Parties and Alternative Lists*. Boulder, CO: Westview Press.

Muller-Rommel, Ferdinand. 1990. "New Political Movements and 'New Politics' Parties in Western Europe." In *Challenging the Political Order: New Social and Political Movements in Western Democracies*, ed. Russell J. Dalton and Manfred Kuechler. New York: Oxford.

Muller-Rommel, Ferdinand, and Geoffrey Pridham, ed. 1991. *Small Parties in Western Europe: Comparative and National Perspectives*. London: Sage Publications.

Narkiewicz, Olga A. 1990. *The End of the Bolshevik Dream: Western European Communist Parties in the Late Twentieth Century*. London: Routledge.

Nassmacher, Karl-Heinz. 1989. "Structure and Impact of Public Subsidies to Political Parties in Europe: The Examples of Austria, Italy, Sweden, and West Germany." In *Comparative Political Finance in the 1980s*, ed. Herbert E. Alexander. Cambridge: Cambridge University Press.

Niedermayer, Oskar. 1986. "Methodological and Practical Problems of Comparative Party Elites Research: The EPPMLE Project," *European Journal of Political Research* 14:253-259.

Niedermayer, Oskar, and Hermann Schmitt. 1983. "Sozialstruktur, Partizipation und Politischer Status in Partieiorganisationen." *Politische Vierteljahresschrift* 24:293-310.

Neumann, Sigmund, ed. 1956. *Modern Political Parties: Approaches to Comparative Politics*. Chicago: University of Chicago Press.

Ostrogorski, Moisei. [1902] 1964. *Democracy and the Organization of Political Parties*. Vol. II of *The United States*. Garden City, New York: Anchor Books.

Ozbudun, Ergun. 1970. "Party Cohesion in Western Democracies: A Causal Analysis." *SAGE Professional Papers in Comparative Politics*. Beverly Hills, CA: Sage Books

Paltiel, Khayyam Zev. 1980. "Public Financing Abroad: Contrasts and Effects." In *Parties, Interest Groups, and Campaign Finance Laws*, ed. Michael J. Malbin. Washington, DC: American Enterprise Institute.

Paltiel, Khayyam Zev. 1981. "Campaign Finance: Contrasting Practies and Reforms." In *Democracy at the Polls*, ed. David Butler, Howard R. Penniman, and Austin Ranney. Washington, DC: American Enterprise Institute.

Panebianco, Angelo. 1988. *Political Parties: Organization and Power*. Cambridge: Cambridge University Press.

Payne, James L. 1979. "Inflation, Unemployment, and Left-Wing Political Parties: A Reanalysis." *American Political Science Review* 73:181-185.

Pedersen, Mogens N. 1983. "Changing Patterns of Electoral Volatility in European Party Systems, 1948-1977: Explorations in Explanation." In *Western European Party Systems: Trends and Prospects*, ed. Peter H. Merkl. New York: Free Press.

Pelinka, Anton. 1983. *Social Democratic Parties in Europe*. New York: Praeger.

Pempel, T.J., ed. 1990. *Uncommon Democracies: The One-Party Dominant Regimes*. Ithaca: Cornell University Press.

Penniman, Howard R. 1981. "Campaign Styles and Methods." In *Democracy at the Polls: A Comparative Study of Competitive National Elections*, ed. David Butler, Howard R. Penniman, and Austin Ranney. Washington, DC: American Enterprise Institute.

Philip, George. 1988. "The Dominant Party System in Mexico." In *Political Parties in the Third World*, ed. Vicky Randall. London: Sage Publications.

Pierre, Jon. 1986. "Attitudes and Behaviour of Party Activists: A Critical Examination of Recent Research on Party Activists and 'Middle-Level Elites'," *European Journal of Political Research* 14:465-479.

Piven, Frances Fox, ed. 1992. *Labor Parties in Postindustrial Societies*. New York: Oxford University Press.

Poguntke, Thomas. 1987. "New Politics and Party Systems: The Emergence of a New Type of Party?" *West European Politics* 10:76-88.

Pomper, Gerald M. 1992. "Concepts of Political Parties." *Journal of Theoretical Politics* 4:143-159.

Pomper, Gerald M., and Susan S. Lederman. 1980. *Elections in America*. New York: Longman.

Powell, G. Bingham, Jr. 1981. "Party Systems and Political System Performance: Voting Participation, Government Stability and Mass Violence in Contemporary Democracies." *American Political Science Review* 75:861-879.

Powell, G. Bingham, Jr. 1986. "Extremist Parties and Political Turmoil: Two Puzzles." *American Journal of Political Science* 30:357-378.

Powell, G. Bingham, Jr. 1987. "The Competitive Consequences of Polarized Pluralism." In *The Logic of Multiparty Systems*, ed. Manfred J. Holler. Dordrecht, The Netherlands: Martinus Nijhoff.

Pribylovskii, Vladimir. 1992. *Dictionary of Political Parties and Organizations in Russia*. Boulder, CO: Westview Press.

Pridham, Geoffrey, ed. 1986. *Coalitional Behavior in Theory and Practice: An Inductive Model for Western Europe*. Cambridge: Cambridge University Press.

Pridham, Geoffrey, and Pippa Pridham. 1981. *Transnational Party Cooperation and European Integration: The Process Toward Direct Elections*. London: George Allen and Unwin.

Przeworski, Adam, and John Sprague. 1986. *Paper Stones: A History of Electoral Socialism*. Chicago: University of Chicago Press.

Pye, Lucien. 1966. "Party Systems and National Development in Asia." In *Political Parties and Political Development*, ed. Joseph LaPalombara and Myron Weiner. Princeton: Princeton University Press.

Quade, Quentin L. 1991. "PR and Democratic Statecraft." *Journal of Democracy* 2:36-41.

Rabinowitz, George, Stuart Elaine Macdonald, and Ola Listhaug. 1991. "New Players in an Old Game: Party Strategies in Multiparty Systems." *Comparative Political Studies* 24:147-185.

Rae, Douglas. 1971. *The Political Consequence of Electoral Laws*. 2nd ed. New Haven: Yale University Press.

Randall, Vicky, ed. 1988. *Political Parties in the Third World*. London: Sage Publications.

Raschke, Joachim. 1983. "Political Parties in Western Democracies." *European Journal of Political Research* 11:109-114.

Reif, Karlheinz, Oskar Niedermayer, and Hermann Schmitt. 1986. "Quantitative = Survey = Attitudes = Issue Stands = Ideology? A Rejoinder to Jon Pierre's 'Attitudes and Behavior of Party Activists," *European Journal of Political Research* 14:685-690.

Reiter, Howard L. 1989. "Party Decline in the West: A Skeptic's View." *Journal of Theoretical Politics* 1:251-348.

Richardson, Bradley M. 1991. "European Party Loyalties Revisited." *American Political Science Review* 85:751-775.

Riker, William. H. 1962. *The Theory of Political Coalitions*. New Haven: Yale University Press.

Rose, Richard, ed. 1974. *Electoral Behavior: A Comparative Handbook*. New York: The Free Press.

Rose, Richard. 1984. *Do Parties Make A Difference?* Chatham, NJ: Chatham House.

Rose, Richard, and Derek Urwin. 1975. "Social Cohesion, Political Parties, and Strains in Regimes." *Comparative Political Studies* 2:7-67.

Rose, Richard. 1970. "Persistence and Change in Western Party Systems, 1945-1969." *Political Studies*. 18:287-319.

Rose, Richard. 1975. *Regional Differentiation and Political Unity in Western Nations*. Beverly Hills, CA: Sage Publications.

Rose, Richard, and Thomas T. Mackie. 1988. "Do Parties Persist or Fail? The Big Trade-off Facing Organizations." In *When Parties Fail: Emerging Alternative Organizations*, ed. Kay Lawson and Peter H. Merkl. Princeton: Princeton University Press.

Rosenstone, Steven J., Roy L. Behr, and Edward H. Lazarus. 1984. *Third Parties in America*. Princeton: Princeton University Press.

Sainsbury, Diane. 1990. "Party Strategies and Party-Voter Linkages: Editor's Introduction." *European Journal of Political Research* 18:1-7.

Sartori, Giovanni. 1976. *Parties and Party Systems: A Framework for Analysis*. Vol. 1. Cambridge: Cambridge University Press.

Scarrow, Howard A. 1986. "Duverger's Law, Fusion, and the Decline of American 'Third' Parties." *Western Political Quarterly* 39:634-647.

Schlesinger, Joseph A. 1991. *Political Parties and the Winning of Office*. Ann Arbor: University of Michigan Press.

Schmidt, Manfred G. 1982. "The Role of the Parties in Shaping Macroeconomic Policy." In *The Impact of Parties: Politics and Policies in Democratic Capitalist States*, ed. Francis G. Castles. London: Sage Publications.

Schmitt, Hermann. 1989. "On Party Attachment in Western Europe and the Utility of Eurobarometer Data." *West European Politics* 12:122-139.

Schoonmaker, Donald. 1988. "The Challenge of the Greens to the West German Party System." In *When Parties Fail: Emerging Alternative Organizations*, ed. Kay Lawson and Peter H. Merkl. Princeton: Princeton University Press.

Schwartz, Mildred. 1991a. "Political Protest in the Western Borderlands: Can Farmers be Socialists?" In *Borderlands Essays in Canadian-American Relations*, ed. Robert Lecker. Toronto: ECW Press.

Schwartz, Mildred. 1991b. "Politics as Moral Causes in Canada and in the United States." *Comparative Social Research* 4:65-90.

Scott, Robert E. 1966. "Political Parties and Policy Making in Latin America." In *Political Parties and Political Development*, ed. Joseph LaPalombara and Myron Weiner. Princeton: Princeton University Press.

Seiler, Daniel Louis. 1986. *De la Comparaison des Partis Politiques*. Paris: Economica.

Selle, Per, and Lars Svasand. 1991. "Membership in Party Organizations and the Problem of Decline of Parties." *Comparative Political Studies* 23:459-477.

Shamir, Michal. 1984. "Are Western Party Systems Frozen? A Comparative Dynamic Analysis." *Comparative Political Studies* 17:35-79.

Silverman, Lawrence. 1985. "The Ideological Mediation of Party-political Responses to Social Change." *European Journal of Political Research* 13:69-93.

Sinclair, Barbara. 1990. "The Congressional Party: Evolving Organizational, Agenda-Setting, and Policy Roles." In *The Parties Respond: Changes in the American Party System*, ed. L. Sandy Maisel. Boulder, CO: Westview Press.

Smith, Gordon. 1989. "A System Perspective on Party System Change." *Journal of Theoretical Politics* 1:349-363.

Smith, Gordon, and Peter Mair. 1989. "Introduction: How are West European Party Systems Changing?" *West European Politics* 12:1-2.

Smith, Gordon, ed. [1989] 1990. *Understanding Party System Change in Western Europe*. London: Frank Cass.

Sorauf, Frank J., and Scott A. Wilson. 1990. "Campaigns and Money: A Changing Role for the Political Parties?" In *The Parties Respond: Changes in the American Party System*, ed. L. Sandy Maisel. Boulder, CO: Westview Press.

Strom, Kaare. 1989. "Inter-Party Competition in Advanced Democracies." *Journal of Theoretical Politics* 1:277-300.

Strom, Kaare. 1990. "A Behavioral Theory of Competitive Political Parties." *American Journal of Political Science* 34:565-598.

Szajkowski, Bogdan, ed. 1986. *Marxist Local Governments in Western Europe and Japan*. Boulder, CO: L. Rienner.

Szajkowski, Bogdan. 1991. *New Political Parties of Eastern Europe and the Soviet Union: A Comprehensive Reference Guide*. London: Longman.

Taagepera, Rein, and Bernard Grofman. 1985. "Rethinking Duverger's Law: Predicting the Effective Number of Parties in Plurality and PR Systems--Parties Minus Issues Equals One." *European Journal of Political Research* 13:341-352.

Taylor, Michael, and Michael Laver. 1973. "Government Coalitions in Western Europe." *European Journal of Political Research* 1:205-248.

Thomas, John Clayton. 1975. "The Decline of Ideology in Western Political Parties: A Study of Changing Policy Orientations." *Sage Professional Papers in Contemporary Political Sociology*, 06-012. Beverly Hills: Sage Publications.

Thomas, John Clayton. 1980. "Ideological Trends in Western Political Parties." In *Western European Party Systems: Trends and Prospects*, ed. Peter H. Merkl. New York: Free Press.

Timmerman, Heinz. 1987. *The Decline of the World Communist Movement: Moscow, Beijing, and Communist Parties in the West*. Boulder: Westview Press.

Turner, Julius, and Edward V. Schneier. 1970. *Party and Constituency: Pressures on Congress*. Baltimore: The Johns Hopkins Press.

von Beyme, Klaus. 1983. "Governments, Parliaments, and the Structure of Power in Political Parties." In *Western European Party Systems*, ed. Hans Daalder and Peter Mair. London: Sage Publications.

von Beyme, Klaus. 1985. *Political Parties in Western Democracies*. New York: St. Martin's.

Waller, Michael, and Meindert Fennema, ed. 1988. *Communist Parties in Western Europe: Decline or Adaptation?* New York: Basil Blackwell.

Ware, Alan. 1987. *Citizens, Parties and the State: A Reappraisal*. Princeton: Princeton University Press.

Ware, Alan. 1989. "Parties, Electoral Competition, and Democracy." *Parliamentary Affairs* 42:1-22.

Weede, Erich. 1990. "Democracy, Party Government and Rent-Seeking as Determinants of Distributional Inequality in Industrial Societies." *European Journal of Political Research* 18:515-533.

Wellhofer, E. Spencer. 1979. "The Effectiveness of Party Organization: A Cross-National Time Series Analysis." *European Journal of Political Research* 7:205-224.

Wellhofer, E. Spencer. 1981. "The Political Incorporation of the Newly Enfranchised Voter: Organizational Encapsulation and

Socialist Labor Party Development." *Western Political Quarterly* 34:399-414.

Wellhofer, E. Spencer. 1990. "Contradictions in Market Models of Politics: The Case of Party Strategies and Voter Linkages." *European Journal of Political Research* 18:9-28.

Welfling, Mary B. 1973. "Political Institutionalization: Comparative Analyses of African Party Systems." *Sage Professional Papers in Comparative Politics*, 01-041. Beverly Hills: Sage.

Wertz, Nikolaus. 1987. "Parties and Party Systems in Latin America." In *The Logic of Multiparty Systems*, ed. Manfred J. Holler. Dordrecht, The Netherlands: Martinus Nijhoff.

Wildenmann, Rudolf. 1986. "The Problematics of Party Government." In *Visions and Realities of Party Government*, ed. Francis G. Castles and Rudoph Wildenmann. Berlin: Walter de Gruyter.

Wilson, Frank L. 1980. "Sources of Party Transformation: The Case of France." In *Western European Party Systems: Trends and Prospects*, ed. Peter H. Merkl. New York: Free Press.

Wilson, James Q. 1962. *The Amateur Democrat*. Chicago: University of Chicago Press.

Wolinetz, Steven B., ed. 1988. *Parties and Party Systems in Liberal Democracies*. London: Routledge.

Wright, William E. 1971. *A Comparative Study of Party Organization*. Columbus, OH: Charles E. Merrill.

Zariski, Raphael. 1960. "Party Factions and Comparative Politics: Some Preliminary Observations." *Midwest Journal of Political Science* 4:27-51.

Zariski, Raphael. 1978. "Party Factions and Comparative Politics: Some Empirical Findings." In *Faction Politics: Political Parties and Factionalism in Comparative Perspective*, ed. Frank P. Belloni and Dennis C. Beller. Santa Barbara, CA: ABC Clio Press.

8

The Not So Simple Act of Voting

Russell J. Dalton and Martin P. Wattenberg

In today's increasingly complex political world, what has been called "the simple act of voting" (Kelley and Mirer 1975) is no longer quite so simple. With more party options to choose from in most of the world's established democracies -- and in the United States many more voting choices to make -- voters' decision-making capabilities are being tested more than ever. Adding to the public's task is the expanding governmental agenda. In addition to their traditional responsibilities of ensuring the economic and physical well-being of their citizens, governments are now regularly being called upon to deal with numerous matters that were not on the political agenda just a generation ago. These include protecting the environment, guaranteeing the rights of consumers, arbitrating moral issues like abortion, and ensuring equality of opportunity for minorities and women.

This chapter provides a broad comparative assessment of research on voting behavior in advanced industrial democracies. This is an extremely large, and rapidly growing literature, all of which cannot fit into a single chapter.[1] Moreover, there are many aspects of electoral behavior that are specific to one nation, or at least not generalizable across most systems. Therefore, we have chosen to focus on the evolution of research on what we feel is the central question of electoral behavior: how voters in advanced industrial democracies deal with the increasingly difficult task of guiding governments via the ballot box.

On the one hand, several developments have significantly helped Western publics to meet this challenge. These societies have experienced an information explosion through the expansion of the mass media, thereby substantially decreasing the costs of obtaining political information (Graber in this volume; Ranney 1983; Semetko et al. 1991; Neuman 1986). It is easy to forget that our contemporary world of instant news and 24-hour cable news services stands in marked contrast to the information environment of even one generation ago. In addition, steady increases in the educational level of Western publics have presumably increased the political skills of contemporary electorates. With more political information available to a more

educated electorate, it might be hypothesized that today's voters no longer need shortcuts or cues to guide their decisions. More citizens now possess the level of political skills and resources necessary to become self-sufficient in politics (Inglehart 1990, chap. 10; Dalton 1984). Instead of depending solely on elites and reference groups, such voters should now be able to deal with intricate political issues and make their own decisions.

On the other hand, any increase in the public's ability to deal with complex political issues has to be balanced against the rise in the complexity of politics itself. Issues such as health care reform, nuclear power, global warming, and national industrial policies challenge the abilities of even the experts. American voters are being asked to make decisions that range from judging the needs for school construction bonds to selecting the president of the United States; Europeans are deciding on town councilors as well as the future of European integration.

The actual balance between the abilities of voters and the demands involved in their making political decisions is a central controversy in electoral research that we will review in this chapter. Still, most analysts believe that voters must rely on some cues and political shortcuts to make their decisions. As Samuel Popkin (1991, 218) writes, "the use of information shortcuts is ... an inescapable fact of life, and will occur no matter how educated we are, how much information we have, and how much thinking we do." Consequently, our review of the electoral behavior literature focuses on the cues that citizens still need to guide their choices. The kinds of cues used by voters may have changed over time, but the process of employing cognitive shortcuts remains intact.

The Nature of Belief Systems

Any discussion of voting behavior is ultimately grounded on basic assumptions about the electorate's political abilities -- the public's level of knowledge, understanding, and interest in political matters. For voters to make meaningful decisions, they must understand the options the polity faces. Citizens must have a sufficient knowledge of the workings of the political system if they intend to influence and control the actions of their representatives. Historically, many theorists maintained that democracy was workable only when the public possessed a high degree of political information and sophistication. Mill, Locke, Tocqueville, and other writers saw these public traits as essential requirements for a successful democratic system.

One of the most striking findings of the first empirical surveys of voter beliefs was the stunning contrast found between the classic image of the democratic citizen and the actual nature of the electorate. The public's political sophistication fell far short of theoretical ideal. For most citizens, political interest and involvement barely extended beyond casting an occasional vote in national or state elections. Furthermore, citizens apparently brought very little understanding to their participation in politics. It was not clear that voting decisions were based on rational evaluations of candidates, parties, and their issue positions. Rather, voting was conditioned by group loyalties and personal considerations. As one early seminal work in the area concluded:

> Our data reveal that certain requirements commonly assumed for the successful operation of democracy are not met by the behavior of the 'average' citizen....Many vote without real involvement in the election....The citizen is not highly informed on the details of the campaign....In any rigorous or narrow sense the voters are not highly rational (Berelson et al. 1954, 307-10).

The landmark in early electoral research, *The American Voter*, reinforced this negative impression of the electorate (Campbell et al. 1960). Campbell and his colleagues documented a lack of ideological awareness or understanding by the American electorate. *The American Voter* concluded that the electorate "is almost completely unable to judge the rationality of government actions; knowing little of the particular policies and what has led to them, the mass electorate is not able either to appraise its goals or the appropriateness of the means chosen to secure these goals" (Campbell et al. 1960, 543). Other research soon extended this negative view of the unsophisticated citizen to other Western democracies (e.g., Converse and Dupeux 1962; Converse 1975; Butler and Stokes 1969). Perhaps the most damning judgment was *The American Voter*'s conclusion that the limited

ideological sophistication of the electorate reflected inherent limits that were not likely to change (Campbell et al. 1960, 253-56).[2]

This image of the uninformed and unsophisticated voter began to reshape our view of the citizenry and democratic politics, but then it confronted a new wave of "revisionist" research. The highly politicized and ideological nature of American campaigns in the 1960s seemed to increase the public's "level of political conceptualization" on indicators similar to those used in *The American Voter* study (Field and Anderson 1969; Nie, Verba, and Petrocik 1976, chap. 7). Other research found that the consistency of the public's issue preferences also had risen in the 1960s (Nie and Andersen 1974; Pierce 1975), indicating that political beliefs were becoming more ideologically structured. In general terms, it was argued that the sophistication of voters was significantly affected by the political environment. In the halcyon days of the 1950s, citizens displayed less interest or involvement in politics; in the politicized decade of the 1960s, citizens seemingly responded by becoming more interested in politics and more sophisticated in their understanding of politics.

The environmental explanation of political sophistication was further supported by cross-national studies indicating that the "level of conceptualization" of the public varies sharply across nations, with the relatively non-ideological American system yielding one of the least ideological publics (Klingemann 1979; Westholm and Niemi 1992). The available longitudinal data from other advanced industrial democracies seemed to parallel these trends: political interest was generally on the rise (van Deth 1990; Almond and Verba 1980; Dalton 1988, chap. 1), and German time series displayed an increasing number of political ideologues over the past two decades (Klingemann 1979; Dalton 1988, chap. 1). Furthermore, in many instances these trends are accelerated in other (non-U.S.) democracies because the socioeconomic transformation of these societies has been even more rapid than in the United States.

The debate moved in a new direction when methodologists began to question the validity of the empirical evidence. Analyses indicated that a major portion of the increased constraint in issue beliefs in U.S. surveys was caused by improvements in question wording and format (Sullivan et al. 1978; Bishop et al. 1978). Other methodological studies questioned the validity of the levels of conceptualization measure used in the original *The Changing American Voter* monograph (Smith 1980; Nie et al. 1979, 366). Using results from an election panel survey in the 1970s, Converse and Markus (1979) showed that the stability of political beliefs, another indicator of the existence of a sophisticated belief system, were relatively unchanged among Americans when compared to panel results of the 1950s. The most direct assault has come from Eric R.A.N. Smith (1989). By redefining the meaning of the concept, Smith argues that the sophistication of the American electorate has remained virtually unchanged in the three decades since *The American Voter*. Whether or not one agrees with Smith's evidence and argumentation, the book itself illustrates the continuing controversy on the basic parameters of this debate.[3]

The "counter-revisionist" literature has itself been questioned in other studies. John Pierce and his colleagues replicated Converse's measurement of Americans' level of conceptualization; they find that the proportion of ideologues among the U.S. electorate remained at higher levels after the turbulent 1960s, suggesting that sophistication had increased, or at least the findings of *The American Voter* came at an unusual low point (Pierce et al. 1982, chap. 7; Klingemann 1979). Other researchers argued that when measurement error is taken into account through the use of sophisticated multi-indicator models, the true stability and consistency of political beliefs is much stronger than simple correlational methods imply (Judd et al. 1981; Judd and Milburn 1980; cf. Converse 1980). Jon Krosnick (1991) shows that a branching method of asking issue positions produces even more reliable issue measures and higher levels of issue constraint than does the seven-point issue scales that are now the standard instrumentation on most election studies. The more things change... (*Plus ça change...*).

The more recent American literature on political sophistication has devoted less attention to assessing the absolute level of the public's political abilities and has instead focused on the manner in which individuals organize and process information. Donald Kinder (1983) advocated this approach to the study of belief systems in his chapter in the first edition of this volume, and it has been reinforced by Luskin's (1987) thoughtful review of the sophistication literature.

Generally identified under the heading of "schema theory," although this may be a misnomer, this research addresses two questions about political thinking. First, instead of viewing belief systems as interconnecting a diverse range of political attitudes (vertical linkage), analysts maintain that there is a network or (hierarchical) structure of beliefs within specific political domains. The conceptual structures used to organize information might also vary across individuals. Thus, the growing literature on schema theory attempts to identify specific cognitive structures (or schema) that are relevant for subsets of individuals; such as a foreign policy schema, or racial schema, or the schema for evaluating political candidates (Conover and Feldman 1984; Hurwitz and Peffley 1987;

Sniderman, Brody, and Kuklinski 1984; Miller, Wattenberg, and Malanchuk 1986; Rohrschneider 1992).

The other use of schema theory focuses on how citizens process political information (e.g., Lau 1986). Schema both assist in organizing existing knowledge and in processing new information. The detail and amount of information incorporated within these structures may vary widely across individuals, but the existence of such structures provides voters with a method of managing information and making political judgments. In other words, even if citizens are not sophisticated on all political topics, they may have logical and structured beliefs within specific domains that enable them to manage the political decisions they must make as citizens. But of course, even the more modest claims of schema theory have not escaped critique (Kuklinski, Luskin, and Bolland 1991).

It is not surprising that this long debate has left many sophisticated political scientists uncertain about the actual sophistication of contemporary publics. Still, this debate has enriched our understanding of the nature of citizen politics. The research literature now yields a more positive assessment of the electorate. Modern electorates do not match the lofty ideals of classic democratic theory. Still, regardless of whether sophistication has increased over time in the United States, our best current measurement methodologies imply that estimates of political sophistication in the era of *The American Voter* were inaccurately low (Niemi and Weisberg 1993a, chap. 4).[4] Moreover, schema theory argues that political sophistication should be studied within specific schematic frameworks, rather than in the global measures of knowledge, constraint, and sophistication introduced by early voting scholars.

The debate on the limited sophistication of the American electorate also generally ignores the cross-national evidence of significantly higher levels of political conceptualization and ideological awareness in non-American systems. Calculating a measure of ideological sophistication similar to that of *The American Voter*, Hans-Dieter Klingemann (1979) finds that Italians are more than twice as likely as Americans to be classified as ideologues, and the Dutch and German electorates also display significantly higher levels of ideological awareness. Similarly, citizens in most other advanced industrial democracies are better able than Americans to explain concepts such as "Left" and "Right" (Fuchs and Klingemann 1990). These Europeans are not cognitively more advanced than Americans, but the political environment in these systems sharply influences how these publics view the political world.

The cross-national evidence underscores the point that political sophistication is not a fixed or a sharply restricted characteristic of mass publics in advanced industrial democracies. In addition, longitudinal surveys of the American public and European publics find that the levels of sophistication displayed by the citizens can change in response to the political environment, reviving V.O. Key's claim that the electorate is partially an echo chamber.

The debate on the political sophistication of contemporary electorates also highlights the assumptions about the nature of political decision making that underlie our models of electoral choice. The lofty ideals of classic democratic theory presumed a rational decision-making process by a fully informed electorate. Even given our more positive assessment about the nature of contemporary electorates, most voters (and even some political scientists) still fall short of the standards of classic democratic theory. However, we also understand that this maximalist definition of the prerequisites for informed decision making is unnecessary. One should not presume that there must be strong constraint across diverse issue domains or citizens must have textbook knowledge about the political process in order to participate in a knowledgable way (e.g., Delli Carpini and Keeter 1991). Instead, our models should look at whether citizens can manage the complexities of politics and make reasonable decisions given their political interests and positions. That is, we emphasize a *satisficing* approach to decision making; these models ask what are the pragmatic ways that individuals actually make their political choices. Through the use of political cues and other decision-making shortcuts, individuals can make reasonable decisions at modest cost and without perfect information.

The logic of satisficing decision making is apparent in the three disciplinary paths -- sociological, psychological, and economic -- that have defined the evolution of electoral behavior research. The next sections of this chapter review the evolution of each approach, and the contemporary controversies of the applicability of each model.

The Classic Studies of Voting Behavior

Most voting behavior research in the first half of the twentieth century employed the *sociological approach*. This was largely because the best available data were census data demographics, which could easily be compared to voting patterns. Thus, when the methodology of survey research first became available, it was natural that demographic variables attracted attention, as their role in shaping voting decisions had already been well established by sociologists.

The pioneers of electoral sociology were led by Paul Lazarsfeld at Columbia University's Bureau of Applied Social Research. Lazarsfeld, Bernard Berelson, and Hazel Gaudet (1944) set out to understand how voting intentions changed during a campaign by interviewing a panel of voters repeatedly during the 1940 election year. Finding that relatively few voters switched back and forth, they fell back upon previously established demographic patterns of voting to explain their findings. In a subsequent study of the 1948 election entitled *Voting*, Berelson, Lazarsfeld, and William McPhee (1954) laid out a comprehensive sociological model of the vote decision. The bulk of their data, as the authors put it, related "either directly to primary groups or to clusters of them in the social strata" (Berelson et al. 1954, 301). The basic assumption was that voting is as much conditioned by who one is as by what one believes. In other words, sociological variables create common group interests that shape the party coalitions and define images concerning which party is most attuned to the needs of various types of people.

Social-group-based voting is an example of satisficing decision making because voters use sociological cues to guide their voting choices. Attention focuses on the party (or parties) that historically have supported the social groups to which a voter belongs. A voter can decide between competing parties based on cues such as the endorsements of labor unions, business associations, religious groups, and the like -- as well as the group appeals of the parties themselves. The stable group base of each party means that many voters develop standing partisan predispositions that endure across elections, further simplifying the decision process.

The sociological perspective of the Columbia scholars was paralleled by European electoral research of the period. For instance, a series of local surveys in Britain began to define the class bases of British electoral politics (Benney et al. 1956; Milne and Mackenzie 1954, 1959). The landmark in European electoral research was Seymour Martin Lipset and Stein Rokkan's (1967) study of party systems and voter alignments. They linked the development of party systems to a historical sequence of political conflicts and their attendant social cleavages. This rich theoretical framework was then integrated with some of the first results from national electoral surveys in Europe. In comparison to the United States, social forces seemed to exert an even stronger influence on the voting choice of Europeans, further underpinning the value of the sociological model. In echoing the historical emphasis of the Columbia researchers, Lipset and Rokkan (1967, 50) voiced their now-famous conclusion that "the party systems of the 1960s reflect, with but few significant exceptions, the cleavage structure of the 1920s."

Although the sociological model of voting provided a useful framework for identifying a set of social cues that structured electoral decisions, the model had several limitations. It was able to explain only a modest proportion of the vote among European electorates, and an even smaller proportion among the less polarized American electorate. In addition, a sociological approach emphasized continuity and stability, and thus had limited value in explaining electoral change.

The weaknesses in the sociological approach led investigators at the University of Michigan to focus more directly on the psychological processes behind the calculus of individual behavior. The publication of *The American Voter* in 1960 introduced an explicitly *social psychological model* of the vote (Campbell et al. 1960). The focal point of this theory was the mediating role of long-term psychological predispositions -- particularly that of party identification -- in guiding citizen action. As the authors stated at the outset, "Our hypothesis is that the partisan choice the individual voter makes depends in an immediate sense on the strength and direction of the elements comprising a field of psychological forces, where these elements are interpreted as attitudes toward the perceived objects of national politics" (Campbell et al. 1960, 9).

Although conceding that sociological characteristics influence the development of party identification, the psychological approach argues that partisanship is more than simply a political reflection of a voter's upbringing and current social status. Correlations between demographic factors and the vote provide interesting information, "yet information pitched at a low level of abstraction" (Campbell et al. 1960, 36). Such social characteristics, moreover, have limited value in providing an evaluative structure the range of different phenomena that citizens encounter. Social class, for instance, does not provide voters with cues on issues that lack a class-referent. Thus, the sociological model has restricted applicability as a method of satisficing decision making, especially in our more varied and changing contemporary political world.

One of the strengths of the psychological model is that it described how most citizens possess a ready guide for judging most political phenomena. The psychological view holds that party identification acts to filter individuals' views of the political world, providing them not only with a means for making voting decisions (support one's own party) but also with a means for interpreting short-term issues and candidacies since parties are central actors in most political conflicts. In addition, psychological variables bear a direct relationship to the vote, as they are more proximally involved in the decision-making process. To routinely support one's preferred party, unless distinct candidate or issue factors

entered the decision field, was both an efficient and probably reasonable way for managing the complexity of politics for most individuals.

The psychological approach of *The American Voter* was rapidly exported to other democratic settings through a series of collaborative cross-national research projects in the late 1950s and 1960s. Converse and Dupeux (1962) compared the characteristics of American and French partisans, and cited their findings as evidence of the functional equivalence of the psychological model in the two societies. Butler and Stokes (1969) integrated sociological and psychological models in their surveys of British voters, and found that a "partisan self-image" helped Britons orient themselves to the complexities of politics. Similar collaborative studies were conducted in Sweden, Italy, Australia, Japan, Germany, the Netherlands, and a host of other democracies (e.g., Budge et al. 1976). The influence of this approach was so pervasive that party identification -- and the theoretical model it represented -- became the central theoretical concept in electoral research.

A third paradigm of electoral research, which we can roughly label an *economic approach*, developed at least partially as a logical extension of the sociological and psychological models. The former models both emphasized relatively stable sources of voter cues as befitting a satisficing model of voting. This third approach argued that citizens could develop simplified ways to use attitudinal factors, such as issue opinions and candidate evaluations, as a basis of their voting decisions.

This perspective was introduced in Anthony Downs's seminal 1957 book, *An Economic Theory of Democracy*. Instead of testing classical notions of democratic practice, Downs reformulates them according to modern economic theory's assumptions of rationality. The fundamental axiom of Downs's theory is that citizens act rationally in politics. When it comes to voting, Downs writes, "this axiom implies that each citizen casts his vote for the party he believes will provide him with more benefits than any other" (p. 36). The key to this decision process is the voter's perception of expected utility. "As a result," Downs asserts, "the most important part of a voter's decision is the size of his *current party differential*, that is, the difference between the utility income he actually received in period t and the one he would have received if the opposition had been in power" (p. 40).

Although this approach asserts that citizens make voting decisions in a calculating manner, taking into account party promises as well as government performance, there is also a pragmatic aspect to this approach that fits our framework of satisficing decision making. For example, Downs devotes an entire chapter to how rational citizens reduce information costs (Downs

1957, chap. 12). Similarly, Downs does not engage in the debate on whether all voters are sophisticated on all issues; instead, he asks whether they possess an informed basis for making policy choices through their vote. For instance, this perspective assumes that people can evaluate past performance (or future promises) of the parties and use this as a basis for decision making. Alternatively, voters might use broad political symbols, such as "liberal" or "conservative" to orient themselves to politics and make their electoral decisions. In short, voters are seen as individual actors using the information they possess on the parties and candidates to evaluate what will be in their best interest.[5]

The next sections of this chapter discuss the development of these three competing paradigms in contemporary electoral research. Although all three processes are obviously at work within any electorate, the relative mix of these forces has fundamental implications for the nature of the public's electoral decisions. Are voters making satisficing decisions based on long-term social or psychological predispositions, or judging between current policy options? To answer this question is to begin to assess the "quality" of the democratic process.

The Decline of Social Cleavage Voting

Ironically, just as Lipset and Rokkan were discussing how Western party systems were frozen around the social cleavages of the 1920s, dramatic changes began to affect these same party systems. The established political parties were presented with new demands and new challenges. European party systems became more fractionalized through the fragmenting of established parties and the creation of new parties. Fluctuations in voting results increased in the United States as well as Europe, with inter-election vote shifts becoming more common at the individual and aggregate level (Crewe and Denver 1985; cf. Bartolini and Mair 1990).

Many scholars directly linked these shifting electoral patterns to ongoing changes in the nature of Western societies -- and thereby the bases of the sociological model of voting (Dalton et al. 1984; Inglehart 1977). For example, virtually all industrial democracies have shared in the increasing affluence of the postwar economic boom. The embourgoisement of the working class narrowed differences in living conditions between class strata and attenuated the importance of class-based political conflict. The growth of the service sector and government employment further reshaped the structure of labor forces, creating new post-industrial societies. These changes in the makeup of

capitalist economies were paralleled by other shifts in the social structure. For instance, modern industrial societies require a more educated labor force and possess the resources to dramatically expand educational access. Changing employment patterns also stimulate increased geographic mobility and urbanization. The traditional closed community life -- be it in a rural farming village or working-class neighborhood -- was gradually supplanted by more open, urban, and cosmopolitan life styles.

These and other social forces profoundly transformed the social composition of contemporary publics from those of the electorates on which our early models of voting behavior were based. In 1948, for example, the number of Americans with only grade school education outnumbered those with some college training by about three to one; by 1988, these proportions had been almost exactly reversed. Similar or even greater educational changes occurred in other democratic societies. The social class, religious, and community bases of social structure have been altered in equally profound ways.

The Class Cleavage

The consequences of these societal changes for the sociological model of voting are most clearly illustrated by the case of the class cleavage. Social scientists have probably devoted more attention to social class than to any other demographic factor. This partially reflects the empirical importance of class cues in explaining the vote, as well as the centrality of class in Marxist theories of politics. At the time of the early voting studies, European political parties were often sharply divided on class-based issues, and even the two U.S. parties projected distinct class appeals during the New Deal period. Early survey evidence found large class voting differences in Britain and many other Northern European democracies (Rose 1974; Lipset and Rokkan 1967). Seymour Martin Lipset's cross-national study of mass politics described the class cleavage as one of the most pervasive bases of party support:

> Even though many parties renounce the principle of class conflict or loyalty, an analysis of their appeals and their support suggests that they do represent the interests of different classes. On a world scale, the principal generalization which can be made is that parties are primarily based on either the lower classes or the middle and upper classes (1960, 230).

Repeating this point, Arend Lijphart's (1981) overview of modern party systems identified the class cleavage as a major dimension of ideological debate in virtually all democracies.

If one of the pillars of the sociological model was the importance of class voting -- the working class leaning toward left-wing parties and the middle class toward conservative parties -- then this pillar has cracked and crumbled over the past generation. There is a now well-known trend of decreasing class voting that is found in virtually every established democratic party system (Dalton et al. 1984; Franklin et al. 1992). The simplest and most frequently used measure of class voting is the "Alford index" which computes the simple difference between middle class and working-class support for left-wing parties (Alford 1963). For instance, in the 1957 West German election the two class strata differed by nearly 40 percentage points in their support for the Social Democratic Party; in recent German elections this difference has averaged about 10% (Dalton 1988). Similar declines are observed for other northern European democracies where class voting was initially strong, such as Britain, Holland, and Sweden. In nations where class voting was initially modest, such as France, it has weakened still further. Even in the unique Japanese party system, where social forces attenuate the class cleavage, class voting differences have also narrowed over the past decade (Watanuki 1991).

In the United States, there was a modest level of class voting during the New Deal period, which reached a peak in Truman's 1948 election. For most postwar elections, however, social class has exerted only a weak influence on the parties' long-term bases of support. The influence of class has ebbed and flowed in presidential elections, but never reached the degree of polarization witnessed during the New Deal (Abramson, Aldrich, and Rhode 1991, 139-141).

In summary, just as Lipset (1960) previously claimed that class voting was a common aspect of electoral politics in most democracies, one can now make an equal claim that a decline of class voting is a common characteristic of these same party systems. Even the class-based rhetoric that has accompanied recent global recessions in the early 1980s and again in the early 1990s has not revived class voting differences in the United States or other Western democracies. This result presents something of a paradox, because social class still has a clear and direct effect on individuals' life chances (Phillips 1990; Thurow 1987; Korpi 1983); the likelihood of university education, future employment, and even lifestyle choices. Yet, there has been an attenuation of the specific linkage between social class and electoral politics.

Given that class voting has been one of the most broadly analyzed aspects of modern electoral research, forecasts of its imminent demise have generated substantial academic discussion and debate. One line of research argues that a crude dichotomous measure of social class does not capture the present complexity of social structure, and thus misses the continued relevance of class cues to voting. John Goldthorpe (1980), for example, proposed a new categorization of social class incorporating notions of job autonomy and authority relationships into traditional class criteria such as income level and manual labor. Other scholars have used occupational titles to create an expanded list of class categories that incorporate new social contexts, such as the new middle class or affluent blue-collar worker (Robertson 1984; Heath et al. 1985, 1991; Pappi 1990).

The reconceptualization of social class implies that social cues now function in more complex and differentiated ways than in the past. Yet the empirical reality remains: even these complex class frameworks have only a modest value in explaining how citizens vote. Rose and McAllister (1986, 50-51) compare several of these alternative models to British voting behavior in the 1983 election and find that all explain a very modest share of the vote.

Another response to the decline of class voting has been to explore criteria other than employment as potential new bases of socioeconomic cleavage. Some researchers have suggested that education might form the basis of a political cleavage separating the information-rich and technologically sophisticated from the information-poor and unskilled voter (Allardt 1968; Huntington 1968). Others have argued that conflicts between the public and private sectors are supplanting traditional class conflicts (Dunleavy and Husbands 1985). Some of the most innovative recent research attempts to define social position in terms of lifestyle characteristics, distinguishing between industrial employees and yuppies, for example (Gluchowski 1987; Hammond 1986; Delli Carpini and Sigelman 1986).

Again, the limitation of these alternative approaches is their power in actually explaining voting behavior. Despite the frequent discussion of education as *the* political cleavage of advanced industrial societies, its impact on voting choice has paralleled the decline of social class voting. There is little empirical evidence, with the possible exception of lifestyle models, that these alternative structures are a significant influence on the electoral choice of many voters.

The Religious Cleavage

If social class was one of the main pillars of the sociological model, then religion was the other. Dating from before the Columbia studies, early empirical research on voting behavior found that religious affiliations were often strongly linked to voting choice.

Supporting that position, Richard Rose and Derek Urwin (1969) compared the social bases of voting in 16 nations and found that "religious divisions, not class, are the main social base of parties in the Western world today" (p. 12). It appeared that religious cues were strongly related to vote choice despite the lack of explicitly religious issues in most campaigns.

Despite the above-mentioned evidence of religious voting, there are indications that the religious cleavage is following the same pattern of decline as social class. In most Western democracies there has been a steady decline in religious involvement over the past 40 years (Harding 1986). In the Catholic nations of Europe, for instance, frequent church attendance has decreased by nearly half since the 1950s. Predominately Protestant countries, such as the United States and the nations of Northern Europe, began with lower levels of church involvement, but nevertheless have followed the same downward trend. By definition, this secularization trend means that fewer voters are integrated into religious networks and exposed to the religious cues that can guide the vote.

In addition to this trend of secularization, the link between religious leaders and political parties has also weakened in most Western democracies. A generation ago, it was routine for a Dutch priest or a German pastor to remind their congregation of what God expected of them at election time. Now, direct church involvement in partisan politics is more often viewed as an intrusion of church influence. The starkest change has occurred in the Netherlands, where in a single generation the rigid system of religiously based "pillars" was replaced by a system of predominately secular social and political relations (Andeweg 1982). To a more modest extent, a similar process of secularization and rapprochement between the churches and Leftist parties attenuated the political relevance of religion in Germany, France, Italy, and other nations where religion was once a strong influence on voting behavior.

One major exception to the secularization trend has been the recent political emergence of evangelical groups in the United States. Groups such as the Moral Majority represented the potential development of a new religious cleavage -- one that cuts across traditional denominations, dividing the electorate according to the extent of the fundamentalism of one's religious beliefs. Christian fundamentalists can best be defined in surveys as having an unquestioning view of the Bible and considering themselves as "born again." Employing television and other means of mass communication, evangelical leaders such as Pat Robertson (a Republican presidential candidate in 1988) have mobilized such people on the basis of new policy issues dealing with matters of morality and traditional family values (e.g., abortion, school prayer, pornography, etc.). Miller and

Wattenberg (1984) isolate a significant subset of the electorate for whom fundamentalist religious beliefs have become politicized. These politicized fundamentalists now form a group of such size and voting cohesion that they have come to play a major role in the Republican coalition, as witnessed by their prominence during the 1992 Republican national convention.[6] Still, longitudinal electoral studies fail to find a significant growth in the relationship between religion and vote choice; the impact of the fundamentalist revival is dwarfed by the ebb and flow of other electoral forces (Wald 1987; Abramson, Aldrich, and Rhode 1991, chap. 5).

The decline of sociologically based voting is most apparent for the class and religious cleavages, but a similar erosion of influence can be observed for most other sociological characteristics. In most Western democracies, urban/rural residence displays only modest differences in voting patterns, and these differences have generally narrowed as the forces of modernization decreased the gap between urban and rural lifestyles. Regional differences have occasionally flared up over the past generation, especially in Britain, Belgium, and Canada, but in most nations region exerts only a minor influence on voting preferences (Rose 1982; Clarke et al. 1980; Inglehart 1977, chap. 9). Despite repeated proclamations of an emerging gender gap, gender remains a minor factor in voting behavior (Klein 1984; Farah and Klein 1989; Falter and Schuman 1990). Perhaps the only exception to the rule of declining social cleavages is the case of race and ethnicity, in which one can identify pockets of solid partisan support -- such as blacks for the Democratic Party in the U.S. (Carmines and Stimson 1989) and the voting patterns of immigrant workers in Europe (Hoskin 1991).

When all the evidence is assembled, one of the most widely repeated findings of modern electoral research is the declining value of the sociological model of voting behavior. The rate and timing of this decline varies across nations, but the end product is the same (Franklin et al. 1992). In party systems like the United States and Japan, where social-group-based voting was initially weak, the decline has occurred slowly. In other electoral systems, such as Germany, the Netherlands, and Italy, where sharp social divisions once structured the vote, the decline has been steady and dramatic.

While the evidence is seldom in dispute, scholars do disagree on how to interpret the decline of socially based voting. The sociological model itself would suggest that cleavage-based voting emerges because parties need such frameworks to structure political competition and voters need such cues to simplify politics and guide their behavior. Thus, if older social cleavages are decaying, then we should look for newly emerging social cleavages to take their place. In the vernacular of this literature, the decline of established cleavages should lead to (or foretell) an eventual *partisan realignment* in which new social divisions come to structure the vote. Realignments have been a regular feature of American electoral politics for well over a century (Sundquist 1973). Similar realignments have occurred in European party systems, such as the ascendence of the British Labour Party in the early twentieth century, or the Gaullist realignment in the French party system of the late 1950s.

The weakness of this realignment scenario is that the old cleavage structure has been decaying for quite some time without a new alignment emerging in its place. In the United States, for example, political analysts have forecast an emerging new alignment at almost every presidential election for the last two decades (Phillips 1969; Miller and Levitin 1976; Chubb and Peterson 1985). Similarly, electoral volatility and partisan instability has increased in most European party systems since the mid-1970s. Recent elections generally perpetuate this fluidity with little evidence that the old system of stable group alignments will be recreated in a new form. If anything, the emergence of green parties in the early 1980s and radical right parties in the early 1990s signals an acceleration of past trends toward partisan fragmentation and volatility.

A contrasting interpretation of these developments has recently been offered by Mark Franklin and his colleagues (1992). They argue that the goal of democratic politics is to resolve political divisions that exist within societies. To the extent that social cleavages reflect broad-based and long-standing social and economic divisions within Western democracies, then the declining electoral relevance of these cleavages signals success in resolving these political divisions. A consensus on the welfare state, for instance, presumably resolved old political conflicts between socioeconomic groups, just as an equalization of living conditions may have eroded urban/rural differences, and so forth.

While this is an appealing explanation, especially as Western democracies bask in their new-found self-esteem with the collapse of the Soviet empire, it suffers from the same problem as earlier "End of Ideology" thesis. Although Western democracies have made substantial progress in meeting their long-term social goals, social and political divisions have *not* come to an end. The global recessions of the 1970s and early 1980s renewed economic problems in most Western industrial countries, and problems of poverty, the homeless, and mounting crime rates persist. Similarly, current political debates over abortion, homosexual rights, and other moral issues reflect the value differences underlying the religious cleavage. Ideology and political conflict have not ended -- they are as much a part of politics as ever.

We favor an explanation that links the decline in the sociological model to the declining relevance of fixed social characteristics for contemporary electoral politics. Social cues may still be a potent influence on voting behavior for people who are integrated into traditional class or religious networks and who share the values of these milieu -- but today there are fewer people who fit within such clear social categories. This partially reflects a fragmentation of life spaces. For instance, Huckfeldt and Kohfeld (1989) find that the constituency of the U.S. Democratic party is now split along class, racial, and value lines. It is a monumental task to unite such diverse constituencies at election time, and even more difficult to sustain agreement during the governing process. A similar fragmentation of constituencies has impacted on social democratic and conservative parties in Europe (Kitschelt n.d.).

The weakening of social characteristics also occurs because fewer people are integrated into stable social structures, such as the working-class milieu and religious networks that originally furnished the basis of the class and religious cleavages. There are simply fewer people who can rely on such ready cues as a surrogate for political decision making.

Furthermore, the broadening of political discourse to involve a wider range of political issues and the increasing exposure to other information sources, especially the electronic media, erodes the value of fixed social characteristics as a guide to electoral choice. Economic conflicts are still salient, for example, but social class is a poor guide to determining one's positions on issues such as tax reform, privatization of government services, or deficit spending. For the majority of the electorate, therefore, social position and the attendant social cues no longer provide a very useful shortcut to political decision making. It is not that voters do not have a social location (of course they do), or that voters cannot identify the parties in terms of traditional class positions (they can)[7] -- but that these cues are of decreasing relevance to contemporary politics.

Once these processes of social change begin to blur the lines of political cleavage, upon which many of the established parties were based, the parties are themselves forced to respond to these developments. As Przeworski and Sprague (1986) show, the numerical demise of the working class forced social democratic parties to soften their class image and look to new sources of support in the middle class. Similarly, attempts to broaden the sources of political support are occurring among conservative parties as they observe their past social bases of support eroding. In other words, the parties are contributing to the demise of cleavage voting by their need to compensate for the changing social bases of advanced industrial societies.

In summary, it is not that cleavages have become entirely irrelevant. They have lost their hold among many voters. And for those voters with continuing cleavage ties, social identities are being fragmented across a range of class, religious, ethnic, and other reference groups. The blurring of party images further erodes the value of social cues as a guide to behavior. Thus social change is ending the simple structure of political cleavages that once framed party competition and provided many voters with an easy method of making their electoral decisions.

Party Identification and Partisan Dealignment

Compared to sociological influences on voting, psychological attitudes are more proximate to the vote and hence more closely related to it. The psychological model maintains that partisanship is continually relevant, because most elections are partisan contests. Citizens must usually make judgments about which party best represents their interests, and these perceptions guide individual voting behavior. Partisanship provides a clear and low-cost voting cue for the sophisticated and unsophisticated voter alike. It is also quite a reliable cue, with a candidate's party affiliation normally indicating a policy program that the candidate espouses.

Surveys generally find a close relationship between partisanship and voting in elections, especially in parliamentary contests. For example, only 11% of British partisans defected from their preferred party in the 1979 election, and only 5% of West German partisans defected in 1983. This is to be expected because the limited voting opportunities in most European nations lessen the separation between partisanship and the vote. In contrast, the American voter is faced with federal, state, and local partisan choices to make simultaneously -- with the parties often standing for different points of view at different levels. Consequently, the separation between party identification and voting is most noticeable in American elections. A similar situation exists in French presidential elections, where the two-candidate runoff is decided by the size of the vote the candidates can attract from parties other than their own. Still, even in the case of these two presidential elections, partisanship has a strong influence on American and French voting patterns. In sum, party ties routinely are one of the strongest predictors of voting behavior.

Besides its clear impact on the vote, scholars have also attributed a great deal of theoretical importance to the role of party identification in guiding citizen behavior. As Almond and Verba (1963, 86) wrote in *The Civic Culture*, "Open and moderate partisanship, then, are essential to a stable democracy. They are the 'feeling correlates' of responsible majority and loyal opposition." Converse and Dupeux (1962) further argued that the likelihood of voters being attracted to "flash" parties and demagogic leaders -- such as the 1950s Poujadists in France or the supporters of Stanislaw Tyminski in the 1990 Polish presidential election -- is increased when many citizens fail to identify with one of the established parties. It is, of course, some sort of economic or cultural shock (such as economic crisis or the fall of communism) that opens the door for demagogic leaders. However, as Converse and Dupeux (1962) note, systems in which many voters do not have long-term partisan attachments are the most likely to be significantly affected.

In sum, widespread party attachments promote continuity in voting and reinforce the stability of the political process. If any change in this situation was foreseen by early researchers of the topic, it was a gradual strengthening of this partisanship model (e.g., Converse 1969).

It therefore came as some surprise when party ties abruptly began to weaken in many Western democracies during the 1970s. This development was initially seen as a temporary development opening the way for a new partisan alignment, but in many nations there has been an enduring erosion in partisan loyalties: a *partisan dealignment*. Credit for first using the term "dealignment" in print goes to Ronald Inglehart and Avram Hochstein (1972) for their article contrasting the patterns of partisan decay in the American system with the growth of partisanship in the French system of the late 1960s. Two years earlier, Walter Dean Burnham (1970) extensively analyzed what he called the "long-term electoral disaggregation" and "party decomposition" in the United States. While neither of Burnham's terms caught on among political scientists, "dealignment" stuck almost immediately.

Whereas realignment involves people changing from one party to another, dealignment concerns people gradually moving away from all parties. Many scholars express concern about potential dealignment trends because they fear the loss of the stabilizing, conserving equilibrium that party attachments provide to electoral systems. This is especially the case in the United States, where political parties have always been uniquely weak in comparison to parliamentary systems.[8] Because dealignment in the United States differs in both form and magnitude from that of the parliamentary democracies, we shall treat it separately.

The Decline of Partisanship in the United States

Mountains of survey evidence attest to Americans' declining concern with partisanship and the role of political parties in U.S. government. Some of the most frequently cited indicators are the rise of split-ticket voting, the decline of party identification, and the increase in neutral attitudes toward the parties -- each of which will be discussed in this section.

Behind all these trends is the pervasive American belief that one should vote for the person, not the party. Even in 1956, when most people were still voting straight tickets, 74% of respondents in a Gallup poll agreed with this general belief; by 1968 this figure had risen to 84% (Dennis 1975). Most recently, a survey by Sabato (1988) found 92% agreeing with the statement, "I always vote for the person who I think is best, regardless of what party they belong to."

With such public opinion data, it can now be said that the principle of putting candidate ahead of party in voting has become a part of the American consensus. One reason is that political parties are not perceived as particularly meaningful in American politics. Indeed, a large percentage of Americans sees little need for parties altogether. Forty-five percent of the 1980 election study sample agreed that "it would be better if, in all elections, we put no party labels on the ballot." Most striking is that 30% agreed with the extreme statement, "the truth is we probably don't need political parties anymore."

Not only have voters increasingly said that they vote for the person rather than the party; they have actually done so with great frequency. Analysis of American voting patterns over the course of the twentieth century clearly reveals a steady trend away from party-line voting. As Burnham (1991) has shown, the shared variance between a state's vote for president and its vote for Senate, House, and governor has declined continuously throughout this century. He finds that at the turn of the century one could almost perfectly predict how a state would vote for Congress and governor by its vote for president. By mid-century a state often followed the same pattern in voting for president as for other offices, but with a fair number of exceptions. By the 1980s, knowing a state's presidential vote was virtually no help in predicting its vote for other offices.

These results are far from academic. They can clearly be seen in the unprecedented level of split party control of both the federal and state governments in recent years. In 1988 only 40% of the states had one party in control of both legislative houses and the governor's office (see Fiorina 1992). Not since the formation of the Republican Party in the 1850s can one find any comparable split in the history of state party politics. Similarly, for the period between 1981 and 1986 different parties controlled the House and Senate for the first time since 1916. Most visible, of course, has been the division in partisan control of the presidency and the Congress since 1952. From 1952 to 1992 the same party controlled the presidency and the House for just 14 out of 40 years.

It would be an overstatement, though, to infer that even a majority of voters are now splitting their tickets between major federal offices. Rather, ticket-splitting between presidential and House voting has risen from 14% in 1960 to a high of 34% in 1980. (Because any vote for Ross Perot is by definition a split-ticket vote, the figure for 1992 will be even higher than in 1980.) Some have argued that such behavior is simply due to the nomination of presidential candidates whom many party identifiers could not support. Yet secular increases can also be found in measures that do not involve presidential voting, such as voting for House and Senate candidates of different parties. A 1990 study of voting behavior in Ohio found that a majority of the electorate voted for different parties in choosing five statewide officials (Beck et al. 1992).

Given the current American preference for voting the person rather than the party, there is good reason to expect that split-ticket voting may reach even higher levels in the future. The attitudinal potential for ticket-splitting has consistently been greater than its incidence, and one can reasonably interpret recent trends as reflecting the tendency for behaviors to eventually come into line with attitudes.

Accompanying the trend toward greater split-ticket voting has been a decline in party identification. Election studies during the period 1952-1964 found that approximately 75% of the electorate identified themselves as either Democrat or Republican. By 1972 the percentage of respondents identifying with one of the parties had dropped to 64%. What once appeared to be a continuing downward spiral no longer seems to be such, but instead a limited period effect in which there was a rapid decline followed by the development of a new, somewhat lower, level of stability. Since 1972 the proportion of the population identifying with one of the parties during presidential elections has held steady at between 63% and 65%. As the number of Democratic identifiers declined during the 1980s, the result was that by 1988 more people identified themselves as independents than anything else (see Wattenberg 1990, 140).

Some scholars have argued that the decline in party identification has been vastly exaggerated, because independents who report that they think of themselves as "closer" to one of the two parties have still been considered nonpartisans (Keith et al. 1992). According to these scholars, the so-called independent leaners are not an uncommitted and unmobilized bloc, but are instead largely "closet" Democrats and Republicans. Although they may prefer to call themselves independents rather than Democrats or Republicans, when it comes to their voting behavior in presidential elections they tend to act no differently than weak party identifiers. If one considers independent leaners as simply partisans by another name, then the proportion of the population identifying with a party can hardly be said to have declined at all over the years.

This argument was first introduced by Keith et al. in a 1977 APSA convention paper, and immediately became influential in the field. Ironically, the book that evolved from the 1977 paper, Keith et al.'s *The Myth of the Independent Voter*, was released for publication in June of 1992 -- just when Ross Perot was leading in the public opinion polls. If ever there was a solid demonstration of the independence of American voters, the Perot phenomenon would be it. Analyzing the 19% of the electorate who voted for Perot, as well as the even greater percentage who at one point intended to vote for him, will no doubt be a prime topic for American voting behavior scholars in the coming years.

One theory concerning the meaning of party identification that is likely to get renewed attention in light of the Perot phenomenon is the multidimensionality of party identification (see Valentine and Van Wingen 1980; Weisberg 1980; Kamieniecki 1985). This perspective holds that the standard party identification measure taps two separate dimensions: 1) preference for the Democrats versus the Republicans; and 2) feelings of political independence. Rather than thinking of independent leaners as "closet partisans," this theory portrays them as people who have genuine feelings of independence, but who also maintain a general party preference. As Weisberg (1980) shows, many people who say they suppport one of the parties also report that they consider themselves political independents. Whereas Keith et al. (1992) regard the increase in independent leaners as inconsequential given their regular support for their preferred party, the multidimensionality theory would lead one to expect these voters to be more prone to support candidates such as Perot.

Yet another theory that could explain the growing volatility of the electorate is the dissipation of party images (see Wattenberg 1990). This theory holds that political parties have been declining in relevance to the American public for several decades due to changes in political communication and the way campaigns are now run. The best, supporting empirical evidence comes from open-ended questions asking people what they like and dislike about the two parties. Since 1952 the proportion of the electorate that can be classified as having a neutral view of both parties has increased gradually from 13% in 1952 to an average of 34% in the 1980s. Virtually all of these individuals said that they neither liked nor disliked *anything* about the Democratic and Republican parties.

In Eisenhower's and Kennedy's eras, such a response pattern typically reflected general political ignorance. Most of these people had little to say about the candidates as well, and few voted. For instance, 84% of them in the 1960 NES sample were classified as "no issue content" on Converse's (1964) classic measure of levels of conceptualization. In contrast, in 1984 only 44% of those who had nothing to say about the parties failed to mention an issue when they were asked about the candidates. In the 1980s such individuals have tuned out the parties but not necessarily the candidates and the issues. Indeed, they are often considered the most important group in American electoral politics --"the floating voters" -- presumably a group that was particularly open to the Perot appeal.

To summarize, many American voters now view parties as a convenience rather than a necessity. Yet, regardless of whether the American public recognizes it or not, parties are necessities for structuring the vote. Political scientists have long recognized the indispensable functions performed by parties, and dealignment has only reinforced this view. As Dalton, Flanagan, and Beck (1984, 462) write, "Unless elections become purely contests of personalities, parties are likely to continue to play an important role in structuring political choices, even in a purely dealigned and issue-oriented electorate." In parliamentary systems, this is far more obvious, and we now turn our attention to these systems.

The Decline of Partisanship Outside the United States

Despite the conceptual and empirical value of party identification in American research, its export to other democracies initially highlighted the uniqueness of the American electoral system. In Britain, for example, Butler and Stokes (1969) found that it was difficult to separate party attachments from present voting intentions. Other scholars similarly found that it was hard to disentangle partisanship and the vote in parliamentary systems (Borre 1984; Baker et al. 1981). In addition, researchers noted that the concept of partisan "independence" was a distinct American political tradition without a clear equivalent in most parliamentary systems (Budge et al. 1976).

Still, most studies agreed that voters held some sort of party allegiances that endure over time and strongly influence other attitudes and behaviors (Miller 1976). The major problem appeared to be one of measurement: finding an equivalent measure of partisanship in multiparty parliamentary systems or in nations where the term "partisan" held different connotations. One could not simply translate the American party identification question into French or German; one had to find a functional equivalent for the concept of partisan attachments.[9] The resulting measures of partisanship appeared to display many of the same political functions as partisanship in the United States. (Baker et al. 1981; Gluchowski 1983; Converse and Pierce 1986; Butler and Stokes 1974).

Having established the validity of partisanship to European electoral research, trend studies in several nations began to find evidence of a weakening of partisan ties that was remarkably similar to the partisan dealignment in the United States. Over 40% of the British public were strong partisans during the late 1960s; this percentage was cut in half within less than a decade (Saarlvik and Crewe 1983; Abramson 1992). Partisan ties initially strengthened in postwar Germany as the party system grew along with the nation's democratic experience, but in the 1980s German attachments to the political parties also began to weaken (Dalton 1992). Longitudinal data from national election studies in France, the Netherlands, Italy, Scandinavia, and Australia display a similar erosion in the strength of party attachments over the past decades (Dalton et al. 1984; McAllister 1992; cf. Schmitt 1989 for an opposing view.)

The symptoms of partisan dealignment are visible in these nations in other ways beyond the public's attachments to the parties. For instance, the erosion of partisanship is visible in the declining stability of voting patterns (Crewe and Denver 1985). In addition, many of these voters have the same doubts about political parties that are harbored by American voters. Peter Gluchowski (1983), for example, found that a significant minority of Germans view parties as mere electoral conveniences. Finally, there has been a decrease in voting turnout in some Western democracies (see below), which is at least partially the result of weakened partisanship.

What is stunning about these findings, as with the weakening of the sociological model, is the relative simultaneity of political trends in various electoral systems. There are several explanations for the spreading pattern of partisan dealignment. One factor involves the declining role of parties as political institutions. Many of the parties' traditional input functions have been taken over by other institutions. A myriad of special-interest groups and single-issue lobbies have developed in recent years, and which are organizing to press their interests without relying on partisan channels. Similarly, the mass media are assuming many of the information and input functions that political parties once controlled. Party leaders are even losing some control over the selection of elected party representatives. The most advanced example is the United States, where the expansion of open primaries and nonpartisan elections undermined the parties' hold on recruitment. The British Labour party has experienced a similar shift in nomination power away from the party in Parliament to party conventions and local constituency groups. And in Israel in 1992, an American-style primary was held to choose the leader of the Labor party, and the Likud followed with a similar primary in 1993. These and other developments lessen the importance of parties in the political process and therefore weaken the significance of parties as political reference points.

Partisan dealignment is also encouraged by the failure of parties to deal successfully with contemporary political controversies, ranging from economic issues to the environment and other quality of life issues. On the one hand, many European parties remain rigidly committed to outdated policies on the economic and welfare issues associated with the traditional class cleavage. On the other hand, the agenda of advanced industrial societies often appears unsuited for mass political parties. Many of these new issues -- such as nuclear energy, minority rights, university reform, or local environmental problems -- are too narrow to affect mass partisan alignments on their own. The rise of single-issue interests does not translate well into partisan attachments, because of the uncertain electoral impact of these issues and the difficulty of accommodating these issues within large political coalitions. In the United States, this has led to a proliferation of citizen interest groups and direct action politics; in Europe this has spawned similar groups as well as a variety of small green and libertarian parties (Mueller-Rommel 1989). Thus the larger established parties are not entirely fulfilling their critical programmatic function of aggregating and articulating political interests.

The decline of partisanship also appears to have a distinct generational component in most nations, suggesting that changes in the political environment are contributing to these trends. In the United States, it may have been the dramatic political events of the 1970s that turned many young people away from political parties. The anti-partisan sentiments stirred by the Vietnam War, Watergate, and similar crises kept new voters from developing the early-life partisan attachments which then could build over time (Beck 1984). Another interpretation is that the events *per se* were not as important as the candidate-centered way in which they were presented (Wattenberg 1990). With an emphasis on the actions of leaders rather than on parties, young voters failed to see any need to affiliate with a party.

In some nations, generational differences in partisanship also may reflect the growing ability of younger and better educated voters to manage the complexity of politics without relying on inherited party leanings. This interpretation of partisan dealignment is supported by the pattern of weakening party ties. For instance, educational level is significantly related to dealignment in Britain. Between 1964 and 1974, the decrease in partisanship among British citizens with advanced education was three times as great as among those with minimal education (Alt 1984; for the United States see Beck 1984; for Germany see Dalton and Rohrschneider 1990). An extension of these analyses presents cross-national evidence of a new kind of nonpartisan in advanced industrial societies (Dalton 1984; Inglehart 1990, chap. 10). These *apartisans* are sophisticated and active citizens who remain unattached to any political party. In contrast to the traditional partisan independents, who were uninformed and uninvolved in politics, apartisans are active participants (though often outside party-related activities such as campaigns and elections). These new independents are also less consistent in their voting patterns because voting behavior is not dependent on long-standing party predispositions. Because apartisans are concentrated among the young, the better educated, and citizens with postmaterial values, the continuing socioeconomic development of advanced industrial societies may reinforce the dealignment trend that has emerged over the past decade.

These on-going debates about the nature and role of party identification suggest several priority areas for future research. First, rather than the static view of partisanship offered by *The American Voter*, current research recognizes the dynamic properties of partisanship. Party attachment is both a socialized political orientation *and* a summation of accumulated electoral experiences through one's adult life (Fiorina 1981; Jennings and Markus 1984; MacKuen et al. 1990; cf. Abramson and Ostrom 1991).[10] In most instances adult electoral experiences reinforce early learning, and partisanship therefore strengthens with the passage of time. But we are witnessing a period when dominant patterns of electoral change often are retarding the development of partisanship. Determining the relative mix of stability and change in forming current partisan attachments has important implications for how we view partisanship as a guide to individual political behavior.

Once we accept that partisanship is a changeable political orientation, this prompts a revival of early research focusing on the functional basis of partisanship. Several scholars have focused on the distinction between affectively-based partisanship, that might be socialized early in life and relatively immune to subsequent change, versus cognitively-based partisanship, that is more likely to reflect current political beliefs (Miyake 1991; Wattenberg 1991; Gluchowski 1983; Richardson 1991).

Similarly, research on the (diminished) functional value of partisanship for the politically informed and issue-oriented apartisans will be an important part of this debate.

Finally, cross-national patterns of societal changes and the generational nature of partisan dealignment suggest that greater partisan fluidity will be a continuing feature of electoral politics in most advanced industrial democracies.[11] Realignment theorists have now waited nearly a generation for a new partisan order to establish itself; how much longer should we wait? We think it is unlikely that contemporary electoral systems will return to the stable, structured patterns of the past, in which social characteristics and an enduring sense of partisanship determined electoral behavior. With less reliance being placed on these simplifying guides for party choice, the question of how satisficing voters actually make their decisions becomes even more important.

The Resurgence of the Rational Voter Model

As the electoral impact of both sociological factors and long-term psychological determinants has eroded, many political scientists have emphasized a corresponding increase in the influence of issue opinions and candidate preferences on voting choices. These short-term factors have often been treated within the framework of the rational voter approach first introduced in Downs's classic *Economic Theory of Democracy*. This approach portrays the average voter as able to assess current political concerns such as party platforms, past performance, and candidate competence better than the voters portrayed in the Columbia and Michigan studies. This section examines the resurgence of the rational voter model, as seen through the evidence for issue and candidate voting.

Issue Voting

The study of issue voting has been closely intertwined with the scholarly debate on the political sophistication of contemporary publics that was discussed earlier in this chapter; researchers thus often differ in their evaluation of the extent of issue voting. In the 1950s the authors of *The American Voter* stressed that only a small percentage of the American electorate relied on issues to decide their votes (Campbell et al. 1960, chap. 6). *The Changing American Voter* challenged this claim, however, arguing that voters in more recent years had become more sophisticated about issues and better able to use policy positions to gauge alternatives (Nie et al. 1976). Their analysis, in turn, has been challenged by many scholars (see Bishop et al. 1979; Sullivan et al. 1978; Smith 1989). In a rejoinder, other research argues that poor question wording and other methodological shortcomings led early researchers to significantly underestimate the role that issues could play in voting behavior whether or not the electorate has changed over time (see Niemi and Weisberg 1993a, chap. 4).

Regardless of whether voters are now more sophisticated about the issues, the unquestioned decline in long-term forces shaping the vote has increased at least the *potential* for issue voting. For if social cues and partisanship are less central in electoral decision making, then voters must be turning to other factors -- such as issues and candidates -- to make their political decisions. Thus, Mark Franklin (1985) showed that the decreasing influence of long-term forces on British voting decisions was counterbalanced by an increased impact of issues on the vote (also Baker et al. 1981, chap. 10; van der Eijk and Niemoeller 1983; Budge and Farlie 1983). In reviewing the findings from a recent comparative study of voting in seven Western democracies, Franklin (1992, 400) goes one step further, concluding: if all the issues of importance to voters had been measured and given their due weight, then the rise of issue voting would have compensated more or less precisely for the decline in cleavage politics."

One problem hampering the comparative study of issue voting, either across time or across nations, is the variability of issues across elections and across voters. One campaign might emphasize economic conflicts, and the next might stress questions of candidate competence. Moreover, there are a variety of issues that might influence the voting choices of contemporary electorates. Elections are seldom dominated by a single issue. Thus the impact of any one issue for the entire public is often modest because not even all the informed voters will be interested in it.

Although the issues of each specific election campaign are different, the general impact of policy preferences on voting behavior can be estimated by examining the relationship between Left/Right (or liberal/conservative) attitudes and the vote. Such ideological positions can be described as a sort of "super issue"; that is, a statement of positions on the issues that are currently most important to each voter (Inglehart 1984). Pamela Conover and Stanley Feldman (1981) see Left/Right images at the core of many political schema (also see Kerlinger 1984; Murphy et al. 1981; Rohrschneider 1992). Dieter Fuchs and Hans-Dieter Klingemann (1990) find that the citizens' interpretation of Left and Right changes over time to reflect the changing nature of political agenda. Furthermore, Downs

conceived of such political labels as a way to reduce information costs, rather than the fully informed ideological orientations presumed by his critics (Stokes 1966). As he explained (Downs 1957, 98), "With this shortcut a voter can save himself the cost of being informed upon a wide range of issues." The labels of "Left" and "Right" help voters in interpreting a wide range of political phenomena. The ability to think of oneself in Left/Right terms does not imply that citizens possess any sophisticated abstract framework or theoretical dogma. For many individuals, Left/Right attitudes are simply a kind of summary statement of their positions.

Studies in numerous countries consistently find that most citizens can position themselves along a Left/Right scale, and these attitudes are linked to specific policy views (Klingemann 1979; Inglehart 1984). In addition, when asked to place the major parties on such a scale, the mean placements are fairly accurate portrayals of actual party positions (also see Castles 1982). While some voters clearly guess at the Left/Right questions, there is much evidence to support the expected pattern of left-wing voters supporting leftist parties and vice versa.

Beginning with this observed relationship, research has moved in two different directions to extend these analyses. One approach has examined the changing meaning of "Left," "Right," and other political symbols to Western publics, in order to trace the changing bases of issue competition in Western democracies (e.g., Fuchs and Klingemann 1990). Most prominent in this literature has been the argument that the basis of issue voting is gradually but systematically shifting from the economic and security issues that arose from the class cleavage and social divisions to the new post-material issues of advanced industrial societies (Inglehart 1990; Dalton et al. 1984; Miller and Levitin 1976). Indeed, the rise of these cross-cutting issue interests is inevitably linked to the erosion of previous social cleavages (Knutsen 1987).

Ironically, this research on "new" issues has been paralleled by a revived interest in government economic performance as a basis for voting choice. Downs does mention performance considerations, but only as secondary considerations in assessing utility income. In his model, "performance ratings enter a voter's decision making whenever he thinks both parties have the same platforms and current policies" (Downs 1957, 44). Rational choice theorists who followed Downs have often reversed priorities, concentrating on the lowered information costs associated with performance as opposed to ideological factors. Given the public's limited attentiveness to politics, these theorists argue that it is sensible for most voters to pay more attention to results than to means. Fiorina (1981, 5) puts it best when he states that citizens "typically have one comparatively hard bit of data: they know what life has been like during the incumbent's administration. They do not need to know the precise economic or foreign policies of the incumbent administration in order to judge the results of those policies." In other words, performance-based voting offers people a reasonable shortcut for ensuring that unsuccessful policies are dropped and successful policies continued.

Of course, one counterargument is that policies may be reversed as seeming failures when in fact they had little to do with subsequent developments. Nevertheless, this literature argues that it is only important that voters dispense electoral rewards and punishments--regardless of whether the policies and the outcomes are truly connected. Benjamin Page (1978, 222), for example, writes that "even if the Great Depression and lack of recovery were not at all Hoover's fault ... it could make sense to punish him in order to sharpen the incentives to maintain prosperity in the future." Acknowledging that blame may be placed unfairly, he notes, "To err on the side of forgiveness would leave voters vulnerable to tricky explanations and rationalizations; but to err on the draconian side would only spur politicians on to greater energy and imagination in problem solving."

Therefore, what is crucial to performance voting is that voters have a target for their blame when the government falters in some respect. Typically, this is due to poor economic performance, and the literature on economic voting has burgeoned in recent years. Much evidence exists to document the importance of macroeconomics on micropolitics, both in the United States (Tufte 1978; Kiewiet 1983; Rosenstone 1983; Markus 1988) and Europe (Lewis-Beck 1988; Clark and Whitely 1990; Norpoth and Lewis-Beck 1991; Norpoth 1992).

If the importance of economically based evaluations of parties and candidates seems non-controversial, the evidence on the exact scope and nature of this influence remains a point of debate. One point of debate concerns whether voters base their political evaluations on their own personal economic situation (egocentric voting) or the performance of the broader national economy (sociotropic voting). Most of the evidence seems to suggest that voters follow the sociotropic model, which implies that policy outcomes rather than narrow self-interest is the driving force behind performance voting (Kinder and Kiewiet 1981; Kiewiet 1983; Lewis-Beck 1988). Researchers also disagree on whether voters evaluate past economic performance retrospectively or base their judgments on prospective expectations for the economy's future performance (see Fiorina 1981; Miller and Wattenberg 1985; MacKuen, Erickson, and Stimson 1992).

It is now the accepted wisdom that incumbent parties are virtually impossible to beat during strong economic upturns and extremely vulnerable during recessionary periods. So important is the state of the economy that it can override other policy considerations. For example, many analysts have argued that right-wing governments in Great Britain and the United States were elected to office in 1979 and 1980, respectively, not for ideological reasons but merely because they were the only instrument available for defeating incumbents who had failed to deliver the economic goods (Crewe and Searing 1988; Wattenberg 1991). Four years after coming to power, both Margaret Thatcher and Ronald Reagan were able to win reelection on the basis of improved economic performance (and the Falklands War in the case of Thatcher) -- in spite of continuing policy differences with the majority of their country's voters.

While such a scenario for electoral change may not conform to democratic theory's emphasis on policy evaluation, it is defended as entirely rational by proponents of retrospective voting (Key 1966; Fiorina 1981). Does it make sense, they would ask, to pay much attention to the positions of an ineffective administration that seemingly cannot make good on its promises and program? Retrospective voting theorists emphasize that the only really effective weapon of popular control in a democratic regime is the electorate's capacity to throw a party from power.

Candidate Evaluations

While issues have always been thought of as desirable influences on the vote, candidate evaluations have traditionally been viewed less positively by electoral analysts. Voting on the basis of personality characteristics has often been viewed in the literature as "irrational" (cf. Converse 1964; Page 1978). The popular cynical view of candidates is that they are attractively packaged commodities devised by image makers who manipulate the public's perceptions by emphasizing traits with special appeal to the voters. People's judgments about alternative candidates are, in this view, based on superficial criteria such as the candidate's style or looks (e.g., Sullivan and Masters 1988). Indeed, Rosenberg and McCafferty (1987) show that it is possible to manipulate a candidate's personal appearance in a way that affects voters' choices. Holding a candidate's issue stands and party identification constant, they find that when good pictures are substituted for bad ones, a candidate's vote-getting ability is significantly increased. Although a laboratory setting may not be representative of the real world, Rosenberg and McCafferty (1987, 44) conclude that "with appropriate pretesting and adequate control over a candidate's public appearance, a campaign consultant should be able to significantly manipulate the image projected to the voting public."

Recently, a very different approach to candidate assessments has begun to appear in the literature. This emerging theory holds that candidate evaluations are not necessarily superficial, emotional, or purely short-term. Voters may focus on the personal qualities of a candidate to gain important information about characteristics relevant to assessing how the individual will perform in office (Kinder et al. 1980; Kinder 1986; Miller et al. 1986; Rahn et al. 1990). This new approach is largely based on the premise that individuals organize their thoughts about other people into broad preexisting categories. These category "prototypes" are then used in making judgments when only limited factual information is available. Kinder et al. (1980), for example, explore the features that may define an ideal president. They find that people can choose attributes they believe would make for an ideal president, but that these prototypic conceptions are related only to ratings of the incumbent president.

Miller et al. (1986) also present data to support a rational voter interpretation of candidate evaluations. They argue that "candidate assessments actually concentrate on instrumental concerns about the manner in which a candidate would conduct governmental affairs" (p. 536). Analyzing open-ended like/dislike data about the candidates from the American National Election Studies, they find that the three most important dimensions of candidate image for Americans are integrity, reliability, and competence. Such criteria are hardly irrational, for if a candidate is too incompetent to carry out policy promises, or too dishonest for those promises to be trusted, it makes perfect sense for a voter to pay more attention to personality than policies. Interestingly, both Glass (1985) and Miller et al. (1986) find that college-educated voters are the most likely to view the candidates in terms of their personal attributes.

The importance of performance-relevant criteria, such as competence and integrity, has also been shown for leader evaluations in the parliamentary systems of Canada (Brown et al. 1988), Australia and New Zealand (Bean n.d.). Whereas early electoral research on parliamentary systems tended to suggest that the impact of party leader images on voting behavior was very minor (Butler and Stokes 1969; Aitkin 1977), more recent research has found significant effects. Bean and Mughan (1989) find that the perceived effectiveness of party leaders was moderately important in the British election of 1983 and possibly decisive in the Australian election of 1987. This "Americanization" of parliamentary elections can also be found somewhat at the level of constituency candidates. Cain, Ferejohn, and Fiorina (1987) find

some evidence for the "personal vote" in Great Britain, although to a much lesser extent than in the United States--where incumbency advantage has recently risen to all-time heights at the congressional level (Fiorina 1989). In Japan's unique multi-member constituencies, Bradley Richardson (1988) has found that partisanship clearly outweighs candidate images in voting behavior, but nevertheless the role of candidates is substantial.

Perhaps the best place to look for candidate effects in voting behavior in the near future is in the newly democratizing countries of Eastern Europe. Unfamiliar with the concept of competing political parties, much less many of the individual parties themselves, the voters of these fledgling democracies have little to guide their decisions. One factor for them to fall back on is thus the most visible feature of the new parties--their leaders. This is especially likely to be the case when parties form around leaders as opposed to leaders emerging from a party organization. The fact that many of the new Eastern European democracies provide for the direct election of a president will no doubt facilitate a focus on the individual leaders such as Vaclav Havel and Lech Walesa. Like American voters, who have been set adrift without the anchoring of partisanship, we expect the citizens of Eastern Europe to focus their choices on the character and competence of the contenders for leadership posts. Certainly, this should be an important focus for comparative voting behavior studies in the near future.

Who Votes?

The preceding sections of this chapter have examined the factors influencing people's decisions on how to vote, but there is an earlier decision that citizens must make: whether to vote in the first place. The dramatic events of the past few years suggest that the value of the ballot is seen differently depending on the individual and the political context. In Eastern Europe, citizens swarmed to the polls when first given the chance to vote in free elections, with turnout rates as high as 93% in East Germany in 1990. In contrast, in the well-established industrialized democracies the opportunity to vote is all too often taken for granted by many citizens. This is particularly true in the United States, where turnout in 1992 was a mere 55%.

To put these recent events into perspective, Table 1 presents the rates in voting turnout for the 21 industrialized democracies from the 1950s to the 1980s. One obvious feature in these data is the sharp cross-national differences in participation levels that exist among democratic polities. In the United States and Switzerland, for instance, participation in national elections involves barely half of the eligible adults; in several European nations participation is nearly universal.

Table 1.   Changes in Turnout From the 1950s to 1980s

	1950s	1960s	1970s	1980s[a]
Australia	90	93	93	91
Austria	94	93	93	90
Belgium	88	86	86	87
Canada	74	77	73	73
Denmark	82	87	86	86
Finland	86	85	78	75
France	75	75	81	70
Germany (West)	84	85	90	86
Iceland	89	90	89	88
Ireland	74	74	76	74
Israel	78	80	78	78
Italy	90	90	89	84
Japan	76	80	78	78
Luxembourg	88	84	84	83
Netherlands	93	93	83	84
New Zealand	91	88	85	89
Norway	78	83	82	83
Sweden	78	86	90	90
Switzerland	68	63	53	47
United Kingdom	80	76	75	74
United States	61	62	54	52

Source: Mackie and Rose (1990) and data collected by the authors.

[a] Figures represent the average in each decade for each country for elections to the lower house in the case of parliamentary systems and the presidency in the U.S.

Low levels of turnout in the United States have been in evidence throughout most of the twentieth century and are often cited as proof of the electorate's limited political involvement. But a more complex set of factors is at work (Powell 1980, 1986; Jackman 1987; Verba et al. 1978). Voter registration systems and other electoral procedures are a major influence on transatlantic differences in turnout. Most European citizens are automatically included on the roster of registered voters, and these electoral registers are updated by the government. Thus a much larger percentage of the European public is registered to participate in elections. In contrast, most Americans must take the initiative to register themselves to vote, which for one reason or another many eligible voters fail to do. By most estimates, participation in American elections would increase by at least ten percentage points if the European system of registration was adopted (Wolfinger and Rosenstone 1980). Turnout also is encouraged by the scheduling of most European elections on weekends, when more voters can find the time to visit the polls. In addition, most European electoral systems are based on proportional representation (PR) rather than plurality-based single-member districts, as in the United States. Proportional representation is generally believed to stimulate turnout because any party, large or small, can increase its representation in the legislature as a direct function of its share of the popular vote.

G. Bingham Powell (1980, 1986) and Markus Crepaz (1990) demonstrate that political competition is another strong influence on turnout rates. Sharp social or ideological cleavages between parties tend to stimulate turnout. The more polarized European party systems generally encourage higher voting rates than found in the United States. When European voters go to the polls they are deciding on whether or not their country will be run by parties with socialist goals or alternatively by conservative and, in some cases, religious parties. The consequences of their votes for redistribution of income and the general orientation of the government are far greater than the impact the ordinary American voter can expect. Robert Jackman (1987) has conducted complementary analyses which show that the structural incentives for voting strongly affect turnout rates. He finds that the number of party choices and the structure of legislative power in a system are direct predictors of turnout.

A final difference between the United States and most other democracies is that the American government asks its citizens to vote far more often. While the typical European voter may be called upon to cast two or three ballots in a four-year period, many Americans are faced with a dozen or more separate elections in the space of four years. Furthermore, Americans are expected to vote for a much wider range of political offices. With one elected official for about every 500 citizens, and elections held somewhere virtually every week, it is no wonder that it is so difficult to get Americans to the polls. In contrast, local, regional, and even national elections in Europe and Japan normally consist of casting just a single ballot for a single office; the extensive list of elected offices and long ballots common to American elections are unknown in Western Europe and Japan. Thus, a distinctive aspect of American politics is the demands it places upon the voter to make political decisions on an array of political offices, government bond and tax proposals, and other policy initiatives. Making decisions in low-information contests, such as voting for local non-partisan offices, is a distinct challenge for American voters. It is probably no coincidence that the one European country that has a comparable turnout level to the United States -- Switzerland -- has also overwhelmed its citizens with voting opportunities, calling 89 national elections in the period between 1947 and 1975 (for other reasons why Swiss turnout is so low, see Powell 1982, 119).

Rather than counting only the number of people who vote in national elections, an alternative measure of participation suggests we focus on the amount of electing being done by the public (Crewe 1981). When the context of American elections is considered, the amount of electing is actually quite high. No country can approach the United States in the frequency and variety of elections, and thus in the amount of electoral participation that actually takes place. No other country elects its lower house as often as every two years, or its president as frequently as every four years. No other country popularly elects its state governors and town mayors, or has as wide a variety of nonrepresentative offices (judges, sheriffs, attorneys general, city treasurers, and so on) subject to election. Only one other country (Switzerland) can compete in the number and variety of local referenda, and only two (Belgium and Turkey) hold party "primaries" in most parts of the country.[12] Even if differences in turnout rates are taken into account, American citizens do not necessarily vote less often than other nationalities; most probably, they do more voting (Crewe 1981, 262).

The other significant pattern in Table 1 is the trend in participation rates over time. Comparing the two end points, one finds that ten of the countries have experienced turnout declines of more than 2%, eight have had virtually stable turnout levels, and three have witnessed a turnout increase of more than 2%. Thus, if there is any predominant pattern in voting participation in recent decades, it is one of declining turnout.

The decline in electoral participation presents a paradox. Education, access to political information, political interest, and sophistication have generally been rising in recent decades, and it has long been established that such indicators are related to turnout. Why then is participation in national elections declining if the public's general level of political involvement is increasing?

Each of the three main theories of voting behavior -- sociological, psychological, and economic -- can offer an answer to this puzzle. Sociological factors are linked to life conditions and other factors that increase (or decrease) one's ability to cope with the demands of electoral politics. For instance, as citizens age they accumulate experience with political issues, as well as a greater stake in the community. Thus, turnout rates are linked to the age composition of the electorate. Psychological factors can provide the motivation to go to the polls. Interest in politics is strongly related to turnout, though turnout has been declining while interest has been rising.

Probably the least useful theory in understanding turnout is the economic one. Given the infinitesimal chance that an individual has to actually decide an election, the benefits of voting are so small that they will always be outweighed by the costs (Wuffle 1984). The economic model generally functions by assuming that by exercising one's citizen duty one contributes to the maintenance of the regime (Enelow and Hinich 1990; Riker and Ordeshook 1968). Still, the general notion of costs and benefits is relevant in understanding why the U.S. has lower turnout than most democracies because the costs of participation are higher due to registration requirements.

The most extensive research on the reasons behind declining turnout has been done in the United States. One source of the decline has been the changing age structure of the American electorate, in part through demographic changes in the population and partially through a lowering of the voting age (Shaffer 1981; Teixeira 1992; Miller 1992). An even more significant factor was the public's changing orientation toward politics -- decreases in feelings of political efficacy and party identification that occurred over the past 20 years (Abramson and Aldrich 1982; Teixeira 1987; Rosenstone and Hansen 1993). Such disconnection from electoral politics naturally inhibits participation in the process.

While the specifics of the American case are well researched, a single-nation focus misses the point that such turnout declines are a common feature across advanced industrial democracies. Decreasing turnout does not mean that citizens are generally disengaging from politics, however, since there have been increases in other forms of political action (Barnes and Kaase 1979; Jennings and van Deth 1990; Verba et al. 1978). Voting is an area where elites and political organizations traditionally were able to mobilize even disinterested citizens to turn out at the polls. High turnout levels often reflect the organizational skills of political groups rather than the public's concern about the election (Uhlaner 1989). Moreover, citizen input through this participation mode is limited by the institutionalized structure of elections, which narrows (and blurs) the choice of policy options and limits the frequency of public input.

Contemporary electorates may not rely on voting and campaign activity as the primary means of expanding their involvement in politics. Citizen participation has increased in areas where activity is citizen initiated, less structured, and more policy oriented. Thus, referenda are preferred over elections, and citizen-interest-group activity over campaign work. The use of referenda has, in fact, increased dramatically in Western democracies in recent years (Butler and Ranney 1981). Similarly, the activity of citizen lobbies, single-issue groups, and citizen action movements is increasing in nearly all Western democracies (Barnes and Kaase 1979; Jennings and van Deth 1990; Ginsberg and Shefter 1990). Many Europeans believe that electoral participation might be reinvigorated by expanding the public's decision-making responsibilities to include primaries, preference-ranking mechanisms for party-list voting, or candidate ranking within party lists. However, it must be noted that such participatory opportunities have not served to increase turnout in the United States.

Overall, the limits of voting have led some critics to claim that by focusing mass participation on voting, parties and political elites are seeking to protect their privileged position in the policy process and actually limit citizen influence (Burnham 1980). Even if this skepticism is merited, voting will remain an important aspect of democratic politics, as much for its symbolic value as for its instrumental influence on policy. Voting is the one activity that binds the individual to the political system and legitimizes the rest of the democratic process.

The Changing Nature of Citizen Politics

The implicit argument of this chapter has been that one of the most difficult tasks that individuals perform is what some political scientists call "the simple act of voting." The choice of candidates and parties involves judgments about the course of society, evaluations of the performance of the incumbents, and projections about the future.

The debate about whether the public is up to this challenge is probably an unending theme in political research. The public is somewhat more informed and knowledgeable about politics because of the expansion of the mass media and the rising levels of education. At the same time, however, the process of electoral decision

making has become more difficult due to the proliferation of complex and often technical issues, such as nuclear power or industrial policy. Like Alice's experience in Wonderland, the voting public has had to run just to keep up.

While the debate about the abilities of the electorate is still ongoing, our description of the research literature has clear implications for the changing nature of electoral politics in advanced industrial democracies. Politics in most Western democracies traditionally has been highly structured and slow to change. Social institutions such as the unions and churches were major political actors, influencing both political elites and their membership. Because individuals were often ill-prepared to deal with the complexities of politics, they relied on the political cues of external reference groups in reaching political decisions. We have seen, however, that the decline of social-group-based voting is one of the common developments affecting virtually all advanced industrial democracies. This is one of the (nearly) indisputable findings from the last generation of electoral research. One's social position no longer determines one's political position as it did when social alignments were solidly frozen.

One possible benefactor from the erosion of social group cues could have been the political parties. Electoral politics is, after all, the primary mechanism of citizen participation in most democracies. And yet, the changing characteristics of Western publics have, in many instances, turned people away from partisan politics. The erosion of party influence involves their role as interest articulators. The established parties have been hesitant to respond to the public's expanding issue interests. Indeed, the rise of single-issue groups and non-ideological issues does not translate well into mass party politics. This has given rise to the fragmentation of old parties and the creation of new parties. Moreover, other institutions -- ranging from citizen lobbies to public-opinion-polling institutes -- have assumed some of the parties' prior role as representatives of popular interests.

Long-term electoral trends thus display an erosion of partisan attachments as a source of voting cues. Strength of party attachment has weakened in several Western democracies over the past generation. Even more common is the decrease in party-line voting and the increase in partisan volatility, split-ticket voting, and other phenomena that indicate the public is no longer voting according to a party line. Perot's strong showing in the 1992 American presidential election provides a graphic illustration of how weakened party ties open up the potential for substantial electoral volatility.

In summary, the trends we have described in this chapter lead to what we would call the "individualization of politics." One development is the shift away from the previous style of decision making based on social group and/or party cues toward a more individualized and inwardly oriented style of political choice. Instead of depending upon party elites and reference groups, more citizens now attempt to deal with the complexities of politics and make their own political decisions. What is developing is an eclectic and egocentric pattern of political decision making. Rather than socially structured and relatively homogeneous personal networks, contemporary publics are more likely to base their electoral decisions on policy preferences, performance judgments, or candidate images.

The relationship between the individual and the media both contributes to these trends and reinforces them (Semetko et al. 1991; Miller 1990). The contemporary media provide voters with a greater variety of information sources, and potentially a more critical perspective of established political actors such as parties, labor unions, and industries. Access to a diverse media environment enables the public to become active *selectors* of information rather than passive *consumers* of political cues provided by others. In addition, the ability to see candidates and parliamentary leaders up close and personal on television has caused more attention to be paid to the personal attributes of politicians, such as competence and integrity. The expansion of the 1992 American presidential campaign into new media forums illustrates this point, and similar developments can be observed in other Western democracies, albeit in more modest form, as new communications technologies change the patterns of information flow.

The individualization of politics also displays itself in the increasing heterogeneity of the public's issue interests. Issues of environmentalism, women's rights, and lifestyles choices have been added to the already full agenda of advanced industrial democracies. In addition, schema theory argues that citizens are becoming fragmented into a variety of distinct *issue publics* (also see RePass 1971; Budge and Farlie 1983; Franklin 1992). Rather than politics being structured by a group benefits framework, which often reflected socially derived cues, citizens now tend to focus on specific issues of immediate or personal importance.

These developments have the potential to either improve or weaken the "quality" of the democratic process and the representation of the public's political interests. The nature of contemporary political beliefs means that public opinion is simultaneously becoming more fluid and less predictable. This uncertainty forces parties and candidates to become more sensitive to public opinion, at least the opinions of those who vote. Motivated issue voters are more likely to at least have their voices heard, even if they are not accepted. Furthermore, the ability of politicians to have unmediated communications with voters can strengthen the link between politicians and the people. To some extent, the individualization of electoral choice revives earlier images of the informed independent voter that we once found in classic democratic theory.

At the same time, there is a potential dark side to these new forces in electoral politics. The rise of single-issue politics handicaps a society's attempts to deal with political issues that transcend specific interests, such as the U.S. budget deficit. A focus on issue publics also leaves the electorally inactive disenfranchised. Too great an interest in a single issue, or too much emphasis on recent performance, can produce a narrow definition of rationality that is as harmful to democracy as "frozen" social cleavages. In addition, direct unmediated contact between politicians and citizens opens the potential for demagoguery and political extremism. Both extreme right-wing and left-wing political movements probably benefit from this new political environment, at least in the short term.

The early empiricists called for a mix of stability and change in mass politics as an essential feature of democracy (Almond and Verba 1963; Berelson et al. 1954). Today, the balance of this mix has changed significantly for most contemporary democracies. It is unlikely that we will ever see the old electoral style of the past repeated, for the nature of electoral politics has permanently changed.

Notes

We would like to thank Robert Huckfeldt, Robert Luskin, and several of the anonymous reviewers for their advice and comments on this chapter; we also want to thank James Hankin for his assistance in preparing this chapter.

1. In order to understand the dynamics of electoral choice, the interested reader should also consult the separate chapters on public opinion (Paul Sniderman) and political communication (Doris Graber) in this volume.

2. Faced with this empirical evidence, some scholars attempted to recast democratic theory to make a virtue of the public's apparently limited abilities. Berelson and his colleagues (1954, 315), for instance, maintained that the smooth functioning of democratic process required that most citizens remain politically aloof, providing some latitude for elites to act and avoiding excessive political conflict. Similarly, Almond and Verba (1963) cautioned that a democratic political culture required a mix of attentive and inattentive citizens that would enable the system to avoid the hyper-politicization and polarization that characterized unstable democracies, such as the Weimar Republic. For a critique of this argument see Barber (1984) and Dalton (1988).

3. Smith's analyses emphasize how much people say about politics, using the number of responses to the open-ended likes/dislikes question, rather than content of these responses. By substituting quantity for the quality of response, Smith ignores what sophistication is supposed to measure (see Luskin 1987).

4. For example, the methodological studies of the 1970s showed that the seven-point scales, now the preferred methodology of the

U.S. National Election Studies, yield higher levels of constraint than did *The American Voter*'s scales (e.g., Sullivan et al. 1978), and Krosnick's (1991) new methodology yields even more reliable and stable issue measurement.

    5. Downs's work has been used to justify much more demanding "rational choice" models of voter decision making that assume high levels of information and sophistication that are unmet by contemporary electorates. Unfortunately, Downs's sensitivity to the pragmatic limits of citizen action are often missing from this later work.

    6. The 1988 *New York Times* exit poll found that white fundamentalist or evangelical Christians made up 9% of the electorate and voted 81% Republican.

    7. Germans, for example, are increasingly able to identify the party leanings of unions, business, and the churches -- at the same time that the social characteristics linked to these cleavages are having a decreasing impact on party choice (Dalton 1992, chap. 8).

    8. From the European perspective, observers such as Philip Williams have been left wondering "how in the 1980s American political parties can be said to have lost power when they hardly ever had any" (quoted in Epstein 1986, 5).

    9. For instance, the German version of the party identification question specifically cues the respondent that it is asking about long-term partisan leanings: "Many people in the Federal Republic lean toward a particular party for a long time, although they may occasionally vote for a different party. How about you?"

    10. See the excellent review of this literature in Niemi and Weisberg (1993b).

    11. Bradley Richardson's (1991) research on the linkage between partisanship and social cleavage attachments suggests that the decline of cleavage alignments reinforces the trend of partisan dealignment (also see Franklin 1992).

    12. A simple comparison of the electoral experiences of a typical European and American voter highlights this difference in the amount of voting. For example, between 1985 and 1990 a resident of Cambridge, England, was called to the polls to make four decisions; a resident of Irvine, California, could have cast several hundred votes in the same period. In one 1990 trip to the polls a voter in Irvine was asked to make 59 separate decisions on the ballot.

Bibliography

Abramson, Paul R. 1992. "Of Time and Partisan Instability in Britain." *British Journal of Political Science* 22:381-395.

Abramson, Paul R., and John H. Aldrich. 1982. "The Decline of Electoral Participation in America." *American Political Science Review* 76:502-21.

Abramson, Paul R., John H. Aldrich, and David W. Rohde. 1991. *Change and Continuity in the 1988 Elections*. Washington, DC: Congressional Quarterly Press.

Abramson, Paul R., and Charles W. Ostrom, Jr. 1991. "Macropartisanship: An Empirical Reassessment." *American Political Science Review* 85:181-92.

Aitkin, Don. 1977. *Stability and Change in Australian Politics*. New York: St. Martins.

Alford, Robert. 1963. *Party and Society: The Anglo-American Democracies*. Chicago: Rand McNally.

Allardt, Erik. 1968. "Past and Emerging Political Cleavages." In *Party Organization and the Politics of the New Masses*, ed. O. Stammer. Berlin: Institute of Political Science at the Free University.

Almond, Gabriel, and Sidney Verba. 1963. *The Civic Culture*. Princeton: Princeton University Press.

Almond, Gabriel, and Sydney Verba, ed. 1980. *The Civic Culture Revisited*. Boston: Little Brown.

Alt, John. 1984. "Dealignment and the Dynamics of Partisanship in Britain." In *Electoral Change in Advanced Industrial Democracies*, ed. Russell Dalton, Scott Flanagan, and Paul Allen Beck. Princeton: Princeton University Press.

Andeweg, Rudy. 1982. *Dutch Voters Adrift*. Ph.D. diss. University of Leiden.

Baker, Kendall, Russell Dalton, and Kai Hildebrandt. 1981. *Germany Transformed: Political Culture and the New Politics*. Cambridge, MA: Harvard University Press.

Barber, Benjamin. 1984. *Strong Democracy*. Berkeley: University of California Press.

Barnes, Samuel, Max Kaase, et al. 1979. *Political Action: Mass Participation in Five Western Democracies*. Beverly Hills, CA: Sage.

Bartolini, and Peter Mair. 1990. *Identity, Competition, and Electoral Availability*. Cambridge: Cambridge University Press.

Bean, Clive. n.d. "The Electoral Influence of Party Leader Images in Australia and New Zealand." *Comparative Political Studies*.

Bean, Clive, and Anthony Mughan. 1989. "Leadership Effects in Parliamentary Elections in Australia and Britain." *American Political Science Review* 83:1165-79.

Beck, Paul Allen. 1984. "The Dealignment Era in America." In *Electoral Change in Advanced Industrial Democracies*, ed. Russell Dalton, Scott Flanagan, and Paul Allen Beck. Princeton: Princeton University Press.

Beck, Paul Allen et al. 1992. "Patterns and Sources of Ticket-Splitting in Subpresidential Voting." *American Political Science Review* 86:916-928.

Benney, M. et al. 1956. *How People Vote*. London: Humanities Press.

Berelson, Bernard, Paul Lazarsfeld, and William McPhee. 1954. *Voting: A Study of Opinion Formation in a Presidential Campaign*. Chicago: University of Chicago Press.

Bishop, George et al. 1978. "Effects of Question Wording and Format on Political Attitude Consistency." *Public Opinion Quarterly* 42:81-92.

Borre, Ole. 1984. "Critical Electoral Change in Scandinavia." In *Electoral Change in Advanced Industrial Democracies*, ed. Russell Dalton, Scott Flanagan, and Paul Beck. Princeton: Princeton University Press.

Brown, Steven D. et al. 1988. "In the Eye of the Beholder: Leader Images in Canada." *Canadian Journal of Political Science* 21:729-55.

Budge, Ian, Ivor Crewe, and Dennis Farlie, eds. 1976. *Party Identification and Beyond: Representations of Voting and Party Competition*. New York: Wiley.

Budge, Ian, and Farlie, Dennis. 1983. *Explaining and Predicting Elections: Issue Effects and Party Strategies in Twenty-three Democracies*. New York: Allen & Unwin.

Burnham, Walter Dean. 1970. *Critical Elections and the Mainsprings of American Politics*. New York: Norton.

Burnham, Walter Dean. 1980. "The Appearance and Disappearance of the American Voter." In *Electoral Participation*, ed. Richard Rose. Beverly Hills: Sage Publications.

Burnham, Walter Dean. 1991. "Critical Realignment: Dead or Alive." In *The End of Realignment*, ed. Byron Shafer. Madison: University of Wisconsin Press.

Butler, David, and Austin Ranney, eds. 1981. *Referendums: A Comparative Study of Practice and Theory*. Washington, DC: American Enterprise Institute.

Butler, David, and Donald Stokes. 1969. *Political Change in Britain: Forces Shaping Electoral Choice*. New York: St. Martin's.

Butler, David, and Donald Stokes. 1974. *Political Change in Britain: The Evolution of Electoral Choice*. 2nd ed. New York: St. Martin's.

Cain, Bruce, John Ferejohn, and Morris Fiorina. 1987. *The Personal Vote*. Cambridge: Harvard University Press.

Campbell, Angus, Gerald Gurin, and Warren Miller. 1954. *The Voter Decides*. Evanston: Row, Peterson and Co.

Campbell, Angus et al. 1960. *The American Voter*. New York: Wiley.

Campbell, Angus et al. 1966. *Elections and the Political Order*. New York: Wiley.

Carmines, Edward, and James Stimson. 1989. *Issue Evolution*. Princeton: Princeton University Press.

Castles, Frances. 1982. *The Impact of Parties*. Beverly Hills: Sage Publications.

Chubb, John, and Paul Peterson, eds. 1985. *New Directions in American Politics*. Washington, DC: Brookings Institution.

Clarke, Harold, and Paul Whiteley. 1990. "Perceptions of Macroeconomic Performance, Government Support and Conservative Party Strength in Britain." *European Journal of Political Research* 18:97-120.

Clarke, Harold et al. 1980. *Political Choice in Canada*. New York: McGraw Hill.

Conover, Pamela, and Stanley Feldman. 1984. "How People Organize the Political World." *American Journal of Political Science* 28:95-126.

Converse, Philip E. 1964. "The Nature of Belief Systems in Mass Publics." In *Ideology and Discontent*, ed. David Apter. New York: Free Press.

Converse, Philip E. 1969. "Of Time and Partisan Stability." *Comparative Political Studies* 2:139-71.

Converse, Philip E. 1972. Change in the American Electorate. In *The Human Meaning of Social Change*, ed. Angus Campbell and Philip Converse. New York: Russell Sage.

Converse, Philip E. 1975. "Some Mass-elite Contrasts in the Perception of Political Spaces." *Social Science Information* 14:49-83.

Converse, Philip E. 1980. "Comment: Rejoinder to Judd and Milburn." *American Sociological Review* 45:644-46.

Converse, Philip E., and Gregory Markus. 1979. "Plus ça Change...The New CPS Election Panel Study." *American Political Science Review* 73:32-49.

Converse, Philip E., and Georges Dupeux. 1962. "Politicization of the Electorate in France and the United States." *Public Opinion Quarterly* 26:1-23.

Converse, Philip E., and Roy Pierce. 1986. *Representation in France*. Cambridge, MA: Harvard University Press.

Conway, M. Margaret. 1985. *Political Participation in the United States*. Washington, DC: Congressional Quarterly Press.

Crepaz, Markus. 1990. "The Impact of Party Polarization and Postmaterialism on Voter Turnout." *European Journal of Political Research* 18:183-205.

Crewe, Ivor. 1981. "Electoral Participation." In *Democracy at the Polls: A Comparative Study of Competitive National Elections*, ed. David Butler et al. Washington, DC: American Enterprise Institute.

Crewe, Ivor, and D. T. Denver, eds. 1985. *Electoral Change in Western Democracies*. New York: St. Martin's.

Crewe, Ivor, and Donald Searing. 1988. "Mrs. Thatcher's Crusade: Conservatism in Britain, 1972-1986." In *The Resurgence of Conservatism in the Anglo-American Countries*, ed. B. Cooper et al. Durham, NC: Duke University Press.

Dalton, Russell. 1984. "Cognitive Mobilization and Partisan Dealignment in Advanced Industrial Democracies." *Journal of Politics* 46:264-84.

Dalton, Russell. 1988. *Citizen Politics in Western Democracies*. Chatham, NJ: Chatham Publishers.

Dalton, Russell. 1992. *Politics in Germany*. New York: Harper Collins.

Dalton, Russell, Scott Flanagan, and Paul Beck, eds. 1984. *Electoral Change in Advanced Industrial Democracies*. Princeton: Princeton University Press.

Dalton, Russell, and Robert Rohrschneider. 1990. "Wählerwandel und die Abschwächung der Parteineigungen." In *Wahlen und Waehler*, ed. Max Kaase and Hans-Dieter Klingemann. Opladen: Westdeutscher Verlag.

Delli Carpini, Michael X., and Scott Keeter. 1991. "Stability and Change in the U.S. Public's Knowledge of Politics." *Public Opinion Quarterly* 55:583-612.

Delli Carpini, Michael X., and Lee Sigelman. 1986. "Do Yuppies Matter? Competing Explanations of Their Political Distinctiveness." *Public Opinion Quarterly* 50:502-18.

Dennis, Jack. 1975. "Trends in Public Support for the American Party System." *British Journal of Political Science* 5:187-230.

Downs, Anthony. 1957. *An Economic Theory of Democracy*. New York: Harper.

Dunleavy, Patrick, and Christopher Husbands. 1985. *British Democracy at the Crossroads*. London: Allen and Unwin.

Eijk, Cees van der, and B. Niemoeller. 1983. *Electoral Change in the Netherlands: Empirical Results and Methods of Measurement*. Amsterdam: CT Press.

Enelow, James, and Melvin Hinich, eds. 1990. *Advances in the Spatial Theory of Voting*. Cambridge: Cambridge University Press.

Epstein, Leon. 1986. *Political Parties in the American Mold*. Madison: University of Wisconsin Press.

Falter, Juergen, and Siegfried Schuman. 1990. "Vive le (tres) Difference!" In *Wahlen und Wähler: Analysen aus Anlass der Bundestagswahl 1987*, ed. Max Kaase and Hans-Dieter Klingemann. Opladen: Westdeutscher Verlag.

Farah, Barbara, and Ethel Klein. 1989. "Public Opinion Trends." In *The Election of 1988*, ed. Gerald Pomper. Chatham, NJ: Chatham House.

Field, John, and Ronald Anderson. 1969. "Ideology in the Public's Conceptualization of the 1964 Election." *Public Opinion Quarterly* 33:380-98.

Fiorina, Morris. 1981. *Retrospective Voting in American National Elections*. New Haven: Yale University Press.

Fiorina, Morris. 1989. *Congress: Keystone of the Washington Establishment*, 2nd ed. New Haven: Yale University Press.

Fiorina, Morris. 1992. *Divided Government*. New York: Macmillan.

Flanagan, Scott et al. 1991. *The Japanese Voter*. New Haven, CT: Yale University Press.

Franklin, Mark. 1985. *The Decline of Class Voting in Britain: Changes in the Basis of Electoral Choice, 1964-1983*. Oxford: Oxford University Press.

Franklin, Mark. 1992. "The Decline of Cleavage Politics." In *Electoral Change: Responses to Evolving Social and Attitudinal Structures in Western Countries*, ed. Mark Franklin et al. New York: Cambridge University Press.

Franklin, Mark et al. 1992. *Electoral Change: Responses to Evolving Social and Attitudinal Structures in Western Countries*. New York: Cambridge University Press.

Frears, J. R. 1991. *Parties and Voters in France*. New York: St. Martin's Press.

Fuchs, Dieter, and Hans-Dieter Klingemann. 1989. "The Left-Right Schema." In *Continuities in Political Action*, ed. M. Kent Jennings and Jan van Deth. Berlin: DeGruyter.

Ginsberg, Benjamin, and Martin Shefter. 1990. *Politics by Other Means*. New York: Basic Books.

Glass, David. 1985. "Evaluating Presidential Candidates: Who Focuses on their Personal Attributes." *Public Opinion Quarterly* 49:517-34.

Gluchowski, Peter. 1983. "Wahlerfahrung und Parteiidentifikation." In *Wahlen und Politisches System: Analysen aus Anlass der Bundestagswahl 1980*, ed. Max Kaase and Hans-Dieter Klingemann. Opladen: Westdeutscher Verlag.

Gluchowski, Peter. 1987. "Lebensstile und Wandel der Wählerschaft in der Bundesrepublik Deutschland." *Aus Politik und Zeitgeschichte* (March 21): 18-32.

Goldthorpe, John. 1980. *Social Mobility and Class Structure in Modern Britain*. Oxford: Clarendon Press.

Hammond, John. 1986. "Yuppies." *Public Opinion Quarterly* 50:487-501.

Harding, Stephen. 1986. *Contrasting Values in Western Europe*. London: Macmillan.

Heath, Anthony, Roger Jowell, and John Curtice. 1985. *How Britain Votes*. New York: Pergamon Press.

Heath, Anthony et al. 1991. *Understanding Political Change: The British Voter 1964-1987*. New York: Pergamon Press.

Hoskin, Marilyn. 1991. *New Immigrants and Democratic Society*. Boulder: Praeger.

Huckfeldt, Robert, and Carol Kohfeld. 1989. *Race and the Decline of Class in American Politics*. Urbana: University of Illinois Press.

Huntington, Samuel. 1968. "Post-industrial Politics: How Benign Will It Be?" *Comparative Politics* 6:147-77.

Hurwitz, Jon, and Mark Peffley. 1987. "How Are Foreign Policy Attitudes Structured?" *American Political Science Review* 81:1099-120.

Inglehart, Ronald. 1977. *The Silent Revolution: Changing Values and Political Styles among Western Publics*. Princeton: Princeton University Press.

Inglehart, Ronald. 1984. "Changing Cleavage Alignments in Western Democracies." In *Electoral Change in Advanced Industrial Democracies*, ed. R. Dalton, S. Flanagan, and P. Beck. Princeton: Princeton University Press.

Inglehart, Ronald. 1990. *Culture Shift in Advanced Industrial Society*. Princeton: Princeton University Press.

Inglehart, Ronald, and Avram Hochstein. 1972. "Alignment and Dealignment of the Electorate in France and the United States." *Comparative Political Studies* 5:343-72.

Jackman, Robert W. 1987. "Political Institutions and Voter Turnout in the Industrialized Democracies." *American Political Science Review* 81:405-24.

Jennings, M. Kent, and Gregory Markus. 1984. "Partisan Orientations over the Long Haul." *American Political Science Review* 78:1000-18.

Jennings, M. Kent, Jan van Deth, et al. 1990. *Continuities in Political Action*. Berlin: de Gruyter.

Judd, Charles, and Michael Milburn. 1980. "The Structure of Attitude Systems in the General Public." *American Sociological Review* 45:627-43.

Judd, Charles et al. 1981. "Political Involvement and Attitude Structure in the United States." *American Sociological Review* 46:660-69.

Kamieniecki, Sheldon. 1985. *Party Identification, Political Behavior, and the American Electorate*. Westport, CT: Greenwood.

Keith, Bruce et al. 1977. "The Myth of the Independent Voter." Paper presented at the annual meeting of the American Political Science Association, Washington, DC.

Keith, Bruce, et al., 1992. *The Myth of the Independent Voter*. Berkeley: University of California Press.

Kelley, Stanley, and Thad Mirer. 1975. "The Simple Act of Voting." *American Political Science Review* 68:572-91.

Kerlinger, Fred. 1984. *Liberalism and Conservatism*. Hillsdale, NJ: Lawrence Erlbaum.

Key, V. O. 1966. *The Responsible Electorate*. Cambridge: Belnap Press.

Kiewiet, D. R. 1983. *Macroeconomics and Micropolitics*. Chicago: University of Chicago Press.

Kinder, Donald, and D. R. Kiewiet. 1981. "Sociotropic Politics." *British Journal of Political Science* 11:129-61.

Kinder, Donald. 1983. "Diversity and Complexity in American Public Opinion." In *Political Science: The State of the Discipline*, ed. Ada Finifter. Washington, DC: American Political Science Association.

Kinder, Donald. 1986. "Presidential Character Revisited." In *Political Cognitions*, ed. Richard R. Lau and David O. Sears. Hillsdale, NJ: Lawrence Erlbaum.

Kinder, Donald et al. 1980. "Presidential Prototypes." *Political Behavior* 2:315-37.

Kitschelt, Herbert. n.d. *The Transformation of European Social Democracy*.

Klein, Ethel. 1984. *Gender Politics*. Cambridge: Harvard University Press.

Klingemann, Hans-Dieter. 1979. "Measuring Ideological Conceptualization." In *Political Action*, ed. Samuel Barnes, Max Kaase, et al. Beverly Hills: Sage Publications.

Knutsen, Oddbjorn. 1987. "The Impact of Structural and Ideological Cleavages on West European Democracies." *British Journal of Political Science* 18:323-52.

Korpi, Walter. 1983. *The Democratic Class Struggle*. London: Routledge.

Krosnick, Jon. 1991. "The Stability of Political Preferences." *American Journal of Political Science* 35:547-76.

Kuklinski, James, Robert Luskin, and John Bolland. 1991. "Where Is the Schema? Going Beyond the "S" Word in Political Psychology." *American Political Science Review* 85:1341-57.

Lau, Richard. 1986. "Political Schemata, Candidate Evaluations, and Voting Behavior." In *Political Cognition*, ed. Richard Lau and David O. Sears. Hillsdale, NJ: Lawrence Erlbaum.

Lazarsfeld, Paul, Bernard Berelson, and Hazel Gaudet. 1944. *The People's Choice*. New York: Columbia University Press.

Lewis-Beck, Michael. 1984. "France: The Stalled Electorate." In *Electoral Change in Advanced Industrial Democracies*, ed. Russell Dalton, Scott Flanagan, and Paul Beck. Princeton: Princeton University Press.

Lewis-Beck, Michael. 1988. *Economics and Elections*. Ann Arbor: University of Michigan Press.

Lijphart, Arend. 1981. "Political Parties." In *Democracy at the Polls: A Comparative Study of Competitive National Elections*, ed. David Butler et al. Washington, DC: American Enterprise Institute.

Lipset, Seymour Martin. 1961. *Political Man: The Social Bases of Politics*. Baltimore: Johns Hopkins University Press.

Lipset, Seymour Martin, and Stein Rokkan. 1967. *Party Systems and Voter Alignments*. New York: Free Press.

Luskin, Robert. 1987. "Measuring Political Sophistication." *American Journal of Political Science* 31:856-99.

Mackie, Thomas, and Richard Rose. 1990. *International Handbook of Electoral Statistics*. New York: Facts on File.

McAllister, Ian. 1992. *Political Behavior: Citizens, Parties and Elites in Australia*. Sydney: Longman Cheshire.

McKuen, Michael B., Robert Erikson, and James Stimson. 1990. "Macropartisanship." *American Political Science Review* 89:1125-42.

MacKuen, Michael B., Robert Erickson, and James Stimson. 1992. "Peasants or Bankers? The American Electorate and the U.S. Economy." *American Political Science Review* 86:597-611.

Markus, Gregory B. 1988. "The Impact of Personal and National Economic Conditions on the Presidential Vote: A Pooled Cross-Sectional Analysis." *American Journal of Political Science* 32:137-54.

Milbrath, Lester, and M. L. Goel. 1977. *Political Participation*. New York: Rand McNally.

Miller, Arthur, and Martin Wattenberg. 1984. "Politics and the Pulpit: Religiosity and the 1980 Elections." *Public Opinion Quarterly* 48:301-17.

Miller, Arthur, and Martin Wattenberg. 1985. "Throwing the Rascals Out." *American Political Science Review* 79:359-72.

Miller, Arthur, Martin Wattenberg, and Oksana Malanchuk. 1986. "Schematic Assessments of Presidential Candidates." *American Political Science Review* 80:521-40.

Miller, Warren. 1976. "The Cross-national Use of Party Identification as a Stimulus to Inquiry." In *Party Identification and Beyond: Representations of Voting and Party Competition*, ed. Ian Budge et al. New York: Wiley.

Miller, Warren. 1992. "The Puzzle Transformed: Explaining Turnout Declines." *Political Behavior* 14:1-43.

Miller, Warren E., and Teresa Levitin. 1976. *Leadership and Change: The New Politics and the American Electorate*. New York: Winthrop.

Miller, William et al. 1990. *How Voters Change: The 1987 British Election Campaign in Perspective*. New York: Oxford University Press.

Miller, William. 1990. *Media and Voters: The Audience, Content and Influence of Press and Television at the 1987 General Election*. New York: Oxford University Press.

Milne, R., and H. C. Mackenzie. 1954. *Straight Fight*. London: Hansard Society.

Milne, R., and H. C. Mackenzie. 1959. *Marginal Seat*. London: Hansard Society.

Miyake, Ichiro. 1991. "Partisanship and Voting Behavior." In *The Japanese Voter*, ed. Scott Flanagan et al. New Haven, CT: Yale University Press.

Mueller-Rommel, Ferdinand. 1989. *The New Politics: The Rise and Success of Green Parties and Alternative Lists*. Boulder: Westview Press.

Murphy, Detlef et al. 1981. "Haben "links" und "rechts" noch Zukunft?" *Politische Vierteljahresschrift* 22:398-414.

Neuman, W. Russell. 1986. *The Paradox of Mass Politics: Knowledge and Opinion in the American Electorate*. Cambridge: Harvard University Press.

Nie, Norman, and Kristi Andersen. 1974. "Mass Belief Systems Revisited." *Journal of Politics* 36:541-91.

Nie, Norman, Sidney Verba, and John Petrocik. 1976. *The Changing American Voter*. Cambridge, MA: Harvard University Press.

Nie, Norman, Sidney Verba, and John Petrocik. 1979. *The Changing American Voter*, enlarged ed. Cambridge, MA: Harvard University Press.

Niemi, Richard G., and Herbert F. Weisberg, eds. 1993a. *Classics in Voting Behavior*. Washington, DC: Congressional Quarterly Press.

Niemi, Richard G., and Herbert F. Weisberg, eds. 1993b. *Controversies in Voting Behavior*, 3rd ed. Washington, DC: Congressional Quarterly Press.

Norpoth, Helmut. 1992. *Confidence Regained: Economics, Mrs. Thatcher, and the British Voter*. Ann Arbor: University of Michigan Press.

Norpoth, Helmut, and Michael Lewis-Beck, eds. 1991. *Economics and Politics* Ann Arbor: University of Michigan Press.

Norpoth, Helmut, and Dieter Roth. 1992. "The Grateful Electorate." In *Germany Votes 1990: Unification and the Creation of the New German Party System*, ed. Russell Dalton. Oxford: Berg Publishers.

Page, Benjamin. 1978. *Choices and Echoes in Presidential Elections*. Chicago: University of Chicago Press.

Pappi, Franz Urban. 1990. "Klassenstruktur und Wählerverhalten im sozialen Wandel." In *Wahlen und Wähler: Analysen aus Anlass der Bundestagswahl 1987*, ed. Max Kaase and Hans-Dieter Klingemann. Opladen: Westdeutscher Verlag.

Phillips, Kevin. 1969. *The Emerging Republican Majority*. New York: Anchor.

Phillips, Kevin. 1990. *The Politics of Rich and Poor*. New York: Harper Perennial.

Pierce, John. 1975. "The Relationship Between Linkage Salience and Linkage Organization in Mass Belief Systems." *Public Opinion Quarterly* 39:102-10.

Pierce, John, Kathleen Beatty, and Paul Hagner. 1982. *The Dynamics of American Public Opinion*. Glenview: Scott Foresman.

Popkin, Samuel. 1991. *The Reasoning Voter*. Chicago: University of Chicago Press.

Powell, G. Bingham. 1980. "Voting Turnout in Thirty Democracies." In *Electoral Participation*, ed. Richard Rose. Beverly Hills, CA: Sage.

Powell, G. Bingham. 1982. *Contemporary Democracies: Participation, Stability and Violence*. Cambridge, MA: Harvard University Press.

Powell, G. Bingham. 1986. "American Voting Turnout in Comparative Perspective." *American Political Science Review* 80:17-44.

Przeworski, Adam, and John Sprague. 1985. *Paper Stones: A History of Electoral Socialism*. Chicago: University of Chicago Press.

Rahn, Wendy M. et al. 1990. "A Social-Cognitive Model of Candidate Appraisal." In *Information and Democratic Processes*, ed. John Ferejohn and James Kuklinski. Urbana: University of Illinois Press.

Ranney, Austin. 1983. *Channels of Power: The Impact of Television on American Politics*. New York: Basic Books.

RePass, David. 1971. "Issue Saliency and Party Choice." *American Political Science Review* 65:389-400.

Richardson, Bradley M. 1988. "Constituency Candidates Versus Parties in Japanese Voting Behavior." *American Political Science Review* 82:695-718.

Richardson, Bradley. 1991. "European Party Loyalties Revisited." *American Political Science Review* 85:751-75.

Riker, William, and Peter Ordeshook. 1968. "A Theory of the Calculus of Voting." *American Political Science Review* 62:25-42.

Robertson, David. 1984. *Class and the British Electorate*. Oxford: Basil Blackwell.

Rohrschneider, Robert. 1992. "Environmental Belief Systems in Western Europe: A Hierarchical Model of Constraint." *Comparative Political Studies*.

Rose, Richard. 1974. *Electoral Behavior: A Comparative Handbook*. New York: Free Press.

Rose, Richard. 1982. *The Territorial Dimension in Politics*. Chatham, NJ: Chatham House.

Rose, Richard, and Derek Urwin. 1969. "Social Cohesion, Political Parties and Strains in Regimes." *Comparative Political Studies* 2:7-67.

Rose, Richard, and Ian McAllister. 1986. *Voters Begin to Choose: From Closed-class to Open Elections in Britain*. Beverly Hills: Sage Publications.

Rose, Richard, and Ian McAllister. 1990. *The Loyalties of Voters: A Lifetime Learning Model*. Newbury Park, CA: Sage Publications.

Rosenberg, Shawn, and Patrick McCafferty. 1987. "The Image and the Vote: Manipulating Voter's Preferences." *Public Opinion Quarterly* 51:31-47.

Rosenstone, Steven. 1983. *Forecasting Presidential Elections*. New Haven: Yale University Press.

Rosenstone, Steven, and John Hansen. 1993. *Mobilization, Participation, and American Democracy*. New York: Macmillan.

Saarlvik, Bo, and Ivor Crewe. 1983. *Decade of Dealignment*. New York: Cambridge University Press.

Sabato, Larry. 1988. *The Party's Just Begun*. Glenview: Scott Foresman.

Schmitt, Hermann. 1989. "About Party Attachments in Europe." *West European Politics* 2.

Semetko, Holli A., Jay G. Blumler, Michael Gurevitch, and David H.
    Weaver. 1991. *The Formation of Campaign Agendas: A
    Comparative Analysis of Party and Media Roles in Recent
    American and British Elections*. Hillsdale, NJ: Lawrence
    Erlbaum.

Shaffer, Stephen. 1981. "A Multivariate Explanation of Decreasing
    Turnout in Presidential Elections." *American Journal of
    Political Science* 25:68-95.

Smith, Eric R.A.N. 1980. "The Levels of Conceptualization." *American
    Political Science Review* 74:685-96.

Smith, Eric R.A.N. 1989. *The Unchanging American Voter*. Berkeley:
    University of California Press.

Sniderman, Paul, Richard Brody, and James Kuklinski. 1984. "Policy
    Reasoning and Political Values: The Problem of Racial
    Equality." *American Journal of Political Science* 28:75-94.

Stokes, Donald. 1966. "Spatial Models of Party Competition." In
    Elections and the Political Order, ed. Angus Campbell et al.
    New York: Wiley.

Sullivan, Denis, and Roger Masters. "Happy Warriors: Leaders' Facial
    Displays, Viewers' Emotions and Political Support."
    American Journal of Political Science 32:345-68.

Sullivan, John et al. 1978. "Ideological Constraint in the Mass Public."
    American Journal of Political Science 22:233-49.

Sundquist, James. 1973. *The Dynamics of the Party System*.
    Washington, DC: Brookings Institution.

Teixeira, Ruy. 1992. *The Disappearing American Voter*. Washington,
    DC: Brookings Institution.

Thurow, Lester. 1987. "A Surge in Inequality." *Scientific American*
    256:30-37.

Tufte, Edward. 1978. *Political Control of the Economy*. Princeton:
    Princeton University Press.

Uhlaner, Carole. 1989. "Rational Turnout: The Neglected Role of
    Groups." *American Journal of Political Science* 33:390-422.

Valentine, David C., and John R. Van Wingen. 1980. "Partisanship,
    Independence, and the Partisan Identification." *American
    Politics Quarterly* 8:165-86.

Van Deth, Jan. 1990. "Interest in Politics." In *Continuities in Political
    Action*, ed. M. Kent Jennings and Jan van Deth. New York:
    de Gruyter.

Verba, Sidney, and Norman Nie. 1972. *Participation in America:
    Political Democracy and Social Equality*. New York: Harper
    & Row.

Verba, Sidney, and Norman Nie. 1978. *Participation and Political
    Equality: A Seven Nation Comparison*. New York:
    Cambridge University Press.

Wald, Kenneth. 1987. *Religion and Politics in America*. New York: St.
    Martins.

Watanuki, Joji. 1991. "Social Structure and Voting Behavior." In *The
    Japanese Voter*, ed. Scott Flanagan et al. New Haven, CT:
    Yale University Press.

Wattenberg, Martin. 1990. *The Decline of American Political Parties
    1952-1988*. Cambridge, MA: Harvard University Press.

Wattenberg, Martin. 1991. *The Rise of Candidate Centered Politics*.
    Cambridge, MA: Harvard University Press.

Weisberg, Herbert F. 1980. "A Multidimensional Conceptualization of
    Party Identification." *Political Behavior* 2:33-60.

Westholm, Anders, and Richard Niemi. 1992. "Political Institutions
    and Political Socialization." *Comparative Political Studies*
    25.

Wolfinger, Raymond, and Steven Rosenstone. 1980. *Who Votes?* New
    Haven: Yale University Press.

Wuffle, A. 1984. "Should You Brush your Teeth on November 6,
    1984? A Rational Choice Perspective" *PS: Political Science
    and Politics* 17:577-81.

9

The New Look in Public Opinion Research

Paul M. Sniderman

Research on public opinion in the 1970s tended, in its basic contours and style, to be continuous with the research of the 1960s, and indeed, very largely with that of the 1950s. One fundamental paradigm -- minimalism as it has been called -- dominated the work of the two decades. Mass publics, it was contended, were distinguished by (1) minimal levels of political attention and information; (2) minimal mastery of abstract political concepts such as liberalism-conservatism; (3) minimal stability of political preferences; (4) and quintessentially, minimal levels of attitude constraint. Research was mainly organized around the four poles of minimalism, with continuity very much the theme of overviews of research of this period (Abramson 1983; Converse 1975; Kinder 1983; Kinder and Sears 1985). Not that complete agreement prevailed by any means (e.g., Achen 1975; Pierce and Rose 1974; Converse 1975; above all, Nie, Verba and Petrocik 1979) -- but there was all the same consensus, if not on the answers to give, on the questions to ask.[1] In contrast, innovation -- new directions, new methods, new perspectives -- distinguishes the research of the last decade. I mean therefore to use this review essay as a platform to call attention to works that are, in point of view or in methodological approach, novel and fresh.

It would be wrong to imply that there was no continuity of concern or approach; still more so to suggest that the work of the 1980s disproved that of the 1960s and 1970s. Instead, the changes characteristic of the last decade illustrate a more interesting lesson to draw about the nature of scientific progress. The research of the 1960s and 1970s was very much preoccupied with whether the paradigm of minimalism should be accepted or not. In contrast, the research of the 1980s managed to get beyond minimalism precisely by accepting its fundamental thrust: ordinary citizens tend to pay attention to politics only fitfully, and possess in consequence a thin, rather than thick, knowledge of it.

It needed to be said that the ordinary citizen ordinarily pays only cursory attention to politics, and that there are in consequence a number of issues about which he or she does not have a considered opinion to offer. But viewed through the lens of minimalism, politics

shrunk in size, indeed threatened to disappear. Research on public opinion, given the dominance of its emphasis in the 1960s and 1970s on the limits of popular understanding, wound up repeating the curious point that the study of public opinion and politics was not, and should not be, concerned with politics. The thrust of minimalism as a research program in public opinion was instead to emphasize the frequency with which ordinary citizens failed to form even an opinion about many political issues and, still more commonly, to document the frequency with which they failed to put their ideas about politics together consistently. The primary message of minimalism was thus, to exaggerate only slightly, that ordinary citizens tended to be muddle-headed (lacking constraint), or empty-headed (lacking genuine attitudes) -- or both. The task of the public opinion analyst, it followed, was not to reveal what the public thought about an issue of public policy, but rather to repeat, for issue after issue, that the ordinary citizen was unlikely to have given it much thought.

In contrast, what defines the new look in public opinion research is the movement of politics from the wings to center-stage. Offering an account of public opinion entails weighing how the preferences and choices of ordinary citizens, uninterested as they often are in public affairs, can be conditioned by the political process itself. Consider, by way of a nearly ideal-typical example, Carmines and Stimson's (1989) landmark study of race and American politics. In an analysis remarkable for its range and coherence, their two-step argument begins with elite politics. With Goldwater's capture of the Republican presidential nomination in 1964, they argue, the party system turned on its axis. The Republican party, once the party of racial liberalism, emerged as the party of racial conservatism, and the Democratic party, only a few years earlier the bastion of southern segregationists, became the party of racial liberalism (see also Huckfeldt and Kohfeld 1989). And with this change at the elite level, Carmines and Stimson maintain, the issue of race moved to the center of the political thinking of ordinary citizens in the mid-1960s, imposing unprecedented constraint on mass belief systems. So viewed, the dynamics of public opinion are connected in a deep way with the dynamics of politics itself.

To understand the connection between the dynamics of public opinion and politics is a problem in political analysis. The study of public opinion too often has been treated as a branch of applied psychology, with progress to be made by importing the latest theory in personality or social psychology. Without minimizing the value of interdisciplinary scholarship, I want to insist both that the intellectual traffic has to run in both directions and that the point of departure has to be a recognition that it is specifically *political* behavior that stands in need of explanation. By way of example, consider a classic problem in public opinion -- the so-called "rally around the flag" effect. It has long been established (e.g., Mueller 1973) that the American public tends to swing to the president's side in a crisis. Indeed, even when he makes an obvious hash of things -- the Bay of Pigs fiasco, for example -- the president can wind up the winner in public opinion polls, with markedly more citizens saying that he is doing a good job during and (immediately) after the crisis than before it. There has been no reticence in offering psychological explanations of why citizens "rally around the flag." Brody and Shapiro (1989; Brody 1991), however, defining the problem as political rather than psychological, called attention to the public's responses: sometimes presidents benefit from a surge of support in a crisis, but sometimes not (see also Lee 1977; Sigelman and Conover 1981). Focusing on the variability of the public's response in different crises, Brody and Shapiro developed an original and elegant argument centered on the intervening role of opinion leadership. Rallying around the flag, they argue, is not driven primarily by emotional and irrational outbursts of patriotism; rather it is conditioned by the intervening reactions of media and political elites. If opinion leaders uniformly support, or at least refrain from criticizing, the president's actions, the public will support them, too; on the other hand, if there is prompt and large-scale criticism, there will be no "rally around the flag." The Brody-Shapiro argument thus directs emphasis away from reductionist psychological explanations to an explicitly political analysis centered on the dynamics of elite consensus and cleavage.

It cannot be too strongly emphasized that it is politics that we need to take into account in explaining public opinion, and that in giving an account of public opinion it is politics that we are attempting to explain. Hence the interest in the reciprocal connection between politics and public opinion. Illustrating one side of the coin, Page and Shapiro (1992, 1983), in a study of longitudinal trends in public opinion which eclipses any predecessor in scope and detail, argue that changes in public policy themselves are frequently a response to changes in public opinion (see also Burstein 1979). Illustrating the other side, Johnston, Blais, Brady, and Crete (1992), in the most original study of elections and voting since *The American Voter*, have driven home the impact of campaigns and campaign events on the dynamics of issue preferences and voting choices. It would be metaphysical to argue over whether the causal arrow runs from public opinion to elite politics, or the other way around. Manifestly, elite politics gets played out against the context of public opinion, and public opinion is constrained by elite choices.

There have been efforts before to insist on the centrality of politics in the study of public opinion. Nie and his colleagues (1979) in particular took issue with minimalism, arguing that its portrait of the minimally engaged and attentive citizen was a reflection of the irrelevance of the politics of the 1950s, contending instead that a more coherently organized politics would evoke a deeper and more coherent engagement with politics on the part of citizens. Research of the last decade, however, has hammered away at the Nie argument, confirming the continuing validity of the image of citizens as "low involvement" spectators of politics. Most synoptically, Smith (1989), concentrating on levels of conceptualization but taking account also of attitude consistency and political knowledge, has made a strong case for a "no change" thesis. Moreover, Bennett (1988) has begun a comprehensive assessment of levels of citizen awareness. He has shown that levels of political knowledge and attention are not altogether flat with respect to time -- in fact, there seems to be some responsiveness to levels of political stimulation, with citizens being more politically knowledgeable, for example, in presidential than in off-election years. But he has also demonstrated that minimal levels of political attention and information are a chronic feature of liberal democratic politics. Then, too, in a series of exemplary studies comparing samples drawn in 1954 and 1989, Delli Carpini and Keeter (1989, 1991) have scrutinized levels of public knowledge of public affairs, demonstrating that increases in awareness, insofar as they have occurred, are modest. Indeed, taking account of the increases in educational opportunity since 1954, it is Delli Carpini and Keeter's suggestion that the level of awareness about politics and public affairs may have actually declined (see also Neuman 1986).

What marks the new look in public opinion, then, is the denial not of the classic premise of minimal levels of information and attention of mass publics, but rather of the conclusion of minimal coherence and reasonableness in their thinking commonly drawn from it. Counter-intuitively, the emphasis on mass publics' minimal levels of information has given way to an emphasis on how they overcome informational shortfalls. A concern to document the lack of organization of mass belief systems has been succeeded by a desire to discover the means by which they achieve a measure of coherence. An emphasis on the irrationality -- variously understood -- of ordinary citizens has been superseded by a more balanced recognition of their admittedly imperfect discharge of the duties of citizenship. I do not mean to leave the impression that the research of the last decade has been following a coordinated master plan. Certainly it is a mistake to attempt to crowd everyone under one tent: there are always and everywhere outliers. But there is also, from time to time, a central tendency, a common or characteristic research emphasis or style. And the dominant tone of the new look in public opinion is advertised in the titles of a wave of large-scale analyses of public opinion and politics which have just appeared or are just about to appear -- *Managing Complexity* (Elkins n.d.); *The Reasoning Voter* (Popkin 1991); *The Rational Public* (Page and Shapiro 1992); and *Reasoning and Choice* (Sniderman, Brody, and Tetlock 1991).

There is always a danger of exaggerated alternatives, and I do not mean at all to suggest that the image of ill-informed citizen has been replaced by that of the conscientious citizen. Perhaps the best way to indicate the thrust of the new look in public opinion is to highlight a problem central to it -- Simon's puzzle, as I have called it (Sniderman, Brody, and Tetlock 1991), in deference to Herbert Simon's pioneering work on decision making with limited information and processing capacity. Manifestly, on a range of issues -- affirmative action, legalization of abortion, increasing taxes, cutting social services -- substantial numbers of citizens know what they favor. The puzzle is, how can they manage this given the intermittent attention they pay to politics and the shallow fund of political knowledge they can consequently draw upon?

Take Simon's puzzle seriously -- accept, that is, that citizens characteristically are minimally involved in politics *and* that they nonetheless manage to make coherent sense of much of it -- and one has a new angle of attack on the nature of public opinion. There has thus been a new emphasis on how ordinary citizens can make sense of politics not by industriously accumulating information -- which they are not disposed to do except in the most uncommon circumstances -- about it but by selectively allocating their interest in it -- which they can easily manage and still maintain their ordinary routines. Elkins (n.d.), for example, has pressed the theme of specialization. Citizens, he argues, pick and choose the issues they care about. It only appears as if scarcely anybody knows scarcely anything if everybody is required to be knowledgeable about everything. A parallel argument, focusing more narrowly on the variations in

the personal importance of different issues, has been made by Krosnick (1990a). And the upshot of both is an insistence on the need to think in terms not of a mass public but of a myriad of issue publics.

Focusing of interest is one way to compensate for attentional and informational shortfalls. More provocatively, it has become common to argue that citizens can overcome their informational shortfalls and make sense of politics by taking advantage of judgmental shortcuts, or heuristics (Popkin 1991; Ferejohn and Kuklinski 1990; Sniderman, Brody and Tetlock 1991). For example, Brady and Sniderman (1985) have shown that substantial numbers of ordinary citizens can make sense of where liberals and conservatives stand on major issues -- regardless of whether or not they can make sense of liberalism and conservatism as abstract political philosophies; and they can do this by taking advantage of the "likability" heuristic -- a rule of thumb that yields approximately accurate predictions of where politically salient groups stand on major issues. A pair of features of judgmental short-cut such as the likeability heuristic deserves to be underlined. First, to take advantage of the heuristic to predict the issue commitments of liberals and conservatives individuals need know only where they stand on an issue, weighted by the difference in how they feel about liberals and conservatives -- information they can easily have on hand even if they do not pay close and deep attention to politics. Second, it is *not* at all being asserted that people make up their minds about who stands for what politically simply on the basis of attributing to political groups they like positions on issues like their own. Rather the whole point of a judgmental shortcut like the likability heuristic is that by taking advantage of it people make inferences -- in this case about what others believe -- that are approximately right.[2]

It would be a mistake to take an emphasis on the use of heuristics as an argument on behalf of the ordinary citizen as an intuitive political theorist. And in speaking of citizens taking advantage of judgmental shortcuts, or heuristics, there is plainly a risk of a merely verbal solution to the problem of mass publics' knowledge of politics. If the question one wants to provide an answer for runs roughly like this -- how is it possible for the ordinary citizen, given how little he or she knows about politics nonetheless to figure out where he or she stands politically? -- and if the answer one puts forward runs roughly like this -- citizens manage to compensate for informational shortfalls by taking advantage of heuristics -- then this surely prompts another question in turn -- namely, how do they manage, knowing as little as they do about politics, to come up with clever shortcuts to compensate for informational shortfalls?

Citizens can organize and effectively simplify political choices just insofar as those choices are organized and simplified for them by the political process itself.[3]   In the American party system, liberal is opposed to conservative, Democrat to Republican, with the pairs of opposites -- and this is the crucial point -- themselves paired. It is thanks to this simplicity of the structure of political conflict that substantial numbers of ordinary citizens can compensate for informational shortfalls by taking advantage of a judgmental shortcut like the likability heuristic (Brady and Sniderman 1985). From another angle, it has become increasingly evident that the public's weighing of political choices is tied to the framing of these choices; indeed, the burgeoning research on issue "framing" has driven home the extent to which responses of citizens to problems of public policy are contingent on the semantic description of policy problems and issue alternatives (e.g., Iyengar 1991; Iyengar and Kinder 1987; Kinder and Sanders 1990; Sniderman, Wolfinger, Mutz, and Wiley 1991). It cannot be said that the notion of issue "framing" has been given a rigorous interpretation, although particular attention should be paid to a quite original exploration, initiated by Jacoby (1990), aimed at gauging the relative aperture of the alternatives in terms of which political issues are posed in public opinion studies.

The presumption that the making of political choices consists in an interaction of situationally defined alternatives and enduring individual characteristics is a prominent feature of the new look in public opinion research; a feature which illustrates the intimate interdependence of substance and methodology. For the new look owes much to the fusing of experimental design and survey research particularly through computer-assisted interviewing. To be sure, experiments have been part of the arsenal of public opinion analysts for at least a generation (e.g., Schuman and Presser 1981). But they have operated under a double constraint in survey research, partly because of self-selected focus on narrowly methodological rather than broadly substantive questions, partly because of the severe restrictions of the classic "split ballot," paper-and-pencil technique. The requirement of producing physically distinct versions of a questionnaire, one for every version of a question wording, order or format, imposed a ceiling on the complexity of experimental designs, as a rule restricting the number of parallel forms to two. Now, in large part thanks to the computer-assisted interviewing, complex experiments can be unobtrusively embedded in public opinion surveys, throwing new light on how citizens arrive at their political positions. More broadly, thanks to the new flexibility in the conventional public opinion interview, there has been a burst of innovations, among them, experiments on "priming" and "agenda-setting" (Iyengar and Kinder 1987; Iyengar 1991); "source

manipulations," assessing the power of political figures and reference groups to shape public opinion (Smith and Squire 1990; Johnston et al. 1992; Sniderman, Piazza, Tetlock, and Feld 1991); the so-called "stop-and-think" manipulations, to ferret out considerations underlying political preferences (Feldman and Zaller 1992; Zaller and Feldman 1992); and the "counter-argument" technique -- deliberate attempts to talk people out of the positions they have just taken on public issues through counter-arguments (Piazza, Sniderman, and Tetlock 1989).

In canvassing the new flexibility in public opinion interviews, I would especially stress the subtlety of the interplay of substance and methodology, of change and continuity. Commentators who have trafficked in Kuhnian notions of paradigms and paradigm shifts have much to answer for, not the least being the swaggering presumption that new analytical and operational approaches make their way by displacing old ones. The dialectic of scientific advance is more subtle. In fact, some of the classical themes of a minimalist perspective have been further cemented through the development of new and more flexible interview procedures. Consider the notion of non-attitudes, the idea that substantial numbers of citizens take a position on an issue in the course of a public opinion interview, not in order to express a belief they have formed, but on the contrary to conceal the fact that they have not troubled to form one (Converse 1964). The notion of non-attitudes, fairly obviously, can serve as a summary metaphor for the minimalist perspective on public opinion; and one of the most compelling validations of the continuing utility of the notion of non-attitudes has been supplied by Fletcher and his colleagues (Fletcher and Chalmers 1991; Bassili and Fletcher 1991), in a striking new line of studies combining counter-argument techniques and breakthrough developments for the measurement of reaction time.

I want to underline the substantive contributions of the new methodological practice of fusing experimental design and survey research, but an overall grace note is in order. The analysis of public opinion had become standardized, routinized. Public opinion research consisted for a generation of the analysis of standard data sets, the design of which had in the largest measure been fixed two generations earlier. There is now a new element of originality. It is difficult to exaggerate the ingenuity and verve of the best of the new experimental studies. It should be mandatory to read, for example, Kuklinski's "deliberation" manipulation, which assesses the impact of reflection on support for free speech (Kuklinski et al. 1991), and his still more ingenious "list" experiment (Kuklinski and Hurley 1991), which permits -- for the first time in public opinion surveys -- the unobtrusive measurement of racial resentment.

The new methodology, moreover, operates in the service of supplying a more nuanced account of political thinking on the part of ordinary citizens. A part of the nuance, as I have been emphasizing, arises from a recognition of the variations from one situation to another in the responses of the very same individual. But another part arises from a new appreciation of the variations among individuals, particularly depending on the extent to which they are aware, educated, or politically informed. The approach to the study of public opinion dominant through the 1970s had rested on a central, albeit unspoken, premise. Citizens, it was assumed, tend to make up their minds in more or less the same way; indeed, so much so that only one causal model is required -- one set of causal factors, the same for all members of the public, arranged in one causal sequence, the same for all. But if one begins to take politics seriously in the study of public opinion, the assumption of causal homogeneity loses its persuasiveness. Why take for granted that different members in the public make up their minds about political issues in the same way? Surely the person who takes politics seriously will weigh his or her political choices differently than the one whose interest in public affairs is altogether superficial.

I do not mean they will always go about the business of decision making differently -- there may well be a tendency to commonality when information is plentiful (Rahn et al. 1990) -- but the politics of key issues -- race and AIDS, among them -- can take on the complex character they have precisely because key segments of the public go about making up their minds in systematically different ways (Sniderman, Brody, and Tetlock 1991). This notion of causal heterogeneity (Rivers 1988) will come up at various points, most notably in the discussion of political ideology and the so-called "innocence of ideology" thesis, and so I want here only to put it on the record. It may sound innocent to say that the politically sophisticated and the politically indifferent make up their minds about political choices in different ways, but this is, I am obliged to say, an example of a wolf's claim in sheep's clothing. If correct, standard accounts of public opinion are misspecified. For the controlling assumption in these accounts has been that ordinary citizens, whether highly involved in politics and well informed about it or completely detached from politics and ill-informed about it, go about making up their minds in the same ways -- that is, they take account of the same considerations, and attach the same weight to them. If one wants to understand how politics engages citizens, it is indispensable to appreciate that they come to terms with it in different ways depending on the information and assumptions they bring to it.

Having sketched some of the broad themes of the new look in public opinion research, I want now to spell out some of the details. From a minimalist perspective, it made only modest sense to ask how mass belief systems are organized, since the point precisely to appreciate was how ill-organized they tend to be; just as it made similarly modest sense to ask how a change in one of their elements could induce a change in another, since exactly the point to grasp was how tenuous connections among mass belief system elements tended to be. However, once one is willing to take seriously the notion of belief *systems*, a pair of master-problems stand out. The first is to characterize the structure of mass belief systems; the second, to give an account of their dynamics. The analysis of the structure of belief systems requires identification of their principal parts and how they are connected one to another. The analysis of the dynamics of belief systems requires examination of changes in belief both over time and across situations. The analysis of dynamics, so understood, is a natural extension of the analysis of structure, for both involve a common emphasis on the role of context in political thinking.

Given the new centrality of politics to public opinion research, I want to organize the discussion of the structure and dynamics of mass belief systems by re-visiting the "innocence of ideology" thesis. Then, in calling attention to a (relatively) neglected element of belief systems, namely values, I shall concentrate on two domains in which personal and political values are complexly implicated -- political tolerance and race. For that matter, in considering the dynamics of political belief systems, I shall stress the new contextual rather than the more familiar temporal variations, since I want to call attention to the light that the dynamics of political belief can throw on the dynamics of politics itself.

Manifestly, the twin problems of the structure and the dynamics of mass belief systems are not exhaustive. To give a fuller sense of the range of issues at the center of research on public opinion over the last decade, I want to devote the last section to a discussion of citizenship. A variety of specific themes fall under the heading of citizenship, including the role of groups in individual citizens' thinking, the problem of political legitimacy, contrasting conceptions of democracy, justice as a principle in political thinking, and -- not least important -- the re-conceptualization of public opinion at the macro rather than at the individual level.

Structure of Mass Belief Systems

No organizational net, however tightly woven, will scoop up everything. I mean accordingly to concentrate on central themes of research over the last decade or so, chief among them ideology and values.

The "Innocence of Ideology" Thesis

Reviewing research on public opinion a decade ago, Kinder (1983) took as the master question, How far are Americans' ideas of politics shaped by ideological conceptions? After making concessions on specific points -- particularly exaggerated estimates of the prevalence of "non-attitudes" -- Kinder's verdict was that Americans are "innocent of ideology": they do not make use of the larger and more abstract political ideas that make up ideologies like liberalism and conservatism in organizing their political responses, even if they could make use of them -- which far and away most of them cannot.

The innocence of ideology thesis is only one plank of the minimalist platform, yet it raises deep questions, normative as well as empirical, about the competence of citizens to act as citizens. To say that they lack ideological ideas is not to say that they lack political ideas altogether. But it is to say that citizens cannot take part in the discussion of political choices in the terms that the people who make these choices, political elites, evaluate and debate them. It is as though public discourse in democracies is carried out in two different languages, with citizens unable to make sense of the one in which consequential public judgments are framed, debated, and manipulated.

Kinder's assessment of the record of research on the ideological competence of mass publics is a measured one. But in asking whether Americans are innocent of ideology, the problem lies not in the answers he and others have offered but, more fundamentally, in the way they posed the question.[4]

The question, as Kinder frames it, is whether Americans are innocent of ideology. Putting the question this way suggests that the task is to characterize the competence and habits of the public taken as a whole. And, indeed, in representing the organization of mass belief systems, it has been taken for granted that measurements of their organization (e.g., constraint coefficients) should be computed for the mass public taken as a whole. Opposing verdicts might be rendered, with the public being judged by some to be innocent of ideology and by others capable of it under propitious circumstances (e.g., Nie, Verba, and Petrocik 1979), but the essential premise, accepted by people on all sides of the debate over the thesis of ideological innocence, is the appropriateness of making judgments about the public as a whole.

But why suppose that everyone adopts a position, or makes a choice, for the same reasons? And more specifically, why suppose, given the striking differences in political information and sophistication *within* the mass public, that the citizen who is politically aware and attentive makes up her mind in the same way as the political ignoramus? Consider the classic problem of the bearing of ideology on issue preferences in mass publics. From the minimalist perspective, this is a two-variable problem, a question of covariation, the task being to measure the covariation of overall political orientation and specific issue position. From the new perspective, it is a three-variable problem, a question of interaction, for the question to ask has become, "Under what conditions is ideology related to policy preference?" In particular, evidence has thus accumulated of a systematic interaction between political sophistication and political reasoning. Luskin (1987), in a finely filigreed account of political sophistication, documents the variation in density, range, and constraint of political cognitions with political sophistication, variously measured, while Krosnick and his colleagues (1990b) have initiated a genuinely interdisciplinary research program centered on the notion of political expertise, driving home that how people reason about a problem depends on how much they know about it.

It may now seem self-evident that how people work their way through a political choice hinges on their level of political information or sophistication, but the implications of this change in perspective are far from clearly established. Two theses can be distinguished -- weak and strong. The weak thesis holds that the belief systems of the more politically aware and sophisticated are more organized than those of the less aware and sophisticated. The strong thesis holds that the belief systems of the less politically aware are not only less but also differently organized than those of the more politically aware.

The weak thesis was put by Stimson (1975) in an inexcusably neglected article. Yoking together measures of political information and education into an overall index of "cognitive ability," Stimson focused on the co-variation of attitude constraint and political sophistication, demonstrating that the preferences of the politically aware members of the mass public were well-organized by any reasonable standard, those of the politically unaware ill-organized. And the consequences of this go deep. For Stimson's findings make plain that any effort to characterize the mass public *as a whole* will be systematically misleading: it will misrepresent the thinking of the more politically aware citizens, or of the less aware, or of both.

There cannot be just one portrait of the public, because if there is a systematic interaction between the organization of political opinions and the level of political sophistication, there is more than one pattern. In an original variation on the sophistication interaction hypothesis, Knight (1985) crystallized an important line of research, demonstrating that the degree of organization of belief systems (as indexed by constraint coefficients), plus the centrality of ideology as a decision criterion in voting, varies provocatively with citizens' levels of conceptualization (see also Cassel 1984). Jacoby (1986, 1988, 1991), in particular, following up Knight's lead in a series of well-crafted studies, has strongly buttressed the sophistication interaction hypothesis, showing (among other things) that ideology plays a differentially important role depending on individuals' levels of conceptualization and that the complexity of political reasoning -- as indexed by levels of conceptualization -- cannot be reduced to individual differences in formal education. Moreover, in a parallel but independent line of research, Lodge and his colleagues (Norpoth and Lodge 1985; Hamill and Lodge 1986; see also Lau and Sears 1986) have demonstrated the role of political sophistication in encoding and retrieving politically relevant cues. Taking advantage of experimentally designed studies of recognition and distinguishing between schematics (those who are expert or at any rate knowledgeable about politics) and aschematics (those who are neither), Lodge and his colleagues show that the former are markedly more likely to recognize and to understand political concepts and leaders. What is more, they have developed a causal model of ideological sophistication, out of which falls the tantalizing result that cognitive ability (as assessed by education and a vocabulary and abstract symbols test) powerfully influences ideological sophistication but that political experience (as assessed by political interest, media usage, and political activity) does not.

All these studies add up to strong confirmation of the weak version of the sophistication thesis. There is also evidence, although weaker, in behalf of the strong version of the thesis. The strong version, like the weak, holds that the more politically aware and sophisticated citizens are, the better organized their political ideas and preferences. However, the strong version of the sophistication interaction hypothesis holds that the less politically aware and sophisticated, in addition to being more vulnerable to failing to organize their thinking, may also organize it in different ways. In consequence, they are not only less likely to have reasons for the positions they take on public issues, but in some politically consequential situations, they may also have *different* reasons for the positions they take than the politically aware and sophisticated (cf. Moon 1990).

I want to offer an example of the strong version of the sophistication hypothesis, if only to make plain what is being argued here. Consider the positions white Americans take on government assistance for blacks. Viewed at a distance, several considerations fairly plainly lie behind decisions to support or oppose such assistance for blacks, among them, their propensity to favor or oppose such governmental action in general and, of course, their feelings toward blacks. It is thus perfectly obvious that the more politically liberal whites are, the more disposed they are to approve of an array of welfare and assistance programs for blacks, just as it is perfectly obvious that the more they dislike blacks, the more likely they are to disapprove of such programs. So defined, the view at a distance is correct -- except that it obscures a crucial detail. The importance of both ideology and affect toward blacks as factors fixing positions on issues of race varies systematically: the better educated whites are, the larger the role of ideology and the less consequential that of affect toward blacks; conversely, the less educated, the larger the role of affect and the less consequential that of ideology (Sniderman, Brody and Kuklinski 1984; Moon 1990). And so far as this holds, the forces shaping the politics of race -- indeed, the very meaning of the contest over one and the same public policy -- can differ in character across the American public (Sniderman and Piazza 1992).

It is to be emphasized that whichever version -- strong or weak -- of the interaction hypothesis is adopted, the "innocence of ideology" thesis is misspecified. Simply put, it is systematically misleading to declare that mass publics *en bloc* are "innocent of ideology," because it is systematically misleading to characterize the political reasoning of mass publics *en bloc*.

Values

It made little sense to explore the structure of mass belief systems when the principal point was to repeat that they are poorly organized. Only if one concedes that ordinary citizens can figure out where they stand politically does the question even arise of how they can organize and make connections among their various beliefs and feelings and aims.

Traditionally, the study of public opinion has concentrated on the smallest units of belief, located at the fringes of political belief systems -- specific opinions about particular issues. But ignoring the larger elements, nearer the core of political belief systems, has favored an exaggerated impression of the political incompetence of the general public. It is as though people were judged not to know much about their economic assets, all in all, because they do not know how much small change they carry in their pockets on any given day. People may be fuzzy about narrow, transient opinions, yet clear-sighted about their basic values.

Analytically, values have a perfectly obvious explanatory appeal because they are obvious consistency generators: rather than ginning up separate reasons why people may take consistent stands on issues of welfare, health and education, crime and standard of living, it is more economical to invoke a value like equality.

Feldman (1988), for example, puts the argument in terms of a consistency conundrum. On the one hand, a small mountain of evidence demonstrates that mass publics do not organize their issue preferences consistent with a "crowning posture" or "superordinate value," such as liberalism-conservatism; on the other hand, ordinary citizens frequently do figure out where they stand politically. How then, Feldman asks, is it possible for them consistently to work out their reactions to political choices given that they do not do so constrained by a single, overarching posture or value?

By relying on "core beliefs and values," he answers. And what are examples of such core beliefs and values? Equal opportunity, economic individualism, and a belief in free enterprise are the three that Feldman singles out, showing that two at least play an organizational role, constraining policy preferences, presidential performance evaluations, and candidate preferences, not simply at the zero order, but net of both demographic variables and more familiar political orientations, such as party identification.

Rasinski (1987) independently makes a similar analytic move. There are, he argues, two principal anchors of judgments of social justice -- equity and egalitarianism. Equity refers to the importance attached to effort, egalitarianism to the importance attached to assisting the disadvantaged and less fortunate. Drawing on a number of independent samples, Rasinski shows that judgments on a range of social policies as well as on the perceived fairness of presidential candidates -- all tend to be rooted in deeper-lying considerations of equity and equality.

Both these studies are inventive in the measures of values they deploy, and persuasive in making a first-order case for the role of deeper-lying values as consistency generators. Yet, it needs to be emphasized that this conception of the role of values is a narrow one, and does not push the causal explanation to a markedly deeper level: people are said to favor more egalitarian policies because they are egalitarian -- not a stunning explanatory gain. By way of illustrating the deeper role of values in the structuring of political belief systems, I want to suggest that, paradoxically, ordinary citizens' political preferences appear ill-organized, their opinions on specific issues seemingly having little to do with one another, in part because their opinions are organized by deeper-lying values.

Consider the structure of political belief systems as represented at the height of minimalism (Converse 1964). A fully formed belief system is two-tiered. The bottom tier consists of specific opinions, covering an array of political issues. The top tier is made up of an abstract, superordinate concept -- usually, but not necessarily, liberalism-conservatism. The idea of this arrangement, of course, is to suggest that insofar as

specific opinions on particular issues exhibit coherence and consistency it is because they follow -- indeed, have been deduced -- from a superordinate ideology. Or rather, from a minimalist perspective, the point of representing political belief systems as capped by ideology is to drive home why the opinions of ordinary citizens show such minimal constraint. For the whole thrust of minimalism as a perspective on public opinion is to make plain the implausibility of supposing that the average citizen would be able or motivated to "deduce" rigorously the positions he or she should take on a gamut of specific issues in light of a large, complex, and abstract ideology like liberalism or conservatism. And as Levitin and Miller (1979), among others, have ably shown, the covariation of ideology and issue preferences in mass publics is thin indeed.

Thanks to a pioneering line of studies by Peffley and Hurwitz (1985; Hurwitz and Peffley 1987), however, the structure of belief systems can be seen in different terms -- as triple rather than double tiered. People, the Peffley-Hurwitz model suggests, do not move from political abstractions to specific issue preferences in one fell swoop. Rather, they move in smaller steps -- first, working their way from a superordinate value (like liberalism-conservatism) to an intermediate one (such as general economic attitudes); then, moving from the intermediate value to an opinion about a specific issue. The idea of constraint, it follows, must be construed in two quite different ways. Introducing the term, Converse (1964) represented it analytically in terms of vertical linkages -- between "crowning postures" and specific policy preferences -- but construed it operationally in terms of horizontal linkages -- between pairs of specific issues. Driving home this distinction between types of constraint, Peffley and Hurwitz demonstrate that the weak "horizontal" linkages recorded in previous studies are quite compatible with strong "vertical" linkages. Still more broadly, they show how it is possible for both the links between end points in a chain of inference and also the constraint across issue positions to be weak *even though each and every link in the chain is strong*. It becomes possible, in turn, to see how the minimal levels of constraint routinely observed for issue preferences in mass publics, rather than being testimony to an "innocence of ideology," can be compatible with the operation of ideology.

A model recommends itself partly by disposing of old questions, partly by raising new ones. If there is a second tier in mass belief systems of general orientations or values, intermediate between a "crowning posture" and specific issue preferences, then the question becomes how these orientations or values are themselves interrelated. Curiously, though people manifestly have more than one value, it has been customary to consider values only one-at-a-time. I think particularly in this respect of the work of Inglehart on post-materialism (e.g., 1977, 1990). I know of no one who has more assiduously pursued a line of argument in the field of public opinion, illuminating the politics of half a dozen countries; and notwithstanding criticism of some of his broader theses on political culture and generational change (e.g., Flanagan 1987, 1982, 1980; Clarke and Dutt 1991). This measure of materialist and post-materialist values surely captures something telling. But here, given our special concern with the problem of multiple values, one aspect of his approach stands out.

Inglehart is, above all, concerned with a particular value orientation -- "postmaterialism" in his terms -- and the object of his research program is to show how the political sentiments and choices of ordinary citizens have increasingly come to be shaped by it. But what is crucial is his way of framing the question. In focusing on post-materialist and materialist values, Inglehart sets out a set of values -- for example, controlling inflation or protecting free speech -- classifying people as post-materialist or materialist depending on which of the competing values they designate as personally the most important. But proceeding this way constrains analysis of the connections among values. And what I want to suggest is that once one concedes that people have more than one value, then in order to understand the role of values in belief systems, it is not enough to explore the relation between specific opinions and deeper values -- *taken one at a time*. It is necessary to take account of the relations of values to one another.

The proposition that people have multiple values I want to dub "value pluralism."[5] People, manifestly, care about more than one thing -- indeed, are, simultaneously and sincerely attached to values that clash. So one and the same person can care for both liberty and order, or for that matter, for both materialism and post-materialism. Regrettably, we know little either about the structural organization of values -- that is, their relation one to another -- or their relation, taken more than one at a time, to specific opinions and attitudes. There is, however, a striking line of studies on value pluralism. The central proposition, roughly put, is this: belief systems differ not only in the priority attached to core, or terminal, values (Rokeach 1973), but also in the degree to which these terminal values are, and are acknowledged to be, in conflict or tension (Tetlock 1986a, 1986b). So viewed, when high priority is attached to only one value or to one consistent set of values, belief systems may be classified as "monistic." Alternatively, when high priority is attached to values acknowledged to be capable of conflicting with one another belief systems are "pluralistic." The causal story that Tetlock urges is that

proponents of pluralistic ideologies, by virtue of having to adjudicate among competing values, are more likely than holders of monistic ideologies to appreciate the range of considerations one has to take into account, the complexity of their interconnections, and the trade-offs deserving consideration; hence the proponents of pluralistic ideologies are likely to be more complex in their thinking.

The focus on integrative complexity, unlike a host of companion studies in social psychology, has consequential political implications because it calls attention to the connection between the structure of political thinking and the substance of political thought. There is of course a long line of studies relevant here, beginning with the argument advanced by Adorno and his colleagues (1950) that the political right is distinctively predisposed to think in either-or terms, dividing up the world into friend-and-foe, to interpret the world in conspiratorial and Manichean terms, to be rigid, intolerant of ambiguity, intolerant through and through, hostile and prejudiced towards others whose beliefs, appearance, background or manners were different or merely unfamiliar (Altemeyer 1988). The "rigidity-of-the-right" hypothesis in turn met with a powerful critique. Shils (1954), Eysenck (1954), and Rokeach (1960), among others, contended that ideologues shared intemperateness and sectarianism, whether they were on the left or the right. Then the revisionist position was itself revised, the scholarly pendulum moved back to the original position, as Brown (1986) and a host of others contended that there was a fundamental asymmetry between ideology on the right in the form of fascism and ideology on the left in the form of communism. On this view, there is an authoritarianism on the right but not an authoritarianism of the left (see also DiRenzo 1974; Barker 1963; but also Ray 1983).

Tetlock's special contribution has been to break out of this seesaw argument. Reanalyzing the in-depth interviews of British M.P.'s conducted by Putnam (1973), Tetlock demonstrated that of four ideological groups, extreme conservatives and extreme socialists were the least integratively complex in their thinking, moderate socialists and conservatives the most and the former still more than the latter (Tetlock 1984). The validity of the symmetry position has subsequently been replicated by McClosky and Chong (1985), who have added the intriguing methodological observation that the apparent rigidity of the extreme right-wing believer in previous studies arises from the greater difficulty of inducing extreme left-wing believers to participate in public opinion surveys.

There is something appealing in the idea of value pluralism as propounded by Tetlock, to a student of political theory as well as of public opinion. The whole thrust of the position is to suggest that awareness of multiple considerations promotes complexity of reasoning and moderation of positions. So conceived, the value pluralism model presents a formulation in social-psychological terms of a classic argument from political theory on the nature of pluralism as a democratic value (Berlin 1969). But familiar as this argument is, a central aspect of it has gone unexplored.

Consistent with the idea of value pluralism, it is commonplace to speak of the tradeoffs of values that political choices impose -- between liberty and equality, for example, or between liberty and order -- to talk, that is, of political choices taking the form of balancing or weighing competing values. But this representation of choice deserves attention. Consider an issue of civil liberties -- say, a specific question of whether a demonstration against the Vietnam war should be permitted, given that it is to be held in a part of a town strongly committed to the war, deeply offended by protests against it, and quite likely in consequence to respond with outrage and, possibly, even violence. (cf. Gibson and Bingham 1985). It is common to speak as though a decision about an issue like this turns on the weighing of competing values: a commitment to free speech, say, as against an appreciation of the risks of violence and the importance of order. But this way of speaking of natural pairs of competing values, however familiar, can be systematically misleading. For the decisive point is that these ostensibly competing values are, in fact, negatively correlated: the more importance a person attaches to the value of freedom of speech, the less he or she attaches to the value of order, and vice versa. And insofar as such values as liberty and order are negatively correlated, the pair tends to be self-reinforcing rather than self-contradictory (McClosky and Brill 1983; McClosky and Zaller 1985; Sniderman, Fletcher, Russell, Tetlock, and Gaines 1991). Indeed, it is in part thanks to the coherence of people's values -- to their placing a high value on liberty and a low one on order, and a high value on order and a low on liberty -- that they react consistently to civil liberties issues even in the heat of specific controversies.

A crucial feature of the architecture of political belief systems is thus the tendency of people to strive for consistency, if not at the level of specific issues, then at any rate at the level of values. And the failure to appreciate this striving for value consistency, imperfect though it is, has given rise to a series of pseudo-problems. For example, it is often said that a racial policy such as affirmative action requires the citizen to balance off the competing claims of liberty and equality. In fact, the more committed a person is to the value of liberty, the more likely he or she is to support affirmative action (say, in the form of support for freedom of speech), the more committed he or she will tend to be to the value of equality (say, in the form of acting to see that the worst off are better off). In short, the people who are most likely to attach importance to core values are precisely those who are most likely to have organized their values in a way that minimizes the conflict of values that many political analysts have emphasized.

Value coherence should not be overstated. Even granted a predisposition to consistency, people can find themselves in situations that activate competing values. Indeed, in sorting out the competing theoretical claims of value pluralism vs. value consistency, the issue is not deciding which is true, and which false, but rather specifying the conditions under which one or the other holds. A rough, but serviceable, rule is this: value consistency tends to be the rule for "top-of-the-head" responses; an appreciation of the tension among values, and a willingness to engage in value trade-offs, is more characteristic of behavior in situations that unequivocally activate competing values, permit some time for a weighing of alternatives before having to manifest a response, and encourage a self-critical mental set -- for example, when one expects to justify one's views to someone whose own views are unknown and one is not constrained by past statements or commitments (Tetlock 1983; Tetlock, Skitka, and Boettger 1989).

It deserves emphasis that values count twice over in political analysis, as both explicans and explicandum, and by way of underlining this duality I want to comment particularly on two domains -- political tolerance and race.

Political Tolerance

The relevance of politics -- even to the conceptualization of political tolerance -- has been driven home by the pioneering research of Sullivan, Piereson, and Marcus (1979, 1982). Invoking the origins of the doctrine of political toleration in the religious controversies of the seventeenth century, they argue that tolerance consists in a willingness to put up with ideas or people or acts that one dislikes or fears. The research program of Sullivan and his colleagues (see also Sullivan et al. 1985; Barnum and Sullivan 1989; Shamir 1991) is easily the most imaginative rethinking of the idea of political tolerance since Stouffer's (1955) seminal study -- and one of the most elegant, for that matter, given that their original operational definition falls so naturally, even self-evidently, out of their conceptual definition. This is the so-called "content-controlled" method, which requires that respondents first identify (usually from a fixed list) a group they dislike, then face a set of standard interrogatories on their willingness to support rights of members of *this* particular group.

The content-controlled method has proven controversial (e.g., Gibson 1992; Mueller 1988; Sniderman, Tetlock, Glaser, Green, and Hout 1989), but the controversy has been excited, not by exotic methodological qualms, but rather by the implications of alternative conceptualizations of political tolerance for the theory and practice of democratic politics. Consider the role of education in a democratic society. The classic studies of political tolerance, which had concentrated on tolerance of groups on the left (communists, socialists, atheists), had suggested strongly that education is an engine of tolerance: the more formal schooling a person has had, the wider the range of both political groups and political acts that he or she is willing to accept as legitimate (Stouffer 1955; Nunn, Crockett, and Williams 1978). In contrast, the findings of Sullivan and his colleagues suggest a far more modest role for education. It is a major determinant, they argue, not of how tolerant one is, but of whom one is prepared to tolerate. The better educated, in the Sullivan view, have misleadingly given the appearance of being markedly more tolerant politically only because classic studies of tolerance (e.g., Stouffer 1955) have focused on groups on the left -- which, as it happens, are the groups that the less educated are more likely to dislike (Sullivan et al. 1982, 114ff; but see Bobo and Licari 1989; Gibson 1992). Analogously, in the Sullivan view, liberals have misleadingly given the appearance of being markedly more tolerant than conservatives in the classic studies of political tolerance, but this reflects not a stronger principled commitment to the value of tolerance on the part of liberals, but only their natural inclination to accept as legitimate groups on the same side of the political fence as themselves -- which, as it happens, were the groups on which the classic studies of tolerance focused.

Being myself a participant in some of these skirmishes (Sniderman, Tetlock, Glaser, Green, and Hout 1989), I don't want to pretend to an above-the-fray disinterestedness. But it is important to underline how deep, both conceptually and normatively, the issues go. There is, at the core, one issue in particular which merits mention -- the so-called unity thesis. The Sullivan approach takes as its central premise the disjunction of political tolerance and nonpolitical forms of tolerance. Individuals should be said to be tolerant politically, according to the Sullivan view, if and only if they dislike a group and nonetheless support the political rights of its members. Whatever sense this makes for political tolerance, it makes no sense for other forms of tolerance. Who would insist that, in order for a person to be characterized as racially "tolerant," it is necessary that he or she dislike blacks? Surely, the notion of tolerance in a variety of its forms -- with respect to gays, for example, or to women, or to Jews -- carries with it the

understanding that disliking, or fearing, or holding in contempt a person because of the color of his skin, or sexual orientation, or religious convictions -- is in and of itself a manifestation of intolerance. These conceptual tangles to one side, proponents of the unity thesis thus hold that the various aspects of tolerance, political as well as nonpolitical, are tied together causally: on this view, factors that increase political tolerance (e.g., education) tend to have a spillover effect, encouraging a variety of specific forms of tolerance, including racial and religious tolerance.

The fate of the unity thesis matters on more than one front, but not the least important is its buttressing of the role of values in political reasoning. Although the dominant theme in research on tolerance remains the limits of popular understanding of, and commitment to, civil liberties and civil rights (McClosky and Brill 1983; Sullivan et al. 1979; Gibson 1992), a new theme has been emerging in counterpoint. A substantial fraction of the general public, it is now being argued (Bobo and Licari 1989; Sniderman, Tetlock, et al. 1989) has formed a genuine -- albeit imperfect -- commitment to the value of tolerance, and their commitment to the value of tolerance is a primary -- although obviously not the sole -- determinant of their reactions to specific issues of civil liberties (see also Sullivan et al. 1983).

The classic studies of political tolerance (e.g., Stouffer 1955; McClosky 1964) had focused on the sources of support for political tolerance as a value. Studies of the last decade have broadened this focus to incorporate the consequences of political tolerance as well as its causes. It can be shown to matter, in ways not previously appreciated, whether citizens place a high value on political tolerance or not. For example, in a quite original line of argument, Gibson (1992) has shown that a natural concomitant of a person's desire to restrict the range of permissible behavior of others is a willingness to restrict the range of his or her own permissible behavior. There is thus a perverse dialectic of intolerance: wishing to restrain others, to confine them to a narrow and safe ambit, the citizens prone to intolerance restrain themselves, confine themselves to a narrow ambit of what they may say and do. More programmatically, Gibson and his colleagues have proposed a contextualized analysis of the politics of tolerance, focusing on actual (and not merely hypothetical) clashes of views over civil liberties, such as the dispute in Skokie, Illinois over the first amendment rights of a group of Nazis (Gibson and Bingham 1985), or the clash in Houston over the rights of homosexuals (Gibson 1987). By contextualizing his studies, by grounding them in specific events and particular controversies, Gibson revived a practice of "firehouse" studies, surveys focusing on events in the headlines, a practice initiated in the heyday of McCarthyism with Stouffer's (1955) heroic study of political tolerance, *Communism, Conformity and Civil Liberties*.

Contextualizing the study of political values like tolerance helps take politics out of the background. Among the several senses in which this is true, one I would particularly stress is the following. As students of politics, what we care about is how citizens will react in actual controversies; indeed, one reason the concept of values seems analytically compelling is precisely because it provides a way to account for how citizens hold their ground in the face of significant pressure to qualify or abandon their positions on issues of civil liberties. It would exaggerate to say that a compelling case has been made for "values as stabilizers," although the evidence now at hand suggests the hypothesis deserves to be taken seriously. The outbreak of AIDS, for example, supplied a grotesque, but instructive, opportunity to assess citizen responses under stress; and taking advantage of a serendipitous "before-and-after" design, Sniderman and his colleagues demonstrated the extent to which citizens would maintain their commitment to the value of tolerance -- and specifically in this instance, to the civil liberties of homosexuals -- even when confronted suddenly, unexpectedly, and undeniably by a deadly threat (Sniderman, Wolfinger, Mutz, and Wiley 1991).

Specific threats to one side, the premise of research on political tolerance has been that a fundamental distinction needs to be drawn between mass publics and political elites. Inattentive to politics, ignorant of political ideas, the ordinary citizen, according to classic studies of political tolerance (Stouffer 1955; McClosky 1964), tends to have only a superficial commitment to democratic values. In contrast, political elites tend to have a markedly deeper commitment to the whole array of civil liberties and civil rights; indeed, so much so that McClosky, in a famous phrase, declared that they "serve as the major repositories of the public conscience and as carriers of the Creed" (1960, 374).

I want to refer to the idea that democratic polities keep their bearings in crises thanks to the special devotion of the politically articulate and influential to civil liberties as the thesis of democratic elitism. Needless to say, the label is for convenience only, and is not intended to be in any way pejorative. The thesis of democratic elitism has become part of the stock of received knowledge, partly because of the excellence of the original studies (Stouffer 1955; McClosky 1964), partly because of the repeated corroboration of subsequent studies, one or two exceptions (Israel, for example) notwithstanding (Stouffer 1955; McClosky 1964; Nunn, Crockett, and Williams 1978; McClosky and Brill 1983; and Sullivan et al. 1982).

Broadly, two explanations of elite-mass differences have been staked out. On the one hand, it is suggested that political elites are more likely to serve as faithful "repositories of the public conscience," because they have been more thoroughly exposed and have more deeply learned civil liberties by virtue of their involvement in politics -- the "political socialization" hypothesis. Alternatively, it is contended that they are more deeply committed to democratic values because of other characteristics associated with their elite status -- for example, education -- having nothing inherently to do with politics -- the "selective recruitment" hypothesis. Each hypothesis has had its supporters: McClosky and his colleagues being perhaps the most unqualified advocates of the political socialization hypothesis (McClosky 1964; McClosky and Brill 1983), and Jackman (1972), one of the earliest and most effective exponents of the selective recruitment hypothesis. The truth, to judge from Sullivan, Walsh, Shamir, Barnum, and Gibson's (1992) overarching analysis of four countries, appears to be a mix of the two.

But if the fact of greater elite commitment to democratic values is not in dispute, the meaning of the fact continues to be debated. For example, Gibson (1992), in a re-analysis of Stouffer's original data, has shown that there is a marked correlation between the "repressiveness" of a state's public policy and the mean level of elite intolerance but not the mean level of public intolerance -- a finding which suggests that the legal McCarthyism of the period was undertaken in response to the demands less of ordinary citizens than of political elites.[6] Beyond this, the thesis of democratic elitism presupposes that the decisive contrast is between the values of political elites and those of mass publics, suggesting that if a choice between the two has to be made, elites are a better bet to back democratic values in any specific controversy than are ordinary citizens. But in liberal democracies, the choice is not between the views of the public at large and those of elites taken as a whole: it is instead between groups of elites, organized around political parties and competing for political power through elections. Partly because of the incentives of electoral competition, partly because of the constraints of political ideology, there tend to be pronounced cleavages in beliefs about civil liberties among partisan elites; so pronounced that the key to the politics of civil liberties can be just which group of partisan elites wins office. To take a specific example, McClosky (1960), in a classic study, showed that Democratic and Republican activists -- as a composite -- were more committed to civil liberties than the general population. But the choice of who will be president or senator is not between political activists and ordinary citizens: it is between Democratic and Republican aspirants for public office, and there is a marked difference between the two in support for democratic values in specific controversies. To translate the terms slightly, Democratic activists tend to be predominantly liberal, Republican activists overwhelmingly conservative, and as Sniderman, Fletcher (1991), drawing on McClosky's published results, have shown, conservative elites are no more committed to civil liberties than are ordinary citizens who are conservative - - *and significantly less committed than ordinary citizens who are liberal* (see also Gibson and Duch 1991). The classic contrast between elites and mass publics is, in consequence, systematically misleading. So far as the normative thrust in formulating and implementing civil liberties policies, what counts is not a mythical choice between an "average" political elite and an "average" citizen but rather the consistent and striking difference in the importance attached to civil liberties between the actual groups of elites competing for political power. The electoral system operates to choose among, not to average across, competing sets of elites, and the fallacy of democratic elitism consists precisely in its indifference to which set of elites prevails.

The Politics of Race

Another expression of the new interest in the stuff of politics is the burgeoning research on race as an issue in contemporary American life. The impetus to this research field was supplied in a significant degree by Sears and his colleagues. In a research program now extending over two decades, they have developed a distinctive account of the politics of race -- the "symbolic politics" perspective. Since this symbolic politics perspective is intended as a systematic perspective on issues of race, I shall set out some of its central tenets, although it should be borne in mind that there are differences in emphasis and nuance from one researcher to another.

The starting point, and a continuing focus, is a strategic contrast between a "self-interest" account on the one side, and a "symbolic politics" account on the other. A quasi-paradigmatic explanatory perspective emphasizing rational choice and utility maximization has recently emerged. It represents voters as making judgments both about policies and politicians on the basis of their tangible self-interest (e.g., Downs 1957; Page 1978; Fiorina 1981). As against this rational choice perspective, Sears and his colleagues (e.g., Sears, Lau, Tyler, and Allen 1980; Kinder and Sears 1981; McConahay 1982; Lau, Brown, and Sears 1978) juxtapose a "symbolic politics" perspective. The heart of the symbolic politics argument is a triple-barreled contention: first, that a limited number of affective orientations or predispositions (e.g., party identification, liberal or conservative ideology, racial prejudice) are

central to the political thinking of ordinary citizens; second, that these affective orientations tend to have been acquired in childhood and maintained ever since; and third, that responses to new policy issues are made on the basis of "the similarity of symbols posed by the policy issue to those long-standing predispositions" (Sears et al. 1980, 671). The central thrust of the symbolic politics research program, accordingly, has been to conduct horse races between measures of self-interest on the one side and of symbolic predispositions on the other, to determine which accounts for the lion's share of the variance in either policy preferences or voting choices. A considerable amount of political terrain has been traversed in this fashion, including a variety of policy domains (e.g., national health insurance, busing, government-guaranteed jobs, law and order); of indicators of self-interest (including employment, short-run trends in family finances, medical insurance, having a child in public school, and so on, the relevant indicator of self-interest varying appropriately with the particular policy domain); and symbolic predispositions (including ideological self-identification, party identification, and racial prejudice). And the findings have been impressively consistent across a range of policies and data sets. The impact of self-interest tends to be modest, not only in the mass public as a whole but in strategic segments of it one might have expected to be especially motivated to make up their minds on the basis of their material well-being. On the other hand, symbolic predispositions have characteristically exerted a substantial impact both on policy preferences and voting choices. Without denying that immediate tangible self-interest can play a role in shaping political belief and perhaps, still more, political behavior, the symbolic politics perspective has made a valuable contribution in demonstrating that its impact is more narrow and more circumscribed than had ever been supposed.

The symbolic politics model represents a general approach to the study of public opinion, accenting the limited number of enduring and general predispositions organizing political thinking. A specific implementation of the general model, applied to the politics of race, is the "symbolic racism" perspective. Briefly, the symbolic racism argument runs as follows. Old-fashioned racism - - overt, crude, offensive on its face -- has largely disappeared. Which is not to say that racism has disappeared. It has instead become less obvious, more subtle. This new, more subtle racism -- or "symbolic racism" or "modern racism," as it is variously called -- consists in a conjunction or fusion of prejudice and a quintessential American value, individualism. From the symbolic racism perspective, a genuine alliance of prejudice and individualism has been effected: white Americans resist racial equality in the name of self-reliance, achievement, individual initiative, and they do so not merely because the value of individualism provides a socially acceptable pretext but because it provides an integral component of the new racism.

The symbolic racism argument has, not surprisingly, proven controversial (e.g., Schuman, Steeh, and Bobo 1985; Weigel and Howes 1985; Bobo 1983; and Sniderman and Tetlock 1986a, 1986b; but see also Kinder 1986; McConahay 1986; and Sears 1988). It is all the more important, therefore, to distinguish two very different grounds on which arguments have been conducted. One concerns the politics of race specifically; the other, the nature of political thinking generally.

To take the issue of race itself first, it is important to underline how far-reaching is the argument of symbolic racism. Its principal claim is that racism is the product not of an historical or external contingency, nor is it an expression of a regrettable but universal aspect of human nature; it is instead the result of the "finest and proudest of American values" (Sears 1988, 54). Racism is, in this view, as American as apple pie or Horatio Alger. Empirically, the nub of the issue is the relation between individualism and contemporary racism, with evidence accumulating in two opposing piles. On the one side, a series of studies have shown that sentiments, which deliberately confound anti-black affect and a reference (direct or indirect) to the value of individualism (e.g., "If blacks would only try harder, they would be just as well off as whites"), are strongly correlated with the positions whites take on a number of racial issues (e.g., Sears et al. 1979; Sears et al. 1980; and Kinder and Sears 1981). On the other side, a series of studies have shown that individualism (measured directly) has little to do either whites' attitudes toward blacks or their position on public policies dealing with blacks (e.g., Kluegel and Smith 1983; Sniderman, Piazza, Tetlock, and Kendrick 1991; Sniderman and Piazza 1992). No consensus on the issue has yet been reached (but see Sears 1988; and Sears and Kosterman 1991).

There is, though, a deeper level at which the symbolic politics argument deserves to be engaged. It offers a general model of political thinking maximally in contrast with the minimalist perspective. To offer a stylized account, minimalism puts its emphasis on the transitoriness of public opinion, with large numbers of ordinary voters unable even to remember the position they took on an issue the election before. In contrast, the symbolic politics perspective rests on a radical persistence hypothesis. Taking as its theme the Jesuit adage that whoever controls the education of the child controls the thinking of the adult, the symbolic politics perspective holds that citizens respond to contemporary issues on the basis, not of "the current informational environments," but of the social and political circumstances and sentiments that prevailed when they were children (Sears

1983, 80). It cannot be said that there is anything like the evidence required to demonstrate persistence on this scale,[7] although it is important to distinguish between failing (so far) to establish the validity of a hypothesis and demonstrating its falsity. Moreover, I want to concentrate on the nature of political thinking viewed from a symbolic politics perspective. Central to this picture of political thinking is a limited number of symbolic predispositions acquired in childhood, and not significantly modified or updated since. Weighting so heavily the role of childhood sentiments and needs as determinants of adult beliefs and choices, the symbolic politics argument represents a revival of a classic tradition in public opinion accenting the irrationality of mass publics (cf. Lippmann 1922; Adorno et al. 1950).

The symbolic politics perspective deserves serious attention because it represents an effort to work out a model of political thinking that is general, coherent, and distinctive. By way of underlining both its coherence and distinctiveness, I want to contrast it with the research program on "issue pluralism," which represents a very different perspective on the politics of race (Sniderman, Tetlock, Carmines, and Peterson n.d.; Sniderman and Piazza 1992). The "issue pluralism" perspective offers a policy-centered account of the thinking of ordinary Americans about issues of race. To say that the account is policy-centered is not to deny that whites base their reactions to issues of race in part on enduring dispositions such as racial stereotypes and political ideology: but the vital point is that which dispositions matter, and how much they matter, varies from one racial policy to another. It was once supposed that when whites were asked to respond to racial policies, what mattered to them was not *what* was to be done by way of policy but rather for *whom* it was to be done: as Converse put it in a classic expression, different racial policies

> would tend to boil down for many respondents to the same single question: 'Are you sympathetic to Negroes as a group, are you indifferent to them, or do you dislike them?' The responses would be affected accordingly. (1964, 235)

This rings true as an account of the politics of race in the 1950s and 1960s. But the premise of the issue pluralism approach is that the politics of race have changed, and it is of course a change-oriented argument that the symbolic politics perspective, with its commitment to the fixity of controlling predispositions acquired early in life, is not well positioned to deal with. How has the issue of race changed? According to the issue pluralism argument, there no longer is *one* issue of race, but a number of them, and notwithstanding some common elements, their politics are distinct. Broadly speaking, a trio of policy agendas can be distinguished --

social welfare, equal treatment, and race consciousness, all concerned with race, each politically distinct nonetheless. From this point of view, the crucial fact to recognize is that the politics of racial welfare policies and those of affirmative action are by no means the same, and the politics of fair housing is different yet again (Sniderman, Tetlock, Carmines, and Peterson n.d.; Carmines and Merriman n.d.; Sniderman and Piazza 1992). There is in this emphasis on the distinctiveness of policy agendas the thread of a larger argument, being made independently and on fronts having nothing to do with race. Thus, Hamill, Lodge and Blake (1985), taking advantage of the language of schema theory, drive home the point that the schema used to structure policy attitudes are domain specific. Moreover, Hurwitz and Peffley (1987, 1990; and Peffley and Hurwitz n.d.), have seized on the natural contrast between how people think about foreign and domestic policy concerns, illustrating the distinctive values (or "postures") structuring responses to foreign policy issues, demonstrating in the process the utility of domain-specific analyses.

The symbolic politics and issue pluralism approaches, though manifestly different, are not mutually exclusive across-the-board. It is too easy to go astray by insisting that one or the other is true. The question is instead which, for any given problem, is more useful. Given the underidentification of theories across-the-board, truth is utility in context. Moreover, both approaches agree on a vital point: that it is useful to take seriously the structure of mass belief systems. Having concentrated to this point on the structure of political belief systems, I want now to turn to their dynamics.

Dynamics

Temporal vs. Contextual

Public opinion, through the 1960s and 1970s, was largely conceived in static terms. There was, to be sure, a prominent strand of panel studies of the dynamics of political attitudes (Jennings and Niemi 1974, 1981; Converse and Markus 1979). But notwithstanding the important contributions of these studies, the problem of change was given strict construction. Relying on panel studies embedded in either a cross-electoral or generational design, it became commonplace to equate the dynamics of political belief with the natural decay of political opinions over extended periods of time.

Given this history, and with an eye to expanding the range of variation relevant to political analysis, I want to introduce a distinction between two ways of construing dynamics. Dynamics may refer -- indeed, in the heyday of minimalism, it nearly always referred -- to changes in belief over time. But it may also refer to variations in belief across situations. This second sense of dynamics -- contextual rather than temporal -- has come increasingly to the fore.

Given the new prominence of politics, I want to illustrate how the notion of dynamics -- construed as contextual rather than temporal variation -- throws light on political thinking. I remarked earlier on the shifting fortunes of the "rigidity-of-the-right" hypothesis, which holds that there is an asymmetric relation between ideology and extremism (the right being more prone to rigidity), and the "ideologue" hypothesis, which holds that the relation is symmetric (both left and right being vulnerable). Tetlock, however, has shown that it is a mistake to think only in trait terms, as though people who fell on the far right -- or far left -- were marked by distinctive personality characteristics or cognitive styles *regardless of their political circumstances*. In particular, Tetlock argued, people's readiness to recognize and respect the complexity of political choices under debate had much to do with a pair of features of the political context -- first, whether they could be held accountable politically for the choice, and second, whether a particular choice was important to them given their political orientation and value priorities. What emerges from this contextualist account is a demonstration that the political left *or* right can be disposed to more (or less) complex political reasoning depending on political circumstance and context (Tetlock 1981, 1983, 1985a, 1985b, and 1988).

A quite different way of representing the contextual character of political judgments is suggested by the longstanding argument over whether people rely on "pocketbook" or "sociotropic" judgments in evaluating leaders. The scholarly debate has concerned which judgment type dominates the other, but as Mutz (1992a) has cleverly shown, framing the analytic issue in either-or terms is a mistake. When media coverage is heavy, personal experiences are 'depoliticized' and people rely more on perceptions of collective experience derived from mass media; on the other hand, when media coverage is low (and among those low in exposure to it), people are more likely to rely on personal experiences as the source of information underlying their political preferences. Two points in particular deserve to be made. First, at the level of the phenomena themselves, Mutz's findings, which jibe nicely with those of Weatherford (1983) and Conover and her colleagues (1991, 1992), suggest that people who are not tied into the beliefs and experiences of the larger collective through regular media consumption will "default" to more parochial sources of information such as personal experience as a basis for their political judgments. Second, at a more 'meta'-level, Mutz's focus on the conditional character of political judgments in situations of high and low media coverage can serve as a mini-sermon, in itself, on the importance of not staging simple contests between "alternative" hypotheses and focusing instead on the conditions under which one or the other may be the more useful.

Variation across situations thus operates as one dimension defining the dynamics of political belief. Variations across individuals define a second dimension. It follows that specification of the rate and processes of diffusion of political preferences, across the general public, is very much at the center of analysis of the dynamics of public opinion. There is not a well-developed set of conventions about how to talk about variation in diffusion rates and processes within mass publics, and so by way of a talking-point, I want to call attention to a model of persuasion and attitude change -- the so-called "two-step reception-yielding model," first formulated nearly a generation ago (McGuire 1964; Converse 1964).

The heart of the two-step model is a distinction between reception and yielding. To be persuaded to adopt a belief or opinion about an issue, according to the two-step model, it is necessary *first* to be exposed to it, *then* to be motivated to accept it. Interpretations of the two-step model usually are quite straightforward (McClosky and Zaller 1985; Zaller 1992), though not less valuable on that account. But taking seriously the sequential character of the process -- first exposure, then acceptance -- yields striking results. The best known of these is Converse's (1962) classic argument on the floating voter. Arguing that the probability of receiving a persuasive political message is positively related to a voter's level of information, but that the probability of yielding to it is negatively related to their informational level, Converse made a specimen case for the curvilinearity of persuasive effects with those who are neither high nor low in information being most likely to defect in an election. More broadly, the two-step model helps illuminate a classic paradox in social influence and democratic theory -- the paradox of conformity. The paradox is a general one, but it is useful to focus on a specific expression of it -- the connection between personality and commitment to democratic values. A lack of self-confidence and self-esteem increases the desire to conform to social norms. On the other hand, a lack of self-confidence and self-esteem interferes with a person learning the values of the larger society. Hence the paradox: the very factor that motivates people to want to conform -- a lack of a feeling of self-worth and a desire for acceptance -- leads them to deviate (DiPalma and McClosky 1970; Sniderman 1975).

The two-step model to one side, there is a heightened attention to the interdependence of political elites and mass publics. Public opinion, in this view, takes on coherence and politically relevant properties precisely because it is shaped by elite politics. Smith and Squire (1990) have come up with an especially elegant demonstration of the interdependence of mass beliefs and elite actions. Focusing on public reactions to judicial nominations and tax referenda, they document the impact of calling attention to the political sponsors of public acts, demonstrating, for example, that the public's response takes on a markedly more political character when ordinary citizens (and particularly the less educated) know the political provenance of judicial nominations or tax policy recommendations (see also Zaller 1992).

These results can be read as an exercise in simple persuasibility, but this mistakes the thrust of the analysis. It is more instructive to observe that ordinary citizens appear to miss the point politically *sometimes* because the questions put to them in conventional public opinion surveys are framed in ways that obscure or omit the political context. For example, Sigelman, Sigelman and Walkosz (1990) offer a striking account of the nuances in the judgments of ordinary citizens about the responsibilities of leadership (especially whether leaders should comply with an "instructed delegate" or an "independent trustee" model), putting into effect an exceptionally nuanced experimental design. For political judgments to be recognized as political they must be rooted in a political context.

It should be emphasized that in highlighting the contextual character of political responses the overriding objective is to call attention to the dynamics of politics. Thus, Sniderman, Piazza, Tetlock, and Feld (1991) have investigated whether more public support for racial policies can be generated by an appeal to the law as a persuasive symbol, demonstrating that a non-trivial fraction of the public can be induced to support a racial policy like set-asides by means of an appeal to law as a persuasive symbol. More striking, if one cares about real politics, is the analysis of who is more persuasible on this issue. It turns out that an appeal to law as a persuasive symbol is most effective in changing the minds of those who start off less rather than more sympathetic to racially liberal policies. It can pay politically to preach to sinners -- or at any rate to those who start off on the opposite side of an issue.

My sense of the initial stream of studies on political persuasion and attitude change is that they represent a new field of study in the making. Politics is about how you get people who start off in one corner of a room to move to another. What is necessary now is systematically to investigate who can be talked out of what political positions, and why. In pursuing this, I should emphasize the need to avoid an application of the latest fashion in social psychology. It is politics and political behavior we are attempting to get a grip on, and explanations must take this as their starting point.

I have offered a number of illustrations of the theme "politics matters," but I should like to offer one more in the context of political persuasion and attitude change. Fairly obviously, the position any given citizen takes on a political issue may be influenced by his or her perceptions of the positions others take on the issue. Far less obviously, as Mutz (1992b) has shown, the direction of a response to the social influence process can vary with the degree of commitment to the initial position taken on the issue, with the weakly committed moving in the direction of the perceived majority while those strongly committed tend to move in the direction opposite that of the cue (Mutz 1992b). Notice Mutz's double-barreled message of social influence and political reasoning. First, on her causal story, the result of social influence exerted in favor of one side of a political issue can be an increase in the proportions strongly committed on both sides of the issue. Second, again on her causal story, social influence on political reasoning is *not* a reflexive process whereby people blindly follow a bandwagon, adopting the position of others reflexively either in order to relieve their personal anxiety or to obtain social approval. Rather, the notion is that when people hear the positions others have taken on an issue they respond by thinking about the reasons that might have led all those others to hold their views; and by bringing cue-consistent thoughts to the fore, they are essentially engaged in a self-persuasion process, with their own views moving in the direction of arguments that otherwise would not have come to mind. This, then, is a thumbnail sketch of a number of themes we have been talking about, among them, the capacity of citizens for deliberation and the importance of the substance of politics in organizing the thinking of citizens about politics.

By way of balance I want to call attention to a more traditional account of the dynamics of political preferences. Taking advantage of a National Election Pilot Study, Zaller and Feldman (1992) asked people what ideas they had in mind about an issue either before or after choosing a position on it. Underlining the number of responses produced on opposing sides of an issue like government's responsibility to assure people that they have a good standard of living, they read this as evidence that a fundamental feature of the steady state of mass belief systems is instability and inconsistency. Respondents do not express fixed preferences; they construct their judgments, on the spot, sampling stochastically from among the miscellany of ill-organized and somewhat conflicting associations they carry about mixed with an over-sample of considerations stimulated by the particular question put to them. The Zaller-Feldman "sampling model" represents a step forward in the treatment of the dynamics of political belief, not least because the metaphor of sampling allows for a degree of explicitness not reached before. But it also reaches back. Its predominant emphasis is on the vagaries, instabilities, and inconsistencies of the survey response. Its controlling presumption is the appropriateness of a common account of how citizens *taken as a whole* reason about political choices. Its principal objective is to re-focus attention on the fringes of belief systems -- the smaller, more distal, more specific particles, in the form of discrete issue preferences and top-of-the-head justifications of these preferences -- not the core of political belief systems -- the larger, more central, and more enduring elements, in the form of personal and political values.[8]

A different analytic tack has been taken in the development of "on-line" accounts of impression formation. It had been customary to assume, until recently, that voters' evaluations of candidates are formed roughly as follows. Voters make a number of separate judgments about a candidate -- whether he or she is honest, broadly likeminded, sincere, competent, and so on. This mix of judgments, some positive and some not, is then stored in long-term memory, and subsequently retrieved following some algorithm or other when it comes time to vote, or to provide a summary evaluation of candidates. In contrast, Lodge and his colleagues, stimulated by the work of Hastie and his colleagues (Hastie and Park 1986; Hastie and Pennington 1989), have developed a research program focusing on on-line processing. As against memory-based judgments, which hinge on retrieval of already stored information, on-line impressions are formed as a person receives fresh information. The intake of fresh information, as a moment's reflection will suggest, requires smoothing out. Hence the notion of a "judgment operator" (Hastie and Park 1986). The judgment operator keeps, as it were, a running tally in working memory, and when voters encounter new information about candidates, the judgment operator is activated and updated. The distinction between on-line and memory-based impression formation, which falls out of the notion of a judgment operator, is an important one.

There is, returning to the sophistication-interaction hypothesis, a pivotal -- and quasi-paradoxical -- problem in modelling the dynamics of political belief systems. The belief systems of the politically sophisticated exhibit a pair of features that appear contradictory at first impression. On the one hand, the more politically aware and sophisticated a person is, the more likely he or she is to show ballast in their political beliefs: rather than gyrating erratically in response to any gust around them, their political convictions, their political likes and dislikes, show impressive continuity over time. On the other hand, it is equally plain that the politically aware also distinguish themselves by the extent and rapidity with which they update their political preferences. The hypothesis of on-line impression formation centered on a "judgment operator" provides an attractively simple mechanism first for modelling the inertial component in political preferences -- and the study of the dynamics of political belief will not progress far without nailing down, by way of a baseline, a continuity component -- and second for modelling the intake of new information. It is also worth remarking, in considering the compatibility of the Lodge model of on-line impression formation and the Zaller-Feldman sampling model, that the "judgment operator" model fits better the more politically aware and sophisticated individuals are (Lodge, Stroh, and Wahlke 1990; McGraw, Lodge, and Stroh 1990), suggesting that the two approaches can be integrated under some version of the "sophistication interaction" hypothesis.

There are points to be made in favor of both approaches, though the balance of advantages depends on whether it is useful to stay within the world of minimalism or to move beyond it. It is not obvious that it pays to take as a primary focus of analysis the reasons people may give for the positions they take on political issues -- as opposed to the positions themselves -- if only because there is good reason to doubt that people are adept at analyzing or remembering the reasons for their preferences or choices (Nisbett and Wilson 1977). Indeed, just because of this, the account of Lodge and his colleagues has a natural verisimilitude. They depict after all, a world in which individuals can remember where they are politically without having to remember exactly how they got there. It is possible to know what one believes without being able to say, on the spot, exactly how one came to form or maintain these beliefs.

However this may be, we cannot make sense of how substantial numbers of citizens make sense of politics if we suppose that they manage this drawing solely on their own resources. I have already remarked on the interdependence of citizens' judgmental shortcuts and the structuring of the political choices that confront them. Now, moving from large contexts to small, I want to say a word about the nature of the public opinion interview as a conversation.

The Public Opinion Interview as a Conversation: A Gricean Perspective

The importance of variation in the immediate context of the interview has long been recognized. It is, for example, well-established (Schuman and Presser 1981; Sudman and Bradburn 1982) that even seemingly trivial changes in the wording, ordering, or formatting of questions can affect the responses made in the course of a public opinion interview. But more often than not, such sources of variation in public opinion responses have been viewed as measurement error, to be purged before a substantive account can be given. In contrast, the new look in public opinion research is marked by a shift in perspective; a shift nicely caught by Tourangeau and Rasinski (1988, 301), who remark of themselves that they "try to find the substantive meat in what others may well regard as methodological poison."

A signature feature of the new look in public opinion research is thus the treatment of variation within the interview, not as methodological noise to be suppressed or isolated, but rather as substantive variance to be analyzed and explained. More specifically, it is necessary to recognize that a public opinion interview is a conversation. Respondents have *in part* appeared erratic and inconsistent in their political preferences because analysis has proceeded as if they are talking to themselves. But two people -- respondent plus interviewer -- are talking to each other. What we are trying to make sense of is not a monologue but a dialogue.

In treating the public opinion interview as a conversation, I want to invoke a broadly Gricean perspective. Conversations, Grice (1989) maintained, have a logic; and just insofar as a public opinion interview approximates a conversation, it follows that the positions taken in an interview, the emphasis and qualifications attached to them, the readiness to stand by them or to give them up are constrained not merely by formal logic but also by the informal logic of conversations. Rather than responding mechanically to the presence (or absence) of artificially manipulated symbols, respondents tend to be guided by a number of general maxims -- for example, that they should say what is true, that they should try to be informative and to avoid mere repetition in giving answers, and that in determining what it means to be responsive to a question, they have to give weight to what the questioner has already said -- or failed to say.

A public opinion interview is a form of conversation. It is worth underlining that just because conversations have their own logic to respondents -- viewed only as speaking to themselves -- they can appear illogical, their opinions may appear to be readily, almost indefinitely, pliable (e.g., Schuman and Presser 1981; Schuman, Steeh, and Bobo 1985). But in addition, remembering that the public opinion interview is a conversation helps dispel some of the mystery of when respondents both change *and* do not change. Consider, for example, "source" effects -- the consequences of attributing a position to a positively valenced source, a neutral source, or a negatively valenced source. There is certainly no shortage of theoretical reasons (Janis and Hovland 1959) to expect that the attribution of a position on a political issue to a high prestige source, for example, would induce a significant number of respondents to endorse it. But as it turns out, attribution of a position to a range of *diffusely* prestigious sources (e.g., "thoughtful people" or "concerned citizens") -- rather than specifically politically prestigious sources -- makes no difference to the positions citizens take on a range of issues (Piazza, Sniderman, and Tetlock 1989). *Pace* Grice, however, it makes a substantial difference if respondents are presented with relevant reasons for changing their mind. Thus, taking racial politics as an example precisely because of the common presumption that here, if anywhere, citizens have their feet firmly planted, one can show that on a number of racial issues (though not all) a large chunk of the public (approaching one in every two) can be induced to give up their positions in the face of a counter-argument (Sniderman and Piazza 1992).

It is, I want to suggest, of fundamental importance that respondents start from the premise that they are being given a relevant reason to modify their political views, even if it does not necessarily follow that they modify their views for *that* reason. And in construing the notion of relevance, it needs to be emphasized that a public opinion interview is not a conversation about anything and everything: it is, and is recognized to be, a conversation about public affairs. And because a public opinion interview is a conversation of a certain kind, then reasons of a certain kind matter. Respondents declare their preferences in the context of what they think is good and what is right, expressing what they regard as not only desirable but justifiable. Stoker (1992), in my view, has ingeniously caught the special mixture of preference and justification that marks the public discussion of public affairs in a contemporary democracy.

It will pay to take seriously the idea that public opinion interviews represent conversations of a special kind. To do this requires re-thinking the interview itself. The conventional public opinion interview is designed to assess the individual differences in political preferences relative to a specific and relatively idiosyncratic social situation. The controlling aim has been not merely to standardize but ideally to eliminate pressure on respondents to favor a given response. But this is, if one stops to think about it, an odd situation in which to find oneself. In real life people tend to find themselves subject to a variety of forms and degrees of social influence. And if we want to know what people believe and how they act once they have shown the interviewer to the door or hung up the phone, then we shall have to put them

quite deliberately into a variety of circumstances in the course of the interview itself -- and this can only be done by re-working the conventional public opinion interview to incorporate suitably complex experimental designs. For example, in an investigation of racial double standards, the characteristics of the person who had lost a job were manipulated, with race, gender, age, marital-parental and work history being systematically varied: only a single question was asked -- but one which took on 96 different forms (Sniderman, Tetlock, Piazza, and Kendrick 1991). It is in the end essential to sample both individuals and situations, for people's behavior is a function of the circumstances in which they find themselves as well as the dispositions and aptitudes they bring to these circumstances.

Citizenship

I want, finally, to single out for particular mention a number of intellectual forays into new territory. Without giving a false impression of a common purpose to these expeditions, I think it is useful all the same to call attention to the way they are mapping out new aspects of the idea of citizenship.

Citizenship in liberal democracies has been given, over the last generation, a construction that has been both conspicuously narrow and impressively unbending. Perhaps because of the ascendancy of individualism in the American political culture, perhaps because of the hegemony of survey research in the study of public opinion, the basic unit of political analysis has been the individual. New lines of research, however, are getting underway which propose to assign ontological parity, if not priority, to groups.

It is not that calling attention to the role of groups is itself novel. On the contrary, the role of groups is a long-standing theme in public opinion research, the major chord having emphatically been struck by the so-called Columbia school in the 1940s (Lazarsfeld, Berelson, and Gaudet 1944; Berelson, Lazarsfeld, and McPhee 1954), a minor chord less conspicuously by the so-called Michigan school (Campbell, et al. 1960), with the literature on "group consciousness" (Miller, Gurin, Gurin, and Malanchuk 1986; Conover and Feldman 1984) offering recent variations on the minor chord in particular. It has, however, become clearer that exploring the role of groups in political thinking offers an especially well-located platform for the study of strategic calculation in political thinking. Lupia (n.d.), for example, has shown how citizens learn to take positions on public propositions by taking into account the groups endorsing and opposing them. There is, on this revisionist view of political thinking, no imputation that a person's likes (or dislikes) strategic political groups are "emotional" or "irrational," and certainly not that they are invariant over time. On the contrary, it is explicitly supposed that ordinary citizens, by focusing on their likes and dislikes of strategic groups, have in their hands a powerful tool for mapping the structure of issue conflict.

Beyond this, there has been an imaginative re-thinking of the idea of legitimacy norms, keying on the role of groups in political thinking. In a conspicuously fresh and appealing approach, Dennis (1987) contrasts three norms of legitimate forms of political activity -- majoritarianism, individualism, and pluralism. As Dennis argues, pluralism, the notion that groups enjoy and confer legitimacy on political activity, is hemmed in, in the American ethos, on both sides -- by majoritarianism on the one pole, and individualism on the other. It is, I think, original and clever to suggest that an account of what citizens take to be fair can be specified, not in terms of their "values," but instead on the basis of what they believe the role of groups in political life ought to be.

There is, obviously, nothing novel in an interest in the issue of political legitimacy, its place on the modern research agenda being established by a trio of pioneering studies (Easton and Dennis 1969; Greenstein 1965; Finifter 1970). An enormous parade of research on trust in government and political alienation subsequently got underway during the years of discord in the late sixties and early seventies (e.g., Miller 1974; Citrin 1974; Abramson 1983). Then the parade unexpectedly halted, an odd straggler or two aside (e.g., Sniderman 1981; but see Weatherford 1992).

Unexpectedly perhaps, but not inexplicably. The argument over legitimacy had become posed in increasingly hyperbolic terms, and with one camp taking the position that the decline in trust in government in the 1960s signalled a fundamental crisis in the American political system (Miller 1974), and with the opposing camp contending that the wave of public cynicism amounted to no more than hot air, akin to baseball fans shouting "Kill the umpire" (Citrin 1974). The research agenda of the 1960s and 1970s, in retrospect, ran aground on two reefs. The more pronounced the emphasis on extreme political attitudes and behavior, the more pronounced the methodological mismatch: the standard national general population sample is ill-suited for the study of rare behavior, which through political disaffection and protest tends to be on a national, cross-sectional basis -- even at its height. Normatively, rather than presupposing that political cynicism and protest was necessarily a threat to governance, it became increasingly evident that a democratic politics not only need not be put at risk by periodic waves of political protest, but may even profit from periodic outbursts of distrust and protest: who, after all, could have taken the idea of

democratic citizenship seriously if after the political debacles of the 1960s and 1970s -- the race riots, assassinations, undeclared wars, prominent politicians unfrocked -- ordinary citizens had lost not a jot or a tittle of trust and confidence in their political leaders (Sniderman 1981)?

An interest in issues of legitimacy, however, has re-emerged, now framed to highlight aspects of democratic citizenship in a fresh way. For example, Finifter and Finifter have offered a sensitive reappraisal of citizens' political identities and attachments to a political order, examining the interplay of exit from one polity and engagement with another (Finifter and Finifter 1989). Departure from one political society, and identification with another, has been seen as a fundamentally discontinuous process -- the replacement of one political identity with another. In contrast, Finifter and Finifter, examining American migrants who have taken up Australian citizenship, accent the element of continuity, showing how the political engagement of these new citizens proceeds in part from their previous political attachments and ideological orientation, in interaction with *political* features (e.g., the relative strength of political parties in their new state) of their new environment.

Finifter and Finifter (1991) are in the process of drawing a portrait of citizenship from a fresh perspective, looking particularly at Americans who not only left America but decided to become Australian citizens. The world of general population surveys is the world of the commonplace, and it should not come as a surprise that when special purpose samples are constructed to enlist respondents with relatively rare attributes, the picture of political loyalty changes. Finifter and Finifter present a finely spun analysis of the array of specific motives and incentives offered by new citizens as the basis of their new citizenship, categorized for convenience into two large classes of reasons: "intrinsic" reasons, that is, reasons that are "self-directed, endogenously related to citizenship, and community-oriented" and "extrinsic" reasons -- that is, reasons that are "dependent on external contingencies, are exogenously related to citizenship and are self-oriented." Without minimizing the issue of external validity -- the politics of the years of discord in the 1960s and 1970s supply a special context to the study of citizenship -- it does not seem unreasonable to expect that our sense of the dynamics of identification with the political order will be deeper when this study is done.

In the meantime, the research agenda on legitimacy has been extended thanks in part to the ironies of the competition between research agendas. Rational choice conceptions, having gained enormous prominence over the last decade, have come to be a foil for competitive perspectives, the irony being that the empirical pay-off of rational choice -- for the study of mass opinion -- has chiefly been in consequence of critical reactions to it.[9] Thus, in a quite self-conscious reaction to rational choice's emphasis on the contemporaneous and immediate rewards and punishments shaping behavior, there has been a resurgence of interest in the normative antecedents of a variety of types of politically relevant behavior including rule following (Tyler 1990), decision acceptance (MacCoun and Tyler 1988), voting behavior (Rasinski and Tyler 1988), and general political activity (Rasinski 1988). Studies have further linked normative judgments of legitimacy and trust to normative judgements about the political world. Tyler, Rasinski, and MacGraw (1985), for example, demonstrated that general evaluations of the justice of government social and economic policies influenced citizens' trust in government, independently of any effects of self-interest. Beyond this, a number of studies have demonstrated that the effects of personal experiences with governmental authorities on attitudes about the legitimacy of government are based on evaluations of the justice of those experiences, not the favorability of their outcomes (Lind and Tyler 1988). These include studies of legal trial procedures (e.g., Lind, Kurtz, Musante, Walker, and Thibaut 1980), of other nontrial procedures used in resolving legal disputes, such as plea bargaining (Houlden 1980; Casper, Tyler, and Fisher 1988) and mediation (Adler, Hensler, and Nelson 1983; MacCoun and Tyler 1988), studies of police officer dealings with citizens (Tyler 1988, 1990; Tyler and Folger 1980), and studies of citizen experiences with political officials (Tyler and Caine 1981). These studies, and an array of others, provide a deepening elaboration of the idea that in making evaluations of political outcomes, citizens often are undertaking an effort to determine what is fair, and not simply what is to their advantage; an idea that deserves consideration not least because it underlines the role of political process -- perceptions of how things came to be decided -- in the shaping of judgments both of political outcomes and political authorities and institutions (Tyler and Lind 1992).

Cutting in quite a different direction, there is a research project on the nature of citizenship in the United States and Great Britain that demands mention because of its freshness and imaginativeness. Rather than relying on either the standard public opinion survey or the conventional in-depth interview, Conover, Crewe, and Searing (1991, 1992) have taken advantage of focus groups -- group conversations rather than individual assessments, primed by a common set of inquiries, followed up catch-as-catch can. Scrutinizing these group conversations, Conover and her colleagues describe the discourse of democratic politics in Great Britain and in the United States, the two countries holding down -- for heuristic purposes -- the two poles of communitarian and contractual democracy. Their account of these conversations contrasts the rights of citizens understood, in the United States, as civil rights and, in Great Britain, as social rights. From this they unfold a fan of distinctions, contrasting rights and benefits, equality of opportunity vs. entitlement to assistance, as well as more obliquely contrasting conceptions of citizen duties, all of which -- to the credit of the investigators -- line up only imperfectly with respect to their initial contrast of communitarian and contractual democracy.

A final line of argument requires mention. Its distinctiveness lies not in what it examines, but the level at which it conducts its examination. An assemblage of scholars -- chief among them, Stimson (1991), Wright, Erikson, and McIver (1987) (also Erikson, Wright, and McIver 1989; and Erikson, McIver, and Wright 1987) and Page and Shapiro (1992, 1983) -- working independently but also taking account of each other's work, are putting together a distinctive and powerful new view of public opinion. Their work is marked by a trio of interlinked features. First, it moves away from a concern with variations among individuals, making instead a strategic choice to work at the aggregate level. The emphasis is on aggregating over discrete individuals, and to a lesser extent over distinct issues, to capture, in Stimson's phrase, the public mood. Second, as against the analysis of cross-sections in citizens taken as individuals, the focus is instead on the analysis of variations of the public taken as a whole or in large blocs, either over time or across consequential political units -- for example, states. And third, the aim of the game is to give an account certainly of the making, and possibly also of the implementation, of public policy.

The work of scholars contributing to this new point of view throws a searching new light. Page and Shapiro (1992) and Stimson (1991) emphasize the aggregate analysis of swings in the public's preferences over time, in the process sharpening notions of change and trend and introducing to the analysis of policy formation the rhythms of public moods. In contrast, Erikson, Wright, and McIver (1987) focus on the variations in public opinion and policy across states, in the process exposing how, once the dynamics of parties' responsiveness to public opinion and the exigencies of office are taken into account, linkages between partisan politics, political ideology, and public policy become evident. Putting to one side details of specific studies, it is, I think, a good bet that this aggregate approach will have powerful impact over the next decade, not least because it goes beyond an interest in public opinion in its own right to focus on the connections between public preferences and public policy.

A Last Word

The idea of the new in science is, or ought to be, nuanced. Research in public opinion over the last decade or so has exhibited a fresh and distinctive flavor, and I have tried to convey this. But viewed over a longer perspective, what is just as evident is the continuing exploration of the implications for democratic politics of the constraints on information and information processing of mass publics. From this angle, what is most original and telling in research in public opinion has manifestly come about by responding to what was most original and telling in the work of the classic analysts of public opinion -- Converse, McClosky, Stouffer, and Verba, among them.

Notes

For facilities at which to work, and colleagues with which to work, I want to thank the Survey Research Center and the Institute of Personality and Social Research, both of the University of California at work. Colleagues too numerous to mention have been generous with suggestions and criticism. I am, however, chiefly in debt to Anthony Tyler, a colleague of mine at the Institute of Personality and Social Research: his assistance was indispensable.

1. Among the several excellent research summaries, Abramson (1983) stands out for the scope of his treatment -- covering party loyalties, feelings of political efficacy, political trust, and political tolerance -- and the detail of his independent analysis.

2. For the record, the feature of the likability heuristic that operates to yield accurate attributions is the weighting of issue attributions by the *difference* in people's feelings toward polar groups like liberals and conservatives. For the hook-up between individual organization and political organization, see the argument on bipolarity below.

3. I am deviating, it should be noted, from what has been the dominant view, both in the study of public opinion and psychology, which has stressed how the perceptual world is a buzzing, booming Jamesian chaos. It seems to me utterly implausible to concede (as I do) that the average citizen pays little attention to politics and then go on to argue that he or she is nonetheless miraculously adept at figuring out effective simplifications. Following Gibson (1979), I am inclined to think that people can effectively pick up information from their environment insofar as that environment is organized.

4. Converse (1964), who first raised the innocence of ideology thesis, put the issue in more nuanced terms, calling attention to the marked variations in informational level and organizational patterns *within* mass publics.

5. The research of Philip Tetlock has had a major impact on the terms in which this section is put, even when the specific assertions depart at points from his. See Tetlock, 1986a and 1986b.

6. This analytic move, aggregating by states, is ingenious on Gibson's part, though it carries with it heavy risks, not least because the original samples were not designed with this maneuver in mind.

7. A particularly strategic contribution, comparing the stability of so-called symbolic and non-symbolic attitudes, has been made by Krosnick (1990a), showing that non-symbolic attitudes are as stable as symbolic ones once differences in reliability of measurement are taken into account. It should also be remarked that the proponents of the symbolic politics model are committed to a strong version of a persistence model, asserting that people hold central political orientations (such as party identification and ideology) *without updating them to any significant degree.*

8. Feldman and Zaller (1992), it should be remarked, take the same variability in response reviewed in Zaller and Feldman (1992) but construe it as evidence not of a lack of crystallized attitudes but rather as evidence of complexity in political reasoning. It will be interesting to see how the interpretations are reconciled in the course of this research program.

9. No criticism is intended here of rational choice: merely a contention that its value for the study of *mass public opinion* remains largely a matter of asseveration, not demonstration. For a major step forward in interweaving rational and causal accounts at the individual level, see Brady and Ansolabehere, 1989.

Bibliography

Abramson, Paul R. 1983. *Political Attitudes in America*. San Francisco: W. H. Freeman.

Achen, Christopher H. 1975. "Mass Political Attitudes and the Survey Response." *American Political Science Review* 69:1218-1231.

Adler, Jane W., Deborah R. Hensler, and Charles E. Nelson. 1983. *Simple Justice: How Litigants Fare in the Pittsburgh Court Arbitration Program*. Santa Monica, CA: RAND.

Adorno, Theodor W., Else Frenkel-Brunswik, Daniel J. Levinson, and R. Nevitt Sanford. 1950. *The Authoritarian Personality*. New York: Harper.

Altemeyer, Bob. 1988. *Enemies of Freedom: Understanding Right-wing Authoritarianism*. San Francisco: Jossey-Bass.

Apostle, Richard A., Charles Y. Glock, Thomas Piazza, and Marijean Suelze. 1983. *The Anatomy of Racial Attitudes*. Berkeley, CA: University of California Press.

Barker, Edwin N. 1963. "Authoritarianism of the Political Right, Center, and Left." *Journal of Social Issues* 1(2): 63-74.

Barnum, David G., and John L. Sullivan. 1989. "Attitudinal Tolerance and Political Freedom in Britain." *British Journal of Political Science* 19:136-146.

Bassili, John N., and Joseph F. Fletcher. 1991. "Response-time Measurement in Survey Research: A Method for CATI and a New Look at Nonattitudes." *Public Opinion Quarterly* 55:329-344.

Bennett, Stephen Earl. 1988. "'Know-nothings' Revisited: The Meaning of Political Ignorance Today." *Social Science Quarterly* 69:476-490.

Bennett, Stephen Earl. 1992. "Changing Levels of Political Information in 1988 and 1990." Unpublished manuscript.

Bennett, Stephen Earl, Robert Oldendick, Alfred J. Tuchfarber, and George F. Bishop. 1979. "Education and Mass Belief Systems: An Extension and Some New Questions." *Political Behavior* 1:53-72.

Berelson, Bernard R., Paul F. Lazarsfeld, and William N. McPhee. 1954. *Voting: A Study of Opinion Formation in a Presidential Campaign*. Chicago: University of Chicago Press.

Berlin, Isaiah. 1969. *Four Essays on Liberty*. New York: Oxford University Press.

Bobo, Lawrence. 1983. "Whites' Opposition to Busing: Symbolic Racism or Realistic Group Conflict?" *Journal of Personality and Social Psychology* 45:1196-1210.

Bobo, Lawrence, and Frederick Licari. 1989. "Education and Political Tolerance: Testing the Effects of Cognitive Sophistication and Target Group Affect." *Public Opinion Quarterly* 53:285-308.

Brady, Henry E., and Paul M. Sniderman. 1985. "Attitude Attribution: A Group Basis for Political Reasoning." *American Political Science Review* 79:1061-1078.

Brady, Henry E., and Stephen Ansolabehere. 1989. "The Nature of Utility Functions in Mass Publics." *American Political Science Review* 83:143-163.

Brody, Richard A., and Catherine R. Shapiro. 1989. "Policy Failure and Public Support: The Iran-contra Affair and Public Assessments of President Reagan." *Political Behavior* 11:353-369.

Brody, Richard A. 1991. *Assessing the President: The Media, Elite Opinion and Public Support*. Stanford, CA: Stanford University Press.

Brown, Roger W. 1986. *Social Psychology*. 2nd ed. New York: The Free Press.

Burstein, Paul. 1979. "Public Opinion, Demonstrations, and the Passage of Anti-Discrimination Legislation." *Public Opinion Quarterly* 43:157-172.

Campbell, Angus, Philip E. Converse, Warren E. Miller, and Donald E. Stokes. 1960. *The American Voter*. New York: John Wiley and Sons.

Carmines, Edward G., and James A. Stimson. 1982. "Racial Issues and the Structure of Mass Belief Systems." *Journal of Politics* 44:2-20.

Carmines, Edward G., and James A. Stimson. 1989. *Issue Evolution: Race and the Transformation of American Politics*. Princeton, NJ: Princeton University Press.

Carmines, Edward G., and W. Richard Merriman, Jr. n.d. "The Changing American Dilemma: Liberal Values and Racial Policies." In *Prejudice, Politics, and the American Dilemma*, ed. Paul M. Sniderman, Philip E. Tetlock, and Edward G. Carmines. Stanford, CA: Stanford University Press.

Casper, Jonathan D., Tom R. Tyler, and Bonnie Fisher. 1988. "Procedural Justice in Felony Cases." *Law and Society Review* 22:483-507.

Cassel, Carol A. 1984. "Issues in Measurement: The 'Levels of Conceptualization' Index of Ideological Sophistication." *American Journal of Political Science* 28:418-432.

Citrin, Jack. 1974. "Comment: The Political Relevance of Trust in Government." *American Political Science Review* 68:973-988.

Clarke, Harold D, and Nitish Dutt. 1991. "Measuring Value Change in Western Industrialized Societies: The Impact of Unemployment." *American Political Science Review* 85:905-920.

Conover, Pamela Johnston, and Stanley Feldman. 1984. "Group Identification, Values, and the Nature of Political Beliefs." *American Politics Quarterly* 12:151-175.

Conover, Pamela Johnston, Ivor Crewe, and Donald D. Searing. 1991. "The Nature of Citizenship in the United States and Great Britain: Empirical Comments on Theoretical Themes." *Journal of Politics* 53:800-832.

Conover, Pamela Johnston, Ivor Crewe, and Donald D. Searing. 1992. "Does Democratic Discussion Make Better Citizens?" Paper presented at the 1992 annual meeting of the American Political Science Association, Chicago.

Converse, Philip E. 1962. "Information Flow and the Stability of Partisan Attitudes." *Public Opinion Quarterly* 26:578-599.

Converse, Philip E. 1964. "The Nature of Belief Systems in Mass Publics." In *Ideology and Discontent*, ed. David E. Apter. New York: Free Press.

Converse, Philip E. 1975. "Public Opinion and Voting Behavior." In *Handbook of Political Science*, ed. Fred I. Greenstein and Nelson W. Polsby. Reading, MA: Addison-Wesley.

Converse, Philip E., and Gregory B. Markus. 1979. "Plus Ca Change...: The New CPS Election Panel." *American Political Science Review* 73:32-49.

Crosby, Faye, Stephanie Bromley, and Leonard Saxe. 1980. "Recent Unobtrusive Studies of Black and White Discrimination and Prejudice: A Literature Review." *Psychological Bulletin* 87:546-563.

Delli Carpini, Michael X., and Scott Keeter. 1991. "Stability and Change in the U.S. Public's Knowledge of Politics." *Public Opinion Quarterly* 55:583-612.

Delli Carpini, Michael X., and Scott Keeter. 1989. "Political Knowledge of the U.S. Public: Results from a National Survey." Paper prepared for the annual meeting of the American Association for Public Opinion Research, St. Petersburg, FL.

Dennis, Jack. 1987. "Groups and Political Behavior: Legitimation, Deprivation and Competing Values." *Political Behavior* 9:323-372.

DiPalma, Giuseppe, and Herbert McCloskey. 1970. "Personality and Conformity: The Learning of Political Attitudes." *American Political Science Review* 64:1054-1073.

DiRenzo, Gordon J. 1974. *Personality and Politics*. Garden City, NY: Anchor Books.

Downs, Anthony. 1957. *An Economic Theory of Democracy*. New York: Harper-Row.

Easton, David, and Jack Dennis. 1969. *Children in the Political System: Origins of Political Legitimacy*. New York: McGraw-Hill.

Elkins, David J. n.d. *Managing Complexity: Sophisticated Citizens and Voting in Canada*. Vancouver: University of British Columbia Press.

Erikson, Robert S., John P. McIver, and Gerald C. Wright. 1987. "State Political Culture and Public Opinion." *American Political Science Review* 81:797-813.

Erikson, Robert S., Gerald C. Wright, and John P. McIver. 1989. "Political Parties, Public Opinion, and State Policy in the United States." *American Political Science Review* 83:729-750.

Eysenck, H. J. 1954. *The Psychology of Politics*. London: Routledge and Kegan Paul.

Eysenck, H.J. 1982. "Left Wing Authoritarianism: Myth or Reality?" *Political Psychology* 3:234-238.

Feldman, Stanley. 1988. "Structure and Consistency in Public Opinion: The Role of Core Beliefs and Values." *American Journal of Political Science* 32:416-440.

Feldman, Stanley, and John Zaller. 1992. "The Political Culture of Ambivalence: Ideological Responses to the Welfare State." *American Journal of Political Science* 36:268-307.

Ferejohn, John A., and James H. Kuklinski, eds. 1990. *Information and Democratic Processes*. Urbana and Chicago: University of Illinois Press.

Finifter, Ada W. 1970. "Dimensions of Political Alienation." *American Political Science Review* 64:389-410.

Finifter, Ada W., and Bernard Finifter. 1989. "Party Identification and Political Adaptation of American Migrants in Australia." *Journal of Politics* 51:599-630.

Finifter, Ada W., and Bernard Finifter. 1991. "Pledging Allegiance to a New Flag: Citizenship Change and its Psychological Aftermath among American Migrants in Australia." Unpublished manuscript.

Fiorina, Morris P. 1981. *Retrospective Voting in American National Elections*. New Haven: Yale University Press.

Fiske, Susan, and Shelley Taylor. 1991. *Social Cognition*. 2nd edition. New York: McGraw Hill.

Flanagan, Scott C. 1987. "Changing Values in Industrial Societies Revisited: Towards a Resolution of the Values Debate." *American Political Science Review* 81:1303-1319.

Flanagan, Scott C. 1982. "Changing Values in Advanced Industrial Society: Inglehart's Silent Revolution from the Perspective of Japanese Findings." *Comparative Political Studies* 14:403-444.

Flanagan, Scott C. 1980. "Value Change and Partisan Change in Japan: The Silent Revolution Revisited." *Comparative Politics* 11:253-278.

Fletcher, Joseph F., and Marie-Christine Chalmers. 1991. "Attitudes of Canadians Toward Affirmative Action: Opposition, Value Pluralism and Nonattitudes." *Political Behavior* 13:67-95.

Gibson, James J. 1979. *The Ecological Approach to Visual Perception.* Boston: Houghton-Mifflin.

Gibson, James L. 1987. "Homosexuals and the Ku Klux Klan: A Contextual Analysis of Political Tolerance." *Western Political Quarterly* 40:427-448.

Gibson, James L. 1988. "Political Intolerance and Political Repression During the McCarthy Red Scare." *American Political Science Review* 82:511-529.

Gibson, James, L. 1992. "Alternative Measures of Political Tolerance: Must Tolerance Be 'Least Liked'?" *American Journal of Political Science* 36:560-577.

Gibson, James L., and Richard D. Bingham. 1985. *Civil Liberties and Nazis: The Skokie Free-Speech Controversy.* New York: Praeger.

Gibson, James L., and Raymond M. Duch. 1991. "Elitist Theory and Political Tolerance in Western Europe." *Political Behavior* 13:191-212.

Greenstein, Fred I. 1965. *Children and Politics.* New Haven, CT: Yale University Press.

Grice, Herbert Paul. 1989. *Studies in the Way of Words.* Cambridge, MA: Harvard University Press.

Hamill, Ruth, Milton Lodge, and Frederick Blake. 1985. "The Breadth, Depth, and Utility of Class, Partisan, and Ideological Schemata." *American Journal of Political Science* 29:850-870.

Hamill, Ruth, and Milton Lodge. 1986. "Cognitive Consequences of Political Sophistication." In *Political Cognition,* ed. Richard R. Lau and David O. Sears. Hillsdale, NJ: Lawrence Erlbaum.

Hastie, Reid, and Bernadette Park. 1986. "The Relationship Between Memory and Judgement Depends on Whether the Task is Memory-Based or On-Line." *Psychological Review* 93:258-268.

Hastie, Reid, and Nancy Pennington. 1989. "Notes on the Distinction Between Memory-Based Versus On-Line Judgements." In *On-Line Cognition in Person Perception,* ed. John N. Bassili. Hillsdale, NJ: Lawrence Erlbaum.

Houlden, Pauline. 1980. "The Impact of Procedural Modifications on Evaluations of Plea Bargaining." *Law and Society Review* 15:267-291.

Huckfeldt, Robert, and Carol Weitzel Kohfeld. 1989. *Race and the Decline of Class in American Politics.* Urbana, IL: University of Illinois Press.

Hurwitz, Jon, and Mark A. Peffley. 1987. "How are Foreign Policy Attitudes Structured? A Hierarchical Model." *American Political Science Review* 81:1099-1120.

Hurwitz, Jon, and Mark A. Peffley. 1990. "Public Images of the Soviet Union: The Impact on Foreign Policy Attitudes." *Journal of Politics* 52:3-28.

Inglehart, Ronald. 1977. *The Silent Revolution: Changing Values and Political Styles among Western Publics.* Princeton, NJ: Princeton University Press.

Inglehart, Ronald. 1990. *Culture Shift in Advanced Industrial Society.* Princeton, NJ: Princeton University Press.

Iyengar, Shanto. 1991. *Is Anyone Responsible? How Television Frames Political Issues.* Chicago: University of Chicago Press.

Iyengar, Shanto, and Donald R. Kinder. 1987. *News that Matters: Television and American Opinion.* Chicago: University of Chicago Press.

Jackman, Mary R. 1978. "General and Applied Tolerance: Does Education Increase Commitment to Racial Integration?" *American Journal of Political Science* 22:302-324.

Jackman, Mary R. 1981. "Education and Policy Commitment to Racial Integration." *American Journal of Political Science* 25:256-269.

Jackman, Robert W. 1972. "Political Elites, Mass Publics, and Support for Democratic Principles." *Journal of Politics* 34:753-773.

Jacoby, William G. 1986. "Levels of Conceptualization and Reliance on the Liberal-Conservative Continuum." *Journal of Politics* 48:423-432.

Jacoby, William G. 1988. "The Sources of Liberal-Conservative Thinking: Education and Conceptualization." *Political Behavior* 10:316-332.

Jacoby, William G. 1990. "Variability in Issue Alternatives in American Public Opinion." *Journal of Politics* 52:579-606.

Jacoby, William G. 1991. "Ideological Identification and Issue Attitudes." *American Journal of Political Science* 35:178-205.

Janis, Irving L., and Carl I. Hovland. 1959. "An Overview of Persuasibility Research." In *Personality and Persuasibility,* ed. Carl I. Hovland and Irving L. Janis. New Haven, CT: Yale University Press.

Jennings, M. Kent, and Richard G. Niemi. 1974. *The Political Character of Adolescence: The Influence of Families and Schools.* Princeton, NJ: Princeton University Press.

Jennings, M. Kent, and Richard G. Niemi. 1981. *Generations and Politics: A Panel Study of Young Adults and Their Parents.* Princeton: Princeton University Press.

Johnston, Richard L., Andre Blais, Henry E. Brady, and Jean Crete. 1992. *Letting the People Decide.* Stanford, CA: Stanford University Press.

Kinder, Donald R. 1983. "Diversity and Complexity in American Public Opinion." In *Political Science: The State of the Discipline,* ed. Ada W. Finifter. Washington, DC: American Political Science Association.

Kinder, Donald. 1986. "The Continuing American Dilemma: White Resistance to Racial Change Forty Years after Myrdal." *Journal of Social Issues* 42:151-172.

Kinder, Donald R., and David O. Sears. 1981. "Prejudice and Politics: Symbolic Racism Versus Racial Threats to the Good Life." *Journal of Personality and Social Psychology* 40:414-431.

Kinder, Donald R., and David O. Sears. 1985. "Public Opinion and Political Action." In *Handbook of Social Psychology,* vol. 2, ed. Gardner Lindzey and Elliot Aronson. New York: Random House.

Kinder, Donald R., and Lynn M. Sanders. 1990. "Mimicking Political Debate with Survey Questions: The Case of White Opinion on Affirmative Action for Blacks." *Social Cognition* 8:73-103.

Kluegel, James S., and Eliot R. Smith. 1983. "Affirmative Action Attitudes: Effects of Self-Interest, Racial Affect, and Stratification Beliefs on Whites' Views." *Social Forces* 61:797-824.

Knight, Kathleen. 1985. "Ideology in the 1980 Election: Ideological Sophistication Does Matter." *Journal of Politics* 47:828-853.

Krosnick, Jon A. 1990a. "Government Policy and Citizen Passion: A Study of Issue Publics in Contemporary America." *Political Behavior* 12:59-92.

Krosnick, Jon A. 1990b. "Expertise and Political Psychology." *Social Cognition* 8:1-8.

Kuklinski, James H., and Norman L. Hurley. 1991. "What You Imagine Affects What You Think" Paper presented at the annual meeting of the Midwest Political Science Association, Chicago, IL.

Kuklinski, James H., Ellen Riggle, Victor Ottati, Norbert Schwarz, and Robert S. Wyer, Jr. 1991. "The Cognitive and Affective Bases of Political Tolerance Judgements." *American Journal of Political Science* 35:1-27.

Lau, Richard R., Thad A. Brown, and David O. Sears. 1978. "Self-Interest and Civilians' Attitudes toward the Vietnam War." *Public Opinion Quarterly* 42:464-48

Lau, Richard R., and David O. Sears, eds. 1986. *Political Cognition.* Hillsdale, NJ: Lawrence Erlbaum.

Lazarsfeld, Paul F., Bernard R. Berelson, and Hazel Gaudet. 1944. *The People's Choice: How the Voter Makes Up His Mind in a Presidential Campaign.* New York: Duell, Sloan, and Pearce.

Lee, J. R. 1977. "Rallying 'Round the Flag: Foreign Policy Events and Presidential Popularity." *Presidential Studies Quarterly* 7:252-256.

Levitin, Teresa E., and Warren E. Miller. 1979. "Ideological Interpretations of Presidential Elections." *American Political Science Review* 73:751-771.

Lind, E. Allan, Susan Kurtz, Linda Musante, Laurens Walker, and John W. Thibaut. 1980. "Procedure and Outcome Effects on Reactions to Adjudicated Resolutions of Conflicts of Interest." *Journal of Personality and Social Psychology* 39:643-653.

Lind, E. Allan, Robert J. MacCoun, P. A. Ebener, W. L. F. Felsteiner, D. R. Hensler, J. Resnik, and Tom R. Tyler. 1989. "The Perception of Justice: Tort Litigants' Views of Trial, Court-Annexed Arbitration, and Judicial Settlement Conferences." Santa Monica, CA: RAND.

Lind, E. Allan, and Tom R. Tyler. 1988. *The Social Psychology of Procedural Justice.* New York: Plenum Press.

Lippmann, Walter. 1922. *Public Opinion.* New York: Harcourt-Brace.

Lodge, Milton, Patrick Stroh, and John Wahlke. 1990. "Black-box Models of Candidate Evaluation." *Political Behavior* 12:5-18.

Lupia, Arthur. n.d. "The Effect of Information on Voting Behavior and Electoral Outcomes: An Experimental Study of Direct Legislation." *Public Choice.*

Luskin, Robert C. 1987. "Measuring Political Sophistication." *American Journal of Political Science* 31:856-899.

MacCoun, Robert J., and Tom R. Tyler. 1988. "The Basis of Citizens' Perceptions of the Criminal Jury." *Law and Human Behavior* 12:333-352.

McClosky, Herbert. 1964. "Consensus And Ideology in American Politics." *American Political Science Review* 18:361-382.

McClosky, Herbert, Paul J. Hoffman, and Rosemary O'Hara. 1960. "Issue Conflict and Consensus among Party Leaders and Followers." *American Political Science Review* 54:406-427.

McClosky, Herbert, and Alida Brill. 1983. *Dimensions of Tolerance: What Americans Believe about Civil Liberties.* New York: Russell Sage Foundation.

McClosky, Herbert, and John Zaller. 1985. *The American Ethos: Public Attitudes Toward Capitalism and Democracy.* Cambridge: Cambridge University Press.

McClosky, Herbert, and Dennis Chong. 1985. "Similarities and Differences between Left-Wing and Right-Wing Radicals." *British Journal of Political Science* 15:329-363.

McConahay, John B. 1982. "Self-interest Versus Racial Attitudes as Correlates of Anti-Busing Attitudes in Louisville: Is It the Buses or the Blacks?" *Journal of Politics* 44:692-720.

McConahay, John B. 1986. "Modern Racism, Ambivalence and the Modern Racism Scale." In *Prejudice, Discrimination, and Racism,* ed. John F. Dovidio and Samuel L. Gaertner. Orlando, FL: Academic Press.

McGraw, Kathleen, Milton Lodge, and Patrick Stroh. 1990. "Processes of Candidate Evaluation: On-Line or Memory Based?" Unpublished manuscript.

McGuire, William J. 1964. "Inducing Resistance to Persuasion: Some Contemporary Approaches." In *Advances in Experimental Social Psychology,* ed. Leonard Berkowitz. Orlando, FL: Academic Press.

Miller, Arthur H. 1974. "Political Issues and Trust in Government: 1964-1970." *American Political Science Review* 68:951-972.

Miller, Arthur H., Patricia Gurin, Gerald Gurin, and Oksana Malanchuck. 1986. "Group Consciousness and Political Participation." *American Journal of Political Science* 25:494-511.

Moon, David. 1990. "What You Use Depends on What You Have: Information Effects on the Determinants of Electoral Choice." *American Politics Quarterly* 18:3-24.

Mueller, John E. 1973. *War, Presidents, and Public Opinion.* New York: Wiley.

Mueller, John E. 1988. "Trends in Political Tolerance." *Public Opinion Quarterly* 52:1-25.

Mutz, Diana C. 1992a. "Mass Media and the Depoliticization of Personal Experience." *American Journal of Political Science* 36:483-508.

Mutz, Diana C. 1992b. "Impersonal Influence: Effects of Representations of Public Opinion on Political Attitudes." *Political Behavior* 14:89-122.

Neuman, Russell. 1986. *The Paradox of Mass Publics: Knowledge and Opinion in the American Electorate.* Cambridge, MA: Harvard University Press.

Nie, Norman H., Sidney Verba, and John R. Petrocik. 1979. *The Changing American Voter.* Cambridge, MA: Harvard University Press.

Nisbett, Richard E., and Timothy DeCamp Wilson. 1977. "Telling More Than We Can Know: Verbal Reports on Mental Processes." *Psychological Review* 84:231-257

Norpoth, Helmut, and Milton Lodge. 1985. "The Difference Between Attitudes and Nonattitudes in the Mass Public: Just Measurements?" *American Journal of Political Science* 29:291-307.

Nunn, Clyde Z., Harry J. Crockett, Jr., and J. Allen Williams, Jr. 1978. *Tolerance for Nonconformity.* San Francisco: Jossey-Bass.

Page, Benjamin I. 1978. *Choices and Echoes in Presidential Elections: Rational Man and Electoral Democracy.* Chicago: University of Chicago Press.

Page, Benjamin I., and Robert Y. Shapiro. 1992. *The Rational Public: Fifty Years of Trends in Americans' Policy Preferences.* Chicago: The University of Chicago Press.

Page, Benjamin I., and Robert Y. Shapiro. 1983. "Effects of Public Opinion on Public Policy." *The American Political Science Review* 77:175-190.

Peffley, Mark A., and Jon Hurwitz. 1985. "A Hierarchical Model of Attitude Constraint." *American Journal of Political Science* 29:871-890.

Peffley, Mark A., and Jon Hurwitz. n.d. "International Events and Foreign Policy Beliefs: Public Response to Changing Soviet-American Relations." *American Journal of Political Science.*

Piazza, Thomas, Paul M. Sniderman, and Philip E. Tetlock. 1989. "Analysis of the Dynamics of Political Reasoning: A General Purpose Computer-assisted Methodology." In *Political Analysis,* ed. James A. Stimson. Ann Arbor, MI: University of Michigan Press.

Pierce, John C., and Douglas D. Rose. 1974. "Non-attitudes and American Public Opinion: The Examination of a Thesis." *American Political Science Review* 68:626-649.

Popkin, Samuel. 1991. *The Reasoning Voter*. Chicago: The University of Chicago Press.

Putnam, Robert D. 1973. *The Beliefs of Politicians: Ideology, Conflict, and Democracy in Britain and Italy*. New Haven, CT: Yale University Press.

Rahn, Wendy M., John H. Aldrich, Eugene Borgida, and John L. Sullivan. 1990. "A Social-Cognitive Model of Candidate Appraisal." In *Information and Democratic Processes*, ed. John A. Ferejohn and James H. Kuklinski. Urbana and Chicago: University of Illinois Press.

Rasinski, Kenneth A. 1987. "What's Fair Is Fair -- Or Is It? Value Differences Underlying Public Views about Social Justice." *Journal of Personality and Social Psychology* 53:201-211.

Rasinksi, Kenneth A. 1988. "Economic Justice, Political Behavior, and American Political Values." *Social Justice Research* 2:61-79.

Rasinski, Kenneth A., and Tom R. Tyler. 1988. "Fairness and Vote Choice in the 1984 Presidential Election." *American Politics Quarterly* 16:5-24.

Ray, John J. 1983. "Half of All Authoritarians are Left-Wing: A Reply to Eysenck and Stone." *Political Psychology* 4:139-143.

Rivers, Douglas. 1988. "Hetereogeneity in Models of Electoral Choice." *American Journal of Political Science* 32:737-757.

Rokeach, Milton. 1960. *The Open and Closed Mind: Investigations into the Nature of Belief Systems and Personality Systems*. New York: Basic Books.

Rokeach, Milton. 1973. *The Nature of Human Values*. New York: The Free Press.

Schuman, Howard, and Stanley Presser. 1981. *Questions and Answers in Attitude Surveys: Experiments on Question Form, Wording, and Context*. New York: Academic Press.

Schuman, Howard, Charlotte Steeh, and Lawrence Bobo. 1985. *Racial Attitudes in America: Trends and Interpretations*. Cambridge, MA: Harvard University Press.

Sears, David O. 1983. "The Persistence of Early Political Predispositions." In *Review of Personality and Social Psychology*, ed. Ladd Wheeler and Philip Shaver. Beverly Hills, CA: Sage.

Sears, David O. 1988. "Symbolic Racism." In *Eliminating Racism*, ed. Phyllis A. Katz and Dalmas A. Taylor. New York: Plenum.

Sears, David O., Carl P. Hensler, and Leslie K. Speer. 1979. "Whites' Opposition to 'Busing': Self-interest or Symbolic Politics?" *American Political Science Review* 73:369-384.

Sears, David O., Richard R. Lau, Tom R. Tyler, and Harris M. Allen, Jr. 1980. "Self-interest vs. Symbolic Politics in Policy Attitudes and Presidential Voting." *American Political Science Review* 74:670-684.

Sears, David O., and Jack Citrin. 1982. *Tax Revolt: Something for Nothing in California*. Cambridge, MA: Harvard University Press.

Sears, David O., and Rick Kosterman. 1991. "Is it Really Racism? The Origins and Dynamics of Symbolic Racism." Paper presented at the Annual meeting of the Midwestern Political Science Association, Chicago, Illinois.

Shamir, Michal. 1991. "Political Intolerance Among Masses and Elites in Israel: A Reevaluation of the Elitist Theory of Democracy." *Journal of Politics* 53:1018-1043.

Shils, Edward A. 1954. "Authoritarianism: 'Right' and 'Left'." In *Studies in the Scope and Method of 'The Authoritarian Personality*," ed. Richard Christie and Marie Jahoda. Glencoe, IL: The Free Press.

Sigelman, Lee, and Pamela Conover. 1981. "The Dynamics of Presidential Support During International Conflict Situations: The Iranian Hostage Crisis." *Political Behavior* 3:303-318.

Sigelman, Lee, Carol K. Sigelman, and Barbara J. Walkosz. 1990. "The Public and the Paradox of Leadership: An Experimental Analysis." *American Journal of Political Science* 36:366-385.

Simon, Herbert A. 1957. *Models of Man: Social and Rational*. New York: Wiley.

Smith, Eric R.A.N. 1989. *The Unchanging American Voter*. Berkeley: University of California Press.

Smith, Eric R.A.N., and Peverill Squire. 1990. "The Effects of Prestige Names in Question Wording." *Public Opinion Quarterly* 54:97-116.

Sniderman, Paul M. 1975. *Personality and Democratic Politics*. Berkeley, CA: University of California Press.

Sniderman, Paul M. 1981. *A Question of Loyalty*. Berkeley, CA: University of California Press.

Sniderman, Paul M., Richard A Brody, and Philip E. Tetlock. 1991. *Reasoning and Choice: Explorations in Political Psychology*. New York: Cambridge University Press.

Sniderman, Paul M., Richard A. Brody, and James H. Kuklinski. 1984. "Policy Reasoning and Political Values: The Problem of Racial Equality." *American Journal of Political Science* 28:74-94.

Sniderman, Paul M., and Michael G. Hagen. 1985. *Race and Inequality: A Study in American Values*. Chatham, NJ: Chatham House.

Sniderman, Paul M., and Philip E. Tetlock. 1986a. "Symbolic Racism: Problems of Motive Attribution in Political Analysis." *Journal of Social Issues* 42:129-150.

Sniderman, Paul M., and Philip E. Tetlock. 1986b. "Reflections on American Racism." *Journal of Social Issues* 42:173-187.

Sniderman, Paul M., Philip E. Tetlock, James M. Glaser, Donald P. Green, and Michael Hout. 1989. "Principled Tolerance and the American Mass Public." *British Journal of Political Science* 19:25-45.

Sniderman, Paul M., Thomas Piazza, Philip E. Tetlock, and Ann Kendrick. 1991. "The New Racism." *American Journal of Political Science* 35:423-447.

Sniderman, Paul M., Barbara Kaye Wolfinger, Diana C. Mutz, and James E. Wiley. 1991. "Values under Pressure: AIDS and Civil Liberties." In *Reasoning and Choice*, ed. Paul M. Sniderman, Richard A. Brody, and Philip E. Tetlock. New York: Cambridge University Press.

Sniderman, Paul M., Thomas Piazza, Philip E. Tetlock, and Peter J. Feld. 1991. "The American Dilemma: The Role of Law as a Persuasive Symbol." In *Reasoning and Choice*, ed. Paul M. Sniderman, Richard A. Brody, and Philip E. Tetlock. New York: Cambridge University Press.

Sniderman, Paul M. Joseph E. Fletcher, Peter H. Russell, Philip E. Tetlock, and Brian J. Gaines. 1991. "The Fallacy of Democratic Elitism: Elite Competition and Commitment to Civil Liberties." *British Journal of Political Science* 21:349-370.

Sniderman, Paul M., Philip E. Tetlock, Edward G. Carmines, and Randall S. Peterson. n.d. "The Politics of the American Dilemma: Issue Pluralism." In *Prejudice, Politics, and the American Dilemma*, ed. Paul M. Sniderman, Philip E. Tetlock, and Edward G. Carmines. Stanford, CA: Stanford University Press.

Sniderman, Paul M., and Thomas Piazza. 1992. *The Scar of Race*. University of California, Berkeley. Unpublished manuscript.

Stimson, James A. 1975. "Belief Systems: Constraint, Complexity, and the 1972 Election." *American Journal of Political Science* 19:393-417.

Stimson, James A. 1991. *Public Opinion in America: Moods, Cycles and Swings*. Boulder: Westview Press.

Stoker, Laura. 1992. "Interests and Ethics in Politics." *American Political Science Review* 86:369-380.

Stouffer, Samuel. 1955. *Communism, Conformity and Civil Liberties*. New York: Doubleday.

Sudman, Seymour, and Norman M. Bradburn. 1982. *Asking Questions*. San Francisco: Jossey-Bass.

Sullivan, John L., James E. Piereson, and George E. Marcus. 1979. "An Alternative Conceptualization of Political Tolerance: Illusory Increases 1950's-1970's." *American Political Science Review* 73:781-794.

Sullivan, John L., James E. Piereson, and George E. Marcus. 1982. *Political Tolerance and American Democracy*. Chicago: The University of Chicago Press.

Sullivan, John L., Michal Shamir, Patrick Walsh, and Nigel S. Roberts. 1985. *Political Tolerance in Context: Support for Unpopular Minorities in Israel, New Zealand, and the United States*. Boulder, CO: Westview Press.

Sullivan, John L., Pat Walsh, Michal Shamir, David G. Barnum, and James L. Gibson. 1992. "Why Are Politicians More Tolerant? Selective Recruitment and Socialization Among Political Elites in New Zealand, Israel, Britain, and the United States." Unpublished paper.

Tetlock, Philip E. 1981. "Personality and Isolationism: Content Analysis of Senatorial Speeches." *Journal of Personality and Social Psychology* 41:737-743.

Tetlock, Philip E. 1983. "Accountability and Complexity of Thought." *Journal of Personality and Social Psychology* 45:74-83.

Tetlock, Philip E. 1984. "Cognitive Style and Political Belief Systems in the British House of Commons." *Journal of Personality and Social Psychology* 46:365-375.

Tetlock, Philip E. 1985a. "Integrative Complexity of American and Soviet Foreign Policy Rhetoric: A Time-series Analysis." *Journal of Personality and Social Psychology* 49:1565-1585.

Tetlock, Philip E. 1985b. "Accountability: A Social Check on the Fundamental Attribution Error." *Social Psychology Quarterly* 48:227-236.

Tetlock, Philip E. 1986a. "A Value Pluralism Model of Ideological Reasoning." *Journal of Personality and Social Psychology* 50:819-827.

Tetlock, Philip E. 1986b. "Structure and Function in Political Belief Systems." In *Attitude Structure and Function*, ed. Anthony Pratkanis, S. Buckler, and Anthony Greenwald. Hillsdale, NJ: Lawrence Erlbaum.

Tetlock, Philip E. 1988. "Monitoring the Integrative Complexity of American and Soviet Policy Statements: What Can Be Learned?" *Journal of Social Issues* 44:101-131.

Tetlock, Philip E. 1991. "People as Politicians: An Alternative Metaphor in the Study of Judgement and Choice." *Theory and Psychology* 1:85-104.

Tetlock, Philip E., Linda Skitka, and Richard Boettger. 1989. "Social and Cognitive Strategies of Coping with Accountability: Conformity, Complexity, and Bolstering." *Journal of Personality and Social Psychology* 57:632-641.

Tourangeau, Roger, and Kenneth A. Rasinski. 1988. "Cognitive Processes Underlying Context Effects in Attitude Measurement." *Psychological Bulletin* 103:299-314.

Tyler, Tom R. 1988. "What Is Procedural Justice? Criteria Used By Citizens to Assess the Fairness of Legal Procedures." *Law and Society Review* 22:103-136.

Tyler, Tom R. 1990. *Why People Obey the Law*. New Haven, CT: Yale University Press.

Tyler, Tom R., and Robert Folger. 1980. "Distributional and Procedural Aspects of Satisfaction with Citizen-Police Encounters." *Basic and Applied Social Psychology* 1:281-292.

Tyler, Tom R., and Andrew Caine. 1981. "The Influences of Outcomes and Procedures on Satisfaction with Formal Leaders." *Journal of Personality and Social Psychology* 41:642-655.

Tyler, Tom R., Kenneth Rasinski, and Kathleen McGraw. 1985. "The Influence of Perceived Injustice on the Endorsement of Political Leaders." *Journal of Applied Social Psychology* 15:700-725.

Tyler, Tom R., and Lind E. Allan. 1992. "A Relational Model of Authority in Groups." In *Advances in Experimental Social Psychology*, ed. Mark Zanna. New York: Academic Press.

Weatherford, M. Stephen. 1983. "Economic Voting and the 'Symbolic Politics' Argument: A Reinterpretation and Synthesis." *American Political Science Review* 77:158-174.

Weatherford, M. Stephen. 1992. "Measuring Political Legitimacy." *American Political Science Review* 86:149-168.

Weigel, Russell H., and Paul W. Howes. 1985. "Conceptions of Racial Prejudice: Symbolic Racism Reconsidered." *Journal of Social Issues* 41:117-138.

Wright, Gerald C., Jr., Robert S. Erikson, and John P. McIver. 1987. "Public Opinion and Policy Liberalism in the American States." *American Journal of Political Science* 31:980-1001.

Zaller, John, and Stanley Feldman. 1992. "A Simple Theory of the Survey Response: Answering Questions Versus Revealing Preferences." *American Journal of Political Science* 36:579-616.

Zaller, John. 1992. *The Nature and Origins of Mass Opinion*. New York: Cambridge University Press.

10

Expanding Disciplinary Boundaries: Black, Latino, and Racial Minority Group Politics in Political Science

Paula D. McClain and John A. Garcia

Introduction

Political science as a discipline historically has not seriously concerned itself with the politics of America's various minority groups,[1] particularly black and Latino politics. In fact, there was tacit, if not expressed, agreement that some groups within the American political spectrum were not legitimate subjects for political scientists to study. Matthew Holden, Jr. (1983) reports that at a 1941 conference on the Interdisciplinary Aspect of Negro Studies, Ralph J. Bunche, the first black American to receive a Ph.D. (1934) in political science,[2] lamented that the publication prospects in political science for works on the political behaviors of Negroes were somewhat limited. Bunche continued:

> In some field[s] this [publishing] is relatively easy. Anthropologists deal with the Negro as a respectable topic, and the journals of anthropology take such articles without hesitation. In respect to my own field, which concerns the status of the Negro, except insofar as papers having to do with colonial problems and the like are involved, there isn't a very cordial reception for papers dealing with the Negro (quoted in Holden 1983, 34).

Professor Emmett E. Dorsey, the late chair of the department of political science at Howard University, was quoted by Walton (1986, xi) to have said, as late as 1964, "Negro politics was long considered an offbeat field of political science." Many viewed it as an "academic graveyard for any young scholar who sought academic respectability..." (p. xi). Holden (1983, 34) has characterized the attitude within political science, as well as other social science disciplines, as an attitude of non-interest in "all this stuff about Negroes." Further,

Holden observes that political scientists "did not perceive those black-white relationships in American society to raise *critical intellectual problems* for scholars, in contrast to raising 'social problems' for social activists." The attention paid to the problems of Latinos within the American political system, as well as Latino-white relationships, was equally nonexistent.

This chapter principally traces and examines the development of the fields of black and Latino politics and their entrance into the realm of appropriate topics for political scientists to study. Current trends and future directions of the two subfields are also explored. Two other emergent fields of study, American Indian politics and Asian-American politics, are addressed as well, but not to the same depth and extent as the other two areas. Our brief discussion of these two subfields is not meant as a comment on the importance and significance of the areas, but is reflective of the paucity of research thus far.

An undertaking of this kind is replete with pitfalls. Principal among them is how one surveys a body of literature to provide a descriptive history of the development of the subfields, while at the same time establishing the analytical and methodological linkages between the various historical periods.[3] Moreover, the importance of political events to the intellectual development and growth of black and Latino politics must also be acknowledged and integrated. Thus one's organizational approach is important.

We have chosen to discuss the subfields separately, focusing on concepts and/or theoretical approaches that characterize the literature at various points in time. There is a tendency within the discipline to assume that similarities in racial minority group status within the United States result in similarities of experiences and behaviors; consequently, blacks, Latinos, Asian Americans, and American Indians are merged under the category of minority group politics. Yet, while there may be similarities in racial minority group status, there are fundamental differences in their experiences, orientations, and political behaviors. Nevertheless, while we handle the subfields separately, an attempt is made to identify linkages between the various subfield areas.

The first part of the chapter is concerned with the field of black politics. Black politics is the oldest of the subfields; therefore it has the largest body of literature. This section is organized in two ways -- the theoretical paradigms that dominated particular generations of research, and the various topical areas which employed those paradigms. Part two examines the field of Latino politics. This section is also structured around theoretical paradigms that have been employed in the research, and the principal concepts that have dominated the literature, but the literature is not explicitly delineated in generational terms.

Part three provides brief overviews of the emerging fields of American Indian and Asian-American politics. This section reviews the subject areas most often covered, and, where possible, the theoretical frameworks employed. Part four discusses the potential patterns of inter-minority group interaction that may result in coalitional or competitive behavior. Additionally, the four subfields are summarized and similarities and differences among them are highlighted.

Part I.   Black Politics: Race and Political Science

Matthews (1969, 113) noted that while the "Negro problem was the most important unresolved domestic problem confronting the nation," American political scientists did not engage in research on race politics or race relations. The resistance of political science to issues of race cannot be viewed in isolation but must be viewed through the lens of the external environment in American society and its effect on changes in the discipline (Walton et al. n.d., 6). Walton et al. contend that political science's attitude toward race was influenced by the theories of social Darwinism, as reflected in the work of John R. Burgess. Burgess "...applied the concept of social Darwinism to political science and jurisprudence," concluding that only Aryan nations were capable of political organization (Walton et al. n.d.).

This particular perspective on the political capabilities of various racial groups influenced the direction of development of the discipline of political science, as reflected in the pages of the early professional journals. Matthews (1969) found that between 1906 and 1963 only 13 articles with the word "Negro," "civil rights," or "race" in the title appeared in the *American Political Science Review*. Wilson (1985, 604) contends that political science classically studies elites, decision-

makers, and the uses of power, and since blacks are not usually found among the elite power brokers, "political science doesn't study black politics." Katznelson (1971, 56) suggests that social (political) scientists only became seriously interested in race relations after "American blacks, using the most effective tactic available to the powerless, that of disruption," were able to make inputs into the political system.

This obstinacy of the discipline to the inclusion of black politics as legitimate political science sparked an intellectual as well as a political battle. The intellectual battle, begun by Ralph J. Bunche and the first generation of black political scientists in the 1940s, continued into the 1980s, culminating in the recognition of black politics as a field of study on the American Political Science Association's listing of specialties. The political battle erupted at the 1970 meeting of the American Political Science Association in Los Angeles over the role of black political scientists and their research within the discipline. The on-site boycott of the meeting resulted in the creation of the Committee on the Status of Blacks in the Profession within the American Political Science Association. Moreover, the 1970 boycott led to the official formation of the National Conference of Black Political Scientists as a separate organization.[4]

First Generation Research: The Modern Beginnings

Walton, McLemore, and Gray (1990) identify the early intellectual basis of black politics as stemming from the pamphlets written during the early 1800s by Freemen of Color, e.g., David Walker and Henry Highland Garnet and Martin R. Delany, exhorting blacks to fight against the oppression of slavery, and from the early memoirs of black congressmen during Reconstruction. Walton, discussing the importance of these early works, suggests that "[w]hile these writers about the American political system may have not known that they were laying the very bases and foundations for black politics as an intellectual area, they did know -- particularly the former black elected officials -- that the black political experience in government was worthwhile noting..." (Walton et al. 1990, 197). While there were numerous writings on various aspects of the black political experience, the intellectual grounding of black politics as an academic field, as we presently conceive it, may be traced to the scholarship of Harold F. Gosnell and the scholarship, as well as activities, of Ralph Johnson Bunche.

While William F. Nowlin's *The Negro in American National Politics* appeared in 1931 and represented the first major work by a black political scientist (Walton et al. 1990), Gosnell's 1934 *American*

Political Science Review article, "Political Meetings in Chicago's Black-Belt," and 1935 book, *Negro Politicians: The Rise of Negro Politics in Chicago,* were the first works by a mainstream political scientist on the political struggles of African Americans. Gosnell's focus on blacks in Chicago was a logical extension of his interest in urban and machine politics, and he used empirical data to analyze the political behavior of African Americans. Gosnell's intent was to "throw light upon a number of hypotheses that might be formulated regarding the role of minority groups in the democratic process" (Gosnell [1935] 1967, 12).

Gosnell purposefully avoided utilizing any of the existing political science paradigms as a theoretical framework to guide his study; instead he posited a series of research questions predicated on the assumption that minority status and oppressive conditions would result in a variety of political relationships between white power structures and the Chicago black community. Moreover, these same conditions would result in certain types of political relationships between various groups within the black community. *Negro Politicians* systematically probed, over a five-year period, various facets of the black political experience in Chicago, e.g., office holding, relationship to machine, civil service positions, appointive positions, and so forth. Essentially, the book was a black community study that developed a broad portrait of black Chicago politics. Moreover, Gosnell made no attempt to generalize his findings beyond Chicago.

Ralph J. Bunche's contributions to the modern foundation of black politics followed three paths -- scholarship, university administration, and political activism. As a young instructor in the Division of Social Science at Howard University, Bunche published a little-known, yet extremely significant, article in 1928, entitled "The Negro in Chicago Politics." This article represents the beginning of Bunche's scholarly writings on the political condition of African Americans. In expressing the importance of studying the political behavior of blacks, Bunche states:

> The negro electorate of Chicago affords an interesting study....Any minority group which can and does control a mayoralty election in the nation's second largest municipality must be of more than passing interest to the student of political affairs (1928, 261).

> It would seem that the growing activity and influence of the negro electorate portends a new era of negro political development. The twelve millions of negroes in this country, approximating one-tenth of the total population, must inevitably wield a more proportionate and equitable degree of influence in the political affairs -- local, state, and national -- of the nation (1928, 64).

Bunche's 1928 article predates Gosnell's work, and a check of the references of *Negro Politicians* indicates that Gosnell was aware of Bunche's early work.

Several themes were prominent throughout Bunche's work -- strategies for overcoming political exclusion, as well as the recognition that the interaction of economic conditions and race were critically important in understanding the situation of the American Negro. (This latter perspective represents the early development of a Marxist analysis of black politics with origins in what has recently been dubbed the Howard School of Thought [Henry 1992].) These themes are evident in a 1935 article, "A Critical Analysis of the Tactics and Programs of Minority Groups," and a 1936 piece, "A Critique of New Deal Social Planning as It Affects Negroes." In particular, the 1935 article describes the various approaches by Negro organizations, e.g., racial separatism, economic passive resistance, interracial conciliation, and so forth. Kirby (1990) suggests that Bunche placed all of the "Negro ideologies on the Negro question" into the category of "accommodationism."

In 1939, the Republican National Committee asked Bunche to conduct research on why the black voters defected from the party in the two previous national elections (Rivlin 1990, 8-9). Additionally, between 1939 and 1940, Bunche became part of the Carnegie study, "The Negro in America," directed by Gunnar Myrdal, and produced a number of memoranda on Negro leadership, ideologies and tactics of Negro organizations, the political status of Negroes, and conceptualizations of the Negro problem, much of which was incorporated into the original study. In 1941, he published an article, "The Negro in the Political Life of the United States," which was based on his research for the Myrdal study.

Several of Bunche's themes were prominent in Myrdal's 1944 *An American Dilemma: The Negro Problem and Modern Democracy* -- Negro leadership styles and the hypocrisy of American democracy in its treatment of Negro citizens. The concept of Negro leadership styles produced one of the first dominant paradigms to guide the scholarship on black politics -- the protest versus the accommodation approach to black political leadership.[5] At the same time, the hypocrisy of American democracy led to the development of a theoretical framework, referred to as the moral dilemma perspective, for assessing race relations in the United States. Clearly the moral dilemma approach has been important in the development of the race relations literature. Notwithstanding, its use in the research on black politics has been limited, partly because of criticism from Cox (1948) and others that Myrdal ignored the problem of power dynamics in American society. Hence, it will not be discussed.

The publication of V.O. Key's *Southern Politics* in 1949 also played an important role in the early paradigmatic themes that evolved in the next generation of black politics research. Of note is the evolution and refinement by Key of several concepts and theories originated by Bunche in his manuscript "The Political Status of the Negro." Key references the Bunche unpublished manuscript on several occasions (Walton n.d.). In *Southern Politics*, Key discussed the importance of black concentration to the political fabric of the South and the centrality of the "Negro question" to Southern politics -- "...the presence of the Negro has created conditions under which the political process operates" (Key 1949, 671). However, he gave little attention to black voting because, at the time, he saw it as being of little consequence to the politics of the South -- "[s]o few have been Negro voters in the South that to estimate their number seems futile" (Key 1949, 517). Key's admonition of the futility of studying the black vote, coupled with Bunche's and Myrdal's categorizations of black leadership, generated a body of research referred to as Negro leadership studies. The leadership studies initially defined the field of black politics and set the early boundaries -- blacks could not vote; therefore the focus of scholarly research must be shifted elsewhere.

Second Generation Research: Protest/Accommodation Paradigm

Several seminal works on black politics (Wilson 1960; Ladd 1966; and Matthews and Prothro 1966) crafted in the protest-accommodation paradigm formed the foundation of the Negro leadership research (Wilson 1961; Walker 1963; Killian and Smith 1960; Dunbar 1961; Tilman and Phillips 1961; and Burgess 1962). The general concept of leadership in these studies was ambiguous and reflected a wide variety of definitions (Smith 1982, 3). Smith (1982, 4) argues that while there was no consensus on the definition of Negro leadership, the literature seemed to agree that "(a) leadership involved affecting the attitudes and behavior of Negroes insofar as social and political goals and/or methods are concerned; and (b) Negro leadership is not limited to Negroes but may and indeed does include whites." The three seminal works, two of which are principally black leadership studies, are James Q. Wilson's *Negro Politics: The Search for Leadership* (1960); Everett C. Ladd, *Negro Political Leadership in the South* (1966); and Donald R. Matthews and James W. Prothro, *Negroes and the New Southern Politics* (1966).

Wilson's *Negro Politics*, like Gosnell's earlier work, was on black Chicago politics. Unlike Gosnell's work, however, Wilson's portrait of black political leadership was unflattering and extremely critical. Walton et al. (1992) suggest that Wilson started from a preconceived set of conclusions about black Chicago, then proceeded to work backwards from the conclusions. Wilson perceived the black community as having no political life that was not a reflection of white politics within the city. For the most part, Wilson saw Negro community leaders as ineffective, partly because Negro leadership could not agree on goals, which for Wilson were categorized as welfare goals and status goals.

Each of these goal orientations was attached to a particular leadership style -- the militant or protest style (status goals) versus the moderate or bargainer style (welfare goals). While all of Negro leadership was ineffective, the moderate leaders' (in Bunche's term, the accommodationists) welfare goals would produce more tangible improvements for the community, even though, as Wilson acknowledges, "they are on a segregated basis." On the other hand, the militant leaders pursuing status goals would bring blacks closer to integration but produce less tangible improvements for the community.

Ladd's *Negro Political Leadership in the South* examined the thesis that Negro leadership is primarily a response to particular societal conditions. The major portion of the book focused on race leadership and only incidentally on political leadership. Ladd concluded that Negro political leadership was issue-based leadership that through successive racial confrontations would produce important changes in the Negro leadership personnel. Building on the categories developed by Myrdal (1944) and adapted by Wilson (1960), Ladd identified three types of Negro leaders: (1) Conservative leaders who are established older men who focus on welfare goals for Negro people; (2) militant leaders who are principally younger men with low incomes and an uncompromising commitment to status goals for Negroes; and (3) moderate leaders who are of all ages and balance welfare and status goals. Unlike Wilson, Ladd sees utility in all three of these styles, depending on the response of the white community to the demands of blacks.

Matthews and Prothro's *Negroes and the New Southern Politics* departed from the restricted focus on black leadership as the core of black politics. Their study centered on "Negro political participation and its consequences" (Matthews and Prothro 1966, vii). Using behavioral research techniques, they examined black voting and other aspects of political participation, controlling for demographic characteristics (regardless of levels of political information, blacks with high incomes engaged in political activity more often than blacks with low incomes), black political organizations (must be created and maintained if blacks are to become a significant force in southern politics), and black leadership styles. For Matthews and Prothro, leadership was reciprocal in nature -- in order for someone to lead, others had to consent to follow. Thus those people most thought of as leaders by black citizens were, in fact, the leaders. Based on the community identification of black leaders, Matthews and Prothro developed their categories -- traditional, moderate, and militant -- which were heavily influenced by Wilson's original formulation (Matthews and Prothro 1966, 189; note 22). Nevertheless, it should be noted that Matthews and Prothro were the first to study the black student sit-ins and protest activity as black political leadership and to estimate their influence on black political behavior in general.

Criticisms of the protest/accommodation dichotomy, particularly as utilized by Wilson, were numerous. For some, the Negro leadership studies put black politics on a path that focused exclusively on the personality and style of certain individuals, rather than on behaviors of the larger black community. Moreover, the criticism was leveled that some of these works utilized theoretical frameworks developed from research on groups who had access to the political system and, therefore, that they were devoid of the black experience in the United States.

Several political, as well as intellectual events, signaled the demise of the leadership studies as the primary form of black politics research. These events were the passage of the 1965 Voting Rights Act, the urban riots of the 1960s, and the ascendancy of pluralism as the dominant paradigm in political science. The Voting Rights Act provided an important avenue for black political participation, particularly for southern blacks. With the right to vote came the intellectual opportunity to examine questions about black voting behavior and black elected officials. The urban riots focused attention on the frustrations and conditions of urban blacks, and the use of protest to address policy concerns (Sears and McConahay 1973; Lipsky 1968, 1970; Eisinger 1974). Likewise, pluralism and black politics research, growing out of the New Haven studies (Dahl 1961), became inextricably entwined. The pluralist notions of the lessening of group identity and interests over time through assimilation into the political mainstream found its expression in the ethnic politics model.

Ethnic Politics Approach

The ethnic politics model attempted to draw parallels/comparisons between the political progress of white ethnics in urban cities and American blacks, in urban areas as well as the South (Litt 1970; Glazer and Moynihan 1963). The argument developed in this approach is that ethnic integration is unavoidable in a pluralistic democracy. Through electoral competition and economic development, immigrant ethnic groups would find themselves assimilated into the mainstream of both the urban political and economic life. Vigorous electoral participation was a guarantee of political power, and continued economic development was the key to economic assimilation. Attendant to political and economic assimilation was the eventual disappearance of ethnic identity and ethnicity as an organizing principle for political activity.

Mack Jones (1972) was particularly critical of the predominance of the ethnic politics approach as a framework for examining the black political experience. He argued that superficial comparisons of blacks with white ethnics ignored the unique and peculiar condition of African Americans in the United States. Moreover, the comparison resulted in the accomplishments of the white ethnic group, without the historical and extant constraints imposed on blacks, serving as the standard against which the political progress of blacks was measured.

Jones was not the only critic of pluralism in general and the ethnic politics approach in particular as appropriate frameworks for black politics. Other examinations of black politics have drawn similar conclusions about the two approaches (McLemore 1972; Holden 1973; Morris 1975; Barker and McCorry 1980; Pinderhughes 1987), which are captured by Hamilton's (1981, 168, quoted in Pinderhughes 1987, 38) declaration, "The political situation of black Americans always posed a special problem for the pluralist system." Manley (1983, 368) recently suggested that "pluralism...fails to account for the reality of political and economic inequality in the United States."

Dissatisfaction with the theoretical approaches, and the direction of research in and development of the field of black politics, gave rise to a new generation of research by black political scientists. The work of Mack Jones, coupled with that of Hanes Walton, Jr., and Matthew Holden, Jr., pushed, or some might argue pulled, the fledgling field of black politics into a new era. The research of this period sought to move black politics toward definition and rigorous theoretical development, while simultaneously attempting to direct the field away from the "ambiguous concepts" of the protest/accommodation paradigm and the ethnic politics/pluralism approach.

Third Generation Research: Power Relations Paradigm and Field Definition

The appearance in 1967 of the book, *Black Power: The Politics of Liberation in America*, by Stokely Carmichael and Charles V. Hamilton served as the bridge between the second and third generation black politics research. Carmichael and Hamilton offered a forceful critique of pluralism-ethnic politics and coalition theory and their relationship to black political power in the United States. They argued that blacks should control their own organizations and communities and only enter into coalitions with others (whites) from a position of strength and power, variously defined (Carmichael and Hamilton 1967, chaps. 2 and 3). They stated that "[b]lack power recognizes...the ethnic basis of American politics as well as the power-oriented nature of American politics" (p. 47). The concept of power was central to their proposals for achieving broadened political participation of blacks in the American political process. This book, while activist in orientation, gave rise to the power relations paradigm in the scholarly black politics literature.

Jones (1972), following the lead of Carmichael and Hamilton, constructed a frame of reference for the study of black politics that he felt was consonant with the black political experience in the United States, one that would facilitate the understanding of blacks in the American political system. Jones concluded that within the United States there is essentially a power struggle between blacks and whites, with whites trying to maintain their superordinate position vis-à-vis blacks. Consequently, "since the political system is the arena in which societal conflicts are definitely resolved, black politics should be thought of as a manifestation of the power struggle between these two groups" (Jones 1972, 9).

Jones, however, adds one very important caveat to this power struggle -- the ideological justification for the superior position of whites is the institutionalized belief in the inherent superiority of that group. Using this conceptualization of the power dynamic as the orienting concept, a theoretical framework, augmented by the concepts of dominant and submissive groups, was developed that could be subdivided into a schematic of goal directed patterns of activity and policy proposals. Jones explicitly sought to refine the "ambiguous concepts -- status and welfare goals, race man, militant" that evolved from the black leadership studies era (Jones 1972, 17).

The power dynamic paradigm, while forceful, was not successful in totally redirecting research in black politics away from the use of traditional political science frameworks and toward the search for alternative frameworks. Walton (1972a), drawing from Jones, also sought to introduce the black/white political conflict system as a framework for analysis, but like Jones's attempt, met with little success. Walton, however, was successful in broadening the definition of what activities and behaviors among black Americans constituted the field of black politics.

Redefining Black Politics

Prior to the 1970s, Walton (1972a, 9) observed, the study of black politics, which he defined as "the attempts of one group of individuals in the American political system to implement their preferences as public policy," had been constricted by what he saw as a very narrow conceptualization of the field. From Walton's perspective, politics encompasses a variety of activities and behaviors, e.g., actions of legislative assemblies, political parties, and other aspects of modern government, yet "the beginning and end of studies on black politics have been primarily from the electoral angle" (Walton 1972a, 2). Most previous studies of black politics started from the assumption that "if blacks could not vote, they had little chance to have any meaningful effect on the political process" (p. 2). Consequently, Walton concluded, "students of black politics tend to feel that the alternative devices (e.g., lobbying, pressure groups, demonstrations, etc.) derive much of their value and significance from the existence of the vote" (p. 2).

The study of black politics, suggested Walton, was much more than electoral participation, and scholars should broaden their definition. Black politics as a field of inquiry should encompass the range of nonelectoral activities, e.g., community organizations and protest activities, in which black Americans participate and which affect their daily existence (Walton 1973). Moreover, Walton suggested that in addition to expanding the research focus beyond the vote, black politics should not be viewed as a monolith, but that patterns of behavior and activities should be expected to vary depending on regional as well as urban location.

The effort to broaden the definition of the field of black politics was joined by Matthew Holden, Jr. (1973). Holden focused on the organizational aspects of, what he labeled, the black "quasi government" and the potential public policy outputs and implications of the "quasi government's" activities. According to Holden's view of the field,

> black politics actually takes place through a fairly well-defined and stable set of relationships which one may call the black 'quasi government.' One can observe the stability of this quasi government by

observing patterns of interdependence between institutions in black communities both local and nationwide; by observing the consistency of symbolism in black politics; and by observing the remarkable stability in groups of people who provide leadership (Holden 1973, 3).

The success of Walton and Holden in broadening the definition of the field of black politics and shifting the spotlight beyond the ability to vote, coupled with a series of political events, generated a fourth generation of research covering a broad spectrum of black political life.

Fourth Generation Research: Multiplicity of Topics and Approaches

This present generation of research is characterized by its diversity of scope and heterogeneity of approaches. Research on various aspects of black political life is abundant.

Urban Politics. The election of big-city black mayors and city council persons, beginning in 1967, resulted in increased attention to black political aspirations and successes in urban politics. The early mayoral research identified the similarities and differences in the election of black mayors in predominately white versus predominately black big cities (Preston 1976, 1983, 1987, 1990; Preston et al. 1987; Jones 1978; Nelson and Meranto 1977), while the later research focuses on the question of what difference have big-city black mayors made in urban politics (Nelson 1990; Rich 1989; Persons 1985, 1987, 1993; Perry 1990). Research on black representation on city councils found a significant relationship between the size of the black population and black success in winning council seats; significantly increased chance of election when elections were held by district rather than at-large; and a modest significant relationship between black socioeconomic resources and city council representation (Cole 1974; Karnig, 1976, 1979a, 1979b; Karnig and Welch 1980; Karnig and McClain 1985; McClain and Karnig 1990; Pinderhughes 1987; Browning, Marshall, and Tabb 1984, 1990; Engstrom and McDonald 1981, 1982; Robinson and Dye 1978). Recent research based on 1980s data argues that although at-large systems still have negative effects on the ability of blacks to be elected to city councils, the effects may be lessening (Welch 1990) or have disappeared entirely (Bullock and MacManus 1987). This last assertion has been hotly contested.

Voting Rights and Public Policy. The electoral opportunities created by the enactment of the Voting Rights Act of 1965 and its extensions led to research on their effect on election of local black officials and empowerment of black electorates, particularly in the South (Grofman and Davidson 1992; Gomes and Williams 1992), and various provisions of the Acts themselves (Foster 1983, 1984a, 1984b, 1985, 1986; Pinderhughes 1990). Some of the literature suggested that many southern jurisdictions found ways around the Act by adopting massive resistant strategies to nullify the impact of the black vote (Parker 1990). The passage of various civil rights statutes also drew attention to a variety of public policy issues of concern to or affecting blacks (Barnett and Hefner 1976), for example, to name but a few, health care (Rice and Jones 1984; Jones and Rice 1987), implementation of civil rights statutes (Walton 1989), urban violence (McClain 1992), and public employment (Preston 1984). More recently, the public policy research has begun to focus on the black administrators who increasingly have responsibility for crafting and implementing public policies that directly affect black Americans (Karnig and McClain 1989; Smith 1984; Henderson 1978, 1979).

Presidential Politics. Research on black participation in presidential politics has argued that blacks have successfully used strategic voting in presidential elections to leverage their influence but have failed in many instances to have their policy interests satisfied (Walters 1988; Henderson 1987; Walton 1992). Jesse Jackson's 1984 and 1988 presidential campaigns spawned debate within the literature over the advantages (Barker 1988; Barker and Walters 1989; Morris 1990) or disadvantages (Reed 1986) of Jackson's candidacy. Moreover, the question of whether or not Jackson had an effect on black voter registration and turnout in 1984 and 1988, and on the Democratic party, has also been hotly debated (Tate 1991, 1992). Census Bureau data on voter registration and turnout in the 1988 presidential election indicate that black voter registration and turnout were higher in 1984 than in 1980, but black registration and turnout levels in 1988 dropped below 1980 levels (United States Bureau of the Census 1989).

Political Socialization and Attitudes. Political socialization research identified black school children as feeling less politically efficacious and trusting than white school children. Abramson (1977) found that studies of black political socialization tended to use one of four explanatory theories for racial differences in political efficacy and trust. The first, the political education explanation, contended that racial differences resulted from differences in political education within American schools (Greenberg 1970; Orum and Cohen 1973; Rodgers 1974). Social deprivation, the second explanation, argued that racial differences resulted from social structural conditions that contributed to low feelings of self-confidence among blacks (Rodgers 1974; Abramson 1972; Lyons 1970). The third explanation, intelligence, suggested that differences resulted from differences in intelligence. While this explanation was based on suggestions that, apart from age, intelligence was the best predictor of sense of political efficacy, little research support was found for intelligence as an explanation of racial differences in political attitudes. Finally, the political reality explanation argued that racial differences in political attitudes resulted from differences in the political environment in which blacks and whites live (Prestage 1968; Sears and McConahay 1973; Rodgers and Taylor 1971). Although political socialization was the focus of research in the early 1970s, little research on the topic has been conducted since then.

The small black sample size in national surveys (Walton 1985) limited research on aspects of black political attitudes; however, a significant body of literature emerged nonetheless. Research in the 1970s found that overall blacks tended to participate less than whites: yet, when differences in socioeconomic status were taken into account, blacks tended to participate more (Verba and Nie 1972; Olsen 1970). However, more recent research has found that blacks tend to participate at the same rate as whites of comparable socioeconomic status, but a new dimension, level of black political empowerment, appears to have a strong effect on levels of black political participation (Bobo and Gilliam 1990). In addition, in early research, a strong group consciousness or ethnic identity was identified as being a strong catalyst to increased black political participation, although it was much more important in explaining behaviors of lower-class blacks than it was for middle-class blacks (Shingles 1981). For the most part, recent research contends that the majority of blacks remain strongly group-oriented (Tate 1993), but that changes in the socioeconomic and political situation of blacks may have reduced the importance of black consciousness as a principal factor in black political participation (Bobo and Gilliam 1990), or that racial consciousness is more multi-faceted than previously thought and manifests itself on several dimensions (Dawson, Brown, and Allen 1990).

Studies of ideological orientations among blacks have concluded that the assignment of liberal or conservative labels to the opinions of black Americans often results in more confusion about black opinion than clarification that the labels are intended to convey. The reasons are that black public opinion is not consistent; black opinion may fall on the conservative end on personal behavior social issues, e.g., abortion and prayer in school, but on the liberal continuum on increased government involvement in rectifying societal ills (Welch and Foster 1987; Seltzer and Smith 1985a, 1985b; Smith and Seltzer 1992; Sigelman and Welch 1991). The National Black Election Study (NBES), collected during the 1984 and 1988 national elections, has overcome the problem of small black sample sizes and provided the

vehicle for expanded study on the numerous facets of black political behavior (Allen, Dawson, and Brown 1989; Dawson, Brown, and Allen 1990; Welch and Foster 1992; Tate 1991).

The NBES data portray a black electorate overwhelmingly identified with the Democratic party, but not as strongly attached as popular wisdom would have one believe; however, intensity of attachment was stronger in 1988 (Tate 1992) than was true in 1984 (Gurin, Hatchett, and Jackson 1989). The history of African American relationships with the major political parties and third parties in American politics suggests a tenuous and contentious union on a number of dimensions (Walton 1972a, 1972b, 1975). The realignment of blacks from the Republican to the Democratic party occurred over a hundred year span, and the NBES data reveal an electorate not enamored with the notion of forming a separate black third party (Gurin, Hatchett, and Jackson 1989).

Black Women and Gender Issues. The growing research on black women and politics, and the salience of gender issues for African Americans, has provided a much needed and different dimension to black politics (Prestage 1991, 1984, 1977; Darcy and Hadley 1988; Bryce and Warrick 1977). The research cautions that generalizations based on studies primarily of black males do not necessarily hold for black females. For instance, while the urban research has found that the election of blacks, primarily males, to city councils is facilitated by single-member systems, electoral structure does not substantially affect black women's representation. Black women are under-represented on city councils in all electoral systems -- single-member, multi-member, and at-large systems (Herrick and Welch 1992). In addition, the salience of gender issues and differences in political behavior between black males and females have also been explored. Research, as well as census voting and registration data, suggests that black females register and vote in higher numbers than do black males (Williams 1987), that more black females than white females consider themselves feminists (Mansbridge and Tate 1992), and that the interaction of race, class, and gender produces a dynamic for black women's political behavior that is absent in the behaviors of white females (King 1973; Lewis 1982; Palley and Preston 1979). However, the limited evidence thus far does not support the existence of a black gender gap in voting (Welch and Sigelman 1989; Lansing 1977). Nevertheless, the convergence of race and gender in the Anita Hill-Clarence Thomas hearings has directed attention to issues of sexism and gender equality within the African American electorate (Mansbridge and Tate 1992).

Congress and Courts. The increase in the number of black Congresspersons, which is related to the issues of redistricting and reapportionment (Grofman 1990; Hill 1992), and the creation of the Congressional Black Caucus directed attention to Congress (Barnett 1975, 1977, 1984; Levy and Stoudinger 1976, 1978; Smith 1981, 1988). Much research has also appeared in areas of the court system and black America (Hamilton 1973b; Barker and McCorry 1980), particularly on decisions by the U.S. Supreme Court (Barker 1973, 1992a; Barker and Combs 1987). Once again, the recent confirmation hearings of Clarence Thomas to the Supreme Court have refocused attention on judicial selection and the future direction of the Court (Barker 1992b).

Approaches in Fourth Generation

While broadening the breadth of the research in black politics, the fourth generation research also resulted in the re-emergence (some question whether it actually disappeared) of pluralism as one of the primary frameworks in black politics research. Dawson and Wilson (1991, 200) suggest that while many of the challengers of pluralism found that the paradigm was "inadequate to rectify the massive problems facing the black community," they nonetheless worked on the same terrain as the classic pluralists. However, the ethnic politics approach, prominent in the Second Generation, has been almost universally rejected as an appropriate framework for analysis in black politics.

Another approach for examining black politics, with origins in the race and class analysis of Bunche, that matured in the Fourth Generation, is Marxist analysis (Marable 1983; 1985; Robinson 1983). Race, as identified by Dawson and Wilson (1991, 205), has never been central to Marxist analysis; however, when the latter is applied to the study of black politics, the view of the role of blacks in society has been fixed and non-contradictory. According to Dawson and Wilson, the Marxist paradigm has traditionally viewed "...African-Americans as being economically marginal, politically backward, and noncentral to the major questions of class conflict and accommodation facing the American working class" (p. 205). Black Marxist scholars who study black politics, they argue, have taken a slightly different perspective suggesting that "organizations based on opposition to racial and sexual oppression not only have a progressive role to play in the period before successful transformation of society and seizure of state power, but would have a progressive role to play in the postrevolutionary period" (p. 205).

A more recent approach is rational choice theory and formal modeling. While still on the periphery, rational choice theory has begun to find its way into the research on black politics, particularly in explanations of group behavior and group consciousness (Dawson and Wilson 1991, 212). This foray has not been without controversy as many scholars believe that rational choice, with its focus on individual actors, eliminates the contextual aspects so important to an understanding of black politics in the American milieu.

The plethora of approaches and topics covered under the rubric of black politics in this generation has led to the Dickensian paradox -- it was the best of times, it was the worst of times. The tremendous increase in the literature coupled with the respectability and acceptance of the field as "legitimate" political science gives those in the field reasons to rejoice. Yet this very circumstance of abundance and acceptability has led to a renewed questioning -- What is really the locus and focus of the field of black politics? Is having blacks as the population under study in any category of political science research a sufficient condition to lead one to conclude that it qualifies as black politics? Or are there necessary conditions that also must be met for the research to be considered as falling under the rubric?

Who's on First? Current Status of Black Politics

The above questions are extremely difficult to address. The argument could be made that one defines black politics by subject matter, i.e., various aspects of black political life and the centrality of race in American politics. However, some scholars who have focused on issues of race in American politics stridently argue that their work should be placed in categories other than black politics -- "we shall have much to say about race, but the issue itself is not our principal focus" (Carmines and Stimson 1989, xiii).

For others, however, Carmines and Stimson's assessment of their work as other than black politics would be appropriate. Mack Jones (1990), in a speech during the twentieth anniversary commemoration of the founding of the National Conference of Black Political Scientists, lamented that initially the field of black politics was conceptualized as one whose purpose was "critically examining the politics internal to the black community and assessing its relevance for the ultimate objectives of the [black] struggle [for freedom]" (Jones 1990, 6). He argues that black political scientists, and one could infer he would include black politics, have been mainstreamed. There is an absence of discussion about alternative frameworks through which to view black political behavior and a lack of challenge to the principal assumptions of political science as they apply to the study of African Americans.

The current controversy surrounding the concept "deracialization" is an example of Jones's charge that black politics has been mainstreamed. Once again, political events have led to a fierce debate over the scholarly boundaries of the academic subfield of black politics. Originally developed by Hamilton (1973a, 1977) in the 1970s and calling for the Democratic party to emphasize issues that appealed across racial lines, deracialization, as currently used, refers to an electoral strategy by black candidates which avoids "explicit reference to race-specific issues, while at the same time emphasizing those issues that are perceived as racially transcendent" (McCormick and Jones 1993, 76). This strategy permits black candidates to appeal to and mobilize a broader segment of the population for purposes of winning or maintaining elective office.

For some, the victory of L. Douglas Wilder as governor in Virginia and Norman Rice as mayor of Seattle signaled the maturation of black politics. Perry (1991) opines that some have suggested that deracialization represents the future of black politics. He argues that the principal force behind contemporary black politics has been the election of black public officials from majority black districts, but that situation is about to end. There are few remaining majority black districts that have not elected black officials; thus if the number of black elected officials is to increase, they must be elected from majority white districts (Perry 1991, 182).

For others, however, deracialization is contrary to the fundamental essence of black politics (Starks 1991) and signals the death of black politics (Smith 1990). Starks (1991, 216) suggests that deracialization diverts "from the substance of what constitutes African-American politics -- using electoral politics as a lever to maximize group power in the fight against racism, exclusion, and marginalization while promoting African-American-specific policy preferences within the political system." Walters (1992) forcefully questions whether deracialization should even be identified as black politics, while Smith (1990, 160) sees an analogy to the deracialization of black politics in the adaptation of black music by black artists to cross over to mainstream white society. He states:

> The new black politics initiated in the late 1960s, like the music of the era, was conceived as a social change agent, the continuation of movement politics by other means. It would indeed be sad if the conditions for its success require it to become a "deracialized" mainstream shell of itself.

This particular debate, which goes to the fundamental foundation -- What is black politics? -- will undoubtedly continue and grow in intensity over the next decade.

What standard does one use to assess the status of a field? There are a variety of ways; however, the one that seems to be the most appropriate is: Can one discern, based on several generations of research, the development of a cumulative body of knowledge about black politics? The answer is a resounding -- maybe! In some subject areas, for instance, black mayors and city council members, there is a cumulative body of knowledge based on the testing and retesting of hypotheses over a period of time. However, in others, for instance, black political behavior, the knowledge is disparate and evolving. There is no one dominant theoretical framework that delineates the field, a plus for the development of different perspectives on the African American political condition. But, more importantly, there is no serious questioning of the utility of standard political science frameworks for understanding the black political condition (Jones 1992), a negative for the perspective that the black experience in the United States must be incorporated into frameworks for analysis of their politics. Based on a review of the extant literature in the fourth generation, it could be argued that the orientations of the individual researchers, rather than the questions under study, determine the choice of theoretical framework.

These intellectual battles, instead of being dysfunctional for the field of black politics, may prove to be dialectic. Black politics as a field is clearly not in a moribund condition; its dynamism has generated argument over the definition of black politics as an area of study. Whether or not individuals will agree on the precise boundaries of the field is open for debate. Nevertheless, even if consensus were reached, changes in the political environment and political condition of African Americans, as well as the introduction of new paradigms and methodologies would compel renewed discourse. Ideally, however, the discourse within the field of black politics over content and theoretical frameworks will continue to be spirited and ongoing.

The question of a catholic or parochial definition of the field should be constantly argued. Ralph J. Bunche would certainly have been in agreement with sustained debate. It seems fitting and appropriate to end this section of the chapter by drawing on a quote by the modern founder of the field that addresses the limitless potentialities of black politics. Bunche ends his first article on black politics in 1928 thusly:

> It would seem that the growing activity and influence of the negro electorate portends a new era of negro political development. [Negroes]...must inevitably wield a more

proportionate and equitable degree of influence in the political affairs -- local, state, and national -- of the nation. Perhaps not in this generation, nor in the next, but ultimately (1928, 264).

Clearly, the centrality of race to American politics suggests that there is more research that needs to be done and, inevitably, will continue to be done.

Part II: Latinos and Politics in the U.S.

Introduction

We will now focus our discussion of race and ethnicity in the U.S. on the Latino, or Hispanic, populations. Generally, the term Hispanic/Latino refers to individuals whose cultural heritage traces back to a Spanish-speaking country in Latin America but also includes individuals with links to Spain or the southwestern region of the U.S. when under Spanish or Mexican rule (Bean and Tienda 1987, 2-3). We begin our discussion with a brief history of the political science discipline and the inclusion of the study of Latinos as well as the participation of Latino political scientists. The development of the study of Latinos and the political system is examined in the next section. Finally, we focus on specific political concepts, activities, and patterns examined by political scientists and describe the status of the subfield and future directions and implications.

A Brief Institutional History

The development of Latino politics and involvement of Latino scholars in the political science profession have been recent phenomena. The themes of exclusion, marginality, and absent bodies of knowledge are central issues in any discussion of Latino politics. The origins of the subarea of Latino politics under the field of racial and ethnic politics are associated with the report of the Ad Hoc Committee on Mexican Americans in the Profession (1970). This committee was concerned about the absence of scholarly and analytical works on the Mexican origin population living in the United States. A related concern was the lack of significant recruitment and training of Mexican Americans in the political science profession. Obviously, the lack of participation by Mexican Americans within the academy was associated with the paucity of research on America's second largest minority group.

The Ad Hoc Committee concluded:

There is something wrong with political science when we (1) fail to adequately interpret the political presence of eight or more million people, and (2) when we fail to recruit and train more than a handful of their representatives. This, of course, means a substantial loss of our body of knowledge and beyond this, it may represent a serious insensitivity, on our part, to the contemporary problem of mankind (Ad Hoc Committee on Mexican Americans in the Profession 1970, 352).

In 1970, there were only four Mexican American Ph.D.s in the country, and two of these individuals were employed in the federal government. Articles dealing with the Mexican origin population in the U.S. were virtually non-existent until the 1970s.[6] Recently, Manuel Avalos (1991) published an article in *PS* focusing on the status of Latinos in the profession, particularly on recruitment, retention, and scholarly publications. He referred to an earlier report by the Western Political Science Association (WPSA) on the status of Chicanos (J.A. Garcia 1975) in which the Committee noted the need for more courses, students, and faculty in the area of Chicano politics in most schools in the western region. The WPSA report concluded that most political science departments were not interested in altering or reassessing their policies regarding student and faculty recruitment.

In addition, questions were raised by departments as to the merits and legitimacy of Chicano politics as an area of inquiry. Avalos looks at these issues in the contemporary period by analysis of publications focusing on Latino politics in the major political science journals from 1964 to 1988. Over this time period, one article was published in the *Journal of Politics*; none, however, have appeared in the *American Political Science Review* or the *American Journal of Political Science*. By contrast, the *Western Political Quarterly* published nine articles in the area during the same time period. Obviously, the WPSA Best Paper Award in Chicano Politics (initiated in 1975) contributed to the number of articles published. Overall, the total percentages of all articles on race, gender, and ethnicity in the major political science journals ranged from 1.9% (APSR) to 6.8% (JOP) to 6.2% (WPQ).[7] Within political science, the analysis and conceptualization of Latino political attitudes and behavior, and political issues important to the Latino population, received virtually no attention.[8]

Certainly, race and ethnicity are both important subjects to study in the development of this nation. Within political science, race and ethnicity have been utilized as key independent variables in the study of community power, voting behavior, political attitudes, and political mobilization (Banfield and Wilson 1963; Parenti 1967; Lineberry and Fowler 1967). Yet, specific focus on Latino groups has not been the subject of articles commonly found in the major journals of political science.

Latino politics moves from the analysis of Chicanos to an "umbrella" alignment of different Spanish origin groups. The more recent development has been the recognition of the broader configuration of Hispanics/Latinos, which includes persons of Spanish origin from many national origins. Designating a subfield of Latino politics also raises concerns -- is it more realistic to deal with specific national origin groups or to treat persons of Spanish origin as a viable, cohesive political community in the United States? Yet the common thread exists in the delineation of a population with distinct histories and experiences in the United States, a cultural milieu with a strong resistance to assimilation, and structural relations which are characterized by subordination, marginality, and discrimination (Alvarez 1973; Jennings and Rivera 1984; Estrada et al. 1981).

The history of Latinos in the profession is characterized by the motivation for recognition as an important segment of American society. This emphasis has encouraged more systematic analysis by political scientists. In addition, the increased presence and participation by Latinos in the profession have served to expand the conceptual and theoretical perspectives and discussions of power, authority, social change, and participation.

Chicano Politics: Origins in the Southwest

The analysis of Latino politics is one which parallels the rise of the Chicano movement of the mid-sixties. The petulance of youth and the frustration over the lack of timely social change (Muñoz 1989) serve as primary motivators for protest politics and direct action efforts by Chicanos in the Southwest. Alvarez (1973) defines this process as an evolutionary one in which growing populations become more aware of the inconsistencies between the American creed and the realities of Chicanos in urban barrios and rural communities (Barrera 1979). The themes of internal colonialization (Almaguer 1971; Blauner 1969), exploitation and resistance (Estrada et al. 1981), and racial and class segmentation (Barrera 1977) characterize scholarly analyses of Chicanos' political and social life.

This characterization of the Mexican origin people focused on both an indigenous and an immigrant population (Acuna 1981).

The Treaty of Guadalupe Hidalgo became the starting point for formal relations between Chicanos and the U.S. political system. Political relations were characterized by subordination, legal manipulation of property rights, and overt hostility. During the Manifest Destiny period, Chicanos were relegated to being an elastic labor force in an expanding agricultural and mining economy (Barrera 1979). Gomez-Quinones (1990) characterizes these developments as efforts by the Mexican community north of the Rio Bravo to engage in an economic and cultural struggle, although this community was viewed as passive, apolitical, politically ineffective, and non-participatory.

In particular, the theory of internal colonialization served as a major analytic framework for the study of Chicano politics. The conquest of Mexico converted a significant portion of the Mexican republic into the southwestern portion of the United States. The internal colonialization process included: an external administration of governance; racial oppression and racial ideology of domination; colonialized individuals as a source of labor; and economic exploitation as the basis of the colonizer-colonized relationship (Moore 1970). Thus the goal of politics for Chicano communities became de-colonialization, that is, a politics of liberation from external controls and domination -- economic and political.

Accompanying this analytical framework were theoretical perspectives focusing more on the economic relationships between the Mexican origin population and the U.S. capitalist system (Barrera 1979; Katznelson 1973). The reason for the economic expansion of the U.S. during the middle of the nineteenth century was seen as expanding borders to find more territory, develop the natural resources therein, and open trade routes. The defeat of Mexico left the Mexican people as a "proletariat" to develop the new industrial and economic sectors. Segmentation of this population involved economic arrangements and dependencies that were legalized and institutionalized over the latter half of the nineteenth century.

More contemporary analysis of the Latino experience has used an economic and Marxist interpretation for Puerto Ricans (Bonilla and Campos 1981) to understand their migration to the U.S. and their experiences in the U.S. economy. The emphasis on economics and politics in Latino populations has been a continual theme in the development of this area of study. Particular attention to the patterns of international migration has emphasized the economic inter-dependencies between the United States and countries in Latin America (Pedraza-Bailey 1985; Portes and Bach

1985). The concepts of reserved labor pools, elastic labor force, labor segmentation, and secondary labor markets have been central to the understanding of the Latino experience. Immigration becomes both a critical condition and a frame of reference for Latino politics. It is important because many nationality groups, under the Latino umbrella, have been more recent immigrants in the past three decades. The distinction between native-born and "foreign-born" Latinos reflects cultural ties, behaviors, and political linkages (J.A. Garcia and de la Garza 1985). The issues of naturalization, legal status (undocumented, permanent resident alien, etc), political loyalty to the U.S., and acculturation and assimilation are relevant to the examination of Latino politics (de la Garza et al. 1991; J.A. Garcia 1987; Jennings and Rivera 1984). We will discuss this aspect of Latino politics further in the section on specific political issues. However, immigration is less a formal issue for Puerto Ricans, as commonwealth status conveys U.S. citizenship. Nevertheless, the distinction between Puerto Ricans born on the mainland U.S. vs. those born in Puerto Rico has real implications for the adaptation process (J. A. Garcia 1986a).

Our discussion will now focus on critical areas involving Latinos and the political system. These include the concepts of assimilation, acculturation, and cultural pluralism; culture and identity; nativity and political integration; political participation and behavior; and political attitudes and values.

Dimensions of Latino Politics

Assimilation, Acculturation, and Cultural Pluralism

The models of internal colonialism and Marxism provide critical foundations to define the political status and origins of Chicano politics. The models' perspectives look at the dynamic processes of social change, adaptation, and ethnic persistence. Theoretically, the concepts of assimilation and acculturation (Gordon 1964; Keefe and Padilla 1987) serve to examine the impact of life in the U.S. for the Mexican origin population, and other Latinos. Wolfinger (1965) and Parenti (1967) have focused on the persistence of ethnicity in American politics, particularly in the electoral arena. While the ethnic groups they focused on were European in origin, the dynamics of assimilation and acculturation were critical factors to explain ethnic persistence. Gordon's (1964) differentiation of the many dimensions of assimilation (i.e., cultural, marital, economic, political, etc.) clarifies the ways in which groups accommodate the mainstream culture; yet there were also cultural expressions of resistance to assimilation. Works by Amado Padilla (1980a, 1980b)

were directed toward the examination of cultural changes among the Mexican origin populations and how cultural distinctiveness can and does continue. The issue is not whether assimilation has occurred but, more, how cultural survival has taken place in light of cultural, marital, and identificational assimilation.

F.C. Garcia and de la Garza's (1977) work on the Chicano experience uses three models -- pluralism, elitism, and internal colonialism -- to evaluate various dimensions of Chicano politics. Culture and ethnic identity serve as two critical ingredients in how the Chicano community views itself in the larger society, as well as how they are viewed by the non-minority population. The idea of cultural pluralism and its political manifestations (Foster 1982) has been developed in the comparative politics field; here cultural diversity and minority institutions are recognized by establishment political institutions and the legal system. Questions of nation building, political integration, ethnic conflict, and social and political stratification serve as critical issues related to ethnic persistence (Horowitz 1985).

More recent works on pluralism (Walzer et al. 1982) discuss the concept of corporate pluralism, in which formal relations are established with the state apparatus assigning political roles to ethnic "corporations." The effect of this type of recognition would be to institutionalize cultural differences and, potentially, intensify these differences. Yet, the concept of pluralism and the state usually entails the government protecting the collective and individual rights of minority groups and the state expanding its official celebrations (Walzer et al. 1982, 19-20). In addition, the passage and implementation of public policies now more reflect the needs and interests of ethnic communities. For Latino groups, public policies that use race and ethnic status as determinants for protected group status or special programs are examples of policy demands and responses.

Often, the success of assimilation could be reversed by differential treatment and designation by social agents such that a "dis-assimilation" process occurs (Hayes-Bautista 1974). That is, minority group members, whether they choose to or not, are differentiated by institutional actions and programs. As a result, these individuals reexamine their historical and cultural origins and begin to reinstitute a sense of ethnicity. In the Hayes-Bautista (1974) work, Chicano medical students are seen to be supported by special educational and other support systems by the medical school. As a result of institutional perceptions of minority status, these Chicano students are treated differently by this educational institution, and this treatment makes them intensify their own minority group loyalties.

Thus discussions of pluralism within a Latino context involve historical analyses of the initial contact between the cultural group and the American political and economic system and reactions to this contact. Secondly, ethnic persistence must be studied in relation to the state's responses to race and ethnicity (laws, public policies, and cultural recognition). Finally, the diligence of ethnic communities must be explored in terms of mobilization, leadership, organizations, and a discernible political and economic agenda. While no one conceptual framework or paradigm dominates the field of Latino politics, the dimensions of critical structural analysis, self-determination, and equality serve as a major "corpus" that is at the heart of any study of Latinos in the United States. In most cases, research in these areas has been limited to specific Latino national origin groups, and an overall analysis of Latinos as a distinctive "ethnic" group is not viewed as viable because of key historical and structural differences (F.C. Garcia et al. 1991a). Therefore, whether or not a unified and distinctive Latino community exists is a major research question in this subfield.

Latino Politics: Culture and Identity

Associated with a discussion of pluralism has been the concept of ethnic identity and its possible dysfunctional role in nation building and allegiance. Works by J.A. Garcia (1982), Portes and Mozo (1985), and Padilla (1980a, 1980b) address factors (individual, experiential, and structural) that influence ethnic identity (J.A. Garcia 1986b) and the effect of identity in the political process. At times, structural conditions and prevailing attitudes can force citizens to choose an ethnic identity and establish rigid distinctions among different ethnic identities.

Analysis of the Latino experience in the U.S. centers on the role of cultural values, attitudes, and behaviors that identify a social structure, networks, and lifestyle. These factors can affect residential patterns, views about government and politics, and political behaviors. A substantial amount of intellectual and analytical energy has been directed by social scientists and others to identify and define the cultural milieu of Mexican Americans, Puerto Ricans, and Cubans (Keefe and Padilla 1987; Levine 1979; Rogler et al. 1980; Arce 1981). This focus on ethnicity and identity revolves around the interplay between cultural origins in one's "mother country" and life experiences in the United States. Cultural patterns such as Spanish language use, ethnic holiday celebrations, and primary social networks comprised of fellow Latinos serve to establish group boundaries and community. Thus the existence of ethnic identity resides in the manifestation of cultural persistence

among Latinos and the types of interactions Latinos have with the political system. The concept of multiplicity of ethnicities suggests ethnic attitudes, knowledge, behaviors, and preferences; thus it is a broader concept than merely ancestry and national origin.

The multidimensionality of ethnic identity (J.A. Garcia et al. 1992) has its link with politics through the concept of "ethnic political consciousness" (Miller et al. 1981; Antunes and Gaitz 1975; Gutierrez and Hirsch 1973). The persistence of ethnic group identification is a precursor to political consciousness. The additional dimensions of social change orientations and collective action also are part of the combinations that dictate motivations for political action (Gurin et al. 1980). In the 1960s and early 1970s, the use of ethnic labels with attached meanings by Mexican origin individuals was purported to be associated with specific political ideologies and political activities -- whether conventional or unconventional (Gutierrez and Hirsch 1973; Foley et al. 1988). A sense of urgency and political activism characterizes Chicano militants. Protest, direct action, and immediate social change are their political expressions. Ethnic identity serves as the basis of psychological grounding, group attachment, and motivation for political involvement.

The thrust of ethnic identity research in the 1980s was analyzing parallel developments of identification among Puerto Ricans (Rodriquez 1989; Rogler et al. 1980) and Cubans (Portes, Parker, and Cobos 1980; M.T. Garcia and Lega 1979). In addition, the concept of Latino identity (Padilla 1984) was introduced as a situational identity. That is, national origin identity among the Latino subgroups continues to persist; yet there now existed a functional utility to define group identity in broader terms. The political capital gained by defining Latinos as an umbrella term for all persons of Spanish origin helps to expand the size of the group and hence defines a larger national constituency to be represented. Latino identity means creating a new sense of identity to expand the community base for Latinos. Implicit in this concept was the assumption of common cultural attributes and behaviors (i.e., language, shared histories, and traditions) across Latino nationality groups. Also, similar characteristics of community status were implied by shared common experiences of immigration, occupational positions, residential location, and discrimination against Latinos. Thus a Latino identifier is used for its political capital as representing a growing population and emerging political agenda.

The basis for a Latino community has been established by Padilla (1985). His study develops the concept of "situational identity," in which Latinos recognize the political utility of defining group boundaries in broader terms. As a result, Latino identity can be acquired by emphasizing common cultural values and practices and similar socioeconomic and political conditions. Yet the actual dynamics of how and whether a Latino community exists is just now being subjected to systematic analyses. The National Latino Political Survey (de la Garza et al. 1992a) represents the first national probability survey of persons of Mexican, Puerto Rican, and Cuban origin living in the United States. One of the primary foci of this survey is to analyze the foundations for a cultural and political community. Early results (J.A. Garcia et al. 1991) suggest that the primacy of national origin status and identity is still the dominant mode, rather than a pan-ethnic identity. There is some awareness among Latino group members of the other Latino groups in terms of common concerns, issues, and cultural origins. Certainly, the evolution of Latino groups as cultural and, potentially, political communities becomes one of the questions for investigation. Correspondingly, the implications for Latino community building and greater involvement in the political process would be influenced by organizational efforts, leadership cadres, and heightened political partisanship.

Latinos and the Political System

Much attention has been given to the growth in the Latino population in the United States. The expected rise in the Latino population as the nation's largest minority, early in the twenty-first century, is recognized as contributing to their growing political impact. Yet there exists a body of literature that reveals their levels of political participation to be low. Most of the works have focused on Mexican Americans, and have been restricted geographically to the southwestern United States. Only recently have political analyses of Cubans and Puerto Ricans been added to the research literature on Latinos (Welch and Sigelman 1990; Fitzpatrick and Parker 1981).

Political Participation

For the most part, the research studies have been limited to political participation, especially electoral and organizational participation (McCleskey and Merrill 1973; Levy and Kramer 1972; F.C. Garcia and de la Garza 1977; Miyares 1980). Lower levels of voter registration and turnout have been the political pattern since the collection of voting data by the Census Bureau (Calvo and Rosenstone 1989). Registration and turnout differentials between Latinos and Anglos and African Americans range from 10 to 25 percentage points. Wrinkle and Miller (1984) present data from southern Texas to indicate that much of the registration differential between Mexican Americans and Anglos is related to socioeconomic status and the significant presence of non-citizens in the former group.

More generally, explanations for lower levels of registration and turnout among Latinos include higher levels of political cynicism and alienation (Buzan 1980; Comer 1978; Welch et al. 1973); lower rates of naturalization among its resident alien population (J.A. Garcia 1981a; Pachon 1987); structural barriers to registration and voting (Brischetto 1982; Jennings 1977); low levels of information and interest in the U.S. political system (Portes, Clark, and Lopez 1982); and lower socioeconomic status (Verba and Nie 1972; de la Garza and Brischetto 1983). There has been some oscillation in Latino voter registration and turnout in presidential elections during the 1980s, while there has been a slight decline for African-American registration and turnout rates.

Within the Latino umbrella, there are some inter-group differences in terms of voting. Mexican Americans continue to lose some of their voting potential since a substantial portion of their population are non-citizens (J.A. Garcia and de la Garza 1985). Recent organizational efforts to promote and inform Latino nationals of the naturalization process, however, have had some positive impacts (Pachon 1987). Regarding Cuban refugees, their unique political status and strong anti-communist orientations have served to produce high naturalization rates (Portes and Mozo 1985; Portes 1984). Because over 80% of the Cuban population residing in the United States was born in Cuba, naturalization remains a salient issue for Cubans. The Puerto Rican population enjoys American citizenship status due to commonwealth origins. Yet very different voting patterns exist among the Puerto Ricans who live in the U.S. and those who live in Puerto Rico. Greater voting participation occurs in the Commonwealth than in the United States (Falcon 1985). Explanations for this phenomenon have included the cultural and political isolation and alienation of Puerto Ricans in the U.S. compared with the relative political affinity and efficacy among Puerto Ricans in their home country (Jennings and Rivera 1984; Falcon 1985).

Naturalization among Mexican Americans, Cubans, and other Latinos has been the focus of the Latino National Immigration Survey (LNIS) under the direction of Harry Pachon and the National Association of Latino Elected Officials (NALEO). This probability telephone survey of Latino immigrants in 45 metropolitan areas explores the extent of and reasons for or against naturalization and the extent of political involvement (Pachon et al. 1990). The slower rate of naturalization among Latinos is attributed to lack of knowledge about the naturalization process, distrust of the Immigration and Naturalization Service (INS), no perceived benefits of naturalization, and distance from the political system. The area of naturalization is a critical issue for most

Latino groups, and they are now actively promoting naturalization, because the connection between naturalization and Latino political empowerment is recognized (Pachon 1987).

Political Mobilization

Voter political mobilization is determined by individual characteristics (i.e. social class, participatory attitudes, economic status, leisure time opportunities, and ethnic identity) and structural conditions and catalytic agents (i.e., organizations and leaders). The linkage between the Latino population and the political system is bridged by organizations, community, and national leaders. These organizations have represented a variety of institutions, ranging from organizations that focus on social and cultural adaptation to those advocating a third party (Williams et al. 1973; Sassen-Koob 1979; Acuna 1981; I.M. Garcia 1989). Organizations like the Mexican American Legal Defense and Education Fund, American GI Forum, National Council of La Raza, Cuban National Planning Council, and Puerto Rican Legal Defense and Education Fund focus on civil rights issues, community empowerment, and public policy issues like education, immigration, and bilingualism (Sierra 1987; Allsup 1982; San Miguel 1987).

The resilience of Latino organizations has been affected by the availability of economic and human resources within the Latino community, stability and continuity of organizational leadership, strength of organizational bases, and extent of controversy and resistance by the majority population. The more recent challenges confronted by Latino organizations have been the expansion of their constituencies across established national origin boundaries and the redefinition of their political agenda to include more diverse communities. The former deals with the existing organizations that are confined to specific Hispanic groups rather than advocacy and representation of a broader-based Latino constituency.

The latter area centers on the effectiveness of organizational leadership to present a policy agenda to both Latino communities and policy-makers. Organizational adaptation has been affected by the expansion of more inclusive group membership and a national agenda-setting strategy. For the most part, the elements of that evolving national policy agenda include education (access, quality, bilingualism); immigration (access and impact on residential and undocumented Latinos); political recognition of group status; and economic growth and development (F.C. Garcia et al. 1992).

The area of political mobilization, beyond the examination of formal organizations, has also been a critical arena for the study of Latino politics. Ortiz (1980) shows the importance of urban political systems for Latinos since they represent the critical battleground for political struggles over important economic and political issues. Browning, Marshall, and Tabb's work (1979) uses the concept of political incorporation to examine the involvement of African Americans and Latinos in San Francisco Bay Area local governments. Leadership styles, mobilization strategies, political strengths, and institutional responses are defined by the current state of incorporation for each minority group. For Latinos, the incorporation process entails internally oriented mobilization and the achievement of recognition as a political player in the local political arena (Browning, Marshall, and Tabb 1979).

Similarly, Rogler (1968) and Jennings and Rivera (1984) discuss the urban condition and political arena for Puerto Ricans, concentrated in the northeastern section of the United States. Racial and economic isolation and a sense of estrangement serve as major obstacles for effective mobilization. International migration of other Latino groups, (i.e., Dominicans, Colombians, Salvadorans, etc.) into the northeastern U.S. has resulted in more competitive inter-group relations with local governments and political organizations. Local arenas become grounds for political empowerment and conflict resolution (Bonilla and Campos 1981; Ortiz 1980).

For Cubans, their concentration in southern Florida has served to enhance their economic mobility through business activity in ethnic enclaves and conversion of acquired socioeconomic attainment obtained in Cuba (Portes, Clark, and Lopez 1982; Moreno 1990). Early waves of Cuban refugees had advanced human capital resources, and their location in southern Florida allowed them to start small businesses and employ fellow Cubans. Quick and substantial political success for Cubans has been credited to higher socioeconomic status, salient participatory political attitudes, and economic penetration into the local economy (Pedraza-Bailey 1985; Portes and Mozo 1985).

Political Ideology and Values

With regard to ideology and partisanship, Latinos have been characterized as moderate to liberal, with Cubans being the most conservative. Yet recent studies by F.C. Garcia et al. (1991a) show a more moderate to conservative ideological self-placement by Latinos. In this study, Mexican Americans most closely reflect the ideological spectrum of Anglos, while greater percentages of Puerto Ricans and Cubans fall toward the conservative end of the continuum. When specific attitudes and roles for governmental intervention are introduced, Latinos seem to be more in favor of greater governmental involvement than Anglos (F.C. Garcia et al. 1991a). Salient policy issues for Latinos tend to focus on domestic economic issues (i.e., employment, inflation, economic development), public safety (i.e., police relations, crime, drugs), and civil rights (i.e., discrimination, access, etc.).

A recent work by de la Garza et al. (1991) examines some core political values (i.e., economic individualism, political tolerance, trust in government, and patriotism) among Mexican Americans, Puerto Ricans, Cubans, and Anglos. In most of the areas, differences between Latino groups and Anglos are very slight. In fact, Latinos, with the exception of Puerto Ricans, have higher levels of trust and patriotism than their Anglo counterparts (de la Garza et al. 1992a). Earlier works by F.C. Garcia (1973) and Lamare (1977, 1982) support the thesis that Mexican American children and youths are supportive of the U.S. political system. Levels of cynicism enter into the process when individuals accept the "American creed" and experience contradictions (Gutierrez and Hirsch 1973, 1974). The result is heightened activism and unconventional political behavior.

The acceptance of a core of shared political values is more the case between Latino groups and Anglos when sociodemographic factors are controlled (de la Garza et al. 1991). Yet there are some differences -- Cubans tend to be more trusting of government, less politically tolerant, and more supportive of economic individualism than Mexican Americans and Puerto Ricans. As a group, Puerto Ricans are farther away from "internalization" of core political values. These results reinforce the need for inter-group analysis of specific national origin groups under the Latino umbrella.

Political Partisanship and Voting

The conventional wisdom is that the partisanship of Chicanos and other Latinos is Democratic party affiliation (Levy and Kramer 1972; McCleskey and Merrill 1973). More recent surveys by de la Garza et al. (1984) and Brischetto (1988) indicate continued Democratic affiliation among Mexican Americans and Puerto Ricans (over 65%); Cuban party identification is overwhelmingly Republican. It has been suggested that Republican positions against communism and for an individual self-help philosophy have appealed to Cuban voters (Moreno 1990). On the other hand, traditional Democratic support for social and welfare programs and civil rights programs has kept the loyalty of Mexican Americans and Puerto Ricans (F.C. Garcia et al. 1991a; de la Garza and Brischetto 1984). Finally, Latinos exhibit "a bifurcated" electorate in presidential vs. state and local elections. That is, Republican presidential candidates have received a proportionately greater

percentage of Latino votes (i.e., among Mexican Americans and Puerto Ricans) than their partisan affiliations would suggest.

The Latino voting behavior literature tends to depict Latinos as voting less than Anglo voters and African Americans. Besides the important factors of socio-economic status, other factors such as the ethnic consciousness model or ethnic community thesis contribute to the understanding of Latino voter turnout (Lovrich and Marenin 1976; Welch et al. 1973). A critical dimension of Latino voting has to do with ethnic voter polarization (J.A. Garcia 1977; de la Garza 1974). Latinos tend to vote for candidates of the same ethnic background. They demonstrate greater interest in elections when Latino candidates are running, although the level of Latino group bloc voting is not as high as that among African American voters (Cain and Kiewiet 1984; Wrinkle and Miller 1984). Recent work by F.C. Garcia et al. (1992) suggests that the factors of socioeconomic status, ethnicity, political ideology, and partisanship play different roles for and have different effects on Mexicans, Puerto Ricans, and Cubans. Party identification remains a factor for Latinos in presidential and congressional elections.

A more recent occurrence in politics is the presence of Latino voters as a swing voting bloc in urban areas. Latinos are urban dwellers (over 85%) and tend to be concentrated in central cities. Mayoral elections in Chicago, New York, Houston, and Los Angeles have established the pattern of a swing vote between white and black candidates (Salces 1978; Falcon et al. 1991). As a result, issues of coalition formation, inter-group networks, and inter-minority cooperation have become very salient issues for minority communities (Davidson and Gaitz 1973; Jackson 1988; Jackson and Preston 1991; Villareal and Hernandez 1991). The question of inter-group coalitions will be discussed in a later section of this chapter.

The other factors affecting voting patterns are structural conditions and rules of the game (Gomez-Quinones 1990; Brischetto 1982; Wolfinger and Rosenstone 1980; Lineberry and Fowler 1967). Factors such as registration systems, poll taxes, literacy tests, off year vs. even year elections, multi-member vs. single member districts, and at-large vs. ward elections have a direct bearing on registration and turnout levels and minority representation (Taebal 1978; Davidson and Gaitz 1973). Recent research on structural and legal factors has focused on bilingualism and access to the ballot box and challenging at-large election systems (F.C. Garcia 1988). Changes to district- or ward-based systems and reapportionment (MacManus and Cassel 1984; Brischetto 1982) have contributed to gains in Latino political representation (J.A. Garcia 1986b; Guerra 1987).

Discussions on the Voting Rights Act and its extensions have centered on maintenance of the bilingual provisions as a critical component to increase registration levels among Latinos. However, results from the limited research have identified a weak association between language provisions and increased registration rates.

Latinas and Gender Issues

Sierra and Sosa-Riddell (n.d.) see a virtual absence of literature on political behaviors, attitudes, and experiences of Latinas. They argue that the scholarly focus within Latino politics on electoral participation results in the exclusion of other types of activism in which Chicanas are more actively involved, e.g., community-based organizations, labor unions, and grass-roots mobilizations. Moreover, when gender has been included in analyses as one of several determinants of political behavior, few significant differences have been identified; therefore, "...the political orientations and electoral behavior of Chicana women have not commanded much attention" (Sierra and Sosa-Riddell n.d., 7). In addition, Sierra and Sosa-Riddell suggest that the underrepresentation of Chicana scholars in political science also contributes to the lack of scholarly attention to the Chicana experience. Nevertheless, they identify an evolving literature on Chicana politics that has found exceptions to the conventional wisdom of the absence of gender differences.

Although Brischetto and de la Garza (1983) distinguished no significant gender differences in voter registration, turnout, and working in political campaigns among Mexican Americans in East Los Angeles, when controls for marital status were introduced, married men were more likely than married women to register and vote. Yet the opposite was true for unmarried individuals -- women were more likely to register and vote than were men. Using national exit poll data for the 1980, 1984, and 1988 presidential elections, Welch and Sigelman (1992) found Latina women to be more liberal and pro-Democratic than Latino men, although the differences were fairly small and inconsistent. Sierra and Sosa-Riddell (n.d.) identified one study that found that Mexican American women's voter registration and turnout rates increased so dramatically over a ten-year period that their participation rates surpassed those of Mexican American males (MacManus et al. 1986).

Latino Politics and Policy Issues

Latino politics, particularly since 1965, could be portrayed as internally focused endeavors of infrastructure building (i.e., organizational base and structures, political awareness and identity, and leadership cadres) with a strategy to impact the political arena at the local and state levels. The 1980s were a period of expansion, both in terms of group numbers (i.e., Latinos rather than specific national origin groups) and involvement in national politics. The "Latino" umbrella became more of a medium and formal governmental designation than a social and political reality for the masses of Spanish origin persons. The politics of Latinos has only recently focused on creating a broader national Latino community. With this community established, a common and consensual agenda can be developed by national organizations and a network of diverse Latino leaders.

Some of the policy arenas that might be included in the agenda are immigration reform (Sierra 1987; Polinard et al. 1984); education access and quality (San Miguel 1987; Meier and Stewart 1991); political representation and access (de la Garza and DeSipio 1993; Hero 1991); and economic well-being/social welfare policies. Recent work by de la Garza et al. (1992c) suggests that variation among Latinos regarding less restrictive immigration policy is based on degree of political incorporation into American society. For the most part, Latinos generally support greater governmental spending on domestic policy areas and Latino focused policies, while they are less supportive of national defense and foreign aid spending (F.C. Garcia et al. 1991a). Cubans tend to have lower levels of support for domestic governmental funding than do Mexican Americans and Puerto Ricans. The question of a definable policy agenda and the degree of consensus among Latino elites and masses is still less clear, given the lack of regularly collected public opinion data from Latinos (de la Garza and Brischetto 1987).

Connected to Latino public opinion, policy agendas, and political representation are the behavior of elites and policy outcomes. Gains in Latino political representation have been noted during the 1980s (J.A. Garcia 1986b), yet little research has been done on the policy effects of this increased representation. Mindiola and Gutierrez (1988) examined the policy outcomes in the Texas legislature and outcomes related to activities of Chicano legislators. Conclusions suggested marked expansion of legislative initiatives by Chicano legislators on both Chicano focused issues and on social areas with a high impact on Mexican Americans.

Welch and Hibbing (1984) noted that Hispanics who have been elected to Congress tend to have liberal voting records which are similar to the voting records of all Congressional representatives with a sizable Latino constituency. They attribute the Latino representatives' motivation for political involvement and advocacy on behalf of Latinos to early socialization experiences (de la Garza and Vaughn 1984). Elites who experience differential treatment because of their ethnicity are more likely to be active on behalf of other Latinos. The role of elites in affecting the policy agenda and outcomes for Latinos represents another under-researched area.

Latino Politics, the Discipline, and a Future Agenda

Our discussion of Latino politics began with the activism of a small group of Chicano political scientists raising issues of under-representation and non-involvement by Chicanos and a paucity of research directed toward the Mexican American community. Over the past twenty years, the recruitment and retention of Latinos in the discipline and the legitimacy of research on Latinos are still salient issues for political scientists. Recently, the name of the APSA Committee on the Status of Chicanos was changed to the Committee on the Status of Latinos. Originally, the Chicano Caucus agreed to expand the scope of the Committee, yet retain the designation of Chicanos along with the recognition of other Latinos. The objective was to maintain a historical link to the APSA by the Chicano Caucus.

In preparing this general survey on Latino politics, we noted an extensive body of research. Recently, F.C. Garcia et al. (1991b) published *Latinos and Politics: A Selected Research Bibliography*, in which over one thousand citations are identified with annotations on various aspects of Latino politics. Two major conclusions were determined through this compilation. The extensive literature on Latino politics is found, mostly, in a variety of social science journals, with only very minimal inclusion in political science journals. As a result, research on Latino politics is relatively invisible in our discipline. Moreover, invisible within the Latino politics research, as identified by Sierra and Sosa-Riddell (n.d.), is research on Latina women as political actors.

The second conclusion lies with the breadth of perspectives and variables that are examined. The discussion of Latino politics considers culture, historical relationships, economic factors, and individual ascriptive characteristics. Thus, the investigation of Latino politics takes a more interdisciplinary approach than many other subfields in the discipline. As a result, scholars of Latino politics deal with concerns of the legitimacy of their research as well as the substance of their inquiries.

Substantively, research on Latino politics has shifted from an examination of the politics of the Mexican American community to a more inclusive investigation of more diverse Spanish origin groups and the politics of Latino subgroups combined. Also, specific studies of the Latino subgroups continue to demand attention by scholars. A central issue for the study of Latino politics lies with the configuration of the "national" Latino community and factors that contribute to its development and operation as a cohesive community.

Does a cohesive and identifiable Latino community exist such that its political mobilization and policy agenda have an impact on the U.S. political process? The issues of community of culture and interests (J.A. Garcia and Pedraza-Bailey 1990) among the Latino subgroups remain a central focus of inquiry. That is, the pervasiveness of perceived and practiced cultural values and behaviors among Latino subgroup members serves as one element for national community building. The community of interest dimension pertains to common conditions and situations such that Puerto Ricans share common experiences and perspectives with Mexican Americans, Cubans, and other Latino national origin groups. These common experiences could be differential treatment in the labor market, educational institutions, social organizations, and governmental institutions and policies. Realization of a viable Latino political community will depend on further organizational development and leadership skills. In addition, institutional responses and social movements reacting to the growth of Latino communities may also serve as motivations for greater Latino mobilization (Smith 1990). The research agenda on Latino politics centers on the translation of significant population growth among all Latino groups into a more cohesive and focused political force.

More specific areas of Latino political research would include electoral strategies for Latino candidates at the state and national level; expansion of the Latino electoral base by incorporating the sizable non-citizen element; Latina political attitudes and behaviors and the salience of gender issues; coalitional strategies involving inter-Latino communities (i.e., across national origin groups) and other minorities for common political concerns; examination of the political activation process for individual Latinos; the interplay of culture and political participation; and structural conditions and political involvement. Thus the future of Latino politics entails continued systematic examination of these political phenomena, as well as theoretical and conceptual frameworks in which to understand and analyze race and ethnicity in a political context.

Part III: American Indian and Asian-American Politics

We now turn to a condensed examination of the fields of American Indian and Asian-American politics. As we asserted at the beginning of the chapter, the brevity of the discussion is not meant as a comment on the importance of the areas, but simply reflects the limited research in these two developing fields.

American Indian Politics

American Indian politics is a nascent, yet solidly grounded, field of study. Like Latino politics, it should be understood that the broad term, American Indian politics, covers a variety of tribes, each with its own history and different structural relationships with the U.S. government. Chaudhuri (1989, 190) argues that the relationships between American Indians and the U.S. governmental process "...touches on practically every operational point in democratic theory." Yet in the vast array of research on American Indians "political scientists are part of the last group of scholars to enter into the vineyards of Indian affairs scholarship." Although anthropology has long studied American Indians, one of the major criticisms of that work has been that it "...show[s] almost no evidence of any Indian perspective, nor [is it] useful for highlighting the policy issues involved..." (Chaudhuri 1989, 192). Deloria (1969, 81) is more forthright in his criticism of and disdain for the work of anthropologists, charging that "behind each policy and program with which Indians are plagued, if traced completely back to its origin, stands the anthropologist."

Central to the development of the field is the work of Vine Deloria, Jr. His 1969 seminal protest work *Custer Died for Your Sins: An Indian Manifesto* was one of the first works on American Indian politics. Deloria forcefully argues that the politics of American Indian peoples includes not only the relationship of the various tribes to the U.S. government but also the various political histories that have shaped the worldview of the tribes (Deloria 1969, 11). Tribes were organized into confederacies throughout the country, and many tribes exercised the principles of democracy *prior* to contact with whites (Deloria 1969, 11-12). Numerous aspects of American Indian affairs are explored. In the end, Deloria calls for a redefinition of Indian affairs on the part of the U.S. government, in light of the fact that urban Indians far outnumber reservation Indians. This redefinition "would concentrate its attention on the coordination among the non-reservation peoples and the reservation programs..." (Deloria 1969, 257).

Chaudhuri (1989, 193) maintains that in dealing with American Indian politics one needs to distinguish between "issues that are common to the tribes and those that are region-specific or tribe-specific." Moreover, distinctions must be made between reservation (rural or urban) and urban Indians. Chaudhuri (1982), in discussing Indian law, also argues that central to any

discussion of Indian politics are the questions: Who is an Indian? Who is subject to Indian law?

While political science has dealt with issues of ethnic consciousness relative to political participation, the heart of the "Indianness" question lies not with Indian peoples themselves but with the federal government. In fact, the answer is entangled with and central to the relationship of the U.S. government with the various Indian peoples. Chaudhuri (1982, 13) states:

> Historically, of course, Indians knew they were Indians, and self-identification is still a matter of great pride as identity is traced through descent, lineage, clan and acceptance in specific tribes. But the Anglo-American preoccupation with formal definition poses a whole host of problems.

Problems occur because federal, state, and tribal definitions of Indian identification have wide variations. In fact, Chaudhuri (1982, 13) states, "the legal definition of Indian-ness is complexly contextual."

The question of who is subject to Indian law also depends on the relationship of the tribe to the federal government and whether or not the federal government recognizes the tribe (Chaudhuri 1982, 11). There are various forms of federal recognition based on the legal nature of the land status of the tribe (treaty based reservations); reservations directly created by Congress; and reservations created by, or tribes recognized by, states. In addition to federally recognized Indians, there are "hundreds of bands of Indians in the U.S. who do not have federally designated trust land" (Chaudhuri 1982, 12) but are Indian peoples nonetheless and are recognized as such by other Indian peoples.

Whereas black and Latino politics has utilized variants of standard political science frameworks for analyses of the groups' political behavior, this does not appear to be as prevalent within the field of American Indian politics. The assumption has been that not only do these frameworks not apply to the study of Indian peoples but that the historical relationship of Indian peoples to the American governmental structure is so singular that, in many ways, Indian peoples are truly outside of the American political system. Therefore, the generalizations developed about citizen participation of other groups in the political process simply do not fit. Chaudhuri (1989, 190) summarizes this position:

> American Indians historically were outside of the social contract because Indians were in America before there was a contractual America. Consequently, beginning with the legitimacy of the social contract, every other democratic concept including consent, rights, obligations, taxation, voting, education,

privileges, immunities, and property could be examined in the context of U.S.-Indian relations.

Deloria (1981, 149) emphasizes that Indian peoples do not want to be a part of pluralist American society. The great fear of Indians, he says, "is that they will in the years ahead move from their plateau of small nationhood to the status of another ethnic group in the American melting pot."

A focus on specific issue areas characterizes the research in this field. Natural resources and resource policy are essential to Indian politics (Deloria 1981, 1984; Van Patten, 1982), primarily "because all the resources of America were, at one time or another, associated with Indian tribes" (Chaudhuri 1989, 193). U.S. Indian policy, such as termination of federal responsibility to the Indian, is also a focal point of much of the research in the field (Deloria and Lytle 1983; Cadwalaer and Deloria 1984; Deloria 1985; Chaudhuri 1982, 1989; Gross 1989; Deloria 1991).

The issue of social/political movement activity, particularly the concept of pan-Indianism is another thread through the research (Deloria 1969; Nagel 1982; Van Patten 1982; Mason 1984; Gross 1989). The black civil rights movement had an impact on Indian peoples producing comparative work on the similarities and differences in the black, Latino, and Indian situation (Deloria 1969). A focus on institutions (tribal + government and sovereignty) is also present in the research (Melody 1976: Deloria and Lytle 1984; Holm 1985; O'Brien 1989), as well as the Indian presence in the federal bureaucracy (Sigelman and Carter 1976).

Little research has been done on political behavior and attitudes of Indian peoples (Peterson 1957; Deloria 1974; McCool 1982; Murdock 1983). Peterson (1957), in an early effort to analyze the political participation of American Indians, recognized the difficulty of defining and studying American Indian political participation because "[t]he problem has always been one of relating Indian political forms to the general governmental framework of the United States..." (p. 116). The fact should also be noted that native-born American Indians were not officially granted U.S. citizenship until the Citizenship Act of 1924, and thus, except in special circumstances, were denied the right to vote. Even with the passage of the Act, many states through their constitutions continued to deny Indians the right to vote (Peterson 1957).

McCool's article on Arizona Indians is one of the few pieces on the voting patterns of Indians (Deloria 1982) in nontribal elections, national and state. A survey of reservation precincts found significant differences in party affiliation across tribes. For example, over time, the Navajos have shifted from Republican to Democratic and during the Reagan years slightly back to the Republicans in national elections; yet they remained fiercely Democratic in Arizona state politics. On the other hand, since the 1956 presidential election, the Papagos have consistently voted Democratic. Even though McCool's article could be classified as traditional political science, he does not approach the subject from a traditional political science perspective. As he points out: "No other minority group voting data is comparable to the Indian experience, however, nor can the same generalizations be made about Indian voting" (McCool 1982, 111).

Research on the effects of electoral structure on the election of American Indians to political office is virtually nonexistent. However, a recent article by Engstrom and Barrilleaux (1991) examined the effects of cumulative voting on the school board elections in Sisseton School District, the headquarters of the Sisseton-Wahpeton Sioux tribe in South Dakota. Engstrom and Barrilleaux found that the cumulative voting system provided the vehicle for the Sisseton-Wahpeton Sioux to elect an individual to the school board in the at-large election system. Furthermore, their data indicated a high degree of understanding and approval of the cumulative system among the Sioux, providing them with a realistic opportunity to elect a candidate of their choice to the board.

So far, at least from the extant literature, the debate over the boundaries of the field, like that raging in black politics, does not appear to be present. Possibly, the infancy of the field has arrested the jurisdictional controversy that is certain to arise. While the number of scholars writing in the area is modest, there is a robustness to the field.

Asian-American Politics

The newest field to emerge in the minority group politics arena is Asian-American politics. While Asian Americans have been routinely elected to office in Hawaii, and interest in electoral politics can be traced to the early twentieth century, the scholarly research is a very recent phenomenon (Nakanishi 1986, 1-2). One of the earliest works by a political scientist was Yung-Hwan Jo's (1980) anthology, *Political Participation of Asian Americans*. As with Latino and American Indian politics, the term Asian-American politics encompasses a multiplicity of ethnic-origin groups -- Japanese, Korean, Chinese, Filipinos, Southeast Asians, Pacific Islanders, and East Indians (Kitano 1981).

Nakanishi (1986, 3) suggests that Asian-American politics should explore those areas that are considered to be traditional political science, such as electoral participation, voting behavior, resource mobilization for campaigns, and election and appointment to political office. In addition, Nakanishi argues that the field should also include examinations of the barriers which have prevented Asian Americans from significant participation in and influence on political parties and governmental decision making. Moreover, like the argument made by Walton (1972a) in broadening the definition of black politics, Nakanishi's argument maintains that Asian-American politics must also focus on nonelectoral activities, e.g., community organizations, internal community political structures, and political protest, as well as labor protest activity (Nakanishi 1991, 31). In essence, Nakanishi (1986, 21) argues for an "intentionally all-encompassing" definition of the field. This broader conceptualization of Asian-American politics takes into account historical circumstances that created structural and legal barriers to Asian-American participation in the political system. Moreover, according to Nakanishi (1991, 33), it guards against unwarranted generalizations being drawn from "political behavior based solely on their relatively low rates of electoral participation."

The emerging, yet limited, research in political science thus far tends to address traditional political science questions -- political behavior, partisanship, policy preferences and political attitudes, and urban politics.

Political Behavior. The research to this point is relatively consistent. Asian-American voter registration and participation are extremely low (Stokes 1988), a pattern that still exists after controls for a variety of other factors are introduced (Uhlaner, Cain, and Kiewiet 1989). Between-group comparisons suggest that Japanese, Koreans, and Filipino Americans are less likely to register and vote, while Chinese Americans are more likely to register and vote (Stokes 1988). Additionally, Asian men are more likely than women to register, contribute money, work in groups, and contact news media (Uhlaner et al. 1989).

Partisanship. In the aggregate, Asian Americans appear to be more Republican than Democratic, with Chinese Americans being more Republican than other groups (Stokes 1988; Cain and Kiewiet 1986; Cain, Kiewiet, and Uhlaner 1991). However, some feel that partisan attachment is weakly held and either party could benefit from Asian-American support, conceivably giving Asian Americans swing voting potential, depending on each party's position on key public policy issues, such as English-only (Nakanishi 1991).

Policy Preferences and Political Attitudes. California data indicate that Asians were less likely to favor bilingual education and ballots than were Latinos and were more supportive of a ban on handguns and less supportive of prayer in schools than were whites, blacks, and Latinos (Cain and Kiewiet 1986).

Urban Politics. The only study we were able to identify that examined the factors that contribute to the election of Asians to city councils concluded that (1) the percentage of the city population that was Asian was a crucial element; (2) electoral structure had no significant effect on Asian electoral success; and (3) Asians' chances of gaining a council seat improve the greater their median family income relative to white income, and Asian education had a significant effect (Alozie 1992).

Other Areas. Much of the extant research has also been comparative with black and Latino political outcomes, behaviors, and attitudes (Parrillo 1982; Cain and Kiewiet 1986; Uhlaner, Cain, and Kieweit 1989; and Cain, Kiewiet, and Uhlaner 1991), and some have directed attention to the effect international events in home countries have had on the behaviors of U.S. citizens who trace their ethnic origin to those countries (Chang 1988).

"Model Minority" Concept

Given the recent appearance of the field in political science, it is difficult to discern if there are controversies emerging. However, the "model minority" label that has been attached to Asian Americans has been highly controversial and severely criticized (Suzuki 1977; Chun 1980 cited in Nakanishi 1991) "because of its simplistic implication that other minority groups can overcome racial and other discriminatory barriers by following the example of Asian [Americans]." The term "model minority" was first used to refer to Japanese Americans in a 1966 article by William Petersen in the *New York Times Magazine* (Petersen 1966 cited in Roger 1988). Petersen, at the time a faculty member at the University of California at Berkeley, was upset with the student radicalism and counter-culture of the 1960s. As a way of criticizing African Americans and Latinos, he held up Japanese American socioeconomic success as a "model" for how minorities could make it in the United States without much government assistance. Roger (1988) argues that Petersen used the term "model" in two ways:

> [F]irst, as a way of praising the superior performance of Japanese Americans; and second, as a way of suggesting that other ethnic groups should emulate the Japanese American example. The unstated major premise of Petersen's argument was that Horatio-Alger-bootstrap-raising was needed for success by such "non-achieving" minorities as blacks and Chicanos, rather

than the social programs of Lyndon Johnson's Great Society (Roger 1988, 318).

Petersen, assuming a lack of "Americanness" on the part of Japanese Americans, attributed their success to their links "with an alien culture" (Petersen 1966 quoted in Roger 1988, 319). Roger contends that once the "insidious theme" of the "model minority" concept took hold, it has been perpetuated by a host of conservative publicists and academics, particularly the conservative black economist Thomas Sowell (p. 318). Critics of this concept argue that it misleads society into believing that discrimination against Asians has not been extensive or, if it existed, it is a thing of the past. (Even though rejected by scholars of Asian-American politics, the "model minority" concept is emerging, in the work of Thomas Sowell [1975, 1978] and other conservative scholars, as the new ethnic politics approach against which to measure the political progress of blacks and Latinos. As with the original ethnic politics model, this one is almost certain to be soundly rejected by black politics scholars as well.)

Part IV: Inter-minority Group Relations: Coalition or Competition?

The various subfields have developed separately but in parallel fashions. Black politics as the oldest field has formed the comparative base for the fields of Latino, American Indian, and Asian-American politics. While in many instances the comparisons have proved useful, in many more instances, the differences in historical relationships with the dominant white community and the resultant governmental structure have yielded very different experiences and different political objectives and behaviors.

However, the similarities in status have led to a great deal of research on the potential for political coalitions between various groups, principally blacks and Latinos (Henry 1980; Sonenshein 1990; Muñoz and Henry 1990). The assumptions of the coalition research is that the relationship between these two groups will be one of mutual respect and shared political goals and ideals. In some instances, status similarities have led to coalition politics between blacks and Latinos. The emphasis on poverty issues in the 1960s promoted unions between blacks and Latinos, particularly Mexican Americans (Estrada et al. 1981), and there is ample indication of coalition building between blacks and Latinos (see Browning, Marshall, and Tabb 1984, 1990).

Over time, nevertheless, the policy preferences of the two groups diverged. Policies designed to foster equal access and equity were often in conflict; Falcon (1985), for example, notes that blacks were concerned with desegregation and were not supportive of bilingual education because they feared a diversion of resources from black concerns. Recently, blacks have not been supportive of issues that Latinos have considered important -- the "English Only Movement," employer sanctions, and immigration reform. These policy differences, as well as the increasing tensions present in many urban communities, have resulted in a pattern of interaction between the various minority groups that is one of conflict, confrontation, and competition, rather than coalition. This competition, rather than stemming from status differences, is the product of status similarities of the two groups, both striving for finite political and social resources. This set of dynamics has spawned a small, but increasing, array of research on the possible competition that may arise between blacks and Latinos when each has different goals, when there is distrust or suspicion between the two groups, or when the size of one group is such that it becomes unnecessary to form coalitions with other minority groups to gain political success (McClain 1993; McClain and Karnig 1990; Falcon 1988; Warren, Corbett, and Stack 1990; Meier and Stewart 1990).

Coalition behavior, therefore, can be viewed as situational and cooperative activities between two or more distinguishable groups with their own political resources who share *similar* conditions, experiences, and agendas. Coalitional efforts, accordingly, are specific, focused, and usually short-lived. Thus another line of research is to explore the conditions under which coalitions form, how they function, and what outcomes are achieved, examining not just the common objective that initiated the coalition but the establishment of networks across groups for future coalitional efforts (Jackson and Preston 1991; Guerra 1987).

Conclusion

We now return to our initial question -- What is the status of racial minority group politics in political science? Overall, we must conclude that the fields of black, Latino, American Indian, and Asian-American politics are continuing to develop, albeit at different rates and with different emphases. In brief summary, each field may be characterized, historically and contemporarily, by a set of critical concepts, pressing issues, and methodological controversies.

Black politics research in its first generation focused on the interaction of economic factors and race, as well as the importance of blacks to the politics of the South, northern urban centers, principally Chicago, and styles of leadership exhibited within black communities. The second generation research was dominated by the protest/accommodation paradigm found primarily in Negro leadership studies.

A push for definition and rigorous theoretical development consonant with the black experience in the United States epitomizes the scholarship in the third generation. This body of work challenged the use of the ethnic politics paradigm for examining black politics and pushed for the development of frameworks grounded in a power relations dynamic. For all of the effort in the third generation, the preponderance of the research in the current generational phase is more closely tied to mainstream political science than to the scholarship of previous generations. Moreover, the research more readily utilizes traditional political science frameworks for explanations of black political behavior. The mainstreaming of black politics is the source of controversy and fierce debate among African-American political scientists.

Initially, Latino politics was synonymous with Chicano politics, and the development of the field paralleled the rise of the Chicano movement in the 1960s. The themes of internal colonization, exploitation and resistance, and racial and class segmentation were prevalent in the early research. Additionally, Marxist analysis provided the early theoretical paradigm for much of the research. Moreover, the majority of the research was published in journals of social science disciplines other than political science.

The focus of present research has shifted to ethnic identity and its effects on the political behavior of the various ethnic origin groups that fall under the Latino politics umbrella. The advent of Hispanics as a larger ethnic category has prompted examinations of inter-group differences on various political dimensions. The importance of Latino organizations is another theme that characterizes the current body of research. While black politics rejected the ethnic politics model, Latino politics has incorporated it into its array of theoretical frameworks. Unlike the field of black politics, however, questions of and concerns for research legitimacy persist for Latino scholars and Latino politics.

Central to the field of American Indian politics is the nature of the relationship of the various tribes, i.e., sovereignty, to the U.S. government and the question of redefinition of Indian affairs in the presence of the preponderance of non-reservation Indians. The research in the field has not been characterized by the use of traditional political science frameworks for explanation of the politics of Indian peoples. Of the four fields covered, American Indian politics, more than any other, has specifically avoided their use, finding the frameworks inappropriate, given the unique historical circumstances of Indian peoples in the United States.

The newest field, Asian-American politics, is in the process of defining the content and boundaries of the field. The direction appears to be moving toward a broad definition of the field that takes into account historical circumstances that created barriers to Asian-American participation in the political system, as well as electoral and non-electoral activities. The controversial issue is the "model minority" concept, which obscures the racism and discrimination experienced by Asian Americans.

The process of reconstructing the history of the development of these fields brought two points sharply into focus which must be underscored -- the reaction of political science to the fields and the role of minority political scientists in the development of the fields. Despite the historical and continuing centrality of race and ethnicity to the American political fabric, political science has demonstrated a marked reluctance to acknowledge as legitimate the study of the politics of America's various racial minority groups. To rephrase Emmett E. Dorsey's comments on Negro politics, assuming that the sentiments could be assumed to have been similar relative to other racial minority groups, political science viewed these fields as "offbeat," and any young political scientist interested in a career would steer clear of research in these areas.

Fortunately, a number of scholars ignored the warning and made racial minority politics their intellectual specialty. It is evident from the historical development of the fields of black and Latino politics, and more recently American Indian and Asian-American politics, that the impetus for the legitimization has come, to a large extent, from racial minority political scientists themselves. While political science has been more accommodating of late to the study of the politics of America's racial minorities, there is still the struggle to convince the discipline to view the fields as separate entities with distinct and very different intellectual histories and foundations. For example, black politics is different from the other three areas in that ethnic differences within the group are not a prominent dimension, as in Latino politics, which subsumes Mexican Americans, Puerto Ricans, Cubans, and other ethnic Latinos.

Also evident is that there are more differences between the fields than there are similarities. While having some things in common, e.g., group minority status, racial minorities differ in their political attitudes and behaviors. For example, presently blacks are primarily Democratic and overwhelmingly vote as such in presidential elections; Mexican Americans identify as Democrats, but many more vote for Republican presidents than one would think; Cubans are primarily Republicans; and Puerto Ricans are Democrats. Asian Americans are mostly Republican, except for Japanese Americans who are more Democratic, and, to date, there has been no major study that has examined partisan identification among the various American Indian peoples. Ideological differences are also in evidence. African Americans are difficult to pinpoint ideologically because they may be liberal on government involvement in certain areas but conservative on some social issues. Mexican Americans are just as likely to be moderate as conservative, while Cubans are conservative on foreign policy issues but somewhat liberal on some social issues. Asian Americans are more conservative on economic issues but liberal on many social issues. Consequently, it should be recognized that generalizations developed from the study of urban African Americans should not be expected to hold for southwestern Mexican Americans. Moreover, it should not be assumed that a scholar whose specialty is black politics is automatically an authority on Latino politics, or vice versa.

The first edition of this book, published in 1983, did not contain a chapter on racial minority group politics. Our task for this edition, therefore, necessitated the reconstruction of the history as well as a delineation of current themes and directions prevailing in each field. Projecting into the future, what would we expect this chapter to contain and how would it be structured in the third edition?

First, we anticipate that the developments in each field, particularly black and Latino politics, will require separate chapters, clearly signifying their acceptance by the discipline. Second, some of the questions currently plaguing the fields will have been resolved, but in keeping with the dynamism of the areas, new ones will have surfaced. For instance, scholars in black politics will once again seriously question the appropriateness of traditional political science explanations for the political attitudes and behaviors of African Americans. Latino politics will no longer suffer from lingering concerns about legitimacy, and inter-group political differences will be more sharply focused. Many more scholars will focus on the politics of American Indian peoples but, heeding the mistakes made by anthropologists, will approach the subject from frameworks that account for the uniqueness of the situation of Indian peoples in the United States. In addition, the "model minority" paradigm in Asian-American politics will have gone the way of the ethnic politics approach in black politics.

Finally, and most importantly, the chapters in the third edition will, we hope, no longer talk about the small numbers of minority political scientists in political science generally and the even smaller number writing in the various areas specifically. For it is our hope that the numbers of black, Latino, American Indian, and Asian-American political scientists, expecially females, will increase as the discipline's recognition and commitment to the study of the politics of America's racial minority groups grow.

Notes

We would like to thank Steven Tauber, research assistant in the Woodrow Wilson Department of Government and Foreign Affairs at the University of Virginia, for his invaluable assistance in locating much of the research referenced in this chapter.

1. There is debate over whether the concept of "minority" politics is a theoretically useful category for conceptualizing and organizing the political experiences of all non-white groups in the United States. We acknowledge this controversy, but do not intend to enter the debate in this chapter, which would require more time and space than has been allocated.

2. It should be noted that Bunche was the first black American male to receive a Ph.D. in political science. The first black American female was Jewel Limar Prestage, who received her Ph.D. in 1954 from the University of Iowa.

3. We have purposely confined our discussion of black and Latino politics to attitudes and behaviors related to the United States domestic political arena. While there is a modest literature on black and Latino participation in foreign policy, we decided not to include that dimension. Although one could argue that foreign policy issues should be a concern of the subfields, to date it has not been an overriding concern in either area.

4. In 1969, a preparatory conference was called at Southern University to discuss professional problems of black political scientists within the discipline, in general, and within the American Political Science Association, in particular, as well as to discuss the political science curricula at historically black colleges and universities (Jones 1990)

5. Between Bunche's work and the Negro leadership studies of the 1960s, several of Bunche's students, principally Robert E. Martin, continued to research and publish in the emerging field of Negro politics. Martin conducted early empirical research on black voting in the Agricultural Adjustment Programs. Given the unreceptivity of political science journals to Negro politics, Martin's studies were published in other disciplinary journals (Martin 1938, 1942, 1951, and 1953).

6. Popular knowledge among many Latino scholars contends that a reference to Douglas Week's article in the 1930s supposedly appeared in the *American Political Science Review*. Our search for this reference for the documentation of this chapter proved unsuccessful.

7. Latino politics, during this time period, is synonymous with Chicano politics.

8. If Avalos had included the *Social Science Quarterly*, especially since 1970, he would have noted the significant inclusion of articles on Mexican Americans. In many respects, the early development of Chicano politics emanated from an interdisciplinary perspective and many social science disciplines. Given the central mission of the *Social Science Quarterly*, there was a greater receptivity by this journal and its editor for submissions in this field.

Bibliography

Abramson, Paul R. 1972. "Political Efficacy and Political Trust Among Black School Children." *Journal of Politics* 34:1243-1275.

Abramson, Paul R. 1977. *The Political Socialization of Black Americans: A Critical Evaluation of Research on Efficacy and Trust.* New York: Free Press.

Acuna, R. 1981. *Occupied America: A History of Chicanos.* 2nd ed. New York: Harper and Row.

Ad Hoc Committee on Mexican Americans in the Profession. 1970. "Report of the APSA Committee." *PS: Political Science & Politics* 3:739.

Allen, Richard L., Michael C. Dawson, and Ronald Brown. 1989. "A Schema-based Approach to Modeling an African-American Racial Belief System." *American Political Science Review* 83:421-441.

Allsup, C. 1982. *The American G.I. Forum: Origins and Evolution*. Austin, TX: Center for Mexican American Studies, University of Texas at Austin.

Almaguer, T. 1971. "Toward the Study of Chicano Colonialism." *Aztlan* 2:7-22.

Alozie, Nicholas O. 1992. "The Election of Asians to City Councils." *Social Science Quarterly* 73:90-100.

Alvarez, R. 1973. "The Psycho-Historical and Socioeconomic Development of the Chicano Community in the United States." *Social Science Quarterly* 53:920-942.

Antunes, G., and C.M. Gaitz. 1975. "Ethnicity and Participation: A Study of Mexican Americans, Blacks and Whites." *American Journal of Sociology* 80:1192-1211.

Arce, C.H. 1981. "A Reconsideration of Chicano Culture and Identity." *Daedalus* 110:177-192.

Avalos, M. 1991. "The Status of Latinos in the Profession: Problems in Recruitment and Retention." *PS: Political Science & Politics* 24:241-246.

Banfield, E., and J.Q. Wilson. 1963. *City Politics*. Cambridge: Harvard and M.I.T. University Presses.

Barker, Lucius J. 1973. "Black Americans and the Burger Court: Implications for the Political System." *Washington University Law Quarterly* (Fall):747-777.

Barker, Lucius J. 1988. *Our Time Has Come*. Urbana: University of Illinois Press.

Barker, Lucius J. 1992a. "Thurgood Marshall, the Law and the System: Tenets of an Enduring Legacy." *Stanford Law Review* 44:1237-1247.

Barker, Lucius J. 1992b. "Defining the Court: The Confirmation and First Term of Justice Clarence Thomas." Paper presented at the annual meeting of the American Political Science Association, Chicago.

Barker, Lucius J., and Michael Combs. 1987. "Courts and Future of Black Politics: Section Five of the Voting Rights Act, an Example." In *The New Black Politics: Black Voting and Political Power*, 2nd ed., ed. Michael Preston et. al. New York: Longman.

Barker, Lucius J., and Jesse J. McCorry, Jr. 1980. *Black Americans and the Political System*. 2nd ed. Cambridge, MA: Winthrop Publishers.

Barker, Lucius J., and Ronald W. Walters, eds. 1989. *Jesse Jackson's 1984 Presidential Campaign*. Urbana: University of Illinois Press.

Barnett, Marguerite R. 1975. "The Congressional Black Caucus." In *Congress Against the People*, ed. H. Mansfield. New York: Praeger.

Barnett, Marguerite R. 1977. "The Congressional Black Caucus: Symbol, Myth, and Reality." *Black Scholar* 9:17-26.

Barnett, Marguerite R. 1984. "The Congressional Black Caucus: Illusions and Realities of Power." In *The New Black Politics*, ed. Michael B. Preston, Lenneal J. Henderson, and Paul Puryear. New York: Longman.

Barnett, Marguerite R., and James Hefner, eds. 1976. *Public Policy for the Black Community*. New York: Alfred.

Barrera, M. 1977. "Class Segmentation and the Political Economy of the Chicano, 1900-1930." *The New Scholar* 6:167-181.

Barrera, M. 1979. *Race and Class in the Southwest: A Theory of Racial Inequality*. Notre Dame, IN: University of Notre Dame Press.

Bean, Frank, and M. Tienda. 1987. *The Hispanic Population of the United States*. New York: Russell Sage Foundation.

Blauner, R. 1969. "Internal Colonialism and Ghetto Revolt." *Social Problems* 16:393-408.

Bobo, Lawrence, and Franklin D. Gilliam, Jr. 1990. "Race, Sociopolitical Participation, and Black Empowerment." *American Political Science Review* 84:377-393.

Bonilla, F., and R. Campos. 1981. "A Wealth of Poor: Puerto Ricans in the New Economic Order." *Daedalus* 110:133-176.

Brischetto, Robert R., ed. 1982. *Bilingual Elections at Work in the Southwest*. A Mexican American Legal Defense and Educational Fund Report. San Antonio: Mexican American Legal Defense Fund.

Brischetto, Robert R., and Rodolfo O. de la Garza. 1983. *The Mexican American Electorate: Political Participation and Ideology*. Occasional Paper No. 3. Austin: Southwest Voter Registration and Education Project, San Antonio: Hispanic Population Studies Program of The Center for Mexican American Studies, University of Texas at Austin.

Brischetto, Robert R. 1988. *The Political Empowerment of Texas Mexicans, 1974-1988*. San Antonio: Southwest Voter Registration and Education Project.

Browning, Rufus P., Dale Rogers Marshall, and David H. Tabb. 1979. "Minorities and Urban Electoral Change: A Longitudinal Study." *Urban Affairs Quarterly* 15:206-228.

Browning, Rufus P., Dale Rogers Marshall, and David H. Tabb. 1984. *Protest Is Not Enough*. Berkeley: University of California Press.

Browning, Rufus P., Dale Rogers Marshall, and David H. Tabb. 1990. *Racial Politics in American Cities*. New York: Longman.

Bryce, Herrington J., and Allan E. Warrick. 1977. "Black Women in Electoral Politics." In *A Portrait of Marginality*, ed. Marianne Githens and Jewel L. Prestage. New York: David McKay Company.

Bullock, Charles III, and Susan MacManus. 1987. "Staggered Terms and Black Representation." *Journal of Politics* 49:543-552.

Bunche, Ralph J. 1928. "The Negro in Chicago Politics." *National Municipal Review* 18 (May):261-264.

Bunche, Ralph J. 1935. "A Critical Analysis of the Tactics and Programs of Minority Groups." *Journal of Negro Education* 4 (July):308-320.

Bunche, Ralph J. 1936. "A Critique of New Deal Social Planning as It Affects Negroes." *Journal of Negro Education* 5 (January):59-65.

Bunche, Ralph J. 1941. "The Negro in the Political Life of the United States." *Journal of Negro Education* 10 (July):567-84.

Bunche, Ralph J. n.d. "The Political Status of the Negro." Unpublished manuscript.

Burgess, M. Elaine. 1962. *Negro Leadership in a Southern City*. Chapel Hill: University of North Carolina Press.

Buzan, B.C. 1980. "Chicano Community Control, Political Cynicism and the Validity of Political Trust Measures." *Western Political Quarterly* 33:108-119.

Cadwalaer, Sandra L., and Vine Deloria, Jr. 1984. *The Aggressions of Civilization: Federal Indian Policy Since the 1880s*. Philadelphia: Temple University Press.

Cafferty, P.S.J., and C. Rivera-Martinez. 1981. *The Politics of Language: The Dilemma of Bilingual Education for Puerto Ricans*. Boulder, CO: Westview Press.

Cain, Bruce E., and D. Roderick Kiewiet. 1984. "Ethnicity and Electoral Choice: Mexican-American Voting Behavior in the California 30th Congressional District." *Social Science Quarterly* 65:315-327.

Cain, Bruce E., and D. Roderick Kiewiet. 1986. "California's Coming Minority Majority." *Public Opinion* 9 (February-March):50-52.

Cain, Bruce E., D. Roderick Kiewiet, and Carole J. Uhlaner. 1991. "The Acquisition of Partisanship by Latinos and Asian Americans." *American Journal of Political Science* 35:390-442.

Calvo, M., and S. Rosenstone. 1989. *Hispanic Political Participation*. Southwest Voter Registration Project. San Antonio: Southwest Voter Research Project.

Carmichael, Stokely, and Charles V. Hamilton. 1967. *Black Power: The Politics of Liberation in America*. New York: Vintage Books.

Carmines, Edward G., and James A. Stimson. 1989. *Race and the Transformation of American Politics*. Princeton: Princeton University Press.

Chang, Edward. 1988. "Korean Community Politics in Los Angeles: The Impact of the Kwangju Uprising." *Amerasia Journal* 14:51-67.

Chaudhuri, Joyotpaul. 1982. "American Indian Policy: An Overview of the Legal Complexities, Controversies, and Dilemmas." *Social Science Journal* 19:9-21.

Chaudhuri, Joyotpaul. 1989. "Indians and the Social Contract." *National Political Science Review* 1:190-200.

Chun, Ki-Taek. 1980. "The Myth of Asian American Success and Its Educational Ramifications." *IRCD Bulletin* 15:1-12

Cole, Leonard. 1974. "Electing Blacks to Municipal Office: Structural and Social Determinants." *Urban Affairs Quarterly* 8:17-39.

Comer, J.C. 1978. "'Street Level' Bureaucracy and Political Support: Some Findings on Mexican Americans." *Urban Affairs Quarterly* 14:207-227.

Cox, Oliver Cromwell. 1948. *Caste, Class and Race: A Study in Social Dynamics*. Garden City, NY: Doubleday.

Dahl, Robert. 1961. *Who Governs?* New Haven: Yale University Press.

Darcy, Robert, and Charles D. Hadley. 1988. "Black Women in Politics: The Puzzle of Success." *Social Science Quarterly* 69:629-645.

Davidson, C., and C.M. Gaitz. 1973. "Ethnic Attitudes as a Basis for Minority Cooperation in a Southwestern Metropolis." *Social Science Quarterly* 53:738-748.

Dawson, Michael C., and Ernest J. Wilson III. 1991. "Paradigms and Paradoxes: Political Science and African American Politics." In *Theory and Practice of Political Science*, ed. William Crotty. Evanston: Northwestern University Press.

Dawson, Michael C., Ronald E. Brown, and Richard L. Allen. 1990. "Racial Belief Systems, Religious Guidance, and African-American Political Participation." *National Political Science Review* 2:22-44.

de la Garza, R.O. 1974. "Voting Patterns in Bicultural El Paso: A Contextual Analysis of Chicano Voting Behavior." *Aztlan* 5:235-260.

de la Garza, R.O. 1982. "Chicano-Mexicano Relations: A Framework for Research." *Social Science Quarterly* 63:115-130.

de la Garza, R.O., and R.R. Brischetto. 1983. *The Mexican American Electorate: Information Sources and Policy Orientations*. The Mexican American Electorate Series, Occasional Paper No. 2. San Antonio: Southwest Voter Registration and Education Project, and Austin: Hispanic Population Studies Program of the Center for Mexican American Studies, University of Texas at Austin.

de la Garza, R.O., and R.R. Brischetto. 1984. *The Mexican American Electorate: An Explanation of Their Opinions and Behavior*. The Mexican American Electorate Series, Occasional Paper No. 4. San Antonio: Southwest Voter Registration and Education Project, and Austin: Hispanic Population Studies Program of the Center for Mexican American Studies, University of Texas at Austin.

de la Garza, R.O., and R.R. Brischetto, eds. 1987. *Ignored Voices: Public Opinion and the Latino Community*. Austin: Center for Mexican American Studies, University of Texas.

de la Garza, R.O., R.R. Brischetto, and J. Weaver. 1984. *The Mexican Electorate: An Explanation of Opinions and Behaviors* (monograph). San Antonio: Southwest Voter Education Project.

de la Garza, R.O., and L. DeSipio. 1993. *From Rhetoric to Reality: Latinos and the 1988 Elections*. Boulder, CO: Westview Press.

de la Garza, R.O., L. DeSipio, F.C. Garcia, J.A. Garcia, and A. Falcon. 1992a. *Latino Voices: Mexican, Puerto Rican, & Cuban Perspectives on American Politics*. Boulder, CO: Westview Press.

de la Garza, R.O., A. Falcon, F. Chris Garcia, and John A. Garcia. 1992b. "The Effects of Ethnicity on Political Culture: A Comparison of Puerto Rican and Anglo Political Values." Center for American Political Studies, Harvard University. Typescript.

de la Garza, R.O., A. Falcon, F. Chris Garcia, and John A. Garcia. 1992c. "Ethnicity and Attitudes toward Immigration Policy: The Case of Mexicans, Puerto Ricans, and Cubans in the U.S." Paper presented at the annual meeting of the American Political Science Association, Chicago.

de la Garza, R.O., A. Falcon, F.C. Garcia, and J.A. Garcia. 1991. "Mexican Immigrants, Mexican Americans, and the American Political Culture." In *Immigration and Public Policy*, ed. Edmonson and Fixx. Washington, DC: Urban Institute.

de la Garza, R.O., and D. Vaughn. 1984. "The Political Socialization of Elites: A Generational Analysis." *Social Science Quarterly* 65:290-307.

Deloria, Vine, Jr. 1969. *Custer Died for Your Sins: An Indian Manifesto*. New York: Macmillan Company.

Deloria, Vine, Jr. 1974. *Behind the Trail of Broken Treaties: An Indian Declaration of Independence*. New York: Delacorte Press.

Deloria, Vine, Jr. 1981. "Native Americans: The American Indian Today." *Annals of the American Academy of Political and Social Sciences* 454:139-149.

Deloria, Vine, Jr. 1982. "American Indians: Landmarks on the Trail Ahead." *Social Science Journal* 19:1-8.

Deloria, Vine, Jr. 1984. "Land and Natural Resources." In *Minority Report*, ed. Leslie W. Dunbar. New York: Pantheon Books.

Deloria, Vine, Jr. ed. 1985. *American Indian Policy in the Twentieth Century*. Norman: University of Oklahoma Press.

Deloria, Vine, Jr. 1991. "Federal Policy and the Perennial Question." *American Indian Quarterly* 15(Winter):19-21.

Deloria, Vine, Jr., and Clifford M. Lytle. 1983. *American Indians, American Justice*. Austin: University of Texas Press.

Deloria, Vine, Jr., and Clifford M. Lytle. 1984. *The Nations Within: The Past and Future of American Indian Sovereignty*. New York: Pantheon Books.

Dunbar, Leslie. 1961. "Reflections on the Latest Reform of the South." *Phylon* 22 (Fall):249-57.

Eisinger, Peter. 1974. "Racial Differences in Protest Participation." *American Political Science Review* 68:592-607.

Engstrom, Richard, and Charles J. Barrilleaux. 1991. "Native Americans and Cumulative Voting: The Sisseton-Walpeton Sioux." *Social Science Quarterly* 72:388-393.

Engstrom, Richard, and M.D. McDonald. 1981. "The Election of Blacks to City Councils." *American Political Science Review* 75:344-354.

Engstrom, Richard, and M.D. McDonald. 1982. "The Underrepresentation of Blacks on City Councils." *Journal of Politics* 44:108-109.

Estrada, L., F.C. Garcia, R.F. Macias, and L.A. Maldonado. 1981. "Chicanos in the United States: A History of Exploitation and Resistance." *Daedalus* 110:103-131.

Falcon, A. 1985. *Black and Latino Politics in New York City: Race and Ethnicity in a Changing Urban Context*. Discussion Paper. New York: Institute for Puerto Rican Policy.

Falcon, A. 1988. "Black and Latino Politics in New York City." *In Latinos in the Political System*, ed. F. Chris Garcia. Notre Dame, IN: Notre Dame University Press.

Falcon, A., Rodolfo de la Garza, F. Chris Garcia, John A. Garcia. 1991. "Modes of Political Participation of Mexican Americans, Puerto Ricans, and Cuban Americans." Paper presented at the annual meeting of the American Political Science Association, Washington, DC.

Fitzpatrick, J.P., and L.T. Parker. 1981. "Hispanic Americans in the Eastern United States." *Annals of the American Academy of Political and Social Sciences* 454:98-110.

Foley, D.E., C. Mota, D.E. Post, and I. Lozano. 1988. *From Peons to Politicos: Class and Ethnicity in a South Texas Town, 1900 to 1987*. Rev. ed. Austin: University of Texas Press.

Foster, C.R. 1982. "Political Culture and Regional Ethnic Minorities." *Journal of Politics* 44:560-568.

Foster, Lorn S. 1983. "The Voting Rights Act: Black Voting and the New Southern Politics." *Western Journal of Black Studies* 7:120-129.

Foster, Lorn S. 1984a. "The Voting Rights Act: Political Modernization and the New Southern Politics." *Southern Studies* 23:266-288.

Foster, Lorn S. 1984b. "Section Five of the Voting Rights Act and Its Effects upon Southern School Boards." *Negro Educational Review* 35:25-34.

Foster, Lorn S. 1985. "Political Symbolism and the Enactment of the 1982 Voting Rights Act." In *The Voting Rights Act: Consequences and Implications*, ed. Lorn Foster. Westport, CT: Praeger.

Foster, Lorn S. 1986. "Section Five of the Voting Rights Act: Implementation of an Administrative Remedy." *Publius* 16:17-24.

Garcia, F.C. 1973. "Orientations of Mexican-American and Anglo Children Toward the U.S. Political Community." *Social Science Quarterly* 53:814-829.

Garcia, F.C., ed. 1988. *Latinos and the Political System*. Notre Dame, IN: University of Notre Dame Press.

Garcia, F.C., and de la Garza, R.O. 1977. *The Chicano Political Experience: Three Perspectives*. North Scituate, MA: Duxbury Press.

Garcia, F.C., R.O. de la Garza, J.A. Garcia, and A. Falcon. 1991a. "Ethnicity and Ideology: Mexican, Puerto Rican and Cuban Origin Populations in the United States." Paper presented at the annual meeting of the American Political Science Association, Washington, DC.

Garcia, F.C., R.O. de la Garza, J.A. Garcia, A. Falcon, and C.J. Abeyta. 1991b. *Latinos and Politics: A Selected Research Bibliography*. Center for Mexican American Studies. Austin: University of Texas Press.

Garcia, F.C., R.O. de la Garza, J.A. Garcia, A. Falcon, and C.J. Abeyta. 1992. "The Effects of Ethnic Partisanship on Electoral Behavior: An Analysis and Comparison of Latino and Anglo Voting in the 1988 Presidential Elections." Paper presented at the annual meeting of the American Political Science Association, Chicago.

Garcia, I.M. 1989. *United We Win: The Rise and Fall of the La Raza Unida Party, Tucson, AZ*. Tucson, AZ: Mexican American Studies and Reseach Center, University of Arizona.

Garcia, J.A. 1975 "Report on the Status of Chicanos in the Profession, Western States Universities." Report to the Western Political Science Association.

Garcia, J.A. 1977. "Chicano Voting Patterns in School Board Elections: Bloc Voting and Internal Lines of Support for Chicano Candidates." *Astibos* (Winter 1976-1977):1-14.

Garcia, J.A. 1981a. "Political Integration of Mexican Immigrants: Explorations into the Naturalization Process." *International Migration Review* 15:608-625.

Garcia, J.A. 1981b. "Yo Soy Mexicano: Self-Identity and Sociodemographic Correlates." *Social Science Quarterly* 62:88-98.

Garcia, J.A. 1982. "Ethnicity and Chicanos: Measurement of Ethnic Identification, Identity, and Consciousness." *Hispanic Journal of Behavioral Sciences* 4:295-314.

Garcia, J.A. 1986a. "Caribbean Migration to the Mainland: A Review of Adaptive Experiences." *Annals of the American Academy of the Political and Social Sciences* 487:114-125.

Garcia, J.A. 1986b. "VRA and Hispanic Political Representation." *Publius* 16:49-66.

Garcia, J.A. 1987. "The Political Integration of Mexican Immigrants: Examining Some Political Orientations." *International Migration Review* 21:372-389.

Garcia, J.A., and R.O. de la Garza. 1985. "Mobilizing the Mexican Immigrant: The Role of Mexican-American Organizations." *Western Political Quarterly* 38:551-564.

Garcia, J.A., R.O. de la Garza, A. Falcon, and F.C. Garcia. 1991. "Ethnicity and National Origin Status: Patterns of Identities Among Latinos in the U.S." Paper presented at the annual meeting of the American Political Science Association, Washington, DC.

Garcia, J.A., and S. Pedraza-Bailey. 1990. "Hispanicity and the Phenomenon of Community of Culture and Interests Among Latinos in the U.S." Paper presented at the annual meeting of the American Political Science Association, San Francisco.

Garcia, John A., F. Chris Garcia, R. de la Garza, and A. Falcon. 1992. "The Multi-Dimensionality of Ethnicity: Examining the Cases of Mexicans, Puerto Ricans, and Cubans." Paper presented at the annual meeting of the American Political Science Association, Chicago.

Garcia, M.T., and L. Lega. 1979. "Development of a Cuban Ethnic Identity Questionnaire." *Hispanic Journal of Behavioral Science* 1(3):247-261.

Glazer, Nathan, and Daniel P. Moynihan. 1963. *Beyond the Melting Pot*. Cambridge, MA: M.I.T. Press.

Gomes, Ralph C., and Linda Faye Williams. 1992. *From Exclusion to Inclusion: The Long Struggle for African American Political Power*. Westport, CT: Greenwood Press.

Gomez-Quinones, Juan. 1990. *Chicano Politics: Reality and Promise*. Albuquerque: University of New Mexico Press.

Gordon, M.M. 1964. *Assimilation in American Life*. New York: Oxford University Press.

Gosnell, Harold F. 1934. "Political Meetings in Chicago's Black-Belt." *American Political Science Review* 28:254-258.

Gosnell, Harold F. [1935] 1967. *Negro Politicians: The Rise of Negro Politics in Chicago*. Chicago: University of Chicago Press.

Greenberg, Edward S. 1970. "Children and Government: A Comparison Across Racial Lines." *Midwest Journal of Political Science* 14:249-275.

Grofman, Bernard. 1990. *Voting Rights, Voting Wrongs*. New York: Twentieth Century Fund.

Grofman, Bernard, and Chandler Davidson. 1992. *Controversies in Minority Voting*. Washington, DC: Brookings Institution.

Gross, Emma R. 1989. *Contemporary Federal Policy Toward American Indians*. Westport, CT: Greenwood Press.

Guerra, Fernando J. 1987. "Ethnic Officeholders in Los Angeles County." *Sociology and Social Research* 71:89-94.

Gurin, P., A. Miller, and G. Gurin. 1980. "Stratum Identification and Consciousness." *Journal of Social Psychology* 40:30-47.

Gurin, Patricia, Shirley Hatchett, and James S. Jackson. 1989. *Hope and Independence: Blacks' Response to Electoral and Party Politics*. New York: Russell Sage Foundation.

Gutierrez, Armando, and H. Hirsch. 1973. "Militant Challenge to the American Ethos." *Social Science Quarterly* 53:83-85.

Gutierrez, Armando, and H. Hirsch. 1974. "Political Maturation and Political Awareness: Case of Crystal City Chicanos." *Aztlan* 5:295-312.

Hamilton, Charles V. 1973a. "Full Employment as a Viable Issue." In *When the Marching Stopped: An Analysis of Black Issues In the 70s*. New York: National Urban League.

Hamilton, Charles V. 1973b. *The Bench and the Ballot: Southern Federal Judges and Black Voters*. New York: Oxford University Press.

Hamilton, Charles V. 1977. "De-Racialization: Examination of a Political Strategy." *First World* 4 1-3-5.

Hamilton, Charles V. 1981. "New Elites and Pluralism." In *The Power to Govern*, ed. Richard M. Pious. *Proceedings of the Academy of Political Science* 34:167-73.

Hayes-Bautista, D.E. 1974. "Becoming Chicano: A 'Dis-Assimilation' Theory of Transformation of Ethnic Identity." Ph.D. diss. University of California, San Francisco.

Henderson, Lenneal J. 1978. "Administrative Advocacy and Black Urban Administrators." *Annals of the American Academy of the Social and Political Sciences* 439:68-79.

Henderson, Lenneal J. 1979. *Administrative Advocacy: Black Administrators in Urban Bureaucracies*. Palo Alto: R and E Research Associates.

Henderson, Lenneal J. 1987. "Black Politics and American Presidential Elections." In *The New Black Politics*, ed. Michael B. Preston, Lenneal J. Henderson, and Paul Puryear. New York: Longman.

Henry, Charles P. 1980. "Black and Chicano Coalitions: Possibilities and Problems." *Western Journal of Black Studies* 43 4:222-232.

Henry, Charles P. 1992. "Ralph Bunche and the Howard School of Thought." Paper presented at the annual meeting of the National Conference of Black Political Scientists, Houston, TX.

Hero, Rodney. 1991. *Latinos and the U.S. Political System*. Philadelphia: Temple University Press.

Herrick, Rebekah, and Susan Welch. 1992. "The Impact of At-Large Elections on the Representation of Black and White Women." *National Political Science Review* 3:62-74.

Hill, Walter. 1992. "Redistricting in the 1990s: Opportunities and Risks for African Americans." In *From Exclusion to Inclusion: The Long Struggle for African American Political Power*, ed. Ralph C. Gomes and Linda Faye Williams. Westport, CT: Greenwood Press.

Holden, Matthew, Jr. 1973. *The Politics of the Black "Nation."* New York: Chandler Publishing.

Holden, Matthew, Jr. 1983. *Moral Engagement and Combat Scholarship*. McLean, VA: Court Square Institute.

Holm, Tom. 1985. "The Crisis in Tribal Government." In *American Indian Policy in the Twentieth Century*, ed. Vine Deloria. Norman, OK: University of Oklahoma Press.

Horowitz, Donald L. 1985. *Ethnic Groups in Conflict*. Berkeley, CA: University of California Press.

Jackson, Byran. 1988. "Ethnic Cleavages and Voting Patterns in U.S. Cities: An Analysis of the Asian, Black and Hispanic Communities of Los Angeles." Paper presented at the Conference on Comparative Ethnicity at the University of California, Los Angeles.

Jackson, Byran, and Michael Preston, eds. 1991. *Racial and Ethnic Politics in California*. Berkeley: Institute for Governmental Studies, University of California.

Jennings, J. 1977. *Puerto Rican Politics in New York City*. Washington, DC: University Press of America.

Jennings, J., and M. Rivera, eds. 1984. *Puerto Rican Politics in Urban America*. Westport, CT: Greenwood Press.

Jo, Yung-Hwan, ed. 1980. *Political Participation of Asian Americans: Problems and Strategies*. Chicago: Pacific/Asian American Mental Health Research Center.

Jones, Mack H. 1972. "A Frame of Reference for Black Politics." In *Black Political Life in the United States*, ed. Lenneal J. Henderson. San Francisco: Chandler Publishing Company.

Jones, Mack H. 1978. "Black Political Empowerment in Atlanta: Myth and Reality." *Annals of the American Academy of Political and Social Sciences* 439:90-117.

Jones, Mack H. 1990. "NCOBPS: Twenty Years Later." *National Political Science Review* 2:3-12.

Jones, Mack H. 1992. "Political Science and the Black Political Experience: Issues in Epistemology and Relevance." *National Political Science Review* 3:25-29.

Jones, Woodrow, Jr., and Mitchell F. Rice. 1987. *Health Care Issues in Black America*. Westport, CT: Greenwood Press.

Karnig, Albert K. 1976. "Black Representation on City Councils." *Urban Affairs Quarterly* 11 (December):223-242.

Karnig, Albert K. 1979a. "Black Resources and City Council Representation." *Journal of Politics* 41 (February):134-149.

Karnig, Albert K. 1979b. "Black Development and City Size." *Social Forces* 57:1194-1121.

Karnig, Albert K., and Paula D. McClain. 1985. "The New South and Black Economic and Political Development: Changes from 1970 to 1980." *Western Political Quarterly* 38 (December):537-550.

Karnig, Albert K., and Paula D. McClain. 1989. *Urban Minority Administrators*. Westport, CT: Greenwood Press.

Karnig, Albert K., and Susan Welch. 1980. *Black Representation and Urban Policy*. Chicago: University of Chicago Press.

Katznelson, Ira. 1971. "Power in the Reformulation of Race Research." In *Race, Change, and Urban Society*, ed. Peter Orleans and William R. Ellis, Jr. Beverly Hills: Sage Publications.

Katznelson, Ira. 1973. "Participation and Political Buffers in Urban America." *Race* 14:465-80.

Keefe, S.E., and A.M. Padilla. 1987. *Chicano Ethnicity*. Albuquerque: University of New Mexico Press.

Key, V.O., Jr. 1949. *Southern Politics*. New York: Vintage Books.

Killian, Lewis M., and Charles U. Smith. 1960. "Negro Protest Leaders in a Southern Community." *Social Forces* 38 (March):253-257.

King, Mae C. 1973. "The Politics of Sexual Stereotypes." *Black Scholar* (March-April):12-23.

Kirby, John B. 1990. "Race, Class, and Politics: Ralph Bunche and Black Protest." In *Ralph Bunche: The Man and His Times*, ed. Benjamin Rivlin. New York & London: Holmes and Meier.

Kitano, Harry H.L. 1981. "Asian-Americans: The Chinese, Japanese, Koreans, Filipinos, and Southeast Asians." *Annals of the American Academy of Political and Social Sciences* 454:125-138.

Ladd, Everett C. 1966. *Negro Political Leadership in the South*. Ithaca: Cornell University Press.

Lamare, James. 1977. "The Political World of the Rural Chicano Child." *American Politics Quarterly* 5:83-108.

Lamare, James. 1982. "The Political Integration of Mexican American Children: A Generational Analysis." *International Migration Review* 16:169-182.

Lansing, Marjorie. 1977. "The Voting Patterns of American Black Women." In *A Portrait of Marginality*, ed. Marianne Githens and Jewel L. Prestage. New York: David McKay Company.

Levine, B.B. 1979. "Sources of Ethnic Identity for Latin Florida." Caribbean Review 8:30-33.

Levy, Arthur B., and Susan Stoudinger. 1976. "Sources of Voting Cues for the Congressional Black Caucus." *Journal of Black Studies* 7:29-46.

Levy, Arthur B., and Susan Stoudinger. 1978. "The Black Caucus in the 92nd Congress: Gauging Its Success." *Phylon* 39:322-332.

Levy, M.R., and M.S. Kramer. 1972. *The Ethnic Factor*. New York: Simon and Schuster.

Lewis, Shelby F. 1982. "A Liberation Ideology: The Intersection of Race, Sex, and Class." In *Women's Rights, Feminism and Politics in the United States*, ed. Mary L. Shanley. Washington, DC: American Political Science Association.

Lineberry, R.L., and E.P. Fowler. 1967. "Reformism and Public Policies in American Cities." *American Political Science Review* 61:701-716.

Lipsky, Michael. 1968. "Protest as a Political Resource." *American Political Science Review* 62:1144-1158.

Lipsky, Michael. 1970. *Protest in City Politics*. Chicago: Rand McNally.

Litt, Edgar. 1970. Ethnic Politics in America. Glenview, IL: Scott, Foresman.

Lovrich, N.P. Jr., and O. Marenin. 1976. "Comparison of Black and Mexican-American Voters in Denver: Assertive vs. Acquiescent Political Orientations and Voting Behavior in an Urban Electorate." *Western Political Quarterly* 29:284-294.

Lyons, Salley R. 1970. "The Political Socialization of Ghetto Children: Efficacy and Cynicism." *Journal of Politics* 32:288-304.

MacManus, Susan, and C. Cassel. 1984. "Mexican Americans in City Politics: Participation, Representation, and Policy Preferences." *Urban Interest* 4:57-69.

MacManus, Susan A., Charles S. Bullock III, and Barbara P. Grothe. 1986. "A Longitudinal Examination of Political Participation Rates of Mexican American Females." *Social Science Quarterly* 67:604-612.

Manley, John. 1983. "Neopluralism: A Class Analysis of Pluralism I and Pluralism II." *American Political Science Review* 77:368-383.

Mansbridge, Jane, and Katherine Tate. 1992. "Race Trumps Gender: The Thomas Nomination in the Black Community." *PS: Political Science and Politics* 23:488-492.

Marable, Manning. 1983. *How Capitalism Underdeveloped Black America: Problems in Race, Political Economy, and Society*. Boston: South End.

Marable, Manning. 1985. *Black American Politics: From the Washington Marches to Jesse Jackson*. London: Verso.

Martin, Robert E. 1938. *Negro Disfranchisement in Virginia*. Washington, DC: Howard University Studies in the Social Sciences.

Martin, Robert E. 1942. "War on Poll Tax Front." *Opportunity* 20:100.

Martin, Robert E. 1951. "The Referendum Process in the Agricultural Adjustment Programs of the United States." *Agricultural History* 25 (January):34-47.

Martin, Robert E. 1953. "The Relative Political Status of the Negro in the United States." *Journal of Negro Education* 22 (Summer):363-379.

Mason, W. Dale. 1984. "You Can Only Kick So Long: American Indian Movement Leadership in Nebraska 1972-1979." *Journal of the West* 23 (July):21-31.

Matthews, Donald R. 1969. "Political Science Research on Race Relations" In *Race and the Social Sciences*, ed. Irwin Katz and Patricia Gurin. New York: Basic Books.

Matthews, Donald R., and James W. Prothro. 1966. *Negroes and the New Southern Politics*. New York: Harcourt, Brace and World.

McClain, Paula D. 1992. "Reconceptualizing Urban Violence: A Policy Analytic Approach." *National Political Science Review* 3:9-24.

McClain, Paula D. 1993. "The Changing Dynamics of Urban Politics -- Black and Hispanic Municipal Employment: Is There Competition?" *Journal of Politics* 55:399-414.

McClain, Paula D., and Albert K. Karnig. 1990. "Black and Hispanic Socioeconomic and Political Competition." *American Political Science Review* 84:535-545.

McCleskey, Clifton, and B. Merrill. 1973. "Mexican American Political Behavior in Texas." *Social Science Quarterly* 53:785-798.

McCool, Daniel. 1982. "Voting Patterns of American Indians in Arizona." *Social Science Journal* 19 (July):101-113.

McCormick, Joseph P. II, and Charles E. Jones. 1993. "The Conceptualization of Deracialization: Thinking Through the Dilemma." In *Dilemmas of Black Politics*, ed. Georgia A. Persons. New York: HarperCollins.

McLemore, Leslie Burl. 1972. "Toward a Theory of Black Politics -- The Black and Ethnic Models Revisited." *Journal of Black Studies* 2 (March):323-331.

Meier, Kenneth J., and Joseph Stewart, Jr. 1990. "Interracial Competition in Large Urban School Districts: Elections and Public Policy." Paper presented at the annual meeting of the American Political Science Association, San Francisco.

Meier, Kenneth J., and Joseph Stewart, Jr. 1991. *The Politics of Hispanic Education*. Albany, NY: State University of New York Press.

Melody, Michael Edward. 1976. *The Sacred Hoop: The Way of the Chiricahua, Apache, and Teton Lakota*. Ph.D. diss. University of Notre Dame.

Miller, A., P. Gurin, G. Gurin, and O. Malanchuk. 1981 "Group Consciousness and Political Participation." *American Journal of Political Science* 25:494-511.

Mindiola, T., and A. Gutierrez. 1988. "Chicanos and the Legislative Process: Reality, Illusion in the Politics of Change." In *Latinos and the Political System*, ed. F. Chris Garcia. Notre Dame, IN: University of Notre Dame Press.

Miyares, M. 1980. *Models of Political Participation of Hispanic-Americans*. New York: Arno Press.

Moore, Joan W. 1970. "Colonialism: The Case of the Mexican Americans." *Social Problems* 17:463-72.

Moreno, D. 1990. "Political Empowerment of Cuban-Americans." Paper presented at the Inter-University Conference on Latinos in the United States. California Polytechnic University, Pomona.

Morris, Lorenzo. 1990. *The Social and Political Implications of the 1984 Jesse Jackson Presidential Campaign*. Westport, CT: Praeger.

Morris, Milton D. 1975. *The Politics of Black America*. New York: Harper and Row.

Muñoz, Carlos, Jr. 1989. *Youth, Identity, and Power*. London: Verso Press.

Muñoz, Carlos, Jr., and Charles P. Henry. 1990. "Coalition Politics in San Antonio and Denver: The Cisneros and Peña Mayoral Campaigns." In *Racial Politics in American Cities*, ed. Rufus P. Browning, Dale Rogers Marshall, and David H. Tabb. New York: Longman.

Murdock, Margaret Maier. 1983. "Political Attachment Among Native Americans: Arapahoe and Shoshoni Children and the National Political System." *Social Science Journal* 20:41-58.

Myrdal, Gunnar. 1944. *An American Dilemma*. New York: Harper and Brothers.

Nagel, Joane. 1982. "The Political Mobilization of Native Americans." *Social Science Journal* 19 (July):37-45.

Nakanishi, Don T. 1986. "Asian American Politics: An Agenda for Research." *Amerasia Journal* 12:1-27.

Nakanishi, Don T. 1991. "The Next Swing Vote? Asian Pacific Americans and California Politics" In *Racial and Ethnic Politics in California*, ed. Byran O. Jackson and Michael B. Preston. Berkeley: Institute of Governmental Studies, University of California.

Nelson, William E. 1990. "Black Mayoral Leadership: A Twenty-Year Perspective." *National Political Science Review* 2:188-195.

Nelson, William E., and Philip J. Meranto. 1977. *Electing Black Mayors*. Columbus: Ohio State University Press.

Nowlin, William F. 1931. *The Negro in American National Politics*. Boston: Stratford.

O'Brien, Sharon. 1989. *American Indian Tribal Government*. Norman: University of Oklahoma Press.

Olsen, Marvin C. 1970. "Social and Political Participation of Blacks." *American Sociological Review* 35:682-697.

Orum, Anthony M., and Roberta S. Cohen. 1973. "The Development of Political Orientations Among Black and White Children." *American Sociological Review* 38:62-74.

Ortiz, I.D. 1980. "The Political Economy of Chicano Urban Politics." *Plural Societies* 11:41-54.

Pachon, H.P. 1987. "Naturalization: Determinants and Process in the Hispanic Community." *International Migration Review* 21:299-310.

Pachon, H.P, L. Desipio, and R. Gold. 1990. "Future Research on Latino Immigrants and the Political Process." Paper presented at Latino Research Perspectives on the 1990s (Inter-University Program on Latino Research), Pomona, CA.

Padilla, A. 1980a. "The Role of Cultural Awareness and Ethnic Loyalty." In *Acculturation: Theory, Models and Some New Findings*, ed. Amado Padilla. Boulder, CO: Westview Press, 47-84.

Padilla, A. ed. 1980b. *Acculturation: Theory, Models and Some New Findings*. Boulder, CO: Westview Press.

Padilla, F.M. 1984. "On the Nature of Latino Ethnicity." *Social Science Quarterly* 65:651-664.

Padilla, F.M. 1985. *Latino Ethnic Consciousness: The Case of Mexican Americans and Puerto Ricans in Chicago*. Notre Dame, IN: University of Notre Dame Press.

Palley, Marian Lief, and Michael B. Preston. 1979. *Race, Sex, and Policy Problems*. Lexington, MA: Lexington Books.

Parenti, M. 1967. "Ethnic Politics and the Persistence of Ethnic Identification." *American Political Science Review* 61:717-726.

Parker, Frank R. 1990. *Black Votes Count*. Chapel Hill, NC: University of North Carolina Press.

Parrillo, Vincent N. 1982. "Asian Americans in American Politics." In *America's Ethnic Politics*, ed. Joseph S. Roucek and Bernard Eisenberg. Westport, CT: Greenwood Press.

Pedraza-Bailey, S. 1985. *Political and Economic Migrants in America: Cubans and Mexicans*. Austin: University of Texas Press.

Perry, Huey L. 1990. "Black Political and Mayoral Leadership in Birmingham and New Orleans." *National Political Science Review* 2:154-160.

Perry, Huey L. 1991. "Deracialization as an Analytical Construct." *Urban Affairs Quarterly* 27 (December):181-191.

Persons, Georgia A. 1985. "Reflections on Mayoral Leadership: The Impact of Changing Issues and Changing Times." *Phylon* 46 (September):205-218.

Persons, Georgia A. 1987. "The Philadelphia MOVE Incident as an Anomaly in Models of Mayoral Leadership." *Phylon* 48 (Winter):249-260.

Persons, Georgia A. 1993. *Dilemmas of Black Politics: Issues of Leadership and Strategy*. New York: HarperCollins.

Peterson, Helen. 1957. "American Indian Political Participation." *Annals of the American Academy of Political and Social Sciences* 311 (May):116-126.

Pinderhughes, Dianne M. 1987. *Race and Ethnicity in Chicago Politics*. Urbana: University of Illinois Press.

Pinderhughes, Dianne M. 1990. "Governing Governing: Voting Rights in the Twentieth Anniversary of the Voting Rights Act of 1965." Paper presented at the annual meeting of the American Political Science Association, San Francisco.

Polinard, Jerry, R. Wrinkle, and R. de la Garza. 1984. "Attitudes of Mexican Americans Toward Irregular Mexican Immigration." *International Migration Review* 18:782-799.

Portes, A. 1984. "The Rise of Ethnicity: Determinants of Ethnic Perceptions Among Cuban Exiles in Miami." *American Sociological Review* 49:383-97.

Portes, A., and R.L. Bach. 1985. *Latin Journey*. Berkeley: University of California Press.

Portes, A., J.M. Clark, and M.M. Lopez. 1982. "Six Years Later: The Process of Incorporation of Cuban Exiles in the United States." *Cuban Studies/Estudios Cubanos* 11-12:1-24.

Portes, A., and R. Mozo. 1985. "The Political Adaptation Process of Cubans and Other Ethnic Minorities in the United States: A Preliminary Analysis." *International Migration Review* 19:35-63.

Portes, A., R.N. Parker, and J.A. Cobos. 1980. "Assimilation or Consciousness: Perceptions of U.S. Society Among Recent Latin American Immigrants to the United States." *Social Forces* 59:200-224.

Prestage, Jewel L. 1968. "Black Politics and the Kerner Report: Concerns and Direction." *Social Science Quarterly* 49 (December):453-464.

Prestage, Jewel L. 1977. "Black Women State Legislators: A Profile." In *A Portrait of Marginality*, ed. Marianne Githens and Jewel L. Prestage. New York: David McKay Company.

Prestage, Jewel L. 1984. "Political Behavior of American Black Women: An Overview." In *The Black Woman*, ed. La Frances Rodgers-Rose. Beverly Hills, CA: Sage.

Prestage, Jewel L. 1991. "In Quest of African American Political Woman." *Annals of the American Academy of the Political and Social Sciences* 515 (May):88-103.

Preston, Michael B. 1976. "Limitations of Black Urban Power: The Case of Black Mayors." In *The New Urban Politics*, ed. Louis Massotti and Robert Lineberry. Cambridge, MA: Ballinger.

Preston, Michael B. 1983. "The Election of Harold Washington: Black Voting Patterns in the 1983 Chicago Mayoral Race." *PS: Political Science and Politics* 16:486-88.

Preston, Michael B. 1984. *The Politics of Bureaucratic Reform: The Case of the California State Employment Service*. Urbana: University of Illinois Press.

Preston, Michael B. 1987. "The Election of Harold Washington: An Examination of the SES Model in the 1983 Chicago Mayoral Election." In *The New Black Politics*, 2nd ed., ed. Michael Preston, Lenneal Henderson, and Paul L. Puryear. New York: Longman.

Preston, Michael B. 1990. "Big City Mayors: An Overview." *National Political Science Review* 2:131-144.

Preston, Michael B., Lenneal J. Henderson, and Paul Puryear. 1987. *The New Black Politics*. 2nd ed. New York: Longman.

Reed, Adolph, Jr. 1986. *The Jesse Jackson Phenomenon*. New Haven: Yale University Press.

Rice, Mitchell R., and Woodrow Jones, Jr. 1984. *Contemporary Public Policy Perspectives and Black Americans*. Westport, CT: Greenwood Press.

Rich, Wilbur C. 1989. *Coleman Young and Detroit Politics*. Detroit: Wayne State University Press.

Rivlin, Benjamin, ed. 1990. *Ralph Bunche*. New York: Holmes and Meier.

Robinson, Cedric J. 1983. *Black Marxism: The Making of the Black Radical Tradition*. London: Zed Press.

Robinson, Theodore, and Thomas Dye. 1978. "Reformism and Black Representation on City Councils." *Social Science Quarterly* 59:153-161.

Rodgers, Harrell R., Jr. 1974. "Toward Explanation of Political Efficacy and Political Cynicsm of Black Adolescents: An Exploratory Study." *American Journal of Political Science* 18:257-282.

Rodgers, Harrell R., Jr., and George Taylor. 1971. "The Policeman as an Agent of Regime Legitimation." *Midwest Journal of Political Science* 15:72-86.

Rodriquez, C. 1989. *Puerto Ricans: Born in the USA*. Boston and London: Unwin and Hyman.

Roger, Daniel. 1988. *Asian America: Chinese and Japanese in the United States Since 1850*. Seattle: University of Washington Press.

Rogler, L.H. 1968. "The Growth of an Action Group: The Case of a Puerto Rican Migrant Voluntary Association." *International Journal of Comparative Sociology* 9:223-34.

Rogler, L.H., R.S. Cooney, and V. Ortiz. 1980. "Intergenerational Change in Ethnic Identity in the Puerto Rican Family." *International Migration Review* 14:193-214.

Salces, L.M. 1978. "Spanish Americans' Search for Political Representation: The 1975 Aldermanic Election in Chicago." *Journal of Political and Military Sociology* 6:175-187.

San Miguel, G. 1987. *"Let Them All Take Heed": Mexican Americans and the Campaign for Educational Equality in Texas 1910-1981*. Austin: University of Texas Press.

Sassen-Koob, S. 1979. "Formal and Informal Associations: Dominicans and Colombians in New York." *International Migration Review* 13:314-332.

Sears, David O., and J.B. McConahay. 1973. *The Politics of Violence: The New Urban Blacks and the Watts Riot*. Boston: Houghton Mifflin.

Seltzer, Richard, and Robert C. Smith. 1985a. "Race and Ideology: A Research Note Measuring Liberalism and Conservatism in Black America." *Phylon* (June):98-105.

Seltzer, Richard, and Robert C. Smith. 1985b. "Race and Civil Liberties." *Social Science Quarterly* 66 (March):155-62.

Shingles, Richard. 1981. "Black Consciousness and Political Participation." *American Political Science Review* 75:76-91.

Sierra, Christine M. 1987. "Latinos and the New Immigration: Responses from the Mexcian American Community" In Renato Rosaldo Lecture Series Monograph. Tucson. Mexican American Studies and Research Center, University of Arizona.

Sierra, Christine M., and Adalijiza Sosa-Riddell. n.d. "Chicanas as Political Actors: Rare Literature, Complex Practice." *National Political Science Review* 4.

Sigelman, Lee and Robert Carter. 1976. "American Indians in the Political System: A Note on the Bureau of Indian Affairs." *Administration and Society* 8 (November):343-354.

Sigelman, Lee, and Susan Welch. 1991. *Black Americans' Views of Racial Inequality: The Dream Deferred*. Cambridge and New York: Cambridge University Press.

Smith, Robert C. 1981. "The Black Congressional Delegation." *Western Political Quarterly* 34:203-221.

Smith, Robert C. 1982. *Black Leadership: A Survey of Theory and Research*. Washington, DC: Institute for Urban Affairs, Howard University.

Smith, Robert C. 1984. "Black Appointed Officials: A Neglected Area of Research in Black Political Participation." *Journal of Black Studies* 14 (March):369-388.

Smith, Robert C. 1988. "Financing Black Politics: A Study of Congressional Elections." *Review of Black Political Economy* 17 (Summer):5-30.

Smith, Robert C. 1990. "Recent Elections and Black Politics: The Maturation or Death of Black Politics." *PS: Political Science and Politics* 23:160-62.

Smith, Robert C., and Richard Seltzer. 1992. *Race, Class, and Culture*. Albany: State University of New York Press.

Smith, Tom. 1990. "Ethnic Survey." *GSS Topical Report No. 19*. Chicago: National Opinion Research Center (University of Chicago).

Sonenshein, Raphael L. 1990. "Biracial Coalition Politics in Los Angeles." In *Racial Politics in American Cities*, ed. Rufus P. Browning, Dale Rogers Marshall, and David H. Tabb. New York: Longman.

Sowell, Thomas. 1975. *Race and Economics*. New York: D. McKay.

Sowell, Thomas, ed. 1978. *Essays with Data on American Ethnic Groups*. Washington, DC: Urban Institute.

Starks, Robert T. 1991. "A Commentary and Response to 'Exploring the Meaning and Implications of Deracialization in African American Urban Politics.'" *Urban Affairs Quarterly* 27 (December):216-222.

Stokes, Bruce. 1988. "Learning the Game." *National Journal* 20:2649-2654.

Suzuki, Bob. 1977. "Education and Socialization of Asian Americans." *Amerasia Journal* 4:23-51.

Taebel, Delbert. 1978. "Minority Representation on City Councils." *Social Science Quarterly* 59:142-152.

Tate, Katherine. 1991. "Black Political Participation in 1984 and 1988 Presidential Elections." *American Political Science Review* 85:1159-1176.

Tate, Katherine. 1992. "The Impact of Jesse Jackson's Presidential Bids on Blacks' Relationship with the Democratic Party." *National Political Science Review* 3:184-197.

Tate, Katherine. 1993. *From Protest to Politics: The New Black Voters in American Elections*. Cambridge, MA: Harvard University and the Russell Sage Foundation.

Tilman, Cothran, and William Phillips. 1961. "Negro Leadership in a Crisis Situation." *Phylon* 22 (Summer):107-118.

Uhlaner, Carole J., Bruce Cain, and D. Roderick Kiewiet. 1989. "Political Participation of Ethnic Minorities in the 1980s." *Political Behavior* 11 (September):195-231.

United States Bureau of the Census. 1989. "Voting and Registration in the Election of November 1988 (Advance Report)." *Current Population Reports*. Series P-20, No. 435, February.

Van Patten, James J. 1982. "The American Indian" In *America's Ethnic Politics*, ed. Joseph Roucek and Bernard Eisenberg. Westport, CT: Greenwood Press.

Verba, S., and N. Nie. 1972. *Participation in America*. New York: Harper and Row.

Villareal, Roberto, and Norman Hernandez, eds. 1991. *Latinos and Political Coalitions*. New York: Greenwood Press.

Walker, Jack L. 1963. "Protest and Negotiation: A Case Study of Negro Leadership in Atlanta, Georgia." *Midwest Journal of Political Science* 7:99-124.

Walters, Ronald W. 1988. *Black Presidential Politics in America: A Strategic Approach*. Albany: State University of New York Press.

Walters, Ronald W. 1992. "Two Political Traditions: Black Politics in the 1990s." *National Political Science Review* 3:198-208.

Walton, Hanes, Jr. 1972a. *Black Politics*. Philadelphia: J.B. Lippincott Co.

Walton, Hanes, Jr. 1972b. *Black Political Parties: An Historical and Political Analysis*. New York: Free Press.

Walton, Hanes, Jr. 1973. *The Study and Analysis of Black Politics*. Metuchen, NJ: Scarecrow Press.

Walton, Hanes, Jr. 1975. *Black Republicans: The Politics of Black and Tans*. Metuchen, NJ: Scarecrow Press.

Walton, Hanes, Jr. 1985. *Invisible Politics*. Albany: State University of New York Press.

Walton, Hanes, Jr. 1986. "Foreword." In *Black Voices in American Politics*, ed. Jeffery M. Elliott. San Diego: Harcourt, Brace, Jovanovich."

Walton, Hanes, Jr. 1989. *When the Marching Stopped*. Albany: State University of New York Press.

Walton, Hanes, Jr. 1992. *The Native Son Presidential Candidate: The Carter Vote in Georgia*. New York: Praeger.

Walton, Hanes, Jr. n.d. "Ralph Bunche Minus African American Politics." *National Political Science Review* 4.

Walton, Hanes, Jr., Leslie Burl McLemore, and C. Vernon Gray. 1990. "The Pioneering Books on Black Politics and the Political Science Community, 1903-1965." *National Political Science Review* 2:196-218.

Walton, Hanes, Jr., Leslie Burl McLemore, and C. Vernon Gray. 1992. "The Problem of Preconceived Perceptions in Black Urban Politics: The Harold F. Gosnell, James Q. Wilson Legacy." *National Political Science Review* 3:217-229.

Walton, Hanes, Jr., Cheryl Miller, and Joseph McCormick, II. n.d. "Race and Political Science: The Dual Traditions of Race Relations Politics and African-American Politics." In *Political Science and Its History: Research Programs and Political Traditions*, ed. John Dryzek, James Farr, and Stephen Leonard.

Walzer, M., E.T. Kantowicz, J. Higham, and M. Harrington. 1982. *The Politics of Ethnicity*. Cambridge, MA: Harvard University Press.

Warren, Christopher L., John G. Corbett, and John F. Stack, Jr. 1990. "Hispanic Ascendancy and Tripartite Politics in Miami." In *Racial Politics in American Cities*, ed. Rufus P. Browning, Dale Rogers Marshall, and David H. Tabb. New York: Longman.

Welch, Susan. 1990. "The Impact of At-Large Elections on the Representation of Blacks and Hispanics." *Journal of Politics* 52:1050-1076.

Welch, Susan, J.C. Comer, and M. Steinman. 1973. "Political Participation Among Mexican Americans: An Exploratory Examination." *Social Science Quarterly* 53:799-813.

Welch, Susan, and Lorn Foster. 1987. "Class and Conservatism in the Black Community." *American Politics Quarterly* 15:445-470.

Welch, Susan, and Lorn Foster. 1992. "The Impact of Economic Conditions on the Voting Behavior of Blacks." *Western Political Quarterly* 45:221-236.

Welch, Susan, and J. Hibbing. 1984. "Hispanic Representation in the U.S. Congress." *Social Science Quarterly* 65:328-335.

Welch, Susan, and Lee Sigelman. 1989. "A Black Gender Gap?" *Social Science Quarterly* 70:120-123.

Welch, Susan, and Lee Sigelman. 1990. "The Politics of Hispanic Americans: Insights from National Surveys, 1980-1988." Unpublished manuscript.

Welch, Susan, and Lee Sigelman. 1992. "A Gender Gap Among Hispanics? A Comparison with Blacks and Anglos." *Western Political Quarterly* 45:181-199.

Williams, J.A., N. Babchuck, and D.R. Johnson. 1973. "Voluntary Associations and Minority Status: A Comparative Analysis of Anglo, Black, and Mexican Americans." *American Sociological Review* 38:637-646.

Williams, Linda. 1987. "Black Political Progress in the 1980s: The Electoral Arena." In *The New Black Politics: The Search for Political Power*, 2nd ed., ed. Michael B. Preston, Lenneal Henderson, and Paul Puryear. New York: Longman.

Wilson, Ernest J. III. 1985. "Why Political Scientists Don't Study Black Politics, but Historians and Sociologists Do." *PS: Political Science and Politics* 18:600-607.

Wilson, James Q. 1960. *Negro Politics*. New York: Free Press.

Wilson, James Q. 1961. "The Strategy of Protest: Problems of Negro Civic Action." *Journal of Conflict Resolution* 5:291-303.

Wolfinger, Raymond E. 1965. "The Development and Persistence of Ethnic Voting." *American Political Science Review* 59:896-908.

Wolfinger, Raymond E., and Steven J. Rosenstone. 1980. *Who Votes?* New Haven: Yale University Press.

Wrinkle, R.D., and L.W. Miller. 1984. "A Note on Mexican American Voter Registration and Turnout." *Social Science Quarterly* 65:308-314.

11

Citizens, Contexts, and Politics

Robert Huckfeldt and John Sprague

Politics is about winners and losers, influence and coercion, exchange and bargaining, coalitions and factions, conflict and compromise. All these topics involve individuals and groups tied together in complex relationships that defy easy disaggregation and reaggregation. Yet, when we address the topic of citizen politics in the mass, the temptation appears overwhelming to shift the level of understanding and analysis to that of independent individuals -- individuals abstracted from time, place, and setting. Indeed, opinions, interests, preferences, attitudes, beliefs, and values are readily defined with respect to individually defined circumstance. Rich people are Republicans, black people are Democrats, educated people participate more, and so on, but such an analysis frequently lacks the capacity to reconstruct a compelling account of political life. Contextual analysis provides one antidote to this common analytic disjuncture between individuals and politics -- to the gap in our understanding between micro and macro analyses of political life. Contextual theories of politics are built on an assertion of behavioral interdependence: the actions of individual citizens are to be understood as the intersection between individually defined circumstance and the circumstances of surrounding individuals. The distinguishing irreducible element of a contextual analysis is that, in addition to measures of individual properties and preferences, the political behavior of individuals is characterized as contingent on the environment. Measurements on the environment, as well as theoretical arguments based on the environment, occupy fundamental positions in the logical structure underlying theories of individual political behavior that appeal to explanatory contextual hypotheses.

A number of consequences follow from this thesis. Contextual theories of politics are inherently multi-level -- they require cross-level inference -- and hence have consequences for the ways in which politics is conceived at multiple levels of analysis and meaning. First, this means that the political choices of individuals are best and most fully understood in relationship to the surrounding environment. But, second, it also means that politics in the mass is not simply an additive consequence of individually discrete interests and impulses. Rather, mass politics is understood as the end product of these intersections between groups and individuals within a particular time period and a particular place.

This paper presents a comprehensive view of contextual analysis. We elaborate the idea of behavior in context as an explanatory concept, as well as the intellectual roots that give rise to multi-level contextual analysis. Contextual analysis is construed here as a line of attack upon the more general problem of cross-level inference, and we argue that ecological fallacies arise only when a contextual effect is present. Finally, attention is given to alternative mechanisms of interdependence -- to alternative micro theories of contextual influence.

Modern Intellectual Roots

The modern intellectual roots of contextual analysis can be located in the work of Emile Durkheim, Herbert Tingsten, V.O. Key, and the early election studies of several Columbia University sociologists -- most notably, but not exclusively, Berelson, Lazarsfeld, and McPhee (1954), followed in the same tradition by Ennis (1962), Segal and Meyer (1974), and others. These efforts articulated several themes that continue to provide a focus for contextual theories: behavioral interdependence, multiple levels of observation, and problems of cross-level inference. These themes were set in a somewhat broader context by Harold Lasswell (1966 originally published 1939), and Lasswell's relevance to the theoretical aspects of contextual analysis is repeatedly touched on by Eulau (1986) in a work that includes systematic development of contextual analysis.

The general topic of contextual analysis is vast and spreads across many fields. This review is selective and focuses on the usefulness of context in the analysis of political behavior. In sociology and particularly in the sociology of education there has been extensive work, both theoretical and empirical, elaborating the opportunities and also the problems presented by the idea that behavior is not independent of the context in which it occurs. The modern canon in sociology is best dated from the seminal writing of Blau (1960a), early inference models by Davis, Spaeth, and Huson (1961), work by the French sociologist Boudon (1963), critiques by Hauser (1974), Hannan's monograph on aggregation (1971), and continuing down to the present in the perhaps controversial thesis about the underclass currently under intense intellectual and scholarly scrutiny (Wilson 1987). Related to the concerns of sociology have been those of criminologists, where a long tradition of contextual analysis has been operative since the work of Burgess and his colleagues at Chicago on delinquency in the early part of this century. A recent, and chilling, example is Rose and McClain (1990, 47-102). And if comprehensive searches are conducted, examples may be turned up of contextual analyses of religion, gerontological issues, health issues, and even of burial practices (Isambert 1960). These riches are mentioned here to emphasize that this review by and large ignores these other areas in order to provide essential focus on politics in context. We return to Durkheim, Tingsten, Key, and the early Columbia University sociologists.

In his classic study of suicidal impulses, Durkheim (1951, originally published 1897) examined perhaps the most individualistic of all acts -- taking one's life -- and argued that such behavior could best be understood as socially contingent. That is, the same person with the same characteristics and predispositions was more or less likely to engage in the act, depending upon social surroundings -- in this case, he argued, the extent to which Catholics and Protestants were surrounded by those of similar or divergent faith and confession. Contextual analysis in particular, and structural analysis in general, has moved far beyond the initial work of Durkheim, but he made the crucial observation that it is meaningful to understand social (and hence political) reality as occurring simultaneously and interdependently at multiple levels, and these multiple levels lie at the heart of contextual analysis even today (Harder and Pappi 1969; Boyd and Iversen 1979; Iversen 1991).

Durkheim's analysis of suicidal impulses has been praised for its path-breaking ingenuity in the use of empirical evidence, but his efforts were limited by data availability -- a curse that continues to afflict the possibilities of contextual analysis. Cross-level inference lies at the heart of contextual analysis, and such inference is furthered by observation at multiple levels. Most commonly this involves observing individuals at the same time that we observe the collective properties of the aggregates within which individuals are imbedded. Such data are not typically available, and they are frequently obtained through good luck and heroic effort on the part of particular social scientists. The earliest efforts at cross-level inference involved measurement at a single level but inference across levels. This usually meant that social scientists observed in the aggregate but theorized about individuals whose behavior varied as a function of the environment -- an enterprise that was called into question by a subsequent concern with ecological fallacies (Robinson 1950; Goodman 1953, 1959; Hannan 1971; Hannan and Burstein 1974; Alwin 1976; Achen 1986; Shively 1969, 1974; Hanushek, Jackson, and Kain 1974).

One of the earliest and most influential efforts at this sort of cross-level inference can be seen in Tingsten's (1937) analysis of socialist and working class voting patterns in Stockholm during the 1920s and 1930s. Figure 1 is a graphical presentation of Tingsten's data on working class support for the socialists, and it shows that the socialist vote increases in working class precincts. But the significance of these data extends far beyond this simple observation. First, notice that the data of Figure 1 are best described by an s-curve (a logistic distribution fits these data with extraordinary accuracy). If the probabilities of socialist support among workers and nonworkers were constant, i.e., if each person had a fixed individual level probability of supporting the socialists, given his or her class membership status, then the data should be clustered around a straight line. (We have imposed the line of perfect proportionality, or uniform returns to scale, $Y = X$, as an aid in studying the plots.) Tingsten recognized the import of these data and offered several suggestions to account for the s-curve pattern. The important point here is that individual propensity to vote socialist cannot be constant across precincts and also yield the pattern exhibited in Figure 1. Furthermore, the nonconstancy is systematic, i.e., in precincts with high working class densities the socialists get a disproportionate share of the vote and the converse holds in precincts with low working class densities.

Figure 1 provides data at only a single aggregate level and even though these Stockholm precincts are very small aggregate units, we are thus forced to theorize regarding the individual level effects that might generate such a pattern. In contrast, Tingsten also offers evidence regarding turnout among Stockholm workers that does not require such an inferential leap because it provides what is, in essence, observations at two levels. As luck would have it, Swedish census officials reported the individual level rate of participation among those classified as working class by precinct; Tingsten had the good theoretical sense to consider that rate as a (linear) function of working class densities within the precinct. In considering these class-specific turnout rates, we are not required to infer the behavior of workers on the basis of the population at large. We observe this rate directly and see that it varies as a function of working class

Figure 1: TINGSTEN'S PRECINCTS

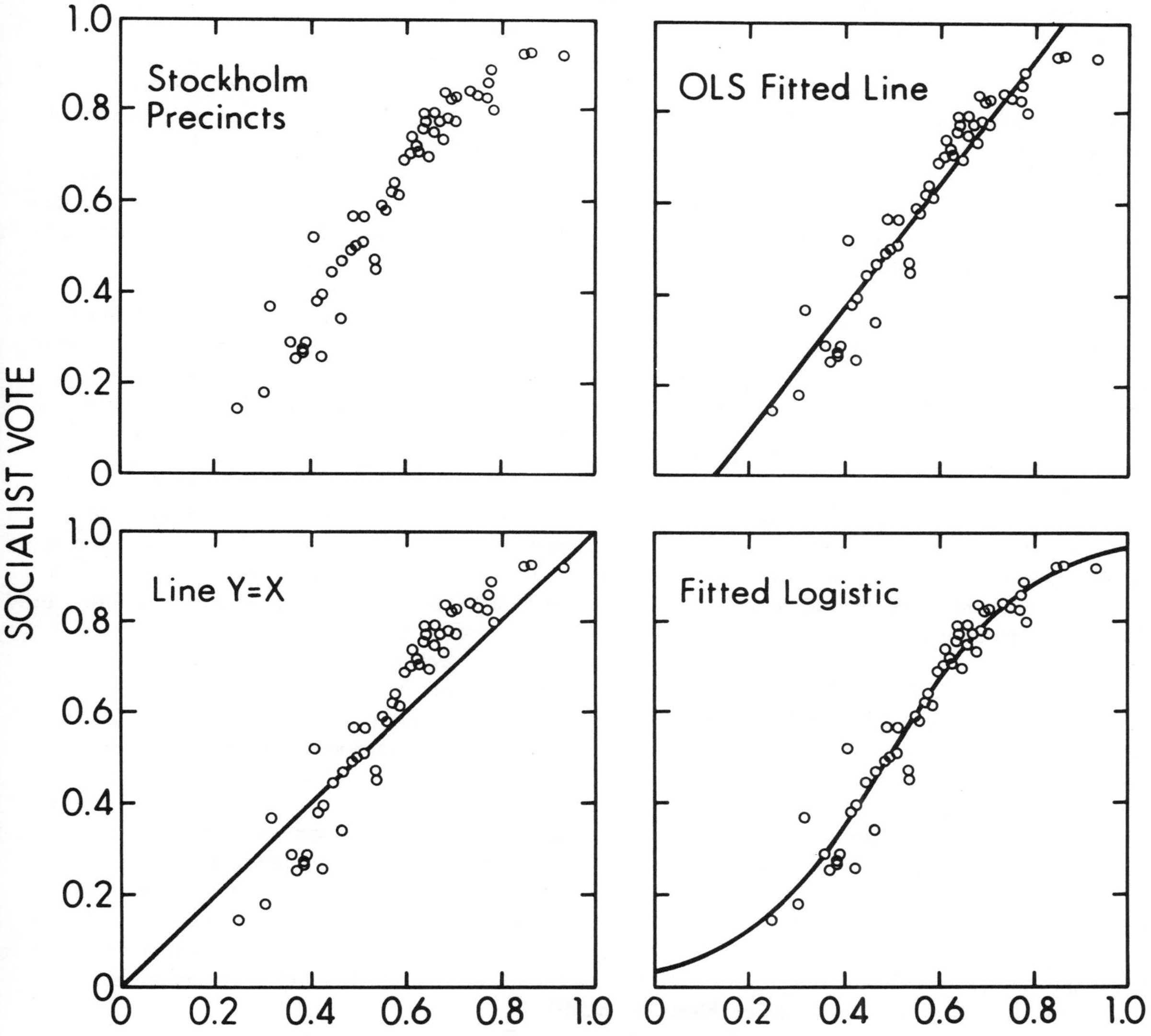

densities. There is no ecological inference problem or compositional measurement problem in these data. And thus Tingsten's work signifies a breakthrough. His combination of aggregate observation with individual level inference explicitly recognized the nonadditive consequences that derive from behavioral interdependence, and his analysis of voting turnout is the earliest cross-level analysis with individual level measurement that we have been able to identify in the literature.

Geographically it is a great distance, but conceptually only a step, from Tingsten and Stockholm to V.O. Key and the American South. Key's work consistently displays a sensitivity to multiple levels of analysis and meaning, but nowhere is this more true than in *Southern Politics* (1949). One of the most compelling analyses of structural influence in political life comes in Key's demonstration that white racial hostility in the South varied as a function of black population concentrations. He demonstrated, for example, that southern whites were more likely to participate in politics if they lived in counties with higher concentrations of black citizens -- a pattern that often continues to the present (Alt 1992). Indeed, Key explains much of the internal variations in southern politics according to the presence or absence of black populations. It is not an exaggeration to say that the central theme of *Southern Politics* revolves around this disjuncture between the politics of the black belt counties and the politics of counties where white populations were numerically dominant.

By contemporary standards, Key's (1949) methodology was fairly primitive and limited by the availability of data, although surely of extraordinary originality. But his insights have stood the test of time and replication, both inside and outside the South, in studies conducted by Matthews and Prothro (1963), Sears and Kinder (1971, 1985), Wright (1976, 1977), Giles and Evans (1985), Bobo (1983, 1988a), and Huckfeldt and Kohfeld (1989). White racial hostility is a common feature of American political life, and it frequently varies as a direct function of blacks' presence in the population.

Furthermore, when Key investigated the problem of racial hostility in the post-World War II South, he saw it through the lens of politics and purpose. In particular, he saw it in terms of a white population that was taking political steps to realize its own interests. According to Key (1949, 5) the central problem in the black belt was "the maintenance of control by a white minority." Thus, in Key's analysis, political self-interest is the concept used to explain racial hostility -- even racial hostility that is contextually contingent. By avoiding an explanation rooted in the social psychology of prejudice, Key shows us that contextual analyses of politics are not necessarily

wed to social psychology. Rather, a contextual analysis might be thoroughly political in its focus upon interests and the mobilization of interests. This is theoretically significant for contextual analyses since it offers a conjunction of motivated behavior, driven by a social condition, with political consequences. In his analysis Key weds rationality and social context as jointly required to give an adequate theoretical account of the politics under analysis.

A final building block for the foundation of contextual analysis was laid when, first, Lazarsfeld introduced the sample survey as a tool of serious social science and, second, the Columbia sociologists used it to demonstrate the importance of social influence in election campaigns. While Tingsten and Key used aggregate data to make inferences regarding the behavior of individuals, the Columbia sociologists used individual level data to make inferences regarding social processes and the dependence of individual behavior upon larger social aggregates. The most sophisticated empirical analysis of the early Columbia tradition occurs in the work of Berelson, Lazarsfeld, and McPhee (1954) -- a 1948 community-based presidential election study located in Elmira, New York. While the authors do not explicitly state the problem as one involving multiple levels of analysis and observation, and while nearly all of their observation is at the level of individuals, it is clear that they place the distinction between the individual and the aggregate at the forefront of their theoretical efforts. In their own words (1954, 122): "Whatever the psychological mechanisms, the social and political consequence is much the same: the development of homogeneous political preferences within small groups and along lines of close social ties connecting them. During a campaign political preferences are 'contagious' over the range of personal contacts." While Tingsten and Key recognized the importance of behavioral interdependence in making inferences from aggregates to individuals, the Columbia sociologists recognized its importance in making inferences from individuals to aggregates. In both instances, the foundation was being laid for a contextual, multi-level understanding of politics.

Too much has probably been made of the disjuncture between the Columbia and Michigan schools of electoral research. Certainly the authors of *The American Voter* gave clear recognition to the importance of both individuals and groups within democratic politics. It is still the case, however, that the Columbia school established a tradition of electoral research that has operated concurrently and yet apart from the dominant Michigan tradition. What sets this Columbia tradition apart? The Columbia sociologists largely ignored the issue of national representativeness in their effort to locate the structures and environments of the individual citizen. The Michigan social psychologists, although not ignoring the importance of contexts, structures, and environments, traded off a local focus in order to obtain a representative picture of the national American electorate. Some accommodation of these traditions can be found in Popkin (1991).

What then is the legacy of these earlier efforts? First, individuals are viewed as interdependent, and individual choice is seen as partially contingent upon the choices or presence of other individuals. Second, the socially contingent nature of political choice leads to a conception of political behavior that is characterized by multiple levels: individuals are to be understood within the larger social aggregates of which they are part, and aggregate behavior is to be understood as more than the simple accumulation of individually determined preferences. Third, and finally, there is a methodological imperative -- measurement which informs political relationships is to be taken at multiple levels if cross-level inferences are to be rooted in observation. But even if observation occurs at a single level, attention is directed to the cross-level consequences of interdependence.

Cross-Level Inference and Contextual Analysis

Two events that occurred during the post-war era redirected the research focus of contemporary political science. The first was the adoption of the national random sample survey as a means of data collection in serious scholarly research on mass political behavior, especially voting behavior. Prior to this time, empirical studies of electoral politics relied most heavily upon aggregate data obtained from the public record -- election returns and census data. There were, of course, notable exceptions to this reliance upon aggregate data: the early Columbia studies (Lazarsfeld, Berelson, and Gaudet 1968 originally published 1944), the imaginative efforts of Harold Gosnell, especially his experiment in stimulating voter participation (1927), and others as well. But with the increased availability of Michigan-based survey data, and particularly with the establishment and growth of the American National Election Study series, the focus of electoral politics research began to shift from the electorate to the voter, from the aggregate to the individual. Thus, at the beginning of the 1950s, a methodological innovation made it possible for political scientists to adopt the framework of individual psychology as a primary element in their arsenal of explanatory devices.

At the same time that mass political psychology became a methodological alternative, the practice of political sociology was rendered suspect among many scholars. The catalytic event for the eclipse of political sociology among political scientists was the publication of W.S. Robinson's (1950) critique of aggregate data analysis and cross-level inference in his exposé of the ecological fallacy. Robinson's argument continues to provide a conundrum for many political scientists. Indeed, 40 years after its publication, a small group of methodologists are still struggling at coming to grips with its implications (Erbring and Young 1979; Achen 1986; Shively 1987; Hanushek, Jackson, and Kain 1974).

We do not intend to recapitulate the entire argument surrounding Robinson's original article and its later critiques and extensions. But the general problem lies at the core of contextual analysis, and to the extent that the ecological fallacy poses a problem, contextual analysis provides the solution. Our discussion begins by borrowing the logic of Przeworski and Teune (1970) but proceeds to carry that logic to its natural culmination.

For purposes of demonstration, suppose that the empirical issue concerns the relationship between individual income and support for a particular Republican gubernatorial candidate. That is, we are interested in the manner in which citizen support for the candidate in an election varied as a function of citizen income level. A number of research strategies are open to us. We might simply regress the candidate's vote proportion within counties on the mean income level within the counties. Alternatively, taking Robinson's admonition seriously, we might contract a polling firm to conduct a random sample of citizens, and in that survey we might ask respondents how strongly they support or oppose the candidate. Remember that in both instances we are interested in the behavior of individual citizens. Is the aggregate strategy as bad as the ecological fallacy makes it seem? Is the survey of individual citizens the solution to our problem?

Consider first the aggregate strategy. What stands in the way of inferring individual behavior on the basis of aggregate data? For purposes of illustration, we select three hypothetical counties with three respondents in each county and construct scenarios on that basis. In order to facilitate comparison, we assume (1) the survey question provides an unbiased estimate of the individual probability that each respondent voted for the candidate and (2) correspondence between aggregate measures for the counties and respondent means within the counties.

Figure 2 is a scatterplot of candidate support on income: each observation is an individual respondent, and each county sample is enclosed by an ellipse. In each panel of Figure 2, a line is drawn to represent the regression of the county mean for candidate support on the county income mean, and thus we can easily compare the aggregate relationship for the county means with the individual relationships within counties. Only in the first panel would we correctly infer a positive individual level relationship within counties on the basis of the positive aggregate relationship. In the second panel we would infer a positive relationship when, in fact, the relationship within the counties was flat, and in the third panel we would infer a positive relationship when the individual relationship within counties was negative.

There is, of course, nothing new to any of this. These are simply variations on the scenarios that drove many political scientists to reject aggregate analysis and embrace individual level data as a cure. But are they a cure? Do individual level data solve these problems?

Returning to the three panels of Figure 2, what would happen if we estimated a single individual level model on the basis of pooled individual level data for the three counties? Figure 2 is redrawn as Figure 3, absent the county means, but with lines drawn to represent the individual level regression of y on x for the pooled sample. What is the result? As before, for each panel, we would obtain a positive slope, even though such an individual level relationship held only within the counties of the first panel.

None of this is anything more than conjecture and line drawing, but it serves to illustrate an important point: the potential for an ecological fallacy is not logically different from the attendant potential of an individual level fallacy (Brown 1991). Suppose that the third panel of Figure 3 is accurate. Is it meaningful to argue that higher income is related to a higher level of support when, in fact, the relationship is reversed within counties? In this particular instance, the pooled individual level model corresponds to the aggregate model, but one model would produce an ecological fallacy, the other would produce an individual level fallacy, and both would be wrong.

The scenarios of Figures 2 and 3 are only the tip of the iceberg. We could continue to generate a long string of observational perversities with respect to relationships within, between, and across the three counties. Fortunately, Boyd and Iversen (1979) have provided a canonical and straightforward formulation for examining a range of possibilities. Following Boyd and Iversen consider first a simple individual level model:

$$y_{ij} = a_j + b_j x_{ij} \qquad (1)$$

where y_{ij} and x_{ij} are the candidate support scores and the income levels for the ith individual in the jth context. Even if the requisite individual level data are available, there may be some profound dangers in ignoring the contextual dependence of a_j and b_j on their local environments by simply regressing y on x using the pooled individual level data. (For example, the intercept varies as a function of $x.j$ in both the second and third

panels of Figures 2 and 3.)

The simplest Boyd-Iversen solution is to express both the slope and the intercept of the individual level model as a linear formulation of the group means.

$$a_j = a' + a''x.j \qquad (2)$$
$$b_j = b' + b''x.j \qquad (3)$$

Substituting equations 2 and 3 into equation 1 produces the single equation form.

$$Y_{ij} = a' + a''x.j + b'x_{ij} + b''x.jx_{ij} \qquad (4)$$

The resulting multi-level model can be estimated in several different ways (Boyd and Iversen 1979; Alwin 1976; also Iversen 1991), but most important for present purposes, notice what the model demands in terms of evidence. Not only are observations on individuals required, but also observations on the aggregates of which they are a part.

The important point of this exercise is that contextual theories of politics grant no particular epistemological status to the ecological fallacy. Rather, the ecological fallacy and the individual level fallacy are both examples of specification error (Hanushek, Jackson, and Kain 1974). As a logical matter, it is no more dangerous to infer individual behavior from aggregate level data than to infer any one person's behavior from individual level data. Indeed, if a'' and b'' are both zero, then either aggregate or individual level data will provide equally revealing inferences regarding the behavior of individuals. It is only when contextual effects are present (a'' < > 0 and/or b'' < > 0) that either the ecological fallacy or the individual level fallacy pose a problem. Stated somewhat differently, ecological fallacies and individual level fallacies are both the result of unspecified contextual effects.

Contexts, Structures, and Environments

What is a contextual effect? How does context differ from structure or environment? Various labels have been applied to individually exogenous factors that serve to influence individual behavior, and the broadest definition of a contextual effect is tied to any such factor extrinsic to the individual. According to such a definition, a contextual effect operates when individual behavior depends upon some individually external factor after all individual level determinants have been taken into account. That is, a contextual effect exists when factors intrinsic to the individual cannot account for

Figure 2 : POSSIBLE AGGREGATION FALLACIES

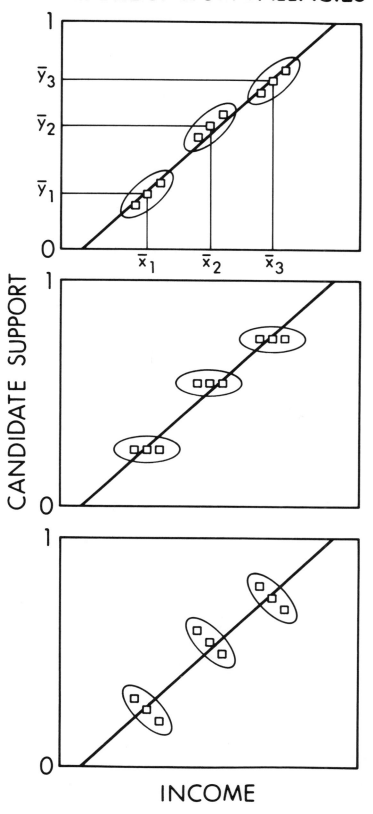

CANDIDATE SUPPORT

INCOME

Figure 3: POSSIBLE INDIVIDUALISTIC FALLACIES

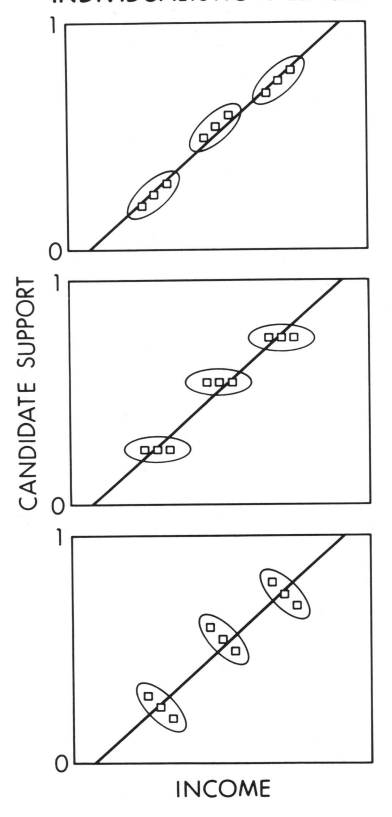

CANDIDATE SUPPORT

INCOME

systematic variations in behavior across environments (Hauser 1974).

Such a definition is certainly appropriate for many purposes, but it is broad, including within its coverage a wide range of disparate environmental factors: institutional variations, media coverage, and social network effects. A more focused definition, building upon the work of Przeworski and Teune (1970) and Eulau (1986), suggests a distinction that establishes contextual effects as a subset of environmental effects (Huckfeldt 1986, 13). Przeworski and Teune (1970, 56) define contextual factors as aggregates of individual properties and argue that the importance of these factors arises through social interaction. Eulau defines an environmental effect as any behavioral influence that arises from factors external to the individual. Contextual effects as construed here are due to social interaction within particular environments, and social contexts are created as a result of these interactions. (For a somewhat different approach, see Books and Prysby 1991.)

The primary advantage of more narrow definitions of context is that they serve to build upon the intellectual foundation laid by Durkheim, Tingsten, Key, and the Columbia sociologists -- a foundation that was renewed by Blau (1956, 1957, 1960a, 1960b), Davis (1966), and Davis, Spaeth, and Huson (1961). Blau was fundamentally concerned with the individual consequences arising due to location in populations with different social compositions. He identified such effects as structural effects, but their similarity to the contextual effects of Eulau and Przeworski and Teune is clear (Blau 1957, 64). In their extension of Blau's work, Davis and his colleagues (Davis, Spaeth, and Huson 1961) argue that calling such effects structural effects confuses these factors with the broader range of phenomena generally included within the boundaries of social structure. For example, the fact that more highly educated people tend to earn more money can be seen as an effect of social structure, but that is not what either Blau or Davis has in mind when they speak of structural effects, and thus Davis and his colleagues adopt the term compositional effects.

Where does this leave us? An environmental effect is any effect on individual behavior that arises because of extra-individual factors. In contrast, a contextual effect is any effect on individual behavior that arises due to social interaction within an environment. We adopt that view here. Both effects are more generally seen as being structural consequences of individual standing and location within particular social and political orders, and thus they can be seen as components of social and political structure.

In the discussions that follow, we will not always constrain ourselves to contextual effects thus defined but will incorporate more general considerations of other environmental influences as well. Moreover, our definition of contextual effects leaves several issues unaddressed. What constitutes social interaction? And how are contexts and contextual effects different from networks and network effects?

Contexts, Networks, and Social Interaction

When we argue that contextual effects on political behavior operate through social interaction, we are not saying very much. Social interaction can be characterized along a variety of dimensions: intimacy, frequency, political content, the extent to which the interaction is purposeful or recreational, the extent to which it is voluntary or coerced. At one extreme, social interaction occurs when lovers hold hands while they stroll in the park. At another, it also occurs when one neighbor sees a political yard sign on another neighbor's lawn. The relative political impact of these various interactions is an open question. But it would be a gross error to believe that social interaction is politically relevant only when it occurs among intimates who interact on a voluntary basis (Huckfeldt and Sprague 1991). In this impersonal sense, then, we can say that the county level racial hostility effects documented by Key were due to a process of social interaction. In yet a different way, the autoworker who involuntarily shares a workplace location with a co-worker whom he finds obnoxious may still learn a great deal about politics, one way or another, through an ongoing and continual process of social interaction.

For many purposes it is useful to contrast voluntary and involuntary social interaction and to use that distinction to characterize the difference between networks and contexts (Huckfeldt and Sprague 1987). Contexts are not the same as networks at a conceptual level. And at the level of measurement, it is a mistake to think of contexts as simply an easy measure of networks, obtained on the cheap. It is probably best to illustrate these matters with an example -- the classic study of associational patterns among autoworkers conducted by Finifter (1974). Finifter investigated friendship patterns at the factory and produced an important result. In these overwhelmingly Democratic workplaces, Republicans were more selective than Democrats in their choice of workplace friendships. This result is consistent with theoretical arguments and empirical work from quite different quarters (Coleman 1964; Huckfeldt 1983; Noelle-Neumann 1984). Taking this result as prototypical of many contextual effect situations produces further ramifications.

In Finifter's study it is useful to think of the factory as an environment with an attendant context created by the distribution of political preferences among a population that is located within a particular set of factory walls. In this sense, then, the context is imposed upon the people who work at the factory. Once they decide to take the job, or once a person decides to attend a church or live in a neighborhood or bowl in a league, they have little control over the people they encounter as part of their activities within the boundaries of the environment. Thus, contexts are external to individuals, even if the composition of the context depends upon the mix of people contained within it (Huckfeldt and Sprague 1987).

This is not to say that citizens are necessarily the helpless victims of a social reality that lies beyond their control. Finifter's Republican autoworkers were surrounded by Democrats, and their response was to create friendship groups that served as protective environments. If we think of a friendship group as one part of a social network, this means that networks are subject to individual control in a way that contexts are not. Indeed, the network can be seen as the end result of efforts made by individuals to impose their own preferences upon their social contexts, and the composition of networks is subject to the multiple, interdependent, cascading choices of people who share the same social space -- the people who compose the context.

At the same time, these associational choices are best seen as operating probabilistically (Huckfeldt 1983; Huckfeldt and Sprague 1988). Personal choice is not determinant in the construction of a social network for two reasons. First, the choice of an associate operates within the constraints imposed by a context. To present an extreme example, a 1988 Dukakis voter was unable to discuss politics with another Dukakis voter if she was located in a context where everyone else supported Bush. Alternatively, if there is only one Republican working at the automobile factory, he will either eat lunch with other Democrats or he will eat alone. And thus, the probability that the choice of politically like-minded discussants will be realized is subject to the distribution of politically like-minded discussants within the context. Choosing a place of residence is self-selection, of course, but it also is constraining and leads to non-self-selected information exposure (T. Brown 1981, 1988). Similarly, employment may be freely chosen, but once work is begun many subsequent choices are circumscribed by the particular workplace setting -- the dilemma of Finifter's Republican autoworkers.

A second reason that associational choice is probabilistic is that it responds to multiple preferences, with different weights, many of which are unformed or at best poorly formed. All of us want friends who are smart, pleasant, great bridge players, Dodger fans (the authors are of different minds on this point), and politically enlightened. But only political scientists are likely to put an overwhelmingly important weight on political enlightenment. Indeed, many citizens have uninformed and perhaps unformed political preferences that become articulate only after associates are chosen and persuasion and education and social learning occurs.

To say that associational choice is probabilistic is not to say that it is unimportant or inconsequential. An important area of research in contextual analysis is the investigation of the relationship between contexts and networks and the role that various selection criteria play in translating contexts into networks. Indeed, the evidence suggests that political minorities are more aggressive in their exercise of choice, even as they face the daunting and inevitably defeating task of maintaining political cohesion (Miller 1956; Finifter 1974; Huckfeldt 1983; Huckfeldt and Sprague 1987).

In summary, social networks and friendship groups are the interdependent products of individual choice operating probabilistically within the boundaries of externally imposed contexts. The context presents a menu of choices that is inherently stochastic as well: if you move into a Democratic neighborhood, the odds are that you may live next door to a Democrat and his yard signs and bumper stickers (Huckfeldt and Sprague 1992), but maybe not. The important point is not that choice and control are lacking, or that individual preference is socially determined (Key and Munger 1959), but rather that choice operates probabilistically within an externally imposed, systematically biased, and necessarily stochastic environment. Hence, even voluntary forms of social interaction typically reflect the composition of a larger, involuntarily imposed social context -- the context is contingent and hence also the choices made within it.

Principal Findings in the Contextual Analysis Tradition

This is not the place for an extended literature review detailing the extensive substantive findings of contextual research. Such reviews are certainly available, and interested readers might consult the works of Books and Prysby (1991) or Huckfeldt (1986). A vast literature on school effects was noted above. Our goal here is to outline several basic thrusts found in the empirical literature which we believe to be of special theoretical relevance as a motivation for the systematic discussion that follows -- a reason, perhaps, for the reader to pay attention to the sequel.

An overarching methodological lesson emerges from considering many of the works cited above, here, and below. Cross-level effects frequently exhibit interaction in the statistical sense. Hence, to the extent that contextual effects are interactively operative in an investigatory situation, individual effect models are necessarily not linearly additive. The fair implication is that substantive explanatory or statistical models that ignore contextual effects, under conditions where contextual effects can be persuasively established, are, in a technical sense, not correctly specified. This conclusion rests on considering a broad array of substantive results.

Social Interaction and Context

Patterns of social relationships are neither wholly stochastic nor wholly determined on the basis of individual choice. As a result, the likelihood of social contact with various social and political groups lies between a prediction based wholly on environmentally bounded, random interaction and an alternative prediction based wholly on individually constructed social and political worlds. (See Putnam 1966; Huckfeldt 1983, 1986; Huckfeldt and Sprague 1987, 1988.)

Political Minorities and Context

The stochastic nature of social interaction creates a political bias favorable to political majorities and, thus, rather than being cohesive and resolute, political minorities suffer from the debilitating consequences of social bombardment by political messages that run counter to their own political inclinations. Such a consequence flows directly and inevitably from the reality of, and perception of, social interaction with political content. In order to survive the loaded dice of social interaction within a bounded environment saturated with stochastically biased information - skewed partisan messages - political minorities may resort to withdrawal from the surrounding context. (See Berelson, Lazarsfeld, and McPhee 1954; Miller 1956; Putnam 1966; Finifter 1974; Huckfeldt 1983; Huckfeldt and Sprague 1987, 1988.)

Multiple Levels of Social and Political Reality

While it is often convenient from a measurement standpoint to characterize the social context at a single level -- counties, neighborhoods, churches, workplaces -- it is clear that these multiple levels of meaning and reality impinge on each other to interact in politically significant ways. The effect of the neighborhood depends on the county, the consequences of the church depend on the neighborhood, and so on. People reside and live day to day in complex social and political spaces that are ineluctably interdependent and that serve to mold and shape particular political realities. (See Wald, Owen, and Hill 1988, 1990; Fuchs 1955; Segal and Meyer 1974; Huckfeldt and Sprague 1990, 1991, 1992.)

Individual Discretion and Control

The accumulated evidence offers scant support for a view that interprets individual citizens as the passive victims of an environmentally determinate process. Instead, individual discretion, individual characteristics, and individual behavior serve to define the position of the individual citizen with respect to environmental circumstances. This is perhaps most obvious with respect to migration and residential relocation: for often complex and apolitical reasons people choose where they will reside, but, willy nilly, these choices expose them to particular political messages. Organizational memberships also serve to shield individuals from some sources of environmental influence (the neighborhood) and expose them to others (the county). As yet another example, the regularity with which people attend their churches may determine the extent to which they are affected by the climate of political opinion that is present among parishioners. Finally, a wealth of research shows that the strength of various contextual effects depends on individual characteristics, and some evidence even suggests that the direction of contextual effects depends on individual status. (See T. Brown 1981, 1988; Finifter and Finifter 1989; Cox 1974; Segal and Meyer 1974; Huckfeldt 1983; Huckfeldt, Plutzer, and Sprague 1993; Giles and Dantico 1982.)

Individual and Environmental Contingencies

The net yield of work on the effects of context is a conception of political behavior as contingent on a variety of interdependencies among social and political structures and individual properties and behavior. The social context is not a single context but rather a series of intersecting, overlapping, and mutually interdependent arenas of political information -- both targeted and accidental political messages. Individual characteristics and individual choice play crucial roles in locating the individual within these complex webs of social relationships and informational environments. Individual characteristics will in part determine how the information is sampled and processed, or even noticed at all. At the same time individual choice should not be viewed in a simple-minded fashion. Adults do not make fundamental life choices regarding church, home, and residential area on the basis of party identification. Rather, partisanship and political preference provide yet another set of contingencies conditioning the manner in which social and political influence is realized. Contextual theories of politics and political behavior are built on the stochastic and contingent nature of social and political life. Such theories allow no simple, mechanical determinism either at the level of the environment or at the level of the individual. From this perspective, politics and political behavior emerge as located at the multiple points of intersection between individual citizens and the contexts wherein they live and work. (See Boudon 1986.)

Micro Theories of Contextual Influence

The individual provides the ultimate unit of analysis in any contextual theory of politics, and individual choice is viewed as located at the intersection between individual purpose, individual cognition, individual predisposition, and individual preference, on the one hand, and environmental opportunities and constraints, on the other hand (Przeworski 1985). Citizens are always understood within a particular setting -- a setting that attaches probabilistically to the menu of choices that is available to the individual. Indeed, this joining of biased environments to rational individual political decision making was modeled in a persuasive fashion by McPhee and his co-workers three decades ago in his dynamic model of the voting process, a model specifically designed to incorporate the idea of the influence of a stochastically biased information environment (probabilistically) sampled by the individual citizen (McPhee and Smith 1962; McPhee and Ferguson 1962; McPhee, Smith, and Ferguson 1963; McPhee 1963).

At the same time, contextual theories of politics resist radical methodological reductionism and with it the idea that any explanation of political phenomena must be judged by its ability to get inside the heads of the individual voter. In other words, a contextual analysis of politics is not coincident with the effort to reduce politics, always, to its smallest discrete units. Such an effort is inconsistent with the premise of contextual analysis that the interdependence of individuals is the key to a compelling explanatory reconstruction of political behavior. And thus politics can be understood from the vantage point of the individual psyche, but only as individual psyches interact to produce political outcomes. Correspondingly, once a contextual analysis of politics is subsumed under the effort to understand based solely on individual motivation, it ceases to engage in a multi-level analysis and hence ceases to be contextual.

The importance of micro theories to contextual analysis is not that they explain individual behavior, but rather that they more fully articulate the nature of

interdependence among citizens and hence add to our understanding of politics as a corporate outcome -- the level at which politics has meaning and substance (Eulau 1986). This task -- the specification of behavioral interdependence -- lies at the heart of contextual analysis. The questions become: Under what conditions does one citizen affect another? And what are the circumstances that give rise to interdependent behavior? Stated somewhat differently, what are the individual and corporate mechanisms that translate the context into a force operating upon individual behavior?

There is no silver bullet that serves as the answer to all these questions -- there is no official micro theory of contextual influence. This is particularly the case because there are a range of divergent forms of contextual influence and appeals to an explanatory contextual hypothesis. V.O. Key (1949) and Matthews and Prothro (1963) demonstrated that southern whites were more likely to engage in racial oppression if county populations were more heavily black in their racial composition. Butler and Stokes (1969) demonstrated that British workers were more likely to vote Conservative if they lived among middle-class populations. Langton and Rapoport (1975) demonstrated that Santiago workers were more likely to be class conscious if they lived among other workers. Carmines and Stimson (1989) demonstrated that a reorganization of civil rights voting cleavages in the Congress led to a reorganization of these cleavages in the population at large. All of these can be seen as contextual effects, but there the similarity ends. Some of these contextual effects involve assimilation between individuals and groups, while others involve conflict as the product of group intersection (Huckfeldt 1986). Some of these contextual effects involve fundamental social and political loyalties, while others involve more ephemeral judgments and attachments. We could extend the list to include even more disparate effects due to the context, e.g., civil burials in Paris which might be viewed as a religious consequence of political belief and class (Isambert 1960), but the point is that no single mechanism of influence is responsible for them all. Rather, a range of alternative mechanisms is inevitably involved. We address the main alternatives here, and our consideration begins with the null model.

The Null Model

A null model warns us against the contextual fallacy of wrongly and prematurely imputing a contextual effect (Hauser 1974; Alwin 1976; Prysby 1976; Burstein 1978; Weatherford 1982; Stipak and Hensler 1982; Boyd and Iversen 1979; Iversen 1991). Such a mistake can be made in a number of ways. If low-status individuals living in low-status contexts are more likely to be Democrats than low-status individuals living in high, status contexts, it may be due to a social interaction effect. But it might alternatively be due to higher income levels among lower status people living among higher status individuals, or it might be that we have better measures on contextual status than we have on individual status. In short, before a contextual effect can be asserted, Hauser (1974) argues, individual level alternatives must be constructed and considered.

Hauser's admonition is fair enough, even though a contextual argument might make a similar counter point: individual level effects should be subject to the same scrutiny. During the past 15 years, contextual analyses have become more conceptually and statistically sophisticated in entertaining alternative, rival, individual level explanations for the behaviors in question. Perhaps more important, to the extent that political scientists have become more attentive to the mechanisms of interdependence that drive contextual effects, important individual level explanations are less likely to be ignored (Huckfeldt 1984; Huckfeldt and Sprague 1992).

A second serious issue in the formulation of an appropriate null model turns on the interpretation of measurements taken at the individual level. Many measures of individual characteristics are better conceived as indicators of a collective social experience, e.g., religious confession, or even as indicators of a broad range of regular social experience, e.g., education. Educational level, that most powerful of social background measures in social and political research, surely proxies in central tendency many things besides knowledge and word skills. Is education more important as an indicator of (1) cognitive efficiency, or (2) a person's knowledge base, or (3) a person's class membership, or (4) a person's social experience -- the sorts of persons one interacts with in varying social contexts? Two further examples may fix ideas -- inherited party and inherited religion. What is the measurement level of such individual properties? How are they to function in explanations? Suppose one's father was a Democrat and a Catholic and the individual identifies herself as a Democrat and a Catholic. Measurement is easy. Theoretical interpretation is, however, not so clear. It is difficult to argue that being brought up in a Catholic and Democratic household is an intrinsic property of the individual. It is surely an indicator of his or her experience. Indeed, interest in such measures rests on arguments about the context in which religion and politics is learned, perhaps precisely the theoretical opposite of individual property effects. By no means do we intend to suggest that individual level factors should not be taken into account but only that the meaning of

many individual level factors is, on reflection, not always straightforward.

There remains a literature devoted to demonstrating that the null model is always correct. Two examples are perhaps sufficient: Tate (1974) and Kelley and McAllister (1985). The general analytic strategy of such pieces is to combine contextual level measures with an exhaustive list of individual level measures in a regression set up to assess whether or not the effects of contextual measures wash out statistically. The two studies just identified find that the contextual effects disappear. By contrast, Abowitz (1990) uses a similar approach and finds that contextual effects on political participation are not effectively controlled by individual level measures. Similarly, Straits (1990) reevaluates an old and robust result of Glaser (1959) on spousal effects on voting and finds the result still persuasive. There are a number of substantive studies that identify contextual effects, but readers should also be aware of a thread of extreme skepticism in the methodological literature on contextual effects, the classic statement of which is found in a series of articles by Hauser (see Hauser 1974 for a summary).

The Self-Selection Model

At one point in time, self-selection was seen as a negation of contextual influence (Hauser 1974). The contextual argument might be people who live in the midst of group X tend to act in ways similar to group X. And the self-selection counter argument would be people who act in ways similar to group X locate themselves in the middle of group X, and thus the behavior predates the location in social structure. Problems such as these befog a great deal of causal reasoning in the social sciences. Absent a longitudinal design, there is little hope for resolving these issues, although some progress has been made in incorporating time-ordered measurements into a dynamic explanation of contextual influence (Huckfeldt and Sprague 1990; C. Brown 1991; T. Brown 1988; Kohfeld and Sprague 1990).

A solution to the problem of confounding effects from self-selection goes deeper than time-ordered measurement, however, and the issue is exacerbated by the primitive conceptualization of contextual influence implied by the formulation above. Presumably, people choose contexts not just because they are comfortable but because they are viewed as being potentially consequential in the future, long after the original choice is made. But there is nothing inconsistent between explanations that appeal to contextual effect theoretical hypotheses and the idea that people choose contexts. The contextual explanation offered above is anchored in an important idea, but it is a crude statement of contextual influence. More sophisticated contextual arguments take account of the fact that people choose environments as well as being influenced by them (Huckfeldt and Sprague 1987, 1988). Contextual effects also may operate quite objectively, more or less, without any occasion for choice at all (Kohfeld and Sprague 1990).

Moreover, is the self-selection argument really a repudiation of contextual influence? If a citizen behaves similarly to group X, why would he feel the need to be surrounded by members of group X? The plausible answer is that he might be uncomfortable being surrounded by people who behave differently. That is, he might be influenced by them. One important aspect of self-selection surely must be the two-sided motivation to avoid (always probabilistically) influence on you or your family arising from some contexts, while encouraging (always probabilistically) influence from other contexts -- the contexts you choose. Self-selection into particular contexts is rational because contexts are influential, not because they are not (Westefield n.d.).

Furthermore, when a context is chosen for its suitability on some characteristic or set of characteristics, there is no guarantee that it will be suitable on all relevant characteristics. Politically relevant social contexts come to us in lumpy fashion like physical plant capital for economists. You cannot get just a little bit of a context but rather you get the whole thing. Finifter's Republican workers provide an excellent example. The factory setting was unavoidable and full of Democrats, and, consequently, the Republican workers developed a systematic strategy of friendship choice (Finifter 1974).

There are other problems with simple versions of the self-selection argument as well. To what extent do people choose their locations in the social structure? How many of us really choose our workplace colleagues, our coreligionists, our neighbors? To the extent that we are able to exercise control over our surroundings, do we use political criteria in exercising such choice? Or do we choose a job because it pays well? A church because our parents raised us in it? A neighborhood because it has good schools? And then we take the politics that accompanies the choice. Thad Brown has shown (1981, 1988) that residential choice is independent of partisanship -- choose a residence on the basis of good schools or convenience to your job and then put up with the Socialist next door.

Once again, a contextual theory of politics confronts the intersection between individual choice and environmentally circumscribed alternatives. And citizens certainly exercise choice when they confront the alternative sources of political information that are available to them. This creates a potential tension between individual preference and the political content of social interaction. The important point is that any theory of contextual influence must incorporate the possibility of such a tension -- it must take account of citizen efforts at self-selection.

Taking account of self-selection in econometric work has been a topic of rapid development in the past decade. The locus classicus is Maddala (1983) on limited dependent variables (also see Achen 1986). Self-selection is a problem in sampling described as incidental truncation, and the solution is clear in principle. Model the self-selection process along with the substantive model of interest. A succinct review is Greene (1990, 715-753; also Achen 1986). Another form of this problem arises when the discussion context is putatively measured directly by obtaining interviews with members of respondents' social network, and the problem in analysis becomes one of sorting out, methodologically, the inherent reciprocities (Huckfeldt and Sprague 1987, 1991; Gilbert 1990; Kenny 1989). In this latter situation statistical strategies can be employed to alleviate the simultaneity. We have not identified contextual analyses employing explicit modeling of self-selection processes in the literature, except for treatment of simultaneity.

Finally, when contextual analysis becomes elaborate and very explicit theory is invoked, the self-selection argument emerges, we believe, as largely irrelevant. A particular example may drive this remark home. Kohfeld and Sprague (1990) disentangled the parameter identification problem in assessing the deterrent effects of police behavior on criminals (burglars) by resort to drastic spatial and time disaggregation of criminal event records and police arrest records. A dynamic model of police and criminal interaction in a metric of weeks, with appropriate lags and some other side conditions, was identified and estimated. The study was able to demonstrate large amplification and attenuation effects on the deterrence parameter as demography was varied -- a theoretically expected contextual effect. Changes in police and criminal dynamic interactions over a short time period cannot be driven by demographic changes that are altered only slowly. It is difficult to formulate a criticism of this demonstration of contextual effect based on self-selection arguments. Did the criminals (burglars) choose to live in certain neighborhoods in order to enhance their response to police arrest behavior? The question may not be absurd, but it certainly is peculiar.

We suspect that many of the self-selection criticisms that appear plausible in the abstract (and when simplified) break down when applied to theoretically well grounded, statistically well designed, and carefully reasoned contextual analyses. In any event, if self-selection is a serious contender as a competing explanatory hypothesis, the appropriate methodology is clear. Statistically model the selection process along with the contextual model. This procedure should allow the investigator to draw conclusions with respect to both the significance of self-selection and the significance of contextual effects in the particular investigation.

Reference Group Models

Interestingly, reference group explanations for contextual influence have decreased in popularity during the same period of time in which their popularity has generally increased among scholars of mass political behavior (Kelley 1952; Davis 1966; C. Brown 1981; Lau 1989; Kenny 1989; Erikson, Lancaster, and Romero 1989; Penning 1988). Explanations of mass behavior have increasingly turned to group-anchored opinions and attitudes. But scholars of contextual influence have become less likely to point toward reference group formation as the tie between individual behavior and the social context. Why?

First, many reference group arguments for contextual influence are especially vulnerable to counter arguments based on self-selection. Is the appropriate question: why do individuals who live among workers identify as workers? Or is it: why do people who identify as workers live among workers? Stated in this manner, it may become difficult to decide which question needs to be answered first.

Second, a combination of scholarly efforts has pushed contextual arguments in the direction of political information and behavioral mechanisms of transmission as opposed to the transmission of social loyalties. An explicit focus of the late 1970s and the early 1980s posed a choice between behavioral contagion on the one hand and social transmission on the other (Sprague and Westefield 1979a, 1979b; Erbring and Young 1979; Huckfeldt 1983). In the discussion of these choices, behavioral transmission tends to win out. Erbring and Young refer to social composition arguments as being rooted in social telepathy -- a label reflecting their dissatisfaction with the specification of the interdependence mechanism. And at an empirical level, support tends to be stronger for arguments rooted in behavioral transmission (Huckfeldt 1984), with one important exception.

Racial hostility has repeatedly been shown to depend on context, but it is difficult to construct a contextual explanation for racial conflict that does not depend upon some sort of explicit or implicit reference group explanation (Key 1949; Heard 1952; Matthews and Prothro 1963; Wright 1976, 1977; Giles and Evans 1985; Sears and Kinder, 1971; Bobo 1983, 1988b; Huckfeldt and Kohfeld 1989). The argument generally flows along these lines: whites who interact with blacks tend to become more racially conscious, threatened, and hostile. And they are likely to act politically in ways that reflect this hostility. Why? Whites identify with whites, they compare their status with blacks whom they believe pose a threat, and they react accordingly. A variation on this general argument is that whites observe the Democratic voting behavior of blacks, they believe that their interests run counter to those of blacks, and they vote in an opposite direction (Huckfeldt and Kohfeld 1989).

Either variation points toward the importance of racial reference groups as the mechanisms of contextual effects, but this reference group function is very different from social telepathy. In an early and influential work Kelley (1952) usefully contrasted two different functions of reference groups -- the normative and comparative functions. The normative function is being called upon when a reference group argument asserts that people who live among workers tend to identify as workers and accept working class norms. The comparative function is being called upon when a reference group argument asserts that whites who live among blacks compare their own status (or interest) with that of blacks and react accordingly.

Behavioral Contagion and Social Learning Models

Behavioral contagion as a micro mechanism of contextual influence is articulated best in terms of a social learning process (Sprague 1982; McPhee 1963). According to this view, citizens are rewarded or punished for political viewpoints that agree or conflict with the viewpoints of other people whom they encounter. The process is repetitive in time and subject to the reinforcement schedule that is probabilistically characteristic of a particular context. That is, white voters in Mississippi experienced distinctive reinforcement schedules in the 1984 presidential election when roughly 85% of them voted for Ronald Reagan. Black voters in Mississippi encountered dramatically different reinforcement schedules in 1984 when roughly 90% of them voted for Walter Mondale.

For some people, learning theory conjures up images of Skinnerian rats being manipulated in a maze, but such a connotation need not be attached to learning theory as it is applied to politics. Citizens certainly make efforts to control their own reinforcement schedules -- there were probably some white Mondale voters in Mississippi who were able to surround themselves with associates who also voted for Mondale. And, thus, the schedule of reinforcement can be seen to vary across both individuals and contexts.

Moreover, a learning theory maintains its focus upon individuals as their own preferences and predispositions collide with those of other individuals. Reconsider McPhee's (1963) vote simulator, which serves as a starting point for Sprague's (1982) work: (1) An individual receives a piece of information from the larger (biased) political environment; (2) He then forms a response based upon his own predisposition; (3) He shares that response with others; (4) The others then reward or punish that response with agreement or disagreement; (5) If disagreement occurs, he samples his (biased) information context broadly conceived, reconsiders his opinion, and shares it once again; (6) And so it goes.

This model has several important advantages. First, it allows both individual predisposition and context to be incorporated within a micro theory of contextual influence. Context enters as the information environment and also as the specialized population from which the individual samples associates with whom to share opinions and responses. Individual predispositions enter as the citizen processes information, formulates an initial response to external political stimuli, and responds to disagreement. The motor that drives the model is disagreement. Only through disagreement does change occur, and, thus, to the extent that people are part of politically homogeneous populations, we see less change. It is not insignificant that recent efforts aimed at examining the political content of social interaction show levels of political disagreement that are perhaps surprisingly high (Huckfeldt and Sprague 1987).

Another advantage of a learning theory model is that it leads directly to a series of expectations regarding the circumstances under which contextual influence should be most pronounced (Sprague 1982). First, the efficiency of learning increases as the delay in reinforcement decreases and the frequency of reinforcement increases. On this basis we might expect that routine, ongoing, social contacts should be especially influential (McClosky and Dahlgren 1959; Straits 1990). Second, continuous reinforcement over a short period of time produces dramatic effects that decay rapidly at the end of reinforcement. Hence, individually idiosyncratic political opinions that are exposed to social influence during an election campaign should be especially subject to change, but the opinions are likely to become individually idiosyncratic once again at the end of the campaign period (see Berelson et al. 1954). Third, individual motivation plays a crucial role in learning efficiency -- motivated citizens make efficient learners. And thus it is not at all clear that only disinterested, uninformed citizens should be subject to social influence (Huckfeldt and Sprague 1990). As Converse (1962) and Orbell (1970) remind us, however, incoming information must compete with stored information, and thus the long-term and short-term consequences of motivation are complex and interdependent.

Rational Choice and Cognition Models

Rational choice theory is sometimes read as excluding the possibility of contextual effects and hence excluding contextual analysis, but there is nothing about social influence that is inherently at odds with a rational choice interpretation of politics. Contextual theories do not argue that citizens are irrational but only that they are interdependent. As Key (1949) shows us, one aspect to the evil logic of the old South was that the racial context stimulated a racial hostility effect among whites through their own perceived self-interest. Moreover, various forms of interdependence can be instrumental for many citizens in many circumstances.

Anthony Downs (1957) argued that citizens are faced with an important dilemma when they seek to become informed about politics. They need information to realize where their interests lie, but information is costly. Indeed, even modest information costs can swamp the benefit that is likely to be obtained through politics, once individual acts are discounted by the likelihood that they will have political consequence. Given such a problem, rational citizens seek to reduce their information costs -- they seek to obtain political information on the cheap -- and one effective way to realize that goal is by obtaining information from other individuals. Information obtained in this fashion may, of course, be biased and partial to others similarly situated, but nonetheless useful (Calvert 1985).

Socially obtained information results in several efficiencies. First, the information comes tailor made. If a citizen wants to know about the current status of nuclear arms reductions talks, he may or may not find relevant information in the newspaper or on the television news, but he can formulate an explicit informational request to an associate who might know. Second, citizens might exercise control over the source. Most citizens have little control over the bias of the evening newspaper or the network news. But they are likely to exercise more control over the bias of their personal information sources. That is, citizens can request information from people who, based on their joint history in some common context, are known to have general viewpoints similar to their own.

A variation on the Downsian view is offered by various cognitive models of decision. Inspired by the early work of Simon (1957), this general viewpoint recognizes the inherent limitations upon the capacities of citizens to make informed choices in complex areas and focuses on the short-cuts citizens employ to make reasonable and informed decisions (Ottati and Wyer 1990; Lodge and Hamill 1986; Hamill, Lodge, and Blake 1985; Lodge, McGraw, and Stroh 1989). One short cut is to obtain information from trusted sources (Carmines and Kuklinski 1990), and one of the trusted sources might be another citizen (Mondak 1990). Thus a cognitive model of decision making might potentially complement a contextual theory of politics and indeed might offer a micro theory to explain contextual effects.

A point of potential divergence between these various viewpoints and a contextual theory of politics lies in the underlying conception of choice and control over political information. Downs's views informational choice as being determinant: he implicitly assumes that people have the freedom to choose their own sources of information with certainty, and thus social influence becomes a direct reflection of the citizen's own prior beliefs. Correspondingly, many cognitive models stress the extent to which individuals engage in selective information seeking and interpretation (Ottati and Wyer 1990; Lodge and Hamill 1986; Hamill, Lodge, and Blake 1985; Lodge, McGraw, and Stroh 1989), thereby screening and reinterpreting incoming information within the general context of their own preexistent orientation (or schema). And thus it is not clear that influence occurs at all, at least to the extent that the target of influence exercises direct or indirect control over the message that is received. Such conceptions of information processing have the potential to deny interdependence -- to deny (1) that an individual's behavior is fundamentally predicated upon the behavior of other individuals, and (2) that explanations of an individual's behavior must look beyond the individual in question.

Microsociological Models

Most advocates of a micro theory for contextual effects look toward psychology or economics as sources of inspiration in constructing a mechanism to explain structural influences upon individual behavior. As Raymond Boudon (1986) informs us, however, the individualistic tradition in sociology also supplies a micro theoretical alternative, with roots that trace to the work of Weber (1966). This tradition is sociological in its emphasis upon the extra-individual factors that impinge on individual behavior, but its unit of analysis is the individual, and it incorporates some form of methodological individualism as a micro theory of human behavior.

Microsociological reasoning can be illustrated with respect to personal influence in politics. What makes for political influence in personal relationships?

The implicit (social psychological) assumption carried over from many political socialization studies is that intimacy is responsible for personal influence on political orientations, even though socialization research offers little support for such an assertion (Jennings and Niemi 1968; Tedin 1974). Even without empirical support, a reliance upon intimacy continues to drive a great deal of reasoning regarding social influence and contextual effects (Eulau and Rothenberg 1986). Following the lead of Burt (1987), we refer to arguments relying upon intimacy as social cohesion models. In contrast, a microsociological explanation would point toward the social locations of both the target and the source of influence. For example, a structural equivalence explanation pursues the notion that a citizen should have more influence over another to the extent that they share the same locations in social structure (Burt 1987; Huckfeldt and Sprague 1991). Such reasoning provides an entirely different vantage point from which to assess contextual effects in politics.

Consider neighborhood effects from the cohesion perspective: why should citizens be influenced by the politics of the neighborhood when we know that, in the modern world, neighbors are seldom friends but merely residents of the same social space? Certainly, neighborhood effects are difficult to explain from a social cohesion perspective. But reconsider neighborhood effects from the vantage point of structural equivalence: neighborhoods may be important because residents share common structural locations. If this is the case, it is not cohesion, discussion, and persuasion that are at issue but rather information. When I see the yard signs and bumper stickers in my neighborhood, I am being informed regarding the political preferences that are appropriate for someone who is like me (Huckfeldt and Sprague 1992).

What is the individual level motive force for conformity? Burt (1987) argues a form of status anxiety in his reanalysis of the Coleman, Katz, and Menzel (1966) study of diffusion patterns in the medical community's adoption of a medical innovation. Boudon (1986) draws on Weber (1966) to urge the adoption of a rational actor motivation and a conception of contextually bounded rationality. Our own position is that different motives are better equipped to explain different behaviors. In the case of yard signs and bumper stickers, it seems reasonable to assume that their informational value is best explained on the basis of shared interests. When we drive down the streets of our neighborhoods and see Democratic yard signs, or when we see co-workers wearing Democratic campaign buttons, or when we see Democratic bumper stickers in the workplace parking lot, we are being informed regarding the political preferences of people with whom we share interests. The influence of such information is independent of intimacy -- indeed it may not even be verbally transmitted -- but it is entirely reasonable that citizens pay heed.

Viewed more generally, how does the microsociological model of political information processing differ from that of the economist or the cognitive psychologist? First and foremost, a microsociological argument views choice and control over information as being incomplete and probabilistic (Huckfeldt 1983; Huckfeldt and Sprague 1988). It is not that people do not intend to collect information about politics that corresponds with their own political biases and predispositions, but rather that they are frequently unable. This means, in turn, that (1) socially obtained political information (indeed all political information) is not simply a reflection of prior preference, (2) people obtain discrepant information that has influence potential (Sprague 1982), and hence (3) individual citizens are interdependent.

Why might the choice and control of political information operate probabilistically? First, the control over information is probabilistic because the search for information is expensive. Remember what we are addressing. The location of an informal source of information means finding someone with whom to discuss matters of interest, or at least someone from whom to gather information. If choice operates deterministically, citizens would not share their concerns with others until they have located the correct bias. If the correct bias is hard to find, the search must continue. Who is willing to pay the social cost of such an extended search? People who demand conformity in surrounding social relationships are the most likely candidates, either because of their own lack of tolerance for discrepant views or their own commitment to a particular bias or their being rejected by others when conversation exposes their differences from others (Finifter 1974). This means, of course, that the extent to which choice is probabilistic depends upon the strength of an underlying preference. Some people are more discriminating than others, but no one exercises complete and total control over incoming information because, if for no other reason, they must determine the bias of potential information sources in the first place in order to discriminate.

Second, informational choice is probabilistic with respect to any particular preference because it responds to multiple preference dimensions. We often discuss politics with the same people with whom we discuss baseball and fly casting. This is not to say that social relationships are not specialized but only that specialization adds to the cost of information search, and thus one more way to economize is to make a single source serve multiple functions. Some specialization is inevitable -- most of us have good friends with whom we would never discuss politics. But specialization comes at a price. In general, life is easier when one contact serves as a source of information for fly casting and politics. Thus, when we choose a contact, we are often implicitly optimizing in several directions and compromising among them all, further attenuating individual control and increasing the probabilistic component of choice with respect to any single underlying preference.

Third, informational choice is incomplete because so much of it is obtained inadvertently. When we see a respected co-worker wearing a campaign pin, we have collected an important piece of information. We know that someone with good judgment, and with a particular set of interests, has decided to support a particular candidate. We did not ask him for his opinion -- we did not even exercise choice in collecting the information -- but the import of such information should not be ignored.

Fourth, control over informally supplied information from social sources is also incomplete because the basis of informational choice is absent -- the underlying preference upon which choice rests is incomplete. In other words, we should not forget that it is possible to ask honest, naive questions with little preconception regarding how such information might be reconciled with some preexisting political bias. None of this is meant to deny the existence or importance of a bias either on the part of the sender or receiver of the information (Huckfeldt and Sprague 1991). Rather, it is only meant to suggest that such biases are incomplete and capable of being informed. And since they are incomplete, they cannot serve as iron-clad criteria in the discrimination among all information sources.

Finally, informational choice is probabilistic because some information is better than no information. Citizens are able to take account of the source's own bias when they evaluate information, or at least they believe that they can. And thus it makes eminently good sense to collect information even if it comes from a wrong-headed source. This does not mean that such information does not have an impact, or that social influence is nullified, but only that people may indeed purposefully expose themselves to information that comes from a source that runs counter to their own bias.

If citizen control over information operates deterministically, then the composition of the incoming stream of information becomes inconsequential for the composition of the information that is ultimately obtained. To the extent that citizens enforce their political predispositions upon informational choice, the menu of informational alternatives no longer matters. Citizens simply wait it out -- they refuse to choose an information source until they find one that they like, even if this means never locating an information source. Such a model of information control produces its own byproducts, of course. To the extent that citizens exercise such control, they are more likely to extend their search for information, to be unable to locate reliable information sources, and thus to be politically isolated (Huckfeldt 1983).

Alternatively, to the extent that informational choice is probabilistic, the incoming stream of information becomes a crucial consideration. What affects the content and composition of this incoming stream? The answer lies in media exposure and in the multiple bases of social experience to which citizens are exposed, and a steadily accumulating body of evidence points to the importance of these various bases of experience for political information and the formation of political preference.

The Multiple Bases of Social Experience

The political influence of social experience is best understood relative to the various bases of this experience. At one and the same time, citizens live in households, among immediate neighbors, located in the middle of larger neighborhoods, surrounded by a city, a county, a state, and a region. Coupled with these relatively inescapable geographically based environments are a whole series of less geographically dependent environments: workplaces, churches, taverns, bowling leagues, little leagues, health clubs, and so on. And each of these environments, whether it be geographically or nongeographically based, serves to establish constraints and opportunities acting upon social interaction.

None of these environments is necessarily more important than any other in influencing citizen behavior. In particular, it is a mistake to believe that more intimately defined environments are more important than environments that are larger and more impersonal. Indeed, the work of Erikson, Wright, and McIver (1989) and Wright and Berkman (1986) demonstrates quite persuasively that the state is the most appropriate environmental unit for many purposes of political analysis. The important point is that opportunities for social interaction are circumscribed by availability, availability is influenced by a range of environments defined at various levels, and thus social experience arises in a particular place and time.

Just as individual choice is not determinant in the selection of information sources, neither is the environment. Citizens do not simply roll over and accept whatever comes along in terms of social interaction opportunities. All of us avoid association with some individuals while we pursue it with others. And thus individual social experience is best seen as the end result of a complex interplay between individual choice and environmental supply. Just as the environment is composed of multiple and intersecting dimensions of experience (work, neighborhood, church, tavern), so also is individual associational preference multi-dimensional, responding to a range of different goals and objectives. To the extent that social experience carries political content, these life domains become important to the diffusion of political information and to the resulting preferences and choices of citizens.

In short, individual discretion plays an important role in defining social space and thereby determining social exposure. Learning theory points toward the importance of exposure, and a range of empirical findings show that, for example, organizational involvement can serve both to shield individuals from and expose individuals to contextual influence (Putnam 1966; Segal and Meyer 1974; Cox 1974). In point of fact, social contexts are created at least in part by an individual's construction of a social space. And thus the social context reflects a series of socially structured decisions regarding where to live, work, worship, drink beer, bowl, and so on. The social context experienced by any individual is the point of intersection between all these environments. As an empirical matter, we will be fortunate if we can obtain contextual measures on one or two environments at a time (Wald, Owen, and Hill 1988, 1990), but the inconveniences of measurement should not obscure the underlying theoretical issues.

Conclusion: Putting the Puzzle Back Together

Of what value is a micro theory of contextual influence? We have already denied that its utility must be evaluated in terms of explaining individual behavior, but rather that it lies in the specification of interdependence. Of what value is the specification of interdependence?

An important dimension of contextual analysis is the effort to deduce the aggregate consequences of interdependence. These efforts are typically modeling enterprises that ask a series of "what if" questions. If the mechanism of contextual influence is social learning or behavioral contagion or social reference groups, what are the consequences for the form and dynamic of public opinion (Sprague 1982; Huckfeldt 1983; MacKuen 1990; MacKuen and C. Brown 1987)? What difference does it make if the source of working class consciousness is to be located in exposure to the working class or in exposure to class-conscious working class behavior (Przeworski and Soares 1971; Przeworski 1974)? If citizens are affected both by the groups to which they belong and by the groups to which they do not belong, what are the consequences for the observation and measurement of contextual influence (Sprague 1976)? If compliant, law-abiding behavior on the part of citizens depends on the distribution of that behavior among others, what are the consequences for the organized coercive efforts of governments to maintain public order and control (Salert and Sprague 1980; Huckfeldt 1989; Huckfeldt 1990)? How does the micro environment shape the development of public attitudes toward law (Franklin and Kosaki 1989)? How does the competitive campaign environment affect the dynamics of money raising and candidate interaction (McBurnett and Kenny 1992)? How does class consciousness affect the potential of social democratic parties to expand the class basis of their support (Przeworski and Sprague 1987)? If political competition occurs between racial groups within the same party coalition, what are the consequences for racial polarization between parties (Huckfeldt and Kohfeld 1989)?

These modeling enterprises occur in various modes using various methodologies. Some are aimed at fitting models to aggregate data (Brown 1991). Others are aimed at exploring aggregate dynamic consequences (Przeworksi and Sprague 1987; Huckfeldt and Kohfeld 1989). But in every instance they are concerned with the political consequences of interdependence among citizens. In short, the specification of interdependence is not an end in itself. Rather, it serves as a vehicle that makes it possible to move back and forth between levels of analysis. Lacking a specification of interdependence, we are unable to move from the individual back to the aggregate. The analytic journey that culminates in an individual level analysis of political behavior becomes a one-way trip. We develop a more complete understanding of the individual psyche and individual motives, but we are unable to relate these parts to the whole. But interdependent electorates, rather than individual voters, shape the course of democratic politics, and it is the task of contextual hypotheses and theories to specify and explain those politically relevant interdependencies.

Bibliography

Abowitz, Deborah A. 1990. "Sociopolitical Participation and the Significance of Social Context: A Model of Competing Interests and Obligations." *Social Science Quarterly* 71:543-566.

Achen, Christopher H. 1986. *The Statistical Analysis of Quasi-Experiments.* Berkeley: University of California Press.

Alt, James. 1992. "Race and Voter Registration in the South Before and After the Voting Rights Act." In *Controversies in Minority Voting: A Twenty-five Year Perspective on the Voting Rights Act of 1965,* ed. Bernard N. Grofman and Chandler Davidson. Washington, DC: Brookings.

Alwin, Duane F. 1976. "Assessing School Effects: Some Identities." *Sociology of Education* 49:294-303.

Berelson, Bernard R., Paul Lazarsfeld, and William N. McPhee. 1954. *Voting: A Study of Opinion Formation in a Presidential Election.* Chicago: University of Chicago Press.

Blau, Peter M. 1956. "Social Mobility and Interpersonal Relations." *American Sociological Review* 21:290-295.

Blau, Peter M. 1957. "Formal Organization: Dimensions of Analysis." *American Journal of Sociology* 65:58-69.

Blau, Peter M. 1960a. "Structural Effects." *American Sociological Review* 25:178-193.

Blau, Peter M. 1960b. "A Theory of Social Integration." *American Journal of Sociology* 65:545-556.

Bobo, Lawrence. 1983. "Whites' Opposition to Busing: Symbolic Racism or Realistic Group Conflict?" *Journal of Personality and Social Psychology* 45:1196-1210.

Bobo, Lawrence. 1988a. "Attitudes Toward the Black Political Movement: Trends, Meaning, and Effects on Racial Policy Preferences." *Social Psychology Quarterly* 51:287-302.

Bobo, Lawrence. 1988b. "Group Conflict, Prejudice, and the Paradox of Contemporary Racial Attitudes." In *Eliminating Racism: Profiles in Controversy,* ed. Phyllis A. Katz and Dalmas A. Taylor. New York: Plenum Press.

Bobo, Lawrence, and Franklin D. Gilliam. 1990. "Race, Sociopolitical Participation, and Black Empowerment." *American Political Science Review* 84:377-393.

Books, John W., and Charles L. Prysby. 1991. *Political Behavior and the Local Context.* New York: Praeger.

Boudon, Raymond. 1963. "Proprietes Individuelles et Proprietes Collectives: Une Probleme d'Analyse Ecologique." *Revue Française de Sociologie* 4:275-299.

Boudon, Raymond. 1986. *Theories of Social Change: A Critical Appraisal.* Trans. J.C. Whitehouse. Berkeley: University of California Press.

Boyd, Lawrence H., Jr., and Gudmund R. Iversen. 1979. *Contextual Analysis: Concepts and Statistical Techniques.* Belmont, CA: Wadsworth.

Brown, Courtney. 1981. "Group Membership and the Social Environment: Multiple Influences on Political Attitudes and Behaviors." Ph.D. diss. Washington University.

Brown, Courtney. 1991. *Ballots of Tumult: A Portrait of Volatility in American Voting.* Ann Arbor: University of Michigan Press.

Brown, Thad A. 1981. "On Contextual Change and Partisan Attitudes." *British Journal of Political Science* 11:427-448.

Brown, Thad A. 1988. *Migration and Politics: The Impact of Population Mobility on American Voting Behavior.* Chapel Hill: University of North Carolina Press.

Burstein, Leigh. 1978. "Assessing Differences Between Grouped and Individual-Level Regression Coefficients: Alternative Approaches." *Sociological Methods and Research* 7:5-28.

Burt, Ronald S. 1987. "Social Contagion and Innovation: Cohesion Versus Structural Equivalence." *American Journal of Sociology* 92:1287-1335.

Butler, David, and Donald Stokes. 1969. *Political Change in Britain* New York: St. Martin's Press.

Calvert, Randall L. 1985. "The Value of Biased Information: A Rational Choice Model of Political Advice." *Journal of Politics* 47:530-555.

Campbell, Angus, Philip E. Converse, Warren E. Miller, and Donald E. Stokes. 1960. *The American Voter.* New York: John Wiley.

Carmines, Edward G., and James H. Kuklinski. 1990. "Incentives, Opportunities, and the Logic of Public Opinion in American

Political Representation." In *Information and Democratic Processes,* ed. John A. Ferejohn and James H. Kuklinski. Urbana and Chicago: University of Illinois Press.

Carmines, Edward G., and James A. Stimson. 1989. *Issue Evolution: Race and the Transformation of American Politics.* Princeton: Princeton University Press.

Coleman, James S. 1964. *Introduction to Mathematical Sociology.* New York: Free Press.

Coleman, James S., Elihu Katz, and Herbert Menzel. 1966. *Medical Innovation: A Diffusion Study.* Indianapolis: Bobbs-Merrill.

Converse, Phillip E. 1962. "Information Flow and the Stability of Partisan Attitudes." *Public Opinion Quarterly* 26:578-599.

Cox, Kevin R. 1974. "The Spatial Structuring of Information Flow and Partisan Attitudes." In *Social Ecology,* ed. Mattei Dogan and Stein Rokkan. Cambridge: M.I.T. Press. First published as "Quantitative Ecological Analysis in the Social Sciences" in 1969.

Davis, James A. 1966. "The Campus as a Frog Pond: An Application of the Theory of Relative Deprivation to Career Decisions of College Men." *American Journal of Sociology* 72:17-31.

Davis, James A., Joe L. Spaeth, and Carolyn Huson. 1961. "A Technique for Analyzing the Effects of Group Composition." *American Sociological Review* 26:215-225.

Downs, Anthony. 1957. *An Economic Theory of Democracy.* New York: Harper and Row.

Durkheim, Emile. [1897] 1951. *Suicide.* Trans. John A. Spaulding and George Simpson. New York: Free Press.

Ennis, Phillip H. 1962. "The Contextual Dimension in Voting." In *Public Opinion and Congressional Elections,* ed. William N. McPhee and William A. Glaser. New York: Free Press.

Erbring, Lutz, and Alice A. Young. 1979. "Individuals and Social Structure: Contextual Effects as Endogenous Feedback." *Sociological Methods and Research* 7:396-430.

Erikson, Robert S., Thomas D. Lancaster, and David W. Romero. 1989. "Group Components of the Presidential Vote, 1952-1984." *Journal of Politics* 51:337-346.

Erikson, Robert S., Gerald C. Wright, and John P. McIver. 1989. "Political Parties, Public Opinion, and State Policy in the United States." *American Political Science Review* 83:729-750.

Eulau, Heinz. 1986. *Politics, Self, and Society: A Theme and Variations.* Cambridge: Harvard University Press.

Eulau, Heinz, and Lawrence S. Rothenburg. 1986. "Life Space and Social Networks as Political Contexts." In *Politics, Self, and Society: A Theme and Variations,* ed. Heinz Eulau. Cambridge: Harvard University Press.

Finifter, Ada W. 1974. "The Friendship Group as a Protective Environment for Political Deviants." *American Political Science Review* 68:607-625.

Finifter, Ada W., and Bernard M. Finifter. 1989. "Party Identification and Political Adaptation of American Migrants in Australia." *Journal of Politics* 51:599-630.

Franklin, Charles H., and Liane C. Kosaki. 1989. "Republican Schoolmaster: The U.S. Supreme Court, Public Opinion, and Abortion." *American Political Science Review* 83:751-771.

Fuchs, Lawrence H. 1955. "American Jews and the Presidential Vote." *American Political Science Review* 49:385-401.

Gilbert, Chris. 1990. "Religious Environments and Political Actors." Ph.D. diss. Washington University.

Giles, Micheal, and Marilyn K. Dantico. 1982. "Political Participation and Neighborhood Social Context Revisited." *American Journal of Political Science* 26:144-150.

Giles, Micheal, and Arthur S. Evans. 1985. "External Threat, Perceived Threat, and Group Identity." *Social Science Quarterly* 66:50-66.

Glaser, William A. 1959. "The Family and Voting Turnout." *Public Opinion Quarterly* 23:563-570.

Goodman, Leo A. 1953. "Ecological Regression and Behavior of Individuals." *American Sociological Review* 18:663-664.

Goodman, Leo A. 1959. "Some Alternatives to Ecological Correlation." *American Journal of Sociology* 65:610-625.

Gosnell, Harold F. 1927. *Getting Out the Vote: An Experiment in the Stimulation of Voting.* Chicago: University of Chicago Press.

Greene, William H. 1990. *Econometric Analysis.* New York: Macmillan.

Hamill, Ruth, Milton Lodge, and Frederick Blake. 1985. "The Breadth, Depth, and Utility of Class, Partisan, and Ideological Schemata." *American Journal of Political Science* 29:850-870.

Hannan, Michael T. 1971. *Aggregation and Disaggregation in Sociology.* Lexington, MA: D.C. Heath.

Hannan, Michael T., and Leigh Burstein. 1974. "Estimation from Grouped Observations." *American Sociological Review* 39:374-392.

Hanushek, Eric A., John E. Jackson, and John F. Kain. 1974. "Model Specification, Use of Aggregate Data, and the Ecological Correlation Fallacy." *Political Methodology* 1:89-107.

Harder, Theodor, and Franz Urban Pappi. 1969. "Multiple Regression Analysis of Survey and Ecological Data." *Social Science Information* 8:43-67.

Hauser, Robert M. 1974. "Contextual Analysis Revisited." *Sociological Methods and Research* 2:365-375.

Heard, Alexander. 1952. *A Two Party South?* Chapel Hill: University of North Carolina Press.

Huckfeldt, Robert. 1983. "Social Contexts, Social Networks, and Urban Neighborhoods: Environmental Constraints on Friendship Choice." *American Journal of Sociology* 89:651-659.

Huckfeldt, Robert. 1984. "Political Loyalties and Social Class Ties: The Mechanisms of Contextual Influence." *American Journal of Political Science* 28:399-417.

Huckfeldt, Robert. 1986. *Politics in Context: Assimilation and Conflict in Urban Neighborhoods.* New York: Agathon.

Huckfeldt, Robert. 1989. "Noncompliance and the Limits of Coercion: The Problematic Enforcement of Unpopular Laws." In *Formal Theories of Politics: Mathematical Modelling in Political Science,* ed. P.E. Johnson. A special issue of *Mathematical and Computer Modelling* 12:533-546.

Huckfeldt, Robert. 1990. "Structure, Indeterminacy, and Chaos: A Case for Sociological Law." *Journal of Theoretical Politics* 2:413-433.

Huckfeldt, Robert, and Carol W. Kohfeld. 1989. *Race and the Decline of Class in American Politics.* Urbana: University of Illinois Press.

Huckfeldt, Robert, Eric Plutzer, and John Sprague. n.d. "Alternative Contexts of Political Behavior: Churches, Neighborhoods, and Individuals." *Journal of Politics.*

Huckfeldt, Robert, and John Sprague. 1987. "Networks in Context: The Social Flow of Political Information." *American Political Science Review* 81:1197-1216.

Huckfeldt, Robert, and John Sprague. 1988. "Choice, Social Structure, and Political Information: The Informational Coercion of Minorities." *American Journal of Political Science* 32:467-482.

Huckfeldt, Robert, and John Sprague. 1990. "Social Order and Political Chaos: The Structural Setting of Political Information." In *Information and Democratic Processes,* ed. John Ferejohn and James Kuklinski. Urbana: University of Illinois Press.

Huckfeldt, Robert, and John Sprague. 1991 "Discussant Effects on Vote Choice: Intimacy, Structure, and Interdependence." *Journal of Politics* 53:122-158.

Huckfeldt, Robert, and John Sprague. 1992. "Political Parties and Electoral Mobilization: Political Structure, Social Structure, and the Party Canvass." *American Political Science Review* 86:70-86.

Isambert, François-A. 1960. "Enterrements Civils et Classes Sociales." *Revue Française de Sociologie* 1:298-313.

Iversen, Gudmund R. 1991. *Contextual Analysis*. Newbury Park, CA: Sage.

Jennings, M. Kent, and Richard G. Niemi. 1968. "The Transmission of Political Values from Parent to Child." *American Political Science Review*. 62:169-184.

Kelley, Harold H. 1952. "Two Functions of Reference Groups." In *Readings in Social Psychology*, ed. Guy E. Swanson, Theodore M. Newcomb, and Eugene L. Hartley. New York: Henry Holt.

Kelley, Jonathan, and Ian McAllister. 1985. "Social Context and Electoral Behavior in Britain." *American Journal of Political Science*. 29:564-586.

Kenny, Christopher B. 1989. "The Consequences of Political Discussion in Mass Political Behavior." Ph.D. diss. Washington University.

Key, V.O., Jr., with the assistance of Alexander Heard. 1949. *Southern Politics: In State and Nation*. New York: Alfred A. Knopf.

Key, V.O., and Frank Munger. 1959. "Social Determinism and Electoral Decision: The Case of Indiana." In *American Voting Behavior*, ed. Eugene Burdick and Arthur J. Brodbeck. New York: Free Press.

Kohfeld, Carol W., and John Sprague. 1990. "Demography, Police Behavior, and Deterrence." *Criminology* 28:111-136.

Langton, Kenneth P., and Ronald Rapoport. 1975. "Social Structure, Social Context, and Partisan Mobilization: Urban Workers in Chile." *Comparative Political Studies* 8:318-344.

Lasswell, Harold D. [1939] 1966. "General Framework: Person, Personality, Group, Culture." In *The Analysis of Political Behavior: An Empirical Approach*, ed. Harold D. Lasswell. Hamden, CT: Archon Books, Shoestring Press.

Lau, Richard R. 1989. "Individual and Contextual Influences on Group Identification." *Social Psychology Quarterly* 52:220-231.

Lazarsfeld, Paul F., Bernard Berelson, and Hazel Gaudet. [1944] 1968. *The People's Choice: How the Voter Makes Up His Mind in a Presidential Campaign*. 3rd ed. New York: Columbia University Press.

Lodge, Milton, and Ruth Hamill. 1986. "A Partisan Schema for Political Information Processing." *American Political Science Review* 80:505-519.

Lodge, Milton, Kathleen M. McGraw, and Patrick Stroh. 1989. "An Impression-Driven Model of Candidate Evaluation." *American Political Science Review* 83:399-419.

MacKuen, Michael. 1990. "Speaking of Politics: Individual Conversational Choice, Public Opinion, and the Prospects for Deliberative Democracy." In *Information and Democratic Processes*, ed. John A. Ferejohn and James H. Kuklinski. Urbana and Chicago: University of Illinois Press.

MacKuen, Michael, and Courtney Brown. 1987. "Political Context and Attitude Change." *American Political Science Review* 81:471-490.

Maddala, G.S. 1983. *Limited Dependent and Qualitative Variables in Econometrics*. Cambridge: Cambridge University Press.

Matthews, Donald R., and James W. Prothro. 1963. "Social and Economic Factors and Negro Voter Registration in the South." *American Political Science Review* 57:24-44.

McBurnett, Michael, and Christopher B. Kenny. 1992. "A Dynamic Model of the Effect of Campaign Spending on Congressional Vote Choice." *American Journal of Political Science* 36:923-937.

McClosky, Herbert, and Harold E. Dahlgren. 1959. "Primary Group Influence on Party Loyalty." *American Political Science Review* 53:757-776.

McPhee, William. 1963. "Note on a Campaign Simulator." In *Formal Theories of Mass Behavior*, ed. William N. McPhee. London: Collier-Macmillan.

McPhee, William N., and Jack Ferguson. 1962. "Political Immunization." In *Public Opinion and Congressional Elections*, ed. William N. McPhee and William A. Glaser. New York: Macmillan.

McPhee, William N. and Robert B. Smith. 1962. "A Model for Analyzing Voting Systems." In *Public Opinion and Congressional Elections*, ed. William N. McPhee and William A. Glaser. New York: Macmillan.

McPhee, William N., with Robert B. Smith and Jack Ferguson. 1963. "A Theory of Informal Social Influence." In *Formal Theories of Mass Behavior*, ed. William N. McPhee. London: Collier-Macmillan.

Miller, Warren. 1956. "One-Party Politics and the Voter." *American Political Science Review* 50:707-725.

Mondak, Jeffery J. 1990. "Determinants of Coattail Voting." *Political Behavior* 12:265-288.

Noelle-Neumann, Elisabeth. 1984. *The Spiral of Silence: Public Opinion -- Our Social Skin*. Chicago: University of Chicago Press.

Orbell, John M. 1970. "An Information-Flow Theory of Community Influence." *Journal of Politics* 32:322-338.

Ottati, Victor C., and Robert S. Wyer, Jr. 1990. "The Cognitive Mediators of Political Choice: Toward a Comprehensive Model of Political Information Processing." In *Information and Democratic Processes*, ed. John A. Ferejohn and James H. Kuklinski. Urbana and Chicago: University of Illinois Press.

Penning, James M. 1988. "The Political Behavior of American Catholics: An Assessment of the Impact of Group Integration vs. Group Identification." *Western Political Quarterly* 41:289-308.

Popkin, Samuel L. 1991. *The Reasoning Voter: Communication and Persuasion in Presidential Campaigns*. Chicago: University of Chicago Press.

Prysby, Charles L. 1976. "Community Partisanship and Individual Voting Behavior: Methodological Problems of Contextual Analysis." *Political Methodology* 3:183-198.

Przeworski, Adam. 1974. "Contextual Models of Political Behavior." *Political Methodology* 1:27-61.

Przeworski, Adam. 1985. "Marxism and Rational Choice." *Politics and Society* 14:379-409.

Przeworski, Adam, and Glaucio A.D. Soares. 1971. "Theories in Search of a Curve: A Contextual Interpretation of Left Vote." *American Political Science Review* 65:51-68.

Przeworski, Adam, and John Sprague. 1987. *Paper Stones: A History of Electoral Socialism*. Chicago: University of Chicago Press.

Przeworski, Adam, and Henry Teune. 1970. *The Logic of Comparative Social Inquiry*. New York: Wiley-Interscience.

Putnam, Robert D. 1966. "Political Attitudes and the Local Community." *American Political Science Review* 60:640-654.

Robinson, W.S. 1950. "Ecological Correlations and the Behavior of Individuals." *American Sociological Review* 15:351-357.

Rose, Harold M., and Paula D. McClain. 1990. *Race, Place, and Risk: Black Homicide in Urban America.* Albany, NY: State University of New York Press.

Salert, Barbara, and John Sprague. 1980. *The Dynamics of Riots.* Ann Arbor: Inter-University Consortium for Political and Social Research, Methodology Monograph Series.

Sears, David O., and Donald R. Kinder. 1971. "Racial Tensions and Voting in Los Angeles." In *Los Angeles: Viability and Prospects for Metropolitan Leadership,* ed. Werner Z. Hirsch. New York: Praeger.

Sears, David O., and Donald R. Kinder. 1985. "Whites' Opposition to Busing: On Conceptualizing and Operationalizing Group Conflict." *Journal of Personality and Social Psychology* 48:1141-1147.

Segal, David R., and Marshall W. Meyer. 1974. "The Social Context of Political Partisanship." In *Social Ecology,* ed. Mattei Dogan and Stein Rokkan. Cambridge, MA: M.I.T. Press. First published as "Quantitative Ecological Analysis in the Social Sciences" in 1969.

Shively, W. Phillips. 1969. "'Ecological' Inference: The Use of Aggregate Data to Study Individuals." *American Political Science Review* 63:1183-1196.

Shively, W. Phillips. 1974. "Utilizing External Evidence in Cross-Level Inference." *Political Methodology* 1:61-73.

Shively, W. Phillips. 1987. "Cross-Level Inference as an Identification Problem." University of Minnesota. Photocopy.

Simon, Herbert A. 1957. *Models of Man: Social and Rational.* New York: Wiley.

Sprague, John. 1976. "Estimating a Boudon Type Contextual Model: Some Practical and Theoretical Problems of Measurement." *Political Methodology* 3:333-353.

Sprague, John. 1982. "Is There a Micro Theory Consistent with Contextual Analysis?" In *Strategies of Political Inquiry,* ed. Elinor Ostrom. Beverly Hills: Sage.

Sprague, John, and Louis P. Westefield. 1979a. "Contextual Effects from Behavioral Contagion." Paper presented at the annual meeting of the Western Political Science Association, Portland, OR.

Sprague, John, and Louis P. Westefield. 1979b. "An Interpretive Reconstruction of Some Aggregate Models of Contextual Effects." Paper presented at the annual meeting of the Southern Political Science Association, Gatlinburg, TN.

Stipak, Brian, and Carl Hensler. 1982. "Statistical Inference in Contextual Analysis." *American Journal of Political Science* 26:151-175.

Straits, Bruce C. 1990. "The Social Context of Voter Turnout." *Public Opinion Quarterly* 54:64-73.

Tate, C. Neal. 1974. "Individual and Contextual Variables in British Voting Behavior: An Exploratory Note." *American Political Science Review* 68:1656-1662.

Tedin, Kent L. 1974. "The Influence of Parents on the Political Attitudes of Adolescents." *American Political Science Review* 68:1579-1592

Tingsten, Herbert. [1937] 1963. *Political Behavior: Studies in Election Statistics.* Trans. Vilgot Hammarling. Totowa, NJ: Bedminster.

Wald, Kenneth, Dennis E. Owen, and Samuel S. Hill. 1988. "Churches as Political Communities." *American Political Science Review* 82:531-548.

Wald, Kenneth, Dennis E. Owen, and Samuel S. Hill. 1990. "Political Cohesion in Churches." *Journal of Politics* 52:195-215.

Weatherford, M. Stephen. 1982. "Interpersonal Networks and Political Behavior." *American Journal of Political Science* 26:117-143.

Weber, Max. 1966. "On the Concept of Sociology and the Meaning of Social Conduct." *Basic Concepts in Sociology.* Trans. H.P.

Secher from *Wirtschaft und Gesellschaft.* New York: Citadel Press.

Westefield, Louis P. n.d. *Personal Communication.*

Wilson, William Julius. 1987. *The Truly Disadvantaged: The Inner City, the Underclass, and Public Policy.* Chicago: University of Chicago Press.

Wright, Gerald C. 1976. "Community Structure and Voting in the South." *Public Opinion Quarterly* 40:200-215.

Wright, Gerald C. 1977. "Contextual Models of Electoral Behavior: The Southern Wallace Vote." *American Political Science Review* 71:497-508.

Wright, Gerald C., and Michael B. Berkman. 1986. "Candidates and Policy in United States Senate Elections." *American Political Science Review* 80:567-588.

12

Political Communication: Scope, Progress, Promise

Doris Graber

Introduction

What is "political" communication? It is the construction, sending, receiving, and processing of messages that are likely to have a significant impact on politics. The impact may be direct or indirect, immediate or delayed. Direct messages may relate to political activities, such as an appeal for votes, or an appeal for support of a policy, or for compliance with a particular law. In the indirect mode, messages may create images of reality that then affect political thinking and action by political elites and mass publics. The message senders may be politicians, journalists, members of interest groups, or private, unorganized citizens. Their identity does not matter. The same holds true for message receivers. The key element is that the message has a significant political effect on the thinking, beliefs, and behaviors of individuals, groups, institutions, and whole societies and the environments in which they exist (Berelson 1948; Lasswell 1969).

Karl Deutsch has called political communication "The Nerves of Government," suggesting that political messages are the stimulus that produces political behavior. He might just as well have called it the lifeblood or mother's milk of politics because communication is the essential activity that links the various parts of society together and allows them to function as an integrated whole. The substance and form of political messages circulating in a polity, and the images that they evoke, determine the thrust and quality of political life. This is why the study of political communication is an extremely important subfield of political science.

One may question whether political communication is a genuinely distinct field of study, or merely a particular context in which one examines various communication phenomena. This is a legitimate question. The answer is that it needs to be treated as a distinct research focus because communication in political contexts presents many unique challenges for scholars that require specialized knowledge of subject matter and of particular research techniques. Because of its significance to a full understanding of politics, and because of past neglect, much effort is needed to explore all the facets of the subfield.

Political communication is a field with fluid boundaries that is interdisciplinary as well as intercultural. It is interdisciplinary because the questions raised by it require political scientists to draw on sister disciplines, including communication, psychology, and sociology. It is intercultural because political communication features vary among cultures so that it is important as well as instructive to examine them from various cultural perspectives (Gurevitch and Blumler 1990).

Looking at the subfield from a historical perspective, it is one of the oldest. Scholars from early times on have studied political communication. Confucius (551-479 B.C.) and Aristotle (384-322 B.C.) taught about aspects of political communication. Cicero (106-43 B.C.) and Pliny (62-113 A.D.) concerned themselves with the persuasive powers of political oratory. Niccolo Machiavelli argued in *The Prince* in 1513 that rulers must study human nature so that they can successfully communicate with their subjects in order to manipulate their thoughts and emotions. Machiavelli provided detailed suggestions about the manner in which princes might do that.

Princes and other practitioners of the art of politics have been keenly interested in political communication from early times on, knowing well that success in politics demands that politicians master the art of political communication so that they can influence their constituents' views about the political world. They have attempted to foster the construction of favorable images in the minds of their subjects through various types of verbal and nonverbal messages, including the symbolism of majestic architectural creations and elaborate public ceremonies, and public speeches. They have also sought to mold human minds through brainwashing tactics and terror, particularly during periods of internal struggles and external wars. They have used propaganda of various types and public relations tactics and political advertising as gentler forms of political persuasion. They have attempted to shape the flow of political communication through laws designed to control communication flows, including mass media offerings, in their society. Control over mass media, which generally are the most prolific sources of political messages, has ranged from government ownership and operation of various mass media institutions to various forms of explicit censorship of the news media, as well as censorship through informal social pressures.

The Study of Political Communication

Although political communication is one of the oldest areas of political studies, as a subsdisciplinary area of political science it is one of the youngest. Despite its youth, it has made remarkably fast progress in exploring a variety of topics such as analyzing communication by political leaders, examining images created by the mass media and other sources, and probing how people process information. Political communication researchers have laid the groundwork for comparative research, examining audience behavior in diverse societies and studying the motivations of communicators cross-culturally.

Though progress has been fast and furious, it has been uneven. Certain areas have received the lion's share of attention while others have been neglected. Among the areas that have been widely researched is electoral politics. Political scientists have been greatly interested in the impact of various types of communications during campaigns and elections. Since most election messages are shaped and transmitted by the mass media, a great deal of attention has also been given to their role. Neglected areas include the role played by political communication in political socialization, the significance of informal dissemination of information via 'leaks,' and the impact of communication factors on the conclusion of international agreements. But it seems petulant to complain about uneven progress in a field that has made such rapid strides in a brief period of time.

How does one review such a growing, highly fragmented field? There is, of course, no ideal answer. The order adopted here rests on a paradigm developed by Harold Lasswell for the study of communication factors. Lasswell suggested that it was important to seek answers to five questions. One needs to know who (meaning the sender), says what (meaning a message), in what channel (meaning the mode of transmission), to whom (meaning the message receiver) with what effect (meaning the attitudinal and behavioral consequences of the message) (Lasswell 1969). Accordingly, this essay will deal with senders and receivers of political messages, with message meanings and modes of transmission, and with message

effects. In addition, the conceptual bases of the subfield will be reviewed, as well as its major research methods.

As is true of most interdisciplinary fields, a survey of research that encompasses the full array of work in all of the component fields would be unwieldy. At the same time, ignoring work by scholars from other disciplines would deprive readers of the chance to experience the richness of the field. As a workable compromise, this essay focuses primarily on the work done by political scientists, but it will also sample major studies from communication, sociology, and psychology. Space limitations also make it necessary to trim the edges of the field somewhat. For this reason, some areas of study that overlap substantially with other subfields have been excluded. Examples are problems of language heterogeneity in political communities, which are amply covered in reviews of ethnic politics and international relations, and comparative studies of documents, such as the comparative analysis of the English and Japanese versions of the Japanese constitution, which are covered by constitutional law experts (Weinstein 1990; Inoue 1991; Lukes 1987).

Because of the richness of the field, the essay focuses primarily, though not exclusively, on developments of recent decades. Only selected publications will be cited in the text as illustrations of various types of research trends. The bibliography ranges much more widely. But though it presents several hundred sources, it merely scratches the surface of published books and, especially, articles. The number of publications, in itself, is testimony to the vigor of the subfield that includes many scholars who do not ordinarily consider themselves political communication researchers, but whose needs to fully explain their own subfields draw them into the realm of political communication.

Conceptual Underpinnings

As might be expected from an interdisciplinary field, the conceptual underpinnings of political communication studies are diverse and largely borrowed from sister disciplines, especially psychology and communications. Most theories relate to individual-level phenomena, especially the persuasive effects of messages on individuals. For example, hypotheses regarding attention to political messages draw heavily on selective choice theories and uses and gratifications theories. Selective choice theories try to explain why people do not pay attention to most of the information to which they are exposed. According to such theories, people feel uncomfortable -- experiencing cognitive dissonance -- when exposed to ideas that call the validity of their own ideas into question or offend their feelings and tastes (Festinger 1957). To avoid discomfort, people select information that is congruent with their existing beliefs and shut out discordant messages. Currently, the selectivity phenomenon is regarded as far less prevalent and potent than originally believed. The reason is that numerous studies of the phenomenon, most of them in the election context, have supported the theory only weakly or even contradicted it (Weiss 1969). Nonetheless, selectivity theories are still widely used to explain selective attention (Graber 1988).

Proponents of uses and gratifications theories contend that individuals are active information selectors who ignore messages that are not relevant to their concerns or that are unattractively presented. They pay attention only to messages that are useful and gratifying, provided that the expense in time and effort seems reasonable. The uses to which people put messages and the gratifications they derive from them may be emotional or intellectual. For example, people may pay attention to messages that help them in voting or in gaining a sense of political adequacy. Uses and gratification theories have been tested repeatedly and refined in line with the findings (Rosengren et al. 1985).

When political communication studies started in the mid-1940s they were based largely on 'hypodermic' theories. In contrast to the view that audiences are active, earlier hypodermic theories were predicated on the notion of audience passivity. Exposure to a media message was equated with its absorption by the receiver in its original form. Armed with such hypodermic theories, political scientists began to investigate the impact of mass media stories on voting decisions. They expected media impact to be profound. Unfortunately for the progress of political communication research, the voting studies, including work by Lazarsfeld et al. (1944), Berelson et al. (1954), Campbell et al. (1954, 1960), and Campbell (1966), did not find the expected effects. Consequently, hypodermic theories became discredited and 'minimal effects' theories came into vogue. According to these minimal effects theories, applied primarily to mass media messages, election news was insignificant, compared to other choice criteria such as party or group allegiance. The minimal effects argument tied in well with persuasion theories about the weaknesses of impersonal messages that cannot address the needs of specific individuals, elicit direct feedback, or even assure the attention of the audience. Disappointed political scientists therefore largely abandoned political message research, especially when it involved mass media messages.

The study of mass media influence on elections resumed in the late 1960s and early 1970s, largely because the notion of media impotence in election contests clashed with appearances and the intuitions of practicing politicians (Nie et al. 1976; Miller and Levitin 1976; Patterson and McClure 1976). These renewed investigations, rather than looking for universal effects, tried to discover under what conditions effects might occur. For instance, interested voters and political experts might be more and differently affected by media than disinterested citizens and political novices. This new approach to research, which confirmed such differential effects, coincided with major social and political changes that affected the interaction between media and politics. Party influence on candidate selection had declined sharply. The slack provided a real opportunity for television -- the newly popular mass communication medium -- to become an important force. It therefore comes as no surprise that studies since the revival of interest in the impact of mass media messages have overturned many of the earlier minimal effects findings.

The new studies have created a strong base of research findings that establish that the mass media influence elections in many important ways. Nonetheless, many political scientists continue to belittle media impact because it rarely is the sole cause of observed effects and because they have been disappointed in their search for statistically significant numbers of voting shifts attributable to media messages. They have slighted the significance of impacts on voter attitudes and feelings or on the conduct of campaigns. Even when media effects are statistically negligible, they may be politically significant in a close election or referendum where a small number of votes can change the outcome.

Many scholars also fail to credit media messages with indirect effects. For instance, if the political climate created by media influences turnout, as appears to be the case, and turnout then influences election outcomes, these outcomes deserve to be attributed at least partially to media influence (Abramson et al. 1990). Similarly, stories about the economy or world affairs that are published during an election campaign may influence the interpretation and impact of election news even when these stories say nothing about the election (Graber 1987b).

The predominant theoretical approach to analyzing the impact of media messages on the electorate is agenda-setting. The credit for starting agenda-setting research accrues chiefly to two communications scholars, Donald Shaw and Maxwell McCombs, who publicized the approach in a 1977 study of North Carolina voters (Shaw and McCombs 1977). However, there are important political science godfathers. They include Bernard Cohen (1963), who pointed out that the mass media are powerful in focusing audience attention on selected topics, even though they may not determine what the audience will think about these topics. Norton Long (1958, 256) ascribed to newspapers "a great part in determining what most people will be talking about, what most people will think the facts are, and what most people will regard as the way problems are dealt with...to a large extent it sets the civic agenda."

Agenda-setting theorists contend that it is far less likely that attitudes and behaviors will be changed by media messages than that the audience's knowledge base for making decisions will change. When media call attention to selected issues and events -- one of their chief functions -- they affect the audience's priorities of concerns. Researchers should therefore study to what extent media messages change the knowledge and priorities that enter into the audience's decision making or 'prime' audiences to view events in light of the context suggested by prior stories (Iyengar 1991).

Rather than focusing on the effects of mass media in specific contexts, some scholars took a broader view and theorized about their more general social effects. Harold Lasswell, in his pathbreaking essay on "The Structure and Function of Communication in Society" (1969) pointed out that media perform three functions that are of major importance to society. They acquaint audiences with ongoing events as part of their agenda-setting role. They also interpret the meaning of messages, thereby shaping the perspectives from which the world will be viewed. In the process, they also socialize individuals into their cultural settings. These functions suggest three major areas of political communication research: the need to examine what types of political images mass media select for wide dissemination, the importance of assessing the interpretations suggested by mass media stories and, finally, the need to assess the impact of media messages on political socialization. Political scientists have done comparatively little to follow up on these suggestions. Sociologists, psychologists, and communications scholars have helped in filling some of the gaps (Nimmo and Sanders 1981; Swanson and Nimmo 1990).

Aside from theories employed in mass media studies, various persuasion theories and mass society theories have been used to analyze the impact of psychological warfare and propaganda messages (Neuman 1991; Beniger 1986). Many of these studies were sparked by an interest in understanding how Hitler, Mussolini, Stalin, and other leaders of modern dictatorships had used propaganda to achieve their goals. Wartime concerns about the effects of indoctrination of troops on their performance on the battlefield and in prisoner-of-war camps also spurred numerous investigations.

The theories discussed thus far are in the prevailing objective, positivist vein of current social science research. A set of subjective theories, some of them very critical of current politics, have also come into vogue, particularly in the communication discipline. Adherents of this 'interpretist,' or 'deconstructionist,'

perspective deny that reality exists in the positivist sense. Rather, reality arises from the shared perceptions developed by people who communicate with each other. What matters most from a subjective perspective is how people perceive and conceptualize their world, quite aside from the world depicted through empirical studies. Therefore, communications studies should focus on perceptual elements. For example, instead of studying the text of a message, scholars should investigate how the text is perceived.

When interpretists think in the 'critical' vein, their research turns to the social consequences of communication, especially the role it plays in subordinating various groups in society, such as women and minorities (Hall 1989). Critical theorists look for message constructions that lead to quiescence and submissiveness by mass publics who are then repressed by dominant groups because of their acquiescence (Edelman 1964, 1988). Messages circulating in organizations serve to instill a submissive spirit in the workforce and perpetuate a repressive capitalist system (Putnam and Pacanowski 1983). Elections are viewed as dramatized rituals that legitimate the existing power structure, rather than genuine expressions of the public's wishes (Ginsberg 1986; Nimmo and Combs 1990). Critical researchers believe that scholars should be political activists who advocate changes in communication patterns designed to liberate workers and create a socialist society.

Besides the individual-level theories discussed thus far, the subfield has also made use of group-level and systems-level theories. Since their use has been far more limited, they will be discussed briefly when relevant research is discussed below. Overall, the various theories that pervade the subfield add up to an embarrassment of riches. There is no single trend. As is true of evolving fields, there still are unbridgeable disagreements about many fundamental issues. Theorists disagree about the focus of research and whether it should be predominantly objective or subjective. They advocate an array of perspectives from which political communication should be studied, ranging from research that focuses on individuals, groups, or entire institutions to studies of the total system in which various institutions are embedded.

Research Methods

Methodologically, political communication research is also diverse, ranging from primarily qualitative to primarily quantitative methods. The most widely used research technique for examining political messages is content analysis. The predominant methodology for examining message effects is survey research, although experimental designs are being used with increasing frequency.

Content Analysis

Content analysis can be either quantitative or qualitative. Preferably, it is a mixture of both. Using trained human coders to identify textual elements still is the most common approach, although computer coding is becoming more effective and more widely used. The two methods can also be combined, taking advantage of the strengths of each. When voluminous data sets need to be analyzed, content analysis is a very time consuming, tedious, and costly technique. For this reason, few political scientists have used it, mostly in its simplest forms. Like other research methods, content analysis has several serious deficiencies that impair the validity of its results. For example, different investigators do not ordinarily use uniform coding categories in their studies. Therefore research is not as comparable as would be desirable. Another problem is the significance assigned to high and low frequency of coded items. In general, high frequency of mention is equated with high significance, while rare mention is equated with lack of significance. Yet, in reality, a single message that points to a major political blunder may have far more significant consequences than hundreds of messages indicating satisfactory performance.

The validity of content analyses is also impaired when text is only partially or incompletely examined. For example, in newspaper research, investigators often check only headlines and front pages on the flawed assumption that they reflect all significant stories. Similarly, an entire story is often coded as a single topic even though coding by paragraphs, for example, would show that most stories contain multiple topics. Such restricted approaches to content analysis severely distort the actual content. Content analysis that codes news content fully and pays heed to non-verbal information in televised news is almost non-existent.

Most content analyses deal with denotations of words and phrases and themes, rather than with their connotations. Connotation research has been avoided because all messages are polysemic, conveying multiple meanings to various audiences. Notwithstanding this difficulty, ascertainment of connotational constructions cannot be skirted if scholars want to know what meanings are actually conveyed to particular audiences (Cohen 1989). The possibility of multiple interpretations of messages does not mean that senders cannot convey consensual connotations. It merely means that senders must know how their audiences are likely to interpret messages and tailor them accordingly. Content analysts also should probe the contexts in which messages were received because it affects interpretation. This is rarely done. The consequences can be disastrous.

Coding of audio-visual information has presented major problems in the past because of the richness of pictorial detail offered by television and related media. These problems can be overcome by focusing coding on the meanings conveyed by audio-visuals rather than coding discrete pictorial elements. However, thus far, very few political scientists have tackled audio-visual coding techniques or have included the meanings conveyed by the visual aspects of messages in their analysis of political messages (Sullivan and Masters 1988; Graber 1988). This is a major omission in understanding the important audio-visual political messages conveyed to Americans, particularly in the context of elections. The establishment of archives for audiovisual materials has made them much more readily accessible to researchers. Among the major ones are the archives for television news broadcasts located at Vanderbilt University, the archives for C-SPAN broadcasts at Purdue University, and archives for political commercials at the University of Oklahoma.

Surveys, Interviews, and Experiments

For surveys and interviews designed to assess the impact of various political messages on audiences, both cross-sectional and panel designs have been used. Panel designs are gaining in favor because they are better suited for tracking attitudinal changes over time (Patterson and McClure 1976; Patterson 1980; Miller and Levitin 1976; Nie et al. 1976). Sample sizes have ranged from several thousand respondents interviewed in a single wave or multiple waves, to intensive work done with small panels or even single individuals (Neuman et al. 1992; Gamson 1992).

Survey research designs employed in impact studies have had a number of serious weaknesses. Investigators usually are not able to confirm that their respondents have actually been exposed to the information stimuli whose impact is being tested. In the majority of instances, investigators do not even examine these stimuli in detail and do not ask to what specific messages the respondents have been exposed. Secondly, survey researchers rarely know what information respondents already held prior to exposure to the stimuli under investigation. Hence there is no baseline for measuring message-induced changes in perception and behavior. Researchers rarely ask open-ended questions that allow respondents to report what they have learned from the messages to which they have been exposed and how these messages meld with their own mental states and feelings. Better ways to ascertain meanings that respondents construct from questions and answers are urgently needed, but none seem currently in the offing despite more careful pretesting, more open-ended questions, and better interviewer training.

While survey research remains the dominant mode for investigating message impact, several other approaches have made inroads. They are based on the idea that understanding message impact requires looking closely at the ways in which individuals process them. Such thinking has led to intensive analyses of small numbers of individuals, using depth interviews of small groups of people, focus groups, and various psychological testing devices (Graber 1988; Iyengar and Kinder 1987; Neuman et al. 1992; Gamson 1992; Rosenberg 1988). Among intensive analysis techniques, Q-methodology appears to be particularly well-suited for political communication research. It measures clusters of subjective reactions to information stimuli, based on individual scores rather than on a mean drawn from a large population. The technique enables researchers to detect types of individuals most likely to exhibit particular patterns of reactions to specific messages (Brown 1980; Nimmo and Savage 1976). Interesting results have been obtained also through ethnographic studies, in which researchers observe how people communicate about political matters in natural settings. However, political scientists have largely shunned this approach as too impressionistic.

Political scientists are turning increasingly to purely experimental studies to probe media impact. Mostly such studies have involved exposing small groups of people to carefully selected information stimuli. Investigators have then measured their subjects' retention of the information or assessed attitudes and opinions, or changes in them, generated by the messages (Meadow and Sigelman 1982; Iyengar et al. 1982; Iyengar and Kinder 1987; Rosenberg 1988; Neuman et al. 1992). Such research has helped in discovering message and context factors that aid or deter learning. It has shown that cognitive skills and high interest in messages contribute significantly to effective information processing although, at best, much information fails to be internalized and all is reshaped to fit into each individual's thinking structures. It has also disclosed the prevalence of priming and framing phenomena whereby prior messages or associations suggested by messages become potent interpretation contexts (Gamson 1992; Iyengar 1991).

The principal advantage of experimental studies is the researcher's ability to control the stimuli to which research subjects are exposed. These controls avoid the stimulus adulteration that occurs in natural settings where many stimuli are present and interact with political messages. The chief problem posed by experimental research is the fact that the context is artificial. Message impact may be quite different in controlled laboratory settings than in natural situations. Experimental studies and small group intensive research both run the risk of being unrepresentative of external realities. Their findings cannot be attributed to larger populations without further testing. Nonetheless, they represent attractive, low-cost alternatives to large-scale surveys. If successful, they often serve as pilots that pretest hypotheses for studies done on a larger scale. Findings from experimental research and depth interviews may also broaden the insights gained from larger surveys and fill gaps. For example, extensive probing of the thinking behind a respondent's answers to survey questions, which is possible in small-scale research, can help in interpreting survey responses. A combination of these complementary research approaches is therefore ideal, though expensive.

Investigation of political symbolism has relied on yet another set of research tools, most of them qualitative. They include dramaturgical analysis and fantasy theme analysis, which involves exploring the dramatic and fantastic themes in political life, and hermeneutics, which is the study of the verbal construction of social meanings. They also include ethnomethodology, which is the study of explanations people give about their daily experiences, and symbolic interactionism, which assesses how people use symbols to communicate with one another. Nimmo and Combs (1990), for example, have used a dramatist perspective to examine election communication. Elections were conceptualized as dramatic rituals played for the audience of prospective voters to show the protagonists locked in a heroic struggle. Audiences perceive these rhetorical visions as reality and gear their expectations of future performance to these visions.

Advances in the techniques for cross-cultural and comparative studies are also shedding important new light on communication processes (Blumler and Gurevitch 1988). Election messages and depictions of public officials have been compared in various countries (Hallin and Mancini 1984; Semetko et al. 1991). They have cast the spotlight on variations in different countries in the discretion enjoyed by journalists in setting the daily news agenda. They have also revealed the impact of differences in party structure and media organization on stories about candidates and elections. Using television news as the media stimulus, Tamar Liebes (1992) compared coverage of the Intifada and the Gulf War on U.S. and Israel television. She concluded that journalists in both countries sanitized the activities of their own military while demonizing the enemy's activities.

Is there anything new on the methodological horizon? The answer seems to be that the basic research approaches used in recent decades will remain intact, but that they will continue to undergo constant refinement. As has happened in the past, new statistical analysis procedures, such as Probit, Logit and Lisrel analysis, will bloom and fade, as will survey and interview techniques in message effect studies. Electronic monitoring devices and computer simulations are likely to grow in importance in research into brain functions. Human coders of political messages will be increasingly replaced by computers which can now be programmed to detect words and their synonyms as well as contextual and network patterns that determine the meanings that the words convey. There will be more research that employs a multiplicity of methods in data gathering and analysis, part of it borrowed from other disciplines and subdisciplines. Currently loosely defined concepts, such as 'attention' to messages, will undergo clarification. However, giant methodological leaps will probably remain in the realm of wishful thinking.

As future research progresses, new paths of inquiry that have not been pursued in the past should be explored along with retesting old findings to ascertain their validity under changing technological and political conditions (Abramson et al. 1988). For example, the opportunities for narrowcasting created through cable television and satellite technology may fracture mass consensus on many political issues and may herald changes in media message effects that need to be investigated (Neuman 1991). Future research should encompass a better melding of quantitative and qualitative research methods, more interdisciplinary cooperation, and more attention to both micro-level and macro-level effects of political messages.

We are now ready to turn to political communication research targets and findings.

What Is the Message?

Political messages are a crucial aspect of politics because the bulk of politically relevant information is conveyed through messages about happenings, rather than through direct experiences. Things that occurred in the past and projections of future events are only available through indirect messages (Boulding 1956). As Kenneth Burke (1966, 5) has noted, most of our reality is verbally created. "And however important to us is the tiny sliver of reality each of us has experienced firsthand, the whole overall 'picture' is but a construct of our symbol system." For abstractions like 'democracy' or 'justice,' and a large number of political phenomena, there is no empirical referent. Understanding depends completely on verbal symbols that lack extra-verbal reality. This is true of a large number of political phenomena.

The kind of information that one gains from politically relevant messages provides guidelines to politicians and private citizens about the current state of politics and about the kinds of messages that achieve

particular political objectives, if the time and audience are suitable. Leaders may gain or lose office and power depending on their oratorical skills, including their ability to classify political phenomena. Freedom fighters' halos may tarnish when they are dubbed 'terrorists.' When opposition to the state is called 'treason' it is treated differently than when it bears the label 'civil disobedience.' All sorts of helpful conceptual linkages can be constructed when it becomes important to legitimate actions. For example, government-sponsored job creation may fare differently in the political arena depending on whether it is linked to morality, to overall economic health, to psychological welfare, to partisan fortunes, or to other causes. Mass audiences may be informed or misled, empowered or subjugated in the wake of the images that have been created (Corcoran 1990).

The Scope of Content Studies

The list of renowned humanists and social and behavioral scientists who have examined the impact of verbal pronouncements on politics is long. It includes Harold Lasswell and associates who authored *The Language of Politics: Studies in Quantitative Semantics* (1965), Edward Sapir who wrote about *Culture, Language and Personality* (1962), and Kenneth Burke who described *Language as Symbolic Action* (1966). It also includes Ernst Cassirer who wrote *Language and Myth* (1946), Alfred North Whitehead who studied *Symbolism: Its Meaning and Effect* (1958), and Susanne Langer's thoughts expressed in *Philosophy in a New Key: A Study in the Sociology of Reason, Rite, and Art* (1951). Other members of the club are Kenneth Boulding who wrote about *The Image: Knowledge in Life and Society* (1956), and Murray Edelman who interpreted political reality, as expressed through political symbols in his widely cited book on *The Symbolic Uses of Politics* (1964).

In the wake of political culture changes in the United States, there has been a great deal of interest in verbally and visually created images of selected politically disadvantaged groups, such as American blacks, or urban squatters, or women (Entman 1992; Van Dijk 1988). Images of social phenomena, like poverty or terrorism, have also received attention (Van Dijk 1988; Alali and Elke 1991). Some scholars have undertaken comparative studies of images. For instance, media images of the Soviet Union and Soviet leaders in the American press have been compared to media images of the United States and its leaders in the Soviet press (Dennis et al. 1991). Students of political linguistics have investigated what meanings the various images conveyed to the audience and to the stereotyped group.

In recent years most content research has focused on political messages relating to real-world political events in mass media stories. However, the focus is expanding so that more scholars now study messages from the realm of entertainment, including fictional movies, situation comedies, and docudramas (Lichter et al. 1991; Parenti 1992). Much of this work seeks to identify how various groups in society, such as business people, or physicians, or unionized workers are depicted. It also tries to discern the ideological perspectives underlying fictional presentations. Frequently, the conclusion is that media perpetuate the status quo by implicitly and explicitly depicting it as legitimate and desirable and by ignoring other possible scenarios (Manheim 1991; Morley 1990). Alternatively, the conclusion has been that the media endanger the status quo by allowing the non-traditional, often left-wing preferences of media personnel to color their presentations (Lichter et al. 1986; Herman and Chomsky 1988). Sociologists, psychologists, and communications scholars have led the way in exploring the content of visual and verbal messages about deviant behaviors and have speculated about the consequences.

Up to now, most image research has remained largely descriptive. There have been few systematic attempts to discern what features are routinely depicted when disadvantaged groups or political leaders, or political phenomena, are discussed and what features are omitted and what political consequences ensue. Scholars have devoted little attention to determining the usefulness of various types of information for making political decisions. For example, we do not know very well whether the kinds of qualities that are stressed for various political leaders are genuinely relevant to understanding the leader's character and performance. More systematic understanding of the information needed to assess politicians during their candidacies and their incumbencies might lead to improvements in their publicized images, a more adequate information supply and improvements in government.

Similarly, American political scientists have rarely examined the reality images that politicians try to convey. Historians, rhetoricians, and communications scholars have done most of this work with a slight assist from political scientists (Edelman 1964; Entman 1989; Bennett 1988; Rothman 1992). In sociology, ethnomethodologists have studied news as a mode of reality construction (Tuchman 1978). They have examined the ideological slants of that reality. Political scientists have not followed in their footsteps, aside from general statements about political orientations and an occasional study of the slant of coverage of a particular event, such as the Watergate affair (Lang and Lang 1983).

Drawing Inferences from Content

Political scientists and other social scientists have made numerous systematic attempts to draw helpful inferences from political messages. For example, the content of political messages has been used to ascertain the values and mores embedded in the social context in which the message has been disseminated (Bennett and Edelman 1985; Paletz and Guthrie 1987). In the 1950s and 1960s, a group of prominent social scientists collaborated in what came to be known as the Hoover Institution's RADIR studies. The initials stand for Revolution And Development of International Relations. The studies rested on the assumption that the knowledge and value structures and priorities prevalent in various nations could be inferred from the images disseminated through their mass media. If these mental environments were known, one could forecast future political developments in these nations (Lasswell et al. 1952; Pool 1952, 1959). Although there are many cautions, presumably "the sequence of movements in history can be conveniently read by scanning the dominant symbols of successive periods" (Lasswell et al. 1952, 505).

The RADIR scholars examined mass media output from five countries over a sixty-year period. They checked 25,000 editorials in prestige newspapers in France, Germany, England, Russia (and the successor Soviet Union) and the United States between 1890 and 1950. They found 416 distinctive verbal symbols relating to the status of the society and therefore deemed worthy of tracing. On the basis of this massive body of evidence, the RADIR group concluded that there were considerable differences among countries and time periods in the nature and frequency of the use of political symbols. Totalitarian societies, for example, concentrated on a much smaller array of symbols than their democratic counterparts.

Karl Deutsch (1957, 1967) thought that it would be possible to trace cohesiveness and value sharing among nations through an analysis of their communication flows and an analysis of mass media and elite images (Deutsch 1957, 1967). He and Richard Merritt analyzed the impact of unfavorable publicity on national images (Deutsch and Merritt 1965). Follow-up on this type of work has been meager. Moreover, most later studies have been largely descriptive without any attempt to analyze the political inferences that might be drawn from verbal images (Adams 1981, 1982).

Studies of message content can also be used to provide data from which psychologically oriented social scientists can infer the psychological characteristics, beliefs, motivations and strategies of political leaders (DeMause 1986; Robinson and Levy 1986; Winter and Carlson 1988). Even when the psychological characteristics remain obscure, valuable inferences can be drawn about power configurations by knowing which political personalities are cited and in what connections their messages are reported. Public figures whose messages are widely quoted are often able to determine the labels and classifications of people and phenomena in their political environment. This greatly enhances their political influence because names and classifications may determine how people and phenomena will be treated.

Strategic Uses of Communication

Election Campaigns

The forms that political messages take hinge on their strategic goals and the political contexts in which they must circulate. Researchers have paid most attention to strategies used in the electoral context. Campaign messages have been examined mostly at the presidential level, but studies of congressional campaigns are increasing. The pickings have been slim when one dips below that level to state campaigns, even at the gubernatorial level, and to local campaigns, including mayoral races (Goldenberg and Traugott 1984, 1987; Vermeer 1982, 1987; Graber 1983). Because this has been such an active research area, substantial progress has been made and is continuing. Since later studies often refine earlier ones, the current body of knowledge remains in flux (Arterton 1978; Robinson 1981, 1987; Robinson and Sheehan 1983; Patterson 1980; Nie et al. 1976; Nimmo and Combs 1990; Nimmo and Savage 1976; A. Miller et al. 1985; Ranney 1983; Nimmo 1981; Adams 1983; Graber 1986).

Political scientists have been especially interested in the substance and frequency of messages about political candidates, deeming them crucial to a candidate's electoral success or failure. However, the precise role played by media-created images seems to vary depending on the contexts in which elections take place. As Bartels (1988) has noted, contrary to classic public choice theory, elections are dynamic situations where individual preferences often change, making collective decisions unpredictable. Researchers concur that winner and loser images are very important because the American public loves winners; but no magic formulae for constructing successful candidate images have as yet been discovered (Orren and Polsby 1987). The concern about winning and losing has focused a large portion of election coverage on horse race aspects of the election. Prophecies about winning and losing become important factors in the contest because they are often self-fulfilling. Similarly, news stories create expectations so that subsequent events are then judged in light of these expectations. A candidate who does better than expected wins more approbation

than a rival who obtained more votes or more favorable ratings in public opinion polls, but did not exceed expectations.

Content analyses have revealed the major characteristics of the news supply available to the public for voting decisions. Stories about candidate qualities and qualifications are more prevalent than stories about the candidates' stands on issues. In presidential campaigns, the balance has hovered around two to one. In general, news stories depict only a limited number of the personal and professional attributes of candidates. Personal qualities, such as trustworthiness, strength of character, leadership abilities, and compassion are stressed most (Patterson 1980; Weaver et al. 1981; Graber 1986; Robinson and Sheehan 1983).

Messages about issues are generally superficial. They focus on current problems and avoid discussions of complexities. Genuinely significant points that bear on the candidates' ability to govern are often sacrificed to the desire to tell interesting tales. This is why news people try to frame most issues as conflicts among the candidates. Television stories emphasize issues for which good pictures are available.

Few political scientists have investigated coverage of specific issues during election campaigns, such as the dealings of the United States with Iran or the formulation of energy policy. Their analyses routinely point to major deficiencies that impair public understanding of the issue in question (Sahr 1983). Scholars who have scrutinized political debates, particularly during presidential election years, have bemoaned the time and format constraints that prevent adequate issue discussions during these events. Nonetheless, most researchers agree that the debates attract large audiences and therefore serve as an important last minute rehearsal for voters, particularly undecided ones, who need help in reviewing the campaign (Kraus 1988; Jamieson 1990). Debate studies have been most prominent at the presidential level, with most studies limited to post-Labor Day debates. The limitation is unfortunate because it seems likely that pre-Labor Day debates may have a greater impact because they occur before voter opinions have hardened. It would also be useful to study debates at the subnational level and comparatively in American and foreign contexts.

When questions arose about the impact of political advertising, numerous researchers turned their attention to this long neglected array of messages (Devlin 1989; Diamond and Bates 1988; Jamieson 1992). Advertising content has been examined, with particular emphasis on the balance between issues and images and on the messages conveyed by visual images. Issue content in longer advertisements often has been quite high compared to issue content of television news stories.

Political commercials also appear to be an important source of information for disinterested, poorly informed voters (Owen 1991; Kaid et al. 1985). Nesbit (1988) has noted the importance of a candidate's video style, which is a combination of verbal and nonverbal content of visuals and film and video production techniques. Apparently, incumbents and challengers employ different video styles in their attempts to sway voters, as do male and female candidates. Challengers, for example, often need to be more aggressive, striving for a 'fighter' image, to overcome the advantages of incumbency. What matters most is the lasting image created by the candidate's video performance, rather than the specific information conveyed to the audience. The position of candidates in relation to the camera and candidate facial expressions have been especially closely scrutinized (Masters and Sullivan 1989; Kepplinger 1990).

Public Information Campaigns

Besides election campaigns, messages in several other types of politically important campaigns have also been studied. Scholars of comparative government have considered information campaigns in developing countries essential for rapid development (Pye 1963; Pool 1963). In the 1960s, these scholars believed that major political processes such as political socialization, and political participation and free circulation of information throughout the country all hinged on the nature and quality of the country's political communication system. If information flowed properly and generated adequate feedback, political systems could be steered towards growth and development. Characteristics of sound information flows included clear and timely messages about internal as well as external happenings, encoded in ways that were comprehensible to intended recipients. Daniel Lerner (1958), for example, studied mass communication in the Middle East believing it taught people how to empathize with and adopt new lifestyles. Gabriel Almond (1960, 46) considered political communication the "crucial boundary maintenance function" because all political functions are performed through communications.

But, as with other effects, it soon became clear that media effects were much more elusive than had been anticipated because they hinged on a variety of contextual factors. Although development scholars were ultimately disappointed about the efficacy of communication to produce rapid growth, interest in campaigns to improve the life of mass publics has continued. In recent decades, it has been largely directed to public health issues. AIDS, population control, anti-smoking, anti-alcohol, and drug campaigns are examples. Typically, messages constructed for such campaigns try to persuade target publics to adopt behaviors that will lessen risks. Behavioral changes

advocated in the messages range from simple steps recommended in a no-littering and Smokey-the-Bear fire prevention campaign, to very difficult behavior modifications required in anti-smoking or AIDS prevention campaigns. Objectives range from composing messages that will arouse the attention of target audiences to behavior-reinforcing messages that are needed after the suggested behavior has been adopted.

Success rates have run the gamut from nearly complete success to nearly total failure. The quality of the campaigns, the receptiveness of the audience, and the ability to get at the root of the problem have been important determinants in the outcome. Knowledgeable audience members are more likely to learn campaign messages than people who lack information into which these messages can be incorporated. Consequently, as 'knowledge-gap' theories predict, the knowledge-rich are likely to become richer while the knowledge-poor fall further behind (Tichenor et al. 1980). Given the importance of such campaigns to public welfare, increased research attention is likely so that factors that produce campaign successes can be more fully understood (Rice and Atkins 1989).

In the decades surrounding World Wars I and II, persuasive messages, including propaganda and psychological warfare messages, were widely studied. The landmark work on government-sponsored propaganda in totalitarian societies is a three-volume collection edited by Harold Lasswell, Daniel Lerner, and Hans Speier in 1980. It provides a historical account of worldwide propaganda activities. Wartime analysis of the content of German radio news is also an important example (George 1959). The U.S. government commissioned such research to infer conditions inside Germany from the thrust of the propaganda messages. Postwar analysis confirmed 85% of the inferences. Later studies have focused primarily on Soviet, Nazi, and Chinese propaganda (Liu 1971; Zeman 1973). Psychological warfare and brainwashing have been studied largely by psychologists. Jay Lifton, for example, examined mental manipulations in China and Fagen did the same thing with respect to Cuba (Lifton 1963; Fagen 1969). There has been a lull in that kind of academic research. However, in the wake of the many controversies about political advertising, interest in persuasive communications appears to be rising again (O'Keefe 1990; Kern 1989; Jamieson 1992).

The Art of Wheeling and Dealing

While it would seem to be exceedingly important for political leaders at all levels of government to know how to structure their messages effectively, the political science community has given relatively little guidance. Scholars have been reluctant to research this matter, fearing accusations of fostering misleading propaganda and mind manipulation and even brainwashing to control audiences. That specter has been raised repeatedly, exposing how ill-defined the boundary lines are between ethical and unethical uses of persuasive messages in political discourse (Edelman 1971; Parenti 1986).

William Riker (1983) has recommended political science research of 'heresthetics,' -- the manipulation of the structure of preferences and alternatives within which decisions are made. Politicians should try to construct suitable environmental contexts for political negotiations and bargaining that will strengthen one contender and weaken the opposition. This is not the same as political rhetoric which seeks to persuade through its own force. Studies that deal with the message environment that is involved in deterrence policies belong to this genre. Creating an impression of invincibility or impending doom for the opponent can lead to major political victories (Jervis et al. 1985).

In the same vein, a few political scientists and economists have used game theory concepts to analyze political negotiations (Schelling 1968; Corsi 1981; Druckman and Harris 1990). Some have examined the ways in which agendas are prepared during negotiations and how initial arguments structure subsequent discourse (Ikle 1964; Welton et al. 1988). Comparisons have been made between what was said and how it was said and what could possibly have been said but was omitted. Since excuses and justifications require important strategic considerations in public discourse, blame avoidance strategies have garnered attention (McGraw 1990, 1991). Much more needs to be done.

Research on the role of language strategies in more general political wheeling and dealing has been sparse. The effectiveness of messages has been studied, but usually in a general, rather than a strategic, context. Information flow studies, for example, have stressed the need for timeliness, clarity, completeness, and accuracy in message construction so that the senders' intentions are correctly transmitted to receivers at the appropriate time (Deutsch 1966; Wilensky 1966). Opportunities to misunderstand and be misunderstood are legion in a society where the contexts in which messages are framed and received vary greatly and may be in constant flux. Congressional hearings during the Reagan administration exposed many instances of incomplete, inaccurate, and unreliable foreign affairs information circulating at the highest levels of government.

Analysis of communication flows during political encounters, such as legislative sessions or executive branch deliberations, could reveal under what circumstances information is likely to be withheld or misinformation circulated for strategic purposes. During the Reagan presidency, for example, National Security Council personnel withheld information from the president about diversion of proceeds from arms sales to Iran to Nicaragua's anti-communist rebels. Similarly, Congress was kept uninformed and misled by false testimony. Important documents were shredded so that they would be unavailable once an investigation had gotten under way. Structural reforms to minimize such occurrences depend on greater insights into past problem situations (Knoke and Kuklinski 1987; Kessel 1983, 1984).

Politicians' Rhetoric

Turning to more ordinary circumstances, there has been a moderate degree of interest in analyzing the rhetoric of political executives, primarily at the presidential level (Hart 1984; Tulis 1987; Edelman 1988; Jamieson 1988). It has been based on the assumption that presidential messages are potent political stimuli because they emanate from the top official of the country. The power or lack of power of the message sender thus transfuses to the message. One needs to know the senders' political role and orientations to accurately interpret message meanings.

A number of scholars have focused on the use of presidential rhetoric as a political tool to overcome congressional opposition (Kernell 1993; Tulis 1987). Instead of trying to negotiate with congressional leaders, as was past practice, presidents appeal to the country by 'going public' via the electronic media. If the president is popular, the public is likely to rally around him, making it difficult for the Congress to deny approval. Even before presidents go public, the possibility of such action may persuade members of Congress to succumb to presidential wishes (Edwards 1983; Foote 1988; Graber 1982; Simon and Ostrom 1989).

Far less attention has been given to the rhetoric of politicians below the presidency. Internal communications in public sector agencies have rarely been examined (Graber 1992b). Herbert Kaufman's (1967) study of the U.S. Forest Service, which describes how communication policies helped to create high morale among agency personnel, is a welcome exception. The role played by governmental public relations personnel in spreading the government's messages via mass media has also been given some attention. A study by Stephen Hess (1984) described how government press officers within the United States national government operate when they prepare messages for press use. Martin Linsky (1986) has reported a series of cases in which policies were aided or hampered by public relations efforts. Manheim and Albritton (1984) investigated how effectively foreign governments used public relations firms to change media coverage in desired ways. These studies break new ground but much more needs to be done to fully investigate and assess how honestly and effectively governments use media to foster governmental purposes.

The data about influence patterns reflected in media coverage have remained hazy because it is often difficult to identify the sources of unattributed messages. Scholars have largely failed to establish which officials are frequent sources of news stories, and how much control such sources have over the substance and slant of news. Success rates in gaining support and cooperation from journalists seem to vary widely, depending on factors such as the power of the source desiring access, the journalistic appeal of the story, and competing claims for news coverage. Story significance and the source's need to have it covered are lesser considerations (Goldenberg 1975; Protess et al. 1991).

Political scientists disagree about whether media content is shaped primarily by proponents reflecting the right or left side of the ideological spectrum. Scholars like Robert and Linda Lichter and Stanley Rothman (1986) have argued that media elites who work for the leading news media lean to the political left, relying on sources holding kindred views. Scholars like Lance Bennett (1988), Michael Parenti (1986), and Benjamin Ginsberg (1986), to name but a few, consider media to be the minions of big business and right-wing politicians. They fault the media for using news selection to strengthen white middle class values and suppress competing left-wing views. Some critics, such as Michael Parenti (1986, 1992) and Edward Herman and Noam Chomsky (1988) contend that these choices are made deliberately to perpetuate capitalist exploitation of the masses in line with the ideological preferences of media owners. They also claim that the media have intentionally suppressed facts about dangerous products and technologies to protect the profits of large corporations (Cirino 1972; Schiller 1973). Still other scholars see the media as apostles of the status quo, reflecting the views of the political establishment. As proof, they cite the fact that government officials are the predominant sources interviewed by journalists and that media, while critical of specific policies and politicians, rarely challenge the main principles that undergird American political institutions (Sigal 1983; Bennett 1988; Entman 1989; Bagdikian 1990).

Charges have been plentiful that messages transmitted in the political arena are biased. Numerous scholars have therefore tried to identify bias, particularly in the election context (Hofstetter 1976, 1978; Kressell 1987; Sorauf 1987). These efforts have been hampered because there is no agreed-upon definition of bias or standards for spotting it. Various imbalances in mass media coverage that may constitute bias have been documented, such as uneven coverage of various candidates and selective treatment of issues. They seem to result predominantly from normal news production

factors, rather than from deliberate, politically motivated behavior. Nonetheless, they can have a profound impact on electoral fortunes. More bias research seems therefore desirable. But it cannot be done successfully without developing reliable, widely accepted, measures to identify bias.

Underlying the vigorous debate about the ideological thrust of media messages is the assumption that these messages color the ideological thrust of political life (Bennett 1988; Entman 1989; Edelman 1988). This is an interesting and important assumption. However, little has been done by political communication scholars to flesh out the bare theoretical bones and demonstrate the extent of news story influence on the ideological orientations of leaders and mass publics.

Transmission Networks and Modes

Information Flows

Rather than looking at the content of messages, a number of scholars have looked at the passage of information through political systems to discern where messages originate, how they travel through networks of receivers and are transformed during their passage through the system, and how they are ultimately received and lead to decisions. Karl Deutsch's pathbreaking study of *The Nerves of Government: Models of Political Communication and Control* (1966) remains the prime example. Initially, the study of communication flows was used most widely by scholars of comparative government who were interested in factors that might influence political and economic development of the many newly independent nations that were emerging in the 1960s (Easton 1965; Fagen 1966; Pye 1963). When interest in these studies flagged in the face of disappointingly slow political and economic growth in the Third World, and dwindling foundation support for this type of research, communication system analysis by political scientists withered.

The earlier studies of information flows through internal and external networks show that the configuration of transmission channels is very significant. Messages cannot reach their destination if communication channels are unavailable or if they lack the capacity to handle the flow of essential messages. Systems must be able to access organizational memories and to avoid distortions that result when messages are filtered through 'screens' of various prejudices and preferences of the message receivers. The limits in the capacity of channels often become acutely apparent during political crises, such as wars or revolutions or major natural or manmade disasters. Overload problems are compounded by the fact that few organizations have developed satisfactory ways for screening incoming messages so that information that deserves priority can be identified and channeled accordingly.

Studies of communication networks have shown that the paths that formal and informal messages take have crucial political consequences (Heclo 1977; Kessel 1983, 1984; Huckfeldt and Sprague 1987; Knoke and Kuklinski 1987). Routing decisions often hinge on communication technologies. For example, congressional communications patterns have been altered by the computer revolution (Frantzich 1982). Generally speaking, people who are at the hub of communications in a political unit and receive comparatively large amounts of information are, or become, the formal or informal leaders of the political unit. If important information fails to reach them, their decisions suffer. People who are not connected to the networks through which essential information flows may be unable to participate effectively in decision making. If units within political systems are improperly connected, messages may miss their appropriate targets. This has been a serious problem in impoverished societies where outlying areas often are not adequately connected to communication hubs where most of the political decisions are made.

Channels of communication may vary in the numbers of people that they connect and in the character of the information flow that they carry. Official channels are often supplemented by a network of unofficial channels that may carry substantive official information, unofficial leaks, as well as gossip. From a democratic perspective, one of the most serious problems in even the most democratic societies is the scarcity of channels through which citizens can communicate with public officials. Disadvantaged groups in particular often find it difficult to route their concerns appropriately so that they receive consideration. Voting usually serves as the only publicly provided avenue through which all groups of the citizenry can send a message to officials. But, except for referenda, elections are a poor channel to voice specific concerns and complaints.

Mass Media Modes

The bulk of political messages that have been described or analyzed have been transmitted in a verbal, visual, or oral mode. Non-verbal messages, such as the emotions conveyed through architectural symbols, like imposing public buildings and interior settings, have been largely ignored, with a few notable exceptions (Goodsell 1988; Ferguson and Ferguson 1988). Communications scholars have paid far more attention to message differences related to the characteristics of various modes

of message transmission, focusing most heavily on comparisons of audio-visual messages with printed messages (Neuman et al. 1992).

Characteristically, political scientists have examined this facet of communication studies mostly in the electoral context (Schram 1987; McCubbins 1992). They have found that television and newspapers cover similar arrays of topics but vary in the transmission of intellectual and emotional content. The brevity of television stories necessitates condensing and simplifying story texts. Pictures, which are often loaded with emotional stimuli, supplement and reinforce the brief verbal messages. To conserve time, television newscasters usually create stereotypical images of candidates during the early campaign stages. Later stories are then tailored to these stereotypes (Robinson and Sheehan 1983). When the stereotypes misrepresent reality or when candidates have changed their policy stands, this can create serious problems (Arterton 1984). A few political scientists have focused their research on the impact of the candidates' facial expressions (Lanzetta et al. 1985; Rosenberg and McCafferty 1987; Rosenberg et al. 1986; Kepplinger 1990). More general studies of audio-visual aspects of information transmission -- such as analysis of the content of visual messages, and assessments of the quality of comprehension and recall -- have been rare (Graber 1988, 1990; Neuman et al. 1992).

Information Processing Channels

How do individuals accept and process information to extract meanings from the flood of messages that reach them? This intriguing question has inspired much research into information processing in the 1980s and 1990s (Kraus and Perloff 1985; Lau and Sears 1986; Graber 1988; Sniderman et al. 1991; Piazza et al. 1989). The desire to model the basic cognitive processes through which information is channeled, processed, and used by the human brain is a natural outgrowth of findings that message stimuli are not absorbed unchanged by audiences. Instead, the relationship is transactional. Audiences interpret incoming information in line with their own cognitions and feelings. The outcome is a multiplicity of perceptions springing from the same stimulus. The precise impact of messages depends on whether receivers have relevant mental schemata stored in memory and on the fit between incoming message images and these schemata (Graber 1988; Miller et al. 1985; Lau and Sears 1986; Fiske and Kinder 1981; Conover and Feldman 1986, 1989; Hamill and Lodge 1986, Lodge et al. 1991).

Research suggests that processing varies depending on the type of information and on a multitude of audience factors. The latter include cultural variables, context variables, personality variables, as well as the processors' political memories, political sophistication, and interest in politics. Because multiple interacting audience variables must be considered, information processing needs to be studied in a variety of contexts. Nonetheless, election messages have continued to be the primary research focus. Researchers have been interested in information processing differences among people of differing partisan orientations and sophistication. They have studied how people pare down information that is of interest to them so that it can be managed more readily and how they incorporate it into their thought processes. Scholars have also examined the inferences drawn from this type of information (Conover and Feldman 1986).

While little progress has been made in measuring information processing directly, various experiments and computer simulations are shedding light on how the human brain functions (Piazza et al. 1989; Boynton and Lodge n.d.). For example, Milton Lodge tested political decision making in the laboratory with human subjects while G.R. Boynton simulated the identical situation through a computer program. The comparison of computer decisions with human decisions was designed to assess the extent to which man and machine thinking processes use similar stepwise progressions and produce similar results.

The Scope of Message Effects

Election Messages

The study of political communication is based on the premise that political messages have some kinds of political effects, on ordinary citizens, on political elites and, at the systems level, on general operations and policies. It remains arguable, however, what precisely these effects are under a variety of circumstances. As Bernard Berelson commented somewhat ambiguously (1948, 192), "Some kinds of communications on some kinds of issues, brought to the attention of some kinds of people under some kinds of conditions, have some kinds of effects." Researchers have found it difficult to isolate message effects from other influences with which they are intertwined. It has been particularly troublesome to distinguish the impact of messages about events from the impact of these events themselves.

Again, as throughout political communication studies, elections have received most attention in the study of communication effects, with a focus on the perceptions and attitudes of individual voters, and, most importantly, their electoral choices. Judging from the vast share of research resources devoted to the field, one might expect that a firm body of knowledge has been

created. Not so. While much has been learned, major debates continue about fundamental issues. The scope of information on which average voters base their voting decisions in presidential elections is one example (Ferejohn and Kuklinski 1990). Some scholars have concluded that American voters, thanks to mass media messages, have acquired a steadily expanding base of knowledge for voting decisions (Nie et al. 1976; Popkin 1991). Others claim that voters cast uninformed votes and that political sophistication continues to be low (Keeter and Zukin 1983; Smith 1989).

Studies of television, newspaper, and news magazine coverage of recent presidential elections show that the information supplied by the major media is inadequate for the kind of rational decision making that democratic theorists favor. The bulk of the news deals with candidate qualities so that voters often find it difficult to base their vote on adequate issue information. As mentioned, presidential debates ease the situation only slightly, because the format allows only cursory discussion. Voters also find it difficult to compare contenders because news stories cover various traits and competencies unevenly across the field of candidates. Moreover, the information reaching voters usually comes from multiple sources and therefore presents contradictory information about individual candidates. Adherence to journalistic criteria of objectivity prevents journalists from making explicit value judgments in ordinary news stories. Accordingly, audiences are deprived of guidelines for judging contradictory messages.

Extensive publication of public opinion polls muddies the informational waters even further. The fact that published poll data seem definitive because they carry precise numbers misleads audiences into believing that they represent an established situation, rather than a time-bound glimpse. When that happens, a bandwagon effect may set in so that putative winners gain support at the expense of putative losers. It is uncertain to what extent this effect is offset by a 'sympathy' effect that favors the underdog (Tannenbaum and Kostrich 1983). Political scientists have also speculated that negative messages about politicians contribute to the rising political cynicism of the American public. However, this remains speculation. Negative portrayals of political candidates have been blamed for making it increasingly difficult for public officials to govern with public support after elections and to win a second term in office (Ranney 1983; Semetko et al. 1991). Again, more research is needed to establish this as a firm scientific datum, rather than an incompletely tested hypothesis.

Most scholars would agree with Dan Nimmo's conclusion (1981, 257), "In sum, the verdict concerning the part played by the mass media in relation to individuals' voting behavior is that they are influential informers and impotent persuaders. Just what aspects of mass communication inform -- or persuade, however, is not clear." The impact of election messages apparently hinges on many factors, including the substance of the message, the appropriateness of its forms, the setting in which it occurs, and the voters' receptivity. Nimmo's conclusion runs counter to the claims made by public relations professionals that voters are highly susceptible to media persuasion, even with respect to election commercials. Such claims receive only mixed support. Richard Joslyn (1984) contends that exposure to political commercials can actually produce voting defections, but other scholars disagree (Meadow and Sigelman 1982).

In the late 1980s and early 1990s, interest in the effects of negative advertising mounted, sparked by criticism of such advertising in presidential elections (Kern 1989; Kaid et al. 1986; Jamieson 1992). Research was also stimulated by candidates and their handlers eager to know the impact of such advertising. There has been concern that advertising messages constitute powerful priming that shapes the political climate and guides the thinking and feeling that goes into the audience's decision making. The specter of Orwellian manipulation looms, but the verdict is still pending, because some scholars have found a backlash against negative advertising and its partisan sponsors (Arterton 1992; Garramone et al. 1990). It is also questionable how much information can be conveyed through the extremely brief messages squeezed into thirty-second commercials (Just et al. 1990). The knowledge that people are active rather than passive message receivers who construct their own meanings from messages, and that there are ways to immunize publics against persuasive messages, may give further comfort (Pfau and Burgoon 1988).

Political Learning and Socialization

Learning

Aside from studies of the effects of election messages on individuals, research on other individual-level impacts has been rather sparse. It is particularly surprising that there has been relatively little research on the extent and substance of factual knowledge that individuals garner from mass media messages and political events, and on the impact of various types of political messages on political socialization and resocialization.

Several studies have examined learning variations springing from differences in message transmission modes, such as the use of audiovisuals compared to the use of printed text (Robinson and Levy 1986; Neuman 1991). Other studies have sought to dissect the learning process on a single medium that contains multiple

coordinated or uncoordinated information stimuli (Tiemens et al. 1988). Television, for example, often combines visual images with non-verbal and spoken sounds, and written messages that may be disparate or even inconsistent. Studies that try to determine the interaction effects of such complex stimuli are still in their infancy. Studying what and how people learn from audio-visual messages is especially important in an age when exposure to visual media constitutes the most common form of contact with political information (Rosenberg et al. 1986; Keeter 1987; Graber 1988).

'Priming' and framing effects have also been investigated. Priming studies try to determine to what extent concepts to which a respondent has been alerted through prior information influence judgments about subsequently received information. The effects appear to be profound (Iyengar and Kinder 1987). For example, evaluations of presidents vary substantially depending on whether the preceding discussion has touched on successful or unsuccessful policies. If this is so, concern about the priming effects of political advertising may be well justified. Framing effects can be powerful as well. News framed as a series of discrete events, rather than a cohesive pattern, fails to suggest that someone is responsible for these events. For example, when homelessness is framed as a series of stories about individual cases, government responsibility for the problem does not become readily apparent. Television news, which routinely uses such an episodic format, thus discourages people from holding public officials responsible for political conditions (Iyengar 1991).

Does attention arousal and subsequent processing of information vary when message content stirs emotions or elicits empathy or presents conflict and violence? Observers have been concerned that such cues may steer people away from rational judgments during important political activities such as voting and during times of serious national and international conflicts. Thus far, the impact of non-rational appeals on thinking and behavior has remained controversial (Morello 1988; Rapport and Alexander 1989).

Public Opinion Development

Individual learning and opinion formation lay the groundwork for the development of publicly shared opinions. The role played by political messages in this process remains of continuing interest. Scholars are still seeking answers to basic questions about the triggering mechanisms that arouse widespread attention to particular issues, produce stereotyped images and lead to mass opinion trends (Iyengar and Kinder 1987; Page et al. 1987; Page and Shapiro 1991; Zaller 1992). Public opinion polling has also been examined as an opinion-shaping force, not only as a device to measure opinions. Researchers now realize that the focus of poll questions and the way they are asked can shape respondents' thinking by pinpointing particular perspectives and facets of the issue in question (Ratzan 1989). When polls are subsequently publicized, the same opinion-shaping forces that affect poll respondents' answers, ripple out to the public. The effects may even be enhanced because views gain legitimacy when they seem to be widely shared. This is the reverse side of the 'spiral of silence' phenomenon that Elizabeth Noelle-Neumann (1984) has documented by showing that people keep silent when they think that their views are unpopular. Widespread silence then condemns these messages to neglect and even scorn.

Socialization

Political socialization involves communicating societal traditions, values, and beliefs to people at various phases of the life cycle so that they can function appropriately as citizens of their society. Study of communication factors in political socialization has many facets, ranging from scrutiny of classroom texts and mass media content to studying the work of public information agencies and propaganda ministries. Some of this work, as mentioned, was done by scholars interested in Third World development (Pye 1963; Fagen 1966; Davies 1977; Dawson, Prewitt, and Dawson 1977), but otherwise media influences have rated only a few lines in political socialization studies, including those dealing with adult socialization. By contrast, public opinion studies generally acknowledge that media play a major role in socialization and opinion formation (Jennings and Niemi 1981; Corbett 1991).

In the closing decade of the twentieth century, it seems particularly important to analyze the role of mass media and other messages in the casual and formal political resocialization that is going on in countries that are switching from Marxist ideologies to various forms of Western-style democracy. Apparently the concerted efforts made throughout much of this century to indoctrinate people into Marxist ideologies did not meet with the high degree of success that had been reported (Bahry and Silver 1990). Can the resocialization campaigns that attempt to lead mass publics towards democratization and economic development do any better?

Elite Decision Making

Turning to messages involving political elites, three areas have received the lion's share of attention. They are the rhetoric of leaders, which has been discussed already; information processing by political elites, and decision making, especially in small groups. Information processing by political elites has been examined indirectly by analyzing patterns of themes in their messages and constructing 'cognitive maps.' These maps presumably represent the individual's core beliefs and approaches to analyzing and solving problems. They are the bases of 'operational codes' that guide decisions and actions (Jervis 1970; Axelrod 1976).

Political decision-making studies have paid considerable attention to the information flows in foreign policy decisions (Kennedy 1969; Allison 1971; Janis 1989). Scholars have focused on information management when major decisions must be made, including the ways in which information is collected, processed, and channeled to reach the appropriate receivers in timely fashion. They have also analyzed various common problems, many of them psychological, that lead to information distortion and faulty decisions (George 1980; Etheredge 1985). These problems are particularly evident when decisions are made by small groups of people at times of crisis (Janis and Mann 1977; George 1980; Etheredge 1985). Irving Janis (1989), for example, showed how U.S. policy makers bungled policies designed to overthrow Cuba's Communist government. Communication in decision-making groups generated psychological pressures that impaired the quality of deliberations and reinforced flawed policy plans.

By and large, studies of decision making by elites have probed the psychological processes involved in decision making far more extensively than has been the case for comparable voting decision studies. Jonathan Roberts (1988), for example, in a study of decision making during international crises, examined the personalities of decision makers, their feelings and subjective perceptions, their levels of fatigue and stress, their mental and physical health, as well as the use of drugs and other mind-altering stimuli that might impinge on communication and decision making. All of these factors may play a part in voting decisions as well and therefore deserve consideration in that important context.

Macro-Level Institutions and Policies

Much of the effects research has taken place at the micro-level investigating message effects on individuals. However, when one begins to talk about communication effects on elites, one enters the outskirts of the macro-level effects arena. Macro-level studies look beyond individuals to the impact of messages on political processes and situations. In these studies, macro-level phenomena are often attributed to message effects without empirical testing which would be impossible in many situations.

Once more, election research predominates. Scholars have noted that coverage of election campaigns by the mass media has changed the conduct of these campaigns. Campaign rallies, including the presidential nominating conventions, are staged as television spectacles and timed to reach large mass media audiences. The ability to present an attractive image on television and to handle reporters expertly has become an important skill that is likely to determine which candidates will enter a race and which will win (Arterton 1984). Research has revealed significant relations between news stories, including the publication of opinion poll data, and campaign contributions and election outcomes (Graber 1989; Joslyn 1984; Owen 1991). Favorable publicity attracts money and support, but may also lead to more intensive scrutiny when candidates attain frontrunner status. Scholars have also examined the political consequences of making New Hampshire and Iowa political hotspots that receive disproportionate amounts of media coverage because their contests occur first during the primary season (Orren and Polsby 1987). Such 'front-loading' of campaigns jeopardizes the chances of candidates who have not yet become familiar to voters. They may be forced out of the race prematurely. The waning influence of political parties in electoral contests has also been attributed in part to the rising influence of the mass media. "Would you ever vote for a person you had never seen on television?" is no longer a facetious question.

The impact of the relationship between journalists and the president and Congress has been studied. Apparently, it affects how these institutions function because politicians gear their activities to gaining good publicity and avoiding bad press. The fact that presidents are able to garner more media attention than Congress has strengthened the presidency at the expense of Congress. However, a central position in the media limelight can be a mixed blessing (Hess 1986, 1981; Robinson and Appel 1979; Cook 1990). Several authors have concentrated on the president's press relations, often with a specialized focus, such as television news or presidential news conferences (Grossman and Kumar 1981; Smith 1990; Smoller 1990). Others have highlighted the general impact of communication on the presidency (Edwards 1983; Kernell 1993; Maltese 1992). Presidency scholar Richard Neustadt's study of *Presidential Power* (1960) relates the president's effectiveness to access to information and control of information flows. He states categorically that "presidential power is the power to persuade."

The judiciary has received less attention from communications scholars than the presidency and Congress. Most of the studies of courts have focused on media coverage of the U.S. Supreme Court and selected Supreme Court decisions and on the social consequences of crime news coverage (Devol 1976; Graber 1980; Campbell 1990). Researchers have rarely examined the impact of reporting about the Supreme Court and its decisions on public knowledge and attitudes about the court and its work (Newland 1964). However, there have been attempts to investigate how newly emerging media, such as television, alter law because a transformed political culture changes the rules of the game (Katsh 1991).

While most research of the systems-level impact of political communication has focused on major political entities, such as nations, political parties or political leaders, there are important exceptions. They include research on media coverage of politically disadvantaged groups like racial and ethnic minorities, the handicapped, women, the elderly, or perpetrators and victims of crime (Cohen and Young 1973; Van Dijk 1988; Downing 1990). How these groups are depicted and perceived appears to have major psychological and political consequences for the perceivers and the perceived, including their respective self-images. The study of the publicized images of such groups deserves more attention because it may reveal serious political problems for which solutions are possible.

In the past, communication by, between, and inside public agencies has rarely been considered despite a burgeoning literature on organizational communication in the private sector. Even studies that deal with the problems of individual public agencies rarely consider communication problems despite their frequency and severity (Graber 1992b). As mentioned, the public relations area is a notable exception, including lobbying messages and public service campaigns (Crompton and Lamb 1986; Hess 1984).

The impact of publicized stories on the success or failure of particular policies has been documented infrequently. We know very little to what extent stories about environmental pollution or homeless people or life in Japan or the travels of foreign heads of state have affected public policies. For example, what role did the media play in the civil rights movement and in the integration of minorities into political life (Goldenberg 1975; Lipsky 1970; Gitlin 1980; Wolfsfeld 1991)? Has the rise of truly national media altered national politics? When a story about shenanigans in financial institutions is broadcast nationwide, how great a danger does it pose for the country's economic soundness? Can it, for instance, frighten bank customers and thereby produce a massive withdrawal of funds that further weakens shaky financial institutions?

There is much political folklore about such matters, but it remains to be substantiated. The study of the Watergate incident by Kurt and Gladys Lang (1983) is an example of the comprehensive analysis that needs to be done. The study reported the interplay of the president, Congress, and the news media during the course of the incident. Other examples are Barbara Nelson's (1984) comprehensive analysis of agenda setting for the child abuse issue and Martin Linsky's (1986) research of the multiple interacting factors, including media coverage, that affect the activities of public agencies.

The impact of mass media messages on foreign policy has been scrutinized more extensively and from a variety of vantage points. Studies of the impact of media coverage on the course and conduct of foreign affairs have been most common (Cohen 1963; Braestrup 1983; Hallin 1989; Berry 1990). Conclusions, often based on case studies, range from viewing the media as government's full partner or rival to assigning media messages a minor supportive or oppositional role. A few scholars have interviewed foreign policy officials for their assessments of media impact (O'Heffernan 1991). Others have studied presidential use of news media to promote the president's foreign policy or the impact of newspaper coverage on public perceptions of foreign affairs. When these events occur in remote, exotic locations, media impact is likely to be profound (Kern et al. 1983; Welch 1972).

In the late 1950s and early 1960s, several scholars toyed with the idea of using media messages to control international conflict. Karl Deutsch suggested that it might be possible to establish official media monitoring enterprises to give early warnings of mounting tensions. Preventive steps might then be taken (Deutsch et al. 1957, 201-202). "It should be possible to say whether the amount of attention given to a specific conflict area or to the image of a particular 'enemy' country is reaching the danger point, in the sense that continuing hostile attention in the mass media may harden public opinion to such a degree as eventually to destroy the freedom of choice of the national government concerned." Charles Osgood explored the possibility of using media strategically to reduce world tensions in *An Alternative to War and Surrender* (1962). Osgood suggested that his GRIT plan (*Graduated Reciprocation In Tension*-reduction), would reduce international tensions. Since tensions are endemic in international affairs, the need for tension reduction exists always, even when no major wars loom. Consequently, a Center for War, Peace, and the News Media, housed at New York University, specializes in this research area. It has issued numerous publications, including bibliographies (Dorman et al. 1988; Manoff et al. 1988). The possibilities of tension and violence reduction through control of mass media messages have also been raised in domestic policy contexts (Wolfsfeld 1984; Tichenor et al. 1980).

Maintaining Democracy

Do media help or hinder democratic politics by educating citizens and alerting them to governmental misbehavior? This has been an important concern since Thomas Jefferson argued that media were essential for maintaining democracy. Little has been done to put his theories to empirical tests. The role of mass media messages in calling attention to governmental misbehavior and major policy failures has received ample scrutiny since the days of muckraking in the Progressive Era, but other aspects of the question have been neglected (Protess et al. 1991; Lang and Lang 1983; Sabato 1991).

Media have fulfilled their watchdog role, but not with great distinction (Entman 1989; Bennett 1988, 1992). Sometimes, they simply serve as transmission channels for messages created and shaped by public and private sources. At other times, the media's main contribution lies in alerting important audiences. However, there are a number of well publicized instances where media institutions became more entrepreneurial and engaged in investigative journalism, often followed by government remedial action (Protess et al. 1991). Though these ventures have been helpful, they are relatively scarce, unsystematic attempts, guided and limited primarily by the desire to produce good stories.

Few studies have examined media impact on democratic institutions in general. Many of these have suggested that media, as currently operating in the United States, may be bad for a healthy democracy. Media have been accused of making audiences cynical about government by constantly stressing its shortcomings (Robinson 1976). They have been charged with trivializing and slanting politics, undermining political learning, and making citizens apathetic, disinterested, and unduly compliant (Manheim 1991; Bennett 1988; Entman 1989). Jeffrey Tulis (1987) and others have documented that presidential rhetoric has deteriorated because presidents try to deliver messages in ever briefer, catchy soundbites (Hallin 1990; Hinckley 1990). Others contend that the need to attract media attention has led politicians of all stripes to focus on trivial, catchy matters at the expense of serious issues. "Show horses" win elections, while "work horses" are abandoned by their constituents. Therefore the quality of political life has been steadily deteriorating (Cook 1990).

Though media coverage may be deleterious to the nation's political health, lack of coverage can also be harmful. The Kerner commission report in 1968, for example, condemned the media for insufficient attention to the problems of black citizens. It blamed the riots of the 1960s on flaws in the media (National Advisory Commission on Civil Disorders 1968). Similarly, a presidential commission that investigated the nuclear mishap at Three Mile Island charged that inadequate media coverage worsened the impact of the problem (President's Commission 1979).

As mentioned, several political scientists have explored the possibility of using the news media to spur political development, based on research showing substantial correlations between mass media growth and economic growth in developing countries. Although their hopes were disappointed and most lost interest in these investigations, public optimism has persisted about the power of mass media to provide the knowledge base on which modernization and democratic governance must rest. In the wake of the restructuring of Communist nations in Eastern Europe and Asia, questions of the role that the media will and should play in that process have come to the fore with renewed vigor. Questions relate to the nature of media impact, and the kinds of media organizations most conducive to democratization objectives. For example, it is important to know what part media messages played when Eastern Europe's Communist governments collapsed in domino fashion in the 1990s (Dennis et al. 1990).

More generally, how does the nature of governmental structures and policies influence the shaping of news? Although such questions fall squarely within the purview of traditional political science, the answers remain a matter of much conjecture and insufficient proof (Pool 1983; Abramson et al. 1988). In the U.S. context, the neglect is partly due to the extraordinary difficulty of designing and executing such studies. Another factor is the misconception that the reciprocal influences of media and government are best studied abroad, especially in countries with authoritarian governments, because a constitutional wall separates American media from government control (Fagen 1969; Liu 1971; Mickiewicz 1988).

Most studies of governmental mechanisms for regulating mass media institutions in the United States have been done by historians, communication scholars and lawyers. There is general agreement that all governments constrain the freedom of expression to some degree, and that some limits are needed and must be enforced by the state because self-controls are not effective enough over the long run. But it is disputed where the limits lie and where they should lie. The impact of constitutional provisions and laws like the First Amendment or the British Official Secrets Act on each nation's political life remains ill-defined (Lichtenberg 1991). We do not know how much of the impact is related to each particular political culture and how much could be transplanted into other political cultures. Much has been said and written on that score, but more often in the popular rather than the scholarly literature. Aside from law books and law reviews, the literature on First Amendment rights and other laws related to political

communication, even in the United States, remains sparse.

Among the few political science studies that deal with media policy making in a U.S. setting, Krasnow, Longley, and Terry's *The Politics of Broadcast Regulation* (1982) provides a sophisticated mix of theory, description, and analysis. Neuman, McKnight and Solomon (n.d.) discuss policy needs and the political obstacles to policy advances. Many more such studies are needed to cover the broad spectrum of laws that directly or indirectly affect the interrelation of media institutions with other political and economic institutions. They are particularly essential now to guide policies to cope with the revolutionary changes in information transmission technologies and to assist the nations that are moving from totalitarianism to more open systems. In recognition of such needs, the Congressional Office of Technology Assessment (OTA) and the National Telecommunication and Information Administration (NTIA) have commissioned and published several studies to guide public officials in making communication policies (NTIA 1988, 1990; OTA 1986, 1987, 1988, 1990).

Conclusions

What overall assessments can we make about the state of the subfield of political communication? Looking back at the intellectual journey that we have completed, what features stand out? Obviously, the field is broad and scholars have tried to do it justice by researching many diverse areas. It is equally obvious that the breadth of the field has left much terrain unexplored or insufficiently explored. There have been numerous tentative probes into some areas, such as media use for political development, which were later abandoned. Not everyone is pleased about the breadth of development. What some welcome as diversification, others see as premature fragmentation of the field. They point out that the depth of research individually and collectively, and even data collection, has suffered because researchers are dispersed. As is often true of newly active research areas, the soundness of evidence leaves something to be desired. Current scholarship is better in description of messages -- what they are and who communicated with whom -- than in explaining the reasons for these messages and their effects. But even when it comes to descriptions, our collective ignorance remains enormous.

Election communication is the only area where description is at least satisfactory and where major progress has been made in theories and analyses. Even there, much remains to be done. But the heavy focus on election communication and, to a certain extent, on mass media messages, is the reason why scholars have been spread very thin in research of other aspects of this broad subdiscipline. What is needed is more tillers in the vineyard. This should not be an unsurmountable obstacle since the concerns of political communication scholars are central to the concerns of scholars in many other subfields of political science and its sister disciplines. If current trends of subfield boundary jumping continue and even accelerate, the outlook seems bright for substantial progress in this burgeoning subfield.

Bibliography

Abramson, Jeffrey B., F. Christopher Arterton, and Gary R. Orren. 1988. *The Electronic Commonwealth: The Impact of New Media Technologies on Democratic Politics*. New York: Basic Books.

Abramson, Paul R., John H. Aldrich, and David W. Rohde. 1990. *Change and Continuity in the 1988 Elections*. Washington, DC: Congressional Quarterly Press.

Adams, William C., ed. 1981. *Television Coverage of the Middle East*. Norwood, NJ: Ablex.

Adams, William C., ed. 1982. *Television Coverage of International Affairs*. Norwood, NJ: Ablex.

Adams, William C., ed. 1983. *Television Coverage of the 1980 Presidential Campaign*. Norwood, NJ: Ablex.

Alali, A. Odasuo, and Kenoye Kelvin Elke, eds. 1991. *Media Coverage of Terrorism: Methods of Diffusion*. Newbury Park, CA: Sage.

Allison, Graham. 1971. *Essence of Decision: Explaining the Cuban Missile Crisis*. Boston: Little, Brown.

Almond, Gabriel A., and James S. Coleman, eds. 1960. *The Politics of Developing Areas*. Princeton: Princeton University Press.

Almond, Gabriel A., and G. Bingham Powell Jr. 1966. *Comparative Politics: A Developmental Approach*. Boston: Little Brown.

Anderson, John R. 1983. *The Architecture of Cognition*. Cambridge: Harvard University Press.

Ansolabehere, Stephen, Roy L. Behr, and Shanto Iyengar. 1991. "Mass Media and Elections: An Overview." *American Politics Quarterly* 19:109-139.

Aristotle. 335-322 B.C. *Rhetoric*.

Arterton, F. Christopher. 1978. "Campaign Organizations Confront the Media-Political Environment." In *Race for the Presidency: The Media and the Nominating Process*, ed. James D. Barber. Englewood Cliffs, NJ: Prentice-Hall.

Arterton, F. Christopher. 1984. *Media Politics: The News Strategies of Presidential Campaigns*. Lexington, MA: D.C. Heath.

Arterton, F. Christopher. 1987. *Teledemocracy: Can Technology Protect Democracy?* Beverly Hills, CA: Sage.

Arterton, F. Christopher. 1992. "The Persuasive Art in Politics." In *Under the Watchful Eye: Managing Presidential Campaigns in the Television Era*, ed. Mathew D. McCubbins. Washington, DC: CQ Press.

Ashford, Adam. 1991. *The Politics of Official Discourse in Twentieth-Century South Africa*. New York: Oxford University Press.

Axelrod, Robert. 1976. *Structure of Decision: The Cognitive Maps of Political Elites*. Princeton, NJ: Princeton University Press.

Bagdikian, Ben H. 1990. *The Media Monopoly*. Boston: Beacon Press.

Bahry, Donna, and Brian Silver. 1990. "Soviet Citizen Participation on the Eve of Democratization." *American Political Science Review* 84:821-847.

Barber, Susanna. 1987. *News Cameras in the Courtroom: A Free Press-Fair Trial Debate*. Norwood, NJ: Ablex.

Barner-Barry, Carol, and Robert Rosenwein. 1985. *Psychological Perspectives on Politics*. Englewood Cliffs, NJ: Prentice Hall.

Bartels, Larry M. 1988. *Presidential Primaries and the Dynamics of Public Choice*. Princeton, NJ: Princeton University Press.

Bendor, Jonathan, Serge Taylor, and Roland Van Gaalen. 1987. "Politicians, Bureaucrats, and Asymmetric Information." *American Journal of Political Science* 31: 4:796-828.

Beniger, James R. 1986. *The Control Revolution: Technological and Economic Origins of the Information Society*. Cambridge: Harvard University Press.

Bennett, W. Lance. 1988. *News: The Politics of Illusion*. 2nd ed. New York: Longman.

Bennett, W. Lance. 1990. "Toward a Theory of Press-State Relations in the United States." *Journal of Communication* 40:103-125.

Bennett, W. Lance. 1992. *The Governing Crisis: Media, Money, and Marketing in American Elections*. New York: St. Martin's Press.

Bennett, W. Lance, and Murray Edelman. 1985. "Toward a New Political Narrative." *Journal of Communication* 35:156-171.

Berelson, Bernard. 1948. "Communication and Public Opinion." In *Communications in Modern Society*, ed. Wilbur Schramm. Urbana: University of Illinois Press.

Berelson, Bernard, Paul Lazarsfeld, and William McPhee. 1954. *Voting: A Study of Opinion Formation in a Presidential Campaign*. Chicago: University of Chicago Press.

Berry, Nicholas O. 1990. *Foreign Policy and the Press: An Analysis of the New York Times' Coverage of U.S. Foreign Policy*. New York: Greenwood.

Best, James J. 1986. "Who Talked to the President When? A Study of Lyndon B. Johnson." *Political Science Quarterly* 103:531-545.

Blumler, Jay G., and Michael Gurevitch. 1988. "The Cross-National Perspective." In *Social Conflicts and Television News: A Cross-National Study of Presentation and Perception*, eds. Akiba Cohen, Hanna Adoni, and Charles R. Bantz. Newbury Park, CA: Sage.

Bollinger, Lee C. 1991. *Images of a Free Press*. Chicago: University of Chicago Press.

Boulding, Kenneth. 1956. *The Image: Knowledge in Life and Society*. Ann Arbor: University of Michigan Press.

Boynton, G. R. 1991. " When Senators and Publics Meet at the Senate Environmental Protection Subcommittee." *Discourse and Society* 2:131-155.

Boynton, G. R. and Milton H. Lodge. n.d. unpublished research.

Braestrup, Peter. 1983. *Big Story: How the American Press and Television Reported and Interpreted the Crisis of TET 1968 in Vietnam and Washington*. New Haven: Yale University Press.

Brown, Steven R. 1980. *Political Subjectivity: Applications of Q Methodology in Political Science*. New Haven: Yale University Press.

Burke, Kenneth. 1966. *Language as Symbolic Action*. Berkeley: University of California Press.

Campbell, Angus. 1966. *Elections and the Political Order*. New York: Wiley.

Campbell, Angus, Gerald Gurin, and Warren Miller. 1954. *The Voter Decides*. Evanston, IL: Row, Peterson.

Campbell, Angus, Philip E. Converse, Warren E. Miller, and Donald E. Stokes. 1960. *The American Voter*. New York: Wiley.

Campbell, Douglas S. 1990. *The Supreme Court and the Mass Media: Selected Cases, Summaries, and Analyses*. New York: Praeger.

Caputo, Richard K. 1988. *Management and Information Systems in Human Services*. New York: Haworth.

Casmir, Fred, and Nobleza Asuncion-Lande. 1989." Intercultural

Communication Revisited: Conceptualization, Paradigm Building, and Methodological Approaches." In *Communication Yearbook,* ed. James A. Anderson. Newbury Park, CA: Sage.

Cassirer, Ernst. 1946. *Language and Myth.* New York: Harper.

Cirino, Robert. 1974. *Power to Persuade: Mass Media and the News.* Toronto: Bantam Books.

Cohen, Akiba A., ed. 1989. "Future Directions in Television News Research." *American Behavioral Scientist* 33:135-268.

Cohen, Akiba A., Hanna Adoni, and Charles R. Bantz. 1990. *Social Conflict and Television News.* Newbury Park, CA: Sage.

Cohen, Bernard C. 1963. *The Press and Foreign Policy.* Princeton, NJ: Princeton University Press.

Cohen, Stanley, and Jock Young. 1973. *The Manufacture of News: Social Problems, Deviance, and the Mass Media.* London: Constable.

Conover, Pamela J. 1984. "How People Organize the Political World: A Schematic Model." *American Journal of Political Science* 28:95-126.

Conover, Pamela J., and Stanley Feldman. 1986. "The Role of Inference in the Perception of Political Candidates." In *Political Cognition,* ed. Richard R. Lau and David O. Sears. Hillsdale, NJ: Erlbaum.

Conover, Pamela J., and Stanley Feldman. 1989. "Candidate Perception in an Ambiguous World: Campaigns, Cues, and Inference Processes." *American Journal of Political Science* 33:912-40.

Cook, Timothy E. 1990. *Making Laws and Making News: Media Strategies in the U.S. House of Representatives.* Washington, DC: Brookings Institution.

Copeland, Gary A., and Karen Johnson-Cartee. 1990. "Southerners' Acceptance of Negative Political Advertising and Political Efficacy and Activity Levels." *Southeastern Political Review* 18:415-427.

Corbett, Michael. 1991. *American Public Opinion: Trends, Processes, and Patterns.* New York: Longman.

Corcoran, Paul E. 1990."Language and Politics." In *New Directions in Political Communication,* eds. David L. Swanson and Dan Nimmo. Newbury Park, CA: Sage.

Corsi, Jerome R. 1981. "Terrorism as a Desperate Game: Fear, Bargaining, and Communication in the Terrorist Event." *Journal of Conflict Resolution* 25:47-85.

Crompton, John L. and Charles W. Lamb, Jr. 1986. *Marketing Government and Social Services.* New York: Wiley.

Davies, James C. 1977. "Political Socialization: From Womb to Childhood." In *Handbook of Political Socialization.* ed. Stanley A. Renshon. New York: Free Press.

Davis, Richard. 1992. *The Press and American Politics: The New Mediator.* New York: Longman.

Dawson, Richard E., Kenneth Prewitt, and Karen S. Dawson. 1977. *Political Socialization.* Boston: Little Brown.

Day, Louis A. 1990. *Ethics in Media Communications: Cases and Controversies.* Belmont, CA: Wadsworth.

DeMause, Lloyd. 1986. "Why Did Reagan Do It?" *Journal of Psychohistory* 14:107-118.

Dennis, Everette E., George Gerbner, and Yassen N. Zassoursky, eds. 1991. *Beyond the Cold War: Soviet and American Media Images.* Newbury Park, CA: Sage.

Denton, Robert E. Jr., ed. 1991. *Ethical Dimensions of Political Communication.* New York: Praeger.

Denton, Robert E. Jr., and Dan F. Hahn. 1986. *Presidential Communication.* New York: Praeger.

Deutsch, Karl W. 1953. *Nationalism and Social Communication.* Cambridge: Massachusetts Institute of Technology Press.

Deutsch, Karl W. 1967. *The Nerves of Government: Models of Political Communication and Control.* New York: Free Press.

Deutsch, Karl W., et al. 1957. *Political Community and the North Atlantic Area.* Princeton, NJ: Princeton University Press.

Deutsch, Karl W., and Richard L. Merritt. 1965. "Effects of Events on National and International Images." In *International Behavior,* ed. Herbert Kelman. New York: Holt, Rinehart and Winston.

Devlin, L. Patrick, 1989. "Contrasts in Presidential Campaign Commercials of 1988." *American Behvioral Scientist* 33:389-414.

Devol, Kenneth S. 1976. *Mass Media and the Supreme Court.* New York: Hastings House.

Diamond, Edwin, and Stephen Bates. 1988. *The Spot.* Cambridge, MA: MIT Press.

Dorman, William, Robert Karl Manoff, and Jennifer Weeks. 1988. *American Press Coverage of U.S.-Soviet Relations, the Soviet Union, Nuclear Weapons, Arms Control, and National Security: A Bibliography.* New York: Center for War, Peace, and the News Media, New York University.

Downing, John D. H. 1990. "U.S. Media Discourse on South Africa: The Development of a Situation Model." *Discourse and Society* 1:39-60.

Drechsel, Robert E. 1983. *News Making in the Trial Courts.* New York: Longman.

Druckman, Daniel, and Richard Harris. 1990. "Alternative Models of Responsiveness in International Negotiations." *Journal of Conflict Resolution* 34:234-251.

Easton, David. 1965. *A Framework for Political Analysis.* New York: Prentice-Hall.

Edelman, Murray. 1964. *The Symbolic Uses of Politics.* Urbana: University of Illinois Press.

Edelman, Murray. 1971. *Politics as Symbolic Action.* Chicago: Markham.

Edelman, Murray, 1988. *Constructing the Political Spectacle.* Chicago: University of Chicago Press.

Edwards, George C. III. 1983. *The Public Presidency.* New York: St. Martin's Press.

Entman, Robert M. 1989. *Democracy without Citizens: Media and the Decay of American Politics.* New York: Oxford University Press.

Entman, Robert M. 1989. "How the Media Affect What People Think: An Information Processing Approach." *Journal of Politics* 51:347-370.

Entman, Robert M. 1992. "Blacks in the News: Television, Modern Racism, and Cultural Change." *Journalism Quarterly* 69:341-361.

Erber, Ralph, and Richard R. Lau. 1990. "Political Cynicism Revisited: An Information-Processing Reconciliation of Policy-Based and Incumbency-Based Interpretations of Changes in Trust in Government." *American Journal of Political Science* 34:236-253.

Erbring, Lutz, Edie N. Goldenberg, and Arthur H. Miller. 1980. "Front-Page News and Real-World Cues: A New Look at Agenda-Setting by the Media." *American Journal of Political Science* 24:16-49.

Ericsson, Karl A., and Herbert A. Simon. 1984. *Protocol Analysis: Verbal Reports as Data.* Cambridge: Massachusetts Institute of Technology.

Etheredge, Lloyd. 1985. *Can Governments Learn?* New York: Pergamon.

Fagen, Richard R. 1966. *Politics and Communication: An Analytic Study.* Boston: Little Brown.

Fagen, Richard R. 1969. *The Transformation of Political Culture in Cuba.* Stanford, CA: Stanford University Press.

Fan, David. 1988. *Predictions of Public Opinion from the Mass Media.* New York: Greenwood.

Farnham, Barbara. 1990. "Political Cognition and Decision-Making." *Political Psychology* 11:83-111.

Feldman, Martha S. 1989. *Order without Design: Information Production and Policy Making.* Stanford, CA: Stanford University Press.

Feldman, Stanley, and Lee Sigelman. 1985. "The Political Impact of Prime-Time Television: 'The Day After.'" *Journal of Politics* 47:556-578.

Ferejohn, John A., and James H. Kuklinski, eds. 1990. *Information and Democratic Processes.* Urbana: University of Illinois Press.

Ferguson, Sherry Devereaux, and Stewart Ferguson. 1988. "The Physical Environment and Communication." In *Organizational Communications* 2nd ed., ed. Sherry Ferguson and Stewart Ferguson. New Brunswick, NJ: Transaction.

Festinger, Leon. 1957. *A Theory of Cognitive Dissonance.* Evanston, IL: Row Peterson.

Fiske, Susan, and Donald Kinder. 1981. "Involvement, Expertise, and Schema Use: Evidence from Political Cognition." In *Personality, Cognition, and Social Interaction,* ed. Nancy Cantor and John F. Kihlstrom. Hillsdale, NJ: Erlbaum.

Foote, Joe S. 1990. *Television Access and Political Power: The Networks, the Presidency, and the "Loyal Opposition."* New York: Praeger.

Francois, William E. 1990. *Mass Media Law and Regulation.* 5th ed. Ames: Iowa State University Press.

Frantzich, Stephen. 1982. *Computers in Congress: The Politics of Information.* Beverly Hills, CA: Sage.

Friedenberg, Robert V., ed. 1990. *Rhetorical Studies of National Political Debates, 1960-88.* New York: Praeger.

Fulbright, J. William. 1971. *The Pentagon Propaganda Machine.* New York: Vintage Books.

Gamson, William. 1992. *Talking Politics.* New York: Cambridge University Press.

Gamson, William A., and Andre Modigliani. 1989. "Media Discourse and Public Opinion on Nuclear Power: A Constructionist Approach." *American Journal of Sociology* 95:1-37.

Gandy, Oscar H., Jr. 1989. "The Surveillance Society: Information Technology and Bureaucratic Social Control." *Journal of Communication* 39:61-76.

Garramone, Gina M., Charles K. Atkin, Bruce E. Pinkleton, and Richard T. Cole. 1990. "Effects of Negative Political Advertising on the Political Process." *Journal of Broadcasting and Electronic Media* 34:299-311.

George, Alexander L. 1959. *Propaganda Analysis.* Evanston, IL: Row, Peterson.

George, Alexander L. 1980. *Presidential Decisionmaking in Foreign Policy: The Effective Use of Information and Advice.* Boulder, CO: Westview.

Gerbner, George, Hamid Mowlana, and Kaarle Nordenstreng, eds. 1991. *The Global Media Debate: Its Rise, Fall, and Renewal.* Norwood, NJ: Ablex.

Ginsberg, Benjamin. 1986. *The Captive Public: How Mass Opinion Promotes State Power.* New York: Basic Books.

Gitlin, Todd. 1980. *The Whole World Is Watching.* Berkeley: University of California Press.

Gitlin, Todd. 1987. "Prime Time Ideology: The Hegemonic Process in Television Entertainment." In *Television: The Critical View.* 4th ed., ed. H. Newcomb. New York: Oxford University Press.

Glasgow University Media Group. 1976. *Bad News.* London: Routledge and Kagan Paul.

Glasgow University Media Group. 1980. *More Bad News.* London: Routledge and Kagan Paul.

Goldenberg, Edie. 1975. *Making the Papers.* Lexington, MA: D.C. Heath.

Goldenberg, Edie, and Michael W. Traugott. 1984. *Campaigning for Congress.* Washington, DC: Congressional Quarterly Press.

Goldenberg, Edie, and Michael W. Traugott, eds. 1987. "Mass Media in Legislative Campaigns." *Legislative Studies Quarterly* 12:317-339.

Goodsell, Charles T. 1981. "Looking Once Again at Human Service Bureaucracy." *Journal of Politics* 43:763-778.

Goodsell, Charles T. 1981. *The Public Encounter: Where State and Citizen Meet.* Bloomington: Indiana University Press.

Goodsell, Charles T. 1988. *The Social Meaning of Civic Space.* Lawrence: University Press of Kansas.

Goodsell, Charles T., Raymond E. Austin, Karen L. Hedblom, and Clarence C. Rose. 1981. "Bureaucracy Expresses Itself: How State Documents Address the Public." *Social Science Quarterly* 62:576-591.

Gordon, Andrew C., and John P. Heinz, eds. 1979. *Public Access to Information.* New Brunswick, NJ: Transaction.

Graber, Doris A. 1976. *Verbal Behavior and Politics.* Urbana: University of Illinois Press.

Graber, Doris A. 1980. *Crime News and the Public.* New York: Praeger.

Graber, Doris A., ed. 1982. *The President and the Public.* Philadelphia: Institute for the Study of Human Issues.

Graber, Doris A. 1983. "Hoopla and Horse-Race in 1980 Campaign Coverage: A Closer Look." In *Massenmedien und Wahlen,* ed. Winfried Schulz and Klaus Schönbach. München: Ölschläger.

Graber, Doris A. 1986. "Mass Media and Political Images in Elections." In *Research in Micropolitics,* Vol. 1, ed. Samuel L. Long. New York: JAI Press.

Graber, Doris A. 1987a. "Kind Pictures and Harsh Words: How Television Presents the Candidates." In *Elections in America,* ed. Kay Lehman Schlozman. Boston: Allen & Unwin.

Graber, Doris A. 1987b. "Framing Election News Broadcasts: News Context and Its Impact on the 1984 Presidential Election." *Social Science Quarterly* 68:552-568.

Graber, Doris A. 1988. *Processing the News: How People Tame the Information Tide.* 2d ed. New York: Longman.

Graber, Doris A. 1990. "Seeing Is Remembering: How Visuals Contribute to Learning from Television News." *Journal of Communication* 40:134-155.

Graber, Doris A. 1992a. *Mass Media and American Politics.* 4th ed. Washington, DC: Congressional Quarterly Press.

Graber, Doris A. 1992b. *Public Sector Communication: How Organizations Manage Information.* Washington, DC: Congressional Quarterly Press.

Graber, Doris A. 1993. *Mass Media and American Politics.* 4th ed. Washington, DC: CQ Press.

Gronbeck, Bruce E. 1989. "Mythic Portraiture in the 1988 Iowa Presidential Caucus Bio-Ads." *American Behavioral Scientist* 33:351-364.

Grossman, Michael B., and Martha J. Kumar. 1981. *Portraying the Presidents: The White House and the News Media.* Baltimore: The Johns Hopkins University Press.

Gunter, Barrie. 1987. *Poor Reception: Misunderstanding and Forgetting Broadcast News.* Hillsdale, NJ: Erlbaum.

Gurevitch, Michael, Tony Bennett, James Curran, and Janet Woollacott, eds. 1982. *Culture, Society, and the Media.* London: Methuen.

Gurevitch, Michael, and Jay G. Blumler. 1990. "Comparative Research: The Extending Frontier." In *New Directions in Political Communication,* ed. David L. Swanson and Dan Nimmo. Newbury Park, CA: Sage.

Habermas, Jurgen. 1970. *Towards a Rational Society: Student Protest, Science, and Politics.* Boston: Beacon.

Hall, Stuart. 1989. "Ideology and Communication Theory." In *Rethinking Communication: Vol. 1. Paradigm Issues,* ed.

Brenda Dervin, Lawrence Grossberg, Barbara J. O'Keefe, and Ellen Wartella. Newbury Park, CA: Sage.

Hallin, Daniel C. 1989. *The "Uncensored War."* Los Angeles: University of California Press.

Hallin, Dan. 1990. "Sound Bite News." In *Blurring the Lines,* ed. Gary Orren. New York: The Free Press.

Hallin, Dan, and Paolo Mancini. 1984. "Speaking of the President: Political Structure and Representational Form in U.S. and Italian Television News." *Theory and Society* 13:829-850.

Hamill, Ruth, and Milton Lodge. 1986. "Cognitive Consequences of Political Sophistication." In *Political Cognition,* ed. Richard R. Lau and David O. Sears. Hillsdale, NJ: Erlbaum.

Hart, Roderick P. 1984. *Verbal Style and the Presidency: A Computer-Based Analysis.* Orlando: Academic Press.

Heclo, Hugh, 1977. *A Government of Strangers.* Washington, DC: Brookings.

Helm, Lewis M., Ray Eldon Hiebert, Michael R. Naver, and Kenneth Rabin. 1981. *Informing the People.* New York: Longman.

Heritage, John, and David Greatbatch. 1986. "Generating Applause: A Study of Rhetoric and Response at Party Political Conferences." *American Journal of Sociology* 92:110-157.

Herman, Edward S., and Noam Chomsky. 1988. *Manufacturing Consent: The Political Economy of the News Media.* New York: Pantheon Books.

Hershey, Marjorie Randon. 1984. *Running for Office: The Political Education of Campaigners.* Chatham, NJ: Chatham House Publishers.

Hess, Stephen. 1981. *The Washington Reporters.* Washington, DC: Brookings.

Hess, Stephen. 1984. *The Government/Press Connection.* Washington, DC: Brookings.

Hess, Stephen. 1986. *The Ultimate Insiders: U.S. Senators in the National Media.* Washington, DC: Brookings.

Hess, Stephen. 1988. *The Presidential Campaign.* Washington, DC: Brookings.

Hess, Stephen. 1991. *Live From Capitol Hill: Studies of Congress and the Media.* Washington, DC: Brookings.

Hinckley, Barbara. 1990. *The Symbolic Presidency: How Presidents Portray Themselves.* New York: Routledge.

Hofstetter, C. Richard. 1976. *Bias in the News.* Columbus: Ohio State University Press.

Holsti, Ole. 1969. *Content Analysis for the Social Sciences and Humanities.* Reading, MA: Addison-Wesley.

Hoxie, Gordon, ed. 1986. "The Media and the Presidency." *Presidential Studies Quarterly* 16:11-116.

Huckfeldt, Robert, and John Sprague. 1987. "Networks in Context: The Social Flow of Political Information." *American Political Science Review* 81:1197-1216.

Ikle, Fred Charles. 1964. *How Nations Negotiate.* New York: Praeger.

Inoue, Kyoko. 1991. *MacArthur's Japanese Constitution: A Linguistic and Cultural Study of Its Making.* Chicago: University of Chicago Press.

Iyengar, Shanto. 1991. *Is Anyone Responsible? How Television Frames Political Issues.* Chicago: University of Chicago Press.

Iyengar, Shanto, and Donald R. Kinder. 1987. *News That Matters: Television and American Opinion.* Chicago: University of Chicago Press.

Jamieson, Kathleen Hall. 1990. *Eloquence in an Electronic Age: The Transformation of Political Speechmaking.* New York: Oxford University Press.

Jamieson, Kathleen Hall. 1992. *Packaging the Presidency: A History and Criticism of Presidential Campaign Advertising.* 2d ed. New York: Oxford University Press.

Jamieson, Kathleen Hall, and David S. Birdsell. 1990. *Presidential Debates: The Challenge of Creating an Informed Electorate.* New York: Oxford University Press.

Janis, Irving L. 1989. *Crucial Decisions: Leadership in Policymaking and Crisis Management.* New York: Free Press.

Janis, Irving L., and Leon Mann. 1977. *Decision Making: A Psychological Analysis of Conflict, Choice, and Commitment.* New York: Free Press.

Janowitz, Morris. 1980. *The Community Press in an Urban Setting: The Social Elements of Urbanism.* 3d ed. Chicago: University of Chicago Press.

Jennings, M. Kent, and Richard Niemi. 1981. *Generations and Politics: A Panel of Young Adults and Their Parents.* Princeton, NJ: Princeton University Press.

Jervis, Robert. 1970. *The Logic of Images in International Relations.* Princeton, NJ: Princeton University Press.

Jervis, Robert, Richard Ned Lebow, and Janice Gross Stein. 1985. *Psychology and Deterrence.* Baltimore: Johns Hopkins University Press.

Joslyn, Richard A. 1984. *Mass Media and Elections.* Reading, MA: Addison-Wesley.

Just, Marion, Ann Crigler, and Lori Wallach. 1990. "Thirty Seconds or Thirty Minutes: What Viewers Learn from Spot Advertisements and Candidate Debates." *Journal of Communication* 40:120-133.

Kaid, Lynda Lee, and J. Foote. 1985. "How Network Television Coverage of the President and Congress Compare." *Journalism Quarterly* 62:59-65.

Kaid, Lynda Lee, Dan Nimmo, and Keith R. Sanders, eds. 1986. *New Perspectives on Political Advertising.* Beverly Hills, CA: Sage.

Katsh, M. Ethan. 1991. *The Electronic Media and the Transformation of Law.* New York: Oxford University Press.

Kaufman, Herbert. 1967. *The Forest Ranger: A Study in Administrative Behavior.* Baltimore: Johns Hopkins Press.

Kaufman, Herbert. 1977. *Red Tape: Its Origins, Uses, and Abuses.* Washington, DC: Brookings.

Kaufman, Herbert. 1981. *The Administrative Behavior of Federal Bureau Chiefs.* Washington, DC: Brookings.

Keeter, Scott. 1987. "The Illusion of Intimacy: Television and the Role of Candidate Personal Qualities in Voter Choice." *Public Opinion Quarterly* 51:344-358.

Keeter, Scott, and Cliff Zukin. 1983. *Uninformed Choice: The Failure of the New Presidential Nominating System.* New York: Praeger.

Kellner, Douglas. 1990. *Television and the Crisis of Democracy.* Boulder, CO: Westview.

Kennedy, Robert F. 1969. *Thirteen Days.* New York: Norton.

Kepplinger, Hans Mathias. 1990. "The Impact of Presentation Techniques: Theoretical Aspects and Empirical Findings." In *The Psychological and Semiotic Processing of Televised Political Advertising,* ed. Franc Biocca. Hillsdale, NJ: Erlbaum.

Kern, Montague. 1989. *30-Second Politics: Political Advertising in the Eighties.* New York: Praeger.

Kern, Montague, Patricia W. Levering, and Ralph B. Levering. 1983. *The Kennedy Crises: The Press, the Presidency, and Foreign Policy.* Chapel Hill: University of North Carolina Press.

Kernell, Samuel. 1993. *Going Public: New Strategies of Presidential Leadership.* 2nd ed. Washington, DC: Congressional Quarterly Press.

Kessel, John H. 1983. "The Structure of the Carter White House." *American Journal of Political Science* 27:431-463.

Kessel, John H. 1984. "The Structure of the Reagan White House." *American Journal of Political Science* 28:231-258.

Kessel, John H. 1988. *Presidential Campaign Politics: Coalition Strategies and Citizen Response.* 3d. ed. Homewood, IL: Dorsey Press.

Knoke, David, and James H. Kuklinski. 1987. *Network Analysis.* Beverly Hills, CA: Sage.

Korzenny, Felipe, and Stella Ting-Toomey. 1990. *Communicating for Peace: Diplomacy and Negotiation.* Newbury Park, CA: Sage.

Kosicki, Gerald M., and Jack M. McLeod. 1990. "Learning from Political News: Effects of Media Images and Information-Processing Strategies." In *Mass Communication and Political Information Processing,* ed. Sidney Kraus. Hillsdale, NJ: Erlbaum.

Krasnow, Erwin G., Lawrence D. Longley, and Herbert A. Terry. 1982. *The Politics of Broadcast Regulation,* 3d ed. New York: St. Martin's Press.

Kraus, Sidney. 1988. *Televised Presidential Debates and Public Policy.* Hillsdale, NJ: Erlbaum.

Kraus, Sidney, and Richard M. Perloff, eds. 1985. *Mass Media and Political Thought.* Beverly Hills, CA: Sage.

Kressel, Neil J. 1987. "Biased Judgments of Media Bias: A Case Study of the Arab-Israel Dispute." *Political Psychology* 8:211-226.

Krone, Kathleen J., Frederic M. Jablin, and Linda L. Putnam. 1987. "Communication Theory and Organizational Communication: Multiple Perspectives." In *Handbook of Organizational Communication,* ed. Frederic M. Jablin, Linda L. Putnam, Karlene H. Roberts, and Lyman W. Porter. Newbury Park, CA: Sage.

Krosnick, Jon A., and Donald R. Kinder. 1990. "Altering the Foundations of Popular Support for the President through Priming." *American Political Science Review* 84:497-512.

Kubey, Robert, and Mihaly Csikszentmihalyi. 1990. *Television and the Quality of Life: How Viewing Shapes Everyday Experience.* Hillsdale, NJ: Erlbaum.

Kuklinski, James H., Robert C. Luskin, and John Bolland. 1991. "Where Is the Schema? Going Beyond the 'S' Word in Political Psychology." *American Political Science Review* 85:1341-1356.

Lang, Gladys Engel, and Kurt Lang. 1983. *The Battle for Public Opinion: The President, the Press, and the Polls during Watergate.* New York: Columbia University Press.

Lang, Kurt, and Gladys Engel Lang. 1990. "Collective Memory and the News." In *Mass Communication and Political Information Processing,* ed. Sidney Kraus. Hillsdale, NJ: Erlbaum.

Langer, Susanne. 1951. *Philosophy in a New Key: A Study in the Sociology of Reason, Rite, and Art.* Cambridge: Harvard University Press.

Lanoue, David J., and Peter R. Schrott. 1991. *The Joint Press Conference: The History, Impact and Prospects of American Presidential Debates.* New York: Greenwood.

Lanzetta, John T., Denis G. Sullivan, Roger D. Masters, and Gregory J. McHugo. 1985. "Emotional and Cognitive Responses to Televised Images of Political Leaders. In *Mass Media and Political Thought,* ed. Sidney Kraus and Richard M. Perloff. Beverley Hills, CA: Sage.

Lasswell, Harold D. 1969. "The Structure and Function of Communication in Society." In *Mass Communications,* ed. Wilbur Schramm. Urbana: University of Illinois Press.

Lasswell, Harold D., Nathan Leites et al. 1965. *The Language of Politics: Studies in Quantitative Semantics.* Cambridge: Massachusetts Institute of Technology Press.

Lasswell, Harold D., Daniel Lerner, and Ithiel de Sola Pool. 1952. *The Comparative Study of Symbols.* Stanford: Stanford University Press.

Lasswell, Harold D., Daniel Lerner, and Hans Speier. 1980. *Propaganda and Communication in World History.* 3 vols. Hawaii: University of Hawaii Press.

Lau, Richard R. 1986. "Political Schemata, Candidate Evaluations, and Voting Behavior." In *Political Cognition,* ed. Richard R. Lau and David O. Sears. Hillsdale, NJ: Erlbaum.

Lau, Richard R., and David Sears, eds. 1986. *Political Cognition: The 19th Annual Symposium on Cognition.* Hillsdale, NJ: Erlbaum.

Laudon, Kenneth C. 1986. *Dossier Society: Value Choices in the Design of National Information Systems.* New York: Columbia University Press.

Lavrakas, Paul J., and Jack K. Holley, eds. 1991. *Polling and Presidential Election Coverage.* Newbury Park, CA: Sage.

Lawler, Peter, and Robert Schaefer. 1990. *American Political Rhetoric.* 2d. ed. Savage, MD: Rowman and Littlefield.

Lazarsfeld, Paul, Bernard Berelson, and Hazel Gaudet. 1944. *The People's Choice.* New York: Columbia University Press.

Lerner, Daniel. 1958. *The Passing of Traditional Society.* Glencoe, IL: The Free Press.

Levitin, Teresa E., and Warren E. Miller. 1979. "Ideological Interpretations of Presidential Elections." *American Political Science Review* 73:751-771.

Lichtenberg, Judith, ed. 1991. *Democracy and the Mass Media.* Cambridge: Cambridge University Press.

Lichter, S. Robert, Linda S. Lichter, and Stanley Rothman. 1991. *Watching America: What Television Tells Us about Our Lives.* New York: Prentice Hall.

Lichter, S. Robert, Stanley Rothman, and Linda S. Lichter. 1986. *The Media Elite.* New York: Adler and Adler.

Liebes, Tamar. 1992. "Our War/Their War: Comparing the Intifadeh and the Gulf War on U.S. and Israeli Television." *Critical Studies in Mass Communication* 9:44-55.

Lifton, Robert Jay. 1963. *Thought Reform and the Psychology of Totalism.* New York: Norton.

Linsky, Martin. 1986a. *Impact: How the Press Affects Federal Policymaking: Six Case Studies.* New York: Norton.

Linsky, Martin, Jonathan Moore, Wendy O'Donnell, and David Whitman. 1986. *How the Press Affects Federal Policy Making: Six Case Studies.* New York: Norton.

Lippmann, Walter. 1922. *Public Opinion.* New York: Macmillan.

Lipsky, Michael. 1970. *Protest in City Politics.* Chicago: Rand McNally.

Liu, Alan P. L. 1971. *Communications and National Integration in Communist China.* Berkeley: University of California Press.

Lodge, Milton, and Ruth Hamill. 1986. "A Partisan Schema for Political Information Processing." *American Political Science Review* 80:505-519.

Lodge, Milton, Kathleen M. McGraw, and Pamela J. Conover. 1991. "Where Is the Schema? Critiques." *American Political Science Review* 85:1358-1380.

Long, Norton. 1958. "The Local Community as an Ecology of Games." *American Journal of Sociology* 64:246-528.

Lukes, Igor. 1987. "Managing U.S.-Soviet Arms Control Initiatives: Do We Speak the Same Language?" *Comparative Strategy* 6:165-184.

Machiavelli, Niccolo. 1513. *The Prince.*

Maltese, John Anthony. 1992. *Spin Control: The White House Office of Communications and the Management of Presidential News.* Chapel Hill: University of North Carolina Press.

Mandelbaum, David, ed. 1962. *Culture, Language, and Personality: Selected Essays.* Berkeley: University of California Press.

Manheim, Jarol B. 1991. *All of the People, All the Time: Strategic Communication and American Politics.* Armonk, NY: M.E. Sharpe.

Manheim, Jarol B., and Robert B. Albritton. 1984. "Changing National Images: International Public Relations and Media Agenda-Setting." *American Political Science Review* 78:641-657.

Manoff, Robert Karl, and Gerd Ruge, eds. 1988. *Between the Summits: An International Conference on Media Coverage of Soviet-American Relations, Nuclear Issues, and Everyday Life.* New

York: Center for War, Peace, and the Media, New York University.

Masters, Roger D., and Denis G. Sullivan. 1989. "Nonverbal Displays amd Political Leadership in France." *Political Behavior* 11:121-153.

McCubbins, Mathew D. 1992. "Party Decline and Presidential Campaigns in the Television Age." In *Under the Watchful Eye: Managing Presidential Campaigns in the Television Era.* ed. Mathew McCubbins. Washington, DC: CQ Press.

McGraw, Kathleen, M. 1990. "Avoiding Blame: An Experimental Investigation of Political Excuses and Justifications." *British Journal of Political Science* 20:119-142.

McGraw, Kathleen M. 1991. "Managing Blame: An Experimental Test of the Effects of Political Accounts." *American Political Science Review* 85:1133-1157.

McGraw, Kathleen M., and Neil Pinney. 1990. "The Effects of General and Domain-specific Expertise on Political Memory and Judgment Processes." *Social Cognition* 8:9-30.

McGraw, Kathleen M., Neil Pinney, and David Neumann. 1991. "Memory for Political Actors: Contrasting the Use of Semantic and Evaluative Organizational Strategies." *Political Behavior* 13:165-189.

Meadow, Robert G., and Lee Sigelman. 1982. "Some Effects and Noneffects of Campaign Commercials: An Experimental Study." *Political Behavior* 4:163-175.

Mickelson, Sig. 1989. *From Whistle Stop to Sound Bite: Four Decades of Politics and Television.* New York: Praeger.

Mickiewicz, Ellen. 1988. *Split Signals: Television and Politics in the Soviet Union.* New York: Oxford University Press.

Miller, Arthur, Edie N. Goldenberg, and Lutz Erbring. 1979. "Type-set Politics: Impacts of Newspapers on Public Confidence." *American Political Science Review* 73:67-84.

Miller, Arthur A., Martin P. Wattenberg, and Oksana Malanchuk. 1985. "Cognitive Representations of Candidate Assessments." In *Political Communication Yearbook, 1984,* ed. Keith R. Sanders, Lynda Lee Kaid, and Dan Nimmo. Carbondale: Southern Illinois University Press.

Miller, Warren E., and Teresa E. Levitin. 1976. *Leadership and Change.* Cambridge: Winthrop.

Montgomery, Kathryn C. 1990. *Target: Prime Time: Advocacy Groups and the Struggle Over Entertainment Television.* New York: Oxford University Press.

Morley, David. 1990. "The Construction of Everyday Life: Political Communication and Domestic Media." In *New Directions in Political Communication: A Resource Book,* ed. David Swanson and Dan Nimmo. Newbury Park, CA: Sage.

Morello, John T. 1988. "Argument and Visual Structuring in the 1984 Mondale-Reagan Debates: The Medium's Influence on the Perception of Clash." *Western Journal of Speech Communication* 52:277-290.

Morrison, Donald, ed. 1988. *The Winning of the White House, 1988.* New York: Time Inc.

Mosher, Steven W. 1990. *China Misperceived: American Illusions and Chinese Reality.* New York: Basic Books.

Mumby, Dennis K. 1988. *Communication and Power in Organizations: Discourse, Ideology, and Domination.* Norwood, NJ: Ablex.

Nacos, Brigette Lebens. 1990. *The Press, Presidents, and Crises.* New York: Columbia University Press.

National Advisory Commission on Civil Disorders. 1968. *Report.* Washington, DC: Government Printing Office.

National Telecommunication and Information Administration. 1988. *Telecom 2000: Charting the Course for a New Century.* Washington, DC: NTIA.

National Telecommunication and Information Administration. 1990. *Comprehensive Study of Domestic Telecommunications Infrastructure.* Washington, DC: NTIA.

Nelson, Barbara. 1984. *Making an Issue of Child Abuse: Political Agenda Setting for Social Problems.* Chicago: University of Chicago Press.

Nesbit, Dorothy Davidson. 1988. *Videostyle in U.S. Senate Campaigns.* Knoxville: University of Tennessee Press.

Neuman, W. Russell. 1991. *The Future of the Mass Audience.* Cambridge, MA: Cambridge University Press.

Neuman, W. Russell, Marion Just, and Ann Crigler. 1992. *Common Knowledge: News and the Construction of Political Meaning.* Chicago: University of Chicago Press.

Neuman, W. Russell, Lee McKnight, and Richard Solomon. n.d. *The Gordian Knot: Political Gridlock and the Communication Revolution.* Cambridge: MIT Press.

Neustadt, Richard E. 1960. *Presidential Power.* New York: John Wiley.

Newland, Chester A. 1964. "Press Coverage of the United States Supreme Court." *Western Political Quarterly* 17:15-36.

Nie, Norman H., Sidney Verba, and John R. Petrocik. 1976. *The Changing American Voter.* Cambridge: Harvard University Press.

Nimmo, Dan P. 1964. *Newsgathering in Washington: A Study in Political Communication.* New York: Atherton Press.

Nimmo, Dan P. 1981. "Mass Communication and Politics." In *Handbook of Political Behavior,* vol. 4, ed. Samuel L. Long. New York: Plenum Press.

Nimmo, Dan P., and James E. Combs. 1990. *Mediated Political Realities.* 2d ed. New York: Longman.

Nimmo, Dan P., and Robert Savage. 1976. *Candidates and Their Images.* Pacific Palisades, CA: Goodyear.

Nimmo, Dan P., and Keith R. Sanders, eds. 1981. *Handbook of Political Communication.* Beverly Hills, CA: Sage.

Noelle-Neumann, Elisabeth. 1984. *The Spiral of Silence: Public Opinion and Our Social Skin.* Chicago: University of Chicago Press.

Office of Technology Assessment. 1986. *Federal Government Information Dissemination in an Electronic Age.* Washington, DC: Government Printing Office.

Office of Technology Assessment. 1987. *Defending Secrets. Sharing Data: New Locks and Keys for Electronic Information.* Washington DC: Government Printing Office.

Office of Technology Assessment. 1988. *Informing the Nation: Federal Information Dissemination in an Electronic Age.* Washington, DC: Government Printing Office.

Office of Technology Assessment. 1990. *Critical Connections: Communication for the Future.* Washington, DC: Government Printing Office.

O'Heffernan, Patrick. 1991. *Mass Media and American Foreign Policy.* Norwood, NJ: Ablex.

O'Keefe, Daniel J. 1990. *Persuasion: Theory and Research.* Newbury Park, CA: Sage.

Orren, Gary R., and Daniel Hallin. 1992. *Blurring the Lines: Elections and the Media in America.* New York: The Free Press.

Orren, Gary R., and Nelson W. Polsby, eds. 1987. *Media and Momentum: The New Hampshire Primary and Nomination Politics.* Chatham, NJ: Chatham House.

Osgood, Charles. 1962. *An Alternative to War or Surrender.* Urbana: University of Illinois Press.

Owen, Diana. 1991. *Media Messages in American Presidential Elections.* New York: Greenwood.

Page, Benjamin, and Robert Shapiro. 1991. *The Rational Public.* University of Chicago Press.

Page, Benjamin I., Robert Y. Shapiro, and Glenn R. Dempsey. 1987. "What Moves Public Opinion?" *American Political Science Review* 81:23-43.

Paglin, Max D., ed. 1990. *A Legislative History of the Communications*

Act of 1934. New York: Oxford University Press.

Paletz, David, and K. Kendall Guthrie. 1987. "The Three Faces of Ronald Reagan." Journal of Communication 37:7-23.

Parenti, Michael. 1986. Inventing Reality: The Politics of the Mass Media. 5th ed. New York: St. Martin's Press.

Parenti, Michael. 1992. Make-Believe Media: The Politics of Entertainment. New York: St. Martin's Press.

Patterson, Thomas E. 1980. The Mass Media Election: How Americans Choose Their President. New York: Praeger.

Patterson, Thomas E., and Robert D. McClure. 1976. The Unseeing Eye: The Myth of Television Power in National Elections. New York: Putnam.

Payne, J. Gregory, John Marlier, and Robert A. Baucus. 1989. "Polispots in the 1988 Presidential Primaries." American Behavioral Scientist 33:365-381.

Pfau, Michael, and Henry C. Kenski. 1990. Attack Politics: Strategy and Defense. New York: Praeger.

Pfau, Michael, and Michael Burgoon. 1988. "Inoculation in Political Campaign Communication." Human Communication Research 15:91-111.

Piazza, Thomas, Paul M. Sniderman, and Philip E. Tetlock. 1989. "Analysis of the Dynamics of Political Reasoning: A General-Purpose, Computer-Assisted Methodology." In Political Analysis, ed. James A. Stimson. Ann Arbor: University of Michigan Press.

Pool, Ithiel de Sola. 1952. The Prestige Papers: A Survey of Their Editorials. Stanford, CA: Stanford University Press.

Pool, Ithiel de Sola. 1959. Symbols of Internationalism. Stanford, CA: Stanford University Press.

Pool, Ithiel de Sola. 1963. "The Mass Media and Politics in the Modernization Process." In Communication and Political Development, ed. Lucian W. Pye. Princeton, NJ: Princeton University Press.

Pool, Ithiel de Sola. 1983. Technologies of Freedom. Cambridge: Harvard University Press.

Popkin, Samuel L. 1991. The Reasoning Voter: Communication and Persuasion in Presidential Campaigns. Chicago: University of Chicago Press.

Powe, Lucas A., Jr. 1991. The Fourth Estate and the Constitution: Freedom of the Press in America. Berkeley: University of California Press.

Powell, Lynda. 1989. "Analyzing Misinformation: Perception of Congressional Candidates' Ideologies." American Journal of Political Science 33:272-293.

Pratkanis, Anthony, and Elliot Aronson. 1992. Age of Propaganda: The Everyday Use and Abuse of Persuasion. New York: W.H. Freeman.

President's Commission on the Accident at Three Mile Island. 1979. Report of the Public's Right to Information Task Force. Washington, DC: Government Printing Office.

Protess, David L., Fay Lomax Cook, Jack C. Doppelt, James S. Ettema, Margaret T. Gordon, Donna R. Leff, and Peter Miller. 1991. The Journalism of Outrage: Investigative Reporting and Agenda Building in America. New York: Guilford Press.

Putnam, Linda L., and T. Jones. 1982. "Reciprocity in Negotiations: An Analysis of Bargaining Interactions." Communication Monographs 49:171-191.

Putnam, Linda L., and Michael E. Pacanowsky, eds. 1983. Communication and Organizations: An Interpretive Approach. Beverly Hills, CA: Sage.

Pye, Lucian W., ed. 1963. Communications and Political Development. Princeton, NJ: Princeton University Press.

Ranney, Austin. 1983. Channels of Power: The Impact of Television on American Politics. Washington, DC: American Enterprise Institute for Public Policy Research.

Rapport, David C., and Yonah Alexander, eds. 1989. The Morality of Terrorism: Religious and Secular Justifications. New York: Columbia University Press.

Ratzan, Scott C. 1989. "The Real Agenda Setters: Pollsters in the 1988 Presidential Campaign." American Behavioral Scientist 32:451-463.

Rice, Ronald E., and Charles K. Atkin, eds. 1989. Public Communication Campaigns, 2d ed. Newbury Park, CA: Sage.

Riker, William H. 1983. "Political Theory and the Art of Heresthetics." In Political Science: The State of the Discipline, ed. Ada W. Finifter. Washington, DC: American Political Science Association.

Roberts, Jonathan. 1988. Decision-Making during International Crises. New York: St. Martin's Press.

Robinson, John P., and Mark R. Levy. 1986. The Main Source: Learning from Television News. Beverly Hills, CA: Sage.

Robinson, Michael J. 1976. "Public Affairs Television and the Growth of Political Malaise." American Political Science Review 70:409-442.

Robinson, Michael J., and Margaret Sheehan. 1983. Over the Wire and on TV: CBS and UPI in Campaign '80. New York: Basic Books.

Robinson, Michael J., and K. R. Appel. 1979. "Network News Coverage of Congress." Political Science Quarterly 96:407-418.

Rosenberg, Shawn W. 1988. Reason, Ideology, and Politics. Princeton, NJ: Princeton University Press.

Rosenberg, Shawn W., and Patrick McCafferty. 1987. "The Image and the Vote: Manipulating Voters' Preferences." Public Opinion Quarterly 51:31-47.

Rosenberg, Shawn W., Lisa Bohan, Patrick McCafferty, and Kevin Harris. 1986. "The Image and the Vote: The Effect of Candidate Presentation on Voter Preference." American Journal of Political Science 30:108-127.

Rosengren, Keith E., Lawrence A. Wenner, and Philip Palmgreen, eds. 1985. Media Gratifications Research: Current Perspectives. Beverly Hills, CA: Sage.

Rothman, Stanley, ed. 1992. The Mass Media in Liberal Democratic Societies. New York: Paragon House.

Rozell, Mark J. 1989. The Press and the Carter Presidency. Boulder, CO: Westview Press.

Ryan, Charlotte. 1991. Prime-Time Activism: Media Strategies for Organizing. Boston: South End Press.

Sabatier, Paul, and David Whiteman. 1985. "Legislative Decision Making and Substantive Policy Information: Models of Information Flow." Legislative Studies Quarterly 1:395-421.

Sabato, Larry J. 1991. Feeding Frenzy: How Attack Journalism Has Transformed American Politics. New York: The Free Press.

Sahr, Robert C. 1983. "Energy as a Non-Issue in 1980 Coverage." In Television Coverage of the 1980 Presidential Campaign, ed. William C. Adams. Norwood, NJ: Ablex.

Savage, Robert L., and Dan Nimmo, eds. 1989. Politics in Familiar Contexts: Projecting Politics through Popular Media. Norwood, NJ: Ablex.

Schelling, Thomas C. 1968. The Strategy of Conflict. London: Oxford University Press.

Schiller, Herbert. 1973. The Mind Managers. Boston: Beacon Press.

Schlesinger, Philip. 1991. State and Nation: Political Violence and Collective Identities. Newbury Park, CA: Sage.

Schonbach, Peter. 1990. Account Episodes: The Management or Escalation of Conflict. Cambridge: Cambridge University Press.

Schram, Martin. 1987. The Great American Video Game: Presidential Politics in the Television Age. New York: William Morrow.

Schramm, Wilbur L. 1964. *Media and National Development: The Role of Information in Developing Countries.* Stanford, CA: Stanford University Press.

Sears, David O., and Jack Citrin. 1982. *Tax Revolt: Something for Nothing in California.* Cambridge: Harvard University Press.

Semetko, Holli A., Jay G. Blumler, Michael Gurevitch, David H. Weaver, Steve M. Barkin, and G. Cleveland Wilhoit. 1991. *The Formation of Campaign Agendas: A Comparative Analysis of Party and Media Roles in Recent American and British Elections.* Hillsdale, NJ: Lawrence Erlbaum Associates.

Shaw, Donald L., and Maxwell E. McCombs. 1977. *The Emergence of American Political Issues: The Agenda-Setting Function of the Press.* St. Paul, MN: West.

Sigal, Leon. 1983. *Reporters and Officials: The Organization and Politics of Newsmaking.* Lexington, MA: D.C. Heath.

Simon, Dennis M., and Charles W. Ostrom Jr. 1989. "The Impact of Televised Speeches and Foreign Travel on Presidential Approval." *Public Opinion Quarterly* 53:58-82.

Simon, Herbert A. 1957. *Administrative Behavior: A Study of Decision Making Processes in Administrative Organizations.* 2d ed. New York: Macmillan.

Smith, Carolyn. 1990. *Presidential Press Conferences: A Critical Approach.* New York: Praeger.

Smith, Eric R.A.N. 1989. *The Unchanging American Voter.* Berkeley: University of California Press.

Smith, Larry David, and Dan Nimmo. 1991. *Cordial Concurrence: Orchestrating National Party Conventions in the Telepolitical Age.* New York: Praeger.

Smoller, Frederic T. 1990. *The Six O'Clock Presidency: A Theory of Presidential Relations in the Age of Television.* New York: Praeger.

Sniderman, Paul, Richard A. Brody, and Philip E. Tetlock. 1991. *Reasoning and Choice: Explorations in Political Psychology.* New York: Cambridge University Press.

Snowball, David. 1991. *Continuity and Change in the Rhetoric of the Moral Majority.* New York: Praeger.

Sorauf, Frank J. 1987. "Campaign Money and the Press: Three Soundings." *Political Science Quarterly* 102:25-42.

Stempel, Guido H. III, and John W. Windhauser, eds. 1990. *The Media in the 1984 and 1988 Presidential Campaigns.* New York: Greenwood.

Stephens, David. 1984. "President Carter, the Congress, the NEA: Creating the Department of Education." *Political Science Quarterly* 98:641-663.

Stevens, John M., and Robert P. McGowan. 1985. *Information Systems and Public Management.* New York: Praeger.

Stone, Deborah. 1989. "Causal Stories and the Formation of Policy Agendas." *Political Science Quarterly* 104:23-35.

Stuckey, Mary E. 1990. *Playing the Game: The Presidential Rhetoric of Ronald Reagan.* New York: Praeger.

Sullivan, Denis G., and Roger D. Masters. 1988. "Happy Warriors: Leaders' Facial Displays, Viewers' Emotions and Political Support." *American Journal of Political Science* 32:345-368.

Surette, Ray, ed. 1984. *Justice and the Media: Issues and Research.* Springfield, IL: Charles C. Thomas.

Swanson, David L., and Dan Nimmo, eds. 1990. *New Directions in Political Communication: A Resource Book.* Newbury Park, CA: Sage.

Sylvan, Donald A., Ashok Goel, and B. Chandrasekaran. 1990. "Analyzing Political Decision Making from an Information-Processing Perspective: JESSE." *American Journal of Political Science* 34:74-123.

Tannenbaum, Percy, and Leslie J. Kostrich. 1983. *Turned-On TV/Turned-Off Voters: Policy Options for Election Projections.* Beverly Hills, CA: Sage.

Tetlock, Philip E. 1983. "Policy-Makers' Images of International Conflict." *Journal of Social Issues* 39:67-86.

Tetlock, Philip E., and Richard Boettger. 1989. "Cognitive and Rhetorical Styles of Traditionalist and Reformist Soviet Politicians: A Content Analysis Study." *Political Psychology* 10:209-232.

Tichenor, Phillip J., George A. Donohue, and Clarice N. Olien. 1980. *Community Conflict and the Press.* Beverly Hills, CA: Sage.

Tiemens, Robert K., Malcolm O. Sillars, Dennis C. Alexander, and David S. Werling. 1988. "Television Coverage of Jesse Jackson's Speech to the 1984 Democratic National Convention." *Journal of Broadcasting and Electronic Media* 32:1-22.

Tuchman, Gaye. 1978. *Making News: A Study in the Construction of Reality.* New York: The Free Press.

Tulis, Jeffrey. 1987. *The Rhetorical Presidency.* Princeton, NJ: Princeton University Press.

United States Government. 1968. *Report of the National Advisory Commission on Civil Disorders.* New York: Bantam Books.

Van Dijk, Teun A. 1988. *News Analysis: Case Studies of International and National News in the Press.* Hillsdale, NJ: Erlbaum.

Van Dijk, Teun A. 1988. *News as Discourse.* Hillsdale, NJ: Erlbaum.

Van Dijk, Teun A. 1991. *Racism and the Press.* London: Routledge.

Vermeer, Jan Pons. 1982. *For Immediate Release: Candidate Press Releases in American Political Campaigns.* Westport, CT: Greenwood Press.

Vermeer, Jan Pons, ed. 1987. *Campaigns in the News: Mass Media and Congressional Elections.* Westport, CT: Greenwood Press.

Weaver, David A., Doris A. Graber, Maxwell E. McCombs, and Chaim H. Eyal. 1981. *Media Agenda-Setting in a Presidential Election: Issues, Images, and Interest.* New York: Praeger.

Weinstein, Brian, ed. 1990. *Language Policy and Political Development.* Norwood, NJ: Ablex.

Weiss, Walter. 1969. "Effects of the Mass Media of Communication." In *The Handbook of Social Psychology*, 2nd ed., vol. V, ed. Gardner Lindzey and Elliot Aronson. Reading, MA: Addison-Wesley Publishing Co.

Welch, Susan. 1972. "The American Press and Indochina, 1950-56." In *Communication in International Politics,* ed. Richard L. Merritt. Urbana: University of Illinois Press.

Welton, Gary L., Dean G. Pruitt, and Neil B. McGillicuddy. 1988. "The Role of Caucusing in Community Mediation." *Journal of Conflict Resolution* 32:181-202.

Whitehead, Alfred North. 1958. *Symbolism: Its Meaning and Effect.* New York: Macmillan.

Wilensky, Harold L. 1967. *Organizational Intelligence: Knowledge and Policy in Government and Industry.* New York: Basic Books.

Williams, Frederick, Ronald E. Rice, and Everett M. Rogers. 1988. *Research Methods and the New Media.* New York: Free Press.

Winter, David G., and Leslie A. Carlson. 1988. "Using Motive Scores in the Psychobiographical Study of an Individual: The Case of Richard Nixon." *Journal of Personality* 56:75-103.

Witherspoon, Patricia Dennis. 1991. *A Study of Communication between Presidents and Their Senior Staff.* New York: Praeger.

Wolfsfeld, Gadi. 1984. "Collective Political Action and Media Strategy: The Case of Yamit." *Journal of Conflict Resolution* 28:363-381.

Wolfsfeld, Gadi. 1991. "Media, Protest, and Political Violence: A Transactional Analysis." *Journalism Monographs* #127.

Wyer, Robert S., and Thomas K. Srull. 1989. *Memory and Cognition in Its Social Context.* Hillsdale, NJ: Erlbaum.

Yamagishi, Toshio, Mary R. Gillmore, and Karen S. Cook. 1987. "Network Connections and the Distribution of Power in

Exchange Networks." *American Journal of Sociology* 93:833-851.

Zaller, John. 1989. "Bringing Converse Back In: Information Flow in Political Campaigns." *Political Analysis* 1:181-234.

Zaller, John. 1991. "Information, Values, and Opinion." *American Political Science Review* 85:1215-1237.

Zaller, John. 1992. *The Nature and Origins of Mass Opinion.* New York: Cambridge University Press.

Zeman, Z.A.B. 1973. *Nazi Propaganda.* London: Oxford University Press.

Zuckerman, Alan S., and Darrell M. West. 1985. "The Political Bases of Citizen Contacting: A Cross-National Analysis." *American Political Science Review* 79:117-131.

Political Institutions of the State

13

Legislatures: Individual Purpose and Institutional Performance

Michael L. Mezey

For students of the United States Congress, the primary unit of analysis is the individual legislator and the things that he or she does. Typically, legislative behavior is explained in terms of the purposes of the legislator, and questions of structure and performance are approached from the perspective of members' goal-seeking behavior. Although individual behavior also is a concern of those who study legislatures other than the Congress, it is not as central to that body of research as it is to congressional research. Instead, comparative legislative studies usually begin with the legislature as the unit of analysis. Questions of institutional performance and the relationship between the legislature and other political institutions are at the heart of the inquiry, and structural and behavioral issues tend to be explained in institutional rather than individual terms.

Like trains proceeding on parallel tracks but in opposite directions, the Congress approach and the comparative approach visit most of the same topics, but in a different order and therefore from a different perspective. Because the volume of research on the Congress is so large relative to the comparative literature, it makes sense to order a review of legislative research in terms of the individual behavior approach that has characterized work on the Congress rather than the institutional approach that has characterized much of the comparative literature. The implications of this disjunction between congressional and comparative legislative research can be taken up at a later point.

The discussion of the legislative research literature will proceed, therefore, through the following five topics: 1) the behavior of legislators outside the institution; 2) their behavior inside the legislature; 3) the effect of legislative structure on behavior; 4) the performance of the legislature; and 5) the status of the institution in the larger political system.[1]

Behavior Outside the Legislature

At one time, most of the scholarly work on the Congress was done at a distance, relying for the most part on public records or journalistic accounts. During the 1950s, however, a new breed of political scientists, working more in the tradition of anthropology, went to Washington to observe the Congress, to interview its participants, and to begin the process of developing explanations for the behavior that they observed. Out of their work emerged a "textbook Congress" characterized by a strong committee system, powerful committee chairs, a rigid adherence to the seniority system and to other unwritten rules of the legislative game, and party leadership based for the most part on personality and persuasion rather than on sanctions and coercion. A similar research style was followed by those who studied European legislatures, although their conclusions were, of course, different from those of their American counterparts.[2]

These studies of what went on inside the legislature accounted for most of the legislative research literature through the 1960s and continues to be an important interest of scholars working in this field. Beginning in the early 1970s, however, a new perspective emerged, among Congress scholars as well as some comparativists, that sought to explain behavior inside the legislature in terms of the relationship between legislators and their constituencies. This "outside" approach directed increased attention toward what legislators did when they were outside the legislature and away from the seat of government.

The Mayhew Approach

The connection between representatives and the represented always had interested normative political theorists (see Pitkin 1967) and a few more empirically inclined political scientists had sought to assess the relationship between legislative roll call voting behavior and either the demographic characteristics of constituencies (MacRae 1958) or rough measures of district opinion (Miller and Stokes 1963). But in a book and an article, both published in 1974, David Mayhew suggested a different perspective on representation.

In *Congress: The Electoral Connection*, Mayhew (1974a) argued that what legislators did both inside and outside the Congress could be explained by their re-election concerns. Specifically, members engaged in credit-claiming, advertising, and position-taking activities as a way to ensure their re-election. Credit claiming involved performing particularized services for individual constituents and working for resource allocation decisions that benefited the constituency as a whole. Advertising referred to activities that made legislators widely known among their constituents, that established a "brand name" loyalty among them. And position-taking involved votes, explanations of votes, and other statements designed to establish one's solidarity with the constituency.

The success of this strategy was indicated by the fact that districts in the House of Representatives that could be classified as "marginal" -- won in the previous election by narrow majorities -- were "vanishing." Incumbent re-election rates, which had been around the 90% mark for most of the post-World War II period, approached or exceeded 95% in some years, but Mayhew's key point was not so much an improvement in the incumbent success rate, but the fact that their margins of victory indicated that most incumbents were not having very difficult re-election races (Mayhew 1974b).

The textbook Congress of decentralized power, strong committees, and weak party leadership described by the research of the 1960s was, Mayhew argued, designed to serve members' re-election needs. The re-election goals of legislators explained how they acted inside the Congress, the manner in which congressional power was distributed, and the nature of the decisions taken. Members responded to the perceived needs and desires of their constituents, power was decentralized so that members could act independently of party leaders on behalf of these local interests, and policies that might well be inefficient in their use of resources were nonetheless enacted because they spread electoral advantages to as many members as possible.

Books by two other scholars, Morris Fiorina (1977) and Richard Fenno (1978), published during the same period gave further detail and structure to the Mayhew themes. Fiorina explained the phenomenon of the vanishing marginals by arguing that legislators ensured their re-election by intervening with the bureaucracy to gain favors for individual constituents as well as favorable treatment in the disbursement of federal funds for the constituency as a whole. And they

guaranteed their role in such activities by their consistent support for legislation creating an activist government with a wide array of favors and money to disburse. Thus, as Mayhew suggested, the re-election goals of legislators had consequences for what they did in Washington.

Fenno's contribution was to describe in rich detail exactly what legislators did in their constituencies. By following a group of House members as they traveled in their districts, Fenno identified various types of "home style" designed to gain the trust of constituents. Credit claiming, position-taking, and advertising were all apparent in Fenno's discussion of representatives constantly in touch with their constituents, interested in their concerns, willing to explain their own actions in Washington in terms of those concerns, and working to build trust both to ensure re-election and to permit them to pursue other goals, such as power and good public policy.

Although the approach suggested by Mayhew, Fiorina, and Fenno altered the research agenda for students of the Congress, an interest in the constituency activities of legislators had been apparent in the work of several scholars studying legislatures outside the United States. As early as 1960 and 1961, interviews with legislators in the Indian state of Orissa and in Austria had found that these legislators spent most of their time running errands for their constituents (Bailey 1960; Crane 1961). Others had written about the "surgeries" that British MPs conducted at which they heard and tried to deal with constituent problems (Barker and Rush 1970; Dowse 1972), and still others had written about the constituency activities of legislators in Tanzania (Hopkins 1970), Colombia (Hoskin 1971), and Thailand (Mezey 1972).

The purpose of this is not to say who got there first, but rather to underline the fact that the representational activities that became central to congressional research during the 1970s seemed to be pursued by members of all legislatures. This constancy of constituency concerns, especially when compared with the much more variable policy-making roles of legislatures, suggested that representation was a more appropriate dimension for comparative legislative analysis than lawmaking. A prerequisite for such an approach, however, was a concept of representation broad enough to include the various activities that had been identified in these different research sites. Eulau and Karps (1977) took on that task. Following Pitkin, they used "responsiveness" rather than representation, and disaggregated the term into four categories: service, allocation, policy, and symbolic responsiveness. Service meant responding to individual constituent requests, and allocation to the resource needs of the constituency as a whole. Policy responsiveness looked to the effect of constituent policy preferences on legislative decisions, and symbolic responsiveness referred to those activities that conveyed the impression if not the substance of the other three forms of responsiveness.

The Agenda and the Data

The research agenda suggested by this "outside" approach was enormous. In the case of the Congress, had the marginal legislators really vanished? Did incumbency explain congressional election outcomes and, if so, how much of the incumbency advantage was explained by representational activities of the sort described by Mayhew, Fiorina, and Fenno, and how much was explained by other factors such as the weakening of political parties, the growth of political action committees, or the strategic decisions taken by those who ran against incumbents? Were legislators really single-minded seekers of re-election or did they have other goals that drove them? Could the structure and operation of Congress be traced in its entirety to the re-election goals of members? Was all of this peculiar to the U.S. House of Representatives, or did it extend in whole or in part to the Senate, to state legislatures, or to legislatures in other nations?

Work on this agenda moved faster and further in research on the United States Congress than on other legislatures in part because more political scientists were interested in the Congress and in part because there was during the 1970s a veritable explosion of new data provoked in part by the theoretical and empirical questions posed by the outside model. In 1972, the first edition of the *Almanac of American Politics* was published, and subsequent biennial editions contained, for each legislator, election data, roll call votes on key issues, interest group ratings, and information on constituency characteristics. Beginning in 1981, Congressional Quarterly's *Politics in America* provided similar data and, over the years, the *Congressional Quarterly Weekly Reports* grew in size and comprehensiveness. In 1980, the first edition of *Vital Statistics on the U.S. Congress* was published containing a wealth of time series data on elections, campaign contributions, staff, and workload.

Beginning in 1974, the Federal Election Commission began to collect data on campaign contributions and expenditures by congressional candidates along with information on the campaign finance activities of political action committees. These found their way in aggregate form into the other reference volumes, while some scholars mined the raw data when it became available. In 1978, the Survey Research Center began to include questions on congressional voting in its national surveys. In 1978 and

1980 a congressional district sampling design was used and, beginning in 1988, a series of surveys were designed to look at Senate elections. Finally, Congress itself contributed to the data explosion by its decision in the reform era of the 1970s to allow recorded teller votes, thereby increasing the number of roll calls available for analysis, to open most of its committee meetings to the public, and to record committee votes.

Some new data also became available to those interested in comparative legislative research. Survey research data existed in several European countries, and the Center for Comparative Legislative Studies at the University of Iowa went forward with survey-based comparative projects on several legislatures in Europe, Asia, and Africa. The Research Committee on Legislative Studies of the International Political Science Association was formed and brought together scholars working on legislatures in different parts of the world. The Consortium for Comparative Legislative Studies funded and otherwise encouraged country research on legislatures many of which had never before been studied.[3] In every edition, *Parliaments of the World*, published by the Inter-Parliamentary Union, contained more detailed information on more legislatures. Nonetheless, truly comparative data proved elusive and therefore most of the new research on legislative elections and constituency service dealt with the Congress.

An Increase in Service?

Comparing survey data from 1958 and 1978, Fiorina (1982) concluded that there had been an increase in the proportion of constituents who expected help from their legislators either with individual problems or with broader constituency projects. On the legislator's side, the magnitude of constituency service activities only could be estimated, but all sources indicated a heavy and increasing service case load and a higher level of importance attached to constituency service by members (Johannes 1984; Parker 1986; Cain, et al. 1987). What was easier to document than the expansion of constituency service itself was the expansion of resources that could be devoted to it; increases were detected in staff size, the number of staff people permanently stationed in the district rather than in Washington, mailings from legislators to their constituents, and the number of days during the year that legislators spent in their districts (see Mayhew 1974b; Parker 1986, 18; Jacobson 1987a, 43).

Measuring Marginality

Attempts to connect indicators of constituency service activities to the vanishing marginals had to deal first with the measurement problem posed by the dependent variable. As political scientists sought to operationalize the concept of marginality, attention focused on incumbent re-election rates, margin of victory in previous election campaigns, and the meaning of the incumbency effect itself. The problem with congressional re-election rates was that they had always been quite high, and therefore it was arguable whether or not the slight rise in the 1970s was significant (Jacobson 1987b). If one focused on margin of victory, the question was what percentage of the vote made a district marginal, with cut-off points of 55% and 60% used in most analyses (Mayhew 1974b). Although margins in both congressional and state legislative elections definitely were rising (Garand 1991), Jacobson showed that vulnerability to defeat had not decreased. Thus, an "incumbent elected in the 1970s with between 60% and 65% of the vote was just as likely to lose in the next election as an incumbent in the 1950s who had been elected with 55 to 60 percent of the vote" (Jacobson 1987b, 130).[4]

A more complicated methodological question was the measurement of the "incumbency effect" -- that is, how much of a candidate's margin of victory was explained simply by the fact of incumbency. This involved distinguishing the votes that a candidate received because of partisan affiliation and because of local or national issues from the "personal" vote received because of the candidate's own qualities or activities.

One approach was to analyze survey data and through regression analysis attempt to distinguish between the variance in the vote explained by attitudes toward the candidate and that explained by other variables, particularly partisanship (Cain et al. 1987; Jacobson 1992). Although this method detects ample evidence of a personal vote for the incumbent, the variability of the results from one survey to another suggests that this is not a particularly reliable way to measure incumbency advantage.

Others have relied on the analysis of aggregate election returns, focusing on the "sophomore surge" -- the difference between a candidate's first election in an open seat race and the candidate's first re-election campaign -- and the "retirement slump" -- the difference in the vote for the incumbent in his last re-election campaign and the vote for his party's candidate in the next open seat campaign (Cover and Mayhew 1977; Alford and Hibbing 1981; Garand and Gross 1984; Breaux 1990). Gelman and King (1990) have suggested that these techniques are biased measures of the incumbency effect because they are based on the small number of districts in each election that have open seats or are being contested for the first time by first term legislators. Their "unbiased" estimate of incumbency effect, using all contested races and controlling for previous votes and partisan swing, produces a somewhat higher estimate of incumbency advantage than other approaches (see also Jacobson 1990a, 30-32).

Not surprisingly then, the consensus of all of this work is that there is indeed an incumbency advantage, but that its magnitude depends on how it is conceptualized and measured. Explanations for the incumbency advantage have focused on redistricting, on the use by incumbents of the perquisites of office to increase their name recognition, on the effect that the waning influence of political parties has on voter behavior, on the representational activities that legislators perform, and on the nature of the opposition that incumbents face.

Service and Incumbency

The hypothesis that incumbency was a product of redistricting was rejected (Ferejohn 1977; Cover 1977; Born 1985; Glazer et al. 1987), and the name recognition hypothesis faltered when no significant increase was found in the frequency with which voters could recall the name of their legislators (see Fiorina 1989, 99). And although the increase in service activities and the resources devoted to those activities had been documented, and although it seems eminently reasonable to believe that members use their enhanced perquisites of office to their electoral advantage, a direct connection between these changes and either re-election rates or election margins has not been conclusively demonstrated. Johannes and McAdams (1988) find in the 1984 National Election Study data no connection between the vote and a recollection of the incumbent having performed service activities. Percentage of the vote won in a district is also found to be unrelated to various measures of constituency service and attentiveness gathered from congressional offices. The only exception appears to be staff size; Cain et al. (1987) find a strong correlation between staff size and voting for incumbents, and Holbrook and Tidmarch (1991) find a connection in state legislative races between the size of staff and sophomore surge. Rivers and Fiorina (1989) suggest that the allocation of resources such as time and staff serve to strengthen the incumbent's reputation for service, and that it is reputation for service rather than service itself that is connected with re-election rates.

The impact of constituency attentiveness on election outcomes may be conditioned by the electoral context. Parker (1986) finds that increased attentiveness results in improved electoral performance for those members of Congress representing states or districts where the opposition party is particularly strong. Similarly, King (1991) argues in a methodological piece that the partisan predisposition of voters in the district affects the level of constituency service that members perform. These findings fit nicely with Jacobson's conclusion that although victory margins of members have increased, their electoral security has not, and with Hibbing's (1991, chap. 6) finding that increased tenure in the House is not associated with lower levels of district activity. Thus, all members are "running scared," and they attend to constituency service as a way to insulate themselves from the swings in electoral behavior that may well characterize the next election. Arguably, such activities have their most visible payoff for those legislators facing the greatest level of electoral uncertainty, that is, members representing districts with contrary partisan predispositions.

Political Parties

One of the first hypothetical explanations for the vanishing marginals pointed to the weakening role of political parties in American politics in general and in congressional elections specifically (Ferejohn 1977). In the first edition of *Congress: Keystone of the Washington Establishment*, Fiorina dismissed the hypothesis, but twelve years later, he concluded that the decline in party loyalties among the American electorate and the weakening of local party organizations require candidates to establish their own direct ties to their constituents based on reputation and service (Fiorina 1989, 112-15).

On the other hand, recent research by Paul Herrnson (1986, 1989) suggests a revitalized role for political party organizations in congressional campaigns. Although recognizing the candidate-centered nature of congressional elections, Herrnson finds that to an increasing extent national congressional campaign committees provide technical services, research, and funding connections for candidates, and state and local party organizations help candidates gauge public opinion and mobilize the electorate. He also finds that Republican organizations, particularly at the national level, have been more active in this respect than Democratic organizations.

Issues

Even if parties are playing a greater role in organizing campaigns than had been thought, party identification is clearly playing less of a role in structuring the decisions of voters (Jacobson 1992, 109ff). The decline of party may mean an increase in the personal vote of incumbents, but it also can mean that issues are becoming more important factors in voters' decisions.

In a number of articles published in the 1970s, Robert Erikson and Gerald Wright maintained that issues are more important in House and Senate elections than analyses that focus entirely on incumbency and party

would suggest (Erikson 1971; Wright 1980). Working with National Election Study data, Alan Abramowitz and Jeffrey Segal (1990, 576) conclude an analysis of the 1988 elections by noting that although incumbency and party identification were the most important factors in explaining congressional voting, "evaluations of national economic conditions and attitudes toward government spending had significant effects on voting for Senate candidates and attitudes toward government spending, abortion, and assistance to blacks had significant effects on voting for House candidates." However, they find that issues had a larger impact on Senate races than on House races, particularly those Senate races characterized by a sharp ideological contrast between the candidates (see also Wright and Berkman 1986).

What still isn't clear is whether issue voting is retrospective, as Fiorina (1981) has argued, or prospective. Although most political scientists continue to accept Fiorina's emphasis on retrospective voting, Lockerbie (1991) provides recent evidence that prospective evaluations may have been underestimated and retrospective evaluations overestimated. He also points to the effect that retrospective evaluations have on prospective evaluations.

National issues as well as partisan factors are involved in assessments of the influence presidential candidates have on the electoral fortunes of their party's congressional candidates. As party loyalty among the electorate has declined, split ticket voting has become more common, and the effect of "presidential coattails" has diminished (Calvert and Ferejohn 1983; Campbell 1986). In off-year elections, the president's party generally loses seats in the Congress, but there is little consensus on the reasons for this. Some have argued for the withdrawing of presidential coattails, others for an explanation focusing on differences in turnout between presidential and off-year elections, and others on the possibility of a vote against the president because of perceived poor performance. Robert Erikson (1988) finds all of these explanations wanting and argues instead that the midterm electorate has a propensity to engage in negative, or protest voting, thus penalizing the president's party simply for being the party in power (see also Alesina and Rosenthal 1989).

Challenger Quality

Gary Jacobson concludes a recent review of work on congressional elections with the observation that incumbent success continues to be attributable in large measure to "inexperienced challengers lacking adequate funds and resonant issues" (Jacobson 1990a, 133). Jacobson and Kernell (1983) first suggested this perspective in their discussion of the strategic decisions of politicians. They describe politicians as rational actors who make decisions in the context of their career goals. Potential challengers with political experience and a current office would be unlikely to risk their careers on a race that they had little chance to win. Ironically, it was exactly such experienced politicians who, if they entered the race, would have the best chance to win. What then do individual candidates consider as they decide whether or not to enter a race?

Perhaps the first point to make is that all inexperienced challengers are not necessarily weak challengers. Green and Krasno (1988) create a measure of challenger quality that includes factors such as celebrity or occupational status, previous candidacies for office, and party activism as well as previous office-holding experience. And Canon (1990) notes that in certain situations, inexperienced candidates do get nominated and do win elections. In implicit contradiction to the strategic challenger model, Canon further suggests that most amateurs know that they have no chance to win, but enter anyway, driven by a number of personal and ideological goals beyond rational calculations of electoral benefit. This view is supported by earlier research (Maisel 1982) on the decision to enter primary campaigns. Assessments of the likelihood of winning are important, but so is a desire to air views or to provide an alternative to the incumbent. Although a majority of those who enter primaries do so with neither the consultation nor the encouragement of party leaders, primary winners were more likely than losers to have had such consultation and support. Recent research with a small group of primary candidates suggests that most had considerable prior experience with the formal party organization at the local or state level (Kazee and Thornberry 1990).

Still, for the strongest potential challengers, the decision will be not to run against an entrenched incumbent unless there are other variables that encourage them to make the race. For example, McAdams and Johannes (1987) find that the incumbent's record of constituency attentiveness is less important than his ideological position in attracting or discouraging a strong challenger. Moderate incumbents in particular seem to scare off strong challengers, with liberal Republicans and conservative Democrats facing the weakest challengers. Jacobson and Kernell (1990), drawing on data from the 1986 congressional elections, show that strong challengers capitalize on favorable national issues while weak challengers do not. However, Krasno and Green (1988) argue that district level political forces rather than the national political climate have the most consistent impact on the emergence of quality challengers (see also Canon 1990, chap. 4)

The other dimension to candidate quality is money. Research on congressional as well as state legislative elections demonstrates that the amount of money spent by challengers has a crucial impact on election outcomes (Jacobson 1990b; Gierzynski and Breaux 1991). Although the consensus is that the level of challenger funding is the key variable, Green and Krasno (1988) maintain that, properly modeled, incumbent spending is just as important. And incumbents typically are well funded because of the strategic decisions of those who contribute to campaigns. Those with funds want to contribute to winners, and interest groups particularly want to contribute to incumbents whom they view as powerful (Grenzke 1989b). Challengers are well funded only if they are thought to have a good chance to win, a conclusion that interest groups are more likely to reach if the candidate has had previous political experience and is in an electoral situation that seems to offer some prospect of success (Jacobson 1990a, 96-102). That few challengers find themselves in such a position is suggested by Alan Abramowitz's (1990a) analysis of the elections of 1986 and 1988. He shows that House challengers are increasingly disadvantaged by rising campaign costs and a declining ability to attract funds. The quality challenger perspective also helps us to understand the more uneven record of incumbent success in U.S. Senate elections. First, senators are more likely than representatives to attract strong challengers (Jacobson and Wolfinger 1990; Squire 1990). A strong record of constituency service will not necessarily protect an incumbent senator, especially one running in a large state, from a strong challenger. Certainly, incumbent senators do not ignore service; on the contrary, the evidence is that they too have become increasingly attentive to their districts (Parker 1986). But the sheer size of the constituency, the much greater media attention to senatorial campaigns than to House campaigns, the greater likelihood that election outcomes will be influenced by issues and national political forces, and the greater likelihood that challengers will be experienced and well funded, means that such a record of service may be overwhelmed (Abramowitz 1988, 1990b; Fiorina 1989, 115-18; Miller 1990; Wright 1990). This interpretation is supported by the finding of a stronger incumbency advantage for senators from smaller, more heterogeneous states than from larger states (see Hibbing and Brandes 1983; Westlye 1983).

The Electoral Connection in Comparative Perspective

The linkage between constituency activities and re-election was plausible in the case of the Congress because national political parties seemed to have relatively little to do with election campaigns. Legislators who wished to return to the Congress had to establish their own strong ties to their constituents. As the single member in Congress from their district, individual citizens and local interests would go to them with their problems; to the extent that members responded well, they would cement their ties with the district and increase their likelihood of re-election.

But what of countries with strong political parties that play a more dominant role in selecting candidates, in financing their campaigns, and in structuring the choices of voters and where individual candidates and their campaigns count for less? Why would legislators be responsive in a service or allocational sense in such political systems? Would there be any political payoff for such activities? Similarly, what about proportional representation systems in which several legislators represented the same constituency? Would citizens come to any or all of these legislators with service demands, would legislators feel obliged to respond, and, again, what would they gain from responding?

Electoral Systems and Parties

A comparative study of Kenya, Korea, and Turkey, relying on interview data with legislators, with elites, and with mass publics, suggests that the electoral system might be a factor. Relatively high levels of constituency service and allocational activity were found in Korea and Kenya, countries with single member district systems, while legislators in Turkey, a country with proportional representation, reported somewhat lower levels of such activities. On the other hand, constituents in all three countries attached the highest priority to the constituency service aspect of the MP's role, a finding that seems to be repeated in virtually every Third World country, regardless of the strength of its parties or the nature of its electoral system (see Kim et al. 1984, chaps 5 and 6; Cohen 1977; Barkan 1979; Valenzuela and Wilde 1979; Mezey 1985, 740-44).

One comparative study, drawing on interviews with American state legislators, found that the level of constituency service activities varied across and within states and that no conclusive link could be established between such activities and electoral victory margins. However, legislators from single member districts placed a "substantially greater" emphasis on service than legislators from multi-member districts (Jewell 1982, 146-47).

Finally, a comparison of the Congress and the British House of Commons, which necessarily holds the electoral system (single member district in both cases) constant, tests the effect of the stronger British party system on constituency service activity. Relying on interviews with legislators and survey data on constituent attitudes in both countries, Cain et al. (1987) document, in Great Britain, an increase in constituency service activities from the mid-1960s to the late 1970s, an increase in constituent awareness of these activities, and an apparent increase in the frequency with which evaluations of service form the basis for constituent evaluation of MP job performance. MPs who engage in constituency service are also better known and more favorably evaluated than those who do less. And some connection between such activities and electoral success is found, although not to the extent indicated by the United States data (see also Norton and Wood 1990). Cain et al. conclude that, like their American counterparts, MPs are driven to perform constituency service by the desire for a personal vote and that this tendency has become more pronounced as the British party system has weakened. The status and votes that MPs acquire in their districts as a result of constituency service allow them to gain a degree of independence from national party leaders. On occasion, the party now finds that they need the member and his popularity as much as the member needs the party.

This suggestion of an electoral connection in Great Britain is supported by David Wood's (1987) finding that a significant number of Conservative MPs viewed lobbying on behalf of local industries as an important part of their job and that this was particularly so for legislators from politically marginal districts. However, Donald Searing (1985) argues that for those British MPs who are especially active in regard to service activities the desire to secure a personal vote is less important than the sense of satisfaction that they gain from being of service.

In addition to the United Kingdom and the United States, evidence of a personal vote has been found in several other single-member district systems including Australia, New Zealand, Canada, and Korea (see Bean 1990; Anagnason 1983; Krashinsky and Milne 1986; Park 1988). And in Brazil, Barry Ames (1987) found that during the 1947-1964 period when the legislature was an active participant in the budgetary process, members who planned on seeking re-election were especially interested in maximizing expenditures in their districts.

In some countries with proportional representation, the service link between legislators and their constituents seems weaker. In the Netherlands, for example, where there are no local constituencies and all candidates run on nationwide lists, voters say that they are unlikely to go to MPs with problems or complaints and MPs, in describing their roles, place very little emphasis on dealing with voters' problems (see Gladdish 1991, 100-102). In Germany, where some legislators are elected from single-member districts and others from party lists, service and pork barrel activities are more common among the former (Lancaster and Patterson 1990).

When proportional representation systems use local lists and candidate preference options, service activities are more evident. In Ireland, the single transferable vote version of proportional representation encourages voters to indicate their preferences among candidates, and in one study a plurality of voters indicated that constituency service was the most important criterion in their preference decisions (Farrell 1985). Irish parliamentarians apparently respond to these expectations as suggested by re-election rates that rival those of their American counterparts (Darcy and Marsh, 1990).

In Belgium, where voter preferences are recorded but seldom affect election outcomes, legislators still act as ombudsmen for their constituents, intervening with government ministers and officials, introducing locally relevant bills, and attending local functions (MacMullen 1985). A similar commitment to casework emerges from interviews with Israeli legislators all of whom are elected from national lists (Uslaner 1985). Partisan factors may be one explanation for such activity in multi-member proportional representation systems. After all, names still appear on party lists, and some percentage of the vote for the party's list will be attracted by the presence of names that are known locally. Whereas the incentive for performing constituency service activities in single member district systems may well be the rational legislator's desire to maximize a personal vote, in multi-member systems the incentive may well be provided by rational parties encouraging their incumbents to act in ways that will maximize the party's vote. This will be especially the case in systems where parties design their national lists to appeal to particular constituencies within the party. Legislators in Israel, for example, are aware of these *de facto* constituencies, and direct their service activities at these groups (Uslaner 1985).

Electoral Consequences

The consequences of constituency activity have not been studied as persistently as they have been in the United States, and the research that does exist leaves one uncertain about the magnitude and importance of a personal vote compared with party and issue factors. In Japan, for example, a system with multi-member constituencies but a tradition of aggressive constituency campaigning by individual candidates, party still accounts for significantly more of the variance in votes than candidate or constituency factors (Richardson 1988). In Canada, where incumbency has been shown to be a

factor, national issues still remain important. There, Happy (1989) finds that retrospective evaluations in regard to the economy have a significant and negative impact on votes for incumbents.

Behavior Inside the Legislature

Definitions and Measures of Behavior

To what does behavior in the legislature refer and how can it be measured? The most durable response to both questions has been the roll-call vote. The casting of a vote is clearly behavior, and clearly important behavior because a defining feature of legislatures is that they make decisions through a voting process. It also is easily measurable behavior. Because legislatures are public bodies that keep records of how their members vote, it is relatively simple to gather roll call voting data, develop indices that distinguish among the voting records of different legislators, and then search for variables that explain why they vote as they do.

Although there is much in the way of legislative behavior that is not captured by the roll call vote and there are limitations to what roll-call data can tell us about the congressional decision-making process, scholars have stuck with these data because they are "hard" and they are available in a number of different legislative settings, often over an extended period of time (see VanDoren 1990; Kingdon 1989, 10-11). Other measures of behavior are in contrast softer and therefore more difficult to quantify, more difficult to gather for a large number of legislators, and do not necessarily come in comparable categories across time and space. These include the speeches that legislators give, the bills and amendments that they introduce, the questions that they ask of the government in parliamentary systems, and the positions that they take and the strategies that they follow during less public phases of the decision-making process (but see Hibbing 1991, chap. 5).

This emphasis on roll call data has hindered comparative research. In many countries a legislator's vote is determined by his party leader or by executive elites outside the legislature. In other systems, legislatures have little apparent policy-making influence, and therefore the votes that members cast are not of interest. The more consequential aspects of legislative behavior in these systems are exactly those activities that are less public and less easily measured. Thus, the "softer" nature of research on many non-American legislatures is in part explained by the absence or irrelevance of the "hard" roll call data that students of the Congress favor.

Roles and Goals

A different category of behavioral data comes from the responses of legislators to questions about how they perceive their legislative roles and how they decide what to do in the legislature. Although role perceptions are supposed to explain behavior, they are often used as measures of behavior. The pathbreaking study in this genre was the analysis by Wahlke et al. (1962) of the roles of legislators in four American states. Through interviews with legislators, various orientations toward the purposes and processes of the legislature, toward the constituency, and toward representational style were identified. These categories have been replicated in a number of legislative settings. Interviews tapping purposive role orientations of legislators in African, Latin American, and Asian nations revealed the importance that these legislators attached to the performance of constituency service activities. This finding revived the interest of scholars in legislatures that had been ignored because their members did not seem to have any influence on the law-making process (Hopkins 1970; Hoskin 1971; Mezey 1972; Mezey 1985, 740-44). Research on role orientations associated with representational style has been conducted in the United States House of Representatives (Davidson 1969; Kozak 1984) and in legislatures in at least eleven other nations in Europe, Asia, Africa, and Latin America (see Mezey 1979, 172).

Although widely gathered, role orientation data have not been linked with actual legislative behavior. That is, the consequences of different role perceptions for what the individual legislator does are not clear. Nor is it clear what different collective role patterns mean for the legislature as a whole. A role consensus within one legislature different from that in another legislature may tell us something about the functions of each legislative body. But role consensus is difficult to find (Kim and Patterson 1988), and the functional implications of different role orientation patterns remain ambiguous (see Jewell 1985, 125).

Recent work on the United States Congress has retained the purposive perspective of role analysis but abandoned the role orientation categories in favor of a discussion of legislative goals. This work has divided between Mayhew's emphasis on the re-election goal and models that see legislators motivated by a more complex mix of goals. The multiple goal approach can be traced to Joseph Schlesinger's (1966) suggestion that behavioral differences could be traced to differences in ambitions. Legislators with progressive ambitions hoped to move to higher office; those with static ambitions planned to stay where they were; and others with discrete ambitions wished to complete their terms and leave office.

Politicians, Schlesinger argued, adjusted their behavior to their ambitions.

Richard Fenno (1973) talked about goals rather than ambition and suggested that legislators pursued three goals -- re-election, power, and good public policy -- and that the relative importance of each goal might vary during a member's career (Fenno 1978). This perspective was refined a bit further by Richard Hall (1987) who, drawing upon Dodd's (1977) analysis of the power goal, distinguished the goal of making a personal mark on public policy from the goal of good public policy. John Kingdon, in his comprehensive analysis of legislative decision making, used Fenno's categories differently phrased -- satisfying constituents, intra-Washington influence, and good public policy -- but seemed to agree with Mayhew that "the congressman considers the constituency interest first" (Kingdon 1989, 248).

Also in accord with Mayhew is much of the scholarship categorized under the rubric of "the new institutionalism" (March and Olsen 1984). Emerging from the public choice literature, this approach views legislators as rational actors with electorally induced preferences among policy alternatives. Public choice analysis develops models of decision making that assume that these preferences are heterogeneous among members of a collective body such as a legislature or a committee. Each legislator has an ideal preference based upon constituency and electoral factors, and behaves in a manner that optimizes that preference. However, what they are able to accomplish depends upon a number of factors: their uncertainty about the preferences of other participants, the voting strategies that they follow and believe that their colleagues are following, and the institutional factors that structure the choices that they and their colleagues must make.[5]

Constituency Influence

Speculating about the influence of constituency and electoral factors on legislative behavior has proven to be easier than empirically mapping that influence. One problem has been measuring constituency views. In the era before survey research, scholars used demographic data on the constituency as a surrogate for attitude data (Turner 1951; MacRae 1958; Froman 1963). Obviously, the attribution of attitudes to constituents based upon the constituency's aggregate demographic characteristics is at best problematic. The breakthrough in this area occurred with the work of Warren Miller and Donald Stokes (1963) who, using survey data, estimated constituency opinion in 116 congressional districts and coupled those estimates with the voting records and preferences of the House members who represented these districts. They found rather weak correlations between roll call voting behavior and constituent attitudes and a similarly weak relationship between the views of representatives as expressed in interviews and the views of their constituents. Although criticized on methodological grounds having to do primarily with the small sample sizes upon which their assessments of constituency opinion were based (Fiorina 1974; Erikson 1978), the main contours of the Miller-Stokes findings never have been convincingly refuted and have been applied in at least one other national setting.

Using a similar model and techniques, Converse and Pierce (1986, chap. 19) find that the relationship between constituent views and the roll-call votes of members of the French National Assembly resembles what Miller and Stokes found for members of the U.S. House. They detect a slight connection between the relatively rare defections from party discipline that occur in the French National Assembly and district views, but not surprisingly, the most salient of their findings was that party was the strongest predictor of how French deputies vote.[6]

The empirical finding of weak correlations between constituency views and the behavior of legislators was puzzling in light of interview data suggesting that legislators always considered constituency opinion when deciding how to vote (see Kingdon 1989). One way to solve this puzzle was to ask how legislators conceived of constituency opinion. Although political scientists and legislators agreed that citizens ordinarily were not aware of very many public issues, legislators could not always anticipate those issues about which constituents ultimately might care. And when voters did care, as Miller and Stokes demonstrated with the high salience issue of civil rights, a stronger connection between constituency opinion and roll call voting obtained.

However, constituency also could be a factor on low saliency issues. In these cases, legislators said that even though their constituents might not be aware of how they voted, it was possible that a future opponent might turn the vote into an issue in the next campaign (Kingdon 1989, 60). Thus, a legislator's decisions could be influenced less by current constituency opinion than by an assessment of future constituency opinion and the retrospective judgments that citizens might make after the vote. Arnold (1990, chap. 3) argues that citizens are more likely to make these retrospective evaluations when they can trace the specific effects of a public policy decision back to the legislator. Such tracing requires, among other things, an identifiable action on the part of the legislator, such as a roll call vote. On this reasoning, the legislator will be less likely to be affected by the prospective views of constituents -- their attitude toward the issue when the legislator votes -- then by their retrospective views -- how they will evaluate the vote after it is cast.

But even if legislators know how their constituents will respond to their vote, they still might vote contrary to constituency wishes. Legislators think that they can deviate from constituency views on occasion, but that a "string of votes" against the expressed views of their constituents is riskier (Kingdon 1989, 41-43). Fenno (1978) argued that legislators might take such a risk if they thought that they could explain their vote in a satisfactory manner and if, through their attentiveness to the constituency, they had established a level of trust that would lead constituents to accept their explanation. Such explanations become particularly important when legislators vote in a sophisticated, or strategic manner -- that is, when they cast a vote against constituency views in order to achieve a final outcome that their constituents would prefer (see Denzau et al. 1985). The difficulty of making such an explanation, however, may well limit the number of cases in which members will vote strategically (Wilkerson 1990).

A second approach to the puzzle of relatively weak links between constituency opinion and roll call voting behavior focuses on the definition of constituency. Observers of the United States Senate noted that it was quite common for two senators representing the same state (and thus the same geographic constituency) to be from different parties and exhibit different voting patterns. Fiorina (1974) explained this phenomenon by suggesting that senators vote in accordance with the preferences of their own constituents, defined as their co-partisans. Thus, senators from the same geographic constituency could be representing different ideological segments of the constituency (see also Poole and Rosenthal 1984). This insight, combined with Fenno's (1978) parsing of the term "constituency" into a number of different components (personal, primary, re-election, and geographic) suggested that analyses of constituency influence had to specify which constituency was being discussed.

Preliminary support for this view came from Stone's (1979) finding that the relationship between the attitudes and votes of legislators and the attitudes of their partisans in the constituency was stronger than the relationship with the attitudes of the constituency as a whole. Converse and Pierce (1986) reached a similar conclusion in their study of representation in France. That various constituencies might be incorporated into the same geographic constituency was also suggested by the finding that heterogeneous states were more likely than homogeneous states to have mixed party representation in the Senate (Bullock and Brady 1983).

The availability of fresh constituency opinion data from recent National Election Surveys has permitted a better test of these ideas. Drawing on such data Shapiro et al. (1990) conclude that the strongest explanatory variable for senators' voting records is the weighted opinions of their co-partisans in the constituency, but that the attitudes of independent constituents also have an effect. Gerald Wright (1990) agrees that the views of independent voters are important, but he discounts the influence of co-partisans. Instead, he emphasizes the impact of the ideology of elites in the senator's state party -- convention delegates and county chairs -- on the voting behavior of senators.

Interest Groups and Attentive Constituents

Wright's finding in regard to local elites makes the point that all constituents are not equal. Students of public opinion had long recognized the important role of attentive constituents -- those who followed public policy issues and the activities of legislators and who might also serve as opinion leaders for other less informed citizens. Darrell West's (1988) study of legislative voting on the 1981 Reagan economic package shows that the opinions of activist constituents, defined as those who wrote or phoned about the issue, explained more of the variance in roll call voting than district opinion as measured by 1980 NES data.

Although relatively little research has been done on attentive publics, a great deal of literature exists on organized interest groups, a special class of attentive publics. These groups and the political action committees that they organize to contribute to congressional campaigns are typically viewed in the popular press as having a particularly strong influence on congressional decision making, but attempts to demonstrate such a connection have produced mixed results. Some have found a connection between votes and campaign contributions (Frendreis and Waterman 1985); others find it on low visibility rather than salient issues (Schroedel 1986), and still others have concluded that there is no connection at all (Welch 1982; Owens 1986; Grenzke 1989a). Wright (1985) finds that PAC contributions occasionally explain a significant amount of the variance in voting behavior and then only when other cues are particularly weak. In another research effort, he concludes that the number of lobbying contacts that legislators have with an interest group explains more about their policy choices than campaign contributions explain (J. Wright 1990). Hall and Wayman (1990) take a different approach, directing attention away from roll-call votes and toward participation in committee deliberations and more generally toward the resources that legislators devote to a particular issue. They argue that the purpose of campaign contributions is to mobilize the committed to activity and to demobilize opponents, rather than to change legislators' minds on the issue itself. On this reasoning, a correlation between contributions and voting behavior would not appear.

Although it is important to recognize the impact of organized and attentive publics, the activities of such groups are still constrained by the views of disorganized and inattentive interests. Arnold (1990, 64-71) discusses the calculations that legislators must make as they choose between the usually unambiguous views expressed by attentive publics and the possibility that inattentive publics might be roused to attention by organized interests or by "instigators" with a contrary view. In a more formal approach to the issue, Denzau and Munger (1986) argue that constituent preferences are represented even when they are disorganized. That is because interest groups concentrate their efforts on legislators whose constituents have no preferences on the policy that concerns the group rather than on those legislators likely to be constrained by constituency opinion.

In countries with stronger party systems, attentive publics and interest groups often seek direct representation in the legislature. In France, for example, it is possible to hold a parliamentary seat and a local elective office simultaneously. In 1988, nearly half of the members of the Chamber of Deputies were sitting mayors (Frears 1990). Group representatives also serve as legislators. During the period 1972-1987 more than half of the German Bundestag performed either full-time or honorary functions for associations and societies with an interest in government policy; these members often served on the parliamentary committee dealing with the concerns of their group (Muller-Rommel 1990). A similar pattern of interest group representation is found in Austria (Pelinka 1985). In Great Britain more than half of the Labor Party MPs serving during the 1980s were union sponsored and, in 1987, more than 80% of all MPs registered as having some pecuniary involvement with an outside interest group (Shaw 1990). A survey of interest groups found that 75% regularly contacted individual MPs, with the most common request being to put down a parliamentary question or arrange a meeting for the group (Rush 1990).

Political Parties

Parties can influence legislative behavior in a variety of ways. Authoritarian parties control the actions of legislators who are members of the party through their national party apparatus (see Nelson 1982). In other political systems, external party organizations may be less important, but the parliamentary party is highly disciplined. And finally, there are political systems where party organizations have little or no influence on what legislators do (see Mezey 1975). In the case of the United

States Congress, it is difficult to imagine a member considering the views of his party's national committee on a pending issue. In Italy, however, members view themselves as representatives of their party rather than their constituency and so national party positions count for a great deal (Pridham 1985).

As for legislative parties, they have been assumed to be stronger in parliamentary systems than in the United States. In the case of the British Parliament, for example, the traditional wisdom had been that party discipline was absolute and that those who rebelled against the leadership, especially in situations when they might deprive a government of its majority, risked sanctions running the gamut from expulsion from the party to a permanent career on the backbench. However, the most persistent student of dissent in the House of Commons demonstrates that this textbook description has not applied, at least since 1970. Members are much more willing to vote against their party leaders, and they have done so even when the effect of such dissent was to endanger the government's majority (Norton 1980, 1985). A more recent analysis even suggests that rebellious members may not necessarily be cutting themselves off from future cabinet posts (Piper 1991). Some of this deviation from the party line is done with electoral considerations in mind; Mughan (1990) finds that the incidence of rebellion is likely to increase as a party loses popularity, and as it nears the next general election. The connection between rebellion and electoral concerns lends further credence to the notion of a personal vote as a factor in British parliamentary elections.

Data such as these should not obscure the fact that party discipline remains the key element in structuring legislative decision making in most parliamentary systems. In Scandinavian legislatures, for example, Damgaard (1990) points out that even though legislators are locally elected, "they primarily consider themselves as representatives of their party." Even in Britain, Richard Rose (1986, 30) reminds us that "by comparison with the mid-19th century House of Commons, party cohesion and discipline are far stronger today than in the past." And when Hibbing and Marsh (1987) analyzed those votes in the British House of Commons on which party leaders did not impose the whip, they discovered that party remained the most important influence on these voting decisions.

On the other hand, discipline is not simply imposed from the top down; rather, party positions often emerge from discussions among leaders and backbenchers, and party leaders refrain from making proposals that will provoke opposition among their followers. Therefore, party discipline may be partially the product of anticipated reaction -- that is, leaders deciding not to propose policies that they know their followers will oppose (see Mezey 1979; Laegrid and Olson 1985).

While the theme of party discipline in parliamentary systems may be somewhat overdrawn, there is also evidence that the theme of weak party leaders, independent legislators, and strong committees that dominated much of the thinking about the American Congress during the 1960s and 1970s is in need of some modification. Analyses had tracked the decline of party voting during the 20th century and the rise of both cross-cutting and bipartisan coalitions (Brady et al. 1979; Collie 1988a).[7] But after 1980, party discipline in the House rose and party leaders improved their capacity to lead. This happened because sectional differences within the Democratic party diminished and because the rules of the House changed to allow the majority party to control the agenda if it was so inclined (Rohde 1992). According to Barbara Sinclair (1983), leaders adopted a service orientation toward rank and file members as a way to increase the prominence of the party, included as many members as possible in the coalition-building process, and used the rules of the House to carefully structure the choices made on the floor. Bills were referred to several committees as a way to enhance leadership control of legislation (Davidson et al. 1988), and the use of special rules increased (Bach and Smith 1988). In David Canon's (1989a) view, these leadership changes in the House are institutionalized in the sense that they transcend the leadership of one Speaker. But a longer perspective warns against viewing changes of this sort as permanent; as Cooper and Brady (1981a) have noted, leadership styles and strategies are influenced by institutional contexts and the nature of party strength (see also Peters 1990).

There are also some indications of increased party unity in the Senate (Rohde 1992). This isn't surprising because party strength in both chambers is affected by the same set of external forces (Hurley and Wilson 1989) even though different variables will explain more of the variance in one chamber than in the other (Patterson and Caldeira 1988). However, the task of party leadership in the Senate continues to be daunting. Fenno (1989a) suggests that the Senate of the 1950s and 1960s about whose folkways Donald Matthews (1960) wrote was a "communitarian" body in which group norms were respected and the committee system was all powerful. But the modern Senate, in Fenno's view, has evolved into a dominantly individualistic body in which committees and leaders have much less influence than they had in the past and assignments to prestigious committees are more equitably distributed to satisfy senators who wish to be involved in a number of policy areas (see Sinclair 1988).

Senate leaders, unlike their House counterparts, have not responded with new procedures to control this norm of increased participation (Smith 1989, chap. 4). Multiple referral of bills has not become a leadership tool in the Senate; rather, leaders use it to serve the needs of individual senators (Davidson 1989). Unanimous consent agreements have become complex documents meticulously negotiated so that the concerns of many individuals are addressed; they seem to allow leaders to move the business of the Senate forward, but they also enable individual senators to get a great deal of what they want (Krehbiel 1986; Smith and Flathman 1989).

Executive Influence

Discussions of the influence of political executives on legislative decision making divide between parliamentary systems in which legislative decision making is often assumed to be controlled by the executive and presidential systems in which power is shared between an executive and a legislature structurally independent of one another. The first point that needs to be made is that all parliamentary systems are not alike. As Richard Rose (1986) shows, British governments during the 1970s saw more than 93% of what they proposed pass the House of Commons, but the comparable figure for Canada was 64%. On the other hand, in Great Britain, approximately 30% of the private member bills proposed each session are passed (Marsh and Read 1988), while in Canada the comparable figure, at least through the 1960s, was only 2% (Mezey 1979, 88). Also, governments must contend regularly with actual or anticipated backbench opposition, and high success rates may occur because the government decides not to push legislation that will cause conflict among its supporters in the legislature or even unduly arouse the opposition party if the government's majority is fragile enough (see King 1976).

In the United States, presidents always have had a difficult time influencing legislative decision making (see Fisher 1991). Connected with their legislative co-partisans by only the most tenuous ties and often confronting a Congress controlled by the opposition party, presidents nonetheless require congressional support for nearly all of their policy initiatives. Their success in gaining such support has been uneven. The personal vote that enables legislators to maintain their distance from party leaders works just as effectively against the president. Of course, there are instances when the influence of the president is strongly felt (Lockerbie and Borelli 1989); presidents do have advantages when dealing with members of their own party (Bond and Fleisher 1990, chap. 4) and may exert more influence on foreign and defense policy than on domestic policy (Shull 1991). Nonetheless, the tension between the distributional policy outcomes favored by Congress and the more national perspective of the president are omnipresent (Mezey 1989). On most issues, most of the

time, presidential influence is felt "at the margins" (See Edwards 1989).

Discussions of presidential strategies for influencing legislators have for the most part relied on anecdotal or case study data (see Wayne 1978; Edwards 1980). A more rigorous game theoretic analysis by Terry Sullivan (1990) finds that presidential compromises produce relatively few votes for the president in Congress; rather, presidential success depends upon the conversion of the president's own partisans, who decide to give support largely because of strategic considerations. Cary Covington (1987) comes to a substantively similar conclusion, finding archival evidence that presidents devote their efforts to mobilizing their "core supporters" most of whom are their co-partisans.

Decision-Making Models

How do legislators decide, given the multiplicity of pressures and the large number of decisions that they must take? By the end of the 1970s, researchers had arrived at models that assumed that legislators looked for ways to simplify the decision-making process. They could do so by assessing opinions of the various actors who are important to them (Kingdon 1973), by relying on the cues of colleagues whom they respect (Matthews and Stimson 1975), or simply by voting as they had on similar issues in the past (Asher and Weisberg 1978). Legislators with intense policy preferences choose cues from policy specialists, but on issues with constituency implications, cues are sought from those with information about district preferences (Hurwitz 1988). More recently, Arnold (1991) has returned to the Mayhew and Kingdon perspective, arguing that all decisions begin with assessments of whom in the constituency cares or might care about the vote and whether or not those who care can trace the consequences of the vote back to the legislator. Those seeking to mold majority coalitions understand this calculus and derive a number of procedural and substantive strategies from it that will weaken or break the traceability chain, thereby insulating the legislator from electoral reprisals.

Another view of the decision-making process comes from the policy-voting perspective introduced by Clausen (1973) and utilized as well by Sinclair (1982). Their approach argues that legislator decision-making varies according to the issue, with some external and internal actors more important for certain issue categories than others. In recent years, this perspective has been challenged by Keith Poole and his colleagues (Poole 1981; Poole and Daniels 1985a; Poole and Rosenthal 1985b; Poole 1988) who have argued that roll-call voting in the United States Congress can be characterized by a single left-right dimension that has persisted since the creation of the republic. This means that the ideology of legislators explains a great deal about how they vote, particularly in certain foreign and defense policy areas where it appears to explain more about voting behavior than either party or constituency (McCormick and Black 1983; McCormick 1985; Lindsay 1990; Overby 1991).

As is so often the case with roll-call studies, methodological questions arise. In this case, those taking the multidimensional perspective favor cluster analysis and those arguing for a unidimensional solution use multidimensional unfolding analysis (Koford 1989). At this point, the multidimensional school, represented by Clausen and Wilcox (1991), has conceded that the liberal/conservative dimension may in fact incorporate some of the separate dimensions identified by Clausen but that other dimensions remain distinct. More importantly, they argue that the process of change in Congress is more accurately tracked by a multiple dimension approach, and that such an approach allows the deviation of individual and group voting records from ideological consistency to be explained in terms of policy substance. For his part, Poole (1988) suggests that the multidimensional and single dimensional approaches are theoretically reconcilable under a "belief system" rubric which, he argues, characterizes individual members as well as legislative parties, the latter defined as individuals with similar patterns of constraints over issues.

Students of the Congress have not been very interested in voting behavior in parliaments outside the United States because they assume that these legislatures are characterized by strong disciplined political parties neatly arrayed on a left-right continuum. Although spatial analyses of voting have suggested that this is the case in, for example, the Netherlands (Wolters 1984), in other countries there have been multidimensional findings. In Ireland, for example, Sinnott's (1989) multidimensional analysis of preference data from a sample of parliamentarians uncovers a two-dimensional policy space -- left-right/nationalism and confessionalism -- along with substantial intraparty variation. Shaffer (1991) also finds a two-dimensional solution -- left/right and urban protest-rural traditionalism -- in his analysis of roll calls in the Norwegian Storting.

Structure and Behavior

How legislators reconcile or decide among the external and internal actors that seek to influence their voting decisions is in part a product of the structure of the legislature. In this case, structure incorporates the various decision-making arenas in a legislature and the formal and informal rules that constrain behavior within these arenas.

Committees

Modern research on the United States Congress has emphasized the committee arena ever since Richard Fenno reminded a generation of scholars of Woodrow Wilson's aphorism that Congress in its committee rooms was Congress at work. Because all legislatures have committees, these bodies also have been discussed cross-nationally. The difference has been that studies of the United States Congress have focused on the individual behavior and collective norms that characterized committees and on their relationship with their parent chamber while research in other countries has been concerned primarily with the power or importance of the committee system in the context of what is usually a stronger party system. Such studies typically have paid little attention to what happens inside committees (see Lees and Shaw 1979; Eulau and McCluggage 1985).

In regard to the internal workings of committees, the research approach pioneered by Fenno (1966) in his study of the Appropriations Committee viewed committees as social systems characterized by varying degrees of integration. Fenno's work on committees eventually moved to an emphasis on the goals of members and the joint impact of these goals and the environment within which the committee operated on its decisions and decision rules (Fenno 1973). More recent research, utilizing the rational choice perspective, models committee decision making in terms of the interaction between member goals and parent body constraints in the form of procedural rules.

Formal analyses of committee power begin with the benefits of the committee system for individual legislators. Drawing on Mayhew's view that legislative structure follows from the electoral motivations of legislators, these models argue that a committee's power is based on its control of policy initiatives that lay within its jurisdiction and therefore on its capacity to allow individual members to secure gains calculated in terms of electoral benefits. Legislators not on the committee defer to the views of those who are, either because they respect their expertise or because they expect this deference to be reciprocated when their own committee proposals come before the legislature. Such mutual deference allows legislators to maximize the electoral benefits that they gain from committee decisions. In this manner, legislative structure produces a stable decision point, or equilibrium, among the competing electorally driven demands of legislators (see Shepsle 1979). In a later paper, Shepsle and Weingast (1987) developed a more complete model of committee power that gives special prominence to the sequence of legislative policy making. They argue that members defer to committees not only because of the committee's agenda-setting power but also because of the committee's power, at the conference stage of deliberation, to make final changes in the bill and then confront their colleagues with a straight up or down vote.

This view of committees as autonomous bodies composed of members with policy views quite different from those of the modal member of Congress has come under increasing criticism. Krehbiel (1990) finds little support for the hypothesis that the views of committee members are more extreme or more homogeneous than those of the legislature as a whole. And, in an earlier piece, Krehbiel (1987) suggests a number of ways in which the parent body can undermine the conference role of the committees. Smith (1988) argues that the Shepsle/Weingast model fails to take into account the different strategies that committees follow, strategies that are influenced by the goals of the committee members. And a more recent analysis of the House Appropriations Committee challenges the assumption that committees are autonomous from party leadership, arguing instead that committees are agents of party leadership and that the membership on the committee as well as the actions of the committee have become increasingly responsive to the views of party caucuses (Kiewiet and McCubbins 1991). Gerald Strom (1990, chap. 7) also suggests that committee decisions are heavily influenced by what they anticipate will be acceptable on the floor.

In contrast to a perspective on committee power which focuses on how committees can advance members' re-election goals, Krehbiel argues for a view of committee power based on the informational benefits that the Congress and its members gain from specialized committees. He believes that the electoral benefits (or distributional) explanation needs to be tempered by an understanding of the need that legislators have for information that will reduce their uncertainty about the link between policy and "outcomes," the latter defined as the effects of the policy adopted. From this perspective "committees earn the compliance of their parent chamber by convincing the chamber that what the committee wants is in the chamber's interest" (Krehbiel 1991, 256). This accords with the idea that legislators are motivated by multiple goals, that re-election is simply one of these goals, and that good public policy and making one's mark on legislation are also important goals. In this vein, Hall (1987), in a study of member participation on the House Education and Labor Committee, finds both electoral and non-electoral motivations for participation, with electoral motivations more prominent in public arenas and the legislator's desire to leave his mark on public policy more important behind the scenes. Strahan (1990), in his study of the Ways and Means Committee, also finds less evidence of distributional policy making and more evidence of the concern with policy substance that Krehbiel's analysis emphasizes.

Finally, some have taken the increased activity on the floor of the Congress, in particular an upsurge in amending activity, as an indicator that the power of committees over the content of legislation has eroded (Bach 1986; Smith 1989). But Weingast (1992) argues that much of the new amending activity is a reflection of subcommittee or committee efforts to hold its coalition together either by fighting opposition amendments with neutralizing counter-amendments, or by accepting amendments that are harmless or that are necessary to maintain majority support. He concludes that increased amending activity says less about the decline of committees and more about the decline of norms that had previously mandated that deals be worked out in committee rather than on the floor.

Parties and Committees

In parliamentary systems, deliberations within the legislative party tend to be more important than what happens in committees. Such an inverse relationship between the importance of committee arenas and the importance of party arenas (see Shaw 1979) is illustrated in recent research on the committee system in the British House of Commons. One study, drawing on interviews with MPs, finds that backbenchers have used the recently strengthened committees to monitor and criticize their party's leaders and policies. Thus, MPs see the committees as instruments for strengthening their own role at the expense of the party organization (Jogerst 1990). For this reason, British governments always have worked to keep parliamentary committees weak. On the other hand, in Germany and Italy, strong parties and strong committees co-exist. In both countries, they provide a more private arena than the chamber floor for government and opposition bargaining (see Saalfeld 1990; Di Palma 1977).

With certain exceptions, most of the bargaining in parliamentary systems takes place within and between political parties. Because data on intra-party bargaining is difficult to retrieve, more research has been done on the process of inter-party bargaining. Formal models of legislative decision making have familial connections with this research as it relates to the formation of cabinets in parliamentary systems. Long before formal models were applied to the American Congress, scholars had constructed game theoretic models with parties rather than individual legislators as actors, in an attempt to understand the conditions under which coalitions form and the size and durability of those coalitions. Unlike models of legislator behavior that needed to accommodate difficult problems such as a large number of legislators, information uncertainty, and repeated plays (i.e., many decisions among the same group of actors), the cabinet coalition application was easier because there were fewer actors (parties), much less information uncertainty, and a decision-making process that might not need to be repeated until the next election. These factors allowed for the construction of formal deductive models of coalition behavior that were good predictors of the composition and size of the coalitions that would be formed in multi-party systems and of how coalitions would apportion cabinet portfolios and other goods among themselves (Groennings et al. 1970; Dodd 1976). But critics of these models have suggested that they neglect questions of coalition politics, alliance strategies, the nature of decision making within political parties, and the effects of different ideologies and motivations on party behavior (see Dodd 1984; Pridham 1986; Bogdanor 1983).

On the Floor

In contrast to intra-party deliberations, what happens on the floor of the legislature happens in public. Thus, there is a wealth of literature on the floor behavior of legislators, particularly in the United States Congress. The function of floor discussion raises some interesting comparative questions. Steven Smith makes the distinction between debate, which is arguing from fixed positions, and deliberation, which involves a more reasoned discussion of various options with a view to seeking consensus. Although Smith (1989, chap. 8) concludes that the House emphasizes debate over deliberation while the Senate does the reverse, most analyses of the American Congress take a deliberative perspective in light of the determinative impact of congressional decisions on public policy.

In other nations where, because of party discipline, legislative outcomes are seldom in doubt, floor discussions can be more accurately characterized as debates, but this too has a function. For example, one study of the Parliament of the French Fifth Republic concludes that debate is used as a way to move issues off the private agenda of cabinets and bureaucrats into the public realm (Baumgartner 1987). Although debate in Congress might well have the same agenda setting impact as in other countries, there has been virtually no systematic exploration of this point. One exception is Kingdon (1984) who finds little connection between committee hearings on a particular subject and the prominence of that subject on the policy agenda.

Rules

The operation of the legislature in its various decision-making arenas is governed by a set of written and unwritten rules that determine how the institution does its work. Matthews' (1960) pathbreaking study of folkways in the United States Senate identified a set of unwritten rules of behavior, or norms, that governed the behavior of its members. These and other Senate norms were empirically explored in a series of articles by Ralph Huitt (see Huitt and Peabody 1969). Subsequent research traced the decline of many of these norms, including reciprocity, interpersonal trust, specialization, and apprenticeship (Asher 1975; Smith 1989; Uslaner 1990), although more recent research by Hibbing (1991) suggests that the death of the apprenticeship norm may have been exaggerated.

Rasmussen (1988) has investigated the behavioral norms of the House of Commons, especially those surrounding the maiden speech of members. He found widespread violation of the norms and, most importantly, few sanctions applied to violators by party leaders. In a comparative study of Belgium, Italy, and Switzerland, Loewenberg and Mans (1988) find that norms regarding courtesy and party have equivalent meanings in all three countries, but the extent to which each is subscribed varies across and within countries. Courtesy appears to be a reflection of the culture of the nation, while norms of party allegiance tend to vary by party within nations.

The problem with a focus on norms is that the concept is largely descriptive rather than explanatory. Norms are indicated by behavioral conformity, but what explains that conformity? Barbara Sinclair (1991) suggests that norms rise and fall as the balance between the costs and benefits of compliance change. A similar marginal utility analysis is offered by Krehbiel (1986) to explain why senators conform with the norm of not objecting to unanimous consent agreements.

Despite its theoretical weaknesses, the focus on unwritten norms of behavior was a change from the more traditional and descriptive research approaches centered on written rules of procedure that at one time had been typical of scholarship on legislatures the world over. More recently, American political scientists have displayed a renewed interest in the formal rules of the Congress. This has been sparked in part by the observed tendency in the House to move more decisions to the floor of the chamber and, in the Senate, toward greater individualism and therefore a decline in committee authority. In these contexts, rules are seen as instruments for managing and stabilizing a more uncertain decision-making environment (Bach and Smith 1988; Smith 1989; Bach 1990). Rational choice theorists have been interested in the impact of rules on the choices that legislators make. Weingast (1989), for example, shows that open rules, properly modeled, can protect the majority preferences of committee members.

Legislative Performance

Functionalism

At one time, functionalism was the major theoretical tool for treating the legislature as a collective institution and for assessing its impact on the larger political system. This approach suggested that legislatures and their members performed various representational and system maintenance functions in addition to the law-making function on which students of Congress tended to concentrate (Kornberg and Musolf 1970; Mezey 1979; Loewenberg and Patterson 1979). Functionalism provided common dimensions for the comparative treatment of legislatures and facilitated the discussion of the things that legislators did that were not connected with lawmaking. Although rich in description, functionalism did not lead to theory; it yielded nothing in the way of testable propositions that would help to explain the differences and similarities in legislative performance that were observed cross-nationally.

Legislatures and Change

Legislatures can be viewed as agents for change in a political or social system or as defenders of the status quo. In Mayhew's discussion of the Congress as well as more conventional analyses focusing on separation of powers, it is argued that the local orientations of members, conflicting electoral cycles, the decentralized committee system, and weak party leadership produce slow, inefficient, and ineffective public policy making favoring either the status quo or at most incremental change (see Sundquist 1981; Mezey 1986; Brady 1988; Fiorina 1989). Others, subscribing to the view of members motivated by multiple goals, give more attention to the legislatures' quest for good public policy (Maass 1983; Krehbiel 1991).

In the case of developing nations, Samuel Huntington (1968) suggested that their legislatures were largely conservative bodies that disproportionately represented the privileged and therefore were resistant to demands for political and social change. Others, however, have viewed individual legislators in Third World countries as important agents of change particularly in their role of linking citizens with central decision-making authorities (see Smith and Musolf 1979). John Sloan (1989) compares more democratic Latin American countries that have strong legislatures with more authoritarian countries with weaker legislatures and concludes that the former are more flexible and can achieve many development goals more effectively than the latter (see also Sloan and Tedin 1987). In Eastern Europe, legislatures seem to have been key arenas for change as the authoritarian political systems that characterized those nations broke down (Hahn 1990). In China, the legislature has not played such a role, but there is some evidence that its prominence has increased (see O'Brien 1988, 1989, 1990).

Universalism

Mayhew (1974a, 88) suggested that in its policy-making activities, Congress followed the principle of "universalism" which meant a preference for distributive policies characterized by specific benefits and generalized costs. This tendency is reflected in the congressional taste for entitlements and formula grants (Arnold 1981) and for logrolling arrangements that achieve near consensual support. Such policies, however, are inefficient because their aggregate costs exceed their aggregate benefits; legislators nonetheless prefer such programs because of uncertainty about how their constituents would fare with more efficient policies (Collie 1988b). Such universalism is encouraged when decisions are made on the floor rather than in committees (Owens and Wade 1984) and by considerations of fairness to the various participants (Collie 1989). Even when Congress delegates authority to the bureaucracy, they do so in a manner that ensures that final policy decisions adhere to the preferences of the median legislator (McCubbins 1985).

There have been at least two types of response to the universalism argument. Some formal theorists argue that policy outcomes are governed by a competitive bargaining process that produces a minimum winning coalition rather than a universalistic coalition. Such collective choice models suggest that the most efficient projects will be selected (Ferejohn et al. 1987). However, empirical support for either universalism or minimum winning coalition arguments is difficult to find. As Collie (1988b) points out, roll call studies usually eliminate consensual votes, thereby emphasizing conflict rather than universalism. Also, such studies are not restricted to distributive policies, and few votes are actually decided by consensus. On the other hand, the minimum winning coalition perspective is equally difficult to defend because coalitions larger than those necessary to carry the day regularly appear. These oversized coalitions, which seem most typical of congressional action, can be explained, Baron and Ferejohn (1989) argue, by combining spatial modeling with game theory (see Krehbiel 1988).

A second response to the universalism argument is to point out that Congress on occasion *is* the source of major policy changes of a non-incremental and often non-universal sort. David Brady (1988, 12-16) argues that under normal conditions the Congress is disposed toward either the status quo or toward incremental policy decisions. This is so because congressional parties are "weak and divided" and the preferences of their members are "heterogeneous and conflicting." These factors prevent parties from assembling coalitions that can overcome the structural features that Mayhew highlighted. Typically this means an absence of major policy changes in the Congress. Atypically, according to Brady, critical elections nationalize political issues, unite the different elements of the party, and thereby "increase the party's ability to legislate" and "decrease the committee system's ability to thwart policy initiatives." Even though Brady's overall perspective on Congress is consistent with Mayhew's, in a recent book Mayhew (1991) challenges Brady's argument. Divided government, he says, does not necessarily retard major policy initiatives, and lawmaking surges are not necessarily connected with electoral realignments.

Bureaucracy

The research of the 1960s and 1970s explained the lack of legislative attentiveness to oversight activities by noting that the electoral incentives to engage in such activities usually were slight. Critics argued that the Congress in effect abdicated decision-making authority to the bureaucracy; only when there was a major incident would Congress react. Essentially, Congress engaged in "fire alarm" oversight -- when they had to -- or when there was political advantage to be gained by doing so (Scher 1963; Ogul 1976; Lowi 1979; McCubbins and Schwartz 1984). And, as Fiorina suggested, electoral advantage could be gained by a collaborative rather than an adversarial relationship with the bureaucracy. Scholars identified subgovernments composed of legislators on subcommittees, the bureaucrats whom they were supposed to be overseeing, and affected interest groups all working together to produce mutually beneficial policy, with the legislator's payoff being calculated primarily in terms of funds and favors for constituents (Dodd and Schott 1979; Hamm 1985).

More recent research by Joel Aberbach (1990) raises some questions about this electoral interpretation of oversight activity. He detects an increase in congressional oversight activities that he attributes to a number of factors: congressional responsiveness to citizen frustration with the increased size and complexity of government; the limited number of things that legislators can do through conventional legislative means to attract and satisfy constituents, given the restrictions on government action imposed by large budget deficits and the scarcity of economic resources; the increased staff and committee resources that legislators have available to devote to oversight; and the increased rivalry between a conservative president and a more liberal Congress.

Others argue that effective control of bureaucratic "agents" by their congressional "principals" may not manifest itself in visible oversight activities. Rather, legislators make their expectations clear when they delegate power, and the regular reports that they require from bureaucrats ensure that these expectations are met. Thus, what appears to be abdication and little visible oversight may in fact be the executive knowing, anticipating, and responding to the wishes of the legislature (see Weingast and Moran 1983; Weingast 1984; Kiewiet and McCubbins 1991).

There has not been a great deal of comparative research on legislative oversight. Aberbach et al. (1981), using interviews with legislators and bureaucrats in several western democracies, find that in Britain, the Netherlands, and Sweden contacts between bureaucrats and legislators are mediated through senior ministers, whereas in Italy, West Germany, and the United States direct contact is more typical. In the latter cases, executive fragmentation and strong committees produce legislatures with more prominent policy-making roles and therefore direct linkages with legislators are important to bureaucrats. Recent comparative research on legislative oversight in regard to monetary policy in the United States, Great Britain, France, and Germany supports the view that legislators are motivated to engage in oversight primarily by constituency concerns, but considerations of the institutional balance of power between the legislature and the executive are also important (Woolley and LeLoup 1989; LeLoup and Woolley 1991).[8]

The Status of the Legislature

Discussions of the power and prominence of the legislature compared with that of political executives such as presidents and prime ministers fall into two broad categories. One tradition examines the institutional factors that explain legislative strength such as constitutional provisions and their history, the power of competing institutions such as parties and executives, and the nature of internal legislative resources such as committees and staff (see Blondel 1973). A second tradition focuses on political factors, particularly the nature, sources, and level of public support for the legislature and its members (see Mezey 1979).

Institutional Factors

Discussions of legislative power always have had a strong constitutional and historical flavor to them. But even though the power of a legislature rests to some extent on the basic law of the nation and the political traditions that surround that law, it is also the case that constitutional provisions do not explain everything. Further, in less stable political systems, constitutions are subject to change, and in many nations there is a substantial gap between what appears on constitutional paper and what actually takes place.

The policy-making power of a legislature is indicated by its capacity to constrain the actions of the executive. For example, the Congress usually rejects or significantly amends more than half of what the president proposes; the House of Commons, in contrast, regularly accepts most of what the Cabinet proposes. But as we have seen, constraint also can be imposed prior to final votes by private discussions among party leaders and followers, by threats of revolt on the floor, and by the prospect of politically damaging debate.

Anthony King (1976) cautions against simplistic notions of executive domination in parliamentary systems, arguing that the legislative-executive relationship takes multiple forms. These include the government's relationship with the opposition leadership, with its own backbenchers, and with backbenchers of both parties. Each relationship affords a different set of opportunities for the exercise of legislative power. One such opportunity is provided by situations of minority government, a phenomenon that Kaare Strom (1990) shows is more frequent than conventional wisdom would suggest. His view is that minority governments strengthen parliamentary control and that opposition parties also allow such governments to form because they anticipate reaping future electoral benefits.

Two additional factors with implications for the legislature's policy-making prominence are committee systems and professional staff. Both speak to independent sources of information as a prerequisite for legislative influence. The congressional committee system originated in part from a desire to restrain the growing influence of the president on public policy (Cooper 1970), and the Congress's continued strength as a public policy-making body is connected by most observers with the strength of its committee system. Comparatively, the greater impact of the German and Italian parliaments on public policy decisions compared with the House of Commons and the French Chamber of Deputies can be attributed in part to the presence in the former two bodies of strong committee systems. Proposals for strengthening the House of Commons and other similarly situated legislatures almost invariably begin with proposals to strengthen the committee system (Crick 1968; Norton 1990; Arkins 1990).

Although legislators employ staff members to help them deal with their constituents, other staff, particularly those assigned to committees, assist them with their legislative responsibilities. Staff members provide legislators with expert information and advice on complex public policy issues, help them to draft legislation, and are even the source of some public policy initiatives. This policy-making role that congressional staff play has been criticized; in some cases, staff are accused of acting independently of their superiors, and in other instances of prompting legislators to consider and pass legislation that they might otherwise have ignored (Malbin 1980). More recent research by Christine DeGregorio (1988) suggests that this critique is overdrawn and that the most aggressive subcommittee staff people act at the behest, and under the control of, their legislative masters. Although the role of staff may be debated, it still seems clear from comparative studies that the absence of professional staff is an impediment to the exercise of legislative power (see Mezey 1979; Blischke 1981; Arter 1984; Hammond 1985; Lock 1988).

Strong committees and large staff resources also may attract skilled and experienced politicians to the legislature. Nelson Polsby (1968) demonstrated that as the strength of the House committee structure grew, turnover in membership declined. In recent years, the percentage of members who have held no previous public office prior to their election has remained at about 25% for the House and about 10% for the Senate (Canon 1989b). Similarly, Shepsle (1988) has argued that as the power of the congressional committee system erodes people of talent will have fewer incentives to stay in the Congress (Cooper and West 1981; Hibbing and Moore 1991). Ultimately, this might result in a decline in the policy-making prominence of the Congress. Legislatures that are weak and vulnerable to attacks on their constitutional prerogatives are characterized by a large number of members without previous political experience and relatively high membership turnover rates (Mezey 1979, 249-51; Kim et al. 1984).

Legislatures and Support

Public support for the legislature is another component of legislative strength. In the United States, relatively high levels of support for individual members and relatively low levels of support for the Congress as an institution have been observed (Parker and Davidson 1979). Although members of Congress have been re-elected at overwhelming rates, evaluations of the job performance of the Congress as a whole have declined (see Davidson and Oleszek 1990, 422). Similar findings of higher support for MPs and lower support for the Parliament have been observed in Great Britain (Norton 1990).

An explanation for these findings may be found in the constituency-oriented activities of legislators. As Mayhew argues, legislators create and support a congressional structure that serves their electoral needs;

their high re-election rates testify to the success of this strategy. However, this structure may well produce poor public policy (Mezey 1986). This poor performance, combined with the isolated scandals about individual members that tend to attract a disproportionate amount of press attention, creates a public impression that the Congress is performing poorly. Members themselves contribute to this perception by deflecting public criticism of themselves toward the Congress, in effect running against Congress (Fenno 1978). However, recent research by Richard Born (1990), using National Election Study data over a number of years, suggests that evaluations of the Congress are strong predictors of how constituents feel about their own member and therefore attempts by members to distance themselves from the institution may be futile.

This approach relies on what Easton (1965) referred to as specific support -- support based on performance. Wahlke (1971) argues that because citizens tend to know very little about what their political leaders are doing, measures of specific support are not as important as measures of support that are unrelated to performance. Such diffuse support is measured by support for the continued existence and powers of the legislature rather than by favorable evaluations of what the legislature is doing. Over the long term, specific and diffuse support are connected. Boynton and Loewenberg (1974) found, for example, that diffuse support for the German Bundestag increased as a result of the economic successes of the post-war government. And a more recent analysis suggests that perceptions of poorer government performance have led to a decline in trust for the Bundestag (Saalfeld 1990).

In Korea, Turkey, and Kenya, it is found that among more modernized sectors of these societies constituent satisfaction with the performance of the legislature is connected with diffuse support for the legislative institution, and satisfaction with the performance of individual legislators has little impact on diffuse support (Kim et al. 1984). Similarly, in Sweden a relatively high level of support for the parliament as an institution along with an increasing cynicism about its members has been noted (Arter 1990).

The Development of Legislatures

A legislature's status in its political system may vary. That is, the prominence of a legislature and the degree to which it is supported by the public may change over time. Drawing on the political development literature in general and on Huntington (1965) specifically, Polsby (1968) used the concept of institutionalization to describe the process by which the House of Representatives became more complex, autonomous, coherent, adaptive, and universal. In so doing, he argued, the House increased its power and prominence in the political system and became a stable body in the sense that its status relative to other political institutions did not change substantially with changes in membership or in its political environment.

The theme of institutionalization has since been pursued by Gerlich (1973) in a discussion of several European parliaments, by Opello (1986) in a case study of Portugal's Parliament, and by Hibbing (1988) in an analysis of the British House of Commons. Hibbing replicates Polsby's categories and finds only spotty evidence of the institutionalization of that body. This finding leads him to question the assumption that the institutionalization process is unidirectional and monotonic, and he concludes that much depends on which indicators one selects and which time period one is examining. He also agrees with Cooper and Brady's (1981a) view that institutionalization is more descriptive than explanatory in the sense that it leaves open the question of what external factors explain the particular facets of institutionalization.

Explaining change is of course more difficult than describing change. Fred Riggs (1975) emphasizes the connection between the conditions under which a nation's legislature first emerged and its current status in the political system, while Sisson and Snowiss (1979) discuss the importance of a supportive ideology involving constitutionalism and individual rights in the creation and maintenance of strong legislative institutions. Organization theory, with its focus on the relationship between organizations and their environments, offers perhaps the strongest potential theoretical approach to understanding legislative change (see Cooper 1977; Hedlund 1985), although as Hibbing (1988, 710) notes, "no one has undertaken the work of empirically relating measures of environmental change to indicators of legislative change."

Conclusions: Behavior, Institutions, and Theory

Purposive Politicians

The reigning perspective for those who study the United States Congress centers on the constituency and electoral concerns of individual members and the impact of those concerns on their behavior and on the structure, performance, and status of the institution. Although the importance of constituency factors cannot be denied, there does remain the strong sense that electoral concerns explain only part of what legislators do. Fenno's view that legislators are driven by policy and power goals as well as by re-election concerns, and that the relative importance of these different goals will vary over the course of a legislative career, continues to resonate as a fuller description of what legislators are about. In Fenno's short books on individual United States senators, the genuine policy commitments of those whom he is studying emerge as a consistent theme (see Fenno 1989b). Keith Krehbiel, in his critique of the view that legislators are driven exclusively by constituency concerns, argues that although a random list of bills passed during any congressional session might reveal some constituency dimension to many of them, "the claim that most or even many of them are predominantly distributive stretches the imagination" (Krehbiel 1991, 252-3).

Even when one discusses activities that are constituency related, it is not at all clear that these are motivated entirely by electoral concerns. As previously noted, Searing found that for many British MPs, constituency service activities yielded little in the way of electoral rewards; instead, members reported that they derived personal satisfaction from helping people. Interviews with members of Third World legislatures, institutions with notoriously high turnover rates and great vulnerability to military coups, also suggest that the electoral dividends of constituency service may be less certain than the personal status that legislators gain in their communities by doing favors for constituents.

Purposive models therefore need to give equal time to non-electoral factors and probably need to be expanded to include non-political factors as well. It would be useful in this connection to return to Schlesinger's notion of ambition theory and to remember that not all legislators have static ambitions -- the desire to stay where they are. Many may be hoping to move on, and others may be more willing than we think to risk loss of office in order to achieve policy goals. It is convenient but inaccurate to think of legislators solely as professional politicians driven to stay in office because the alternative is unemployment. Rather, legislators who leave office often do quite well; those who stay in office may have to be content with doing good.

What still has yet to be demonstrated in a convincing manner is the impact of service, distributional policies, credit claiming, and home style on the re-election of members of Congress. Surely these factors count for something, but we still do not know, and may never know, how much they count, and how much they count in comparison with party, issues, and national events. What we do know is that challenger quality does count in congressional elections. This knowledge should cause us to direct less attention at incumbents and what they do and more at political parties, their methods for recruiting candidates, the personal motivations that drive people toward seeking a political career, and issues of campaign finance. Certainly, the political strength of incumbents and the campaign funds at their disposal will be important in these decision-making processes. But as David Canon (1990) has shown, challengers with a great deal to recommend them do turn up, and often for apparently hopeless races.

The role of political parties also needs to be reconsidered. The Mayhew perspective assumed that the weakness of political parties in the electoral arena meant that legislators interested in re-election would have to take care of themselves. But apparently the role of national political parties in such matters is increasing. Will that altered role affect the behavior of members of Congress in their constituencies? Certainly, in some countries, as parties have weakened, the service activities of legislators have increased. Is the inverse going to be true? Elaine Swift's (1987) discussion of the nineteenth century Congress suggests that the answer may well be no. She demonstrates that careerist behavior, calculated in terms of advertising and credit claiming, seemed to be unaffected by changes in the strength of political parties that occurred during that century. And as has been noted, in several countries with stronger party systems than the American case, legislators continue to engage in service activities, albeit less for their own personal electoral advantage than for the advantage of their parties.

All of this calls into question Mayhew's hypothesis that questions of congressional structure and procedure are dominated by the electoral motives of members of Congress. Just as constituency activities and strong parties can co-exist, Cooper and Young (1989) demonstrate that changes in procedures for bill introduction cannot be explained entirely in terms of the electoral self-interest of members. Rather, context mediates between procedure and self-interest and, more importantly, contextual factors exist apart from and beyond the control of members and their self-interest.

Institutional Performance

The purposive model, with its focus on individual behavior, has diverted the attention of Congress scholars from the broader institutional questions that are more frequently addressed by comparativists. More research needs to be done on the question of what difference the legislature makes for the political system and for the policies that it pursues. Are all legislatures inclined toward universal and therefore more inefficient policies? If the congressional policy-making process is slow, incremental, and dominated by monied interest groups, does that suggest that the hypothesis that legislatures are inherently conservative bodies disposed to support the economic and social status quo apply as much to the Congress as to Third World legislatures? If so, would that reaffirm the point of view of those who have always looked to the executive as the catalyst for major political change? Does a legislative policy-making process that fosters universal, often inefficient policies, along with a politics of blame avoidance, affect the level of public support for the legislature as a whole? Do stronger legislative parties and more centralized legislative power lead to more efficient and effective policy performance by the legislature? And if parties decline, as they seem to be doing in some European nations, will that result in poorer legislative performance?

Comparing Legislatures Across Space and Time

To answer these questions we must look at more than one legislature, just as we must look at more than one legislator if we are to understand legislative behavior. And to look at how legislatures affect, and are affected by, political and social change, we must look at longer time periods. But the fact is that most of the legislative literature is firmly rooted in time and place, and for much of the subfield the place is Washington, D.C., and the time frames are usually current. The research decision to deal only with the Congress is often dictated by practical considerations: comparative research is more difficult and expensive to do. But ethnocentric factors also come into play. Most legislative scholars in the United States have congressionally centered research agendas because they view themselves as Americanists and they view the Congress as a uniquely important institution.

Comparative efforts are further impeded by the institutionally centered and often less quantitative approach that characterizes much of the research conducted on legislatures outside the United States. This is more than simply a matter of research training or taste. The implicit comparative argument is that legislative behavior is shaped by the status of the legislature and its role relative to other institutions such as the executive and political parties. The congressional argument is that institutional and structural factors follow from the goals and purposes of self-interested politicians. The comparative argument insists on the importance of context; the congressional argument persistently pushes contextual questions to the periphery.

All of this presents significant impediments to comparative research. And it should be obvious that only when we move toward comparative research will we be able to move toward theories of legislative behavior. As Samuel Patterson (1989, 461) reminds us, the "overarching theoretical and empirical requirements of political science are invariant as to country." Even if

comparative data are unavailable, "patterns of behavior and generalizations found to hold in one system ought to inform, or be tested in, another system." And even if one's research is confined to a single country, generalizations can be strengthened by testing them across time (Cooper and Brady 1981b).

A comparative and diachronic -- and therefore a more theoretically promising -- approach to legislative studies has not been characteristic of the research that has dominated the field. The "normal science" studies that constitute much of the research cited in this chapter reduce the complexity of the legislature by identifying falsifiable hypotheses, looking for data with which to test these hypotheses, and through these findings refining or advancing to some small degree the state of knowledge in a narrow subfield. This work is what doctoral students are encouraged to do; it is the work that most continue to do after their doctorates; and it characterizes the bulk of the literature published in our leading scholarly journals. Although this work is clearly valuable, its value is just as clearly limited. With each article on each topic, the questions seem to get narrower, the issues more arcane, and the findings less relevant to all but the small group of scholars pursuing that specific line of research. Ironically, congressional scholars seem to have replicated one of the major failings of the Congress itself: extreme specialization at the cost of a view of the "big picture." To use a well-worn metaphor, such work produces lots of trees, but few perspectives on what the forest as a whole looks like (Rieselbach 1983). And such a larger view is what theory is all about.

More recent attempts at theorizing have come from those who have sought to develop formal models of aspects of the legislative process. In contrast to the normal scientist, the formal modelers reduce complexity through a series of rules and assumptions, much in the manner of economists who model national economic systems. Such work compels both those who do it and those who read it to think rigorously about legislative decision-making processes. But the impact of this work has been restricted by technical and notational paraphernalia that are unfamiliar to most political scientists, by what some have seen as its tendency to minimize political factors (see Rieselbach 1992), by the difficulty that many of its practitioners have encountered in testing these stylized laboratory models against the more disorderly real political world, and by its refusal to move beyond the Congress.

All of this is unfortunate, because formal theories of legislative behavior hold out the hope of being truly generalizable. The idea that structure influences collective decision making is intrinsically comparative because all legislatures are collective decision-making bodies. For example, modeling decision making within a party caucus where members are bound to support on the floor decisions taken by the caucus majority should not be more difficult than modeling decision making within a congressional committee. Similarly, the implications of decision-making sequences in parliamentary systems that place committee decisions after floor discussion should be at least as interesting as the power congressional committees may gain from their placement at the conference stage of deliberation. The point is that formal modelers have unnecessarily restricted their efforts to the Congress. The data-gathering reasons that influence the "America first" approach of normal science practitioners do not apply to those who design deductive models. And the cost of this decision is great because it is through such models that theories of legislative (as opposed to congressional) behavior may come.

In summary, normal science, in its quest for narrow questions with narrow answers typically avoids comparative and/or diachronic analysis; and formal models, at least at this nascent stage in their development, have dealt only with the Congress. This means that legislative research remains theoretically impoverished. Its lack of comparative focus is part of the problem; one can no more have a theory of legislatures that applies only to the United States Congress, than a theory of relativity that applies only to Chicago. Even a theory of Congress has proven elusive; few congressional scholars have had the inclination to put the various narrow studies together, and those who have attempted to do so have operated more at the level of description and speculation than explanation. This work has produced various "perspectives" or ways of looking at legislative behavior, but little in the way of theory.

Work on these perspectives, one hastens to add, still needs to be encouraged because as they synthesize and interpret the narrower work associated with normal science they can start us toward theory. Such efforts are at once creative, risky, and important. They involve imaginative leaps, and bold, often controversial pronouncements. They invite criticism from those committed to normal science, but if successful, such work can change the way all of us, including normal scientists, think about the field. Mayhew's *The Electoral Connection* is such a work. Drawing primarily on the empirical work of others, he attempted to step back from the "trees" and look at more general patterns. Although frequently criticized for its descriptive and non-empirical approach, there should be little debate about the extent to which it has shaped the thinking and the research agendas of a generation of legislative scholars.

Notes

1. What follows is a far from complete review of a large body of literature. Given space limitations and my editor's mandate to

incorporate research on legislatures outside the United States, I have had to make some difficult choices. These include the exclusion of virtually all of the research on state and other sub-national legislatures, as well as the slighting of several important areas of congressional research. Even work that I have included is sometimes summarized too briefly. Thus, apologies in advance to those who have been left out, to those who think that their work deserves more space than I have provided, and to those who think that they would have liked to know more. For the latter group, the most complete treatment of the literature is still found in *The Handbook of Legislative Research* (1985). I also can recommend other literature review articles that I have found helpful, including Collie (1988b), Krehbiel (1988), Ogul and Rockman (1990), Patterson (1989), and Rieselbach (1992). I am grateful to Aage Clausen, Ada Finifter, Malcolm Jewell, David Mayhew, and Marvin Overby for their comments on earlier drafts of this manuscript.

2. The essence of this research on the Congress can be gathered from the essays in Peabody and Polsby (1963), from Ralph Huitt's essays in Huitt and Peabody (1969), and from Matthews (1960). On European legislatures, see Jennings (1957) on the British Parliament, Loewenberg (1967) on the German Bundestag, and Williams (1968) on the French Parliament.

3. Much of this research is collected in anthologies. See Kornberg and Musolf (1970); Boynton and Kim (1975); Eldridge (1977); Smith and Musolf (1979) See also Kim, et al. (1984)

4. For a critique of Jacobson's view, see Hibbing and Bauer, 1989; also see Jacobson (1990a, 40) for a rejoinder.

5. There is a great deal of literature in this area. For an introduction, see Shepsle 1979; Krehbiel 1988; G. Strom 1990.

6. For a critical discussion of Converse and Pierce, see Eulau (1987) and Wahlke (1987).

7. See Cox and McCubbins (1991) for a recent critique of this view.

8. For excellent reviews of the literature on legislative-bureaucratic relations, see Rockman (1985) and Ogul and Rockman (1990).

Bibliography

Aberbach, Joel D. 1990. *Keeping a Watchful Eye: The Politics of Congressional Oversight.* Washington, DC: The Brookings Institution.

Aberbach, Joel D., Robert D. Putnam, and Bert A. Rockman. 1981. *Bureaucrats and Politicians in Western Democracies.* Cambridge: Harvard University Press.

Abramowitz, Alan I. 1988. "Explaining Senate Election Outcomes." *American Political Science Review* 82:385-403.

Abramowitz, Alan I. 1990a. "Incumbency, Campaign Spending, and the Decline of Competition in U.S. House Elections." Prepared for delivery at the Annual Meeting of the American Political Science Association, San Francisco, CA.

Abramowitz, Alan I. 1990b. "Campaign Spending in U.S. Senate Elections." In *The Changing World of the U.S. Senate,* ed. John Hibbing. Berkeley, CA: IGS Press.

Abramowitz, Alan I., and Jeffrey A. Segal. 1990. "Beyond Willie Horton and the Pledge of Allegiance: National Issues in the 1988 Elections." *Legislative Studies Quarterly* 15:565-580.

Alesina, Alberto, and Howard Rosenthal. 1989. "Partisan Cycles in Congressional Elections and the Macroeconomy." *American Political Science Review* 83:373-398.

Alford, John R., and John R. Hibbing. 1981. "Increased Incumbency Advantage in the House." *Journal of Politics* 43:1042-1061.

Ames, Barry. 1987. "The Congressional Connection: The Structure of Politics and the Distribution of Public Expenditures in

Brazil's Competitive Period." *Comparative Politics* 19:147-171.

Anagnoson, J. Theodore. 1983. "Home Style in New Zealand." *Legislative Studies Quarterly* 8:157-176.

Arkins, Audrey. 1990. "Legislative and Executive Relations in the Republic of Ireland." In *Parliaments in Western Europe,* ed. Philip Norton. London: Frank Cass and Co.

Arnold, R. Douglas. 1979. *Congress and the Bureaucracy.* New Haven: Yale University Press.

Arnold, R. Douglas. 1990. *The Logic of Congressional Actions.* New Haven: Yale University Press.

Arter, David. 1984. *The Nordic Parliaments: A Comparative Analysis.* New York: St. Martin's Press.

Arter, David. 1990. "The Swedish Riksdag: The Case of a Strong Policy-Influencing Assembly." In *Parliaments in Western Europe,* ed. Philip Norton. London: Frank Cass and Co.

Asher, Herbert B. 1975. "The Changing Status of the Freshman Representative." In *Congress in Change: Evolution and Reform,* ed. Norman J. Ornstein. New York: Praeger Publishers.

Asher, Herbert B., and Herbert F. Weisberg. 1978. "Voting Change in Congress: Some Dynamic Perspectives on an Evolutionary Process." *American Journal of Political Science* 22:391-425.

Bach, Stanley. 1986. "Representatives and Committees on the Floor: Amendments to Appropriations Bills in the House of Representatives, 1963-1982." *Congress and the President* 13:41-53.

Bach, Stanley. 1990. "Suspension of the Rules, the Order of Business, and the Development of Congressional Procedures." *Legislative Studies Quarterly* 15:49-64.

Bach, Stanley, and Steven S. Smith. 1988. *Managing Uncertainty in the House of Representatives: Adaptation and Innovation in Special Rules.* Washington, DC: Brookings Institution.

Bailey, F.G. 1960. "Traditional Society and Representation: The Case of Orissa." *Archives Europeanes de Sociologie* 1:121-141.

Barkan, Joel D. 1979. "Bringing Home the Pork: Legislator Behavior, Rural Development, and Political Change in East Africa." In *Legislatures in Development,* ed. Lloyd D. Musolf and Joel Smith. Durham: Duke University Press.

Baron, David P., and John A. Ferejohn. 1989. "Bargaining in Legislatures." *American Political Science Review* 83:1181-1206.

Bauer, Monica, and John R. Hibbing. 1989. "Which Incumbents Lose in House Elections: A Reply to Jacobson's 'The Marginals Never Vanished.'" *American Journal of Political Science* 33:262-271.

Baumgartner, Frank R. 1987. "Parliament's Capacity to Expand Political Controversy in France." *Legislative Studies Quarterly* 12:33-54.

Barker, Anthony, and Michael Rush. 1970. *The Member of Parliament and His Information.* London: George, Allen and Unwin.

Bean, Clive. 1990. "The Personal Vote in Australian Federal Elections." *Political Studies* 38:253-268.

Blischke, Werner. 1981. "Parliamentary Staffs in the German Bundestag." *Legislative Studies Quarterly* 6:533-558.

Blondel, J. 1973. *Comparative Legislatures.* Englewood Cliffs, NJ: Prentice-Hall.

Bogdanor, Vernon, ed. 1983. *Coalition Government in Western Europe.* London: Heinemann Educational Books.

Bond, Jon R., and Richard Fleisher. 1990. *The President in the Legislative Arena.* Chicago: University of Chicago Press.

Born, Richard. 1985. "Partisan Intentions and Election Day Realities in the Congressional Redistricting Process." *American Political Science Review* 79:305-319.

Born, Richard. 1990. "The Shared Fortunes of Congress and Congressmen: Members May Run From Congress, But They

Can't Hide." *Journal of Politics* 52:1223-1241.

Boynton, G. Robert, and Gerhard Loewenberg. 1974. "The Development of Public Support for Parliament in Germany, 1951-59." *British Journal of Political Science* 3:169-189.

Brady, David W. 1988. *Critical Elections and Congressional Policy Making.* Stanford: Stanford University Press.

Brady, David W., Joseph Cooper, and Patricia A. Hurley. 1979. "The Decline of Party in the U.S. House of Representatives." *Legislative Studies Quarterly* 4:381-408.

Breaux, David. 1990. "Specifying the Impact of Incumbency on State Legislative Elections: A District Level Analysis." *American Politics Quarterly* 18:270-286.

Bullock, Charles S., III, and David W. Brady. 1983. "Party, Constituency, and Roll-Call Voting in the U.S. Senate." *Legislative Studies Quarterly* 8:29-44.

Cain, Bruce, John Ferejohn, and Morris Fiorina. 1987. *The Personal Vote: Constituency Service and Electoral Independence.* Cambridge: Harvard University Press.

Calvert, Randall L., and John A. Ferejohn. 1983. "Coattail Voting in Recent Presidential Elections." *American Political Science Review* 77:407-419.

Campbell, James E. 1986. "Predicting Seat Gains from Presidential Coattails." *American Journal of Political Science* 30:165-183.

Canon, David T. 1989a. "The Institutionalization of Leadership in the U.S. Congress." *Legislative Studies Quarterly* 14:415-443.

Canon, David T. 1989b. "Political Amateurism in the United States Congress." In *Congress Reconsidered,* 4th ed., ed. Lawrence C. Dodd and Bruce I. Oppenheimer. Washington, DC: Congressional Quarterly Press.

Canon, David T. 1990. *Actors, Athletes, and Astronauts: Political Amateurs in the United States Congress.* Chicago: University of Chicago Press.

Clausen, Aage. 1973. *How Congressmen Decide: A Policy Focus.* New York: St. Martin's Press.

Cohen, Lenard J. 1977. "Conflict Management and Political Institutionalization in Social Yugoslavia: A Case Study of the Parliamentary System." In *Parliaments in Plural Societies,* ed. A. F. Eldridge. Durham: Duke University Press.

Collie, Melissa P. 1988a. "The Rise of Coalition Politics: Voting in the U.S. House, 1933-1980." *Legislative Studies Quarterly* 13:321-342.

Collie, Melissa P. 1988b. "The Legislature and Distributive Policy Making In Formal Perspective." *Legislative Studies Quarterly* 13:427-458.

Collie, Melissa P. 1989. "Electoral Patterns and Voting Alignments in the U.S. House, 1886-1986." *Legislative Studies Quarterly* 14:107-128.

Converse, Philip E., and Roy Pierce. 1986. *Political Representation in France.* Cambridge: Harvard University Press.

Cooper, Joseph. 1970. *The Origins of the Standing Committees and the Development of the Modern House.* Houston: Rice University Press.

Cooper, Joseph. 1977. "Congress in Organizational Perspective." In *Congress Reconsidered,* ed. Lawrence C. Dodd and Bruce I. Oppenheimer. New York: Praeger.

Cooper, Joseph, and David W. Brady. 1981a. "Institutional Context and Leadership Style: The House from Cannon to Rayburn." *American Political Science Review* 75:411-425.

Cooper, Joseph, and David W. Brady. 1981b. "Toward a Diachronic Analysis of Congress." *American Political Science Review* 75:988-1006.

Cooper, Joseph, and William West. 1981. "Voluntary Retirement, Incumbency, and the Modern House." *Political Science Quarterly* 96:279-300.

Cooper, Joseph, and Cheryl D. Young. 1989. "Bill Introduction in the Nineteenth Century: A Study of Institutional Change." *Legislative Studies Quarterly* 14:67-106.

Cover, Albert D. 1977. "One Good Term Deserves Another: The Advantage of Incumbency in Congressional Elections." *American Journal of Political Science* 21:523-542.

Cover, Albert D., and David Mayhew. 1977. "Congressional Dynamics and the Decline of Competitive Congressional Elections." In *Congress Reconsidered*, ed. Lawrence C. Dodd and Bruce I. Oppenheimer. New York: Praeger.

Covington, Cary R. 1987. "Mobilizing Congressional Support for the President: Insights from the 1960s." *Legislative Studies Quarterly* 12:77-96.

Cox, Gary W., and Mathew D. McCubbins. 1991. "On the Decline of Party Voting in Congress." *Legislative Studies Quarterly* 16:547-570.

Crane, Wilder. 1961. "The Errand-Running Function of Austrian Legislators." *Parliamentary Affairs* 15:160-169.

Crick, Bernard. 1968. *The Reform of Parliament*. London: Weidenfeld and Nicolson.

Damgaard, Erik. 1990. "The Strong Parliaments of Scandinavia." Unpublished manuscript.

Darcy, R., and Michael Marsh. 1990. "Strategic Candidates in Irish Elections." Prepared for delivery at the Annual Meeting of the American Political Science Association, San Francisco.

Davidson, Roger H. 1969. *The Role of the Congressman*. New York: Pegasus.

Davidson, Roger H. 1989. "Multiple Referral of Legislation in the U.S. Senate." *Legislative Studies Quarterly* 14:375-392.

Davidson, Roger H. 1992. "The Emergence of the Postreform Congress." In *The Postreform Congress*, ed. Roger H. Davidson. New York: St. Martin's.

Davidson, Roger H., and Walter J. Oleszek. 1990. *Congress and its Members*. 3rd ed. Washington, DC: Congressional Quarterly Press.

Davidson, Roger H., Walter J. Oleszek, and Thomas Kephart. 1988. "One Bill, Many Committees: Multiple Referrals in the U.S. House of Representatives." *Legislative Studies Quarterly* 13:3-28.

DeGregorio, Christine. 1988. "Professionals in the U.S. Congress: An Analysis of Working Styles." *Legislative Studies Quarterly* 13:459-476.

Denzau, Arthur, and Michael Munger. 1986. "Legislators and Interest Groups: How Unorganized Interests Get Represented." *American Political Science Review* 80:89-106.

Denzau, Arthur, William Riker, and Kenneth Shepsle. 1985. "Farquharson and Fenno: Sophisticated Voting and Home Style." *American Political Science Review* 79:1117-1134.

Di Palma, Giuseppe. 1977. *Surviving Without Governing: The Italian Parties in Parliament*. Berkeley: University of California Press.

Dodd, Lawrence C. 1976. *Coalitions in Parliamentary Government*. Princeton: Princeton University Press.

Dodd, Lawrence C. 1977. "Congress and the Quest for Power." In *Congress Reconsidered*, ed. Lawrence C. Dodd and Bruce I. Oppenheimer. New York: Praeger.

Dodd, Lawrence C. 1984. "The Study of Cabinet Durability." *Comparative Political Studies* July: 55-161.

Dodd, Lawrence C., and Richard L. Schott. 1979. *Congress and the Administrative State*. New York: Wiley

Dowse, R. E. 1972. "The M.P. and His Surgery." In *The Backbencher and Parliament*, ed. D. Leonard and Valentine Herman. London: St. Martin's

Easton, David. 1965. *A Systems Analysis of Political Life*. New York: Wiley.

Edwards, George C., III. 1980. *Presidential Influence in Congress*. San Francisco: W. H. Freeman.

Edwards, George C., III. 1989. *At the Margins: Presidential Leadership of Congress*. New Haven: Yale University Press.

Eldridge, A. F., ed. 1977. *Parliaments in Plural Societies*. Durham: Duke University Press.

Erikson, Robert S. 1971. "The Electoral Impact of Congressional Roll-Call Voting." *American Political Science Review* 65:1018-1032.

Erikson, Robert S. 1978. "Constituency Opinion and Congressional Behavior: A Re-Examination of the Miller-Stokes Representation Data." *American Journal of Political Science* 22:511-535.

Erikson, Robert S. 1988. "The Puzzle of Midterm Loss." *Journal of Politics* 50:1011-1029.

Erikson, Robert S., and Gerald C. Wright, Jr. 1980. "Policy Representation of Constituency Interests." *Political Behavior* 1:91-106.

Eulau, Heinz. 1987. "The Congruence Model Revisited." *Legislative Studies Quarterly* 12:171-214.

Eulau, Heinz, and Paul Karps. 1977. "The Puzzle of Representation: Specifying Components of Responsiveness." *Legislative Studies Quarterly* 2:233-254.

Eulau, Heinz, and Vera McCluggage. 1985. "Standing Committees in Legislatures." In *Handbook of Legislative Research*, ed. Gerhard Loewenberg, Samuel Patterson, and Malcolm Jewell. Cambridge: Harvard University Press.

Farrell, Brian. 1985. "Ireland: From Friends and Neighbours to Clients and Partisans: Some Dimensions of Parliamentary Representation under PR-STV." In *Representatives of the People? Parliamentarians and Constituents in Western Democracies*, ed. Vernon Bogdanor. Brookfield, VT: Gower.

Fenno, Richard F., Jr. 1962. "The House Appropriations Committee as a Political System." *American Political Science Review* 56:310-324

Fenno, Richard F., Jr. 1966. *The Power of the Purse: Appropriations Politics in Congress*. Boston: Little, Brown.

Fenno, Richard F., Jr. 1973. *Congressmen in Committees*. Boston: Little, Brown.

Fenno, Richard F., Jr. 1978. *Home Style: House Members in Their Districts*. Boston: Little, Brown.

Fenno, Richard F., Jr. 1989a. "The Senate Through the Looking Glass: The Debate Over Television." *Legislative Studies Quarterly* 14:313-348.

Fenno, Richard F., Jr. 1989b. *Dan Quayle: The Making of a U.S. Senator*. Washington, DC: Congressional Quarterly Press.

Ferejohn, John A. 1977. "On the Decline of Competition in Congressional Elections." *American Political Science Review* 71:166-176.

Ferejohn, John A., Morris Fiorina, and Richard D. McKelvey. 1987. "Sophisticated Voting and Agenda Independence in the Distributive Politics Setting." *American Journal of Political Science* 31:169-193.

Fiorina, Morris P. 1974. *Representation, Roll Calls, and Constituencies*. Lexington, MA: Heath.

Fiorina, Morris P. 1977. *Congress: Keystone of the Washington Establishment*. New Haven: Yale University Press.

Fiorina, Morris P. 1981. *Retrospective Voting in American National Elections*. New Haven: Yale University Press.

Fiorina, Morris P. 1982. "Congressmen and Their Constituents: 1958 and 1978." In *The United States Congress: Proceedings of the Thomas P. O'Neill, Jr. Symposium*, ed. Dennis Hale. Chestnut Hill, MA: Boston College.

Fiorina, Morris P. 1989. *Congress: Keystone of the Washington Establishment*. 2nd ed. New Haven: Yale University Press.

Fisher, Louis. 1991. *Constitutional Conflicts Between Congress and the President*. 3rd ed. rev. Lawrence, KS: University Press of Kansas.

Frears, John. 1990. "The French Parliament: Loyal Workhorse, Poor Watchdog." In *Parliaments in Western Europe*, ed. Philip Norton. London: Frank Cass and Co.

Frendreis, John P., and Richard W. Waterman. 1985. "PAC Contributions and Legislative Voting Behavior." *Social Science Quarterly* 66:401-412.

Froman, Lewis A., Jr. 1963. *Congressmen and Their Constituencies*. Chicago: Rand McNally.

Garand, James C. 1991. "Electoral Marginality in State Legislative Elections, 1968-1986." *Legislative Studies Quarterly* 16:7-28.

Garand, James C., and Donald Gross. 1984. "Changes in the Vote Margins for Congressional Candidates: A Specification of the Historical Trends." *American Political Science Review* 78:17-30.

Gelman, Andrew, and Gary King. 1990. "Estimating Incumbency Advantage Without Bias." *American Journal of Political Science* 34:1142-1164.

Gerlich, Peter. 1973. "The Institutionalization of European Parliaments." In *Legislatures in Comparative Perspective*, ed. Allan Kornberg. New York: David McKay.

Gierzynski, Anthony, and David Breaux. 1991. "Money and Votes in State Legislative Elections." *Legislative Studies Quarterly* 16:203-218.

Gladdish, Ken. 1991. *Governing From the Center: Politics and Policy-Making in the Netherlands*. DeKalb, IL: Northern Illinois University Press.

Glazer, Amihai, Bernard Grofman, and Marc Robbins. 1987. "Partisan and Incumbency Effects of 1970s Congressional Redistricting." *American Journal of Political Science* 31:680-707.

Green, Donald Philip, and Jonathan Krasno. 1988. "Salvation for the Spendthrift Incumbent." *American Journal of Political Science* 32:844-907.

Grenzke, Janet. 1989a. "PACs and the Congressional Supermarket: The Currency is Complex." *American Journal of Political Science* 33:1-24.

Grenzke, Janet. 1989b. "Candidate Attitudes and PAC Contributions." *Western Political Quarterly* 42:254-264.

Groennings, Sven, E. W. Kelly, and Michael Leiserson, eds. 1970. *The Study of Coalition Behavior*. New York: Holt, Rinehart and Winston.

Hahn, Jeffrey W. 1990. "As Elections Move East: Boss Gorbachev Confronts His New Congress." *Orbis* 34:163-178.

Hall, Richard L. 1987. "Participation and Purpose in Committee Decision-Making." *American Political Science Review* 81:105-128.

Hall, Richard L., and Frank Wayman. 1990. "Buying Time: Moneyed Interests and the Mobilization of Bias in Congressional Committees." *American Political Science Review* 84:797-820.

Hamm, Keith E. 1985. "Legislative Committees, Executive Agencies, and Interest Groups." In *Handbook of Legislative Research*, ed. Gerhard Loewenberg, Samuel Patterson, and Malcolm Jewell. Cambridge: Harvard University Press.

Hammond, Susan Webb. 1985. "Legislative Staffs." In *Handbook of Legislative Research*, ed. Gerhard Loewenberg, Samuel Patterson, and Malcolm Jewell. Cambridge: Harvard University Press.

Happy, J.R. 1989. "Economic Performance and Retrospective Voting in Canadian Federal Elections." *Canadian Journal of Political Science* 22:377-387.

Hedlund, Ronald D. 1985. "Organizational Attributes of Legislative Institutions: Structure, Rules, Norms, Resources." In *Handbook of Legislative Research*, ed. Gerhard Loewenberg,

Samuel Patterson, and Malcolm Jewell. Cambridge: Harvard University Press.

Herrnson, Paul S. 1986. "Do Parties Make a Difference? The Role of Party Organizations in Congressional Elections." *Journal of Politics* 48:589-615.

Herrnson, Paul S. 1989. "National Party Decision Making, Strategies, and Resource Distribution in Congressional Elections." *Western Political Quarterly* 42:301-324.

Hibbing, John R. 1988. "Legislative Institutionalization with Illustrations from the British House of Commons." *American Journal of Political Science* 32:681-712.

Hibbing, John R. 1991. *Congressional Careers: Contours of Life in the U.S. House of Representatives*. Chapel Hill, NC: University of North Carolina Press.

Hibbing, John R., and Sara L. Brandes. 1983. "State Population and the Electoral Success of U.S. Senators." *American Journal of Political Science* 27:809-819.

Hibbing, John R., and David Marsh. 1987. "Accounting for the Voting Patterns of British MPs on Free Votes." *Legislative Studies Quarterly* 12:275-297.

Hibbing, John R., and Michael K. Moore. 1991. "Is Serving In Congress Fun Again? Voluntary Retirements and Congressional Careers Through the 1980s." Prepared for delivery at the Annual Meeting of the American Political Science Association, Washington, DC.

Holbrook, Thomas M., and Charles M. Tidmarch. 1991. "Sophomore Surge in State Legislative Elections." *Legislative Studies Quarterly* 16:49-64.

Hopkins, Raymond. 1970. "The Role of the M.P. in Tanzania." *American Political Science Review* 64:754-771.

Hoskin, Gary W. 1971. "Dimensions of Representation in the Colombian National Legislature." In *Latin American Legislatures: Their Role and Influence*, ed. Weston Agor. New York: Praeger.

Huitt, Ralph K., and Robert L. Peabody, eds. 1969. *Congress: Two Decades of Analysis*. New York: Harper and Row.

Huntington, Samuel P. 1968. *Political Order in Changing Societies*. New Haven: Yale University Press.

Hurley, Patricia A., and Rick W. Wilson. 1989. "Partisan Voting Patterns in the U.S. Senate, 1877-1986." *Legislative Studies Quarterly* 14:225-250.

Hurwitz, Jon. 1988. "Determinants of Legislative Cue Selection." *Social Science Quarterly* 69:212-223.

Jacobson, Gary C. 1987a. "Running Scared: Elections and Congressional Politics in the 1980s." In *Congress: Structure and Policy*, ed. Mathew D. McCubbins and Terry Sullivan. Cambridge: Cambridge University Press.

Jacobson, Gary C. 1987b. "The Marginals Never Vanished: Incumbency and Competition in Elections to the U.S. House of Representatives." *American Journal of Political Science* 31:126-141.

Jacobson, Gary C. 1990a. *The Electoral Origins of Divided Government: Competition in U.S. House Elections, 1946-1988*. Boulder: Westview Press.

Jacobson, Gary C. 1990b. "The Effects of Campaign Spending in House Elections: New Evidence for Old Arguments." *American Journal of Political Science* 34:334-362.

Jacobson, Gary C. 1992. *The Politics of Congressional Elections*. 3rd ed. New York: Harper Collins.

Jacobson, Gary C., and Samuel Kernell. 1983. *Strategy and Choice in Congressional Elections*. 2nd ed. New Haven: Yale University Press.

Jacobson, Gary C., and Samuel Kernell. 1990. "National Forces in the 1986 U.S. House Elections." *Legislative Studies Quarterly* 15:65-88.

Jacobson, Gary C., and Raymond E. Wolfinger. 1990. "Information and Voting in California Senate Elections." In *The Changing World of the U.S. Senate*, ed. John Hibbing. Berkeley, CA: IGS Press.

Jennings, Ivor. 1957. *Parliament*. London: Cambridge University Press.

Jewell, Malcolm E. 1982. *Representation in State Legislatures*. Lexington, KY: The University Press of Kentucky.

Jewell, Malcolm E. 1985. "Legislators and Constituents in the Representative Process." In *Handbook of Legislative Research*, ed. Gerhard Loewenberg, Samuel Patterson, and Malcolm Jewell. Cambridge: Harvard University Press.

Johannes, John R. 1984. *To Serve the People: Congress and Constituency Service*. Lincoln: University of Nebraska Press.

Jogerst, Michael A. 1990. "Select Committees of the British House of Commons and the Changing Role of MPs." Prepared for delivery at the Annual Meeting of the American Political Science Association, Washington, DC.

Kazee, Thomas A., and Mary C. Thornberry. 1990. "Where's The Party: Congressional Recruitment and American Party Organizations." *Western Political Quarterly* 43:61-80.

Kiewiet, D. Roderick, and Mathew D. McCubbins. 1991. *The Logic of Delegation: Congressional Parties and the Appropriations Process*. Chicago: University of Chicago Press.

Kim, Chong Lim, Joel D. Barkan, Ilter Turan, and Malcolm Jewell. 1984. *The Legislative Connection: Representation in Kenya, Korea, and Turkey*. Durham: Duke University Press.

Kim, Chong Lim, and G. Robert Boynton, eds. 1975. *Legislative Systems in Developing Countries*. Durham: Duke University Press.

Kim, Chong Lim, and Samuel C. Patterson. 1988. "Parliamentary Elite Integration in Six Nations." *Comparative Politics* 20:379-399.

King, Anthony. 1976. "Modes of Executive-Legislative Relations: Great Britain, France, and West Germany." *Legislative Studies Quarterly* 1:37-65.

King, Gary. 1991. "Constituency Service and Incumbency Advantage." *British Journal of Political Science* 21:119-128.

Kingdon, John W. 1973. *Congressmen's Voting Decisions*. New York: Harper and Row.

Kingdon, John W. 1984. *Agendas, Alternatives, and Public Policies*. Boston: Little Brown.

Kingdon, John W. 1989. *Congressmen's Voting Decisions*. 3rd ed. Ann Arbor: The University of Michigan Press.

Koford, Kenneth. 1989. "Dimensions in Congressional Voting." *American Political Science Review* 83:949-962.

Kornberg, Allan, and Lloyd D. Musolf, eds. 1970. *Legislatures in Developmental Perspective*. Durham: Duke University Press.

Kozak, David C. 1984. *Contexts of Congressional Decision Behavior*. Lanham, MD: University Press of America.

Krashinsky, Michael, and William J. Milne. 1986. "The Effect of Incumbency in the 1984 Federal and 1985 Ontario Elections." *Canadian Journal of Political Science* 19:337-343.

Krasno, Jonathan S., and Donald Philip Green. 1988. "Preempting Quality Challengers in House Elections." *Journal of Politics* 50:920-936.

Krehbiel, Keith. 1986. "Unanimous Consent Agreements: Going Along in the Senate." *Journal of Politics* 48:541-564.

Krehbiel, Keith. 1987. "Why Are Congressional Committees Powerful?" *American Political Science Review* 81:929-935.

Krehbiel, Keith. 1988. "Spatial Models of Legislative Choice." *Legislative Studies Quarterly* 13:259-320.

Krehbiel, Keith. 1990. "Are Congressional Committees Composed of Preference Outliers?" *American Political Science Review* 84:149-164.

Krehbiel, Keith. 1991. *Information and Legislative Organization*. Ann Arbor: University of Michigan Press.

Laegreid, Per, and Johan P. Olsen. 1986. "The Storting: A Last Stronghold of the Political Amateur." In *Parliaments and Parliamentarians in Democratic Politics*, ed. Ezra N. Suleiman. New York: Holmes and Maier.

Lancaster, Thomas D., and W. David Patterson. 1990. "Comparative Pork Barrel Politics: Perceptions from the West German Bundestag." *Comparative Political Studies* 22:458-477.

Lees, John D., and Malcolm Shaw, eds. 1979. *Committees in Legislatures: A Comparative Analysis*. Durham: Duke University Press.

LeLoup, Lance T., and John T. Woolley. 1991. "Legislative Oversight of Monetary Policy in France, Germany, Great Britain, and the United States." In *Legislatures in the Policy Process: The Dilemmas of Economic Policy*, ed. David Olson and Michael Mezey. Cambridge: Cambridge University Press.

Lindsay, James M. 1990. "Parochialism, Policy, and Constituency Constraints: Congressional Voting on Strategic Weapons Systems." *American Journal of Political Science* 34:936-960.

Lock, Geoffrey. 1988. "Information for Parliament." In *The Commons Under Scrutiny*, eds. Michael Ryle and Peter Richards. London: Routledge.

Lockerbie, Brad. 1991. "Prospective Economic Voting in U.S. House Elections, 1956-1988." *Legislative Studies Quarterly* 16:239-262.

Lockerbie, Brad, and Stephen A. Borelli. 1989. "Getting Inside the Beltway: Perceptions of Presidential Skill and Success in Congress." *British Journal of Political Science* 19:97-106.

Loewenberg, Gerhard. 1967. *Parliament in the German Political System*. Ithaca, New York: Cornell University Press.

Loewenberg, Gerhard, and Samuel Patterson. 1979. *Comparing Legislatures*. Boston: Little, Brown.

Loewenberg, Gerhard, and Thomas C. Mans. 1988. "Individual and Structural Influences on the Perception of Legislative Norms in Three European Parliaments." *American Journal of Political Science* 32:155-177.

Lowi, Theodore J. 1979. *The End of Liberalism: The Second Republic of the United States*. New York: W. W. Norton and Co.

MacMullen, Andrew. 1985. "Citizens and National Parliamentarians in Belgium: Sectional Representation in a Multi-Party System." In *Representatives of the People? Parliamentarians and Constituents in Western Democracies*, ed. Vernon Bogdanor. Brookfield, VT: Gower.

MacRae, Duncan. 1958. *Dimensions of Congressional Voting*. Berkeley: University of California Press.

McAdams, John C., and John R. Johannes. 1987. "Determinants of Spending by House Challengers, 1974-1984." *American Journal of Political Science* 31:457-483.

McAdams, John C., and John R. Johannes. 1988. "Congressmen, Perquisites, and Elections." *Journal of Politics* 50:412-439.

McCormick, James. 1985. "Congressional Voting on the Nuclear Freeze Resolutions." *American Politics Quarterly* 13:122-134.

McCormick, James, and Michael Black. 1983. "Ideology and Senate Voting on the Panama Canal Treaty." *Legislative Studies Quarterly* 8:45-63.

McCubbins, Mathew D. 1985. "The Legislative Design of Regulatory Structure." *American Journal of Political Science* 29:721-748.

McCubbins, Mathew D., and Thomas Schwartz. 1984. "Congressional Oversight Overlooked: Police Patrols Versus Fire Alarms." *American Journal of Political Science* 28:165-179.

Maass, Arthur. 1983. *Congress and the Common Good*. New York: Basic Books.

Maisel, Louis Sandy. 1982. *From Obscurity to Oblivion: Running In the Congressional Primary*. Knoxville: The University of Tennessee Press.

Malbin, Michael J. 1980. *Unelected Representatives: Congressional Staff and the Future of Representative Government.* New York: Basic Books.

March, James G., and Johan P. Olson. 1984. "The New Institutionalism: Organizational Factors in Political Life." *American Political Science Review* 78:734-749.

Marsh, David, and Melvyn Read. 1988. *Private Members' Bills.* Cambridge: Cambridge University Press.

Matthews, Donald. 1960. *U.S. Senators and Their World.* New York: Vintage Press.

Matthews, Donald R., and James A. Stimson. 1975. *Yeas and Nays: Normal Decision-Making in the U.S. House of Representatives.* New York: Wiley.

Mayhew, David R. 1974a. *Congress: The Electoral Connection.* New Haven: Yale University Press.

Mayhew, David R. 1974b. "Congressional Elections: The Case of the Vanishing Marginals," *Polity* 6:295-317.

Mayhew, David R. 1991. *Divided We Govern: Party Control, Lawmaking, and Investigations, 1946-1990.* New Haven: Yale University Press.

Mezey, Michael L. 1972. "The Functions of Minimal Legislature: Role Perceptions of Thai Legislators." *Western Political Quarterly* 25:686-701.

Mezey, Michael L. 1975. "Legislative Development and Political Parties: The Case of Thailand." In *Legislative Systems in Developing Countries,* ed. Chong Lim Kim and G. Robert Boynton. Durham: Duke University Press.

Mezey, Michael L. 1979. *Comparative Legislatures.* Durham: Duke University Press.

Mezey, Michael L. 1985. "The Functions of Legislatures in the Third World." In *Handbook of Legislative Research,* ed. Gerhard Loewenberg, Samuel Patterson, and Malcolm Jewell. Cambridge: Harvard University Press.

Mezey, Michael L. 1986. "The Legislature, the Executive and Public Policy: The Futile Quest for Congressional Power." *Congress and the Presidency* 13:1-20.

Mezey, Michael L. 1989. *Congress, the President and Public Policy.* Boulder: Westview Press.

Miller, Arthur H. 1990. "Public Judgments of Senate and House Candidates." *Legislative Studies Quarterly.* 15:525-542.

Miller, Warren E., and Donald E. Stokes. 1963. "Constituency Influence in Congress." *American Political Science Review* 57:45-56.

Mughan, Anthony. 1990. "Midterm Popularity and Governing Party Dissension in the House of Commons, 1959-79." *Legislative Studies Quarterly* 15:341-356.

Müller-Rommel, Ferdinand. 1990. "Interest Group Representation in the Bundestag." In *The U.S. Congress and the German Bundestag: Comparisons of Democratic Processes,* ed. Uwe Thaysen, Roger H. Davidson, and Robert Gerald Livingston. Boulder: Westview Press.

Nelson, Daniel. 1982. "Communist Legislatures and Communist Politics." In *Communist Legislatures in Comparative Perspective,* ed. Daniel Nelson and Stephen White. Albany: State University of New York Press.

Norton, Philip. 1980. *Dissension in the House of Commons: 1975-1979.* Oxford: Clarendon Press.

Norton, Philip. 1985. "Behavioural Changes: Backbench Independence in the 1980s." In *Parliament in the 1980s,* ed. Philip Norton. Oxford: Basil Blackwell.

Norton, Philip. 1990. "Parliament in the United Kingdom: Balancing Effectiveness and Consent?" In *Parliaments in Western Europe,* ed. Philip Norton. London: Frank Cass and Co.

Norton, Philip, and David Wood. 1990. "Constituency Service by MPs: Does It Contribute to a Personal Vote?" *Parliamentary Affairs* 43:196-208.

O'Brien, Kevin J. 1988. "China's National People's Congress: Reform and Its Limits." *Legislative Studies Quarterly* 13:343-374.

O'Brien, Kevin J. 1989. "Legislative Development and Chinese Political Change." *Studies in Comparative Communism* 22:57-75.

O'Brien, Kevin J. 1990. "Is China's National People's Congress a Conservative Legislature?" *Asian Survey* 30:782-794.

Ogul, Morris S. 1976. *Congress Oversees the Bureaucracy.* Pittsburgh: University of Pittsburgh Press.

Ogul, Morris S., and Bert A. Rockman. 1990. "Overseeing Oversight: New Departures and Old Problems." *Legislative Studies Quarterly* 15:5-24.

Opello, Walter C., Jr. 1986. "Portugal's Parliament: An Organizational Analysis of Legislative Performance." *Legislative Studies Quarterly* 11:291-320.

Overby, L. Marvin. 1991. "Assessing Constituency Influence: Congressional Voting on the Nuclear Freeze, 1982-83." *Legislative Studies Quarterly* 16:297-312.

Owens, John E. 1986. "The Impact of Campaign Contributions on Legislative Outcomes in Congress: Evidence from a House Committee." *Political Studies* 34:285-295.

Owens, John R., and Larry L. Wade. 1984. "Federal Spending in Congressional Districts." *Western Political Quarterly* 37:404-423.

Owens, John R., and Larry L. Wade. 1988. "Economic Conditions and Constituency Voting in Great Britain." *Political Studies* 36:30-51.

Park, Chan Wook. 1988. "Constituency Representation in Korea: Sources and Consequences." *Legislative Studies Quarterly* 13:225-242.

Parker, Glenn R. 1986. *Homeward Bound: Explaining Changes in Congressional Behavior.* Pittsburgh: University of Pittsburgh Press.

Parker, Glenn R., and Roger H. Davidson. 1979. "Why Do Americans Love Their Congressman So Much More Than Their Congress?" *Legislative Studies Quarterly* 4:53-61.

Patterson, Samuel C. 1989. "Understanding the British Parliament." *Political Studies* 37:449-462.

Patterson, Samuel C., and Gregory A. Caldeira. 1988. "Party Voting in the United States Congress." *British Journal of Political Science* 18:111-131.

Peabody, Robert L., and Nelson W. Polsby, eds. 1969. *New Perspectives on the House of Representatives.* Chicago: Rand McNally.

Pelinka, Anton. 1985. "The Case of Austria: Neo-Corporatism and Social Partnership." In *Representatives of the People? Parliamentarians and Constituents in Western Democracies,* ed. Vernon Bogdanor. Brookfield, VT: Gower.

Peters, Ronald M., Jr. 1990. *The American Speakership: The Office in Historical Perspective.* Baltimore: Johns Hopkins University Press.

Piper, R. Richard. 1991. "British Backbench Rebellion and Government Appointments, 1945-1987." *Legislative Studies Quarterly* 16:219-238.

Pitkin, Hanna F. 1967. *The Concept of Representation.* Berkeley: University of California Press.

Polsby, Nelson W. 1968. "The Institutionalization of the U.S. House of Representatives." *American Political Science Review* 62:144-168.

Poole, Keith. 1981. "Dimensions of Interest Group Evaluation of the U.S. Senate, 1969-1978." *American Journal of Political Science* 25:49-67.

Poole, Keith. 1988. "Recent Developments in Analytic Models of Voting in the U.S. Congress." *Legislative Studies Quarterly* 13:117-133.

Poole, Keith, and R. Steven Daniels. 1985. "Ideology, Party, and

Voting in the U.S. Congress, 1959-1980." *American Political Science Review* 79:373-399.

Poole, Keith, and Howard Rosenthal. 1984. "The Polarization of American Politics." *Journal of Politics* 46:1061-1079.

Poole, Keith, and Howard Rosenthal. 1985. "A Spatial Model for Legislative Roll Call Analysis." *American Journal of Political Science* 29:357-384.

Pridham, Geoffrey. 1985. "Parliamentarians and their Constituents in Italy's Party Democracy." In *Representatives of the People? Parliamentarians and Constituents in Western Democracies,* ed. Vernon Bogdanor. Brookfield, VT: Gower.

Pridham, Geoffrey. 1986. "An Inductive Theoretical Framework for Coalitional Behaviour: Political Parties in Multi-Dimensional Perspective in Western Europe." In *Coalition Behavior in Theory and Practice: An Inductive Model for Western Europe,* ed. Geoffrey Pridham. Cambridge: Cambridge University Press.

Rasmussen, Jorgen. 1988. "Will I Like it the First Time? The Maiden Speech in the British House of Commons." *European Journal of Political Research* 16:527-544.

Richardson, Bradley M. 1988. "Constituency Candidates Versus Parties in Japanese Voting Behavior." *American Political Science Review* 82:695-718.

Rieselbach, Leroy. 1983. "The Forest for The Trees: Blazing Trails for Congressional Research." In *Political Science: The State of the Discipline,* ed. Ada W. Finifter. Washington, DC: The American Political Science Association.

Rieselbach, Leroy. 1992. "Purposive Politicians Meet the Institutional Congress: A Review Essay." *Legislative Studies Quarterly* 17:95-111.

Riggs, Fred W. 1975. *Legislative Origins: A Comparative and Contextual Approach.* International Studies Association, Occasional Paper Number 7. Pittsburgh, PA: International Studies Association.

Rivers, Douglas, and Morris P. Fiorina. 1989. "Constituency Service, Reputation, and Incumbency Advantage." In *Home Style and Washington Work: Studies of Congressional Politics,* ed. Morris P. Fiorina and David Rohde. Ann Arbor: University of Michigan Press.

Rockman, Bert A. 1985. "Legislative-Executive Relations and Legislative Oversight." In *Handbook of Legislative Research,* ed. Gerhard Loewenberg, Samuel Patterson, and Malcolm Jewell. Cambridge: Harvard University Press.

Rohde, David W. 1992. "Electoral Forces, Political Agendas, and Partisanship in the House and Senate." In *The Postreform Congress,* ed. Roger Davidson. New York: St. Martin's Press.

Rose, Richard. 1986. "British MPs: More Bark than Bite." In *Parliaments and Parliamentarians in Democratic Politics,* ed. Ezra N. Suleiman. New York: Holmes and Maier.

Rush, Michael. 1990. "Pressure Politics." In *Parliament and Pressure Politics,* ed. Michael Rush. Oxford: Clarendon Press.

Saalfeld, Thomas. 1990. "The West German Bundestag After Forty Years: The Role of Parliament in a Party Democracy." In *Parliaments in Western Europe,* ed. Philip Norton. London: Frank Cass and Co.

Scher, Seymour. 1963. "Conditions for Legislative Control." *Journal of Politics* 25:526-551.

Searing, Donald. 1985. "The Role of the Good Constituency Members and the Practice of Representation in Great Britain." *Journal of Politics* 47:348-381.

Schlesinger, Joseph A. 1966. *Ambition and Politics: Political Careers in the United States.* Chicago: Rand McNally.

Schroedel, Jean Ruth. 1986. "Campaign Contributions and Legislative Outcomes." *Western Political Quarterly* 34:371-389.

Shaffer, William R. 1991. "Interparty Spatial Relationships in

Norwegian Storting Roll Call Voting." *Scandinavian Political Studies* 14:59-83.

Shapiro, Catherine R., David W. Brady, Richard A. Brody, and John A. Ferejohn. 1990. "Linking Constituency Opinion and Senate Voting Scores: A Hybrid Explanation." *Legislative Studies Quarterly* 15:599-622.

Shaw, Malcolm. 1979. "Conclusion." In *Committees in Legislatures: A Comparative Analysis,* ed. John D. Lees and Malcolm Shaw. Durham: Duke University Press.

Shaw, Malcolm. 1990. "Members of Parliament." In *Parliament and Pressure Politics,* ed. Michael Rush. Oxford: Clarendon Press.

Shepsle, Kenneth A. 1979. "Institutional Arrangements and Equilibrium in Multi-Dimensional Voting Models." *American Journal of Political Science* 23:27-59.

Shepsle, Kenneth A. 1988. "Representation and Governance: The Great Legislative Trade-Off." *Political Science Quarterly* 103:461-484.

Shepsle, Kenneth A., and Barry R. Weingast. 1987. "The Institutional Foundations of Committee Power." *American Political Science Review* 81:85-104.

Shull, Steven A. 1991. *The Two Presidencies: A Quarter Century Assessment.* Chicago: Nelson Hall.

Sinclair, Barbara. 1982. *Congressional Realignment 1925-1978.* Austin: University of Texas Press.

Sinclair, Barbara. 1983. *Majority Party Leadership in the U.S. House.* Baltimore: Johns Hopkins University Press.

Sinclair, Barbara. 1988. "The Distribution of Committee Positions in the U.S. Senate: Explaining Institutional Change." *American Journal of Political Science* 32:276-301.

Sinnott, Richard. 1989. "Locating Parties, Factions, and Ministries in a Policy Space: A Contribution to Understanding the Party-Policy Link." *European Journal of Political Research* 17:689-705.

Sloan, John W. 1989. "The Policy Capabilities of Democratic Regimes in Latin America." *Latin American Research Reports* 24:113-126.

Sloan, John W., and Kent L. Tedin. 1987. "The Consequences of Regime Type for Public Policy Outputs." *Comparative Political Studies* 20:98-124.

Smith, Joel, and Lloyd D. Musolf, eds. 1979. *Legislatures in Development: Dynamics of Change in New and Old States.* Durham: Duke University Press.

Smith, Steven S. 1988. "An Essay on Sequence, Position, Goals, and Committee Power." *Legislative Studies Quarterly* 13:151-176.

Smith, Steven S. 1989. *Call To Order: Floor Politics in the House and Senate.* Washington, DC: The Brookings Institution.

Smith, Steven S., and Marcus Flathman. 1989. "Managing the Senate Floor: Unanimous Consent Agreements Since the 1950s." *Legislative Studies Quarterly* 14:349-374.

Squire, Peverill. 1990. "Challengers in U.S. Senate Elections." In *The Changing World of the U.S. Senate,* ed. John Hibbing. Berkeley, CA: IGS Press.

Stone, Walter J. 1979. "Measuring Constituency-Representative Linkages: Problems and Prospects." *Legislative Studies Quarterly* 4:623-639.

Strahan, Randall. 1990. *New Ways and Means: Reform and Change in a Congressional Committee.* Chapel Hill: University of North Carolina Press.

Strom, Gerald S. 1990. *The Logic of Lawmaking: A Spatial Theory Approach.* Baltimore: Johns Hopkins University Press.

Strom, Kaare. 1990. *Minority Government and Majority Rule.* Cambridge: Cambridge University Press.

Sullivan, Terry. 1990. "Bargaining With the President: A Simple Game and New Evidence." *American Political Science Review* 84:1167-1196.

Sundquist, James L. 1981. *The Decline and Resurgence of Congress.* Washington, DC: The Brookings Institution.

Swift, Elaine W. 1987. "The Electoral Connection Meets the Past: Lessons from Congressional History." *Political Science Quarterly* 102:625-645.

Turner, Julius. 1951. *Party and Constituency: Pressures on Congress.* Baltimore: Johns Hopkins University Press.

Uslaner, Eric M. 1985. "Casework and Institutional Design: Redeeming Promises in the Promised Land." *Legislative Studies Quarterly* 10:35-52.

Uslaner, Eric M. 1990. "What Sustains Congressional Norms?" Prepared for delivery at the Annual Meeting of the American Political Science Association, San Francisco.

Valenzuela, Arturo, and Alexander Wilde. 1979. "Presidential Politics and the Decline of the Chilean Congress." In *Legislatures in Development,* ed. Lloyd D. Musolf and Joel Smith. Durham: Duke University Press.

VanDoren, Peter M. 1990. "Can We Learn the Causes of Congressional Decisions From Roll-Call Data?" *Legislative Studies Quarterly* 15:311-340.

Wahlke, John C. 1971. "Policy Demands and System Support: The Role of the Represented." *British Journal of Political Science* 1:271-290.

Wahlke, John C. 1987. "Legislative Behavior, 1967-1968." *Legislative Studies Quarterly* 12:215-226.

Wahlke, John C., Heinz Eulau, W. Buchanan, and W. Ferguson. 1962. *The Legislative System.* New York: Wiley.

Wayne, Stephen J. 1978. *The Legislative Presidency.* New York: Harper and Row.

Weingast, Barry R. 1984. "The Congressional-Bureaucratic System: A Principal-Agent Perspective. With Applications to the SEC." *Public Choice* 44:147-191.

Weingast, Barry R. 1989. "Floor Behavior in the U.S. Congress: Committee Power Under the Open Rule." *American Political Science Review* 83:795-816.

Weingast, Barry R. 1992. "Fighting Fire With Fire: Amending Activity and Institutional Change in the Postreform Congress." In *The Postreform Congress,* ed. Roger Davidson. New York: St. Martin's.

Weingast, Barry R., and Mark J. Moran. 1983. "Bureaucratic Discretion or Congressional Control? Regulatory Policymaking by the Federal Trade Commission." *Journal of Political Economy.* 91:765-800.

Welch, W.P. 1982. "Campaign Contributions and Legislative Voting: Milk Money and Dairy Price Supports." *Western Political Quarterly* 30:478-495.

West, Darrell M. 1988. "Activists and Economic Policymaking in Congress." *American Journal of Political Science* 32:662-680.

Westlye, Mark C. 1983. "Competitiveness of Senate Seats and Voting Behavior in Senate Elections." *American Journal of Political Science* 27:253-283.

Wilcox, Clyde, and Aage Clausen. 1991. "The Dimensionality of Roll Call Voting Reconsidered." *Legislative Studies Quarterly* 16:393-406.

Wilkerson, John D. 1990. "Re-election and Representation in Conflict: The Case of Agenda Manipulation." *Legislative Studies Quarterly* 15:263-282.

Williams, Phillip M. 1968. *The French Parliament: Politics in the Fifth Republic.* New York: Praeger.

Wolters, Menno. 1984. *Interspace Politics.* Holland: Drukkerij Van de Ridder.

Wood, David M. 1987. "The Conservative Member of Parliament as Lobbyist for Constituency Economic Interests." *Political Studies* 35:393-409.

Woolley, John T., and Lance T. LeLoup. 1989. "The Adequacy of the Electoral Motive in Explaining Legislative Attention to Monetary Policy: A Comparative Study." *Comparative Politics* 22:63-82.

Wright, Gerald C., Jr. 1978. "Candidate's Policy Position and Voting in U.S. House Elections." *Legislative Studies Quarterly.* 3:445-464.

Wright, Gerald C., Jr. 1990. "Policy Voting in the U.S. Senate: Who Is Represented?" In *The Changing World of the U.S. Senate,* ed. John Hibbing. Berkeley, CA.: IGS Press.

Wright, Gerald C., Jr., and Michael B. Berkman. 1986. "Candidates and Policy in United States Senate Elections." *American Political Science Review* 80:567-588.

Wright, John R. 1985. "PACs, Contributions, and Roll Calls: An Organizational Perspective." *American Political Science Review* 79:400-414.

Wright, John R. 1990. "Contributions, Lobbying, and Committee Voting in the U.S. House of Representatives." *American Political Science Review* 84:417-438.

14

Public Law and Judicial Politics

Martin Shapiro

The Status of the Field

Public law, judicial politics, or law and politics today enjoys a highly problematic status as a subfield of political science. Even its name is in doubt. Once one of the five or six major subdisciplines, it has, to some degree, avoided the fragmentation of some of the others. It remains one of the larger subdisciplines in numbers of practitioners and publications. Yet it has become one of the more minor fields in terms of status within the discipline. Few, if any, public law political scientists are numbered among the stars of the discipline as Corwin and Cushman once were. Many departments have reduced judicial politics to a sub-subfield of American politics. During much of the 1980s, a striking proportion of the top departments, including Harvard, Yale, Chicago, Michigan, and Stanford had no senior person devoted to principally to teaching in the field. Through promotion, some senior lateral hiring, and the joint appointment of law faculty to political science departments, the situation is now somewhat improved. Nevertheless, several generations of Ph.D's are depleted, and in only a handful of major departments is there more than one senior person of national reputation devoting full time to political-science-based (as opposed to law-based) instruction in law and politics.

Vigorous efforts are being made to fill the gap by the Law and Courts Organized Section of APSA. A committee of the section, chaired by Austin Sarat, prepared a major report on the state of the discipline, and, in conjunction with the section, the *Review of Politics* has announced it will devote one issue a year for three years to law and politics studies (see the "Special Issue on Public Law," Summer 1992).

Public Law as Constitutional Law: Supreme Court Alone

Intellectual change typically is overdetermined and full of chicken and egg problems. A number of paradoxes associated with the decline of the subfield can be noted even though describing them falls short of a causal explanation. The central paradox involves constitutional law and the Supreme Court. Until the 1950s, "public law" was usually thought of as containing three distinct entities that together formed the field while each also performed a vital service to another major field. The three were constitutional law, administrative law, and international law, linked respectively to American politics, public administration, and international relations. Moreover, another small but distinct field, "government regulation of business," called heavily on the services of public law political scientists.

Then, in a bipolar, cold war world, particularly as interpreted by the dominant Morgenthau school of international relations scholars, international law came to seem a meaningless facade. The number of international law teachers and scholars in political science declined to near zero. Even those international relations specialists seeking non-Clauswitzian facets somewhere in the family of nations, now concerned themselves, not with international law, but international organization.

Under the impact of the "behavioral revolution" the policy studies areas of political science such as government regulation fell away. Public administration became administrative behavior and organization, with administrative law, like all law, treated as one of those formal screens which investigators had to penetrate in order to discover real political behavior.

In American politics, too, behaviorism tended to denigrate formal legal and constitutional structures and language as mere appearances behind which real and quantifiable political behavior lurked. Yet the power of the Supreme Court to declare laws unconstitutional was too big and too dramatic to permit as great a decline in constitutional law as occurred in administrative and international law. Constitutional law remained as the eroded but still visible remnant of what had been "public law." Even in the remnant, however, much of "constitutional law" became "judicial behavior," and most of judicial behavior became the analysis of the votes of the justices of the Supreme Court in particular cases. In the eyes of most political scientists public law was reduced to the study of the Supreme Court's Constitutional Law Opinions and Votes

Reduced in this way, public law encounters the paradox that it studies only one thing, and the thing is so big as to be unimportant to most political scientists. Supreme Court decisions declaring laws unconstitutional were few and far between even in the Warren court years, and they seem to come as bolts from the blue. American politics and public administration specialists immersed in the everyday, routine politics of Congress, the presidency, and the federal bureaucracy naturally treated constitutional judicial review as a kind of random act of God -- sporadic incidents to which the legislative-executive system they studied had to adjust occasionally Reduced to constitutional law, law and courts were read out of the normal nitty gritty politics of pluralist bargaining and compromise that American politics people studied. And constitutional law and/or judicial behavior people were seen by American politics scholars as being, to mix metaphors, a set of Kremlinologists who sat in a corner trying to divine the intentions of the Olympian justices. Moreover, they did their divining either by an arcane lawyer-babble of case names or an equally arcane Guttman-scaling of judicial attitudes. So American politics people stopped talking to constitutional law and judicial behavior people, because they spoke only in a weird non-political-science language and because they studied things that had almost nothing to do with the everyday politics that American politics people studied.

This constitutional law-Supreme Court orientation also has curious cause and effect relations with certain internal tendencies in both the American and comparative politics fields. Nearly all congressional and American bureaucratic studies have always consisted of input and through put analysis. While economists routinely assess the performance of complex organiza-tions by studying their outputs, political scientists almost never seek to understand the performance of Congress by reading its statutes or of executive branch organizations by reading the regulations and rules they produce. Comparativists, even those principally concerned with law-making processes and institutions, are almost invariably totally ignorant of the actual laws of the countries they study and of the courts of those countries. No doubt a major reason for this law avoidance is that law is complex and technical. Yet if Americanists and comparativists turned to their public law colleagues for technical help, there was no help to be had. Public law people only did constitutional law. They knew nothing about statutes or administrative regulations. And they knew nothing about foreign law or courts either because until very recently most foreign countries had little or no constitutional judicial review. Thus, politics people

defined law out of what they did and could not even ask law and politics people to do what politics people should have been doing themselves.

Public law and/or judicial behavior thus dwindled into a marginalized constitutional law-Supreme Court ghetto of little interest to other political scientists. And public law, judicial behavior graduate students were taught that what they ought to do was to stay in that ghetto and concentrate on learning its esoteric languages.

Two Breaks in the Constitutional Law Barrier: Urban Courts and Private Law

One early break in the ghetto wall occurred during the urban politics episode of American political science. Empirically oriented urbanists looking at what was really going on in cities kept running into local courts and judges. Because most of these political scientists were not public law trained, they did not know that they were supposed to ignore these courts and judges because they did not do constitutional law. Thus, a major opening occurred from constitutional law-Supreme Court-only studies.

A second, but so far much narrower, break occurred as some political scientists reconsidered the "public" in public law. The distinction between public and private law is drawn from nineteenth century European civil law. That distinction makes very good sense in a laissez faire era in which the state is a neutral policeman of private relationships themselves established by private contracts. Private law is then the essentially unchanging rules of the game of private enterprise enforced by an apolitical court in the absence of any government interest. Public law governs the internal processes of government bodies and their relations to one another and to the citizens. It embodies the public interest and is an instrument of public policies. Public law and government, as the distinguished name of the Columbia department tells us, go together. The political scientist has no interest in private law.

Once political science defines itself as dealing with the authoritative allocation of values, and the modern state is seen not as a neutral policeman but a positive achiever of welfare, the public law/private law distinction becomes less tenable. The "private" law of property and contract authoritatively allocate most of the values in a capitalist society. As the Supreme Court constitutionalized criminal procedure, somehow it became appropriate even for public law political scientists to study criminal law and courts, although criminal law sits uneasily on the boundary between public and private. And as urbanists studied the trial courts that loomed so large in city politics, eventually they had to discover that such courts had civil as well as criminal divisions. So there has been a slight movement from public to private, as well as from Supreme Court to trial courts, most notably in Herbert Jacob's work on divorce (Jacob 1988) and Baum and Cannon's (1981) on tort. See also Scheppele (1988). Meanwhile, studies of the criminal justice process, essentially in local courts, continue to appear regularly (Heinz, Jacob, and Lineberry 1983; Nardulli, Eisenstein, and Flemming 1988; Casper and Diamond n.d.). The politics of criminal justice policy also attracted researchers (Scheingold 1991; Dalton 1985).

The political science study of one crucial area of private law, i.e., property, has been much distorted by constitutional law blinders. When the New Deal Supreme Court read property out of the Constitution, political scientists who defined their trade as constitutional law stopped studying property. Although still somewhat distorted by constitutional law concerns, there is now a significant return to property studies (Brigham 1990b; Coyle 1993; Shapiro 1986; Paul and Dickson 1990; Nedelsky 1990).

Three Major Movements "Outward" from Constitutional Law-Supreme Court Studies

(1) International Law Returns

Trial courts and private law have always been there. Political scientists were just slow to recognize them. The three largest political science movements "outward" from the constitutional Supreme Court have occurred because of massive changes in the real world that even "public law" political scientists could not go on ignoring indefinitely. The most recent change is in the international realm, and so the change it is engendering in political science law studies is still embryonic. If international law dwindled in an age of cold war bipolarity, it should follow that it might revive as that international condition changed. Because good old constitutional law had become so preoccupied with rights, it was natural that a few political scientists would bleed over from constitutional rights to international human rights. Given the post-Gorbachev world, it is also natural that some international relations specialists would see the need to shift from an exclusive preoccupation with power to some attention to the treaty law that is actually beginning to again define international relationships. Even here, however, the public law legacy will prove a handicap. Some political scientists are studying multinationals and international trade policy. Both public and private international law (the law of international business

transactions) play major roles in these areas. But even as law-oriented political science moves to take up international law again (Renteln 1990; Forsythe 1990), its preoccupation with public law and with individual rights analogical to our first ten amendment rights will prevent it from promptly rendering the assistance it ought to be giving to political scientists studying international political economy.

(2) Comparative Law as Comparative Constitutional Law

A second major change in the real world has led to a rather easy and natural, but still strangely small, movement of public law outward into broader concerns. If public law reduced itself to the study of constitutional judicial review, it would follow that if constitutional judicial review traveled, so would public law. Courts with constitutional judicial-review powers were established in many nations after World War II. As the actual impact of some of these courts has increased, the political science study of comparative constitutional law and courts has begun to flourish a little (McWhinney 1986; Beer 1992, 1984; Ellerman, Gawron, and Rogowski 1987). It is a bit difficult for political science to ignore such things as the German constitutional court, which has had major impacts on policy and governmental structure; the Israeli constitutional court, which has, in effect, written an Israeli constitution; and the French Constitutional Council, which today reviews nearly every major piece of French legislation. Indeed, major political science works on German (Kommers 1989) and French (Stone 1992) constitutional law and courts have recently appeared. Yet most comparative politics scholars remain woefully uninformed about constitutional law and courts. The group of comparative constitutional law political scientists remains small and rather isolated from the main body of comparativists. However, just as American constitutional law specialists have spread outward and downward, there is some comparative scholarship by political scientists or those heavily influenced by political analysis of law into non-constitutional comparative law areas (Willborn 1989; Stetson 1982; Goldberg 1990). Attempts are also being made to undertake general comparative analysis of courts comparable to systematic comparative work on legislatures, executives and bureaucracies (Shapiro 1981; Damaska 1986; Waltman and Holland 1988).

Vigorous attempts are being made by the Research Committee on Comparative Judicial Studies of the International Political Science Association to end the isolation of law from comparative politics, particularly in a series of major publications (Schmidhauser 1987; Jackson and Tate 1993; Symposium on "The Comparative

Study of Judicial Review" in *Policy Studies Journal* 1990, 19, 74-171). *Comparative Political Studies* currently contemplates a special issue on comparative judicial review. *The International Political Science Review* will shortly publish one symposium on judicial elites and another on judicialization of politics. *West European Politics* will devote an issue to judicial policy making. Mary Volcansek has been particularly active with a long string of recent publications -- only two of which are noted here (1992, 1990).

At this very moment, not only is constitutional judicial review flourishing in some countries, but the writing of new constitutions is a booming industry worldwide. Surely, political science ought to have a very marked comparative advantage in this enterprise given that it is supposed to know about both political development and constitutional law. In fact, because almost all political scientists who do constitutional law are Americanists and almost all of them who do political development or comparative institutions or systems know nothing about constitutional law, American law school constitutional lawyers, rather than political scientists, tend to be central to this new export trade. Nevertheless it hardly seems possible that American political scientists who say they are students of constitutional law can continue to ignore the international constitution epidemic. Nor does it seem possible that political scientists who are country specialists can continue to carefully shield their graduate students' eyes from constitutional law when the countries they are studying themselves see constitutions and constitutional courts as pressing political questions.

American and Comparative Electoral Law Studies

One major exception to the aversion of Americanists and comparativists to law is to be found in the area of electoral laws. *Baker v. Carr* has engendered an endless stream of litigation over districting, now vividly augmented by the Court's anti-gerrymandering decision in *Bandemer v. Davis*. One product of this judicial initiative has been a group of Americanists who do districting studies connected to litigation (Grofman 1985). Partially in connection with the new binge of constitution writing, some comparativists have now been working on electoral laws too (Lijphart 1990).

Comparative Law and the European Community

Exactly the same story may be told about the European Community. American political science has had a hard time recognizing the Community. In spite of the name they take, most comparative politics people are not comparativists but single-country specialists. Even our "Europeanists" are nearly all French, German,

British, or Italian politics specialists. The Community was not a country so it didn't get studied by "comparativists." Most comparativists no doubt thought the Community somehow belonged in international relations and left it to "them." But it doesn't really belong there, and "they" did little about it. The Community is a federalism. But the small federalism subfield of political science was basically a set of Americanists. Compound all this by the refusal of public law people to do anything other than the American Supreme Court and everybody else in political science to know anything about law at all. The result was that American political science knew nothing of the European Court of Justice, although it is arguably the most significant judicial instrument of political development in the twentieth century. After some pioneering work by Scheingold, Haas, and others, American political science largely ignored the Community. It can hardly continue to do so now. Comparative politics is being dragged kicking and screaming into Community studies, notably by the Brookings volume (Sbragia 1992) which contains a chapter on the Court of Justice. A small number of American political scientists of public law and/or federalism persuasions -- most notably for the public law community, Sam Krislov and Don Kommers --were incorporated into a major European comparative study of Community and American law (Cappelletti, Seccombe, and Weiler 1986-89). Other political science work on the Court of Justice is beginning to appear (Volcansek 1992). Yet the greatest expertise on the intersection of law and politics in the Community to be found in the United States is not in the work of political scientists but in that of law professors such as Joseph Weiler (1986).

Comparative Non-Constitutional Law

Moreover, the whole small realm of political science comparative law is still very excessively constitutional law and constitutional court centered. While in Community law the distinction is somewhat artificial, much of what is of political interest in that law is administrative rather than constitutional. Nearly all British law comparable to American constitutional law is called administrative law in Britain. Yet the amount of comparative administrative law research in political science is minuscule, even now that administrative law is reviving as a subfield of public law (Sterett 1990). As to political science comparative study of other key bodies of law, such as environmental regulation, David Vogel's (1987) work stands nearly alone (but see Kagan 1989), and it is probably no coincidence that he is a political scientist on a business school faculty.

(3) Administrative and Regulatory Law Returns

Vogel's work on comparative regulation is a kind of link between the second and third great change in the real world I am attempting to highlight. That third change lies in the realm of the American politics of regulation. The 1960s, 1970s, and 1980s presented us with a major outburst of new government regulation of health, safety, the environment, education, and civil rights. At the same time there was an enormous surge of judicial activism, not only in the Supreme Court's constitutional decisions but in the decisions of all the rest of the American courts and in all kinds of regulatory law cases.

Not entirely coincidentally, a major change was occurring in political science itself. Perhaps Congress specialists could go on forever blithely ignoring the huge product that Congress was spewing forth, but it was difficult for all of political science to do so. Policy replaced behavior as the voguish catchword of our trade. The most important branch of policy studies immediately became implementation. And students of implementation, mostly trained in American politics and/or public administration, soon came upon law and courts all over the implementation game. Any implementation action immediately set off a series of lawsuits. A major tool of implementation itself was the lawsuit or the threat of suit. Those political scientists who were concerned not only with the implementation but with the making of policy now discovered that the old policy-making iron triangle of interest group-congressional committee-executive agency had become a rectangle with courts (most often the D.C. Circuit) at the fourth corner. Most of the new regulatory policy statutes entailed large amounts of supplementary law making by "informal rule-making," that is, executive agency enacted regulations. Judicial review of that rule making had grown to incredibly intrusive proportions. That review was not constitutional. The question asked by the reviewing court was not: "Is the regulation constitutional?" but instead "Is the regulation in accord with its parent statute and with the Administrative Procedures Act?"

The bodies of regulatory and administrative law -- statutes, regulations, court decisions, and redecisions -- involved here were extremely technical, voluminous, and complex. But because the political scientists confronted by them thought of themselves as policy specialists and not "public law" people, they did not think they had to blind themselves to non-constitutional law. And because there was so much law and it was so central, they did not think they could do what American politics and public administration people had been doing for years, blind themselves to all law. As policy studies, or to use the old name, government regulation, became a centerpiece of political science, public law necessarily again began to grow outward from constitutional law to at least really public law, to concern itself with all the law and all the courts that were involved in public policy (Bryner 1987; O'Brien 1987; Rebell and Block 1982; Williams and Matheny 1992).

A Realm Between

Even here, however, the growth has been small compared to the great continuing weight of constitutional scholarship. There is a strong and easily identifiable return of administrative law to its old place as a recognized subfield of public law and a significant component of public administration (Carter and Harrington 1991; Cooper 1983; Shapiro 1988; Rohr 1986). Particular attention ought now to be paid to a particular "realm between" constitutional law and normal regulatory law. Certain statutes, for instance, the Administrative Procedures Act, the anti-trust statutes, and the civil rights acts are so sweeping and, by their general wording, leave so much to judicial interpretation, that they are semi-constitutional in character and may invite a different style of judicial action than either constitutional provisions or routine statutes, a style that emphasizes "prudential" interpretation (Bryner and Thompson 1988; Shapiro 1986).

Law and Policy Studies

A number of widely read case studies of policy development and implementation treat all relevant law and all relevant courts as a routine part of long, complex policy stories involving legislatures, executives, parties, interest groups, etc., that ought to be handled routinely by whatever political scientist is telling the story rather than shunted off to some separate law specialist. These policy stories may be about environmental, or transportation, or civil rights, or occupational health and safety law rather than only constitutional law (Rabkin 1989). They have produced some of the most important "public law" books of the 1980s (Katzmann 1986, 1980; Melnick 1983; Mezey 1988; Mutch 1988). Indeed Melnick's book is clearly one of the most important books of the 1980s for the future development of "public law," because it is the first to routinely treat all levels of courts and all kinds of law as integral parts of the politics of policy making (see also Melnick n.d.; Mashaw and Harfst 1990).

From the Supreme Court to All Courts

Such stories almost always involve both trial and intermediate appellate courts as well as the Supreme Court, and often state as well as federal courts (Orren 1991). The federal courts of appeal, and district courts which loom very large in regulatory law, little of which reaches the Supreme Court, are the subject of a small number of political science studies (Barrow and Walker 1988; Cooper 1988; Howard 1982; Wasby 1987; Wenner 1992). Policy implementation studies lead naturally to the federal district courts in an age of "institutional remedies" when district court orders seek to implement anti-discrimination and other national policies at local levels. Urban studies gave us a body of work on state trial courts. If political science did state trial courts and the U.S. Supreme Court, it followed naturally that it ought to do something about state supreme courts (Glick 1992). In this area recent developments in the old standby, national constitutional law, have encouraged more study of state supreme courts (Ducat, Wyckoff, and Flango 1991; Fino 1987). As an increasingly Republican Supreme Court has become increasingly noncompliant to the constitutional rights agenda of the left, the rights industry has shifted some of its productive energies to state constitutional law and thus to state supreme courts (Friedelbaum 1988; Sheldon 1988). The attention of constitutional law-Supreme Court political scientists is then painlessly drawn from the U.S. Supreme Court to state supreme courts. Constitutional, criminal justice, urban politics, and policy studies also move attention onward to lower state courts (Porter and Tarr 1982; Gates and Johnson 1991; Culver and Stumpf 1992; Feeley 1983; Cole 1986). Political scientists have also contributed to the study of alternative dispute resolution (Harrington 1985).

Public Choice and the Return to Administrative and Regulatory Law

Along with policy studies, the great rising star of recent political science has been public or rational choice, which requires no description here given its pride of place elsewhere in this volume. Given the virulence of the virus it could hardly be thought that even constitutional law could escape infection. Yet constitutional law's almost complete isolation from the rest of political science has meant, as has been typical of past epidemics, that it has been among the last areas of political science to experience the new methodology and has been least affected by it. Rational choice is, however, having quite a dramatic impact on political science concern for administrative law. "Principal-agent" problems are of central concern to rational choice

analysts. These problems are especially acute in the process of implementation of federal statutes. The principal, that is Congress, itself has typically issued a complex, ambiguous, and somewhat self-contradictory directive. The agent is an independent and coequal executive branch. Congressional oversight of administration thus becomes a key principal-agent arena. Again, precisely because public choice political scientists have not been trained in public law, they do not know that they are forbidden to look at non-constitutional law. Free of these blinders, they have quickly seen that the administrative procedures enacted into law by Congress in the Administrative Procedures Act and in most program-creating statutes are one of the major avenues by which the principal seeks to control its agents. And once this point is seen, in a twinkling it can be seen that the courts, which engage not in constitutional but in administrative judicial review enforcing these procedures, are also big players in this agency game. Thus today we have the usual paradox that, while most public law scholars hang back, it is rational choice Congress, bureaucracy, government regulation scholars who are working at forced draft to acquire administrative law expertise and to move administrative law and administrative, as opposed to constitutional, judicial review toward the center of American politics studies. It is also typical of public law *and* American politics political scientists that this new work is far better known among academic lawyers than among political scientists (McCubbins 1985; McCubbins, Noll, and Weingast 1988, 1989, 1990; Calvert, McCubbins, and Weingast 1989).

Statutory Interpretation in the Movement Beyond Constitutional Law

Similar forces and roughly the same group of scholars are moving political science toward actually looking at the substantive laws Congress passes. In the search for all the various devices by which congressional principal controls executive agent, it must eventually occur to someone that Congress just might sometimes seek to control its agents by telling them what to do in the language of the statutes it enacts. Moreover, in the same decisions in which courts uphold or strike down agency actions on the basis of whether the agencies followed the procedural language of statutes, the same judge approves or disapproves agency actions on the basis of whether they followed the substantive language of the statutes. Thus the study of administrative law and administrative judicial review inevitably leads to the study of the substantive law that Congress enacts. Attracted by agency problems, Congress specialists may finally be pushed to the last resort, actually reading the statutes that Congress enacts.

Meanwhile rational choice concerns, policy studies, and the more general incursions of economics into political science, are among the several forces leading public law political scientists to some concern for statutory interpretation. Law and economics types have pushed a so-called "economic" theory of legislation which is really the old Bentley-Truman pluralist theory dressed in economic language. Because the vast outburst of proactive regulatory statutes of the 1960s, 1970s, and 1980s have been accompanied by a proliferation of deregulation-oriented Republican presidents, statutory interpretation has become a key political battleground. Depending on the theory and practice of statutory interpretation, particularly of the D.C. Circuit and the Supreme Court, either the Democratic regulatory vigor of the initial statutes could be preserved through hard Republican executive times or Republican presidential economic sense could temper the rhetorical excesses of Democratic green position takings. As real world politics brought statutory interpretation to center stage, academics seized upon the subject. Economic theories of legislation generate theories of statutory interpretation (McCubbins, Noll, and Weingast 1992). Older conventional theories of statutory interpretations are revived. Literary theory of textual interpretation is commandeered. And again the disciplinary dialectic is typical. Academic lawyers, who for years had abandoned statutory interpretation as unworthy of attention, returned to it quickly as it became politically relevant. Given that real political relevance was the spur, one might have thought that political scientists would have beaten them to it. But statutory interpretation is about statutes, not constitutions. And it is practiced more by "lower" courts than by the Supreme Court. So, naturally, public law political scientists were late to awaken to statutory interpretation. They are barely awakening now. And typically again, they tend to drift into statutory interpretation as a kind of obscure cousin of the real glamour subject: constitutional interpretation. Studies in constitutional interpretation are enjoying a great revival to be described in a later portion of this chapter. Nevertheless, some public law political scientists, and some academic lawyers with political science ties, are now working on statutory interpretation (Rodriguez 1989; Sunstein 1989; Ball 1988).

Interest Groups and Non-Constitutional Law

There is a fairly long tradition of studying interest group litigation activities as a facet of constitutional law. At least this movement directed our attention outward from the constitutional Supreme Court as such to some other legal actors. There is no reason to limit ourselves, however, to constitutional litigation in the Supreme Court. Interest groups and many courts interact in many areas of both constitutional and nonconstitutional law and in judicial politics more generally. Interest group studies are now beginning to reflect this realization (Caldeira and Wright 1988; Epstein 1985; O'Connor and Epstein 1985; Shapiro 1990a; Maveety 1991).

Beyond the Three Major Movements Outward From Constitutional Law-Supreme Court Studies

Interdisciplinary Studies by Political Scientists

So far we have been looking at a movement "outward" and "downward" from constitutional law and Supreme Court toward all law and all courts. And we have tracked that movement largely as one within "public law" or "judicial politics" itself or at least within political science as a self-contained discipline. Much of the movement in public law political science, however, has been even further outward, beyond the edges of the discipline.

Initially the very term "public law" was a claim by political science to do the law that the law schools did not do. They did common law, which denied there was such a thing as public law. In practice, however, political science departments and law schools both taught constitutional, administrative, and international law. Armed with the more acute sense of the political, which gave them a major comparative advantage in the age of New Deal judicial realism, political scientists like E. S. Corwin, T. R. Powell, J. A. C. Grant, and Robert Cushman were dominant players in the constitutional law game shared with lawyers. Many political scientists continue to do constitutional doctrinal analysis and, in this sense, political science constitutional law has always been and is now interdisciplinary, calling on skills in both legal and political analysis.

Beyond this root interdisciplinariness, however, there has developed a newer, major interdisciplinary thrust. This movement has been shared by both the law and political science disciplines. The law schools are full of "law and..." movements: law and economics, law and philosophy, law and literature, etc. Law professors working in constitutional and administrative law do not speak of themselves as in "law and politics," but that is only because they have so internalized political science teachings about political institutions and processes that they no longer think in terms of "and." Moreover, the critical legal studies and feminist legal studies movements in the law schools are themselves interdisciplinary in character.

The parallel movement in political science has a number of facets. Recent movements in public law political science toward philosophy (Barber 1984; Smith 1985) and toward literature are intimately connected to developments in political science constitutional law studies and will be considered further in the later sections on constitutional law. Here the central phenomenon to be considered is the law and society movement. In one sense, within political science, that movement is part of the outward and downward vectors we have already traced. It directed political scientists away from the Supreme Court and constitutional law and toward everyday courts and everyday law. From its initiation, political scientists like Victor Rosenblum, Sam Krislov, and Joel Grossman played major roles in the law and society movement. For a substantial number of public law, judicial politics political scientists, the annual Law and Society Association meetings, and the *Law and Society Review* and other interdisciplinary journals, are more significant than American Political Science Association [APSA] annual meetings and the *American Political Science Review* [APSR].

Initially in this presentation reference was made to a number of paradoxes that have tended to marginalize public law as a subfield of political science. One of the most central of these paradoxes is that precisely because political scientists have been highly successful at interdisciplinary legal studies, their status as political scientists comes into question. A political scientist who publishes in the APSR and the *Western Political Quarterly* and goes to APSA and Western Political Science Association meetings is indubitably a political scientist. What is a political scientist who publishes in the *Law and Society Review* and goes to Law and Society Association meetings? Precisely because most senior political scientists who are not in public law think of it as nothing more or less than constitutional law-Supreme Court studies, a young political scientist who is interdisciplinary and studying British judicial review of administrative decisions or work site implementation of OSHA rules (Rees 1988; see also Bardach and Kagan 1982) is in some danger of being told he or she is not a political scientist at all.

Yet it would be fatal for any serious political science commitment to the study of law and courts to denigrate interdisciplinary work in these areas. Such work is now central to the study of law and courts and constitutes the leading edge of law school scholarship. A political scientist who claimed to be a law and courts specialist and who knew nothing about law and economics or post-utilitarian moral philosophy or legal ethnography or alternative dispute resolution would simply be viewed as a fool by other law and courts specialists. Conversely, political scientists bring to interdisciplinary legal studies a claim to comparative advantage comparable to all the other disciplinary claims. The political dimension of law is sufficiently obvious that the political scientist is clearly bringing as important and unique a contribution to inquiry about law as is an economist or sociologist. The political scientist's identity as political scientist ought not and need not be lost in the course of interdisciplinary work.

The range of interdisciplinary law and society work by political scientists is great. Rather than endlessly inflating the bibliography, I urge those interested to scan such leading interdisciplinary journals as *Law and Society Review*, *Law and Social Inquiry*, *Judicature*, and *Law and Policy* for work by political scientists. Feeley, Sarat, Krislov, Harrington, and a number of others contribute frequently. There are many other such journals including *Law, Economics and Organizations* and *Law and Politics*. The Jurisprudence and Social Policy Program at Berkeley is producing interdisciplinarily trained Ph.D.s and sending them into political science departments, among others, and so are various public policy schools and programs.

The point is that, using any definition of politics and any set of boundaries of the concerns of political science that you care to, all sorts of law, lawyers, courts and judges, not to mention law-crafting legislators and bureaucrats, pop up as major phenomena. Most of them are not the Supreme Court and constitutional law. And most of them are best understood through combining a number of modes of analysis -- some of which come from political science and some of which don't.

Political Science and the Interdisciplinary Study of Lawyers

Lawyers constitute one subject of interdisciplinary studies of particular concern to political science. In many political systems, lawyers constitute a fairly distinct political elite and, in most, a significant transmission belt for both public policies and political ideologies. Political scientists have been making some contributions in this area (Zemans and Rosenblum 1981; Kritzer 1990; Sarat and Felsteiner 1986, 1989; Kagan and Rosen 1985; Shapiro 1990b; Cain and Harrington n.d.; Provine 1986).

Another Brand of Interdisciplinary Political Science Studies

The law and society movement is not the only home of interdisciplinary political scientists studying law and courts. In part informed by various bodies of contemporary European social theory, and in part by the general suspicion of objectivism and positivism as innately conservative that has gripped much of the American academy for the last three decades (Silbey and Sarat 1987), a number of political scientists have been central players in the "Amherst Seminar." The quotation marks are because the seminar has become a kind of symbol or shorthand for interdisciplinary work on law, lawyers, and courts whose subjects, boundaries, and field methods are about the same as those of the law and society movement but whose presuppositions and purposes are somewhat different. Focusing on law as a constitutive act, the Amherst group sees the study of law and courts not as a purely exterior observation of things that are "out there," but as itself part of the process of making the "there." At the most Heideggerian edge, this position becomes "What we say about the law is the law." Most often, however, the central thrust is that law is less determined by society and more self-creating than most social scientists have normally appreciated and that, therefore, those studying law ought to see themselves as part of the process of making law (see the replies to Trubek and Easer 1989 by various members of the Amherst group presented in *Law and Social Inquiry* 1990, 15, 135-180).

The New Institutionalism and Normative Theory: Interdisciplinary Studies in Law and Philosophy

Political science has recently been in the grip of "the new institutionalism" or "bringing the state back in." Quite obviously this movement brings renewed prominence to law and courts that are central institutions and central expressions of the state (Hall and Brace 1989; Nardulli 1991). We have already noted one aspect of the new institutionalism in the concern of rational or public choice analysts to deal with law and courts as significant aspects of principal-agent relationships. Another tack is taken by those who treat widely held stable values or ideologies as institutions that constrain and partly determine political choice. In this guise, the new institutionalism provides a new urgency to the study of the normative aspect of law.

"Political jurisprudence" has often served as a convenient tag for the 1960s through 1980s work of political scientists who worked on law and courts and sought to distinguish their work from the doctrinal analysis done by academic lawyers. This political jurisprudence emphasized the political nature of law, and an exterior perspective on law as opposed to the academic lawyer's interior participation in the improvement of law. In both these aspects, it was echoed by the later blooming critical legal studies movement. Largely positivist in approach, political jurisprudence tended to leave normative legal theory to others while never denying that

the values incorporated into and surrounding legal systems were themselves important facts to be studied. The relationship between political jurisprudence and the new institutionalism is a major agenda item for the 1990s. Early stages in the encounter may be traced in Stumpf (1983, 1988), Smith (1988), and the exchange between Sotirios Barber, Rogers Smith, and myself in volume three of *Studies in American Political Development* (1989).

"Legal theory" or "jurisprudence" has always been a recognized facet of the public law subfield. Public law political scientists have typically been either public law-American politics or public law-political theory types. Treated as political discourse, the opinions of the Supreme Court are a central body of American political theory. There are, of course, enormous overlaps between political and legal theory. Nevertheless, political theorists without public law training or interests are likely to ignore some portions of legal theory and some major aspects of the history of legal thought. Thus a specialization in legal theory is discernible, but the legal theory scholar is likely to straddle public law and political theory subfields. And both as legal and political theorist, that scholar is also likely to straddle political science and philosophy.

Starting in roughly 1960, moral philosophy or ethics has undergone an enormous post-utilitarian or "post-consequentialist" change. Moral philosophers now again assert that statements of right and wrong other than and better than "the greatest good of the greatest number" can be made. Normative political theory revives in such works as John Rawls's. Normative legal theory revives in such works as Ronald Dworkin's (Brubaker 1985). Legal theory political scientists join political theory political scientists in reading Rorty and other normative philosophers. Other segments of this book describe the currently flourishing state of normative political theory in the political theory subfield of political science. A parallel development inevitably must occur in public law as we return to normative legal theory (Fiskin 1983; Berns 1983).

The return to normative legal theory in public law political science is in one sense an aspect of the new institutionalism which takes values seriously as political phenomena (Epstein, Walker, and Dixon 1989). In another sense, this return is a manifestation of the law and philosophy movement also to be found in the law schools (Scheppele and Waldron 1991). So here again, some public law political scientists must be interdisciplinary in order to do their jobs well.

The new institutionalism is then a vehicle for two interdisciplinary movements in public law political science, rational choice linked to economics, and normative legal theory linked to moral philosophy. The new institutionalism's third major interdisciplinary thrust is toward history. As a field, American politics is currently experiencing considerable interest in American political history. The annual volume, *Studies in American Political Development*, is a major expression of this interest. It has already published some work in judicial politics. Legal history, including constitutional history, has been flourishing as a subdiscipline of history, and it may make little difference in most instances whether the producer of a given piece of work is a historian or a political scientist (Nash 1983; Jillson 1988; and the work cited elsewhere in the chapter on the origins of judicial review).

Things have come to such a pass, along both law and courts dimensions, that it is now actually possible that someone could be considered a public law specialist who has not written a constitutional law-Supreme Court dissertation and has never taught a constitutional law course.

Constitutional Law -- Supreme Court Studies in Many Forms

For the bulk of the readers of this volume, however, all the things said so far are mere idiosyncratic preliminaries to getting down to the real business of constitutional law-Supreme Court that continues to preoccupy most political scientists who identify themselves as public law or judicial politics specialists. Indeed, it is noteworthy, that with the outstanding exception of Maveety (1991), almost no recent work on the Supreme Court treats of both its constitutional and non-constitutional cases. All of the standard currents in the mainstream continue to flow.

Behavioral Studies

Behavioral studies of the attitudes, votes, and small-group participation of Supreme Court justices and other "jurimetric" studies continue (Brenner and Spaeth 1990; Segal and Cover 1989; Handberg and Tate 1991; Segal and Spaeth 1993; Baum 1989). These studies now extend to lower federal court judges and state judges, most notably in Goldman and Lamb (1985). Although, from the beginnnings, these quantitative studies included concern for judges' votes in non-constitutional areas, they continue to present themselves largely as a methodological advance on conventional constitutional law studies. H. W. Perry (1991) has produced an outstanding analytical study of Supreme Court agenda setting. Analytical data studies will be much facilitated in the future by the recent development of extensive new data bases (Palmer 1990; Spaeth n.d.) Some of this work

moves toward the construction of more formalized theories of judicial decision making (Caldeira 1985).

Doctrinal Analysis and Advocacy

The distinction between scholarship and advocacy has always been uncertain or nonexistent in most of the legal scholarship produced in law schools. Much of that scholarship consists of doctrinal analysis that purports to yield the correct or a good, better, or best statement of the law. The central strategy is a massive and deliberate confusion of is and ought. The previous cases are examined to show that, properly interpreted, the body of existing law really adds up to the law as the author thinks it ought to be. In short, most such writing consists of expanded and embroidered legal briefs. The key question in understanding such work is "Who's the client?" In constitutional law scholarship of this sort, the writer really begins by deciding what he or she wants the constitution to mean and then works backwards shaping an interpretation of past history and legal doctrine and a policy analysis that will culminate in that meaning.

Political scientists who are constitutional law scholars have always participated in this brand of advocacy scholarship. Some of it openly presents itself as direct lobbying of courts and/or legislatures (Shapiro 1985; Levinson 1985; Schuck and Smith 1985). Most of it presents itself as a search for what the correct law is, which usually turns out coincidentally to be the law the writer thinks best (Alfange 1983; Binion 1983; Carmen 1985; Randall 1989). A bit of it adopts an exterior perspective, or "constitutional politics" approach in which the political scientist seeks to describe the various doctrinal moves made by various participants in a process that over time moves constitutional law, or rather the Supreme Court, from one policy position to another (Downs 1985, 1989). The task is not to arrive at the correct law but to engage in the standard positivist task of political science, describing who gets what, how, and why (Way 1989; Mendelson 1990; Scigliano 1988).

Post-Modern Constitutional Scholarship

Both the traditional legal scholarship of advocacy and the newer, positivist, constitutional politics scholarship is now being challenged by various "post-modern" approaches, including some feminist legal scholarship. (Much feminist legal scholarship is more conventionally positivistic. See Cook et al. 1987; cf. Binion 1991.) This post-modern scholarship either consciously denigrates the distinction between objectivity and subjectivity or adopts a "discourse-deliberation" or "practice" approach to constitutional law (Brigham 1990a;

Carter 1989; McCann 1986). The political scientist as constitutional scholar ought not to be either an external, objective describer of constitutional maneuver or a mere constitutional champion of particular social interests. Instead he or she ought to be a participant in the public discourse that continuously constitutes and reconstitutes constitutional and other law designed to achieve a more flourishing citizen in a more flourishing state (Carter and Harrington 1990; Carter and Gilliom 1989; Carter 1985; Levinson 1988; Bumiller 1988). Cass Sunstein (1990) and Bruce Ackerman (1991), both of whom are academic lawyers holding joint appointments in law schools and political science departments, and Sandy Levinson who is both a lawyer and a political scientist, are crucial figures in this movement. It is at the core of the Amherst interdisciplinary group.

Constitutional Interpretation

This movement is also to be found, often under the label "constitutional interpretation," among other political scientists of less post-modern bent (Murphy, Fleming, and Harris 1986). The renewed interest in textual interpretation of the Constitution is in part a natural reaction to the reductionism that characterized behaviorism and in part a piece of the new institutionalism (O'Brien 1991b). It is also in part the scholarly side of the partisan struggle to control the Supreme Court in which Republican and Democrat are translated into originalist and nonoriginalist, or mainstream versus natural law à la the Bork and Thomas hearings. Its intellectual vitality, however, is derived from the revivals of moral philosophy and of political philosophy that were alluded to earlier. Constitutional interpretation becomes a vehicle for doing real normative constitutional theory (Hirsh 1992; Baer 1983; Macedo 1990; Meister 1989; Arkes 1990; Miller 1985). And this constitutional interpretation political theory ranges from the Straussians and their "founding moment" to the champions of community, the reconstructors of liberal democratic theory, and a wide variety of egalitarians and social democrats (Smith 1985; Jacobsohn 1986; Kammen 1988).

Quite obviously, too, this renewed interest in textual interpretation is a facet of the current law and literature vogue and of the intellectual prominence of the array of European social theory from Heidegger to Habermas, Foucault, and Bordieu that focuses on language or communications practice. The constitution is a text and ought to be amenable to the whole gamut of literary interpretative techniques that have infested English departments for some time and are now colonizing law faculties. All political scientists know that constitutional law is not only or even principally the constitutional text but is most centrally the interpretive practice of the Supreme Court and of the lawyers surrounding it. Why shouldn't political scientists' attentions return from scoring justices' votes to taking constitutional language seriously (Levinson and Mailloux 1988)?

The Eternal Question: The Legitimacy of Judicial Review

The new concern with constitutional interpretation is inextricably mixed with that constant of American constitutional concerns, the legitimacy of judicial review itself (Fisher 1988). New descriptive and prescriptive works on the role of the Supreme Court in American politics are added to the stream (Brigham 1987; Jennings n.d.; Lasser 1989; McDowell 1982; Steamer 1986; Wiecek 1988; Halpern and Lamb 1982; Carter 1985; Morgan 1984). Interesting new work has recently appeared on the origins and evolution of judicial review (Snowiss 1990; Goldstein 1986; Wolfe 1986). There is a now long-established tradition of study of the impact of Supreme Court decisions, which continues and broadens into more general studies of the capacity of the Supreme Court to achieve implementation of its decisions, most notably in Rosenberg's (1991) recent work (see also Dometrius and Sigelman 1988; Songer 1988). Constitutional implementation studies have also been influenced by the "outward" and "downward" movements since the pioneering work of Jack Peltason, so that we get studies of district court implementation of anti-discrimination decisions (Cooper 1988; Bullock and Lamb 1984), and even some consideration of the implementation of non-constitutional decisions (Johnson and Cannon 1984).

Following up earlier and current work by Murphy and Tannenhaus (1990), studies of public opinion and the Court continue to appear (Caldeira and Gibson 1992), as do works on interest group efforts to lobby the Court (O'Neill 1985). Led by Mason and Swisher, political scientists have long made a specialty of studies of individual justices as a tool of political analysis of judicial review. That work continues (Ball and Cooper 1992; Davis 1989; Murphy 1988; Silverstein 1984; Strum 1984; Lamb and Halpern 1993; Stephenson 1991). American politics specialists are now producing a great deal of analysis of divided government. The Supreme Court appointment process has been a uniquely dramatic public demonstration of that division, and public law political scientists, following pioneering work by Henry Abraham (1992), have begun to write about it (Danelski 1990; Shapiro 1990a; Grossman and Wasby 1990; O'Brien 1991b).

The Study of Law and Courts in Political Science

Thus, the outward and downward movement away from the constitutional law Supreme Court is counterbalanced by a major new vigor in constitutional scholarship. Moreover, the movement from advocacy scholarship toward an essentially positivist exterior perspective on law and courts has been balanced by a new self-confidence about normative constitutional theory or interpretation. Finally, a post-modernist jurisprudence tends to deny the distinctions between description and prescription, objectivity and subjectivity, and scholarship and participation. In this light, the political scientist is simply a participant in the interpretative community contributing to constitutional discourse.

The question may then arise of whether the political scientist has any special claim to expertise in this interpretive community. Those most exhaustively trained and most daily active in this discourse are lawyers. Those who provide its critical foundations are moral philosophers. Those who know most about what it is supposed to be doing, namely, interpreting text and constructing language, are literary theorists and theorists of social communication. The stance that law might well have a rich interior life of its own, but that the job of political science was one of exterior perspective showing how politics invaded law, and the degree to which law and courts were institutions of politics, allowed political scientists to claim that what they knew of politics gave them a unique competence to study law or at least certain aspects of law. Political scientists who claim that they are participants in the interpretative community of law, busy constituting the law through deliberative discourse, may have difficulty making any comparable assertion. Much may depend on the degree to which they can establish that law is not an entirely or even largely autonomous mode of discourse on the one hand or simply a branch of moral discourse on the other, but has some especially important political dimension that gives the expert in political discourse some claim to a separate and prominent role in legal studies.

The problem of a place for law-and-courts political scientists can be clearly seen in political science faculties. At the moment, a long-standing bipolarity of public law is reasserting itself. As we have noted, traditionally most public law scholars were either public law-American politics people or public law-political theory people with very small numbers connected to public administration or international relations. At a certain point in the history of political science such a collapse occurred in every other aspect of public law that it became, as it is now in many departments, a constitutional law-Supreme Court subfield of American

politics. Today the revived interest in constitutional interpretation and constitutional theory is recreating the political theory wing of public law.

Meanwhile the outward and downward and interdisciplinary movements have created some political scientists who are neither constitutional law leaning toward American politics nor constitutional law leaning toward political theory. There are non-constitutional (or rather all of public law rather than a little of public law) political scientists leaning toward American politics-policy-administration-regulation. They can conveniently fit into departments that treat judicial politics as a subfield of American politics or can fit easily into the public administration subfield, if political science departments can bring themselves to understand that a public law person need not be someone who sits in a corner mumbling *Dred Scott* and *Roe v. Wade*.

More serious is the problem that if public law is a subfield of American politics so that hiring is dominated by American politics faculty, there will be no access to political science departments for comparative judicial politics scholars. Most of those currently in this specialty are part-time converts from good old American constitutional law. But where can real "made from scratch" comparative law people go? American politics will not want them. Most departmental comparative politics groups will know so little about law that they will not want to "waste" a slot on a law type that they could use to get an Ethiopian or Estonian specialist. Only where public-law judicial politics has been retained as an independent subfield, or a set of particularly sophisticated comparative politics people exists, is comparative law and courts likely to have much of a chance.

It is to be hoped that international relations and state and local government or urban groups will fairly readily recognize their law needs given the renewed role of treaties in international relations and the pervasiveness of litigation and quasi-judicial administrative proceedings in state and local policy making. Certainly there is already a renewed acknowledgement of administrative law as an essential component of public administration studies. Yet in all these fields it is far easier to lobby for hiring someone in the public law subfield who will do international law or administrative law or state and local courts than it is to use one of your own precious slots for a law person. Thus, to perhaps a lesser degree but nevertheless quite tangibly, it will be harder for a department that treats public law as a subfield of American politics to develop the law support it needs in international relations, state and local government, and public administration than for a department with a separate judicial politics subfield.

The public law-judicial politics subfield today is flourishing along a larger set of dimensions than it ever has in the past. The degree to which this flourishing will benefit political science as a whole depends upon the extent to which political science departments stop seeing their situation as one in which they are forced to spend one American politics slot on somebody to teach the constitutional law courses that pre-law students demand. Instead they might start seeing their real scholarly needs for dealing with law and courts, which pervade nearly every aspect of the politics they study.

In spite of all the talk about the conflict between research and teaching, in American universities teaching agendas set research agendas far more than is commonly understood. So long as political science departments think they *must* teach a constitutional law course and need not necessarily teach any other law courses, the judicial politics research agenda will remain excessively directed toward the constitutional law Supreme Court. Departments should learn that there is no single necessary undergraduate political science course in law and courts. Where courses on Congress and the president, or legislatures and executives are taught, there ought to be a comparable course on federal courts or courts in general that covers the same range of policies, processes, and behaviors as is covered in those other courses. Where comparative politics groups recruit faculty with an eye toward teaching not only country courses but courses on comparative parties, political economy, development, etc., then one of the courses to be contemplated is a comparative law and courts course. Departments that think they can give policy courses with only a constitutional law-Supreme Court person on hand, rather than one who looks at all kinds of law and courts, are wrong. Departments that teach bureaucracy and regulation courses need courses in administrative and regulatory law because that law is a major part of bureaucratic and regulatory politics. No undergraduate will die, or worse yet, fail to get into law school, because he or she hasn't had a constitutional law course. Departments ought to begin telling their students the truth -- that law schools don't care at all about undergraduate constitutional law courses. A course on the legal thought of Bentham and Weber sure beats tracing the Supreme Court's move from the fair trial rule to selective incorporation. If one course there must be, then a course on comparative law and courts or on the whole law and politics of the U.S., not just the small and peculiar constitutional part of it, would certainly be better for the students' intellectual health and the departments' research agenda than a constitutional law course. The movement in the subdiscipline is toward a set of people who treat all of law and courts as interwoven with all the rest of politics. It is time that other political scientists demand public law scholars and teachers who can speak to them, not to John Marshall.

Bibliography

Abraham, Henry. 1992. *Justices and Presidents*. 3rd ed. New York: Oxford University Press.

Ackerman, Bruce. 1991. *We the People*. Cambridge: Harvard University Press.

Alfange, Dean, Jr. 1983. "Congressional Regulation of the 'States Qua States' From National League of Cities to EEOC v. Wyoming." *Supreme Court Review* 215-282.

Arkes, Hadley. 1990. *Beyond the Constitution*. Princeton: Princeton University Press.

Baer, Judith. 1983. *Equality Under the Constitution: Reclaiming the 14th Amendment*. Ithaca: Cornell University Press.

Ball, Howard. 1988. "The U.S. Supreme Court's Glossing of the Federal Tort Claims Act: Statutory Construction and Military Veterans Tort Actions." *Western Political Science Quarterly* 41:529-552.

Ball, Howard, and Phillip Cooper. 1992. *Of Power and Right: Justice Black and Douglas and America's Constitutional Revolution*. New York: Oxford University Press.

Barber, Sotirios. 1984. *On What the Constitution Means*. Baltimore: Johns Hopkins University Press.

Bardach, Eugene, and Robert Kagan. 1982. *Going by the Book: The Problem of Regulatory Unreasonableness*. Philadelphia: Temple University Press.

Barrow, Deborah, and Thomas Walker. 1988. *A Court Divided: The Fifth Circuit Court of Appeals and the Politics of Judicial Reform*. New Haven: Yale University Press.

Baum, Lawrence. 1989. "Comparing the Policy Positions of the Supreme Court Justices from Different Periods." *Western Political Quarterly* 42:509-21.

Baum, Lawrence, and Bradley Canon. 1981. "Patterns of Adoption of Tort Law Innovations." *American Political Science Review* 75:975-87.

Beer, Lawrence. 1984. *Freedom of Expression in Japan: A Study of Comparative Law, Politics and Society*. Tokyo: Kodanska International.

Beer, Lawrence, ed. 1992. *Constitutional Systems in Late 20th Century Asia*. Seattle: University of Washington Press.

Berns, Walter. 1982. "Judicial Review and the Rights and Laws of Nature." *Supreme Court Review* 49-84.

Binion, Gayle. 1983. "'Intent' and Equal Protection Reconsidered." *Supreme Court Review* 397-458.

Binion, Gayle. 1991. "Toward a Feminist Regrounding of Constitutional Law." *Social Science Quarterly* 72:207-220.

Brenner, Saul, and Harold Spaeth. 1990. *Studies in U.S. Supreme Court Behavior*. New York: Garland Press.

Brigham, John. 1987. *The Cult of the Court*. Philadelphia: Temple University Press.

Brigham, John. 1990a. "Bad Attitude: The Consequences of Survey Research for Constitutional Practice." *Review of Politics* 52:582-603.

Brigham, John. 1990b. *Property and the Politics of Entitlement*. Philadelphia: Temple University Press.

Brubaker, Stanley. 1985. "Taking Dworkin Seriously." *Review of Politics* 47:45-65.

Bryner, Gary. 1987. *Bureaucratic Discretion: Law and Policy in Federal Regulatory Agencies*. New York: Pergamon Press.

Bryner, Gary, and Dennis Thompson, eds. 1988. *The Constitution and the Regulation of Society*. Provo, UT: Brigham Young University Press.

Bullock, Charles, and Charles Lamb, eds. 1984. *Implementation of Civil Rights Policy*. Monterey, CA: Brooks/Cole Publishing.

Bumiller, Kristin. 1988. *The Civil Rights Society: The Social Construction of Victims*. Baltimore: John Hopkins University Press.

Cain, Maureen, and Christine Harrington. n.d. *Lawyering and Its Limits*.

Caldeira, Gregory. 1985. "The Transmission of Legal Precedent: A Study of State Supreme Courts." *American Political Science Review* 79:178-193.

Caldeira, Gregory, and James Gibson. 1992. "The Etiology of Public Support for the Supreme Court." *American Journal of Political Science* 36:635-64.

Caldeira, Gregory, and John Wright. 1988. "Organized Interests and Agenda Setting in the U.S. Supreme Court." *American Political Science Review* 82:1109-1129.

Calvert, Randall, Mathew McCubbins, and Barry Weingast. 1989. "A Theory of Political Control and Agency Discretion." *American Journal of Political Science* 33:588-611.

Cappelletti, Mauro, Monica Seccombe, and Joseph Weiler, eds. 1986-89. *Integration Through Law: Europe and the American Federal Experience*. 7 Vols. Berlin: de Gruyter.

Carmen, Ira. 1985. *Cloning and the Constitution*. Madison: University of Wisconsin Press.

Carter, Lief. 1985. *Contemporary Constitutional Law-Making: The Supreme Court and the Art of Politics*. Elmsford, NY: Pergamon Press.

Carter, Lief. 1989. "How Liberals Can Philosophize." *Texas Law Review* 67:943-54.

Carter, Lief, and John Gilliom. 1989. "From Foundation to Discourse." In *Judging the Constitution*, ed. Michael McCann and Gerlad Houseman. Boston: Scot, Foresman, Little, Brown.

Carter, Lief, and Christine Harrington. 1990. "Realism in the Authority of Law." *Social Epistemology* 4:4-26.

Carter, Lief, and Christine Harrington. 1991. *Administrative Law and Politics*. 2nd ed. New York: HarperCollins.

Casper, Jonathan, and Sherry Diamond. n.d. "Twenty-Five Years of Jury Research." *Law and Human Behavior*.

Cole, George, ed. 1986. *Criminal Justice: Law and Politics*. Monterey, CA: Brooks/Cole.

Cook, Beverly et al. 1987. *Women in the Judicial Process*. Washington, DC: American Political Science Association.

Cooper, Phillip. 1983. *Public Law and Public Administration*. Palo Alto, CA: Mayfield.

Cooper, Phillip. 1988. *Hard Judicial Choices: Federal District Judges and State and Local Officials*. New York: Oxford University Press.

Coyle, Dennis. 1993. *Property Rights and the Constitution: Mapping Society Through Land Use Regulation*. Albany: State University of New York Press.

Culver, John, and Harry Stumpf. 1992. *The Politics of State Courts*. New York: Longman.

Dalton, Thomas. 1985. *The State Politics of Judicial and Congressional Reform: Legitimizing Criminal Justice Policies*. Westport, CT: Greenwood Press.

Damaska, Mirjan. 1986. *The Faces of Justice and State Authority: A Comparative Approach to the Legal Process*. New Haven: Yale University Press.

Danelski, David. 1990. "Ideology as a Ground for the Rejection of the Bork Nomination." *Northwestern Law Review* 84:900-920.

Davis, Sue. 1989. *Justice Rehnquist and the Constitution*. Princeton: Princeton University Press.

Dometrius, Nelson, and Lee Sigelman. 1988. "Modeling the Impact of Supreme Court Decisions: Nygant v. Board." *Journal of Politics* 50:131-149.

Downs, Donald. 1985. *Nazis in Skokie*. Notre Dame, IN: Notre Dame University Press.

Downs, Donald. 1989. *The New Politics of Pornography*. Chicago: University of Chicago Press.

Ducat, Craig, Mikel Wyckoff, and Victor Flango. 1991. "State Judges and Federal Constitutional Rights." *Research in Law and Policy Studies* 4:241-267.

Ellerman, R., T. Gawron, and R. Rogowski. 1987. *Constitutional Courts in Comparison*. Gummbersback, Germany: Theodor Heuss Akademie.

Epstein, Lee. 1985. *Conservatives in Court*. Knoxville: University of Tennessee Press.

Epstein, Lee, Thomas Walker, and William Dixon. 1989. "The Supreme Court and Criminal Justice Disputes: A Neo-Institutional Perspective." *American Journal of Political Science* 33:825-837.

Feeley, Malcolm. 1983. *Court Reform on Trial: Why Simple Solutions Fail*. New York: Basic Books.

Fino, Susan. 1987. *The Role of the State Supreme Courts in the New Judicial Federalism*. Westport, CT: Greenwood Press.

Fisher, Louis. 1988. *Constitutional Dialogues: Interpretation as Political Process*. Princeton: Princeton University Press.

Fiskin, James. 1983. *Justice, Equal Opportunity and the Family*. New Haven: Yale University Press.

Forsythe, David. 1990. *The Politics of International Law: U.S. Foreign Policy Reconsidered*. Boulder, CO: Lynne Rienner.

Friedelbaum, Stanley, ed. 1988. *Human Rights in the States: New Directions in Constitutional Policy-Making*. Westport, CT: Greenwood Press.

Gates, John, and Charles Johnson, eds. 1991. *The American Courts: A Critical Assessment*. Washington, DC: CQ Press.

Glick, Henry. 1991. "Innovation and Re-Invention in State Policy-Making: Theory and the Evolution of Living Will Laws." *Journal of Politics* 53:835-50.

Glick, Henry. 1992. "Judicial Innovation and Policy Re-Invention: State Supreme Courts and the Right to Die." *Western Political Quarterly* 45:71-92.

Goldberg, Edward. 1990. "The 'Bad Law' Argument in Morgentaler v. The Queen." *Canadian Journal of Women and the Law* 3:584-591.

Goldman, Sheldon, and Charles Lamb, eds. 1985. *Judicial Conflict and Consensus: Behavioral Studies of American Appellate Courts*. Lexington: University of Kentucky Press.

Goldstein, Leslie. 1986. "Popular Sovereignty, the Origins of Judicial Review and the Revival of Unwritten Law." *Journal of Politics* 48:51-71.

Grofman, Bernard. 1985. "Criteria for Districting: A Social Science Perspective." *UCLA Law Review* 33:77-184.

Grossman, Joel, and Stephen Wasby. 1990. "Judge Clement Haynesworth, Jr.: New Perspectives on his Nomination to the Supreme Court." *Duke Law Journal* 1990:74-80.

Hall, Melinda, and Paul Brace. 1989. "Order in the Courts: A Neo-Institutional Approach to Judicial Consensus." *Western Political Quarterly* 42:391-407.

Halpern, Steven, and C. Lamb, eds. 1982. *Supreme Court Activism and Restraint*. Lexington, MA: Lexington Books.

Handberg, Roger, and C. Neal Tate. 1991. "Time Binding and Theory Building in Personal Attribute Models of Supreme Court Voting Behavior." *American Journal of Political Science* 35:460-80.

Harrington, Christine. 1985. *Shadow Justice: The Ideology and Institutionalization of Alternatives to Court*. Westport, CT: Greenwood Press.

Heinz, Anne, Herbert Jacob, and Robert Lineberry, eds. 1983. *Crime in City Politics*. New York: Longman.

Hirsh, Harry. 1992. *A Theory of Liberty: The Constitution and Minorities*. New York: Routledge.

Howard, J. Woodford. 1982. *Courts of Appeals in the Federal Judicial System*. Princeton: Princeton University Press.

Jackson, Donald, and C. Neal Tate, eds. 1993. *Judicial Review and Public Policy in Comparative Perspective*. New York: Macmillan.

Jacob, Herbert. 1988. *Silent Revolution: The Transformation of Divorce Law in the United States*. Chicago: University of Chicago Press.

Jacobsohn, Gary J. 1986. *The Supreme Court and the Decline of Constitutional Aspiration*. Totowa, NJ: Rowman and Littlefield.

Jennings, Terri. n.d. *Judicial Review and Political Responsibility: In Defense of a Political Court*.

Jillson, Calvin. 1988. *Constitution Making: Conflict and Consensus in the Federal Convention of 1787*. New York: Agathon.

Johnson, Charles, and Cannon, Bradley. 1984. *Judicial Policies: Implementation and Impact*. Washington, DC: Congressional Quarterly Press.

Kagan, Robert, ed. 1989. "Special Issue. Law and Regulation: Studies From Great Britain and the Netherlands," *Law and Policy* 11:7-41.

Kagan, Robert, and Robert Rosen. 1985. "On the Social Significance of the Large Law Firm." *Stanford Law Review* 37:399-446.

Kammen, Michael. 1988. *Sovereignty and Liberty: Constitutional Discourse in American Culture*. Madison: University of Wisconsin Press.

Katzmann, Robert. 1980. *Regulatory Bureaucracy: The Federal Trade Commission and Antitrust Policy*. Cambridge: MIT Press.

Katzmann, Robert. 1986. *Institutional Disability: The Saga of Transportation Policy for the Handicapped*. Washington, DC: Brookings.

Kommers, Donald. 1989. *The Constitutional Jurisprudence of the Federal Republic of Germany*. Durham: Duke University Press.

Kritzer, Herbert. 1990. *The Justice Broker: Lawyers and Ordinary Litigation*. New York: Oxford University Press.

Lamb, Charles, and Stephen Halpern. 1993. *The Burger Court: Political and Judicial Profiles*. Urbana: University of Illinois Press.

Lasser, William. 1989. *The Limits of Judicial Power: The Supreme Court in American Politics*. Chapel Hill: University of North Carolina Press.

Levinson, Sanford. 1985. "Gerrymandering and the Brooding Omnipresence of Proportional Representation: Why Won't It Go Away." *UCLA Law Review* 33:257-282.

Levinson, Sanford. 1988. *Constitutional Faith*. Princeton: Princeton University Press.

Levinson, Sanford, and Steven Mailloux, ed. 1988. *Interpreting Law and Literature: A Hermeneutic Reader*. Evanston, IL: Northwestern University Press.

Lijphart, Arend. 1990. "The Political Consequences of Electoral Laws." *American Political Science Review* 84:481-496.

Macedo, Stephen. 1990. *Liberal Virtues: Citizenship, Virtue, and Community in Liberal Constitutionalism*. Oxford: Oxford University Press.

Mashaw, Jerry, and David Harfst. 1990. *The Struggle for Auto Safety*. Cambridge, MA: Harvard University Press.

Mather, Lynn, and Keith Boyum, eds. 1983. *Empirical Theories of Courts*. New York: Longman.

Maveety, Nancy. 1991. *Representation Rights and the Burger Years*. Ann Arbor: University of Michigan Press.

McCann, Michael. 1986. *Taking Reform Seriously: Perspectives on Public Interest Liberalism*. Ithaca: Cornell University Press.

McCubbins, Mathew. 1985. "The Legislative Design of Regulatory Structure." *American Journal of Political Science* 29:721-748.

McCubbins, Mathew, Roger Noll, and Barry Weingast. 1987. "Administrative Procedures as Instruments of Political Control." *Journal of Law, Economics and Organization* 3:243-274.

McCubbins, Mathew, Roger Noll, and Barry Weingast. 1989. "Structure and Process: Politics and Policy: Administrative Arrangements and the Political Control of Agencies." *Virginia Law Review* 75:431-82.

McCubbins, Mathew, Roger Noll, and Barry Weingast. 1990. "Positive and Normative Models of Due Process: An Integrative Approach to Administrative Procedures." *Journal of Law, Economics and Organizations* 6:307-330.

McCubbins, Mathew, Roger Noll, and Barry Weingast. 1992. "Positive Canons: The Role of Legislative Bargains in Statutory Interpretation." *Georgetown Law Review* 80:705-42.

McDowell, Gary. 1982. *Equality and the Constitution: The Supreme Court, Equitable Relief and Public Policy*. Chicago: University of Chicago Press.

McWhinney, Edward. 1986. *Supreme Courts and Judicial Law-Making: Constitutional Tribunals and Constitutional Review*. Dordrecht: Martinus Mijhoff.

Meister, Robert. 1989. "The Logic and Legacy of Dred Scott: Marshall, Taney and the Sublimination of Republican Thought." *Studies in American Political Development* 3:199-260.

Melnick, R. Shep. 1983. *Regulation and the Courts: The Case of the Clean Air Act*. Washington, DC: Brookings Institution.

Melnick, R. Shep. n.d. *The Politics of Statutory Rights: Courts and Congress in the Welfare State*.

Mendelson, Wallace. 1990. "James Madison's Triumph: The Fourteenth Amendment." In *The Constitutional Bases of Political and Social Change in the United States*, ed. Shlomo Slonim. New York: Praeger.

Mezey, Susan. 1988. *No Longer Disabled: The Federal Courts and the Politics of Social Security Disability*. New York: Greenwood Press.

Miller, Arthur. 1985. *Politics, Democracy and the Supreme Court: Essays on the Frontier of Constitutional Theory*. Westport, CT: Greenwood Press.

Morgan, Richard. 1984. *Disabling America: The "Rights" Industry in Our Time*. New York: Basic Books.

Murphy, Bruce. 1988. *Fortas: The Rise and Ruin of A Supreme Court Justice*. New York: William Marrow.

Murphy, Walter, J. E. Fleming, and W. F. Harris. 1986. *Constitutional Interpretation*. Mineola, NY: Foundation Press.

Murphy, Walter, and Joseph Tanenhaus. 1990. "Publicity, Public Opinion, and the Court." *Northwestern Law Review* 84:985-1023.

Mutch, Robert. 1988. *Campaigns, Congress and Courts: The Making of Federal Campaign Finance Law*. New York: Praeger.

Nardulli, Peter, ed. 1991. *The Constitution and American Political Development: An Institutional Perspective*. Urbana: University of Illinois Press.

Nardulli, Peter, James Eisenstein, and Roy B. Flemming. 1988. *The Tenor of Justice: Criminal Courts and the Guilty Plea Process*. Urbana: University of Illinois Press.

Nash, A. E. Keir. 1983. "On Radical Interpretations of American Law: The Relation of Law and History." *Michigan Law Review* 81:274-345.

Nedelsky, Jennifer. 1990. *Private Property and the Limits of American Constitutionalism*. Chicago: University of Chicago Press.

O'Brien, David. 1987. *What Process Is Due*. New York: Russel Sage.

O'Brien, David. 1991a. "The Framers Muse in Republicanism, the Supreme Court, and Pragmatic Constitutional Interpretivism." *Review of Politics* 53:251-288.

O'Brien, David. 1991b. "The Politics of Professionalism: President Gerald R. Ford's Appointment of Justice John Paul Stevens." *Presidential Studies Quarterly* 21:103-126.

O'Connor, Karen, and Lee Epstein. 1985. "Bridging the Gap between Congress and the Supreme Court: Interest Groups and the Erosion of the American Rule Governing Attorney's Fees." *Western Political Quarterly* 38:238-249.

O'Neill, Timothy. 1985. *Bakke and the Politics of Equality*. Middletown, CT: Washington University Press.

Orren, Karen. 1991. *Belated Feudalism: Labor, the Law and Liberal Development in the United States*. Cambridge: Cambridge University Press.

Palmer, Jan. 1990. *The Vinson Court Era: The Supreme Court's Conference Votes*. New York: AMS Press.

Paul, Ellen, and Howard Dickson, eds. 1990. *Liberty, Property and the Future of Constitutional Development*. Albany, NY: SUNY Press.

Perry, H. W. 1991. *Deciding to Decide: Agenda Setting in the United States Supreme Court*. Cambridge, MA: Harvard University Press.

Porter, Mary, and G. Alan Tarr, eds. 1982. *State Supreme Courts: Policy Makers in the Federal System*. Westport, CT: Greenwood Press.

Provine, Doris. 1986. *Judging Credentials: Non-Lawyer Judges and the Politics of Professionalism*. Chicago: University of Chicago Press.

Rabkin, Jeremy. 1989. *Judicial Compulsions: How Public Law Distorts Public Policy*. New York: Basic Books.

Randall, Richard. 1989. *Freedom and Taboo: Pornography and the Politics of a Self Divided*. Berkeley: University of California Press.

Rebell, Michael, and Arthur Block. 1982. *Educational Policy-Making and the Courts: An Empirical Study of Judicial Activism*. Chicago: University of Chicago Press.

Rees, Joseph. 1988. *Reforming the Workplace: A Study of Self-Regulation in Occupational Safety*. Philadelphia: University of Pennsylvania Press.

Renteln, Alison Dundee. 1990. *International Human Rights: Universalism versus Relativism*. Newbury Park, CA: Sage Publications.

Rodriguez, Daniel. 1989. "The Substance of the New Legal Process." *California Law Review* 77:919-953.

Rohr, John. 1986. *To Run a Constitution*. Lawrence, KS: University of Kansas Press.

Rosenberg, Gerald. 1991. *The Hollow Hope: Can Courts Bring About Social Change?* Chicago: University of Chicago Press.

Sarat, Austin, and William Felsteiner. 1986. "Law and Strategy in the Divorce Lawyer's Office." *Law and Society Review* 20:93-126.

Sarat, Austin, and William Felstiner. 1989. "Lawyers and Legal Consciousness: Law Talk in Lawyers' Offices. *Yale Law Journal* 98:1663-1689.

Sbragia, Alberta, ed. 1992. *European Political Institutions and Policy Making After 1992*. Washington, DC: Brookings Institution.

Scheingold, Stuart. 1991. The Politics of Street Crime: *Criminal Process and Cultural Obsession*. Philadelphia: Temple University Press

Scheppele, Kim. 1988. *Legal Secrets: Equality and Efficiency in the Common Law*. Chicago: University of Chicago Press.

Scheppele, Kim, and Jeremy Waldron. 1991. "Contractarian Methods in Political and Legal Evaluation." *Yale Journal of Law and Humanities* 3:195-230.

Schmidhauser, John, ed. 1987. *Comparative Judicial Systems*. London: Butterworths.

Schuck, Peter, and Rogers Smith. 1985. *Citizenship Without Consent: Illegal Aliens in the American Polity*. New Haven: Yale University Press.

Scigliano, Robert. 1988. "The Presidency and the Judiciary." In *The Presidency and the Political System*, ed. Michael Nelson. Washington, DC: CQ Press.

Segal, Jeffrey, and Albert Cover. 1989. "Ideological Values and the Votes of Supreme Court Justices." *American Political Science Review* 83:557-564.

Segal, Jeffrey, and Harold Spaeth. 1993. *The Supreme Court and the Attitudinal Model*. New York: Cambridge University Press.

Shapiro, Martin. 1981. *Courts: A Comparative and Political Analysis*. Chicago: University of Chicago Press.

Shapiro, Martin. 1985. "Gerrymandering, Unfairness and the Supreme Court." *UCLA Law Review* 33:227-257.

Shapiro, Martin. 1986. "The Supreme Court's 'Return' to Economic Regulation." *Studies in American Political Development* 1:91-141.

Shapiro, Martin. 1988. *Who Guards the Guardians: Judicial Control of Administration*. Athens, GA: University of Georgia Press.

Shapiro, Martin. 1990a. "Interest Groups and Supreme Court Appointments." *Northwestern Law Review* 84:935-961.

Shapiro, Martin. 1990b. "Lawyers, Corporations and Knowledge." *American Journal of Comparative Law* 38:683-716.

Sheldon, Charles H. 1988. *A Century of Judging: A Political History of the Washington Supreme Court*. Seattle: University of Washington Press.

Silbey, Susan, and Austin Sarat. 1987. "Critical Traditions in Law and Society Research." *Law and Society Review* 21:165-174.

Silverstein, Mark. 1984. *Constitutional Faiths: Felix Frankfurter, Hugo Black and the Process of Judicial Decision Making*. Ithaca, NY: Cornell University Press.

Smith, Rogers. 1985. *Liberalism and American Constitutional Law*. Cambridge: Harvard University Press.

Smith, Rogers. 1988. "Political Jurisprudence, the 'New Institutionalism' and the Future of Public Law." *American Political Science Review* 82:90-102.

Snowiss, Sylvia. 1990. *Judicial Review and the Law of the Constitution*. New Haven: Yale University Press.

Songer, Donald. 1988. "Alternative Approaches to the Study of Judicial Impact: Miranda in Five State Courts." *American Politics Quarterly* 16:425-546.

Spaeth, Harold. n.d. "United States Supreme Court Judicial Database." Ann Arbor: Inter-University Consortium for Political and Social Research Study 9422.

Steamer, Robert. 1986. *Chief Justice: Leadership and the Supreme Court*. Charleston: University of South Carolina Press.

Stephenson, D. Grier. 1991. *An Essential Safeguard: Essays on the United States Supreme Court and Its Justices*. New York: Greenwood Press.

Sterett, Susan. 1990. "Keeping the Law Up-to-Date: The English Law Commission, Administrative Law and the Idiom of Legalism." *Law and Social Inquiry* 15:731-64.

Stetson, Dorothy M. 1982. *A Woman's Issue: The Politics of Family Law Reform in England*. Westport, CT: Greenwood Press.

Stone, Alec. 1992. *The Birth of Judicial Politics in France*. New York: Oxford University Press.

Strum, Phillippa. 1984. *Louis D. Brandeis: Justice for the People*. Cambridge: Harvard University Press.

Stumpf, Harry, ed. 1983. "Whither Political Jurisprudence: A Symposium." *Western Political Quarterly* 36:533-570.

Stumpf, Harry. 1988. *American Judicial Politics*. San Diego: Harcourt Brace Jovanovich.

Sunstein, Cass. 1989. "Interpreting Statutes in the Regulatory State." *Harvard Law Review* 103:405-508.

Sunstein, Cass. 1990. *After the Rights Revolution: Reconceiving the Regulatory State*. Cambridge: Harvard University Press.

Vogel, David. 1987. *National Styles of Regulation: Environmental Policy in Great Britain and the United States*. Ithaca: Cornell University Press.

Volcansek, Mary. 1990. "Decision Making Italian Style." *West European Politics* 13:33-45.

Volcansek, Mary. 1992. *Judicial Politics in Europe: An Impact Analysis*. New York: Peter Lang.

Waltman, Jerold, and Kenneth Holland, eds. 1988. *The Political Role of Law Courts in Modern Democracies*. London: Macmillan.

Wasby, Stephen. 1987. "Communication in the Ninth Circuit: A Concern for Collegiality." *University of Puget Sound Law Review* 11:73-138.

Way, Frank. 1989. "Religious Disputation and the Civil Courts: Quasi-Establishment and Secular Principles." *Western Political Quarterly* 42:523-543.

Weiler, Joseph. 1986. "Eurocracy and Distrust." *Washington Law Review* 61:1103-42.

Wenner, Lettie. 1992. "Federal Courts and Environmental Management: Harvesting Old Growth Timber." In *Environmental Politics and Policy in the West*, ed. Zachary Smith. College Station, TX: Texas A&M Press.

Wiecek, William. 1988. *Liberty Under Law: The Supreme Court in American Life*. Baltimore: Johns Hopkins University Press.

Willborn, Steven. 1989. *A Secretary and a Cook: Challenging Women's Wages in the Courts of the United States and Great Britain*. Ithaca: Institute of Industrial and Labor Relations.

Williams, Bruce, and Albert Matheny. 1992. *Democracy, Dialogue and Social Regulation*. New Haven: Yale University Press.

Wolfe, Christopher. 1986. *The Rise of Modern Judicial Review: From Constitutional Interpretation to Judge-Made Law*. New York: Basic Books.

Zemans, Frances, and Victor Rosenblum. 1981. *The Making of a Public Profession*. American Press Foundation.

15

Political Executives and Their Officials

Colin Campbell, S.J.

> Unlike most work dealing with style, then, Campbell makes a serious attempt to move beyond the personalization of institutions, and he is explicitly concerned with theory-construction and other building blocks of social science. But [presidential] style, as always, proves to be a stumbling block rather than a vehicle for progress -- promoting conceptual confusion, the endless proliferation of relevant variables, and more complications than any analysis can make sense of (Moe 1990, 44).

The Campbell cited above is none other than your current author. One might legitimately ask whether someone prone to devising frameworks "promoting conceptual confusion..." is the appropriate person for presenting a distillation of the state of political science on the topic of "political executives and their officials." However, this area of inquiry is as old as political science itself. And its major debates have centered precisely on such issues as the complexity of models employed in analyzing executive leaders and their relations with their officials. This does not give one license for conceptual overkill. Yet, it should make us all attentive to the difficulty of reconciling our desire to capture the richness of this subject matter and the need to make sense of it all.

Political science by its nature attempts to focus on moving targets. And, as sub-fields go, executive leadership presents as much flux as any object of political science inquiry. This means that students of political executives constantly find themselves struggling with sharp learning curves as one administration takes over from another or executive leaders face crises or unforeseen circumstances which call upon their adaptive skills (Rockman 1984, 4-7). Also, just about everybody feels compelled to share views about executive leaders. For instance, my barber has become aware of the "lightening rod" theory of why George Bush kept John Sununu so long. My barber expounds his ideas for all comers -- regardless of whether they make their living studying presidents. Other burning issues to political scientists -- such as how Congress allocates committee memberships -- would bore my barber and most of his customers to tears. Whereas other political science fields attract a lot of deference, presidency and executive leadership scholars compete with an overabundance of conventional wisdom. In this field, attentive publics often actually say on their own the types of things that one hears pronounced in panels at the APSA annual meeting.

One finds a tremendous amount of volatility in this field. From an institutional perspective, however, the presidency remains infinitely more vulnerable to the personality of the incumbent at a given moment than either house of Congress would be to the constellation of personalities that occupy it from time to time. Changes in the balance between the president and Congress due to party turnover or the peculiarities of personality can badly miscue even the most shrewd observers. The profession broadly endorsed John F. Kennedy's inattentiveness to organizational structure (Neustadt 1960). Political scientists had convinced themselves that excessive institutional rigor in the policy process had led to overcooking issues during the Eisenhower administration. Fred I. Greenstein's revisionist analysis of Eisenhower, however, contests the early critique of Eisenhower -- arguing that his administration achieved a highly adaptive balance between structural and personalized responses to issues (1982).

When students of the presidency piled on the anti-imperial-presidency bandwagon after Watergate (Nathan 1975), we contributed little foresight of the extreme decentralization that characterized the Carter administration. In the aftermath of Carter's failure as a political executive, we were the first to issue glum prognoses for the future of presidential leadership in the face of Congress's ascendancy (Heclo and Salamon 1981). During the Reagan years, we began to point to the facility with which presidents can short-circuit institutional relationships with other parts of the policy apparatus in Washington -- Congress included -- by going public, pursuing partisan responsiveness, and using foreign affairs, to distract attention from domestic issues (Kernell 1986; Moe 1985; Rose 1988; Campbell 1986). With the end of the Reagan years and the minimalism of the Bush administration, we began to focus upon "divided government" and its constraints on the executive (Sundquist 1988).

Thus, political scientists have tended to extrapolate from the approach and circumstances of each administration in making more general assertions about the state of the presidency which soon fail the test of time. We have taken kernels of truth from analyses of individual presidents and overdrawn their consequences for the development of the presidency.

This chapter takes the broad compass of "political executives" literally. Thus, it will consider in some detail crossnational perspectives on executive leadership. In the U.S., "political executives" would take in most immediately presidents. Strictly speaking, cabinet secretaries -- as unelected appointees who serve at the pleasure of the president on the advice and consent of the Senate -- do not tap autonomous executive authority. Yet, some cabinet members might enjoy greater leverage and maneuverability because of the strength of their personalities, the degree to which the president defers to their expertise and prerogatives, the importance of their department, the salience of the issues they handle to the president's agenda, and/or their ties with sectors of the population whose support the administration requires for legislative and electoral success. Other presidential systems similarly construe executive leadership so that authority tends to focus on the individual who serves simultaneously as head of state and head of government (Riggs 1988, 247-78).

Parliamentary systems divide the political executive. Typically, they provide for a split between the head of state and the head of government with the former assuming the bulk of the ceremonial functions and the latter effectively serving as chief executive (Mackintosh 1977). More important, the head of government shares the day-to-day exercise of executive authority with a cabinet (Hennessy 1986). This body -- either because of a highly legitimized constitutional convention or a specific provision in the country's basic law -- defines the parameters of executive actions and initiatives in collective terms. Cabinet systems vary in the degree to which ministers actually deliberate collectively (Mackie and Hogwood 1985). And, the stylistic preferences of the heads of government can introduce great fluctuations in the role of cabinet dynamics in the process of executive leadership.

Americans might find it tempting to conclude that viewing political executives in the U.S. in light of executive leadership in other countries amounts to introducing beer to a wine tasting. However, a commonality has emerged in the tasks of executive leaders over the past 20 years. The fact that in many respects presidents and prime ministers face similar problems and frequently employ comparable strategies underscores this phenomenon (Rose and Suleiman 1980; Plowden 1987). The electronic era has meant that both, more often than before, catapult to their positions without having passed through the conventional socialization lower down in public life (Campbell and Wyszomirski 1991, 13). Presidents and prime ministers tend much more than before to go above the heads of their cabinet colleagues and legislative supporters to make special pleas directly to the people (Seymour-Ure 1991).

Fewer prime ministers than presidents face divided government. However, some must work as hard as presidents to bring the necessary coalitions together to fulfill comprehensive agendas. Labour prime ministers in Britain must deal with an extremely fractious caucus; both Labour and Conservative prime ministers in the U.K. increasingly find their prerogatives constrained not only by their cabinet colleagues but by their opposite numbers in the European Economic Community (Nugent 1989, 88-109). German chancellors usually can only form coalition governments and must follow the rubrics of collective government mandated by the Basic Law (Mayntz 1987; Berry 1989). Canadian prime ministers might control Parliament. However, any legislation that affects the powers of the provinces must be negotiated through tortuous discussions with provincial governments (Simeon 1972).

To some extent, all advanced democracies have wrestled with similar fiscal constraints to those faced by the United States. Further, they have encountered comparable declines in public support of social programs and government intervention in the marketplace to those experienced in the United States. Thus, the increased difficulty of governance coupled with declining resources and support have introduced conditions every bit as likely to incline prime ministers toward minimalism as those which prevail in the United States.

Johan P. Olsen has done an especially good job of alerting us to the effects of economic conditions on our view of the state and, in turn, what we expect from political executives. His *Organized Democracy* argues that political executives operating within the corporatist-pluralistic model for governance that emerged in Norway during the period of economic expansion and growth of the welfare state lost all sense of proportion (1983, 31-33). Their efforts to respond to societal demands went beyond integration of broad and institutionalized groupings to accommodation of extremely particularistic and ad hoc interests. Following strategies of privatization and deregulation, the conservative-center government of the mid-1980s attempted to recapture the "institutional state" -- a style of governance which attempts to define in clear terms the boundary between the state and various sectors of society.

In a subsequent work, Olsen has further developed his thesis in ways which point up its applicability to the comparative study of executive leadership (1987). Here three points emerge. First, political executives must base their relations with the bureaucratic elite in ways which comport with the formers' preferred model for governance. Instrumental approaches will prevail when general agreement exists over the boundaries of the state; evolutionary modes when the political executive attempts to redefine these boundaries; an emphasis on adaptiveness characterizes the classic corporate-pluralist state as it adjusts to shifts in political power between social groups; and political responsiveness becomes the dominant value for the welfare state which -- like Norway in the 1960s and 1970s -- has become the "supermarket" for society's "great necessities."

Second, political executives can misread their circumstances to the point where a disjunction develops between their leadership style and the received image of the state. Canada's Pierre Elliott Trudeau ceaselessly pressed the sovereign-rational approach in a highly fragmented, consociational and corporate-pluralistic state (Aucoin 1986; French 1980; Hartle 1983). Britain's two Labour prime ministers during the 1970s -- Harold Wilson and James Callaghan -- failed to adequately address the shift of British thinking about the state from corporate-pluralistic to institutional (Keegan and Pennant-Rea 1979; Rose and Peters 1978; Hood and Wright 1981). Thus, their adaptive strategies were left unrewarded.

Third, Olsen's emphasis of administrative style as related to the boundary between the state and society invites us to make a distinction between moderate and radical views of the proper role of government. In other words, we must allow for thinking which crosses the line between reorienting and dismantling the state. As represented by some of the thinking behind Ronald Reagan's and Margaret Thatcher's form of market-oriented governance, a distinct movement emerged in the 1980s toward recrafting the entire context of the state in ways which would limit it to only a fraction of its former functions (Savas 1982; Riddell 1983, chap. 8).

The remainder of this chapter will serve as a guide for those wishing to pursue some of the central issues concerning political executives and their relations with their officials. It will not contain an American bias because your author is a Canadian who has cut his teeth on comparisons of executive leadership in the U.K., Canada, and Australia as well as the United States. However, it will have an Anglo-American bias. It will make appropriate reference throughout to issues and literature emerging from beyond the Anglo-American context. But it cannot lay claim to the same familiarity with the materials. The sections which follow will place the issue of political executives in the wider setting of the current direction of the discipline in this field in the United States. Tremendous pressures have emerged for greater rigor in the analysis of the presidency. We will probe what realistically can be done to address these concerns and the degree to which what we learn might be applied in other systems.

The reader will find that I have not departed from the multi-dimensional approach which occasioned Terry Moe's response noted at the very beginning of this chapter. I will, however, take extra pains to meet his concerns half way and call for a recognition among students of executive leadership that the accessibility of various dimensions of our subject matter to rigorous theory and analysis differ considerably. Investigators should always be able to locate themselves in this matrix and to exercise due restraint -- especially when making connections from one body of knowledge to another.

The Search for Rigor and Trends in the Discipline

One cautionary note might guide our reflections as we consider the search for rigor in the study of executive politics. Above, I have reviewed the swings in the discipline's view of the presidency since the emergence of the behavioral era by reporting the reaction to various incumbents. These gyrations should alert us to a shortfall in the discipline's capacity to retain distance from its highly volatile subject matter.

Some of the swings owe more to episodic events than longer-term distortions in professional vision. In their own ways, Nixon and Carter scared us -- the former because he exposed the vulnerability of the system to imperial behavior, the latter because his performance pointed up the bias toward paralysis in the system -- and we tended to project from these experiences to our view of the presidency. However, other swings stem from changes in political scientists' criteria for assessing governance.

The initial absorption of the discipline with the divided government issue emerged in the late 1940s and early 1950s. The recent focus on divided government often appeals most strongly to authors inclined to interpret Bush's minimalism as reflecting the constraints of the institutional context of the administration. Thus, Bert A. Rockman has attributed Bush's tendency to "syndicate responsibility" to the exigencies of divided government (1991, 13-14); Charles O. Jones has maintained that we cannot understand Bush unless we employ the standard of how he handled "diffused responsibility" rather than examining his performance according to the unrealistic expectations of "party government" (1991, 38); and Paul Quirk has allowed that the institutional context faced by Bush put the onus on his ability to pursue mediation and cooperative negotiation (1991, 72).

This latter-day response to divided government departs from that which prevailed in the 1940s and 1950s. In that period, the discipline took a strongly prescriptive stance based on the view that it should work for the reform of the system. In a 1950 statement, an American Political Science Association committee on political parties called for changes which would foster the development of a responsible two-party system in the United States. Here parties would identify realizable goals and maintain sufficient discipline to actually deliver on their promises. This perspective took root in a fascination at the time with the British parliamentary system.

Unlike the U.S., Britain had moved decisively after the war to advance further the welfare state. Reflecting upon the incapacity of the U.S. system to press the social agenda, scholars became enamored of party discipline. And, their commitment to addressing the need for leadership capable of achieving adequate policies for social maintenance flowed over into other realms later in the 1950s and early in the 1960s. Indeed, James MacGregor Burns -- writing in a period during which the Democrats controlled both houses of Congress -- lamented the intractable nature of the American "four-party" system. Due to the different coalitions of forces which produce even administrations and congresses of the same party, presidents -- Burns believed -- had proved incapable of tackling the big issues -- "urban decline, conservation, tax reform, medical care, government organization" -- even when the same party ostensibly controlled all the levers of power (Burns 1963, 3). One author of Burns' generation -- James L. Sundquist -- continues to press this view (1986, 78-79; 1988, 613-635). Today he focuses his critique more on the need for the type of executive management capable of reestablishing national purpose and direction than upon concern about the stalled social agenda. Yet, his prescriptions for constitutional reform fit squarely within the responsible two-party tradition.

A realpolitik emerged within the profession in response to those disillusioned by the U.S. tendency toward indecisive government. The first of this wave became known as the pluralists. Led by the seminal contributions of Robert A. Dahl and Charles Lindblom, authors within this tradition argued that we should lower the bar and expect much less comprehensive decision-making in the U.S. system (Dahl 1956, 1971; Lindblom 1965). This perspective had a pervasive effect on all fields of the discipline -- including the dissemination of

the view that the system by its nature would provide most presidents with opportunities to make only incremental changes to existing policies. Working from shared analytic perches elsewhere within the behavioral tradition, authors such as Theodore J. Lowi (1969) and Jack Walker (1966, 1969) took issue with the implications of the pluralist analysis. Nonetheless, the approach set the agenda and tone of most empirical research in the field of executive politics throughout the 1960s and 1970s.

Beginning in the 1960s, two-party responsible government began to encounter more direct and damaging assaults from public choice theorists. Such scholars as James Buchanan, Gordon Tullock, and William Niskanen effectively pressed the view that the U.S. should have less government, not more (Buchanan and Tullock 1962; Niskanen 1971). To such authors, the great debates being waged between the proponents of two-party responsible government and incrementalist models missed the point. Given greater knowledge about their options, voters and their representatives would make only those choices that correspond to the highest-ranked selections on their preference schedules. They would not understand, much less support, comprehensive policy programs. Nor would they -- given full knowledge of their options -- tolerate incremental augmentation of programs which do not serve their immediate interests.

Public choice theorists ushered in a new perspective on political leadership which greatly influenced expectations for executive politics. They anticipated by several years the limits of campaign appeals based on candidates' promises of social programs for which ultimately voters had to pay. It was not until the late 1970s that more conventional analysts began to observe that executive politics faced new constraints. Social spending had become such a drag on advanced economies that its net effect no longer contributed that clearly to citizens' disposable income (Rose and Peters 1978, 33-34).

The public choice perspective's link with monetarist economics was reflected in the politics of the two most dominant chief executives of the eighties -- Ronald Reagan and Britain's Margaret Thatcher. Thatcher achieved considerable success in pressing the public choice agenda. She so cut spending that the U.K. government operated in surplus through the latter years of the 1980s. She privatized several government enterprises and introduced a series of reforms designed to make the public service more accountable for its resources. On the other hand, Reagan's experience suggests that the U.S. system lends itself to public choice approaches as poorly as it does to the expansive and comprehensive welfare state. Conflict and inaction plagued the administration throughout over such issues as how deeply supply-side economics should dig into taxes, the extent of cuts in social spending, and the degree to which the Pentagon should "give at the office" and absorb its share of parsimony (Stockman 1986; Roberts 1984).

The Public Choice Thinking: Consequences for the Study of Political Executives

The mixed results of public choice in the U.S. constitute a true paradox. Its proponents developed the approach in response to elements of fragmentation in the U.S. system which made it very hard for executive leaders to reverse the incremental growth of bureaucracy. Niskanen's work addressed most directly the perceived crisis of executive politics in which presidents find it impossible to break down the coalitions of officials, legislators, and interest groups which fuel the proliferation and expansion of government programs. He asserted that the budget-maximizing tendencies of government officials -- appointive as well as career -- stood at the root of the problem (Niskanen 1971, 21-22, 38). The fragmentation of the system sets officials up in a perfect climate in which to pursue their personal utility. This involves seeking higher salaries, better perquisites, greater reputations, and more power; dispensing more patronage; increasing programmatic outputs; and it adds up to immense pressures to expand organizations and increase budgets.

In suggesting how political executives might stem budget maximizing, Niskanen departed from the received wisdom of the time. This held that those seeking to control bureaucracies should acquire more detailed information on the actual operation of policy programs. Niskanen argued, on the other hand, that the surest way to take political executives off the scent of budget maximizers was to get them absorbed by issues associated with comprehensiveness, detail, procedural rationality, and control (Niskanen 1973a, 6-8; cites Wildavsky 1961).

Niskanen proposed a number of structural changes in the budget process which would replace ad hoc mechanisms with automatic rules which would force tough decisions. This automation of budgeting included a committee of congressional leaders which would recommend "target" outlays to both houses and the president, a requirement that Congress would have to offset spending beyond that recommended in the agreed budget with dollar-for-dollar increases in personal income taxes, and the assumption by the Executive Office of the President of a more active role in providing express guidance to the Office of Management and Budget on budget priorities -- thereby, making "the proposed budget a more effective instrument of the political interests of the President" (Niskanen 1973a, 17-19, 55-57). During the chronic fiscal stress which began in the mid-1970s and still persists, Congress and presidents have engaged in an iterative process gradually moving toward the type of budgetary discipline envisioned by Niskanen. Once again, however, the fragmented nature of the system seems to preordain that many pockets of government activity will prove highly resistant even to potential draconian automatization of budgeting.

As mentioned above, public choice has found much more fertile soil in parliamentary systems. This is ironic. Several qualities of such systems already make them less susceptible than the American system to afflictions -- such as budget maximizing bureaucracy -- which so absorb the attention of Niskanen and others. First, political appointees and career civil servants in the U.S. -- especially the latter -- tend to focus their careers much more narrowly than their opposite numbers in parliamentary systems (Heclo 1977, 116-120; 1984, 18-20). For U.S. career officials, movement from one specialized section of a department to another occurs rarely. Much less would we expect transfers from department to department. This inclines U.S. officials toward blinkered perspectives. They, therefore, become much more territorial than their counterparts in parliamentary systems.

Second, parliamentary systems do not have truly transformative legislatures. That is, legislators lack the capacity to mold and reshape laws and budgets independent of the guidance provided by the political executive as embodied in the leadership of the governing party or coalition (Polsby 1975, 277). The absence of long and reasonably secure tenure in specialized fields among bureaucrats and transformative legislatures inhibits the development of strong client-patron relationships in parliamentary systems. In the U.S., the currency that such terms as "sub-government," "iron triangles," and "atomization" have attained suggests the extent to which permanent officials can play both the political executive and Congress off the middle to get their own way (see, for instance, Olson 1982, 50-52; and Aberbach, Putnam, and Rockman 1981, 94-100).

In the English-speaking world, parliamentary systems began implementing public-choice approaches to budgeting in the mid-1970s. As a condition of its 1976 rescue of the pound, the International Monetary Fund prompted the U.K.'s Labour government under James Callaghan to greatly extend the application of "cash limits" to public expenditure (Keegan and Pennant-Rea 1979, 205). Here the Treasury imposed cash limits on the estimates submitted to Parliament (Campbell 1983, 185-186). Departments received from Parliament authority to spend a given amount of cash, not an open-ended remit to pursue specific programs. In theory, this procedure greatly reduced cost overruns. However, few parliamentary systems concentrate budget power in one department to the degree that the U.K. does. The imposition of cash limits -- especially without external pressure -- becomes especially difficult if control over economic policy is divided between a finance department and a budget department -- as is the case in Canada and Australia. It also would encounter much more resistance if ministers have become used to making budget decisions through collective consultation rather than deferring largely to the judgment of the minister responsible for preparing the budget.

Canada in the mid- to late-1970s presented a clear instance of a system whose budgeting process had become extremely fragmented. Since Confederation in 1867, a committee of cabinet -- the Treasury Board -- has given collective review of the expenditure budget. In the 1960s, the cabinet increasingly did its business through specialized policy committees. In the same period, the Treasury Board Secretariat emerged as a department separate from the Finance Department. As well, the cabinet secretariat -- called the Privy Council Office -- began increasingly to present independent advice to the prime minister and cabinet committees rather than simply lending logistical support to the collective decision-making process. Paralysis arose in the executive-bureaucratic arena -- especially in connection with questions which related to the budget. The Treasury Board found it difficult to impose discipline. As a recent offspring of the Finance Department, it lacked standing. Meanwhile, the Privy Council Office remained very much within the expansive mindset of the 1960s -- tending to give moral support to cabinet committees as they continued to dream up expensive government programs and regulations (French 1980).

Through an iterative process beginning in 1978 and involving governments of both the Liberals' Pierre Elliott Trudeau and the Progressive Conservative's Joe Clark, the Government of Canada totally revamped its budget-making apparatus. Public-choice thinking operated behind its moves. Key public servants had become convinced that cabinet committees might be used to break down the corner-fighting tendencies of ministers (Borins 1982; Doern 1982; Van Loon 1983; Campbell 1983, 194-200). Here ten expenditure envelopes with specific sums of cash were distributed among the policy committees of cabinet. If ministers decided to allocate additional funds for a new or existing program, they would have to pay for it with savings found in the salient envelope.

As the theory went, ministers would develop a sense of sectoral responsibility allowing them to identify potential savings in their departments. That is, they would more willingly give up funds if these went to their sector rather than back into the general treasury. This higher-level game theory was lost on ministers who proceeded to

logroll in precisely the way that congressional committees do in the United States. That is, they would trade off their support of one another's programs and offer to the government politically unacceptable savings -- such as eliminating the Royal Canadian Mounted Police Musical Ride, Canada's equivalent of the Washington Monument. By fiscal year 1982-83, the deficit had ballooned to fully 50% of revenue. The experience points up the possibility that -- in fragmented policy arenas, presidential or otherwise -- facile adoption of public choice solutions can actually backfire and exacerbate the incapacity of the system to make tough decisions.

As already noted, the Thatcher government in the U.K. so tightened fiscal policy that it ran surpluses through the latter part of the 1980s. Rational choice perspectives played an important role here. In 1973, William Niskanen published a monograph in the U.K. which hoped to alert Britons to the need to control the growth of bureaucracy (1973b). This work argued that prime ministers should eschew particularistic considerations -- such as personal and regional backgrounds -- in the assignment of cabinet secretaries and insure that they not go native by shuffling them occasionally on a random basis (Niskanen 1973b, 60). In making such proposals, Niskanen displayed a lack of understanding of the dynamics of cabinet systems of government. However, his book's focus on the evils of bureaucracy worked a tremendous effect on Mrs. Thatcher -- who urged all of her ministers to read it when she formed her first government in 1979.

Effectively adapting Niskanen's message to the circumstances of the British executive, Mrs. Thatcher stressed innovations which made budgeting less ad hoc and more automatic (Campbell 1983, 186-189; Wildavsky 1983, 164). She extended cash limits to several previously exempt programs; she created a "Star Chamber" of cabinet -- a group of her most prominent ministers -- to impose spending constraints in cases where the Treasury and line departments had become deadlocked; she abolished Policy Analysis and Review -- that is, interdepartmental studies of programs which as often as not had failed to recommend the tough options necessary to limit the size of the budget.

Some schizophrenia has emerged among those who style the central task of political executives as taming the bureaucracy. Public-choice-oriented political executives have embraced as a primary goal reduction of the bureaucrats' discretion and latitude for independent advocacy. In this respect, they have tried to reestablish the dichotomy between policy and administration which dominated thinking about the relationship between politicians and bureaucrats earlier in this century (Wilson 1941 (reprint); Goodnow 1900, 92-3; Gulick 1937, 10). Yet, many of the same political executives have sought to devise ways of making bureaucracy run more like organizations in the private sector. This would involve more creative and risk-oriented management. Niskanen argued:

> Bureaucrats...would be permitted to offer a wide range of public services....There would be no "strong" departments or "strong" secretaries. The choice of which bureau or combination of bureaus to supply a specific service would be forced to the level of the executive review (1973b, 61).

Peter Aucoin -- a Canadian scholar who has followed closely managerial reform in his country over the past 20 years -- has argued that the automatic decision criteria and the managerialist paradigms of public-choice political executives derive from different and potentially conflicting premises (1990a, 125-126). The former style the problem of the relationship between political executives and bureaucrats as one of control and seek measures through which elected politicians might "tame" the public service by putting it under tighter constraints. Managerialist paradigms, on the other hand, start with the proposition that, intramurally, bureaucracies run overly hierarchically -- thereby, stifling imagination and initiative.

In the U.S., the two premises have not done much hand-to-hand combat. This owes largely to the difficulty of introducing managerialist concepts in a highly fragmented bureaucratic culture (Campbell 1986, 192-93; Hansen and Levine 1988, 267-68). On the other hand, the U.K., Canada, Australia, and New Zealand have all initiated managerialist programs with relatively far-reaching objectives (Aucoin 1989; Boston 1987; Considine 1988; Fry 1988; Scott, Bushnell, and Sallee 1990; Keating and Holmes 1990; Kemp 1990). As with the introduction of automatic budgeting techniques, however, the level of fragmentation in the political/bureaucratic system appears to affect the degree to which political executives can guide public service organizations toward managerialist approaches. Here Britain and New Zealand have achieved the most sweeping changes -- which is not to say that these have all worked; Australia has taken a more paced approach and achieved a great deal, and Canada has moved cautiously and made only modest progress (Aucoin 1990a, 1990b; Hood 1990; Campbell and Halligan 1992).

The New Zealand case represents by far the most conscious use of public choice theory as a justification for managerial reform in bureaucracy. For instance, Graham Scott and Peter Gorringe (1988) -- both Treasury officials -- have explicitly employed agency theory in justifying their department's initiatives toward reorganization of the public service. Relying heavily upon the work of A. A. Alchain (e.g., Alchain and Woodward

1987), they fully embrace the view that bureaucrats serve as the agents of politicians who, in turn, function as the agents of the populace. In this regard, Scott and Gorringe distinguish between strategies for improving "performance" and those attempting to enhance accountability (1988, 6). The latter focus on whether "politicians...buy the right services to achieve social goals like wealth, justice and the relief of suffering." Politicians need not purchase all the services which advance social goals from the bureaucracy.

In all of this, bureaucrats often perceive constraints on their agency. They welcome the opportunities for greater flexibility that managerialism holds out. However, many find themselves tempted to conclude that political executives have thrown them crumbs after sharply curtailing their ability to exercise discretion and to operate as advocates. A civil-service head of a large department in Britain has put it as succinctly as any:

> I said to Treasury, and so did many others, "This is a fine doctrine, but unless you believe it and are prepared to implement it and accept what goes with it, it won't work." ...you can't say to someone, "You're responsible for your budget and you won't get any more money, and you can carry your own account," if at the same time you are saying, "I will determine your staff, what they will be paid, how much you will pay for accommodation...." And, this is exactly how it worked out. The amount of delegation of eventual control was at most five per cent (Campbell 1992).

Public choice theory concerning political executives emerged first in response to the fragmented conditions of governance in the United States. However, policies deriving from public choice have not taken particularly strong root here. That is, political executives pressing public choice approaches have run into the same types of systemic obstacles to coherent policies encountered by those attempting to expand the role of government in the 1960s. Advocates of public choice in some parliamentary systems, on the other hand, have advanced the cause with considerable success. Here the U.K. and New Zealand stand out. In each case, strong majority governments pushed the reforms. The fact that each country has only one department, the Treasury, which controls both economic and budget policy, greatly assisted the process. Australia presents a case of a more fragmented system, with a Labor government highly dependent upon mood swings in the party's parliamentary caucus and divided authority between the economics and budget departments. However, the Labor government negotiated these tricky waters deftly -- largely through the exceptional commitment of time and effort that Bob Hawke (prime minister, 1983-1991) made to deliberations on the budget, and to the discipline of a group of "economic rationalist" ministers and a like-minded cadre of senior officials (Campbell and Halligan 1992).

Some observers have concluded that public choice approaches have gone too far in systems which have accommodated them more readily than others (Pusey 1991). In this respect, it appears that governments can engage in the practice of overtreatment. This prospect arises especially when they start to chalk up fairly substantial surpluses. It also presents itself when it appears that the government has embraced managerialist rhetoric only for cosmetic reasons. That is, some programs designed to give officials more discretion in the use of their resources involve such a small proportion of their ever-shrinking budgets that they serve only the symbolic goals of the government.

The Presidency, Public Choice, and the Unresolved American Debate

Unlike the study of Congress, the U.S. presidency sub-field has remained relatively resistant to scholarship which employs formal theory. Many have attributed this fact to differences in the data base for presidential studies. At any time, there is only one case of "president." Widening the scope to take in executive branch behavior does not help much. The executive branch operates informally and iteratively, and much of what it does and how it functions remains obscured from public view. Congress, on the other hand, provides clear units of behavior such as votes and the allocation of committee assignments.

Nonetheless, formal theory has pervaded mainstream political science and increasingly dominates the journals. Some practitioners of the approach have already cast their eyes upon presidential studies. For instance, Terry Moe -- even though the presidency field is not his main specialty -- has sparked lively debate with a few cogent and strategically placed challenges. One of his recent contributions put the case starkly: "the positive theorists are coming anyway. They are going to invade presidential studies, just as they invaded legislative and electoral studies" (Moe 1993).

The current debate on the role of institutional approaches to presidential studies goes back several decades. In many respects, it concerns the relative effects of individual presidents and the institution of the presidency in American governance. Should we focus our attention on the most volatile part of this equation -- the personality, character, and style of each incumbent? Or should we concentrate on the more tangible and concrete dimensions -- such as the organization and operation of the White House, the Executive Office of the President, along with the many agencies embedded in it, and/or the many organizations which constitute the "line" side of the executive branch?

Any attempt to pursue an integrative approach will immediately involve us in two tasks. First, we as analysts have to devise ways of relating what we know about presidents generally to the organization and operation of the formal apparatus. Second, we have to examine how individual presidents adapt to their own needs and engage the apparatus which they inherit with incumbency. In neither case have presidential studies achieved a high degree of rigor. However, we have spent more effort on the second task than on the first. Indeed, we have not explicitly addressed the first in any systematic way until very recently.

The Apparatus and Two Gearbox Issues

Broadly, Eisenhower stands as a high-water mark for blending the routinized and hierarchical presidency. Here "routinized" refers to the reliance upon structured procedures for conducting the business of the executive branch; "hierarchical" refers to the practice whereby control is sought through pyramidal and centralized organizations. Since 1960, several presidents either have betrayed ambivalence about engaging the standing apparatus to accomplish their objectives (most notably Kennedy and Reagan) and/or they have employed insufficient routinization and hierarchical structure to accomplish their objectives (clearly the case with Carter).

Two concerns have prompted presidents to be ambivalent about the standing apparatus, routinization, and hierarchical structure. First, along the lines pursued by Richard Neustadt's caveats about presidential leadership, incumbents and those advising them about organizational matters began to prize flexibility and adaptability (Neustadt 1960). Thus, Kennedy ran his administration without cabinet meetings (Hess 1976, 10). He also virtually ignored the National Security Council -- a statutorily mandated cabinet-level apparatus patterned after the British executive's collective approach to foreign and defense policy (Hess 1976, 78; Destler 1981, 267; Nelson 1981, 235). Johnson paid slightly more attention than Kennedy to routinization and collective bodies (Hess 1981, 106; Destler 1981, 269-71). However, the core of his approach centered on achieving flexibility and adaptability by creating in the White House and the Executive Office of the President a counterbureaucracy which would generate innovative ideas and force departments to respond to presidential initiatives (Redford and Blisset 1981, 204-14; Rose 1976, 46). Nixon became so frustrated with the seeming intractability of the bureaucracy that two years into his administration he began to pursue the Johnson strategy with a vengeance -- drawing every conceivable issue into the White House and the Executive Office of the President and purging appointees in the departments and agencies who had "gone native" (Nathan 1975).

The second concern which has fueled presidents' ambivalence about the state apparatus and routinization and hierarchical structure became dominant in the aftermath of Watergate. It is one thing for presidents to avoid circumstances in which they, their immediate advisers, and appointees in the departments and agencies become subject to the tendency of career officials to control the agenda, stifle innovation, and expand their empires. This all concerns the gearbox between an administration and the state apparatus that it inherits.

Yet, there is another gearbox at issue here -- the one that connects the president with his ever-expanding apparatus for controlling and guiding the entire state apparatus. As John Hart (1987) has argued, the White House and the Executive Office of the President gradually have taken on the size, complexity, and moment of a "presidential branch" of government. Similarly, Hugh Heclo (1984) has identified a "public careerist" culture among the appointees to line departments and agencies. Operating as a surrogate for the type of permanent mandarinate found in other advanced democracies, this culture produces individuals well schooled in the ways of Washington and just as capable as not of identifying and pressing goals which comport neither with what the president wants nor the permanent bureaucracy will readily embrace.

Even while disentangling their administrations from the imperatives pressing down from the state apparatus and inertia of bureaucratic routinization and hierarchy, presidents since Nixon have wrestled at least as much with their own presidential branch. They want to devise ways of staffing it and organizing it so that it can help them master the rest of the executive branch. However, they frequently have become painfully aware that rise of the presidential branch poses two dangers -- either that of a monster which plays into its "master's" weakness for imperialization or a leviathan which pulls him apart in a death by a thousand conflicting agendas.

Presidents in the post-Nixon era have achieved only limited success in coping with the second gearbox issue. Ford implemented a spokes-in-a-wheel design for the White House which placed considerable value on "multiple advocacy" (Porter 1980; see George 1980 for full discussion of multiple advocacy). Here White House advisers enjoyed relatively equal access to the Oval Office. As well, the president encouraged cabinet secretaries to resolve as many problems as possible among themselves so that he and his staff would be able to focus attention on the major issues of the day. However, Ford modulated his approach and encouraged the use of coordinative structures -- such as the Economic Policy Board -- to midwife multiple advocacy among cabinet secretaries.

Carter pushed the Ford model too far. He refused to appoint a chief of staff until summer 1979; he allowed his White House Staff to function virtually without any routinized procedures and hierarchical structure; he let his cabinet secretaries select appointees for top departmental positions with practically no review in the White House; and he used ad hoc and overly inclusive meetings whenever trying to develop agreed administration positions (Campbell 1986).

Reagan went through three phases. The first and mostly successful stage corresponded with the first term. It involved a modified spokes-in-a-wheel format in which James A. Baker kept government business running on schedule and managed legislative strategy; Edwin Meese III served as Reagan's ideological conscience; and Michael K. Deaver nurtured the president's ego and public image. It also entailed very close scrutiny of nominations of sub-cabinet appointees by the White House and an elaborate system of "councils" of cabinet secretaries which -- while very constricted by the budgetary discipline imposed by the administration -- worked together on the development of administration initiatives. Reagan's second phase lasted from 1984 to 1986 and saw the imposition of hierarchical direction by James A. Baker's replacement -- Donald Regan -- and a marked de-emphasis of cabinet councils. The backlash to Regan, capped by the events of the Iran-Contra Affair, led to his replacement by Howard Baker -- the former Senate Republican leader -- and, ultimately, Kenneth Duberstein -- a Republican operative and former assistant to the president for congressional liaison. Both of the latter managed to run the White House in a nonhierarchical way and neither incurred wrath either inside or outside the Beltway. However, 1986 to 1988 hardly constitutes a period of activist or interventionist leadership.

Bush obviously encountered a great deal more difficulty than he perhaps bargained for in the gearbox between himself and his administration (Campbell 1991). This owed significantly to his selection of John Sununu as chief of staff. First, this move meant that others who might potentially prove tremendous assets in the White House -- such as Robert M. Teeter and Craig Fuller -- ended up not joining the administration. They believed that Sununu would not operate as a team player. Second, it preordained that the administration would not run on the basis of multiple advocacy. Sununu clung to deep ideological commitments which he did not readily concede; he managed in an ad hoc and personalistic fashion; and he brought to the West Wing virtually no experience either in how Washington functions or how a president might consolidate and maintain his electoral appeal. The immediate post-Sununu period saw a flurry of activity associated with the gearbox between the president and the administration.

The Limits of Institutionalism

Undoubtedly, some readers will believe that they have seen some relationship between presidents' experiences with gearbox problems discussed above and presidents' personal styles. Yet, such connections run into increasingly stiff opposition from within mainstream presidential studies. This comes through very clearly in several chapters of a recently published mid-term assessment of George Bush. Most scholars writing in that volume maintain that institutional factors -- especially those associated with divided government -- do most of the work in explaining the organization and operation of the Bush administration.

For instance, Charles Jones takes issue with the premise that presidents must act decisively and energetically the minute they assume office (Jones 1991, 52). He notes that even James P. Pfiffner -- the scholar who has defined in the clearest terms the hitting-the-ground-running imperatives faced by presidents at the outset of an administration (1988) -- absolves Bush for not adopting an aggressive approach to his domestic agenda on the grounds that Bush lacked a mandate for anything besides maintenance of the Reagan legacy (Pfiffner 1990, 70). George C. Edwards III -- looking at the factors which maintained Bush's approval ratings at such heights -- asserts that voters, not analysts, determine what they expect from presidents (1991, 20, 26). Writing before the economy became an issue in fall 1991, Edwards underscores the extent to which voters were not factoring in consideration of whether Bush's performance matched the challenges which many analysts believed the nation faced. The issues which exercised such analysts had not become salient to the electorate.

In the volume mentioned above, Barbara Sinclair takes on even more directly Bush's critics' hand-wringing over whether his personality lends itself to the challenges faced by the nation implying that they do not understand democracy:

> The behavior of the president and members of Congress is shaped and constrained by the context in which they act; what commentators interpret as playing politics or a lack of backbone is, given the context, often the best strategy.... That is, it is the best way to advance the politician's goals of policy results and electoral success. While

some may argue that the goal of electoral success *is* disreputable and that what is needed are principled public officials indifferent to being voted out of office, this argument ignores the crucial role that wanting to be reelected plays in keeping public officials responsive to the wishes of the electorate that chose them (Sinclair 1991, 155).

Even though authors such as Jones, Edwards, and Sinclair carefully style their treatments of Bush as specific to the conditions of his administration, their analyses comport with a two-fold transformation in presidential studies which begins at least with the Reagan administration. The transformation has addressed a simple problem: How can we say nice things about a president who does not fit conventional standards for presidential performance but nonetheless attains high levels of popular support? It has concluded, first, that a president's continued support among the electorate is the only valid measure of his performance and, second, institutional factors rather than personality, style, and character determine what a president ends up doing. I will maintain that both dimensions of this transformation reflect more the degree to which the discipline had become mesmerized by the approval ratings and electoral successes of Reagan and Bush than a scientific breakthrough.

Much of the ongoing debate centers on how we ascertain whether a president has led competently. Terry Moe accurately identifies one strain in the profession which gives, in his view, too much attention to "neutral" competence (1985). This criterion for presidential performance relates to the first of the gearbox issues considered above -- the extent to which an administration effectively engages the permanent state apparatus and gets it to do its bidding. Moe correctly notes that this concept can take on romantic proportions in the minds of some analysts.

More recently, Colin Campbell and Margaret Wyszomirski amplify this view by asserting that the concept of neutral competence remains ill-defined by those who regret the underutilization of the state apparatus which has characterized recent administrations' encounters with the executive branch:

> Their critique might simply be a lament for a neutrally competent ...[civil service] that never existed – one in which officials offered their advice and conducted the affairs of state without any personal commitments of a partisan or political nature (Campbell and Wyszomirski 1991, 15).

This does not mean that presidents have nothing to gain by tapping into the expertise and institutional memory of the permanent bureaucracy. However, they must engage it or ignore it for the right reasons. Administrations that dismiss the capabilities of the executive branch become error prone about small things which, over time, can add up to major crises. Yet, administrations which defer too much to the ongoing bureaucracy and let it ponder interminably the myriad options will lose sight of the big picture and doom themselves to electoral defeat. In either case, such administrations would betray a misunderstanding of the meaning of "neutral." It should not imply that public servants have abandoned all ideas and convictions about the range of possibilities suggesting themselves in a given issue. It simply should convey the notion that their career commitments prescribe a capacity to adapt what they supply -- expertise and knowledge about the system -- to the needs of their new principals each time the executive branch passes from one party to the other.

The term neutral does not connote the provision of value-free analysis. It relates rather to the degree to which career officials adjust their agendas and priorities in ways which reflect changes in the political leadership. In this regard, recent work by Joel D. Aberbach -- based on surveys he has conducted with Bert A. Rockman -- suggests considerably more adaptability of the career public service to the Reagan/Bush agenda than we might expect. Aberbach's research serves as a strong corrective for those who continue to maintain that the bureaucracy remains enamored of the expansive welfare state and hostile to all attempts to constrict it (1991).

Moe's earliest contribution to the debate over assessment of presidents focused on the first gearbox issue -- that centering on the relationship between an administration and the standing state apparatus. He posits a clear linear process whereby successive presidents have turned a blind eye to or positively advanced the de-institutionalization of the executive branch (1985, 258). They have done so because they do not prize what the standing apparatus has to offer. Instead, they have placed the highest value on "responsive competence" (p. 239). They advance this by centralizing their institutional resources in the White House and politicizing the federal bureaucracy -- both of which strategies provide them with an enhanced capacity to "circumvent established organizations and vested interests" (p. 244-45). Insofar as the desire to maintain their political support motivates them, evaluation of presidents from the standpoint of their engagement of the state apparatus becomes -- at best -- a secondary concern.

Moe's 1985 work provided important theoretical bearings to a growing body of scholarship which has reflected the ambivalence of administrations toward the bureaucracy. Thomas Cronin has termed such works "presidentialist" in that they place a great deal of stock in the capacity of presidents to override "complexity, diversity, jurisdictional disputes, and bureaucratic recalcitrance" without becoming bogged down trying to master and restructure the state apparatus (1980, 248). Bert A. Rockman -- writing a year before Moe -- cautions that "policy" competence should form an integral part of presidents' pursuit of "political" competence (1984, 195). Policy competence allows presidents to maintain an historical perspective on their options and the likely consequences of their choices. It also gives rise to presidents' activation of their "managerial capacity" whereby they can "move decisions along, effectively coordinate them, and have a sufficient information base to make them." Thus, even before Moe's articulation of the de-institutionalization thesis, some scholars had raised serious doubts about the degree to which presidents had solved the first gearbox problem by trying to override the state apparatus.

In two more recent works, Moe adjusts his nomenclature so as to accommodate his view that -- whereas the bureaucracy has de-institutionalized -- the presidency itself has institutionalized (1990, 1993). Thus, the strategies -- centralizing of power in the White House and politicizing the bureaucracy -- which reduce the autonomy of the state apparatus also increase the institutional leverage of the presidential branch (1990, 8). Yet, Moe does an inadequate job of defining the boundary between presidential and bureaucratic institutions. For instance, he gives the National Security Council (NSC) as an example of the "agencies" of centralization in the institutionalized presidency.

In fact, the NSC originally took shape under Truman as a U.S. attempt to routinize -- and, therefore, make less subject to the management styles of individual presidents -- interdepartmental consultation on national security issues (Nelson 1981, 230). Since its creation in 1947, the centralizing function of the NSC has ebbed and flowed, depending on factors such as each president's interest in foreign affairs, the forcefulness of key participants -- including the secretaries of defense and state and the director of the CIA -- and their mutual working relations and relative power, and the approach of the principal White House adviser responsible for advising the president on national security affairs (George 1980; Nelson 1981; Destler 1981; Greenstein 1982; Mulcahy and Kendrick 1991). To assert that the NSC has worked a consistent and continually intensifying centralizing function would ignore dramatic differences in its trajectory from president to president. It would also obscure the fact that forceful presidents with strong aptitudes for and interest in foreign affairs would as likely ignore the NSC apparatus as engage it. Indeed, as was the case with Kennedy, they might consciously eschew institutionalization in favor of flexibility (Allison 1971).

One finds an element of ambivalence toward the role of the state in Moe. This fits well within the non-statist tradition of American politics (Rockman 1984, 49-52). It also represents the prevailing stance of presidential studies. It does this insofar as it accepts as a contextual given that presidents should confine their efforts to objectives which they can actually attain -- assuming recurrent paralysis owing to divided government. Along the line pursued by Olsen (1983, 1988), Moe correctly implies that Franklin D. Roosevelt -- through the dual effect of his leadership during the depression and WWII -- bloated expectations for presidential leadership. Without employing Olsen's concept explicitly, Moe argues that Roosevelt turned the presidency into a supermarket for the great necessities:

> ...all presidents would be held responsible for addressing every conceivable social problem -- however gargantuan ... intractable ... far removed from the president's actual sphere of power -- and they would be expected, through legislative leadership and executive control of the administrative apparatus of the government, to take action (Moe 1990, 8).

Yet, Moe fails to accommodate the possibility that models of the state change in their appeal over time. We can no more argue that Roosevelt's approach did not fit his times than we can affirm that it should have prevailed during the relatively cautious and nonexpansive administrations of Eisenhower, Ford, Carter, or Bush. Two difficulties arise if students of the presidency fail to adjust their models to reflect the dominant expectations for the state. First, they can become bound within a specific methodology. Second, they can focus on one dimension of presidential politics to the detriment of their coverage of others.

As we have seen, the 1980s became a definitional decade in advanced democracies. Political executives in virtually every system -- even left-leaning governments such as Australia's -- sunk or swam on their ability to adjust the contours of the state to the more constricted circumstances of the increasingly globalized economy and public disenchantment with the fiscal and regulatory burdens of the interventionist, regulatory/welfare-oriented state. We have noted that public choice theory soon migrated from the U.S. -- where it first emerged -- and actually found more fertile soil in parliamentary systems -- where usually the regulatory/welfare state had become more entrenched than in the U.S. and the political institutions proved more

malleable to decisive leadership (just as they had during the expansion of the interventionist state).

In fact, the lessons from the unintended consequences of simplistic adherence to public choice have now had considerable time to sink in. For example, revolts in two parliamentary systems recently have ousted prime ministers who had spearheaded public choice approaches to governance. Now their replacements -- Britain's John Major and Australia's Paul Keating -- have attempted to salvage each government's political fortunes by, respectively, promoting a "citizens' charter" of baselines below which government services will not fall and "creative" guidance of the market economy. The more governments retreat from the neo-liberal stances which prevailed in the 1980s the more we should begin to anticipate the possibility that public choice will join Keynesian economics in the rogues gallery of theoretical approaches.

This will not at all challenge the gradual adaptation of the discipline to the rigors of formal theory. Formal theory has been the streetcar whereby public choice disseminated through the profession. However, it can just as easily serve scholars operating from different assumptions about the nature of the state. Moe accurately observed that public choice gained appeal as the "new economics" of organizations emerged as a focus of scholarship in the 1980s. This centered attention on the elements of political behavior which follow the conditions of "voluntary actors in the market place" and "the conditions under which they will find it mutually beneficial to cooperate -- that is, to organize their behavior" (1993).

If we have a return -- some might prefer "relapse" -- of interest in and expectations of the interventionist state, overly transactional perspectives might fail to capture forms of expectations for political executives which tap more than public support of the integrity of the market. The demands from rational choice scholars that we focus analysis on issues amenable to formal theory go beyond simply limiting the compass of presidential studies to institutional factors. They also place a straight jacket on an approach capable of enhancing our investigation of many other dimensions of the presidency. They do so by defining formal theory so narrowly that it appears only applicable in market-like, transactional circumstances. In this regard, we would do well to remember that Robert Dahl -- a pluralist -- presented cogent formal theories about democracy before the major public choice works first emerged (Dahl 1956).

Management Style and the Second Gearbox

Much of the definitional thrust of executive leadership through the 1980s focused on the first gearbox problem --

the interface between administrations/governments and the bureaucracy. The second gearbox problem -- that associated with the interrelationship between chief executives and their own administrations received little attention.

Thus, we forgave a multitude of lapses on the grounds that the main game concentrated on the effort to control bureaucracy. We excused Ronald Reagan's lack of engagement in the day-to-day affairs of state and vulnerability to manipulation by the White House staff as part of painting with broad strokes. The president had become so detached from the management of his own administration by his second term that he took no role in consultations which led to James A. Baker, the first-term chief of staff and Donald Regan, the first term treasury secretary, switching jobs (Schieffer and Gates 1989, 192-196).

Only the Iran-contra Affair swung observers around to contemplating the possibility that leadership in the new context of the institutional presidency required more than the president clinging to a few immutable ideas about the world and his aides filling in the details. The Tower Commission minced words neither in its assigning much of the blame for emergence of the scandal to Reagan's "management style" nor its attributing to Donald Regan responsibility for not living up to his control-oriented approach to running the White House (1987). Of Reagan, the commission said:

> The President's management style is to put the responsibility for policy review and implementation on the shoulders of his advisors. Nevertheless,...the President should have ensured that the NSC system did not fail. He did not force his policy to undergo the most critical review of which the NSC participants and the process were capable. At no time did he insist upon accountability and performance review (p. 79-80).

Regarding Regan's role, the commission noted:

> Mr. Regan also shares in this responsibility. More than almost any Chief of Staff of recent memory, he asserted personal control over the White House staff and sought to extend this to the National Security Advisor. He was personally active in national security affairs and attended almost all of the relevant meetings....He, as much as anyone, should have insisted that an orderly process be observed....He must bear primary responsibility for the chaos that descended upon the White House...(p. 81).

A committee of privy councillors documented in indisputable terms the degree to which Mrs. Thatcher's ad hoc utilization of cabinet machinery had contributed to the U.K. not responding in time to prevent the Argentinean invasion of the Falkland Islands (Franks Report 1983). Yet, she was quick to cover her lapse with jingoism and a decisive -- though almost foolishly hazardous -- campaign to recover the islands. Eight years later, George Bush virtually replicated Mrs. Thatcher's negligence by letting the response to Saddam Hussein's bellicose threats fall victim to in-fighting and indecisiveness among his principal foreign affairs advisers (Berman and Jentleson 1991, 118-21; Campbell 1991, 209-10).

The Reagan, Thatcher, and Bush experiences in the foreign policy field suggest the degree to which we should exercise caution in making generalizations about the aptitude that systems display for coordination between chief executives and their advisers and cabinet members. We can certainly anticipate circumstances -- either under presidential or parliamentary government -- in which chief executives achieve a high degree of effectiveness or very little. For instance, in a recent paper introducing the central themes of a Brookings Institution conference on the institutional effects of the two systems, Kent Weaver and Bert A. Rockman point up conditions under which parliamentary systems can be either more or less conducive to strong executive leadership. At one point in the paper, they note that parliamentary systems often allow a "greater potential for concentrated power if a prime minister has a firm majority in the legislature and surrounds him (or her)self with weak and compliant ministers..." (Weaver and Rockman 1990, 9). Later, they probe the opposite possibility: "...cabinet ministers in parliamentary systems may (unlike those in the U.S.) have political standing and power independent of the prime minister, making it difficult to challenge them in their own domains" (Weaver and Rockman 1990, 20-21).

Similarly, Peter Hennessy has recently compared the Oversea and Defence secretariat of the British Cabinet Office unfavorably with the U.S. National Security Council staff on the grounds that the former relies too heavily upon secondees -- mostly from the Ministry of Defence and the Foreign and Commonwealth Office, and the military (Hennessy 1991, 312). He argues that Oversea and Defence should be able to develop its own career structure and bring in people from outside government. In fact, the NSC staff relies heavily on secondees as well. Certainly, it does not have a permanent staff structure. And, its track record of bringing in secondees from outside government has not always proven successful.

On domestic fronts, political scientists have bent over backwards to give chief executives the benefit of the doubt whenever seeming dysfunctions emerge in the management style. A recent edited collection containing ten assessments of Bush by twelve students of executive leadership made several references to John Sununu, all of which characterized his style as confrontational (Campbell and Rockman 1991). Yet, the authors proved loath to attack directly the "lightening rod" theory whereby analysts had concluded that George Bush was simply using Sununu to serve as a focal point for criticism of the administration's tougher stances on the domestic front. Analysts, apparently, found it hard to disentangle the rhetoric early in the administration heralding a new cooperative era with Congress and the evidence of deepening hostility between some White House officials and congressional leaders.

For instance, Paul Quirk -- whose chapter proved broadly critical of Bush's record -- took pains to distance Bush from Sununu's approach and that of the equally confrontational Richard Darman:

> ...Bush was well known and generally liked in Congress. To maintain his relationships and show respect for the institution, he came to Capitol Hill for personal visits with congressional leaders. In a period of a few months he invited every senator and most of the representatives to the White House. Through countless phone calls and handwritten personal notes, he kept in touch with members of Congress of both parties and a host of other Washington acquaintances. Two of Bush's senior aides...Sununu and...Darman...sometimes interfered with the good feelings by taking positions in a manner that members of Congress found arrogant. But after the incessant hostilities of the Reagan years, members of Congress and especially Democrats appreciated the atmosphere of harmony (1991, 75).

However, Quirk's description of Bush's substantive moves vis-à-vis Congress corresponds more with our image of the machinations of Sununu than that of harmony in executive-legislative relations:

> ...Bush failed to take positions and adopt strategies well suited to a cooperative approach....Bush vacillated -- and so was, by turns, flexible and rigid about everything. At times he quickly gave up whatever was needed to get a deal....At other times, Bush refused to make significant concessions....Some of his occasional rigidity was perhaps a matter of acting tough just to show his capacity to do so -- a way of dealing with the "wimp" factor (1991, 75-76).

Either Bush had ceded responsibility for domestic policy to the volatile Sununu and deferred to him because he wanted to stay above the fray or he consciously pursued a duplicitous strategy toward Congress. Whatever the case, a disjunction existed between the administration's putative approach to domestic politics and its actual performance which went largely undetected until the collapse of Bush's approval ratings in fall 1991. This, of course, occasioned Sununu's departure from the West Wing and an effort to revamp the White House.

Focusing on administrations' relationships with the permanent bureaucracy also has lulled observers of political executives in parliamentary governments into giving inadequate attention to the dynamics by which prime ministers have interacted with their political advisers and cabinet colleagues. George Jones -- rejoining an old debate which he has been conducting for several years now with Patrick Weller (Weller 1983; Jones 1983; Weller 1985) -- defended Mrs. Thatcher to the end as not running her cabinet in a "presidential" way (Jones 1991).

Weller has led a growing number of students of executive leadership in Westminster systems who assert that the complexity of modern government and the availability of electronic means for making direct appeals to the public have introduced an era of convergence between the devices employed by prime ministers to get what they want from their governments and those used by presidents with their administrations. In this context, he has construed the growth and specialization of staffs reporting directly to prime ministers as fitting within the evolutionary development of Westminster systems toward more central guidance by the chief executive.

Jones denies such an evolutionary process. Even in the case of Mrs. Thatcher, he argues, cabinet maintained the potential -- assuming the support of Conservative MPs -- to remove her if her approach appeared so much at variance with the conventions of British government. However, Jones's case only takes us so far. In fact, the 1990 leadership challenge which unseated Mrs. Thatcher came initially not from within cabinet but from a group of disenchanted MPs who had rallied around Michael Heseltine whom Mrs. Thatcher had forced from cabinet more than four years earlier. That cabinet did not register their concerns with Mrs. Thatcher until she lost the confidence of her party members in the House of Commons hardly means that the seeds of her own demise had not begun to germinate long before. As *The Times* of London had observed as early as 1984, Mrs. Thatcher had neglected cabinet consultation and manipulated ministers to an unprecedented degree:

> Ministers increasingly voice concern about the way key decisions are taken by Mrs. Thatcher and small groups of ministers

without reference to the full Cabinet -- a practice which they say has contributed to failings in the presentation of policies. One minister said privately last week that Mrs. Thatcher probably has used Cabinet less than any prime minister since the war. Some ministers are calling for a return to genuine cabinet government (*The Times*, March 5, 1984).

Scholars' assessments of Canada's Brian Mulroney present another case in which they have paid too little attention to a chief executive's ability to handle the second gearbox problem. When Mulroney took power in 1984, scholars simply had to consult those who had worked closely with him as leader of the opposition to find that he had abdicated management of the shadow cabinet to Erik Nielsen -- a wily parliamentary strategist (Campbell 1988, 322-328). Part of Mulroney's reliance upon Nielsen stemmed from the need to build bridges with the right wing of the Progressive Conservative Party after a fractious leadership race in 1983. However, during Mulroney's year as leader of the opposition he demonstrated virtually no aptitude for the collective decision-making processes so central to cabinet systems of government. The pattern had established itself so firmly that the leaders of Mulroney's transition team enshrined the principle that the prime minister would require a deputy who would actually run cabinet. This practice even survived the transfer of the deputy prime ministership to another minister in 1986 when Nielsen left the cabinet in the wake of a conflict of interest scandal involving a cabinet colleague.

Through his first term (1984-88), Mulroney mostly received the benefit of the doubt in scholarly assessments of how he was handling the second gearbox problem. Two points emerged. First, a government trying to reverse the expansion of the state should limit the opportunities for officials -- either through their ministers or through direct access to collective decision-making bodies -- to fight for their corners (Campbell 1988, 324). We would expect, thus, that Mulroney's government -- as was the case with Thatcher's -- would rely less on cabinet committee deliberations than had the more expansive and statist Trudeau governments. Second, the prime minister clearly felt awkward with formal cabinet-level meetings and, in fact, rarely attended such sessions. Instead, he preferred bilateral discussions with individual ministers about specific problems -- often conducted on the telephone. As Peter Aucoin asserted, this did not mean that he did not want teamwork in his cabinet. It simply meant that he would limit his direct participation in collective deliberations and, therefore, place less emphasis on collegial dynamics as he sought to establish teamwork:

...Mulroney's leadership style [in contrast with Trudeau's] is transactional rather than collegial. His preference is to deal with individuals on a one-to-one basis rather than on a collective basis. The logic here, of course, is that this transactional style better facilitates the negotiation of compromises among differing points of views than does the collegial process, where the checks and balances more readily lead to stalemates if different points of view are strongly held (Aucoin 1986, 18).

Three difficulties have presented themselves with this approach, and each has persisted throughout the Mulroney years. First, the transactional approach has always operated in conjunction with the collective machinery. This has proven a constant source of confusion and tension. The emphasis given to the transactional approach as against the collective one ebbs and flows notably depending on the perceived electoral vulnerability of the government. In other words, it will adopt more collective approaches when it becomes necessary to mobilize cabinet in a major effort to pull the government out of especially threatening predicaments. Second, players -- cabinet ministers and senior officials alike -- never know for sure which rules will prevail in the resolution of specific issues. Each return to collective processes has involved significant changes of the machinery with which players take some time to familiarize themselves. Further, some ministers will under any circumstances retain -- due to personal ties with the prime minister or their importance to the coalition of interests which sustains the government -- the ability to short-circuit collective processes. This stems from that fact that the prime minister's fundamental approach still invites special pleading outside the confines of cabinet-level bodies.

Third, the consequences of a dysfunctional collective decision-making process have proven somewhat more severe for the legitimacy of Canadian government under Mulroney than they did for that of the U.K. government under Thatcher. A very strong representational imperative weighs down on cabinet operations in Canada (Campbell 1985). This owes largely to the fact that disciplined collective government fits much less well in a federal system attempting to resolve differences emerging from a highly fragmented society than in a unitary system coping with pressures in a relatively homogeneous society.

In Canada's case, the representational imperative has operated behind two especially distinctive patterns in cabinet building in the federal government -- cabinet has swelled to some 40 members and the cabinet committee system has become both intricate and highly institutionalized. Obviously, prime ministers -- especially ones trying to trim nonproductive elements of the state -- should take any opportunities which present themselves for rationalization of the cabinet machinery. However, all indications suggest that the apparatus cannot long be ignored or overridden without serious consequences both in the coordination between ministers and the legitimacy of the government's decisions.

We have focused above on instances in which analysts have suspended their disbelief in their critiques of chief executives' handling of the second gearbox problem. Scholars have done so because they have seen the key task of the chief executive as gaining control of the standing bureaucracy. However, one case presents itself in which the received wisdom -- informed by highly statist social theory -- fails to give due credit to a prime minister. Here Australian social theorists have argued that Bob Hawke and his cabinet became captured by a segment of the career public service which actually had renounced expansive views of the state (Pusey 1991, 154-55). This interpretation sells short the contribution of the political executive to the radical reforms which occurred under Hawke. To be sure, a symbiosis took place between the right of the Labor party and top officials in the central coordinating agencies of the public service. However, this symbiosis would not have held together as long nor accomplished as much without Hawke's aptitude for and commitment to collective cabinet processes (Campbell and Halligan 1992).

The various cases cited in this section suggest that analysts could profitably spend more time assessing how executive leaders handle the second gearbox problem -- the fact that presidents and prime ministers often have to worry as much about their relationship with their "own" as about that with the permanent bureaucracy. Some authors seem to imply that it amounts to an area of executive leadership which takes care of itself. For instance, Terry Moe bases a significant proportion of his portrayal of the potential institutional autonomy of the presidency on the assertion that it does not experience "collective action problems" and functions as a "team" (1992, 50-51). In fact, the internal capacity of administrations and governments for harmony often falls well short of what we might expect.

A Pinch of Personality?

During the era in which institutional factors have taken center stage, we have seen that presidency scholars have become especially hesitant to probe personality and the effects it might work on presidential performance. This is ironic. Whatever the force of institutional factors, we might expect U.S. administrations -- given the presidency's emphasis of monocratic leadership -- to prove somewhat more susceptible to differences in the personalities of incumbents than would cabinet governments. The latter -- however they might have strayed toward the monocratic format -- still call upon chief executives to win the approval of their cabinet colleagues. In addition, prime ministers traditionally have had to pass through a stronger socialization process in "insider" politics (Rockman 1991, 53-54). In fact, we might attribute some of Brian Mulroney's difficulties discussed above to his lack of previous exposure to collective decision-making processes.

In comparison to the presidency literature -- which supplies an abundance of studies centering on the personalities of presidents -- we find relatively little work which explicitly examines prime ministers from the standpoint of personality. This does not mean that scholars do not have available biographies of prime ministers which develop profiles of incumbents' personalities and make links between these and their performance in office (Young 1989; Radwanski 1978; Gwyn 1980; d'Alpuget 1982). However, political scientists normally leave this type of work to journalists who have both the luxury of knowing a great deal more about incumbents' foibles and having to adhere to somewhat relaxed standards for analysis. Some expressly psychoanalytic works have appeared which reviewers have believed to make strained connections between prime ministers' personalities and performance (Little 1985; Anson 1991). Political scientists' efforts to incorporate some material which relates to personality have tended to employ this only within a context in which the leadership style of a prime minister serves as an especially engaging topic (Campbell 1980; Weller 1989).

I have already cited Barbara Sinclair's strong caveat against the introduction of personality issues in the assessment of presidents (1991, 155). Her position fits within the institutionalist perspective which broadly views presidential behavior as stemming much more from the exigencies of office and the maintenance of electoral support than from personality. Moe follows a similar line of argumentation but adds considerations associated with the difficulty of operationalizing personality factors.

Differentiating presidential behavior and the presidency, Moe asserts that -- with the institutionalization of the latter -- the former has become subject to all the individuals that make up the presidency "collectively" and, therefore, "an institutional phenomenon, not a personal one" (1990, 7). He adds, however, that if we did include personality factors in our models this would immensely complicate our analysis:

> The explanatory focus is no longer on general issues of organization and structure, but rather on the behavior of a single person in the full flower of his uniqueness (Moe 1990, 10).

Moe, in fact, believes that our research can take into account what we know about presidents' personalities. This type of work can provide "the empirical foundation that promotes sound judgments about what presidents have actually done and why" (Moe 1993). However, personality does not lend itself to the "coherent theories with the degree of generality and explanatory power" which we seek in rigorous analysis.

We -- as a sub-discipline -- must disentangle what scholars such as Sinclair and Moe have argued. On the one hand, they seem to be asserting that personality lacks salience because institutional factors largely cancel out its effects. On the other, they seem to base part of their reluctance to include personality in analysis on the grounds that its operationalization presents too many difficulties. The first rationale would absolve us of any responsibility to continue to consider personality as a major element of presidential behavior. The second, however, should prompt at least some of us to redouble efforts to develop theoretically cogent ways of incorporating personality factors in our analyses.

A simple illustration should help make the point. During the 1988 primaries, George Bush became subject to a great deal of criticism for not providing a "vision" which would guide his presidency. During the 1988 presidential campaign, he embraced a strategy of attacking his opponent with innuendo and ridicule rather than promoting a discussion of the issues which would have provided him with a mandate. Yet, after the election the spin doctors got to work and built Bush up as an interventionist president who -- now that he no longer had to work in the shadow of Ronald Reagan -- would energetically pursue his own (still undefined) domestic agenda (Campbell 1991, 194-97). As analysts, how much should Bush's record in public life, and campaign performances during the primaries and the election, have informed our efforts to project his presidential style? Or, how much should we have listened to the spin doctors who, in the case of one observer, asserted that Bush had transformed himself from a "pit bull" to a "statesman far removed from the fray of the campaign"? Were we to have believed that George Bush did not, after all, reveal a dark side to his personality during the primaries and the election campaign, or, if he did, that being president meant that he could put it all behind him?

Erwin C. Hargrove has done more than any other scholar to mediate between students of the presidency focusing on institutional factors and those seeking to introduce a systematic consideration of personality (1993). He argues that a great deal of presidential behavior, in fact, does not fit neatly into what we might expect from incumbents' institutional context. Such behavior includes how presidents present themselves to mass audiences, how they devise their initial policy

agenda, how they manage decision processes, and the ways in which they persuade independent power holders in the policy arena.

Hargrove registers a strong and, I believe, legitimate question about how much we can attribute to the institutional constraints of presidents. History, he suggests, presents us with several cases of presidents who engaged in behavior stemming more from their "internal vulnerabilities" than from their objective circumstances (1993). Due to the monocratic structure of the American executive, such tendencies when present pose a greater threat than they would under collective formats for political leadership. Hargrove asks essentially how the system protects us from "inappropriate ego-defensive actions" especially given the "great scope for autonomous action in our 'elective monarchy'"? He does not call for psychoanalytic approaches -- we would normally lack the evidence necessary to adequately probe our hypotheses. Rather he urges us to use biography to identify repetitive patterns in individual presidents' behavior and the contexts in which these tend to occur.

In the literature, the issue of personality links most strongly with the assessment of how presidents will handle the second gearbox problem -- their relationship with their White House staff and the cabinet. We only have to consider the clearer instances in which a dysfunctional match emerged. For instance, Bob Haldeman's hierarchical White House would not have achieved such notoriety had it not fed Nixon's passion for control. Similarly, Donald Regan would not have arrogated to himself so much power had not Ronald Reagan slumped in the second term from a relatively detached to alarmingly disengaged president. And, only an incurable optimist like Reagan would have placed so much trust in one adviser.

The prima facie evidence suggests, thus, that presidential character and style work strong effects on the organization and operation of presidential staff and the cabinet. Yet, presidency scholars have strived with only modest success to find out how exactly the personal qualities of presidents link into organizational and operational issues surrounding administrations. Virtually everyone accepts the existence of a relationship. However, the exact functioning of the gearbox connecting one to the other has largely escaped rigorous empirical inquiry. First, let us examine what we mean by character and style.

In his treatment of presidential personalities and the management of the foreign policy process, Alexander George discusses at length the need to tailor the design and management of the national security process to each individual president:

> ...each president is likely to define his role
> in foreign-policymaking somewhat

differently and to approach it with a different decisionmaking and management style. Hence, too, he will have a different notion as to the kind of policymaking system that he wishes to create around him, feels comfortable with, and can utilize (George 1980, 146).

Presidential self-knowledge rests at the heart of this process and it does not always get it right. As George recounts, Richard Nixon tried at the start of his administration to encourage the type of multiple advocacy that had worked so well under Roosevelt and Kennedy. But he soon abandoned the system in favor of "by far the most centralized and highly structured model yet employed by any president (George 1980, 155)." If Nixon had been able to acknowledge some of his deepest character flaws, he would have recognized that his embracing this highly formal model would simply exacerbate his tendency to seek excessive control.

In my own research, I have pointed out the degree to which Carter overburdened himself by not seeking structures in the White House and cabinet that would serve as checks for his passion to master every conceivable detail before making a decision (Campbell 1986, 60-63, 83-84). As we have noted above, observers have told us that Ronald Reagan gave virtually no personal reflection to the swap between James A. Baker and Donald Regan that saw the latter become White House chief of staff (Schieffer and Gates 1989, 193-195). Had he given some time to the question, he might well have seen that Regan would arrogate power in areas where Reagan -- either because of his view of government or declining interest in his job -- had left a vacuum.

The frequency with which presidents seem to lack adequate self-knowledge comprises just one dimension to the issue of personality. More fundamentally, the issue takes us into the difficult task of defining the parameters of presidential character. A bitter debate broke out among political scientists in the 1970s in response to James David Barber's classification of presidents according to four personality types -- active-positives, active-negatives, passive-positives and passive negatives (Barber 1972, 1977; George 1974; Qualls 1977). According to Barber, active presidents come across as "human cyclones" with boundless energy while passive presidents evoke memories of Calvin Coolidge -- who indulged himself in 11 hours of sleep each night plus a nap in the afternoon. Positive presidents find a great deal of fun in their job while negative ones at best take grim satisfaction in tasks well done.

Most of Barber's problems with the rest of the political science community stem from his assertion that he has developed a predictive model of presidential performance (Barber 1977, 213, 218). At best his model simply helps us understand the psychological factors associated with presidential performance. We can detect some early warning signals of potential behavior. However, we must continually guard against the expectation that a president with particular psychological traits will behave in a specific fashion.

When we turn down the volume in the heated scholarly exchange, however, we find some common ground regarding presidential character. For instance, Richard Neustadt faults Barber for appearing to force presidents into the boxes of his paradigm without sufficient accommodation of differences and nuances (1990, 206-207). However, in trying to diagnose what made the presidential experiences of Nixon and Johnson so unhappy, he does agree with Barber's assertion that both embraced the challenges of office with "relatively intense effort and relatively low emotional reward (1990, 206)." Neustadt argues that both presidents' behavior betrayed deep personal insecurity:

> Back of their bad grace when things went wrong lay insecurity, or so it seems, a stressful inner turmoil that would go away only when things went right. Apparently both men were in the grip of human hungers they endeavored to appease by being President...(Neustadt 1990, 206).

Neustadt maintains that we should have seen the ways in which Johnson abused his Senate staff and Nixon let Bob Haldeman run his campaign staff as harbingers of how they would approach the presidency. Along the same lines, George attributes Nixon's proclivity for formalistic approaches to decision making as rooted in the fact that he had "developed a cognitive style that enabled him to cope with deeply rooted personal insecurities by adopting an extremely conscientious approach to decision-making." Whereas we might quibble with Barber's labelling (that is, the positive-negative dimension), it appears that just about everyone recognizes that presidents range from those with strong self-esteem to those who, for some reason, betray insecurity. Neustadt characterizes Roosevelt and Kennedy as having the former when he says both "approached the office as their natural habitat and drew security from being themselves (1990, 207)."

This leaves us with Barber's active-passive axis. At first blush, it appears that Barber has focused on a dimension which taps solely the degree to which the president has engaged himself in his job. However, it becomes clear that, in Barber's mind, presidents who put activity together with a sense of efficaciousness maintain perspective -- and, their effectiveness -- while those who do not lose both. The former type of president:

...shows an orientation toward productiveness as a value and an ability to use his styles flexibly, adaptively.... He sees himself as developing over time toward relatively well defined personal goals -- growing toward himself as he might yet be (Barber 1972, 12).

There are two problems with this formulation. First, it seems to assume adaptability and growth during the entire length of office when, in fact, presidents -- especially as the job begins to wear on them -- often become less flexible and more turned in on themselves. In this regard, analysts should always ask questions about a president's resilience. For instance, what would Kennedy have looked like as president in January 1969 after completing two terms and weathering the similar problems associated with Vietnam and civil rights that Johnson faced?

Second, we have to take care to delineate different types of activity. For instance, some presidents become cautious in their second term as they begin to think of how they will stand in the history books. But, Reagan, prodded on by his wife, actually gave greater attention to one policy area when he began worrying about the type of legacy he would leave (Cannon 1991, 507-510). Thus, we saw in his final years a number of overtures to the Soviets which contributed immensely to the end of the Cold War. Activity is often in the eye of the beholder.

This assessment, thus, construes activity as a multifaceted dimension. Presidents like Roosevelt, Kennedy, and Johnson earn high ratings as actives because they seek to establish a *new order* either in domestic or international affairs. Thus, Roosevelt brought in the New Deal and then led the U.S. effort to make the world safe for democracy; Kennedy sought to focus American attention on the "New Frontier" and urged that they "ask not what their country can do for them but what they can do for their country;" Johnson advanced civil rights in this nation more than any other president and pressed the "War Against Poverty."

Jimmy Carter embraced no overarching objectives that called for establishment of a new order. Carter's concerns focused much more on pragmatism. His activity was *executive*. The assumption that "there must be a better way" drove him to probe in exhaustive detail how the government worked and how it might become more efficient and effective.

Ronald Reagan -- whom most would rate as a passive president -- in fact proved to be a *being-there* active. He threw himself massively into the symbolic dimensions of the job. But he took no real interest in the executive functions. Further, the new-order goals he presented -- tax cuts, reduced spending, and increased defense expenditure -- played into the minimalist view of

the state's domestic responsibilities and the anxieties about America's decline as a world power which prevailed at the time. Nonetheless, Reagan utilized and exploited the immense prerogatives of the head of state function -- becoming a sort of high priest of the national liturgy. Ultimately, he turned Americans around so that they felt as good about their country as Ronald Reagan did about himself.

This leaves us with the final type of active president. I have developed more fully elsewhere the view that George Bush -- even if we grant that he might have been a new order active in foreign policy -- exemplified the *"let's deal"* active on the domestic side (Campbell 1991). As the president who never provided the nation with a vision of his domestic goals, Bush eschewed so much as a hint of a new-order activeness. He picked and chose the parts of the executive branch in which he took an interest. He was not an executive president. Even in foreign policy, we have all seen that -- although Bush would not shy away from exercising his prerogatives as commander in chief -- he found it difficult to express to the nation why, for instance, he dispatched such a huge U.S. force to the Persian Gulf. He was not, thus, a being-there active.

In linking presidential personality to how incumbents organize and operate their advisory systems, we must look at their management style. Here we refer to the way in which they prefer to do business (Campbell 1986). *Priorities-and-planning* leaders seek an advisory system which will optimize choice and creativity. They will tend to expand White House and Executive Office of the President resources so that they can tap alternate views to those issuing from the various departments and agencies. However, they will not stifle the competition of viewpoints.

Priorities-and-planning presidents will -- minimally--give assignments and/or create units in ways which will optimize choice. They might -- as well -- foster competition between departments and agencies by establishing cabinet councils and task forces that will expose secretaries and their top aides to the purifying fires of face-to-face criticism. Both Roosevelt and Kennedy were priorities-and-planning presidents. However, neither took their approach so far as to establish regularized mechanisms for engaging cabinet secretaries in a collective process of canvassing alternatives. The style requires the president to think big and to enjoy enough self-esteem to enter into the give and take of an open advisory system. Thus, only new-order actives with a high degree of personal security need apply to be priorities-and-planning managers.

Broker-politics presidents seek the countervaillance provided by multiple points of view. But, they tend much less than priorities-and-planning presidents to institutionalize -- either through creating advisory positions or utilizing collective decision-making bodies -- the process whereby they obtain alternative advice. As well, they shy away from "big picture" scenarios. They prefer instead to work from relatively modest game plans. They will tend, thus, to channel their energies more into resolving crises than probing issues which do not cry out for immediate attention. Reactive-active presidents -- such as Eisenhower and Bush -- would find in broker politics a good fit between their personality and style. So would executive presidents like Carter. *Administrative-politics* presidents neither seek to tap a multiplicity of views nor to institutionalize countervaillance. They prefer to devolve as many issues as possible down to departments. Thus, they see themselves as engaging in the process only in cases where problems prove too difficult to resolve lower down. Jimmy Carter organized his White House and cabinet systems as if he were an administrative-politics president. But his passion for detail undercut the appropriateness of this approach. That is, a serious disjunction emerged between the frequency with which the president immersed himself in issues and the relatively meager institutional apparatus available to handle the resultant case load. Normally, we would expect a being-there president to embrace administrative politics. Until Fred Greenstein's revisionist assessment of Eisenhower, presidency scholars had pegged Eisenhower as following administrative politics (1982). This owed in large part to the "hidden hand" quality of much of Eisenhower's pursuit of broker politics.

Finally, *survival-politics* presidents appear mostly to resort to this approach only when the other styles have failed. If they started out fostering countervaillance, they increasingly cut down on the number of advisers whom they consult and their reliance upon collective consultative bodies. If they sought to devolve decisions to departments, they would turn more and more to specific advisers or units in the White House or the Executive Office of the President. These would increasingly operate as a counterbureaucracy to departments and agencies. Nixon gradually slid into survival politics even though he started in broker politics. Carter adopted survival politics in summer 1979 when concerns about the intractability of the American policy process and reelectability concentrated his mind on giving some direction to his administration.

Conclusion

This chapter began by locating the political executive sub-discipline within the wider context of political science. It asserted at the outset that the members of the sub-

discipline have always encountered considerable difficulty reconciling analysts' desire for simple explanatory theories and the innate complexity and unpredictability of political executives' behavior and performance. It focused its assessment of the state of the sub-discipline on Anglo-American systems. This allowed us to give special attention to factors emerging from one presidential and four considerably different parliamentary systems. But, it avoided the inevitable overload which would occur if we had sought an inventory of the entire canvas of executive leadership. And, several of the lessons which emerge from this analysis might prove of use to those more intimately concerned with political executives outside the compass of this review.

First, following upon Olsen's important work, analysts within any setting should give greater attention to secular changes which have altered publics' expectations for executive leadership and, in turn, political executives' views of their own roles. Similarly, they should eschew the tendency to overcompensate for the strengths and/or failings of current political executives by projecting immutable changes in the nature of the entire system.

Second, we should become more aware of the degree to which one researcher's rigor is another's subjectivity. The pursuit of the divided government thesis presents a case in point. In its 1960's U.S. incarnation, it emerged from a school of political science which had become disenchanted with the indolence of the system in addressing social problems. The more recent institutionalist variant has employed the concept -- perhaps too eagerly -- to excuse the inaction of presidents in grappling with key domestic issues.

Third, we should keep a cautious eye on the copycat effect in the world of political executives. We forget all too often that presidents and prime ministers and their many men and women view their counterparts in other countries as peers. Presidents and prime ministers tend to borrow ideas from one another -- about inflation, deficits, the size of public services, privatization, and many more issues (see for example, Putnam and Bayne 1984). They and their advisers talk shop about how to organize presidents' and prime ministers' staffs, cabinet, economic policy making, budget review, management reform, and many similar topics. Furthermore, entire units within the World Bank, the IMF, and the OECD proffer advice on such matters and develop working groups designed to advance across-the-board acceptance of reforms. Yet, the copycat effect can become a poison pill. This chapter has dwelt on the degree to which unquestioning acceptance of public choice solutions to the intractable problems facing political executives -- in some systems -- have amounted to overtreatment or simply created side effects worse than the original affliction.

Fourth, this chapter has tried to disentangle two dimensions of the perennial institutionalization issue in the study of political executives. It has identified two, rather than one, gearbox problems. The first of these concerns the political executives who make up an administration or government and their relations with the standing bureaucracy. We found abundant evidence that the institutionalization of the latter works a diminished effect as chief executives and their colleagues heighten efforts to reassert political control. Yet, the tug of war between an administration/government and the bureaucracy forms simply one part of the policy competence equation. Institutionalization inevitably rears its ugly head. And, in the case of the second gearbox problem, it involves the increased complexity, unwieldiness, and even willfulness of the cadre of presidents' and prime ministers' men and women who make up an administration or government. Nobody -- least of all presidents or prime ministers -- can assume that just because two or more gather in a chief executive's name that they actually will work in harmony.

Finally, this chapter attempted to demonstrate the continued utility of examining presidents' and prime ministers' personalities as critical factors contributing to their management style and performance. The case presented here places a strong emphasis on the special salience of the issue to presidential systems -- owing, of course, to their monocratic nature. However, personality has worked distinctive effects in parliamentary systems. This assessment readily admits that inclusion of personality in analyses presents difficult problems of operationalization. However, we can lull ourselves into some seriously error-prone analyses if we rule out personality as a factor altogether or construe it as an optional add-on.

Bibliography

Aberbach, Joel D., Robert A. Putnam, and Bert A. Rockman. 1981. *Bureaucrats and Politicians in Western Democracies.* Cambridge, MA: Harvard University Press.

Aberbach, Joel D. 1991. "The President and the Executive Branch." In *The Bush Administration: First Appraisals*, ed. Colin Campbell and Bert A. Rockman. Chatham, NJ: Chatham House.

Alchain, A. A., and S. Woodward. 1987. "Reflections on the Theory of the Firm." *Journal of Institutional and Theoretical Economics* 143:110-36.

Allison, Graham T. 1971. *The Essence of Decision: Explaining the Cuban Missile Crisis.* Boston: Little, Brown.

Anson, Stan. 1991. *Hawke: An Emotional Life.* Ringwood, Victoria: Penguin.

Aucoin, Peter. 1986. "Organizing Change in the Machinery of Canadian Government." *Canadian Journal of Political Science* 14:3-17.

Aucoin, Peter. 1988. "The Mulroney Government: Priorities, Positional Policy and Power." In *Canada Under Mulroney: An End of Term Report*, ed. A. B. Gollner and D. Salee. Montreal: Vehicule.

Aucoin, Peter. 1989. "Contraction, Managerialism and Decentralization in Canadian Government." *Governance* 1:144-161.

Aucoin, Peter. 1990a. "Administrative Reform in Public Management: Paradigms, Principles, Paradoxes and Pendulums." *Governance* 3:115-137.

Aucoin, Peter. 1990b. "Comment: Assessing Managerial Reforms." *Governance* 3:197-204.

Barber, James David. 1972. *The Presidential Character: Predicting Performance in the White House.* Englewood Cliffs, NJ: Prentice-Hall.

Barber, James David. 1977. "Comment: Qualls's Nonsensical Analysis of Nonexistent Works." *American Political Science Review* 71:212-225.

Berman, Larry, and Bruce W. Jentleson. 1991. "Bush and the Post-Cold War Worlds: New Challenges for American Leadership." In *The Bush Administration: First Appraisals*, ed. Colin Campbell and Bert A. Rockman. Chatham, NJ: Chatham House.

Berry, Phyllis. 1989. "The Organization and Influence of the Chancellory during the Schmidt and Kohl Chancellorships." *Governance* 2:339-355.

Borins, Sanford F. 1982. "Ottawa's Expenditure 'Envelopes': Workable Rationality at Last?" In *How Ottawa Spends Your Tax Dollars: National Policy and Economic Development*, ed. G. Bruce Doern. Ottawa: Carleton University Press.

Boston, Jonathan. 1987. "Transforming New Zealand's Public Sector: Labour's Quest for Improving Efficiency and Accountability." *Public Administration* 65:423-442.

Buchanan, James M., and Gordon Tullock. 1962. *The Calculus of Consent: Logical Foundations of Constitutional Democracy.* Ann Arbor: University of Michigan Press.

Burns, James MacGregor. 1963. *The Deadlock of Democracy: Four-Party Politics in America.* Englewood Cliffs, NJ: Prentice-Hall.

Campbell, Colin. 1980. "Political Leadership In Canada: Pierre Elliott Trudeau and the Ottawa Model." In *Presidents and Prime Ministers*, ed. Richard Rose and Ezra Suleiman. Washington: American Enterprise Institution.

Campbell, Colin. 1983. *Governments Under Stress: Political Executives and Key Bureaucrats in Washington, London and Ottawa.* Toronto: University of Toronto Press.

Campbell, Colin. 1985. "Cabinet Committees in Canada: Pressures and Dysfunctions Stemming from the Representational Imperative." In *Unlocking the Cabinet: Cabinet Structures in Comparative Perspective*, ed. Thomas T. Mackie and Brian Hogwood. London: Sage.

Campbell, Colin. 1986. *Managing the Presidency: Carter, Reagan and the Search for Executive Harmony.* Pittsburgh: University of Pittsburgh Press.

Campbell, Colin. 1988. "Mulroney's Broker Politics: The Ultimate in Politicized Incompetence?" In *Canada Under Mulroney: An End of Term Report*, ed. A. B. Gollner and D. Salee. Montreal: Vehicule.

Campbell, Colin. 1991. "The White House and Presidency under the 'Let's Deal" President." In *The Bush Administration: First Appraisals*, ed. Colin Campbell and Bert A. Rockman. Chatham, NJ: Chatham House.

Campbell, Colin, and Margaret Jane Wyszomirski. 1991. "Introduction." In *Executive Leadership in Anglo-American Systems*, ed. Colin Campbell and Margaret Jane Wyszomirski. Pittsburgh: University of Pittsburgh Press.

Campbell, Colin, and Bert A. Rockman, eds. 1991. *The Bush Administration: First Appraisals.* Chatham, NJ: Chatham House.

Campbell, Colin, and John Halligan. 1992. *Leadership in an Age of Constraint: The Australian Experience*. Sydney: Allen & Unwin.

Campbell, Colin. 1992. "Public Service and Democratic Accountability." In *Ethics in Public Service*, ed. Richard A. Chapman. Edinburgh: University of Edinburgh Press.

Cannon, Lou. 1991. *President Reagan: The Role of a Lifetime*. New York: Simon & Shuster.

Considine, Mark. 1988. "The Corporate Management Framework as Administrative Science: A Critique." *Australian Journal of Public Administration* 47:4-17.

Dahl, Robert A. 1956. *A Preface to Democratic Theory*. Chicago: University of Chicago Press.

Dahl, Robert. 1971. *Polyarchy: Participation and Opposition*. New Haven: Yale University Press.

d'Alpuget, Blanche. 1982. *Robert J. Hawke: A Biography*. Melbourne: Schwartz.

Destler, I. M. 1981. "National Security II: The Rise of the Assistant (1961-1981)." In *The Illusion of Presidential Government*, ed. Hugh Heclo and Lester M. Salamon. Boulder, CO: Westview.

Doern, Bruce. 1982. "Liberal Priorities 1982: The Limits of Scheming Virtuously." In *How Ottawa Spends your Tax Dollars*, ed. Bruce Doern. Toronto: James Lorimer & Company.

Edwards III, George C. 1991. "George Bush and the Public Presidency: The Politics of Inclusion." In *The Bush Administration: First Appraisals*, ed. Colin Campbell and Bert A. Rockman. Chatham, NJ: Chatham House.

Franks Report. 1983. "Falkland Islands Review, Report of a Committee of Privy Councillors." London: Her Majesty's Stationery Office.

French, Richard D. 1980. *How Ottawa Decides: Planning and Industrial Policy-Making, 1968-1980*. Toronto: Lorimer.

Fry, Geoffrey. 1988. "The Thatcher Government, the Financial Management Initiative and the 'New Civil Service.'" *Public Administration* 66:1-20.

George, Alexander. 1974. "Assessing Presidential Character." *World Politics* 26:234-282.

George, Alexander. 1980. *Presidential Decisionmaking in Foreign Policy: The Effective Use of Information and Advice*. Boulder, CO: Westview.

Goodnow, Frank J. 1900. *Politics and Administration*. New York: Macmillan.

Greenstein, Fred I. 1982. *The Hidden-Hand Presidency: Eisenhower as Leader*. New York: Basic Books.

Gulick, Luther. 1937. "Science, Values and Public Administration." In *Papers in the Science of Administration*, ed. Luther Gulick and L. Urwick. New York: Institute of Public Administration.

Gwyn, Richard. 1980. *The Northern Magus: Pierre Elliott Trudeau and Canadians*. Toronto: McClelland and Stewart.

Hansen, Michael, and Charles H. Levine. 1988. "The Centralization-Decentralization Tug-of-War in the New Executive Branch." In *Organizing Governance: Governing Organizations*, ed. Colin Campbell and B. Guy Peters. Pittsburgh: University of Pittsburgh Press.

Hargrove, Erwin C. 1993. "Presidential Personality and Leadership Style." In *Researching the Presidency: Vital Questions, New Approaches*, ed. George Edwards, John Kessel and Bert A. Rockman. Pittsburgh: University of Pittsburgh Press.

Hart, John. 1987. *The Presidential Branch*. New York: Pergamon.

Hartle, Douglas. 1983. "An Open Letter to Richard Van Loon (with a Copy to Richard French)." *Canadian Public Administration* 26:84-94.

Heclo, Hugh. 1977. *A Government of Strangers: Executive Politics in Washington*. Washington, DC: Brookings.

Heclo, Hugh. 1984. "In Search of a Role: America's Higher Civil Service." In *Bureaucrats and Policy Making: A Comparative Overview*, ed. Ezra Suleiman. New York: Holmes & Meier.

Heclo, Hugh, and Lester M. Salamon, eds. 1981. *The Illusion of Presidential Government*. Boulder, CO: Westview.

Hennessy, Peter. 1986. *Cabinet*. Oxford: Basil Blackwell.

Hennessy, Peter. 1991. "The Whitehall Model: Career Staff Support for Cabinet in Foreign Affairs." In *The Bush Administration: First Appraisals*, ed. Colin Campbell. Chatham, NJ: Chatham House.

Hess, Stephen. 1976. *Organizing the Presidency*. Washington, DC: Brookings.

Hood, Christopher. 1990. "De-Sir Humphreyfying the Westminster Model of Bureaucracy: A New Style of Governance?" *Governance* 3:205-214.

Hood, Christopher, and Maurice Wright. 1981. "From Decrementalism to Quantum Cuts." In *Big Government in Hard Times*, ed. Christopher Hood and Maurice Wright. Oxford: Martin Robertson.

Jones, Charles O. 1991. "Meeting Low Expectations: Strategy and Prospects of the Bush Presidency." In *The Bush Administration: First Appraisals*, ed. Colin Campbell and Bert A. Rockman. Chatham, NJ: Chatham House.

Jones, George W. 1983. "Prime Ministers' Departments Really Create Problems: A Rejoinder to Patrick Weller." *Public Administration* 61: 79-84.

Jones, George W. 1991. "Presidentialization in a Parliamentary System?" In *Executive Leadership in Anglo-American Systems*, ed. Colin Campbell and Margaret Jane Wyszomirski.

Keating, Michael, and Malcolm Holmes. 1990. "Australia's Budgetary and Financial Management Reforms." *Governance* 3:168-185.

Keegan, William, and R. Pennant-Rea. 1979. *Who Runs the Economy? Control and Influence in British Economic Policy*. London: Maurice Temple Smith.

Kemp, Peter. 1990. "Next Steps for the British Civil Service." *Governance* 3:186-196.

Kernell, Samuel. 1986. *Going Public: New Strategies of Presidential Leadership*. Washington, DC: Congressional Quarterly.

Lindblom, Charles E. 1965. *The Intelligence of Democracy: Decision-Making through Mutual Adjustment*. New York: Free Press.

Little, Graham. 1985. *Political Ensembles: A Psychological Approach to Politics and Leadership*. Oxford: Oxford University Press.

Lowi, Theodore J. 1969. *The End of Liberalism: Ideology, Policy, and the Crisis of Public Authority*. New York: Norton.

Mackie, Thomas T., and Brian Hogwood, eds. 1985. *Unlocking the Cabinet: Cabinet Structures in Comparative Perspective*. London: Sage.

Mackintosh, John P. 1977. *The British Cabinet*, 3rd ed. London: Stevens and Sons.

Mayntz, Renate. 1987. "West Germany." In *Advising the Rulers*, ed. William Plowden. Oxford: Basil Blackwell.

Moe, Terry M. 1985. "The Politicized Presidency." In *The New Direction in American Politics*, ed. John E. Chubb and Paul E. Peterson. Washington, DC: Brookings.

Moe, Terry M. 1990. "Presidential Style and Presidential Theory." A paper presented at the Presidency Research Conference, Pittsburgh.

Moe, Terry M. 1993. In *Researching the Presidency: Vital Questions, New Approaches*, ed. George C. Edwards III, John Kessel, and Bert A. Rockman. Pittsburgh: University of Pittsburgh Press.

Mulcahy, Kevin V., and Harold F. Kendrick. 1991. "The National Security Adviser: A Presidential Perspective." In *Executive*

Leadership in Anglo-American Systems, ed. Colin Campbell and Margaret Jane Wyszomirski. Pittsburgh: University of Pittsburgh Press.

Nathan, Richard. 1975. *The Plot That Failed: Nixon and the Administrative Presidency*. New York: Wiley.

Nelson, Anna Kasten. 1981. *National Security I: Inventing a Process (1945-1960)*. In *The Illusion of Presidential Government*, ed., Hugh Heclo and Lester M. Salamon. Boulder, CO: Westview.

Neustadt, Richard E. 1960. *Presidential Power: The Politics of Leadership*. New York: Wiley.

Neustadt, Richard E. 1990. *Presidential Power and Modern Presidents: The Politics of Leadership from Roosevelt to Reagan*. New York: Free Press.

Niskanen, William A. 1971. *Bureaucracy and Representative Government*. New York: Aldine and Atherton.

Niskanen, William A. 1973a. *Structural Reform of the Federal Budget Process*. Washington, DC: American Enterprise Institute.

Niskanen, William A. 1973b. *Bureaucracy: Servant of Master? Lessons From America*. London: Institute of Economic Affairs.

Nugent, Neill. 1989. *The Government and Politics of the European Community*. London: Macmillan.

Olsen, Johan P. 1983. *Organizing Democracy: Political Institutions in a Welfare State, The Case of Norway*. Oslo: Universitetsforlaget.

Olsen, Johan P. 1988. "Administrative Reform and Theories of Organization." In *Organizing Governance, Governing Organizations*, ed. Colin Campbell and B. Guy Peters. Pittsburgh: University of Pittsburgh Press.

Olson, Mancur. 1982. *The Rise and Decline of Nations: Economic Growth, Stagflation, and Social Rigidities*. New Haven: Yale University Press.

Pfiffner, James P. 1988. *The Strategic Presidency: Hitting the Ground Running*. Chicago: Dorsey.

Pfiffner, James P. 1990. "Establishing the Bush Presidency." *Public Administration Review* 50:64-73.

Plowden, William, ed. 1987. *Advising the Rulers*. Oxford: Basil Blackwell.

Polsby, Nelson W. 1975. "Legislatures." In *Government Institutions and Processes*, vol. 5 of *Handbook of Political Science*, ed. Fred I. Greenstein and Nelson W. Polsby. Reading, MA: Addison-Wesley.

Porter, Roger B. 1980. *Presidential Decision-Making: The Economic Policy Board*. Cambridge: Cambridge University Press.

Pusey, Michael. 1991. *Economic Rationalism in Canberra: A Nation Building State Changes Its Mind*. Cambridge: Cambridge University Press.

Putnam, Robert D., and Nicholas Bayne. 1984. *Hanging Together: The Seven-Power Summits*. Cambridge: Harvard University Press.

Qualls, James H. 1977. "Barber's Typological Analysis of Political Leaders." *American Political Science Review* 71:182-211.

Quirk, Paul J. 1991. "Domestic Policy: Divided Government and Cooperative Presidential Leadership." In *The Bush Administration: First Appraisals*, ed. Colin Campbell and Bert A. Rockman. Chatham, NJ: Chatham House.

Radwanski, George. 1978. *Trudeau*. Toronto: Macmillan.

Redford, Emmette S., and Marlan Blissett. 1981. *Organizing the Executive Branch: The Johnson Presidency*. Chicago: University of Chicago Press.

Riddell, Peter. 1983. *The Thatcher Government*. Oxford: Martin Robertson.

Riggs, Fred W. 1988. "The Survival of Presidentialism in America: Para-constitutional Practices." *International Political Science Review* 9:247-278.

Roberts, Paul Craig. 1984. *The Supply-Side Revolution: An Insider's Account of Policymaking in Washington*. Cambridge, MA: Harvard University Press.

Rockman, Bert A. 1984. *The Leadership Question: The Presidency and the American System*. New York: Praeger.

Rockman, Bert A. 1991. "The Leadership Style of George Bush." In *The Bush Administration: First Appraisals*, ed. Colin Campbell and Bert A. Rockman. Chatham, NJ: Chatham House.

Rockman, Bert A. 1991. "The Leadership Question: Is There an Answer?" In *Executive Leadership in Anglo-American Systems*, ed. Colin Campbell and Margaret Jane Wyszomirski. Pittsburgh: University of Pittsburgh Press.

Rose, Richard. 1976. *Managing Presidential Objectives*. New York: Free Press.

Rose, Richard. 1988. *The Postmodern Presidency: The White House Meets the World*. Chatham, NJ: Chatham House.

Rose, Richard, and B. Guy Peters. 1978. *Can Government Go Bankrupt?* New York: Free Press.

Rose, Richard, and Ezra Suleiman, eds. 1980. *Presidents and Prime Ministers*. Washington, DC: American Enterprise Institution.

Savas, E. S. 1982. *Privatizing the Public Sector: How to Shrink Government*. Chatham, NJ: Chatham House.

Schieffer, Bob, and Gary Paul Gates. 1989. *The Acting President: Ronald Reagan and the Supporting Players Who Helped Him Create the Illusion That Held America Spellbound*. New York: E. P. Dutton.

Scott, Graham, and Peter Gorringe. 1988. "Reform of the Core Public Sector: The New Zealand Experience." A paper delivered to the Bicentennial Conference of the Royal Australian Institute of Public Administration, Melbourne, Australia.

Scott, Graham, Peter Bushnell, and Nikitin Sallee. 1990. "Reform of the Core Public Sector: New Zealand Experience." *Governance* 3:138-167.

Seymour-Ure, Colin. 1991. "The Role of Press Secretaries on Chief Executives: The U.S.A., the U.K., Canada and Australia." In *Executive Leadership in Anglo-American Systems*, ed. Colin Campbell and Margaret Jane Wyszomirski. Pittsburgh: University of Pittsburgh Press.

Simeon, Richard. 1972. *Federal-Provincial Diplomacy: The Making of Recent Policy in Canada*. Toronto: University of Toronto Press.

Sinclair, Barbara. 1991. "Governing Unheroically (and Sometimes Unappetizingly): Bush and the 101st Congress." In *The Bush Administration: First Appraisals*, ed. Colin Campbell and Bert A. Rockman. Chatham, NJ: Chatham House.

Stockman, David A. 1986. *The Triumph of Politics: How the Reagan Revolution Failed*. New York: Harper & Row.

Sundquist, James L. 1986. *Constitutional Reform and Effective Government*. Washington, DC: Brookings.

Sundquist, James L. 1988. "Needed: A Political Theory for the New Era of Coalition Government in the United States." *Political Science Quarterly* 103:613-635.

Tower Commission. 1987. "President's Special Review Board." *The Tower Commission Report* (*New York Times* edition). New York: Bantam.

Van Loon, R. J. 1983. "The Policy Expenditure Management System in the Canadian Federal Government: The First Five Years." *Canadian Public Administration* 26:255-285.

Walker, Jack L. 1966. "A Critique of the Elitist Theory of Democracy." *American Political Science Review* 60:285-295.

Walker, Jack L. 1969. "The Diffusion of Innovations Among the American States." *American Political Science Review* 63:880-889.

Weaver, Kent, and Bert A. Rockman. 1990. "Introduction: Assessing the Effects of Institutions." A paper prepared for presentation at a conference titled "Political Institutions and Their Consequences," The Brookings Institution, Washington, DC.

Weller, Patrick. 1983. "Do Prime Ministers' Departments Really Create Problems?" *Public Administration* 61:59-78.

Weller, Patrick. 1985. *First Among Equals: Prime Ministers in Westminster Systems*. London: Allen and Unwin.

Weller, Patrick. 1989. *Malcolm Fraser PM: A Study of Prime Ministerial Power in Australia*. Ringwood, Victoria: Penguin.

Wildavsky, Aaron. 1961. "Political Implications of Budgetary Reform." *Public Administration Review* 21:183-190.

Wildavsky, Aaron. 1983. "From Chaos Comes Opportunity: Movement Toward Spending Limits in American and Canadian Budgeting." *Canadian Public Administration* 26:163-181.

Wilson, Woodrow. 1941 (reprint). "The Study of Administration." *Political Science Quarterly* 16:481-506.

Young, Hugo. 1989. *One of Us: A Biography of Margaret Thatcher*. London: Macmillan.

16

Public Administration: The State of the Field

Donald F. Kettl

The scholarly study of bureaucracy and the administrative process has long been a contentious business. Scholars, in fact, have pointedly chosen to label the field in different ways. For traditionalists, the term of choice is "public administration." Many political scientists prefer "bureaucracy" instead, while others embrace "the new economics of organization" or "the new institutionalism." "Implementation" has its followers, while some scholars in public policy schools pursue "public management" and explicitly separate themselves from political science, in both traditional and new forms. Scholars from these different approaches rarely cite each other. They frequently suggest, at least implicitly, that those from other approaches have little to contribute to the really important questions. Of course, they rarely agree on what those important questions are. If anything characterizes the study of public administration, it is fragmentation.

Important questions in public administration, not surprisingly, have long revolved around problems of boundary-drawing. Woodrow Wilson, in "The Study of Administration" (1887), drew public administration's most famous boundary in stipulating a distinction between politics and administration. The Wilsonian politics-administration dichotomy has long dominated the way scholars have attacked the basic questions in the field. It has also directed the way they have answered them. It has allowed some public administrationists to distance themselves from indelicate political battles, and political scientists to immunize themselves against administrative complexity. The dichotomy ultimately has led many within political science to abandon the unruly child of public administration. It has also played into the cause of elected officials who were eager to use "administration" to pursue political ends and to blame administrators for political failures. The politics-administration dichotomy has fueled the struggle but not enhanced the debate. The challenge of drawing these boundary lines led to often difficult battles -- indeed, estrangement -- between public administration and political science.

The different approaches, as a result, are struggling for the very soul of the field. Some of the conflict comes from fundamental disagreement over defining the basic questions. Some comes from stark differences in method, which especially distances newer, mathematically based approaches from older, descriptive approaches. Most fundamentally, however, the controversy flows from three fundamental problems.

First, different approaches to the study of administration usually come from one of two conflicting traditions in American politics -- and each tradition leads to a very different perspective on the role of administration in American democracy (see Table 1). Some students of administration come to the subject with a fundamentally Hamiltonian bent. Like Alexander Hamilton, they seek a vigorous state vested with a strong administrative apparatus. They see the task of administration as carrying out publicly defined goals effectively; they see an energetic government doing good. Other students of administration, however, are fundamentally Madisonians. Like James Madison, they are wary about too much government action, and they are cautious about the concentration of governmental -- especially administrative -- power. Like Madison, they see in a delicate balance of power the best protection against tyranny. The competition of political interests, in their view, lessens the risk that bureaucracy can abuse individual liberty.[1]

Second, different scholars have pursued very different ends in their study of administration. Some scholars have sought to build a body of theory that would explain the role administration plays in society. Their central goal has been to establish the study of administration firmly among the respected social sciences. Other scholars have recognized the importance of theory-building, but for them theory was just a step toward a more important goal: understanding the administrative process so that its functions can be improved. The distinction is based on the traditional theory-practice issue, but it is more than that. The two approaches differ sharply in how important finding practical solutions to administrative problems ought to be. They also differ on how important these problems ought to be in defining the central questions for the study of administration. Some

**Table 1. Strange Bedfellows:
Political Heritage in the Major Approaches**

Heritage

Hamiltonian	Madisonian
• Public administration • Public management	• Bureaucratic politics • Implementation • Economic theories • Bureaucracy

scholars have been content to reason abstractly, while others insist that theory speak directly to practical problems.

The Hamiltonian and Madisonian traditions enrich much of the study of American government, but perhaps no other area of political science so regularly finds itself in such deep conflict over the theory-practice problem. Since the very beginning of the American Political Science Association, public administrationists have threatened to bolt from the fold. Yet, as political science nears the end of its first century, the issue of public administration's relationship with political science remains central. This relationship defines not only public administration's intellectual home; it also defines which questions will be preeminent.

Because of these fundamental differences, public administration has long struggled with a third basic problem -- the accumulation of knowledge. Other fields, from voting behavior to comparative politics, have integrated disparate approaches, accumulated knowledge, and built theory. For several generations, public administration followed this course. Since World War II, however, public administration has lurched from one fad to another, stumbled among several policy disappointments, and found itself fragmented because of alluring new approaches in sister disciplines. As a result, the field has shown a constant tendency to reinvent itself, only to discover that "new" approaches frequently rehash old ideas.

Thus, it is no exaggeration to say that public administration is in crisis -- and that, in fact, it has been in crisis since 1950 (Ostrom 1973; Waldo 1990). Important questions plague the field. Should there be a relationship between theory and practice? Does the pursuit of theory tend to have higher status and win the intellectual high ground? Is there room for the development of practical solutions to administrative

problems in the evolving scientism of political science? Does political science maintain any interest in what public administration has to say? Do other disciplines, from the interdisciplinary study of policy analysis (Weimer and Vining 1992) to the scholarly pursuit of organization theory in sociology and social psychology (Perrow 1986a), sometimes contribute more to basic administrative questions than public administration? Ultimately, does public administration still have -- and need -- a home in political science?

To each of these questions, I say "yes." Neither the study nor practice of administration -- or of politics -- can be complete without a theory that links them. As John Gaus (1950) argued, "A theory of public administration means in our time a theory of politics also." To that I would add, "No theory of politics is complete without a theory of administration." If administration is central to government, as Wilson argued in the less-cited portion of his famous 1887 paper, neither political science nor public administration can be complete without embracing the other.

Nevertheless, tensions among competing approaches to administration, and between these approaches and political science, have plagued the attempt to build a theory of administration. To examine these questions, I begin with a study of the field's creation. I consider how and why the field became fragmented. I continue by analyzing the emerging problems that theories of administration and politics must address and then conclude by examining public administration's greatest dilemma -- how to elicit effective performance and political accountability in the public sector. I conclude by examining the issues that, in the end, tie political science and public administration together.[2]

An Uneasy Marriage

Public administration developed as a field through four stages: the assertion that administration plays a central role in government (from 1887 until 1915); the era of scientific management and administrative principles (from 1915 to 1940); a period of critical self-examination (from 1940 to 1969); and a generation of centrifugal forces (from 1969 to the present).[3]

The Centrality of Administration: 1887 Until 1915

Although Woodrow Wilson is generally credited as the father of the *study* of American public administration, it really was Alexander Hamilton a century earlier who established the *practice* of American public administration[4] (see Van Riper 1987; see also White 1948, 1951, 1954, 1958). Hamilton's famous reports on public credit and manufactures, written during his tenure as Secretary of Treasury, set the stage for policy making and administration for decades. Nevertheless, American administrative process evolved without a self-conscious view of itself or of its mission until Wilson formulated it in "The Study of Administration" (1887).

Wilson's work, as well as that of other early leaders like Goodnow (1900), defined the Progressive tradition. The Progressives were interested in two things. First, by establishing a professional administration they wanted to build a new American state (Short 1923; Skowronek 1982). They sought a strong and energetic government, a government that used science to pursue efficiency. Second, they sought to distance administration from the political spoils and scandals that had undercut administrative effectiveness, especially in the last half of the nineteenth century. Wilson and Goodnow are both remembered most for their commitment to separating politics from administration, Wilson for articulating it and Goodnow for developing it into a doctrine. "If I see a murderous fellow sharpening a knife cleverly," Wilson wrote, "I can borrow his way of sharpening the knife without borrowing his probable intention to commit murder with it; and so, if I see a monarchist dyed in the wool managing a public business well, I can learn his business methods without changing one of my republican spots" (Wilson 1887, 220; see also Doig 1983). Wilson suggested that administrators could create a set of tools that could be used for any public purpose.

Even though the politics-administration dichotomy suggests a highly stylized and inaccurate view of the role of administration in American government

(Henry 1987), it has established the importance both of the executive establishment and the systematic study of the field. If Wilson and Goodnow are best known for arguing the policy-administration dichotomy, however, they deserve to be equally known for believing in the centrality of administration in the political process (compare Holden 1991). The American Political Science Association's first president, Frank J. Goodnow, devoted his presidential address in 1904 to "the work of the American Political Science Association" and set out the fundamental questions to which he believed the new association ought to address itself (1905, 37): "the expression of the State will," "the context of the State will as expressed," and "the execution of the State will." He saved discussion of public administration, in fact, for his penultimate point. In Goodnow's view, APSA ought to address itself to helping government achieve "what is the best attainable" (p. 46). Public administration was the crucial link between the abstract study of politics and the process of improving the way the political system worked.

The importance of administration lay at the very core of the creation of the new American Political Science Association [APSA]. Five of the first eleven presidents of the association came from public administration and played important roles in framing the new discipline.[5] One of them -- Woodrow Wilson -- went on to even higher office. As subheadings in the first *American Political Science Review*'s book review section shows, public administration was one of five fields comprising the new discipline of political science; the others were comparative government (in the form of the study of colonies), public law (comprised of constitutional law and jurisprudence), international law, and political theory. From its very beginning, public administration was one of the critical foundations of political science, and political science was the natural home of public administration.

Despite their affinity, public administration and political science soon nearly divorced. Public administration promoted a "training movement," devoted to preparing students for government service with a curriculum independent of political science. Others in the APSA argued the association should devote its efforts to building theory. Did practical training belong -- or could it perhaps comfortably fit -- within a discipline devoted to the development of theory? Or did political science's more practical side belong in a separate discipline, in which its approaches could be integrated with those of related disciplines? The "training movement" proved short-lived, because mainline public administrationists saw their home in the new APSA and were committed to maintaining it. The truce proved uneasy, though. Many public administrationists were unhappy about sharing the discipline with more theoretical political scientists, and some political scientists found practice-oriented public administration an undesirable partner.

Problems recurred constantly. Public administrationists never felt that political science recognized the importance of education for the public service. The natural corollary of the Wilson/Goodnow movement toward a professional administration was to train professionals to staff it. Many political scientists, struggling on a different front to establish the discipline as a social science to be taken as seriously as economics, focused their attention instead on developing advanced theories.

Scientific Management: 1915-1940

Having established the importance of administration in the American system, and having uneasily accepted political science as their home, public administrationists began to develop their craft. The gospel of separating politics from administration, which Goodnow and Wilson preached, became a strategy instead for separating administration from politics. Following the "scientific management" approach charted by Frederick W. Taylor (1911), analysts sought the "one best way" to perform administrative work efficiently, free from the meddling of partisan politics. As Roscoe Martin described:

> In the atmosphere provided by scientific management, a mechanistic concept of public administration came to prevail widely and in important circles. Administration was separated severely from the legislative body, toward which its spokesmen frequently manifested not only impatience but also profound distrust. "Politics" was anathema -- not the politics practiced by administrators, but the politics of the "politicians." The emphasis seemed to be on answers, not on questions (1952, 67).

Advocates of the scientific management approach to public administration saw virtually no barrier to its ability to improve government -- if only managers could be protected from political meddling. They advanced the creation of new regulatory institutions, such as the Federal Reserve Board, new tax systems, such as the income tax, and new budgetary processes, such as the executive budget. It was an era of remarkable success and self-confidence.

Despite its rocky first years within political science, public administration gained remarkable prestige in government and, in fact, within political science. By 1940, one-fifth of all political science doctoral degrees

were in public administration (Martin 1952, 662). President Roosevelt had just implemented the recommendations of the Brownlow Committee (1937), which had proposed sweeping changes to transform the presidency. The committee's three members -- Louis Brownlow, Charles Merriam, and Luther Gulick -- occupied the pantheon of public administration (Karl 1963). Brownlow had helped establish the city manager movement, while Merriam was a vigorous proponent of scientific management. Background papers prepared for the committee, notably Gulick's "Notes on the Theory of Organization" (1937), came to define the field's orthodoxy for a generation. Meanwhile, young committee staff members were soon to establish themselves as the leaders of public administration's next generation.[6] As a field, public administration had things to say to government, and it did not hesitate to say them. When World War II broke out, it was scarcely surprising that many of the nation's leading public administrationists went off to Washington to help manage the war effort.

Public administration reached its high point during World War II. Its leading scholars had helped found APSA and had trained government managers. They had generated a "scientific" approach to management that tried to elbow politicians aside. They had developed principles to guide executive officials, and they had put them to work in the Roosevelt administration.[7] They had gained important seats in the central councils of American government and continued to play an important role within political science.

Critical Self-Examination: 1940-1969

Soon after the war ended, the focus of political science itself began to change. Political scientists began developing new theoretical approaches that undermined the scientific management approach to public administration. Norton Long (1949) contended that political power, not administrative efficiency, was necessary for effective administrative practice. Even as political science sought to discover how to become more scientific, Robert A. Dahl (1947) argued that the study of administration would never be able to achieve that goal. A new behavioralism, devoted to the understanding of how *individuals* (like voters) instead of *institutions* (like bureaucracies) behaved, began displacing more traditional approaches. The questions were not ones that public administration either recognized as important or was equipped to answer. Statistical methods were a whole new language for most public administrationists -- and not one they understood well or could speak clearly (Fesler 1975; Schick 1975).

For their part, many public administrationists returned to their universities from Washington with a fresh sense of realism. Simple principles of efficiency, based on scientific management, seemed unacceptably shallow. They developed instead a new perspective on public administration based on the relationship between administration and democracy (Appleby 1945; Waldo 1984). They also struggled for new principles to replace the old -- and for ways to train public servants to face the nation's new challenges, which seemed not well answered by traditional theory. The idea of training reappeared, but this time the separatist tendencies were far stronger.

Meanwhile, Herbert Simon helped create a new management science. He argued (1946) that the old public administration produced principles which were frequently conflicting and hence useless. His attacks on traditional administration were against a straw-man target instead of the rich theories that public administration had developed. Nevertheless, his criticisms reflected growing dissatisfaction with the old theories at the same time that other theorists were defining a new, politically aware approach to public administration (Fesler 1975). Even more important, Simon redefined the *process* of decision making as the critical problem of administration, instead of finding the best organizational *structure* (Simon 1947; March and Simon 1958). With its traditional approaches under attack, public administration suddenly found that its intellectual foundation was slipping (White and McSwain 1990).

Just before World War II, leading public administrationists created "an association of public administration for public administrators" (Pugh 1988, 17). The movement, spearheaded by Syracuse University's William Mosher, soon led to the creation of the new American Society for Public Administration [ASPA]. ASPA's organizational meeting was held at APSA's 1939 annual meeting, and more than 150 APSA political scientists decided to join the new organization. Leonard D. White, well-known for his authorship of the leading public administration textbook (1926), became the editor-in-chief of the new association's journal, *Public Administration Review*. Even though ASPA's first meetings were held in conjunction with APSA's annual meeting, the new association soon decided to split completely from APSA. Otherwise, its founders feared, ASPA would never be more than a section of the political science association and its goal of establishing a society for public administrators -- as opposed to those who studied public administration -- would never be realized (Pugh 1988). War-time restrictions on travel and heavy demands on ASPA's founders to help manage the war effort slowed ASPA's early progress. With the end of the war, however, the separatist movement sparked by ASPA's creation took firm hold.

The three trends -- the rise of a new political science, the separate creation of a new management science, and the separation of ASPA from APSA -- aggravated the tensions between public administration and political science. Political science as a discipline strongly fought the separatist tendencies. "We recommend that the tendency toward splintering the field of political science be stopped at once," the association's Committee for the Advancement of Teaching vigorously argued in 1951 (p. 129; see also Martin, 1952). Its Committee for the Advancement of Teaching wrote:

> A few fields are mentioned again and again as constituting the core of political science. They are: political theory, public law, international relations, public administration, and politics, either as subjects unto themselves or as set forth in courses in American or comparative governments. It is noteworthy that the two fields that have had a tendency to become separated from political science -- international relations and public administration -- are considered by these respondents [teachers of political science around the country surveyed for the study] to be at the very heart of the discipline (APSA 1951, 126).

The battle against separatism, however, was a losing one. Political science was moving toward new theoretical questions that public administration was ill-equipped to answer. The drive of many within public administration to link its practice and its study helped drive some scholars out of political science and into ASPA (Caldwell 1965, 58). As Allen Schick observed, "Public administration had come apart and could not be put back together" (1975, 157).

In 1904, public administration had been a critical pillar in Goodnow's vision of political science. In 1951, it was one of the "core fields" of political science. By 1962, when APSA issued "Political Science as a Discipline" (1962, 417, 421), a special report on instruction, public administration was mentioned only in passing as a subfield of American government. The report discussed teaching in public administration as part of a broader look at "professional fields of instruction," along with other approaches including law, business administration, school administration, social work, and foreign affairs. The American Society for Public Administration was drawing important public administration scholars away from political science, while some scholars in political science wondered whether public administration properly belonged within political science. Public administration had lost both of its traditional anchors, its theoretical base and its disciplinary home. Dwight Waldo wrote sadly:

412 Public Administration

It is now unrealistic and unproductive to regard public administration as a subdivision of political science....The truth is that the attitude of political scientists (other than those accepting public administration as their "field") is at best one of indifference and is often one of undisguised contempt or hostility. We are now hardly welcome in the house of our youth (quoted in Schick 1975, 160).

Centrifugal Forces: 1969-Present

Many competing answers rose up in the struggle to replace orthodoxy. In the leading textbook of the era, Leonard D. White noted, "There are many ways to study the phenomenon of public administration. . . . All of these approaches are relevant and from all of them come wisdom and understanding" (4th ed, 11; quoted by Storing 1965, 50). While some of this diversity reflected a lively intellectual search for new ideas, some students of administration saw it as a "complacent, undiscriminating eclecticism" (Storing 1965, 50). If *any* approach could be useful, then no approach could be *central*. So great was the movement away from central theoretical questions, in fact, that White, perhaps the leading student of administration from the 1920s to the 1950s, ended his career not with grand theories but with careful histories (White 1948, 1951, 1954, 1958). It was almost as if he felt compelled to begin again at the beginning, to rebuild the field on a new foundation of fresh interpretations.

During the 1950s and early 1960s, public administration suffered from more than just the rejection of the politics-administration dichotomy. It suffered from the lack of a theoretical guide and a comfortable disciplinary home. It had come to the realization that politics mattered, but did not know *how*. Meanwhile, much of political science had convinced itself that public administration was stuck in old questions and crippled by outmoded methods.

The decline in public administration's status could scarcely have been greater. From a place of supreme confidence, reflected in the Brownlow Committee report, it was in uneasy search for itself. From having an important role in the APSA's governance and in the production of its young scholars, it had faded to the background. Public administration fell into a state of critical self-examination and faced a serious intellectual crisis (see Ostrom 1973).

Public administrationists have disagreed among themselves about the prospects for resolving this crisis, especially within the discipline of political science. Dwight Waldo's 1987 John M. Gaus Lecture -- delivered upon bestowal of the association's most prestigious award

to leading senior scholars in the field -- argued that "*estrangement* is perhaps too mild to characterize the relationship of public administration to other fields of political science." Waldo regretfully suggested that, for most political scientists, "public administration concerns the lower things of government, details for lesser minds" (1990, 74; emphasis in original). Herbert Kaufman, in his 1990 Gaus Lecture, worried that public administration and political science were reaching "the end of alliance." For Waldo and Kaufman, the battle was over; public administration was and ought to be separate from political science.

Allen Schick had presented a far different opinion years before. "[P]ublic administration can no more escape political science than it can escape politics," as Schick put it. "Until it makes peace with politics, public administration will wander in quest of purpose and cohesion" (1975, 160). In a third Gaus Lecture, James W. Fesler agreed with Schick. The worlds of governance and of political science "should not be far apart," he contended (1990, 85).

These disagreements reflect great uneasiness about whether the rift between public administration and political science can -- or indeed should -- be healed. The answer to this puzzle lies in developing a theory of administration that, as Gaus suggested, is a theory of politics also.

New Approaches

Graham Allison's "Conceptual Models of the Cuban Missile Crisis" (1969) undermined traditional studies of public administration more than any other work of the behavioral era. Instead of focusing on how to structure bureaucracies to produce desired outputs, he sought to explain why certain structures produced observed outputs. In doing so, they rejected traditional public administration and reached past political science. His was perhaps the first product of an interdisciplinary environment, then being nurtured at Harvard by Richard Neustadt, to understand policy problems.

Allison contended that three different models helped explain the crisis. In Model I, the "rational actor" model, the crisis policy makers attempted to develop the best, most rational answer to the problem of nuclear-armed missiles in Cuba. In Model II, the "standard operating procedures" model, the rules of the diplomatic and military bureaucracies led to predictable behavior that sometimes frustrated policy makers. In Model III, the "bureaucratic politics" model, political bargaining among top officials explained outcomes.

Allison was very careful not to say that any of his models represented the "correct" explanation of the crisis. He presented them as complementary, not exclusive alternatives. Some scholars who read his work, however, took a different lesson from it. They viewed Model I as a proxy for the rational approach of economics, and they rejected it as unrealistic. They saw Model II as a proxy for conventional, principles-bound public administration, and they discounted it as woefully inadequate. They saw in Model III a new and lively approach to public policy based centrally in political science. Model III took a problem -- explaining outcomes -- and solved it by applying the central political process -- bargaining -- to the behavior of top officials.

Allison's work, perhaps unintentionally, had two important effects on the study of administration. First, for readers who saw far more virtue in Model III than in Models I and II, it further widened the split between politics and administration. Because the focus on political bargaining at the top seemed more illuminating -- and exciting -- than the study of administrative processes toward the bottom, it became easier for some political scientists to dismiss the study of administration in favor of Model III. Traditional public administration seemed even more remote from issues like the Cuban Missile Crisis and decision making in organizations. A lively literature devoted to bureaucratic politics sprang up soon after the publication of Allison's article and his subsequent book (Allison 1969, 1971; Halperin 1974; Steinbruner 1974).

Second, and far more subtly, Allison's work launched the study of new phenomena in the administrative world. The traditional approach to public administration was devoted to the *organization* as the unit of analysis: how it was structured; what processes and problems administrators had to solve; and how the entire process could work more efficiently. Like the broader movement in political science, Allison's three models focused attention instead on the *behavior* of political actors, of which administrators were only one group. Unlike the behavioral movement, he concentrated on power relations among actors. These actors bargained among themselves to shape policy decisions; the actors with the most political power won. In the bureaucratic politics perspective, administration was a "political resultant," not the search for efficiency.

Within the political science community, the bureaucratic politics perspective thus provided a fresh look at administration. It established a forum for studying administration outside traditional public administration channels, and it focused on a unit of analysis different from the ones that public administrationists had studied. The new approach was most important because of its departure from the Hamiltonian vision of bureaucratic power and efficiency that had characterized public administration for its first

century. Bureaucratic politics was implicitly Madisonian, full of competing interests that struggled to shape administrative action. Following close on the bureaucratic approach were four new approaches: implementation, public management, economic theories, and public bureaucracy. They had little in common but their rejection of traditional public administration.

Implementation

The 1960s brought the Great Society, ambitious promises, and major disappointments. Many political scientists found public administration sorely lacking: It neither produced success nor explained failure. If program results did not live up to their ambitions, administrative failures seemed to be the cause -- and if existing administrative patterns were not working, it was time to reexamine the old principles. Part of the reason was also theoretical: public administration seemed to many observers to leave major gaps in the explanation of the process. A new "public policy" approach grew up within political science, an approach that explicitly sought to build a bridge between old administrative theory and the new administrative realities forcefully brought home by the Great Society programs (Jones 1976). The bridge was a new theory -- implementation -- designed to be the "missing link" between policy making and policy outcomes (Hargrove 1975).

"There is (or there must be) a large literature about implementation in the social sciences," Pressman and Wildavsky wrote. "It must be there; it should be there; but it fact it is not" (1973, 166).[8] Traditional public administration scholars were surprised to read this bold statement, for they believed that the entire field was dedicated to precisely this question. Leonard D. White, in the first edition of his public administration textbook, wrote, "Public administration is the management of men and materials in the accomplishment of the purposes of the state." John M. Gaus, a giant in public administration, added in the margin of his own copy of White's text: "and a reconsideration of the policy being implemented." Charles O. Jones has concluded, "Unquestionably Gaus viewed administration as comprehensively as Pressman and Wildavsky define implementation" (Jones 1977).[9]

What was truly new about implementation was not its focus but its rejection of traditional public administration prescriptions for the study of administration. Unlike public administration's concentration on the organization, implementation fixed instead on the *program* as the basic unit of analysis. It borrowed as well from the systems approach then gaining ground in the economists' study of public policy analysis: Goals and resources are put into the political system;

outcomes, often at variance with the original goals, result. Government agencies and their employees are means to an end, not an end in themselves. All too often, in the view of most of the early implementation scholars, they are, in fact, the source of the problem.

From this foundation, the implementation movement evolved through three stages (Goggin, Bowman, Lester, and O'Toole 1990). In the first stage, launched by Pressman and Wildavsky's study, implementation was singularly devoted to the study of government failure, with failure understood as the inability of a public program to achieve its legislative goals. Problems were everywhere. (See Derthick 1972; Bardach 1977; Berman 1978; Elmore 1978; Van Horn 1979.) The causes of failure were legion, rooted especially in fundamental pathologies of public bureaucracy (Hogwood and Peters 1985).

Pressman and Wildavsky identified three major problems. First, in their view, programs were plagued by the "complexity of joint action" (1973, 107). With so many steps in the policy process, the opportunities for disgruntled interests to derail or deflect implementation were endless. Second, there was the problem of control. Implementation tended to take a top-down view, and policy makers at the top had great difficulty in regulating the behavior of implementers at the bottom through the long and complex policy chain.[10] Finally, the implementation environment was complex, with many opportunities for participants to play games that distorted and delayed implementation (Bardach 1977).

The behavior of government bureaucrats posed, for implementation theorists, a special problem. Bureaucrats delay, obstruct, vacillate, hesitate, and regulate. They get caught up in their own routines and orthodoxies, becoming blinded to new signs and signals. Bureaucracy demonstrates "a preference for procedure over purpose" (Pressman and Wildavsky 1973, 133). In fact, of all the impediments to success, early students of implementation rated bureaucracy the worst. "No one is clearly in charge of implementation," Ripley and Franklin conclude. It was little wonder, therefore, that program performance so often fell short of expectations (1986, 12).

Two important weaknesses characterized much work in implementation's first stage, however. First, the results were largely creatures of the cases scholars studied. Scholars were naturally drawn to interesting problems, but the most interesting puzzles often tended to be failure stories. The failure focus resulted in a depressing body of literature that promoted the perception that lack of success was the norm. The focus on failures explained neither how to achieve success nor why many programs, from the early space program to the construction of flood control dams, were so manifestly successful.

Second, there was a more subtle bias toward studying intergovernmental programs. Nearly 80 percent of all of the entries for programs and organizations in one standard implementation textbook are for program and organizations that have an important intergovernmental dimension.[11] Such an overwhelming focus on intergovernmental programs is far out of proportion to the role that such programs actually play in American public policy. Most of the national policy initiatives of the Great Society and of the next decade were intergovernmental, so scholars naturally were drawn to these programs. Most administrative activity, however, was not intergovernmental. Implementation theory that concentrated on studies of intergovernmental activity resulted in a distorted view of the administrative process.

These problems inspired a clever subtitle for Pressman and Wildavsky's now-classic book (1973): *How Great Expectations in Washington Are Dashed in Oakland; Or, Why It's Amazing That Federal Programs Work At All.* The implementation approach argued that Washington's goals too often went unrealized in the states and cities. That approach, however, did not often take account of one central fact: that the primary objective of many of the programs was to adapt broad national goals to specific local conditions. A secondary objective frequently was to shift power from the national government to the cities and, especially, to citizens in their neighborhoods. Conflicts over how to spend the money were the natural result of this process (Kettl 1980).

Inferences about "success" and "failure" were far too simpleminded, out of step with the shifts in political power and the complex organizational arrangements in many of these programs. A success to a neighborhood group might seem like a failure to a federal official. Judgments about program results, moreover, often changed over time. Delayed programs sometimes became eventual successes, and some early successes turned sour. Even a program brought to a standstill, such as construction of a new highway, may well be a success for an interest which did not want it finished.

By the mid-1980s, a second stage of implementation research emerged to tackle these problems. Marked by important syntheses by Ingram and Mann (1980), Mazmanian and Sabatier (1983), and Ripley and Franklin (1986), scholars searched for systematic variations among public programs. These authors contended that success was possible, that conditions for successful implementation varied over time and across levels of government, and that the political context of implementation significantly affected results. As critics have pointed out, however, the second-stage analyses *illustrated* but could not *prove* the value of their formulations. The case studies on which their conclusions were based were never replicated, and their theoretical propositions were not validated. The studies produced useful synthesis but, in the end, few firm conclusions about which variables were most important in determining program success (Goggin, Bowman, Lester, and O'Toole 1990).

The third stage combined both top-down and bottom-up perspectives on implementation with theories about communication to seek an integrated theory of implementation. It is explicitly more scientific, seeking a systematic understanding of how different conditions produce different results (O'Toole 1986, 1989a, 1989b; Goggin, Bowman, Lester, and O'Toole 1990; Ingram 1990). This work represents an important advance past the first two stages, but it is still in its infancy: a broad sketch with only some details is just beginning to appear. It offers insights into how managers are likely to affect the odds of success and a plan for more research to improve the state of implementation theory. It is handicapped, however, by what preceded it: a cynical sense of inevitable failure that discouraged many scholars from even exploring implementation.

Implementation did, however, establish a very different approach to administration. Like bureaucratic politics, it implicitly rejects the Hamiltonian vision of bureaucratic power. With its Madisonian vision of competing interests, implementation has helped to explain why success in government programs seems so elusive. It has not provided the interdisciplinary approach that the early founders of the public policy movement hoped it would. It has, however, capitalized on declining public confidence in government effectiveness by explaining the difficulty of making government work. If the approach has not matured theoretically, it has nevertheless leveled a far more serious blow to traditional public administration than the bureaucratic politics approach ever delivered.

Public Management

From the seeds of the bureaucratic politics approach came a new public management movement. Unlike bureaucratic politics, it was more Hamiltonian, devoted to the study of administrative leadership and power. Unlike implementation, public management was devoted to finding prescriptions for making public programs work better.

The public management approach has developed in two tracks: as a counterbalance to policy analysis in the public policy schools; and, in the field of institutional theory, as an elaboration of Simon's theory of decision making.

Public Management in the Policy Schools

The public management movement emerged in the 1970s with the development of public policy schools. It began with a focus on the importance of the environment and of strategy-setting by top executives (Bryson 1988). It borrowed the business school case method as the basic research and teaching tool. In fact, the public management movement has its foundation on writing *about* public managers *by* former public officials. At Harvard, the movement grew from work by Richard Neustadt (1960; Neustadt and Fineberg 1978) and his students Mark Moore (Moore and Stephens 1981; Fleishman, Liebman, and Moore 1991) and Philip Heymann (1987). At Berkeley, a separate public management movement built on the Pressman and Wildavsky implementation approach. Together, they conceived of public management as an intellectual balance for the policy analysis approach developing at the public policy schools. If policy analysis was to help government officials make better decisions, public management would help them achieve better results.

Public management has since become a term for all manner of administrative studies, from organization theory and behavior to old-style public administration dressed up in new clothes to avoid the old problems. Scholars sometimes find it easier to win grants and publish materials under the more lively sounding public management banner than under the tattered public administration flag. Top-rank research universities, which had rejected the vocational overtones of public administration, sometimes found public management a more high-minded approach.

The irony, of course, is that the public policy school approach to public management has innumerable echoes from public administration's past. It is essentially Hamiltonian, as practical minded as public administration ever was. Its approach builds on the same case-study tool that characterized public administration in the post-World War II years (Stein 1952), and for which public administration was roundly criticized because case studies were believed to be unscientific (see Behn 1988; Barzelay 1991). It seeks principles that many political scientists rejected in the late 1940s as outmoded. The main difference with traditional public administration is its heavy focus on top leaders, its argument that it is onto something new, and its rejection of the public administration work that preceded it. Two Kennedy School public management experts pointedly argue that "public managers are negotiators" and "public managers are leaders." By contrast, "public administrators are experts" (Barzelay and Kaboolian 1990, 600).

This approach to public management offers great potential, especially in coupling management strategy with the manager's political environment, but progress has been halting. It grows from Simon's argument (1947) that decision making is the central administrative act. Like implementation, however, the public management movement has largely been a creature of what its students have studied. The case studies have been interesting but the knowledge gained from them is rarely cumulative. Insights drawn from them have often been more the result of the experiences of the authors than of their theoretical contributions. Nevertheless, this approach to public management has produced absorbing studies devoted to new visions for improving government (Lynn 1981, 1987; Barzelay 1993). Despite the self-conscious attempt to distance itself from public administration, moreover, the similarities -- in both method and basic questions -- are striking.

Institutional Theory

During the 1980s, public management theory developed a separate branch, christened "institutional theory," quite independent of the Harvard/Berkeley public policy school approach. The institutional theorists started from Simon's decision-making theory, but from there they departed significantly from the public management scholars. Unlike the public management approach, institutional theorists were more focused on the behavior of organizations. Unlike traditional public administrationists, institutional theorists built more on interdisciplinary work, especially research by organizational sociologists like James D. Thompson (1967) and Philip Selznick (1949, 1957). They build on previous work as diverse as Herbert Kaufman's classic study of the forest ranger (1960) and Wamsley and Zald's analysis of the political economy of organizations (1973). With the "new institutionalists" of political science (Skowronek 1982), they share the belief in the importance of institutions in government and the importance of bureaucracy as a political institution (March and Olsen 1984, 1989; Powell and DiMaggio 1991).

Wamsley and Zald defined the central questions to which the institutional theorists have devoted themselves:

> How does the level of required coordination among the units of an organization and the constitutional norms about the interrelations among units affect the degree of centralization of the internal policy? What are the conditions under which internal succession systems emerge, essentially limiting the choices of the nominally

superior appointing officer? How do variations of accounting systems limit the surveillance of external actors? How do accounting systems shape perceptions of power and allocate resources to avoid accountability? How does the mode of funding interact with agency goals so as to displace agencies from pursuit of their original goals? (1973, 81)

These critical questions contain echoes of traditional public administration issues, such as centralization vs. decentralization, accountability, oversight of career officials by political appointees, budgetary control, and organizational norms. They present the traditional questions in a new light, however. The institutional theorists have devised far more rigorous experiments to test their hypotheses. They have also worked far harder to aggregate their findings. The result is an impressive body of work that offers sustained attention to the critical issues of public management (see, for example, Rainey, Backoff, and Levine 1976; Bozeman 1987; Rainey 1983, 1991; Romzek and Dubnick 1987; Perry 1989; Provan and Milward 1991; LaPorte and Consolini 1991; and Milward, Provan, and Else 1993).

While still in its adolescence (Scott 1987), institutional theory offers some of the most useful new contributions to administration. Organizations lie at the center of their work. They are Hamiltonians at heart, seeking to invigorate bureaucracies and make them effective. Although the institutional theory approach is in relative infancy, it has already produced some of the most stimulating work in public management. It offers a connection between the critical questions that public administration defined in the past and at least the foundation for developing useful answers.

Economic Theories

Out of economics came a third approach to studying administration. This approach sought to derive a cogent set of predictions from a limited set of assumptions, based fundamentally on a theory of rational action. The economic theories begin with the assumption that participants in the political process, including administrators, seek to maximize their utility (Buchanan and Tullock 1962; Tullock 1965; Downs 1967; Niskanen 1971; Romer and Rosenthal 1978). As they gain more experience, they are likely to become more risk-averse because they have more to lose and because they become more entrapped in the organization's routines. Bureaucrats are therefore less likely to be entrepreneurs and more likely to become "conservers" as their careers develop. Whole bureaucracies likewise tend to become more conserver-dominated as they age (Downs 1967). Administrators seeking to maximize their utility also work to increase their power and their discretion (Niskanen 1971; Blais and Dion 1991).

The assumption of utility-maximizing bureaucrats has produced a host of formal models of bureaucracy (Bendor 1988). Four branches of theory have dominated: principal-agent theory; bureaucratic-outcomes theory; institutional-choice theory; and transaction-cost theory.

Principal-Agent Theory

The economic theories build upon a basic argument that the critical relationship is the one between elected officials and administrators. As policy makers, elected officials are the *principals* in the relationship. Administrators act as their *agents* in implementing policy. The central problems of such principal-agent relationships are how principals can choose the best agents, how faithfully agents are likely to pursue their principals' policies, and how principals can improve the odds that their agents' actions will coincide with their desires. Information asymmetries, where agents know more about their tasks and about their own behavior than principals, complicate the relationship. Principals have a difficult time telling agents what they ought to do because agents know more about the technical details. Principals therefore find it hard to pick good agents or to discover precisely what their agents are doing and how well they are doing it. When agents know more about their behavior than the principal ever can, and when agents are self-interested, then shirking and opportunism can result (Moe 1984; Arrow 1985; Bendor 1990).

Agency theory offers basic insights into the problems of managerial control and organizational effectiveness (White 1985). It helps explain implementation problems, such as why the Department of Energy had such difficulty in managing the contractors that manufactured the nation's nuclear weapons. It is difficult for principals to know enough to choose good contractors as agents (the "adverse selection" problem). It is also hard for the department to know enough about what its contractor-agents are doing and thus whether their performance matches the department's goals (the "moral hazard" problem). Agency theory identifies the flow of information as the critical problem. Principals can improve their selection of agents if they can learn more about them before hiring them. Principals can reduce information asymmetries by altering their agents' incentives and by improving the monitoring of their agents' behaviors.

Bureaucratic Outcomes Theory

Agency theory has been most powerful, however, in two applications: theories of bureaucratic outcomes, and theories of institutional choice. In the bureaucratic outcome approach, researchers have set out to reform the bureaucratic politics literature. Bureaucratic politics, along with much early public choice literature, has suggested that American bureaucracies resist change. Controllers, like members of Congress, have little incentive for oversight because the rewards are few (Mayhew 1974). The bureaucratic-outcomes approach, however, argues from the experiences of the Reagan years and from sophisticated quantitative analysis that the course of bureaucracies can indeed be changed. The argument goes like this (see, for example, Wood and Waterman 1991): Institutions headed by elected officials, such as the presidency and Congress, create bureaucracies; that is, bureaucracies can be viewed as agents for the principals' -- elected officials' -- wishes. The principals design incentives and sanctions to enhance their own control. When the principals detect bureaucratic behavior that does not match their policy preferences, they use these incentives and sanctions to change that behavior. Among the important sanctions are the president's appointment power and the budgetary leverage that the two branches share. Bureaucrats' behavior can thus be influenced by shaping their incentives and sanctions.

Using quantitative data gathered from a number of federal agencies, researchers demonstrated that agency outcomes vary with political preferences, especially changes in presidential administrations (see Moe 1982; Weingast and Moran 1983; Moe 1985a; Wood and Waterman 1991). From that they conclude that "elected leaders can and do shape bureaucratic behavior in systematic ways" (Wood and Waterman 1991, 801).

There is a fundamental irony, of course, in using rational-choice models, first proposed as a way to explain bureaucratic intransigence, to demonstrate bureaucratic responsiveness. In rejecting the obviously too simple assumptions of the most basic rational-choice approach and the arguments about immovable bureaucracies, however, the bureaucratic outcomes approach has struggled with a more fundamental problem. The tests of the model are statistical, and the dependent variables employed tend to be *process*, rather than *outcome* measures, such as the number of seizures by drug enforcement agencies or the level of enforcement activity by regulatory agencies. Separating activity from results is an old problem in measuring bureaucratic performance. In drug enforcement, for example, thousands of small dealers can be put out of business without affecting the large suppliers; a large number of seizures can produce high levels of activity without demonstrating effectiveness. Likewise, hundreds of small anti-trust cases can pale by comparison with one single case, such as the divestiture of AT&T, which took years to accomplish but had profound implications.[12] Covariance between independent variables, such as presidential administrations, and process measures, such as the number of seizures or inspections, may in fact say very little about bureaucratic outcomes. That weakens the argument for a clear principal-agent connection between the preferences of elected officials and the activities of government bureaucracies. Furthermore, it underlines the critical information problems that undercut inferences about the whole process.

Institutional-Choice Theory

The impact of institutional-choice theory has been far greater. It seeks to examine the basic questions of bureaucratic politics -- the three-way interactions among bureaus, politicians, and interest groups. Unlike bureaucratic politics, however, it attempts to model these interactions formally. It borrows heavily from agency theory in postulating the bureaucracy as agent of political forces and in incorporating serious information asymmetries. It assumes that the players are self-interested, but it also builds on Simon's (1947) argument about bounded rationality. Participants would like to maximize their utility -- to optimize -- but they cannot because of information constraints. Thus, they must satisfice and adapt their choices to the constraints they face. The result is a tight argument, based on mathematical (but not necessarily statistical) models, that produces a pluralist outcome: the power of bureaucracies is the result of the equilibrium that contending political forces produce (Bendor and Moe 1985; Knott and Miller 1987; Moe 1989).

Institutional-choice theory thus completes the steps, in rigorous form, first made by bureaucratic politics. It replaces the traditional public administration view of bureaucracy-as-actor, as independent variable, with a new view of bureaucracy-as-acted-upon, as dependent variable. Organizations are not designed to promote efficiency but, rather, to reflect the power of political interests. Thus, it is scarcely surprising that bureaucratic structures often do not seem designed to promote efficiency or that they often produce ineffective results. Institutional-choice theory contends that they are not fundamentally designed to do so. Rather, they are the result of rules, implicit and explicit, that are the result of political forces. These rules can be discovered, influenced, and changed. Any attempt to reform bureaucracy thus must take account not just (and perhaps not even) efficiency but, rather, the constellation of political forces that will create the rules under which the

bureaucracy must operate. Some studies in this tradition, such as Chubb and Moe's controversial study on reform of local schools (1990), build on economic theories to recommend more choice as a way to make bureaucracies more responsive.

Transaction-Cost Theory

Transaction-cost analysis has revolutionized organization theory but has surprisingly little impact within political science or public administration. Based on path-breaking work by Nobel laureate Ronald Coase (1937) and important elaborations by Oliver Williamson (1975), this theory sees the environment as a network of organizations (compare Landau 1991). It begins by assuming that self-interested individuals work within organizations to promote their own individual goals. The environment, however, is uncertain. To stabilize it, organizations tend to develop long-term relationships with other organizations, notably suppliers, which cannot easily be replaced if the relationship becomes strained. Other organizations in the network gain bargaining power because of this interdependence.

All of these factors combine to create boundaries on rational behavior. In such interdependent organizational networks, the high level of uncertainty makes it hard to predict outcomes. Instead, administrators consider the costs of their transactions among organizations and conclude that it is most rational for their organizations to become bigger. When they cannot grow larger, they seek to integrate other organizations in the network into their organization. To minimize the costs of transactions among organizations, the theory thus argues that it is most efficient to substitute *authority* relationships *within the organization* for the uncertain *market* relationships in the *outside networks*. Vertical integration, not market competition, is the result.

Despite the enormous impact of transaction-cost analysis on generic organization theory, it has yet to be applied widely within the public sector (Rainey 1991, 44). Nevertheless, the potential appears significant. Researchers have discovered that many government organizations work through networks. Local mental health programs, for example, are managed through complex interrelationships among government bureaus and nonprofit organizations (Milward, Provan, and Else 1993). At the federal level, contracting out has proliferated, in everything from telecommunications policy to toxic waste cleanup. The management networks have become ever more complex and interdependent as a result (Kettl 1993). While these examples are suggestive, links between such service networks and transaction-cost economics have yet to be drawn.

Summary

These theories have appeal because they provide a foundation for understanding the unresponsiveness that nearly everyone has criticized in bureaucracies. When they have been incorporated into conservative political rhetoric, they have also helped help explain why bureaucracies, bureaucratic power, and public budgets have tended to grow over time. From the right, they have produced a voluminous literature of why privatization, by replacing governmental power with market competition, can improve governmental effectiveness (Savas 1987; Hanke 1987; Donahue 1989; compare Salamon 1981; Smith 1983; Seidman and Gilmour 1986; Moe 1987; Salamon 1989). From the left, they have generated calls for beefing up government by making it more entrepreneurial (Osborne and Gaebler 1992). Few fundamental ideas in public administration have ever struck more intellectual sparks.

The economic approach has come under heavy criticism, especially from theorists who contend that the basic focus on rationality robs the study of organizations of their very life. Economic theories of organization, Charles Perrow contends, represent "a challenge that resembles the theme of the novel and movie *The Invasion of the Body-Snatchers*, where human forms are retained but all that we value about human behavior -- its spontaneity, unpredictability, selflessness, plurality of values, reciprocal influence, and resentment of domination -- has disappeared" (1986b, 41). Terry M. Moe agrees, contending that bureaucracies tend to be omitted as major features of these models. Instead, they appear "as black boxes that mysteriously mediate between interests and outcomes. The implicit claim is that institutions do not matter much" (Moe 1987, 475).

One tenet common to all of the modern theories of organization is that institutions -- especially bureaucratic ones -- *do* matter. What varies is how. The more formal economic models of bureaucracy answer this problem by actually reducing bureaucracies to black boxes, which allows the creation of sophisticated models of how, for example, Congress can dominate bureaucracy (see, for example, Weingast and Moran 1983). In the process of building such models, however, some of what we *do* know about bureaucratic behavior is cast aside. In seeing the bureaucracy as a black box, for example, some formal models ignore the self-evident political importance of bureaucratic decisions (Moe 1991). Some branches of economic theory stray far from practice. Many are hard to test empirically and even harder to follow as practical prescriptions. Lowi contends that they rob the study of administration of its very life and emotion (1992). The rational-choice theories do raise interesting questions often missing from more traditional approaches.

Potentially useful cross-fertilization rarely occurs, however. Those who promote rational choice view the methods pursued by other approaches as inadequate. Students of other approaches argue that the assumptions of the rational-choice models are untenable.

The rational-choice branch of economic theory has produced a schism between traditional public administration and newer approaches in political science. In part, this is because economic theory of bureaucracy begin from assumptions of rationality and highly structured relationships that traditional public administrationists find implausible. In part, this is because the abstract mathematical language of formal economic theories is inaccessible to many scholars trained in traditional public administration. Most of all, this is because the formulations, while elegant, speak little to the politics in administration. Having struggled for generations to escape the simplistic allure of the politics-administration dichotomy, public administrationists have struggled ever since to combine administration with a theory of politics. The formal theories run in the opposite direction.

The other branches of economic theory, notably transaction-cost economics, as well as its close cousins in institutional theory, offer far more promise. They have a rich sense of the complexity and uncertainty of the administrative environment. These theories are still underdeveloped, and their full potential has yet to emerge. Because they are fundamentally Madisonian, moreover, they contrast with the Hamiltonian vision of much of traditional public administration. The often stark differences between the two visions sometimes make conversations difficult, but the insights of the theories suggests that the conversation is well worth pursuing.

Public Bureaucracy

Although the behavioral revolution shook political science to its roots, it never completely obliterated the study of public administration within the discipline. A small, eclectic, but gifted group of political scientists have since focused centrally on the role of bureaucracy in government. They concentrated not on administration but on bureaucracy, not on agencies but on institutions, not on micro-principles but on mega-phenomena. Norton Long's classic article, "Power and Administration" (1949), is the classic text for the public bureaucracy movement: It asserts that the influence of bureaucracies grows from their ability to build political support.

From Long's foundation came Theodore J. Lowi's challenge to create a "juridical democracy" designed to replace the power that the interest-group/bureaucracy alliance had forged (1969). Hugh

Heclo elegantly traced the linkages between political executives and the rest of the Washington establishment (1977). He warned that a "government of strangers," based in the very structure of American bureaucracy, posed serious problems for government performance. Francis E. Rourke found in the bureaucracy's attentive and mass publics the source of much independent bureaucratic power (1984; see also 1991). The public bureaucracy movement is defined preeminently by James Q. Wilson's synthesis, *Bureaucracy* (1989), as well as by his earlier work (1967, 1973, 1978). Supporting Wilson's view is work by his students and colleagues, such as books by Derthick (1990), DiIulio (1987), and Kelman (1990).

Three basic principles define the public bureaucracy movement. First, public bureaucracy theorists assert that bureaucracy matters. For traditional students of public administration, this assertion often seems strange. Woodrow Wilson's fundamental argument a century before had been precisely the same, and public administrationists had worked hard to develop its implications. Public bureaucracy scholars, however, are writing not for public administrationists but for other political scientists. As political science moved away both from the study of institutions, the public bureaucracy movement has labored to remind political science of the importance of each. Unlike public administration, its proponents are devoted to theory, not practice.

Second, they place bureaucracy within a network of political forces. Heclo's theory of "issue networks" is a classic statement of how bureaucracies are woven into the cloth of interest-group politics (1978). These networks provide independent sources of political power for bureaucracies. This argument challenges traditional public administration, which sees the delegation of authority from elected officials as the foundation for administration.

Third, they assert that bureaucracies are important because of their role in the state. They are institutions with independent sources of power and influence on the conduct of public policy. The public bureaucracy movement, in short, seeks to use a base in political science to explain the growing power of bureaucracy in the United States. The movement resonates with a troubled note: How, given bureaucracy's independent power, can it be made accountable in a democracy?[13] The intersection of these two issues -- the independent *political* power of bureaucracies and the legal base of bureaucratic power in *law* -- has helped fuel a rebirth of interest in administrative law. The issue was an important field in traditional public administration, but with work by Mashaw (1983, 1985) and Melnick (1983), for example, it has produced important new insights into the challenges that such independent political power poses

for bureaucratic accountability (Finer 1941; Friedrich 1940; Burke 1986).

The work of the public bureaucracy scholars builds on many of the same fundamental issues raised by early public administration scholars. In writing about James Q. Wilson's *Bureaucracy*, however, David H. Rosenbloom notes that "in an odd way, his intellectual path and that of public administration seem to parallel each other more, and to intersect less, than one might reasonably expect" (Rosenbloom 1991, 191). In fact, many public administrationists fail to recognize and cite the work of the public bureaucracy scholars. They, in turn, often self-consciously separate themselves from traditional public administration by writing under the banner of bureaucracy, instead of administration (Hill 1992b).

The differences between bureaucracy and public administration are at once profound and trivial. At its most basic, the difference is between Madisonian and Hamiltonian views of American politics that are rooted in the Federalist papers. In *Bureaucracy*, for example, Wilson self-effacingly suggests to his readers that, if they "want to get immediately to the 'bottom line,'" they "can spare themselves the hundreds of pages that follow and turn immediately to Federalist Paper number 51, written two centuries ago by James Madison" (p. 28). Federalist 51, of course, is Madison's famous exposition of the fundamental principles at the core of republican government. These principles about power relationships in a democracy lie at the core of the theory of public bureaucracy. Traditional public administration, on the other hand, builds on Hamilton's argument for a strong executive.

The public bureaucracy movement, furthermore, can never quite embrace public administration because public administration can never quite seem to escape the old politics-administration dichotomy. Public bureaucracy begins by stipulating the essentially *political* nature of bureaucracy, while vestiges of the *instrumental* nature of bureaucracy -- the use of administrative tools to reach certain policy ends -- lurk in every cranny of public administration. This conflict is one which the two approaches have never managed to reconcile.

In *Bureaucracy*, Wilson contends that if we want to learn about government agencies, we must stick "as close as possible to what actually happens in real bureaucracies" (p. xii). This feet-on-the floor orientation separates public bureaucracy theory from many of the economic theories and links it with public management, in particular. To learn what happens, Wilson favors a bottom-up view. "By looking at bureaucracies from the bottom up, we can assess the extent to which their management systems and administrative arrangements are well or poorly suited to the tasks the agencies actually perform" (p. 12). Organization matters because it determines the relationship between government agencies and their clients and, in the end, the success of the agency. Complicating this relationship, however, are the difficulties in managing the functions of and relationships between different levels of the bureaucracy -- operators (the rank-and-file employees), managers, and agency executives. The behavior of bureaucrats at each of these levels, and thus the agency's overall performance, are the result of incentives created by both the organization's structure and political influences from the outside. Structure matters, but political power matters more (Nivola 1991).

For many students of bureaucracy, therefore, the study of public agencies is most fascinating because it serves as a prism for the central questions Madison raised in Federalist #51. Government performance matters, but the study of performance sits uneasily beside a fascination with the great forces of American politics. It is the former issue that defines the common ground between bureaucracy and public administration. It is the latter that defines the differences.

The bureaucracy approach sees administration in an untidy, pluralist way. It also fears the accumulation of bureaucratic power and worries about the effects of such power on bureaucratic effectiveness. Like some economic theorists, in fact, public bureaucracy scholars worry that the incentives of the political system pervert bureaucratic performance. They often end up favoring many of the same prescriptions -- such as privatization, decentralization, deregulation -- if for different reasons (Wilson 1989; Derthick and Quirk 1985; Kelman 1990). Bureaucracy might be troublesome, but "you can have less bureaucracy only if you have less government. Many, if not most, of the difficulties we experience in dealing with government agencies arise from the agencies being part of a fragmented and open political system," Wilson concludes (1989, 376). In fact, when problems of bureaucratic performance arise, they tend to be due not to bureaucratic malfeasance but to fundamental problems of governance in American democracy (Wilson 1989; Derthick 1990).

The bureaucracy scholars have thus brought the study of administration to a position both ultimately consistent with and fundamentally in conflict with public administration's early theorists. Like Wilson and Goodnow, they argue for the importance of administration, both for making democracy work and for shining a light on democracy's critical processes. Unlike the early theorists, however, they contend that bureaucracy can be understood and can function only as a piece of the larger fabric of politics. One can no more separate politics from administration than one can

separate, say, politics from Congress or the presidency. Thus, despite their close links, the fundamental Hamiltonian-Madisonian differences segregate the two approaches from each other and hinder useful cross-fertilization that might otherwise occur.

Strange Bedfellows

This review of administrative theories reveals two features. First, the fundamental issues to which each approach has devoted itself have been remarkably the same. Each approach has sought to reconcile the different sources of administrative power: delegation, how elected officials grant bureaucrats the authority to make decisions on their behalf; bureaucratic expertise, how professional know-how gives administrators authority independent of delegated power; and politics, how relations with outside forces can give bureaucrats a source of power independent of the others. Scholars who have studied administrative systems in other nations have come upon the same basic questions. As Aberbach, Putnam, and Rockman found in a major survey of western democracies, the relationship between party politicians and professional bureaucrats, in fact, stands at the center of many issues in the modern state (1981). Bureaucratic power depends on the relationship between outside groups and government officials, as Crozier discovered in his study of French bureaucracy (1964; see also Riggs 1964, 1991; Heady 1979; Peters 1989, 1992). Different historical and constitutional traditions in different countries, moreover, significantly affect the role of the executive (Rohr 1991, 1992).

Second, even though the basic questions are similar, there has been remarkably little accumulation of knowledge. The reasons are complex. In part, public administration's original focus on the politics-administration dichotomy has struck many scholars from other approaches as completely unrealistic. Because they focused on the first formulation instead of subsequent revisions, these scholars dismissed much of what public administration had to say. In part, public administration's relatively soft qualitative methods struck scholars trained in statistical methods and formal modeling as woefully inadequate. In part, some scholars rejected public administration's effort to link theory and practice. They believed that important mega-theoretical issues, such as the role of administration in the state, were neglected in the push to find practical solutions to management problems. They also suspected that practical training was not so high a calling as theory building. In many universities, the pursuit of theoretical elegance has often received more support than the more mundane training of future public servants. Traditional public administration has suffered because its pragmatic interests have often been seen as low-status, low-priority items.

Finally, the fundamental Hamiltonian/Madisonian differences underlining many of the basic disputes in the field have rarely been confronted. Some approaches, like traditional public administration and public management, have in Hamiltonian fashion sought to discover how to make administration more effective. Other approaches, notably bureaucratic politics, implementation, and some parts of the economic and public bureaucracy theories, have been far more concerned about the risks of administrative power and have sought to contain it. With such basic disagreements, cross-fertilization has proven difficult, even though the approaches have much to say to each other.

As a result, the public policy school version of public management and the public bureaucracy approach developed independently, even though they were using many of the same methods to investigate many of the same questions of traditional public administration. Traditional public administration, meanwhile, meandered somewhat aimlessly even though some of the formal economic approaches and, especially, institutional theory offer extremely useful answers to questions that have hamstrung public administration for a generation.

Cross-fertilization among these approaches is critical. It can avoid needless repetition. It could add rigor to those parts of administrative research, especially in parts of public management and public administration that have been criticized for their methodology. It could provide fresh answers to old questions. It could help clear up internal contradictions that muddy policy prescriptions. For example, economic theories lead in different directions: toward greater reliance upon competitive markets and decentralization, in principal-agent theory; and toward more centralization and less reliance upon external markets, in transaction-cost analysis. Most important, it could point out the blinders that ageless assumptions, especially those coming from Hamiltonian or Madisonian predispositions, create.

The third stage of implementation research (Goggin, Bowman, Lester, and O'Toole 1990) provides a most useful model for cross-fertilization. In early implementation research, as in most of the public management and some bureaucratic politics literature, bureaucracy was yet one more impediment to success. Innovative researchers have begun taking a more positive view of bureaucracy's instrumental role and have tied it more closely to the course of program implementation. Through game theory and other creative techniques, the second generation of implementation theory has begun moving the approach from its preoccupation with failure to the search for sources of success. Its successes have been built on a careful integration of basic questions with

a survey of what can be gleaned from public administration. This model promises important implications for other approaches as well. Scholars engaged in this form of research have much to learn from public administration -- and public administration has much to learn from them.

Shared Questions

Despite the differences among these approaches, each approach tends to ask questions closely related to the others: How can we design organizational structures that produce the desired results efficiently? How can we create incentives for bureaucrats to do the same? How can we make good decisions within bureaucracies and gauge the results of those decisions? What are the networks of organizations -- and of political forces -- that shape administrative behavior? And, ultimately, how can that behavior be made accountable to politically responsible officials? These questions lead to important insights.

1. The difficulty of reconciling traditional public administration with political science. As long as the discipline has existed, public administration has not occupied a stable position. Part of the reason is the conflict between education for the public service, which has always preoccupied public administration, and the more theoretical and academic concerns of political science. More fundamentally, however, public administration and public management have been based in the Hamiltonian tradition, while the other approaches have grown from the Madisonian perspective. Much of the conflict between political science and public administration, including the public service education issue, can be traced to this critical difference.

2. Different approaches for different problems. The administrative literature has been a contentious one, with different approaches vying for the prime role. The analysis of the role and heritage of bureaucracy in each model, however, suggests that different approaches to administration yield different answers that are appropriate for different problems. From an overall "systems" point of view, public administration and public management have focused on the organization, either looking predominantly inward (public administration) or outward (public management). Implementation research, by contrast, tends to focus on policy outcomes. Bureaucratic politics, economic theories, and bureaucracy seek linkages between the bureaucracy and the wider political environment. Each approach has its primary value in attacking a characteristic set of questions. Put differently, different questions are best answered by different approaches.

3. Combination of approaches for crosscutting questions. Most important and interesting administrative questions, of course, do not reside neatly within one of these cells. Rather, administrative problems increasingly spill across two or even three of the issues. That leads to a clear conclusion: obtaining a full picture of administrative issues usually requires several different analytical approaches. One approach has the virtue of asking an important question that other approaches would neglect.

4. Combining approaches rarely produces stable answers. Our experience, both pragmatically and theoretically, is that such cross-fertilization is difficult. Each major approach has taken great pains to separate itself from the others. Just as the Hamiltonian and Madisonian traditions have long struggled for the soul of American politics, it is unlikely that competing approaches to administration based on these disparate traditions are likely to find an easy accommodation. Cross-fertilization among the approaches is essential; common ground among them is unlikely. From the inevitable conflict, however, can still come useful insights, just as the struggles between Hamiltonian and Madisonian traditions have yielded useful -- if often untidy -- patterns of governance.

5. Profound normative and educational differences. The inevitable struggles among the disparate approaches produce starkly different normative prescriptions, from strengthening bureaucracy to weakening its hand, from encouraging market competition to improving the power of government executives. These normative differences likewise produce widely varying approaches to education. Some approaches, especially the organizational ones, seek to give clear guidance to impart to future government managers. Others, such as those focused on the political environment, seek theoretical understanding of why bureaucracies behave as they do, but are largely divorced from public service education. Even approaches pursuing the same goal -- notably the organizational approaches of public administration and public management -- have sharply different views of what is important, how what is important can be learned, and how to transfer that learning to students. Cross-fertilization undoubtedly would bear much fruit, but the search for common normative or educational ground is likely to be contentious. Subdisciplines, as well as whole professional schools, have been founded on the principle of exceptionalism, not commonality. That fundamental self-definition would be hard to shake.

The Politics-Administration Dichotomy Reinterpreted

These comparisons and contrasts mirror the ancient dichotomy between politics and administration on which the field cut its teeth. The study of administration, of course, has moved far beyond the early search for a clear line between politics and administration -- that is, for a Hamiltonian vision based on bureaucracy as an independent actor. In discarding that well-meaning but poorly focused search, however, other approaches have risked committing the same error. Within the rich politics of the American political system, it is no more possible to solve the problem of bureaucracy by embracing the Madisonian tradition than by following the Hamiltonian vision. Americans' strange love-hate affair with bureaucracy is the direct result of America's conflicting traditions about what role bureaucracy ought to play. We want bureaucracy to be powerful enough to do -- effectively and efficiently -- what needs to be done. We also want its power carefully constrained so that it poses no threat to personal liberty (Goodsell 1985).

The academic study of administration began by asserting that the phenomenon was worthy of study in its own right. In making the case, early public administrationists overdrew that argument by ignoring important complexities, especially Madisonian influences and the effects of other political forces on bureaucratic power. The reform efforts, however, sometimes replicated the mistakes of early public administration by ignoring the Hamiltonian traditions and the independent power of bureaucracy. Having solved the first problem of Wilson, Goodnow, and the other early founders of public administration -- that administration had become too important to ignore -- public administration could not solve the second -- the troubled relationship between administration and politics. Administration is both a dependent and an independent variable, a product of Hamiltonian and Madisonian traditions. It is virtually impossible to study administration without viewing administration as the result of one of the competing political traditions. It is certainly impossible to produce an adequate theory based on one set of choices. Thus, only a catholic approach, fully informed by the cross-fertilization of competing traditions, is likely to advance our understanding of administration. That is the lesson that the struggles over the politics-administration dichotomy ultimately teaches.

Notes

I am deeply indebted to the following colleagues who generously read the manuscript and made many, many suggestions for improvement: Kenneth Bickers, Martha Derthick, James Fesler, Ada Finifter, George Frederickson, Alice Honeywell, Patricia Ingraham, Charles O. Jones, Anne Khademian, Laurence Lynn, Rob Meyer, H. Brinton Milward, Laurence J. O'Toole, Paul Quirk, Andrew Reschovsky, Francis Rourke, Karl Scholz, Michael Wiseman, and two anonymous reviewers. They asked far better questions than I had the wit or space to answer. I will attempt to explore some of these issues more fully in a forthcoming book, to be published by the Johns Hopkins University Press.

1. In this paper, I will use "bureaucracy" to refer to the government's administrative apparatus. "Administration" will include "bureaucracy" as well as the broader political and social processes surrounding it.

The differences between Hamilton and Madison's approaches are reflected in basic tensions between Hamiltonian and Jeffersonian administrative theories. For a fascinating look at this question, see Caldwell (1988).

2. Readers interested in comparing other analyses of the state of administration can consult Chandler (1987), Perry (1989), Lynn and Wildavsky (1990), Stillman (1991), Rainey (1991), and Hill (1992a).

3. The first three of these historical periods match an analysis developed by Martin (1952).

4. Not everyone, however, credits Wilson with the influence usually ascribed to him. See Van Riper (1987). The best guide to this, and most other questions involving the literature of public administration, is Martin (1989).

5. They were, in addition to Goodnow, A. Lawrence Lowell, Woodrow Wilson, W.W. Willoughby, and Ernst Freund.

6. Members of the staff included: Joseph P. Harris, director; G. Lyle Belsley; A.E. Buck; Laverne Burchfield; Robert H. Connery; Robert E. Cushman; Paul T. David; William Y. Elliott; Herbert Emmerich; Merle Fainsod; James W. Fesler; Katherine Frederic; Patterson H. French; William J. Haggerty; James Hart; Arthur N. Holcombe; Arthur W. Macmahon; Harvey C. Mansfield; Charles McKinley; John F. Miller; John D. Millett; Floyd W. Reeves; Leo C. Rosten; Spencer Thompson; Mary C. Trackett; Schuyler C. Wallace; and Edwin E. Witte (see President's Committee on Administrative Management 1937, viii; and Fesler 1987).

7. For a useful catalog of the enduring administrative principles, see Hood and Jackson (1991).

8. In fact, there already was a small but important literature on implementation when Pressman and Wildavsky wrote their path-breaking book. See Bailey and Mosher (1968) and Murphy (1971).

9. I am indebted to Charles O. Jones for finding and sharing this nugget.

10. A notable exception to the top-down approach is Elmore (1982).

11. These figures were calculated by the author from the index in Ripley and Franklin (1986).

12. I am indebted to Steven Kelman for making this point.

13. A very useful history of the public bureaucracy movement is Hill (1992b).

Bibliography

Aberbach, Joel D., Robert D. Putnam, and Bert A. Rockman. 1981. *Bureaucrats and Politicians in Western Democracies*. Cambridge: Harvard University Press.

Allison, Graham T. 1969. "Conceptual Models and the Cuban Missile Crisis." *American Political Science Review* 63:689-718.

Allison, Graham T. 1971. *Essence of Decision: Explaining the Cuban Missile Crisis*. Boston: Little, Brown.

American Political Science Association, Committee for the Advancement of Teaching. 1951. *Goals for Political Science*. New York: William Sloane Associates.

Appleby, Paul H. 1945. *Big Democracy*. New York: Alfred A. Knopf.

Arrow, Kenneth J. 1985. "The Economics of Agency." In *Principals and Agents: The Structure of Business*, ed. John W. Pratt and Richard J. Zeckhauser. Boston: Harvard Business School Press.

Bailey, Stephen K., and Edith K. Mosher. 1968. *ESEA: The Office of Education Administers a Law*. Syracuse: Syracuse University Press.

Bardach, Eugene. 1977. *The Implementation Game: What Happens After a Bill Becomes a Law*. Cambridge: MIT Press.

Barzelay, Michael. 1991. "The Single Case Study as Intellectually Ambitious Inquiry." Paper prepared for delivery at the National Public Management Research Conference, Syracuse, NY.

Barzelay, Michael. 1993. *Breaking Through Bureaucracy: A New Vision for Managing in Government*. Berkeley: University of California Press.

Barzelay, Michael, and Linda Kaboolian. 1990. "Structural Metaphors and Public Management Education." *Journal of Policy Analysis and Management* 9:599-610.

Behn, Robert. 1988. "The Nature of Knowledge About Public Management: Lessons for Research and Teaching from Our Knowledge About Chess and Warfare." *Journal of Policy Analysis and Management* 7:200-12.

Bendor, Jonathan. 1988. "Review Article: Formal Models of Bureaucracy." *British Journal of Political Science* 18:353-95.

Bendor, Jonathan. 1990. "Formal Models of Bureaucracy: A Review." In *Public Administration: The State of the Discipline*, ed. Naomi B. Lynn and Aaron Wildavsky. Chatham, NJ: Chatham House.

Bendor, Jonathan, and Terry Moe. 1985. "An Adaptive Model of Bureaucratic Politics." *American Political Science Review* 79:755-74.

Berman, Paul. 1978. "The Study of Macro- and Micro-Implementation." *Public Policy* 26:157-84.

Blais, André, and Stéphane Dion, eds. 1991. *The Budget-Maximizing Bureaucrat: Appraisals and Evidence*. Pittsburgh: University of Pittsburgh Press.

Bozeman, Barry. 1987. *All Organizations Are Public: Bridging Public and Private Organization Theories*. San Francisco: Jossey-Bass Publishers.

Brownlow Committee (The President's Committee on Administrative Management). 1937. *Report of the President's Committee: Administrative Management in the Government of the United States*. Washington: Government Printing Office.

Bryson, John M. 1988. *Strategic Planning for Public and Nonprofit Organizations: A Guide to Strengthening and Sustaining Organizational Achievement*. San Francisco: Jossey-Bass.

Buchanan, James M., and Gordon Tullock. 1962. *The Calculus of Consent: Logical Foundations of Constitutional Democracy*. Ann Arbor: University of Michigan Press.

Burke, John P. 1986. *Bureaucratic Responsibility*. Baltimore: Johns Hopkins University Press.

Caldwell, Lynton K. 1965. "Public Administration and the Universities: A Half-Century of Development." *Public Administration Review* 25:52-60.

Caldwell, Lynton K. 1988. *The Administrative Theories of Hamilton and Jefferson: Their Contribution to Thought on Public Administration*, 2nd ed. New York: Holmes & Meier.

Chandler, Ralph Clark, ed. 1987. *A Centennial History of the American Administrative State*. New York: Free Press.

Chubb, John E., and Terry M. Moe. 1990. *Politics, Markets, and America's Schools*. Washington, DC: Brookings Institution.

Coase, R.H. 1937. "The Nature of the Firm." *Economica* 4:386-405.

Crozier, Michel. 1964. *The Bureaucratic Phenomenon*. Chicago: University of Chicago Press.

Dahl, Robert A. 1947. "The Science of Public Administration: Three Problems." *Public Administration Review* 7:1-11.

Derthick, Martha. 1972. *New Towns In-Town: Why A Federal Program Failed*. Washington: Urban Institute.

Derthick, Martha. 1990. *Agency Under Stress: The Social Security Administration in American Government*. Washington, DC: Brookings Institution.

Derthick, Martha, and Paul J. Quirk. 1985. *The Politics of Deregulation*. Washington: Brookings Institution.

DiIulio, John J., Jr. 1987. *Governing Prisons: A Comparative Study of Correctional Management*. New York: Free Press.

Doig, Jameson W. 1983. "'If I See a Murderous Fellow Sharpening a Knife Cleverly...': The Wilsonian Dichotomy and the Public Authority Tradition." *Public Administration Review* 43:292-304.

Donahue, John D. 1989. *The Privatization Decision: Public Ends, Private Means*. New York: Basic Books.

Downs, Anthony. 1967. *Inside Bureaucracy*. Boston: Little, Brown.

Elmore, Richard. 1978. "Organizational Models of Social Program Implementation." *Public Policy* 26:185-228.

Elmore, Richard. 1982. "Backward Mapping: Implementation Research and Policy Decisions." In *Studying Implementation: Methodological and Administrative Issues*, Walter Williams et al. Chatham, NJ: Chatham House.

Fesler, James W. 1975. "Public Administration and the Social Sciences: 1946 to 1960." In *American Public Administration: Past, Present, Future*, ed. Frederick C. Mosher. University: University of Alabama Press.

Fesler, James W. 1987. "The Brownlow Committee Fifty Years Later." *Public Administration Review*, 47:291-96.

Fesler, James W. 1990. "The State and its Study: The Whole and Its Parts." In *Public Administration: The State of the Discipline*, ed. Naomi B. Lynn and Aaron Wildavsky. Chatham, NJ: Chatham House Publishers.

Finer, Herman. 1941. "Administrative Responsibility in Democratic Government." *Public Administration Review* 1:335-50.

Fleishman, Joel L., Lance Liebman, and Mark H. Moore, eds. 1981. *Public Duties: The Moral Obligations of Government Officials*. Cambridge: Harvard University Press.

Friedrich, Carl J. 1940. "Public Policy and the Nature of Administrative Responsibility." In *Public Policy*, ed. Carl J. Friedrich and E. S. Mason. Cambridge: Harvard University Press.

Gaus, John. 1950. "Trends in the Theory of Public Administration." *Public Administration Review* 10:161-68.

Goggin, Malcom L., Ann O'M. Bowman, James P. Lester, and Laurence J. O'Toole, Jr. 1990. *Implementation Theory and Practice: Toward a Third Generation*. Glenview, IL.: Scott, Foresman/Little, Brown.

Goodnow, Frank J. 1900. *Politics and Administration: A Study in Government*. New York: Russell and Russell.

Goodnow, Frank J. 1905. "The Work of the American Political Science Association." *Proceedings of the American Political Science Association, 1904*. Lancaster, PA: Wickersham Press.

Goodsell, Charles T. 1985. *The Case for Bureaucracy: A Public Administration Polemic*, 2d ed. Chatham, NJ: Chatham House Publishers.

Gulick, Luther. 1937. "Notes on the Theory of Organization." In *Papers on the Science of Administration*, ed. Luther Gulick and L. Urwick. New York: Institute of Public Administration.

Halperin, Morton H. 1974. *Bureaucratic Politics and Foreign Policy*. Washington, DC: Brookings Institution.

Hanke, Steve H., ed. 1987. *Prospects for Privatization*. New York: Academy of Political Science.

Hargrove, Erwin C. 1975. *The Missing Link: The Study of the Implementation of Social Policy*. Washington, DC: Urban Institute.

Heady, Ferrel. 1979. *Public Administration: A Comparative Perspective*, 2d ed. New York: Marcel Dekker.

Heclo, Hugh. 1977. *A Government of Strangers: Executive Politics in Washington*. Washington, DC: Brookings Institution.

Heclo, Hugh. 1978. "Issue Networks and the Executive Establishment." In *The New American Political System*, ed. Anthony King. Washington, DC: American Enterprise Institute.

Henry, Nicholas. 1987. "The Emergence of Public Administration as a Field of Study." In *A Centennial History of the American Administrative State*, ed. Ralph Clark Chandler. New York: Free Press.

Heymann, Philip B. 1987. *The Politics of Public Management*. New Haven: Yale University Press.

Hill, Larry B., ed. 1992a. *The State of Public Bureaucracy*. Armonk, NY: M.E. Sharpe.

Hill, Larry B. 1992b. "Taking Bureaucracy Seriously." In *The State of Public Bureaucracy*, ed. Larry B. Hill. Armonk, NY: M.E. Sharpe.

Hogwood, Brian W., and B. Guy Peters. 1985. *The Pathology of Public Policy*. Oxford: Clarendon Press.

Holden, Matthew. 1991. *Continuity and Disruption: Essays in Public Administration*. Photocopy.

Hood, Christopher, and Michael Jackson. 1991. *Administrative Argument*. Aldershot, England: Dartmouth Publishing.

Ingram, Helen. 1990. "Implementation: A Review and Suggested Framework." In *Public Administration: The State of the Discipline*, ed., Naomi B. Lynn and Aaron Wildavsky. Chatham, NJ: Chatham House Publishers.

Ingram, Helen, and Dean E. Mann. 1980. "Policy Failure: An Issue Deserving Analysis." In *Why Policies Succeed or Fail*, ed. Helen Ingram and Dean E. Mann. Beverly Hills, CA: Sage.

Jones, Charles O. 1976. "Policy Analysis: Academic Utility for Practical Rhetoric." *Policy Studies Journal* 4:281-86.

Jones, Charles O. 1977. *An Introduction to the Study of Public Policy*, 2nd ed. Duxbury, MA: Duxbury.

Karl, Barry D. 1963. *Executive Reorganization and Reform in the New Deal: The Genesis of Administrative Management, 1900-1939*. Cambridge: Harvard University Press.

Kaufman, Herbert. 1960. *The Forest Ranger: A Study in Administrative Behavior*. Baltimore: Johns Hopkins University Press.

Kaufman, Herbert. 1990. "The End of an Alliance: Public Administration in the Eighties." In *Public Administration: The State of the Discipline*, ed. Naomi B. Lynn and Aaron Wildavsky. Chatham, NJ: Chatham House Publishers.

Kelman, Steven. 1990. *Procurement and Public Management: The Fear of Discretion and the Quality of Government Performance*. Washington, DC: American Enterprise Institute.

Kettl, Donald F. 1980. *Managing Community Development in the New Federalism*. New York: Praeger.

Kettl, Donald F. 1993. *Private Markets, Public Interests*. Washington, DC: Brookings Institution.

Knott, Jack H., and Gary J. Miller. 1987. *Reforming Bureaucracy: The Politics of Institutional Choice*. Englewood Cliffs, NJ: Prentice-Hall.

Landau, Martin. 1991. "On Multiorganizational Systems in Public Administration." *Journal of Public Administration Research and Theory* 1:5-18.

LaPorte, Todd R., and Paul M. Consolini. 1991. "Working in Practice but Not in Theory: Theoretical Challenges of 'High-Reliability Organizations.'" *Journal of Public Administration Research and Theory* 1:19-47.

Long, Norton. 1949. "Power and Administration." *Public Administration Review* 9:257-64.

Lowi, Theodore J. 1969. *The End of Liberalism*. New York: W.W. Norton.

Lowi, Theodore J. 1992. "The State of Political Science: How We Become What We Study." *American Political Science Review* 86:1-7.

Lynn, Laurence E., Jr. 1981. *Managing the Public's Business*. New York: Basic Books.

Lynn, Laurence E., Jr. 1987. *Managing Public Policy*. Boston: Little, Brown.

Lynn, Naomi B., and Aaron Wildavsky, eds. 1990. *Public Administration: The State of the Discipline*. Chatham, NJ: Chatham House Publishers.

March, James G., and Johan P. Olsen. 1984. "The New Institutionalism: Organizational Factors in Political Life." *American Political Science Review* 78:734-49.

March, James G., and Johan P. Olsen. 1989. *Rediscovering Institutions: The Organizational Basis of Politics*. New York: Free Press.

March, James G. and Herbert Simon. 1958. *Organizations*. New York: John Wiley.

Martin, Roscoe C. 1952. "Political Science and Public Administration: A Note on the State of the Union." *American Political Science Review* 46:660-76.

Martin, Daniel W. 1989. *The Guide to the Foundations of Public Administration*. New York: Marcel Dekker.

Mashaw, Jerry L. 1983. *Bureaucratic Justice: Managing Social Security Disability Claims*. New Haven: Yale University Press.

Mashaw, Jerry L. 1985. *Due Process in the Administrative State*. New Haven: Yale University Press.

Mayhew, David. 1974. *Congress: The Electoral Connection*. New Haven: Yale University Press.

Mazmanian, Daniel A., and Paul A. Sabatier. 1983. *Implementation and Public Policy*. Glenview, IL: Scott, Foresman.

Melnick, R. Shep. 1983. *Regulation and the Courts: The Case of the Clean Air Act*. Washington, DC: Brookings Institution.

Milward, H. Brinton, Keith G. Provan, and Barbara Else. 1993. "What Does the Hollow State Look Like?" In *Public Management Theory*, ed. Barry Bozeman. San Francisco: Jossey-Bass.

Moe, Ronald C. 1987. "Exploring the Limits of Privatization." *Public Administration Review* 47:453-60.

Moe, Terry M. 1982. "Regulatory Performance and Presidential Administration." *American Journal of Political Science* 26:197-224.

Moe, Terry M. 1984. "The New Economics of Organization." *American Journal of Political Science* 20:734-49.

Moe, Terry M. 1985a. "Control and Feedback in Economic Regulation: The Case of the NLRB." *American Political Science Review* 79:1094-1116.

Moe, Terry M. 1985b. "The Politicized Presidency." In *The New Direction in American Politics*, ed. John E. Chubb and Paul E. Peterson. Washington, DC: Brookings Institution.

Moe, Terry M. 1987. "An Assessment of the Positive Theory of 'Congressional Dominance.'" *Legislative Studies Quarterly* 12:475-520.

Moe, Terry M. 1989. "The Politics of Bureaucratic Structure." In *Can the Government Govern?*, ed. John E. Chubb and Paul E. Peterson. Washington, DC: Brookings Institution.

Moe, Terry M. 1991. "Politics and the Theory of Organization." *Journal of Law, Economics, and Organization*. 7:106-29.

Moore, Mark H., and Darrel W. Stephens. 1991. *Beyond Command and Control: The Strategic Management of Police Departments*. Washington, DC: Police Executive Research Forum.

Murphy, Jerome T. 1971. "Title I of ESEA: The Politics of Implementing Federal Educational Reform." *Harvard Educational Review* 41:35-63.

Neustadt, Richard E. 1960. *Presidential Power: The Politics of Leadership*. New York: John Wiley & Sons.

Neustadt, Richard E., and Harvey V. Fineberg. 1978. *The Swine Flu Affair: Decision-Making on a Slippery Disease*. Washington, DC: U.S. Department of Health, Education, and Welfare.

Niskanen, William A. 1971. *Bureaucracy and Representative Government*. Chicago: Aldine Publishers.

Nivola, Pietro S. 1991. "Interbranch and International Dimensions." *Public Administration Review* 51:199-201.

Osborne, David, and Ted Gaebler. 1992. *Reinventing Government: How the Entrepreneurial Spirit is Transforming the Public Sector*. Reading, MA: Addison-Wesley.

Ostrom, Vincent. 1973. *The Intellectual Crisis in American Public Administration*. University: University of Alabama Press.

O'Toole, Laurence J., Jr. 1986. "Policy Recommendations for Multi-Actor Implementation: An Assessment of the Field." *Journal of Public Policy* 6:181-210.

O'Toole, Laurence J., Jr. 1989a. "Goal Multiplicity in the Implementation Setting: Subtle Impacts and the Case of Wastewater Treatment Privatization." *Policy Studies Journal* 18:1-20.

O'Toole, Laurence J., Jr. 1989b. "Alternative Mechanisms for Multiorganizational Implementation: The Case of Wastewater Management." *Administration and Society* 21:313-39.

Perry, James L., ed. 1989. *Handbook of Public Administration*. San Francisco: Jossey-Bass Publishers.

Perrow, Charles. 1986a. *Complex Organizations: A Critical Essay*, 3rd ed. New York: Random House.

Perrow, Charles. 1986b. "Economic Theories of Organization." *Theory and Society* 15:11-45.

Peters, B. Guy. 1989. *The Politics of Bureaucracy*, 3d ed. New York: Longman.

Peters, B. Guy. 1992. "Comparative Perspectives on Bureaucracy in the Policy Process." In *The State of Public Bureaucracy*, ed. Larry B. Hill. Armonk, NY: M.E. Sharpe.

"Political Science as a Discipline." 1962. Statement by the Committee on Standards of Instruction of the American Political Science Association. *American Political Science Review* 56:417-21.

Powell, Walter W., and Paul J. DiMaggio, eds. 1991. *The New Institutionalism in Organizational Analysis*. Chicago: University of Chicago Press.

President's Committee on Administrative Management. 1937. *Report with Special Studies*. Washington, DC: Government Printing Office.

Pressman, Jeffrey L., and Aaron Wildavsky. 1973. *Implementation*. Berkeley: University of California Press.

Provan, Keith G., and H. Brinton Milward. 1991. "Institutional-Level Norms and Organizational Involvement in a Service-Implementation Network." *Journal of Public Administration Research and Theory* 1:391-417.

Pugh, Darrell L. 1988. *Looking Back -- Moving Forward*. Washington: American Society for Public Administration.

Rainey, Hal. 1983. "Public Agencies and Private Firms: Incentives, Goals, and Individual Roles." *Administration and Society* 15:207-42.

Rainey, Hal. 1991. *Understanding and Managing Public Organizations*. San Francisco: Jossey-Bass Publishers.

Rainey, Hal G., Robert W. Backoff, and Charles H. Levine. 1976. "Comparing Public and Private Organizations." *Public Administration Review* 36:233-46.

Riggs, Fred W. 1964. *Administration in Developing Countries -- The Theory of Prismatic Society*. Boston: Houghton Mifflin.

Riggs, Fred W. 1991. "Public Administration: A Comparativist Framework." *Public Administration Review* 51:473-77.

Ripley, Randall B., and Grace Franklin. 1986. *Policy Implementation and Bureaucracy*, 2nd ed. Chicago: Dorsey Press.

Rohr, John A. 1991. "Ethical Issues in French Public Administration: A Comparative Study." *Public Administration Review* 51:283-97.

Rohr, John A. 1992. "French Constitutionalism and the Administrative State: A Comparative Textual Study." *Administration and Society* 24:224-58.

Romer, Thomas, and Howard Rosenthal. 1978. "Political Resource Allocation, Controlled Agendas, and the Status Quo." *Public Choice* 33:27-43.

Romzek, Barbara, and Melvin J. Dubnick. 1987. "Accountability in the Public Sector: Lessons from the Challenger Tragedy," *Public Administration Review* 47:227-38.

Rosenbloom, David H. 1991. "From the Editor in Chief." *Public Administration Review* 51:191.

Rourke, Francis E. 1984. *Bureaucracy, Politics, and Public Policy*, 3rd ed. Boston: Little, Brown.

Rourke, Francis E. 1991. "American Bureaucracy in a Changing Political Setting." *Journal of Public Administration Research and Theory* 1:111-29.

Salamon, Lester M. 1981. "Rethinking Public Management: Third-Party Government and the Changing Forms of Government Action." *Public Policy* 29:255-75.

Savas, E.S. 1987. *Privatization: The Key to Better Government*. Chatham, NJ: Chatham House Publishers.

Schick, Allen. 1975. "The Trauma of Politics: Public Administration in the Sixties." In *American Public Administration: Past, Present, Future*, ed. Frederick C. Mosher. University: University of Alabama Press.

Scott, W. Richard. 1987. "The Adolescence of Institutional Theory." *Administrative Science Quarterly* 32:493-511.

Seidman, Harold, and Robert Gilmour. 1986. *Politics, Position, and Power: From the Positive to the Regulatory State*, 4th ed. New York: Oxford University Press.

Selznick, Philip. 1949. *TVA and the Grass Roots: A Study of Politics and Organization*. Berkeley: University of California Press.

Selznick, Philip. 1957. *Leadership and Administration: A Sociological Interpretation*. New York: Harper and Row.

Short, Lloyd Milton. 1923. *The Development of National Administrative Organization in the United States*. Baltimore: Johns Hopkins University Press.

Simon, Herbert. 1946. "The Proverbs of Administration." *Public Administration Review* 6:53-67.

Simon, Herbert. 1947. *Administrative Behavior*. New York: Macmillan.

Skowronek, Stephen. 1982. *Building A New American State: The Expansion of National Administrative Capacities, 1877-1920*. Cambridge: Cambridge University Press.

Smith, Bruce L.R. 1983. "Changing Public-Private Sector Relations: A Look at the United States." *Annals of the American Academy of Political and Social Sciences* 466:149-64.

Stein, Harold. 1952. *Public Administration and Policy Development: A Case Book*. New York: Harcourt, Brace.

Steinbruner, John D. 1974. *The Cybernetic Theory of Decision: New Dimensions of Political Analysis*. Princeton: Princeton University Press.

Stillman, Richard J., II. 1991. *Preface to Public Administration: A Search for Themes and Direction*. New York: St. Martin's Press.

Storing, Herbert J. 1965. "Leonard D. White and the Study of Administration." *Public Administration Review* 25:38-51.

Taylor, Frederick W. 1911. *Principles of Scientific Management*. New York: Harper and Brothers.

Thompson, James D. 1967. *Organizations in Action: Social Bases of Administrative Theory*. New York: McGraw-Hill.

Tullock, Gordon. 1965. *The Politics of Bureaucracy*. Washington: Public Affairs Press.

Van Horn, Carl E. 1979. *Policy Implementation in the Federal System: National Goals and Local Implementors*. Lexington, MA: Lexington Books.

Van Riper, Paul P. 1987. "The American Administrative State: Wilson and the Founders." In *A Centennial History of the American Administrative State*, ed. Ralph Clark Chandler. New York: Free Press.

Waldo, Dwight. 1984. *The Administrative State: A Study of the Political Theory of American Public Administration*, 2nd ed. New York: Holmes and Meier.

Waldo, Dwight. 1990. "A Theory of Public Administration Means in Our Time a Theory of Politics Also." In *Public Administration: The State of the Discipline*, ed. Naomi B. Lynn and Aaron Wildavsky. Chatham, NJ: Chatham House Publishers.

Wamsley, Gary L., and Mayer N. Zald. 1973. *The Political Economy of Organizations: A Critique and Approach to the Study of Public Administration*. Lexington, MA: Lexington Books.

Weimer, David L., and Aidan R. Vining. 1992. *Policy Analysis: Concepts and Practice*, 2nd ed. Englewood Cliffs, NJ: Prentice-Hall.

Weingast, Barry R., and Mark J. Moran. 1983. "Bureaucracy Discretionary Congressional Control? Regulatory Policymaking by the Federal Trade Commission." *Journal of Political Economy* 91:765-800.

White, Harrison C. 1985. "Agency as Control." In *Principals and Agents: The Structure of Business*, ed. John W. Pratt and Richard J. Zeckhauser. Boston: Harvard Business School Press.

White, Leonard D. 1926. *Introduction to the Study of Public Administration*. New York: Macmillan.

White, Leonard D. 1948. *The Federalists*. New York: Macmillan.

White, Leonard D. 1951. *The Jeffersonians: A Study in Administrative History, 1801-1829*. New York: Macmillan.

White, Leonard D. 1954. *The Jacksonians: A Study in Administrative History, 1829-1861*. New York: Macmillan.

White, Leonard D. 1958. *The Republican Era: A Study in Administrative History, 1869-1901*. New York: Macmillan.

White, Orion F., Jr., and Cynthia J. McSwain. 1990. "The Phoenix Project: Raising a New Image of Public Administration from the Ashes of the Past." *Administration and Society* 22:3-38.

Williamson, Oliver E. 1975. *Markets and Hierarchies: Analysis and Antitrust Implications*. New York: Free Press.

Wilson, James Q. 1967. "The Bureaucracy Problem." *The Public Interest* 6:3-9.

Wilson, James Q. 1973. *Political Organizations*. New York: Basic Books.

Wilson, James Q. 1978. *The Investigators: Managing the FBI and Narcotics Agents*. New York: Basic Books.

Wilson, James Q. 1989. *Bureaucracy*. New York: Basic Books.

Wilson, Woodrow. 1887. "The Study of Administration." *Political Science Quarterly* 2:197-222.

Wood, B. Dan, and Richard W. Waterman. 1991. "The Dynamics of
        Political Control of the Bureaucracy." *American Political
        Science Review* 85:801-28.

Nations and Their Relationships

17

Comparative Politics

Ronald Rogowski

Comparative politics in the 1980s was characterized chiefly by five interrelated trends.[1] In approximate order of importance, these were:

(1) A far greater attention to the economic aspects of politics, including the ways in which governmental policy affects economic growth or decline (Bates 1981; Zysman 1983; Olson 1982; North 1981; Katzenstein 1985),[2] the structural constraints on econ- omic policy (Hall 1986), and the effects of economic hardship on political cleavages and coalitions (Gourevitch 1986).

(2) Increased interest in the international context of domestic politics and institutions, encompassing new explanations, not only in the perhaps obvious domain of trade policy (e.g., Milner 1988), but in governmental growth (Cameron 1978), social revolutions (Skocpol 1979), political cleavages (Gourevitch 1986; Rogowski 1989; Frieden 1991a), and forms and styles of governance (Katzenstein 1985).[3]

(3) An altered and sharpened focus on interest groups, particularly in the context of various kinds of corporatism (Berger 1981; Schmitter 1981; Olson 1982; Katzenstein 1985).

(4) A revival of interest in state structures and their performance (Evans et al. 1985; Powell 1982; Lijphart 1990), treated perhaps most intriguingly as a trade-off between "markets" and "hierarchy" (Williamson 1975, 1985). For obvious reasons, this line of work has assumed new importance with the collapse of the centrally planned economies.

(5) Further work on nationalism and ethnic cleavages (Laitin 1986; Horowitz 1985).

I shall focus on each of these topics in turn, endeavoring at the end to draw the strands together and to speculate about the directions of future work.

Economics and Politics: The "New Political Economy"

The oil price shock of 1973 threw into doubt the comfortable postwar assumption that, at least in the industrialized West, ever-increasing prosperity would bring an "end of ideology" and convergence on a single liberal model of governance. The ensuing deep recession evoked widely varying governmental responses and highlighted longer-term differences in economic performance. Among the economically advanced nations, the continuing Japanese "miracle" and the quite respectable growth of the continental European economies contrasted sharply with the dismal record of the U.S. and U.K. and the increasingly evident catastrophe of the Soviet Union and Eastern Europe.[4] For the market economies, the simple statistics of average annual growth in real GDP per capita, both for the whole interval 1960 to 1980 and for the years after the oil price shock, spoke volumes (OECD 1982):

Average Annual Growth in Real GDP Per Capita (%)

	1960-80	1973-80
Japan	6.5	2.7
France	3.8	2.4
Italy	3.7	2.2
Germany	3.2	2.4
U.S.	2.3	1.3
U.K.	2.0	0.9

While official statistics for the USSR, based as they were on "Net Material Product," non-market prices, and propagandistic exaggeration, were not comparable, even they showed an annual total (not per capita) growth rate for the early 1980s of only about 3% (International Monetary Fund 1991, 3); and, by some informed estimates, real per capita Soviet output in this period grew by less than 0.5% annually[5] -- despite the great benefits that the USSR, as a major exporter of petroleum, drew from the post-1973 price increases.

Among the less developed economies, the differences were even more stark. Africa had experienced declining growth of per capita output since 1960 and, after 1980, actual reductions;[6] much of the remaining Third World had stagnated economically;[7] but a few dramatic exceptions -- principally Taiwan, South

Korea, Hong Kong, and Singapore -- had grown so rapidly as to have defined a new category of "newly industrialized countries," or NICs (Haggard 1990).[8]

These disparities in economic growth had obvious implications for national prestige and power and for the survival of individual leaders. Research on voting increasingly generalized to the other Western democracies the U.S. finding that national election outcomes hinged on economic performance;[9] and prolonged failure in the economic realm destabilized governments of every stripe. Understandably, comparativists began to focus on such questions as: What explained the successes? What tensions and cleavages were unleashed by failure? How, and in what circumstances, had previously damaged economies managed to turn themselves around?

Governmental Policy

In a first subcategory of work, such scholars as Robert Bates, Peter Katzenstein, John Zysman, and Douglass North emphasized the ways in which governmental policy affected economic growth. Bates's (1981) pathbreaking work on what, to the ill-informed, would have seemed a soporific topic, namely post-independence African agricultural policy, demonstrated conclusively, if sometimes obliquely (a) that the African economic disaster was self-inflicted and (b) that, in general, policies either of Soviet-style rapid industrialization at the expense of the countryside or of more moderate import-substituting industrialization (ISI) were doomed.[10] With but two significant exceptions (Côte d'Ivoire and Kenya), the independent governments of land-rich Africa had ruthlessly taxed domestic farmers to gain the investment capital that would supposedly permit rapid industrialization; and they had attempted to stimulate industrial growth through tariffs, quotas, and an overvalued currency. Instead, these policies had yielded -- in ways that Bates showed to have been absolutely predictable from the most rudimentary economics -- black markets, smuggling, declines in agricultural production, flight from the land, monopolistic and uncompetitive industries, massive corruption, and an increasing reliance on imported foodstuffs.

An early side effect of Bates's crucial book was near-total abandonment of two important streams of previous theorizing about development, namely (a) culturalism and (b) the "dependency" and "world-systems" analyses. On the one hand Lipset (1963, chap. 3), McClelland (1961), and others working in the Parsonian tradition had sought to link long-term economic performance to cultures that valued, and role-structures that rewarded, individual achievement. Against the weight of tradition, they contended, governmental policy could achieve little. On the other hand, Cardoso and Faletto (1979), Gunder Frank (1967), I. Wallerstein (1974), and others had asserted in essence that the causes of particular regions' chronic underdevelopment lay outside themselves: under capitalist exchange, "core" economies could prosper only to the extent that "peripheral" ones yielded up primary goods at starvation wages; the "dependence" of the latter was thus "structural" and could be alleviated only by rapid autarkical industrialization or (as Wallerstein argued most strongly) by a socialist world revolution. Against the culturalists, Bates seemed to show that policy mattered enormously and was not simply an artifact of culture.[11] Against the dependency theorists, he demonstrated the utter folly of most efforts at autarkical industrialization.[12]

To James Buchanan (1980), Mancur Olson, Jr. (1982), and other comparative economists, what Bates described was but one manifestation of a far more general phenomenon first identified by Anne O. Krueger (1974), namely governmental policies that awarded (and thus encouraged the pursuit of) what economists call *rents*.[13] Olson was particularly forceful in contrasting such *redistributive* policies (which sought merely to reallocate slices of a fixed "pie") with *productive* ones (which sought to enlarge it).

The award of rents via discretionary government control of scarce resources, according to these analysts, reduces social output in at least two ways. Most obviously, by distorting incentives it redirects some factors into less productive uses. Krueger argued, however, that the *pursuit* of rents might harm society more: if government can grant rents, private actors will expend resources trying to influence government -- again, to the neglect of actual production. From this standpoint, a mercurial and discretionary government is especially deleterious.[14]

Failure, however, proved easier to explain than success, particularly in the advanced industrial societies.[15] Olson attributed virtually all variation in economic performance, in the poorer and the richer countries alike, to the relative prevalence of rent-seeking (Olson 1982, esp. 175-177), but others were less certain. Were the successful advanced economies, in Asia or in Europe, in fact characterized by less governmental intervention and lobbying?

In a highly influential essay at the end of the 1970s, Peter Katzenstein (1978) had looked closely at the quite different ways in which the major industrial states had responded to the oil crises of 1973. Britain and the U.S., in this instance as in others, had relied chiefly on "voluntarist" agreements and on monetary and fiscal policy; Japan had invoked a much broader array of policy instruments, including detailed administrative regulation and allocation of capital; the continental European states had assumed an intermediate position, with France closer to the Japanese model, Germany and Italy closer to the Anglo-American one. It might have been asserted (although Katzenstein did not do so) that the more interventionist policies had enjoyed greater success.[16]

John Zysman (1983), working in part with Laura Tyson (Zysman and Tyson 1983), offered a partial and controversial answer. He contended that the traditional economics of trade (including particularly the Heckscher-Ohlin Theorem) erred in assuming that technology was universally available and that comparative advantage resulted purely from exogenously given factor endowments. Rather, Zysman asserted, technological advantage and imperfect markets could endure, and comparative advantage could be "created":

> in advanced industrial economies, comparative advantage...[must] be understood as the cumulative effect of firm capacities and government policy choices and not simply as the effect of resource endowments....(Zysman 1983, 40).

In particular, learning-by-doing, together with economies of scale and scope, implied that favorable governmental policies -- guarantees of stable home demand, provision of human and physical infrastructure, simultaneous encouragement of sectors with shared economies of scope (e.g., industries characterized by "high-volume standardized production") -- could impart lasting competitive advantage and consistently more rapid economic growth. While Zysman readily conceded that such efforts could be perverted into rent-seeking, notably by support of failing industries rather than of genuine "national champions," he insisted that government had a productive, indeed probably an indispensable, role in economic success.

Douglass North (1981) adopted the most general, if in some ways also the most elusive, perspective. Government, he insisted, did not merely award rents or stimulate production. Essentially, its various policies defined and enforced *property rights*, in the sense advanced earlier and less comprehensively by Coase (1960) and by Alchian and Demsetz (1973). The simple analysis of rent-seeking had failed to note that government was prior to, and conditioned, the market. By specifying rights to use, to exclude, to inherit, and to sell, rulers determined who brought what to market. By imposing suboptimal property rights, or by leaving ownership insecure, governments inhibited savings and growth; by approaching more closely to optimal property rights, they increased output.

More originally and provocatively, North asserted that a society's particular endowments of land, labor, and capital determined a uniquely best set of property rights.[17] Hence a "best" set of policies for Japan might differ radically from the "best" for the U.S., Belgium, or a less developed country. One particularly intriguing implication was that societies would inevitably "outgrow" their property rights as they accumulated capital or people; those that failed to adapt would decline.

Katzenstein's (1985) pathbreaking work on the smaller European democracies was in the spirit of North's theory but moved beyond it in significant ways. States such as Austria, Belgium, and Sweden, he observed, had discovered in policies of economic openness, "flexible adjustment," and democratic corporatism (defined roughly as a property right of each major interest to influence economic policy) the secret of economic success *for their particular situation* of extreme trade-dependence.[18] At the same time, however, their situation was becoming general: rapidly increasing international trade (discussed more fully below) meant that even large countries would have to forgo protectionism and to adapt quickly to changing external markets, exactly as the trade-dependent smaller advanced economies had done long before. "The large states," as Katzenstein put it laconically, "are shrinking." Not Japan's much-vaunted *dirigisme* but the small states' "reactive and flexible policy of industrial adjustment" seemed to him the wave of the future (1985, 21, 27).

Social Sources of Policy

If policy and property rights mattered, so, plainly, did the question of how they were shaped; and work on this issue constituted a second major subcategory in political economy. All students agreed, perhaps none so emphatically as North,[19] that here no system of "natural selection" guaranteed that the fittest would quickly prevail: grossly suboptimal policies and property rights -- in Spain from the seventeenth century, in Britain from the late nineteenth century, in the Communist societies throughout their existence, in post-colonial Africa -- had often continued, with attendant economic decline, for decades if not centuries. How was such evident folly to be explained, particularly in a world characterized (at least in the Realist tradition in international relations) by mortal interstate competition? One class of answers, to be addressed in a subsequent section, emphasizes characteristics of *states*; those to be discussed here focus on aspects of *civil society*.

Bates invoked Mancur Olson's (1965) early work on collective action: agriculture was victimized in most African societies chiefly because farmers were numerous, poor, and ill-organized; where a coterie of wealthy farmers could provide leadership, as in Kenya, policy was very different (Bates 1981, chap. 5, 126-127).[20] Even within countries, large-scale farmers were taxed less onerously.

For Katzenstein (1985, chap. 4), countries' options in economic policy were constrained by their history, indeed almost by their culture. Europe's smaller countries were small because they had lacked the strong feudal aristocracy that made for territorial expansion in the early modern period; they had been dominated by urban mercantile elites. This history had endowed them with a weak political Right, a more self-confident and moderate bourgeoisie, less zeal about the imposition of religious and linguistic uniformity, and less intense class conflict. Those features, in turn, had nurtured patterns of cross-group and cross-class cooperation, norms of proportionality (including early adoption of proportional representation in parliamentary elections), and an ethos of social partnership and "low-voltage" politics. All of this had permitted, perhaps uniquely, the policy procedures and outcomes that by the 1980s characterized these societies.

At the same time, the deviant case of modern Austria suggested how a country might adapt from a much less favorable starting-point (1985, 186-189).[21] As ruler of the Austro-Hungarian Empire, Austria had been a large state with a strong landed aristocracy, weak urban elites, a powerful Right, and intense class conflict. Civil war, annexation by Hitler, and military defeat and occupation had followed. Influenced profoundly by those disastrous experiences, it emerged after 1945 as

> perhaps the most typically "consociational" regime in Europe...exhibit[ing] with particular clarity the coincidence of deep social cleavages and intense elite collaboration (1985, 188).

Its policy making, in short, had come to resemble that of the Netherlands or of Scandinavia. Perhaps evolution was Darwinian (or even Lamarckian) after all, but with an uncomfortably long lag.

John Zysman (1983, chap. 2) saw policy as more constrained, but by economic rather than political history: more specifically, by the financial markets that a country's particular industrial revolution had bequeathed it. As Gerschenkron (1962, chap. 1) had first observed, early developers such as Britain and the U.S. had developed "thick" markets in private credit (stock and bond exchanges) and, consequently, a merchant banking system that provided only short-term credit. Late developers -- notably France, Germany, Italy, and Japan (Gerschenkron had added: pre-revolutionary Russia) -- had required a massive and simultaneous "push" of investment in a situation of initially "thin" credit markets; hence, their entrepreneurs had relied extensively on

industrial or universal banks that extended long-term loans and often took equity positions in specific firms. Frequently the state was also involved, directly or indirectly, in the mobilization and allocation of investment capital.

Out of this gestation, Zysman argued, three kinds of financial markets were born, based respectively on: (1) private exchange in equity and debt (the U.K. and U.S.); (2) bank-dominated lending (Germany; others would add Italy); (3) state-dominated allocation of credit (France, Japan). Only in the last situation was state-orchestrated adjustment politically easy or likely. Where banks held sway, tripartite negotiations among capital, labor, and government were the likely instrument of change. Among the early developers, where capital continued to be allocated privately, all efforts at large-scale restructuring, and particularly attempts at state intervention, were likely to provoke insurmountable political conflict.

Peter Hall's (1986) richly detailed study of recent economic policy making in Britain and France argued with equal force, despite some theoretical confusion,[22] that policy was powerfully constrained by social structure and tradition. Not only financial but labor markets tended to remain broadly fixed over generations, to affect economic growth, and to limit policy options.[23] Britain's long economic decline, Hall agreed, was to be blamed chiefly on its inherited financial structure of merchant rather than industrial banks and the consequent absence of leverage to restructure outmoded industry at critical junctures (pp. 38-40). But in labor markets, too, early industrialization had left its mark in the form of a skilled work force, powerful craft unions, and deep resistance to labor-saving innovations; together, these factors encouraged employers to adhere to tradition and avoid new investment (pp. 44-45). Even the radically reforming government of Margaret Thatcher, at least by 1986 when Hall wrote, had been able to achieve surprisingly little with respect to these underlying factors (chap. 5, esp. 132-133).[24]

North and Olson offered far more sweeping perspectives. For North, suboptimal policies and property rights were normally a consequence of either (a) private-sector monopoly power (e.g., a militarily indispensable aristocracy wins exclusive rights to own certain lands) or (b) high costs of monitoring or enforcement (e.g., a grant of monopoly is more cheaply administered than a tax). For purposes of current research, these categories seemed too general: it was hard to see, for example, how they could explain the differences between British and French, or Japanese and U.S., economic policy or performance.

Olson's theory, although it was widely challenged and frequently rejected,[25] was richer and clearer in its empirical implications. As I discuss in greater detail below, it attributed destructive economic policies to the proliferation of a particular kind of pressure group, namely the "distributional," or rent-seeking, coalition, and asserted that such coalitions ordinarily pervaded a society more the longer it remained free and independent. Japan, France, Italy, and Germany grew more rapidly because, having been occupied, subjected to totalitarian rule, and (except for Japan) integrated into a larger unit (the European Community), they had been "cleansed" of powerful distributional coalitions; Britain, the U.S., New Zealand, and Australia grew slowly precisely because, having avoided those tribulations, they experienced more intense rent-seeking.

Recent events offer fertile new ground for inquiry. In the Soviet systems, policy and property rights were plainly suboptimal, indeed ultimately suicidal; repeated serious attempts at reform failed;[26] and efforts to reform policy making (e.g., through democratization) brought down the entire edifice. As stubbornly as in the post-1945 British economy or at General Motors or IBM today, manifestly self-destructive policies resisted all efforts to reverse them. In many Third World countries, however, policy (and, usually, institutions) has changed over the last decade away from what Bates described toward something markedly more favorable to economic growth (Clark 1992, A14).

Economic Death and Political Transfiguration

A third line of work in political economy, associated chiefly with the name of Peter Gourevitch (1986), investigated the political consequences of economic failure. Comparing coalitions and policy choices in five countries (France, Germany, Sweden, the U.K., and the U.S.) in response to three major economic downturns (1873-96, 1929-49, and 1971-present), Gourevitch contended that the policies advocated in each case could be comprehended in five broad categories: (a) classical liberalism (laissez-faire); (b) socialization and planning; (c) protectionism; (d) Keynesian demand stimulus; and (e) sector-specific intervention, more recently called "industrial policy" (chap. 2).

Such a perspective offered radical simplification and startling comparison. Despite the striking differences in political base, ideology, and method, for example, the U.S. New Deal, Swedish Socialism, and German National Socialism all endorsed policies of demand stimulus (pp. 128-129). Moreover, it proved possible to specify the enduring preferences, or at least the aversions, of major social groups with respect to these options: agriculture and labor had rejected laissez-faire in virtually every crisis; business had similarly spurned socialization. Domestically oriented producers in business, agriculture, and sometimes labor were sympathetic to protection (but often also to demand

stimulus); those who depended on international markets sought non-protectionist remedies (and worried that demand stimulus, by raising wages, might make their products uncompetitive). Actual policy choice was linked to the particular coalition of interests that formed in support of the given option. With respect to demand stimulus in the 1930s, for example, the coalition of urban masses and agriculture, with support from some elements of business, proved crucial.

Gourevitch concluded early in his analysis, however, that one could not simply predict policy from preferences. Indeed, typically in such a crisis, and demonstrably in the 1930s,

> policy preferences...evolved rapidly ....
> Ideological commitments toward the
> "proper" role of government disintegrated,
> and so did political commitments of long
> standing (p. 159).

To understand a specific outcome required a knowledge not only of "production profile" and pre-existing associational structure, but of state structure, economic ideology, political leadership, and international system. What resulted was, as Gourevitch conceded in his conclusion,

> not...a "scientific" testing of alternative
> explanations...[but] a historical sociology of
> the trajectories of national responses to
> external changes (p. 221).

Nonetheless, a clear finding of the study was the lasting impact of the specific choices that had been made in each crisis. The protectionist "deals" of the nineteenth century solidified existing regimes in France, Germany, Sweden, and the United States; the success of demand stimulus in the 1930s in Sweden and the U.S., coupled with memories of the preceding misery, gave the Left in both countries a long-term lease on power. In his concluding focus on the post-1971 crisis and its resultant worldwide wave of "neo-liberalism," Gourevitch suggested that policy choices were again underway whose consequences would extend over decades.

The International Context

Increasingly in the 1980s, students of comparative politics began to grasp how profoundly domestic conflicts and institutions were shaped by states' international surroundings: by what Gourevitch, in a 1978 essay that may fairly be said to have re-opened this whole direction of inquiry, had called simply the influences of "war and trade" (Gourevitch 1978, 883).[27]

War

In an important historical study that appeared in the previous decade, Perry Anderson (1974) had shown how even the European absolutist states of the seventeenth and eighteenth centuries had been shaped -- partially in the West European cases, predominantly in those of Eastern Europe and Russia -- by the necessities of military competition and survival. The logic was simple: given the military and extractive technology of the age, only absolutist governments could field the armies that survival required. Those states whose rulers imposed absolutist rule (e.g., Austria, Prussia, Russia, Sweden) survived; those where such efforts failed (e.g., Poland), unless they were sheltered by natural defenses (e.g., England), disappeared from the map of Europe.

Douglass North (1981, 30, 135-139) reminded his readers that changes in military technology had often altered both states' optimal geographic extent and their modes of internal governance: the rise of ancient Greek democracy and, subsequently, of the great empires of Macedonia and Rome, was linked to the use of the phalanx in combat; the rise of feudalism and the parcellization of sovereignty, to the predominance of armored knights; the dilution of feudal power and the return of larger states, to the emergence of the pike, the longbow, and gunpowder.

Even the great social revolutions of the modern era in France, Russia, and China, Theda Skocpol (1979) contended in a sweeping comparative study, had all been precipitated by an external cause, namely, the failure of the existing state in its most fundamental task of defense. Defeat or Pyrrhic victory in major external wars had led in each case both to domestic recrimination and to a fatal weakening of internal mechanisms of control.

Trade

In the 1980s as in the previous decade (see Migdal 1983, 324), work on the international-domestic tie centered more on trade than on war. Trade connects directly to the issues of growth and crisis discussed earlier, because trade and consequent specialization are among the most powerful engines of growth; and many of history's most painful economic downturns, from that of declining Rome to the Depression of the 1930s, were compounded (we now believe) by a collapse of interregional trade. Moreover, as Richard Rosecrance (1986) has argued, trading prowess may by now have replaced martial virtue as the principal bestower of influence in international relations.[28] At the same time, openness to trade evidently exposed a country to more severe economic buffeting from an unpredictable international economy.

The years since 1948 have been marked by an accelerating growth of international trade, and of individual economies' dependence on such trade, that by now eclipses all analogous episodes in recorded history.[29] On average over that period, the volume of world trade has doubled about every eleven years, growing 1.4 times as rapidly as output. In the average (industrialized) member state of the Organization for Economic Co-operation and Development (OECD), trade rose from 24.4% of GDP in 1960 to 36.8% in 1989 (OECD 1991, 71-72, Tables 6.12 and 6.13; population-weighted means). From various perspectives, analysts of comparative politics have sought to determine the consequences of this expansion.

David Cameron (1978) established a close connection among the OECD states between trade-dependence and expansion of the public sector: state revenues as a share of GDP grew in direct proportion to the share of GDP that was initially devoted to international trade.[30] Presumably the explanatory link was the political need for government to cushion its subjects against international economic shocks. Katzenstein's work buttressed this presumption: the highly trade-dependent small European democracies were indeed characterized by generous public benefits intended to meet, and to hasten adjustment to, the dislocations of ever-changing international markets.[31]

Others sought to link trade-dependence to particular forms of governance and political contestation. By the 1980s, Geoffrey Ingham's (1974, 42) finding, that both labor and business tended to organize more thoroughly and more centrally in those industrial economies that depended heavily on exports, was widely accepted.[32] Katzenstein noted, further, that the smaller and more trade-dependent European democracies had better-organized political parties and closer ties between parties and interest groups (1985, 90). Douglas Hibbs established that, since 1945, strikes had declined far more in the small, open European economies than in the larger and more self-sufficient ones, presumably because conflict in the former cases had more self-evidently disastrous consequences (Hibbs 1978, 162; cited in Katzenstein 1985, 88). Several scholars attempted to establish a linkage between trade-dependence and democratic corporatist governance (see below).

Stein Rokkan had called attention to the fact that the smaller democracies had adopted proportional representation (PR) earlier, with less conflict, and in the end with fewer exceptions, than their bigger fellows (1970, 76, 80, 89; cited in Katzenstein 1985, 100, 151). Katzenstein and I suggested, from slightly different directions, a specific symbiosis between PR and reliance on external trade: PR diminished conflict, made policy more predictable and thus investment more secure, and (to the extent that it employed large constituencies) dissipated regional pressure for protection (Katzenstein 1985, 100-101, 150-156; Rogowski 1987). Empirically, the correlation between trade and PR seemed stronger than that between geographical smallness and PR; and one could venture the prediction that, as even large states' reliance on trade increased, PR would spread (Rogowski 1987).[33]

A third line of work sought to link changes in international trade with the country-specific systems of what Rokkan and others had called "cleavage and coalition," i.e., the lines of politically relevant division and alliance. That fluctuations in international trade help some groups and harm others is self-evident; so, presumably, is the tendency of the victims to demand, and of the beneficiaries to oppose, policies that offset those changes of fortune. An example familiar at least since Charles Kindleberger's seminal essay of 1951 is the flood of American wheat onto European markets in the 1870s after the extension to the Great Plains of the U.S. and Canadian railway systems and the introduction of cheaper ocean shipment through iron steamships. Grain farmers throughout Europe demanded tariff protection.[34] European workers, as represented in trade unions and parties of the Left, agitated against what they regarded as a food tax.[35] In places as diverse as Germany, France, Italy, and Sweden, the farmers (usually in coalition with protectionist industrial interests) prevailed, and tariffs were imposed; in Britain, Belgium, Denmark, and the Netherlands, trade in grain remained substantially free.

Less obvious, but evident on even cursory reflection, are the longer-term effects on wealth, power, and regime of such market shifts and political responses. To take a much-studied contrast from that same period: in Britain, rents and land prices fell precipitously to reflect decreased returns; in Germany, land prices remained high. In Britain, there ensued what Kindleberger (1951) called "the liquidation of agriculture as the most powerful economic group"; in Germany, the landed *Junker* continued their ancient domination. Finally, as Alexander Gerschenkron (1943) argued, tariffs even nurtured German opposition to democracy. Urban consumers, representing a constantly growing share of the populace, wanted free trade but lacked political power. Democratization, it became clear, would mean an end to tariffs. Yet Germany's traditional elites had come to depend so heavily on protection that any liberalization of trade would have meant their ruin. Out of purest self-preservation, they therefore grew increasingly anti-democratic -- exactly at the same time as British elites, having moved into non-agricultural investments, were accepting democratic rule.

The lesson seems clear: changes in international markets precipitate domestic conflicts that may reach far beyond the direct arena of trade policy. What proves extraordinarily difficult is to develop a convincing general theory that can explain and predict the preferences that shape, and the alliances that settle, those conflicts.

For the nineteenth century, for example, there is general agreement that divisions over trade policy followed principally *factoral* lines:[36] owners of land, labor, or capital generally held the same preferences in a given country irrespective of their particular line of activity, so that (for example) German farmers and industrialists eventually embraced protectionism almost regardless of their specific products or investments. By about 1900, that solidarity had begun to fray: while heavy industry sought tariff protection in almost every country, light, consumer-oriented industries -- chemicals, electrical equipment, home appliances -- joined workers in support of free trade. Within industry, in other words, *sectoral* divisions began to appear.

By the 1970s, Stephen Magee (1978) has suggested from U.S. evidence, sectoral divisions had begun to dominate within labor as well: workers in import-threatened industries (steel, automobiles) supported protection, while ones in export-oriented branches (computers, pharmaceuticals) endorsed free trade. Working from broader comparative data, Charles Lipson (1983, 244 and 259) contends that protectionist demands in the industrial countries have been "highly product-specific," limited to "labor-intensive" sectors that are wage-sensitive, produce-standardized, price-competitive goods, use relatively standard technologies, and are under the direction of national firms. At the other extreme, producers of differentiated goods with high research and development, relatively short product lives, and often increasing returns to scale have powerfully supported freer trade. Helen Milner (1988), looking closely at particular sectors in France and the U.S. during two critical periods of controversy, has concluded that trade preferences must often be disaggregated to the level of the firm.

In light of these contradictory data, Peter Gourevitch and Jeffry Frieden have argued for a general analytic primacy of *sectors*; I have contended that, in general, we do better to focus on *factors* (Gourevitch 1986, 55; Frieden 1991a, 29-35; Rogowski 1989, 18-19). Economic theories of international trade make clear, however, that the argument is essentially over "specificity," or fixedness, of assets. To the extent that factors of production (including human and physical capital) can be moved easily from one employment to another, the Stolper-Samuelson Theorem (1941) applies: locally abundant factors will generally benefit, and locally scarce ones will be harmed, by an expansion of trade. Land was abundant in North America in the nineteenth century and scarce in Europe; labor was abundant in Europe and scarce in North America. Nothing could be more natural than that farmers were free-trading in America and protectionist in Europe; or that workers were free-trading in Europe and protectionist in America.

To the extent, however, that factors are "trapped" in specific applications -- a worker is trained only for automobile production, a plant is suited exclusively for the output of shoes, a plot of land can grow nothing but rye -- then trade that threatens *that investment*, even if good for the factor as a whole, will arouse at least short-term demands for protection in the affected sectors.[37] The U.S., for example, is abundant in capital; hence industrial owners will in general support free trade. Automobile manufacturers, however, have *specific* capital: plants that cannot readily be adapted to other uses, and that Japanese and Korean competition is rapidly making worthless. Hence we are not surprised to learn that firms in this sector demand protection against imports.

The degree to which assets are in fact specific, and whether their specificity changes over time, remains an important, but essentially empirical, research question.

Finally, one must ask whether the growing internationalization of the economy has directly constrained policy. As virtually every account of the early Mitterand government has emphasized (e.g., Hall 1986, chap. 8; Gourevitch 1986, 185-190; Moravcsik 1991, 29-30 and sources there cited), its phase of socialist experimentation -- extensive nationalization, "redistributive Keynesianism," and aggressive expansion of employment -- had to be abandoned chiefly because the international economic ramifications, in a far more trade-dependent economy, could not be borne. A chastened Prime Minister Mauroy declared after two years of socialist rule: "Quite simply, a real left-wing policy can be applied in France only if the other European countries also follow policies of the Left." (*L'Express*, 8 April 1983; quoted in Hall 1986, 201).

Gourevitch has broadened this lesson to assert that growing interdependence pushes all governments toward a revival of classical liberalism and reliance on the market. Citing a "shift rightward" that "no observer would have thought possible in the 1970s," and noting that "governments of quite different partisan colorations have adopted similar [neo-liberal] policies," Gourevitch (1986, 215) offers the explanation that "worldwide competitive pressures have [everywhere] given leverage to investors and managers, who under present conditions particularly want a reduction in costs." Frieden points more specifically to the rapid increase in international mobility of capital as the reason for the rightward shift, and in particular for the dramatic reduction, in every industrialized country, in taxes on the highest incomes (Frieden 1991b). Presumably the shift toward the market in the Third World, and perhaps even in the formerly communist countries, can be explained in part by the same increase in competitive pressures.

Interest Groups and Corporatism

By the late 1970s, many students of comparative politics saw in democratic corporatism -- defined by one leading author as the "incorpora[tion of]...formally designated interest associations...within the process of authoritative decision making and implementation" (Schmitter 1981, 295) -- "the foundation for advanced industrial growth and adaptation" and the "mechanism that could assure survival and even growth in a fast-paced, open international economy" (Migdal 1983, 316-317). In a landmark volume edited by Suzanne Berger (1981),[38] Philippe Schmitter (1981) offered perhaps the most cogent and empirically persuasive statement to date of the overall position; and Charles Maier (1981) expanded the perspective developed in his book on post-World War I Europe to trace the antecedents of present-day arrangements back to the plebiscitarian experiments and the tariff struggles of the last half of the nineteenth century -- thus further specifying corporatism as the natural means of governance in a mature, internationally open, industrial democracy.[39]

Katzenstein's work, as already indicated, proceeded precisely in this vein. A system of powerful, centralized interest groups, accepting an ideology of social partnership and continually bargaining with one another, seemed uniquely well suited to encourage adjustment and growth in an export-oriented industrial economy. Whether in the "social" variant of corporatism, with strong labor movements and weak, decentralized, locally owned businesses; in the "liberal" variant, with weak working-class movements and strong, centralized, multinational business communities; or in the seemingly unique Swedish case, which combined strong multinational business with powerful labor; the recipe, in his view, worked almost equally well (1986, chap. 3).[40] Seeming to confirm Katzenstein's insight, John Ikenberry (1989) subsequently offered evidence to show that, even in the United States, increasing trade-dependence was engendering a pronounced corporatism in the realm of foreign economic policy, notably in the "fast-track" procedure for ratification of trade agreements.

Schmitter (1981, esp. 297 and 307), it should be recalled, had sounded a more cautionary note. Including in his analysis many of the larger industrial democracies, he had noted that the combination (at least on the working-class side) of high rates of associational membership with disunity or weak centralization led to high levels of instability and conflict rather than to any form of "social partnership"; Britain and Italy were prominent examples.[41]

Mancur Olson, Jr. (1982) dissented far more sharply from the emerging corporatist consensus. While admitting that "encompassing" organizations -- ones that embraced a large share of a given country's work force or industries -- might contribute to social peace and increase productive efficiency, he held that the great majority of pressure groups were "distributional" (i.e., rent-seeking) in the sense outlined earlier. To the extent that such groups pervaded an economy, Olson contended, it was less efficient and more protectionist, innovated less, grew more slowly, had higher "normal" unemployment that particularly burdened the young and the unskilled, experienced greater inequality, inflation, and political instability, and was subject to more intense business cycles.[42]

A theory more contradictory to Katzenstein's could hardly be imagined. Corporatism, except where (as in Sweden) virtually all groups were encompassing, was predicted to lead to low growth, high conflict, little social compensation, and a substantially closed economy.[43] Olson and Schmitter, on the other hand, agreed on crucial points: to Olson, for example, the most detrimental combination would be one of powerful but non-encompassing organizations -- exactly what Schmitter had diagnosed as the problem in Britain and Italy.

Alvarez, Garrett, and Lange (1991) have recently offered a more nuanced perspective, suggesting that the economy grows most rapidly, and inflation and unemployment are best controlled, in *either* of two cases: where strong and encompassing labor unions co-exist with a leftist government; or where weak unions face a rightist government. Gauging economic performance somewhat more subtly than many earlier efforts (e.g., taking into account vulnerability to international economic shocks), they advance strong empirical evidence in support of their contention. Paradoxically, however, they do not pursue the important lines of inquiry opened by Schmitter and M. Wallerstein.

Following Schmitter (and indirectly Olson), it would be worthwhile to examine the countries in which unions, relative to the share of the work force they organize, are either weakly centralized or disunited. We might expect these to be among the worst economic performers on many dimensions. By one plausible measure that derives from Alvarez, Garrett, and Lange's work, such cases would include (in descending order) Italy, the U.K., Australia, Canada, and France.[44]

The implications of Michael Wallerstein's work (1989) are even more intriguing. If, as Wallerstein argued, union power itself varies inversely with the size of a country's work force, it would seem to follow from

the work of Alvarez, Garrett, and Lange that on average large countries will perform better under rightist, and small countries better under leftist, governments; and that electorates, which presumably seek to reward economic success, will therefore be drawn over time to those respective alternatives. Moreover, governments that seek re-election through economic success will likely endeavor to shape labor markets accordingly: Leftist governments will strengthen unions; rightist ones will weaken them -- a result entirely consonant with Wallerstein's other main finding, that the cumulative time in office of the Left correlates positively with union strength, controlling for the effect of work-force size.[45]

Obviously, much fruitful research remains to be done in this area. Efforts to test Olson's work have perhaps focused too much on his predictions about economic growth, too little on his rich array of hypotheses about inflation, unemployment, instability, inequality, and protectionism.

State Structures

As Skocpol (1985, 3) has observed, comparativists began to rediscover the state sometime in the early 1970s. One powerful influence was Samuel P. Huntington's *Political Order in Changing Societies* (1968),[46] which took as its leitmotif the fatal weakness of most Third World states. A second was the growing emphasis among students of international relations on the autonomous position even of "weak" states, such as the U.S., in the making of foreign policy; here Stephen Krasner's 1976 article in *World Politics* and his 1978 book, *Defending the National Interest*, were seminal. A third factor was renewed interest in the historical processes of European state-building, culminating in Charles Tilly's edited volume on *The Formation of National States in Western Europe* (1975).[47]

Fundamentally, this group of scholars asserted that state elites were in significant degree autonomous from society, that state policies did not simply reflect social preferences or pressures, and that differences in state structure and recruitment therefore accounted for much of the observed variation in policy and outcome.[48] To take a representative example: Margaret Weir and Theda Skocpol (1985) attribute much of the policy variation among Britain, Sweden, and the U.S. in the 1930s (and subsequently) to (a) the centralization of economic policy making in Britain and Sweden, as against its dispersal in the U.S.; and (b) the British Treasury's long-standing ties to the City of London, vs. the Swedish tradition of central administrative boards with deep respect for professional (e.g., economists') judgments. In the U.S., unorthodox ideas about demand stimulus could readily percolate into parts of the inchoate policy-making apparatus, obtaining early but insecure influence. In Britain, the Treasury remained resolutely orthodox until almost the end of World War II; but, once converted to Keynesianism, became almost equally impervious to such subsequent heterodoxies as monetarism. In Sweden, expert opinion was quickly heard and implemented.

With respect to economic growth, the impressive success of Japan and the NICs led many to believe that growth-stimulating policy could be achieved only by strong, autonomous, "smart" states.[49] North's (1981) and Olson's (1982) depictions of how powerful pressure groups distort economic policy could also be read as arguments for state autonomy.[50] Katzenstein (1978, 313-316, 320-321) suggested that the more detailed, supple, and authoritative Japanese (and, to a lesser extent, French) foreign economic policy was a consequence of the greater strength and centralization of those particular states. Students of both developing and advanced countries came to focus on the issue of state "strength" or "capacity."[51] In all of this, there was often an almost Freudian hint of "penetration envy" on the part of Americans accustomed to regarding their own state as weak.   Analyses based on state capacity work best if one can assume that relevant state structures change slowly, thus serving as the "bedrock" variable that can explain persistent differences between nations. Weir and Skocpol take for granted that basic patterns of governance from the eighteenth and nineteenth centuries persist into the twentieth; Katzenstein sees the strength and autonomy of the Japanese and French states as a legacy of the absolutism which, in each case, ended feudalism and commenced economic development; Krasner asserts that "the weakness of the American polity is deeply embedded in the country's history."[52]

Studies both of historical trends and of recent national policy making, however, have tended to rebut historical determinism and to undermine sweeping assessments of state capacity. Anderson (1974) showed how quickly absolutism had sometimes been constructed (e.g., in Prussia under the Great Elector); Skowronek (1982), how even the "weak" U.S. regime had been able to build capacity when necessity demanded it; Zysman (1983, 315), that the vaunted Japanese system was "not a cultural inheritance but an explicit political creation of the postwar years." Both Zysman (1983, 295-299, 299n) and Gourevitch (1986, 190-192, 198-199) concluded that differences in state capacity could not explain the intertemporal or cross-national variations in policy that they observed. Moreover, Zysman suggests, on close inspection assessments of state capacity often blur:

...France is a strong state in terms of energy policy but in the social services the

bureaucracy is trapped in a morass; in welfare policy France is a weak state (p. 297).[53]

Milner (1987), going farther, suggests that the vaunted autonomy of the French state as a whole is greatly overrated in the traditional literature; and, even more problematically, the Communist regimes (presented by Huntington as an enviable example of developing-country institutionalization) turn out to have been sinkholes of influence-peddling and corruption.

The state, it appears, is at best an intervening variable, which itself responds (or fails to respond) to social pressures and needs. Further advance requires a theoretical explanation of the ongoing interaction between the state and its domestic and international environment, along the lines suggested by Migdal's (1988) essay in comparative history.

One possible route to such a theory, only now beginning to be explored, is to extend to the world of government the insights of Oliver Williamson (1975, 1985) and others -- the so-called "new institutional economics" -- on transaction costs and the organization of the firm.[54] Among the relevant insights of this literature are: (a) that organizational forms are best interpreted as solutions to problems of information and supervision; (b) that competition creates incentives to adopt maximally efficient forms of organization; and (c) that hierarchies replace markets, or vice-versa, to the extent that one or the other form more efficiently resolves problems of information and organization. North (1981, 37ff.) explicitly took this literature as his starting-point for a "neoclassical theory of the state"; Stinchcombe (1990, chap. 9) has applied it creatively to such issues as university governance; and, most importantly for present purposes, Weingast and Marshall (1988) have extended parts of it to the analysis of congressional procedures.

Much more can probably be done. Two brief examples indicate the possibilities. (1) The various forms of claimancy (chiefly debt vs. equity) and attendant voting power in corporations, and the reasons for their use, have been extensively discussed (Alchian and Demsetz 1972, 788-789, 789n; Williamson 1985, chap.12, esp. 304-309). (The "leveraged buy-outs" of the 1980s, for example, were chiefly a way of increasing managerial autonomy by using non-voting bonds to replace shares of stock that carried voting rights.) Similar considerations should govern the expansion or contraction of governmental participation, more specifically of democratic rule; and Bates and Lien (1985) have argued, in essence, that they do. (2) Chandler, Williamson, and others have persuasively analyzed the emergence of the multidivisional form of corporate organization in the 1920s as an effective answer to problems of informational overload and strategic planning.[55] Quite similar logic should apply to: (a) legislatures' centralization of authority in cabinets or "control" committees; (b) the displacement of cabinets by personal staffs of prime ministers or presidents; and (c) the devolution of independent authority to central banks, courts, and regulatory agencies.[56]

A separate, more modest, and quite fruitful approach to the state in this period was simply to test empirically the many assertions about specific institutions' effects -- on policy, on groups, on civil peace or disorder.[57] In his prizewinning work on *Contemporary Democracies*, Bingham Powell (1982) examined statistically how constitutional variations (parliamentary vs. presidential regimes, proportional vs. majoritarian electoral systems), in the context of country size, level of modernization, and pre-existing cleavages of ethnicity and class, affect such aspects of state performance as participation, stability and effectiveness of government, fractionalization and extremism of political parties, and avoidance of organized protest and revolt. Dovetailing with the work on PR in trade-dependent economies, the proportional parliamentary systems emerged absolved from much of their reputation for poor performance; and, in perhaps his most striking finding, Powell gave a new lease on life to the widely discredited notion of political business cycles[58] by showing that single-party domination of a country's executive was strongly associated with atypical election-year expansions of real disposable income.[59]

In a similar but narrower vein, Arend Lijphart (1990) re-tested Douglas Rae's (1971) pioneering hypotheses on the effects of electoral laws, using a larger data set and more discriminating measures. Perhaps his most counterintuitive finding was a considerable weakening of "Duverger's Law," the hoary link between electoral system and number of parties. Plurality and majority systems turned out to average just under three "effective" parties normally contesting elections; systems of proportional representation averaged just over four (1990, 490).

A particularly promising avenue of institutional inquiry involves efforts to link economic performance to features of regimes. An early, rather simple hypothesis, now widely accepted, asserted an inverse relationship between central bank independence and inflation.[60] More recently Grilli, Masciandaro, and Tabellini have claimed that all recent cases of extreme indebtedness and inflation occurred "in countries governed by highly proportional electoral systems" (Grilli et al. 1991, 4). Majority and plurality parliamentary systems, they argue, assure greater price stability; strong presidential regimes (France and the U.S.) do even better. Other economists have pursued similar claims, sometimes with an imperfect understanding of the political institutions.[61] Better

empirical testing, preferably by comparativists, is required.

Nationalism and Ethnic Conflict

The intensity of ethnic cleavage and conflict in the 1980s, not only in the less developed countries (e.g., India) but in Europe (Belgium, the United Kingdom, Spain), North America (Quebec), and most sharply in what had been Yugoslavia and the USSR, remained as a standing rebuke to prevailing theories in comparative politics.[62] Crawford Young's (1976, esp. 6-11) pioneering discussion seemed increasingly prescient.

According to Parsonian theory, modernization entailed greater universalism and less orientation to ascriptive criteria; yet conflict arose in the most modern nations, led sometimes by their most advanced regions (e.g., Catalonia).[63] Marxism held that ethnic and national loyalties were a form of false consciousness that would be superseded under Socialism; but decades of allegedly Socialist rule, and indeed of intense effort to create a "new Soviet man," had evidently succeeded only in intensifying ethnic loyalties.

On a quite different tack, Karl Deutsch (1961; 1969, 73) and Clifford Geertz (1963) both suggested (albeit from contrasting perspectives) that rapid social change might itself re-activate ethnic (for Geertz, "primordial") loyalties;[64] but the correlation between change and ethnic conflict was imperfect, and the loyalties involved were often as much self-chosen, improvised, or even invented, as they were primordial.[65] Working from such observations, others contended that most ethnic conflict was entirely tactical, an effort to restrict competition for especially desirable sectors and professions (notably in the civil service) to a limited subgroup.[66] As David Laitin (1986) trenchantly noted in his study of Nigerian cleavages, such a theory was powerless to explain cases in which tactically tempting ethnic or religious distinctions *failed* to generate political conflict (1986, esp. chaps. 1 and 6; cf. Young 1976, 516-517). Worse, it explicitly assumed that rank-and-file followers of ethnic movements (who could never realistically expect to achieve such jobs) were behaving irrationally;[67] and it stretched credulity by supposing that visions of slightly better jobs motivated the indescribably cruel conflicts, replete with ritual maimings and slaughter of the innocent, between Tamils and Sinhalese, Sikhs and Hindus, Armenians and Azerbaijanis, Serbs and Croats, et cetera ad nauseam.[68]

Several authors attempted in the 1980s to offer more convincing accounts of these important phenomena. Three main lines of argument emerge.

Ranked vs. Unranked Ethnicities

It is useful to distinguish between what Donald Horowitz (1985, 21-36) has called "ranked" and "unranked" systems of ethnicity. In the former (sometimes also called "segmented" or "plural" societies), ethnic groups stand in clear relations of super- and subordination to one another; and their positions are often linked, in ways described earlier in anthropology by Furnivall and others (1948; cf. Smith 1969), to particular occupational positions. In unranked systems (also denominated, particularly in European usage, "pillarized"), each ethnic group spans the whole available range of occupations and statuses.

Ranked systems tend to remain stabler over long periods of time, or to be agitated only by attempts to raise particular groups (e.g., castes) in the given hierarchy (Horowitz 1985, 34). When such systems do break down, however, typically by upward mobility from the subordinate group or a change in technology that "de-skills" the superordinate caste, some of the bloodiest and most revolutionary ethnic conflicts ensue, typically ignited by desperate efforts of the higher-ranked group (or its most threatened elements) to maintain their position: Horowitz (1985, 30, 34-35) advances as examples the revolutions in Rwanda (1959) and Zanzibar (1964) and the repeated pogroms against Hutu by Tutsi in Burundi. Black-white conflict in South Africa and the pre-1965 U.S. South, Catholic-Protestant warfare in Northern Ireland, even Francophone-Anglophone discord in Canada, probably also qualify.[69]

In contrast, the "pillars" of unranked systems, Horowitz notes (citing approvingly Michael Hudson's analysis of pre-civil war Lebanon), are "incipient whole societies" that relate to each other "as if they were states in an international environment" (Horowitz 1985, 31). Exactly as in the classical international balance of power, conflict in such systems is more continual but ordinarily less mortal; only where one "nation" tries to assimilate or subjugate another (as in Lebanon) is major warfare likely (Horowitz 1985, 31, 35; Rogowski 1985, 100). Where that danger is avoided (the Netherlands, Switzerland, by now probably Belgium), ethnic divisions may actually erode peacefully over time.

In the most intense conflicts, Horowitz shows with a wealth of evidence, one or more groups typically express the belief that they are in danger of permanent subjection or actual extinction: with surprising frequency, the parallel of the North American Indians is invoked (Horowitz 1985, 175-181). That threat is perhaps most apparent in the case of a de-skilled or penetrated elite within a *ranked* system: deprived of its former monopoly of privilege (e.g., in landownership, industrial management, the professions), it often lacks other skills, including (notably among colonial or caste elites) the most rudimentary ones required for self-sufficiency (Rogowski 1985, 94). It may also arise, as Horowitz (179, 186ff) emphasizes, when one previously unranked group progresses much more (or less) rapidly than others, thus moving toward monopoly of (or exclusion from) key positions in the modern economy.

In ranked systems, again, a powerful revolutionary sentiment is unleashed when a formerly servile group comes to understand that all skills are in fact open to them: that French-Canadians, or Indians under the *raj*, or African Americans can manage, administer, judge, or research on an equal basis with their previous overlords.

From this standpoint, Soviet nationalities policy was foolish. While long maintaining a fully ranked system of Russian, or at least Slav, dominance in the military and the all-Union *nomenklatura* (Laitin 1991, 158), it provided full educational opportunities through the university level (and thus a full range of presumably modern skills) to each of the major non-Russian nationalities.

The Colonial Inheritance

Laitin, Horowitz, and others have placed much emphasis on the ethnic groups' colonial or imperial inheritance. In Nigeria, according to Laitin, British colonial rule had been "hegemonic" in the Gramscian sense and had thus indelibly structured perceptions of ethnicity and of "natural" alliance among ethnic groups. Only this legacy, he believed, could explain the continuing absence of religious conflict in Nigerian politics.

Horowitz (esp. chap. 4) has emphasized how colonial or imperial elites allocated occupations among specific groups and labelled them as "backward" or "advanced." Although Gramsci is not prominently cited, Horowitz clearly believes as firmly as Laitin that the colonialists exercised cultural hegemony: the invidious distinctions that they planted, particularly among unranked groups, inflict lasting psychological wounds (images of poor self-worth and weakness) and structure post-colonial conflict as a particularly vicious ethnic rivalry. Only the psychological dimension, involving group legitimacy and self-worth, Horowitz (181-184, chap. 5) believes, can explain the passion and cruelty of the competition.

In his recent work on the politics of language, and even more on ethnic conflict in the former USSR, Laitin has stressed the original ties between local and central elites: Were the former accepted by the latter as full equals -- "most favored lords," in Laitin's phrase (1988, 296-297; 1991, 143-148) -- or were they patronized as strictly provincial rulers? By a logic too intricate to reproduce here, Laitin predicts that the cases of full incorporation (typical of western European nation-building) will have produced either total assimilation or, where ethnicity does revive (e.g., Catalonia), intense conflicts only within the regional elite. Where acceptance of local elites was halting or absent (as under European colonial rule in India and Africa), ethnicity revives easily under a coalition of old and new elites; but intense conflict often ensues between the locally dominant and locally subordinate ethnic groups, with the latter often preferring continued central rule. Among the territories of the former Soviet Union, Laitin believes, Ukraine exemplifies the former pattern; Central Asia, the latter. Georgia and Estonia assume an intermediate position.

Laitin's argument links readily to Horowitz's, and both gain credence from recent Soviet events. Where colonial rulers see their subjects as most alien, they will be least ready to accept even local elites as equal; and they will be most inclined to draw invidious distinctions about the degree to which their various subject peoples meet the high standard of civilization to which they, the conquerors, have already attained. On the evidence so far, it is precisely the most "colonial" areas of the Soviet empire that have experienced the most vicious interethnic conflict, often on precisely the lines that Horowitz would have led us to expect: e.g., the Armenians are regarded as more "advanced" than the Azerbaijanis, who therefore see themselves as economically threatened.[70]

International Factors

Connecting to an earlier part of this survey, international factors in ethnic revivals have been noted by several authors. In the nineteenth century, international markets and the threat of international conflict both argued for large states. Today, freer trade and a relaxation of tensions encourage the formation of smaller, more ethnically homogeneous units (Rogowski 1985, 380-381). Horowitz (1985, 35) notes that international pressure now virtually prohibits ranked systems of ethnicity -- consider only the South African case -- and Laitin concedes that international diplomatic recognition of successor republics has played a crucial role in the breakup of the USSR and Yugoslavia (1991, 176).

At a slightly deeper level, one may suggest, the mere availability of wider and more lucrative international markets -- for Scottish oil, Quebec timber and hydroelectric power, Uzbek cotton, or Baltic entrepreneurship[71] -- may have nourished ethnic grievances and encouraged ethnic separatism.

Conclusion

Twin tendencies run as an unbroken thread through the entire preceding discussion: the growing reliance on economic, and the relegation of sociological, modes of analysis in comparative politics. Those areas in which the most has been accomplished, namely political economy, the study of the international-domestic linkage, and the analysis of pressure groups, are those most characterized by extensive borrowing from, and collaboration with, economists. The area now best poised to make a similar advance, the study of the state, is being prodded by economists to do so. The domain that remains least satisfactorily explained, despite its evident importance, is the one to which the least economic analysis has been applied, namely that of ethnic conflict and nationalism. So far as the study of comparative politics was concerned, Brian Barry (1970) was either prescient or successfully hortatory when, two decades ago, he weighed the previously dominant sociological approaches in the balance and found them wanting.

What of the future? While no one can rule out a sociological revival (see Eckstein 1988; Inglehart 1988) or the emergence of some yet more powerful alternative approach, the likeliest prospect is that the economic perspective will continue to dominate. Relatedly, the most exciting and promising future work is likely to center on the issue of economic growth and performance: what policies and property rights most favor growth in particular circumstances; what institutions best guarantee the maintenance of those policies; and what aspects of domestic civil society or of the international environment favor the adoption and survival of such institutions? Why are anti-growth policies so often chosen? These questions are of particular moment for the post-Communist societies, but they agitate also the Third World (e.g., India, Mexico) and the industrialized West (debates about central bank independence in Italy, New Zealand, and the European Community; about the electoral system in Japan and the United Kingdom; about how to enforce fiscal discipline and whether to adopt a conscious industrial policy in the United States).

A second major area of future inquiry is likely to revolve around economic internationalization. More open trade in goods and services, easier movement of factors, the widening and deepening of such regional regimes as the European Community and (if it comes to pass) the North American Free Trade Area (NAFTA) affect institutions, constrain policies, and re-shape political alignments. Our models for explaining and predicting those effects are in their infancy; but the baby seems lusty and has nourishment close to hand, chiefly from economics and the comparative histories of U.S., Italian, and nineteenth-century German unification.

Third, we are likely to see much more important work on state structures, from both historical and deductive perspectives. Here the goal will be to explain not the consequences but the causes of state organization and evolution: why power is concentrated or delegated differently; what common forces lead to the broad convergence of regimes that we see among the industrialized states; why, historically, regime-types often ebb or flow in tandem across states (e.g., absolutism in the seventeenth century, democratization in the nineteenth and twentieth).

While I am eager to be proved wrong, I suspect that corporatism's vein of good work is almost played out and that studies of nationalism will continue to disappoint. In the former case, some powerful theory seems to have reached a dead end and to have little new to say; in the latter, it is hard to discern the basic, powerful strands of theory on which alone a better explanatory edifice might arise.

These speculations about the future, however, should be treated with the skepticism that any practitioner of comparative politics deserves. We are, after all, a field whose most signal accomplishment in the past decade has been its utter failure to predict the two most important domestic changes of the last half of the twentieth century, namely, the abandonment of communism as an ideology and the collapse of the centrally planned economies as institutions. In the coming decade, we can only do better.

Notes

This chapter has benefitted greatly from critical readings and bibliographic suggestions by Ada Finifter, my colleague Michael Lofchie, and two anonymous readers. For bibliographic and research assistance, I am most grateful to David D'Lugo. As the customary formula has it, the viewpoints and the errors remain wholly my responsibility.

1. Every individual perspective on a field is necessarily idiosyncratic, even parochial, to some degree. To state the main predelictions that inform this essay: I focus above all on works that seem to me to have advanced the field theoretically, thus relegating or omitting many contributions that are chiefly descriptive, or whose theoretical ambitions remain unfulfilled; and I am by training and orientation a student of the First World, who runs some risk of overlooking valuable work on regions outside Europe, North America, and Oceania. I have nevertheless endeavored (doubtless without total success) to include research on Africa, Asia, and Latin America that has had a major impact on theoretical discourse.

2. The naming of authors is intended, in each case, to be illustrative rather than exhaustive.

3. As some of the citations make clear, this trend entailed further substantial erosion of the traditional boundary between the subdisciplines of international relations ("IR") and comparative politics.

That trend had already been noted by Joel Migdal (1983) (following Peter Gourevitch) in the previous edition of this book.

4. Only a small part of these disparities can be accounted for by "convergence effects," i.e., the tendency of initially poorer countries to grow more rapidly (see, for a useful summary, Barro and Sala-i-Martin, 1992). Every effort to regress post-1960 economic growth among the OECD states on their 1960 per-capita GDP leaves a large positive residual for Japan and large negative ones for the U.S. and the United Kingdom.

5. Abram Bergson (1991, 33) suggests that Soviet GDP per capita in 1980 was 44% that of the U.S.; in 1985, 42%. Letting 1980 U.S. output = 100 and extrapolating from the 1973-80 U.S. annual growth rate (1.3%), 1985 U.S. output would be $(1.013)^5 \times 100 = 106.7$; 42% of that would amount to 44.8. Dividing that by 44 (the 1980 Soviet base output) yields 1.018; and that to the 1/5 power gives us an annualized growth rate for Soviet per capita GDP of about 0.4%.

6. For sub-Saharan Africa as a whole, per capita GDP grew by 1.3% annually in the 1960s; by 0.7% annually in the 1970s; and then fell in each of the ensuing three years (beginning 1981) by more than 3%. For twelve of thirty-six countries on which data were available, real per capita GDP was lower in 1981 than it had been in 1970 (World Bank 1984, 11).

7. In every major Latin American country, real per capita GDP was lower in 1985 than it had been in 1980; in Argentina, Peru, and Venezuela, it was lower in 1985 than it had been in 1973. (Balassa et al. 1986, Table 1.2).

8. Taiwan's per capita GDP, for example, grew at an annual rate of 8.1% between 1963 and 1972 and 6.6% between 1973 and 1980, as against OECD (population-weighted) averages of 3.9% and 1.7%, respectively, for those same periods (Amsden 1985, 80, Table 3.1; OECD 1982, Table 3.2).

9. In "at least nine countries..., lower inflation, lower unemployment, and higher rates of growth of disposable income [have been shown to] increase popular support for incumbent elected politicians" (Alt and Chrystal 1983, 150).

10. The first point was no news to Africanists, it having been argued forcefully for some time by Michael Lipton (1976). Bates however made the case conclusively and tied it to larger theoretical concerns; and he reached a much larger audience.

11. That policy matters is now almost universally accepted. For influential treatments, (see World Bank 1984, esp. chaps. 2 and 4; and Balassa et al. 1986).

12. Interestingly, many Soviet scholars were arriving at precisely the same conclusion in this period: see Hough (1986).

13. In economic parlance, we should be clear, a "rent" is any above-market return to a factor of production. Familiar examples of governmentally awarded rents are agricultural subsidies, minimum wages, and restrictions on entry (e.g., in taxis and cable television). Bhagwati (1982) and others prefer the term "directly unproductive profit-seeking."

14. Thus the more discretionary American government that Theodore Lowi (1979) contended had arisen since the New Deal would have particularly damaged U.S. economic growth.

15. Japan, of course, was much studied at both a popular and a scholarly level: examples, respectively, are Ezra Vogel (1979) and Chalmers Johnson (1982). Both the "lessons" and the possibility of their export remained unclear, however. See for example the dissenting view of David Friedman (1988).

16. In the two "horrible years" of 1974 and 1975, U.S. real GDP per capita declined on average by 1.7% annually; British, by 0.9%; Japanese, German, and Italian, by 0.6%. French GDP per capita rose on average by 1.2% annually. Calculated from OECD (1982, Table 3.2).

17. Property rights in land, for example, came to be worth enforcing only after population achieved a certain threshold density (North 1981, 80-82).

18. Trade share has been shown to vary in proportion to the inverse cube root of population (in millions); thus a country that numbers 8 million (cube root = 2) will have roughly twice the trade share of GNP as one that numbers 64 million (cube root = 4) (Taagepera and Hayes 1977).

19. "...'efficient' property rights are unusual in history.... As a result,...technological progress has been slow throughout most of history" (1981, 6).

20. In his current work on coffee-growing in Colombia, Bates (privately circulated ms.) concedes that the Olsonian "latent group" cannot offer a complete explanation: in Colombia, small coffee-growers triumphed politically over both latifundists and an initially hostile state.

21. For reasons not fully clear, however, Katzenstein doubted that the U.S. could adapt similarly: "We cannot apply the 'lessons' of the small European states for the simple reason that we cannot remake our history" (p. 207).

22. Without pausing to think about negative degrees of freedom, Hall suggests (1986, 259) that "five sets of structural variables," each "var[ying] along several dimensions," will be required to explain his two cases. Indeed, "any further reduction would fail to capture the full range of factors affecting their policies."

23. More recent work raises doubt about the immutability of financial markets. In separate studies of struggles to establish independent central banks, John Goodman (1991) and Lawrence Broz (1992) show that significant changes have occurred quickly.

24. Zysman (1983, 225-227), writing earlier, was even less sanguine about the Thatcher experiment.

25. Among the many critiques are Pryor (1983), Rogowski (1983), Cameron (1988), and Gray and Lowery (1988).

26. See especially Schroeder (1988) and Wolf (1991).

27. Students of international relations began also to explore the link between domestic and international politics, albeit with a predictably different focus on international regimes and the projection of national power. Among the most influential writings were Keohane and Nye (1977) and Ruggie (1983).

28. Rosecrance's views can be usefully contrasted with those of Keohane and Nye (1977, esp. chap. 2), who had protrayed "complex interdependence" as an ideal type, unlikely to be achieved in the real world; cf. Keohane and Nye 1987, 731.

29. For more detailed statistics, and a comparison with earlier expansions, see Rogowski (1989, 88-90).

30. More precisely, Cameron estimated the following regression equation for the OECD states: state revenues/GDP 1975 - state revenues/GDP 1960 = 1.315 + .184(trade/GDP 1960) (r=.819, r^2=.671).

31. Nonetheless there were very substantial differences in direction of outlays between Katzenstein's "social" and "liberal" corporatisms (1985, 115-121).

32. Michael Wallerstein (1989, 491-492), however, hypothesized persuasively, from a rational-choice perspective, that unionization rates were an artifact of the size of a country's work force, moderated by leftist political dominance; trade had no independent effect. Katzenstein's (1985, 89-91) arguments on the point also emphasized smallness rather than trade-dependence.

33. The United Kingdom and Japan are at present the most interesting test cases for the prediction.

34. U.S. and Canadian grain-growers, unsurprisingly, supported free trade with equal militancy.

35. U.S., Canadian, and Australian workers generally voted in favor of protectionist parties in this period.

36. Most notably, this is clearly implied by the pathbreaking comparative work on this period by Barrington Moore, Jr. (1967).

37. Two fundamental papers on the specific-factors approach are Ronald W. Jones (1971) and Michael Mussa (1974).

38. Several of the contributions are discussed incisively in Migdal (1983, 317). Also influential were Schmitter and Lehmbruch (1979) and Lehmbruch and Schmitter (1982).

39. Corporatist institutions have of course been observed also in other, often non-democratic contexts, including particularly Latin America. I focus here on the theoretical effort to link a particular kind of corporatism to economic pressures and outcomes.

40. Katzenstein (p. 118) warned, however, that social corporatism's propensity to expand public employment seemed likely to hinder investment and competitiveness.

41. Katzenstein had no occasion to disaggregate these two characteristics, since (as Schmitter's data reveal) among the smaller European democracies they are strongly collinear: almost everywhere that labor organizes a high share of the work force (Sweden, Austria, Norway, Denmark) it is united and centralized; where labor organization is less "dense" (the Netherlands, Switzerland), labor is also more divided, less centralized, or both. The sole (and partial) exception is Belgium, with rather "dense" organization but somewhat low unity Schmitter (1981, 294, 297).

42. Olson's logically admirable argument is too intricate to be recapitulated briefly here; I have attempted to summarize it in Rogowski 1983, 715-717.

43. On the other hand, five of the seven countries that Katzenstein studied (all except Sweden and Switzerland) had suffered foreign occupation or totalitarian rule during World War II; and three (Belgium, Denmark, and the Netherlands) had joined the European Community. Hence Olson would expect them to have a weak interest-group structure in the first place.

44. Alvarez, Garrett, and Lange combine measures of "density" and "centralization" into a single standardized "labor organization index" ("Government and Macroeconomic Performance," p. 353). The two measures are indeed strongly correlated (r=.79; centralization = .055 + .012 (density)), but of interest are the negative outliers: Italy, for example, is predicted by the regression to have a centralization score of .55 (density = 41), but in reality its centralization is .33. Britain's expected value is .59, its real one .43; and so on.

45. Wallerstein's best-supported OLS estimation (p. 491; R^2 = .80) is: unionized% of workforce = 83.4 - 6.35 (ln work force in thousands) + .30 (Wilensky cumulative index of Left party participation since 1919).

46. Cf. Skocpol's (1985, 31) appreciation of this "path-breaking state-centered book."

47. Also highly influential was Perry Anderson's *Lineages of the Absolutist State* (1974). Theoretical debates among Marxist scholars were also influential at the time (see, for example, Krasner's preface to *Defending the National Interest*, xii) but have in recent years receded sharply from attention.

48. The manifesto of the approach, not only in the study of foreign policy, was chapter 1 of Krasner (1978).

49. On Japan, see Johnson (1982); on the NICs, inter alia Amsden (1985); Evans 1979; and Stephan Haggard 1990.

50. North's detailed treatments of Dutch and English economic success in the early modern period (pp. 152-157), however, supported a more nuanced view.

51. See for example Evans (1985b) and Migdal (1988). The most cogent definition of state strength was offered by Krasner (1978, 55-61).

52. Weir and Skocpol (1985); Katzenstein (1978, 323-330); Krasner (1978, 66).

53. The point had been conceded earlier by Krasner (1978, 58) and Skocpol (1985, 17-18). It is made forcefully, with respect to the developing countries, by Migdal (1988, xviii-xix).

54. A helpful introduction to the political applications of this work is Moe (1984). Other major contributors have been Coase (1960), Alchian and Demsetz (1972), Chandler (1977), and Klein, Crawford, and Alchian (1978).

55. See, for example, Williamson (1985, chap. 8) and sources there cited. These efforts at explanation carry an evident danger of functionalism — because the institution arose, it must have been more efficient — but the danger can be, and I think in the literature cited here has been, successfully resisted.

56. Gary Cox's (1986, 208-211) account of nineteenth-century MPs' delegation of quasi-judicial tasks (enclosures, rights-of-way) seems to me to be entirely in this spirit. For a more direct effort at application, see Weingast and Moran (1983).

57. Demonstrating such effects, of course, proves nothing about state autonomy. If, for example, PR leads to more stable government but itself is determined by some aspect of civil or international society, institutions still have little independent effect.

58. William Nordhaus (1975) had originally asserted that democratic governments stimulated the economy before an election, and often depressed demand immediately after, resulting in economic perturbations that were at best unhelpful to long-term economic growth. The most influential statement of the hypothesis was in Edward Tufte (1978). Valerie Bunce (1980) subsequently contended that the Soviet and East European governments also stimulated consumer-goods output to win support for new leaders immediately after a change of power. On closer inspection, as Alt and Chrystal (1983, chap. 5) observed in their pioneering and far-ranging textbook on *Political Economics*, evidence for these plausible hypotheses was almost wholly lacking for the democratic states; and Philip Roeder (1985) cast similar doubt on Bunce's assertions.

59. In parliamentary systems where a single party held a majority throughout the period of analysis, real disposable income increased in 78% of the election years but in only 39% of the non-election years; in systems with strong presidencies, the respective figures were 71% for election years, 47% for years without an election. In no other category of systems did the difference between election and non-election years exceed 10% (Powell 1982, 210).

60. See the discussion in Alt and Chrystal (1983, 47-49). An important intervening effort is Richard C. K. Burdekin and Leroy O. Laney (1988).

61. See, for example, Roubini and Sachs (1989); Alesina (1989, esp. 78-86); and Alesina and Summers (1991).

62. Two recent review essays, by Newman (1991) and Laitin (1991), discuss the theoretical issues with particular acuity. Also helpful is the critique by Donald L. Horowitz (1985, chap. 3).

63. Gourevitch (1979) argued that separatist sentiment was likeliest to arise in regions that were economically dynamic but politically subservient.

64. See the discussions in Newman (1991, 454-455), Horowitz (1985, 99-101), and Laitin (1986, 97-98).

65. Notable are David Laitin's (1986, 145-146) analysis of the "instrumental management" of Yoruba identity and Nelson Kasfir's (1979) discussion of the invented "Nubian" ethnicity in Uganda.

66. The clearest, or at least the most provocative, statement of the view came from the pen of Albert Breton (1964). Other prominent representatives of the "conflict" tendency include Fredrik Barth (1969), Howard Melson and Robert Wolpe (1970), and Walker Connor (1973).

67. For explicit statements of the assumption, see Breton (1964) and the sources cited in Horowitz (1985, 101-105). See also Newman (1991, 458).

68. The events that accompanied the partition of India in 1947 are a fair sample: see Larry Collins and Dominique Lapierre (1975, esp. chap. 13). On the other hand, the two World Wars spilled even more blood, for equally little tangible gain to individual participants.

69. One may of course quibble about whether the conflict in Northern Ireland is ethnic. The distinct ancestry of the two groups (the Protestants having originally been Scottish and English settlers) supports an affirmative answer. See the incisive discussion of the larger

definitional issue in Horowitz (1985, chap. 1, esp. 41ff). On the peculiar situation of settler elites, see Ian Lustick (1985).

70. As early as 1968, John Armstrong called attention to the advanced educational and occupational status of the Armenian population of the USSR: 94 of every 10,000 were full-time students in higher education (among Russians, the figure was 90; among Azerbaijanis, 75); 43 of every 10,000 were "scientific workers" (Russians, 33; Azerbaijanis, 24); and 30 in every 1000 were "specialists with higher education" (Russians, 21; Azerbaijanis, 18). Armstrong went on to note that, "like all mobilized diasporas, the Armenians arouse resentment....the Azerbaijanis and some other Turkic groups have a tradition of bitter animosity to Armenians" (Armstrong 1990, 25, 27, 60).

71. Laitin (1991, 162) notes that the Estonian national movement "was propelled...[in part] by the expectation of rapid growth under capitalism in an independent state."

Bibliography

Alchian, Armen A., and Harold Demsetz. 1972. "Production, Information Costs, and Economic Organization." *American Economic Review* 62:777-795.

Alchian, Armen A., and Harold Demsetz. 1973. "The Property Rights Paradigm." *Journal of Economic History* 33:16-27.

Alesina, Alberto. 1989. "Politics and Business Cycles in Industrial Democracies." *Economic Policy* 8:57-98.

Alesina, Alberto, and Lawrence H. Summers. 1991. "Central Bank Independence and Macroeconomic Performance: Some Comparative Evidence." Harvard University and NBER, mimeo.

Alt, James E., and K. Alec Chrystal. 1983. *Political Economics*. Berkeley: University of California Press.

Alvarez, Michael R., Geoffrey Garrett, and Peter Lange. 1991. "Government Partisanship, Labor Organization, and Macroeconomic Performance." *American Political Science Review* 85:539-556.

Amsden, Alice H. 1985. "The State and Taiwan's Economic Development." In *Bringing the State Back In*, ed. Peter B. Evans, Dietrich Rueschemeyer, and Theda Skocpol. Cambridge: Cambridge University Press.

Anderson, Perry. 1974. *Lineages of the Absolutist State*. London: NLB.

Armstrong, John A. [1968] 1990. "The Ethnic Scene in the Soviet Union: The View of the Dictatorship." *Journal of Soviet Nationalities* 1:14-65.

Balassa, Bela, Gerardo M. Bueno, Pedro-Pablo Kuczynski, and Mario Enrique Simonsen. 1986. *Toward Renewed Economic Growth in Latin America*. Washington, DC: Institute for International Economics.

Barro, Robert J., and Xavier Sala-i-Martin. 1992. "Convergence." *Journal of Political Economy* 100:223-251.

Barry, Brian. 1970. *Sociologists, Economists, and Democracy*. Chicago: University of Chicago Press.

Barth, Fredrik, ed. 1969. *Ethnic Groups and Boundaries: The Social Organization of Cultural Difference*. London: Allen & Unwin.

Bates, Robert H. 1981. *Markets and States in Tropical Africa: The Political Basis of Agricultural Policies*. Berkeley: University of California Press.

Bates, Robert H., and Da-Hsiang Donald Lien. 1985. "A Note on Taxation, Development, and Representative Government." *Politics & Society* 14:53-70.

Berger, Suzanne, ed. 1981. *Organizing Interests in Western Europe: Pluralism, Corporatism, and the Transformation of Politics.* Cambridge: Cambridge University Press.

Bergson, Abram. 1991. "The USSR Before the Fall: How Poor and Why." *Journal of Economic Perspectives* 5:29-44.

Bhagwati, Jagdish N. 1982. "Directly Unproductive, Profit-seeking (DUP) Activities." *Journal of Political Economy* 90:259-273.

Breton, Albert. 1964. "Economics of Nationalism." *Journal of Political Economy* 72:376-386.

Broz, J. Lawrence. 1992. "Wresting the Scepter from London: The International Political Economy of the Founding of the Federal Reserve." Ph.D. diss. UCLA.

Buchanan, James M. 1980. "Rent-Seeking and Profit-Seeking." In *Toward a Theory of the Rent-Seeking Society*, ed. James M. Buchanan, Robert D. Tollison, and Gordon Tullock. College Station, TX: Texas A & M University Press.

Bunce, Valerie. 1980. "The Succession Connection: Policy Cycles and Political Change in the Soviet Union and Eastern Europe." *American Political Science Review* 74:966-77.

Burdeking, Richard C. K., and Leroy O. Laney. 1988. "Fiscal Policymaking and the Central Bank Institutional Constraint." *Kyklos* 41:4, 647-61.

Cameron, David. 1978. "The Expansion of the Public Economy: A Comparative Analysis." *American Political Science Review* 72:1243-1261.

Cameron, David. 1988. "Distributional Coalitions and Other Sources of Economic Stagnation: On Olson's *Rise and Decline of Nations*." *International Organization* 42:561-603.

Cardoso, Fernando Henrique, and Enzo Faletto. [1971] 1979. *Dependency and Development in Latin America.* Trans. Marjory Mattingly Urquidi. Berkeley: University of California Press.

Chandler, Alfred. 1977. *The Visible Hand: The Managerial Revolution in American Business.* Cambridge: The Belknap Press of Harvard University Press.

Clark, Lindley H. 1992. "Why the Third World Is Embracing Free Trade." *Wall Street Journal*, 20 February, sec A.

Coase, A. H. 1960. "The Problem of Social Cost." *Journal of Law and Economics* 3:1-44.

Collins, Larry, and Dominique Lapierre. 1975. *Freedom at Midnight.* New York: Simon and Schuster.

Connor, Walker. 1973. "Politics of Ethnonationalism." *Journal of International Affairs* 27:1-21.

Cox, Gary. 1986. "The Development of a Party-Orientated Electorate in England, 1832-1918." *British Journal of Political Science* 16:187-216.

Deutsch, Karl W. 1961. "Social Mobilization and Political Development." *American Political Science Review* 55:493-514.

Deutsch, Karl W. 1969. *Nationalism and Its Alternatives.* New York: Knopf.

Eckstein, Harry. 1988. "A Culturalist Theory of Political Change." *American Political Science Review* 82:789-804.

Evans, Peter B. 1979. *Dependent Development: The Alliance of Multinational, State, and Local Capital in Brazil.* Princeton, NJ: Princeton University Press.

Evans, Peter B., Dietrich Rueschemeyer, and Theda Skocpol, eds. 1985. *Bringing the State Back In.* Cambridge: Cambridge University Press.

Evans, Peter B. 1985. "Transnational Linkages and the Economic Role of the State: An Analysis of Developing and Industrialized Nations in the Post-World War II Period." In *Bringing the State Back In*, ed. Peter B. Evans, Dietrich Rueschemeyer, and Theda Skocpol. Cambridge: Cambridge University Press.

Feenstra, Robert C., ed. 1983. *The Theory of Commercial Policy: Essays in International Political Economy.* Cambridge: MIT Press.

Frieden, Jeffry. 1991a. *Debt, Development, and Democracy: Modern Political Economy and Latin America, 1965-1985.* Princeton, NJ: Princeton University Press.

Frieden, Jeffry. 1991b. "Invested Interests: The Politics of National Economic Policies in a World of Global Finance." *International Organization* 45:425-452.

Friedman, David. 1988. *The Misunderstood Miracle: Industrial Development and Political Change in Japan.* Ithaca: Cornell University Press.

Furnivall, J. S. 1948. *Colonial Policy and Practice.* London: Cambridge University Press.

Geertz, Clifford. 1963. "The Integrative Revolution: Primordial Sentiments and Civil Politics in the New States." In *Old Societies and New States*, ed. Clifford Geertz. New York: The Free Press.

Gerschenkron, Alexander. 1943. *Bread and Democracy in Germany.* Berkeley and Los Angeles: University of California Press.

Gerschenkron, Alexander. 1962. *Economic Backwardness in Historical Perspective: A Book of Essays.* Cambridge, MA: Belknap Press of Harvard University Press.

Goodman, John B. 1991. "The Politics of Central Bank Independence." *Comparative Politics* 23:329-349.

Gourevitch, Peter A. 1978. "The Second Image Reversed: The International Sources of Domestic Politics." *International Organization* 32:881-912.

Gourevitch, Peter A. 1979. "The Re-emergence of 'Peripheral Nationalisms': Some Comparative Speculations on the Spatial Distribution of Political Leadership and Economic Growth." *Comparative Studies in Society and History* 21:303-322.

Gourevitch, Peter A. 1986. *Politics in Hard Times: Comparative Responses to International Economic Crises.* Ithaca: Cornell University Press.

Gray, Virginia, and David Lowery. 1988. "Interest Group Politics and Economic Growth in the U.S. States." *American Political Science Review* 82:109-131.

Grilli, Vittorio, Donato Masciandaro, and Guido Tabellini. 1991. "Political and Monetary Institutions and Public Financial Policies in the Industrial Countries," mimeo.

Gunder Frank, André. 1967. *Capitalism and Underdevelopment in Latin America.* New York: Monthly Review Press.

Haggard, Stephan. 1990. *Pathways From the Periphery: The Politics of Growth in the Newly Industrializing Countries.* Ithaca, NY: Cornell University Press.

Hall, Peter A. 1986. *Governing the Economy: The Politics of State Intervention in Britain and France.* New York: Oxford University Press.

Hibbs, Douglas A., Jr. 1978. "On the Political Economy of Long-Run Trends in Strike Activity." *British Journal of Political Science* 8:153-176.

Horowitz, Donald L. 1985. *Ethnic Groups in Conflict.* Berkeley: University of California Press.

Hough, Jerry F. 1986. *The Struggle for the Third World: Soviet Debates and American Options.* Washington, DC: The Brookings Institution.

Huntington, Samuel P. 1968. *Political Order in Changing Societies.* New Haven: Yale University Press.

Ikenberry, G. John. 1989. "Manufacturing Consensus: The Institutionalization of American Private Interest in the Tokyo Trade Round." *Comparative Politics* 21:289-309.

Inglehart, Ronald. 1988. "The Renaissance of Political Culture." *American Political Science Review* 82:1203-1230.

Ingham, Geoffrey K. 1974. *Strikes and Industrial Conflict*. London: Macmillan.

International Monetary Fund, World Bank, OECD, and European Bank for Reconstruction and Development. 1991. *The Economy of the USSR: Summary and Recommendations*. Washington, DC: World Bank.

Johnson, Chalmers. 1982. *MITI and the Japanese Miracle: The Growth of Industrial Policy, 1925-75*. Stanford, CA: Stanford University Press.

Jones, Robert. 1971. "A Three Factor Model in Theory, Trade and History." In *Trade, Balance of Payments and Growth*, ed. J. Bhagwati et al. Amsterdam: North-Holland.

Kasfir, Nelson. 1979. "Explaining Ethnic Participation." *World Politics* 31:365-388.

Katzenstein, Peter. 1978. "Domestic Structures and Strategies of Foreign Policy." In *Between Power and Plenty: Foreign Economic Policies of Advanced Industrial States*. Madison: University of Wisconsin Press. (The volume appeared originally as the Autumn 1977 issue of *International Organization*.)

Katzenstein, Peter. 1985. *Small States in World Markets*. Ithaca, NY: Cornell University Press.

Keohane, Robert O., and Joseph S. Nye, Jr. 1977. *Power and Interdependence: World Politics in Transition*. Boston and Toronto: Little, Brown and Co.

Keohane, Robert O., and Joseph S. Nye, Jr. 1987. "*Power and Interdependence* Revisited." *International Organization* 41:725-753.

Kindleberger, Charles P. 1951. "Group Behavior and International Trade." *Journal of Political Economy* 59:30-46.

Klein, Benjamin, Robert G. Crawford, and Armen A. Alchian. 1978. "Vertical Integration, Appropriable Rents, and the Competitive Contracting Process." *Journal of Law and Economics* 21:297-326.

Krasner, Stephen. 1976. "State Power and the Structure of International Trade." *World Politics* 28:317-347.

Krasner, Stephen. 1978. *Defending the National Interest: Raw Materials Investments and U.S. Foreign Policy*. Princeton, NJ: Princeton University Press.

Krasner, Stephen D., ed. 1983. *International Regimes*. Ithaca, NY: Cornell University Press. (The volume appeared originally in two issues of *International Organization*: vol. 35, no. 4; vol. 36, no. 2.)

Krueger, Anne. 1974. "The Political Economy of the Rent-Seeking Society." *American Economic Review* 64:291-303.

Laitin, David. 1986. *Hegemony and Culture: Politics and Religious Change among the Yoruba*. Chicago and London: University of Chicago Press.

Laitin, David D. 1988. "Language Games." *Comparative Politics* 20:289-302.

Laitin, David D. 1991. "The National Uprisings in the Soviet Union." *World Politics* 44:139-77.

Lehmbruch, Gerhard, and Phillipe C. Schmitter, eds. 1982. *Patterns of Corporatist Policy-Making*. Beverly Hills, CA: Sage.

Lijphart, Arend. 1990. "The Political Consequences of Electoral Laws, 1945-85." *American Political Science Review* 84:481-96.

Lipset, Seymour Martin. 1963. *The First New Nation*. New York: Basic Books, Inc.

Lipson, Charles. 1983. "The Transformation of Trade: The Sources and Effects of Regime Change." In *International Regimes*, ed. Stephen Krasner. Ithaca, NY: Cornell University Press.

Lipton, Michael. 1976. *Why Poor People Stay Poor: Urban Bias in World Development*. Cambridge, MA: Harvard University Press.

Lowi, Theodore. 1979. *The End of Liberalism: The Second Republic of the United States*. 2nd ed. New York: W. W. Norton & Co.

Lustick, Ian. 1985. *State-building Failure in British Ireland & French Algeria*. Berkeley: Institute of International Relations, University of California, Berkeley.

Magee, Stephen P. 1978. "Three Simple Tests of the Stolper-Samuelson Theorem." In *Issues in International Economics*, ed. Peter Oppenheimer. London: Oriel Press.

Maier, Charles. 1981. "'Fictitious Bonds...of Wealth and Law': On the Theory and Practice of Interest Representation." In *Organizing Interests in Western Europe: Pluralism, Corporatism, and the Transformation of Politics*, ed. Suzanne Berger. Cambridge: Cambridge University Press.

Maier, Charles. 1975. *Recasting Bourgeois Europe: Stabilization in France, Germany, and Italy in the Decade After World War I*. Princeton, NJ: Princeton University Press.

McClelland, David C. 1961. *The Achieving Society*. Princeton, NJ: Van Nostrand.

Melson, Howard, and Robert Wolpe. 1970. "Modernization and the Politics of Communalism: A Theoretical Perspective." *American Political Science Review* 64:1112-1130.

Migdal, Joel S. 1983. "Studying the Politics of Development and Change: The State of the Art." In *Political Science: The State of the Discipline*, ed. Ada W. Finifter. Washington, DC: American Political Science Association.

Migdal, Joel S. 1988. *Strong Societies and Weak States: State-Society Relations and State Capabilities in the Third World*. Princeton, NJ: Princeton University Press.

Milner, Helen. 1987. "Resisting the Protectionist Temptation: Industry and the Making of Trade Policy in France and the United States during the 1970s." *International Organization* 41:639-666.

Milner, Helen. 1988. *Resisting Protectionism: Global Industries and the Politics of International Trade*. Princeton, NJ: Princeton University Press.

Moe, Terry. 1984. "The New Economics of Organization." *American Journal of Political Science* 28:739-777.

Moore, Barrington, Jr. 1967. *Social Origins of Dictatorship and Democracy*. Boston: Beacon Press.

Moravcsik, Andrew. 1991. "Negotiating the Single European Act: National Interests and Conventional Statecraft in the European Community." *International Organization* 45:19-56.

Mussa, Michael. 1974. "Tariffs and the Distribution of Income: The Importance of Factor Specificity, Substitutability, and Intensity in the Long and Short Run." *Journal of Political Economy* 82:1191-1203.

Newman, Saul. 1991. "Does Modernization Breed Ethnic Conflict?" *World Politics* 43:451-78.

Nordhaus, William. 1975. "The Political Business Cycle." *Review of Economic Studies* 42:169-90.

North, Douglas. 1981. *Structure and Change in Economic History*. New York and London: W. W. Norton & Co.

Olson, Mancur C. 1965. *The Logic of Collective Action: Public Goods and the Theory of Groups*. Cambridge, MA: Harvard University Press.

Olson, Mancur C. 1982. *The Rise and Decline of Nations: Economic Growth, Stagflation, and Social Rigidities*. New Haven: Yale University Press.

Organization for Economic Co-operation and Development (OECD). 1982. *Economic Outlook: Historical Statistics, 1960-1980*. Paris: OECD.

Organization for Economic Co-operation and Development (OECD). 1991. *Economic Outlook: Historical Statistics, 1960-1989*. Paris: OECD.

Powell, Bingham. 1982. *Contemporary Democracies*. Cambridge, MA: Harvard University Press.

Pryor, Frederic. 1983. "A Quasi-test of Olson's Hypotheses." In *The Political Economy of Growth*, ed. Dennis C. Mueller. New Haven: Yale University Press.

Rae, Douglas. 1971. *The Political Consequences of Electoral Laws*. 2nd ed. New Haven: Yale University Press.

Roeder, Philip. 1985. "Do New Soviet Leaders Really Make a Difference? Rethinking the 'Succession Connection'." *American Political Science Review* 79:958-76.

Rogowski, Ronald. 1983. "Structure, Growth, and Power: Three Rationalist Accounts." *International Organization* 37:713-738.

Rogowski, Ronald. 1985. "Causes and Varieties of Nationalism: A Rationalist Account." In *New Nationalisms of the Developed West: Toward Explanation*, ed. Edward A. Tiryakian and Ronald Rogowski. Boston: Allen and Unwin.

Rogowski, Ronald. 1987. "Trade and the Variety of Democratic Institutions." *International Organization* 41:203-223.

Rogowski, Ronald. 1989. *Commerce and Coalitions*. Princeton, NJ: Princeton University Press.

Rokkan, Stein. 1970. *Citizens, Elections, Parties: Approaches to the Comparative Study of the Processes of Development*. Oslo: Universitetsforlaget.

Rosecrance, Richard. 1986. *The Rise of the Trading State: Commerce and Conquest in the Modern World*. New York: Basic Books.

Roubini, Nouriel, and Jeffrey Sachs. 1989. "Political and Economic Determinants of Budget Deficits in the Industrial Democracies." *European Economic Review* 33:903-933.

Ruggie, John Gerard. 1983. "International Regimes, Transactions, and Change: Embedded Liberalism in the Postwar Economic Order." In *International Regimes*, ed. Stephen Krasner. Ithaca, NY: Cornell University Press.

Schmitter, Philippe. 1981. "Interest Intermediation and Regime Governability in Contemporary Western Europe and North America." In *Organizing Interests in Western Europe: Pluralism, Corporatism, and the Transformation of Politics*, ed. Suzanne Berger. Cambridge: Cambridge University Press.

Schmitter, Philippe C., and Gerhard Lehmbruch, eds. 1979. *Trends toward Corporatist Intermediation*. Beverly Hills, CA: Sage.

Schroeder, Gertrude E. 1988. "Property Rights Issues in Economic Reforms in Socialist Countries." *Studies in Comparative Communism* 21:175-188.

Skocpol, Theda. 1979. *States and Social Revolutions: A Comparative Analysis of France, Russia, and China*. Cambridge: Cambridge University Press.

Skocpol, Theda. 1985. "Bringing the State Back In: Strategies of Analysis in Current Research." In *Bringing the State Back In*, ed. Peter B. Evans, Dietrich Rueschemeyer, and Theda Skocpol. Cambridge: Cambridge University Press.

Smith, M. G. 1969. *The Plural Society in the British West Indies*. Berkeley and Los Angeles: University of California Press.

Skowronek, Stephen. 1982. *Building a New American State: The Expansion of National Administrative Capacities, 1877-1920*. Cambridge: Cambridge University Press.

Stolper, Wolfgang Friedrich, and Paul A. Samuelson. 1941. "Protection and Real Wages." *Review of Economic Studies* 9:58-73.

Stinchcombe, Arthur L. 1990. *Information and Organizations*. Berkeley: University of California Press.

Taagepera, Rein, and James P. Hayes. 1977. "How Trade/GNP Ratio Decreases with Country Size." *Social Science Research* 6:108-132.

Tilly, Charles, ed. 1975. *The Formation of National States in Western Europe*. Princeton, NJ: Princeton University Press.

Tufte, Edward. 1978. *Political Control of the Economy*. Princeton, NJ: Princeton University Press.

Vogel, Ezra. 1979. *Japan as Number One*. Cambridge: Harvard University Press.

Wallerstein, Immanuel. 1974. *The Modern World-System I*. New York: Academic Press.

Wallerstein, Michael. 1989. "Union Organization in Advanced Industrial Democracies." *American Political Science Review* 83:481-501.

Weingast, Barry R., and Mark J. Moran. 1983. "Bureaucratic Discretion or Congressional Control? Regulatory Policymaking by the Federal Trade Commission." *Journal of Political Economy* 91:765-800.

Weingast, Barry R., and William Marshall. 1988. "The Industrial Organization of Congress; or, Why Legislatures, Like Firms, Are Not Organized as Markets." *Journal of Political Economy* 96:132-163.

Weir, Margaret, and Theda Skocpol. 1985. "State Structures and the Possibilities for Keynesian' Responses to the Great Depression in Sweden, Britain, and the United States." In *Bringing the State Back In*, ed. Peter B. Evans, Dietrich Rueschemeyer, and Theda Skocpol. Cambridge: Cambridge University Press.

Williamson, Oliver. 1975. *Markets and Hierarchies: Analysis and Antitrust Implications; A Study in the Economics of Internal Organization*. New York: The Free Press; London: Collier Macmillan Publishers.

Williamson, Oliver. 1985. *The Economic Institutions of Capitalism: Firms, Markets, Relational Contracting*. New York: The Free Press; London: Collier Macmillan Publishers.

Wolf, Thomas A. 1991. "The Lessons of Limited Market-Oriented Reform." *Journal of Economic Perspectives* 5:45-58.

World Bank. 1984. *Toward Sustainable Development in Sub-Saharan Africa: A Joint Program of Action*. Washington, DC: The World Bank.

Young, Crawford. 1976. *The Politics of Cultural Pluralism*. Madison: University of Wisconsin Press.

Zysman, John. 1983. *Governments, Markets, and Growth: Financial Systems and the Politics of Industrial Change*. Ithaca, NY: Cornell University Press.

Zysman, John, and Laura Tyson, eds. 1983. *American Industry in International Competition*. Ithaca, NY: Cornell University Press.

18

Global Political Economy

James A. Caporaso

Introduction

Global political economy is not unified by a shared theoretical approach or encompassing methodology. Rather, it is a collection of orientations, perspectives, theories, and methods addressed to understanding the relations between diverse political and economic phenomena at the global level. The world does not look the same from a bank office in Zurich, a *maquiladora* (border factory) in Mexico, a shantytown in Peru, a rice paddy in Sri Lanka, and a trade office in Washington, D.C. Academics are not above the fray. Neorealists, institutionalists, structuralists, Marxists, deconstructionists, and modern-day mercantilists frame the world differently too.

Without belaboring the obvious, let me briefly describe some of the key axes of disagreement: the actors; the dominant metaphor; and the constitutive principle relating politics and economics. Different theories presuppose the importance of different actors, or even whether actors in the ordinary sense are important at all (Galtung 1971). Thus, individuals, firms, interest groups, epistemic communities, technocrats, bureaucrats, states, and international organizations are variously posited as the central actors. Neoclassical political economy favors individuals and firms; Marxian political economy favors classes and production relations; dependency theory focuses on transnational alliances of capital (financial and industrial); and realist theory places states at the center.

Each approach is defined by a dominant metaphor and associated theoretical principles. Three such metaphors are the market, the polity, and class processes. Neoclassical economics places the market and voluntary exchange at the center. The portals to politics are guarded by the idea of market failure. Realism and neorealism expand on the role of the state and related ideas of power and domination. The connections with economics are controlled by state officials who set parameters to voluntary exchange and who seek to use wealth to enhance relative power. Politics structures the realm of economics. Class processes are the domain of Marxian political economy. The production, realization, and appropriation of value are thematized. Politics appears either directly in production relations, in the power exercised by owners of capital and bosses (Marglin 1974), or in the ways in which the state advances the systemic interests of capital, i.e., those interests which capitalists cannot advance individually. Crossing the divides that separate these approaches is not an easy task.

Finally, there are different constitutive principles of global political economy, different ways of framing or organizing the connections between politics and economic forces. While they do not correspond in a precise way with theories of international political economy, the differences among them are important. One constitutive principle takes economics as the primary subject matter and looks at associated political activities. What is economic is trade, technology, debt, and what is political are the activities of bargaining, power, and collective problem solving in each arena, in short, the "politics of trade" (investment, debt, etc.) approach. This approach emphasizes the management of international economic problems.

A second constitutive principle conceives economics and politics as analytically coequal subsystems and theorizes about their interactions. Economics is variously conceived as markets, production, and wealth; politics as states, institutions, and power. Global political economy now involves theorizing about the relations between markets and states or power and wealth at the global level.

The third constitutive principle is that of reduction of politics or economics to the other. I do not use the term reduction the way Waltz does (1959, 1979), as the explanation of facts at one level by reference to the facts and relations situated at a different (lower) level. By reduction I refer to the subsumption or assimilation of facts of a political (or economic) nature by concepts of an economic (or political) nature. Reduction here is a conceptual but not a theoretical enterprise. It involves reclassifying and reinterpreting phenomena previously seen as autonomous. The public choice component of neoclassical economics reinterprets politics as economic insofar as it focuses on political agents rationally pursuing their interests under political constraints. In a similar fashion, some Marxian political economists see politics in the very processes of production and exchange otherwise thought of as economic. "The economy *is* political" might be a Marxian slogan just as "the political *is* economic" might serve for public choice theory. This constitutive principle involves a meta-theoretical conception of how politics and economics connect that is very different from approaches seeking to explain economics and politics independently defined.

Any attempt to write about the entire field of global political economy faces a dilemma at the start. Does the author choose to write about as many approaches as possible or to develop a few selected themes in more depth? The former approach risks becoming a catalogue of approaches, sometimes very specific. The latter risks ignoring important work lying outside the controversial main theoretical traditions. Nevertheless, a choice is necessary. This chapter lies more toward the second horn of the dilemma. To convey a sense of the important theoretical controversies, it is necessary to provide detail and depth, even at the expense of horizontal coverage. This means that important literatures are omitted, including world systems theory, public choice, international coordination of economic policies, and post-structural theories. What follows is a critical discussion of four approaches: neoclassical, realist, liberal, and Marxian. In the conclusion, I present a broad assessment and point to areas where future research is needed.

The Neoclassical Approach

The central institution of neoclassical economic theory is the market, a system of voluntary exchange relations among legally independent property owners. The market coordinates wants and capacities of numerous individuals and conveys information about relative scarcities and relative preferences through prices. Within the market, the theoretical status of private agents is that of property owners who may seek to improve their positions through voluntary exchange.

In the neoclassical approach, political economy can be approached in a number of ways. One important connection is via the institution of the market and market failure. A central claim about markets is that they provide for efficient outcomes. This means that if property rights are well-defined, given any initial distribution of endowments and a set of preferences, efficient (Pareto-optimal)[1] outcomes will result. To the extent that markets allow wants to be satisfied (subject to

resource and technological constraints) there is little need for politics. However, markets sometimes fail, i.e., they systematically underproduce and overproduce certain goods.

When markets fail to satisfy the ends of private agents, the political process may provide an alternative. Market failure provides a major theoretical entry point between economics and politics. When the scope of a market failure involves more than one national jurisdiction, we have a stylized example of a "problem" for international political economy (Olson 1980, 10).

Classical and neoclassical economics provide a wide array of theoretical insights relevant for global political economy. Developments in modern neoclassical theory are suggestive of a number of ways to connect politics and economics besides market failure. There is the theory of commercial policy which has both normative and empirical components. Normative commercial policy is concerned with the best (optimal) policy to follow given the objective of maximizing national welfare. The empirical component, concerned with the actual (observed) forces impacting commercial policy, takes economics closer to interest groups and political institutions, phenomena more familiar to political scientists. The literatures on rent-seeking and directly unproductive profit-seeking activities explore distributional struggles rather than aggregate efficiency. Through the concepts of property rights and transaction costs, economists have helped to bridge the gap between the institutional worlds of economics and political science, dominated respectively by the market and the state. Finally, the public choice approach does not rely on markets and market failure for links between economics and politics. Instead, the assumption of rational, self-interested behavior is applied to a variety of non-market settings, including political ones.

All of the above approaches can't be reviewed here. Instead, I will focus on two categories of market failure -- international externalities and public goods -- and strategic trade theory.

Market Failure: Externalities and Public Goods

The concepts of externalities and public goods provide openings for integrating politics and economics at the global level. At the broadest level, an externality occurs when the action of one individual affects others who are not parties to the transaction. Externalities may be positive, e.g., when a breakthrough in pharmaceutical research quickly spreads to countries besides the originating one. Sometimes, arguments for the rapid growth of newly industrializing countries rest on implicit external benefits, e.g., "riding" the product cycle and benefitting from the technological innovations of the most advanced. Sometimes externalities are negative. International pollution (rivers, acid rain), ozone depletion, global warming (which may help some countries), and overexploiting common property resources are examples of the negative force of externalities.

There are a number of responses to the existence of international externalities. One response, advocated by defenders of the market, is to let the affected parties bargain among themselves about how to distribute costs and benefits. If country B (or a group of countries) suffers from the external effects of country A's actions, B may try to buy out A's harmful behavior. An example of this is supplied by the Japanese suggestion that the Western, industrialized countries buy out Brazilian rights to deplete their own rain forest. This strategy is inspired by the theory which Coase set forth in his classic "The Problem of Social Cost" (1960).

Other responses are possible that require more in the way of active political and institutional change. The dispute could be submitted to an international tribunal, a board of arbitration, or a court such as the International Court of Justice or European Court of Justice. It is also possible to submit conflicts to national courts with the consent of the relevant parties.

Finally, if potential conflicts exist among countries, they may attempt to create economic zones or jurisdictions such that the domain of the zone is coterminous with the scope of the relevant externality. Perhaps more likely is the creation of some institutional arrangement to regulate the activities giving rise to externalities -- a treaty or agreement to control the export of inflation, pollution, unemployment, or a permanent international organization (World Health Organization, International Telecommunication Union, etc.).

Let us now shift the attention to public goods. Public goods have two characteristics: non-excludability and non-rivalness. The former property says that if a good (say defense, law and order, clean air) exists for anyone within a given area or jurisdiction, it exists for all. Within such an area (say a country), it is impossible to exclude certain people from the benefits of protection, even though only part of the population may have made an effort to provide for it. An urban taxpayer benefits no more or less than a mountain dweller who eludes the IRS. The latter characteristic, non-rivalness or jointness of supply, implies that consumption of a good by one will not decrease the amount available for others. Enjoying clean air and secure borders is not at the expense of others, at least up to a point where congestion creates interference. Economic efficiency alone, then, would seem to dictate that, once the good exists, additional members should be permitted to consume it. The

marginal benefit is positive; marginal cost is low or zero. Variations in excludability and rivalness allow us to construct a typology of goods and to locate the position of public goods.

The intersection of goods which are excludable and rival define conventional private goods, the main subject matter of economic theory. Public goods, by contrast, are neither excludable nor rival. Individuals within a given jurisdiction cannot be prevented from consuming the good once it exists regardless of whether they contributed to its production. Cell #3 (non-excludable but rival) identifies common property resources (the mineral seabed, the earth's atmosphere, high-seas fishing resources). Here the goods in question are subtractable (i.e., rival) but it is difficult, costly, or impossible to exclude. Cell #2 refers us to situations where it is possible to exclude but where the goods in question are non-rival.

There are numerous examples of international public goods: nuclear deterrence, as provided by the North Atlantic Treaty Organization (NATO), clean oceans, rules for the disposal of nuclear wastes, and an international program of public health to eliminate infectious diseases. Not all of the above examples exist in fact, and the degree of publicness of a good is a complicated empirical question. But a public good is one which, if it did come into existence, would have certain properties. In a sense, a public good is an extreme case of an externality, where nearly all the benefit is non-capturable, hence there is little individual incentive to provide it.

The supply (or undersupply) of public goods at the international level is a thriving field of research. General treatments are provided by Conybeare (1980, 1984), Frey (1984a, 1984b), Loehr and Sandler (1978), and Sandler (1980). Applied work has been carried out in many fields, including the North Atlantic Treaty Organization (Murdoch and Sandler 1982, 1984; Olson and Zeckhauser 1966; and O'Neal and Elrod 1989), trade (Conybeare 1987; Lipson 1982), and hegemony and stability (Kindleberger 1973; Keohane 1980; Lake 1991; and Snidal 1985).

Political scientists are fond of saying that economic exchange does not take place in a vacuum but have been woefully short of ideas about just how to infuse political content into economic transactions. The provision of international public goods, including the organization and institutions required for provision, should be thought of not as isolated instances of politics and international organization dotting the global landscape but as part of the foundation for that landscape. As Gill and Law remark, these goods are "...effectively the politico-economic conditions for, and aspects of, a liberal international economy..." (1988, 45). Similarly, David

TABLE 1

Types of Goods

	rivalness	
	yes	no
excludability yes	private goods	spite goods
no	common property goods	public goods

Lake treats public goods as part of the international economic infrastructure of international politics (Lake 1991).

There are many directions in which externality and public goods theory and research can go. First, one can investigate the circumstances under which international public goods are likely to be supplied or not. In realist and neorealist theory, the international system is represented as anarchic and as lacking in both centralized power and common values. This would not seem to be a promising starting point for public goods provision. Yet there are numerous ways for public goods to be provided short of a central government and sanctions. One facilitating condition concerns the distribution of power. To the extent that power is concentrated -- the limiting case would be a hegemonic power -- public goods can be more easily provided.

This simple proposition, linking the distribution of economic power and public goods provision, is the theoretical core of hegemonic stability theory. Just a little over two decades old, if we consider Gilpin (1971) and Kindleberger (1973) as the founders, this theory has exerted considerable sway in the United States. Part of the reason for its appeal is that it connects a fragment of realism (distribution of power, albeit economic power) with international public goods. Its promise cuts two ways at once: it provides a way of connecting realism and neoclassical economics; and it attempts to show how international governance is possible absent international government.

Research on hegemonic stability theory went through three phases. During the first phase (1971 to 1980), the theory was introduced and secured on the analytical foundation of public goods theory. A hegemon is important, Kindleberger (1973) argued, because a single leader helps to solve collective action problems. This is true whether acting in isolation or as part of a privileged group. The second phase runs from 1980 to the late eighties. It corresponds to the development of the original insights and to their empirical testing (by supporters, skeptics, and agnostics) in various issue areas, such as trade, monetary policy, and petroleum (see Keohane 1980, 1982; Cowhey and Long 1983; Lawson 1983; Evans 1989). The third phase overlaps with the second. It is distinguished in that the primary concerns are theoretical (Snidal 1985; Lake 1991). I will elaborate on these concerns below.

These theoretical developments were, and continue to be, important. Keohane (1984) untied the knot connecting hegemony and public goods (and regimes). International openness, regimes, and public goods were all possible without hegemony. Similarly, Ostrom (1990) made important headway demonstrating that international self-governance structures were possible in "Global Commons" situations. Both scholars built upon and extended basic economic theory concerned with self-enforcing agreements.

In 1985 Duncan Snidal wrote an important article, "The Limits of Hegemonic Stability Theory." In it he argued that hegemonic stability theory was not so much right or wrong as underspecified. It did not provide enough (theoretical) information to be properly tested, information relating to the importance of size (absolute and relative) and the distributional implications of the theory.

Snidal's first move was to distinguish between two strands of hegemony, benevolent and coercive. The benevolent hegemon pioneers the creation of international public goods and pays for their costs, while others enjoy the benefits while free-riding. The hegemon is exploited at the same time that it also enjoys the public good. The coercive hegemon forces weaker states to make contributions (Snidal 1985, 589), that is, to pay for provision of the good. The two models are distinguished by the role of the hegemon and by different distributional implications. They are united in that both are concerned with collective goods (Snidal 1985, 590). Snidal's superb analysis leaves us with an important unresolved question. Does the coercive hegemon act against the interests of others compared to the *status quo ante* or does it "merely" assure that others pay for their share of the gains?

The most recent attempt to extend hegemonic stability theory is provided by David Lake (1991). In "The Theory of Hegemonic Stability: An Interim Report," Lake correctly points out that Snidal's distinction between coercive and benevolent models has to do with the distribution of gains. All parties gain. This is almost axiomatic since public goods are at issue. Weaker states gain less in the coercive model, more in the benevolent model. But everyone gains. The main issue concerns the ways the dominant state uses (or does not use) its power. From Lake's standpoint, the critical point is that interests (preferences) aren't questioned in both models. Everyone wants the same things. What differs is ability to affect provision and ability to engage in opportunistic behavior.

Lake moves the discussion forward by distinguishing between neoliberal models of hegemonic stability, which are based on common preferences, and neorealist models based on different preferences over outcomes such as international trade and exchange. While the full import of this distinction cannot be discussed here, it clearly broadens the terms of debate. It does so not by diluting concepts but by refining our subject matter in more precise ways. Lake's approach allows us to see divergent behaviour as resulting from pursuit of conflicting interests as well as opportunities.

A second direction in which research could go involves investigating free-riding and burden-sharing. It is a popular concern of security analysts working on NATO, at least this side of the Atlantic. Since Olson and Zeckhauser wrote their pioneering article, "An Economic Theory of Alliances" (1966), free-riding and burden-sharing within alliances have inspired much follow-up research (e.g., Knorr 1985; Murdoch and Sandler 1982, 1984; O'Neal and Elrod 1989; Oppenheimer 1979; and Russett and Sullivan 1971).

Research on burden-sharing within NATO is marred by a weakness sometimes characteristic of the literature on public goods as a whole. This has to do with the difficulty of unambiguously identifying a public good. What is it about NATO, or some outcome associated with it, that is public in nature? Unless a clear answer to this question is forthcoming, the rationale for the burden-sharing cum free-riding perspective breaks down and a model based on the pursuit of separate interests becomes more appropriate.

The generally accepted answer to what is public about NATO is nuclear deterrence. Without doubt, NATO's role in this regard displays attributes of public goods. But the empirical world is more complicated. Under the doctrine of massive retaliation, deterrence was more public (i.e., applied to all NATO members with less discrimination) than after McNamara's Ann Arbor speech in 1962. Here the concepts of flexible response, graduated deterrence, and damage-limitation came into play. The distinctions between "strategic" and "theater" weapons caused further worries among Europeans and led to charges that Europe would become a combat zone for "limited" war while the U.S. and Canada would remain secure. Without trying to resolve the historical quarrel, the conceptual point remains -- the identification of public goods is no easy task. This requires us to do a certain amount of conceptual and empirical spadework before constructing models of burden-sharing and shirking. This work is inevitably of an interpretive nature, requiring us to think not only of force structures but also of plans and strategies, intentions, geopolitical situations, and historical contingencies. In general, the further we move from hardware to software (e.g., from missiles in silos to computer programs for targeting), from overall force structures to strategy and tactics, the greater the ambiguity about what is public and private.

The model of Conybeare and Sandler (1990) is more realistic in that it makes an effort to distinguish and then theorize about pure public goods (deterrence), impure public goods (damage-limitation), and private goods (infrastructure). Building on these distinctions, they construct a joint product model of alliance behavior as resulting from three sets of forces.

The preceding point about public goods has to do with the appropriate conceptual categorization of the subject matter of global political economy. The same point could be applied to issue areas besides security, for example, trade, finance, monetary relations, the resources of the oceans, and so on. Without a precise understanding of the ways that international trade, investment, and deep seabed mining display public and private characteristics and are rival or excludable or both, we can make little progress theoretically. Before we ask our concepts to do theoretical work (i.e., to explain variation in other concepts), they should be unambiguously connected to empirical referents.

The third and last point concerns theoretical work that needs to be done to advance our understanding of the role of externalities and public goods in global political economy. At times, the relationship between particular issues (e.g., trade), game structures (e.g., prisoners' dilemma), institutional forms (e.g., regimes), and outcomes (e.g., cooperation, allocative results) is very confused. Is free trade a public good (as many hegemonic stability theorists assume), a private good, or a mixed good, offering private benefits as well as important externalities? What are the consequences of conceptualizing trade as a public good or prisoners' dilemma? Does it make a difference for our theories?

Basic theoretical work is needed to clarify the differences among different incentive structures (or games) and to draw out their theoretical implications. Important work has already been done clarifying the differences among games of assurance, prisoners' dilemma, chicken games and others (Stein 1982). Duncan Snidal (1985) has drawn out the consequences of differences in the structure of coordination versus prisoners' dilemma games for cooperation and international organization. Conybeare (1984) has probed prisoners' dilemma and public goods conditions and argued that conceptualizing an issue (such as trade) one way or the other has consequences for theory and policy.

Other scholars are attempting to link particular environmental and incentive configurations to other variables, especially to institutional structure and cooperative-uncooperative outcomes. Elinor Ostrom and her colleagues (1992) have shown that binding cooperation is possible even without central government sanctions. And Lisa Martin (1992a) has theorized the importance of different interest configurations for the *form* of international institutions.

In particular, Martin has demonstrated how the utility of multilateral norms and institutions varies with the type of problem faced. Robert Keohane (1990b) argues that international institutions are sometimes exclusive by nature (NATO, the EC), sometimes conditionally open (G.A.T.T.), and sometimes unconditionally open (the World Health Organization). He argues a correspondence between degree of openness and the underlying configuration of interest. Exclusive institutions revolve around distributional issues and are often motivated by rent-seeking. Conditionally open institutions are usually a response to free-riding and unconditionally open structures predominate under coordination incentives (1990, 751-53). There is little reason to exclude countries from membership in the World Health Organization (WHO). A common under-standing of disease, medical technology, and treatments benefits all. By contrast, membership in the G.A.T.T. carries a price tag, since non-members could exploit collective benefits while pursuing autonomous commercial policies themselves.

Strategic Trade Theory

Strategic trade theory, or the "new international economics," is a body of thought about how firms and governments think and act with respect to trade in the modern world (Brander and Spencer 1981, 1985; Grossman and Richardson 1986; Krugman 1986, 1987; and Stegemann 1989). Orthodox trade theory, in both its classical (Ricardian) and neoclassical (Heckscher-Ohlin-Samuelson) variants, suggests that governments should do very little beyond providing a healthy domestic and inter-national environment for specialization and exchange. In addition, prescribed governmental policy is non-strategic. There is a best trade policy to follow regardless of what other countries do. With factor endowments, tastes, and technology specified exogenously, the broad lines of comparative advantage are settled. Specialization and exchange take place to exploit comparative cost differences. The assumption of a competitive market means that each firm is a price-taker, that no firm can affect the output and pricing behavior of other firms, and that any "rents" existing in the system will be quickly competed away.

Until recently (10-15 years ago), theories of international trade were organized around the assumption of perfect competition (Stegemann 1989, 73). As Lake points out, neoclassical theories of trade are characterized by "...constant returns to scale which are fully internalized by the firm" (1991, 18). These assumptions discouraged economists from examining the effects of externalities, dynamic phenomena such as learning effects, and scale economies.

How then do we account for the new departures in trade theory? Perhaps empirical observation that some firms behave in a strategic fashion provided part of the impetus. More likely, as Stegemann argues, is that the literature on industrial organization found its way into trade theory. Industrial organization deals with the consequences of different sectoral characteristics, such as size, concentration, capital intensity, mobility, etc. This

literature becomes part of the theoretical foundation of strategic trade theory.

Before proceeding, one point should be clarified. Analysts sometimes attribute different motives (objectives) to governments in strategic trade theory. States are thought of as predatory or motivated by relative rather than absolute gain (wealth-maximization). States may in fact behave in predatory fashion but not necessarily because their goals have fundamentally changed. The basic goal is still national wealth-maximization. Instrumental preferences may change to accommodate different ways of reaching the basic goal. Stegemann is quite correct to point out that national welfare is central to mercantilist, neoclassical, and strate-gic views of trade. What distinguishes strategic trade theory is the view that the classical harmony between national and global welfare may break down (Stegemann 1989, 80).

A common thread running throughout the literature on strategic trade theory is that market imperfections of several kinds allow welfare-improving (national -- not global) state intervention(Sherman 1991, 1). These imperfections include monopolies, increasing returns to scale, learning-by-doing effects, and spillovers generated by research and development. Brander and Spencer (1981) initiated research in the area of modeling trade policy in a market supplied by a foreign monopolist while Krugman's work (1986, 1987) focuses more on externalities associated with learning, scale economies, and research and development. These developments are important challenges to neoclassical trade theory in that they raise the possibility that profit-shifting (as opposed to wealth-producing) activities may be possible. But it is precisely at this point that the academic sparks begin to fly.

Let us explore in more detail how strategic trade works. In addition to profit-shifting activities, strategic trade has three other characteristics. These have to do with the creation of comparative advantages, the role of governments as actors, and the importance of sectoral policy, as opposed to macroeconomic policy.

First, "the creation of comparative advantage." Just what does this phrase mean? This is best answered by going back to orthodox trade theory as the reference point. According to this theory, firms within countries face constraints established by forces outside themselves. There are a certain amount of natural resources, a labor pool, and a stock of capital inside the country. Although the amount within any category is not unchanging, there is little short-term variation, and this is outside the control of economic and political agents.

This view of fixed and naturally given comparative advantage is increasingly being replaced by a more fluid conception in which relative advantages can change significantly in the short-run in response to governmental and firm strategies. The idea of human capital (or skilled, knowledge-intensive labor), advanced technology, and research and development all provide cases in point. Labor can be looked at in terms of the physical stock of men and women of working age in a country and can be categorized in terms of different levels of strength, skill, abstract knowledge, and so on. Alternatively, labor can be viewed as a resource subject to transformation by governmental and corporate policies. One way of transforming the work force is through educational policies, either to raise the literacy level in a country or to target specific vocational skills. A variety of work-training programs provided by the public and private sectors might also be relevant. By pursuing such policies, particular countries could acquire a comparative advantage in specific skilled labor categories.

Much the same argument could be made for technology, research, and development. The idea that national technological advantages are temporary and prone to dissipate under pressure of market solvents can be increasingly questioned. In addition, research and development, because they create significant, nonappropriable external benefits, are more and more subject to strategic manipulation both at the level of the firm and governments.

States may play a central role in strategic trade, though this is one of the most controversial aspects of the strategic trade literature (Krugman 1987, 139-40; Stegemann 1989, 89-95). In orthodox trade theory, the role of the state is minimal. Of course the positive theory of trade policy has long recognized protectionist policies, e.g., the demand for protection on the part of failing, uncompetitive industries. The exceptions in normative trade theory allow for protecting "infant industries" and optimal tariffs. However, this permission is carefully qualified, and the burden of proof is placed on those arguing intervention. All in all, governments play only a small part in international trade.

The key actors in strategic trade theory are large, oligopolistic firms and governments. In strategic trade theory, governments are not only interventionist in an empirical sense. It is also argued that sometimes they should be so in the sense that intervention can increase national welfare. Interventionist trade policies may be the rule in those industries where there are large economies of scale, learning effects, and spillover effects from one industry to another. Scale and learning effects are important because they suggest advantages to those firms which get there first, establish their positions, then engage in preemptive market strategies (Gilpin 1987, 217). Spillover effects are important because they suggest the interlocked nature of the benefits of industrial production. Some of these benefits are captured (as income); others escape as externalities. A strategic trade

theory would try to assure that, to the extent possible, these spillovers transpire among national firms and industries.

The role of government intervention to correct for externalities is neither new nor unique to trade. The justification for government intervention in profit-shifting activities is different. In the standard model of duopoly, we have two producers in two different countries with each producer exporting to a third market. In this model, developed by Brander and Spencer (1981, 1985), firms behave like Cournot duopolists, each setting its export level on the basis of what the other does. The Cournot equilibrium therefore corresponds to the Nash equilibrium, i.e., the best one can do given what the other will do (Stegemann 1989, 81).

A sophisticated firm can question treating the behavior of a competitor as given. Why not assume an independent stance, and make the other adjust? In other words, there may be first-mover advantages. But the problem is that this strategy makes sense for both firms, and therefore for neither. Without a way of making its strategy credible, both firms will be nudged back into the Nash equilibrium. Firms by themselves cannot provide credible commitments because the other firm can simply cut prices and ride out the attempt to garner larger profits. The ultimate justification for government intervention is that governments can provide such credible commitments. By paying a subsidy to a national firm to enter a market first, governments can deter entry and shift profits to national firms. Since governments cannot be put out of business, at least not so easily as firms, their commitment to underwrite the firm is more credible (see Stegemann 1989, 81-84; Krugman 1987, 134-37).

Finally, strategic trade implies industrial and sectoral policy as opposed to exclusive reliance on macro policy. Macro policy includes money supply, exchange rate policy, balance of payments adjustments, and demand management. These policies are not intended to affect relative incentives to produce across different sectors of the economy. A focus on strategic trade, however, implies favoring some sectors over others, particularly those producing the highest rents, i.e., returns above those possible if resources are employed in the next best way. Thus, selective subsidies to leading edge industries, export promotion of particular sectors, low-interest loans, and differential tax-breaks for capital depreciation in strategic sectors might all be employed as policies consistent with a strategic trade outlook.

It would still be this side of understatement to say that strategic trade theory has sparked heated controversies within the academy and in policy circles. A survey of world trade conducted by *The Economist* carried a caption that read "Krugman proposes, Bhagwati disposes" (September 22, 1990). Bhagwati has led the charge, or rather countercharge, advancing the plausible proposition that strategic trade theory is the ideology of protectionist forces.[2] This leads Bhagwati to worry that resistance to the supply of protection in the executive branch of the U.S. government will be weakened (Bhagwati 1989, 17).

Apart from these opening salvos, criticisms of strategic trade theory have centered on four themes: (1) infrequency with which the assumptions of the new trade theory are satisfied; (2) lack of robustness of the theory; (3) the stringent informational requirements; and (4) encouragement of rent-seeking.

While many economists recognize the widespread existence of learning effects, technological spillovers, and economies of scale, some (perhaps quite a few) are reluctant to admit the pervasiveness of firms with sufficient market power to alter world prices. Yet this is just what the theory requires for firms to pursue strategies that deter market entry, alter the terms of trade, or affect global market shares. Thus it is not clear how widespread the existence conditions of strategic trade theory are (Haberler 1990, 25). Yet the scope of these conditions determines the applicability of strategic trade theory to commercial policy.

A related issue concerns the robustness of the theory. Apart from the issue of how often the assumptions hold, we need to ask how continuous departures affect the performance of the core theoretical propositions. Presumably, classical and neoclassical trade theory are quite robust, in that conclusions hold even under large departures from the conditions contained in the theoretical assumptions. Just the opposite is the case, argue the critics, with strategic trade theory. A number of papers (Eaton and Grossman 1986; Grossman 1986; and Markusen and Venables 1988) attempt to demonstrate lack of robustness.

A third criticism centers on the stringent informational requirements of strategic trade theory. Political agents engaged in commercial policy need to know about market structure, reaction functions of other firms, the nature of scale economies, learning by doing effects, and the short- and long-term consequences of research and development spending. Regarding scale economies and learning-by-doing, it is not enough to know simply that such effects exist, and what the directions are, but what some crucial parameters are, such as the slopes of the curves, how steeply they rise, when they reach their plateaus, etc. On this general point, critics of strategic trade theory join industrial policy critics in arguing that sectoral targeting and interventions are difficult and almost always produce results inferior to the market.

Finally, critics argue that commercial policy based on strategic trade theory will encourage rent-seeking and revenue-seeking (Krueger 1974; Bhagwati 1983). Both activities (the former is a struggle for the windfall premiums associated with import quotas; the latter is the counterpart for revenues) involve socially wasteful expenditures of resources (if only the labor time used up in lobbying) that provide incomes by diverting wealth from other sectors of the economy.

The upshot of these criticisms is that there is a large gap between strategic trade theory and normative commercial policy. Even those who recognize the merit of strategic trade ideas, such as Krugman, are very cautious about the proper policy conclusions. The consensus seems to be that the conditions supporting a successful strategic trade policy are fragile. The costs of organizing are high and, if interest groups are part of the political process behind the formulation of policy, firm- or industry-specific rents rather than national welfare are likely results. Information requirements are high, governments are not likely to possess the information, and, if they do, they are not likely to act purely on informational considerations. In the hurley-burley world of politics, interest groups will be motivated by a variety of short- and long-term goals rather than by national welfare. Krugman perhaps understates when he says: "Governments do not act in the national interest, especially when making detailed microeconomic interventions" (Krugman 1987, 142).

Numerous empirical studies of strategic trade theory have been carried out but will not be reviewed here. For examples and surveys, see Cline (1986), Gasiorek, Smith, and Venables (1989), and Baldwin (1988). The general finding is that trade behavior in particular sectors does not reflect strategic behavior and when it does, it does not result in net gains. But these studies are equivocal and do not allow disciplined inferences about many propositions in strategic trade theory. Some of these studies virtually equate strategic trade with protectionism, an equation that is not at all forced by the theory (Krugman 1987). Other studies rely on weak designs. Demonstrating that automobiles or computers do not reflect the principles of strategic trade theory is not conclusive, unless one can argue that these sectors are "crucial cases." Instead, designs that employ multiple cross-sectoral variation in properties such as scale economies, externalities, and learning-by-doing effects are required. A more promising approach is provided by Milner and Yoffie (1989) who use strategic trade theory to account for patterns of conditional protection.

To the extent strategic trade theory becomes recognized as playing a central role, it erodes some obstacles to integrating politics and economics. An economic theory of trade built on the premises of imperfect competition, oligopolistic market structure, externalities, and the need for non-economic actors to back up (make credible) strategies of firms, provides obvious entry points for politics. Political scientists have long questioned neoclassical assumptions about market competition, low (or nonexistent) barriers to entry, the assumption of no long-term rents, and, in general, the entire worldview that decisions about the international division of labor are best left to the market.

While the primary benefits of strategic trade theory are likely to lie in trade theory itself, there is considerable potential for cross-fertilization between development theory and trade theory. At a minimum, innovations in strategic trade theory offer a fresh look at infant industry arguments and specialization in accord with naturally bestowed comparative advantage.

Finally, strategic trade theory is very suggestive of aspects of dependency theory, an association which is likely to be strenuously resisted. Although the methodological tools of strategic theory are rejected by dependentistas, in favor of historical-structural analysis, similarities at the level of perceived structure and operation of the international system are considerable. Cardoso and Faletto (1971, 1978) have long viewed the world system as oligopolistic rivalry among firms and states, have never believed that politics could be separated from economics, and have accepted the long-term, self-reproducing superiority of industries in dominant countries as a fact of life. This last point is dependency theory's way of saying that long-term rents exist (or continuously reproducible rents, within and across sectors). Furthermore, Brewster (1973) and Sunkel (1973) firmly believe in the importance of intersectoral linkages (spillovers) while Mytelka (1978) and Gereffi (1978) emphasize the continuing importance of economies of scale, learning by doing, and the role of the knowledge industry in maintaining technological superiority.

I have argued that market failure is the master concept linking politics with economics within the neoclassical tradition. The reach of this concept is broader than is sometimes supposed and could be extended to include not only externalities, public goods and strategic trade, but also international property rights and international organization. Insofar as markets do not spontaneously produce their own existence conditions -- secure property rights, communications and infrastructure, and minimal global institutions -- a failure of sorts exists. Nevertheless, the market failure approach is limited as I hope to show by remarking on externalities and strategic trade.

One limitation is that the externalities paradigm cuts a narrower path to international political economy than one might think. Since the world is very interdependent, one might think that externalities are correspondingly high. While there is some truth in this, the political relevance of externalities is diminished in two ways. First, not all effects transmitted from one country to another are externalities. International externalities define a subset of international interdependencies. If a firm in country A produces a product that puts a firm in country B out of business, and this result was effected through the market, there is no externality. Similarly, if adverse terms of trade or volatile commodity earnings are the result of movements in supply and demand, they are not externalities either. To avoid misunderstanding, the fact that externalities have a clearly limited domain is not a conceptual defect. My point is simply that the externalities paradigm does not include much that may otherwise be considered political. Much work in international political economy concerns how political phenomena (e.g., power bargaining, autonomous state actions) affect market processes or how the market creates outcomes that are politically contested by market and non-market players. In *Structural Conflict: The Third World Against Global Liberalism* (1985), Stephen Krasner takes as an important theme the political contestation over markets and market outcomes themselves. Both Gruber (1992) and Krasner (1991) remind us that much of the subject matter of international relations has to do with relative capabilities and winning and losing -- not with overcoming Pareto-suboptimality.

Realist Approaches

According to many accounts, realism, and more recently, neorealism[3] is the dominant approach in international relations theory, though not necessarily in global political economy. In "Thucydidean Realism," Michael Doyle identifies a number of surveys in which evidence is given for this proposition (Doyle 1990, 223). In *The Power of Power Politics*, John Vasquez reports that over 90% of the hypotheses tested by behaviorists are realist in origin (Vasquez 1983, 162-170). However, since its central research agenda is guided by power, anarchy, and security, realism's reach into the realm of international economics is uncertain. In this section I will show some of the ways politics and economics are connected within realism.

I define realism in terms of its theorization or assumptions about (1) relevant actors (states), (2) environment (anarchy), (3) capacities ("powers") of the units, and (4) motivations. It seems that something must be said (or assumed) about all four points before the realist system can be set into motion. In brief, the central actors are nation-states. Non-state actors are downplayed or theorized as dependent entities; for example, multinational corporations are seen as operating in a space defined by state policies. Power, however defined, identifies the capabilities of states. Because relative power is so crucial to the success of many other ends, power is also a goal. The environment within which states interact is anarchic, i.e., without centralized rule and power. And finally, with regard to motives, states are variously seen as pursuing security, power, and wealth. Security, especially survival, is the most important motivation and is treated as a scarce good, the improvement of the security of some states coming at the expense of others. When conflicts are acute, security can be thought of as dominating other goals, but when security concerns decline, a variety of other goals may push toward the foreground.[4]

Realist theory is structural theory, i.e., theory about the importance of third-image factors. For Kenneth Waltz (1979), there are three central components of international structure. First, there is the ordering principle, anarchy, which defines how units relate to one another. Second, there is the distribution of capabilities, i.e., how power is spread across states. Third, there is the differentiation principle. Within states, differentiation of functions is high; across states, it is low. Classical realist theory tends to take anarchy and states themselves as givens and looks at consequences of exogenous variation in the distribution of capabilities.[5] How does the change in the power of one country, either through domestic growth processes or alliances, affect the preferences, opportunities, and policies of others? Faced with such changes, will a state choose to ally with the weaker grouping (balance), join the stronger alliance (bandwagon), stay neutral, pursue a divide-and-rule strategy, or increase its arms (Walt 1987)?

Part of the difference between realists and nonrealists lies not in what is excluded or included, but in what each takes as exogenous versus problematic. With respect to what is fixed and what is allowed to vary, world order and regional integration theorists are outside the realist mainstream, since it is precisely the idea of anarchy that they make problematic. Integration theorists often take distribution of capabilities as a given and look at the way in which anarchic structures and the nature of states can be transformed. Successful regional integration constitutes a mitigation (or perhaps transformation) of anarchy. The work of Karl Deutsch on national and international community building focuses on "core areas," as reflecting the distribution of capabilities (including administrative and social capabilities -- not just military ones). Deutsch's dependent variables are pluralistic and amalgamated security communities, concepts defining different degrees of centralized decision making within a regional system where the expectation that violence will be used to address conflicts has been reduced. States within Deutschian security communities are not asocial, perpetually insecure, and necessarily threatened by

relative power changes (Deutsch 1953; Deutsch et al. 1957).

Realism and Economics

Security questions lie at the center of the realist research program. The central issue concerns the relationship between the international distribution of power and state behavior. How do states, within anarchy, respond to power changes? Thus diplomacy, alliances, divide-and-rule strategies, and arms races are important components of realist research. With the exception of the focus on arms races, where national military capabilities are expressed as a reaction function to the capabilities of others, national power is fixed by forces outside realist theory. The explanatory task is to account for how power combines across countries and the implications for perceptions of insecurity, conflict, war, and peace.

Every theory must take some things as exogenous. This allows us not to have to explain everything at once. Given the interest in explaining war and peace, realism does not have to take on the additional burden of explaining variations in national power. Yet, to connect to economics, realism must move beyond security issues narrowly defined. In the remainder of this section, I explore four theoretical links: (1) the use of state power to structure international economic exchange; (2) the effect of international economic exchange (especially asymmetries in trade patterns) on the power of states; (3) the effect of the systemic distribution of military power on economic exchange; and (4) finally, the connection between realism and institutions.

State Capacity to Structure Economic Exchange

Realists stress the capacity of state agents to structure exchange relations at the international level. In this they differ from neoclassical economists who see exchange dictated by relative factor proportions and cross-national preference patterns -- and interdependence theorists, who see technology as the basic determinant of exchange. In either case, states are faced with international exchange patterns that are given, outside their control. Realists attempt to turn the tables, arguing that what others treat as independent is really dependent. Disagreements center on which ways to draw the causal arrows -- not on which variables are salient.

There are numerous specific ways in which this argument is made. The most general claim involves the rejection of the twin proposition that technology and economics are autonomous and that their growth erodes state sovereignty. As Thomson and Krasner (1989) assert, "Realists argued first that growing interdependence has been a function of political power and political choice, not of exogenous technological change" (1989, 196). Further, states are the necessary, if not sufficient, condition for international exchange, since it is states that establish secure property rights across countries. Without a medium of exchange, convertability, and secure rights for foreign investments and goods in transit, international trade could hardly have taken root (Thomson and Krasner 1989, 197-98). States have "consolidated sovereignty," to use Thomson and Krasner's phrase. States thus exert control over their economies, including economic activities in foreign countries, in ways they didn't previously. Vernon and Spar point out that U.S. courts did not consider foreign activity of U.S. firms as subject to U.S. law before 1909 (1989, 114).

A corollary point is that the mix of autonomy-interdependence is not a technological given, but is influenced by state preferences. Realists refer not just to extreme cases (Albania, Burma, and the People's Republic of China) but to any country concerned with minimizing vulnerabilities and risks at the same time that it strives to enjoy the benefits of international specialization. While autonomy is one of the traditional concerns of dependency theory, scholars demonstrate that the tradeoffs also face advanced countries. Vernon and Kapstein worry that over 20% of the ingredients of U.S. weapons come from outside the country (1991, 5). In the same issue of *Daedalus*, Moravcsik argues that military planners have traditionally supported free trade, perhaps surprisingly, but the rationale is that trade helps to secure financing from abroad and it allows economies of scale not afforded by the domestic market (1991, 23-25).

Finally, apart from the ratio of trade to gross national product, states also play a role in affecting trade partners and the composition of trade. The issue of trade partners is taken up in the discussion of security externalities. Here I just mention the case of the former Soviet Union, Eastern Europe, and the Council on Mutual Economic Assistance (CMEA). If technical forces were adequate to explain patterns of exchange, CMEA countries would not have formed a separate world system largely cut off from the advanced capitalist world. While the extent of regional autarky is controversial (see Chase-Dunn 1982), Szymanski argues strongly that Soviet participation in the capitalist world economy was severely limited so as to reduce vulnerability. Trade was designed to cover shortfalls or to provide non-essential items. Economic exchange was thus similar to the long-distance trade in luxury items that Wallerstein discusses under pre-capitalist systems (Szymanski 1982, 58, 66).

Finally, states are sensitive to the product lines in which countries specialize. Strategic trade predicts that states will foster industries associated with large externalities. Different products vary in associated wages, profits, demand-elasticities, spinoffs, and value added. Also, most states have a food and raw materials policy. After World War I and up to the common agricultural policy of the European Community (EC), most Western European countries had independent agricultural policies, despite the large gains to be had by cross-national specialization in food and manufactures. One suspects that comparative cost differences between food and industry were much larger than those across different manufacturing sectors.

International Exchange, Power, and Vulnerability

The preceding section dealt with the ways in which states structure the realm of international economic exchange. Exchange patterns were the dependent variables. The second realist theme turns the tables and asks how international exchanges affect state power and vulnerability. National power can be thought of as constituted by two kinds of capabilities: attribute and exchange capabilities. Attribute capabilities refer to properties of states, or the national economy or society, e.g., size of army, air force, navy, gross national product, etc. Exchange capabilities refer to resources that flow out of the connections among countries. These connections are varied and might include trade, aid, technology flows, foreign investment, financial movements, debt, migration, and knowledge transfer. The general idea is that economic exchanges confer advantages (or liabilities) on countries and to the extent that such ties are asymmetric and not easily replaced, they provide a source of leverage, hence power.

Albert Hirschman (1945) was one of the first to recognize fully the political potential implicit in classical arguments about the gains from trade. The "gains from trade" describe the incremental consumption that occurs through trade compared to the baseline of domestic production. Formulated in opportunity cost terms, it becomes clear that the classical concept "gains from trade," when inverted, approximates the vulnerability of a country to another (Hirschman 1945, 18).[6]

Hirschman opened a conceptual door left slightly ajar by Ricardo. The opportunity costs idea, concretized in the form of trade among countries, points the way to a connection between power and exchange theory. If power implies the capacity to reward and punish, and if exchanges define flows of valued objects, numerous policy implications result. If A is dependent on B, if the costs of shifting, substituting, or doing without are also high, B will have power over A.

Hirschman's insights were suggestive of refinements in thinking about power (Baldwin 1979; Caporaso 1978). Bargaining power may be defined as the ability to control the outcomes of specific events. A different order of control is suggested by "structural power," the power to manipulate the choices, capabilities, and payoffs that other actors possess. As Hirschman put it, the purpose of these strategies is not immediately to exert one's will in a specific contest, but rather to shape the matrix of incentives in such a way as to "...make the pursuit of power a relatively easy task" (Hirschman 1978, 46).

The economic strategy of Germany, during the Third Reich, of creating "exclusive complementarities" with Eastern and Central European countries, attempted to put these countries in a dependent position. Similarly, when the Soviet Union sold oil and other natural resources to Eastern Europe below world market prices, it did so in part to increase the opportunity cost of changing suppliers (see Marrese 1986). And when twelve countries form an economic union with internally free trade and common external tariffs, they deprive nonmembers of the power to exploit divisions among them that are implicit in all social dilemmas.

The insights pioneered by Hirschman have not been vigorously pursued by realism. Yet, a diverse body of scholars is working on the connections between international exchange and power. They include dependency theorists (Cardoso and Faletto 1978; Dos Santos 1970; Sunkel 1973), national security strategists (Knorr and Trager 1977; Knorr 1975), peace researchers (Galtung 1971), and international political economy analysts (Strange 1988, 1989, 1991). In addition, there is a substantial amount of research and theory development on economic sanctions, which in many ways is a logical extension of international influence structures (Doxey 1972; Galtung 1967). The most comprehensive and insightful books in this area are Baldwin's *Economic Statecraft* (1985) and Martin's *Coercive Cooperation* (1992b).

While this literature is impressive in scope, much of it is not consistently motivated by what I take to be Hirschman's central project -- the development of a theory of structural power. In *National Power and the Structure of Foreign Trade* (1945), Hirschman sets out to construct a theory of international influence networks that is importantly different from power in realist theory. Considered as a capability, realism treats power as an attribute of a country or distribution of countries. Bipolarity and multipolarity are distributional parameters.[7] Considered as a behavior (the activity of power), realism treats power as a relation. Hirschman wants to extend the capability aspect of power by pursuing the implications of the ways (mostly economic) in which countries are connected (by trade, investments, technology, and so on). To the extent that these relations identify gains which, if lost, could not easily be recouped

through partner or product substitution, they identify vulnerabilities. Vulnerabilities can be exploited; they are sources of power.

Power for Hirschman is not an attribute or distributional parameter. It is more tied to network and exchange theory than to attribute theory. The threat of using power is a threat to withdraw something rather than to deliver something. Understanding international influence networks is an important project that will help to round out the realist conception of power.

Systemic Distribution of Power and Economic Exchange

The first realist theme attempted to connect state power and exchange by referring to state actions aimed at limiting or expanding the realm of exchange. The state acted as a sort of architect creating barriers and opportunities to exchange. But what motivates states? What inclines leaders to seek liberalization or protection, autonomy or interdependence, overall efficiency or minimum vulnerability? One answer lies within domestic politics. States are agents of society and pursue goals in line with internal domestic pressures. A second answer lies at the structural (third-image) level. Since realism is a theory about the importance of international structure, I pursue the structural vein.

Two elements of structure are anarchy and the distribution of power. Both Waltz (1979) and Grieco (1988, 1990) have written extensively about the dampening effect of anarchy on international exchange. Within anarchy, states must be sensitive to relative as well as absolute gains. The distribution of gains -- not just total gains from trade -- must be brought into the calculation of whether and how to specialize and cooperate.

While anarchy doubtlessly produces levels of exchange below the prediction based on world government, by itself it is incapable of explaining important variations in levels of exchange and exchange partners. It explains why the average level of exchange is low and why profitable opportunities for exchange go unrealized. Anarchy is too global a property to explain temporal and partner variations. Without appealing to attribute similarities (e.g., sharing democratic principles, common ethnic or religious membership), structural theory can point to the influence of changes in international economic or political structure as determinants of exchange.

Two such international structural theories are hegemonic stability theory and the theory of security externalities developed by Joanne Gowa (1989). Hegemonic stability theory was discussed in a previous section and won't be elaborated here. Its major thesis is that the systemic distribution of power (economic power) affects the provision of international public goods. One such good is a free trade regime. Hegemonic stability theory attempts to explain trade liberalization -- hence the level of exchange -- by the degree of concentration of power.

For hegemonic stability theorists, the *systemic* distribution of power is confined to those who share purposes regarding public goods. After World War II, hegemony applied to countries within the advanced capitalist world. Shares of resources were calculated as fractions of the total resources within the Organization for Economic Cooperation and Development (OECD). The worldwide distribution of political-military power was bipolar at the same time that the U.S. was hegemonic within the OECD.

Joanne Gowa, in "Bipolarity, Multipolarity, and Free Trade" (1989), addresses the important issue of the global distribution of power and its relationship to trade. She criticizes the view that the prisoners' dilemma structure is responsible for the scarcity of open international markets. Instead she focuses on the security externalities (roughly the consequences of trade for defense and war-making) that result from open trade arrangements (Gowa 1989, 1246).

Gowa's theory joins a fragment of Hirschman's argument (1945) about the supply effects of trade to the military benefits of trade on trade partners. Because of these external benefits, countries cannot be indifferent to their trade partners. Because exchange among countries not only makes more goods available for consumption, but also allows countries to shuffle (substitute) domestic resources in more efficient combinations, it inevitably affects military capability.

Because trade takes place in an anarchic international system, countries must pay attention to relative as well as absolute gain. This directs attention to distributional themes rather than just growth and allocative efficiency. A number of specific predictions flow from Gowa's theory. First, countries are more likely to trade with allies than with neutrals or enemies. This preference is due to more than affective ties, common values, and communitarian considerations. Indeed, the prediction would also apply to cases where countries ally purely out of convenience, even in the face of great differences in domestic structure and national values. Second, trade is more likely to be open (free trade) under bipolarity than under multipolarity. The argument for this prediction is not obvious. Security externalities characterize bloc settings of various kinds. The critical factor is the degree of certainty with which one knows (military) friend and foe. Gowa presents two arguments for the greater openness (within poles) of bipolar systems, one based on the lesser exit costs of alliances in a multipolar world and the second based on

incentives for great powers to forgo their market power (Gowa 1989, 1249-252).

Structural international relations theory predicts that multipolar systems are more fluid than bipolar systems, fluidity defined in terms of the rate of change in membership from one alliance to another (Snyder 1984). This proposition has been confirmed empirically by Duncan and Siverson (1982). Perhaps the lower rate of exit from bipolar alliances is due to the greater cost of exit -- a country is less likely to find a compatible ally just on statistical grounds in a bipolar world. The relative stability of bipolarity leads countries to attach greater importance to the future (a low discount rate) than under multipolarity.

A third prediction, which Gowa does not make but which seems perfectly consistent with her analysis, is that regional integration is more likely to occur if it takes place within a more comprehensive military alliance. This point was made very early by Stanley Hoffmann (1963) and later by Kenneth Waltz (1979). The European Coal and Steel Community and the European Economic Community were and are both nested within a more comprehensive military organization, the North Atlantic Treaty Organization. This fact may help to explain why the EEC countries have integrated further than the member states of the European Free Trade Association, which has a sizeable number of neutrals (e.g., Sweden, Switzerland, Austria).

Both hegemonic stability theory and Gowa's theory of security externalities attempt to relate the international distribution of power to economic exchange. There are important differences in how this is done. First, hegemonic stability theory focuses on economic power while Gowa focuses on military power. The former approach looks at shares of trade, investment, and industrial output while the latter examines the ingredients of military power. Second, the two approaches sometimes differ in what they take to be the systemic level. Hegemonic stability theory sometimes refers to the distribution of economic power within a bloc (e.g., within the OECD world) and sometimes within the system as a whole (nineteenth century hegemony). Gowa, by contrast, is interested in the global distribution of power. Finally, hegemonic stability theory yields predictions relevant to liberalization-protectionism while the theory of security externalities predicts trade partners.

Realism and Institutions

In this section I briefly discuss realism's account of institutions. I do not elaborate the theory, leaving that for a later section. Instead, I use this opportunity as a way of anticipating and connecting with the subsequent treatment of liberalism, within which a more complete theory of institutions is taking shape.

In one sense, realism's theory of institutions is straightforward. International institutions are expressions of power. The Security Council of the United Nations, for example, recognizes World War II's victors by giving permanent membership and veto power to the U.S., England, France, the Soviet Union, and China. The Bretton Woods system, along with the International Monetary Fund and World Bank, recognizes the liberal international purposes of the United States.

This approach, however appealing, leaves some unanswered questions. Two stand out. The first question concerns the incremental explanatory power of the view that institutions reflect power (Krasner 1983). If institutions *only* reflect power, aren't they theoretically redundant and therefore dispensable in an explanatory sense? The second question asks how such an institutional account can explain the apparently voluntary nature of many international organizations and the great diversity of institutional forms. Can the World Health Organization, the Council of Mutual Economic Assistance, and the North Atlantic Treaty Organization be understood as reflections of power in the same way?

These questions are raised not because realism is incapable in principle of answering them, but because realism will have to break new ground to do so. To respond to the charge of redundancy, realists can point to the role of institutions in adding to the strengths of the powerful, increasing the efficiency with which they pursue goals. Institutions can reduce transaction costs and make it easier to coordinate policies among allies.

The second question, concerning the voluntary nature of many international organizations, raises the issue of how to characterize the interests among states. Classical realism thought in terms of conflictual and harmonious or zero-sum and non-zero-sum relations. Before modern game theory filtered into international relations, the range of interest structures (prisoners' dilemmas, coordination, chicken) was very limited. Without understanding the significance of mixed-motive games for international relations, it was impossible to develop a theory of cooperation. Realism had to first break loose from its zero-sum moorings. In a realist world where power is primary, and interests are zero-sum, institutions would either be irrelevant or limited to enhancing the efficiency of domination. In a harmonious world where agents costlessly transact, institutions would be unnecessary for the most part. What is locally rational (i.e., in a state's interest without coordination) would be beneficial for others.

In the subsequent discussion on liberalism, the significance of different interest structures is pursued.

Liberalism and Global Political Economy

The strongest contemporary challenge to realism comes from an unexpected quarter -- not Marxism or world systems theory -- but rather from liberalism, an approach whose roots lie more in domestic than international politics. Liberalism has "no canonical description" (Doyle 1986, 1152) and no generally accepted text compared to Waltz's *Theory of International Politics* (1979). It picks up on the importance of international society among functionalists and international pluralists, the role of common understandings salient to world order and epistemic community theorists, and the importance of institutions and regulations for resolving collective action problems among institutionalists.

What precisely is liberalism's challenge? At one level the challenge presents itself as a dispute about the goals (or implications of different goals) of state leaders (Grieco 1988, 1990; Snidal 1991; Powell 1991). Realists such as Grieco have argued that relative gains are central while institutionalists (Keohane 1984, 1990a) and some game theorists (Powell 1991; Snidal 1991) have argued in favor of contextually defined absolute gains. This is directly related to the debate about the scope of cooperative exchange. Realists argue that the realm of cooperative exchange is limited; liberals that it is much larger and capable of expanding.

While the relative-absolute gains debate has been prominent, there are other differences. Liberalism predicts outcomes (war, peace, cooperation) that are not structurally derived,[8] i.e., not determined by the existing or changing distribution of power. Structural (third-image) explanation is central to realism. Liberalism thus points to the importance of unit-level factors (e.g., form of government), emphasizes the private (non-governmental) and sociological aspects of international relations, along with state power, and sees possibilities for cooperation and progress in contrast to the endemic conflict and eternal cycles of realism (Keohane 1990a, 174).

What makes the challenge so acute is that liberalism accepts many (not all) of realism's ground rules -- the importance of states, power politics, and anarchy -- and comes to different conclusions. The differences are not so much a product of fundamentally different worldviews as of contrasting ways of reasoning. It is not true, as both Keohane (1990a) and Moravcsik (1992) point out, that liberalism is a normative and idealistic theory. It has a positive content that has been useful in critiquing (and forcing revisions in) realism.

Nevertheless, there are important differences in assumptions and analytical starting points. Liberalism exploits a two-way tension between state and society. The state is recognized as an actor but one that is embedded within a domestic and international society. Liberals insist on the importance of civil society (Moravcsik 1992, 6-9; Zacher and Matthew 1992) and on the connections between society, state, and individual. Domestic and transnational social forces can create constraints on states and can lead them to change policies. The European Community's White Paper outlining moves toward further integration and the collapse of communism in Eastern Europe owe a debt (probably smaller in the second case) to transnational social and economic forces.

Another important difference between liberalism and realism concerns the nature of interests. Realism takes state interests, at least the primary interest of security and relative power, as fixed, relative, and dominating other interests such as wealth. States desire power, in particular, relative power. This is not a matter of psychological taste so much as physical survival. Preferences are structurally determined. Anarchy, insecurity, and relative power are part of one coherent ensemble. It is this ensemble which liberalism tries to detach and analyze. Realists see a causal chain running from anarchy to the security dilemma, to the concern for relative power to limited cooperation. Liberals accept anarchy as a descriptive characterization of the global system but do not draw the same conclusions as realists.

In the remainder of this section I briefly describe different strands in liberal global political economy, discuss neoliberal institutionalism in more detail, and, finally, try to identify some research directions ahead.

Liberalism's varied intellectual heritage (Smith, Kant, Locke, Madison, Hume) suggests diverse theoretical strands:[9] Republican, commercial, sociological, and institutional.

Republican liberalism suggests the importance of limited, constitutional government, of democratic rights, elections, freedom from state intrusion into the "private" sphere, and control of the rulers by the ruled. Michael Doyle's starting point is that "...neither the logic of the balance of power nor the logic of hegemony explains the separate peace maintained for more than 150 years among states sharing one particular form of governance -- liberal principles and institutions." (Doyle 1986, 1157). While there are numerous empirical and theoretical issues to be resolved (see Schweller 1992; Lake 1992; Russett 1990), pointing to the association between liberal democracy and peace is a provocative starting point for future research.

A second variant is commercial liberalism. The starting point is civil society, a world of self-interested economic agents engaged in specialized production and exchange. Barring political obstacles (a big condition from our standpoint), Smith and Ricardo secured the foundation of gains from trade. Countries, by specializing in areas where they had a relative advantage, can gain by exchanging with other countries similarly motivated. This familiar economic story has a political implication. Specialized production and exchange, even according to purely technical criteria, lead to interdependence, vulnerability (often uneven) and political leverage. As Nye points out (Nye 1988, 238), sophisticated versions of liberalism provide a process-level theory linking international interactions to domestic society and politics. Commercial liberalism not only creates webs of interdependence that constrain states and create opportunities, it may also lead to redefinitions of self-interest. As Nye (1988) argues, realism recognizes learning as a response to changing payoffs. No change of identity, of the unit of account, or of connection between means and ends is involved. But regional integration theory is precisely a change of all these.

The third strand of liberalism is sociological (Nye 1988; Zacher and Matthew 1992). Sociological liberalism stresses the nature of group life in pluralistic industrial societies. Individuals, operating through a variety of groups -- occupational, professional, scientific, public-interest-oriented -- spawn contacts across national lines that may lead to redefinitions of interest, new knowledge, and even new identities.

Sociological liberalism adds a new dimension to international political economy. State to state interaction is important, but sociological liberals see these interactions taking place within a milieu in which domestic and transnational contacts and coalitions of interests and identities are prominent too. These coalitions may affect perceptions of state interests (as arguably cross-border coalitions of business interests do in the European Community) and provide vehicles (or obstacles) and resources for pursuing state goals. Indeed, state goals and social contacts may go hand in hand, as when the Federal Republic of Germany's *Ostpolitik* included social contacts among its goals, e.g., twinning cities, tourism, and cultural exchange.

Joseph Nye (1988) is quite right to point to the transformative potential of sociological liberalism (indeed, of liberalism in general). Nye identifies non-power incentives and the capacity to communicate as strengths of liberal theory, and correspondingly, as areas of weakness in realism (Nye 1988, 250).

The final version of liberalism is liberal institutionalism, or neoliberal institutionalism, as Robert Keohane has labelled it (1989). The starting point of the program is a dissatisfaction with the ability of extant theories to explain important variations in international outcomes. Neither realism, nor Marxism, nor process-level theories provide adequate explanations. Hegemonic stability theory provides a partial explanation but offers few refinements useful for explaining regional and cross-issue variations. As Keohane notes, if Marxism and realism were true, "we would not observe variations in cooperation from one time period to another, or issue by issue, that were unexplained by the dynamics of capitalism or by changes in international structure." (Keohane 1990a, 171).

The basic theoretical claim of neoliberal institutionalism is simple -- international institutions make a difference in explaining cooperative and noncooperative outcomes. The approach accepts states, anarchy, and power distribution as important. It does not see all of international politics as either purely conflictual or perfectly harmonious. Instead, liberal institutionalists start from mixed-motive games, where elements of conflict and cooperation exist. In these circumstances, institutions may make behavior more transparent (e.g., making defection visible), reduce uncertainty and transaction costs, lengthen the frame of interaction (thus enhancing the value of reputation), link issues, and provide monitoring and limited enforcement mechanisms. In short, institutions can foster cooperative gains in circumstances where they might not have been realized. There is some theoretical value added here since institutional claims are not based on changing the interests, the actors, the anarchical environment, or the power distribution.

The liberal's world is one of absolute gain, i.e., gains are judged against the pre-exchange baseline of utility separately for each actor. Agents are better off if they improve their pre-exchange conditions, independently of what others do. Realist skepticism about this proposition centers on the pervasiveness of relative gains. If states are in a security dilemma, and if economic gains are relevant for power, states must judge improvement by a relative yardstick. They must ask not only "am I better off?" but "how does my gain compare with that of others?" As a result, large absolute gains may be forgone because of adverse distributional implications.

As broad propositions, few would doubt either the relativity of power or the link between unequal economic gain and power. The controversial question is how much scope to give to relative and absolute gains. To what extent are states motivated by one or the other? What are the conditions determining which goals states pursue? Are preferences exogenous, given by complex domestic politics, or structurally determined?

Realists such as Grieco (1988, 1990) and Mearsheimer (1990) see power and anarchy as pervasive facts of international life. For Mearsheimer (1990) shifts in the distribution of capabilities have consequences for insecurity and conflict. While he does not concentrate on the implications for economic exchange (except for a brief analysis of the EC), this connection seems obvious.

Grieco has tackled the problem more directly arguing that liberals have exaggerated the scope of cooperative exchange. While the issue can't be discussed in detail here, the battle lines have been clearly drawn between those who feel that relative gains are salient and pervasive, making cooperation difficult, fragile, or impossible, and those who believe joint gains are extensive, robust, and growing.

In the face of the realist critique, three responses are possible. The first is to question seriously the descriptive accuracy of relative gains as a motive for states. It asks how widespread relative gains-seeking is. The second accepts relative gains as an assumption and explores the consequences for cooperation. The third accepts both relative and absolute gains as analytical categories and theorizes the conditions under which each holds. The first project is mainly empirical and descriptive; the second is formal and deductive; the third is synthetic and theoretical.

The first approach, though disarmingly simple, is actually fraught with ambiguities. How does one observe motives? They cannot be directly observed, and they are resistant to the standard attitudinal measures (questionnaires, content analysis). While motives can often be inferred from behavior, there are special difficulties in this case. Snidal is correct to point out that intense bargaining over distribution of gains is not evidence that states pursue relative gains (1991, 703). Any agent interested in absolute gain will also be interested in bargaining over the way gains are distributed. Bargaining behavior is therefore theoretically equivocal. It does not distinguish relative from absolute gains.

The other two approaches hold promise. Snidal (1991) accepts as an assumption the relative-gains motive and asks to what extent its existence hinders cooperation. The simple answer is that the conditions under which cooperation is hindered are limited to a world of just two states (or bipolarity) and pure relative gains (no mixed interests). Snidal remarks that "Only in the very special case of the two-state interaction, with high concern for relative gain and near disregard for absolute gains, is the realist case compelling" (Snidal 1991, 701).

Robert Powell's article (1991) reflects the third approach. Part of Powell's motivation is with the overall theoretical coherence of global political economy. If structural realism and neoliberal institutionalism make fundamentally different assumptions about state preferences, political economy and security studies are not easily unified within a single theory. Security studies are likely to be preoccupied by "us-them" and "win-lose" situations, economic exchange with joint gains and cooperation. Powell reasons that if differences in preferences are fundamental, i.e., are not simply local expressions of a basic theoretical principle, we may have to look to domestic politics for their causes. This undermines the structural project of realism and (fpartly) liberalism.

Powell takes a cue from neoclassical economics which has succeeded in unifying theories of market shares and profit-maximization (1991, 1304). He develops a model where the pursuit of relative and absolute gains is tied to changing external constraints. The units do not change. The underlying goals of states are invariant. Instead, derived preferences change in response to changes in the structure of the environment. Powell's approach is unifying in the sense that both motives (preferences) are particular contextual expressions of one underlying model.

Space limitations prevent a fuller discussion of liberalism. Let me simply mention a few points of broad significance. The movements toward democracy and markets in many parts of the world, the collapse of state communism in Eastern Europe and the Soviet Union, and the reunification of East and West Germany are important, challenging developments. Without depreciating state power and systemic factors, liberalism's focus on domestic and transnational social forces and coalitions provides an insightful vantage point. Risse-Kappen's (1991) critique of "peace through strength" points to the importance of societal forces as does Kaldor's (1991, 1) notion of "detente from below." Along the same lines Timothy Ash (1990) reminds us that the whole reintroduction of "Mitteleuropa" into our modern cold war and post-cold-war vocabulary was animated by a Czech émigré in Paris (Kundera) and a playwright in Prague (Havel). While these phenomena may or may not have been determinative, they were and are a part of the story. Liberalism's domestic focus does not make it less relevant for understanding international politics and economics. Some argue that liberalism's focus on rights and free exchange is appropriate within sovereign political communities but not among them; in short, that liberalism's organizing principles do not travel well. This argument overlooks the similarities between domestic and international politics and denies the international system a capacity to transform itself (Modelski 1990). Judith Shklar (1989) reminds us that liberalism within domestic societies was born in fear (and bloodshed, intolerance, insecurity). The analogy is appropriate to the changing international system.

Marxian International Political Economy

With Marxism, it would seem that there are many possible vantage points from which to view political economy. Marxists have argued the existence of politics in the silent process by which surplus value is appropriated from direct producers, the expansion of capital and the historical manner in which the modern unequal division of labor came about, unequal exchange, the role of the state in managing the interests of capital, the mobilization of class bias, and bargaining between labor and capital for respective shares of the surplus (Caporaso and Levine 1992, chap. 3).

The analytical core of Marxism has, perhaps confusingly, been represented as both class process and power-bargaining (Wolff and Resnick 1987, 145). Classical Marxism (the Marxism of *Capital* and *Theories of Surplus Value*) is generally understood as a theory about capital accumulation, classes, and class processes. The production of value by workers and the class processes by which surplus value is appropriated and distributed, are central themes. As Marxian theory has evolved, power concepts have played a greater role. Sometimes, power is treated as central, as the critical variable that does the explanatory work. Classes are important to the extent that they are vehicles for exerting power. According to this approach, large, wealthy firms and states influence smaller firms and states. Class processes give way to the market power of firms, union strength, and state power exercised in the interest of particular classes. While this approach may be useful, and is prominent in dependency theory, it offers little that is distinctively Marxian. Thus the linking of politics and economics at the international level is not without obstacles for Marxism.

In this section, I will discuss three Marxian or Marxian-inspired approaches to international political economy: the internationalization of capital, or imperialism; unequal exchange theory; and Gramscian conceptions of hegemony.

Internationalization of Capitalism and Imperialism

The core of Marx's *Capital* ([1867] 1967) is an endogenous theory of capitalist development. Unlike the neorealist system, where states are in equilibrium until upset by exogenous power shifts, capitalism is in constant motion, propelled by its own inner dynamic. While my intent here is to focus on current developments in Marxian theory and research, it may be helpful to sketch the basic model of capital accumulation.

Starting with a simple model of a closed capitalist economy, one based on private ownership of productive capital, free wage labor, and market competition, Marx tried to demonstrate capital's laws of motion, that is, the time path that capitalism would follow. In this model, C stands for constant capital, V for variable capital (labor), and S for surplus. The accounting scheme employed is:

$$C + V + S = \text{total output (or value).}$$

This accounting expression is an algebraic identity -- not a prediction equation. Marx broke down a society's total output into three categories: (1) how much it takes to replace C (depreciation of capital costs); (2) how much it takes to reproduce V (wage costs); and (3) a residual category, the surplus. Society goes through three stages. In the first stage, C and V are just barely replaced. This is simple reproduction. In the second, C and V are augmented, and S increases proportionately. This is equivalent to the quantitative expansion of factor inputs (longer working day, more machines) but no change of technology. Both C/V (organic composition of capital) and S/C+V (rate of profit) stay the same. During phase three, there are changes in technology (capital expenditures increase relative to labor, so C/V goes up). Here the rate of profit changes also.

Marx's argument is that increases of C/V ultimately lead to a lowering of the rate of profit. Marx argued that long-term decline in profits would lead to the search for foreign markets and cheaper foreign inputs, particularly labor. Imperialism, then, could be seen as the extension of capitalist exchange and production relations into the foreign realm.

Current Marxian theory and research seem less interested in deducing imperialism from capitalism's laws of motion and more interested in exploring a variety of motives for capital expansion. The internationalization of capital is an empirical fact. Firms may go abroad to increase profits, to hold on to market shares, or to fend off economic decline at home. Modern Marxian scholarship recognizes diverse motives and seeks to explore the consequences for the expansion of capital (Hymer 1979; Murray 1971; Picciotto 1990; Poulantzas 1974; Radice 1984; Warren 1971).

Under the conceptual umbrella of "the internationalization of capital," various research emphases are possible: (a) the political infrastructure of global capital; (b) the expansion of capital and the less developed world; and (c) capital's global cooperation problem.

The Political Infrastructure of Global Capital

The formation of the European Economic Community (EEC) in 1958 and its expansion to a membership of twelve countries provides one focus for Marxist scholarship. Not only does the EEC facilitate the coordination of economic policies, it also provides a framework for the international expansion of capital.

Scholars in the Soviet Union and East Europe were quick to see the internationalization of capital aspects of European integration. Western Marxist writers have been equally sensitive to the pressures of global competition and have interpreted integration as a response to these pressures. In addition, some writers (Cocks 1991; Lambert 1990) have highlighted the political and legal framework of European integration. Peter Cocks sees European integration as a method of state-building, an effort to create the political infrastructure and means of legitimation needed for capital to move freely at the regional level (Cocks 1991, 35-36). The market, i.e., an expanded regional market, is not seen as the natural result of breaking down national-political obstacles to the movement of capital. Positive measures are required, including "... a correspondingly enlarged legal system that protects private property and enforces contracts and second, an adequate supply of labor" (Cocks 1991, 36).

While Cocks's concern with the political infrastructural requirements of capital is important, others have taken this as a given and have criticized the weak political institutions and political practices of the European Community. To understand this debate, Marxists distinguish two senses of politics. Politics can refer to the basic political conditions of exchange, e.g., private property rights, a judicial system to enforce contracts, a framework of legal liability, and so on. Politics can also mean organized contests for public office, coalition-building, and authoritative rule. The idea of democratic politics implies institutionalized party competition and electoral accountability. John Lambert, a critic of the European Community, accepts economic integration as a fact (1990). Lambert sees capital as moving freely within a European space, responding to constantly shifting opportunities. Yet, this economic activity is for the most part unaccountable to organized democratic forces. Some scholars (Picciotto 1990) see this imbalance as reflective of the enormous structural advantages of capital over labor (and consumers), starting with its superior mobility. Picciotto is pessimistic about recreating the political shell of parliamentarism at the international level. Others (Lambert 1990; S. Williams 1991) clearly recognize the advantage of capital but see the possibilities of correcting the imbalance through organized European political action.

The Internationalization of Capital and the Less Developed World

The relationship between the advanced capitalist countries (ACCs) and the less developed countries (LDCs) identifies an important topic of research. The primary research question relates to development, defined *inter alia* as the expansion of material output, structural diversification of the economy, improvement of well-being, eradication of poverty, increasing equity, and the evolution of responsive democratic institutions. Neoclassical economics approaches development from the standpoint of instituting market incentives. Thus, putting in place private property rights and a structure of relative prices that reflect real scarcities is critical. Realism, despite its great-power focus, has attempted to extend its theory to cover relations with LDCs (see Krasner 1985; Lake 1987). Marxian theories have approached the less developed world from the standpoint of the expansion of global capitalism. The focus is more on classes and economic processes (commodity production, exchange, realization of surplus value) than on national economies.

A necessary caveat to this section is that what is or is not Marxian is controversial. If we adopt a narrow stance, an understanding of the expansion of capital to the LDCs is Marxian only when it can be shown to result from the logic of competitive capital accumuluation, particularly changes in the composition of capital and the rate of profit. With a broader stance, numerous approaches emphasizing the contact of advanced capital with the less developed world might qualify as Marxian. In addition, the literature is voluminous and difficult to summarize. It includes theories of imperialism, world systems theory, and dependency theory, each with Marxian and non-Marxian strands.

Instead of focusing on particular schools, I will briefly describe three ideas relevant to capital expansion into the less developed world: foreign expansion and incorporation lead to underdevelopment; expansion and incorporation lead to peripheral capitalist development; and expansion leads to associated dependent development.

Did the expansion of capitalism, including private ownership of productive assets, markets, and wage labor, have a positive or negative effect on what came to be called the Third World? A. G. Frank (1962) conceptualizes the world as one integrated system, composed of juridically separate states, but functioning as one coherent whole. For him development and underdevelopment are two sides of the same coin, the advancement of the First World coming at the expense of the Third World. Countries are not simply "undeveloped." Instead, they are "underdeveloped."

Frank's argument is a variant of Paul Baran's (1973) surplus drainage mechanism. In their contact with ACCs, surplus from LDCs gets channeled into the rich zones of the world economy. A variety of mechanisms may be responsible for this: unequal exchange (trade), profit repatriation, interest payments, and royalty and licensing fees (see Warren 1980, 140-43). Data on these processes are difficult to come by and are often subject to many interpretations. For example, Bill Warren (1980, 141) is very critical of the practice of many surplus-drainage theorists of subtracting the amount of capital leaving a country from the amount entering and concluding that the difference represents an absolute loss.

The second view is that the foreign expansion of capital creates local accumulation and peripheral capitalist development. The contact between advanced capital and LDCs destroys many aspects of traditional ways of life -- customs, kinship units, handicraft forms of production, etc. Pre-capitalist forms of production are replaced with capitalist forms. Both the technical forces of production and capitalist production relations come to dominate. Notwithstanding the negative aspects of these changes, capitalist transformation is seen as progressive. For a full treatment of this approach, see Bill Warren, *Imperialism: Pioneer of Capitalism* (1980).

The third approach argues that foreign capital neither retarded the periphery nor propelled the Third World along a path of economic growth similar to that presumably experienced by Europe. The associated dependent development school, identified most closely with Fernando H. Cardoso (1973), argues that foreign capital stimulates economic growth in the periphery but that this growth is propelled by the rhythms of core capital, is nonautonomous, and produces a variety of distortions: internal inequality, marginalization of key sectors, and structural disintegration of the economy. This last (disintegration) implies not that the economy is falling apart but that it is both sectorally and functionally disconnected. This in turn undermines efforts to control the economy by manipulating the key instruments of macroeconomic policy, e.g., interest rates, tax policy, money supply (see Brewster 1973; Sunkel 1973).

Dependency theory has had many critics (Packenham 1992; Almond 1990). However, in this writer's opinion, dependency theory died out more from neglect than frontal criticism. By the middle of the 1980s, little work was being done in the United States on dependency theory.

There is no space to evaluate these views of the effects of foreign capital expansion here. Yet, is it interesting to ask how each approach might respond to the appearance of the newly industrializing countries (or semi-periphery) in the global economy. The first approach (Frank's development of underdevelopment) simply cannot explain the NICs. The NICs pursued policies based on a strong export-orientation and invited foreign capital on favorable terms. Their key policy was to integrate into the international capitalist system and to pursue absolute gains rather than to spend resources bargaining over distributional issues. The success of the NICs is a refutation of the first theory.

The second approach accepts, even anticipated, the spread of capitalist development throughout the periphery. Peripheral capitalism is seen as a necessary and progressive phase of a larger historical process.

Moralizing as to whether this is good or bad is beside the point according to proponents. The third approach, that of Cardoso and Wallerstein (who are very different in other ways), recognizes the growth of the semi-periphery but sees it as both derivative and limited. Neoclassical economists and classical Marxists such as Warren have no difficulty accepting (even expecting) many more members of the semi-periphery and the passage from there to the core. The space at various levels of the global hierarchy is not limited. Contrast this expansive view to the view of Wallerstein, who argues that only a fraction of poor countries can fit into a growing world market (1979, 76) and that, when the world economy experiences a downturn, the weakest (poorest) suffer first (1979, 88). Wallerstein treats economic growth as a scarce good (with rival properties) for which bargaining power is relevant. This contrasts with the view that economic growth is essentially non-rival, that contact with those doing well improves one's own chances, and that voluntary exchange rather than power is the appropriate instrument of improvement.

Global Cooperation Problems for Capital

A third application within the internationalization of capital umbrella concerns the coordination of separate capitals internationally. The relation of owners of capital to one another is of a dual nature. On the one hand, capitalists are competitors. They strive to outperform one another in global markets, and, if they are successful enough, they will drive competitors out of business. On the other hand, they share interests with respect to labor and international infrastructural goods (currency stability, tax policies of governments, predictable political environment, labor laws, regulations regarding capital mobility etc.). Since these goods are public in substantial ways, they generate collective action problems. While the literature on international regimes has studied the cooperation problem in many issue areas, few have researched the capital cooperation problem (Duvall and Wendt 1987).

Along these lines, Picciotto's article (1990) raises interesting research possibilities. Picciotto does not approach the problem of cooperation from the standpoint of noncooperative game theory. Neither does he see the formation of international organizations or regimes as crucial. Instead, he tries to formulate a logic of international corporate culture. This culture is a collection of understandings, codes, and informal agreements. While it doubtless owes something to international institutions such as the World Bank and the International Monetary Fund, it works primarily from the ground up, relying on conventions stitched together by central bankers, key leaders of business interest groups, and members of national finance ministries. The solution to the problem of cooperation is "...a nationally based but internationally coordinated corporate capitalism" (Picciotto 1990, 33).

Theories of Unequal Exchange

Given the tremendous inequality in incomes and life circumstances among countries in the world today, it is not surprising that liberal and Marxian economists have addressed themselves to understanding the process of development and underdevelopment. According to Immanuel Wallerstein (1974), the period from 1450 to 1800 allowed for the eradication of feudalism and fostered primitive accumulation of capital in the core. It is only with the nineteenth century that what is today called "the widening gap" emerged. From the fifteenth to the eighteenth century differences in wealth between Europe and the other centers of civilization -- China, India, and the Middle East -- were not great (Bairoch 1979). By the late 1970s, the gap between richest and poorest was thirty to one (McGowan and Kordan 1981, 56). One theory which attempts to explain the gap relies on conditions relating to exchange among rich and poor. Terms of trade theories, at least some of them, provide arguments about the transfer of surplus from less to more developed countries.

The terms of trade theory refer to a class of arguments about why certain countries or classes gain systematically through trade while others lose. Strictly speaking, terms of trade theory is about relative -- not absolute -- gains and losses. While some theories can speak to absolute immiseration (see Dutt 1986), the distribution of benefits is generally at issue rather than the entire Ricardian theory of comparative advantage. Given this broad definition of the concept, Frank, Prebisch, Emmanuel, Singer, and Lewis can all be interpreted as terms of trade theorists.

Operationally, the terms of trade are defined as a ratio of export to import prices,[10] using a standard definition of goods and employing the assumption of constant technology. The basic descriptive claim is that poor countries (or those that produce primary goods), will suffer a long-term decline in their terms of trade, giving up more than they receive in the long haul.

Trevor Bell (n.d.) is correct to argue that neoclassical trade theory has no comprehensive hypothesis about long-term trends in the terms of trade. Instead it deals with the issue in terms of changing relative prices of imports and exports due to exogenous changes in supply and demand. Neoclassical theory is therefore noncommittal about long-term movements in prices.

Whether trade at one point in time embodies equal value for both parties is a metaphysical question under market conditions.[11]

Raul Prebisch, an Argentine economist, advanced a terms of trade argument based on assumptions of differential elasticities of demand and factual claims about the position of less developed countries (LDCs) in the international division of labor (Prebisch 1950, 1969). Prebisch also made an argument about the effect of surplus labor in LDCs, but he is most remembered for the elasticity theory. The argument is simple. Poor countries are poor not because of the absence of productive inputs, or because rising population pressures periodically consume investible surplus, but because of the goods they produce and export in the international division of labor.

LDCs produce raw materials and food goods (non-processed food goods). Advanced countries produce manufactured goods. Prebisch combined these facts[12] with an argument about elasticities, maintaining that as income increases a declining share will be spent on primary goods, a rising share on manufactured goods. This assertion provides a hypothesis about the secular trend in relative demand, missing from neoclassical theory. As demand for manufactured goods outstrips demand for primary goods, prices for the former rise more rapidly. When these respective goods trade in international markets, the secular terms of exchange favor the advanced countries.

In contrast to Prebisch, A. Emmanuel (1972) tries to develop a theory of unequal exchange independently of the exchange system (trade) itself. Technically, trade is treated as the carrier of inequalities whose source lies in domestic production relations. Grounding inequality of exchange in production relations is seen as perhaps the primary task for classically oriented Marxists and neo-Ricardians. As a result, Emmanuel eschews theories which appeal to market power, monopolistic advantage, rents from control over technology, or differential elasticities in product markets. Instead, he posits the fundamental cause of unequal exchange to be the differential rewards to labor in different countries.

The assumptions of *Unequal Exchange* include the mobility of capital globally but the immobility of labor, an assumption which is largely true. While international movements of people (hence labor power) are not unimportant, these movements are overwhelmed by movements of physical and financial capital. Since capital is mobile, rates of profit equalize. Labor, however, is protected by state boundaries. Advanced countries are labor-scarce and have strong, well-organized labor movements. This was more true in 1972 when Emmanuel wrote *Unequal Exchange* than during the eighties. Other countries (LDCs) are labor-abundant and have organizationally weak labor forces. As a result, the wage bill is higher in advanced countries than in LDCs, higher than would be predicted by productivity differences. The residual implies that part of production costs are due to class struggle.

When countries with strong and weak labor movements trade with one another, the former reap a premium reflecting these institutional differences between countries. The terms of trade reflect these wage-level differences. They do not cause them.

Whereas most terms of trade theorists attribute importance to market imperfections (monopoly power, spillover benefits of processed goods, learning by doing effects), Emmanuel conceives adverse terms of trade and underdevelopment as the inevitable outcome of free trade among more and less developed countries, even under the most competitive conditions. The book is subtitled "A Study of the Imperialism of Trade."

While Emmanuel's effort is ambitious, it contains internal inconsistencies and troubling assumptions. He sees wages as independent and autonomous, rather than as reflecting productivity differences. It is not plausible, on neoclassical or Marxian grounds, that wages cause productivity differences. Second, by his own assumptions, rates of profit (Marx's $S\backslash C+V$) equalize across countries. This logically implies that LDCs cannot do worse than advanced countries in terms of relative surplus value (Weeks and Dore 1979, 71). Given any arbitrary starting point, if the initial cross-country rates of profit are not in equilibrium, the natural flow of capital would be from advanced to less developed countries. As Weeks and Dore point out, this mechanism predicts higher rates of accumulation in LDCs (1979,71), an implication not congenial to unequal development favoring the core.

All in all, *Unequal Exchange* does not wear well with time. As Barratt-Brown pungently put it, the theory of unequal exchange is contrary both to the neoclassical doctrine of comparative costs and to the Marxian argument that the rate of capital accumulation and socially necessary labor time determine prices (Barratt-Brown 1974, 230).

Gramscian Approaches

Classical Marxian theory focuses on the economy, particularly the productive forces and class processes through which value and surplus value are produced. The engines of change in society (and in politics and culture) are located in economic forces, particularly in the pace of capital accumulation. Some have abandoned the notion of economic primacy and have replaced it with a non-reductionist focus on politics and economics (Bowles and Gintis 1986). Other scholars see culture and ideas as important and not simply derivative of economics. It is this strand of thought that I want to discuss briefly here, using the work of Robert Cox (1983, 1986, 1987), Stephen Gill (1990, 1991), and Augelli and Murphy (1988).[13]

The basic idea of Cox's work is that world politics and global political economy cannot be reduced to either a political or economic essence. The neorealist approach is truncated since it omits the social forces (most notably economic) underlying and traversing states and the milieu of beliefs and ideologies in which states are embedded. Neorealism relegates these forces to the second-image level and argues that they can be safely ignored because of the overriding force of security concerns. Cox argues that such a view may have made sense in the eighteenth and early nineteenth centuries when the separation between civil society and the state was cleaner. In today's world, state and society are interpenetrated. We should therefore talk about state-society complexes, or "forms of state" with different underlying social coalitions rather than the state as an abstract category (1986, 5).

Cox's approach is brought out nicely in his treatment of hegemony. Hegemony is not just a power concept. It cannot be accessed simply with reference to states and the distribution of capabilities. Instead, hegemony "...is based on a coherent conjunction or fit between a configuration of material power, the prevalent collective image of world order (including certain norms) and a set of institutions which administer the order with a certain semblance of universality (that is, not just as the overt instruments of a particular state's dominance)" (Cox 1986, 223).

Cox's historical method relies on an analysis of three sets of important factors, none of which can be reduced to the others: social forces, state forms, and ideas. Social forces include, but are not limited to, economic (material) factors. State forms include the many different institutional expressions that authority and organized power can take. And ideas refer to beliefs, common understandings, and the shared codes which allow for predictability and coordinated actions. The importance of the tripartite focus is that it allows one to pose questions and make problematic some things that would otherwise be unquestioned and nonproblematic. Certain leads and lags (Cox 1986, 224) are possible in the cycles of hegemonic rise and decline. Britain had imperial pretensions and beliefs well after her material base had declined. Similarly, there are some who argue that the U.S. is not declining in strict power terms. Rather it is U.S. moral leadership and legitimacy that are questioned. Johnson's failure to raise taxes to finance the Vietnam War and the subsequent shifting of part of the

costs to Europe, Nixon's abrupt suspension of the gold standard, and Reagan's insensitive unilateralism combined to undermine confidence in U.S. leadership.

A second thing that Cox's framework allows is the exploration and possibly explanation of the content of world order or regimes. In a neorealist world, states are modeled as having interests and power but not beliefs. It must be presumed that states have the necessary beliefs about the causal structure of the world, at a minimum, to see the connections among means and ends. But beliefs in a large sense, including purposes, principles, and existential propositions, are not at work. Thus, when it comes to world order, cooperative institutions, or regimes, the best that neorealism can do is provide expectations about when order is more or less likely and something about its form (Martin 1992a).

While I do not have the space to develop related contributions, the work of Augelli and Murphy (1988), Gill (1990, 1991), and Gill and Law (1989) is important. Augelli and Murphy examine the reconstitution of "American" hegemony during the Reagan era, after significant reversals during the late sixties and seventies. Gill and Law (1989) deal with the structural power of capital in both its national and international dimensions. While state structures are important for all these authors, hegemony is not confined to the distribution of power among states. International capital is also important. Capital, especially in the form of foreign direct investment, is not just an abstract factor of production. It is also a social and political presence providing or restricting jobs, income, technology, and knowledge.

The Gramscian approach is less a theory than a conceptual framework within which certain questions can be explored. The three main components of the framework -- material capabilities, ideas, and institutions -- are touchstones to be used in historical analysis, not independent and dependent variables. Nevertheless, the framework is suggestive of different problems and hypotheses. For one thing, the prevailing image differs from the neorealist theory of states and state actions. Cox's view of the world is not state-centered. Hegemony cannot be represented as a distributional parameter, as a share of total system-wide resources controlled by one country. Cox is more interested in which fractions of international capital occupy important locations in the world economy.

Following from the above, evidence for hegemony or hegemonic decline is not provided by the percentage of economic assets controlled by one (or several) powers but in the privileged position of key social forces (particularly international capital) of major capitalist states. Better indicators of hegemony are provided by the increasing importance of the economic summits among the advanced capitalist countries, the anticipated success of the European Community's deregulatory 1992 project, privatization schemes carried out by governments in Western Europe and North America, the collapse of socialism in East Europe, and the continuing influence of international financial institutions in the Third World. By these measures, capitalism, particularly advanced fractions of international capital, are not in decline.

Two final comments relate to the treatment of culture and governance in the Gramscian approaches. The liberal conception of international governance is driven by the provision of international public goods. International politics has to do with those institutions, rules, and collective action procedures associated with the provision of these goods. Realists see a decentralized, state-centric world but recognize the embryo of international governance in international organizations. Inis Claude (1962) arrays international organizations along a continuum from least to most centralized. Politics in the international system is represented as the reconstitution of capacities at another, more global, level.

The focus of Cox and Gill is different. Cox sees key elements of the internationalization of the state in the ascending importance of key national ministries (trade, finance) and in their increasing utilization as points of contact among "national" ministers. In addition, there is an emerging world or transnational class culture, with bankers, capitalists, civil servants and perhaps academics as part of it. Brussels, Paris, London, Geneva and New York and Tokyo may be the centers of this emerging culture, less in the sense of what is headquartered here and more in terms of serving as nodes of contact for key elites, providing the international watering holes reminiscent of Bohemian Grove (Domhoff 1974). Gramscian conceptions of international governance, then, are based neither on collections of states in international organizations nor on "...hierarchical power structures with lines of force running exclusively from the top down..." (Cox 1986, 230).

Finally, while the Gramscian approach is clearly distinct, it does resonate with the works of others. Susan Strange's work on the U.S. empire (1988, 1989) emphasizes strongly U.S. structural resources in capital, technology, and knowledge and is also sensitive to the moral dimension of U.S. foreign policy. William Appleman Williams speaks of "Empire as a Way of Life" (1991), arguing that the privileged position of the U.S. in the world has deep roots in American culture and national experience. Finally, John Ruggie has consistently advocated the importance of ideas and social purpose along with power and interest as conventionally defined (Ruggie 1982, 1992). Using counterfactual thinking, he argues that the systemic ordering principle of the postwar order, liberal multilateralism, is not the one that would have been instituted had Germany or Japan won the war.

There was nothing inevitable about a liberal multilateral world order. It was the product of a distinctive set of social and political forces in the United States.

Conclusion

The preceding review of the global political economy literature is far from comprehensive. Entire fields of work have been omitted, among them world systems theory, dependency theory, long cycle theory, regulation theory, and theories based on foreign economic policy making. I have not omitted these theories because they lack importance. My justification is simply that I place greater value on developing the arguments of a few theories than saying something about all of them.

Taking the neoclassical, realist, liberal, and Marxian approaches as points of departure, a number of gaps and blind spots emerge. These gaps, I argue, characterize scholarly work in mainstream international relations journals in the United States. Most striking are the paucity of articles and books on north-south relations, poverty, and development (or underdevelopment). A research program concerning south-south relations scarcely exists, north-south relations figure a bit more prominently, and north-north relations dominate the agenda, more or less in conformity with Johan Galtung's feudal interaction structure (Galtung 1971). I recognize that research agendas are motivated in part by theoretical concerns, in part by questions that reflect important values. Development and poverty certainly fall into the latter category and often into the first. We should ask ourselves why there is not more work on the global political economy of development.[14]

A second gap, Marxian theories notwithstanding, is the analysis of classes, class conflict, and the consequences of changes in the global political economy for different classes. There is surprisingly little research as opposed to essays and broad speculative work, even within Marxian political economy. Some of the best work examining the connections between the global political economy and domestic classes is done by scholars who cannot be neatly categorized within one of the dominant approaches (see Bergquist 1984; Pahl 1984; and Piore and Sabel 1984). Rupert's (1990a) research on the "production of hegemony" involves an understanding of state-society relations that builds on classes.

A third gap involves underemphasis on the political aspects of international economic involvement in two senses: first, the construction of favorable international economic structures, a project limited to major powers; second, the effects of international economic position on conflict and war. This gap may seem odd in light of the large literature on interdependence. However, interdependence is taken as a datum, i.e., a given, and not as something that is purposefully constructed. Yet the present international economy is not the one expected on the basis of an economic model of comparative advantage and factor endowments. In other words, a large political element is implied in the exchange and production structures of the global (political) economy. The purposeful structuring of the conditions of international economic exchange has not received adequate attention. This makes it seem as if the capitalist world economy is an accident, more or less the result of the external projections of separate national capitalisms.

Apart from these broad gaps, each approach examined here has strengths and weaknesses. Neoclassical political economy has excelled as a policy science, applying its tools and theory to issues of protection, property rights, and foreign investment. It has contributed to our understanding by elaborating the idea of market failure at the international level. Finally, blended with realism, it has supplied a basis for thinking about international institutions.

When I began this paper, there were two areas where I thought neoclassical political economy was weak and not likely to make a contribution. These two areas were unequal exchange and the formation of preferences. The reason for pessimism about unequal exchange rested on competitive markets. The formation of preferences, on the other hand, was thought to be a social matter and that economists were correct to take preferences as given. This assumption proved partly wrong. I have reviewed how Lake interprets strategic trade theory as molding preferences and how Gowa treats international power structures as affecting economic incentives. Ronald Rogowski has shown how aspects of international trade theory (Stopler-Samuelson theorem) can be used to make predictions about the preferences of different domestic groups (1989).

The chief limitation of neoclassical economics is that it molds political economy along lines guided by market failure and efficiency. Yet politics and political economy are not limited to market failure. Politics sometimes involves structuring market activities, determining the scope of markets, regulating their impacts (not just externalities), and engaging in redis-tributional politics that violates ordinary efficiency criteria.

Neoclassical economics has had difficulty coming to grips with power (see Caporaso and Levine 1992; Heilbroner 1988; Gruber 1992). Partly, this is due to conceptualizing economics as voluntary exchange. Economists have attempted to identify the core of an economy by isolating the set of exchanges that are Pareto-superior (where at least one person improves but

no one is worse off). The omission of a theory of power in neoclassical economics is not simply an oversight or something that can be "filled in" with additional work. The gap results from the focus on voluntary exchange and mutually improving transactions. Implicitly, the relevant power idea is "power to" (to organize collectively, to achieve common goals) rather than "power over" (to achieve goals at the expense of others). Politics involves exchange also, though here welfare loss is typical, some would say central. Conflict, antagonisms, domination, and winning and losing characterize politics. The work of Krasner (1985, 1991), Spiro (1993), and Gruber (1992) helps to understand these differences and to retain our focus on some traditional political concerns.

Realism has attempted to theorize global political economy on the basis of the state operating within an anarchic environment pursuing economic goals. It has contributed to our understanding of the political conditions guiding economic exchange and international institutions. Given the anarchy assumption, realism has availed itself of the theory of non-cooperative games, an approach developed largely in economics. Realism has (in part) become economic in its approach as well as its substantive concerns.

On the other hand, some realists, particularly Krasner (1991), have kept traditional power-oriented concerns on the agenda and have sustained the view that these concerns are distinct from economic ones. These distinctions are perhaps most easily seen when it comes to institutional and bargaining phenomena. Economic approaches typically deal with situations marked by Pareto sub-optimality and ask how states can forge arrangements (institutions) to arrive at the Pareto frontier. In "Global Communications and National Power," (1991), Krasner argues that disagreements are more often over which point on the frontier should be chosen, rather than over how to arrive at the frontier. The primary focus is (or should be) distributional conflict rather than market failure (p. 336). The point is general and is not limited to communications. Relative power capabilities are important in situations regarding relative power, the ability to eliminate other actors, and in cases where some states affect the assignment of property rights (not at all rare in international relations) (Krasner 1991, 365).

The chief limitation of realism is its truncated view of social and political life. It largely ignores domestic politics and the social forces (as Cox and Gill term it) that undergird state to state politics. Every theory must omit many things. This is not a criticism that not everything is included. The omission of domestic politics makes it seem as if international politics is simply the collision of predetermined state interests or interests determined by international structure. Civil society disappears. This cuts realists off from understanding the role of business groups, professional groups (say life scientists working on the greenhouse effect), the Catholic Church (in Poland), and the influence of social groups working on their own *Ostpolitik* in the former Federal Republic of Germany -- except to the extent that these groups operate through the state.

Realism's fear seems to be that, if examined, domestic politics will prove to be a Pandora's box of country-specific parameters. This fear seems exaggerated. Domestic politics, and its implications for global political economy, can be theorized, as the work of Rogowski (1989), Putnam (1988), Katzenstein (1978, 1985), Goldstein (1988), Frieden (1991), and Lake (1991) shows.

Marxian global political economy starts on a promising note. It is conceptually comprehensive, attempting to bring together political institutions, social forces, and ideas. At present, however, little systematic theory exists in testable form. Instead, the theory is applied illustratively to various global situations. While Marxism has historical roots, the modern Gramscian approach is very new and the group of scholars working in the tradition very limited.

Modern Marxian political economy has departed from the classical project in two quite distinct directions. The Gramscian turn, exemplified by Cox, Gill, Rupert, and Augelli and Murphy, abandons the development of the forces of production as the (single) engine of change and places ideas on an analytically coequal plane with material forces and state institutions. Rational choice Marxism abandons the project of deducing capital expansion from the laws of motion of capitalism in favor of collective action problems inherent in class conditions. While these foci are valuable (both capitalists and workers confront social dilemmas), analytical Marxism is limited by not having a theory of capitalist development. What was attractive about Marxism is that it said something about the time path of capitalism and the transformation of interests along this path. One does not need to believe in the iron laws of increasing organic composition of capital and falling rate of profit to argue for attention to the historical dimension of capitalism.

In my opinion, Gramscian approaches could be refreshed and sharpened by contact with the more classical strains of Marxism. Forces of production have broadened into a less definable "material interests," and production relations have either disappeared or have been absorbed by "social forces." Perhaps regulation theory has furthered the older notion of relations of production (see Noel 1987). In any case, the Gramscian approach would do well to rethink the role of this important concept.

The Gramscian approaches reviewed here have been organized around the interplay of material interests, state forms, and ideas. This is not the only way to go. Mark Rupert's project (1990b) is to understand (historically) the construction of international civil society. His focus is not directly on states-markets and power-wealth. Instead, he first wants to understand how an international space for "private" capital was created, how labor and capital came to confront one another as juridically free agents within international civil society. Domination has to do not so much with states over states or states over non-state actors, as with global capital over labor. For Rupert, global political economy involves tasks that are radically different from realists and liberals.

There are other directions in which Marxian global political economy might go. If Marxism is concerned with competitive capital accumulation, we can ask about the consequences of accumulation processes at the global level. Few countries have anything remotely resembling closed economies. Almost all "national" economies must insert themselves into the global economy to complete their cycles of accumulation. Some "tie-ins" are for markets, some for physical capital, some for financial capital, and others for labor (skilled or unskilled), and knowledge. Most of these global links do not involve arms-length transactions, although some do more than others. Taking these economic connections seriously will involve understanding better the political forces associated with economic integration, a project central to dependency theory.

Ten years ago it might have been debated whether global political economy was fad or field. The concerns that have dominated research have proved to be durable. Significant research accomplishments have been made in numerous areas, among them institutions, cooperation, public goods theory, strategic trade, and hegemony. Still, significant gaps remain which are not just due to finite resources. Hopefully, this essay has conveyed a sense of progress as well as pointed to some areas where future work is sorely needed.

Notes

I would like to acknowledge the research assistance of Richard Sherman in preparing this chapter. His papers, one of which is cited in the references, provided valuable suggestions in carrying out my research. I also gratefully recognize the support of the Virginia and Prentice Bloedel Chair of Political Science.

Various drafts of this paper have benefitted from the comments of Hayward R. Alker, Jr., Robert O. Keohane, David Lake, Lisa Martin, Richard Sherman, David Spiro, Janice Thomson, and Alexander Wendt. Special appreciation is due to Stephen D. Krasner and an anonymous referee. I did not satisfy all readers and must accept responsibility for the final product.

1. A Pareto-optimal outcome is one that cannot be improved on in the sense that there is no alternative that makes someone better off without making someone else worse off.

2. Many political scientists would welcome the introduction of the concept of ideology into economic theory but as yet it is rare to see it used in either an explanatory or descriptive way. Agents are typically characterized by preferences and by beliefs about the causal structure of the environment (i.e., information) but not "belief systems" that disguise and yet advance the interests of particular groups. In addition, there seems to be no good *a priori* reason why the term ideology should apply only to non-market configurations.

3. The exact difference between realism and neorealism is unclear and bound to be controversial. On one interpretation, neorealism is "merely" a more rigorous version of realism, one grounded on microeconomic foundations. On another not entirely different interpretation, neorealism provides a theoretically unified systemic account of interstate politics. Some claim that neorealism attempts to correct for realism's inability to deal with economic issues (Hollis and Smith 1990, 36-37).

4. This last point concerning the goals of states requires some comment. While much effort has been spent trying to justify the content of utility functions on *a priori* grounds -- witness the debate over absolute vs. relative gains -- there seems little to be gained and much to lose by unduly restricting the range of state motives *a priori*. Why not allow the goals of states to change depending on situational properties? In neoclassical economic theory private agents pursue absolute gains or market shares, cooperative or uncooperative strategies, narrowly egoistic, predatory, or altruistic actions -- all depending on the structure of the environment. Not only would this enhance flexibility of analysis, it would also open the way toward incorporating institutions into realist theory and facilitate a reconciliation with those whose work has been relegated to "mitigation of anarchy" -- the work of those in international law, morality, norms, learning, etc.

5. There are some scholars who are trying to endogenize capabilities in ways that are consonant with realist theory. See Kugler and Domke (1986), Organski and Kugler (1980), and Snider (1988).

6. I stress that this is an approximation rather than an exact relation. The gains from trade do not convert directly to the losses of trade disruption because this simple equation ignores substitution possibilities.

7. Let me try to clarify this point. It might appear that bipolarity and multipolarity are relational concepts since they refer to the way something (power) is distributed across countries. But notice that power itself is a property attached to countries -- not to pairs or larger sets. Attribute power is therefore different from network power, where capabilities are expressed in terms of positions (and roles) in exchange structures. I refer to bipolarity and multipolarity as distributional parameters since they summarize how national attributes are distributed, in much the same way that one could summarize the height of individuals in a group.

8. Not everyone would agree with this assertion. In "Liberalism and International Relations Theory," (1992) Moravcsik argues that liberalism is structural theory (at least partly), but it is the pattern of preferences rather than the distribution of capabilities that counts.

9. See Keohane "International Liberalism Reconsidered" (1990a) for one classification; also see Zacher and Matthew "Liberal International Theory: Common Threads, Divergent Strands" (1992) for a comprehensive view of liberalism which distinguishes different approaches.

10. Technically speaking, this is a definition of the price, or commodity terms of trade. Terms of trade may also be defined with reference to quantities of goods exchanged (gross barter terms of trade) and in terms of quantities of labor and capital contained in the goods exchanged (factoral terms of trade) (see Barratt-Brown 1974, 231).

11. In other words, it makes little sense to ask, in any particular exchange, which party acquired more value. Terms of trade theories logically imply a time dimension, i.e., they have to do with changes in ratios of exchanges over time.

12. At least they were facts during a rather long historical era. Beginning with the 1960s, a rising share of LDC production was accounted for by manufactures. While a large proportion of LDC manufactures was accounted for by a few countries (newly industrializing countries), there is some evidence that manufacturing production is spreading to a sizable number of third-world countries (see Caporaso 1981; Haggard 1990).

13. The question arises as to whether these authors should be classified as Marxian. None focuses exclusively or mainly on the process of competitive capital accumulation or production and distribution of the economic surplus. Much of Robert Cox's work attempts to understand labor as an economic category and social relation. All of these authors attempt to understand ideas, institutions, politics, and economic process as a coherent ensemble, i.e., as organically connected. While the lines of causality are not one-way, the authors attach substantial weight to economic forces.

14. I recognize that certain global political economy approaches are focused (some exclusively) on development issues. Dependency theory and world systems theory come to mind. The limitation applies in particular to neoclassical, liberal, and realist approaches. Important exceptions within the realist tradition include Krasner (1985) and Lake (1987).

Bibliography

Almond, Gabriel A. 1990. *A Discipline Divided: Schools and Sects in Political Science*. Newbury Park, CA: Sage Publications.

Ash, Timothy G. 1990. "Mitteleuropa?" *Daedalus* 119(1):1-21.

Augelli, Enrico, and Craig Murphy. 1988. *America's Quest for Supremacy and the Third World: A Gramscian Analysis*. London: Pinter Publishers.

Bairoch, Paul. 1979. "Ecarts Internationaux des Niveaux de Vie Avant la Revolution Industrielle." *Annales: Economies, Societes, Civilisations* 34(1):145-171.

Baldwin, David A. 1979. "Power Analysis in World Politics: New Trends and Old Tendencies." *World Politics* 31:161-194.

Baldwin, David A. 1985. *Economic Statecraft*. Princeton, NJ: Princeton University Press.

Baldwin, Richard. 1988. "Evaluating Strategic Trade Policies." *Aussenwirtschaft* 43:207-230.

Baran, P. 1973. *The Political Economy of Growth*. Harmondsworth: Penguin.

Barratt-Brown, Michael. 1974. *The Economics of Imperialism*. Middlesex, England: Penguin Books.

Bell, Trevor. n.d. "Theories of Terms of Trade of Less Developed Countries." Denver. Unpublished Manuscript.

Bergquist, Charles, ed. 1984. *Labor in the Capitalist World Economy*. Vol. 7 of *Political Economy of the World System Annuals*. Beverly Hills, CA: Sage Publications.

Bhagwati, Jagdish. 1983. "DUP Activities and Rent Seeking." *Kyklos* 36:634-637.

Bhagwati, Jagdish. 1989. "Is Free Trade Passé After All?" *Weltwirtschafiliches Archiv*, 125(1):17-44.

Bowles, Samuel, and Herbert Gintis. 1986. *Democracy and Capitalism*. New York: Basic Books.

Brander, James A., and Barbara J. Spencer. 1981. "Tariffs and the Extraction of Foreign Monopoly Rents Under Potential Entry." *Canadian Journal of Economics* 14(3):371-389.

Brander, James A., and Barbara J. Spencer. 1985. "Export Subsidies and International Market Share Rivalry." *Journal of International Economics* 18:83-100.

Brewster, Havelock. 1973. "Economic Dependence: A Quantitative Interpretation." *Social and Economic Studies* 22(1):90-95.

Caporaso, James A. 1978. "Dependence, Dependency, and Power in the Global System: A Structural and Behavioral Analysis." *International Organization* 32(1):13-43.

Caporaso, James A. 1981. "Industrialization in the Periphery: The Evolving Global Division of Labor." *International Studies Quarterly* 25(3):347-384.

Caporaso, James A., and David P. Levine. 1992. *Theories of Political Economy*. Cambridge, England: Cambridge University Press.

Cardoso, Fernando H. 1973. "Associated Dependent Development: Theoretical and Practical Inplications." In *Authoritarian Brazil*, ed. Alfred Stepan. New Haven, CT: Yale University Press.

Cardoso, Fernando H., and Enzo Faletto. 1978. *Dependency and Development in Latin America*. Berkeley, CA: University of California Press.

Chase-Dunn, Christopher K. 1982. "Socialist States in the Capitalist World Economy." In *Socialist States in the World System*, ed. Christopher K. Chase-Dunn. Beverly Hills, CA: Sage Publications.

Claude, Inis L., Jr. 1962. *Power and International Relations*. New York: Random House.

Cline, William R. 1986. "U.S. Trade and Industrial Policy: The Experience of Textiles, Steel, and Automobiles." In *Strategic Trade Policy and the New International Economics*, ed. Paul R. Krugman. Cambridge, MA: M.I.T. Press.

Coase, Ronald. 1960. "The Problem of Social Cost." *Journal of Law and Economics* 3:1-44.

Cocks, Peter. 1991. "Toward a Marxist Theory of European Integration." In *International Political Economy*, 2nd ed., ed. Jeffry A. Frieden and David A. Lake. New York: St. Martin's Press.

Conybeare, John A.C. 1980. "International Organization and the Theory of Property Rights." *International Organization* 34(3):307-334.

Conybeare, John A.C. 1984. "Public Goods, Prisoners' Dilemmas, and the International Political Economy." *International Studies Quarterly* 28:5-22.

Conybeare, John A.C. 1987. *Trade Wars: The Theory and Practice of International Commercial Rivalry*. New York: Columbia University Press.

Conybeare, John A.C., and Todd Sandler. 1990. "The Triple Entente and the Triple Alliance 1884-1914: A Collective Goods Approach." *American Political Science Review* 84(4):1197-1206.

Cowhey, Peter F., and Edward Long. 1983. "Testing Theories of Regime Change: Hegemonic Decline or Surplus Capacity?" *International Organization* 37(2):157-188.

Cox, Robert W. 1983. "Gramsci, Hegemony, and International Relations Theory." *Millenium* 10(2):126-155.

Cox, Robert W. 1986. "Social Forces, States, and World Orders: Beyond International Relations Theory." In *Neorealism and Its Critics*, ed. Robert O. Keohane. New York: Columbia Unversity Press.

Cox, Robert W. 1987. *Production, Power, and World Order*. Vol. I. New York: Columbia University Press.

Deutsch, Karl W. 1953. *Nationalism and Social Communication*. Cambridge, MA: MIT Press.

Deutsch, Karl W. et al. 1957. *Political Community and the North Atlantic Area*. Princeton: Princeton University Press.

Domhoff, G. William. 1974. *The Bohemian Grove and Other Retreats: A Study in Ruling Class Cohesiveness*. New York: Harper and Row.

Dos Santos, Theotonioistyisty. 1970. "The Structure of Dependence." *American Economic Review* 60:231-236.

Doxey, Margaret. 1972. "International Sanctions: A Framework for Analysis with Special Reference to the U.N. and Southern Africa." *International Organization* 26(2):525-550.

Doyle, Michael W. 1986. "Liberalism and World Politics." *American Political Science Review*" 80(4):1151-1169.

Doyle, Michael W. 1990. "Thucydidean Realism." *Review of International Studies* 16(3):223-237.

Duncan, George T., and Randolph M. Siverson. 1982. "Flexibility of Alliance Partner Choice in a Multipolar System: Models and Tests." *International Studies Quarterly* 26:511-538.

Dutt, Amitava K. 1986. "Vertical Trading and Uneven Development." *Journal of Development Economics* 20(2):339-359.

Duvall, Raymond, and Alexander Wendt. 1987. "The International Capital Regime and the Internationalization of the State." Paper presented at the German-American Workshop on International Relations Theory, Bad Homburg, Frankfurt, West Germany.

Eaton, Jonathan, and Gene M. Grossman. 1986. "Optimal Trade and Industrial Policy Under Oligopoly." *Quarterly Journal of Economics* 101:383-406.

The Economist. 1990. "The Economics of Managed Trade," September 22, 19-25.

Emmanuel, A. 1972. *Unequal Exchange: A Study of the Imperialism of Trade*. New York: Monthly Review Press.

Evans, Peter B. 1989. "Declining Hegemony and Assertive Industrialization: U.S.-Brazil Conflicts in the Computer Industry." *International Organization* 25(3):207-238.

Frank, Andre Gunder. 1969. *Capitalism and Underdevelopment in Latin America*. Rev. ed. New York: Modern Reader Paperbacks.

Frey, Bruno. 1984a. "The Public Choice View of International Political Economy." *International Organization* 38:199-223.

Frey, Bruno. 1984b. *International Political Economics*. New York: Basil Blackwell.

Frieden, Jeffry A. 1991. "Invested Interests: The Politics of National Economic Policies in a World of Global Finance." *International Organization* 45(4):425-451.

Galtung, Johan. 1967. "On the Effects of International Economic Sanctions with Examples for the Case of Rhodesia" *World Politics* 19(Spring):378-416.

Galtung, Johan. 1971. "A Structural Theory of Imperialism." *Journal of Peace Research* 8:81-117.

Gasiorek, Michael, Alisdair Smith, and Anthony J. Venables. 1989. "Tariffs, Subsidies, and Retaliation." *European Economic Review* 33:480-489.

Gereffi, Gary. 1978. "Drug Firms and Dependency in Mexico: The Case of the Steroid Hormone Industry." *International Organization* 32(1):237-286.

Gill, Stephen. 1990. *American Hegemony and the Trilateral Commission*. Cambridge and New York: Cambridge University Press.

Gill, Stephen. 1991. "Historical Materialism, Gramsci, and International Political Economy." In *The New International Political Economy*, ed. Craig N. Murphy and Roger Tooze. Boulder, CO.: Lynne Rienner Publishers.

Gill, Stephen, and David Law. 1988. *The Global Political Economy*. Baltimore, MD: Johns Hopkins University Press.

Gill, Stephen, and David Law. 1989. "Global Hegemony and the Structural Power of Capital." *International Studies Quarterly* 33(4):475-499.

Gilpin, Robert. 1971. "The Politics of Transnational Economic Relations." *International Organization* 25(3):398-419.

Gilpin, Robert. 1987. *The Political Economy of International Relations*. Princeton, NJ: Princeton University Press.

Goldstein, Judith. 1988. "Ideas, Institutions, and American Trade Policy." *International Organization* 42(1):179-217.

Gowa, Joanne. 1989. "Bipolarity, Multipolarity, and Free Trade." *American Political Science Review* 83(4):1245-1256.

Grieco, Joseph M. 1988. "Anarchy and the Limits of Cooperation: A Realist Critique of the Newest Liberal Institutionalism." *International Organization* 42(3):485-507.

Grieco, Joseph M. 1990. *Cooperation Among Nations: Europe, America, and Non-Tariff Barriers to Trade*. Ithaca, NY: Cornell University Press.

Grossman, Gene M. 1986. "Strategic Export Promotion: A Critique." In *Strategic Trade Policy and the New International Economics*, ed. Paul R. Krugman. Cambridge, MA: M.I.T. Press.

Grossman, Gene M., and David J. Richardson. 1986. *Strategic Trade Policy: A Survey of Issues and Early Analysis*. Special Papers in Economics no. 15, International Finance Section, Department of Economics, Princeton University.

Gruber, Lloyd G. 1992. *Winners and Losers: Toward a Realist Theory of European Integration*. Ph.D. diss. Stanford University.

Haberler, Gottfried. 1990. "Strategic Trade Policy and the New International Economics: A Critical Analysis." In *The Political Economy of International Trade: Essays in Honor of Robert E. Baldwin*, ed. Ronald W. Jones and Anne O. Krueger. Cambridge: Basil Blackwell.

Haggard, Stephan. 1990. *Pathways from the Periphery: The Politics of Growth in the Newly Industrializing Countries*. Ithaca, NY: Cornell University Press.

Heilbroner, Robert. 1988. "Economics Without Power." *New York Review of Books* 35(3):23-25.

Hoffmann, Stanley. 1963. "Discord in Community: The North Atlantic Area as a Partial International System." In *The Atlantic Community: Progress and Prospects*, ed. Francis O. Wilcox and H. Field Haviland, Jr. New York: Frederick Praeger.

Hollis, Martin, and Steve Smith. 1990. *Explaining and Understanding International Relations*. Oxford, England: Clarendon Press.

Hirschman, Albert O. 1945. *National Power and the Structure of Foreign Trade*. Berkeley and Los Angeles: University of California Press.

Hirschman, Albert O. 1978. "Beyond Asymmetry: Critical Notes on Myself as a Young Man and Some Other Old Friends." *International Organization* 32(1):45-50.

Hymer, Stephen H. 1979. In *The Multinational Corporation: A Radical Approach*, ed. Robert B. Cohen et al. New York and London: Cambridge University Press.

Inyatullah, Naeem. 1990. "Realizing Sovereignty." Paper presented at the annual meeting of the American Political Science Association, San Francisco.

Kaldor, Mary, ed. 1991. *Europe from Below*. London: Verso.

Katzenstein, Peter J. 1985. *Small States in World Markets: Industrial Policy in Europe*. Ithaca: Cornell University Press.

Katzenstein, Peter J., ed. 1978. *Between Power and Plenty: Foreign Economic Policies of Advanced Industrial States*. Madison: University of Wisconsin Press.

Keohane, Robert O. 1980. "The Theory of Hegemonic Stability and Changes in International Economic Regimes, 1967-1977." In *Change in the International System*, ed. Ole Holsti, Randolph Siverson, and Alexander George. Boulder, CO: Westview Press.

Keohane, Robert O. 1982. "Hegemonic Leadership and U.S. Foreign Economic Policy in the 'Long Decade' of the 1950s." In *America in a Changing World Economy*, ed. William P. Avery and David P. Rapkin. New York: Longman.

Keohane, Robert O. 1984. *After Hegemony: Cooperation and Discord in the World Economy*. Princeton, NJ: Princeton University Press.

Keohane, Robert O., ed. 1986. *Neorealism and its Critics*. New York: Columbia University Press.

Keohane, Robert O. 1989. *International Institutions and State Power*. Boulder, CO: Westview Press.

Keohane, Robert O. 1990a. "International Liberalism Reconsidered." In *The Economic Limits of Modern Politics*, ed. John Dunn. Cambridge, England: Cambridge University Press.

Keohane, Robert O. 1990b. "Multilateralism: An Agenda for Research." *International Journal* 45(Autumn):731-764.

Kindleberger, Charles P. 1973. *The World in Depression, 1929-1939*. Berkeley, CA: University of California Press.

Knorr, Klaus. 1975. *The Power of Nations: The Political Economy of International Relations*. New York: Basic Books.

Knorr, Klaus. 1985. "Burden-Sharing in NATO." *Orbis* 29:517-536.

Knorr, Klaus, and Frank N. Trager, eds. 1977. *Economic Issues and National Security*. Lawrence, KS: Allen Press.

Krasner, Stephen D. 1991. "Global Communication and National Power: Life on the Pareto Frontier." *World Politics* 43(3):336-366.

Krasner, Stephen D. 1985. *Structural Conflict: The Third World Against Global Liberalism*. Berkeley, CA: University of California Press.

Krasner, Stephen D., ed. 1983. *International Regimes*. Ithaca: Cornell University Press.

Krueger, Anne O. 1974. "The Political Economy of the Rent-Seeking Society." *The American Economic Review* 64:291-303.

Krugman, Paul R., ed. 1986. *Strategic Trade Policy and the New International Economics*. Cambridge, MA: M.I.T. Press.

Krugman, Paul R. 1987. "Is Free Trade Passe?" *Journal of Economic Perspectives* 1:131-44.

Kugler, Jacek, and William Domke. 1986. "Comparing the Strength of Nations." *Comparative Political Studies* 19(April): 39-69.

Lake, David A. 1987. "Power and the Third World: Toward a Realist Political Economy of North-South Relations." *International Studies Quarterly* 31(2):217-234.

Lake, David A. 1991. "The Theory of Hegemonic Stability: An Interim Report." University of California, Los Angeles. Unpublished Manuscript.

Lake, David A. 1992. "Powerful Pacifists: Democratic States and War." *American Political Science Review* 80(4):1151-1169.

Lambert, John. 1990. "Europe: the Nation-State Dies Hard." *Review of Radical Political Economics* 22(1):1-13.

Lawson, Fred. 1983. "Hegemony and the Structure of International Trade Reassessed: A View from Arabia." *International Organization* 37(2):317-337.

Lindbeck, Assar. 1978. "Economic Dependence and Interdependence in the Industrialized World." In *From Marshall Plan to Global Interdependence*, ed. Organization for Economic Cooperation and Development. Paris: OECD.

Lipson, Charles. 1982. "The Transformation of Trade: The Sources and Effects of Regime Change." *International Organization* 36:417-455.

Loehr, William, and Todd Sandler, eds. 1978. *Public Goods and Public Policy*. Beverly Hills, CA: Sage.

Marglin, Stephen. 1974. "What Do Bosses Do?" *Review of Radical Political Economy* 6:60-112.

Markusen, James R., and Anthony J. Venables. 1988. "Trade Policy with Increasing Returns and Imperfect Competition: Contradictory Results from Competing Assumptions." *Journal of International Economics* 24:299-316.

Martin, Lisa L. 1992a. "Interests, Power, and Multilateralism," *International Organization* 46(4):765-792.

Martin, Lisa L. 1992b. *Coercive Cooperation: Explaining Multilateral Economic Sanctions*. Princeton, NJ: Princeton University Press.

Marrese, Michael. 1986. "CMEA: Effective but Cumbersome Political Economy." *International Organization* 40(2):287-327.

Marx, Karl. [1867] 1967. *Capital*. Vol. 1. New York: Modern Library.

McGowan, Patrick J., and Bohdan Kordan. 1981. "Imperialism in World System Perspective: Britain 1870-1914." In *World System Structure: Continuity and Change*, ed. W. Ladd Hollist and James N. Rosenau. Beverly Hills, CA: Sage Publications.

Mearsheimer, John J. 1990. "Back to the Future: Instability in Europe after the Cold War." *International Security* 15(1).

Milner, Helen V., and David B. Yoffie. 1989. "Between Free Trade and Protectionism: Strategic Trade Policy and a Theory of Corporate Trade Demands." *International Organization* 43(2):238-272.

Modelski, George. 1990. "Is World Politics Evolutionary Learning?" *International Organization* 44(1):1-24.

Moravcsik, Andrew. 1991. "Arms and Autarky in Modern European History." *Daedalus* 120(4): 23-45.

Moravcsik, Andrew. 1992. "Liberalism and International Relations Theory." Harvard Center for International Affairs. Working Manuscript.

Murdoch, J.C., and Todd Sandler. 1982. "A Theoretical and Empirical Analysis of NATO." *Journal of Conflict Resolution* 26:237-263.

Murdoch, J.C., and Todd Sandler. 1984. "Complementarity, Free-Riding, and the Military Expenditure of NATO Allies." *Journal of Public Economics* 25:83-101.

Murphy, Craig N., and Roger Tooze, eds. 1991. *The New International Political Economy*. Boulder, CO: Lynne Rienner Publishers.

Murray, R. 1971. "The Internationalisation of Capital and the Nation State." *New Left Review* 67:84-109.

Mytelka, Lynne K. 1978. "Technological Dependence in the Andean Group." *International Organization* 32(1):101-140.

Noel, Alain. 1987. "Accumulation, Regulation, and Social Change: An Essay on French Political Economy." *International Organization* 41(2):561-198.

Nye, Joseph S., Jr. 1988. "Nuclear Learning and U.S.-Soviet Security Regimes." *International Organization* 41(3):371-402.

Olson, Mancur. 1980. "Introduction." In *The Theory and Structures of International Political Economy*, ed. Todd Sandler. Boulder, CO: Westview Press.

Olson, Mancur, and Richard Zeckhauser. 1966. "An Economic Theory of Alliances." *Review of Economics and Statistics* 48:266-279.

O'Neal, John R., and Mark A. Elrod. 1989. "NATO Burden Sharing and the Forces of Change." *International Studies Quarterly* 33(4):435-456.

Oppenheimer, Joe. 1979. "Collective Goods and Alliances." *Journal of Conflict Resolution* 23:387-407.

Organski, A.F.K., and Jacek Kugler. 1980. *The War Ledger*. Chicago, IL: University of Chicago Press.

Ostrom, Elinor. 1990. *Governing the Commons*. Cambridge, England: Cambridge University Press.

Ostrom, Elinor, James Walker, and Roy Gardner. 1992. "Covenants With and Without a Sword: Self-Governance Is Possible." *American Political Science Review* 86(2):404-417.

Packenham, Robert A. 1992. *The Dependency Movement*. Cambridge, MA: Harvard University Press.

Pahl, R.E. 1984. *Divisions of Labour*. Oxford, England: Basil Blackwell.

Picciotto, Sol. 1990. "The Internationalization of the State." *Review of Radical Political Economy* 22(1):28-44.

Piore, Michael J., and Charles F. Sabel. 1984. *The Second Industrial Divide*. New York: Basic Books.

Poulantzas, Nicos. 1974. "The Internationalization of Capitalist Relations and the Nation-State." *Economy and Society* 145-179.

Powell, Robert. 1991. "Absolute and Relative Gains in International Relations Theory." *American Political Science Review* 80(4):1151-1169.

Prebisch, Raul. 1950. *The Economic Development of Latin America and Its Principal Problems*. Lake Success, NY: United Nations Department of Economic Affairs.

Prebisch, Raul. 1969. "Commercial Policy in the Underdeveloped Countries." *American Economic Review* 59(2):251-273.

Putnam, Robert D. 1988. "Diplomacy and Domestic Politics: The Logic of Two-Level Games." *International Organization* 42(3):427-460.

Radice, Hugo. 1984. "The National Economy: A Myth?" *Capital and Class* 22:111-140.

Risse-Kappen, Thomas. 1991. "Did 'Peace Through Strength' End the Cold War?" *International Security* 16(1):162-188.

Rogowski, Ronald. 1989. *Commerce and Coalitions: How Trade Affects Domestic Political Alignments*. Princeton, NJ: Princeton University Press.

Ruggie, John Gerard. 1982. "International Regimes, Transactions, and Change: Embedded Liberalism in the Postwar Economic Order." *International Organization* 36:379-415.

Ruggie, John Gerard. 1992. "Multilateralism: The Anatomy of an Institution." *International Organization* 46(3):561-598.

Rupert, Mark. 1990a. "Producing Hegemony: State/Society Relations and the Politics of Productivity in the United States." *International Studies Quarterly* 34(4):427-456.

Rupert, Mark. 1990b. "Alienation, Capitalism and the Interstate System: Toward a Marxian/Gramscian Critique of IPE." Paper presented for delivery at the 1990 annual meeting of the American Political Science Association, San Francisco.

Russett, Bruce M. 1990. *Controlling the Sword*. Cambridge, MA: Harvard University Press.

Russett, Bruce M., and John D. Sullivan. 1971. "Collective Goods and International Organization." *International Organization* 29:845-865.

Sandler, Todd, ed.. 1980. *The Theory and Structures of International Political Economy*. Boulder, CO: Westview Press.

Schweller, Randall L. 1992. "Democratic Structure and Preventive War: Are Democracies More Pacific?" *World Politics* 44(2):235-269.

Sherman, Richard. 1991. "A Review of Strategic Trade Policy." University of Washington, Seattle. Unpublished Manuscript.

Shklar, Judith N. 1989. "The Liberalism of Fear." In *Liberalism and the Moral Life*. Cambridge, MA: Harvard University Press.

Snidal, Duncan. 1985. "The Limits of Hegemonic Stability Theory." *International Organization* 39:579-614.

Snidal, Duncan. 1991. "Relative Gains and International Cooperation." *American Political Science Review* 85(4):1303-1320.

Snider, Lewis. 1988. "Political Strength, Economic Structure, and the Debt Servicing Potential of Developing Countries." *Comparative Political Studies* 20(4):455-487.

Snyder, Glenn H. 1984. "The Security Dilemma in Alliance Politics." *World Politics* 36:461-495.

Spiro, David. 1993. *Recycling Power: Petrodollar Politcs and the Delegitimation of American Hegemony*. Ithaca: Cornell University Press.

Stegemann, Klaus. 1989. "Policy Rivalry Among Industrial States: What Can We Learn from Models of Strategic Trade Policy?" *International Organization* 43(1):73-100.

Stein, Arthur A. 1982. "Coordination and Collaboration: Regimes in an Anarchic World," *International Organzation* 36(2):299-324.

Stokey, Edith, and Richard Zeckhauser. 1978. *A Primer for Policy Analysis*. New York: W.W. Norton.

Strange, Susan. 1988. "The Future of the American Empire?" *Journal of International Affairs* 42:1-17.

Strange, Susan. 1989. "Toward a Theory of Transnational Empire." In *Global Changes and Theoretical Challenges*, ed. Ernst-Otto Czempiel and James N. Rosenau. Lexington, MA: D.C. Heath.

Strange, Susan. 1991. "An Eclectic Approach." In *The New International Political Economy*, ed. Craig N. Murphy and Roger Tooze. Boulder, CO: Lynne Rienner.

Sunkel, Osvaldo. 1973. "Transnational Capitalism and National Disintegration in Latin America." *Social and Economic Studies* 22(1):132-176.

Szymanski, Albert. 1982. "The Socialist World System." In *Socialist States in the World System*, ed. Christopher Chase-Dunn. Beverly Hills, CA: Sage Publications.

Thomson, Janice E., and Stephen D. Krasner. 1989. "Global Transactions and the Consolidation of Sovereignty." In *Global Changes and Theoretical Challenges*, ed. Ernst-Otto Czempiel and James N. Rosenau. Lexington, MA: D.C. Heath.

Vasquez, John A. 1983. *The Power of Power Politics*. New Brunswick, NJ: Rutgers University Press.

Vernon, Raymond, and Debora L. Spar. 1989. *Beyond Globalism: Remaking American Foreign Economic Policy*. New York: Free Press.

Vernon, Raymond, and Ethan B. Kapstein. 1991. "National Needs, Global Resources." *Daedalus* 120(4): 1-22.

Wallerstein, Immanuel. 1974. *The Modern World System*. New York: Academic Press.

Wallerstein, Immanuel. 1979. *The Capitalist World Economy*. New York: Cambridge University Press.

Walt, Stephen M. 1987. *The Origins of Alliances*. Ithaca, NY: Cornell University Press.

Waltz, Kenneth N. 1959. *Man, the State, and War*. New York: Columbia University Press.

Waltz, Kenneth N. 1979. *Theory of International Politics*. New York: Random House.

Warren, B. 1971. "How International is Capital?" *New Left Review* 68 (July/August): 83-88.

Warren, B. 1980. *Imperialism, Pioneer of Capitalism*. London: New Left Books and Verso.

Weeks, John, and Elizabeth Dore. 1979. "International Exchange and the Causes of Backwardness." *Latin American Research Review* 6(2):62-87.

Williams, Shirley. 1991. "Sovereignty and Accountability in the European Community." In *The New European Community*, ed. Robert O. Keohane and Stanley Hoffmann. Boulder, CO: Westview Press.

Williams, William Appleman. 1991. "Empire as a Way of Life." *Radical History Review* 50(Spring):71-102.

Wolff, Richard D., and Stephen A. Resnick. 1987. *Economics: Marxian versus Neoclassical*. Baltimore, MD: John Hopkins University Press.

Zacher, Mark W., and Richard A. Matthew. 1992. "Liberal International Theory: Common Threads, Divergent Strands," Paper presented to the annual meeting of the American Political Science Association, Chicago, IL.

19

Political Conflict, War, and Peace

Jacek Kugler

World politics can be divided into two main strands. One strand is the broad study of war and peace that encompasses the analysis of competition, conflict and warfare; the second equally broad strand deals with the field of political economy and includes political development, integration, trade, negotiations, and political demography. This chapter focuses on the study of conflict (for political economy see Caporaso in this volume).

War is aptly and generally defined by Malinowski (1968, 28) as an "armed contest between two independent political units, by means of organized military force, in the pursuit of a tribal or national policy." Levy (1983, 51) introduces the more restricted concept of "international war" as "a substantial armed conflict between the organized military forces of independent political units." International war so defined excludes many domestic conflicts that produced enormous casualties such as the American Civil War (1861-1865), the Boxer Rebellion (1899), or the Russian Revolution and Civil War (1917-1921). It also does not include terrorist campaigns such as the protracted conflict in Northern Ireland (1969-1991), or guerrilla activities such as those leading to the fall of Chiang Kai-shek in China (1949) or to the fall of Batista in Cuba (1958). Also excluded are border incursions such as the Sino-Soviet Split (1959-1969). Limited punitive strikes such as Israeli actions against Lebanon (1967-1991) do not fall under this definition of war, or even protracted confrontations such as the Cold War between the United States and the USSR (1946-1989), because they do not qualify as substantial international conflict. The fighting in Yugoslavia illustrates the difficulty of defining war. In the early stages, this is not an international war because competitors are not independent states. Later this conflict also does not qualify as a war because it does not involve organized military directly attached to nations. Thus, using Levy's definition, the Yugoslav conflict has not yet turned into an international war.

Much of the work I report on here deals with Levy's restricted concept of international war, but many generalizations and inferences may apply to conflict in general.[1] Given this conception of war, peace defines all interactions among nations that are a complement to international war. Nations are at peace when no serious contests arise, when disputes are resolved by accommodation or continue to simmer, and, as is frequently the case, when one side yields to the demands of another without resort to force.

The concern with war and peace is so central to world politics that it defined this field for many years. For that reason it is simply impossible to do justice to the whole literature. Let me start this review, therefore, with two important disclaimers. First, in this short space it is not possible to provide a fair summary of all developments in the vast field of international war. Second, even if length were not a constraint, I am a captive of my own interest and research experience. Thus, like a myopic observer looking at an open field through a long funnel, I am aware of minute distinctions among works whose results directly relate to my own research agenda, and still see through this lens, albeit imprecisely, the contributions of distant but directly related predecessors. This intellectual funnel is also a blinder, however, and much of the research on international war that has evolved in directions different from those I chose will not attract recognition and is, unfairly, discarded. Like most reviews, therefore, this is a personal journey through the vast literature on international war that says perhaps as much about my own perspective on war and peace, as about the development of this vibrant branch of world politics.

To provide a guide, let me first outline my general perspective on the field. The study of war and peace is still chaotic because an agreement on a general paradigm to study this subject has not been reached.[2] My review emphasizes the war literature that clearly specifies general propositions, and places such propositions under empirical scrutiny. Such systematic study of war and peace is in the early stages of development, and today's findings will no doubt be seriously revised and perhaps reversed in the next decade. Yet, a body of theory supported by evidence is now available that provides hope for large theoretical gains in the near future. This review centers on a select number of general propositions that have undergone empirical scrutiny.

Paradigms on War

A consensus on a paradigm for the study of war has not emerged, and students of war and peace have not achieved closure on testing procedures. In this sense, the field of war and peace is a "developing" discipline that lacks two key characteristics of a "mature" discipline: agreement on a common paradigm to ground research and consensus on a common empirical basis for the evaluation of competing theories.[3] Because a common paradigm is lacking and because the criteria for falsification are hotly contested, theories of war and peace continue to be judged by the novel insights they suggest, whether or not such insights conform with existing empirical evidence. This review will argue that over the last two decades the most important contribution of the empirical literature on war and peace has been to show that strongly held, popular and academic constructs are usually tenuously consistent and frequently totally inconsistent with observed reality. Indeed, empirical evaluations that support general structures are rare (Midlarsky 1988).

Given this empirical record, the corpus of consistent, cumulative theories about war is thin. At this state of theoretical development it is difficult to determine whether new propositions advanced by the modern scholars supersede those advanced by earlier scholars, and it is hard to decide which theoretical strands should be discarded and which should be kept and expanded. It is not surprising, therefore, that in this vast field of competing theories, support by ardent advocates counts for as much or more than support by evidence. Moreover, perhaps because empirical tests do not conform closely with theoretical expectations, much of the debate is aimed at the philosophy of scientific research rather than at the findings from such research (Gurr 1980; Midlarsky 1989; Kugler and Lemke 1993). One wonders whether this exercise will ultimately simplify or complicate the enterprise of knowledge creation. However, there is little doubt that the debate regarding rules of falsification complicates any attempt to define and review this field.[4]

Given the current development of the study of war and peace, a reviewer is forced to make unpalatable choices. If vague falsification guidelines are accepted, the literature to be reviewed is immense and clouded by internal and external inconsistency. On the other hand, if stringent criteria for rejection are adopted, the surviving literature is tiny and there is little left worth reporting. There is no simple escape from this dilemma. My personal solution is predicated by my interest in general, cumulative, empirical knowledge. In the study of war and peace many propositions are advanced to explain a single event. Indeed, major wars such as World Wars I and II have generated such an enormous body of scholarly work that a listing of alternative explanations alone would require space far larger than this paper. For this reason, I emphasize the necessity of an agreement on empirical criteria for rejection that permits researchers to choose among the already vast array of competing propositions. Thus, I consider works that approach the simple scientific research principles proposed by Lakatos:[5]

> A scientific theory T is **falsified** if and only if another theory T' has been proposed with the following characteristics: (1) T' has excess empirical content over T; that is, it predicts novel facts, that is, facts improbable in the light of, or even forbidden by T; (2) T' explains the previous success of T, that is, all the unrefuted content of T is included (within limits of observable error) in the contents of T', and (3) some of the excess content of T' is corroborated (Lakatos 1978, 32).

In Lakatos' view, a superior scientific theory is simple and makes definite predictions that can be tested by observation. In the absence of a contending theory, systematic, parsimonious statements that account for a given phenomenon are superior to no statements at all. Indeed, like paleontologists who had to wait until the discovery of bone dating techniques to reconstruct a time pattern and develop connections to understand the evolution of a species,[6] students of war and peace could use Lakatos' rules of falsification to evaluate alternative explanations and, based on comprehensiveness, parsimony, and predictive capacity, choose those alternatives that deserve further scrutiny while discarding those options that do not conform to empirical reality. Analysts of world affairs frequently talk about taking such steps but have, thus far, failed to accept them when new propositions are introduced.

Using Lakatos' perspective, I will discuss the progress and potential of contending paradigms that dominate the current study of war and peace.

The Realist Tradition

The classic account of international war comes from the realist tradition in world politics. Realists propose that changing distributions of power among nations are directly related to the likelihood of war.

Despite differences, realists argue that nation states are effective units of analysis, and that through their growth and alliance behavior they set the broad pre-conditions for war and peace. This approach to the study of war has a very long tradition that can be traced from Thucydides (400 B.C.) to Machiavelli (1513), to Hobbes (1651), to Hume (1741), to von Clausewitz (1832), to Morgenthau (1948), to Organski (1958), to Waltz (1979), and to Gilpin (1981).

Two contradictory propositions dominate. The first, and predominant, proposes that a power parity among contenders leads to peace while an imbalance in the distribution of power leads to war. The alternative proposition contends that power preponderance or hegemony leads to peace while parity creates the conditions for war. Much of the war literature has developed along these two competing lines of inquiry. Let me consider each perspective in turn.

The Balance of Power Perspective

Balance of power is the dominant theory that adopts the power parity perspective. As the term implies, balance of power contends that an equal distribution of power leads to peace, whereas a power imbalance brings about the necessary conditions for war. Underlying this bold thesis is the assumption that nations exist in an environment of anarchy where power distributions other than parity, as Waltz (1959, 232) aptly argues, lead to wars "because there is nothing to prevent them." In this anarchic international order, decision makers can seldom manipulate their own domestic growth enough to affect relative power distributions. They can, however, alter relative power distributions through alliances or through expansion into regions where potential opponents threaten to gain power. Hence, war is expected when one side or alliance achieves a power advantage over another. The function of alliances is to preserve parity among contending coalitions and provide the weaker nations with security. Under power parity, a great power and its coalition cannot attack another great power and its allies because the costs of war would be prohibitive. Peace is preserved by the fear of war, and not by an intrinsic desire of contending parties to maintain the status quo.

Balance of power advocates concentrate on severe international war of global proportions. Levy's definition of international war is transformed into total global war by Gilpin's (1981) addition of stringent and complex criteria. He claims that only three global wars -- the Napoleonic Wars, 1803-1815; World War I, 1914-1918; and World War II, 1939-1945 -- have been waged in the last two centuries. Less stringent definitions of major power wars add the Crimean War, 1853-1856; the

Austro-Prussian War, 1866; the Franco-Prussian War, 1870-1871; the Russo-Japanese War, 1905; and the Korean War, 1950-1953 (Levy 1983; Organski and Kugler 1980). Thus, by any count only a handful of global wars have been fought during this period and no more than a score have been waged in all of recorded history (Gilpin 1981; Thompson 1988; Midlarsky 1988).

Attention centers on global wars because the resulting massive destruction of industry and population leaves lasting scars on the productive capacity and population profile of the international community. Global wars also may mark the beginning of many major transformations in the international system (Modelski 1978). Moreover, since the seminal work of Brodie (1946) brought the specter of nuclear conflict into clear focus, the threat of a global nuclear war has been the dominant concern of the peace analysts.

The focus of balance of power is on global war, but implications about lesser encounters are not excluded. Following the dictum of von Clausewitz, most balance of power advocates would argue that "war is the continuation of policy by other means," conceding that asymmetric wars of limited severity cannot be prevented. Thus, minor adjustments among contending coalitions resulting in limited war (i.e., the USSR's 1956 intervention in Hungary, or the United States' 1989 intervention in Panama) that disturb rather than profoundly affect the international order continue to be waged. In contrast, major wars ensue when the equality among large contending coalitions is fundamentally disturbed. After such wars, however, states attempt to avoid dismemberment of key members of contending coalitions to assure that a balance can once more be reimposed.

Despite its wide acceptance and influence, balance of power theory has been exposed to a very limited number of empirical tests, and, with few exceptions, most of these tests have produced negative or contradictory results. The pioneering empirical analysis by Singer, Bremer, and Stuckey (1972) associated power equality with peace in the nineteenth century and with war in the twentieth century. Using Lakatos' criteria such results are spurious or at best suggest a major specification error, however, a flurry of similar investigations preserved the century distinctions and continued to draw contradictory results (Singer 1979, 1980). An overview presented by Siverson and Sullivan (1983) suggested that while Ferris (1973) found systematic support a linkage between power equality and peace, other evaluations reject parity as a condition for peace, or found no systematic relation between power distribution and war. The empirical rejection of balance of power propositions is reinforced by more current findings (Organski and Kugler 1980; Bueno de Mesquita

1981a; Moul 1988; Bueno de Mesquita and Lalman 1988; Houweling and Sicamma 1991; Mansfield 1992). Moreover, explorations of the balance of power theory using formal logic suggest internal inconsistencies in the overall structure. Niou, Ordeshook, and Rose (1989) show that while peace is possible under power equality conditions, very stringent and seldom met conditions -- i.e., full knowledge of the war outcome, or multiple power poles -- must prevail to ensure stability in world politics. Kugler and Zagare (1990) demonstrate that to maintain stability under a power equality, leaders must be unwilling to take risks. Moreover, Bueno de Mesquita and Lalman (1992) reveal that under balance of power assumptions actors must concurrently be risk-acceptant and risk-averse to avoid instability -- a logical impossibility. Thus, despite a long ingrained tradition of accepting power equality as a condition for peace, the lack of empirical support reinforced by logical inconsistency poses grave questions about the validity of this perspective in world politics.

An overview of current events likewise leads us to seriously question the empirical validity of generalizations based on a balance of power model. The collapse of the Warsaw Pact, and the ensuing dismemberment of the USSR, are disturbing events from a balance of power perspective because after the power equality of competing forces was destroyed, and a key actor was dismembered, no war followed. One would anticipate that such events would set in motion the preconditions for major war. Yet most policy observers and practitioners contend that peace has broken out (Mueller 1989). Simply stated, power changes of the magnitude recorded between 1989-1992 are rare and must qualify as systemic changes. Their scope is rivaled only by transformations following World Wars I and II. Yet the destruction of the Soviet Empire and the dismemberment of the Soviet Union itself led to a rapprochement between East and West, have not increased tensions, and have diminished the potential for global war. Such results are inconsistent with the well established expectations of the balance of power theory where war is anticipated when the equilibrium breaks down, and when major actors are dismembered.

The lack of empirical consistency, however, has not affected the influence of the balance of power perspective on national policy, since nuclear deterrence theory retains the same general structure.

The Power Preponderance Perspective

Within the realist tradition, power preponderance theories pose a direct challenge to the conception of balance of power. Power transition, and more recently hegemonic theory, challenge the central inference of

balance of power that power parity leads to peace. Power transition, proposed by Organski (1958) and later modified as hegemonic theory by Gilpin (1981), contends that the international order is not anarchical but hierarchical. Nations recognize their power position in the international hierarchy and acknowledge that their influence will be roughly based on differences in the distribution of power. At the top of the hierarchy is the dominant nation or hegemon, that for most of its tenure as leader of a regime is the single most powerful actor in the international order and controls the status quo.[7] Below the dominant nation are the great powers, with the potential to overtake the dominant country at some future point in time. In the last 200 years this group has included Great Britain, France, Austria-Hungary, Germany, Russia/USSR, the United States, Japan, China and in the future perhaps India (Waltz 1979, Table 8.1; Organski and Kugler 1980). At any point in time, very few nations can hope to become the dominant world power. Below the great powers are the large powers who are influential but who cannot individually contend for regime leadership. This group includes, among others, Italy, the Netherlands, Spain, Canada, Argentina, Indonesia, Brazil, Australia, South Africa and their like. At the bottom of the international hierarchy are the remaining 100-plus nations that exist within or outside the regime established by the dominant power, and cannot directly challenge for control of the global order.

Organski (1958) implied that within hierarchical regimes nations attempt to maximize net gains and do not disregard the stability resulting from the existing status quo. Relations between nations where the choice to wage war is prompted by expectations of marginal gains from war, and offset by disturbances in the regime status quo resulting from such action, are relations of conditional, not total anarchy (Grieco 1988; Kugler and Hussein 1989; Kugler and Organski 1989; Kugler and Zagare 1990; and Snidal 1991). Here the conditional anarchy assumptions of power transition and hegemony differ substantively from the total anarchy postulated by balance of power.

Power preponderance theories reject the notion that nations maximize absolute gains in power or security and exist in total anarchy. If this were true, a dominant power that became a hegemon would seek to become a universal empire. The empirical record of national interaction refutes such an assertion. Consider. After World War II, the United States emerged as the undisputed hegemon and maintained this condition until the early 1950s, yet it did not seek to create a universal empire. Moreover, preponderance has been present in the international system over the last 200 years. Yet, unlike the predictions of balance of power but congruent with power preponderance, dominant nations did not expand to the limit of their capabilities, rather they sought to maintain the status quo by preserving the international order (Gilpin 1981; Kugler and Organski 1987). To ensure the stability of a regime and the maintenance of the status quo, nations seek alliances that are stable and reliable instruments not easily altered.

The power preponderance perspective conceives of the organization of world politics in a manner similar to that of domestic politics. National actors accept their position in the political order and recognize influence based on differences in the power distributions among competing political groups. Competition in the domestic and international systems differs only in degree. Despite the absence of enforceable codes of international law, nations, like domestic political groups, are in constant competition over scarce resources and driven by the search for net gains to be accrued from conflict or cooperation. In sum, the objective of nations is not to maximize power or security; rather the objective is to maximize net gains. Peaceful competition ensues when parties agree that the net gains from war are inferior to the net benefits of the status quo; war emerges when the opposite is true. Power preponderance claims that in the international hierarchical system one or more among the major powers may become a challenger to the dominant power. Thus, a nation dissatisfied with the existing status quo will bide its time until it becomes powerful enough to challenge the status quo.

The conditions for global war emerge when the challenger reaches parity with the dominant nation and seeks to establish a new place for itself in the international order. In sum, power preponderance suggests that power equality creates the necessary but not sufficient conditions for waging a global war by giving contending sides an equal opportunity for success; while gross power inequality assures peace. Less dramatic but still asymmetric power relations lead to limited war (Organski 1958; Claude 1962; Organski and Kugler 1980; Bueno de Mesquita 1981a; Gilpin 1981; Houweling and Sicamma 1988; Kugler and Organski 1989; Kugler and Zagare 1990).

Choucri and North (1975) advanced the proposition that lateral pressure theory is an important complement to power preponderance. Lateral pressure theory contends that the competition for power, influence, and global dominance is the source of war in the international system. The reasons for war are both domestic and international. Nations are driven to war by their desire to expand beyond existing borders. When such expansion tendencies clash with those of other nations of equal size, the probability of global war increases as leaders of influential sectors of competing great powers perceive the economic, political, or security dominance of their country being threatened by the increasing capabilities of challengers. The addition of expansionist tendencies driven by domestic requirements extends the notions of power preponderance. Lateral pressure explains, for example, that the collision of Japan's expansion tendencies with American interests in the Pacific Basin was the reason for the United States intervention in World War II. In sum, lateral pressure theory uses domestic and international events to account for the initiation of major wars.[8]

Empirical evaluations of the proposals advanced by power preponderance have fared relatively well. Organski and Kugler (1980) report that for the last two centuries, where the empirical record is robust, global wars occurred only when a contender achieved parity with the dominant power, and immediately after the transition had occurred. Alliances are shown to be fixed and to determine the outcome in favor of the dominant power, even though that nation is no longer preponderant.[9] The results linking war with a transition prior to the conflict, and the proposition that a speedy overtaking will trigger war, remain unclear. The early studies, associating the timing of major war with the period immediately after the transition (Organski and Kugler 1980), were challenged by evaluations that link such initiations to the period just before a transition (Thompson 1988). Recent empirical work suggests that the transition itself may or may not add specificity to the timing of war. For example, Kim and Morrow (1990) question the need for a transition to precede war, and show that the speed of closure may also be irrelevant. However, new empirical work consistently associates power parity among major nations with war. Lemke (1991) shows that power transition generalizes to regional wars in Latin America. Werner and Kugler (1993) demonstrates that arms buildups combined with a power overtaking account for 80% of major power wars where territory is at stake, and Vasquez (1992) suggests that territorial contiguity combined with a power overtaking enhance dramatically the prospects for major war.

Indirect evidence also suggests that when power parity is present, adherence to the status quo can moderate conflict. Bueno de Mesquita (1990) shows that the 1866 war between Prussia and Austria-Hungary was waged when these nations reached parity. But because these nations had a history of cooperation (against their main foe, France) and valued the status quo, the war did not escalate. However, Prussia in the subsequent Franco-Prussian War of 1870 escalated the war, since regime dominance was at stake. Therefore, while we still lack effective measures of the status quo, this work suggests that parity leads to restricted war when both nations agree on the international status quo, and to major, total war among great nations that have dramatically different visions of the world order. Such was the case between Germany and the United Kingdom prior to both World War I and World War II.

A reason why power preponderance theories have gained ground is that they are consistent with empirical reality and provide general results. Recall that Singer, Bremer, and Stuckey (1972) reported that for the nineteenth century an imbalance of power was associated with global war and for the twentieth century power parity was the precondition for such conflicts. The evolving empirical record seems to have shifted from this position. Organski and Kugler (1980), Bueno de Mesquita (1981a), and Houweling and Sicamma (1988) find no such differences. Formal derivations are also supportive of power preponderance arguments. Kugler and Zagare (1987, 1990) show that under parity when challengers are willing to take risks, war can occur, while peace is preserved when the actors are risk neutral or risk-averse. War and peace, then, are tenuously in balance when parity is achieved and national elites play a critical role in determining the choice between conflict or stability. Indeed, parity conditions imply that elites play a critical role in the preservation of peace. Perhaps because power parity is only the necessary but not sufficient condition for major war, that balance of power advocates such as Morgenthau (1948) attributed war to failures of diplomatic balancing efforts and Jervis (1976) ascribes war to misperception. Indeed, Bueno de Mesquita and Lalman's (1992) formal explorations of the internal logic of realism show that power preponderance is consistent with rational expectations for war initiation both under certainty and uncertainty, while balance of power is not, and Kugler and Zagare (1990) demonstrate that balance of power can maintain peace only when risk takers are not present. However, power preponderance theories only identify the necessary conditions for the initiation of major war and cannot account with any precision for the specific reasons that lead to the initiation or avoidance of war within relatively long periods of parity. Decision-making theories, to be considered later, take a stab at this problem.

The Collective Security Perspective

The reemergence of the collective security perspective is motivated by the decline and dismemberment of the Soviet Union following the collapse of the communist block starting in 1989. The debate is vibrant but not new. Following World War I, President Wilson argued that power hegemony rather than equality preserved peace in world politics (Claude 1962). Frustrated with the dire consequences of anarchical competition among nations, Wilson proposed the creation of a League of Nations to prevent the repetition of global war. The League of Nations would institutionalize a collective security alliance binding major powers to jointly punish, with overwhelming force, all "aggressors" that departed from the legal conventions agreed upon by the League. Because international organizations rather than nations were to decide how to exercise power, President Wilson was incorrectly branded an "idealist" not aware of realist propositions. Wilson was no idealist. The League of Nations he proposed would institutionalize the power hierarchy then in place, and would force all nations to play by the rules established by the major powers. Once national self-determination established the legitimate distribution of contested territories, overwhelming force would be used against any violator of existing agreements. Failure to comply would lead to collective punishment.

Wilson's collective security agreement was specifically designed to ensure peace where balance had failed. In practice, collective security would most likely increase the incidence of asymmetric wars, but such conflicts were deemed a necessary evil required to avoid the much larger and dangerous global war. Even though vestiges of collective security are used to justify asymmetric interventions (Korean War 1950-1953, Kuwait 1991), collective security has not been used to prevent symmetric confrontations among major powers. Claude (1962) argues in support of institutionalized preponderance that empirical tests failed to do justice to the theory. He argues that the League of Nations died because key actors among the major powers did not participate and not because the principle of collective security was untenable. Moreover, the United Nations is an ineffective instrument of collective action not because collective action is impossible but because major powers have granted themselves a veto power in the Security Council, and have denied such privilege to the other members of the international community. The United Nations arrangements are therefore a far cry from Wilson's conception of a hegemonic preponderance that would impose established rules whenever aggression by major or minor powers was detected.

Collective security is frequently confounded with interdependence. Indeed, Keohane and Nye (1977) seem to be applying Wilson's principles to conceptions of the functioning of regimes, when they claim that a hegemon is responsible for distributing collective security within a regime. However, there is a critical difference between Collective Security and Interdependence. Collective Security assumes that nations are interested in preventing all aggression in order to ensure peace in the long run. Thus, if one nation violates the frontiers of another becoming an "aggressor," collective action snaps into place. The alliance of powerful nations would not be deterred from military action against any aggressor, small or large. Interdependence, on the other hand, focuses on aggression by countries outside of a given regime, assuming that the hegemon would protect regime members by punishing any outside action against them. The hegemon, however, would not punish "aggression" by members of the regime against outsiders.

The preconditions for collective security have not been institutionalized. Recall that after 1945 the United States emerged as the world hegemon and consolidated this position by establishing a preponderant alliance under NATO in the west and SEATO in the east. The Soviet Union and China were the only great powers excluded; India remained neutral. The Soviet Union countered with the Warsaw Pact, and initially obtained support from China. Bipolarity was born. After the Sino-Soviet Split where China detached from the Soviet bloc, the Communist world was fractured but remained distinct from the American led alliance. Perceptions of bipolarity remained. Only after 1989, when the Soviet Union withdrew from Eastern Europe and shed parts of the old Russian empire, has the opportunity to test collective security emerged. Will institutions like the European Community expand to incorporate the new states, thus creating a regional collective regime? Will NATO incorporate Eastern Europe, Russia, Ukraine, Byelorussia and many of the new republics, becoming a collective agreement preponderant over all others? Will a broader Atlantic and Pacific alliance anchored by the United States survive or will it splinter with the demise of bipolarity? Will the United Nations evolve into a world collective security regime and become the focal point for a power preponderance that averts major confrontations? Evidence to support or reject such claims is lacking. Yet, the jury is at last in the courtroom and the evidence is starting to unfold.

It is perhaps useful to contrast the implications of the various realist perspectives on nuclear deterrence and proliferation to assess the likelihood of nuclear war in our lifetime.

The Nuclear Perspective: Nuclear Deterrence

Theory is important not only when it is confirmed by evidence but also when it is acted upon. Recall that ancient navigators feared crossing oceans long after their equipment was adequate for this task, because they assumed a flat world and concluded that upon reaching the ocean's edge their crafts would spill into an abyss. The preservation of peace in the nuclear era is not much different from the problem faced by ancient navigators. The fear of the "unthinkable" consequences associated with nuclear war have forced practitioners to adopt untested postures that hopefully can prevent a nuclear holocaust. Nuclear policies are advanced and adopted not because there is experience with the outcomes, but because the theory suggests what choices could reduce the danger of war. Thus, despite very tenuous support for parity assumptions during the prenuclear period, deterrence policies from the logic of Balance of Terror to Mutual Assured Destruction are derived from the balance of power perspective. Unlike the ancient navigators, however, we cannot, and do not wish to, experiment with nuclear weapons to ascertain the validity of our assumptions about deterrence. Such tests would potentially decide not simply the life of a crew, but the life of large portions of humanity and even the human species.

Before 1945, few realists disputed von Clausewitz's conception of war as "the continuation of policy by other means." Yet, following the bombing of Hiroshima and Nagasaki in 1945, Bernard Brodie contradicted this widely accepted axiom and built the cornerstone of deterrence: "Thus far the chief purpose of our military establishment has been to win wars. From now on its chief purpose must be to avert them. It can have almost no other useful purpose" (Brodie 1946, 76). Power politics moved from understanding how to wage wars to illuminating how to prevent them. For this reason, the theory of deterrence plays a critical role in world politics.

Nuclear deterrence theory shifts the focus from power as conventional capabilities to power as nuclear capacity. It is defined as the ability to prevent attack by a credible threat of unacceptable retaliation. The writings of Brodie (1946, 1959), Wohlstetter (1959), Kaufmann (1956), Kissinger (1957) and most recently Intriligator and Brito (1987) and Buzan (1987) among others, helped define deterrence as a separate field (for an excellent historical review, see Freedman 1981).

Massive Retaliation was the first deterrence policy explicitly adopted by the United States. Under Massive Retaliation, a preponderant nuclear defender credibly threatens to devastate non-nuclear opponents when provoked. The expectation is that nuclear terror can credibly compel potential opponents to avoid challenges they would otherwise initiate.

With the advent of nuclear parity, deterrence reverts in its core to the balance of power model proposed in a multilateral context by Hume (1741) and Morgenthau (1948), adapted to a bilateral environment by Waltz (1979) after World War II, and formalized using the tools of social choice by Niou, Ordeshook, and Rose (1989). Balance of Terror and Mutual Assured Destruction, the two dominant nuclear deterrence strategies after Massive Retaliation, explicitly adopt equilibrium principles from balance of power.

The Balance of Terror is achieved when both sides have nuclear capabilities but their arsenals are not large enough to assure retaliation if attacked by the other side first. Wohlstetter (1959) was the first to note that a nation with a limited nuclear arsenal could not avert a preemptive strike by threatening to retaliate, if most of the weapons available would be lost while enduring the first strike. To compensate for this uncertainty, a nuclear nation would have to retaliate when the first warning of an impending attack was detected. Thus, Balance of Terror is tenuously unstable until a credible second strike capability is developed (Bottome 1971). In practice, the specter of unstable deterrence remains through the nuclear period and is brought to life by Eisenhower's concern about the bomber gap, Kennedy's apprehension regarding the missile gap, and Reagan's worries about the "window of vulnerability" to a preemptive first strike.

The basic contention of Mutual Assured Destruction under balance of power assumptions is that equality of nuclear capabilities and secure second strike capabilities on both sides minimize the likelihood of war, because the costs of war become "unacceptable." The logic of Mutual Assured Destruction is devastatingly simple. Well informed, closely matched contenders, capable of destroying an opponent with a retaliatory strike, are aware that war among them will result in enormous damage to themselves and by extension to many other parties. As the capacity to wage a nuclear war increases, deterrence becomes increasingly stable.

William Riker (1962) provided strong impetus to deterrence by deducing that in a zero-sum, multi-actor, interactive environment minimal winning coalitions should form among contending parties. Riker shows that the costs of increasing a coalition beyond the number necessary to win by a small margin are prohibitive. These results provide a strict, logical justification for the automatic creation of equilibriums among contending nuclear poles. Riker's argument reinforces Claude's (1962) suggestion that in the nuclear era there seems to be little need to require purposeful intervention by competing actors to establish equality among competing poles. Thus, following the logic of balance of power, Mutual Assured Destruction assumes anarchy, allows for flexibility of alliances, and ensures stability due to the enormous absolute costs of nuclear war (for a discussion of automatic and purposeful balances see Morgenthau 1948; and Claude 1962).

Intriligator and Brito (1987) are to my knowledge the first scholars who provide a very clear graphic and internally consistent outline that transforms verbal statements derived from the balance of power perspective into structured equations. Their summary provides a temporal connection between the successive deterrence policies.

This structure directly links the period of Balance of Power, when conventional weapons were the only means of destruction, to the period of Massive Retaliation, when the nuclear monopoly held by the United States could compel opponents, to the period of Balance of Terror when limited nuclear arsenals were available to both sides and finally to the period of Mutual Assured Destruction, when nuclear nations could rely on a secure second strike capability.

Like Brodie (1946, 1959), Intriligator and Brito assume that when nations anticipate that the costs of war exceed a threshold above which they are no longer willing to initiate war, they will fight only in self defense. When a second threshold is exceeded, a nation is no longer willing to confront the opponent and it will be deterred from war or yield to demands. Therefore, the possibility of war exists only when costs are "acceptable." Unstable conditions are found first when contending actors only have conventional capabilities and cannot impose sufficient costs to deter opponents. Conventional parity and preponderance are both conditions for war, but the first leads to severe wars. The possibility of war is also given in the areas of transition from the region of Balance of Power to Massive Retaliation and Balance of Terror, from Massive Retaliation and Balance of Terror to Mutual Assured Destruction. During such transitions at least temporarily one actor cannot fully deter the other and war is possible. In the stable area of Massive Retaliation there is still a threat of war. If the preponderant nation fails to adhere to the principle of retaliation only when attacked, a preemptive war would follow. The ultra-stable condition of Mutual Assured Destruction is attained only under redundant nuclear parity. Here all sides will choose to yield rather than fight because the costs of war initiation are "unacceptable." Finally, under the Balance of Terror, nations that fear preemption and do not have enough weapons to assure a retaliatory strike might preempt first. Thus, a Balance of Terror is tenuously unstable.

The critical difference between unstable power parity under a Balance of Power, or Balance of Terror, and stable parity under Mutual Assured Destruction, is the absolute cost of war. Under a Balance of Power, war can be waged because the cost is relatively low. Under the Balance of Terror, war can be waged for fear of preemption. But under Mutual Assured Destruction, costs increase beyond acceptable thresholds and ensure stable deterrence. Paradoxically, further "overkill" provides a cushion against technological breakthroughs or an uneven deployment of new generations of strategic weapons. Nuclear arms races ensure peace. The costs of war are the key difference between the nuclear and pre-nuclear era.

Short of a nuclear confrontation, however, its is impossible to empirically test nuclear deterrence and determine if nuclear weapons have prevented the recurrence of war. By itself, the absence of a nuclear

Figure 1

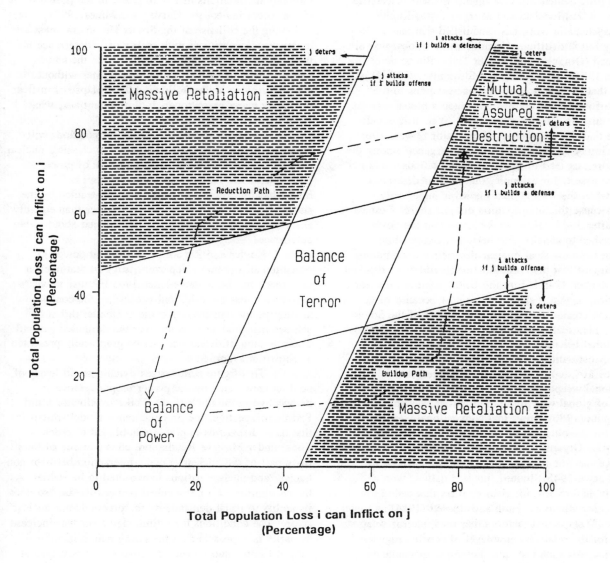

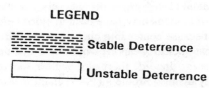

LEGEND

Stable Deterrence

Unstable Deterrence

war after the bombing of Hiroshima and Nagasaki provides little evidence for or against nuclear deterrence (Morgan 1977; Modelski and Morgan 1985; Kugler 1984). Systematic work has established that the necessary but not sufficient conditions for global war are rare indeed (Organski and Kugler 1980; Bueno de Mesquita 1981a; Houweling and Sicamma 1988). It is possible that the addition of nuclear weapons to the arsenals of major powers has prevented a global war, as classical nuclear deterrence suggests. Yet, it is equally plausible that the peace enjoyed by major powers after 1945 is simply due to the lack of convergence among the rare factors that lead to massive confrontations. It is not enough to assert, for example, that nuclear deterrence worked when the United States enjoyed superiority simply because the Soviet Union did not attack Western Europe after 1945. How do we know that the Soviet Union wished to attack? Furthermore, implications following from classical nuclear deterrence assumptions would suggest that the United States should have attacked the USSR after 1945 before the USSR achieved nuclear capabilities, or that it should do so now because of the opportunity created by the dismemberment of the Soviet Empire. Yet, such assumptions are clearly not consistent with national behavior.

Most damaging to the claim of classical nuclear deterrence are studies of war which suggest that conventional weapons can be used to account for the absence of global war in the international system. Bueno de Mesquita (1980) shows that conventional weapons account for the outcome of almost all crises and wars since 1945. Organski and Kugler (1980) find that nuclear deterrence has not affected the way crises have been resolved since 1945. Indeed, nuclear nations won as frequently as they lost in crises or wars that called for nuclear confrontations. Huth and Russett (1984) and later Huth (1988) show that factors other than nuclear weapons account for the relatively low level of conflict registered after 1945. All such tests are, however, inconclusive. Achen and Snidal (1989) argue persuasively that many potential confrontations may have been avoided before they started, because contending nuclear parties already understood that nuclear weapons would be called upon to settle such issues. Indeed, short of a nuclear war one cannot directly dismiss Brodie's (1946) claim that the only acceptable role of nuclear weapons is to prevent nuclear war and not to wage or win such a war. However, one can also make the equally valid claim that the introduction of nuclear weapons raised the stakes in a global war, but did not fundamentally change the behavior of nations. The jury on this issue is still out (for alternative evaluations of the same evidence see Huntington 1982; and Kugler 1984).

There is no doubt that classical nuclear deterrence theory based on the concept of nuclear

retaliation must be identified as a major contribution of international relations theory to peace in the post-war era (for a recent review see Harvey and James 1992). Yet, following the collapse of the Soviet Union one must ask: is deterrence congruent with reality or is deterrence a well established but untested myth? Like the ancient mariners who navigated further and further without encountering an abyss, following the collapse of nuclear bipolarity many practitioners will no doubt ask, what ensures peace under preponderance?

Certainly, many alternative propositions will emerge. Yet, one existing alternative to classical nuclear deterrence is provided by the perspective of power preponderance. If the international system is hierarchically ordered, if actors are constrained by the status quo, and if power asymmetry rather than equality ensures stability, then what can be deduced about stable deterrence?

Kugler and Zagare (1990), using power transition as a point of departure, suggest that nuclear deterrence has been stable since 1945 because power asymmetry was the rule, and because in the contest among the two superpowers, the contender did not achieve marginal superiority over the dominant nation. Their version of deterrence can be graphically presented as shown in Figure 2.

This figure summarizes dynamics and levels of conflict anticipated by the power preponderance perspective in the nuclear era. Like Intriligator's and Brito's perspective, the preponderance model anticipates that large disparities in power would lead to peace. Thus, under Massive Retaliation, characteristic of the early part of the nuclear era, the interaction between non-nuclear and nuclear nations is expected to be stable. As the capabilities of a non-nuclear power increase, so does its ability to resist demands by the preponderant nuclear actor. The conditions for a limited nuclear war increase as parity is approached, if the rising nation is not a satisfied status quo power. Limited conflicts waged at this stage are frequently won by the dominant power. The few decided in favor of the weaker side occur when the costs endured by the challenger are much higher than those suffered by the dominant nation (i.e., Vietnam, Afghanistan). The most serious conflict is anticipated when the challenger overtakes the dominant nation in power terms and matches its ability to destroy (Organski and Kugler 1980; Houweling and Sicamma 1988; for alternate timing see Thompson 1988).

Deterrence under power parity is therefore tenuous.[10] Parity provides the necessary conditions for peace and serious conflict. The challenger can make demands and wage a war with a probability of success that is equivalent to that confronted by the deterrer. The risk of taking such an action is high, but marginal probing by a risk taker should result in some gains that

Figure 2

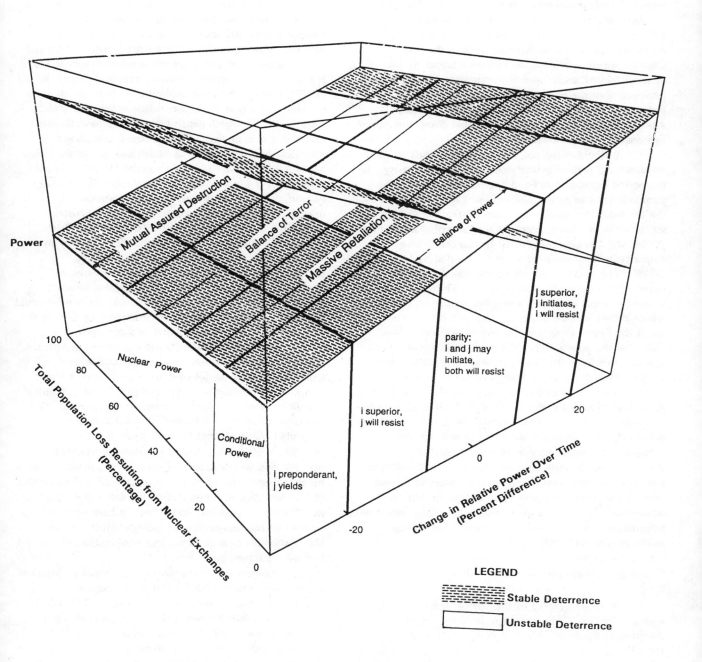

Power

Total Population Loss Resulting from Nuclear Exchanges
(Percentage)

100

80

60

40

20

0

Nuclear Power

Conditional Power

Mutual Assured Destruction

Balance of Terror

Massive Retaliation

Balance of Power

i preponderant, j yields

i superior, j will resist

parity: i and j may initiate, both will resist

j superior, j initiates, i will resist

-20

0

20

Change in Relative Power Over Time
(Percent Difference)

LEGEND

Stable Deterrence

Unstable Deterrence

may eventually lead to escalation if repeated. Deterrence is determined by the joint decision of both nuclear actors not to act -- if one chooses to break the compact, the terror of nuclear weapons cannot deter the initiation and eventual escalation of such conflict (Kugler and Zagare 1987; Powell 1990; Zagare 1990). Parity is the necessary but not the sufficient condition for war. Choices are open to decision makers whether to initiate or to avoid war under specific circumstances. From the perspective of the power preponderance, therefore, the Balance of Power, Balance of Terror, and Mutual Assured Destruction are all policies that share in common one condition: tenuous stability.

In the nuclear era, no country has thus far traversed the path to power parity and nuclear parity. In the period between 1945 and approximately 1960, the preponderance of power and nuclear capabilities held by the United States ensured stability despite the Cold War. Once parity in nuclear weapons was achieved in the mid-1960s, stability was maintained by the continuing disparity in capabilities between the United States and the USSR. The convergence in nuclear capabilities was never accomplished by power parity. Thus, the USSR would have had to initiate a conflict against an opponent whose power was far superior. As new information about the Soviet economy has become available, it is clear that the power of NATO was overwhelmingly superior to that of the Warsaw Pact. Since 1945, the preconditions for a major war have not been met.

The implications for today's world are telling. A nuclear overtaking may be very difficult to achieve by any superpower. Yet, the potential for a nuclear war has not disappeared from the world arena and may be enhanced by nuclear proliferation.[11] Continuing disputes in the Middle East, or confrontations among the emerging splinter republics from the old Soviet Union, may still provide gruesome testimony to the failure of deterrence. In a period of nuclear parity, then, effective negotiations about the status quo rather than nuclear terror are the tools that can prevent war.

Nuclear Proliferation

A second aspect of the nuclear era is the Nth nation dilemma. This process is attracting increased attention as the Soviet Union splinters into its component republics and as nations like Iraq, Iran, or Korea seek to achieve nuclear status. Like the ancient navigators who did not venture far from the coastline, it is impossible for political analysts to ascertain empirically whether nuclear deterrence is stable or tenuous short of a nuclear war. Yet, as more nations achieve nuclear parity with chosen opponents, this question becomes more and more relevant. One may, therefore, assess the validity of the competing perspectives by looking at implications and contrasting them with actual national behavior.

Consider first the balance of power perspective. Logically if one argues that Mutual Assured Destruction is stable, one must conclude that extending the nuclear balance will secure stability for a larger number of nations. Many scholars advocate the carefully managed proliferation of nuclear weapons to allies to reduce the risk of accidents, while enhancing regional peace. Rosen (1977), perhaps the most explicit and eloquent advocate of the introduction of nuclear weapons into the Middle East, argues that such capabilities should have the same salutary effects on the Arab and Israeli contenders, as they have had on the United States and the Soviet Union at the height of the Cold War. Waltz (1981) likewise argues that if Mutual Assured Destruction is stable, expanding the scope of nuclear deterrence should dramatically reduce the likelihood of war whether contenders are large or small. Intriligator and Brito (1981), and Bueno de Mesquita and Riker (1982) are somewhat more reserved, advocating restricted proliferation to allies or nations in danger of being attacked. Such managed nuclear proliferation would reduce the possibility that a regional nuclear contest could transform itself into a world confrontation by linking the defense of a weak nation to that of a superpower.

Nuclear proliferation has not gained acceptance. Nuclear nations have restricted access to nuclear technology and have not seen fit to proliferate nuclear weapons strategically in the hopes of enhancing regional stability. Active prevention seems to be the rule. The coalition of nations led by the United States that frustrated Iraq's attempt to incorporate Kuwait, for instance, was to some degree motivated by the fear that Mr. Hussein would acquire nuclear weapons and threaten his neighbors. Indeed, a major priority of UN inspectors in Iraq has been to remove every nuclear device from that country. However, Israel has not been pressured to remove its nuclear devices to balance efforts in Iraq. Iran's attempts to acquire nuclear weapons are monitored but not yet threatened. Why?

Leaders of nuclear nations that practice MAD as a deterrence strategy do not follow the nuclear proliferation tactic consistent with MAD. This policy inconsistency fails to meet Lakatos' demand that the inferences from a theory should consistently reflect empirical reality. A second alternative is to accept inconsistency. Indeed, many policy analysts who argue that mutual deterrence is viable, reject the logical links to proliferation on common sense grounds (Epstein 1976; Nye 1990). Again, Lakatos' criteria of consistency force us to reject this option, because it allows support for a desirable aspect of a theory while rejecting its undesirable implications.[12] A third alternative is that the behavior does not conform with the theory. Jervis (1984) suggests this line of inquiry, but does not abandon Mutual Assured Destruction as the superior option.

Following the dictates of Lakatos, if the theory itself is flawed, so are the deductions. One reason we act contrary to the fear of falling from the edge of the Earth, is we fear the consequences of a tenuous nuclear deterrence. Consider the implications.

From the perspective of power preponderance, avoiding nuclear proliferation to smaller countries ensures stability. Proliferation is, as practitioners have recognized, a very dangerous practice unlikely to produce lasting peace. As the number of actors who achieve nuclear parity increases, the probability of a regional or a global nuclear war likewise increases. Thus, nuclear deterrence is stable under parity conditions provided that competing actors do not want to challenge the status quo and maximize long-term stability, but may lead to war if such actors, either by accident or design, opt for confrontation. Nuclear weapons are, from this perspective, as dangerous as their conventional counterparts. Maybe nuclear weapons have not been used, thus far, simply because unilateral destruction by supporters of the status quo is unacceptable under conditions of preponderance and the tenuous nuclear parity among the superpowers was short lived? If such deductions are accurate and proliferation leads to regional parity, nuclear war may well be in our future.[13]

I have thus far reviewed the realist perspectives that accept the basic premise that nations, power distributions, and national security are the key elements required to understand world politics. Let me now explore important contributions to the understanding of war that depart from this perspective.

The Global Perspective: The Cycle of War

Basic challenges come from analysts who dispute the core assumption of realism that war emerges from an interaction between nations. Based on extensive observation of historical trends, the English historian Arnold Toynbee (1934-1954) proposed a cycle of war and peace that coincided roughly with a period of a little more than one hundred years. Each cycle started with a global war, was followed by a peaceful period, then a smaller war, a pause, and finally another global war. Toynbee attributed this repetitive pattern to the war weariness of the combatants. He reasoned that the generation directly involved in major war would be reluctant to re-enter a similar war. However, the generation once removed from a global war, enticed by writings that glorified war and encouraged by victories in

smaller wars, would once more view global war as a viable alternative to advance national goals. Toynbee's vision is congruent with the post World War II period, where a major victory by the United States resulted in a long peace punctured only by a draw in the Korean war, then a defeat in Vietnam, and consolidated by the success in Kuwait. Americans and Europeans, Toynbee would argue, have overcome the weariness of global war and might seek to once more create or enter a global war. Toynbee's argument is persuasive; however, the anticipated cycle fails to materialize under systematic scrutiny of the historical record (Blainey 1973; Thompson 1988).

Exploring how a global cycle interacts with war is not without promise. Recent interest centers on whether major war is related to a long cycle of war leadership, or to a Kondratieff economic long-term cycle. In both, a strong relationship is anticipated between the initiation of major wars and the performance of the global economy (Modelski 1978; Goldstein 1985; Thompson 1988). In cycle theory, global war is associated with systemic world fluctuations over which national decision makers have no direct control, and nations are pawns in a larger game. Nations, like surfers, can maneuver in and out of war during the buildup of a wave, but are dragged under by forces beyond their control when the wave breaks, dragging nations into major confrontations.

Goldstein (1985) and Thompson (1988) show that the evidence for and against Kondratieff economic cycles and war is very tentative. In part, this uncertainty is due to a lack of clear specification of economic and political cycles and in part to data limitations. Cycle theory requires long time series where almost no reliable evidence exists, forcing compromises that foster further controversy about the structure of detected cycles. A variant of the long cycle theory was developed by Modelski (1978), then extended and tested by Thompson (1988). These scholars postulate that a regular cycle of war is associated with changes in world leadership over the past five centuries. They center on the global implications of a system dominated by a single state, and focus on the control of sea lines that insure trade dominance. The global power seeks naval dominance to maintain an economic system that strengthens trade. The costs of such leadership are high, allowing new rivals to emerge, leading to succession in world leadership. From this perspective, the two world wars are the result of declining British leadership and the failed attempt by Germany to compete in world markets. Similar patterns are detected when the Netherlands and Portugal lost their superiority as major naval powers, after having colonized much of Africa, Asia, and Latin America. The anticipated American decline should lead to similar instability.

The cycle of world leadership is plausible, but the evidence at hand seems insufficient to accept or reject. First, the focus on naval strength as an indicator of overall power produces further distortions. Major historical powers like Sweden, Russia, Austria-Hungary, Prussia, Poland-Lithuania, and France had no major sea profile and are undervalued despite their historical importance. Further, victory in global wars was decided by land fighting and not naval warfare. Recall that Europe was altered over time by major wars fought on land: the collapse of the Polish-Lithuanian confederation led to the rise of Russia in the East and Prussia in the West; Napoleon's largest battles were fought against Prussia and Russia; the destruction of the Austro-Hungarian Empire was the major outcome of World War I. Sea power had little to do with such transformations. Significantly, except for the period of Pax Britannica, in Midlarsky's (1988) and Kennedy's (1987) historical evaluation of the rise and fall of great powers and the evolution of world wars share little in common with the picture derived from the cycle of world leadership. The actors differ and so do many of the identified confrontations. The main difference can be traced to the definition of power. Thus far, analysis of alternate time series produces sometimes promising and sometimes contradictory results for the cycle theories (Thompson 1988 and 1992).

Many of these criticisms are now being confronted. Rasler and Thompson (1992) have expanded the temporal domain to allow more effective testing. They have redefined power to include naval and conventional military capabilities. They have introduced both domestic fiscal constants and cycle effects to account for long-term transformations that may be associated with major war. The new approach is vibrant and intriguing. If nations are merely pawns in a larger world structure, can war be averted? What is gained by direct national intervention?

The question posed by cycle theory is central in a nuclear world. What are the prospects of averting nuclear war if or when the next wave crashes? Modelski and Morgan (1985) suggest that nuclear deterrence may well be unstable. They find that the ability to manage cycles is not part of nuclear deterrence, that credibility has not been demonstrated to be a significant factor in a historical context, and that the absence of major war thus far coincides with the most benign phase of the power cycle. Modelski and Morgan, like advocates of power preponderance, conclude that nuclear deterrence is at best tenuous.

A different approach to cycle theory considers the relative position of a nation in respect to all others in the international system. Taagepera (1986) shows that all nations and empires have a characteristic relative pattern of rise and decline over time. Kennedy (1987) documents the rise and fall of great empires and associates such changes with military overspending. No nation or empire has persisted forever. This well documented phenomenon of rise and decline characterized the expansion and contraction of Rome, the Mongol Empire, Venice, the Ottoman Empire, Spain, France, the United Kingdom, Russia, and in the distant future perhaps the United States.

Doran links relative power decline to account for cycles of war (Doran and Parsons 1980; Doran 1991). Great nations emerge from the pack of smaller nations and expand to their maximum strength to become a dominant nation when their power is relatively larger than that of others. However, this dominance is followed by a leveling off period, and terminates after a period of decline when a new competitor catches up and overtakes the dominant nation. Using the cycle of relative power, Doran tests the link between stages in a nation's relative cycle and the decisions to initiate war. Relative cycle theory departs fundamentally from other power distribution models because it rejects interaction among states as the main cause of war, and instead purports that domestic factors drive the external actions. The specification of the theory remains somewhat vague regarding the specific phase in the relative power cycle when war is waged. There is also some lack of clarity regarding the severity of war.

Empirical evidence regarding the relative cycle of war is, thus far, mixed. In their early work, Doran and Parsons (1980) suggested a strong relationship between the relative cycle of power and war. Thompson's (1988) follow-up study tends to discount or diffuse the earlier findings. However, Doran (1991) has recently revised and restructured his argument and finds strong empirical congruence. Moreover, Houweling and Sicamma (1991), combining power transitions with the relative power cycle, improve dramatically previous accounts for the waging of major power wars. When these two conditions coincide -- (1) two major nations reach a power balance; and (2) the dominant nation is in relative decline -- major war is waged. Cycle theory recasts the relationship between power and war in ways congruent with power preponderance models and seemingly adds to them. The results are encouraging but preliminary.

The empirical jury on cycles and relative power is still out, but the direction seems promising and new extensions may produce further fruitful results.

The Arms Race Perspective

Just prior to World War II, Richardson (1960a) argued that the result of an unstable arms race is war.

National elites react to the buildup of armaments by opposing nations with buildups of their own. Richardson's logic is disarmingly simple. When competing parties reach an equilibrium in their arms expenditures, a tenuous stability is attained between arms expansion and reduction. An unexpected increase leads to an arms race and war, while an unexpected decrease leads to disarmament and peace. Smoker (1964) asserted that the fear inspired by an arms race would lead to war unless a restraining effect kicked in and forced the two countries to back down. Smoker explicitly expanded the connection between war and arms races, suggesting that the weaker of the competing sides would initiate the war because, unable to compete, the weaker nation is forced to preempt or be left behind.[14] Huntington (1958) suggested a distinction between qualitative and quantitative arms races, indicating that naval arms competition did not lead to war while mobilization did so prior to the two world wars. These intuitively appealing insights have been explored in some depth.

Richardson was unusual among early formal scholars because he compiled the data required to test his propositions. His empirical analysis shows an explosive arms race between Germany and the United Kingdom before 1939, and forecasts the initiation of World War II. Other empirical tests produced less supportive results. Wallace (1979) originally found a very strong relationship between arms races and the escalation of disputes to war. His results seemingly resolved the long-standing conflict regarding the relationship between arms races and war. However, Wallace's study was severely criticized on methodological grounds for breaking down multilateral wars into separate dyads and thus inflating the results (Weede 1980). Furthermore, Wallace's arms race index not only placed inordinate weight on the last two years of the arms race but also failed to adequately capture the interactive component that Wallace believed to be integral to arms races. Follow-up studies on Wallace that explore the relationship between arms races and escalation to war have suggested either weak or very confounded and complex results (Smith 1980; Horn 1987). Siverson and Diehl (1989, 212) conclude after a thorough survey of the literature that "if there is any consensus among arms race studies, it is that some arms races lead to war and some do not." Like Siverson and Diehl, most researchers in the field now concur that the relationship between arms races and war is very weak (Diehl 1983; Diehl and Kingston 1987; Horn 1987). Supporting this perception, Morrow (1989, 502) states that "rather than asking whether arms races lead to war, we should ask which arms races lead to wars."

Recently, arm buildups have emerged as an important focus of research on wars. Studies in this field indicate a significant distinction between arms races, which are based upon the interaction and acceleration effect across countries; and arms buildups, which reflect unusually large defense expenditures by our nation. As Richardson's original equations specified, an arms race required that the level of military expenditures of nation A be determined at least in large part by the level of military expenditures of nation B and vice versa. For every action, there would be a reaction. The model of an unstable arms race suggested that the rate of acquisition would become increasingly faster. Military buildups do not incorporate interactive concepts. They assume, instead, that if nation A begins to increase its military expenditures, nation B can match that threat in many different ways -- only one of which is to match its expenditures to those of its opponent. Thus, one nation's military buildup, or "abnormally" high level of growth, refers to the "normal" buildup of that nation.

Zinnes, Gillespie, and Rubinson (1976) formally show that with minor changes in the structures of Richardson's equations, arms buildups could result from competition among domestic groups. After every over-expenditure or under-expenditure, national elites respond to domestic constraints and return to the equilibrium point following a self-regulating process. Empirical evaluations of arms expenditures show that arms buildups, suggestive of a military industrial complex, seem to dominate; while external factors, suggestive of an interactive arms race, are far less influential (Ostrom and Aldrich 1978; Kugler, Organski, and Fox 1980; Ward 1984; Ostrom and Marra 1986; and McGinnis 1991). Contrary to Richardson's expectations, therefore, empirical analysis strongly suggests that domestic pressures fuel arms buildups, while the external competition has a relatively small impact.

From the perspective of war studies this is unfortunate. The domestic arms buildup model accounts for budgetary allocations, but does not provide direct assistance in understanding the initiation of war. Indeed, war may occur during an arms buildup, an arms reduction, or when arms acquisition policies among competitors are stable. The absence of a direct theoretical link between arms buildups and war encourages ad hoc arguments that posit positive as well as negative relationships between military increases and the escalation of violence. A positive relationship is generally defended on the basis of an "armaments-tensions" circle to which arms buildups allegedly contribute (Singer 1958). Conversely, the peace through strength argument suggests that a military buildup may actually diminish the likelihood of war (Morgenthau 1948).

Recently, Werner and Kugler (1993) persuasively argues that it is necessary to focus on the context of power distribution within which the buildup is taking place in order to understand the theoretical connection to war. Linking the structural conditions of power configurations with the choice by national leaders to initiate an abnormal period of arms acquisitions, Werner finds a very strong and consistent association with war.

The arms races-arms buildup literature is an excellent example of a successful interaction between empirical investigations and effectively specified theories. While the cumulative evidence indicates that the original connection between war and arms races may not be robust, it leads to the specification of arms buildup propositions that are robust. This research led to the discovery that is critical to assess the links between war and arms buildups.

The appeal of arms races is still quite strong in the world of practitioners, and there is delay in transmitting the notion that arms races and war are not directly connected, but that arms buildups seem to be. However, practitioners seem to have dismissed unwarranted implications. President Reagan, for example, advocated the buildup of arms in order to force the Soviet Union to agree to American peace overtures, not to generate war. Mr. Gorbachev initiated many unilateral arms reductions without waiting for an American response or obtaining one. President Bush seems to have adopted a similar strategy. Arms negotiators may perhaps look at these actions and reconsider the implication of Richardson's model that mutual, linked moves are the most effective way to achieve arms reductions.

The Decision Makers' Perspective: Group Preference and War

Students of decision making provide a very different reaction to the realist controversy about the initiation of war. Contributors to this branch of war studies argue that for far too long it was assumed that world politics was played in a field where all nations were like billiard balls of different sizes or that these nations allied according to neutral principles of power maximization, and otherwise conformed to similar rules of behavior. Decision making models stress differences among nations and emphasize, in particular, the vast disparity in the preferences that elites wish to maximize.

Allison's (1969) classic treatment of the Cuban Missile Crisis provided a major impetus for this work. Allison posited that elites and pressure groups had far more to say about the initiation of war than relative power structures. Moreover, he argued that assumptions of a common, self-evident national interest were grossly violated in practice. Finally, Allison offered a set of

general criteria and rules that could help account for war initiation. He suggested that to understand a confrontation and its resolution or escalation to war, one needs to know the goals of elites, the options that are available to manipulate outcomes, and the probability of success the elites attach to each option. With this summary information, decision makers could "rationally" minimize costs by choosing the option that left them least exposed and provided the maximum probability of success. If the first policy failed, the decision makers could choose the next option along the ladder that minimized costs and provided an increased probability of success. If none was available, the crisis ended. Differences in decision patterns emerged. Some elites might choose options that maximized the probability of success while minimizing cost, while others would first minimize costs and then maximize the probability of success. Indeed, a decision maker like Hitler, unlike Kennedy, for example, might have chosen to invade rather than blockade Cuba. Neither, however, would have chosen nuclear war as the first option to settle that crisis. Such rhetoric was simply a bluff.

As an alternative to this "rational actor" model, Allison then developed the more complex "organizational model" that introduced the possibility that different groups within one nation would hold competing goals thus advocating alternative policies. Elites could no longer simply strive for a set goal by minimizing their costs while attempting to maximize the probability of success, but had to struggle with each other. Allison did not provide the formal structures necessary to solve the problem posed by the increased complexity and failed to note that the "organizational model" was simply an extension of his simpler "rational actor" model. However, he opened the door to the introduction of positive political theory to study war (for a critical review of Allison's work see Bendor and Hammond 1992).

Bruce Bueno de Mesquita (1981a) was the first to make systematic use of Allison's insight. He made a major contribution to the field of international politics by introducing to international relations a deductive perspective.

Bueno de Mesquita's (1981a) seminal *The War Trap* forced students of war to consider a formal, deductive specification of the necessary conditions for war and peace. He provided clearly specified variables and empirically tested propositions deduced from explicitly stated assumptions. Bueno de Mesquita assumed that nations are led by single strong leaders, that such actors maximize net gains in confrontations, that risk is a variable connected to individual decision makers, and that divergent preferences for competing goals held with varying degrees of commitment are at the root of war. Unlike realists who considered power as the key variable, Bueno de Mesquita argued that to account for war one must also consider policy goals, commitments, and risk propensity. Power provides elites with the ability to execute policies that seek to maximize their net gains. Power is not the end itself.

This decision making perspective, which has roots in micro-economic theory, generated a very dynamic and still growing literature that concentrates on war initiation. Lalman's (1988) extension allows differentiation between war initiation and escalation. Morrow (1985) extends this analysis to competitive interaction among dimensions such as trade, human rights, and diplomatic recognition. This approach allows scholars to concurrently assess policies while varying the goals of competing elites. The promise of cumulative work is starting to be a reality.

Empirical results are general and supportive. Bueno de Mesquita (1981a) shows that expected utility provides the necessary but not sufficient conditions for war. The incidence of war is over-predicted by a wide margin because the model fails to effectively discriminate between war and non-war before a dispute does occurs. But once a crisis develops, calculations of net gain accurately account for the escalation and termination of disputes. Results are very specific. Once a crisis starts, net gains analysis distinguishes between asymmetric and symmetric wars, anticipates when wars will be limited and when they will escalate, determines when confrontations will remain bilateral and when they will become multilateral, and indicates how a war will terminate (Bueno de Mesquita 1981a, 1985; Bueno de Mesquita and Lalman 1986). This approach is powerful because all wars can be treated without regard to the number of actors, or to questions of major or minor power participation. Moreover, expected utility applies to wars regardless of their intensity, and the logic can be extended from international to domestic confrontations (Muller et al. 1991). The main limitation is that a static picture of evolving confrontations is presented that depends on short-term updates to account for war dynamics. Some of these limitations are now being overcome with game theory, which I consider next.

Game theory provides a separate but related perspective on the problem of war (von Neumann and Morgenstern 1953). Unlike expected utility theory, which assumes independent decisions by each actor, game theory directly considers the interdependence of strategic choice among the participants.

Building on the early contributions of Schelling (1960, 1966), Ellsberg (1959, 1961), Kaplan (1957), Kahn (1960, 1962, 1965), Rapaport (1964), and Snyder (1961, 1972), there has been a flurry of attempts in the past few years to use game theory to understand interstate war. Unlike the early, static modeling efforts, contemporary applications have used recent refinements of equilibrium solution concepts (Brams and Wittman 1981; Fraser and Hipel 1979; Kreps and Wilson 1982; Selten 1975) and breakthroughs in games of incomplete information (Rasmusen 1989) to develop dynamic models that more closely capture the essence of strategic choice. Snidal (1985c), Brams (1985), Zagare (1987), Langlois (1989), Powell (1990), Kilgour (1991), Wagner (1991) and Bueno de Mesquita and Lalman (1992), among others, have developed rich game-theoretic models mapping a variety of conflictual relationships. O'Neill (1989) and Zagare (1990) offer insightful reviews of this extensive literature.

The essential contribution of war is the clarification of the dichotomy between cooperation and conflict. Political transactions are intrinsically conflictual since political demands are imposed by one state on another when a disagreement occurs (Bueno de Mesquita et al. 1985). The weak party cannot walk out, but must accept the offer or resist and pay the consequences of dissent. Thus, like a convicted murderer who cannot escape the sentence for his transgression by refusing to cooperate, a nation cannot avoid the repercussions generated by a challenge by choosing not to yield. Opponents must choose between war, deterrence, or concessions to resolve the impasse.

Cooperation, however, is possible. Recent work on decision making shows that cooperation is the outcome of sophisticated calculations of the future costs of confrontations. Pioneering work by Axelrod (1984) demonstrates that a simple tit-for-tat strategy, within constraints, can be adopted to advance interactive diplomacy and generate cooperation. Applying this conception to arms races, for example, suggests that weapons reductions unilaterally initiated by one nation can reinforce similar behavior in opponents. Powell (1989) further explores the notion of strategic bargaining in a nuclear context and shows that in sequential interactions, the ability to preempt specific choices, particularly under uncertainty, can result in stable outcomes even among risk takers. Likewise, Kilgour and Zagare (1991) and Wagner (1991) extend such arguments and generalize their application, suggesting the beginning of a general strategy of conflict resolution.

Much of this work remains formal, however, and its power rests on the force of the argument rather than empirical evidence. The empirical analysis of game theoretical solutions is in its infancy. Many propositions have been generated, but few have been exposed to empirical tests. Two important exceptions deserve mentioning. Niou, Ordeshook, and Rose (1989) explore the implications of balance of power and show formally and empirically that the conditions for stability under balance are difficult to reconcile with international reality.

Bueno de Mesquita and Lalman (1992) apply game theory to extend their previous expected utility analysis of war and show that the addition of interactive structures greatly aids in the understanding of conflict development and its resolution. They persuasively argue that the analysis of interactive preferences is essential to understand the escalation of crisis to war.

The early results from formal analysis augur well for the future understanding of war. However, current decision-making approaches provide a limited time perspective and the detail required for effective evaluations is taxing. Few systematic data sets do justice to these requirements, which in turn leads to much debate about the validity of the reported findings. Yet, the promise is that ultimately formal models will be able to provide a general theory of conflict initiation, escalation, termination, and particularly management.

Other Perspectives on War

Much of the work on war providing important angles of vision on this phenomenon cannot be directly connected to traditional over-arching explications of war. Such work should not be overlooked, because it points to new directions that need serious investigation. I will, somewhat capriciously, select arguments that have attracted my attention from this vast literature.

Democracy and War

A growing number of studies deals with the connection between democracy and war. The puzzle to be explained is posed by Rummel (1963), who points out that while wars are waged among autocratic or totalitarian regimes with the same frequency as between these regimes and democracies, democracies do not wage war on other democracies. The debate was unearthed by Maoz and Abdolali (1989), who show that the phenomenon of war avoidance by democracies withstands statistical scrutiny after normal controls for factors related to war propensity. The results are robust challengers who have considered without altering the relation of democracy and peace, levels of national wealth, rates of economic growth, territorial contiguity, alliance structures, opportunity, and historical precedent (Morgan and Campbell 1991; Siverson and Emmons 1991). Ember, Ember, and Russett (1992) have even extended the scrutiny for an explanation of this unexpected stability to domestic confrontations among primitive societies, showing that political participation deters war. Recently, Maoz and Russett (1991) propose that the absence of war among democracies is robust and probably due to political constraints imposed on democracies that attempt

to mobilize the population as well as the general norms that distinguish electoral system from authoritarian regimes.

If such results hold, increasing the level of participation would deter war. Thus, establishing functioning democracies may provide a new means of controlling war. Perhaps the growing trend toward democratic rule will contribute more to peace than either nuclear deterrence or arms control. These results challenge assumptions of theories focusing on power distribution or cycles, which assume that countries act in a general manner regardless of the form of government.[15]

Many are skeptical of such findings. Weede and Waltz question the selection of cases. If democracy is defined somewhat more liberally, World War II and the American Civil War were initiated by elected leaders. The collapse of Yugoslavia resulted from domestic and then international confrontations among elected elites. The question is, are they democratic? And if not, what is a democracy? With the emergence of new democratic systems, this line of research will no doubt be expanded.

Consequences of War

Evaluation of the consequences of war has also carved out an independent empirical niche. Organski and Kugler (1980) demonstrate the existence of a "phoenix factor," whereby within 20 years nations recover economic losses and more than overcome the aggregate populations losses incurred by the waging of war. Thus, following conventional wars, actors have reentered the international system and competed at a level similar to that prior to the war, after a single generation.

A political explanation for the phoenix factor flows from Olson's (1982) seminal work on collective goods. Olson argues that devastated, defeated nations, like Germany or Japan after World War II, have a substantial advantage over devastated victors, such as England or France after World War II, and even over relatively untouched contenders, such as the United States after World War II. He claims that the vanquished nations reinvigorate their economies because invaders destroy the political structures and coalitions created to protect specific interests, and allow the pure market place to reemerge. Victors, on the other hand, preserve such coalitions and the inefficiencies associated with their presence.

Empirical evaluations of these propositions produce inconclusive results. Chan (1987), using data from the Far East, shows that the vanquished accrue the beneficial economic effects anticipated by Olson. On the other hand, Kugler and Arbetman (1989b) find no evidence linking the decline of political structures to economic recovery in Western societies. Indeed the contrary seems to be the case. Further exploration of this puzzling pattern is warranted.

War Termination

A related literature deals with the termination of war. Rosen (1972) explored the relationship between the severity of war and the willingness to suffer and shows that all wars end, but some end very differently than others. Urlanis (1971) places an upper boundary on casualties and shows that contenders will terminate a total war if casualties exceed 20% of the population. However, Bueno de Mesquita demonstrates that different calculations based on the importance the competitors attach to the outcome are required in order to understand the termination of limited wars. Work in this vein suggests that there is a calculus of war: contenders do not blindly pursue a lost cause, but withdraw when losses exceed expectations. In Vietnam 50,000 Americans died before the United States withdrew, in Afghanistan 10,000 Russians were killed before the Soviet Union withdrew. These superpowers could have secured victory by escalating either war, but they chose not to. Cioffi-Revilla (1991a) points out that United States' success in Kuwait was assured by effective anticipation of low American casualties. Iusi-Scarborough and Bueno de Mesquita (1988) show that suffering and endurance in war are directly related to the willingness of elites to accept casualties and their calculations are in turn conditioned by expectations of success. The end of war is seemingly predictable.

The Diffusion of War

The analysis of diffusion of war concentrates on the economic, human, and political changes caused by war. Siverson and Starr (1991) show that the diffusion of international wars is directly related to territorial contiguity and alliance structures. Looking at war in its geopolitical context, they employ the concept of diffusion as a tool to understand the systematic effect of war on the international environment and its entities. Siverson's and Starr's empirical analysis demonstrates that opportunity and willingness have independent and important effects on the likelihood of nations entering ongoing wars. According to their study, contiguity provides the opportunity for war expansion and has a significant effect on the timing of war entry of the individual nation. In contrast, alliance commitments, expressing the willingness of actors to expand war, have a greater influence as a spatial factor on the diffusion of war. Thus, the involvement of allies or bordering nations in wars increases the probability that nations at peace will

join the war. Furthermore, Siverson and Starr reveal that the interaction of both factors has an even greater impact on the question of when and where war takes place than either factor alone. Demonstrating that the geopolitical situation provides environmental opportunities and constraints for nations, Siverson and Starr claim that people consider the factors of opportunity and willingness in their utility calculations on initiating or joining wars.

Other Perspectives on War

Numerous findings could be added. Empirical work shows that nations tend to bandwagon after war (Walt 1987). Allies tend to fulfill their commitments, demonstrateing that wars among allies are possible but less intense than wars among unattached nations (Bueno de Mesquita 1981b; Maoz 1983). Enduring rivalries should be considered in anticipating war, suggesting that national elites may choose to initiate international war in order to avoid domestic instability (Rummel 1963; Tanter 1966; Wilkenfeld 1968, 1969). Studies of geopolitical factors long excluded should once more be considered in the study of war (Ward 1992). Important insights about the evolution of wars have also recently emerged. Maoz (1990) shows that war produces important non-linear structures that prevent logical, linear solutions. Since we are working with a paradoxical behavior, our answers may be far to simple. Our methods may be too simple, as well. Much of this new work is loosely connected to the broader frameworks, yet if some of these well-documented insights are incorporated into existing frameworks, they may force us to restructure our thinking. The agenda for future research is very broad.

Data Sources

Like early paleontologists who faced an enormous and bewildering legacy of bones, and developed crude but accurate characteristics that defined species, political scientists are overburdened by multiple, detailed accounts of seemingly distinct events that can be categorized as international wars. The challenge is to create a coherent pattern from this record that accounts for this vast diversity. Fortunately, data collection is one area where research efforts have made major strides in the last three decades. Figure 3 gives a good overview on the achievements of major data-collecting projects.[16]

The systematic study of war owes much to J. David Singer, Melvin Small, and their colleagues at the Correlates of War Project (COW). Following the tradition set by the seminal collections of Sorokin (1937), Wright (1942), and Richardson (1960b), participants in the COW project have collected data on Major/Minor

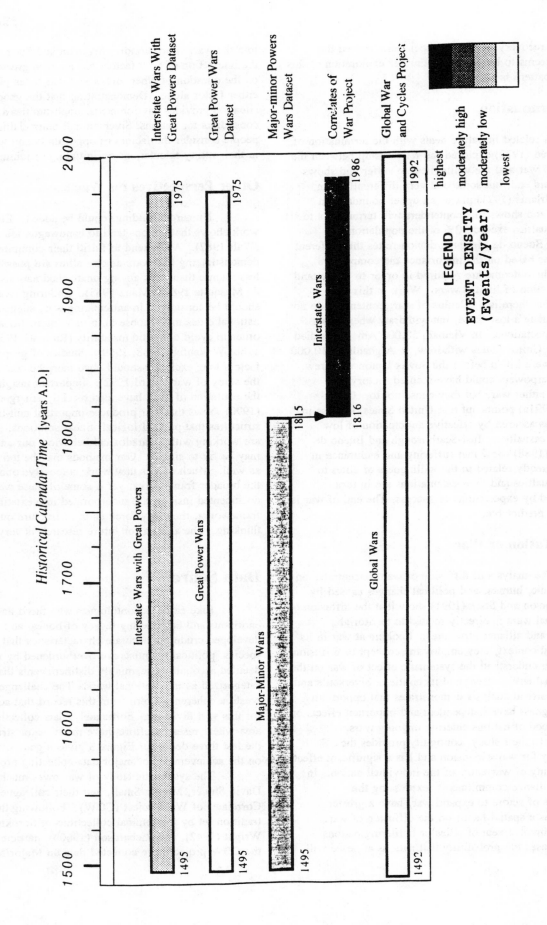

Figure 3

Historical Calendar Time [years A.D.]

Power wars, and Interstate wars that capture many characteristics of the international war phenomenon (Singer and Small 1972; Small and Singer 1982; Singer and Diehl 1990). The COW project provides the first truly comprehensive cross-temporal report on the initiation, frequency, duration, participation in, and severity of wars. In addition, the COW project pioneered in the collection of data on non-militarized disputes, helped in the compilation of behavioral precursors to war, and amassed many elements thought to be potential correlates of international war. A non-exhaustive list includes alliances, military size, arms expenditures, industrial output, national capabilities, systemic polarity, geographic proximity, or indices of diplomatic status inconsistency.[17] Jack Levy has added an extended data set on Great Power Wars, focusing on the most severe conflicts. William Thompson and Karen Rasler have developed a comprehensive collection of socio-economic data surrounding Global Wars. The ambitious Long Range Analysis of War Project headed by Cioffi-Revilla (1991b) is gathering all available information on all wars that have left a historical mark starting in 3000 BC.

Many of the above data collection efforts are being supported or expanded by the Data Development for International Research Program (DDIR) headed by Dina Zinnes and Richard Merritt. Under DDIR's auspices the collection of wars involving great powers was extended back to 1495, a large data set of wars between major and minor powers was compiled, a summary of international military interventions in the nuclear era was completed, and much more. Due to these and other efforts, the world politics community now has access to standard definitions and measures of territorial dispersion of wars, enduring rivalries, numerous alliance indices, event data summaries, and various ways to document international crises.[18]

Despite shortcomings, the growing data collections on war attributes and corollaries finally allow modern scholars to test propositions about war and replicate previous results. Indeed, for the first time since before the birth of Christ, when Thucydides (400 B.C.) and Kautilya (300 B.C.) proposed contending explanations of the causes of war, competing propositions accounting for war are under empirical scrutiny. This empirical scrutiny, once started, will no doubt continue expanding the base of systematic information about war.

Conclusions

My reading of the literature on war and peace suggests that key elements that still permeate much of the modern work on war have been inherited from ancient thinkers. The importance of Thucydides' and Kautilya's[19] work for the analysis of war and peace is not due to the completeness and accuracy of their insights, but rather because this work provides the initial statement from which the systematic study of war evolved.

Lakatos suggests that a theory is superior to another if it can encompass a wider portion of the phenomenon than its alternative. The reason one wishes to identify a common ancestor is that it is easier to summarize a field by tracing its evolution from the origin and concentrating on the most fruitful branches. Like Galileo, whose contributions were critical to the early development of physics, Thucydides provides the study of war and peace with a loose framework upon which many builders can construct vastly different structures. Just as Aristotle's insights about our physical environment were surpassed by Galileo's, extended by Newton and Einstein, and will assuredly be superseded by an as yet unknown physicist;[20] the work of Thucydides has been surpassed by modern scholars without diminishing its impact. Without the foundation laid out long ago by these giants, it is difficult to conceive the evolution of insights on war and peace proposed by Machiavelli, Hobbes, Hume, Clausewitz, Carr, Wright, Morgenthau, von Neumann and Morgenstern, and the modern extension by Organski, Waltz, Allison, Keohane, Gilpin, or Bueno de Mesquita. The study of war is still developing; ancient writers receive as much attention today as do propositions advanced by modern analysis. Theories about war are still not exposed to Lakatos' criteria for theoretical specification or empirical tests. Validity is still ascertained by authority and frequently by consistency alone. Unless we alter this approach, the study of war and peace will remain in its infancy. Refinement requires that we stop relying on important but vague insights that may already have been rejected by evidence, and that we drop arguments that are internally inconsistent even when they can be traced to ancient authority, and that we reject formal deductions whose only claim is consistency. New and plausible insights should be required to survive tests of consistency and basic empirical evaluations.

The scientific understanding of war must tell as much about war as about peace. Indeed, a successful understanding of the puzzle of war initiation, escalation, or diffusion should simultaneously show how peace can be attained, extended, and diffused. To study war, we must study peace. Thus far, however, we have concentrated on specifying the necessary conditions for war. To gain a fuller understanding of war, more attention will have to be paid to conditions that lead to cooperation and allow peace to break out.

I hope to have persuaded the reader that current theories of war are, at best, imprecise. Our best perspectives specify the necessary but not sufficient conditions leading to the initiation, escalation, diffusion, and termination of war. A search to approach sufficiency is afoot in different directions.

Can we say that there is progress in the study of war and peace? The answer is a tentative yes. As part of this exercise, I randomly read articles on international war in leading journals, starting with the end of World War II.[21] In journals from the 1940s and 1950s, I found much precise description but only limited attempts to go beyond the case under scrutiny. It is not surprising that few academics refer to that work today. In the 1960s and 1970s, journal articles remain largely descriptive, but a change is noticeable.[22] Published empirical results seldom supported widely held propositions. Instead, they legitimized radically different theories from the accepted norm. In the 1980s and 1990s the development of alternative perspectives on the causes of war exploded. The legacy of the last two decades shows a growing commitment to theoretical specification and an increasing link to empirical evaluations. The study of war and peace is poised at the verge of generating a consistent paradigm that may guide work in the next decade.

It is my belief that the next generation of scholars will be far more dependent on their own cohorts than on their ancient ancestors. The massive improvements in specification and extensive empirical developments permit rejection of some plausible propositions, while others are preserved because they survive initial tests. As we move into the future, and larger, well-documented data sets become increasingly available to students of politics, one expects that current work will be dramatically revised and superseded. Improvements in formal structures and statistical developments that have started to appear in the last decade will undoubtedly expand and integrate larger sections of the field. This generation can take credit for being the first to face the scientific challenge and explore, admittedly very incompletely, the propositions generated by generations of students of war and peace. The next generation faces the urgent challenge of controlling war that now can escalate to unthinkable levels. That task is challenging and urgent.

Notes

* With special thanks to James Caporaso, James Morrow, Gretchen Hower, Randolph Siverson, Bruce Bueno de Mesquita, Frank Zagare, Claudio Cioffi-Revilla, John Vasquez and Suzanne Werner for their insightful suggestions and to Douglas Lemke and Doris Fuchs, who labored long and hard improving and editing the manuscript and putting together the bibliography. David Hopson and Joel Smith were instrumental in constructing graphics. Sandra Seymour is responsible for the final typing.

1. I use this particular definition of war as a means to narrow my subject area and not because it has more validity than other definitions of war. A most comprehensive, all-inclusive definition is provided by Cioffi-Revilla (1991b), who wishes to catalog all possible conflicts. "War is an occurrence of purpose, collective violence among two or more social groups pursuing conflicting political goals that result in fatalities, with at least one belligerent group being organized under the command of authoritative leadership."

2. Thomas Kuhn (1970) proposed the notion of a paradigm but conceded that it has been used in various ways. In later work he argues that a paradigm "...stands for the entire constellation of beliefs, values, techniques, and so on shared by the members of a given community. On the other, it denotes one sort of element in that constellation, the concrete puzzle-solutions which, employed as models or examples, can replace explicit rules as a basis for the solution of the remaining puzzles of normal science" (Kuhn 1970, 175) Here I employ paradigm in the first sense defined by Kuhn. For an enlightening discussion with world politics applications see Vasquez (1983, 1-12).

3. For a particularly heated discussion of data and paradigm testing in the context of deterrence, see Richard Ned Lebow and Janice Gross Stein (1990) and Paul Huth and Bruce Russett (1990).

4. For a practical review of epistemological problems in political science, see Tilly 1985 and Collier 1991.

5. The more advanced the field, the stronger is the consensus on rules of falsification. Note that Stephen Hawking, despite the enormous complexity of his ideas on time and space, accepts with little discussion Lakatos' criteria and through their application is able to reject complex theoretical alternatives (Stephen W. Hawking, 1988. *A Brief History of Time*. Bantam, 9-13 and 47-49).

6. In no area is the difficulty of establishing a paradigm more apparent than in the study of human evolution. Paleontologists organized their discipline around Darwin's insight that the current expressions of a species, despite differences in size and appearance, evolved from a common extinct ancestor that was less adapted to survival than those still among us. Darwin's notions were and still are in sharp contrast to the theory of human creation held by the Western church. The debate on the evidence is being fought to this day. For example, "scientific" creationists challenge bone dating techniques and attempt to show that species were concurrently created. The modern study of genetics, however, has independently confirmed the validity of species transformation, lending further credence to Darwin's insight.

7. The difference between "hegemon," that is omnipotent over all its allies and foes and "dominant," which is simply the largest among the major powers is important. A dominant power is large, indeed the largest among large, but it is not large enough to impose its preferences on the whole coalition or the rest of the world. Thus, a dominant nation at the top of a hierarchy needs allies to preserve a regime. A "hegemon" is autarchic, requiring no allies to exercise influence over the regime or the world. Empirically, dominance is frequent but hegemony is very rare in the international system, appearing for less than 20 years over the last 200, and usually after devastating wars (Keohane 1984; Strange 1985; Russett 1985; Kugler and Organski 1989).

8. Recent extensive work on Japan and the elaborate evaluation of the interactions among European nations during World War I suggest that this avenue is promising (Choucri and North 1975, 1989).

9. This is a critical difference between power transition and hegemonic theory. Power transition contends that a dominant nation is the largest among major powers but not preponderant over all. Hegemonic theory, on the other hand, suggests that stability is maintained only when the largest power is preponderant, a condition not found in the international system in the last 200 years, with the exception of the brief interlude after World War II when the United States was preponderant mainly because the competition was exhausted by war. This unfortunate specification has detracted from the central

finding that preponderance and not necessarily hegemony is associated with the absence of major war (Gilpin 1981; Russett 1985; Kugler and Organski 1989; Nye 1990).

10. Modelski and Morgan (1985) argue along similar lines, but center their criticism of the stability of deterrence on the global cycle (for details, see pp. 49-50).

11. John Mueller (1989) brings vividly to attention an oversight present in most war theories: the conditions for war are effectively and fully elaborated but those for peace are simply noted. Organski and Kugler (1980), for example, carefully define conditions for war under parity and transition, but fail to elaborate with equal precision the reasons for peace under preponderance. The reverse tendency, however, is present in the treatment of nuclear deterrence. Intriligator and Brito (1989) elaborate extensively the conditions for peace under deterrence, but fail to label the conditions their model suggests will lead to nuclear war. Indeed, their model suggests that since 1945, during transitions from the cone of war to compellence or from compellence to mutual deterrence, a nuclear war would be waged. The lack of a nuclear war under such conditions is -- after the fact -- dismissed or attributed to luck. This emphasis on the partial outcome one wishes to explore is prevalent.

12. Other reasons for nations to oppose nuclear proliferation might exist. Bueno de Mesquita and Riker (1982) and Wu (1990) point out that proliferation would reduce the bargaining power of a nation possessing nuclear weapons versus a prospective nuclear power.

13. For an alternate view of deterrence not based on power distributions, see John Mueller (1989).

14. This argument is used by Intriligator and Brito (1987) to oppose the development of defensive missile systems that could force nuclear nations out of stable Mutual Assured Destruction and into regions of uncertain deterrence (Figure 1).

15. Decision-making approaches would account for such phenomena if it can be proven that dramatically different preferences are held by authoritarian, totalitarian, and democratic populations and elites.

16. For specific information, consult Claudio Cioffi-Revilla's Long Range Analysis of War (LORANOW) Project, University of Colorado at Boulder.

17. Paul Diehl's (1991) bibliographic review of the COW project provides an excellent overview of data expansions.

18. Recently, many of these data collections have been extended under the auspices of the Merriam Laboratory for Analytical Political Research as part of the Data Development for International Relations project. Important extensions include Ted Robert Gurr, *National Capabilities*; Jack Levy, *Great Power Wars;* Manus Midlarsky, *Major-Minor Powers Wars*; John Wilkenfeld, *International Crisis Behavior;* Frederick Parson, *Interventions*; Philip Schaefer, Gary Goertz, and Paul Diehl, *Territorial Change Coding Manual*; and Randolph Siverson with Harvey Starr, *Data on International Borders, 1816-1965*. The quantitative analysis of international events now offers a number of perspectives: Rudolph Rummel's *Dimensionality of Nations* (DON); Charles McClelland's *World Events Interaction Survey* (WEIS), Edward Azar's *Conflict and Peace Databank* (COPDAT), Charles Herman's *Comparative Research on the Events of Nations* (CREON), Charles Taylor and David Jodice's *World Handbook of Political and Social Indicators*, and Ernst Haas, Joseph Nye, and Robert Butterworth's *SHERFACTS* on conflict management. These now provide a very extensive cross-temporal and cross-national basis for empirical research. The data sets are available to the community through the ICPSR at the University of Michigan. In addition, interested readers can obtain current issues of the *DDIR-Update* that reports on data developments for international relations.

19. Perhaps Kautilya, who wrote his classic *Arthasastra* sometime between 321-296 B.C., deserves equal credit with Thucydides. This work parallels in many respects the critical elements of Thucydides' postulates on war. However, I know of no evidence that the Western thinkers who laid the foundations of contemporary war theory, such as Machiavelli, Hobbes, or Morgenthau, discovered the writings of Kautilya.

20. The development of physics is outlined in a clear and brilliant manner by Hawking (1988).

21. *The American Political Science Review, World Politics, Foreign Affairs*, and more recently *The Journal of Conflict Resolution*.

22. This change coincides with the appearance of *The Journal of Conflict Resolution*.

Bibliography

Achen, Christopher, and Duncan Snidal. 1989. "Rational Deterrence Theory and Comparative Case Studies." *World Politics* 41:143-169.

Allison, Graham. 1969. "Conceptual Models of the Cuban Missile Crisis." *American Political Science Review* 63:689-718.

Axelrod, Robert. 1984. *The Evolution of Cooperation*. New York: Basic Books.

Bendor, Jonathan, and Thomas H. Hammond. 1992. "Rethinking Allison's Models." *American Political Science Review* 86:301-322.

Blainey, Geoffrey. 1973. *The Causes of War*. New York: The Free Press.

Bottome, Edgar M. 1971. *The Balance of Terror. A Guide to the Arms Race*. Boston: Beacon Press.

Boulding, Kenneth. 1962. *Conflict and Defense*. New York: Harper.

Brams, Steven. 1985. *Superpower Games*. New Haven, CT: Yale University Press.

Brams, Steven, and Donald Wittman. 1981. "Nonmyopic Equilibria in 2x2 Games." *Conflict Management and Peace Science* 6:39-62.

Brito, Dagobert, and Michael Intriligator. 1982. "Arms Races: Behavioral and Economic Dimensions." In *Missing Elements in Political Inquiry*, ed. John Gillespie and Dina Zinnes. Beverly Hills, CA: Sage Publications.

Brodie, Bernard. 1946. *The Absolute Weapon*. New York: Harcourt Brace.

Brodie, Bernard. 1959. *Strategy in the Missile Age*. Princeton, NJ: Princeton University Press.

Bueno de Mesquita, Bruce. 1980. "Theories of International Conflict." In *Handbook of Political Conflict*, ed. Ted Gurr. New York: The Free Press.

Bueno de Mesquita, Bruce. 1981a. *The War Trap*. New Haven, CT: Yale University Press.

Bueno de Mesquita, Bruce. 1981b. "Risk, Power, and the Likelihood of War." *International Studies Quarterly* 25:541-568.

Bueno de Mesquita, Bruce. 1985a. "The War Trap Revisited." *American Political Science Review* 79:156-177.

Bueno de Mesquita, Bruce. 1985b. "Toward a Scientific Understanding of International Conflict: A Personal View." *International Studies Quarterly* 29:121-136.

Bueno de Mesquita, Bruce. 1988. "The Contribution of Expected Utility to the Study of International Conflict." *Journal of Interdisciplinary History* 18:629-652.

Bueno de Mesquita, Bruce. 1990. "Pride of Place: The Origins of German Hegemony." *World Politics* 43:28-52.

Bueno de Mesquita, Bruce, and David Lalman. 1986. "Reason and War." *American Political Science Review* 80:1113-1131.

Bueno de Mesquita, Bruce, and David Lalman. 1988. "Empirical Support for Systemic and Dyadic Explanations of International Conflict." *World Politics* 41:1-20.

Bueno de Mesquita, Bruce, and David Lalman. 1992. *War and Reason*. New Haven, CT: Yale University Press.

Bueno de Mesquita, Bruce, David Neuman, and Alvin Rabushka. 1985. *Forecasting Political Events*. New Haven, CT: Yale University Press.

Bueno de Mesquita, Bruce, and William H. Riker. 1982. "Assessing the Merits of Selective Nuclear Deterrence." *Journal of Conflict Resolution* 26:283-306.

Buzan, Barry. 1987. *An Introduction to Strategic Studies. Military Technology & International Relations*. New York: St. Martin's Press.

Chan, Steven. 1987. "Growth with Equity: A Test of Olson's Theory for the Asian Pacific-Rim Countries." *Journal of Peace Research* 24:133-149.

Choucri, Nazli, and Robert C. North. 1975. *Nations in Conflict*. San Francisco: W.H. Freeman.

Choucri, Nazli, and Robert C. North. 1989. "Lateral Pressure in International Relations." In *Handbook of War Studies*, ed. Manus Midlarsky. Boston: Unwin Hyman.

Cioffi-Revilla, Claudio. 1991a. "On the Likely Magnitude, Extent, and Duration of an Iraq-UN War." *Journal of Conflict Resolution* 35:387-411.

Cioffi-Revilla, Claudio. 1991b. "The Long Range Analysis of War." *Journal of Interdisciplinary History* 4:603-624.

Claude, Inis. 1962. *Power and International Relations*. New York: Random House.

Collier, David. 1991. "The Comparative Method: Two Decades of Change." In *Comparative Political Dynamics*, ed. Rustow and Erickson. New York: HarperCollins.

Doran, Charles. 1991. *Systems in Crisis*. New York: Cambridge University Press.

Doran, Charles, and Wes Parsons. 1980. "War and the Cycle of Relative Power." *American Political Science Review* 74:947-965.

Diehl, Paul F. 1983. "Arms Races and Escalation: A Closer Look." *Journal of Peace Research* 20:205-212.

Diehl, Paul F. 1991. "The Correlates of War Project: A Bibliographic Essay." Unpublished mimeo.

Diehl, Paul F., and Jean Kingston. 1987. "Messenger or Message? Military Buildups and the Initiation of Conflict." *The Journal of Politics* 49:801-813.

Ellsberg, Daniel. [1959] 1975. "The Theory and Practice of Blackmail." Lecture at the Lowell Institute. Boston. In *Bargaining: Formal Theories of Negotiation*, ed. R. Young. Urbana: University of Illinois Press.

Ellsberg, Daniel. 1961. "The Crude Analysis of Strategic Choice." *American Economic Review* 51:472-478.

Ember, Carol R., Melvin Ember, and Bruce Russett. 1992. "Peace Between Participatory Polities: A Cross-National Test of the 'Democracies Rarely Fight Each Other' Hypothesis." *World Politics*.

Epstein, William. 1976. *The Last Chance: Nuclear Proliferation and Arms Control*. New York: The Free Press.

Ferris, William. 1973. *The Power Capability of Nation States*. Lexington, MA: Lexington Books.

Fraser, Niall M., and Keith Hipel. 1979. "Solving Complex Conflicts." *IEEE Transactions on Systems, Man, and Cybernetics*, SCM-9, 12:805-816.

Freedman, Lawrence. 1981. *The Evolution of Nuclear Strategy*. New York: St. Martin's Press.

Garst, Daniel. 1989. "Thucydides and Neorealism." *International Studies Quarterly* 33:3-28.

Gilpin, Robert. 1981. *War and Change in World Politics*. New York: Cambridge University Press.

Goldstein, Joshua. 1985. "Kondratieff Waves as War Cycles." *International Studies Quarterly* 29:411-444.

Grieco, Joseph. 1988. "Anarchy and the Limits of Cooperation." *International Organization* 42:485-502.

Gulick, Luther. 1955. *Europe's Classical Balance of Power*. Ithaca: Cornell University.

Gurr, Ted, ed. 1980. *Handbook of Political Conflict*. New York: The Free Press.

Harvey, Frank, and Patrick James. 1992. "Nuclear Deterrence Theory: The Record of Aggregate Testing and an Alternative Research Agenda." *Conflict Management and Peace Science* 12:17-45.

Hawking, Stephen. 1988. *A Brief History of Time*. New York: Bantam Books.

Hobbes, Thomas. [1651] 1985. *Leviathan*. New York: Penguin Books.

Horn, Michael. 1987. "Arms Races and the International System." Ph.D. diss. University of Rochester.

Houweling, Henk, and Jan Sicamma. 1988. "Power Transitions as a Cause of War." *Journal of Conflict Resolution* 32:87-102.

Houweling, Henk, and Jan Sicamma. 1991. "Power Transitions and Critical Points as Predictors of Great Power War." *Journal of Conflict Resolution* 35:642-658.

Hume, David. [1741] 1990. "Of the Balance of Power." In *Classics of International Relations*, 2nd ed., ed. John Vasquez. Englewood Cliffs, NJ: Prentice-Hall.

Huntington, Samuel. 1982. *The Strategic Imperative*. Cambridge, MA: Ballinger.

Huntington, Samuel. 1958. "Arms Races: Prerequisites and Results." *Public Policy* 8:41-46.

Huth, Paul. 1988. *Extended Deterrence and the Prevention of War*. New Haven, CT: Yale University Press.

Huth, Paul, and Bruce Russett. 1984. "What Makes Deterrence Work?" *World Politics* 36:496-526.

Huth, Paul, and Bruce Russett. 1990. "Testing Deterrence Theory: Rigour Makes a Difference." *World Politics* 42:466-501.

Intriligator, Michael, and Dagobert Brito. 1981. "Nuclear Proliferation and the Probability of War." *Public Choice* 37:247-260.

Intriligator, Michael, and Dagobert Brito. 1987. "The Stability of Mutual Deterrence." In *Exploring the Stability of Deterrence*, ed. Jacek Kugler and Frank Zagare. Boulder, CO: Lynne Rienner.

Intriligator, Michael, and Dagobert Brito. 1989. "Richardsonian Arms Race Models." In *Handbook of War Studies*, ed. Manus Midlarsky. Boston: Unwin Hyman.

Iusi Scarborough, Grace, and Bruce Bueno de Mesquita. 1988. "Threat and Alignment Behavior." *International Interactions* 14:85-93.

Jervis, Robert. 1976. *Perception and Misperception in World Politics*. Princeton, NJ: Princeton University Press.

Jervis, Robert. 1984. *The Illogic of American Nuclear Strategy*. Ithaca: Cornell University Press.

Kahn, Herman. 1960. *On Thermonuclear War*. Princeton: Princeton University Press.

Kahn, Herman. 1962. *Thinking About the Unthinkable*. New York: Horizon Press.

Kahn, Herman. 1965. *On Escalation: Metaphors and Scenarios*. Rev. ed. Baltimore: Penguin Books.

Kaplan, Morton. 1957. *System and Process in International Politics*. New York: Wiley.

Kaufmann, William. 1956. "The Requirements of Deterrence." In *Military Policy and National Security*, ed. William Kaufmann. Princeton, NJ: Princeton University Press.

Kautilya. [300 B.C.] 1967. *Arthasastra*. Mysore, India: Mysore Printing and Publishing House.

Kennedy, Paul. 1987. *The Rise and Fall of the Great Powers*. New York: Random House.

Keohane, Robert. 1980. "The Theory of Hegemonic Stability and Changes in International Economic Regimes." In *Change in* the *International System*, ed. Ole R. Holsti, Randolph Siverson, and Alexander George. Boulder, CO: Westview Press.

Keohane, Robert. 1984. *After Hegemony*. Princeton, NJ: Princeton University Press.

Keohane, Robert, and Joseph Nye. 1977. *Power and Interdependence*. Boston: Little Brown.

Kilgour, D. Marc. 1991. "Domestic Political Structures and War: A Game Theoretic Approach." *Journal of Conflict Resolution* 35:266-284.

Kilgour, D. Marc, and Frank Zagare. 1991. "Credibility, Uncertainty, and Deterrence." *American Journal of Political Science* 35:305-334.

Kim, Woosang, and James Morrow. 1990. "When Do Power Transitions Lead to War?" Paper delivered at the annual meeting of the Midwest Political Science Association, Chicago.

Kissinger, Henry. 1957. *Nuclear Weapons and Foreign Policy*. New York: Harper and Row.

Kreps, David, and Robert Wilson. 1982. "Sequential Equilibria." *Econometrica* 50(4):863-894.

Kugler, Jacek. 1984. "Terror without Deterrence." *Journal of Conflict Resolution* 28:470-506.

Kugler, Jacek, and Marina Arbetman. 1989a. "Choosing Among Measures of Power: A Review of the Empirical Record." In *Power in World Politics*, ed. Richard Stoll and Michael D. Ward. Boulder, CO: Lynne Rienner.

Kugler, Jacek, and Marina Arbetman. 1989b. "Exploring the 'Phoenix Factor' with the Collective Goods Perspective." *Journal of Conflict Resolution* 33:84-112.

Kugler, Jacek, and Seifeldin Hussein. 1989. "Conditional Anarchy: The Status Quo in World Politics." Paper presented at the annual meeting of the Peace Science Society.

Kugler, Jacek, and Douglas Lemke. n.d. *Parity and War. A Critical Evaluation of 'The War Ledger.'*

Kugler, Jacek, and A. F. K. Organski. 1987. "The End of Hegemony: Says Who?" *International Interactions* 15(2):113-128.

Kugler, Jacek, and A. F. K. Organski. 1989. "The Power Transition: A Retrospective and Prospective Evaluation." In *Handbook of War Studies*, ed. Manus Midlarsky. Boston: Unwin Hyman.

Kugler, Jacek, A. F. K. Organski, and Daniel Fox. 1980. "Deterrence and the Arms Race: The Impotence of Power." *International Security* 4:105-138.

Kugler, Jacek, and Frank Zagare, eds. 1987. *Exploring the Stability of Deterrence*. Boulder, CO: Lynne Rienner.

Kugler, Jacek, and Frank Zagare. 1990. "The Long-Term Stability of Deterrence." *International Interactions* 15:255-278.

Kuhn, Thomas. 1970. *The Structure of Scientific Revolutions*. Chicago: The University of Chicago Press.

Lakatos, Imre. 1978. *The Methodology of Scientific Research Programs*. London: Cambridge University Press.

Lalman, David. 1988. "Conflict Resolution and Peace." *American Journal of Political Science* 32:590-615.

Langlois, Jean-Pierre. 1989. "Modeling Deterrence and International Crises." *Journal of Conflict Resolution* 33:67-83.

Lebow, Richard Ned, and Janice Gross Stein. 1990. "Deterrence: The Elusive Dependent Variable." *World Politics* 42:336-369.

Lemke, Douglas. 1991. "Predicting Peace: Power Transitions in Latin America." Paper presented at the annual meeting of the International Studies Association.

Levy, Jack. 1983. *War in the Modern Great Power System*. Lexington, KY: The University Press of Kentucky.

Machiavelli, Niccolo. [1513] 1950. *The Prince*. New York: Random House.

Malinowski, Bronislaw. 1968. "An Anthropological Analysis of War." In *War*, ed. Bramson and Goethals. New York: Basic Books.

Mansfield, Edward. 1992. "The Concentration of Capabilities and the Onset of War." *Journal of Conflict Resolution* 36:3-24.

Maoz, Zeev. 1983. "Resolve, Capabilities, and the Outcomes of Interstate Disputes." *Journal of Conflict Resolution* 27:195-229.

Maoz, Zeev. 1990. *The Paradoxes of War*. Boston: Unwin Hyman.

Maoz, Zeev, and Nasrim Abdolali. 1989. "Regime Types and International Conflict, 1816-1976." *Journal of Conflict Resolution* 33:3-36.

Maoz, Zeev, and Bruce Russett. 1991. "Normative and Structural Causes of Democratic Peace, 1946-1986." Unpublished mimeo.

McGinnis, Michael D. 1991. "Richardson, Rationality, and Restrictive Models of Arms Races." *Journal of Conflict Resolution* 35:443-473.

Midlarsky, Manus. 1988. *The Onset of World War*. Boston: Unwin Hyman.

Midlarsky, Manus, ed. 1989. *Handbook of War Studies*. Boston: Unwin Hyman.

Modelski, George. 1978. "The Long Cycle of Global Politics and the Nation State." *Comparative Studies in Society and History* 20:214-235.

Modelski, George, and Patrick M. Morgan. 1985. "Understanding Global War." *Journal of Conflict Resolution* 29:391-417.

Morgan, Patrick M. 1977. *Deterrence*. Beverly Hills, CA: Sage Publications.

Morgan, T. Clifton, and Sally Howard Campbell. 1991. "Domestic Structure, Decisional Constraints, and War." *Journal of Conflict Resolution* 35:187-211.

Morgenthau, Hans. [1948] 1960. *Politics Among Nations*. New York: Alfred A. Knopf.

Morrow, James. 1985. "A Continuous Outcome Expected Utility Theory of War." *Journal of Conflict Resolution* 29:473-502.

Morrow, James. 1989. "A Twist of Truth." *Journal of Conflict Resolution* 33:500-529.

Morrow, James. 1991. "Alliances and Asymmetry: An Alternative to the Capability Aggregation Model of Alliances." *American Journal of Political Science* 35:904-933.

Most, Benjamin, and Harvey Starr. 1990. "Theoretical and Logical Issues in the Study of Diffusion." *Journal of Theoretical Politics* 2:391-412.

Moul, William Brian. 1988. "Balances of Power and the Escalation to War of Serious Disputes among the European Great Powers, 1815-1939: Some Evidence." *American Journal of Political Science* 32:241-275.

Mueller, John. 1989. *Retreat from Doomsday*. New York: Basic Books.

Muller, Edward, Henry Dietz, and Steven Finkel. 1991. "Discontent and the Expected Utility of Rebellion." *American Political Science Review* 85:1261-1282.

Nye, Joseph. 1990. *Bound to Lead*. New York: Basic Books.

Niou, Emerson, and Peter Ordeshook. 1991. "Realism and Neoliberalism: A Formulation." *American Journal of Political Science* 35:481-511.

Niou, Emerson, Peter Ordeshook, and Gregory Rose. 1989. *The Balance of Power*. New York: Cambridge University Press.

Olson, Mancur. 1982. *The Rise and Decline of Nations*. New Haven, CT: Yale University Press.

O'Neill, Barry. 1989. "Game Theory and the Study of the Deterrence of War." In *Perspectives on Deterrence*, ed. Paul C. Stern et al., New York: Oxford University Press.

Organski, A. F. K. 1958. *World Politics*. New York: Alfred A. Knopf.

Organski, A. F. K, and Jacek Kugler. 1980. *The War Ledger*. Chicago: The University of Chicago Press.

Ostrom, Charles, and John Aldrich. 1978. "The Relationship Between Size and Stability in the Major Power International System." *American Journal of Political Science* 22:743-771.

Ostrom, Charles, and Robert Marra. 1986. "U.S. Defense Spending and the Soviet Estimate." *American Political Science Review* 80:819-842.

Powell, Robert. 1989. "Nuclear Deterrence and the Strategy of Limited Retaliation." *American Political Science Review* 83:503-520.

Powell, Robert. 1990. *Nuclear Deterrence Theory*. Cambridge, MA: Cambridge University Press.

Rapaport, Anatol. 1957. "Lewis F. Richardson's Mathematical Theory of War." *Journal of Conflict Resolution* 1:249-304.

Rapaport, Anatol. 1960. *Fights, Games, and Debates*. Ann Arbor, MI: University of Michigan Press.

Rapaport, Anatol. 1964. *Strategy and Conscience*. New York: Harper and Row.

Rasler, Karen A., and William R. Thompson. 1992. "Explaining the Cyclicality of Global Warfare." Paper presented at the annual meeting of the Peace Science Society.

Rasmusen, Eric. 1989. *Games and Information*. New York: Basil Blackwell.

Richardson, Lewis F. 1960a. *Arms and Insecurity*. Pittsburgh, PA: The Boxwood Press.

Richardson, Lewis F. 1960b. *Statistics of Deadly Quarrels*. Pittsburgh, PA: The Boxwood Press.

Riker, William H. 1962. *The Theory of Political Coalitions*. New Haven, CT: Yale University Press.

Rosen, Steven. 1972. "War, Power, and the Willingness to Suffer." In *Peace, War, and Numbers*, ed. Bruce Russett. Beverly Hills, CA: Sage Publications.

Rosen, Steven. 1977. "A Stable System of Mutual Nuclear Deterrence in the Arab-Israeli Conflict." *American Political Science Review* 71:1367-1383.

Rosencrance, Richard. 1975. "Strategic Deterrence Reconsidered." *Adelphi Paper #116*. The International Institute for Strategic Studies.

Rummel, Rudolph J. 1963. "Dimensions of Conflict Behavior within and Between Nations." *General Systems* 8:1-50.

Russett, Bruce. 1985. "The Mysterious Case of Vanishing Hegemony." *International Organization* 39:207-231.

Russett, Bruce. 1989. "Democracy, Public Opinion, and Nuclear Weapons." In *Behavior, Society, and Nuclear War*, ed. Phillip E. Tetlock et al. New York: Oxford University Press.

Schelling, Thomas C. 1960. *The Strategy of Conflict*. Cambridge: Harvard University Press.

Schelling, Thomas C. 1966. *Arms and Influence*. New Haven: Yale University Press.

Selten, Reinhard. 1975. "A Re-examination of the Perfectness Concept for Equilibrium Points in Extensive Games." *International Journal of Game Theory* 4:25-55.

Singer, David. 1958. "Threat-Perception and the Armament-Tension Dilemma." *Journal of Conflict Resolution* 2:90-105.

Singer, David. 1979. *The Correlates of War I. Research Origins and Rational*. New York: The Free Press.

Singer, David. 1980. *The Correlates of War II. Testing Some Realpolitik Models*. New York: The Free Press.

Singer, J. David, Stuart Bremer, and John Stuckey. 1972. "Capability Distribution, Uncertainty, and Major Power War." In *Peace, War, and Numbers*, ed. Bruce Russett. Beverly Hills, CA: Sage Publications.

Singer, J. David, and Paul Diehl, eds. 1990. *Measuring the Correlates of War*. Ann Arbor, MI: University of Michigan Press.

Singer, J. David, and Melvin Small. 1972. *The Wages of War: A Statistical Handbook*. New York: Wiley.

Siverson, Randolph, and Paul Diehl. 1989. "Arms Races, the Conflict Spiral, and the Onset of War." In *Handbook of War Studies*, ed. Manus Midlarsky. Boston: Unwin Hyman.

Siverson, Randolph, and Julian Emmons. 1991. "Democratic Political

Systems and Alliance Choices." *Journal of Conflict Resolution* 35:285-306.

Siverson, Randolph, and Harvey Starr. 1991. *The Diffusion of War*. Ann Arbor, MI: University of Michigan Press.

Siverson, Randolph, and Michael Sullivan. 1983. "The Distribution of Power and the Onset of War." *Journal of Conflict Resolution* 27:473-494.

Siverson, Randolph, and Michael R. Tennefoss. 1984. "Power, Alliance, and the Escalation of International Conflict, 1815-1965." *American Political Science Review* 78:1057-1069.

Small, Melvin, and J. David Singer. 1982. *Resort to Arms*. Beverly Hills, CA: Sage Publications.

Smith, T.C. 1980. "Arms Races, Instability, and War." *Journal of Conflict Resolution* 24:253-284.

Smoker, Paul. 1964. "Fear in the Arms Race: A Mathematical Study." *Journal of Peace Research* 1:55-64.

Snidal, Duncan. 1985a. "Coordination versus Prisoners' Dilemma: Implications for International Cooperation and Regimes." *American Political Science Review* 79:923-942.

Snidal, Duncan. 1985b. "The Limits of Hegemonic Stability Theory." *International Organization* 39:579-614.

Snidal, Duncan. 1985c. "The Game Theory of International Politics." *World Politics* 38:25-57.

Snidal, Duncan. 1991. "Relative Gains and the Pattern of International Cooperation." *American Political Science Review* 85:701-726.

Snyder, Glenn H. 1961. *Deterrence and Defense: Toward a Theory of National Security*. Princeton: Princeton University Press.

Snyder, Glenn H. 1972. "Crisis Bargaining." In *International Crises: Insights from Behavioral Research*, ed. Charles F. Hermann. New York: The Free Press.

Sorokin, Pitirim. 1937. *Social and Cultural Dynamics*. New York: American Book Company.

Stein, Arthur, and Bruce Russett. 1980. "Evaluating War: Outcomes and Consequences." In *Handbook of Political Conflict*, ed. Ted Gurr. New York: The Free Press.

Strange, Susan. 1985. "The Persistant Myth of Lost Hegemony." *International Organization* 41:551-574.

Taagepera, Rein. 1986. "Growth and Decline of Empires since 600 A.D." Paper presented at the annual meeting of the International Studies Association.

Tanter, Raymond. 1966. "Dimensions of Conflict Behavior within and Between Nations." *Journal of Conflict Resolution* 10:41-64.

Thompson, William R. 1988. *On Global War*. Columbia, SC: University of South Carolina Press.

Thompson, William R. 1992. "Dehio, Long Cycles, and the Geohistorical Context of Structural Transition." *World Politics* 44.

Thucydides. [400 B.C.] 1954. *History of the Peloponnesian War*. Baltimore, MD: Penguin Books.

Tilly, Charles. 1985. "War Making and State Making as Organized Crime." In *Bringing the State Back In*, ed. Evans, Rueschemeyer, and Skocpol. New York: Cambridge University Press.

Toynbee, Arnold. 1934-1954. *A Study of History*. London: Oxford University Press.

Urlanis, B. 1971. *Wars and Population*. Moscow: Progress Publishers.

Vasquez, John. 1983. *The Power of Power Politics: A Critique*. New Brunswick, NJ: Rutgers University Press.

Vasquez, John. 1992. *The War Puzzle*. Cambridge: Cambridge University Press.

von Clausewitz, Carl. [1832] 1968. *On War*. Baltimore, MD: Penguin Books.

von Neumann, John, and Oskar Morgenstern. 1953. *Theory of Games and Economic Behavior*. Princeton, NJ: Princeton University Press.

Wagner, R. Harrison. 1991. "Nuclear Deterrence, Counterforce Strategies, and the Incentive to Strike First." *American Political Science Review* 85:727-750.

Wallace, Michael. 1979. "Arms Races and Escalation." In *Explaining War*, ed. J. David Singer. Beverly Hills, CA: Sage Publications.

Wallace, Michael. 1982. "Armaments and Escalation, Two Competing Hypotheses." *International Studies Quarterly* 26:37-56.

Walt, Stephen M. 1987. *The Origins of Alliances*. Ithaca: Cornell University Press.

Waltz, Kenneth. 1959. *Man, the State, and War*. New York: Columbia University Press.

Waltz, Kenneth. 1979. *Theory of International Politics*. Reading, MA: Addison-Wesley.

Waltz, Kenneth. 1981. "The Spread of Nuclear Weapons." *Adelphi Paper #171*. The International Institute for Strategic Studies.

Ward, Michael D. 1984. "Differential Paths to Parity." *American Political Science Review* 78:297-317.

Ward, Michael D., ed. 1992. *The New Geopolitics*. New York: Gordon Breach Science Publishers.

Werner, Suzanne, and Jacek Kugler. 1993. "Power Transition and Military Build-ups: Resolving the Relations Between Arms Build-up and War." In *Parity and War: A Critical Evaluation of 'The War Ledger,'* ed. Jacek Kugler and Douglas Lemke.

Weede, Erich. 1980. "Arms Races and Escalation: Some Persisting Doubts." *Journal of Conflict Resolution* 24:285-288.

Wilkenfeld, Jonathan. 1968. "Domestic and Foreign Conflict Behavior of Nations." *Journal of Peace Research* 5:56-69.

Wilkenfeld, Jonathan. 1969. "Some Further Findings Regarding the Domestic and Foreign Conflict Behavior of Nations." *Journal of Peace Research* 6:147-156.

Wittman, Donald. 1979. "How a War Ends: A Rational Approach." *Journal of Conflict Resolution* 23:743-763.

Wohlstetter, Albert. 1959. "The Delicate Balance of Terror." *Foreign Affairs* 37:211-256.

Wu, Samuel. 1990. "To Attack or Not to Attack." *Journal of Conflict Resolution* 34:531-552.

Wright, Quincy. 1942. *A Study of War*. Chicago: The University of Chicago Press.

Zagare, Frank. 1987. *The Dynamics of Deterrence*. Chicago: The University of Chicago Press.

Zagare, Frank. 1990. "Rationality and Deterrence." *World Politics* 42:238-260.

Zinnes, Dina, John Gillespie, and Michael Rubinson. 1976. "A Reinterpretation of the Richardson Arms-Race Model." In *Mathematical Models in International Relations*, ed. John Gillespie and Dina Zinnes. New York: Praeger.

Appendix

Political Science: The State of the Discipline 1983
Edited by Ada W. Finifter

Contributors

HENRY E. BRADY is director of the Data Archive and Technical Assistance Program and associate professor of political science and public policy at the University of California, Berkeley. He is the president of the American Political Science Association's Political Methodology Section. He has written on psychometrics, survey research, and political methodology and on voting behavior, public opinion, and political participation in the United States, Canada, Estonia, and Russia. He is coauthor of *Letting the People Decide: Dynamics of a Canadian Election*, Stanford University Press, 1992.

LARRY M. BARTELS is professor of politics and Stuart Professor of Communications and Public Affairs in the Woodrow Wilson School at Princeton University. He is the vice-president of the APSA's Political Methodology Section. He has written articles on statistical research methods, electoral politics, and public opinion, as well as *Presidential Primaries and the Dynamics of Public Choice* (Princeton University Press, 1988), which won the American Political Science Association's Woodrow Wilson Foundation Award.

COLIN CAMPBELL, S.J. is University Professor in the Martin Chair and director of the Graduate Public Policy Program at Georgetown University. He was founding cochair of the International Political Science Association Research Committee on Structure and Organization of Government and founding coeditor of *Governance: An International Journal of Policy and Administration*. He has had fellowships at York University in Toronto (where he formerly taught), the University of Manchester, and Australian National University. He has twice been a guest scholar at the Brookings Institution. He has published widely in the field of comparative executive leadership. His book, *Managing the Presidency,* won the Presidency Research Section's Richard E. Neustadt Award for the best book published on the presidency in 1986.

JAMES A. CAPORASO, Bloedel Professor of Political Science, University of Washington, is currently treasurer of the American Political Science Association and a past Council member, and former vice-president of the International Studies Association. Most recently, he is coauthor (with David Levine) of *Theories of Political Economy* and has written in the fields of international relations theory and international political economy. He is also the editor of *Comparative Political Studies*.

SUSAN J. CARROLL is an associate professor of political science at Rutgers University and senior research associate at the Center for the American Woman and Politics (CAWP) of the Eagleton Institute of Politics. She is the author of various works on women's political participation including *Women as Candidates in American Politics* (Indiana University Press, 1985). Her most recent research focuses on the impact of women in public office.

DAVID COLLIER is professor and department chair in political science at the University of California, Berkeley. His research focuses on Latin American politics, the study of national political regimes, and comparative method. He is editor and coauthor of *The New Authoritarianism in Latin America*, and coauthor of *Shaping the Political Arena: Critical Junctures, the Labor Movement, and Regime Dynamics in Latin America*.

RUSSELL J. DALTON is professor of political science at the University of California, Irvine, chair of the department of politics and society, and director of the UC Irvine Research Program on Democratization. His scholarly interests include comparative political behavior, political parties, political change in advanced industrial societies, and democratization processes. Among his recent books are *Citizen Politics in Western Democracies* (1988), *Politics in Germany* (1992), and *The Green Rainbow: Environmental Groups in Western Europe* (forthcoming).

ADA W. FINIFTER, professor of political science at Michigan State University, is a past president of the Midwest Political Science Association and has been vice-president of the American Political Science Association. She has written on political alienation, political deviance, public opinion in the United States and the Soviet Union, and political aspects of international migration. She was also the editor of the first edition of this book.

WILLIAM A. GALSTON is professor, School of Public Affairs at the University of Maryland at College Park, and senior research scholar, Institute for Philosophy and Public Policy. He is currently on leave serving as deputy assistant to President Clinton for domestic policy. His scholarly interests include political philosophy, American politics, and public policy. His most recent books include *Liberal Purposes* (Cambridge University Press, 1991) and *Virtue* (New York University Press, 1992).

JOHN A. GARCIA is currently department head and associate professor of political science at the University of Arizona. His primary research interests are minority and urban politics with emphases on political behavior and public policy. He received his Ph.D. from Florida State University.

DORIS A. GRABER, professor of political science at the University of Illinois at Chicago, is a past president of the Midwest Political Science Association and has been a vice-president of the American Political Science Association. Among her recent books are *Processing the News: How People Tame the Information Tide* (1988), *Public Sector Communication: How Organizations Manage Information* (1992), and *Mass Media and American Politics* (1993). She is editor-in-chief of *Political Communication*, an interdisciplinary international journal.

ROBERT HUCKFELDT is professor of political science at Indiana University in Bloomington. His interests lie in the general areas of urban and electoral politics. He is the author or coauthor of *Dynamic Modeling*; *Politics in Context*; *Race and the Decline of Class in American Politics*; and *Citizens, Politics, and Social Communication* (forthcoming).

KENNETH JANDA holds the Payson S. Wild Chair in Political Science at Northwestern University. He is past president of the American Political Science Association's sections on Political Organizations and Parties and on Computers and Multimedia. He is the senior author of *The Challenge of Democracy*, a leading text on American government, but most of his published research is on comparative political parties.

DONALD F. KETTL, professor of political science and public affairs at the University of Wisconsin-Madison, is associate director of the university's Robert M. La Follette Institute of Public Affairs. He has written extensively on the problems of public administration and governmental performance, including *The Politics of The Administrative Process* (with James W. Fesler); *Sharing Power: Public Governance and Private Markets;* and *Government by Proxy.*

JACEK KUGLER, the Elisabeth Rosecrans Professor of International Relations at the Claremont Graduate School, is a past president of the Conflict Processes Section of the American Political Science Association. He has written on the initiation, escalation, and consequence of major wars, the long-term stability of nuclear deterrence, and nuclear proliferation. He has also contributed to political demography, economic development, and modeling of international decisions. In addition to numerous scholarly articles, he has coauthored *The War Ledger; Births, Deaths and Taxes;* and coedited *Exploring the Stability of Deterrence* and the forthcoming *Parity and War.*

DAVID LALMAN is assistant professor of government and politics at the University of Maryland. His work is in the areas of formal and positive theory and international relations.

PAULA D. McCLAIN, professor of government and foreign affairs at the University of Virginia, is past president of the National Conference of Black Political Scientists, former member of the American Political Science Association's Executive Council, and program cochair for the American Political Science Association's 1993 Annual Meeting. Her research is in the areas of urban violence, black politics, racial-minority-group political competition, and urban politics.

MICHAEL L. MEZEY is professor of political science and associate dean of the College of Liberal Arts and Sciences at DePaul University. He is the author of *Comparative Legislatures* (1979), *Congress, the President, and Public Policy* (1989), and numerous articles, papers, and book chapters in the areas of American politics and comparative legislative behavior. He serves on the editorial boards of the *Legislative Studies Quarterly* and the *Journal of Politics* and edits the Book Review section of the *Journal of Politics*.

JOE A. OPPENHEIMER, professor of government and politics at the University of Maryland, specializes in positive and normative political economy. He has written books and articles on public choice, distributive justice, and methods, as well as software to author game theoretic experiments. His latest book, coauthored with Norman Frohlich, is *Distributive Justice: An Experimental Approach to Ethical Theory*.

RONALD ROGOWSKI is professor and former chair of political science at the University of California, Los Angeles. He is currently president of the American Political Science Association's organized section in Comparative Politics and serves on the APSA Council and Administrative Committee. His most recent book is *Commerce and Coalitions* (1989).

ARLENE W. SAXONHOUSE is chair of the department of political science at the University of Michigan. She has published widely in the area of classical political thought and is the author of *Women in the History of Political Thought: Ancient Greece to Machiavelli* (1985) and *Fear of Diversity: The Birth of Political Science in Ancient Greek Thought* (1992).

MARTIN SHAPIRO is professor of law in the interdisciplinary Ph.D. Program in Jurisprudence and Social Policy of the School of Law, University of California, Berkeley. A past president of the Western Political Science Association and past vice-president of the American Political Science Association, he is the author and editor of numerous books and articles on American and comparative law and politics.

PAUL M. SNIDERMAN is professor of political science at Stanford University and research political scientist at the Survey Research Center, University of California at Berkeley. He has written on personality and politics, political alienation, democratic values, and issues of race in American politics. His most recent book, *Reasoning and Choice: Explorations in Political Psychology* (with Richard A. Brody and Philip E. Tetlock), won the 1992 Woodrow Wilson Foundation Award.

JOHN SPRAGUE is professor of political science and chair of the department at Washington University in St. Louis. He has written on the U.S. Supreme Court, lawyers in politics, the dynamics of riots, the history of socialist voting in Western Europe, the social and economic determinants of criminal behavior, and the effects of contexts on both criminal and political behavior.

PIOTR SWISTAK is assistant professor of government and politics at the University of Maryland. His work is in the areas of formal and positive theory, research methods, and public policy.

MARTIN P. WATTENBERG is professor of political science at the University of California, Irvine. His first regular, paying job was with the Washington Redskins in 1977, from which he moved on to receive a Ph.D. at the University of Michigan in 1982. While at Michigan, he authored *The Decline of American Political Parties* (Harvard University Press), soon to be in its fourth edition. Most recently, he has written *The Rise of Candidate-Centered Politics: Presidential Elections of the 1980s,* also published by Harvard.

LINDA M. G. ZERILLI is assistant professor of political science at Rutgers University. She has published widely in the areas of feminist political theory, French feminism, and postmodernism. Her book, *Signifying Culture and Chaos: Woman in Rousseau, Burke, and Mill* is forthcoming from Cornell University Press. She is currently working on a manuscript entitled *Feminist Theory without Solace: The Work of Simone de Beauvoir in Postmodern Context.*

Index of Cited Authors

524

526

530

532

Political Science: The State of the Discipline II was prepared by Joanne Dunkelman, Patricia Spellman, Richard Galentino, and Jane Trimble. The cover was designed by Richard Pottern of Richard Pottern, Inc. The text was set in Times Roman by Joanne Dunkelman of the American Political Science Association. The Kirby Lithographic Company, Inc. of Arlington, Virginia, printed and bound the volume.